PENGUIN REFERENCE

The Penguin Pocket Spanish Dictionary

Josephine Riquelme-Beneyto was born in Elche, Spain, and read philology at universities in Alicante, Arizona, and London. She lives with her family in Surrey and works as a translator, interpreter, teacher, and university lecturer.

THE PENGUIN POCKET SPANISH DICTIONARY
ENGLISH – ESPAÑOL
SPANISH – INGLES

Josephine Riquelme-Beneyto

PENGUIN BOOKS

PENGUIN BOOKS

Published by the Penguin Group
Penguin Books Ltd, 80 Strand, London WC2R 0RL, England
Penguin Group (USA) Inc., 375 Hudson Street, New York, New York 10014, USA
Penguin Group (Canada), 90 Eglinton Avenue East, Suite 700, Toronto,
Ontario, Canada M4P 2Y3 (a division of Pearson Penguin Canada Inc.)
Penguin Ireland, 25 St Stephen's Green, Dublin 2, Ireland
(a division of Penguin Books Ltd)
Penguin Group (Australia), 250 Camberwell Road, Camberwell, Victoria 3124, Australia
(a division of Pearson Australia Group Pty Ltd)
Penguin Books India Pvt Ltd, 11 Community Centre,
Panchsheel Park, New Delhi – 110 017, India
Penguin Group (NZ), 67 Apollo Drive, Rosedale, North Shore 0632, New Zealand
(a division of Pearson New Zealand Ltd)
Penguin Books (South Africa) (Pty) Ltd, 24 Sturdee Avenue,
Rosebank 2196, South Africa

Penguin Books Ltd, Registered Offices: 80 Strand, London WC2R 0RL, England

www.penguin.com

First published 2005
This special sales edition published 2007
1

Copyright © Market House Books Ltd, 2005
All rights reserved

The moral right of the author has been asserted

Set in Stone Sans and ITC Stone Serif
Printed in England by Clays Ltd, St Ives plc

ISBN: 978–0–141–03425–6

Guide to the dictionary

The infinitives of all irregular verbs appearing in the headword list are marked with an asterisk. These and examples of Spanish stemchanging verbs, and the tenses in which such changes occur, can be found in the following verb tables. Composite verbs, such as *deshacer* from *hacer*, are also included under the parent verb.

The Spanish alphabet includes three symbols or combinations of letters that are not found in the English alphabet. These are **ch**, **ll**, and **ñ**, which are treated as individual letters and follow **c**, **l**, and **n** respectively in the alphabetical order.

The plurals of almost all Spanish nouns are formed regularly by the addition of *s* or *es* to the singular form. Occasional irregular plural forms are shown immediately after the part of speech referring to the headword. Some nouns do not change in the plural and these are marked *invar* (invariable).

Adverbs are regularly formed by adding *-mente* to the feminine (or occasionally masculine) form of the adjective, and are not normally shown unless a different translation is called for.

Guía al diccionario

Los plurales irregulares de los sustantivos se hallen junto al encabezamiento. Las categorías siguientes de los plurales se consideran regulares en inglés:

cat/cat**s**, glass/glass**es**, fly/fl**ies**, half/hal**ves**, wife/wi**ves**

Los verbos irregulares en la lista de encabezamientos se señalan por medio de un asterisco y se hallen en las tablas de los verbos.

Los adverbios regulares no se indican. Los adverbios ingleses que se forman añadiendo *-(al)ly* al adjetivo, se consideran regulares. Los adverbios españoles que se forman añadiendo *-mente* al adjetivo femenino (de vez en cuando masculino), se consideran regulares y no se indican sino exigiendo una traducción diferente.

Spanish pronunciation

a cada ['kaða]	g grande ['grande]	t todo ['toðo]
e entre ['entre]	k poco ['poko]	w luego ['lwego]
i libro ['liβro]	l salud [sa'luð]	θ cerveza [θer'βeθa]
o loco ['loko]	m hombre ['ombre]	β hábil ['aβil]
u lunes ['lunes]	n noche ['notʃe]	tʃ muchacho [mu'tʃatʃo]
j nieve ['njeβe]	p lápiz ['lapiθ]	ð ciudad [θju'ðað]
b bueno ['bweno]	r cerca ['θerka]	ʎ calle ['kaʎe]
d desde ['desðe]	rr perro ['perro]	ŋ señor [se'ŋor]
f fácil ['faθil]	s servir [ser'βir]	x ojo, ágil ['oxo], ['axil]

The symbol ' indicates that the following syllable should be stressed.

Prononciación del inglés

a hat [hat]	au how [hau]	p pick [pik]
e bell [bel]	ou road [roud]	r rose [rouz]
i big [big]	eə lair [leə]	s sit [sit]
o dot [dot]	iə fear [fiə]	t toe [tou]
^ bun [b^n]	uə poor [puə]	v vest [vest]
u book [buk]	b back [bak]	w week [wi:k]
ə alone [ə'loun]	d dull [d^l]	z zoo [zu:]
a: card [ka:d]	f find [faind]	θ think [θiŋk]
ə: word [wə:d]	g gaze [geiz]	ð those [ðouz]
i: team [ti:m]	h hop [hop]	ʃ shoe [ʃu:]
o: torn [to:n]	j yell [jel]	ʒ treasure ['treʒə]
u: spoon [spu:n]	k cat [kat]	tʃ chalk [tʃo:k]
ai die [dai]	l life [laif]	dʒ jump [dʒ^mp]
ei ray [rei]	m mouse [maus]	ŋ sing [siŋ]
oi toy [toi]	n night [nait]	

El signo de acentuación ' se coloca directamente delante de la sílaba aguda.
El signo , se coloca delante de la sílaba aguda secundaria.

Abbreviations/Abreviaciones

adj adjective, adjetivo
adv adverb, adverbio
aero aeronautics, aeronáutica
agr agriculture, agricultura
anat anatomy, anatomía
arch architecture
arq arquitectura
art article, artículo
astrol astrology, astrología
astron astronomy, astronomía
auto automobile, automóvil
bot botany, botánica
chem chemistry
coll colloquial
com comercio
comm commerce
conj conjunction, conjunción
culin culinario
derog derogatory
econ economics, economía

elec electricity, electricidad
f feminine, femenino
fam familiar, colloquial
ferr ferrocarril
fig figurative, figurativo
foto fotografía
geog geography, geografía
geol geology, geología
gram gramática
gramm grammar
impol impolite
interj interjection, interjección
interrog interrogative, interrogativo
invar invariable
jur jurisprudencia
m masculine, masculino
mar marítimo
mat matemáticas
math mathematics
mec mecánica
mech mechanics

med medicine, medicina
mil military, militar
mot motoring
n noun
naut nautical
phot photography
pl plural
pol politics, política
prep preposition, preposición
pron pronoun, pronombre
psych psychology
quím química
rail railways
rel religion, religión
s sustantivo
sing singular
tech technology, technical
tecn tecnología
v verb, verbo
V vide (see, vea)
zool zoology, zoología

Spanish verb tables

1. The final consonants preceding the infinitive endings (**-ar**, **-er**, and **-(u)ir**) change, for reasons of euphony, when they occur before certain vowels.

Infinitives	Change	Before
-car	the **c** to **qu**	**e**
-cer	the **c** to **z**	**a** or **o**
-cir	the **c** to **z**	**a** or **o**
-gir	the **g** to **j**	**a** or **o**
-guir	the **gu** to **g**	**a** or **o**
-quir	the **qu** to **c**	**a** or **o**
-gar	the **ga** to **gu**	**e**
-zar	the **z** to **c**	**e**

2. Verbs adding **z**. There are numerous verbs ending in **-ecer** (*e.g.* **parecer**) and other verbs ending in a vowel + **-cer** (*e.g.* **conocer**). When the ending of these verbs is **a** or **o** (specifically, present indicative 1 *sing* and present subjunctive, all persons), a **z** is added before the **c** (*e.g.* **parezco, conozco**).

3. Verbs in the following tables change the vowels in their stems in certain persons and tenses. The sections below are arranged according to the vowel change involved and are followed by a selection of verbs exemplifying the change. Note that composite verbs (*e.g.* **desplegar**) are conjugated in the same way as their base forms (*e.g.* **plegar**).

(i) Stem changes **e** to **ie** in present indicative and present subjunctive 1, 2, 3 *sing* and 3 *pl*, and in imperative *sing*.

acertar, acrecentar, aferrar, apretar, arrendar, ascender, aterrar, aventar, calentar, cegar, cerner, cerrar, comenzar, concertar, confesar, contender, decentar, defender, dentar, desalentar, descender, desempedrar, despernar, despertar, entender, entesar, fregar, gobernar, hacendar, heder, helar, herrar, incensar, invernar, manifestar, mentar, merendar, negar, nevar, pensar, perder, plegar, quebrar, recentar, recomendar, regar, remendar, restregar, reventar, segar, sembrar, sentar, serrar, sosegar, soterrar, temblar, tender, tentar; hender, trascender, trasegar, trasverter, tropezar, verter

(ii) Stem changes **o** to **ue** in present indicative and present subjunctive 1, 2, 3 *sing* and 3 *pl*, and in imperative *sing*.

acordar, acostar, aforar, almorzar, apostar, aprobar, avergonzar, azolar, colar, colgar, contar, costar, doler, encontrar, forzar, holgar, jugar, moler, mostrar, mover, poblar, probar, recordar, renovar, resollar, rodar, rogar, solar, soldar, soler, soltar, sonar, soñar, torcer, tostar, trocar, tronar, volcar, voler, volver

(iii) Stem changes from **e** to **i** in present indicative 1, 2, 3 *sing* and 3 *pl*; preterite 3 *sing* and *pl*; present, imperfect, and future subjunctives, all persons; imperative *sing* and present participle.

colegir, concebir, corregir, derretir, elegir, gemir, henchir, medir, pedir, regir, rendir, repetir, seguir, servir, vestir

(iv) Stem changes **e** to **ie** in present indicative and present subjunctive 1, 2, 3 *sing* and 3 *pl*; imperative *sing*. Stem changes **e** to **i** in preterite 3 *sing* and *pl*; present subjunctive 1, 2 *pl*; imperfect and future subjunctives, all persons; present participle.

advertir, cernir, convertir, diferir, digerir, divertir, hendir, herir, hervir, inferir, ingerir, mentir, preferir, requerir, sentir, sugerir

4. The verbs shown below change in various ways. In the table, 1 and 3 *sing* are shown under the present indicative and 1 *sing* under the preterite and future.

Infinitive	Present Indicative	Preterite	Future	Past Participle
andar	ando, anda	anduve	andaré	andado
caber	quepo, cabe	cupe	cabré	cabido
caer	caigo, cae	caí	caeré	caido
dar	doy, da	di	daré	dado
decir	digo, dice	dije	diré	dicho
dormir	duermo, duerme	dormí	dormiré	dormido
erguir	yergo, yergue	erguí	erguiré	erguido
errar	yerro, yerra	erré	erraré	errado
estar	estoy, está	estuve	estaré	estado
haber	he, ha	hube	habré	habido
hacer	hago, hace	hice	haré	hecho
huir	huyo, huye	huí	huiré	huido
ir	voy, va	fui	iré	ido
oír	oigo, oye	oí	oiré	oido
oler	huelo, huele	olí	oleré	olido
poder	puedo, puede	pude	podré	podido
poner	pongo, pone	puse	pondré	puesto
querer	quiero, quiere	quise	querré	querido
reducir	reduzco, reduce	reduje	reduciré	reducido
reír	río, ríe	reí	reiré	reido
saber	sé, sabe	supe	sabré	sabido
ser	soy, es	fui	seré	sido
tener	tengo, tiene	tuve	tendré	tenido
traer	traigo, trae	traje	traeré	traído
valer	valgo, vale	valí	valdré	valido
venir	vengo, viene	vine	vendré	venido
ver	veo, ve	vi	veré	visto

Verbos irregulares ingleses

Infinitivo	Pretérito	Participo Passado	Infinitivo	Pretérito	Participo Passado
abide	abode	abode	**fall**	fell	fallen
arise	arose	arisen	**feed**	fed	fed
awake	awoke	awoken	**feel**	felt	felt
be	was	been	**fight**	fought	fought
bear	bore	borne *or* born	**find**	found	found
			flee	fled	fled
beat	beat	beaten	**fling**	flung	flung
become	became	become	**fly**	flew	flown
begin	began	begun	**forbid**	forbade	forbidden
behold	beheld	beheld	**forget**	forgot	forgotten
bend	bent	bent	**forgive**	forgave	forgiven
bet	bet	bet	**forsake**	forsook	forsaken
beware			**freeze**	froze	frozen
bid	bid	bidden *or* bid	**get**	got	got
			give	gave	given
bind	bound	bound	**go**	went	gone
bite	bit	bitten	**grind**	ground	ground
bleed	bled	bled	**grow**	grew	grown
blow	blew	blown	**hang**	hung	hung
break	broke	broken		*or* hanged	*or* hanged
breed	bred	bred	**have**	had	had
bring	brought	brought	**hear**	heard	heard
build	built	built	**hide**	hid	hidden
burn	burnt *or* burned	burnt *or* burned	**hit**	hit	hit
			hold	held	held
burst	burst	burst	**hurt**	hurt	hurt
buy	bought	bought	**keep**	kept	kept
can	could		**kneel**	knelt	knelt
cast	cast	cast	**knit**	knitted *or* knit	knitted *or* knit
catch	caught	caught			
choose	chose	chosen	**know**	knew	known
cling	clung	clung	**lay**	laid	laid
come	came	come	**lead**	led	led
cost	cost	cost	**lean**	leant *or* leaned	leant *or* leaned
creep	crept	crept			
cut	cut	cut	**leap**	leapt *or* leaped	leapt *or* leaped
deal	dealt	dealt			
dig	dug	dug	**learn**	learnt *or* learned	learnt *or* learned
do	did	done			
draw	drew	drawn	**leave**	left	left
dream	dreamed *or* dreamt	dreamed *or* dreamt	**lend**	lent	lent
			let	let	let
drink	drank	drunk	**lie**	lay	lain
drive	drove	driven	**light**	lit *or* lighted	lit *or* lighted
dwell	dwelt	dwelt			
eat	ate	eaten	**lose**	lost	lost

Infinitivo	Pretérito	Participo Passado	Infinitivo	Pretérito	Participo Passado
make	made	made	**speak**	spoke	spoken
may	might		**speed**	sped	sped
mean	meant	meant		or speeded	or speeded
meet	met	met	**spell**	spelt	spelt
mow	mowed	mown		or spelled	or spelled
must			**spend**	spent	spent
ought			**spill**	spilt	spilt
pay	paid	paid		or spilled	or spilled
put	put	put	**spin**	spun	spun
quit	quitted	quitted	**spit**	spat	spat
	or quit	or quit	**spilt**	split	split
read	read	read	**spread**	spread	spread
rid	rid	rid	**spring**	sprang	sprung
ride	rode	ridden	**stand**	stood	stood
ring	rang	rung	**steal**	stole	stolen
rise	rose	risen	**stick**	stuck	stuck
run	ran	run	**sting**	stung	stung
saw	sawed	sawn or sawed	**stink**	stank	stunk
				or stunk	
say	said	said	**stride**	strode	stridden
see	saw	seen	**strike**	struck	struck
seek	sought	sought	**string**	strung	strung
sell	sold	sold	**strive**	strove	striven
send	sent	sent	**swear**	swore	sworn
set	set	set	**sweep**	swept	swept
sew	sewed	sewn or sewed	**swell**	swelled	swollen or swelled
shake	shook	shaken	**swim**	swam	swum
shear	sheared	sheared or shorn	**swing**	swung	swung
			take	took	taken
shed	shed	shed	**teach**	taught	taught
shine	shone	shone	**tear**	tore	torn
shoe	shod	shod	**tell**	told	told
shoot	shot	shot	**think**	thought	thought
show	showed	shown	**throw**	threw	thrown
shrink	shrank	shrunk	**thrust**	thrust	thrust
shut	shut	shut	**tread**	trod	trodden
sing	sang	sung	**wake**	woke	woken
sink	sank	sunk	**wear**	wore	worn
sit	sat	sat	**weave**	wove	woven
sleep	slept	slept	**weep**	wept	wept
slide	slid	slid	**win**	won	won
sling	slung	slung	**wind**	wound	wound
slink	slunk	slunk	**wring**	wrung	wrung
slit	slit	slit	**write**	wrote	written
smell	smelt or smelled	smelt or smelled			
sow	sowed	sown or sowed			

English – Español

A

a, an [ə, ən] *art* un, -a.

aback [ə'bak] *adv* **be taken aback** quedar desconcertado.

abandon [ə'bandən] *v* abandonar. *n* abandono *m*.

abashed [ə'baʃt] *adj* avergonzado, confundido.

abate [ə'beit] *v* disminuir. **abatement** *n* disminución *f*.

abattoir ['abatwa:] *n* matadero *m*.

abbey ['abi] *n* abadía *f*. **abbess** *n* abadesa *f*. **abbot** *n* abad *m*.

abbreviate [ə'bri:vieit] *v* abreviar. **abbreviation** *n* abreviación *f*.

abdicate ['abdikeit] *v* abdicar. **abdication** *n* abdicación *f*.

abdomen ['abdəmən] *n* abdomen *m*. **abdominal** *adj* abdominal.

abduct [ab'dʌkt] *v* raptar. **abduction** *n* rapto *m*.

aberration [abə'reiʃən] *n* extravío *m*, engaño *m*. **abberant** *adj* extraviado.

abet [ə'bet] *v* instigar, inducir.

abeyance [ə'beiəns] *n* **in abeyance** en suspenso.

abhor [əb'ho:] *v* aborrecer, odiar. **abhorrence** *n* aborrecimiento *m*, odio *m*. **abhorrent** *adj* aborrecible.

***abide** [ə'baid] *v* residir, habitar; (*tolerate*) aguantar, sufrir. **abide by** atenerse a, cumplir con.

ability [ə'biləti] *n* habilidad *f*, capacidad *f*. **to the best of one's ability** lo mejor que pueda.

abject [,abdʒekt] *adj* abyecto.

ablaze [ə'bleiz] *adj* en llamas.

able ['eibl] *adj* capaz; (*talented*) hábil. **be able** poder.

able-bodied *adj* entero. **able-bodied seaman** marinero de primera *m*. **ably** *adv* hábilmente.

abnormal [ab'no:ml] *adj* anormal. **abnormality** *n* anormalidad *f*.

aboard [ə'bo:d] *adv*, *prep* a bordo (de). **all aboard!** ¡viajeros a bordo! **go aboard** embarcarse.

abode [ə'boud] *n* domicilio *m*.

abolish [ə'boliʃ] *v* abolir. **abolition** *n* abolición *f*.

abominable [ə'bominəbl] *adj* abominable. **abominate** *v* abominar (de). **abomination** *n* abominación *f*.

Aborigine [abə'ridʒini] *n* aborigen *m*.

abortion [ə'bo:ʃən] *n* aborto *m*. **abort** *v* abortar.

abound [ə'baund] *v* abundar.

about [ə'baut] *adv* (*approximately*) alrededor de, más o menos. **all about** por todas partes. *prep* (*place*) alrededor de; (*near*) cerca de; (*concerning*) de, acerca de.

above [ə'bʌv] *adv* encima, arriba. *prep* (*place*) encima de, sobre; (*number*) más de; (*rank*) superior a. **above-mentioned** *adj* susodicho, citado.

abrasion [ə'breiʒən] *n* raspadura *f*. **abrasive** *adj* raspante.

abreast [ə'brest] *adv* de frente. **keep abreast of** *or* **with** ir al paso de.

abridge [ə'bridʒ] *v* abreviar, resumir. **abridgement** *n* abreviación *f*, resumen *m*.

abroad [ə'bro:d] *adv* en el extranjero.

abrupt [ə'brʌpt] *adj* abrupto, brusco.

abscess ['abses] *n* absceso *m*.

abscond [əb'skond] *v* fugarse.

abseil ['abseil] *v* hacer rappel

absent ['absənt] *adj* ausente. **absent-minded** *adj* distraído. **absent oneself** ausentarse. **absence** *n* ausencia *f*. **absentee** *n* ausente *m*, *f*. **absenteeism** *n* absentismo *m*.

absolute ['absəlu:t] *adj* absoluto. **absolutely** *adv* absolutamente; (*interj*) categóricamente. **absolutism** *n* absolutismo *m*.

absolve [əb'zolv] *v* absolver. **absolution** *n* absolución *f*.

absorb [əb'zo:b] *v* absorber. **be absorbed in** enfrascarse en. **absorbent** *adj* absorbente. **absorbing** *adj* sumamente interesante.

abstain [əb'stein] *v* abstenerse (de). **abstention** *n* abstención *f*. **abstinence** *n* abstinencia *f*.

abstemious [əb'sti:miəs] *adj* abstemio.

abstract ['abstrakt; *v* ab'strakt] *adj* abstracto. *n* resumen *m*. *v* extractar. **abstractedly** *adv* distraídamente. **abstraction** *n* abstracción *f*.

absurd [əb'sə:d] *adj* absurdo. **absurdity** *n* absurdidad *f*.

abundance [ə'bʌndəns] *n* abundancia *f*. **abundant** *adj* abundante.

abuse [ə'bju:z; *v* ə'bju:s] *v* abusar (de). *n* abuso *m*; injuria *f*; (*maltreatment*) abuso *m*. **abusive** *adj* abusivo; injurioso.

abyss [ə'bis] *n* abismo *m*. **abysmal** *adj* abismal; profundo.

academy [ə'kadəmi] *n* academia *f*. **academic** *adj* académico.

accede [ak'si:d] *v* acceder.

accelerate [ək'seləreit] *v* acelerar. **acceleration** *n* aceleración *f*. **accelerator** *n* acelerador *m*.

accent ['aksənt] *n* acento *m*. *v* acentuar.

accept [ək'sept] *v* aceptar. **acceptable** *adj* aceptable. **acceptance** *n* aceptación *f*.

access ['akses] *n* acceso *m*. **accessible** *adj* asequible.

accessory [ak'sesəri] *nm, adj* accessorio *m*, (*law*) cómplice *m*, *f*. **accessories** *pl n*. (*mot, etc.*) complementos *m pl*.

accident ['aksidənt] *n* accidente *m*. **by accident** sin querer, por casualidad. **accidental** *adj* accidental.

acclaim [ə'kleim] *v* aclamar, aplaudir. *n* also **acclamation** aclamación *f*, aplauso *m*.

acclimatize [ə'klaimətaiz] *v* aclimatar.

accolade ['akəleid] *n* acolada *f*.

accommodate [ə'komədeit] *v* acomodar; (*lodge*) alojar, hospedar; adaptar; (*provide*) proveer (de). **accommodating** *adj* complaciente. **accommodation** *n* alojamiento *m*.

accompany [ə'kʌmpəni] *v* acompañar. **accompaniment** *n* acompañamiento *m*. **accompanist** *n* acompañante, -a *m*, *f*.

accomplice [ə'kʌmplis] *n* cómplice *m*, *f*.

accomplish [ə'kʌmpliʃ] *v* cumplir. **accomplished** *adj* (*talented*) talentoso. **accomplishment** *n* efectuación *f*; talentos *m pl*.

accord [ə'ko:d] *v* conceder; concordar. *n* acuerdo *m*. **of one's own accord** espontáneamente. **in accordance with** conforme a. **accordingly** *adv* en consecuencia. **according to** según.

accordion [ə'ko:diən] *n* acordeón *m*.

accost [ə'kost] *v* abordar.

account [ə'kaunt] *n* (*bank, etc.*) cuenta *f*; (*narrative*) relato *m*; (*status*) importancia *f*. **on account of** a causa de. **on no account** de ninguna manera. **take into account** tener en cuenta. **account for** dar una explicación de. **accountant** *n* contador, -a *m*, *f* (*chartered*) contador colegiado.

accrue [ə'kru:] *v* crecer.

accumulate [ə'kju:mjuleit] *v* acumular. **accumulation** *n* acumulación *f*.

accurate ['akjurət] *adj* exacto. **accuracy** *n* precisión *f*.

accuse [ə'kju:z] *v* acusar. **accusation** *n* acusación *f*. **the accused** el/la acusado, -a.

accustom [ə'kʌstəm] *v* acostumbrar.

ace [eis] *n* as *m*. **within an ace of** de dos dedos de.

ache [eik] *n* dolor *m*. *v* doler.

achieve [ə'tʃi:v] *v* ejecutar. **achievement** *n* ejecución *f*; (*feat*) hazaña *f*.

acid ['asid] *nm, adj* ácido. **acidity** *n* acidez *f*. **acid rain** lluvia ácida *f*.

acknowledge [ək'nolidʒ] *v* reconocer, aceptar. **acknowledge receipt of** acusar recibo de. **acknowledgement** n reconocimiento m; acuse de recibo m.

acne ['akni] n acné m.

acorn ['eiko:n] n bellota f.

acoustic [ə'ku:stik] adj acústico. **acoustics** pl n acústica f sing.

acquaint [ə'kweint] v informar, avisar. **acquaintance** n (knowledge) conocimiento m; (person) conocido, -a m, f. **be acquainted with** conocer(a).

acquiesce [akwïes] v consentir, conformarse. **acquiescence** n conformidad f. **acquiescent** adj sumiso.

acquire [ə'kwaiə] v adquirir. **acquisition** n adquisición f. **acquisitive** adj adquisitivo; (derog) ahorrativo.

acquit [ə'kwit] v absolver. **acquit oneself** portarse. **acquittal** (law) absolución f.

acrid ['akrid] adj acre.

acrimony ['akriməni] n acrimonia f. **acrimonious** adj áspero.

acrobat ['akrəbat] n acróbata m, f. **acrobatic** adj acrobático. **acrobatics** pl n acrobacia f sing.

acronym ['akrənim] n acrónimo m

across [ə'kros] adv a través, al través. prep a través de, al través de; de través de; al otro lado de, del otro lado de.

acrylic [ə'krilik] adj acrílico.

act [akt] v (theatre) representar; (function) funcionar, marchar; (behave) comportarse; (take action) obrar, tomar medidas; (affect) afectar. n acto m, acción f; obra f; (law) decreto m; (theatre) acto m. **actor** n actor m. **actress** n actriz f.

action ['akʃən] n acción f, hecho m; (mil) acción f, batalla f; (mech) mecanismo m. **bring an action against** entablar demanda contra. **put out of action** inutilizar.

active ['aktiv] adj activo. **activate** v activar. **activist** n activista m, f. **activity** n actividad f; movimiento m.

actual ['aktʃuəl] adj verdadero, efectivo. **actually** adv en realidad.

actuate ['aktjueit] v mover; accionar.

acupuncture ['akjupʌnktʃə] n acupuntura f.

acute [ə'kju:t] adj agudo.

adamant ['adəmənt] adj firme, seguro.

Adam's apple [adəm'zapl] n nuez de la garganta f.

adapt [ə'dapt] v adaptar; ajustar; (play, book) refundir; (music) arreglar. **adaptable** adj adaptable. **adaptation** n adaptación f; refundición f; arreglo m. **adapter** n (theatre) refundidor m; (elec) enchufe de reducción m.

add [ad] v añadir; (increase) aumentar. **add up** sumar. **add up to** subir a. **addition** n el añadir m; (math) suma f, adición f. **additional** adj adicional.

addendum [ə'dendəm] n invar adenda f.

adder ['adə] n víbora f.

addict ['adikt] n partidario, -a m, f; (drugs) toxicómano, -a m, f. **addiction** n adicción f; propensión f; **addictive** adj adictivo; be **addicted to** ser adicto a.

additive ['aditiv] n aditivo m.

address [ə'dres] v (letter) dirigir; (meeting, etc.) pronunciar un discurso ante. **address oneself to** dirigirse a. n (postal) dirección f; (speech) discurso m; (envelope) sobrescrito m. **addressee** n destinatario, -a m, f.

adenoids ['adənoidz] pl n amígdalas vegetaciones f pl.

adept [ə'dept; adj 'adept] nm experto.

adequate ['adikwət] adj adecuado, suficiente.

adhere [əd'hiə] v pegarse; (to a policy) adherirse **adhesion** n adhesión f. **adhesive** adj adhesivo. **adhesive tape** (medical) esparadrapo m; (stationery) cinta adhesiva f, Scotch® m.

adherent [əd'hiərənt] n partidario, -a m, f.

adjacent [ə'dʒeisənt] adj próximo, contiguo.

adjective ['adʒiktiv] n adjetivo m.

adjoin [ə'dʒoin] v lindar (con). **adjoining** adj contiguo.

adjourn [ə'dʒə:n] v aplazar; (session) levantar la sesión. **adjournment** n aplazamiento m; (of a session) suspensión f.

adjudicate [ə'dʒu:dikeit] v adjudicar; (law) juzgar. **adjudication** n adjudicación f; (law) fallo m. **adjudicator** n árbitro m.

adjust [ə'dʒʌst] v arreglar; (tech) ajustar. **adjustment** n arreglo m; ajuste m.

ad-lib ['ad'lib] adv a voluntad, a discreción. v improvisar.

administer [əd'ministə] v administrar; (law) aplicar; (med) suministrar. **administration** n administración f; (ministry) gobierno m. **administrative** adj administrativo. **administrator** n administrador, -a m f.

admiral ['admərəl] *n* almirante *m*.

admire [əd'maiə] *v* admirar. **admirable** *adj* admirable.

admiration *n* admiración *f*.

admit [əd'mit] *v* dar entrada a; (*concede*) conceder; (*acknowledge*) reconocer. **admission** *n* entrada *f*; (*acknowledgement*) confesión *f*.

adolescence [adə'lesns] *n* adolescencia *f*. **adolescent** *n*(*m + f*), *adj* adolescente.

adopt [ə'dopt] *v* adoptar; (*report*) aprobar. **adopted** *adj* (*child*) adoptivo. **adoption** *n* adopción *f*.

adore [ə'do:] *v* adorar. **adoration** *n* adoración *f*.

adorn [ə'do:n] *v* adornar, embellecer. **adornment** *n* adorno *m*.

adrenaline [ə'drenəlin] *n* adrenalina *f*.

adrift [ə'drift] *adv* a la deriva.

adroit [ə'droit] *adj* diestro, hábil.

adulation [adju'leiʃən] *n* adulación *f*.

adult ['adʌlt] *n, adj* adulto, -a.

adulterate [ə'dʌltəreit] *v* adulterar.

adultery [ə'dʌltəri] *n* adulterio *m*. **adulterer** *n* adúltero, -a *m, f*.

advance [əd'va:ns] *v* adelantar; avanzar. *n* progreso *m*, avance *m*, adelanto *m*; (*cash*) anticipo *m*.

advantage [əd'va:ntidʒ] *n* ventaja *f*. **take advantage of** aprovecharse de. **advantageous** *adj* ventajoso.

advent ['advənt] *n* advenimiento *m*. **Advent** *n* Adviento *m*.

adventure [əd'ventʃə] *n* aventura *f*; (*comm*) especulación *f*. **adventurer** *n* aventurero, -a *m f*. **adventurous** *adj* aventurero.

adverb ['advə:b] *n* adverbio *m*.

adversary ['advəsəri] *n* adversario, -a *m, f*.

adverse ['advə:s] *adj* adverso. **adversity** *n* adversidad *f*.

advertise ['advətaiz] *v* anunciar; publicar. **advertisement** *n* anuncio *m*. **advertising** *n* publicidad *f*.

advise [əd'vaiz] *v* aconsejar; avisar. **advisable** *adj* conveniente. **advisedly** *adv* con intención. **adviser** *n* consejero, -a *m f*. **advice** *n* consejo *m*.

advocate ['advəkeit] *v* recomendar.

aerial ['eəriəl] *adj* aéreo. *n* antena *f*.

aerobics [eə'roubiks] *n* aerobic *m*

aerodynamics [eərədai'namiks] *n* aerodinámica *f sing*.

aeronautics [eərə'no:tiks] *n* aeronáutica *f sing*.

aeroplane ['eərəplein] *n* avión *m*.

aerosol ['eərəsol] *n* aerosol *m*.

aesthetic [i:s'θetik] *adj* estético. **aesthetics** *n* estética *f sing*.

affair [ə'feə] *n* asunto *m*; episodio *m*; (*love*) aventura amorosa *f*. **affairs** (*business*) negocios *m pl*.

affect¹ [ə'fekt] *v* (*influence*) influir en; (*move*) conmover.

affect² [ə'fekt] *v* (*pretend*) afectar.

affection [ə'fekʃən] *n* cariño *m*.

affiliate [ə'filieit] *v* afiliarse (a). **affiliation** *n* afiliación *f*.

affinity [ə'finəti] *n* afinidad *f*.

affirm [ə'fə:m] *v* afirmar. **affirmation** *n* afirmación *f*. **affirmative** *adj* afirmativo.

affix [ə'fiks] *v* fijar; añadir; pegar; poner.

afflict [ə'flikt] *v* afligir, aquejar. **affliction** *n* aflicción *f*, dolor *m*.

affluent ['afluənt] *adj* afluente, opulento. **affluence** *n* afluencia *f*, opulencia *f*.

afford [ə'fo:d] *v* tener medios; (*produce*) dar; ofrecer.

affront [ə'frʌnt] *v* afrentar. *n* afrenta *f*, ofensa *f*.

afloat [ə'flout] *adv* a flote.

afoot [ə'fut] *adv* a pie; (*fig*) en proyecto.

aforesaid [ə'fo:sed] *adj* susodicho, mencionado.

afraid [ə'freid] *adj* temeroso, espantado. **be afraid** tener miedo (a *or* de).

afresh [ə'freʃ] *adv* de nuevo.

Africa ['afrikə] *n* África *f*. **African** *n, adj* africano, -a *m f*.

aft [a:ft] *adv* a popa.

after ['a:ftə] *prep* (*time*) después de; (*place*) detrás de; tras. *adv* (*time*) después; (*place*) detrás. *conj* después (de) que. **after all** con todo. **afterwards** *adv* después. **after-effect** *n* consecuencia *f*. **aftershave** *n* loción de afeitar *f*.

afternoon [.a:ftə'nu:n] *n* tarde *f*. **good afternoon!** ¡buenas tardes!

aftershave ['a:ftəʃeiv] *n* aftershave *m*, loción de afeitar *f*

again [ə'gen] *adv* de nuevo, otra vez; además. **again and again** una y otra vez. **now and again** de vez en cuando.

against [ə'genst] *prep* contra; (*touching*)

tocante.

age [eidʒ] *n* edad *f*; (*era*) época *f*. **of age** mayor de edad. **under age** menor de edad. *v* envejecer. **aged** *adj* de la edad de; (*old*) viejo.

agency ['eidʒənsi] *n* agencia *f*; mediación *f*.

agenda [ə'dʒendə] *n* agenda *f*.

agent ['eidʒənt] *n* agente *m, f*; (*comm*) representante *m, f*.

aggravate ['agrəveit] *v* agravar; (*coll*) exasperar. **aggravation** *n* agravamiento *m*; (*coll*) irritación *f*.

aggregate ['agrigət] *n, adj* agregado. *v* agregar, juntar.

aggression [ə'greʃən] *n* agresión *f*. **aggressive** *adj* agresivo. **aggressiveness** *n* belicosidad *f*. **aggressor** *n* agresor, -a *m, f*.

aghast [ə'ga:st] *adj* horrorizado.

agile ['adʒail] *adj* ágil, ligero. **agility** *n* agilidad *f*.

agitate ['adʒiteit] *v* agitar, excitar. **agitate for** luchar por. **agitation** *n* agitación *f*; perturbación *f*.

agnostic [ag'nostik] *n, adj* agnóstico, -a. **agnosticism** *n* agnosticismo *m*.

ago [ə'gou] *adv* hace, ha. **long ago** hace mucho tiempo. **a short time ago** hace poco.

agog [ə'gog] *adj* ansioso.

agony ['agəni] *n* agonía *f*, angustia *f*. **agonize** *v* atormentar.

agree [ə'gri:] *v* estar de acuerdo, convenir (en); (*consent*) consentir (en); (*gram*) concordar; (*correspond*) estar conforme (con). **agreeable** *adj* agradable. **agreement** *n* (*pact*) pacto *m*; (*comm*) contrato *m*.

agriculture ['agrikʌltʃə] *n* agricultura *f*. **agricultural** *adj* agrícola.

aground [ə'graund] *adv* encallado. **run aground** encallar, varar.

ahead [ə'hed] *adv* delante, al frente. **be ahead** estar adelante. **go ahead!** ¡adelante!

aid [eid] *v* ayudar, socorrer. *n* ayuda *f*. **in aid of** en beneficio de. **first aid** primera cura. **go to the aid of** acudir en defensa de.

Aids [eidz] *n* (*med*) Sida *m*

aim [eim] *v* (*weapon*) apuntar (a); (*remark*) dirigir (a). *n* (*weapon*) puntería *f*; (*fig*) propósito *m*, meta *f*, blanco *m*. **aimless** *adj* sin objeto. **aimlessly** *adv* a la ventura.

air [eə] *n* aire *m*; (*music*) aire *m*, tonada *f*;

(*aspect*) aspecto *m*. *v* airear, ventilar.

airbed ['eəbed] *n* colchón de viento *m*.

airborne ['eəbo:n] *adj* en el aire.

aircraft ['eəkra:ft] *n* avión *m*. **aircraft carrier** *n* portaaviones *m invar*.

airfield ['eəfi:ld] *n* campo de aviación *m*.

air force *n* fuerza *f* o flota aérea *f*.

air-hostess *n* azafata *f*.

air lift *n* puente aéreo *m*.

airline ['eəlain] *n* línea aérea *f*.

airmail ['eəmeil] *n* correo aéreo *m*.

airport ['eəpo:t] *n* aeropuerto *m*.

air-raid *n* bombardeo aéreo *m*.

airtight ['eətait] *adj* hermético, herméticamente cerrado.

air traffic controller *n* controlador de tráfico aéreo *m*

airy ['eəri] *adj* aéreo; (*flippant*) frívolo.

aisle [ail] *n* nave lateral *f*.

ajar [ə'dʒa:] *adv* entreabierto, entornado.

alabaster ['aləba:stə] *n* alabastro *m*. *adj* alabastrino.

alarm [ə'la:m] *n* alarma *f*. *v* alarmar. **alarm clock** *n* despertador *m*.

alas [ə'las] *interj* ¡ay!

Albania [al'beinjə] *n* Albania *f*. **Albanian** *n, adj* albanés, -esa.

albatross ['albətros] *n* albatros *m*.

albino [al'bi:nou] *n, adj* albino, -a.

album ['albəm] *n* álbum *m*.

alchemy ['alkəmi] *n* alquimia *f*. **alchemist** *n* alquimista *m*.

alcohol ['alkəhol] *n* alcohol *m*. **alcoholic** *n, adj* alcohólico, -a. **alcoholism** *n* alcoholismo *m*.

alcove ['alkouv] *n* nicho *m*, hueco *m*.

alderman ['o:ldəmən] *n* teniente de alcalde *m*, concejal *m*.

ale [eil] *n* cerveza *f*.

alert [ə'lə:t] *adj* alerta, vivo, despierto. *v* poner sobre aviso, alertar.

algebra ['aldʒibrə] *n* álgebra *f*.

Algeria [al'dʒiəriə] *n* Argelia *f*. **Algerian** *n, adj* argelino, -a.

alias ['eiliəs] *nm, adv* alias.

alibi ['alibai] *n* coartada *f*.

alien ['eiliən] *n, adj* extranjero, -a. **alienate** *v* enajenar, alejar. **alienation** *n* alienación *f*.

alight¹ [ə'lait] *v* desmontar, bajar, apearse.

alight² [ə'lait] *adj* encendido, iluminado, en llamas.

align [ə'lain] *v* alinear. **alignment** *n* alineación *f*.

alike [ə'laik] *adj* igual, parecido, semejante. *adv* igualmente, del mismo modo.

alimentary canal [ali'mentəri] *n* tubo digestivo *m*.

alimony ['aliməni] *n* alimentos *m pl*.

alive [ə'laiv] *adj* vivo, activo. **alive to** sensible de. **alive with** rebosante de.

alkali ['alkəlai] *n* álcalis *m*.

all [ɔ:l] *adj* todo. *pron* todo el mundo. *n* todo *m*, totalidad *f*. *adv* todo, enteramente. **all but** casi. **all right** está bien. **all the more** cuanto más. **all the same** sin embargo.

allay [ə'lei] *v* aliviar, calmar.

allege [ə'ledʒ] *v* alegar, afirmar.

allegiance [ə'li:dʒəns] *n* fidelidad *f*, lealtad *f*.

allegory ['aligəri] *n* alegoría *f*.

allergy ['alədʒi] *n* alergia *f*. **allergic** *adj* alérgico.

alleviate [ə'li:vieit] *v* aliviar. **alleviation** *n* alivio *m*.

alley ['ali] *n* callejuela *f*, paseo *m*. **blind alley** callejón sin salida *m*.

alliance [ə'laiəns] *n* alianza *f*.

allied ['alaid] *adj* aliado.

alligator ['aligeitə] *n* caimán *m*.

alliteration [əlitə'reiʃən] *n* aliteración *f*.

allocate ['aləkeit] *v* asignar, distribuir. **allocation** *n* asignación *f*, repartimiento *m*.

allot [ə'lot] *v* asignar. **allotment** *n* lote *m*.

allow [ə'lau] *v* permitir, admitir. **allow for** tener en cuenta. **allowable** *adj* permisible, legítimo. **allowance** *n* ración *f*; pensión *f*. **monthly allowance** mesada *f*.

alloy ['aloi; v ə'loi] *n* aleación *f*; (*fig*) mezcla *f*. *v* alear, ligar.

allude [ə'lu:d] *v* aludir. **allusion** *n* alusión *f*. **allusive** *adj* alusivo.

allure [ə'ljuə] *v* seducir, fascinar. **allurement** *n* incentivo *m*, anzuelo *m*. **alluring** *adj* halagüeño, tentador.

ally ['alai; v ə'lai] *n* aliado, -a *m, f*, asociado, -a *m, f*. *v* unir.

almanac ['ɔ:lmənak] *n* almanaque *m*.

almighty [ɔ:l'maiti] *adj* omnipotente, todopoderoso.

almond ['a:mənd] *n* (*nut*) almendra *f*; (*tree*) almendro *m*.

almost ['ɔ:lmoust] *adv* casi.

alms [a:mz] *n* limosna *f*. **almsgiving** *n* caridad *f*. **almshouse** *n* hospicio *m*.

aloft [ə'loft] *adv* en alto, arriba.

alone [ə'loun] *adj* solo, único. *adv* solamente, a solas. **leave alone** dejar en paz.

along [ə'loŋ] *prep* a lo largo de. **along with** en compañía de, junto con. **come along!** ¡ven! **alongside** *adv* al lado; (*naut*) al costado de.

aloof [ə'lu:f] *adv* a distancia. *adj* altanero, reservado. **keep aloof** mantenerse alejado. **aloofness** *n* alejamiento *m*.

aloud [ə'laud] *adv* en voz alta, recio, alto.

alphabet ['alfəbit] *n* alfabeto *m*.

alpine ['alpain] *adj* alpino.

Alps [alps] *n* Alpes *m pl*.

already [ɔ:l'redi] *adv* ya.

also ['ɔ:lsou] *adv* también, además.

altar ['ɔ:ltə] *n* altar *m*. **high altar** altar mayor. **altar boy** monaguillo *m*. **altarpiece** retablo *m*.

alter ['ɔ:ltə] *v* cambiar, modificar, corregir, transformar; (*clothes*) arreglar. **alteration** *n* cambio *m*, modificación *f*; (*building*) reforma *f*.

alternate [ɔ:l'tə:nət; v 'ɔ:ltəneit] *adj* alterno. *v* alternar. **alternating current** corriente alterna *f*.

alternative [ɔ:l'tə:nətiv] *n* alternativa *f*. *adj* alternativo. **have no alternative but ...** no poder menos de ....

although [ɔ:l'ðou] *conj* aunque.

altitude ['altitju:d] *n* altura *f*, altitud *f*.

altogether [ɔ:ltə'geðə] *adv* en total, en conjunto, del todo.

altruistic [altru'istik] *adj* altruista. **altruism** *n* altruismo *m*. **altruist** *n* altruista *m, f*.

aluminium [alju'miniəm] *n* aluminio *m*.

always ['ɔ:lweiz] *adv* siempre.

am [am] *V* be.

amalgamate [ə'malgəmeit] *v* amalgamar, combinar, unir; combinarse, unirse. **amalgamation** *n* amalgamación *f*; mezcla *f*.

amass [ə'mas] *v* acumular, amontonar.

amateur ['amətə] *n, adj* aficionado, -a. **amateurish** *adj* de aficionado, superficial.

amaze [ə'meiz] *v* asombrar, sorprender, congrave;fundir. **amazement** *n* asombro *m*.

amazing *adj* asombroso.
ambassador [am'basədə] *n* embajador, -a *m* f.
amber ['ambə] *n* ámbar *m*. *adj* ambarino.
ambidextrous [ambi'dekstrəs] *adj* ambidextro.
ambiguous [am'bigjuəs] *adj* ambiguo. **ambiguity** *n* ambigüedad f.
ambition [am'biʃən] *n* ambición f. **ambitious** *adj* ambicioso.
ambivalent [am'bivələnt] *adj* ambivalente.
amble ['ambl] *v* amblar, andar lentamente. *n* paso de andadura *m*.
ambulance ['ambjuləns] *n* ambulancia f.
ambush ['ambuʃ] *n* emboscada f, asechanza f. *v* emboscar, asechar.
ameliorate [ə'mi:liəreit] *v* mejorar. **amelioration** *n* mejora f.
amenable [ə'mi:nəbl] *adj* tratable, dócil, sujeto.
amend [ə'mend] *v* enmendar, modificar, rectificar. **amendment** *n* enmienda f. **make amends** dar satisfacción, indemnizar.
amenity [ə'mi:nəti] *n* amenidad f, comodidad f.
America [ə'merikə] *n* América f. **American** *n, adj* americano, -a *m, f*.
amethyst ['aməθist] *n* amatista f.
amiable ['eimiəbl] *adj* amistoso, afable.
amicable ['amikəbl] *adj* amigable.
amid [ə'mid] *prep* entre, rodeado por, en medio de.
amiss [ə'mis] *adv* mal, de más, impropiamente. **take amiss** llevar a mal.
ammonia [ə'mouniə] *n* amoníaco *m*.
ammunition [amju'niʃən] *n* municiones f *pl*.
amnesia [am'ni:ziə] *n* amnesia f.
amnesty ['amnəsti] *n* amnistía f.
amoeba [ə'mi:bə] *n* ameba f.
among [ə'mʌŋ] *prep* entre, en medio de.
amoral [ei'morəl] *adj* amoral.
amorous ['amərəs] *adj* amoroso.
amorphous [ə'mo:fəs] *adj* amorfo.
amount [ə'maunt] *n* cantidad f, importe *m*, suma f. *v* **amount to** llegar a, subir a, valer. **gross amount** importe bruto *m*. **net amount** importe neto *m*. **it amounts to this** se reduce a esto.
ampere ['ampeə] *n* amperio *m*.

amphetamine [am'fetəmi:n] *n* anfetamina f.
amphibian [am'fibiən] *nm, adj* anfibio.
amphitheatre ['amfiθiətə] *n* anfiteatro *m*.
ample ['ampl] *adj* amplio, abundante; (*enough*) bastante, suficiente.
amplify ['amplifai] *v* ampliar, amplificar, aumentar. **amplifier** *n* amplificador *m*.
amputate ['ampjuteit] *v* amputar. **amputation** *n* amputación f.
amuse [ə'mju:z] *v* divertir, distraer, entretener. **amuse oneself** divertirse. **amusement** *n* diversión f, entretenimiento *m*, recreo *m*; (*hobby*) pasatiempo *m*. **amusement arcade** recreativos *m pl*. **amusement park** parque de atracciones *m*. **amusing** *adj* divertido, gracioso.
anachronism [ə'nakrənizəm] *n* anacronismo *m*. **anachronistic** *adj* anacrónico.
anaemia [ə'ni:miə] *n* anemia f. **anaemic** *adj* anémico.
anaesthetic [anəs'θetik] *nm, adj* anestésico.
anagram ['anəgram] *n* anagrama *m*.
analogy [ə'nalədʒi] *n* analogía f. **analogous** *adj* análogo.
analysis [ən'aləsis] *n, pl* -ses análisis *m*. **analyst** *n* analista *m, f*. **analytic(al)** *adj* analítico.
anarchy ['anəki] *n* anarquía f. **anarchic** *adj* anárquico. **anarchist** *n* anarquista *m, f*.
anathema [ə'naθəmə] *n* anatema *m*.
anatomy [ə'natəmi] *n* anatomía f. **anatomical** *adj* anatómico.
ancestor ['ansestə] *n* antepasado *m*. **ancestral** *adj* ancestral, hereditario. **ancestry** *n* linaje *m*.
anchor ['aŋkə] *n* ancla f; (*fig*) áncora f. *v* anclar, fijar, fondear.
anchovy ['antʃəvi] *n* anchoa f.
ancient ['einʃənt] *adj* anciano, antiguo. **the ancients** *pl n* los antiguos *m pl*. **from ancient times** de antiguo.
ancillary [an'siləri] *adj* auxiliar.
and [and] *conj* y, e.
anecdote ['anikdout] *n* anécdota f.
anemone [ə'neməni] *n* anémona f.
anew [ə'nju:] *adv* de nuevo, otra vez.
angel ['eindʒəl] *n* ángel *m*. **angelic** *adj* angélico.
anger ['aŋgə] *n* cólera f, ira f, enojo *m*. *v*

enojar, enfadar, encolerizar. **angry** *adj* enojado, enfadado.

angina [an'dʒainə] *n* angina *f*. **angina pectoris** angina de pecho.

angle ['aŋgl] *n* ángulo *m*, rincón *m*; (*viewpoint*) punto de vista *m*.

angling ['aŋgliŋ] *n* pesca con caña *f*. **angler** *n* pescador, -a *m*, *f*.

anguish ['aŋgwiʃ] *n* angustia *f*, agonía *f*, dolor *m*.

animal ['animəl] *n* animal *m*, bestia *f*. *adj* animal. **animal kingdom** reino animal *m*. **animal spirits** brío *m*, energía *f*, exuberancia vital *f*.

animate ['animeit; *adj* 'animət] *v* animar, alentar, vivificar. *adj* viviente, animado. **animated** *adj* animado, vivo. **animated cartoon** dibujo animado.

animosity [ani'mosəti] *n* animosidad *f*, hostilidad *f*.

aniseed ['anisi:d] *n* grano de anís *m*.

ankle ['aŋkl] *n* tobillo *m*.

annals ['anlz] *pl n* anales *m pl*.

annex ['aneks; *v* ə'neks] *n* anexo *m*. *v* anexar, anexionar; unir, juntar. **annexation** *n* anexión *f*.

annihilate [ə'naiəleit] *v* aniquilar. **annihilation** *n* aniquilación *f*.

anniversary [ani'və:səri] *n* aniversario *m*.

annotate ['anəteit] *v* anotar, acotar, glosar. **annotation** *n* anotación *f*, nota *f*.

announce [ə'nauns] *v* anunciar, publicar, proclamar. **announcement** *n* anuncio *m*, aviso *m*, publicación *f*; (*of engagement*) participación *f*. **announcer** *n* annuncidor, -a *m*, *f*; (*radio*) locutor, -a *m*, *f*.

annoy [ə'noi] *v* molestar, irritar, fastidiar. **annoyance** *n* molestia *f*, disgusto *m*. **annoyed** *adj* enojado. **annoying** *adj* fastidioso, enojoso, molesto.

annual ['anjuəl] *adj* anual. *n* (*book*) anuario *m*; (*plant*) planta anual *f*.

annul [ə'nʌl] *v* anular; (*law*) abrogar. **annulment** *n* anulación *f*.

Annunciation [ə,nʌnsi'eifən] *n* (*rel*) Anunciación *f*.

anode ['anoud] *n* ánodo *m*.

anomaly [ə'noməli] *n* anomalía *f*. **anomalous** *adj* anómalo.

anonymous [ə'noniməs] *adj* anónimo.

anorak ['anərak] *n* anorak *m*.

anorexia (*nervosa*) [anə'reksiə] *n* anorexia

(nerviosa) *f*.

another [ə'nʌðə] *adj* otro. *pron* otro, -a *m*, *f*. **one after another** uno después de otro.

answer ['a:nsə] *n* contestación *f*, respuesta *f*; (*solution*) solución *f*; (*math*) resultado *m*. *v* contestar, responder; (*a bell*) acudir; (*door*) abrir. **answer back** replicar. **answer by return** contestar a vuelta de correo. **answerable** *adj* responsable. **answering machine** contestador automático *m*.

ant [ant] *n* hormiga *f*.

antagonize [an'tagənaiz] *v* antagonizar, contender. **antagonism** *n* antagonismo *m*, oposición *f*. **antagonist** *n* antagonista *m*, *f*. **antagonistic** *adj* antagónico.

antecedent [anti'si:dənt] *nm*, *adj* antecedente.

antelope ['antəloup] *n* antilope *m*.

antenatal [anti'neitl] *adj* antenatal.

antenatal [anti'neitl] *adj* prenatal

antenna [an'tenə] *n* antena *f*.

anthem ['anθəm] *n* motete *m*. **national anthem** himno nacional *m*.

anthology [an'θolədʒi] *n* antología *f*.

anthropology [anθrə'polədʒi] *n* antropología *f*.

anti-aircraft [anti'eəkra:ft] *adj* anti-aéreo.

antibiotic [antibai'otik] *nm, adj* antibiótico.

antibody ['anti,bodi] *n* anticuerpo *m*.

anticipate [an'tisipeit] *v* prever, esperar; anticiparse a. **anticipation** *n* anticipación *f*, esperanza *f*, adelantamiento *m*. **in anticipation of** en espera de.

anticlimax [anti'klaimaks] *n* anticlimax *m*.

anticlockwise [anti'klokwaiz] *adj* en dirección contraria a las agujas del reloj.

antics ['antiks] *pl n* cabriola *f sing*, travesura *f sing*, payasadas *f pl*.

anticyclone [anti'saikloun] *n* anticiclón *m*.

antidepressant [antidi'presənt] *adj* antidepresivo

antidote ['antidout] *n* antídoto *m*, contraveneno *m*.

antifreeze ['antifri:z] *n* anticongelante *m*.

antipathy [an'tipəθi] *n* antipatía *f*, aversión *f*.

antique [an'ti:k] *n* antigualla *f*, antigüedad *f*. *adj* antiguo. **antique dealer** anticuario *m*. **antique shop** tienda de antigüedades *f*. **antiquity** *n* antigüedad *f*.

anti-Semitic [antisə'mitik] *adj* antisemitico. **anti-Semitism** n antisemitismo m.

antiseptic [anti'septik] nm, adj antiséptico.

antisocial [anti'soufəl] adj antisocial.

anti-tank [anti'tæŋk] adj antitanque.

antithesis [an'tiθəsis] n, pl -ses antítesis f.

antler ['antlə] n asta f, cuerno m.

antonym ['antənim] n antónimo m.

anus ['einəs] n ano m. **anal** adj anal.

anvil ['anvil] n yunque m.

anxious ['aŋkfəs] adj ancioso, preocupado, inquieto. **anxiety** n inquietud f, ansiedad f, intranquilidad f.

any ['eni] adv cualquier; (some) algún, ningún; (every) todo. pron alguno, -a m, f; cualquiera m, f; ninguno, -a m, f. adv algo. **anybody** or **anyone** pron cualquiera, alguien, nadie. **anyhow** adv de cualquier modo. **anything** n algo m; (negative) nada f. **anywhere** adv dondequiera.

apart [ə'pa:t] adv aparte.

apartment [ə'pa:tmənt] n apartamento m, cuarto m, habitación f; (flat) piso m.

apathy ['apəθi] n apatía f, indiferencia f. **apathetic** adj apático.

ape [eip] n simio m, mono, -a m, f. v imitar.

aperitif [ə'peritiv] nm, adj aperitivo.

aperture ['apətjuə] n abertura f, orificio m, agujero m.

apex ['eipeks] n ápice m.

aphrodisiac [afrə'diziak] n afrodisíaco m.

apiece [ə'pi:s] adv por persona, por cabeza, cada uno.

apology [ə'polədʒi] n disculpa f, apologia f, excusa f. **apologize** v disculparse, pedir perdón; (regret) sentir.

apoplexy ['apəpleksi] n apoplejía f. **apoplectic** adj apoplético.

apostle [ə'posl] n apóstol m.

apostrophe [ə'postrəfi] n (punctuation) apóstrofo m; (speech) apóstrofe m.

appal [ə'po:l] v espantar, aterrar. **appalling** adj espantoso, horrible.

apparatus [apə'reitəs] n aparato m, máquina f.

apparent [ə'parənt] adj aparente; notable, obvio, evidente, claro. **apparently** adv al parecer.

apparition [apə'rifən] n aparición f, fantasma m.

appeal [ə'pi:l] v (law) apelar; (attract) atraer. n (law) apelación f; atractivo m. **appeal**

against suplicar de.

appear [ə'piə] v aparecer; (seem) parecer; (in court) comparecer. **appearance** n aparición f; (aspect) apariencia f, aspecto m; (arrival) llegada f.

appease [ə'pi:z] v aplacar, apaciguar. **appeasement** n aplacamiento m, apaciguamiento m.

appendix [ə'pendiks] n apéndice m. **appendicitis** n apendicitis f.

appetite ['apitait] n apetito m. **have an appetite** tener ganas. **appetizing** adj apetitoso.

applaud [ə'plo:d] v aplaudir. **applause** n aplauso m.

apple ['apl] n (fruit) manzana f; (tree) manzano m. **apple sauce** compota de manzana f.

apply [ə'plai] v dirigirse a, recurrir; aplicar; (use) emplear; (for a job) proponerse a. **apply oneself to** dedicarse a. **appliance** n aparato m. **applicable** adj aplicable. **applicant** n aspirante m, f. **application** n aplicación f.

appoint [ə'point] v nombrar, designar. **be appointed to** colocarse a. **be appointed as** ser nombrado. **appointment** n puesto m, empleo m; (assignation) cita f. **make an appointment with** citar.

apportion [ə'po:fən] v distribuir, repartir.

appraisal [ə'preizl] n valoración f, estimación f. **appraise** v valorizar, tasar.

appreciate [ə'pri:fieit] v apreciar, darse cuenta de; (affection) encarecer; (in value) tener en alza. **appreciation** n apreciación f, aprecio m; (understanding) percepción f; (of shares, etc.) aumento de valor m.

apprehend [apri'hend] v (arrest) prender, capturar; (understand) aprehender, percibir; (fear) temer. **apprehension** n (arrest) aprehensión f; (understanding) comprensión f; (fear) aprensión f. **apprehensive** adj aprensivo.

apprentice [ə'prentis] n aprendiz, -a m f. **apprenticeship** n aprendizaje m.

approach [ə'proutf] v acercarse a, aproximar; (speak to) hablar con. n acercamiento m, aproximación f; (arrival) llegada f; (entrance) entrada f.

appropriate [ə'prouprieit; adj ə'proupriət] v tomar posesión de, apropiar; (assign) asignar, destinar. adj propio, pertinente, correspondiente. **appropriateness** n conveniencia f.

approve [ə'pru:v] v aprobar. **approval** n aprobación f. **on approval** a prueba. **approved** adj bien visto.

approximate [ə'prɒksimeit; adj ə'prɒksimət] v aproximar, aproximarse. adj aproximado. **approximately** adv poco más o menos.

apricot ['eiprikɒt] n (fruit) albaricoque m; (tree) albaricoquero m.

April ['eiprəl] n abril m.

apron ['eiprən] n delantal m; (stage) proscenio m.

apt [apt] adj apto; propenso; (suitable) apropiado.

aptitude ['aptitju:d] n aptitud f.

aqualung ['akwəlʌŋ] n aparato de aire comprimido m.

aquarium [ə'kweəriəm] n acuario m.

Aquarius [ə'kweəriəs] n Acuario m.

aquatic [ə'kwatik] adj acuático.

aqueduct ['akwidʌkt] n acueducto m.

Arab ['arəb] n(m + f), adj árabe. **Arabia** n Arabia f. **Arabic** adj arábigo.

arable ['arəbl] adj arable.

arbitrary ['a:bitrəri] adj arbitrario.

arbitrate ['a:bitreit] v arbitrar. **arbitration** n arbitraje m. **arbiter** or **arbitrator** n árbitro, -a m, f.

arc [a:k] n arco m. **arc lamp** lámpara de arco f.

arcade [a:'keid] n arcada f, galería f.

arch¹ [a:tʃ] n arco m. v arquear.

arch² [a:tʃ] adj (chief) principal; archi-.

archaeology [a:ki'ɒlədʒi] n arqueología f. **archaeologist** n arqueólogo, -a m, f.

archaic [a:'keiik] adj arcaico, arcaizante.

archbishop [a:tʃ'biʃəp] n arzobispo m.

archduke [a:tʃ'dju:k] n archiduque m.

archery ['a:tʃəri] n tiro con arco m. **archer** n arquero, -a m, f.

archetype ['a:kitaip] n arquetipo m.

archipelago [a:ki'peləgou] n archipiélago m.

architect ['a:kitekt] n arquitecto, -a m, f. **architecture** n arquitectura f.

archives ['a:kaivz] n pl archivo m sing.

arctic ['a:ktik] adj ártico. **the Arctic** el Ártico.

ardent ['a:dənt] adj ardiente, apasionado.

ardour ['a:də] n ardor m.

arduous ['a:djuəs] adj arduo.

are [a:] V be.

area ['eəriə] n área f, superficie f; extensión f.

arena [ə'ri:nə] n arena f, liza f.

Argentina [a:dʒən'ti:nə] n Argentina f. **Argentinian** n, adj argentino, -a m, f.

argue ['a:gju:] v debatir, disputar, discutir. **argue against** oponer. **arguable** adj discutible. **argument** n argumento m. **argumentative** adj contencioso.

arid ['arid] adj árido, seco.

Aries ['eəri:z] n (astrol) Aries m.

***arise** [ə'raiz] v elevarse, subir; (revolt) sublevarse; (from bed) levantarse.

aristocracy [ari'stɒkrəsi] n aristocracia f. **aristocrat** n aristócrata m, f. **aristocratic** adj aristocrático.

arithmetic [ə'riθmətik] n aritmética f.

ark [a:k] n arca f. **Noah's Ark** arca de Noé f.

arm¹ [a:m] n (limb) brazo m. **armchair** n sillón m. **arm in arm** de bracete, de bracero. **armpit** n sobaco m. **within arm's reach** al alcance del brazo.

arm² [a:m] n arma f. v armar. **to arms!** ¡a las armas! **take up arms** alzarse en armas. **under arms** sobre las armas.

armistice ['a:mistis] n armisticio m.

armour ['a:mə] n armadura f, arnés m; (ships, vehicles) blindaje m. v blindar, acorazar. **armour-plate** n coraza f. **armoury** n armería f.

army ['a:mi] n ejército m.

aroma [ə'roumə] n aroma m, fragancia f. **aromatic** adj aromático.

around [ə'raund] prep alrededor de, cerca de; a la vuelta de. adv alrededor, en torno, por todas partes.

arouse [ə'rauz] v despertar, excitar.

arouse [ə'rauz] v despertar

arrange [ə'reindʒ] v arreglar, disponer; organizar; (music) adaptar; concertarse. **arrangement** n arreglo m; (agreement) acuerdo m; (music) adaptación f. **arrangements** pl n preparativos m pl.

array [ə'rei] v ataviar, poner en orden de batalla. n (dress) atavío m; (troops) formación f.

arrears [ə'riəz] pl n atrasos m pl. **in arrears** atrasado en pagos.

arrest [ə'rest] v arrestar, detener. n (stop) parada f; (detention) detención f. **under**

arrest bajo arresto.

arrive [ə'raiv] v llegar. **arrival** n llegada f, venida f. **on arrival** al llegar.

arrogant ['arəgənt] adj arrogante, altanero. **arrogance** n arrogancia f.

arrow ['arou] n flecha f, saeta f.

arse [a:s] n (vulgar) culo m, ojete m.

arsenal ['a:sənl] n arsenal m.

arsenic ['a:snik] n arsénico m.

arson ['a:sn] n incendiarismo m, incendio premeditado m.

art [a:t] n arte m; (cunning) artificio m. **art gallery** museo de pinturas m. **artful** adj artero, mañoso.

artery ['a:təri] n arteria f.

arthritis [a:'θraitis] n artritis f.

artichoke ['a:titʃouk] n alcachofa f.

article ['a:tikl] n artículo m; (object) objeto m.

articulate [a:'tikjuleit; adj a:'tikjulət] v articular. adj claro, distinto.

artifice ['a:tifis] n artificio m.

artificial [a:ti'fiʃəl] adj artificial, falso. **artificiality** n lo artificial. **artificial respiration** respiracíon artificial f.

artillery [a:'tiləri] n artillería f.

artisan [a:'ti'zan] n artesano, -a m, f.

artist ['a:tist] n artista m, f. **artistic** adj artistico.

as [az] adv tan. prep, conj como, ya que, según, a medida que; (when) cuando; (since) puesto que; (because) porque; (although) aunque. **as a rule** por regla general. **as far as** en cuanto a. **as from** desde. **as good as** tan bueno como. **as if** como si. **as it were** en cierto modo. **as soon as** en cuanto. **as soon as possible** cuanto antes. **as usual** como de costumbre. **as well** también. **as well as** además de.

asbestos [az'bestos] n asbesto m.

ascend [ə'send] v subir. **ascendancy** n ascendiente m. **be in the ascendant** ir en aumento. **ascension** n subida f. **ascent** n subida f; (slope) cuesta f.

ascetic [ə'setik] adj ascético. n asceta m, f.

ash¹ [aʃ] n (cinder) ceniza f, cenizas f pl. **ashtray** n cenicero m.

ash² [aʃ] n (tree) fresno m.

ashamed [ə'ʃeimd] adj avergonzado.

ashore [ə'ʃo:] adv a tierra. **go ashore** desembarcar.

Ash Wednesday n miércoles de ceniza m.

Asia ['eiʃə] n Asia f. **Asian** n, adj asiático, -a m, f.

aside [ə'said] adv aparte, a un lado. n (theatre) aparte m.

ask [a:sk] v preguntar, pedir, invitar. **ask for trouble** buscársela. **for the asking** sin más que pedirlo.

askew [ə'skju:] adj a un lado.

asleep [ə'sli:p] adj, adv dormido. **fall asleep** dormirse.

asparagus [ə'sparəgəs] n espárrago m.

aspect ['aspekt] n aspecto m, vista f.

asphalt ['asfalt] n asfalto m.

asphyxiate [əs'fiksieit] v asfixiar.

aspire [ə'spaiə] v aspirar. **aspiration** n aspiración f.

aspirin ['aspərin] n aspirina f.

ass [as] n asno m. **asinine** adj asnal.

assail [ə'seil] v atacar. **assailant** n asaltador, -a m, f.

assassinate [ə'sasineit] v asesinar. **assassin** n asesino, -a m, f. **assassination** n asesinato m.

assault [ə'so:lt] n asalto m. v asaltar.

assemble [ə'sembl] v (people) convocar; (things) juntar; (machines) armar. **assemblage** n reunión f. **assembly** n asamblea f **assembly line** linea de montaje f.

assent [ə'sent] v asentir. n asentimiento m.

assert [ə'sə:t] v afirmar, declarar. **assertion** n afirmación f, aserción f; **assertive** asertivo.

assess [ə'ses] v evaluar, asesorar. **assessment** n valoración f.

asset ['aset] n ventaja f. **assets** pl n activo m sing, haber m sing, bienes m pl.

assiduous [ə'sidjuəs] adj asiduo, aplicado.

assign [ə'sain] v asignar, señalar; (law) consignar; (goods) traspasar. **assignment** n asignación f.

assimilate [ə'simileit] v asimilar, incorporarse. **assimilation** n asimilación f.

assist [ə'sist] v asistir, ayudar. **assistance** n ayuda f. **assistant** n ayudante m, f, colaborador m.

associate [ə'sousiət; v ə'sousieit] n socio, -a m, f, compañero, -a m, f, cómplice m, f. v asociar, juntar. **associate with** ir con. **association** n asociación f, sociedad f.

assorted [ə'so:tid] adj surtido, mezclado.

assortment n clasificación f, mezcla f.

assume [ə'sjuːm] v asumir, tomar; (*suppose*) suponer. **assumed** adj fingido. **assuming that** dado que. **assumption** n asunción f.

assure [ə'ʃuə] v asegurar, garantizar. **assurance** n seguridad f, certeza f; (*comm*) seguro m. **assuredly** adv seguramente.

asterisk ['astərisk] n asterisco m.

asthma ['asmə] n asma f.

astonish [ə'stoniʃ] v asombrar. **astonishment** n asombro m.

astound [ə'staund] v aturdir. **be astounded** quedarse muerto.

astray [ə'strei] adv desviado. **go astray** perderse.

astride [ə'straid] adv a horcajadas. prep a horcajadas sobre.

astringent [ə'strindʒənt] adj astringente.

astrology [ə'strolədʒi] n astrologia f. **astrologer** n astrólogo, -a m, f.

astronaut ['astrənɔːt] n astronauta m, f.

astronomy [ə'stronəmi] n astronomia f. **astronomer** n astrónomo, -a m, f. **astronomical** adj astronómico.

astute [ə'stjuːt] adj astuto, agudo. **astuteness** n astucia f, sagacidad f.

asunder [ə'sʌndə] adv separadamente, en dos.

asylum [ə'sailəm] n (*refuge*) asilo m; (*for the insane*) manicomio m.

at [at] prep a, en.

ate [et] V eat.

atheism ['eiθiizəm] n ateismo m. **atheist** n ateo, -a m, f.

Athens ['aθinz] n Atenas f. **Athenian** n(m + f), adj ateniense.

athlete ['aθliːt] n atleta m, f. **athletic** adj atlético. **athletics** n atletismo m sing.

Atlantic [ət'lantik] n Atlántico m. adj atlántico.

atlas ['atləs] n atlas m.

atmosphere ['atməsfiə] n atmósfera f, aire m; (*feeling*) ambiente m. **atmospheric** adj atmosférico. **atmospherics** pl n perturbaciones atmosféricas f pl.

atom ['atəm] n átomo m. **atomic** adj atómico.

atone [ə'toun] v expiar. **atonement** n expiación f.

atrocious [ə'trouʃəs] adj atroz. **atrocity** n atrocidad f.

attach [ə'tatʃ] v atar, adherir, pegar. **attach oneself to** asociarse con. **attachment** n unión f; (*hook*) enganche m; (*friendship*) amistad f.

attaché [ə'taʃei] n agregado m. **attaché case** maletin m.

attack [ə'tak] v atacar. n ataque m; (*mil*) ofensiva f. **attacker** n atacador, -a m, f.

attain [ə'tein] v lograr, alcanzar. **attainable** adj asequible, realizable. **attainment** n logro m. **attainments** pl n prendas f pl.

attempt [ə'tempt] n tentativa f. v procurar, tratar de.

attend [ə'tend] v atender, servir; concurrir; (*the sick*) asistir; (*listen*) escuchar. **attendance** n servicio m, asistencia f; (*audience*) auditorio m. **attendant** n criado, -a m, f, servidor, -a m, f.

attention [ə'tenʃən] n atención f. **call attention to** destacar, hacer presente. **pay attention** prestar atención. **attentive** adj atento, cortés. **attentiveness** n cuidado m.

attic ['atik] n desván m, sotabanco m.

attire [ə'taiə] n atavío m, ropaje m, traje m, adorno m. v ataviar, vestir.

attitude ['atitjuːd] n actitud f, postura f, ademán m.

attorney [ə'təːni] n (*agent*) apoderado, -a m, f; (*solicitor*) abogado, -a m, f. **power of attorney** poderes m pl.

attract [ə'trakt] v atraer, llamar. **attraction** n atracción f, imán m. **attractive** adj atractivo, atrayente.

attribute ['atribjuːt; v ə'tribjuːt] n atributo m. v atribuir. **attributable** adj atribuible. **attribution** n atributo m.

attrition [ə'triʃən] n atrición f.

atypical [ei'tipikl] adj atípico.

aubergine ['oubəʒiːn] n berenjena f.

auburn ['oːbən] adj castaño rojizo.

auction ['oːkʃən] n remate m, almoneda f, subasta f. v rematar, subastar. **auctioneer** n subastador, -a m f.

audacious [oː'deiʃəs] adj audaz, arrojado. **audacity** n audacia f, arrojo m, atrevimiento m.

audible ['oːdəbl] adj audible. **audibility** n audibilidad f.

audience ['oːdjəns] n audiencia f; oyentes m pl.

audiovisual [oːdiou'viʒuəl] adj audiovisual.

audit ['oːdit] v intervenir. n intervención f,

ajuste (de cuentas) *m.* **auditor** *n* inventor, -a *m,f*, contador, -a *m,f.*

audition [oːˈdiʃən] *n* audición *f. v* dar audición.

auditorium [oːdiˈtoːriəm] *n* auditorio *m*, sala de espectáculos *f.*

augment [oːgˈment] *v* aumentar, engrosar; acrecentarse.

august [oːˈgʌst] *adj* augusto.

August [ˈoːgəst] *n* agosto *m.*

aunt [aːnt] *n* tía *f.* **great-aunt** *n* tía abuela *f.*

aura [ˈoːrə] *n* aura *f*; exhalación *f.*

auspicious [oːˈspiʃəs] *adj* propicio.

austere [oːˈstiə] *adj* austero, severo. **austerity** *n* austeridad *f*, severidad *f.*

Australia [oˈstreiljə] *n* Australia *f.* **Australian** *n, adj* australiano, -a *m, f.*

Austria [ˈostriə] *n* Austria *f.* **Austrian** *n, adj* austríaco, -a *m, f.*

authentic [oːˈθentik] *adj* auténtico

author [ˈoːθə] *n* autor, -a *m, f.*

authority [oːˈθorəti] *n* autoridad *f.* **on good authority** de buena fuente. **authoritarian** *adj* autoritario.

authorize [ˈoːθəraiz] *v* autorizar. **authorization** *n* autorización *f.*

autism [ˈoːtizəm] *n* autismo *m*

autistic [oːˈtizætic] *adj* autístico.

autobiography [oːtoubaiˈografi] *n* autobiografía *f.* **autobiographical** *adj* autobiográfico.

autocratic [oːtouˈkratik] *adj* autocrático. **autocrat** *n* autócrata *m, f.*

autograph [ˈoːtəgraːf] *n* autógrafo *m. v* firmar, dedicar.

automatic [oːtəˈmatik] *adj* automático. **automation** *n* automatización *f.*

automobile [ˈoːtəməbiːl] *n* automóvil *m.*

autonomous [oːˈtonəməs] *adj* autónomo.

autopsy [ˈoːtopsi] *n* autopsia *f.*

autumn [ˈoːtəm] *n* otoño *m.* **autumnal** *adj* otoñal.

auxiliary [oːgˈziljəri] *adj* auxiliar. *n* auxiliador *m.*

avail [əˈveil] *v* servir, valer, importar; aprovechar. **avail oneself of** aprovecharse de. **to no avail** en balde.

available [əˈveiləbl] *adj* útil, disponible.

availability *n* utilidad *f*, disponibilidad *f.*

avalanche [ˈavəlaːnʃ] *n* avalancha *f*, alud *m.*

avarice [ˈavəris] *n* avaricia *f*, codicia *f.* **avaricious** *adj* avariento.

avenge [əˈvendʒ] *v* vengar, vindicar. **avenge oneself** vengarse de. **avenger** *n* vengador, -a *m, f.*

avenue [ˈavinjuː] *n* avenida *f.*

average [ˈavəridʒ] *n* promedio *m*, término medio *m. adj* de promedio, corriente. *v* hallar el término medio. **on average** por regla general.

aversion [əˈvəːʃən] *n* aversión *f.* **averse** *adj* opuesto. **be averse to** ser enemigo de.

avert [əˈvəːt] *v* apartar; (*avoid*) evitar.

aviary [ˈeiviəri] *n* avería *f.*

aviation [eiviˈeiʃən] *n* aviación *f.* **aviator** *n* aviador, -a *m, f.*

avid [ˈavid] *adj* ávido, codicioso, voraz. **avidity** *n* avidez *f*, codicia *f.*

avocado [avəˈkaːdou] *n* aguacate *m.*

avoid [əˈvoid] *v* evitar, eludir, evadir. **avoidance** *n* evitación *f.*

await [əˈweit] *v* esperar, aguardar.

*****awake** [əˈweik] *v* despertar; despertarse. *adj* despierto, atento (a). **awakening** *n* despertamiento *m.*

award [əˈwoːd] *n* fallo *m*, premio *m*, recompensa *f. v* otorgar, conceder, conferir.

aware [əˈweə] *adj* enterado, vigilante, consciente. **become aware of** darse cuenta de. **make aware of** hacer saber. **awareness** *n* conocimiento *m.*

away [əˈwei] *adv* a lo lejos, ausente, fuera, en otro lugar.

awe [oː] *n* temor *m*, pasmo *m*; reverencia *f. v* intimidar, atemorizar. **awesome** *adj* pavoroso, imponente.

awful [ˈoːful] *adj* tremendo, atroz, terrible, espantoso. **how awful!** ¡¡qué barbaridad! **awfully** *adv* (*coll*) muy.

awkward [ˈoːkwəd] *adj* difícil; (*clumsy*) desmañado; (*ungraceful*) sin gracia.

awl [oːl] *n* punzón *m*, lezna *f.*

awning [ˈoːniŋ] *n* toldo *m.*

axe [aks] *n* hacha *f.*

axiom [ˈaksiəm] *n* axioma *m.*

axis [ˈaksis] *n* eje *m.*

axle [ˈaksl] *n* eje *m*, peón *m*, árbol *m.*

B

babble ['babl] v balbucear; garlar. n murmullo m, cháchara f.

baboon [bə'bu:n] n babuino m.

baby ['beibi] n bebé m, criatura f, nene m; (*animals*) crío m. **babyhood** n niñez f. **babyish** adj infantil. **baby-sitter** canguro m, f.

bachelor ['batʃələ] n soltero m; (*of Arts or Science*) licenciado m, bachiller m.

back [bak] n (*anat*) **espalda** f; dorso m; (*sport*) defensa f. **back-up** (*computer*) copia de seguridad f; (*support*) apoyo m. adj trasero, posterior, de atrás; (*of pay, etc.*) atrasado. adv atrás; detrás; otra vez, de nuevo. v retroceder; (*support*) apoyar; (*bet on*) apostar a. **back down** abandonar. **back out** echarse atrás; (*retract*) desdecirse.

backache ['bakeik] n dolor de espaldas m.

backbone ['bakboun] n espinazo m.

backdate [,bak'deit] v poner fecha atrasada.

backfire [,bak'faiə] n petardeo m. v petardear.

backgammon ['bak,gamən] n chaquete m.

backhand ['bakhand] n (*sport*) revés m. **back-handed** adj de revés; (*fig*) ambiguo.

backing ['bakiŋ] n forro m; (*support*) apoyo m; (*lining*) refuerzo m; (*betting*) el apostar (a) m.

backlash ['baklaʃ] n reacción f.

backlog ['baklog] n atrasos m pl.

backside ['baksaid] n trasero m, parte trasera f.

backward ['bakwəd] adj atrasado, vuelto hacia atrás. **backwardness** n atraso m, torpeza f. **backward and forward** de acá para allá.

backwards ['bakwədz] adv hacia atrás, al revés.

backwater ['bakwo:tə] n (*pool*) remanso m.

bacon ['beikən] n tocino m.

bacteria [bak'tiəriə] n pl bacteria f pl.

bad [bad] adj malo; (*ill*) enfermo; (*rotten*) podrido; (*debt*) incobrable; (*dangerous*) peligroso; (*coin*) falso; (*pain*) fuerte; (*unlucky*) desgraciado. **bad-tempered** adj de mal genio. **from bad to worse** de mal en peor. **badly** adv mal; (*seriously*) gravemente.

badge [badʒ] n insignia f, marca f, divisa f.

badger ['badʒə] n tejón m. v molestar.

badminton ['badmintən] n volante m, badminton m.

baffle ['bafl] v frustrar, desconcertar, confundir. **baffling** adj desconcertante, difícil; (*person*) enigmático.

bag [bag] n bolsa f, saco m, valija f; (*sewing*) costurera f; (*suitcase*) maleta f. v ensacar; (*coll, esp, game*) matar, tomar. **pack one's bags** liar el petate. **baggage** m equipaje m.

baggy ['bagi] adj holgado.

bagpipes ['bagpaips] n pl gaita f.

bail¹ [beil] n (*law*) fianza f, caución f. v poner bajo fianza.

bail² or **bale** [beil] v **bail out** (*flooded boat*) achicar, baldear; (*from aircraft*) lanzarse en paracaídas.

bailiff ['beilif] n (*law*) alguacil m; (*of estate*) capataz m.

bait [beit] n (*fishing*) cebo m, anzuelo m; (*lure*) añagaza f. v cebar, azuzar; (*annoy*) molestar.

bake [beik] v cocer al horno. **baker's dozen** docena del fraile f. **baker** m panadero, -a m, f. **bakery** n panadería f. **baking powder** levadura en polvo f.

balance ['baləns] n equilibrio m; (*scales*) balanza f; (*comm*) balance m. v equilibrar; (*comm*) saldar.

balcony ['balkəni] n balcón m, galería f; (*theatre*) anfiteatro m.

bald [bo:ld] adj calvo, pelado; (*tyre*) desgastado. **baldness** n calvicie f.

bale¹ [beil] n fardo m, bala f. v embalar.

bale² V **bail²**.

ball¹ [bo:l] n pelota f; globo m, bola f; (*shot*) bala f; (*of wool*) ovillo m; (*of the foot*) planta del pie f. **ball-and-socket joint** articulación esférica f. **ball bearings** cojinete de bolas m sing. **ball-point pen** bolígrafo m.

ball² [bo:l] n (*dance*) baile m. **fancy-dress ball** baile de disfraces. **ballroom** n salón de baile m.

ballad ['baləd] n balada f, romance m, trova f; (*music*) canción f.

ballast ['baləst] n lastre m. v lastrar.

ballet ['balei] n ballet m, danza f. **ballet dancer** bailarín, bailarina m, f.

ballistic [bə'listik] adj balístico. **ballistic**

missile proyectil balístico *m*.

balloon [bə'lu:n] *n* globo *m*. **balloonist** *n* aeronauta *m, f*.

ballot ['balət] *n* votación *f*, sufragio *m*. *v* votar, balotar. **ballot-box** *n* urna electoral *f*.

bamboo [bam'bu:] *n* bambú *m*.

ban [ban] *n* prohibición *f*, interdicción *f*. *v* prohibir, proscribir.

banal [bə'na:l] *adj* trivial, trillado.

banana [bə'na:nə] *n (fruit and tree)* plátano *m*; (*S. Am.*) *(fruit)* banana, *(tree)* banano *m*.

band¹ [band] *n (troop)* grupo *m*, banda *f*; *(music)* orquesta *f*, banda *f*. *v* congregar, unir, asociar.

band² [band] *n (strip)* lista *f*, tira *f*, banda *f*.

bandage ['bandidʒ] *n* venda *f*. *v* vendar.

bandit ['bandit] *n* bandido *m*.

bandy ['bandi] *adj also* **bandy-legged** estevado. *v* trocar.

bang [baŋ] *n* golpazo *m*, detonación *f*, golpe *m*. *v* golpear, estallar.

bangle ['baŋgl] *n* ajorca *f*, pulseta *f*, brazalete *m*.

banish ['baniʃ] *v* desterrar, despedir, exilar, deportar. **banishment** *n* destierro *m*.

banister ['banistə] *n* baranda *f*, pasamano *m*.

banjo ['bandʒou] *n* banjo *m*.

bank¹ [baŋk] *n (of river, etc.)* ribera *f*, orilla *f*, margen *m*.

bank² [baŋk] *n* banco *m*. **bank account** cuenta bancaria *f*. **bank holiday** día festivo *m*. *v* depositar en el banco. **banker** *n* banquero, -a *m, f*.

bankrupt ['baŋkrʌpt] *n* quebrado, -a *m, f*. *adj* insolvente, quebrado. **go bankrupt** hacer bancarrota, declararse en quiebra. **bankruptcy** *n* bancarrota *f*, quiebra *f*.

banner ['banə] *n* bandera *f*, estandarte *m*.

banns [banz] *n pl* amonestaciones *f pl*. **publish the banns** decir las amonestaciones.

banquet ['baŋkwit] *m* banquete *m*. *v* banquetear.

bantam ['bantəm] *n* gallina enana *f*. **bantamweight** *n* peso gallo *m*.

banter ['bantə] *n* burla *f*, chanza *f*. *v* burlarse.

baptize [bap'taiz] *v* bautizar. **baptism** *n* bautismo *m*. **baptist** *n* bautista *m, f*. **baptistry** *n* baptisterio *m*, bautisterio *m*.

bar [ba:] *n* barra *f*; (*soap, chocolate, etc.*) pastilla *f*; (*music*) barra *f*, compás *m*; (*barrier*) barrera *f*; (*refreshments*) bar *m*; (*law*) foro *m*, curia *f*; **bar code** código de barras *m*. *v* atrancar, obstruir, impedir. **barman** *n* mozo de bar *m* **barmaid** *n* camarera *f*.

barb [ba:b] *n* púa *f*; (*fish-hook*) lengüeta *f*.

barbarian [ba:'beəriən] *n, adj* bárbaro, -a *m, f*. **barbaric** *adj* barbárico. **barbarity** *n* barbaridad *f*.

barbecue ['ba:bikju:] *n* barbacoa *f*.

barber ['ba:bə] *n* barbero *m*, peluquero *m*. **barber's shop** barbería *f*, peluquería *f*.

barbiturate [ba:'bitjurət] *n* barbitúrico *m*.

bare [beə] *adj* desnudo, descubierto. *v* desnudar, descubrir. **bare-faced** *adj* descarado. **barefoot** *adj* descalzo. **bareheaded** *adj* sin sombrero. **barely** *adv* apenas.

bargain ['ba:gin] *n (cheap)* ganga *f*; (*agreement*) pacto *m*, ajuste *m*, convenio *m*. *v* negociar, regatear. **bargain sale** saldo *m*. **into the bargain** por más señas.

barge [ba:dʒ] *n* barca *f*, bote *m*, barcaza *f*. **barge in** irrumpir. **barge into** entremeterse.

baritone ['baritoun] *n* barítono *m*.

bark¹ [ba:k] *n (dog)* ladrido *m*. *v* ladrar.

bark² [ba:k] *n (tree)* corteza *f*.

barley ['ba:li] *n* cebada *f*. **barley water** *n* hordiate *m*.

barn [ba:n] *n* granero *m*, pajar *m*.

barometer [bə'romitə] *n* barómetro *m*.

baron ['barən] *n* barón *m*. **baroness** *n* baronesa *f*. **baronet** *n* baronet *m*.

baroque [bə'rok] *adj* barroco.

barracks ['baraks] *pl n* cuartel *m*, barraca *f*.

barrage [ba:ra:ʒ] *n* presa *f*; (*mil*) bombardeo *m*, cortina de fuego *f*.

barrel ['barəl] *n (cask)* barril *m*; (*gun, etc.*) cañón *m*. **barrel organ** organillo *m*.

barren ['barən] *adj (land)* yermo, árido; estéril. **barrenness** *n* aridez *f*; esterilidad *f*.

barricade [bari'keid] *n* barrera *f*, barricada *f*, empalizada *f*. *v* barrear, obstruir.

barrier ['bariə] *n* barrera *f*; impedimento *m*; valla *f*.

barrister ['baristə] *n* abogado, -a *m, f*.

barrow ['barou] *n* carretilla *f*.

barter ['ba:tə] *v* cambiar, trocar. *n* trueque *m*, cambio *m*, tráfico *m*.

base¹ [beis] *n* base *f*, fundamento *m*, pie *m*. *v* fundar, apoyarse, basar. **baseless** *adj* sin base.

base² [beis] *adj* bajo, vil, impuro. **baseness** *n* bajeza *f*, vileza *f*.

baseball ['beisbo:l] *n* béisbol *m*.

basement ['beismənt] *n* sótano *m*.

bash [baʃ] *n* golpe *m*. *v* golpear.

bashful ['baʃful] *adj* vergonzoso, tímido, encogido. **bashfulness** *n* vergüenza *f*, encogimiento *m*.

basic ['beisik] *adj* fundamental; (*chem*) básico.

basil ['bazl] *n* albahaca *f*.

basilica [bə'zilikə] *n* basílica *f*.

basin ['beisin] *n* bacía *f*, jofaina *f*; (*washbasin*) palangana *f*; (*dock*) dársena *f*; (*river*) cuenca *f*.

basis ['beisis] *n* base *f*, fundamento *m*.

bask [bask] *v* calentarse.

basket ['ba:skit] *n* cesta *f*, canasta *f*. **basketball** *n* baloncesto *m*.

Basque [bask] *n, adj* vasco, -a *m, f*; (*language*) vascuence *m*.

bas-relief ['basri,li:f] *n* bajorrelieve *m*.

bass¹ [beis] *n* (*voice*) bajo *m*. **bass clef** *n* clave de fa *f*.

bass² [bas] *n* (*freshwater*) róbalo *m*; (*sea*) lobina *f*.

bassoon [bə'su:n] *n* bajón *m*.

bastard ['ba:stəd] *n* bastardo, -a *m, f*.

baste [beist] *v* (*cookery*) enlardar, pringar; (*sewing*) bastear, hilvanar.

bastion ['bastjən] *n* bastión *m*, baluarte *m*.

bat¹ [bat] *n* maza *f*, palo *m*; (*cricket*) paleta *f*; (*table tennis*) pala *f*. *v* golpear con la paleta.

bat² [bat] *n* (*zool*) murciélago *m*.

batch [batʃ] *n* grupo *m*; (*loaves*) hornada *f*.

bath [ba:θ] *n* baño *m*. *v* bañar, lavar, tomar un baño. **bath-chair** *n* cochecillo de inválido *m*. **bathrobe** *n* albornoz *m*. **bathroom** *n* cuarto de baño *m*. **bathtowel** *n* toalla de baño *f*. **swimming baths** *n pl* piscina *f sing*.

bathe [beið] *v* bañar, bañarse. **bathing cap** gorra de baño *f*. **bathing costume** traje de baño *m*. **bathing pool** piscina *f*. **bathing trunks** pantalones de baño *m pl*.

baton ['batn] *n* (*mil*) bastón de mando *m*; (*police*) porra *f*; (*music*) batuta *f*.

battalion [bə'taljən] *n* batallón *m*.

batter¹ ['batə] *v* apalear, golpear, derribar.

batter² ['batə] *n* (*cookery*) batido *m*, pasta *f*.

battery ['batəri] *n* (*elec*) pila *f*, batería *f*; (*mil*) batería; (*law*) agresión *f*. **storage battery** acumulador *m*. **battery cell** pila de batería eléctrica *f*. **battery farming** cría intensiva *f*, cría avícola intensiva *f*.

battle ['batl] *n* batalla *f*, combate *m*. *v* batallar, luchar. **battlefield** *n* campo de batalla *m*. **battlement** *n* almenaje *m*. **battleship** *n* buque de guerra *m*.

bawdy ['bo:di] *adj* obsceno, escabroso.

bawl [bo:l] *v* vocear.

bay¹ [bei] *n* (*geog*) bahía *f*.

bay² [bei] *v* (*cry*) aullar. **at bay** acorralado.

bay³ [bei] *n* (*tree*) laurel *m*.

bayonet ['beiənit] *n* bayoneta *f*. *v* dar un bayonetazo.

bay window *n* mirador *m*.

bazaar [bə'za:] *n* bazar *m*.

*be [bi:] *v* ser, existir; estar; (*place*) encontrarse, quedar.

beach [bi:tʃ] *n* playa *f*; costa *f*. *v* varar, encallar en la costa.

beacon ['bi:kən] *n* fanal *m*, faro *m*; (*naut*) boya *f*.

bead [bi:d] *n* cuenta *f*, perla *f*, gota *f*. **beads** *n pl* rosario *m sing*.

beagle ['bi:gl] *n* sabueso *m*.

beak [bi:k] *n* pico *m*; punta *f*. **beaked** *adj* picudo.

beaker ['bi:kə] *n* vaso *m*, copa *f*.

beam [bi:m] *n* (*light*) rayo *m*, destello *m*; (*arch*) madero *m*; (*width of a ship*) manga *f*; (*smile*) sonrisa brillante *f*. *v* irradiar; (*smile*) sonreír radiantemente.

bean [bi:n] *n* (*broad*) haba *f*; (*black*) fréjol *m*; (*kidney*) habichuela *f*, alubia *f*, judía *f*.

*bear¹ [beə] *v* soportar, aguantar, sufrir; (*carry*) llevar; (*have*) tener, (*fruit*) dar; (*give birth to*) parir; (*a strain*) resistir. **bear in mind** tener presente. **bearing** *n* porte *m*, aspecto *m*; relación *f*.

bear² [beə] *n* oso *m*.

beard [biəd] *n* barba *f*. *v* enfrentarse con, mesar la barba a. **bearded** *adj* barbudo. **beardless** *adj* imberbe.

bearings ['beəriŋz] *n pl* situación *f sing*, relación *f sing*, camino *m sing*. **lose one's bearings** desorientarse, desatinar. **take**

belt

one's bearings orientarse.

beast [bi:st] n bestia f; res f; (wild) fiera f.
beastly adj bestial; desagradable.

*beat [bi:t] v batir; (games) derrotar, vencer;
(with weapon) golpear; (carpet) sacudir. **beat
down** atropellar. n (med) latido m, pulsación f; golpe m; (music) compás m.

beauty ['bju:ti] n hermosura f, belleza f;
(coll) lo mejor. **beauty spot** lunar m. **beautiful** adj bello, hermoso; guapo. **beautify**
v embellecer.

beaver ['bi:və] n castor m.

because [bi'koz] conj porque. **because of**
a causa de.

beckon ['bekən] v llamar con señas, atraer,
invitar.

*become [bi'kʌm] v convenir; llegar a ser,
ponerse; hacerse. **becoming** adj que sienta
bien, propio, decoroso. **becomingly** adv
con gracia.

bed [bed] n cama f, lecho m; (coal, etc.)
yacimiento m; (flowers) macizo m. **bed and
breakfast** alojamiento y desayuno m. **bedding** n ropa de cama f. **bedroom** n dormitorio m. **bedsitter** n salón con cama m.
bedspread n colcha f.

bedbug ['bedbʌg] n chinche f.

bedraggled [bi'dragld] adj mojado y sucio,
enlodado.

bee [bi:] n abeja f. **bee line** linea recta f.
beehive n colmena f. **bumble-bee** n
abejorro m.

beech [bi:tʃ] n (tree) haya f; (nut) hayuco m.

beef [bi:f] n carne de vaca f. **beefburger** n
hamburguesa (de ternera) f. **roast beef** ros-
bif m.

been [bi:n] V be.

beer [biə] n cerveza f.

beetle ['bi:tl] n (zool) escarabajo m; (tech)
pisón m. **death-watch beetle** carcoma f.
beetle-browed adj cejijunto.

beetroot ['bi:tru:t] n remolacha f.

before [bi'fo:] adv delante; al frente; (time)
antes; (already) ya. prep delante de; frente
de; (time) ante; (rather than) antes de. conj
antes (que). **beforehand** adv de antemano.

befriend [bi'frend] v favorecer, amistar,
proteger, ayudar.

beg [beg] v pedir, suplicar; mendigar. **I beg
your pardon?** ¿cómo dice? **I beg your
pardon!** ¡Vd dispense! **beg the question**
dejar a un lado. **beggar** n mendigo m.

*begin [bi'gin] v comenzar, empezar, iniciar. **to begin with** en primer lugar.
beginner n principiante, -a m, f. **beginning** n principio m.

begrudge [bi'grʌdʒ] v envidiar; conceder
de mala gana.

beguile [bi'gail] v engañar; (charm) encantar.

behalf [bi'ha:f] n **on behalf of** en nombre
de, a favor de.

behave [bi'heiv] v comportarse, manejarse,
portarse; funcionar, obrar. **behaviour** n
comportamiento m, conducta f; funcionamiento m.

behead [bi'hed] v decapitar.

behind [bi'haind] adv atrás, detrás, hacia
atrás; (time) después; (late) con retraso. prep
detrás de, por detrás de. n (coll) trasero m.
fall behind retrasarse. **behind the times**
pasado de moda.

*behold [bi'hould] v mirar, contemplar,
interj ¡aquí está!, ¡he aquí!

beige [beiʒ] adj beige.

being ['bi:iŋ] n ser m, existencia f, estado m.
human being ser humano m. **well-being**
n bienestar m.

Belarus ['belərʌs] n Bielorrusia

belated [bi'leitid] adj tardio.

belch [beltʃ] n eructo m. v eructar, arrojar.

belfry ['belfri] n campanario m.

Belgium ['beldʒəm] m Bélgica f. **Belgian**
n(m + f), adj belga.

believe [bi'li:v] v creer, pensar; opinar.
believer n creyente m, f, fiel m. **belief** n, pl
-s creencia f; opinión f.

bell [bel] n campana f, campanilla f; (electric) timbre m; (hand) esquila f.

belligerent [bi'lidʒərənt] n, adj beligerante,
-a m, f.

bellow ['belou] v bramar, rugir. n bramido
m.

bellows ['belouz] n pl fuelle m sing.

belly ['beli] n barriga f, panza f, vientre m.
bellyful n hartón m.

belong [bi'loŋ] v pertenecer, tocar a.
belong to ser de. **belongings** n pl bienes m
pl.

beloved [bi'lʌvid] n amado, -a m, f, querido, -a m, f. favorito, -a m, f.

below [bi'lou] adv abajo, debajo. prep (por)
debajo de.

belt [belt] n cinturón m, cinto m, faja f;

(tech) correa f; *(geog)* zona f. **v** ceñir, rodear, fajar.

bench [bentʃ] n banco m, banca f, escaño m, *(law)* tribunal m.

*bend [bend] v torcer, doblar; inclinar, encorvar. n recodo m, curva f.

beneath [bi'ni:θ] adv abajo, debajo. *(prep)* bajo, debajo de. **beneath regard** indigno de consideración.

benefactor ['benəfæktə] n bienhechor, -a m, f, patrono, -a m, f.

benefit ['benəfit] n beneficio m, provecho m. v beneficiar. **beneficial** adj ventajoso. **beneficiary** n beneficiario, -a m, f.

benevolent [bi'nevələnt] adj benévolo; caritativo. **benevolence** n benevolencia f, caridad f.

benign [bi'nain] adj benigno.

bent [bent] adj torcido, encorvado; *(on a course of action)* resuelto (a); *(coll)* invertido. n talento m, inclinación f.

bequeath [bi'kwi:ð] v legar; transmitir. **bequest** n legado m.

bereaved [bi'ri:vd] adj afligido. **bereave** v quitar; afligir. **bereavement** n pérdida f, aflicción f.

beret ['berei] n boina f.

berry ['beri] n baya f, grano m.

berserk [bə'sə:k] adj demente.

berth [bə:θ] n camarote m; *(dock)* fondeadero m. v fondear. **give a wide berth to** apartarse de.

beside [bi'said] prep junto a, cerca de. **beside oneself** fuera de sí. **be beside the point** no venir al caso. **besides** adv *(as well)* también; *(moreover)* además.

besiege [bi'si:dʒ] v asediar, sitiar.

bespoke [bi'spouk] adj hecho a medida. **bespeak** v reservar.

best [best] adj, adv mejor. **at best** a lo mejor. **do one's best** hacer todo lo posible. **make the best of** sacar el mayor provecho de. **best man** padrino de boda m. **bestseller** n éxito de librería, éxito de ventas m.

bestow [bi'stou] v conferir, otorgar.

*bet [bet] v apostar; jugar. n apuesta f, postura f. **better, bettor** n apostador, -a m, f. **betting shop** establecimiento de apuesta m.

betray [bi'trei] v traicionar; engañar; revelar. **betrayal** n traición f.

better ['betə] adj, adv mejor. **get better**

mejorarse. **better half** *(coll)* media naranja f. **better off** mejor situado. **so much the better** tanto mejor. v mejorarse.

between [bi'twi:n] prep entre. adv entre los dos. **far between** a grandes intervalos. **between ourselves** entre nosotros.

beverage ['bevəridʒ] n bebida f, brebaje m.

*beware [bi'weə] v tener cuidado de. interj ¡atención!

bewilder [bi'wildə] v desconcertar, aturrullar, aturdir. **bewilderment** n aturdimiento m, anonadamiento m.

beyond [bi'jond] adv más alla, más lejos. prep superior a, fuera de. **beyond doubt** fuera de duda. **beyond measure** sobremanera. **beyond question** indiscutible.

bias ['baiəs] n sesgo m, través m; propensión f, prejuicio m. **cut on the bias** contar al sesgo. v influir; predisponer. **biased** adj predispuesto.

bib [bib] n babero m, pechera f.

Bible ['baibl] n Biblia f. **biblical** adj bíblico.

bibliography [bibli'ogrəfi] n bibliografía f. **bibliographer** n bibliógrafo, -a m, f. **bibliographical** adj bibliográfico.

biceps ['baiseps] n bíceps m.

bicker ['bikə] v disputar, reñir, altercar. **bickering** n altercado m.

bicycle ['baisikl] n bicicleta f.

*bid [bid] v ofrecer, pujar; *(command)* mandar; rogar. n oferta f; *(attempt)* tentativa f. **make a bid for** procurar. **no bid** *(cards)* paso. **bidder** n postor, -a m, f.

bidet ['bi:dei] n bidé m.

biennial [bai'eniəl] adj bienal, bianual.

bifocals [bai'foukəlz] pl n lentes bifocales m pl.

big [big] adj grande; grueso; abultado; importante.

bigamy ['bigəmi] n bigamia f. **bigamist** n bígamo, -a m, f. **bigamous** adj bígamo.

bigot ['bigət] n beatón, -ona m, f, fanático, -a m, f. **bigoted** adj fanático, intolerante. **bigotry** n fanatismo m, intolerancia f.

bikini [bi'ki:ni] n bikini m.

bilingual [bai'lingwəl] adj bilingüe.

bilious ['biljəs] adj bilioso. **bile** n bilis f.

bill¹ [bil] n *(comm)* cuenta f, factura f; *(poster)* cartel m; *(pol)* proyecto de ley m; anuncio m. **billboard** n cartelera f. **bill of lading** conocimiento de embarque m. **bill of sale** escritura de venta f. v enviar una cuenta; anunciar. **bill and coo** arrullar; (*coll*) besuquearse.

bill² [bil] *n* (*beak*) pico *m*.

billiards ['biljədz] *n* billar *m*.

billion ['biljən] *n* (10^{12}) billón *m*; (10^9) mil millones *m pl*.

bin [bin] *n* arcón *m*, hucha *f*; papelera *f*; (*wine*) estante *m*.

binary ['bainəri] *adj* binario.

*bind [baind] *v* atar; ligar, unir; (*bandage*) vendar; (*sheaves*) agavillar, (*books*) encuadernar; (*captive*) aprisionar; (*sewing*) ribetear; (*oblige*) comprometer.

binding ['baindiŋ] *n* (*books*) encuadernación *f*, atadura *f*. *adj* válido; obligatorio.

binge [bindʒ] *n* (*coll*) parranda *f*. **go on the binge** ir de parranda.

binge [bindʒ] *n* (*drinking*) borrachera *f*; (*eating*) comilona *f*, atracón *m*

binoculars [bi'nokjuləz] *n pl* binóculos *m pl*. prismáticos *m pl*. gemelos *m pl*.

biodegradable [,baioudi'greidəbl] *adj* biodegradable

biography [bai'ogrəfi] *n* biografia *f*. **biographer** *n* biógrafo, -a *m*, *f*. **biographical** *adj* biográfico.

biology [bai'olədʒi] *n* biologia *f*. **biological** *adj* biológico. **biologist** *n* biólogo, -a *m*, *f*.

birch [bə:tʃ] *n* abedul *m*. *v* varear.

bird [bə:d] *n* pájaro *m*, ave *f*; (*slang*) chica *f*. **bird's eye view** vista de pájaro *f*. **birdcage** *n* jaula *f*. **birdseed** *n* alpiste *f*.

Biro ['baiərou] *n* bolígrafo *m*

birth [bə:θ] *n* nacimiento *m*, parto *m*; linaje *m*; comienzo *m*. **give birth to** dar a luz; parir. **birth certificate** partida de nacimiento *f*. **birth control** anticoncepcionismo *m*. **birthday** *n* cumpleaños *m*. **birthplace** *n* lugar de nacimiento *m*. **birthrate** *n* natalidad *f*. **birthright** *n* herencia *f*.

biscuit ['biskit] *n* bizcocho *m*, galleta *f*.

bishop ['biʃəp] *n* obispo *m*; (*chess*) alfil *m*.

bison ['baisən] *n* bisonte *m*.

bit¹ [bit] *n* (*drill*) barrena *f*, taladro *m*; (*horse*) bocado *m*. **take the bit between one's teeth** desbocarse.

bit² [bit] *n* pedazo *m*, poco *m*, trocito *m*; (*time*) ratito *m*; (*jot*) jota *f*. **bit by bit** poco a poco. **not a bit** nada de eso.

bit³ [bit] *V* bite.

bitch [bitʃ] *n* (*dog*) perra *f*; (*slang*) zorra *f*.

*bite [bait] *v* morder; (*insect, etc.*) picar. *n* mordedura *f*; picadura *f*. **biting** *adj* (*remark, etc.*) mordaz.

bitter ['bitə] *adj* amargo, áspero. **to the bitter end** hasta la muerte. **bitterness** *n* amargura *f*.

bizarre [bi'za:] *adj* extravagante, grotesco.

black ['blak] *n*, *adj* negro, -a *m*, *f*. **blacken** *v* ennegrecer; (*character*) denigrar.

blackberry ['blakbəri] *n* (*bush*) zarza *f*; (*fruit*) zarzamora *f*.

blackbird ['blakbə:d] *n* mirlo *m*.

blackboard ['blakbo:d] *n* pizarra *f*.

blackcurrant [,blak'kʌrənt] *n* grosella negra *f*.

black eye *n* ojo a la funerala *m*.

blackhead ['blakhed] *n* espinilla *f*.

blackleg ['blakleg] *n* esquirol *m*.

blackmail ['blakmeil] *n* chantaje *m*. *v* hacer chantaje. **blackmailer** *n* chantajista *m*, *f*.

black market *n* mercado negro *m*.

blackout ['blakaut] *n* apagón *m*, apagamiento *m*; (*fainting*) desmayo *m*.

black pudding *n* morcilla *f*.

blacksmith ['blaksmiθ] *n* herrero *m*.

bladder ['bladə] *n* vejiga *f*.

blade [bleid] *n* (*grass*) brizna *f*; (*razor*) hoja *f*; (*propeller*) paleta *f*; (*oar*) pala *f*.

blame [bleim] *n* culpa *f*. *v* culpar. **blameless** *adj* inculpable. **blameworthy** *adj* culpable.

bland [bland] *adj* afable; dulce.

blank [blaŋk] *adj* en blanco; (*empty*) vacío; confuso. *n* blanco *m*, hueco *m*; vacío *m*. **blank cartridge** cartucho para salvas *m*. **blank verse** verso libre *m*, verso suelto *m*.

blanket ['blaŋkit] *n* manta *f*, frazada *f*; (*of dust*) capa *f*. *v* cubrir con manta. *adj* comprensivo.

blare [bleə] *v* vociferar, rugir. *n* trompetazo *m*, fragor *m*; estrépito *m*.

blaspheme [blas'fi:m] *v* blasfemar. **blasphemer** *n* blasfemador, -a *m*, *f*. **blasphemous** *adj* blasfemo. **blasphemy** *n* blasfemia *f*.

blast [bla:st] *n* explosión *f*; (*trumpet*) trompetazo *m*; (*wind*) ráfaga *f* *v* (*rocks*) barrenar; (*wither*) marchitar; (*curse*) maldecir. **full blast** en plena marcha. **blast furnace** alto horno *m*.

blatant ['bleitənt] *adj* descarado, vocinglero, llamativo.

blaze [bleiz] *n* incendio *m*, llamarada *f*, conflagración *f*. *v* llamear, flamear; arder. **blaze a trail** abrir un camino. **blaze of colour** masa de color *f*. **blazer** *n* chaqueta deportiva *f*.

bleach [bli:tʃ] *v* blanquear, descolorar. *n* lejía *f*

bleak [bli:k] *adj* desabrido, desierto, crudo; (*prospect*) sombrío.

bleat [bli:t] *v* balar. *n* balido *m*.

***bleed** [bli:d] *v* sangrar. **bleed to death** morir desangrado. **bleeding** *n* hemorragia *f*.

blemish ['blemiʃ] *n* mácula *f*, defecto *m*, mancha *f*. *v* empañar, manchar.

blend [blend] *v* mezclar, combinar, fundir; (*colour*) matizar. *n* mezcla *f*, combinación *f*.

bless [bles] *v* bendecir; consagrar; favorecer. **blessedness** *n* felicidad *f*. **blessing** *n* bendición *f*; merced *f*; favor *m*.

blew [blu:] *V* **blow²**.

blight [blait] *n* (*plants*) tizne *m*; (*fig*) influencia maligna *f*. *v* atizonar; (*fig*) malograr.

blight [blait] *v* arruinar

blind [blaind] *adj* ciego. *n* pretexto *m*; (*window*) persiana *f*. *v* cegar. **blindness** *n* ceguera *f*. **turn a blind eye** hacer la vista gorda.

blindfold ['blaindfould] *n* venda *f*. *v* vendar los ojos de.

blink [bliŋk] *v* parpadear, pestañear, guiñar. *n* parpadeo *m*, guiño *m*; (*of light*) destello *m*. **blinkers** *pl n* anteojeras *f pl*.

bliss [blis] *n* bienaventuranza *f*, felicidad *f*. **blissful** *adj* bienaventurado, feliz.

blister ['blistə] *n* vesícula *f*, ampolla *f*. *v* ampollar.

blizzard ['blizəd] *n* ventisca *f*.

bloated ['bloutid] *adj* abotagado.

blob [blob] *n* gota *f*, goterón *m*; borrón *m*.

bloc [blok] *n* (*pol*) bloque *m*.

block [blok] *n* bloque *m*; (*butcher's*) tajo *m*; (*houses*) manzana *f*; (*obstruction*) atasco *m*. *v* bloquear, obstruir, cerrar el paso. **block and tackle** polea con aparejo.

blockade [blo'keid] *n* bloqueo *m*. *v* bloquear.

blockade [blo'keid] *n* bloqueo *m*, inmovilización *f*

bloke [blouk] *n* (*coll*) tio *m*, fulano *m*.

blond [blond] *adj* rubio. **blonde** *n* rubia *f*.

blood [blʌd] *n* sangre *f*; (*lineage*) parentesco *m*. **bloodless** *adj* exangüe. **blood donor** donante de sangre *m*, *f*. **blood group** grupo sanguíneo *m*. **blood poisoning** envenenamiento de la sangre *m*. **blood pressure** *n* presión arterial *f*. **bloodshed** *n* matanza *f*. **bloodshot** *adj* inyectado de sangre. **bloodstream** *n* corriente sanguínea *f*. **bloodthirsty** *adj* sanguinario. **bloody** *adj* sangriento; (*slang*) maldito.

bloom [blu:m] *n* flor *f*; florecimiento *m*; (*prime*) lozanía *f*. *v* florecer. **in bloom** en flor. **blooming** *adj* floreciente.

blossom ['blosəm] *n* flor *f*. *v* florecer.

blossom ['blosəm] *n* flor *f*

blot [blot] *n* borrón *m*; mancha *f*. *v* manchar, tachar; (*dry*) secar. **blot out** borrar. **blotter** *n* libro borrador *m*. **blotting paper** papel secante *m*.

blotch [blotʃ] *n* mancha *f*; (*med*) erupción *f*. *v* manchar, ennegrecer.

blouse [blauz] *n* blusa *f*.

blow¹ [blou] *n* (*hit*) golpe *m*, bofetada *f*; (*shock*) choque *m*; (*misfortune*) revés *m*. **come to blows** venir a las manos.

***blow²** [blou] *n* soplido *m*. *v* soplar, hacer viento; (*pant*) jadear; (*fuse*) fundirse; (*music*) tocar. **blow away** disipar. **blow-dry** secar a mano. **blow one's nose** sonarse las narices. **blow out** (*a light*) apagar soplando. **blow up** (*explode*) volar; (*inflate*) inflar.

blubber ['blʌbə] *n* grasa de ballena *f*. *v* gimotear.

blue [blu:] *adj* azul; (*mournful*) deprimido; (*obscene*) verde. **bluebell** *n* campanilla *f*. **bluebottle** *n* moscón *m*. **blueprint** *n* fotocopia *f*, plan *m*

bluff [blʌf] *v* fanfarronear. *n* fanfarronada *f*; (*cliff*) morro *m*, tisco *m*, peñasco *m*. *adj* campechano, brusco.

blunder [blʌndə] *n* desatino *m*, yerro *m*. *v* desatinar; tropezar (con); (*coll*) meter la pata. **blunderer** *n* desatinado *m*.

blunt [blʌnt] *adj* desafilado, embotado; (*abrupt*) franco, descortés; (*plain*) claro. *v* despuntar, desafilar, embotar; (*pain*) mitigar. **bluntness** *n* embotamiento *m*.

blur [blə:] *v* empañar; emborronar. *n* borrón *m*. **blurred** *adj* borroso.

blush [blʌʃ] *v* ruborizarse, enrojecerse. *n* rubor *m*, sonrojo *m*; (*of shame*) bochorno *m*.

boar [bo:] *n* jabalí *m*.

board [bo:d] *n* tabla *f*; (*chess, draughts*) tablero *m*; (*for notices*) tablón *m*; (*table*) mesa *f*; (*food*) comida *f*; (*committee*) junta *f*, tribunal *m*; (*naut*) bordo *m*. *v* (*carpentry*) enmaderar, entablar; (*embark*) embarcarse en.

boast [boust] *n* jactancia *f*, alarde *m*, baladronada *f*. *v* jactarse, presumir. **boastful** *adj* jactancioso.

boat [bout] *n* bote *m*, lancha *f*, barca *f*; buque *m*, barco *m*. *v* navegar, ir en bote. **boatman** *n* barquero *m*. **boatswain** *n* contramaestre *m*.

boater ['boutə] *n* (*hat*) canotié *m*, canotier *m*.

bob [bob] *v* bambolear, menear. *n* balanceo *m*; borla *f*.

bobbin ['bobin] *n* (*sewing-machine, loom*) bobina *f*.

bobsleigh ['bobslei] *n* trineo doble *m*. *v* ir en trineo.

bodice ['bodis] *n* corpiño *m*.

body ['bodi] *n* cuerpo *m*, masa *f*, entidad *f*; (*corpse*) cadáver *m*; (*mot*) carrocería *f*. **body-guard** *n* guardaespaldas *m, f*.

bog [bog] *n* pantano *m*.

bogus ['bougəs] *adj* espurio, fingido, falso.

bohemian [bə'hi:miən] *adj* bohemio.

boil[1] [boil] *v* hervir. *n* hervor *m*. **boil over** irse. **boiler** *n* caldera *f*. **boiling point** punto de ebullición *m*.

boil[2] [boil] *n* divieso *m*, grano *m*, furúnculo *m*.

boisterous ['boistərəs] *adj* borrascoso, bullicioso. **boisterousness** *n* bullicio *m*.

bold [bould] *adj* osado, arrojado, atrevido; resuelto; (*showy*) llamativo; (*typeface*) negrita *f*. **bold-faced** *adj* descarado. **bold-faced type** letra negra *f*. **boldness** *n* temeridad *f*, intrepidez *f*.

Bolivia [bə'liviə] *n* Bolivia *f*. **Bolivian** *adj*, *n* boliviano, -a *m, f*.

bollard ['bola:d] *n* baliza *f*

bolster ['boulstə] *n* travesaño *m*; almohada *f*. *v* estribar, levantar, apoyar.

bolt [boult] *n* (*door*) cerraja *f*, cerrojo *m*; (*for nut*) perno *m*; rayo *m*. *v* (*run*) huir; (*secure*) empernar; (*food*) zampar. **bolt upright** enhiesto. **thunderbolt** *n* rayo *m*.

bomb [bom] *n* bomba *f*. *v* bombardear.

bombard [bəm'ba:d] *v* bombardear. **bombardment** *n* bombardeo *m*.

bonafide [bounə'faidi] *adj* fidedigno.

bond [bond] *n* lazo *m*, unión *f*, vínculo *m*; (*comm*) obligación *f*; (*security*) fianza *f*; (*customs*) depósito *m*. *v* unir, ligar; dar fianza. **bonds** *n pl* cadenas *f pl*. **bondage** *n* esclavitud *f*.

bone [boun] *n* hueso *m*; (*fish*) espina *f*. *v* desosar. **bony** *adj* huesudo. **all skin and bones** estar en los huesos. **pick a bone with** arreglar las cuentas con.

bonfire ['bonfaiə] *n* hoguera *f*.

bonnet ['bonit] *n* capota *f*, gorra *f*; (*mot*) capó *m*.

bonus ['bounəs] *n* extra *m*, prima *f*.

booby trap ['bu:bi] *n* trampa *f*; (*mil*) mina *f*.

book [buk] *n* libro *m*; tomo *m*. *v* (*a seat*) tomar; (*reserve*) reservar; (*engage*) contratar.

bookcase ['bukkeis] *n* librería *f*.

book-ends ['bukendz] *n pl* sujetalibros *m pl*.

booking ['bukiŋ] *n* taquilla *f*.

book-keeper ['buk̩ki:pə] *n* tenedor de libros *m*.

booklet ['buklit] *n* folleto *m*.

bookmark ['bukma:k] *n* marcador *m*.

bookseller ['bukselə] *n* librero, -a *m, f*.

bookshop ['bukʃop] *n* librería *f*.

boom [bu:m] *n* (*noise*) ruido *m*; (*econ*) auge repentino *m*. *v* (*comm*) prosperar, estar en bonanza; sonar, bramar.

boost [bu:st] *v* (*advertise*) dar bombo (a); (*coll*) empujar. *n* (*coll*) empujón *m*.

boot [bu:t] *n* (*shoe*) bota *f*; (*mot*) maleta *f*. **boot (up)** (*comput verb*) iniciar. **get the boot** (*coll*) ser despedido.

booth [bu:ð] *n* cabina *f*, quiosco *m*.

booze [bu:z] *n* (*coll*) bebida alcohólica *f*. *v* (*coll*) emborracharse, coger una turca.

border ['bo:də] *n* confín *m*, frontera *f*; margen *m*; (*sewing*) ribete *m*; (*garden*) arriate *m*. *v* lindar con. **borderline** *n* límite *m*.

bore[1] [bo:] *v* (*hole, etc.*) perforar, horadar, taladrar. *n* taladro *m*, barreno *m*; (*gun*) calibre *m*.

bore[2] [bo:] *v* aburrir, fastidiar. *n* aburrimiento *m*; (*person*) pelmazo *m*. **boredom** *n* tedio *m*, hastío *m*. **boring** *adj* aburrido, tedioso.

bore[3] [bo:] *V* **bear**[1].

born [bo:n] *adj* nacido, nato. **be born**

nacer.

borne [bo:n] *V* **bear¹**.

borough ['bʌrə] *n* municipio *m*.

borrow ['borou] *v* tomar prestado, pedir prestado. **borrower** *n* prestatario, -a *m, f*.

Bosnia ['bozniə] *n* Bosnia *f*; **Bosnian** *adj* bosnio.

bosom ['buzəm] *n* seno *m*; pecho *m*.

boss [bos] *n* amo *m*, jefe, -a *m, f*, patrón, -a *m, f*; (*political*) cacique *m*. *v* dominar, dirigir.

botany ['botəni] *n* botánica *f*. **botanical** *adj* botánico. **botanist** *n* botánico, -a *m, f*.

both [bouθ] *adj, pron* ambos, los dos.

bother ['boðə] *v* molestar; (*worry*) preocuparse, *n* molestia *f*; preocupación *f*.

bottle ['botl] *n* botella *f*, frasco *m*; (*water*) cantimplora *f*; (*wine*) porrón *m*. **bottle bank** contenedor de vidrio *m*. *v* embotellar.

bottom ['botəm] *n* fondo *m*; casco *m*; (*coll*) trasero *m, m*; (*river*) lecho *m*; (*page*) pie *m*; (*chair*) asiento *m*. *adj* más bajo. **bottomless** *adj* sin fondo.

boudoir ['bu:dwa:] *n* tocador *m*, gabinete *m*.

bough [bau] *n* rama *f*.

bought [bo:t] *V* **buy**.

boulder ['bouldə] *n* peñasco *m*, pedrusco *m*.

bounce [bauns] *v* rebotar, botar, saltar; (*cheque*) ser rechazado. *n* rebote *m*, respingo *m*.

bound¹ [baund] *v* (*leap*) saltar, brincar. *n* salto *m*, brinco *m*.

bound² [baund] *n* límite *m*. **within bounds** dentro del límite.

bound³ [baund] *V* **bind**.

bound⁴ [baund] *adj* **bound for** destinado a, con rumbo a.

boundary ['baundəri] *n* lindero *m*, término *m*.

bouquet [bu:kei] *n* ramo *m*, ramillete *m*; perfume *m*; (*wine*) nariz *f*.

bourgeois ['buəʒwa:] *adj* burgués.

bout [baut] *n* turno *m*; (*illness*) ataque *m*.

bow¹ [bau] *v* (*bend*) inclinarse, saludar; (*submit*) someterse (a). *n* inclinación *f*; reverencia *f*.

bow² [bou] *n* (*music, weapon*) arco *m*; (*ribbon*) lazo *m*. **bow-legged** *adj* patiestevado.

bow window ventana arqueada *f*.

bow³ [bau] *n* (*naut*) proa *f*.

bowels ['bauəlz] *n pl* intestinos *m pl*, entrañas *f pl*.

bowl¹ [boul] *n* receptáculo *m*; (*soup*) escudilla *f*; (*washing*) jofaina *f*.

bowl² [boul] *v* tirar; (*cricket*) sacar. **bowl over** (*fig*) desconcertar. **bowls** *pl n* juego de bolos *m sing*.

bowler hat *n* hongo *m*.

box¹ [boks] *n* caja *f*, cajón *m*; (*luggage*) baúl *m*; (*theatre*) palco *m*; (*sentry*) garita *f*, casilla *f*. *v* encajonar. **box office** taquilla *f*. **post-office box** apartado de correos *m*.

box² [boks] *v* (*sport*) boxear. **boxer** *n* boxeador *m*, pugilista *m*. **boxing** *n* boxeo *m*, pugilato *m*.

Boxing Day *n* Día de San Esteban *m*.

boy [boi] *n* muchacho *m*, niño *m*, chico *m*. **boyfriend** *n* novio *m*. **boy scout** muchacho explorador *m*. **boyhood** niñez *f*.

boycott ['boikot] *n* boicot *m*. *v* boicotear.

bra [bra:] *n* sostén *m*.

brace [breis] *n* refuerzo *m*; (*tech*) abrazadera *f*; (*pair*) par *m*. *v* reforzar; refrescar. **braces** *n pl* tirantes *m pl*. **bracing** *adj* tónico.

bracelet ['breislit] *n* pulsera *f*; brazalete *m*.

bracken ['brakən] *n* helecho *m*.

bracket ['brakit] *n* soporte *m*; (*writing*) paréntesis *m*, corchete *m*.

brag [brag] *v* jactarse. *n* jactancia *f*.

braid [breid] *n* (*hair*) extensiones *f* (*pl*); (*clothes*) galón *m*.

Braille [breil] *n* Braille *m*, alfabeto para los ciegos *m*.

brain [brein] *n* cerebro *m*, sesos *m pl*. *v* romper la crisma. **brains** *n pl* talento *m sing*. **brainwash** *v* lavar el cerebro. **brainwave** *n* idea luminosa *f*. **brainy** *adj* sesudo. **rack one's brains** devanarse los sesos.

braise [breiz] *v* estofar.

brake [breik] *n* freno *m*. *v* frenar.

bramble ['brambl] *n* zarza *f*, maleza *f*. **bramble patch** breña *f*, matorral *m*.

bran [bran] *n* salvado *m*.

bran [bran] *adj* salvado

branch [bra:ntʃ] *n* rama *f*; (*of learning*) ramo *m*; (*river*) tributario *m*; (*road, rail*) ramal *m*; (*company*) dependencia *f*. *v* echar ramas, dividirse.

brand [brand] *n* (*manufacture*) marca *f*;

(*animals*) hierro m; (*fire*) tizón m; (*stigma*) estigma m. v marcar; tildar. **brand-new** adj enteramente nuevo.

brandish ['brandiʃ] v blandir.

brandy ['brandi] n coñac m.

brass [brɑːs] n latón m; (*music*) cobre m, metal m; (*coll*) pasta f. **brassy** adj de latón: (*coll*) presuntuoso.

brassière ['brasiə] V **bra**.

brave [breiv] adj valiente, intrépido. v desafiar. **bravery** n valentía f.

brawl [brɔːl] n alboroto m, riña f. v alborotar.

brawn [brɔːn] n carnosidad f. músculo m; (*food*) carne de cerdo adobada f. **brawny** adj musculoso.

brazen ['breizn] adj (*metal*) de latón; (*fig*) desahogado.

Brazil [brə'zil] n (el) Brasil m. **Brazilian** n, adj brasileño, -a m, f. **Brazil nut** nuez del Brasil f.

breach [briːtʃ] n brecha f. v abrir brecha; romper. **breach of promise** infracción f. **breach of the peace** alteración de orden público f.

bread [bred] n pan m. **breadcrumb** n migaja f. **breadcrumbs** n pl pan rallado m sing. **slice of bread** rebanada f.

breadth [bredθ] n anchura f.

*break** [breik] v romper; quebrar; quebrantar; (*burst*) reventar; (*violate*) infringir. **break away** desprenderse. **break down** (*mech*) averiarse; (*cry*) deshacerse en lágrimas. **break in** forzar la entrada. **break out** estallar. **break up** desmenuzar. n ruptura f, rotura f; (*opening*) abertura f; (*interruption*) interrupción f. **breakdown** n colapso m. **break-in** robo m. **breakthrough** n avance m.

breakfast ['brekfəst] n desayuno m. v desayunar.

breast [brest] n pecho m; (*female*) mama f, teta f. **breastbone** n esternón m. **breast pocket** bolsillo de pecho m. **breaststroke** n brazada de pecho f.

breath [breθ] n respiración f, aliento m; (*breeze*) soplo m. **breathless** adj sin aliento. **under one's breath** en voz baja.

breathalyser ['breθəlaizə] n alcohómetro m.

breathe [briːð] v respirar, exhalar, inspirar. **breathing** n respiración f.

*breed** [briːd] v criar, engendrar. n raza f, casta f. **breeding** n cría f, reproducción f; (*upbringing*) crianza f, educación f.

breeze [briːz] n brisa f. **breezy** adj fresco; (*of manner*) animado.

brew [bruː] v (*infuse*) infusionar; (*beer*) fabricar. n poción f. **brewery** n fábrica de cerveza f.

bribe [braib] n soborno m. v sobornar. **bribery** n soborno m.

brick [brik] n ladrillo m. v enladrillar. **bricklayer** n albañil m. **brickyard** n ladrillar m.

bride [braid] n novia f, desposada f. **bridal** adj nupcial. **bridegroom** m novio m, desposado m. **bridesmaid** n dama de honor f, madrina de boda f.

bridge¹ [bridʒ] n puente m. **drawbridge** n puente levadizo m. **suspension bridge** puente colgante m. v pontear.

bridge² [bridʒ] n (*cards*) bridge m.

bridle ['braidl] n brida f, freno m. v enfrenar; picarse.

brief [briːf] adj breve. n resumen m; (*law*) escrito m, relación f. v (*law*) instruir. **briefcase** n cartera f. **briefly** adv brevemente.

brigade [bri'geid] n brigada f.

bright [brait] adj brillante; (*intelligent*) inteligente. **brighten** v hacer brillar; (*make happy*) alegrar; (*polish*) pulir; (*weather*) aclarar. **brightness** n brillantez f; (*intelligence*) talento m.

brilliant ['briljənt] adj brillante. **brilliance** n brillo m, fulgor m.

brim [brim] n (*of a container*) borde m; (*hat*) ala f.

brine [brain] n salmuera f.

*bring** [briŋ] v traer, llevar, conducir. **bring about** causar, ocasionar. **bring down** rebajar. **bring in** introducir. **bring off** lograr, conseguir. **bring out** sacar; publicar. **bring together** reunir. **bring to light** descubrir. **bring up** criar, educar.

brink [briŋk] n borde m. **on the brink of** a dos dedos de.

brisk [brisk] adj animado, vivo.

bristle ['brisl] n cerda f. v erizarse. **bristly** adj erizado.

Britain ['britn] n Gran Bretaña f. **British** adj británico. **Briton** n britano, -a m, f británico, -a m, f.

brittle ['britl] adj quebradizo.

broad [brɔːd] *adj* ancho; *(fig)* lato, amplio; *(accent)* fuerte. **broad-minded** *adj* tolerante. **broaden** *v* ensanchar. **broadly** *adv* en general. **broadness** *n* anchura *f*.

broadcast ['brɔːdkɑːst] *n* emisión *f*, radiodifusión *f*; *v* emitir, radiar. **broadcasting station** *n* emisora *f*.

broccoli ['brɔkəli] *n* bróculi *m*, brécol *m*.

brochure ['brouʃuə] *n* folleto *m*.

broke [brouk] *V* **break**. *adj* (*coll*) pelado, sin blanca.

broken ['broukn] *V* **break**.

broker ['broukə] *n* corredo, -a de bolsa *m*, *f*.

bronchitis [brɔŋ'kaitis] *m* bronquitis *f*.

bronze [brɔnz] *n* bronce *m*.

brooch [broutʃ] *n* broche *m*.

brood [bruːd] *n* (*chickens*) pollada *f*; (*birds*) nidada *f*; (*other animals*) cria *f*. *v* empollar. **brood over** ruminar.

brook [bruk] *n* arroyo *m*.

broom [bruːm] *n* escoba *f*; (*bot*) retama *f*.

broth [brɔθ] *n* caldo *m*.

brothel ['brɔθl] *n* burdel *m*, lupanar *m*.

brother ['brʌðə] *n* hermano *m*. **brother-in-law** *n* cuñado *m*. **brotherhood** *n* fraternidad *f*. **brotherly** *adv* fraternal.

brow [brau] *n* frente *f*; (*hill*) cumbre *f*. **browbeat** *v* intimidar verbalmente.

brown [braun] *adj* castaño, moreno. *v* (*cookery*) dorar; (*tan*) tostar. **brown paper** papel de estraza *m*. **brownish** *adj* pardusco.

Brownie Guide *n* Niña Exploradora *f*

browse [brauz] *v* pacer; (*internet*) navegar. **browser** navegador *m*.

bruise [bruːz] *n* contusión *f*, magulladura *f*. *v* magullar.

brunette [bruːnet] *n* morena *f*.

brush [brʌʃ] *n* cepillo *m*; (*broom*) escoba *f*; (*for painting*) pincel *m*; (*undergrowth*) matorral *m*. *v* cepillar; (*sweep*) barrer; (*touch*) rozar. **brush aside** echar a un lado. **brush off** sacudir(se).

brusque [brusk] *adj* brusco, rudo.

Brussels ['brʌsəlz] *n* Bruselas. **Brussels sprouts** coles de Bruselas *f pl*.

brute [bruːt] *n* bruto *m*, bestia *m*, *f*. **brutal** *adj* brutal, bestial. **brutality** *n* brutalidad *f*.

BSE *n* Encefalopatía Espongiforme Bovina *f*

bubble ['bʌbl] *n* burbuja *f*; borbollón *m*. *v* burbujear, borbollar.

buck [bʌk] *n* gamo *m.*; *(dollar)* dólar *m*. *v* encorvarse. **pass the buck** pasar el muerto. **buck up** animarse.

bucket ['bʌkit] *n* cubo *m*, balde *m*.

buckle ['bʌkl] *n* hebilla *f*. *v* enhebillar; doblarse.

buck-tooth *n* diente saliente *m*.

bud [bʌd] *n* brote *m*. *v* brotar, germinar.

Buddhism *n* Budismo *m*; **Buddhist** *adj* budista.

budge [bʌdʒ] *v* mover, moverse, menearse.

budgerigar ['bʌdʒəriːgɑː] *n* periquito *m*.

budget ['bʌdʒit] *n* presupuesto *m*. *v* presupuestar.

buffalo ['bʌfələu] *n* búfalo *m*.

buffer ['bʌfə] *n* parachoque *m*.

buffet[1] ['bʌfit] *n* (*blow*) bofetón *m*, bofetada *f*. *v* abofetear, golpear.

buffet[2] ['bufei] *n* fonda *f*, bar *m*.

bug [bʌg] *n* chinche *m*; (*computer*) virus *m*. *v* (*coll*) ocultar un micrófono en.

bugger ['bʌgə] *n* sodomita *m*. *v* cometer sodomia. *interj* (impol) ¡joder! **bugger off!** (impol) ¡vete a la mierda! **buggery** *m* sodomía *f*.

buggy ['bʌgi] *n* silla de paseo *f*

bugle ['bjuːgl] *n* corneta *f*. **bugler** *n* trompetero *m*.

***build** [bild] *v* construir; edificar; fundar. **building** *n* edificio *m*. **building site** *n* solar *m*. **built-up area** *n* zona urbana *f*.

bulb [bʌlb] *n* (*elec*) bombilla *f*; (*bot*) bulbo *m*.

Bulgaria [bʌl'geəriə] *n* Bulgaria *f*. **Bulgarian** *n*, *adj* búlgaro, -a *m*, *f*.

bulge [bʌldʒ] *n* hinchazón *f*, bulto *m*. *v* hincharse. **bulging** *adj* hinchado (de).

bulimia [buːlimiə] *n* bulimia *f*

bulk [bʌlk] *n* bulto *m*; masa *f*; (*larger part*) grueso *m*. **in bulk** (*comm*) en bruto. **bulky** *adj* voluminoso.

bull [bul] *n* toro *m*. **bullfight** *n* corrida de toros *f*. **bullfighter** *n* torero *m*. **bull in a china shop** un caballo loco en una cacharreria *m*. **bullring** *n* plaza de toros *f*. **bull's-eye** *n* centro del blanco *m*.

bulldozer ['buldouzə] *n* bulldozer *m*, excavadora *f*.

bullet ['bulit] *n* bala *f*. **bullet-proof** *adj* a prueba de balas.

bulletin ['bulətin] *n* boletin *m*.

bullion ['buliən] n (gold) oro en barras m; (silver) plata en barras f.

bully ['buli] n valentón, -ona m, f, rufián m. v intimidar.

bun ['bʌn] n (cake) bollo m.

bum [bʌm] n (coll) posaderas f pl. v holgazanear.

bump [bʌmp] n (swelling) hinchazón f; (blow) golpe m. v chocar, golpear.

bumper ['bʌmpə] n (mot) parachoques m invar. adj abundante.

bun [bʌn] n buñuelo m; (hair) moño m.

bunch [bʌntʃ] n (flowers) ramo m; (fruit) racimo m; (coll: gang) pandilla f. v agruparse.

bundle ['bʌndl] n fardo m, bulto m. v enfardar, liar.

bungalow ['bʌŋgəlou] n chalet m, casa de un solo piso f.

bungle ['bʌŋgl] v estropear, chapucear. n chapucería f. **bungler** n chapucero, -a m, f. **bungling** adj chapucero.

bunion ['bʌnjən] n juanete m.

bunk [bʌŋk] n litera f; (coll: nonsense) palabrería f. **bunk beds** literas f pl. **do a bunk** pirarse.

bunker ['bʌŋkə] n (refuge) refugio m; (coal) carbonera f; (golf) bunker m, hoya de arena f.

buoy [boi] n boya f. **buoyancy** n fluctuación f. **buoyant** adj boyante.

burden ['bə:dn] n carga f. v cargar.

bureau ['bjuərou] n (desk) escritorio m; (office) oficina f; departmento m.

bureaucracy [bju'rokrəsi] n burocracia f. **bureaucrat** n burócrata m, f. **bureaucratic** adj burocrático.

burglar ['bə:glə] n ladrón, -ona m, f. **burglar alarm** alarma contra ladrones f. **burglary** n robo m. **burgle** v robar.

*****burn** [bə:n] v quemar, incendiar. n quemadura f. **burner** n quemador m. **burning** adj ardiente.

burrow ['bʌrou] n madriguera f. v amadrigar, minar.

*****burst** [bə:st] n estallido m, explosión f. v reventar, estallar. **burst into tears** romper a llorar. **burst open** forzar; abrirse de golpe.

bury ['beri] v enterrar, sepultar. **burial** n entierro m.

bus [bʌs] n autobús m, ómnibus m. dou-

ble-decker bus ómnibus de dos pisos m. **bus station** término m. **bus-stop** n parada de autobús or ómnibus.

bush [buʃ] n arbusto m; (undergrowth) maleza f. **bushy** adj denso, espeso, matoso.

business ['biznis] n negocio m, comercio m; ocupación f. **business hours** horas de trabajo f pl. **businesslike** adj práctico, sistemático. **businessman** n hombre de negocios m. **mean business** estar resuelto. **mind one's own business** no meterse donde no le llaman.

bust[1] [bʌst] n (anat) pecho m; (art) busto m.

bust[2] [bʌst] adj (fam) quebrado, reventado. **go bust** quebrar.

bustle ['bʌsl] n animación f. v menearse, dar prisa (a).

busy ['bizi] adj ocupado; activo, diligente. **busybody** n entrometido, -a m, f.

but [bʌt] conj pero, sino. prep excepto. adv solamente. **but for** a no ser por. **nothing but** nada más que.

butane ['bju:tein] n butano m.

butcher [butʃə] n carnicero, -a m, f. **butcher's shop** carniceria f. v matar, destrozar.

butler ['bʌtlə] n mayordomo m.

butt[1] [bʌt] n (gun) culata f; (cigarette, etc.) colilla f.

butt[2] [bʌt] n (of jokes, etc.) objeto m.

butt[3] [bʌt] v topar, acornear. **butt in** entrometerse.

butter ['bʌtə] n mantequilla f; v untar con mantequilla.

buttercup ['bʌtəkʌp] n ranúnculo m.

butterfly ['bʌtəflai] n mariposa f.

butterscotch ['bʌtəskotʃ] n dulce de azúcar y mantequilla m.

buttocks ['bʌtəks] n pl nalgas f pl.

button ['bʌtn] n botón m. v abotonear. **buttonhole** n ojal m. v (coll) importunar.

buttress ['bʌtris] n estribo m, contrafuerte m; (fig) apoyo m. v estribar.

*****buy** [bai] v comprar. n compra f. **buy up** acaparar. **buyer** n comprador, -a m, f.

buzz [bʌz] v zumbar. n zumbido m. **buzzer** n zumbador m; (bell) timbre m.

by [bai] prep por, de, a; (near) cerca de. adv al lado, cerca; aparte. **by all means** naturalmente. **by and large** en general. **by the way** de paso.

bye-law ['bailo:] n reglamento m.

by-election [ˈbaiiˌlekʃən] n elección parcial f.

bypass [ˈbaiˌpaːs] n desviación f. v desviar.

by-product [ˈbaiprodəkt] n subproducto m.

bystander [ˈbaiˌstandə] n espectador, -a m, f.

byte [bait] n byte m

C

cab [kab] n taxi m; (lorry) cabina f.

cabaret [ˈkabərei] n cabaret m; (show) attracciones f pl.

cabbage [ˈkabidʒ] n col f, repollo m.

cabin [ˈkabin] n cabaña f; (naut) camarote m; (aircraft, etc.) cabina f. **cabin cruiser** n motonave f.

cabinet [ˈkabinit] n (cupboard) armario m; (display) vitrina f; (pol) gabinete m, consejo de ministros m. **medicine cabinet** botiquín m. **cabinet-maker** n ebanista m, f.

cable [ˈkeibl] n (rope, wire) cable m; (message) cablegrama m. **cable address** dirección telegráfica f. **cable car** funicular m. v cablegrafiar. **cable television** televisión por cable f.

cache [kaʃ] n caché m

cackle [ˈkakl] v carcarear. n carcareo m.

cactus [ˈkaktəs] n pl -i or -uses cacto m.

caddie [ˈkadi] n caddy m; (trolley) carrito m.

cadence [ˈkeidəns] n cadencia f.

cadet [kəˈdet] n cadete m.

Caesarean [siˈzeəriən] n cesárea f

café [ˈkafei] n café m, restaurante m.

cafeteria [kafəˈtiəriə] n cafetería f, restaurante de autoservicio m.

caffeine [ˈkafiːn] n cafeína f.

cage [keidʒ] n jaula f. v enjaular.

cake [keik] n pastel m; (soap) pastilla f. **Christmas cake** tarta de Navidad f. **be a piece of cake** (coll) ser pan comido. **sell like hot cakes** (coll) venderse como rosquillas. **take the cake** (coll) llevarse la palma. v endurecerse.

calamine [ˈkaləmain] n calamina f.

calamity [kəˈlaməti] n calamidad f.

calcium [ˈkalsiəm] n calcio m.

calculate [ˈkalkjuleit] v calcular; (guess, suppose) confiar en. **calculated** adj intencional, deliberado. **calculating** adj calculador. **calculation** n cálculo m. **calculator** n calculador m.

calendar [ˈkaləndə] n calendario m. **calendar month** mes civil m.

calf[1] [kaːf] n (zool) becerro m, ternero m.

calf[2] [kaːf] n (anat) pantorrilla f.

calibre [ˈkalibə] n (measurement) calibre m; (talent) capacidad f, talento m.

call [koːl] n llamada f, llamamiento m; (cry) grito m; (visit) visita f. **on call** de guardia. **trunk call** conferencia f. v llamar. **call for** pedir. **call off** cancelar. **call on** visitar. **call up** evocar; convocar.

callous [ˈkaləs] adj insensible, duro.

calm [kaːm] adj calmoso, sosegado, tranquilo. n calma f, tranquilidad f. v calmar, sosegar.

calorie [ˈkaləri] n caloría f.

camcorder [ˈkamkoːdə] n videocámara f

came [keim] V come.

camel [ˈkaməl] n camello m.

camera [ˈkamərə] n máquina fotográfica f. **in camera** a puerta cerrada. **cameraman** n cameraman m.

camouflage [ˈkaməflaːʒ] n camuflaje m. v camuflar.

camp[1] [kamp] n (site) campamento m. **camp-bed** n cama plegable f. (person) campista mf; (van) caravana f, autocaravana f. **holiday camp** campamento de vacaciones m. v acampar.

camp[2] [kamp] adj (coll) afeminado; afectado; homosexual.

campaign [kamˈpein] n campaña f. **advertising campaign** campaña publicitaria f. **election campaign** campaña electoral f. v hacer (una) campaña.

campus [ˈkampəs] n recinto universitario m, campus m, ciudad universitaria f.

*****can**[1] [kan] v (be able) poder; (know how to) saber.

can[2] [kan] n (container) lata f. **can-opener** n abrelatas m invar. v enlatar, conservar en lata. **canned** adj enlatado.

Canada [ˈkanədə] n Canadá m. **Canadian** n(m + f), adj canadiense.

canal [kəˈnal] n canal m.

canary [kəˈneəri] n canario m.

Canary Islands *n pl* (islas) Canarias *f pl.*

cancel ['kansəl] *v* (*contract, decree, etc.*) cancelar; (*cheque, order, invitation*) anular; (*delete*) tachar; (*maths*) eliminar. **cancel out** anularse. **cancellation** *n* cancelación *f*; anulación *f.*

cancer ['kansə] *n* cáncer *m.* **cancerous** *adj* canceroso.

Cancer ['kansə] *n* Cáncer *m.*

candid ['kandid] *adj* franco, sincero.

candidate ['kandidət] *n* candidato, -a *m, f.* **candidacy** *n* candidatura *f.*

candle ['kandl] *n* vela *f*; (*in a church*) cirio *m.* **burn the candle at both ends** hacer de la noche dia. **candlestick** *n* candelero *m.*

candour ['kandə] *n* franqueza *f*, sinceridad *f.*

candy ['kandi] *n* caramelo *m.* *v* escarchar, cristalizar.

cane [kein] *n* caña *f*; (*walking stick*) bastón *m*; (*school*) palmeta *f.* vara *f* **sugar cane** caña de azúcar *f.* **cane furniture** muebles de mimbre *m pl.* *v* castigar con la palmeta *or* vara.

canine ['keinain] *adj* canino. **canine tooth** diente canino *m.*

cannabis ['kanəbis] *n* marijuana *f.*

cannibal ['kanibəl] *n*(*m + f*), *adj* caníbal. **cannibalism** *n* canibalismó *m.*

cannon ['kanən] *n* cañón *m.* **cannonball** *n* bala de cañón *f.*

canoe [kə'nu:] *n* canoa *f.* *v* ir en canoa.

canon ['kanən] *n* canónigo *m.* **canonical** *adj* canónico. **canonize** *v* canonizar. **canonization** *n* canonización *f.*

canopy ['kanəpi] *n* (*awning*) toldo *m*; (*over a bed*) dosel *m*, baldaquin *m.*

canteen [kan'ti:n] *n* (*restaurant*) cantina *f*; (*flask*) cantimplora *f*; (*cutlery*) juego de cubiertos *m.*

canter ['kantə] *n* medio galope *m.* *v* ir a medio galope.

canton ['kantən] *n* cantón *m.*

canvas ['kanvəs] *n* (*fabric*) lona *f*; (*art*) lienzo *m.*

canvass ['kanvəs] *v* solicitar votos de; (*comm*) buscar clientes; (*public opinion*) sondear.

canyon ['kanjən] *n* cañón *m.*

cap [kap] *n* gorra *f*; (*military or bathing*) gorro *m*; (*cover*) tapa *f*; (*bottle*) chapa *f*; (*pen*)

capuchón *m.* *v* (*fig: crown*) coronar; (*do better than*) superar.

capable ['keipəbl] *adj* capaz, hábil. **capability** *n* capacidad *f*, habilidad *f.*

capacity [kə'pasəti] *n* capacidad *f*; (*mot*) cilindrada *f.*

cape[1] [keip] *n* (*cloak*) capa *f*; (*cycling*) impermeable de hule *m.*

cape[2] [keip] *n* (*geog*) cabo *m.*

caper ['keipə] *n* (*jump*) cabriola *f*; (*prank*) travesura *f*; (*cookery*) alcaparra *f.*

capillary [kə'piləri] *n* capilar *m.*

capital ['kapitl] *adj* capital. **capital punishment** pena capital *f.* *n* (*letter*) mayúscula *f*; (*city*) capital *f*; (*money*) fondo de operaciones *m.* **capitalism** *n* capitalismo *m.* **capitalist** *n* capitalista *m, f.* **capitalistic** *adj* capitalista. **capitalize** *v* capitalizar. **capitalization** *n* capitalización *f.*

capitulate [kə'pitjuleit] *v* capitular. **capitulation** *n* capitulación *f.*

capricious [kə'priʃəs] *adj* caprichoso. **caprice, capriciousness** *n* capricho *m.*

Capricorn ['kapriko:n] *n* Capricornio *m.*

capsicum ['kapsikəm] *n* pimiento *m.*

capsize [kap'saiz] *v* volcar, zozobrar.

capsule ['kapsju:l] *n* cápsula *f.*

captain ['kaptin] *n* capitán *m.* *v* capitanear. **captaincy** *n* capitanía *f.*

caption ['kapʃən] *n* encabezamiento *m*; pie *m.* *v* poner pie a.

captive ['kaptiv] *n*, *adj* cautivo, -a. **captivate** *v* cautivar. **captivity** *n* cautividad *f.*

capture ['kaptʃə] *v* capturar; (*place*) tomar; (*market*) acaparar; (*fig*) atraer. *n* captura *f*, apresamiento *m*; (*place*) toma *f.*

car [ka:] *n* coche *m*, automóvil *m*; (*rail*) vagón *m*; (*cable*) cabina *f.* **car boot sale** mercadillo *m*, la mercancía se expone en el maletero del coche y es de segunda mano. **car park** aparcamiento *m.* **car wash** lavado de coches *m.* **dining car** coche comedor *m.* **racing car** coche de carreras *m.* **sleeping car** coche cama *m.*

caramel ['karəmel] *n* caramelo *m*, azúcar quemado *m.*

carat ['karət] *n* quilate *m.*

caravan ['karəvan] *n* (*mot*) remolque *m*; (*travellers*) caravana *f*; (*gipsy*) carromato *m.*

caraway ['karəwei] *n* (*seed*) carvi *m*; (*plant*) alcaravea *f.*

carbohydrate [ka:bə'haidreit] *n* carbohidrato *m*.

carbon ['ka:bən] *n* (*chem*) carbono *m*; **carbón** *m*. **carbon dioxide** bióxido de carbono *m*. **carbon monoxide** monóxido de carbono *m*. **carbon paper** papel carbón *m*.

carbuncle ['ka:bʌŋkl] *n* (*med*) carbunco *m*, carbunclo *m*.

carburettor ['ka:bjuretə] *n* carburador *m*.

carcass ['ka:kəs] *n* (*animal*) res muerta *f*.

card [ka:d] *n* tarjeta *f*; (*visiting*) tarjeta de visita *f*; (*postcard*) tarjeta postal *f*; (*playing card*) carta *f*, naipe *m*; (*membership*) carnet *m*; (*thin cardboard*) cartulina *f*; (*coll*) gracioso, -a *m*, *f*. **cardboard** *n* cartón *m*. **card index** fichero *m*.

cardiac ['ka:diak] *adj* cardiaco *m*.

cardigan ['ka:digən] *n* rebeca *f*.

cardinal ['ka:dənl] *n* (*church, bird*) cardenal *m*. *adj* cardinal, esencial. **cardinal number** número cardinal *m*.

care [keə] *n* cuidado *m*, atención *f*; (*worry*) inquietud *f*; (*responsibility*) cargo *m*. **medical care** asistencia médica *f*. **care of** para entregar a. **handle with care** frágil. **take care!** ¡ojo! *v* importar, preocuparse por. **take care of** guardar, tener cuidado de. **careful** *adj* cuidadoso. **carefulness** *n* cuidado *m*, esmero *m*. **careless** *adj* descuidado, desatento.

career [kə'riə] *n* carrera *f*, curso *m*. *v* correr a toda velocidad.

caress [kə'res] *n* caricia *f*. *v* acariciar.

cargo ['ka:gou] *n* carga *f*, cargamento *m*.

Caribbean [kari'bi:ən] *adj* caribeño

caricature ['karikətjuə] *n* caricatura *f*. *v* caricaturizar.

carnage ['ka:nidʒ] *n* carnicería *f*.

carnal ['ka:nl] *adj* carnal. **carnality** *n* carnalidad *f*.

carnation [ka:'neiʃən] *n* clavel *m*.

carnival ['ka:nivəl] *n* carnaval *m*.

carnivorous [ka:'nivərəs] *adj* carnívoro. **carnivore** *n* carnívoro, -a *m*, *f*.

carol ['karəl] *n* villancico *m*.

carpenter ['ka:pəntə] *n* carpintero *m*. **carpentry** *n* carpintería *f*.

carpet ['ka:pit] *n* alfombra *f*; (*fitted*) moqueta *f*. *v* alfombrar. **carpet-sweeper** escoba mecánica *f*.

carriage ['karidʒ] *n* carruaje *m*, carro *m*; vagón *m*; (*posture*) manera de andar *f*; (*comm*) porte *m*. **carriageway** *n* calzada *f*.

dual carriageway carretera de doble calzada *f*.

carrier ['kariə] *n* portador *m*; (*comm*) empresa de transportes *f*; (*med*) portador, -a *m*, *f*.

carrot ['karət] *n* zanahoria *f*.

carry ['kari] *v* llevar; (*bring*) traer; (*a load*) transportar; (*by pipes*) conducir; (*sustain*) sostener. **carry forward** (*comm*) pasar. **carry out** realizar. **carrycot** *n* cuna portátil *f*.

cart [ka:t] *n* carro *m*; (*handcart*) carro de mano *m*; (*trolley*) carrito *m*. *v* carretear. **cart horse** caballo de tiro *m*.

cartilage ['ka:tilidʒ] *n* cartílago *m*.

cartography [ka:'tografi] *n* cartografía *f*.

carton ['ka:tən] *n* cartón *m*, caja de cartón *f*.

cartoon [ka:'tu:n] *n* caricatura *f*, chiote *m*; (*art*) cartón *m*; (*film*) dibujos animados *m pl*. **cartoonist** *n* caricaturista *m*, *f*, humorista *m*, *f*.

cartridge ['ka:tridʒ] *n* cartucho *m*; (*blank*) cartucho sin bala *m*.

carve [ka:v] *v* (*meat*) trinchar; (*cut*) cortar; (*sculpture*) tallar. **carve up** (*divide*) dividir; (*stab*) acuchillar. **carving knife** cuchillo de trinchar *m*.

cascade [kas'keid] *n* cascada *f*, salto de agua *m*. *v* caer en cascada.

case[1] [keis] *n* caso *m*; (*affair*) asunto *m*. **in any case** en todo caso. **in case** en caso. **in no case** de ningún modo. **in the case of** en cuanto a. **it's not a case of ...** no se trata de. **... just in case** por si acaso. **state the case** exponer los hechos.

case[2] [keis] *n* (*box*) caja *f*; (*rigid*) estuche *m*; (*soft*) funda. **suitcase** *n* maleta *f*. *v* encajonar, embalar.

cash [kaʃ] *n* dinero al constante *m*; (*comm*) pago al contado *m*. **cash account** cuenta de caja *f*. **cash book** libro de caja *m*. **cash discount** descuento por pago al contado *m*. **cash dispenser** cajero automático *m*. **cash on delivery** envío contra reembolso *m*. **cash register** caja registradora *f*. **petty cash** dinero para gastos menores *m*.

cashier[1] [ka'ʃiə] *n* (*bank*) cajero, -a *m*, *f*.

cashier[2] [ka'ʃiə] *v* (*mil*) dar de baja.

cashmere [kaʃ'miə] *n* cachemira *f*.

casing ['keisiŋ] *n* cubierta *f*; (*wrapping*) envoltura *f*; (*cylinder*) camisa *f*.

cell

casino [kə'si:nou] *n* casino *m*.

cask [ka:sk] *n* barril *m*.

casket ['ka:skit] *n* joyero *m*, cofre *m*.

casserole ['kasəroul] *n* (*dish*) cacerola *f*; (*food*) cazuela *f*.

cassette [kə'set] *n* (*tape*) cassette *m*; (*phot*) cartucho *m*.

cassock ['kasək] *n* sotana *f*.

***cast** ['ca:st] *n* (*acting*) reparto *m*; (*throw*) lanzamiento *m*; (*appearance*) aspecto *m*; (*tech*) molde *m*; (*squint*) estrabismo *m*; (*plaster*) escayola *f*. *v* echar, arrojar; (*tech*) moldear, fundir. **castaway** *n* náufrago, -a *m, f*. **cast aside** desechar. **cast down** bajar. **cast iron** hierro colado *m*. **cast off** abandonar; (*naut*) desamarrar.

castanets [kastə'nets] *pl n* castañuelas *f pl*.

caste [ka:st] *n* casta *f*.

castle ['ka:sl] *n* castillo *m*.

castor ['ka:stə] *n* (*wheel*) ruedecilla *f*.

castor oil *n* aceite de ricino *m*.

castrate [kə'streit] *v* castrar. **castration** *n* castración *f*.

casual ['kaʒuəl] *adj* casual, informal; (*carefree*) despreocupado. **casual clothes** ropa de sport *f sing*. **casually** *adv* de paso.

casualty ['kaʒuəlti] *n* accidente *m*; victima *f*; (*mil*) baja *f*.

cat [kat] *n* gato, -a *m, f*. **let the cat out of the bag** descubrir el pastel.

catalogue ['katalog] *n* catálogo *m*. *v* catalogar.

catalyst ['katəlist] *n* catalizador *m*. **catalytic converter** convertidor catalítico *m*.

catapult ['katəpʌlt] *n* catapulta *f*, honda *f*. *v* catapultar.

cataract ['katərakt] *n* catarata *f*.

catarrh [kə'ta:] *n* catarro *m*.

catastrophe [kə'tastrəfi] *n* catástrofe *f*. **catastrophic** *adj* catastrófico.

***catch** [katʃ] *v* (*seize*) agarrar, cojer; (*capture*) prender, atrapar; (*disease*) contraer; (*hook*) engancharse. **catch on** (*coll*) comprender. **catch out** sorprender. **catch up** alcanzar. *n* (*act of catching*) cogida *f*; (*prey*) presa *f*; (*bolt*) pestillo *m*; (*buckle*) hebijón *m*; (*drawback*) trampa *f*; (*trick*) truco *m*. **safety catch** fiador *m*. **catching** *adj* contagioso. **catchy** *adj* pegadizo.

category ['katəgəri] *n* categoría *f*. **categorical** *adj* categórico, rotundo. **categorize** *v* clasificar.

cater ['keitə] *v* proveer de comida. **cater for** atender a. **caterer** *n* proveedor, -a *m, f*. **catering** *n* abastecimiento *m*.

caterpillar ['katəpilə] *n* oruga *f*.

cathedral [kə'θi:drəl] *n* catedral *f*.

cathode ['kaθoud] *n* cátodo *m*. **cathode-ray tube** tubo de rayos catódicos *m*.

catholic ['kaθəlik] *n, adj* católico, -a. *adj* universal; ortodoxo. **catholicism** *n* catolicismo *m*. **catholicity** *n* catolicidad *f*.

catkin ['katkin] *n* candelilla *f*.

cattle ['katl] *n* ganado *m*.

catty ['kati] *adj* malicioso.

caught [ko:t] *V* **catch**.

cauliflower ['koliflauə] *n* coliflor *f*.

cause [ko:z] *n* causa *f*, motivo *m*. *v* causar, provocar. **in the cause of** por.

causeway ['ko:zwei] *n* terraplén *m*.

caustic ['ko:stik] *adj* cáustico, mordaz.

caution ['ko:ʃən] *n* cautela *f*, cuidado *m*; (*warning*) advertencia *f*. *v* (*reprimand*) amonestar; (*warn*) advertir. **cautionary** *adj* amonestador. **cautious** *adj* cauteloso, precavido.

cavalry ['kavəlri] *n* caballería *f*.

cave [keiv] *n* cueva *f*, caverna *f*. **cave in** derrumbarse. **cavernous** *adj* cavernoso.

caviar ['kavia:] *n* caviar *m*.

cavity ['kavəti] *n* cavidad *f*; (*dental*) caries *f invar*.

cayenne [kei'en] *n* pimentón *m*.

CCTV *n* TVCC *f*, video portero *m*

CD *n* CD *m*

CD-ROM [si:di:'rom] *n* CD-ROM *m*

cease [si:s] *v* cesar. **cease-fire** *n* alto el fuego *m*. **ceaseless** *adj* incesante.

cedar ['si:də] *n* cedro *m*.

cedilla [si'dilə] *n* cedilla *f*.

ceiling ['si:liŋ] *n* techo *m*; (*aero*) altura *f*; (*fig*) tope *m*, limite *m*. **hit the ceiling** subirse por las paredes.

celebrate ['seləbreit] *v* celebrar, festejar. **celebrated** *adj* célebre. **celebration** *n* celebración *f*. **celebrant** *n* celebrante *m*.

celery ['seləri] *n* apio *m*.

celestial [sə'lestiəl] *adj* celestial; (*astron*) celeste.

celibate ['selibət] *n(m + f)*, *adj* célibe. **celibacy** *n* celibato *m*.

cell [sel] *n* celda *f*; (*biol*) célula *f*; (*elec*) pila *f*.

cellar ['selə] *n* sótano *m*; (*wine*) bodega *f*.

cello ['tʃelou] *n* violoncelo *m*. **cellist** *n* violoncelista *m*, *f*.

cellular ['seljulə] *adj* celular.

cement [sə'ment] *n* cemento. *v* (*tech*) cementar; (*fig*) cimentar.

cemetery ['semətri] *n* cementerio *m*.

cenotaph ['senətɑːf] *n* cenotafio *m*.

censor ['sensə] *n* censor *m*. *v* censurar; (*delete*) tachar. **censorious** *adj* censorador. **censorship** *n* censura *f*.

censure ['senʃə] *n* censura *f*. *v* censurar. **censurable** *adv* censurable.

census ['sensəs] *n* censo *m*. **take a census of** empadronar.

cent [sent] *n* **centavo** *m*.

centenary [sen'tiːnəri] *nm*, *adj* centenario. **centenarian** *n*, *adj* centenario, -a. **centennial** *adj* centenario.

centigrade ['sentigreid] *adj* centígrado.

centimetre ['sentimiːtə] *n* centímetro *m*.

centipede ['sentipiːd] *n* ciempiés *m invar*.

centre ['sentə] *n* centro *m*. **community centre** centro social *m*. *v* centrar. **central** *adj* central, céntrico. **central heating** calefacción central *f*. **centralize** *v* centralizar. **centralization** *n* centralización *f*.

centrifugal [sen'trifjugəl] *adj* centrífugo.

century ['sentʃuri] *n* siglo *m*.

ceramic [sə'ramik] *adj* cerámico. **ceramics** *n* cerámica *f sing*.

cereal ['siəriəl] *nm*, *adj* cereal.

ceremony ['serəməni] *n* ceremonia *f*. **stand on ceremony** andarse con ceremonias. **ceremonial** *nm*, *adj* ceremonial. **ceremonious** *adj* ceremonioso.

certain ['səːtn] *adj* cierto, seguro. **make certain** asegurarse. **certainly** *adv* desde luego, naturalmente. **certainly not** de ninguna manera. **certainty** *n* certeza *f*. certidumbre *f*, seguridad *f*.

certificate [sə'tifikət] *n* certificado *m*; (*academic*) título *m*, diploma *f*. **birth certificate** partida de nascimiento *f*. **death certificate** partida de defunción *f*. **marriage certificate** partida de matrimonio *f*. **certify** *v* certificar; garantizar.

cesspool ['sespuːl] *n* pozo negro *m*.

chafe [tʃeif] *v* (*rub*) rozar; (*irritate*) irritar; (*for warmth*) frotar; (*fig*) enfadar. *n* rozadura *f*; irritación *f*.

chaffinch ['tʃafintʃ] *n* pinzón *m*.

chain [tʃein] *n* cadena *f*. *v* encadenar. **chain store** sucursal *m*.

chair [tʃeə] *n* silla *f*; (*university*) cátedra *f*; (*meeting*) presidencia *f*. **folding chair** silla plegable *f*. **take the chair** tomar la presidencia. *v* presidir. **chairman** *n* presidente *m*.

chalet ['ʃalei] *n* chalet *m*.

chalk [tʃoːk] *n* (*geol*) creta *f*; (*for writing*) tiza *f*. **not by a long chalk** ni mucho menos. *v* marcar con tiza. **chalk up** apuntarse. **chalky** *adj* cretáceo, yesoso.

challenge ['tʃalindʒ] *n* reto *m*, desafío *m*; (*sentry*) alto *m*; (*incentive*) estímulo *m*; (*law*) recusación *f*. *v* desafiar, retar. **challenger** *n* desafiador, -a *m*, *f*, retador, -a *m*, *f*.

chamber ['tʃeimbə] *n* (*room, legislative body*) cámara *f*; (*tech*) recámara *f*. **chambermaid** *n* doncella *f*, camarera *f*. **chamber music** música de cámara *f*. **chamber pot** orinal *m*.

chameleon [kəmiːliən] *n* camaleón *m*.

chamois ['ʃamwaː] *n* gamuza *f*.

champagne [ʃam'pein] *n* champaña *f*.

champion ['tʃampiən] *n*, *adj* campeón, -ona. *v* defender, hacerse el campeón de. **championship** *n* campeonato *m*.

chance [tʃaːns] *n* casualidad *f*, suerte *f*, azar *m*; oportunidad *f*, ocasión *f*; posibilidad *f*; riesgo *m*. *adj* casual, fortuito. *v* arriesgar; probar; (*happen*) acaecer. **chance upon** tropezarse con.

chancellor [tʃaː'nsələ] *n* canciller *m*. **chancellery** *n* cancillería *f*.

chandelier [ʃandə'liə] *n* araña *f*.

change [tʃeindʒ] *n* cambio *m*; (*money*) suelto *m*; (*clothes*) muda *f*. **for a change** para variar. *v* cambiar; mudar. **changeable** *adj* (*character, weather*) variable; (*inconsistent*) cambiadizo; (*able to be changed*) cambiable. **changing room** vestuario *m*.

channel ['tʃanl] *n* canal *m*; (*of a river*) cauce *m*; (*fig*) vía *f*; (*groove*) ranura *f*. **English Channel** Canal de la Mancha *m*; **Channel tunnel** Eurotúnel *m*.

chant [tʃaːnt] *n* canción *f*, canto *m*. *v* cantar; entonar.

chaos ['keios] *n* caos *m*. **chaotic** *adj* caótico.

chap¹ [tʃap] *v* (*skin*) agrietar. *n* grieta *f*.

chap² [tʃap] *n* (*coll*) tipo *m*, sujeto *m*.

chapel ['tʃapəl] *n* capilla *f*.

chaperon [ˈʃapəroun] n carabina f. v acompañar.

chaplain [ˈtʃaplin] n capellán m.

chapter [ˈtʃaptə] n capítulo m; (rel) cabildo m. **quote chapter and verse** citar literalmente.

charisma [kəˈrizmə] n carisma m

char[1] [tʃaː] v (burn) carbonizar.

char[2] [tʃaː] n (charwoman) asistenta f.

character [ˈkarəktə] n carácter m; (person) personaje m; (role) papel m; (coll) tipo m. **character reference** informe m. **characterize** v caracterizar. **characterization** n caracterización f.

characteristic [ˌkarəktəˈristik] adj característico. n característica f.

charcoal [ˈtʃaːkoul] n carbón de leña m.

charge [tʃaːdʒ] n (responsibility) cargo m; (task) tarea f; (battery, explosive, attack) carga f. **charge account** cuenta a cargo f. **charge card** tarjeta de crédito f. **in charge of** encargado de. **take charge of** hacerse cargo de. v (accuse) acusar; (bill) cobrar; (mil) atacar.

chariot [ˈtʃariət] n carro m.

charity [ˈtʃarəti] n caridad f; (alms) limosna f; (society) sociedad benéfica f. **charitable** adj caritativo.

charm [tʃaːm] n encanto m; (spell) hechizo m. v encantar; hechizar. **charming** adj encantador, simpático.

chart [tʃaːt] n (naut) carta marina f; (map) mapa m; (table) tabla f; (graph) gráfico m. v tabular; trazar.

charter [ˈtʃaːtə] n (law) carta f; (comm) flete m, fletamento m, fletamiento m; (transport) alquiler m. v fletar; alquilar; (grant a charter) conceder carta a. **charter flight** vuelo charter m. **charter member** socio fundador m.

chase [tʃeis] v perseguir; (hunt) cazar. **chase after** ir detrás de. **chase away/off** ahuyentar. n persecución f; caza f.

chasm [ˈkazəm] n sima f, abismo m.

chassis [ˈʃasi] n (mech) chasis m.

chaste [tʃeist] adj casto; (style) sobrio. **chastity** n castidad f.

chastise [tʃasˈtaiz] v castigar.

chat [tʃat] n charla f. **chat room** (internet) chat room m, foro de discusión m. **chat show** chat show m, programa basura m. v charlar. **chatty** adj charlador.

chatter [ˈtʃatə] v chacharear, parlotear; (teeth) castañetear. n cháchara f, parloteo m; castañeteo m. **chatterbox** n charlatán, -ana m, f.

chauffeur [ˈʃoufə] n chófer m, conductor, -a m, f.

chauvinism [ˈʃouvinizəm] n chauvinismo m. **chauvinist** n(m + f), adj chauvinista.

cheap [tʃiːp] adj barato. **dirt cheap** baratísimo. **cheapen** v abaratar.

cheat [tʃiːt] v (swindle) timar, estafar; (deceive) engañar; (at games) hacer trampas; (in exams) copiar. n timador, -a m, f, estafador, -a m, f; tramposo, -a m, f; (trick) trampa f.

check [tʃek] v parar, detener; (restrain) reprimir, refrenar; (inspect) inspeccionar; (facts) comprobar; (mark) marcar; (chess) dar jaque a. **check in** registrarse. **check on** averiguar. **check with** cotejar con. n parada f, detención f; (restraint) restricción f; (control) inspección f; (pattern) cuadro m; (chess) jaque m. **checkmate** v dar el mate; n jaque mate m. **checkpoint** n control m. **check-up** n (med) reconocimiento general m.

cheek [tʃiːk] n carillo m, mejilla f; (coll) cadura f. **turn the other cheek** poner la otra mejilla. **cheekbone** n pómulo m. **cheeky** adj descarado.

cheer [tʃiə] v (shout) vitorear, aclamar; (gladden) alegrar. **cheer on** animar. **cheer up** alentar. n (shout) viva m; (comfort) consuelo m; (joy) ánimo m. **cheers!** interj ¡a su salud! **cheerful** adj alegre, animado. **cheerfulness** n alegría f. **cheerio!** interj ¡hasta luego! **cheerless** adj triste.

cheese [tʃiːz] n queso m. **cheesecake** n pastel de queso m. **cheesecloth** n estopilla f.

cheetah [ˈtʃiːtə] n leopardo cazador m.

chef [ʃef] n jefe de cocina m.

chemical [ˈkemikl] adj químico

chemistry [ˈkemistri] n química f. **chemical** adj químico. **chemist** n químico, -a m, f; farmacéutico, -a m, f. **chemist's shop** farmacia f.

cheque [tʃek] n cheque m. **chequebook** n talonario de cheques m. **cheque card** tarjeta de identificación bancaria f. **traveller's cheque** cheque de viaje m.

cherish [ˈtʃeriʃ] v (love) querer; (nourish) abrigar; (take care of) cuidar.

cherry [ˈtʃeri] n (fruit) cereza f; (tree)

cerezo *m*.

chess [tʃes] *n* ajedrez *m*. **chessboard** *n* tablero de ajedrez *m*. **chessman** *n* pieza de ajedrez *f*.

chest [tʃest] *n* (*anat*) pecho *m*; (*box*) caja *f*. **chest of drawers** *n* cómoda *f*. **chesty** *adj* (*cough*) delicado de los broncios.

chestnut ['tʃesnʌt] *n* (*fruit*) castaña *f*; (*tree*) castaño *m*. *adj* (*hair*) castaño.

chew [tʃu:] *v* masticar. **chewing gum** chicle *m*. **chew the cud** rumiar. **chew up** estropear.

chick pea ['tʃik,pi:] *n* garbanzo *m*.

chicken ['tʃikin] *n* pollo *m*. **chickenpox** *n* varicela *f*. **chicken out** (*slang*) ser una gallina.

chicory ['tʃikəri] *n* (*coffee*) achicoria *f*; (*salad*) escarola *f*.

chief [tʃi:f] *n pl* -s jefe *m*, *f*. *adj* principal. **chiefly** *adv* principalmente; sobre todo.

chilblain ['tʃilblein] *n* sabañón *m*.

child [tʃaild] *n pl* -ren niño, -a *m*, *f*. **childbirth** *n* parto *m*. **childhood** *n* niñez *f*. **childish** *adj* infantil, pueril. **childless** *adj* sin hijos. **child-minder** cuidadora *f*.

Chile ['tʃili] *n* Chile *m*. **Chilean** *n*, *adj* chileno, -a *m*, *f*.

chill [tʃil] *n* frío *m*; (*med*) tiritona *f*; (*shiver*) escalofrío *m*. *adj* frialdad *f*. *v* enfriar. **chilled to the bone** enfriado hasta los huesos. **chilly** *adj* fresco.

chilli ['tʃili] *n* chile *m*.

chime [tʃaim] *v* sonar, repicar. **chime in** intervenir. *n* carillón *m*.

chimney ['tʃimni] *n* chimenea *f*. **chimney pot** cañón de chimenea *m*. **chimney sweep** deshollinador *m*.

chimpanzee [tʃimpən'zi:] *n* chimpancé *m*.

chin [tʃin] *n* barbilla *f*, mentón *m*.

china ['tʃainə] *n* porcelana *f*.

China ['tʃainə] *n* China *f*. **Chinese** *n*, *adj* chino, -a. **the Chinese** los chinos.

chink[1] [tʃiŋk] *n* (*fissure*) raja *f*, grieta *f*.

chink[2] [tʃiŋk] *n* (*sound*) sonido metálico *m*. *v* hacer tintinear.

chip [tʃip] *n* (*fragment*) pedacito *m*; (*in cup, etc*.) desportilladura *f*; (*gambling*) ficha *f*. **chipboard** *n* madera aglomerada *f*. **chips** *pl n* (*cookery*) patatas fritas *f*. *pl v* astillar. **chip in** (*interrupt*) interrumpir; (*contribute money*) poner.

chiropodist [ki'ropədist] *n* pedicuro, -a *m*,

f. **chiropody** *n* quiropodia *f*.

chirp [tʃə:p] *v* (*birds*) gorjear; (*crickets*) chirriar. *n* gorjeo *m*; chirrido *m*. **chirpy** *adj* animado.

chisel ['tʃizl] *n* cincel *m*. *v* cincelar.

chivalry ['ʃivəlri] *n* caballerosidad *f*. **chivalrous** *adj* caballeroso.

chive [tʃaiv] *n* cebolleta *f*.

chlorine ['klo:ri:n] *n* cloro *m*. **chlorinate** *v* tratar con cloro.

chloroform ['klorəfo:m] *n* cloroformo *m*. *v* cloroformizar.

chlorophyll ['klorəfil] *n* clorofila *f*.

chocolate ['tʃokələt] *n* chocolate *m*. **drinking chocolate** chocolate a la taza *m*.

choice [tʃois] *n* elección *f*, selección *f*; preferencia *f*. *adj* (*best*) de primera calidad.

choir ['kwaiə] *n* coro *m*, coral *f*. **choirboy** *n* niño de coro *m*. **choirmaster** *n* director de coro *m*.

choke [tʃouk] *v* (*strangle*) estrangular; (*block*) obstruir. *n* (*mot*) estrangulador *m*.

cholera ['kolərə] *n* cólera *m*.

cholesterol [kə'lestərol] *n* colesterol *m*.

*choose [tʃu:z] *v* escoger, elegir.

chop[1] [tʃop] *n* (*meat*) chuleta *f*; (*blow*) golpe *m*. *v* (*cut*) cortar; (*mince*) picar; (*lop*) tronchar. **chop down** talar. **chopper** *n* hacha *f*; (*slang*) helicóptero *m*.

chop[2] [tʃop] *v* **chop and change** cambiar de opinión. **choppy** *adj* (*sea*) picado.

chops [tʃops] *pl n* (*jaws*) morros *m pl*. **lick one's chops** relamerse.

chopstick ['tʃopstik] *n* palillo *m*.

chord [ko:d] *n* (*music*) acorde *m*; (*anat*) cuerda *f*.

chore [tʃo:] *n* (*unpleasant*) tarea penosa *f*. **chores** *pl n* (*household*) faenas de la casa *f pl*.

choreography [kori'ogrəfi] *n* coreografía *f*. **choreographer** *n* coreógrafo, -a *m*, *f*.

chorus ['ko:rəs] *n* (*refrain*) estribillo *m*; (*singers*) coro *m*. **chorus girl** corista *f*. **choral** *adj* coral. **choral society** orfeón *m*.

chose [tʃouz] *V* **choose**.

christen ['krisn] *v* bautizar; (*nickname*) llamar. **christening** *n* bautismo *m*.

Christian ['kristʃən] *n*, *adj* cristiano, -a *m*, *f*. **Christian name** nombre de pila *m*. **Christianity** *n* cristianismo *m*.

Christmas ['krisməs] *n* Navidad *f*.

Christmas Day dia de Navidad *m*.
Christmas Eve Nochebuena *f*.
chromatic [krə'matik] *adj* cromático.
chrome [kroum] *n* cromo *m*.
chromium ['kroumiəm] *n* cromo *m*.
chromium-plated *adj* cromado.
chronic ['kronik] *adj* crónico; (*coll: dreadful*) terrible.
chronicle ['kronikl] *n* crónica *f*.
chronological [kronə'lodʒikəl] *adj* cronológico.
chrysalis ['krisəlis] *n* crisálida *f*.
chrysanthemum [kri'sanθəməm] *n* crisantemo *m*.
chubby ['tʃʌbi] *adj* gordinflón.
chuck [tʃʌk] *v* (*coll: throw*) tirar; (*give up*) abandonar.
chuckle ['tʃʌkl] *v* reir entre de dientes. *n* risa *f*.
chunk [tʃʌŋk] *n* pedazo *m*; (*large amount*) cantidad grande *f*.
church [tʃəːtʃ] *n* iglesia *f*. **church service** oficio religioso *m*. **churchyard** *n* cementerio *m*.
churn [tʃəːn] *n* mantequera *f*. *v* batir. **churn out** producir en profusión.
chute [ʃuːt] *n* tolva *f*.
cider ['saidə] *n* sidra *f*.
cigar [si'gaː] *n* puro *m*.
cigarette [sigə'ret] *n* cigarillo *m*. **cigarette case** pitillera *f*. **cigarette holder** boquilla *f*. **cigarette lighter** encendedor *m*, mechero *m*. **cigarette paper** papel de fumar *m*.
cinder ['sində] *n* carbonilla *f*, ceniza *f*.
cinema ['sinəmə] *n* cine *m*. **cinematography** *n* cinematografia *f*.
cinnamon ['sinəmən] *n* canela *f*.
circle ['səːkl] *n* círculo *m*; (*theatre*) piso principal *m*. **go round in circles** dar vueltas. *v* rodear; (*surround*) circundar. **circular** *adj*, *n* circular *f*.
circuit ['səːkit] *n* (*route*) circuito *m*; (*perimeter*) perímetro *m*; (*law*) distrito *m*; (*cinemas, theatres*) cadena *f*. **short circuit** cortocircuito *m*. **circuitous** *adj* indirecto.
circulate ['səːkjuleit] *v* circular. **circulation** *n* circulación *f*.
circumcise ['səːkəmsaiz] *v* circuncidar. **circumcision** *n* circuncisión *f*.
circumference [sə'kʌmfərəns] *n* circunferencia *f*.
circumflex ['səːkəmfleks] *n* circunflejo *m*.
circumscribe ['səːkəmskraib] *v* circunscribir. **circumscription** *n* circunscripción *f*.
circumstance ['səːkəmstans] *n* circunstancia *f*. **extenuating circumstances** circunstancias atenuantes *f pl*. **under no circumstances** de ninguna manera. **under the circumstances** en estas circunstancias. **circumstantial** *adj* (*incidental*) circunstancial; (*detailed*) circunstanciado. **circumstancial evidence** testimonio indirecto *m*.
circus ['səːkəs] *n* circo *m*.
cistern ['sistən] *n* cisterna *f*, aljibe *m*.
cite [sait] *v* citar. **citation** *n* citación *f*; (*mil*) mención *f*.
citizen ['sitizn] *n* ciudadano, -a *m*, *f*. **citizenship** *n* ciudadania *f*.
citrus ['sitrəs] *n* cidro *m*. **citrus fruit** *n* agrios *m pl*. **citric acid** ácido cítrico *m*.
city ['siti] *n* ciudad *f*.
civic ['sivik] *adj* cívico.
civil ['sivl] *adj* civil; (*polite*) cortés. **civil engineering** ingeniería civil *f*. **civil rights** derechos civiles *m pl*. **civil servant** funcionario, -a *m*, *f*. **civil service** administración pública *f*. **civil war** guerra civil *f*.
civilian [sə'viljən] *adj* civil, de paisano. *n* paisano, -a *m*, *f*.
civilization [ˌsivilai'zeiʃən] *n* civilización *f*. **civilize** *v* civilizar.
clad [klad] *adj* vestido (de).
claim [kleim] *v* (*damages*) exigir; (*a right*) reclamar; (*assert*) declarar; (*need*) requerir. *n* (*right*) derecho *m*; (*demand*) demanda *f*, reclamación *f*; (*statement*) declaración *f*; (*land*) propiedad *f*. **claimant** (*law*) *n* demandante *m*, *f*; (*pretender*) pretendiente *m*, *f*.
clairvoyant [kleə'voiənt] *n*(*m* + *f*), *adj* clarividente. **clairvoyance** *n* clarividencia. *f*.
clam [klam] *n* almeja *f*.
clamber ['klambə] *v* trepar.
clammy ['klami] *adj* pegajoso.
clamour ['klamə] *n* clamor *m*. *v* clamar, vociferar.
clamp [klamp] *n* abrazadera *f*. **clamp** (*wheel*) cepo *m*. *v* sujetar con abrazadera; poner un cepo. **clamp down on** suprimir.
clan [klan] *n* clan *m*. **clannish** *adj* exclu-

sivista.

clandestine [klan'destin] *adj* clandestino.

clang [klaŋ] *v* sonar estripitosamente. *n* sonido metálico *m*.

clap [klap] *v* aplaudir, dar palmadas. *n* (*with hands*) palmada *f*; (*noise*) ruido seco *m*. **clap of thunder** trueno *m*.

claret ['klarət] *n* clarete *m*.

clarify ['klarəfai] *v* aclarar; (*liquid*) clarificar. **clarification** *n* aclaración *f*; clarificación *f*.

clarinet [klarə'net] *n* clarinete *m*.

clarity ['klarəti] *n* claridad *f*.

clash [klaʃ] *v* (*collide*) chocar; (*cymbals*) golpear; (*interests*) estar en desacuerdo; (*dates*) coincidir; (*colours*) matarse., *n* ruido metálico *m*; (*encounter*) choque *m*; (*interests*) conflicto *m*; coincidencia *f*; disparidad *f*.

clasp [kla:sp] *v* (*grasp*) agarrar; (*fasten*) abrochar. *n* (*hands*) apretón *m*; (*fastening*) cierre *m*; (*belt*) broche *f*.

class [kla:s] *n* clase *f*.

classic ['klasik] *adj* clásico. **classical** *adj* clásico. **classics** *n pl* clásicas *f pl*.

classify ['klasifai] *v* clasificar. **classification** *n* clasificación *f*. **classified advertisement** anuncio por palabras *m*.

clatter ['klatə] *n* estruendo *m*; (*hooves*) chacoloteo *m*. *v* sonar con estrépito; chacolotear.

clause [klo:z] *n* (*law*) cláusula *f*; (*gramm*) oración *f*.

claustrophobia [klo:strə'foubiə] *n* claustrofobia *f*.

claw [klo:] *n* (*talon*) garra *f*; (*cat*) uña *f*; (*crab*) pinza *f*; (*tech*) garfio *m*. *v* agarrar; arañar; (*tear*) desgarrar.

clay [klei] *n* arcilla *f*, barro *m*.

clean [kli:n] *adj* limpio; (*irreproachable*) sin tacha. *v* limpiar. **clean out** (*empty*) vaciar. **clean up** (*tidy*) ordenar; (*win*) ganarse. **clean-cut** *adj* bien hecho, perfilado. **cleaner** (*person*) *n* asistenta *f*. **cleanliness** *n* limpieza *f*. **clean-shaven** *adj* bien afeitado.

cleanse [klenz] *v* limpiar, purificar.

clear [kliə] *adj* claro, transparente; (*conscience*) tranquilo; evidente; (*free*) libre; (*unobstructed*) despejado; (*profit*) neto. *adv* claramente. *v* aclarar; despejar; (*law*) absolver. **clearance** *n* espacio *m*, altura libre *f*, margen *m*; despeje *m*; acreditación *f*. **clearance sale** liquidación *f*.

clef [klef] *n* clave *f*.

clench [klentʃ] *v* apretar, sujetar.

clergy ['klə:dʒi] *n* clero *m*. **clergyman** *n* clérigo *m*.

clerical ['klerikəl] *adj* (*clerk*) de oficina; (*rel*) clerical. **clerical error** error de copia *m*.

clerk [kla:k] *n* oficinista *m*, *f*; (*law*) escribano *m*.

clever ['klevə] *adj* listo; inteligente; (*skilful*) hábil; (*cunning*) astuto. **cleverness** *n* habilidad *f*; ingenio *m*.

cliché ['kli:ʃei] *n* cliché *m*, clisé *m*.

click [klik] *n* chasquido *m*; taconeo *m*; (*computing*) un click en *m*. *v* chascar, chasquear; taconear; (*computing*) hacer click en.

client ['klaiənt] *n* cliente *m*, *f*.

cliff [klif] *n* (*coast*) acantilado *m*; (*crag*) risco *m*.

climate ['klaimət] *n* clima *m*; (*atmosphere*) ambiente *m*. **climatic** *adj* climático.

climax ['klaimaks] *n* punto culminante *m*; climax *m*. *v* llevar al punto culminante.

climb [klaim] *v* subir, escalar; (*plants*) trepar. *n* subida *f*, escalada *f*. **climber** *n* escalador, -a *m*, *f*; (*mountaineer*) alpinista *m*, *f*; (*plant*) planta trepadora *f*.

***cling** [kliŋ] *v* agarrarse; (*stick to*) adherirse a, pegarse a. **clinging** *adj* ceñido; pegajoso.

clinic ['klinik] *n* dispensario *m*; clínica *f*. **clinical** *adj* clínico.

clip¹ [klip] *v* (*trim*) recortar; (*animals*) esquilar; (*ticket*) picar; (*coll: cuff*) abofetear. *n* (*film*) fragmento *m*; (*cuff*) bofetada *f*.

clip² [klip] *v* (*fasten*) sujetar. *n* grapa *f*; sujetapapeles *m invar*; (*hair*) horquilla *f*; (*pen, pencil*) prendedor *m*.

cloak [klouk] *n* capa *f*; (*fig*) manto *m*; (*mil*) capote *m*. **cloak-and-dagger** *adj* de capa y espada. **cloakroom** *n* guardarropa *m*; (*toilet*) servicios *m pl*. *v* encubrir, cubrir, encapotar.

clock [klok] *n* reloj *m*. **against the clock** contra reloj. **alarm clock** despertador *m*. **around the clock** durante 24 horas. **clockwise** *adj* en el sentido de las agujas del reloj. **clockwork** *n* aparato de relojería *m*. *v* registrar.

clog [klog] *n* zueco *m*. *v* atascar, obstruir.

cloister ['kloistə] *n* claustro *m*. *v* enclaustrar.

clone [kloun] *n* clon *m*. *v* clonar

close [klouz; *adj, adv* klous] *v* cerrar; (*block*) tapar; (*end*) acabar; (*account*) saldar; (*dis-*

tance) acortar. **close in** acercarse. *n* conclusión *f*; final *m*. *adj* cercano; íntimo; (*air*) cargado; (*game*) reñido. *adv* cerca. **close-up** *n* primer plano *m*.

closet ['klɔzit] *n* (*WC*) retrete *m*, water *m*; armario *m*.

clot [klɔt] *n* (*blood*) coágulo *m*; (*liquid*) grumo *m*. *v* coagular, cuajar.

cloth [klɔθ] *n* (*rag*) trapo *m*; (*fabric*) paño *m*; (*tablecloth*) mantel *m*.

clothe [klouð] *v* vestir; (*cover*) cubrir.

clothes [klouðz] *pl n also* **clothing** ropa *f sing*; vestidos *m pl*. **clothes basket** cesta de la ropa sucia *f*. **clothes brush** cepillo de la ropa *m*. **clothes line** tendedero *m*. **clothes peg** pinza *f*.

cloud [klaud] *n* nube *f*; (*gas*) capa *f*. *v* nublar; (*darken*) ensombrecer, oscurecer. **cloudburst** *n* chaparrón *m*. **cloudiness** *n* nubosidad *f*. **cloudless** *adj* despejado. **cloudy** *adj* nuboso; nublado.

clove¹ [klouv] *n* (*spice*) clavo *m*.

clove² [klouv] *n* (*of garlic, etc.*) diente *m*.

clover ['klouvə] *n* trébol *m*.

clown [klaun] *n* payaso *m*. *v* hacer el payaso.

club [klʌb] *n* (*association*) club *m*; (*stick*) porra *f*, garrote *m*; (*golf*) palo *m*. *v* (*beat*) aporrear. **clubfoot** *n* pie zopo *m*.

clue [klu:] *n* (*police lead*) pista *f*; (*piece of evidence*) indicio *m*.

clump [klʌmp] *n* (*trees*) grupo *m*; (*flowers*) matar *f*; (*earth*) terrón *m*; (*noise*) pisada fuerte *f*. *v* agrupar; andar con pisadas fuertes.

clumsy ['klʌmzi] *adj* (*awkward*) torpe; (*unskilful*) desmañado; (*tactless*) sin tacto. **clumsiness** *n* torpeza *f*; desmaña *f*.

cluster ['klʌstə] *n* grupo *m*; (*fruits*) racimo *m*. *v* agruparse, arracimarse.

clutch [klʌtʃ] *v* agarrar, apretar. *n* (*grip*) agarrón *m*; (*mot*) embrague *m*. **engage the clutch** embragar.

clutter ['klʌtə] *n* desorden *m*, confusión *f*. *v* desordenar, atentar.

coach [koutʃ] *n* (*carriage*) coche *m*; (*ceremonial carriage*) carroza *f*; (*mot*) autocar *m*; (*tutor*) profesor, -a particular *m*, *f*; (*trainer*) entrenador, -a *m f*, *v* dar clases particulares; entrenar.

coagulate [kou'agjuleit] *v* coagular. **coagulation** *n* coagulación *f*.

coal [koul] *n* carbón *m*, hulla *f*. **coal cellar** carbonera *f*. **coalman** *n* carbonero *m*. **coalmine** *n* mina de carbón *f*. **coalminer** *n* minero de carbón *m*. **coal scuttle** cubo para el carbón *m*.

coalesce [kouə'les] *v* (*unite*) unirse; (*merge*) fundirse.

coalition [kouə'liʃən] *n* coalición *f*.

coarse [kɔ:s] *adj* (*gross*) grosero; (*illmade*) basto. **coarse-grained** *adj* de grano grueso. **coarseness** *n* grosería *f*; basteza *f*.

coast [koust] *n* costa *f*. **the coast is clear** no hay moros en la costa. *v* (*freewheel*) deslizarse cuesta abajo. **coastguard** *n* guardacostas *m invar*. **coastline** *n* litoral *m*.

coat [kout] *n* chaqueta *f*; (*overcoat*) abrigo *m*; (*animal*) pelo *m*. **coat-hanger** *n* percha *f*. **coat of arms** escudo de armas *m*. **coat of paint** mano de pintura *f*. *v* cubrir; dar una mano de pintura; (*cookery*) rebozar. **coating** *n* capa *f*; mano *f*; rebozo *m*.

coax [kouks] *v* engatusar.

cobbler ['koblə] *n* zapatero *m*.

cobra ['koubrə] *n* cobra *f*.

cobweb ['kobweb] *n* telaraña *f*.

cocaine [kə'kein] *n* cocaína *f*.

cock¹ [kok] *n* (*male fowl*) gallo *m*; (*male bird*) macho *m*; (*vulg: penis*) polla *f*. **cocky** *adj* engreído.

cock² [kok] *v* (*gun*) amartillar; (*ears*) aguzar el oído.

cockle ['kokl] *n* berberecho *m*.

cockpit ['kokpit] *n* (*aero*) cabina del piloto *f*; (*cockfighting*) reñidero *m*.

cockroach ['kokroutʃ] *n* cucaracha *f*.

cocktail ['kokteil] *n* cóctel *m*. **cocktail shaker** coctelera *f*.

cocoa ['koukou] *n* cacao *m*.

coconut ['koukənʌt] *n* coco *m*. **coconut palm** cocotero *m*.

cocoon [kə'ku:n] *n* capullo *m*.

cod [kod] *n* bacalao *m*.

code [koud] *n* código *m*; (*signals*) cifra *f*, clave *f*; (*area code*) prefijo *m*. **highway code** código de la circulación *m*. **Morse code** alfabeto Morse *m*. *v* cifrar.

codeine ['koudi:n] *n* codeína *f*.

coeducation [kouedju'keiʃən] *n* coeducación *f*.

coerce [kou'əts] *v* forzar, óbligar.

coexist [kouig'zist] *v* coexistir. **coexistence**

n coexistencia *f*.

coffee ['kofi] *n* café *m*. **black/white coffee** café solo/con leche *m*. **coffee bean** grano de café *m*. **coffee pot** cafetera *f*. **coffee table** mesita de café *f*.

coffin ['kofin] *n* ataúd *m*.

cog [kog] *n* diente *m*; (*wheel*) rueda dentada *f*.

cognac ['konjak] *n* coñac *m*.

cohabit [kou'habit] *v* cohabitar, vivir juntos. **cohabitation** *n* cohabitación *f*.

cohere [kə'hiə] *v* adherirse, pegarse. **coherence** *n* coherencia *f*. **coherent** *adj* coherente.

coil [koil] *n* (*rope*) rollo *m*; (*smoke*) espiral *m*; (*elec*) carrete *m*. **coil spring** muelle en espiral *m*. *v* enrollar, arrollar.

coin [koin] *n* moneda *f*. **toss a coin** echar a cara o cruz. *v* acuñar; inventar. **coinage** *n* moneda *f*.

coincide [kouin'said] *v* coincidir. **coincidence** *n* coincidencia *f*. **coincidental** *adj* coincidente.

colander ['kɔləndə] *n* escurridor *m*.

cold [kould] *adj* frío. **be cold** (*person*) tener frío; (*weather*) hacer frío. **cold front** frente frío *m*. **cold storage** conservación *f*. **cold war** guerra fría *f*. **catch a cold** resfriarse. **cold-blooded** *adj* (*biol*) de sangre fría; (*fig*) insensible.

colic ['kolik] *n* cólico *m*.

collaborate [kə'labəreit] *v* colaborar. **collaboration** *n* colaboración *f*. **collaborator** *n* (*colleague*) colaborador, -a *m, f*; (*pol*) colaboracionista *m, f*.

collapse [kə'laps] *v* derrumbar; (*med*) sufrir un colapso. *n* derrumbamiento *m*; colapso; (*failure*) fracaso *m*. **collapsible** *adj* plegable.

collar ['kolə] *n* cuello *m*; (*dog, etc.*) collar *m*. *v* (*seize*) agarrar por el cuello; (*put a collar on*) acollarar. **collarbone** *n* clavícula *f*.

collate [ko'leit] *v* cotejar. **collation** *n* (*food*) colación *f*; (*texts*) cotejo *m*.

colleague ['koli:g] *n* colega *m, f*.

collect [kə'lekt] *v* (*bring together*) juntar, reunir; (*hobby*) coleccionar; (*funds*) allegar; (*taxes*) recaudar; (*bills*) cobrar; (*gather*) recoger. **collected works** obras completas *f pl*. **collection** (*hobby*) colección *f*; (*charity*) colecta *f*; (*people*) grupo *m*; (*things*) reunión *f*; (*rent, bills*) cobro *m*; (*taxes*) recaudación *f*; (*postal*) recogida *f*. **collective** *adj* colectivo.

collector *n* (*tax*) recaudador, -a *m, f*; (*bills, rent*) cobrador *m*; (*hobbies*) coleccionista *m, f*.

college ['kolidʒ] *n* colegio *m*. **collegiate** *adj* colegiado.

collide [kə'laid] *v* chocar. **collision** *n* choque *m*.

colloquial [kə'loukwiəl] *adj* familiar, popular. **colloquialism** *n* expresión familiar *f*.

Colombia [kə'lombiə] *n* Colombia *f*. **Colombian** *n, adj* colombiano, -a *m, f*.

colon ['koulon] *n* dos puntos *m pl*; (*anat*) colon *m*.

colonel ['kə:nl] *n* coronel *m*.

colony ['koləni] *n* colonia *f*. **colonial** *adj* colonial. **colonialist** *n*(*m + f*), *adj* colonialista. **colonist** *n* colono *m*. **colonization** *n* colonización *f*. **colonize** *v* colonizar.

colossal [kə'losəl] *adj* colosal.

colour ['kʌlə] *n* color *m*. **colour bar** barrera racial *f*. **colour-blind** *adj* daltoniano. **colourful** *adj* animado. **fast colour** color sólido *m*. **in colour** en colores. *v* colorear; (*dye*) teñir.

colt [koult] *n* potro *m*.

column ['koləm] *n* columna *f*. **columnist** *n* columnista *m, f*.

coma ['koumə] *n* coma *m*.

comb [koum] *n* peine *m*; (*honey*) panal *m*. *v* peinar.

combat ['kombat] *n* combate *m*. *v* combatir, luchar contra. **combatant** *n*(*m + f*), *adj* combatiente.

combine [kəm'bain; *n* 'kombain] *v* combinar, reunir. *n* (*comm*) cártel *m*. **combination** *n* combinación *f*, asociación *f*.

combustion [kəm'bʌstʃən] *n* combustión *f*. **combustible** *adj* combustible.

***come** [kʌm] *v* venir, llegar; proceder; salir. **come about** ocurrir. **come across** dar con. **come along!** ¡vamos! **come back** volver. **comeback** *n* restablecimiento *m*. **come off** desprender; (*succeed*) tener éxito. **come out** salir. **come to** (*from faint*) volver en sí; (*total*) ascender a.

comedy ['komədi] *n* comedia *f*. **comedian** *n* cómico *m*.

comet ['komit] *n* cometa *m*.

comfort ['kʌmfət] *n* (*relief*) alivio *m*; (*consolation*) consuelo *m*; (*well-being*) bienestar *m*; (*convenience*) comodidad *f*. *v* aliviar; consolar; animar. **comfortable** *adj* cómodo;

agradable. **comfortably** *adv* cómodamente; confortablemente.

comic ['komik] *adj* cómico, divertido. *n* (*magazine*) tebeo *m*. **comical** *adj* cómico.

comma ['komə] *n* coma *f*. **inverted commas** comillas *f pl*.

command [kə'ma:nd] *n* (*order*) orden *f*; (*authority*) mando *m*; (*mastery*) dominio *m*. *v* mandar, ordenar; dominar. **commandant** *n* comandante *m*. **commander** *n* comandante *m*; (*leader*) jefe *m*. **commander-in-chief** *n* comandante-en-jefe *m*. **commandment** *n* mandamiento *m*.

commandeer [komən'diə] *v* expropiar.

commando [kə'ma:ndou] *n* comando *m*.

commemorate [kə'meməreit] *v* conmemorar. **commemoration** *n* conmemoración *f*. **commemorative** *adj* conmemorativo.

commence [kə'mend] *v* empezar, comenzar. **commencement** *n* comienzo *m*.

commend [kə'mend] *v* (*recommend*) recomendar; (*entrust*) encomendar; (*praise*) alabar. **commendable** *adj* recomendable. **commendation** *n* alabanza *f*, elogio *m*, encomio *m*.

comment ['koment] *n* observación *f*; (*explanation*) comentario *m*. **no comment** sin comentarios. *v* comentar, hacer observaciones. **commentary** *n* comentario *m*, observación *f*. **running commentary** reportaje en directo *m*.

commerce ['komə:s] *n* comercio *m*. **commercial** *adj* comercial; *n* comercial *m*, *f*. **commercial traveller** agente comercial *m*. **commercialism** *n* mercantilismo *m*. **commercialize** *v* comercializar.

commiserate [kə'mizəreit] *v* compadecerse. **commiseration** *n* commiseración *f*.

commission [kə'miʃən] *n* (*profit*) comisión *f*; (*to a post, etc.*) nombramiento *m*; (*assignment*) cometido *m*; (*charge*) encargo *m*; (*crime*) ejecución *f*; (*mil*) grado de oficial *m*. *v* comisionar; encargar; (*mil*) nombrar. **commissionaire** *n* portero *m*. **commissioner** *n* comisionado *m*. **High Commissioner** alto comisario *m*.

commit [kə'mit] *v* (*crime*) cometer; (*entrust*) confiar; (*imprison*) encarcelar. **commit oneself** comprometerse. **commitment** *n* (*assignment*) cometido *m*; (*pledge*) compromiso *m*.

committee [kə'miti] *n* comité *m*, comisión *f*.

commodity [kə'modəti] *n* mercancía *f*, producto *m*, artículo *m*.

common ['komən] *adj* común; público; ordinario; frecuente. **commoner** *n* plebeyo, -a *m*, *f*. **Common Market** Mercado Común *m*. **commonness** *n* frecuencia *f*; vulgaridad *f*. **commonplace** *adj* común, trivial. **commonsense** *adj* lógico. **commonwealth** *n* república *f*.

commotion [kə'mouʃən] *n* disturbio *m*; tumulto *m*.

commune[1] [kə'mju:n] *v* (*communicate*) communicarse; (*meditate*) meditar. **communion** *n* comunión *f*.

commune[2] ['komju:n] *n* comuna *f*. **communal** *adj* comunal.

communicate [kə'mju:nikeit] *v* communicar. **communication** *n* comunicación *f*. **communicative** *adj* comunicativo.

communism ['komjunizəm] *n* comunismo *m*. **communist** *n*(*m* + *f*), *adj* comunista.

community [kə'mju:nəti] *n* comunidad *f*. **community centre** centro social *m*.

commute [kə'mju:t] *v* (*travel*) viajar; (*law*) conmutar. **commuter** *n*, *adj* viajero, -a.

compact[1] [kəm'pakt] *adj* compacto; recogido; conciso; denso. **compact disc** disco compacto *m*, compac disc. *v* condensar; comprimir.

compact[2] ['kompakt] *n* pacto *m*; (*powder*) polvera *f*.

companion [kəm'panjən] *n* compañero, -a *m*, *f*; (*professional*) acompañante *m*, *f*. **companionship** *n* compañerismo *m*.

company ['kʌmpəni] *n* (*comm*) compañíá *f*, empresa *f*; (*companionship*) compañerismo *m*, sociedad *f*.

compare [kəm'peə] *v* comparar. **comparable** *adj* comparable. **comparative** *adj* relativo; (*gram*) comparativo. **comparison** *n* comparación *f*.

compartment [kəm'pa:tmənt] *n* compartimiento *m*, departamento *m*.

compass ['kʌmpəs] *n* (*naut*) brújula *f*; (*extent*) extensión *f*. **compasses** *n pl* (*maths*) compás *m sing*.

compassion [kəm'paʃən] *n* compasión *f*. **compassionate** *adj* compasivo.

compatible [kəm'patəbl] *adj* compatible. **compatibility** *n* compatibilidad *f*.

compel [kəm'pel] *v* compeler, obligar. **compelling** *adj* convincente.

compensate ['kɒmpənseit] v (*make up for*) compensar; (*repay*) indemnizar. **compensation** n compensación f; indemnización f; (*reward*) recompensa f.

compete [kəm'pi:t] v competir. **competition** n competición f; (*contest*) concurso m; (*comm*) competencia f. **competitive** adj competitivo; (*spirit*) de competencia. **competitor** n competidor, -a m, f. (*contestant*) concursante m, f.

competent ['kɒmpətənt] adj competente; (*suitable*) adecuado. **competence** n competencia f, aptitud f.

compile [kəm'pail] v compilar. **compilation** n compilación f. **compiler** n compilador, -a m, f.

complacent [kəm'pleisnt] adj complaciente. **complacence, complacency** n satisfacción de sí mismo f.

complain [kəm'plein] v quejarse. **complaint** n queja f; (*med*) enfermedad f; (*law*) demanda f.

complement ['kɒmpləmənt] n complemento m. v complementar. **complementary** adj complementario.

complete [kəm'pli:t] adj completo; (*finished*) acabado, concluido, terminado; (*entire*) entero. v completar; terminar; (*fill in*) llenar. **completion** n cumplimiento m; terminación f.

complex ['kɒmpleks] adj complejo, complicado. n complejo m. **complexity** n complejidad f.

complexion [kəm'plekʃən] n tez f, cutis m; aspecto m.

complicate ['kɒmplikeit] v complicar. **complicated** adj complicado. **complication** n complicación f.

complicity [kəm'plisəti] n complicidad f.

compliment ['kɒmpləmənt] n cumplido m. **compliments** n pl saludos m pl. **complimentary** adj elogioso; (*gratis*) de favor.

comply [kəm'plai] v conformarse; (*obey*) obeceder.

component [kəm'pəunənt] nm, adj componente.

compose [kəm'pəuz] v componer; calmar. **composed** adj sereno. **be composed of** constar de. **composer** n compositor, -a m, f. **composite** adj compuesto. **composition** n composición f.

compost ['kɒmpɒst] n abono m.

composure [kəm'pəuʒə] n calma f, serenidad f.

compound¹ [kəm'paund; n, adj 'kɒmpaund] v componer; mezclar. nm, adj compuesto. **compound fracture** fractura complicada f.

compound² ['kɒmpaund] n (*enclosure*) recinto cercado m.

comprehend [kɒmpri'hend] v comprender. **comprehensible** adj comprensible. **comprehension** n comprensión f. **comprehensive** adj extenso, amplio. **comprehensive insurance** seguro a todo riesgo m. **comprehensive school** colegio integrado m.

compress ['kɒmpres; v kəm'pres] n (*med*) compresa f. v comprimir; (*condense*) condensar. **compression** n compresión f.

comprise [kəm'praiz] v comprender.

compromise ['kɒmprəmaiz] n compromiso m, arreglo m. v (*agree*) llegar a un arreglo; (*yield*) transigir; (*endanger*) comprometer. **compromising** adj comprometedor.

compulsion [kəm'pʌlʃən] n obligación f; (*coercion*) coacción f; (*impulse*) impulso m. **compulsive** adj compulsivo. **compulsory** adj obligatorio.

computer [kəm'pju:tə] n computador m. computadora f, ordenador m. **compute** v computar, calcular. **computerize** v tratar.

comrade ['kɒmrid] n camarada m, f compañero, -a m, f. **comradeship** n camaradería f.

concave [kɒn'keiv] adj cóncavo. **concavity** n concavidad f.

conceal [kən'si:l] v ocultar. **concealed** adj oculto. **concealment** n encubrimiento m.

concede [kən'si:d] v conceder; (*admit*) reconocer. **concede victory** darse por vencido.

conceit [kən'si:t] n presunción f, vanidad f. **conceited** adj engreido, vanidoso.

conceive [kən'si:v] v concebir. **conceive of** imaginarse. **conceivable** adj concebible.

concentrate ['kɒnsəntreit] v concentrar. n concentrado m. **concentration** n concentración f. **concentration camp** campo de concentración m.

concentric [kən'sentrik] adj concéntrico.

concept ['kɒnsept] n concepto m. **conception** n concepción f; idea f.

concern [kən'sə:n] n asunto m; (*interest*) interés m; (*business*) empresa f (*worry*) preocupación f. v (*have as a subject*) tratar de; (*affect*) afectar; (*be related to*) referirse a.

concerned *adj* preocupado. **concerning** *prep* con respecto a.

concert ['kɒnsət; *v* kən'sə:t] *n* concierto *m*. *v* concertar.

concertina [kɒnsə'ti:na] *n* concertina *f*.

concerto [kən'tʃə:tou] *n* concierto *m*.

concession [kən'seʃən] *n* concesión *f*.

conciliate [kən'silieit] *v* conciliar. **conciliation** *n* conciliación *f*. **conciliator** *n* conciliador, -a *m*, *f*. **conciliatory** *adj* conciliatorio.

concise [kən'sais] *adj* conciso.

conclude [kən'klu:d] *v* acabar, terminar; (*treaty*) concertar; (*deduce*) concluir. **conclusion** *n* conclusión *f*. **conclusive** *adj* conclusivo; concluyente.

concoct [kən'kokt] *v* (*mix*) confeccionar; (*plot*) urdir; inventar. **concoction** *n* (*mixture*) mezcla *f*; (*lies*) fabricación *f*.

concrete ['kɒŋkri:t] *n* hormigón *m*. **concrete mixer** hormigonera *f*. **reinforced concrete** hormigón armado *m*. *adj* concreto; (*tech*) de hormigón.

concussion [kən'kʌʃən] *n* conmoción cerebral *f*. **concuss** *v* conmocionar.

condemn [kən'dem] *v* condenar; (*building*) declarar en ruina. **condemnation** *n* condenación *f*. **condemnatory** *adj* condenatorio. **condemned** *adj* condenado.

condense [kən'dens] *v* (*cut*) abreviar, resumir; (*physics*) condensar. **condensation** *n* condensación *f*; (*vapour*) vaho *m*; (*abbreviation*) resumen *m*. **condenser** *n* condensador *m*.

condescend [kɒndi'send] *v* condescender, dignarse. **condescending** *adj* condescendiente, superior. **condescension** *n* condescencia *f*.

condition [kən'diʃən] *n* condición *f*. estado *m*. *v* condicionar, determinar. **conditional** *adj* condicional. **conditionally** *adv* con reservas. **conditioner** acondicionador *m*. **conditioning** *n* condicionamiento *m*.

condolence [kən'douləns] *n* condolencia *f*, pésame *m*. **condole** *v* condolerse, dar el pésame.

condom ['kɒndəm] *n* condón *m*.

condone [kən'doun] *v* condonar, perdonar.

conducive [kən'dju:siv] *adj* conducivo; (*helpful*) propicio.

conduct ['kɒndʌkt; *v* kən'dʌkt] *n* conducta *f*, comportamiento *m*. *v* (*lead*) conducir;

(*music, business*) dirigir; (*behave*) comportarse. **conductance** *n* conductancia *f*. **conduction** *n* conducción *f*. **conductivity** *n* conductividad *f*.

conductor [kən'dʌktə] *n* (*music*) director, -a *m*, *f*; (*guide*) guía *m*; (*bus*) cobrador, -a *m*, *f*; (*physics*) conductor *m*. **lightning conductor** pararrayos *m sing*.

cone [koun] *n* cono *m*; (*bot*) piña *f*; (*ice cream*) cucurucho de helado *m*. **cone-shaped** *adj* cónico.

confectioner [kən'fekʃənə] *n* confitero, -a *m*. *f*. **confection** *n* dulce *m*. **confectionery** *n* (*sweets*) dulces *m pl*; (*shop*) confitería *f*; (*cake shop*) repostería *f*.

confederate [kən'fedərət] *nm, adj* confederado. *v* confederar. **confederation** *n* confederación *f*.

confer [kən'fə:] *v* consultar, conferir; (*hold a conference*) conferenciar. **conference** *n* consulta *f*; (*meeting*) conferencia *f*; (*talks*) entrevista *f*.

confess [kən'fes] *v* confesar. **confession** *n* confesión *f*. **confessional** *n* (*rel*) confesionario *m*. **confessor** *n* confesor *m*; (*priest*) director espiritual *m*.

confetti [kən'feti] *n* confeti *m*.

confide [kən'faid] *v* confiar. **confidence** *n* (*trust*) confianza *f*; (*secret*) confidencia *f*; (*self-reliance*) seguridad en sí mismo *f*. **confidence trick** estafa *f*. **confident** *adj* lleno de confianza. **confidential** *adj* confidencial. **confidentially** *adv* en confianza.

confine [kən'fain] *n* confín *m*; límite *m*. *v* confinar; limitar; (*med*) estar de parto. **confined** *adj* reducido. **confinement** *n* encierro *m*; (*med*) parto *m*.

confirm [kən'fə:m] *v* confirmar; (*treaty*) ratificar. **confirmation** *n* confirmación *f*; ratificación *f*. **confirmed** *adj* confirmado; (*inveterate*) empedernido.

confiscate ['kɒnfiskeit] *v* confiscar. **confiscation** *n* confiscación *f*.

conflict ['kɒnflikt; *v* kən'flikt] *n* conflicto *m*. *v* luchar; (*clash*) chocar. **conflicting** *adj* contrapuesto.

conform [kən'fo:m] *v* conformarse. **conformist** *n*(*m* + *f*), *adj* conformista. **conformity** *n* conformidad *f*.

confound [kən'faund] *v* confundir; (*foil*) frustrar; (*disconcert*) desconcertar.

confront [kən'frʌnt] *v* hacer frente a; (*present with*) presentarse; (*bring face to face*) enfrentar, confrontar. **confrontation** *n* confrontación f.

confuse [kən'fju:z] *v* confundir; desconcertar; complicar. **confused** *adj* confuso; perplejo. **confusing** *adj* confuso; desconcertante. **confusion** *n* confusión f, desorden m.

congeal [kən'dʒi:l] *v* congelar; coagular.

congenial [kən'dʒi:niəl] *adj* (*pleasant*) agradable; (*suitable*) conveniente; (*similar*) compatible.

congenital [kən'dʒenitl] *adj* congénito.

congested [kən'dʒestid] *adj* congestionado; (*crowded*) superpoblado. **congestion** *n* congestión f; superpoblación f.

conglomeration [kən,glomə'reiʃən] *n* conglomeración f. **conglomerate** *v* conglomerar.

congratulate [kən'grætjuleit] *v* felicitar, dar la enhorabuena. **congratulations** *pl n* felicitaciones f *pl*; *interj* ¡felicidades!

congregate ['koŋgrigeit] *v* congregarse. **congregation** *n* congregación f, asamblea f; (*rel*) feligreses m *pl*.

congress ['koŋgres] *n* congreso m.

conical ['konikəl] *adj* cónico.

conifer ['konifə] *n* conífera f. **coniferous** *adj* conífero.

conjecture [kən'dʒektʃə] *n* conjetura f. *v* conjeturar. **conjectural** *adj* conjetural.

conjugal ['kondʒugəl] *adj* conyugal.

conjugate ['kondʒugeit] *v* conjugar. **conjugation** *n* conjugación f.

conjunction [kən'dʒʌŋkʃən] *n* (*gramm*) conjunción f. **conjunctive** *adj* conjuntivo.

conjunctivitis [kən,dʒʌŋkti'vaitis] *n* conjuntivitis f.

conjure ['kʌndʒə; (*appeal to*) kən'dʒuə] *v* (*magic*) hacer juegos de manos; (*appeal to*) conjurar. **conjurer** *n* ilusionista m, f, prestidigitador, -a m, f. **conjuring trick** juego de manos m.

connect [kə'nekt] *v* (*join*) unir, juntar; (*relate*) relacionar; (*elec*) conectar. **connected** (*joined*) conectado, unido; (*related*) emparentado; (*associated*) relacionado; coherente. **connection** *n* relación f; (*transport*) empalme m; (*elec*) conexión f; (*joint*) unión f; (*relative*) pariente m. **in connection with** con respecto a.

connoisseur [konə'sə:] *n* experto, -a m, f, conocedor, -a m, f.

connotation [konə'teiʃən] *n* connotación f.

conquer ['koŋkə] *v* vencer, triunfar. **conquering** *adj* victorioso. **conqueror** *n* conquistador, -a m f, vencedor, -a m, f. **conquest** *n* conquista f.

conscience ['konʃəns] *n* conciencia f.

conscientious [konʃi'enʃəs] *adj* concienzudo. **conscientious objector** objector de conciencia m. **conscientiousness** *n* escrupulosidad f.

conscious ['konʃəs] *adj* (*aware*) consciente; (*deliberate*) intencional. **be conscious** tener conocimiento. **be conscious of** tener conciencia de. **become conscious** volver en sí. **become conscious of** darse cuenta de. **consciousness** *n* conocimiento m.

conscript ['konskript] *n* recluta m.

consecrate ['konsikreit] *v* consagrar. **consecration** *n* consagración f.

consecutive [kən'sekjutiv] *adj* consecutivo.

consensus [kən'sensəs] *n* consenso m.

consent [kən'sent] *n* consentimiento m. **by common consent** de acuerdo mutuo. *v* consentir (en).

consequence ['konsikwəns] *n* consecuencia f, resultado m. **consequent** *adj* consiguiente. **consequently** *adv* consecuentemente, por lo tanto.

conserve [kən'sə:v] *v* conservar. *n* conserva f. **conservation** *n* conservación f. **conservative** *adj* conservador, moderado. **conservatory** *n* (*plants*) invernadero m; (*music*) conservatorio m.

consider [kən'sidə] *v* considerar; (*think*) pensar (en); (*study*) examinar; (*realize*) darse cuenta de; (*take into account*) tener en cuenta. **considerable** *adj* considerable. **considerably** *adv* considerablemente. **consideration** *n* consideración f; (*payment*) retribución f. **considerate** *adj* considerado.

consign [kən'sain] *v* consignar; (*send*) enviar; (*entrust*) confiar. **consignee** *n* consignatario m. **consignment** *n* consignación f; envío m.

consist [kən'sist] *v* consistir; (*made up of*) constar, componerse. **consistency** *n* (*density*) consistencia f; (*agreement*) conformidad f. **consistent** *adj* de acuerdo; firme. **consistently** *adv* constantemente; consecuentemente.

console¹ ['konsoul] *n* (*table, organ*) consola f; (*support*) ménsula f; mesa de control f;

pupitre *m*.

console² [kən'soul] *v* consolar. **consolation** *n* consuelo *m*. **consolation prize** premio de consolación *m*.

consolidate [kən'solídeit] *v* consolidar. **consolidation** *n* consolidación *f*.

consommé [kən'somei] *n* consomé *m*, caldo *m*.

consonant ['konsənənt] *n* consonante *f*. *adj* conforme.

consortium [kən'so:tiəm] *n* consorcio *m*.

conspicuous [kən'spikjuəs] *adj* visible; (*remarkable*) notable; (*attracting attention*) llamativo.

conspire [kən'spaiə] *v* conspirar. **conspiracy** *n* conspiración *f*. **conspirator** *n* conspirador, -a *m, f*.

constable ['kʌnstəbl] *n* policía *m*, guardia *m*. **constabulary** *n* policía *f*.

constant ['konstənt] *adj* (*continuous*) constante; (*faithful*) fiel, leal. **constancy** *n* constancia *f*; fidelidad *f*, lealdad *f*.

constellation [konstə'leiʃən] *n* constelación *f*.

constipation [konsti'peiʃən] *n* estreñimiento *m*. **constipated** *adj* estreñido.

constitute ['konstitju:t] *v* constituir. **constituency** *n* distrito electoral *m*. **constituent** *n* (*component*) componente *m*; (*pol*) votante *m, f*. *adj* (*component*) constitutivo, constituyente; electoral. **constitution** *n* constitución *f*. **constitutional** *adj* constitucional. *n* (*coll*) paseo *m*.

constraint [kən'streint] *n* (*restriction*) encierro *m*; (*compulsion*) coacción *f*; (*inhibition*) turbación *f*. **constrain** *v* encerrar; (*compel*) constreñir; (*inhibit*) incomodar.

constrict [kən'strikt] *v* (*narrow*) estrechar; (*compress*) oprimir. **constricted** *adj* estrecho. **constriction** *n* constricción *f*.

construct [kən'strʌkt] *v* construir. **construction** *n* construcción *f*; (*structure*) estructura *f*; (*meaning*) interpretación *f*. **constructive** *adj* constructivo. **constructor** *n* constructor *m*.

consul ['konsəl] *n* cónsul *m*. **consular** *adj* consular. **consulate** *n* consulado *m*.

consult [kən'sʌlt] *v* consultar. **consultant** *n* (*adviser*) asesor, -a *m, f*; (*med*) especialista *m*; (*tech*) consejero técnico *m*. **consultation** *n* consulta *f*. **consulting room** consultorio *m*.

consume [kən'sju:m] *v* consumir; (*time*)

tomar; (*food*) comerse; (*drink*) beberse. **consumer** *n* consumidor, *m, f*. **consumer goods** bienes de consumo *m pl*. **consumption** *n* consumo *m*; (*med: tuberculosis*) tisis *f*. **consumptive** *n, adj* (*med*) tísico, -a.

contact ['kontakt] *n* contacto *m*. **contact lens** lente de contacto *f*. *v* ponerse en contacto con.

contagious [kən'teidʒəs] *adj* contagioso. **contagion** *n* contagio *m*.

contain [kən'tein] *v* contener. **container** *n* (*package*) envase *m*; (*receptacle*) recipiente *m*. (*transport*) contenedor *m*. **containment** *n* contención *f*.

contaminate [kən'tamənei:t] *v* contaminar. **contamination** *n* contaminación *f*.

contemplate ['kontəmpleit] *v* contemplar; (*expect*) contar con; (*consider*) considerar. **contemplation** *n* contemplación *f*, meditación *f*; consideración *f*. **contemplative** *adj* contemplativo.

contemporary [kən'tempərəri] *n, adj* contemporáneo, -a *m, f*.

contempt [kən'tempt] *n* desprecio *m*, desdén *m*. **contempt of court** desacato a los tribunales *m*. **bold in contempt** despreciar. **contemptible** *adj* despreciable, desdeñable. **contemptuous** *adj* despreciativo, desdeñoso.

contend [kən'tend] *v* (*struggle*) contender; (*compete*) competir; (*dispute*) disputir; (*affirm*) afirmar. **contender** *n* competidor, -a *m, f*. **contention** *n* contienda *f*; (*argument*) discusión *f*; (*opinion*) opinión *f*. **contentious** *adj* (*person*) pendenciero; (*issue*) discutible. **contentiousness** *n* carácter pendenciero *m*.

content¹ ['kontent] *n* contenido *m*.

content² [kən'tent] *adj* also **contented** contento, satisfecho. **be contented with** contentarse con. **contentment** *n* contento *m*.

contest [kən'test; *n* 'kontest] *v* (*dispute*) disputar; (*question*) impugnar. *n* (*struggle*) contienda *f*; (*competition*) competición *f*; (*controversy*) controversia *f*. **contestant** *n* contrincante *m*; (*election*) candidato, -a *m, f*.

context ['kontekst] *n* contexto *m*.

continent ['kontinənt] *n* continente *m*. **the Continent** el continente europeo *m*. **continental** *adj* continental.

contingency [kən'tindʒənsi] *n* (*possibility*) contingencia *f*, eventualidad *f*; (*event*) acontecimiento fortuito *m*. **contingent** *adj* (*accidental*) fortuito; (*probable*) contingente; (*incidental*) derivado; (*dependent*) subordinado; (*dependent on chance*) aleatorio.

continue [kən'tinju:] *v* continuar, seguir; (*extend*) prolongar. **continual** *adj* continuo. **continually** *adv* constantemente. **continuation** *n* continuación *f*. **continuity** *n* continuidad *f*; (*cinema, radio*) guión *m*. **continuous** *adj* continuo.

contort [kən'to:t] *v* retorcer, torcer. **contortion** *n* contorsión *f*; deformación *f*. **contortionist** *n* contorsionista *m, f*.

contour ['kontuə] *n* (*map*) curva de nivel *f*; (*outline*) contorno *m*.

contraband ['kontrəband] *n* contrabando *m*. *adj* de contrabando.

contraception [kontrə'sepʃən] *n* contracepción *f*. **contraceptive** *nm, adj* contraceptivo. **contraceptive pill** píldora contraceptiva *f*.

contract ['kontrakt; *v* kən'trakt] *n* contrato *m*. *v* (*shrink*) contraer; (*make a contract*) contratar; (*ailment*) coger. **contraction** *n* contracción *f*. **contractor** *n* contratista *m*. **contractual** *adj* contractual.

contradict [kontrə'dikt] *v* contradecir. **contradiction** *n* contradicción *f*. **contradictory** *adj* contradictorio.

contralto [kən'traltou] *n* contralto *m, f*.

contraption [kən'trapʃən] *n* (*coll*) chisme *m*.

contrary ['kontrəri] *adj* contrario. **on the contrary** al contrario.

contrast [kən'tra:st; *n* 'kontra:st] *v* contrastar. *n* contraste *m*. **in contrast** por contraste. **in contrast to** a diferencia de. **contrasting** *adj* contrastante.

contravene [kontrə'vi:n] *v* contravenir. **contravention** *n* contravención *f*.

contribute [kən'tribjut] *v* contribuir (con); (*write*) escribir; (*give information*) aportar. **contribution** *n* contribución *f*; artículo *m*; aportación *f*; (*to conversation*) intervención *f*. **contributive** *adj* contributivo. **contributor** *n* contribuyente *m, f*; (*writer*) colaborador, -a *m, f*. **contributory** *adj* contribuyente.

contrive [kən'traiv] *v* idear, inventar; (*manage*) conseguir. **contrived** *adj* artificial. **contrivable** *adj* realizable; imaginable. **contrivance** *n* aparato *m*; invención *f*; (*resourcefulness*) ingenio *m*.

control [kən'troul] *n* control *m*; autoridad *f*; dominación *f*; (*standard of comparison*) testigo *m*. **remote control** mando a distancia *m*. **controls** *pl n* mandos *m pl*. *v* controlar; tener autoridad sobre; (*direct*) dirigir; (*regulate*) regular; (*vehicle*) manejar. **controller** *n* director, -a *m, f*. **air traffic controller** controlador del tráfico aéreo *m*. **controlling** *adj* predominante; (*decisive*) determinante.

controversy [kən'trovəsi] *n* controversia *f*. **controversial** *adj* discutible.

convalesce [konvə'les] *v* convalecer. **convalescence** *n* convalecencia *f*.

convector [kən'vektə] *n* estufa de convección *f*. **convection** *n* convección *f*.

convenience [kən'vi:njəns] *n* conveniencia *f*; (*comfort*) comodidad *f*; (*advantage*) ventaja *f*; (*useful object*) dispositivo útil *m*. **at your convenience** cuando le sea posible. **public convenience** servicios *m pl*. **convenient** *adj* (*handy*) cómodo; (*suitable*) conveniente; (*place*) bien situado; (*time*) oportuno.

convent ['konvənt] *n* convento *m*.

convention [kən'venʃən] *n* (*usage*) convención *f*; (*assembly*) asamblea *f*; (*international agreement*) convenio *m*. **conventions** *n pl* conveniencias *f pl*. **conventional** *adj* (*not original*) convencional; (*traditional*) clásico.

converge [kən'və:dʒ] *v* convergir, converger. **convergence** *n* convergencia *f*. **converging** *adj* convergente.

converse¹ [kən'və:s] *v* conversar, hablar. **conversant** *adj* versado, familiarizado. **conversation** *n* conversación *f*.

converse² ['konvə:s] *n* lo opuesto *m*. *adj* opuesto, contrario.

convert ['konvə:t; *v* kən'və:t] *n* converso, -a *m, f*. *v* convertir. **conversion** *n* conversión *f*; transformación *f*.

convertible [kən'və:təbl] *adj* convertible; transformable. *n* (*mot*) descapotable *m*.

convex ['konveks] *adj* convexo.

convey [kən'vei] *v* (*carry*) llevar, transportar; (*suggest*) sugerir, dar a entender; (*transmit*) transmitir; (*meaning*) expresar. **conveyance** *n* transporte *m*; transmisión *f*; (*deed*) escritura de traspaso *f*. **conveyancer** *n* notario, -a que hace escritura de traspaso *m, f*. **conveyancing** *n* redacción de una escritura de traspaso *f*.

convict ['konvikt; *v* kən'vikt] *n* presidiario, -

a *m*, *f*. v (*prove guilty*) condenar; (*betray*) traicionar.

conviction [kən'vikʃən] *n* condena *f*; (*belief*) convicción *f*.

convince [kən'vins] *v* convencer. **convincing** *adj* convincente.

convivial [kən'viviəl] *adj* alegre, sociable, festivo.

convoy ['konvoi] *n* convoy *m*. *v* convoyar.

convulsion [kən'vʌlʃən] *n* (*med*) convulsión *f*; (*laughter*) carcajadas *f pl*. **convulse** *v* convulsionar.

cook [kuk] *v* cocinar; (*coll: the books*) falsificar. *n* cocinero, -a *m*, *f*. **cooker** *n* cocina *f*; olla *f*. **pressure cooker** olla de presión *f*. **cookery** *n* arte de cocina *m*; cocción *f*; cocina *f*. **cookery book** libro de cocina *m*. **do the cooking** guisar.

cool [ku:l] *adj* fresco; (*calm*) tranquilo; (*unenthusiastic*) frío. *v* enfriar; calmar. **cooler** *n* enfriador *m*. **cooling** *adj* refrescante. **cooling system** *n* sistema de refrigeración *m*. **coolish** *adj* fresquito. **coolly** *adv* friamente; tranquilamente. **coolness** *n* frescor *m*; frialdad *f*; serenidad *f*; sangre fria *f*.

coop [ku:p] *n* (*poultry*) gallinero *m*. **coop up** encerrar.

cooperate [kou'opəreit] *v* cooperar. **cooperation** *n* cooperación *f*. **cooperative** *adj* cooperativo.

coordinate [kou'o:dineit] *n* coordenada *f*. *adj* igual. *v* coordinar. **coordination** *n* coordinación *f*.

cope[1] [koup] *v* arreglárselas; dar abasto; poder con.

cope[2] [koup] *n* (*rel*) capa pluvial *f*.

Copenhagen [koupən'heigən] *n* Copenhague.

copious ['koupiəs] *adj* copioso, abundante.

copper[1] ['kopə] *n* (*metal*) cobre *m*. *adj* de cobre; (*colour*) cobrizo. **copper plate** plancha de cobre *f*.

copper[2] ['kopə] *n also* **cop** (*slang*) poli *m*.

copulate ['kopju:leit] *v* copular. **copulation** *n* cópula *f*.

copy ['kopi] *n* copia *f*; (*book*) ejemplar *m*; (*pattern*) modelo *m*; (*reportage*) asunto *m*. **carbon copy** copia en papel carbón *f*. **fair copy** copia en limpio *f*. **rough copy** borrador *m*. *v* copiar; imitar. **copyright** *n* propiedad literaria *f*.

coral ['korəl] *n* coral *m*. *adj* coralino.

cord [ko:d] *n* (*string, rope*) cuerda *f*; (*insulated wire*) cordón *m*. **spinal cord** médula espinal *f*. **umbilical cord** cordón umbilical *m*. **vocal cords** cuerdas vocales *f pl*.

cordial ['ko:diəl] *adj*, *nm* cordial. **cordiality** *n* cordialidad *f*.

cordon ['ko:dn] *n* cordón *m*. **cordon off** acordonar.

corduroy ['ko:dəroi] *n* pana *f*.

core [ko:] *n* (*fruit*) corazón *m*; (*geol*) núcleo *m*; (*fig*) centro *m*, esencia *f*. *v* quitar el corazón de.

cork [ko:k] *n* (*bot*) corcho *m*; (*stopper*) tapón *m*. **cork tree** alcornoque *m*. **cork-tipped** *adj* con boquilla de corcho. *v* taponar. **uncork** *v* (*bottle*) descorchar. **corked** *adj* (*bottle*) taponado; (*wine*) que sabe a corcho. **corkscrew** *n* sacacorchos *m invar*.

corn[1] [ko:n] *n* (*wheat*) trigo *m*; (*maize*) maíz *m*; (*cereals*) granos cereales *m pl*. **corn on the cob** maíz en la mazorca *m*.

corn[2] [ko:n] *n* (*med*) callo *m*.

corner ['ko:nə] *n* (*inside angle*) rincón *m*; (*outside angle*) esquina *f*; (*of an object*) pico *m*. **cut corners** tomar atajos. *v* poner en un aprieto; (*accost*) abordar; (*mot*) tomar una curva; (*comm*) monopolizar.

cornet ['ko:nit] *n* corneta *f*; (*ice cream*) cucurucho *m*.

coronary ['korənəri] *adj* coronario. **coronary thrombosis** trombosis coronaria *f*.

coronation [korə'neifən] *n* coronación *f*.

corporal[1] ['ko:pərəl] *adj* corporal. **corporal punishment** castigo corporal *m*.

corporal[2] ['ko:pərəl] *n* (*mil*) cabo *m*.

corporate ['ko:pərət] *n* corporativo *m*

corporation [ko:pə'reifən] *n* corporación *f*; sociedad anónima *f*. **municipal corporation** ayuntamiento *m*. **corporate** *adj* colectivo, corporativo.

corps [ko:] *n* cuerpo *m*. **corps de ballet** cuerpo de ballet. **diplomatic corps** cuerpo diplomático *m*.

corpse [ko:ps] *n* cadáver *m*.

correct [kə'rekt] *adj* (*accurate*) exacto; (*behaviour*) correcto; (*right*) justo. *v* corregir. **correction** *n* corrección *f*. **corrective** *adj* correctivo. **correctness** *n* corrección *f*; exactitud *f*; (*judgment*) rectitud *f*.

correlate ['korəleit] *v* correlacionar. **correlation** *n* correlación *f*.

correspond [korə'spond] *v* corresponder;

(*write*) escribirse. **correspondence** n correspondencia f. **correspondent** n correspondiente m, f; (*newspaper*) corresponsal m, f.

corridor ['korido:] n pasillo m, corredor m.

corroborate [kə'robəreit] v corroborar. **corroboration** n corroboración f.

corrode [kə'roud] v corroer. **corrosion** n corrosión f. **corrosive** adj corrosivo.

corrugated ['korəgeitid] adj ondulado.

corrupt [kə'rʌpt] adj corrupto; corrompido; (*rotten*) estragado; (*perverted*) pervertido; (*bribable*) venal. v corromper; (*bribe*) sobornar. **corruptible** adj corruptible. **corruption** n corrupción f.

corset ['ko:set] n faja f.

Corsica ['ko:sikə] n Córcega f. **Corsican** n, adj corso, -a m, f.

cosmetic [koz'metik] nm, adj cosmético.

cosmic ['kozmik] adj cósmico.

cosmopolitan [kozmə'politən] n(m + f), adj cosmopolita.

***cost** [kost] n costo m, coste m; (*price*) precio m; (*expenses*) gastos m pl. **costs** pl n (*law*) costas f pl. **at all costs** cueste lo que cueste. **cost of living** coste de vida m. **to one's cost** a expensas de uno. v costar; valer. **costly** adj caro.

Costa Rica [kostə'ri:kə] n Costa Rica. **Costa Rican** n(m + f), adj costarriquense; n, adj costarriqueño, -a m, f.

costume ['kostju:m] n traje m. **bathing costume** traje de baño. **costume jewellery** bisutería f.

cosy ['kouzi] adj confortable; (*place*) acogedor.

cot [kot] n cuna f.

cottage ['kotidʒ] n casa de campo f; chalet m. **cottage cheese** requesón m.

cotton ['kotn] n algodón m. adj de algodón. **cotton wool** n algodón hidrófilo m.

couch [kautʃ] n sofá m; (*bed*) lecho m. v (*express*) expresar.

cough [kof] n tos f. v toser. **cough up** (*coll*) cascar.

could [kud] V **can¹**.

council ['kaunsəl] n consejo m; (*assembly*) ayuntamiento m. **council house** vivienda de protección oficial f, VPO f. **town council** concejo municipal m. **councillor** n concejal, -a m, f.

counsel ['kaunsəl] n consejo m; (*lawyer*) abogado, -a m, f; (*legal adviser*) asesor

jurídico, asesora jurídica m, f. v aconsejar.

count¹ [kaunt] v contar, calcular; (*consider*) considerar. **count against** ir en contra de. **count for** valer por. n cuenta f, cálculo m; (*sum*) total m; (*votes*) escrutinio m. **countable** adj contable. **countdown** n cuenta atrás f. **countless** adj incontable.

count² [kaunt] n (*noble*) conde m. **countess** n condesa f.

countenance ['kauntinəns] n semblante m, cara f. v (*approve*) aprobar; (*support*) apoyar.

counter¹ ['kauntə] n (*disc*) ficha f; (*table top*) mostrador m, contador m. **Geiger counter** contador Geiger m. **under the counter** bajo mano.

counter² ['kauntə] adj (*opposed*) contrario, opuesto. v contraatacar; oponerse. **go counter to** ir en contra de.

counterattack ['kauntərə,tak] n contraataque m. v contraatacar.

counterfeit ['kauntəfit] adj falso, falsificado. v falsificar. n falsificación f.

counterfoil ['kauntə,foil] n talón m.

counterpart ['kauntə,pa:t] n contraparte f.

country ['kʌntri] n (*state*) país m; (*out of town*) campo m. **country estate** finca f. **country house** casa de campo f. **countryman** n campesino m; compatriota m. **countryside** n campo m; (*landscape*) paisaje m.

county ['kaunti] n condado m. **county council** diputación provincial f.

coup [ku:] n golpe m. **coup d'état** golpe de estado m.

couple ['kʌpl] n par m; (*married, engaged, etc.*) pareja f. v emparejar; (*associate*) asociar; (*vehicles*) enganchar; (*elec*) conectar; (*copulate*) copular.

coupon ['ku:pon] n cupón m; (*pools*) boleto m.

courage ['kʌridʒ] n valor m, valentía f. **pluck up courage** armarse de valor. **take courage** cobrar ánimo. **courageous** adj valiente.

courgette [kuə'ʒet] n calabacín m.

courier ['kuriə] n guía m, f; agente de turismo m, f; mensajero, -a m, f.

course [ko:s] n (*direction*) dirección f, rumbo m; (*progress*) curso m; (*way, means*) camino m; (*action, conduct*) línea f; (*meal*) plato m; (*track*) pista f; (*golf*) campo m. **in due course** a su debido tiempo. **main course** plato fuerte m. **of course** claro, por supuesto. **set course for** hacer rumbo a. *v* (*hunt*) cazar; (*run: liquid*) correr.

court [ko:t] *n* (*royalty*) corte *f*; (*road*) callejón sin salida *m*; (*law*) audiencia *f*, tribunal *m*; (*sport*) cancha *f*. **court order** orden judicial *f*. **go to court** acudir a los tribunales. *v* (*woo*) cortejar, hacer la corte a; buscar; pedir, solicitar. **courtier** *n* cortesano *m*. **courtly** *adj* cortés. **court-martial** *n* consejo de guerra *m*. **courtship** *n* noviazgo *m*. **courtyard** *n* patio *m*.

courteous [ˈkəːtiəs] *adj* cortés. **courtesy** *n* cortesía *f*.

cousin [ˈkʌzn] *n* primo, -a *m*, *f*. **first cousin** primo, -a carnal *m*, *f*.

cove [kouv] *n* cala *f*; (*slang*) tío *m*.

cover [ˈkʌvə] *n* cubierta *f*; (*lid*) tapa *f*; (*bed*) colcha *f*; (*table*) tapete *m*; (*refuge*) refugio *m*; (*parcel*) envoltura *f*; (*envelope*) sobre *m*; (*pretence*) excusa *f*; (*protection*) amparo *m*. **cover charge** precio del cubierto *m*. **take cover** ponerse a cubierto. *v* cubrir, tapar. **coverage** *n* alcance *m*.

cow [kau] *n* vaca *f*; (*female animal*) hembra *f*. *v* intimidar. **cowboy** *n* vaquero *m*, (*Amer*) gaucho *m*. **cowshed** *n* establo *m*. **cowslip** *n* prímula *f*.

coward [ˈkauəd] *n* cobarde *m*, *f*. **cowardice** *n* cobardía *f*. **cowardly** *adj* cobarde.

cower [ˈkauə] *v* encogerse; agacharse.

coy [koi] *adj* (*shy*) tímido; (*demure*) remilgado.

crab [krab] *n* cangrejo *m*. **crab apple** manzana silvestre *f*. **crabbed** *adj* (*badtempered*) malhumorado; (*writing*) indecifrable.

crack [krak] *n* (*noise*) restallido *m*, chasquido *m*; (*opening*) abertura *f*; (*split*) raja *f*; (*in walls, etc.*) hendidura *f*; (*slit*) rendija *f*; (*blow*) golpe *m*; (*coll: joke*) chiste *m*. **at the crack of dawn** al amanecer. **have a crack at** intentar. *v* restallar, chasquear; golpear; (*break*) romper; (*a nut*) cascar, hender; rajar; (*burst*) reventar; (*give in*) ceder; (*break down*) hundirse; (*coll: joke*) bromear; (*coll: safe*) forzar. **get cracking** darse prisa. **crackpot** *n*, *adj* (*coll*) chiflado, -a *m*, *f*.

cracker [ˈkrakə] *n* (*Christmas*) sorpresa *f*; (*firework*) buscapiés *m invar*; (*biscuit*) galleta *f*.

crackle [ˈkrakl] *n* crepitación *f*, crujido *m*. *v* crepitar, crujir. **crackling** *n* (*cookery*) chicharrón *m*.

cradle [ˈkreidl] *n* cuna *f*; soporte *m*. *v* acunar; (*in one's arms*) mecer; soportar.

craft [kra:ft] *n* (*trade*) trabajo manual *m*; (*skill*) arte *m*; (*guild*) gremio *m*; (*cunning*) astucia *f*, maña *f*; (*ship*) embarcación *f*; (*aircraft*) avión *m*. **craftily** *adv* astutamente. **craftsman** *n* artesano *m*. **craftsmanship** *n* artesanía *f*. **crafty** *adj* astuto, socarrón.

cram [kram] *v* (*fill up*) abarrotar; (*force in*) meter a la fuerza; (*for exam*) empollar.

cramp [kramp] *n* (*med*) calambre *m*. *v* dar calambre a. **cramped** *adj* (*crowded*) apiñado; (*writing*) apretado.

cranberry [ˈkranbəri] *n* arándano *m*.

crane [krein] *n* (*hoist*) grúa *f*; (*bird*) grulla *f*. *v* (*neck*) estirar.

crank [kraŋk] *n* (*tech*) manivela *f*; (*fool*) chiflado, -a *m*, *f*. *v* arrancar con la manivela. **crankcase** *n* cárter *m*. **crankiness** *n* irritabilidad *f*; excentricidad *f*; chifladura *f*. **crankshaft** *n* cigüeñal *m*.

crap [krap] *n* (*slang: nonsense*) disparate; (*impol*) mierda *f*. *v* (*impol*) cagar.

crash [kraʃ] *n* accidente *m*, choque *m*; (*noise*) estrépito *m*; (*aircraft*) caída *f*; (*business*) quiebra *f*. **crash course** curso intensivo *m*. **crash helmet** casco protector *m*. *v* chocar; caer; quebrar; (*make a loud noise*) retumbar. **crash-land** hacer un aterrizaje de emergencia.

crate [kreit] *n* cajón de embalaje *m*. *v* embalar.

crater [ˈkreitə] *n* cráter *m*.

crave [kreiv] *v* (*desire*) ansiar; (*beg*) suplicar; (*attention*) reclamar. **craving** *n* ansia *f*.

crawl [kro:l] *v* arrastrarse, andar a gatas; (*move slowly*) andar lentamente. *n* arrastramiento *m*; marcha lenta *f*.

crayfish [ˈkreifiʃ] *n* ástaco *m*, cangrejo de río *m*.

crayon [ˈkreiən] *n* lápiz de color *m*. *v* dibujar al pastel.

craze [kreiz] *n* (*wild enthusiasm*) locura *f*; (*fad*) manía *f*; (*fashion*) moda *f*. *v* enloquecer. **craziness** *n* locura *f*. **crazy** *adj* loco.

creak [kri:k] *n* crujido *m*. *v* crujir. **creaky** *adj* que cruje.

cream [kri:m] *n* nata *f*, crema *f*. **whipped cream** nata batida *f*. *adj* color crema. *v* (*coll: beat*) batir; (*skim*) desnatar. **cream cheese** queso de nata *m*.

crease [kri:s] *n* (*fold*) pliegue *m*; (*wrinkle*) arruga *f*; (*trousers*) raya *f*. **crease-resistant** *adj* inarrugable. *v* plegar; arrugar; hacer la raya de.

create [kri'eit] v crear. **creation** n creación f. **creator** n creador, -a m, f.

créche [kre...sh] n guardería f.

credentials [kri'denʃəlz] pl n credenciales f pl.

credible ['kredəbl] adj creíble. **credibility** n credibilidad f.

credit¹ ['kredit] n crédito m; (comm) haber m; (prestige) honor m. **credits** pl n (film) ficha técnica f sing. **credit balance** saldo acreedor m. **credit card** tarjeta de crédito f. **credit rating** solvabilidad f. **on credit** a plazos. **we do not give credit** no se fía.

credit² ['kredit] v (believe) creer; (fig) atribuir; (an account) abonar en cuenta. **creditable** adj (believable) digno de crédito; (praiseworthy) encomiable; (well spoken of) de buena reputación. **creditably** adv honrosamente. **creditor** n acreedor, -a m, f.

credulous ['kredjuləs] adj crédulo.

creed [kri:d] n credo m.

***creep** [kri:p] v deslizarse, arrastrarse; (flesh) ponerse a uno la carne de gallina. n (coll) pelotillero, -a m, f. **creepy** adj horripilante.

cremate [kri'meit] v incinerar. **cremation** n incineración f. **crematorium** n horno crematorio m.

crescent ['kresnt] n medialuna f, luna creciente f. adj creciente.

cress [kres] n berro m.

crest [krest] n (on animal's head, wave) cresta f; (hill) cima f, cumbre f; (heraldry) timbre m. **crested** adj crestado. **crestfallen** adj alicaído.

crevice ['krevis] n grieta f; hendedura f.

crew [kru:] n (body of workers) equipo m; (ship, aircraft) tripulación f; (mob) banda f. **ground crew** personal de tierra m.

crib [krib] n (rack) pesebre m; (small cot) cuna f; (coll: exam) chuleta f. v plagiar.

cricket¹ ['krikit] n (insect) grillo m.

cricket² ['krikit] n (sport) criquet m.

crime [kraim] n crimen m; criminalidad f. **criminal** n, adj criminal m, f.

crimson ['krimzn] nm, adj carmesí.

cringe [krindʒ] v agacharse, encogerse. **cringing** adj servil.

crinkle ['kriŋkl] n arruga f. v arrugarse.

cripple ['kripl] n, adj tullido, -a m, f. v (person) tullir; (object) estropear; (fig) paralizar.

crisis ['kraisis] n pl **-ses** crisis f invar.

crisp [krisp] adj fresco; (bread) curruscante; (style) crespo; (snow) crujiente; (talk) animado. v encrespar, rizar. **potato crisp** patata frita a la inglesa f. **crispness** n encrespado m.

criterion [krai'tiəriən] n pl **-a** criterio m.

criticize ['kriti,saiz] v criticar. **critic** (faultfinder) criticón, -ona m, f; (reviewer) crítico, -a m, f. **critical** adj crítico. **criticism** n crítica f.

Croatia [krou'eiʃə] n Croacia f; **Croatian** adj croata.

crochet ['krouʃei] n croché m, ganchillo m. v hacer a ganchillo.

crockery ['krokəri] n loza f, vajilla f.

crocodile ['krokə,dail] n cocodrilo m.

crocus ['kroukəs] n azafrán m.

crook [kruk] n (shepherd's) cayado m; (bishop's) báculo m; (coll) ladrón, -ona m, f; timador, -a m, f.

crooked ['krukid] adj (bent) curvado; (twisted) torcido; (path) sinuoso; (nose) ganchudo; (coll) poco limpio. **crookedness** n sinuosidad f; (coll) falta de honradez f.

crop [krop] n (harvest) cosecha f; (cultivated produce) cultiva f; (whip) fusta f; (bird) buche m; (haircut) corte de pelo m. **crop rotation** rotación de cultivos f. v (graze) pacer; (ears) desorejar; (tail) cortar la cola de; (hair) cortar muy corto. **come a cropper** darse un batacazo.

croquet ['kroukei] n croquet m.

cross [kros] n cruz f; (breeding) cruce f. **make the sign of the cross** santiguarse. adj cruzado; (angry) enfadado. v (move) atravesar; (limbs) cruzar; (oppose) contrariar; (mark) marcar con una cruz. **cross out** tachar. **cross one's mind** ocurrírsele a.

cross-country adj a campo traviesa.

cross-current n contracorriente f.

cross-examination n repregunta f.

cross-eyed adj bizco.

crossfire ['kros,faiə] n fuego cruzado m.

crossing ['krosin] n (intersection) cruce f; (voyage) travesía f; (pedestrian) paso de peatones m.

cross-purposes pl n fines opuestos m pl.

cross-reference n remisión f.

crossroads ['kros,roudz] pl n cruce f sing; (fig) encrucijada f sing.

cross section n sección transversal f.

crossword ['kros,wə:d] n crucigrama m.

crotchet ['krotʃit] n (music) negra f. **crotchety** adj de mal genio.

crouch [krautʃ] v agacharse, encogerse.

crow¹ [krou] n (bird) cuervo m. **as the crow flies** en línea recta. **crowbar** n palanca f.

crow² [krou] v cantar; cacarear. n cacareo m.

crowd [kraud] n muchedumbre f, multitud f. v amontonar; congregarse. **crowded** adj lleno.

crown [kraun] n corona f; (hat) copa f; (hill) cumbre f; (head) coronilla f. **crown jewels** joyas reales f pl. **crown prince** príncipe heredero m. v coronar. **to crown it all** para rematarlo todo. **crowning** adj supremo.

crucial ['kruːʃəl] adj crucial, decisivo.

crucify ['kruːsifai] v crucificar. **crucifix** n crucifijo m. **crucifixion** n crucifixión f.

crude [kruːd] adj (raw) crudo; (steel) bruto; (oil) sin refinar; (vulgar) basto; (ill-made) tosco. **crudeness, crudity** n crudeza f; tosquedad f.

cruel ['kruːəl] adj cruel. **cruelty** n crueldad f.

cruise [kruːz] n crucero m. v hacer un crucero; (patrol) patrullar; (at cruising speed) ir a una velocidad de crucero. **cruiser** n (naut) crucero m.

crumb [krʌm] n migaja f, miga f.

crumble ['krʌmbl] v desmenuzar; desmigar. **crumbly** adj desmenuzable.

crumple ['krʌmpl] v arrugar, ajar. **crumple up** desplomarse.

crunch [krʌntʃ] n crujido m; (coll) punto decisivo m. v crujir; mascar. **crunchy** adj crujiente.

crusade [kruːˈseid] n cruzada f; (fig) campaña f. v hacer una cruzada. **crusader** n cruzado m.

crush [krʌʃ] n aplastamiento m; (crowd) aglomeración f; (squeeze) apretón m. **have a crush on** (coll) estar loco perdido por. v aplastar; apretar; (pulverize) machacar; (overwhelm) abrumar. **crushing** adj aplastante.

crust [krʌst] n (of a loaf) corteza f. **upper crust** la flor y nata f. **crusty** adj de corteza dura; (coll) brusco.

crutch [krʌtʃ] n (support) muleta f; (fig) apoyo m.

crux [krʌks] n quid m.

cry [krai] n grito m. v (call) gritar; (weep) llorar. **cry out** clamar.

crypt [kript] n cripta f. **cryptic** adj secreto; enigmático.

crystal ['kristl] n cristal m. adj de cristal. **crystal clear** cristalino. **crystallize** v cristalizar.

cub [kʌb] n (bear, lion, tiger, wolf) cachorro m; (other animals) cria f. **cub scout** niño explorador m.

Cuba ['kjuːbə] n Cuba f. **Cuban** n, adj cubano, -a m, f.

cube [kjuːb] n (math) cubo m; (sugar, etc.) terrón m. v (math) cubicar. **cube root** raíz cúbica f. **cubic** adj cúbico.

cubicle ['kjuːbikl] n cubículo m; (for sleeping) cubilla f; (for changing) caseta f.

cuckoo ['kukuː] n cuco m, cuclillo m.

cucumber [kjuˈkʌmbə] n pepino m.

cuddle ['kʌdl] n abrazo m. v abrazar. **cuddly** adj mimoso.

cue¹ [kjuː] n (theatre) señal f; entrada f. v indicar.

cue² [kjuː] n (billiards) taco m.

cuff¹ [kʌf] n (shirt) puño m. **cufflinks** pl n gemelos m pl. **off the cuff** de improviso.

cuff² [kʌf] n (hit) bofetada f. v abofetear.

culinary ['kʌlinəri] adj culinario.

culminate ['kʌlmiˌneit] v culminar. **culmination** n culminación f.

culprit ['kʌlprit] n culpado, -a m, f; culpable m, f.

cult [kʌlt] n culto m.

cultivate ['kʌltiˌveit] v cultivar. **cultivated** adj (land) cultivado; (person) culto. **cultivation** n cultivo m.

culture ['kʌltʃə] n cultura f; cultivo m. **cultured** adj culto.

cumbersome ['kʌmbəsəm] adj molesto; (annoying) incómodo.

cunning ['kʌniŋ] adj (sly) taimado; (clever) astuto; (skilful) mañoso. n astucia f; maña f.

cup [kʌp] n taza f; (prize) copa f.

cupboard ['kʌbəd] n armario m.

curate ['kjuərət] n cura m.

curator [kjuəˈreitə] n conservador, -a m, f.

curb [kəːb] v contener, refrenar. n (obstacle) estorbo m; (fig) freno m.

curdle ['kəːdl] v cuajar, cuajarse. **curd** cuajada f.

cure [kjuə] n (*course of treatment*) cura f; (*remedy*) remedio m; v curar; (*fig*) remediar; (*in salt*) salar; (*leather*) curtir. **cure-all** n curalotodo m.

curfew ['kə:fju:] n toque de queda m.

curious ['kjuəriəs] adj curioso. **curiosity** n curiosidad f.

curl [kə:l] n (*hair*) bucle m; (*smoke*) voluta f; (*twist*) torcedura f; serpenteo m. v (*hair*) rizar. **curl oneself up** harcerse un ovillo. **curler** n rulo m. **curly** adj rizado; sinuoso; en espiral.

currant ['kʌrənt] n (*dried grape*) pasa f; (*berry*) grosella f; (*bush*) grosellero m.

currency ['kʌrənsi] n moneda f; (*general use*) uso corriente m.

current ['kʌrənt] n corriente f; curso m. **alternating/direct current** corriente alterna/continua f. adj (*general*) corriente, prevalente; (*now*) actual; (*accepted*) admitido. **current account** cuenta corriente f. **current affairs** actualidades f pl. **current rate of exchange** cambio del día m. **current year** año en curso m. **currently** adv corrientemente; actualmente.

curriculum [kə'rikjuləm] n currículum m

curry ['kʌri] n cari m, curry m. v preparar con cari. **curry powder** curry en polvo m.

curse [kə:s] n maldición f. v maldecir; (*swear*) decir palabrotas; (*blaspheme*) blasfemar.

cursor ['kə:sə] n cursor m

curt [kə:t] adj brusco. **curtness** n brusquedad f.

curtail [kə:'teil] v (*cut short*) abreviar; (*expenses*) reducir. **curtailment** n abreviación f; reducción f.

curtain ['kə:tn] n cortina f; (*theatre*) telón m. **curtain call** llamada a escena f. **draw the curtain** correr la cortina. v poner cortinas en; encubrir.

curtsy ['kə:tsi] n reverencia f. v hacer una reverencia.

curve [kə:v] n curva f; vuelta f. v doblar; encorvar. **curvature** n curvatura f; (*earth*) esfericidad f; (*spine*) encorvamiento m. **curved** adj curvo; doblado.

cushion ['kuʃən] n cojín m, almohadón m. v amortiguar, acolchar.

custard ['kʌstəd] n natillas f pl.

custody ['kʌstədi] n custodia f, guardia f; prisión f. **in custody** bajo custodia. **take into custody** detener. **custodian** n custodio, -a m, f; guardián, -ana m, f.

custom ['kʌstəm] n (*habit*) costumbre f; (*customers*) clientela f sing. **customs** n derechos de aduana m pl. **customary** adj de costumbre. **custom-built** adj hecho de encargo. **customer** n cliente m, f.

*****cut** [kʌt] n corte m; (*wound*) herida f; (*notch*) muesca f; (*reduction*) reducción f; (*med*) incisión f. **short cut** atajo m. **cut-and-dried** previsto. **cut and thrust** la lucha f. v cortar; reducir; (*reap*) segar; (*shorten*) acortar. **cut short** cortar en seco. adj cortado; reducido. **cut-price** adj a precio reducido.

cute [kju:t] adj (*attractive*) mono, lindo; (*clever*) astuto. **cuteness** n monería f; astucia f.

cuticle ['kju:tikl] n cutícula f.

cutlery ['kʌtləri] n cubiertos m pl.

cutlet ['kʌtlit] n chuleta f.

CV n CV m

cyberspace ['saibəspeis] n ciberespacio m

cycle ['saikl] n ciclo m; bicicleta f. v pasar por un ciclo; ir en bicicleta. **cyclical** adj cíclico. **cycling** n ciclismo m. **cyclist** n ciclista m, f.

cyclone ['saikloun] n ciclón m.

cylinder ['silində] n cilindro m. **cylinder block** bloque de cilindros m. **cylindrical** adj cilíndrico.

cymbal ['simbəl] n címbalo m, platillo m.

cynic ['sinik] n, adj cínico, -a m, f. **cynical** adj cínico. **cynicism** n cinicismo m.

cypress ['saiprəs] n ciprés m.

Cyprus ['saiprəs] n Chipre. **Cypriot** n, adj chipriota m, f.

cyst [sist] n quiste m. **cystitis** n cistitis f.

Czech [tʃek] n, adj checo, -a. **Czech Republic** La República Checa f.

D

dab [dab] n (*light blow*) golpe ligero m; (*touch*) toque m; (*bit*) pizca f. v golpear ligeramente; dar unos toques de. adj **be a dab hand at** ser un hacha en.

dabble ['dabl] v (*splash*) salpicar; (*wet*)

mojar. **dabble in** (*water*) chapotear; (*participation*) meterse en.

dad [dad] *n* (*coll*) papá *m*.

daffodil ['dafədil] *n* narciso *m*.

daft [da:ft] *adj* (*coll*) tonto.

dagger ['dagə] *n* daga *f*; puñal *m*.

daily ['deili] *adj* (*taste*) delicado, fino; (*fussy*) difícil. **daintiness** *n* delicadeza *f*; elegancia *f*.

daily ['deili] *adj* diario, cotidiano. *adv* diariamente, cada día. *n* (*coll: newspaper*) diario *m*.

dainty ['deinti] *adj* (*taste*) delicado, fino; (*fussy*) difícil. **daintiness** *n* delicadeza *f*; elegancia *f*.

dairy ['deəri] *n* lechería *f*. **dairy cattle** vacas lecheras *f pl*. **dairy farm** granja de vacas *f*. **dairy products** productos lácteos *m pl*.

daisy ['deizi] *n* margarita *f*.

dam [dam] *n* (*barrier*) dique *m*; (*reservoir*) embalse *m*; (*zool*) madre *f*. *v* construir un dique; embalsar.

damage ['damidʒ] *n* daño *m*; (*fig*) perjuicio *m*. **damages** *pl n* (*law*) daños y perjuicios *m pl*. *v* dañar; perjudicar; (*spoil*) estropear.

damn [dam] *v* (*condemn*) condenar; (*curse*) maldecir. *damn!* (*interj*) ¡mechacis!
damnable *adj* condenable; detestable. **damnation** *n* condenación *f*; (*interj*) ¡maldición! **damned** *adj* condenado; (*coll*) maldito; tremendo. *adv* sumamente.

damp [damp] *adj* húmedo. *n* humedad *f*.
damp course aislante hidráfugo *m*. *v* (*also* **dampen**) humedecer; (*extinguish*) apagar, sofocar; (*discourage*) desanimar; (*sound*) amortiguar. **damper** *n* humedecedor *m*; (*chimney*) regulador *m*. **put a damper on** caer como un jarro de agua fría en.

damson ['damzən] *n* (*fruit*) ciruela damascena *f*; (*tree*) ciruelo damsceno *m*.

dance [da:ns] *n* baile *m*; (*ritual*) danza *f*.
dance band orquesta de baile *f*. **dance floor** pista de baile *f*. **dance hall** sala de baile *f*. *v* bailar. **dancer** *n* bailarín, -ina *m, f*.

dandelion ['dandi,laiən] *n* diente de león *m*.

dandruff ['dandrəf] *n* caspa *f*.

Dane [dein] *n* danés, -esa *m, f*. **Danish** *adj* danés. **Great Dane** perro danés *m*.

danger ['deindʒə] *n* peligro *m*. **danger zone** área de peligro *f*. **dangerous** *adj* peligroso.

dangle ['daŋgl] *v* (*hang*) colgar, dejar colgado; (*swing*) balancear en el aire.

dare [deə] *v* (*challenge*) desafiar; (*have the impudence to*) atreverse. **I dare say** quizás. *n* desafío *m*, reto *m*. **daredevil** *n* temerario, -a *m, f*. **daring** *adj* atrevido; osado. *n* osadía *f*.

dark [da:k] *adj* oscuro; (*hair, complexion*) moreno; (*sombre*) triste; (*menacing*) amenazador; (*mysterious*) misterioso. **Dark Ages** edad de las tinieblas *f*. **dark room** cámara oscura *f*. **grow dark** anochecer. *n* oscuridad *f*. **after dark** después del anochecer. **be in the dark** estar a oscuras. **darken** *v* oscurecer; entristecer. **darkness** *n* oscuridad *f*.

darling ['da:liŋ] *n, adj* querido, -a *m, f*.

darn [da:n] *v* zurcir. *n* zurcido *m*. **darning needle** aguja de zurcir *f*.

dart [da:t] *n* (*missile*) dardo *m*; (*movement*) movimiento rápido *m*. *v* lanzar. **dartboard** *n* blanco *m*. **darts** *pl n* (*sport*) dardos *m pl*.

dash [daʃ] *n* (*rush*) carrera *f*; (*printing*) guión *m*; (*cookery*) poco *m*, gotas *f pl*; (*verve*) brío *m*. *v* (*rush*) precipitarse, ir de prisa; (*hopes*) defraudar. **dash off** (*letter, etc.*) escribir deprisa. **dashboard** *n* salpicadero *m*. **dashing** *adj* gallardo.

data ['deitə] *pl n* datos *m pl*. **database** base de datos *f*. **data processing** proceso de datos *m*.

date¹ [deit] *n* (*calendar*) fecha *f*; época *f*. **be up to date** estar al día. **out of date** anticuado. **to date** hasta la fecha. **date line** meridiano de cambio de fecha *m*. *v* fechar.

date² [deit] *n* (*fruit*) dátil *m*. **date palm** palmera datilera *f*.

dative ['deitiv] *nm, adj* dativo.

daughter ['do:tə] *n* hija *f*. **daughter-in-law** *n* nuera *f*, hija política *f*.

daunt [do:nt] *v* (*dishearten*) desanimar; (*intimidate*) intimidar. **dauntless** *adj* intrépido.

dawdle ['do:dl] *v* (*loiter*) holgazanear; (*waste time*) malgastar; (*walk slowly*) andar despacio.

dawn [do:n] *n* (*fruit*) alba *f*, amanecer *m*; (*fig*) albores *m*, *pl*. **from dawn to dusk** de sol a sol. *v* alborear, amanecer.

day [dei] *n* día *m*; (*of work*) jornada *f*. **all day** todo el día. **every day** todos los días. **the day after tomorrow** pasado mañana. **the day before yesterday** anteayer. **from day to day** de día en día. **good day!** ¡buenos días! **daybreak** *n* amanecer *m*.

daydream n ensueño m; v soñar despierto.
daylight n luz del día f. **in broad daylight** en pleno día. **daytime** día m.
daze [deiz] n aturdimiento m. v aturdir. **be in a daze** estar aturdido.
dazzle ['dazl] n brillo m. v deslumbrar. **dazzling** adj deslumbrante, deslumbrador.
dead [ded] adj muerto; (absolute) absoluto; (insensible) insensible; (battery) descargado; (extinguished) apagado. **deadline** n fecha f. **deadly** adj mortal; (unerring) absoluto; (habit) pernicioso.
deaden ['dedn] v (sound, etc.) amortiguar; (pain) calmar; (feeling) embotar. **deadening** adj (tech) aislante.
deaf [def] adj sordo. **turn a deaf ear** hacerse el sordo. **deaf-and-dumb** (derog) adj sordomudo. **deafen** v ensordecer. **deafening** adj ensordecedor. **deafness** n sordera f.
*deal [di:l] v repartir, distribuir. **deal in** comerciar en. n transacción f, negocio m; (treatment) trato m; (agreement) convenio m; (amount) cantidad f; (cards) reparto m; (wood) abeto m. **it's a deal!** ¡trato hecho! **your deal** te toca. **dealer** m comerciante m, f; (cards) mano f. **dealing** n trato m; (behaviour) conducta f. **dealings** pl n relaciones f pl.
dean [di:n] n (rel) deán m; (academic) decano m.
dear [diə] adj querido; (costly) caro, costoso. **dear me!** ¡Dios mío! **dear sir** estimado señor. **dearly** adv (affectionately) cariñosamente; (costly) caro.
death [deθ] n muerte f; (formal) fallecimiento m. **death certificate** certificado de defunción m. **death duty** derechos de sucesión m pl. **deathless** adj inmortal. **deathly** adj (appearance) cadavérico; (silence) sepulcral. **death penalty** pena de muerte f. **death rate** mortalidad f.
debase [di'beis] v degradar; (coins) alterar. **debasement** n degradación f; alteración f.
debate [di'beit] n debate m, discusión f; controversia f. v discutir; controvertir; considerar. **debatable** adj discutible. **debating society** asociación que organiza debates f.
debit ['debit] n (entry of debt) débito m; (left-hand side of account) debe m. v cargar en cuenta.
debris ['deibri:] n escombros m pl.
debt [det] n deuda f. **run into debt** contraer deudas. **debtor** n deudor, -a m, f.

decade ['dekeid] n decenio m.
decadent ['dekədənt] n(m + f), adj decadente. **decadence** decadencia f.
decaffeinated [di'kafineitid] adj descafeinado
decant [di'kant] v decantar. **decanter** n garrafa f, jarra f.
decapitate [di'kapi,teit] v decapitar. **decapitation** n decapitación f.
decay [di'kei] n descomposición f; (teeth) caries f invar; decadencia f; (physics) desintegración progresiva f. v descomponerse; cariarse; decaer.
decease [di'si:s] n fallecimiento m. v fallecer. **deceased** n, adj difunto, -a.
deceit [di'si:t] n (cheating) engaño m; fraude m; decepción; (lying) mentira f. **deceitful** adj engañoso; fraudulento; mentiroso. **deceitfulness** n lo engañoso m; falsedad f.
deceive [di'si:v] v engañar; defraudar. **deceiver** n embustero, -a m, f.
December [di'sembə] n diciembre m.
decent ['di:sənt] adj decente; (satisfactory) razonable; (coll) bueno, simpático. **decency** n decencia f, decoro m.
deceptive [di'septiv] adj engañoso. **deceptiveness** n apariencia engañosa f.
decibel ['desi,bel] n decibel m, decibelio m.
decide [di'said] v decidir; (line of action) determinar; (conflict) resolver; (choose) optar por. **decided** adj decidido; determinado; resuelto; (difference) marcado.
deciduous [di'sidjuəs] adj de hoja caduca.
decimal ['desiməl] nf, adj decimal. **decimal point** coma de decimales f.
decipher [di'saifə] v descifrar.
decision [di'siʒən] n decisión f. **decisive** adj decisivo; concluyente; (manner) decidido; (tone) tajante. **decisively** adv con decisión.
deck [dek] n (ship) cubierta f; (bus) piso m. **deck chair** tumbona f.
declare [di'kleə] v declarar; proclamar. **declaration** n declaración f; proclamación f. **declaratory** adj declaratorio.
decline [di'klain] n (decrease) disminución f; (life) ocaso m; (decay) decaimiento m; (number) baja f. v negarse (a); (an offer) rehusar; (gramm) declinar; bajar; (med) debilitarse. **declining** adj declinante.
decode [di:'koud] v descodificar
decompose [,di:kəm'pouz] v (break up)

decomponer; (*rot*) pudrir. **decomposition** n decomposición f; putrefacción f.

decorate ['dekə,reit] v decorar, adornar; (*medal*) condecorar; (*paint*) pintar. **decoration** n (*medal*) condecoración f; (*ornament*) adorno m; (*décor*) decoración f. **decorative** *adj* decorativo. **decorator** n decorador, -a m, f.

decoy ['di:koi] n señuelo m.

decrease [di'kri:s] v disminuir, reducir. n disminución f, reducción f. **decreasing** *adj* decreciente.

decree [di'kri:] n decreto m. v decretar; pronunciar.

decrepit [di'krepit] *adj* decrépito.

dedicate ['dedi,keit] v (*book, life, etc.*) dedicar; (*church*) consagrar. **dedication** n (*devotion*) dedicación f; (*inscription*) dedicatoria f. **dedicatory** *adj* dedicatorio.

deduce [di'dju:s] v deducir.

deduct [di'dʌkt] v descontar. **deductible** *adj* deducible. **deduction** n (*discount*) deducción f, rebaja f, descuento m; (*conclusion*) conclusión f, deducción f.

deed [di:d] n acto m, acción f; (*something done*) hecho m; (*feat*) hazaña f; (*law*) escritura f.

deep [di:p] *adj* profundo, hondo. **a hole a metre deep** un pozo de un metro de hondo. **deep in debt** cargado de deudas. **go off the deep end** perder los estribos. n (*sea*) piélago m. **deepfreeze** n congelador m.

deer [diə] n ciervo m.

deface [di'feis] v desfigurar; multilar. **defacement** n desfiguración f; mutilación f.

default [di'fo:lt] n (*debt*) falta de pago f; (*absence*) falta f; (*law*) contumacia f, rebeldía f. **judgment by default** sentencia en rebeldía f. **win by default** ganar por incomparecencia del adversario. v dejar de pagar; condenar en rebeldía; (*a contest*) perder por incomparecencia.

defeat [di'fi:t] n derrota f. v derrotar, vencer. **defeatism** n derrotismo m. **defeatist** n(m + f), *adj* derrotista.

defect ['di:fekt; v di'fekt] n defecto m. v desertar. **defection** n deserción f. **defective** *adj* defectuoso; incompleto; (*gramm*) defectivo. **defectiveness** n imperfección f.

defend [di'fend] v defender. **defence** n defensa f. **self-defence** n autodefensa f.

defenceless *adj* indefenso. **defendant** n (*civil*) demandado, -a m, f; (*criminal*) acusado, -a m, f. **defender** n defensor, -a m, f. **defensible** *adj* defensible; justificable. **defensive** *adj* defensivo. **on the defensive** a la defensiva.

defer [di'fə:] v (*postpone*) diferir; (*submit*) someter; (*delay*) tardar. **deference** n deferencia f. **in deference to** por respeto a. **deferential** *adj* deferente, respetuoso. **deferment** n aplazamiento m; (*mil*) prórroga f. **deferrable** *adj* diferible. **deferred** *adj* diferido; aplazado.

defiant [di'faiənt] *adj* provocativo; (*challenging*) desafiante. **defiance** n desafío m. **in defiance of** con desprecio de.

deficient [di'fiʃənt] *adj* deficiente; (*med*) atrasado.

deficit ['defisit] n déficit m. *adj* deficitario.

define [di'fain] v definir; caracterizar; formular; determinar. **definition** n definición f; (*phot*) claridad f.

definite ['definit] *adj* definido; determinado; claro; definitivo; seguro. **definitely** *adv* claramente; categóricamente; (*without doubt*) seguramente.

deflate [di'fleit] v desinflar; (*comm*) provocar la deflación de; (*hopes*) reducir. **deflation** n desinflado m; (*comm*) deflación f.

deflect [di'flekt] v desviar

deform [di'fo:m] v deformar, desfigurar. **deformation** n deformación f.

defraud [di'fro:d] v defraudar, estafar.

defrost [di:'frost] v deshelar.

deft [deft] *adj* hábil, diestro. **deftness** n habilidad f, destreza f.

defunct [di'fʌŋkt] *adj* difunto.

defuse [di:'fju:z] v desactivar

defy [di'fai] v (*challenge*) desafiar, retar; (*resist*) resistir a.

degenerate [di'dʒenə,reit] v; n, *adj* di'dʒenərit] v degenerar. n, *adj* degenerado, -a. **degeneration** n degeneración f. **degenerative** *adj* degenerativo.

degrade [di'greid] v (*humiliate, reduce in rank*) degradar; (*quality*) rebajar; (*morals*) envilecer. **degradation** n degradación f. **degrading** *adj* degradante.

degree [di'gri:] n (*stop*) grado m; categoría f; (*university*) título m. **bachelor's degree** licenciatura f. **by degrees** poco a poco. **doctor's degree** doctorado m. **to some degree** hasta cierto punto.

dehydrate [di:'haidreit] v deshidratar. **dehydration** n deshidratación f.

de-icer [di:'aisə] n descongelador m.

deign [dein] v dignarse a hacer algo.

deity ['di:əti] n deidad f.

dejected [di'dʒektid] adj descorazonado, desanimado. **dejection** n desaliento m, abatimiento m.

delay [di'lei] n dilación f, retraso m; (wait) demora f. v retrasar f; (postpone) aplazar. **delaying** adj dilatorio.

delegate ['deləgit; v 'deləgeit] n delegado, -a m, f. v delegar. **delegation** n delegación f.

delete [di'li:t] v tachar, borrar. **deletion** n supresión f.

deliberate [di'libərət; v di'libəreit] adj (intentional) deliberado; (unhurried) lento; (premeditated) premeditado; (cautious) prudente. v deliberar; (ponder) reflexionar. **deliberately** adv (on purpose) a propósito; prudentemente; lentamente. **deliberation** n deliberación f; lentitud f; reflexión f.

delicate ['delikət] adj delicado; (food) exquisito; refinado; escrupuloso; (touch) ligero; (health) frágil. **delicacy** n delicadeza f, fragilidad f.

delicatessen [,delikə'tesn] n charcutería f

delicious [di'liʃəs] adj delicioso.

delight [di'lait] n deleite m; encanto m. v deleitar; encantar. **delightful** adj delicioso; encantador.

delinquency [di'liŋkwənsi] n delincuencia f. **delinquent** n(m + f), adj delincuente.

delirious [di'liriəs] adj delirante. **be delirious** delirar. **delirium** n delirio m.

deliver [di'livə] v (hand over) entregar; (goods, post) repartir; (message) dar; (opinion) expresar; (speech) pronunciar; (baby) asistir para dar a luz; (free) liberar. **deliverance** n liberación f. **delivery** n entrega f; reparto m; pronunciación f; lanzamiento m; (med) parto m; manera de expresarse f. **delivery service** servicio a domicilio m. **delivery van** furgoneta de reparto f. **take delivery of** recibir.

delta ['deltə] n delta m.

delude [di'lu:d] v engañar. **delusion** n engaño, m, error m, ilusión f.

deluge ['delju:dʒ] n diluvio m. v inundar; (fig) abrumar.

delve [delv] v cavar. **delve into** ahondar.

demand [di'ma:nd] n (comm) demanda f;

(request) petición f; (for payment) reclamación f. v (require) requerir; (ask urgently) exigir; reclamar. **demanding** adj (tiring) agotador; (absorbing) aborbente; (person) exigente.

demean [di'mi:n] v **demean oneself** rebajarse.

demented [di'mentid] adj demente, loco. **dementia** n demencia f.

democracy [di'mokrəsi] n democracia f. **democrat** n demócrata m, f. **democratic** adj democrático.

demolish [di'moliʃ] v (building) demoler, derribar; (fig) destruir. **demolition** n demolición f, derribo m; destrucción f.

demon ['di:mən] n demonio m, diablo m.

demonstrate ['demən,streit] v demostrar, probar; (show how something operates) mostrar; (pol) hacer la manifestación. **demonstration** n demostración f, prueba f; manifestación f. **demonstrative** adj demostrativo. **demonstrator** n ayudante m, f; (protester) manifestante m, f.

demoralize [di'morə,laiz] v desmoralizar. **demoralization** n desmoralización f. **demoralizing** adj desmoralizador, desmoralizante.

demote [di'mout] v bajar de categoría

demure [di'mjuə] adj recatado.

den [den] n (of animals, etc.) guarida f; (study) estudio m.

denial [di'naiəl] n (refusal) negativa f; (disavowal) negación f; (rejection) rechazamiento m. **self-denial** abnegación f.

denim ['denim] n tela vaquera f.

Denmark ['denma:k] n Dinamarca f.

denomination [di,nomi'neiʃən] n (measure) denominación f; (rel) secta f, confesión f; (coins) valor m; (type) clase f, tipo m. **denominational** adj sectario. **denominator** n (math) denominador m.

denote [di'nout] v denotar.

denounce [di'nauns] v denunciar.

dense [dens] adj (thick) denso; (coll: person) torpe. **densely** adv densamente. **density** n densidad f; torpeza f.

dent [dent] n abolladura f. v abollar.

dental ['dentl] adj dental.

dentist ['dentist] n dentista m, f. **dentistry** n odontología f.

denture ['dentʃə] n dentadura f, postiza f.

denude [di'nju:d] v desnudar.

denunciation [dinʌnsi'eiʃən] *n* denuncia *f*; (*condemnation*) condena *f*; (*criticism*) censura *f*.

deny [di'nai] *v* (*refuse, dispute*) negar; (*request*) denegar; (*give the lie to*) desmentir; (*repudiate*) repudiar.

deodorant [di:'oudərənt] *n* desodorante *m*.

depart [di'pa:t] *v* (*go away*) marcharse; (*set off*) salir; (*deviate*) apartarse. **departed** *adj* pasado; (*dead*) difunto. **departure** *n* marcha *f*; salida *f*; desviación *f*.

department [di'pa:tmənt] *n* (*in a shop*) departamento *m*; (*in a business*) servicio *m*; (*college, university*) sección *f*; (*ministry*) negociado *m*; (*branch*) ramo *m*; (*fig: sphere*) esfera *f*. **department store** gran almacén *m*. **departmental** *adj* departamental.

depend [di'pend] *v* depender. **dependence** *n* dependencia *f*. **dependent** *adj* dependiente; subordinado.

depict [di'pikt] *v* (*art*) **pintar**; (*fig*) describir. **depiction** *n* pintura *f*; descripción *f*.

deplete [di'pli:t] *v* vaciar, agotar. **depletion** *n* agotamiento *m*.

deplore [di'plo:] *v* deplorar, lamentar. **deplorable** *adj* deplorable, lamentable.

deport [di'po:t] *v* expulsar. **deport oneself** comportarse. **deportation** *n* expulsión *f*. **deportment** *n* porte *m*; conducta *f*.

depose [di'pouz] *v* deponer.

deposit [di'pozit] *n* (*bank*) depósito *m*; (*substance*) sedimento *m*, poso *m*; (*pledge*) señal *f*; (*on accommodation*) entrada *f*. *v* depositar; (*money in account*) ingresar; dar de señal. **deposit account** cuenta de depósitos a plazo *f*.

depot ['depou] *n* (*store*) almacén *m*; (*buses*) cochera *f*; (*mil*) depósito *m*.

deprave [di'preiv] *v* depravar. **depravity** *n* depravación *f*.

depreciate [di'pri:ʃiait] *v* (*belittle, money*) despreciar; (*goods*) abaratar; (*price*) bajar. **depreciation** *n* depreciación *f*; abaratamiento *m*; (*fig*) desprecio *m*.

depress [di'pres] *v* (*dishearten*) deprimir; (*weaken*) debilitar; (*lessen*) disminuir; (*lower*) bajar; (*push down*) presionar; (*pedal*) pisar. **depressed** *adj* deprimido; (*indigent*) necesitado; (*comm*) de depresión. **depressing** *adj* deprimente. **depression** *n* (*dejection*) abatimiento *m*; (*geog, med, comm*) depresión *f*.

deprive [di'praiv] *v* privar, desposeer.

deprivation *n* privación *f*; (*loss*) pérdida *f*.

depth [depθ] *n* profundidad *f*; (*colour*) intensidad *f*; (*sound*) gravedad *f*. **be out of one's depth** perder pie; (*fig*) no entender nada.

deputy ['depjuti] *n* delegado, -a *m*, *f*; (*substitute*) suplente *m*, *f*; (*politician*) diputado, -a *m*, *f*. **deputation** *n* delegación *f*. **deputize** *v* diputar; delegar; sustituir.

derail [di'reil] *v* hacer descarrilar. **derailment** *n* descarrilamiento *m*.

derelict ['derilikt] *adj* abandonado. *n* (*neut*) derrelicto *m*; (*person*) deshecho *m*. **dereliction** *n* abandono *m*; (*negligence*) negligencia *f*.

deride [di'raid] *v* ridicular. **derision** *n* mofas *f pl*. **derisive** *or* **derisory** *adj* (*mocking*) mofador; (*petty*) irrisorio.

derive [di'raiv] *v* derivar; (*profit*) sacar. **derivation** *n* derivación *f*. **derivative** *nm*, *adj* derivado.

derogatory [di'rogətəri] *adj* despectivo, rebajante.

descend [di'send] *v* descender, bajar. **descendant** *n*(*m* + *f*), *adj* descendiente. **descent** *n* descenso *m*, bajada *f*; (*slope*) declive *m*; (*lineage*) descendencia *f*.

describe [di'skraib] *v* describir; (*draw*) trazar. **describe oneself as** presentarse como. **description** *n* descripción *f*; (*sort*) clase *f*. **descriptive** *adj* descriptivo.

desert¹ ['dezət] *n* (*land*) desierto *m*.

desert² [di'zə:t] *v* abandonar; (*mil*) desertar de. **deserter** *n* desertor *m*. **desertion** *n* (*mil*) deserción *f*; abandono *m*.

deserts [di'zə:ts] *pl n* **get one's deserts** llevarse su merecido.

deserve [di'zə:v] *v* merecer; ser digno de. **deserving** *adj* digno; (*deed*) meritorio.

design [di'zain] *n* (*intention*) propósito *m*; (*plan*) proyecto *m*; (*drawing*) dibujo *m*; (*style*) estilo *m*. **have designs on** haber puesto sus miras en. *v* (*prepare plans for*) diseñar; dibujar; proyectar; inventar; (*create*) crear; imaginar. **designer** *n* diseñador, -a *m*, *f*; *adj* de diseño. (*draughtsman*) delineante *m*, *f*. **dress designer** modista *m*, *f*. **designing** *adj* intrigante.

designate ['dezig,neit] *v* (*name for a duty*) designar; (*name*) denominar; (*appoint*) nombrar; (*point out*) señalar. *adj* designado; nombrado. **designation** *n* designación *f*; denominación *f*; nombramiento *m*.

desire [di'zaiə] *n* deseo *m*; (*request*) petición *f*. *v* desear; pedir; (*want*) querer. **desirable** *adj* deseable; atractivo. **desirability** *n* lo atractivo; conveniencia *f*. **desirous** *adj* deseoso.

desk [desk] *n* (*office*) escritorio *m*; (*school*) pupitre *m*.

desolate ['desələt; *v* 'desəle:t] *adj* (*waste*) desolado; solitario; desierto; disconsolado. *v* (*lay waste*) asolar; abandonar; desconsolar. **desolating** *adj* desolador. **desolation** *n* desolación *f*; soledad *f*.

despair [di'speə] *n* desesperación *f*, desesperanza *f*. *v* desesperar.

desperate ['despərət] *adj* desesperado; (*resistance*) enérgico; (*urgent*) apremiante. **desperation** *n* desesperación *f*.

despise [di'spaiz] *v* despreciar. **despicable** *adj* despreciable. **despicableness** *n* bajeza *f*.

despite [di'spait] *prep* a pesar de.

despondent [di'spondənt] *adj* desanimado, desalentado. **despondency** *n* desánimo *m*, desaliento *m*.

despot ['despot] *n* déspota *m*. **despotic** *adj* despótico. **despotism** *n* despotismo *m*.

dessert [di'zə:t] *n* postre *m*. **dessertspoon** *n* cuchara de postre *f*.

destine ['destin] *v* destinar. **destination** *n* destinación *f*. **destiny** *n* destino *m*.

destitute ['destitju:t] *adj* indigente, menesteroso. **be destitute** estar en la miseria. **destitution** *n* indigencia *f*, miseria *f*.

destroy [di'stroi] *v* destruir, destrozar. **destroyer** *n* (*naut*) destructor *m*. **destruction** *n* destrucción *f*; ruina *f*. **destructive** *adj* destructivo.

detach [di'tatʃ] *v* despegar; separar. **detachable** *adj* separable; (*collar*) postizo. **detached** *adj* independiente; (*untroubled*) indiferente. **detachment** *n* separación *f*; indiferencia *f*; (*mil*) destacamento *m*.

detail ['di:teil] *n* detalle *m*. *v* detallar; (*itemize*) enumerar; (*mil*) destacar.

detain [di'tein] *v* retener; (*law*) detener. **detention** *n* detención *f*, arresto *m*.

detect [di'tekt] *v* (*discover*) descubrir; (*perceive*) percibir; (*note*) advertir; (*tech*) detectar. **detection** *n* descubrimiento *m*; detección *f*. **detective** *n* detective *m*. **detective story** novela policíaca *f*. **detector** *n* detector *m*. **lie detector** detector de mentiras *m*.

deter [di'tə:] *v* desuadir. **deterrent** *adj* dis-

uasivo. *n* fuerza de disuasión *f*.

detergent [di'tə:dʒənt] *nm, adj* detergente.

deteriorate [di'tiəriə,reit] *v* (*wear out*) deteriorar; (*become worse*) empeorar; (*in value*) depreciar. **deterioration** *n* deterioro *m*; empeoramiento *m*; (*decline*) decadencia *f*.

determine [di'tə:min] *v* (*fix*) determinar; (*cause*) provocar; (*limits*) definir; (*decide*) decidir; resolver. **determination** *n* determinación *f*; resolución *f*; decisión *f*. **determined** *adj* resuelto; decidido; determinado.

detest [di'test] *v* destestar, odiar. **detestable** *adj* detestable, odioso. **detestation** *n* odio *m*.

detonate ['detə,neit] *v* detonar. **detonating** *adj* detonante. **detonation** *n* detonación *f*.

detour ['di:tuə] *n* desvío *m*, desviación *f*; vuelta *f*. **make a detour** dar un rodeo.

detract [di'trakt] *v* (*take away*) quitar, reducir; (*denigrate*) denigrar. **detraction** *n* denigración *f*.

detriment ['detrimənt] *n* detrimento *m*. perjuicio *m*. **detrimental** *adj* perjudicial.

devalue [di:'valju:] *v* devaluar, desvalorizar. **devaluation** *n* devaluación *f*.

devastate ['devə,steit] *v* devastar. **devastating** *adj* devastador. **devastation** *n* devastación *f*.

develop [di'veləp] *v* (*expand*) desarrollar; (*business*) explotar; (*land*) urbanizar; (*resources*) aprovechar; (*promote*) fomentar; (*taste*) adquirir; (*ailment*) contraer; (*tendency*) manifestar; (*talent*) mostrar; (*phot*) revelar. **developer** *n* (*phot*) revelador *m*. **development** *n* desarrollo *m*; evolución *f*; progreso *m*.

deviate ['di:vi,eit] *v* desviarse. **deviation** *n* desviación *f*; (*from truth*) alejamiento *m*; (*sexual*) inversión *f*. **deviationism** *n* desviacionismo *m*. **deviationist** *n* desviacionista *m, f*.

device [di'vais] *n* (*tech*) mecanismo; ingenio; (*scheme*) ardid *m*; estratagema *f*.

devil ['devl] *n* diablo. **devilish** *adj* diabólico. **devil's advocate** abogado del diablo *m*.

devise [di'vaiz] *v* inventar; (*plan*) concebir; (*plot*) tramar.

devoid [di'void] *adj* desprovisto.

devolution [,di:və'lu:ʃən] *n* (*powers*) delegación *f*. **devolve** *v* delegar; transmitir.

devote [di'vout] *v* dedicar. **devoted** *adj*

dedicado; (*loyal*) leal; (*devout*) devoto.
devotion *n* dedicación f; lealtad f; devoción f. **devotional** *adj* piadoso.

devour [di'vauə] *v* devorar. **devouring** *adj* devorador.

devout [di'vaut] *adj* devoto; sincero.
devoutness *n* devoción f.

dew [dju:] *n* rocío m.

dexterous ['dekstrəs] *adj* diestro, hábil.
dexterity *n* destreza f, habilidad f.

diabetes [,diə'bi:ti:z] *n* diabetes f. **diabetic** *n, adj* diabético, -a.

diagnose [,diəg'nouz] *v* diagnosticar.
diagnosis *n* diagnóstico m.

diagonal [daɪ'agənəl] *nf, adj* diagonal.
diagonally' *adv* diagonalmente.

diagram ['daɪə,gram] *n* (*math*) figura, (*chart*) gráfico m; (*sketch*) esquema m; (*explanatory*) diagrama m. **diagrammatic** *adj* esquemático.

dial ['daɪəl] *n* (*clock*) esfera f; (*selector*) botón m; (*telephone*) disco m. *v* marcar. **dialling tone** señal para marcar f.

dialect ['daɪəlekt] *n* dialecto m.

dialogue ['daɪəlog] *n* diálogo m.

diameter [daɪ'amitə] *n* diámetro m. **diametrically** *adv* diametralmente.

diamond ['daɪəmənd] *n* diamante m. **diamond-shaped** *adj* romboidal.

diaper ['daɪəpə] *n* (*US*) pañal m.

diaphragm ['daɪə,fram] *n* diafragma m.

diarrhoea [,daɪə'riə] *n* diarrea f.

diary ['daɪəri] *n* diario m; (*for appointments*) agenda f.

dice[1] [daɪs] *n pl* dados m pl. *v* jugar a los dados. **dice with death** jugar con la muerte.

dice[2] [daɪs] *v* cortar en cubitos.

dictate [dik'teɪt] *v* dictar; (*order*) mandar; (*impose*) imponer. *n* mandato m. **dictation** *n* dictado m. **dictator** *n* dictador m. **dictatorial** *adj* dictatorial. **dictatorship** *n* dictadura f.

dictionary ['dikʃənəri] *n* diccionario m.

did [did] *V* **do**.

*****die** [daɪ] *v* morir, fallecer. **die away** (*sound*) desvanecer. **die down** (*fire*) apagarse; (*wind*) amainar; (*conversation*) decaer. **die out** desaparecer.

diesel ['di:zəl] *nm, adj* diesel. **diesel engine** motor diesel m. **diesel oil** gasoil m.

diet ['daɪət] *n* dieta f, régimen m. *v* estar a

dieta *or* régimen. **dietary** *adj* dietético.
dietetics *n* dietética f. **dietician** *n* dietético, -a m, f.

differ ['difə] *v* ser diferente, ser distinto.
difference *n* diferencia f; (*disagreement*) desacuerdo m. **different** *adj* diferente, distinto. **differential** *nf, adj* diferencial. **differentiate** *v* diferenciar, distinguir.

difficult ['difikəlt] *adj* difícil. **difficulty** *n* dificultad f.

*****dig** [dig] *v* cavar; excavar; (*coal, etc.*) extraer. **dig in** enterrar. **dig into** clavar. **dig up** desenterrar. *n* (*in the ribs*) golpe m; excavación arqueológica f; (*fig*) pinchazo m.

digest ['daɪdʒest; *v* daɪ'dʒest] *n* resumen m. *v* digerir; (*summarize*) resumir; (*fig*) asimilar. **digestible** *adj* digerible. **digestion** *n* digestión f. **digestive** *adj* digestivo. **digestive system** aparato digestivo m.

digit ['didʒit] *n* (*finger, toe*) dedo m; (*math*) dígito m. **digital** *adj* digital.

dignified ['digni,faid] *adj* digno; solemne.
dignify *v* dignificar.

dignity ['digniti] *n* dignidad f. **dignitary** *n* dignatario, -a m, f.

digress [daɪ'gres] *v* desviarse, apartarse.
digression *n* digresión f.

digs [digz] *n pl* (*coll*) pensión f *sing*.

dilapidated [di'lapi,deitid] *adj* (*building*) ruinoso; (*clothes*) muy estropeado. **dilapidate** *v* deteriorar; estropear. **dilapidation** *n* estado ruinoso m.

dilate [daɪ'leɪt] *v* dilatar.

dilemma [di'lemə] *n* dilema m.

diligent ['dilidʒent] *adj* diligente. **diligence** *n* diligencia f.

dilute [daɪ'lu:t] *v* diluir, aguar; (*fig*) atenuar. *adj* diluido, atenuado. **dilution** *n* dilución f.

dim [dim] *adj* oscuro; (*memory*) lejano; (*sound*) sordo; (*sight*) turbio; (*light*) débil; (*vague*) borroso; (*colour*) apagado; (*coll*) tonto. **take a dim view of** ver con malos ojos. *v* (*light*) bajar; (*sight*) nublar. **dimly** *adv* vagamente; poco iluminado.

dimension [di'menʃən] *n* dimensión f.

diminish [di'miniʃ] *v* disminuir.

diminutive [di'minjutiv] *adj* diminuto. *nm, adj* (*gramm*) diminutivo.

dimple ['dimpl] *n* hoyuelo m. *v* formar hoyuelos en.

din [din] *n* estrépito *m*, alboroto *m*.

dine [dain] *v* cenar. **dining car** coche restaurante *m*. **dining room** *n* comedor *m*.

dinghy ['diŋgi] *n* bote *m*.

dingy ['dindʒi] *adj* sucio, sórdido.

dinner ['dinə] *n* (*evening*) cena *f*; (*midday*) comida *f*. **dinner jacket** esmoquin *m*. **dinner party** cena *f*. **dinner table** mesa de comedor *f*.

dinosaur ['dainə,so:] *n* dinosaurio *m*.

diocese ['daiəsis] *n* diócesis *f*. **diocesan** *n*, *adj* diocesano, -a.

dip [dip] *v* (*wet*) mojar; (*immerse*) sumergir; (*someone*) zambullir; (*scoop*) sacar; (*put a hand in*) meter; (*flag*) inclinar; (*headlights*) poner luz de cruce; (*road*) bajar; *n* baño *m*; (*slope*) declive *m*.

diphthong ['difθoŋ] *n* diptongo *m*.

diploma [di'pləumə] *n* diploma *m*.

diplomacy [di'pləuməsi] *n* diplomacia *f*. **diplomat** *n* diplomático, -a *m*, *f*. **diplomatic** *adj* diplomático. **diplomatic corps** cuerpo diplomático *m*. **diplomatic immunity** inmunidad diplomática *f*.

dipstick ['dipstik] *n* varilla graduada *f*.

dire [daiə] *adj* extremo; terrible.

direct [di'rekt] *adj* (*straight*) directo; (*blunt*) tajante; (*frank*) franco. **direct current** corriente continua *f*. **direct debit** domiciliación bancaria *f*. *v* dirigir; (*order*) mandar; (*show the way*) indicar; (*gaze, attention*) señalar. **direction** *n* dirección *f*. **directions** *n pl* instrucciones *f pl*. **directive** *n* instrucción *f*. **directly** *adv* directamente; (*at once*) en seguida. **directness** *n* franqueza *f*.

director *m* director, -a *m*, *f*. **board of directors** consejo de administración *n*. **managing director** director, -a gerente, -a *m*, *f*.

dirt [də:t] *n* suciedad *f*; (*filth*) mugre *f*; (*rubbish*) basura *f*. **dirt-cheap** *adj* baratísimo. **dirty** *adj* sucio; (*obscene: person*) verde; (*language*) grosero. **dirty trick** mala pasada *f*.

disability [disə'biləti] *n* incapacidad *f*. **disable** *v* incapacitar; (*cripple*) lisiar. **disabled** *adj* inválido. **disablement** *n* incapacidad *f*.

disadvantage [,disəd'va:ntidʒ] *n* desventaja *f*. **be at a disadvantage** estar en situación desventajosa.

disagree [,disə'gri:] *v* discrepar; no estar de acuerdo. **disagreeable** *adj* desagradable. **disagreement** *n* desacuerdo *m*.

disappear [,disə'piə] *v* desaparecer. **disappearance** *n* desaparición *f*.

disappoint [,disə'point] *v* decepcionar; defraudar. **disappointing** *adj* decepcionante. **disappointment** *n* decepción *f*; disgusto *m*.

disapprove [,disə'pru:v] *v* desaprobrar; estar en contra. **disapproval** *n* desaprobación. *f*. **disapproving** *adj* desaprobador. **disapprovingly** *adv* con desaprobación.

disarm [dis'a:m] *v* desarmar. **disarmament** *n* desarme *m*.

disaster [di'za:stə] *n* desastre *m*. **disastrous** *adj* desastroso.

disband [dis'band] *v* disolver; (*mil*) licenciar.

disc *or US* **disk** [disk] *n* disco *m*. **disc jockey** discjockey *m*, *f*.

discard [dis'ka:d; *n* 'diska:d] *v* (*cast away*) desechar; (*cards*) descartar; (*fig*) renunciar. *n* descarte *m*.

discern [di'sə:n] *v* discernir. **discernible** *adj* perceptible. **discerning** *adj* perspicaz.

discharge [dis'tʃa:dʒ; *n* 'distʃa:dʒ] *v* descargar; (*debt*) saldar; (*gun*) disparar; (*sack*) despedir; (*law*) absolver; (*duty*) desempeñar; (*prisoner*) liberar; (*patient*) dar de alta; (*bankrupt*) rehabilitar. *n* descarga *f*; (*debt*) descargo; (*gas*) escape *m*; liberación *f*; rehabilitación *f*; absolución *f*; desempeño *m*; alta *f*; disparo *m*.

disciple [di'saipl] *n* discípulo, -a *m*, *f*.

discipline ['disiplin] *n* disciplina *f*. *v* castigar. **disciplinarian** *n* disciplinario, -a *m*, *f*. **disciplinary** *adj* disciplinario.

disclaim [dis'kleim] *v* rechazar; (*law*) renunciar. **disclaimer** *n* (*denial*) denegación *f*; (*law*) renuncia *f*.

disclose [dis'klouz] *v* revelar. **disclosure** *n* revelación *f*; descubrimiento *m*.

disco ['diskou] *n* discoteca *f*

discolour [dis'kʌlə] *v* descolorar; (*stain*) manchar. **discolouration** *n* descoloración *f*.

discomfort [dis'kʌmfət] *n* molestia *f*; incomodidad *f*; malestar *m*. *v* molestar.

disconcert [diskən'sə:t] *v* desconcertar, perturbar. **disconcerting** *adj* desconcertante.

disconnect [diskə'nekt] *v* (*elec*) desconectar; (*separate*) separar. **disconnection** *n* desconexión *f*; separación *f*.

disconsolate [dis'kɒnsələt] *adj* desconsolado. **disconsolateness** *n* desconsuelo *m*.

discontinue [diskən'tinju:] *v* descontinuar, interrumpir; suspender. **discontinuance** *or* **discontinuation** *n* cesación *f*; suspensión *f*. **discontinuity** *n* discontinuidad *f*; interrupción *f*. **discontinuous** *adj* discontinuo.

discord ['disko:d] *n* discordia *f*; (*music*) disonancia *f*. **discordant** *adj* discordante; (*music*) discorde.

discotheque ['diskətek] *n* discoteca *f*.

discount ['diskaunt] *n* descuento *m*; (*reduction*) rebaja *f*. *v* descontar; rebajar; (*disregard*) no hacer caso de.

discourage [dis'kʌridʒ] *v* desanimar. **discourage from** recomendar que no. **discouragement** *n* desánimo *m*. **discouraging** *adj* desalentador.

discover [dis'kʌvə] *v* descubrir; (*realize*) darse cuenta de. **discoverer** *n* descubridor, -a *m, f*. **discovery** *n* descubrimiento *m*.

discredit [dis'kredit] *v* desacreditar; (*disbelieve*) dudar de; (*dishonour*) deshonrar. *n* descrédito *m*; duda *f*. **discreditable** *adj* indigno; vergonzoso.

discreet [dis'kri:t] *adj* discreto; prudente. **discretion** *n* discreción; circunspección *f*. **at your discretion** a su gusto. **discretionary** *adj* discrecional.

discrepancy [di'skrepənsi] *n* discrepancia *f*; diferencia *f*. **discrepant** *adj* discrepante; diferente.

discrete [di'skri:t] *adj* discreto.

discriminate [di'skrimi,neit] *v* distinguir. **discriminate against** discriminar contra. **discriminating** *adj* (*law*) discriminatorio; (*taste*) muy bueno. **discrimination** *n* discriminación *f*; discernimiento *m*; buen gusto *m*. **discriminatory** *adj* discriminatorio.

discus ['diskəs] *n* disco *m*.

discuss [di'skʌs] *v* discutir; hablar de. **discussion** *n* discusión *f*.

disease [di'zi:z] *n* enfermedad *f*. **diseased** *adj* enfermo.

disembark [disim'ba:k] *v* desembarcar. **disembarkation** *n* (*people*) desembarco *m*; (*cargo*) desembarque *m*.

disengage [disin'geidʒ] *v* (*detach*) soltar; (*unhook*) desenganchar; (*free*) liberar; (*mil*) retirar; (*gears*) desengranar; (*clutch*) desembragar. **disengagement** *n* liberación *f*; retirada *f*; desembrague *m*.

disfigure [dis'figə] *v* desfigurar; (*spoil*) afear. **disfigurement** *n* desfiguración *f*; afeamiento *m*.

disgrace [dis'greis] *n* (*disfavour*) desgracia *f*; (*cause of shame*) vergüenza *f*; deshonra *f*; ignominia *f*. *v* deshonrar. **disgraceful** *adj* deshonroso; vergonzoso.

disgruntled [dis'grʌntld] *adj* malhumorado.

disguise [dis'gaiz] *v* disfrazar. *n* disfraz *m*.

disgust [dis'gʌst] *n* repugnancia *f*. *v* repugnar.

dish [diʃ] *n* plato *m*; (*serving vessel*) fuente *f*. *v* servir. **dish out** dar. **dishwasher** *n* lavaplatos *m*.

dishearten [dis'ha:tn] *v* descorazonar, desanimar. **disheartening** *adj* descorazonador.

dishevelled [di'ʃevəld] *adj* despeinado; desarreglado.

dishonest [dis'ɒnist] *adj* fraudulento.

dishonour [dis'ɒnə] *n* deshonra *f*. deshonor *m*. *v* deshonrar.

disillusion [disi'lu:ʒən] *v* desilusionar. *n* desilusión *f*.

disinfect [disin'fekt] *v* desinfectar. **disinfectant** *nm, adj* desinfectante.

disinherit [disin'herit] *v* desheredar. **disinheritance** *n* desheradamiento *m*.

disintegrate [dis'inti,greit] *v* desintegrar. **disintegration** *n* desintegración *f*.

disinterested [dis'intristid] *adj* desinteresado; imparcial. **disinterest** *n* desinterés *m*.

disjointed [dis'dʒɔintid] *adj* desarticulado; (*incoherent*) inconexo.

disk [disk] (*computer*) *n* disk *m*, disco *m*. **disk drive** unidad de disco *f*.

dislike [dis'laik] *v* aborrecer, tener aversión a. *n* aversión *f*, antipatía *f*.

dislocate ['dislə,keit] *v* (*joint*) dislocar; (*plans*) desarreglar. **dislocation** *n* dislocación *f*; desarreglo *m*.

dislodge [dis'lɒdʒ] *v* desalojar. **dislodgement** *n* desalojamiento *m*.

disloyal [dis'lɔiəl] *adj* desleal. **disloyalty** *n* deslealtad *f*.

dismal ['dizməl] *adj* triste; (*face*) sombrío; (*voice*) lúgubre.

dismantle [dis'mantl] *v* desmantelar; desmontar.

dismay [dis'mei] *n* consternación *f*; (*fright*) espanto *m*. *v* consternar; espantar; (*discour-*

age) desalentar.

dismiss [dis'mis] *v* despedir; (*discharge*) licenciar; (*assembly*) disolver; (*mil*) romper filas; (*idea*) descartar. **dismissal** *n* (*employee*) despido *m*; abandono *m*.

dismount [dis'maunt] *v* desmontar.

disobey [disə'bei] *v* desobedecer. **disobedience** *n* desobediencia *f*. **disobedient** *adj* desobediente.

disorder [dis'o:də] *n* desorden *m*; (*riot*) disturbio *m*; (*illness*) trastorno *m*. *v* desordenar. **disorderliness** *n* desorden *m*. **disorderly** *adj* (*person*) desordenado; (*place*) desarreglado; (*meeting*) alborotado.

disorganize [dis'o:gənaiz] *v* desorganizar. **disorganization** *n* desorganización *f*.

disown [dis'oun] *v* repudiar; (*deny*) negar; no reconocer.

disparage [di'sparidʒ] *v* desacreditar; (*belittle*) menospreciar; (*denigrate*) denigrar. **disparagement** *n* descrédito *m*; menosprecio *m*; denigración *f*. **disparaging** *adj* despectivo; menospreciativo; denigrante. **disparagingly** *adv* con desprecio.

disparity [dis'pariti] *n* disparidad *f*. **disparate** *adj* dispar.

dispassionate [dis'paʃənit] *adj* desapasionado; imparcial.

dispatch [di'spatʃ] *n* (*message*) despacho *m*, expedición *f*; (*messenger, parcels*) envio *m*; (*promptness*) diligencia *f*. *v* despachar; enviar; matar.

dispel [di'spel] *v* disipar.

dispense [di'spens] *v* (*drugs*) preparar; (*justice*) administrar; (*distribute*) distribuir; (*laws*) aplicar. **dispense with** prescindir de. **dispensable** *adj* prescindible. **dispensary** *n* dispensario *m*; farmacia *f*. **dispensation** *n* distribución *f*; administración *f*; (*exemption*) dispensa *f*.

disperse [di'spə:s] *v* dispersar. **dispersal** *n* dispersión *f*.

displace [dis'pleis] *v* desplazar; (*oust*) quitar el puesto; (*remove from office*) destituir. **displacement** *n* desplazamiento *m*; destitución *f*; reemplazo *m*.

display [di'splei] *v* exhibir; demostrar. *n* exhibición *f*; demostración *f*; despliegue *m*; (*emotion*) alarde *m*; (*show*) exposición *f*; (*parade*) desfile *m*; (*tech*) representación visual *f*.

displease [dis'pli:z] *v* desagradar, disgustar. **displeasing** *adj* desagradable. **displeasure**

n desagrado *m*, disgusto *m*.

dispose [di'spouz] *v* (*arrange*) disponer; determinar; inclinar; mover. **dispose of** tirar; (*transfer*) traspasar; (*argument*) echar por tierra; (*kill*) liquidar; (*sell*) vender; (*consume*) consumir. **disposable** *adj* disponible; (*to be thrown away*) para tirar. **disposal** *n* (*arrangement*) desposición *f*; eliminación *f*; resolución *f*; traspaso *m*; venta *f*. **disposition** *n* disposición *f*; traspaso *m*; predisposición *f*.

disprove [dis'pru:v] *v* refutar.

dispute [di'spru:v] *n* disputa *f*; discusión *f*; controversia *f*; (*law*) litigio *m*. *v* disputar; discutir; (*question*) poner en duda. **disputation** *n* discusión *f*; controversia *f*.

disqualify [dis'kwolifai] *v* (*render unfit*) incapacitar; (*competitor*) descalificar. **disqualification** *n* incapacidad *f*; descalificación *f*.

disregard [disrə'ga:d] *v* (*neglect*) descuidar; desatender. *n* descuido *m*; indiferencia *f*.

disreputable [dis'repjutabl] *adj* (*shabby*) lamentable; (*not respectable*) de mala fama. **disrepute** *n* descrédito *m*.

disrespect [disrə'spekt] *n* falta de respeto *f*. **disrespectful** *adj* irrespetuoso.

disrupt [dis'rʌpt] *v* (*upset*) trastornar; (*interrupt*) interrumpir; (*break up*) romper; desorganizar. **disruption** *n* trastorno *m*; ruptura *f*; interrupción *f*; desorganización *f*. **disruptive** *adj* perjudicial.

dissatisfy [di'satisfai] *v* no satisfacer. **dissatisfaction** *n* descontento *m*.

dissect [di'sekt] *v* disecar. **dissection** *n* disección *f*.

dissent [di'sent] *n* disensión *f*; (*disagreement*) disentimiento *m*. *v* (*disagree*) disentir. **dissension** *n* disensión *f*.

dissident ['disidant] *n*(*m + f*), *adj* disidente. **dissidence** *n* disidencia *f*.

dissimilar [di'similə] *adj* desigual; distinto. **dissimilarity** *n* desigualdad *f*.

dissipate ['disipeit] *v* derrochar

dissociate [di'sousieit] *v* disociar. **dissociation** *n* disociación *f*.

dissolute ['disalu:t] *adj* disoluto. **dissolution** *n* (*society, marriage, melting*) disolución *f*.

dissolve [di'zolv] *v* disolver; (*disintegrate*) descomponer; disipar; (*law; contract*) rescindir.

dissuade [di'sweid] *v* disuadir. **dissuasion**

n disuasión *f*. **dissuasive** *adj* disuasivo.

distance ['distəns] *n* distancia *f*. *v* distanciar, **distant** *adj* distante, lejano.

distaste [dis'teist] *n* disgusto *m*, aversión *f*. **distasteful** *adj* desagradable.

distemper [di'stempə] *n* (*dogs*) moquillo *m*; (*paint*) temple *m*.

distend [di'stend] *v* distender. **distension** *n* distensión *f*.

distil [di'stil] *v* destilar. **distillation** *n* destilación *f*. **distillery** *n* destilería *f*.

distinct [di'stiŋkt] *adj* (*clear*) claro; (*different*) distinto; (*definite*) bien determinado. **distinction** *n* distinción *f*. **distinctive** *adj* distintivo. **distinctness** *n* claridad *f*; diferencia *f*.

distinguish [di'stiŋgwiʃ] *v* distinguir. **distinguishable** *adj* distinguible. **distinguished** *adj* (*elegant*) distinguido; (*eminent*) eminente.

distort [di'sto:t] *v* torcer; (*fig*) desvirtuar. **distortion** *n* torcimiento *m*; desvirtuación *f*.

distract [di'strakt] *v* (*divert attention*) distraer; (*confuse*) aturdir; (*madden*) enloquecer. **distraction** *n* distracción *f*; aturdimiento *m*; locura *f*.

distraught [di'stro:t] *adj* distraído; enloquecido.

distress [di'stres] *n* aflicción *f*; (*poverty*) miseria *f*; (*danger*) peligro *m*. *v* afligir; angustiar. **distressed** *adj* afligido; en la miseria; en peligro. **distressing** *adj* angustioso.

distribute [di'stribjut] *v* distribuir, repartir. **distribution** *n* distribución *f*; reparto *m*. **distributor** *n* distribuidor, -a *m*, *f*; (*mot*) distribuidor *m*.

district ['distrikt] *n* (*pol*) distrito *m*; (*town*) barrio *m*; (*region*) región *f*. **district manager** representante regional *m*, *f*.

distrust [dis'trʌst] *n* desconfianza *f*. *v* desconfiar. **distrustful** *adj* desconfiado.

disturb [di'stə:b] *v* molestar; perturbar; agitar; preocupar. **disturbance** *n* molestia *f*; perturbación *f*; agitación *f*; preocupación *f*; (*row*) alboroto *m*; (*public disorder*) disturbio *m*. **disturbing** *adv* molesto; perturbador; preocupante.

disuse [dis'ju:s] *n* desuso *m*; abandono *m*.

ditch [ditʃ] *n* (*trench*) zanja *f*; (*roadside*) cuneta *f*; (*irrigation*) acequia *f*; (*drainage*) canal *m*. *v* (*coll: get rid of*) tirar; (*coll: aban-*

don) abandonar.

ditto ['ditou] *n* idem *m*.

divan [di'van] *n* diván *m*.

dive [daiv] *n* zambullida *f*. *v* zambullirse; saltar; bajar en picado; sumergirse. **diver** *n* buzo *m*; saltador, -a *m*, *f*.

diverge [dai'və:dʒ] *v* divergir; desviar. **divergence** *n* divergencia *f*. **divergent** *adj* divergente.

diverse [dai'və:s] *adj* diverso; distinto; diferente; variado. **diversity** *n* diversidad *f*.

divert [dai'və:t] *v* (*reroute*) desviar; (*distract*) distraer; (*amuse*) divertir. **diversion** *n* desviación *f*; diversión *f*.

divide [di'vaid] *v* dividir. **division** *n* división *f*; separación *f*; distribución *f*; sección *f*; (*fig: opinions*) discrepancia *f*; (*fig: discord*) desunión *f*.

dividend ['dividend] *n* dividendo *m*.

divine [di'vain] *adj* divino. *v* adivinar. **divinity** *n* divinidad *f*; teología *f*.

divorce [di'vo:s] *n* divorcio *m*. **sue for a divorce** pedir el divorcio. *v* divorciar; divorciarse de. **divorcee** *n* divorciado, -a *m*, *f*.

divulge [dai'vʌldʒ] *v* divulgar.

dizzy ['dizi] *adj* mareado; (*height, speed*) vertiginoso. **dizziness** *n* mareo *m*, vértigo *m*.

*do [du:] *v* (*act*) hacer; (*deal with*) ocuparse de; (*fulfil*) cumplir con; (*serve*) venir bien; (*feel*) estar, sentirse; (*be suitable*) valer; (*work*) trabajar. **do away with** suprimir. **do for** llevar la casa a; **do up** (*buttons, belt*, etc.) abrocharse; (*laces*) atarse; (*renovate*) renovar. **do well** ir bien, salir bien; recuperarse. **do without** prescindir de. **it doesn't do to** no conviene. **how do you do?** (*after being introduced*) encantado; (*how are you?*) ¿cómo está usted? **make do with** arreglárselas con. **please do** pòr supuesto, por favor.

DNA ADN

docile ['dousail] *adj* dócil. **docility** *n* docilidad *f*.

dock[1] [dok] *n* (*wharf*) dársena *f*; *v* (*ship*) atracar al muelle; (*arrive*) llegar.

dock[2] [dok] *n* (*law*) banquillo de los acusados *m*.

dock[3] [dok] *v* (*cut, shorten*) cortar; reducir; (*coll: deduct*) descontar; (*coll: fine*) multar.

doctor ['doktə] *n* médico, -a *m*, *f*; (*university title*) doctor, -a *m*, *f*. *v* atender; adulterar;

falsificar. **doctorate** n doctorado m.

doctrine ['dɒktrin] n doctrina f. **doctrinaire** adj doctrinario. **doctrinal** adj doctrinal.

document ['dɒkjumənt; v dɒkju'ment] n documento m. v documentar. **documentary** nm, adj documental.

dodge [dɒdʒ] v esquivarse; eludir; (hide) echarse; (avoid) evitar. n (manoeuvre) regate m; (trick) truco m. **dodgy** (coll) adj astuto; (unreliable) incierto.

doe [dou] n cierva f; coneja f

dog [dɒg] n perro m. **beware of the dog** cuidado con el perro. v seguir; perseguir.

dog biscuit n galleta de perro f.

dog days n pl canícula f sing.

dog-eared adj sobado.

dogged ['dɒgid] adj tenaz. **doggedness** n tenacidad f.

doggerel ['dɒgərəl] n aleluyas f pl.

dogma ['dɒgmə] n dogma m. **dogmatic** adj dogmático.

do-it-yourself [,du:itjə'self] adj hágalo usted mismo.

dole [doul] n (alms) limosna f; (unemployment pay) subsidio de paro m. **be on the dole** estar parado. **dole out** repartir.

doleful ['doulful] adj triste. **dolefulness** n tristeza f.

doll [dɒl] n muñeca f.

dollar ['dɒlə] n dólar m.

dolphin ['dɒlfin] n delfín m.

domain [də'mein] n dominio m; (fig) campo m.

dome [doum] n (arch) cúpula f, domo m.

domestic [də'mestik] adj doméstico; (home-loving) hogareño; (market) nacional. **domestic animal** animal doméstico m. **domestic help** doméstico, -a m, f. **domesticate** v domesticar. **domestication** n domesticación f. **domesticity** n domesticidad f.

dominate ['dɒmi,neit] v dominar. **dominant** adj dominante. **domineering** adj dominante.

dominion [də'minjən] n dominio m.

domino ['dɒminou] n dominó m. **play dominoes** jugar al dominó.

don [dɒn] v ponerse. n catedrático m.

donate [də'neit] v donar. **donation** n donativo m.

done [dʌn] V **do**.

donkey ['dɒŋki] n burro m.

donor ['dounə] n donante m, f.

doodle ['du:dl] n garabato m

doom [du:m] n perdición f. v condenar. **doomsday** n día del juicio final m.

door [dɔ:] n puerta f. **next door** en la casa de al lado.

doorbell ['dɔ:bel] n timbre m.

door-keeper n portero m; conserje m.

door-handle n mano de la puerta f.

doorknob ['dɔ:nɒb] n tirador de puerta m.

door-knocker n llamador m.

doormat ['dɔ:mat] n felpudo m.

doorstep ['dɔ:step] n peldaño m; (threshold) umbral m.

doorway ['dɔ:wei] n portal m.

dope [doup] n (coll: drug) droga f; (coll: varnish) barniz m; (coll: information) informes m pl. v drogar.

dormant ['dɔ:mənt] adj letárgico; inactivo; latente.

dormitory ['dɔ:mitəri] n dormitorio m.

dormouse ['dɔ:,maus] n -mice lirón m.

dose [dous] n dosis f invar. v dar la dosis. **dosage** n dosis f invar.

dot [dɒt] n punto m. **dot-com** punto com m. **on the dot** puntualmente. v poner el punto a; (scatter) salpicar.

dote [dout] v chochear. **dote on** estar chocho por. **dotage** n chochez f. **doting** adj chocho.

double ['dʌbl] nm, adj, adv doble. v doblar.

double bass n contrabajo m.

double bed n cama de matrimonio f.

double-breasted [,dʌbl'brestid] adj cruzado.

double-cross [,dʌbl'krɒs] n traición f. v traicionar.

double-edged [,dʌbl'edʒd] adj de dos filos.

double entendre [du:blä'tädr] n expresión con doble sentido f.

double entry n (comm) partida doble f.

doubt [daut] n duda f. **no doubt** in duda. v dudar. **doubtful** adj dudozo; sospechoso. **doubtless** adv indudablemente.

dough [dou] n masa f. **doughnut** n buñuelo m.

dove [dʌv] n paloma f.

dowdy ['daudi] *adj* desaliñado. **dowdiness** *n* desaliño *m*.

down-and-out [daunən'aut] *n* pobres *m* (*pl*). *v* no tener donde caerse muerto

download [daun'loud] *v* bajar

down¹ ['daun] *adv* hacia abajo. *prep* abajo. *adj* descendente, bajo. **down payment** desembolso inicial *m*. *v* derribar; tirar al suelo; (*food*) tragar; (*drink*) vaciar de un trago.

down² [daun] *n* plumón *m*; (*fine hair*) vello *m*; (*upland*) loma *f*.

downcast ['daun,ka:st] *adj* (*sad*) abatido; (*in a downward direction*) bajo.

downfall ['daun,fo:l] *n* ruina *f*; perdición *f*; caída *f*; (*rain*) chaparrón *m*.

downhearted [,daun'ha:tid] *adj* descorazonado.

downhill [,daun'hil] *adj* en pendiente. *adv* cuesta abajo.

downpour ['daun,po:] *n* aguacero *m*, chaparrón *m*.

downright ['daun,rait] *adj* categórico; sincero; evidente; verdadero. *adv* categóricamente; verdaderamente; completamente.

Down's Syndrome *n* Síndrome de Down *m*.

downstairs ['daun,steəz; *adv* ,daun'steəz] *adj* de abajo. *adv* abajo.

downstream [,daun'stri:m] *adj*, *adv* río abajo.

downtrodden ['daun,trodn] *adj* (*fig*) oprimido.

downward ['daunwəd] *adj* descendente. *adv* hacia abajo.

downwards ['daunwədz] *adv* hacia abajo.

dowry ['dauəri] *n* dote *f*.

doze [douz] *v* dormitar. *n* cabezada *f*.

dozen ['dʌzn] *n* docena *f*. **baker's dozen** docena del fraile *f*.

drab [drab] *adj* pardo; monótono.

draft [dra:ft] *n* (*version*) redacción *f*; (*drawing*) esbozo *m*; (*plan*) bosquejo *m*; (*payment*) libramiento *m*; (*bill*) letra de cambio *f*; (*naut*) calado *m*; (*conscription*) quinta *f*. *v* hacer un proyecto; (*draw up*) redactar; esbozar; (*conscript*) reclutar.

drag [drag] *v* arrastrar; (*river, etc.*) dragar. **drag down** hundir. *n* (*tow*) arrastre *m*; (*that which hinders*) estorbo *m*; (*device for dragging rivers, etc.*) rastra *f*; (*theatre*) disfraz de mujer *m*; (*aero*) resistencia aerodinámica *f*; (*tech*:

brake) galga *f*. **what a drag!** ¡qué lata!

dragon ['dragən] *n* dragón *m*. **dragonfly** *n* libélula *f*.

drain [drein] *n* desaguadero *m*; (*sewer inlet*) sumidero *m*; (*strength*) pérdida *f*. *v* desaguar; (*drink empty*) vaciar; (*marshes*) desecar; (*strength*) agotar. **drainage** *n* desagüe *m*; desecación *f*. **draining board** escurridero *m*. **drainpipe** *n* tubo de desagüe *m*.

drama ['dra:mə] *n* drama *m*. **dramatic** *adj* dramático. **dramatics** *n pl* teatro *m sing*. **dramatist** *n* dramaturgo, -a *m*, *f*. **dramatize** *v* adaptar al teatro.

drape [dreip] *v* cubrir con ropa, adornar con colgaduras. *n* colgadura *f*. **draper** *n* pañero, -a *m*, *f*. **drapery** *n* telas *f pl*.

drastic ['drastik] *adj* drástico.

draught [dra:ft] *n* (*air*) corriente de aire *f*; (*plan*) bosquejo *m*; (*drink*) trago *m*. *adj* (*animals*) de tiro. **draughtboard** *n* tablero de damas *m*. **draughtsman** *n* delineante *m*. **draughtsmanship** *n* dibujo lineal *m*.

***draw** [dro:] *n* (*sport*) empate *m*; (*lots*) sorteo *m*; (*lottery*) lotería *f*. *v* (*pull*) tirar de; (*extract*) extraer; (*attract*) atraer; (*art*) dibujar; (*a line*) trazar; (*nail, water, confession, profits.*) sacar; (*comparisons*) hacer; (*breath*) tomar; (*salary*) cobrar; (*cheque*) librar; (*prize*) ganar; sortear; (*close: curtains*) descorrer; (*blinds*) bajar; (*cards*) robar. **draw attention** llamar la atención. **draw up** (*document*) redactar a.

drawback ['dro:bak] *n* (*disadvantage*) desventaja *f*; (*shortcoming*) inconveniente *m*.

drawer ['dro:ə] *n* (*container*) cajón *m*; (*art*) dibujante *m*, *f*.

drawing ['dro:iŋ] *n* (*art*) dibujo *m*; (*extraction*) extracción *f*. **drawing board** tablero de dibujo *m*. **drawing pin** chincheta *f*. **drawing room** salón *m*.

drawl [dro:l] *n* voz lenta *f*. *v* arrastrar las palabras.

drawn [dro:n] *adj* (*weary*) cansado. **drawn to** atraído por.

dread [dred] *n* miedo; terror. *v* temer. **dreadful** *adj* terrible; espantoso.

***dream** [dri:m] *v* soñar; imaginarse. *n* sueño *m*. **bad dream** pesadilla *f*. **daydream** *n* ensueño *m*. **dream up** inventar.

dreary ['driəri] *adj* trioste; monótono; (*boring*) aburrido. **dreariness** *n* tristeza *f*; monotonía *f*.

dredge [dredʒ] v dragar. n draga f.

dregs [dregz] n pl heces f pl.

drench [drentʃ] v empapar, mojar. **drenched to the skin** mojado hasta los huesos.

dress [dres] n (frock) vestido m; (clothing) ropa f; (evening dress: men) traje de etiqueta m, (women) traje de noche m; (wedding) traje de novia m. v vestir. **dress up** poner de tiros largos. **dress up as** disfrazarse de.

dress circle n piso principal m.

dress coat n frac m.

dress designer n modelista m, f.

dresser ['dresə] n aparador m.

dressing ['dresiŋ] n (act) vestir m; (clothes) ropa f; (med) vendaje m; (cookery) aliño m; (agriculture) abono m. **dressing gown** bata f.

dressmaker ['dresmeikə] n modista m, f. **dressmaking** n costura f.

dress rehearsal n ensayo general m.

dress shirt n camisa de frac f.

dressy ['dresi] adj elegante.

dribble ['dribl] n goteo m. v gotear.

drier ['draiə] n secador m; (for clothes) secadora f.

drift [drift] n arrastramiento m; (snow) ventisquero m; (sand) montón m; (naut, aero) deriva f. v ser arrastrado; amontonarse; derivar; (fig) vivir sin rumbo. **drift along** vagar. **drifter** n (vagrant) vagabundo m; (boat) trainera f.

drill [dril] n (tech) taladro m; (dental) fresa f; (mil) instrucción f. v (mil). ejercitar; (bore) taladrar, perforar. **drilling** n instruccion f; perforación f.

*drink [driŋk] v beber; tomar; (toast) brindar por. **drink down** beber de un trago. **drink in** beberse. **drink up** bebérselo todo. n bebida f; (alcoholic) copa f; (water, milk) vaso m; algo de beber. **soft drink** bebida no alcohólica f. **have a drink** tomar algo.

drinkable ['driŋkəbl] adj potable.

drinker ['driŋkə] n bebedor, -a m, f.

drinking ['driŋkiŋ] n beber m; bebida f. **drinking fountain** fuente de agua potable f. **drinking water** agua potable f.

drip [drip] n goteo m; (drop) gota f. v gotear. **drip-dry** adj de lava y pon.

*drive [draiv] v (push onwards) empujar; (control a vehicle) conducir; (carry in a vehicle) llevar; (some distance) recorrer; (force someone out) echar; (compel) obligar. **drive at** (physically) dirigirse hacia; (fig) insinuar. **drive away** irse; alejar. **drive by** pasar (por). **drive in** entrar; clavar. **drive into** chocar contra. **drive on** seguir su camino. **drive up** llegar. n paseo m; excursión f; (journey) viaje m; (fig) vigor m; (mil) ofensiva f; (tennis, golf) drive m; (mot) tracción f; transmisión f; propulsión f; (instinct) instinto m. **driver** n conductor, -a m, f; chófer m, f; (taxi) taxista m, f; (train) maquinista m, f. **driveway** n camino de entrada m.

drivel ['drivl] n tonterías f pl. v decir tonterías.

driving ['draiviŋ] n conducción f. **driving licence** carnet de conducir m. **driving school** autoescuela f. **driving test** examen para sacar el carnet de conducir m.

drizzle ['drizl] n llovizna f. v lloviznar.

drone [droun] n (noise) zumbido m; (voices) murmullo m; (bee) zángano m; (aero) teledirigido m. v zumbar; murmurar.

droop [dru:p] n (shoulders) encorvamiento m; (head) inclinación f. v estar encorvado; inclinarse; (flowers) marchitarse; (eyelids) caerse; (fig) desanimarse; debilitarse.

drop [drop] n gota f; (sweet) pastilla f; (bit) pizca f; (fall) caída f; (in value) disminución f; (in prices) baja f; (in temperature) descenso m. v (release) soltar; (let fall) dejar caer; (tears) derramar; (a friend) dejar; (prices, eyes, voice) bajar; (give up a habit) dejar de; (leave behind) despegarse de. **drop behind** quedarse atrás. **drop dead** caerse muerto. **drop in on** pasar por casa de. **drop off** dormirse.

dropout ['dropaut] n abandono m; marginado, -a m, f.

dropsy ['dropsi] n hidropesía f.

drought [draut] n sequía f.

drown [draun] v ahogar.

drowsy ['drauzi] adj soñoliento. **be drowsy** tener sueño. **drowse** v dormitar.

drudge [drʌdʒ] n esclavo, -a m, f. v currelar. **drudgery** n trabajo penoso m.

drug [drʌg] n droga f; medicamento m. v drogar. **drug addict** drogadicto, -a m, f. **drug addiction** toxicomanía f.

drum [drʌm] n (music) tambor m; (container) bidón m; (ear) tímpano m. v tocar el tambor; (fingers) tamborilear.

drummer n tambor m; batería f. **drumstick** n palillo de tambor m.

drunk [drʌŋk] adj borracho; (fig) ebrio. **get drunk** emborracharse. **drunkard** n borracho, -a m, f. **drunkenness** n embriaguez f.

dry [drai] adj seco; (measure) para áridos; (boring) aburrido; (thirsty) sediento; (wit) agudo; (subject) árido. v secar. **dry-clean** v limpiar en seco. **dry cleaner** tintorero, -a m, f.

dual ['djuəl] adj doble. **dual carriageway** pista doble f. **dual-purpose** adj de dos usos.

dubbed ['dʌbd] adj (named) apodado; (knighted) armado; (film) doblado. **dub** v apodar; armar; doblar.

dubious ['djuːbiəs] adj dudoso; ambiguo; indeciso; discutible; sospechoso.

duchess ['dʌtʃis] n duquesa f.

duck¹ [dʌk] n (bird) pata f; (drake) pato m; (dodging) esquiva f; (in water) zambullida f.

duck² [dʌk] v (crouch) agachar; zambullir.

duckling ['dʌkliŋ] n patito m.

duct [dʌkt] n (anat) canal m; (gas) conducto m; (elec) tubo m.

dud [dʌd] n (coll) desastre m; (mil) projectil fallido m. adj falso; inútil; defectuoso; (cheque) sin fondos.

due [djuː] adj (care, time) debido; (payable) pagadero. **due date** vencimiento m. **be due to** deberse a. n merecido m. adv derecho hacia. **dues** pl n derechos m pl. **duly** adv debidamente; a su debido tiempo.

duel ['djuəl] n duelo m. v batirse en duelo. **duellist** n duelista m.

duet [djuˈet] n dúo m.

duke [djuːk] n duque m.

dull [dʌl] adj monótono; (obtuse) torpe; (slow) tardo; (tedious) pesado; (colour) apagado; (surface) mate; (weather) gris; (sullen) sombrío; (blunt) embotado. v (emotions) enfriarse; (pain) aliviar; (sound) apagar. **dullness** n monotonia f; torpeza f; pesadez f. **dully** adv torpemente; lentamente.

dumb [dʌm] adj mudo; (coll) estúpido. **dumbbell** n pesa f. **dumbfound** v dejar sin habla. **dumbfounded** adj confuso, atónito. **dumbwaiter** n carrito m.

dummy ['dʌmi] n (teat) chupete m; (tailor's) maniquí m; (puppet) muñeco m; (cards) muerto m; (coll) lobo, -a m, f. adj ficticio, falso. v (sport) fintar.

dump [dʌmp] n (rubbish dump) depósito de basura m; (heap) montón m; (scrapheap) vertedero m; (coll: wretched place) tugurio m. v (throw away) tirar; (get rid of) deshacerse de; (unload) descargar. **dumping** n descarga f. **dumpy** adj regordete.

dumpling ['dʌmpliŋ] n masa hervida f.

dunce [dʌns] n tonto, -a m, f. burro m.

dune [djuːn] n duna f.

dung [dʌŋ] n excrementos m pl; (manure) estiércol m.

dungarees [dʌŋgəˈriːz] n pl mono m sing.

dungeon ['dʌndʒən] n calabozo m, mazmorra f.

duplicate ['djuːplikət; v 'djuːplikeit] n copia f, doble m, duplicado m. adj duplicado. v duplicar; multicopiar. **duplicating machine** multicopista f. **duplication** n duplicación f; copia f.

durable ['djuərəbl] adj duradero. **durability** n durabilidad f.

duration [djuˈreiʃən] n duración f.

during ['djuriŋ] prep durante.

dusk [dʌsk] n crepúsculo m. **dusky** adj oscuro; (complexion) moreno.

dust [dʌst] n polvo m. v (clean) limpiar el polvo; (powder) espolvorear. **dustbin** n cajón de basura m. **duster** trapo m; (feather) plumero m. **dustman** n basurero m. **dustpan** n recogedor m. **dusty** adj polvoriento; cubierto de polvo.

duty ['djuːti] n deber m. obligación f; (tax) impuesto m. (at customs) derechos de aduana m pl. **be off duty** estar libre. **on duty** de servicio. **dutiful** adj obediente; deferente. **duty-free** adj libre de derechos de aduana.

duvet ['duːvei] n colcha de plumón f.

DVD n DVD m.

dwarf [dwoːf] n, adj enano, -a. v achicar.

*dwell [dwel] v vivir. **dwell on** (emphasize) insistir en; (a subject) extenderse en. **dwelling** n vivienda f.

dwindle ['dwindl] v disminuir, menguar.

dye [dai] n (colouring substance) tinte m; (colour) color sólido m. v teñir.

dyke [daik] n (ditch) zanja f; (bank) dique m.

dynamic [daiˈnamik] adj dinámico.

dynamite ['dainəˌmait] n dinamita f. v dinamitar.

dynamo ['dainəˌmou] n dínamo f.

dynasty ['dinəsti] *n* dinastía *f*. **dynastic** *adj* dinástico.

dysentery ['disəntri] *n* disentería *f*.

dyslexia [dis'leksiə] *n* dislexia *f*.

dyspepsia [dis'pepsiə] *n* dispepsia *f*. **dyspeptic** *adj* dispéptico.

E

each [i:tʃ] *adj* cada. *pron* cada uno, cada una. **each other** el uno al otro.

eager ['i:gə] *adj* ávido; ansioso; impaciente. **eagerness** *n* ansia *f*; impaciencia *f*.

eagle ['i:gl] *n* águila *f*. **be eagle-eyed** *adj* tener ojos de lince.

ear[1] [iə] *n* oreja *f*; (*fig*) oído *m*. **earache** dolor de oído *m*. **eardrum** *n* tímpano *m*. **earmark** *v* reservar; destinar. **earring** *n* pendiente *m*; **earshot** *n* alcance del oído *m*.

ear[2] [iə] *n* (*grain*) espiga *f*.

earl [ə:l] *n* conde *m*.

early ['ə:li] *adv* temprano; pronto; al principio. *adj* temprano; próximo; pronto.

earn [ə:n] *v* ganar; merecer. **earnings** *pl n* (*income*) ingresos *m pl*; (*salary*) sueldo *m sing*.

earnest ['ə:nist] *adj* sincero; aplicado; serio. **in earnest** en serio.

earth [ə:θ] *n* tierra *f*. **earthenware** *n* alfarería *f*.

earwig ['iəwig] *n* tijereta *f*.

ease [i:z] *n* facilidad *f*; naturalidad *f*; (*comfort*) comodidad *f*; (*from pain*) alivio *m*. *v* facilitar; aliviar; tranquilizar; (*tension*) relajar.

easel ['i:zl] *n* caballete *m*.

east [i:st] *n* este *m*. *adj also* **easterly**, **eastern** oriental; del este; *adv* al este, hacia el este. **eastward** *adj*, *adv* hacia el este.

Easter ['i:stə] *n* Pascua de Resurrección *f*. **Easter egg** huevo de Pascua *m*.

easy ['i:zi] *adj* fácil. **easy chair** sillón *m*. **easy-going** *adj* acomodadizo; indolente. **take it easy!** ¡tómatelo con calma! **easiness** *n* facilidad *f*.

*eat [i:t] *v* comer. **eat up** comerse. **eatable** *adj also* **edible** comestible.

eavesdrop ['i:vzdrop] *v* fisgonear. **eaves-**

dropper *n* fisgón, -onera *m*, *f*.

ebb [eb] *n* reflujo *m*, menguante *m*. *v* menguar; decaer. **ebb tide** marea menguante *f*.

ebony ['ebəni] *n* ébano *m*.

eccentric [ik'sentrik] *n*, *adj* excéntrico, -a. **eccentricity** *n* excentricidad *f*.

ecclesiastical [ikli:zi'astikl] *adj also* **ecclesiastic** eclesiástico.

echo ['ekou] *n* eco *m*; resonancia *f*; repetición *f*. *v* resonar; repetir; imitar.

eclair [ei'kleə] *n* relámpago *m*.

eclipse [i'klips] *n* eclipse *m*. *v* eclipsar.

ecology [i'kolədʒi] *n* ecología *f*. **ecological** *adj* ecológico. **ecologist** *n* ecólogo, -a *m*, *f*.

e-commerce ['i:,komə:s] *n* comercio electrónico *m*

economy [i'konəmi] *n* economía *f*. **economic** *adj also* **economical** económico. **economics** *n* economía *f*. **economist** *n* economista *m*, *f*. **economize** *v* economizar.

ecstasy ['ekstəsi] *n* éxtasis *m*; (*drug*) éxtasis *m*. **go into ecstasies over** extasiarse ante. **ecstatic** *adj* extático.

Ecuador ['ekwədo:] *n* Ecuador *m*. **Ecuadoran, Ecuadorean,** *or* **Ecuadorian** *n*, *adj* ecuatoriano, -a *m*, *f*.

eczema ['eksimə] *n* eczema *m*.

edge [edʒ] *n* borde *m*; (*blade*) filo *m*, corte *m*. **have the edge on** llevar ventaja a. **be on edge** tener los nervios de punta. *v* bordear; mover poco a poco. **edging** *n* (*sewing*) orla *f*; (*path*) borde *m*. **edgy** *adj* nervioso.

edible ['edəbl] *adj* comestible.

Edinburgh ['edinbərə] *n* Edimburgo *m*.

edit ['edit] *v* (*text*) redactar; (*film*) montar; (*direct a paper, magazine*) dirigir. **editor** *n* redactor, -a *m*, *f*. director, -a *m*, *f*. **editorial** *n* editorial *m*; artículo de fondo *m*. **editorial staff** redacción *f*.

edition [i'diʃən] *n* edición *f*; tirada *f*.

educate ['edju,keit] *v* educar. **educated** *adj* culto. **education** *n* educación *f*; (*teaching*) enseñanza *f*; (*specific*) instrucción *f*. **educational** *adj* educativo; (*teaching*) docente.

eel [i:l] *n* anguila *f*.

eerie ['iəri] *adj* misterioso; espantoso.

effect [i'fekt] *n* efecto *m*; resultado *m*; impresión *f*; (*meaning*) significado *m*. **side effect** efecto secundario. **take effect** (*drugs, etc.*) surtir efecto; (*law, etc.*) tener efecto. *v* efectuar. **effective** *adj* (*efficient*) eficaz; (*real*) efectivo; (*in force*) vigente.

effectiveness *n* eficacia *f*; efecto *m*; vigencia *f*.

effeminate [i'feminət] *adj* afeminado.

effervescent [,efə'vesənt] *adj* efervescente. **effervesce** *v* estar en efervescencia.

efficient [i'fiʃənt] *adj* eficaz, eficiente. **efficiency** *n* eficacia *f*, eficiencia *f*.

effigy ['efidʒi] *n* efigie *f*.

effort ['efət] *n* esfuerzo *m*. **effortless** *adj* sin esfuerzo.

egg [eg] *n* huevo *m*. **bad egg** huevo podrido. **boiled egg** huevo pasado por agua. **hard-boiled egg** huevo duro. **newlaid egg** huevo fresco. **poached egg** huevo escalfado. **scrambled eggs** huevos revueltos *m pl*. **eggcup** *n* huevera *f*. **eggshaped** *adj* oviforme. **eggshell** *n* cascarón de huevo *m*. **egg on** incitar.

ego ['i:gou] *n* el ego *m*. *adj* orgullo

egotism ['egətizm] *n* egotismo *m*. **egotist** *n* (*self-important person*) egotista *m*, *f*; (*selfish person*) egoista *m*, *f*.

Egypt ['i:dʒipt] *n* Egipto *m*. **Egyptian** *n*, *adj* egipcio, -a, *m*, *f*.

eiderdown ['aidədaun] *n* edredón *m*.

eight [eit] *nm*, *adj* ocho. **eighth** *n*, *adj* octavo, -a.

eighteen [ei'ti:n] *nm*, *adj* dieciocho. **eighteenth** *n*, *adj* decimoctavo, -a.

eighty ['eiti] *nm*, *adj* ochenta. **eightieth** *n*, *adj* octogésimo, -a.

either ['aiðə] *adj* cada, ambos. *pron* uno u otro; cualquiera de los dos. *adv* tampoco. *conj* o. **either ... or ...** o ... o ....

ejaculate [i'dʒakjuleit] *v* exclamar; (*med*) eyacular. **ejaculation** *n* exclamación *f*; eyaculación *f*.

eject [i'dʒekt] *v* expulsar; echar; (*tenant*) desahuciar. **ejection** *n* expulsión *f*; desahucio *m*. **ejector seat** asiento eyectable *m*.

eke [i:k] *v* **eke out** (*add to*) complementar; (*make last*) escatimar.

elaborate [i'labərət; *v* i'labəreit] *adj* complicado; detallado. *v* elaborar. **elaborate on** ampliar. **elaborately** *adv* cuidadosamente; complicadamente; detalladamente. **elaboration** *n* elaboración *f*; explicación *f*; complicación *f*.

elapse [i'laps] *v* transcurrir.

elastic [i'lastik] *nm*, *adj* elástico. **elastic band** goma elástica *f*. **elasticity** *n* elasticidad *f*.

elated [i'leitid] *adj* jubiloso; exaltado. **elation** *n* júbilo *m*; exaltación *f*.

elbow ['elbou] *n* codo *m*. **elbow grease** fuerza de puños *f*. **elbow room** espacio suficiente *m*.

elder[1] ['eldə] *nm*, *adj* mayor. **elderly** *adj* mayor de edad. **eldest** *adj* mayor.

elder[2] ['eldə] *n* (*bot*) saúco *m*. **elderberry** *n* baya del saúco.

elect [i'lekt] *v* elegir. *adj* elegido. **election** *n* elección *f*. **electoral** *adj* electoral. **electorate** *n* electorado *m*.

electric [ə'lektrik] *adj also* **electrical** eléctrico. **electric blanket** manta eléctrica *f*. **electric fire** estufa eléctrica *f*. **electric shock** electrochoque *m*. **electrician** *n* electricista *m*, *f*. **electricity** *n* electricidad *f*. **electrify** *v* (*rail, industry*) electrificar; (*produce electricity*) electrizar; (*fig*) entusiasmar.

electrocute [i'lektrəkju:t] *v* electrocutar. **electrocution** *n* electrocución *f*.

electrode [i'lektroud] *n* electrodo *m*.

electronic [elək'tronik] *adj* electrónico. **electronics** *n* electrónica *f*.

elegant ['eligənt] *adj* elegante; bello. **elegance** *n* elegancia *f*.

elegy ['elidʒi] *n* elegia *f*.

element ['eləmənt] *n* elemento *m*; factor *m*. **elementary** *adj* elemental; fundamental.

elephant ['elifənt] *n* elefante *m*.

elevate ['eliveit] *v* elevar; (*voice, eyes*) levantar; (*honour*) enaltecer. **elevation** *n* elevación *f*; (*hill*) altura *f*; (*thought*) nobleza *f*.

eleven [i'levn] *nm*, *adj* once. **eleventh** *n* undécimo, -a *m*, *f*; *adj* onceavo.

elf [elf] *n*; *pl* -ves duende *m*. **elfin** *adj* de los duendes.

eligible ['elidʒəbl] *adj* elegible; atractivo.

eliminate [i'limineit] *v* eliminar. **elimination** *n* eliminación *f*.

elite [ei'li:t] *n* élite *f*.

ellipse [i'lips] *n* elipse *f*. **elliptical** *adj* elíptico.

elm [elm] *n* olmo *m*.

elocution [elə'kju:ʃən] *n* elocución *f*; declamación *f*.

elope [i'loup] *v* fugarse. **elopement** *n* fuga *f*.

eloquent ['eləkwənt] *adj* elocuente. **eloquence** *n* elocuencia *f*.

else [els] *adv* más, de otra manera. **or else** si no. **elsewhere** *adv* otro sitio.

elude [i'lu:d] *v* eludir, escapar; (*a blow*) evitar. **elusive** *adj* escurridizo.

emaciated [i'meisieitid] *adj* demacrado. **emaciation** *n* demacración *f.*

e-mail ['i:meil] *n* correo electrónico *m. v* mandar un correo electrónico

emanate ['emǝneit] *v* emanar. **emanation** *n* emanación *f.*

emancipate [i'mansipeit] *v* emancipar. **emancipation** *n* emancipación *f.*

embalm [im'ba:m] *v* embalsamar.

embankment [im'baŋkmǝnt] *n* (*road, rail*) terraplén *m*; (*river*) dique *m.*

embargo [im'ba:gou] *n* prohibición *f.*

embark [im'ba:k] *v* embarcar. **embark on** emprender. **embarkation** *n* (*people*) embarco *m*; (*cargo*) embarque *m.*

embarrass [im'barǝs] *v* desconcertar; molestar. **embarrassment** *n* desconcierto *m*; molestia *f.* **financial embarrassment** apuros de dinero *m pl.*

embassy ['embǝsi] *n* embajada *f.*

embellish [im'belif] *v* embellecer; adornar. **embellishment** *n* embellecimiento *m*; adorno *m.*

ember ['embǝ] *n* ascua *f.*

embezzle [im'bezl] *v* malversar. **embezzlement** *n* malversación *f.* **embezzler** *n* malversador, -a *m.*

embitter [im'bitǝ] *v* (*person*) amargar. **embittered** *adj* amargado; rencoroso.

emblem ['emblǝm] *n* emblema *m.* **emblematic** *adj* emblemático.

embody [im'bodi] *v* personificar; materializar; incluir. **embodiment** *n* personificación *f*; incorporación *f.*

emboss [im'bos] *v* grabar en relieve; (*paper*) gofrar; (*leather, silver*) repujar. **embossed** *adj* (*letterhead*) gofrado.

embrace [im'breis] *v* abrazar; (*encompass*) abarcar; (*opportunity*) aprovecharse de. *n* abrazo *m.*

embroider [im'broidǝ] *v* bordar; (*fig*) adornar. **embroidery** *n* bordado *m*; adorno *m.*

embryo ['embriou] *n* embrión *m.* **in embryo** en embrión. **embryonic** *adj* embrionario.

emerald ['emǝrǝld] *n* esmeralda *f.*

emerge [i'mǝ:dʒ] *v* salir; sacarse. **emergence** *n* salida *f.*

emergency [i'mǝ:dʒǝnsi] *n* emergencia *f*;

(*med*) urgencia *f.* **emergency exit** salida de emergencia *f.* **emergency landing** aterrizaje forzoso *m.* **in case of emergency** en caso de emergencia.

emigrate ['emigreit] *v* emigrar. **emigrant** (*m + f*), *adj* emigrante. **emigration** *n* emigración *f.*

eminent ['eminǝnt] *adj* eminente. **eminence** *n* eminencia *f.*

emit [i'mit] *v* (*light, sound*) emitir; (*cry*) dar; (*heat*) desprender; (*smoke*) echar; (*smell*) despedir. **emission** *n* emisión *f.*

emotion [i'moufǝn] *n* emoción *f.* **emotional** *adj* (*concerning the emotions*) emocional; (*occasion, person*) emotivo. **emotionally** *adv* con emoción. **emotive** emotivo.

empathy ['empǝθi] *n* empatía *f.*

emperor ['empǝrǝ] *n* emperador *m.* **empress** *n* emperatriz *f.*

emphasis ['emfǝsis] *n, pl* -ses (*fig*) énfasis *m*; importancia *f*; (*stress*) acento *m.* **emphasize** *v* subrayar; (*stress*) acentuar. **emphatic** *adj* enfático; enérgico; categórico.

empire ['empaiǝ] *n* imperio *m.*

empirical [im'pirikǝl] *adj* empírico. **empiricism** *n* empirismo *m.*

employ [im'ploi] *v* emplear. *n also* **employment** empleo *m.* **employee** *n* empleado, -a *m, f.* **employer** *n* empresario, -a *m, f*; empleador, -a *m, f.* **employment agency** agencia de colocaciones *f.*

empower [im'pauǝ] *v* autorizar, habilitar.

empty ['empti] *adj* vacío; vacante; desocupado; desierto. *v* vaciar; (*river*) desaguar. **empty-handed** *adj* con las manos vacías. **empty-headed** *adj* casquivano. **emptiness** *n* vacío *m*; vacuidad *f.*

emu ['i:mju:] *n* emú *m.*

emulate ['emju:leit] *v* emular. **emulation** *n* emulación *f.*

emulsion [i'mʌlfǝn] *n* emulsión *f.* **emulsify** *v* emulsionar.

enable [i'neibl] *v* permitir; capacitar.

enact [i'nakt] *v* (*represent*) representar; (*a law*) promulgar; (*decree*) decretar; (*do*) hacer. **enactment** *n* promulgación *f*; decreto *m.*

enamel [i'namǝl] *n* esmalte *m. v* esmaltar.

enamour [i'namǝ] *v* enamorar. **be enamoured of** estar enamorado de.

encase [in'keis] *v* (*enclose*) encerrar; (*box*) encajonar.

enchant [in't∫a:nt] v encantar. **enchanter** n (magician) hechicero m; encantador m. **enchanting** adj encantador. **enchantment** n (charm) encanto m; (magic) hechizo m. **enchantress** n hechicera f; encantadora f.

encircle [in'sə:kl] v cercar, rodear.

enclose [in'klouz] v (shut in) encerrar; (surround) rodear; (in a letter) adjuntar. **enclosed** adj adjunto. **enclosure** n encierro m; carta adjunta f.

encompass [in'kʌmpəs] v cercar; (surround) rodear; (include) abarcar

encore ['oŋko:] interj ¡bis! ¡otra vez! n repetición f. v pedir la repetición; repetir.

encounter [in'kauntə] v encontrarse con; enfrentarse a. n encuentro m.

encourage [in'kʌridʒ] v animar, alentar; estimular; incitar. **encouragement** n ánimo m, aliento m; estimulación f; incitación f. **encouraging** adj alentador; prometedor.

encroach [in'krout∫] v invadir; usurpar. **encroachment** n invasión f; usurpación f.

encumber [in'kʌmbə] v (hamper) estorbar; (load) cargar; (block) obstruir. **encumbrance** n estorbo m; obstáculo m.

encyclopaedia [insaiklə'pi:diə] n enciclopedia f.

end [end] n (tip) punta f; (tail end) cabo m; (finish) fin m, final m. **end product** (comm) producto final m; (result) resultado m. **make ends meet** pasar con lo que se tiene. v acabar, terminar. **ending** n fin m, final m. **endless** adj interminable.

endanger [in'deindʒə] v arriesgar, poner en peligro.

endearing [in'diəriŋ] adj entrañable, simpático

endeavour [in'devə] n esfuerzo m, empeño m. v esforzarse, procurar.

endemic [en'demik] adj endémico.

endive ['endiv] n escarola f, endibia f.

endorse [in'do:s] v (cheque, etc.) endosar; (approve) aprobar. **endorsement** n endoso m; aprobación f; (mot) nota de inhabilitación f.

endow [in'dau] v dotar; (prize, etc.) fundar. **endowment** n dotación f; fundación f.

endure [in'djuə] v (support) aguantar; (last) durar. **endurable** adj soportable. **endurance** n aguante m; resistencia f.

enduring adj resistente; duradero.

enemy ['enəmi] n enemigo, -a m. f.

energy ['enədʒi] n energía f. **energetic** adj enérgico.

enfold [in'fould] v envolver; abrazar.

enforce [in'fo:s] v (discipline) imponer; (law) hacer cumplir.

engage [in'geidʒ] v (employ) ajustar; (pledge) comprometer; (attention) llamar; (keep busy) ocupar; (clutch) embragar. **engaged** adj prometido; ocupado. **get engaged** comprometerse. **engagement** n compromiso m; (appointment) cita f; (encounter) encuentro m. **engagement ring** sortija de pedida f.

engine ['endʒin] n motor m; máquina f. **engine driver** maquinista m, f. **engine room** sala de máquinas f.

engineer [endʒi'niə] n ingeniero, -a m, f; (workman) mecánico m. **engineering** n ingeniería f.

England ['iŋglənd] n Inglaterra f. **English** adj inglés. **the English** los ingleses. **English-speaking** de habla inglesa.

English Channel n Canal de la Mancha m.

engrave [in'greiv] v grabar. **engraver** n grabador, -a m, f. **engraving** n grabado m.

engross [in'grous] v absorber. **engrossing** adj absorbente.

engulf [in'gʌlf] v tragarse; (sink) hundir.

enhance [in'ha:ns] v (prices, etc.) aumentar; (beauty) realzar. **enhancement** n aumento m; realce m.

enigma [i'nigmə] n enigma m. **enigmatic** adj enigmático.

enjoy [in'dʒoi] v (like) gustar; (delight in, have the use of) gozar de; (party) divertirse en. **enjoyable** adj agradable; divertido. **enjoyment** n placer m; diversión f.

enlarge [in'la:dʒ] v ampliar, agrandar; (expand) extender. **enlargement** n aumento m; extensión f; ampliación f. **enlarger** n (phot) ampliadora f.

enlighten [in'laitn] v iluminar; (inform) informar; aclarar. **enlightenment** n aclaración f.

enlist [in'list] v alistar; alistarse; (obtain support) conseguir. **enlistment** n alistamiento m.

enmity ['enməti] n enemistad f.

enormous [i'nɔ:məs] *adj* enorme. **enormity** *n* enormidad *f.* **enormously** *adv* enormemente.

enough [i'nʌf] *adj, adv* bastante. *n* lo bastante. **enough is enough** basta y sobra. **curiously enough** por extraño que parezca. **sure enough** más que seguro. **that's enough** con eso basta.

enquire [in'kwaiə] *V* **inquire**.

enrage [in'reidʒ] *v* enfurecer.

enrich [in'ritʃ] *v* enriquecer; (*soil*) fertilizar. **enrichment** *n* enriquecimiento *m*; fertilización *f.*

enrol [in'roul] *v* inscribir; registrar; matricular; (*mil*) alistar. **enrolment** *n* inscripción *f*; registro *m*; matriculación *f*; alistamiento *m.*

ensign ['ensain] *n* (*flag*) enseña *f*; (*badge*) insignia *f*; (*naut*) bandera de popa *f.*

enslave [in'sleiv] *v* esclavizar. **enslavement** *n* esclavitud *f.*

ensue [in'sju:] *v* seguir; resultar. **ensuing** *adj* siguiente; resultante.

en suite ['ɒnswi:t] con baño incorporado

ensure [in'ʃuə] *v* asegurar.

entail [in'teil] *v* (*involve*) suponer; (*follow as a result of*) acarrear; (*law*) vincular. **entailment** *n* vinculación *f.*

entangle [in'taŋgl] *v* enredar; complicar. **entanglement** *n* enredo *m*; (*fig*) lío *m.*

enter ['entə] *v* entrar en; penetrar; meterse en; registrar; matricular; presentar. **enter for** tomar parte en. **enter into** empezar; establecer; comprender.

enterprise ['entəpraiz] *n* empresa *f*; iniciativa *f.* **enterprising** *adj* emprendedor.

entertain [,entə'tein] *v* (*host*) recibir; (*amuse*) divertir; (*ideas*) abrigar. **entertainer** *n* artista *m, f.* **entertaining** *adj* divertido, entretenido. **entertainment** *n* entretenimiento *m.*

enthral [in'θrɔ:l] *v* encantar. **enthralling** *adj* cautivador.

enthusiasm [in'θu:ziˌazəm] *n* entusiasmo *m.* **enthusiast** *n* entusiasta *m, f.* **enthusiastic** *adj* (*person*) entusiasta; (*praise, etc.*) entusiástico.

entice [in'tais] *v* tentar, seducir. **enticing** *adj* tentador; atractivo. **enticement** *n* atracción *f*; seducción *f.*

entire [in'taiə] *adj* entero, completo. **entirety** *n* totalidad *f.*

entitle [in'taitl] *v* (*authorize*) dar derecho a; (*written work*) titular. **be entitled** tener derecho.

entity ['entəti] *n* entidad *f*, ente *m.*

entrails ['entreilz] *pl n* entrañas *f pl.*

entrance[1] ['entrəns] *n* entrada *f*; ingreso *m.* **entrance examination** examen de ingreso *m.* **entrance hall** vestíbulo *m.* **tradesmen's entrance** entrada de servicio *f.*

entrance[2] [in'tra:ns] *v* arrebatar. **entrancing** *adj* encantador.

entrant ['entrənt] *n* participante *m, f.*

entreat [in'tri:t] *v* suplicar, implorar. **entreaty** *n* súplica *f*, imploración *f.*

entrée ['ɒntrei] *n* entrada *f.*

entrench [in'trentʃ] *v* atrincherar. **entrenchment** *n* atrincheramiento *m*; (*encroachment*) invasión *f.*

entrepreneur [,ɒntrəprə'nə:] *n* empresario *m*; intermediario *m.*

entrust [in'trʌst] *v* (*commit*) confiar; (*someone*) encargar.

entry ['entri] *n* (*entrance*) entrada *f*; (*into profession*) ingreso *m*; (*in a book*) anotación *f*; (*book-keeping*) asiento *m.* **no entry** dirección prohibida *f.*

entwine [in'twain] *v* entrelazar.

enunciate [i'nʌnsiˌeit] *v* enunciar. **enunciation** *n* enunciación *f.*

envelop [in'veləp] *v* envolver. **enveloping** *adj* envolvente.

envelope ['envəˌloup] *n* sobre *m.*

environment [in'vaiərənmənt] *n* ambiente *m.* **environmental** *adj* ambiental, medioambiental, del medio ambiente.

envisage [in'vizidʒ] *v* (*imagine*) imaginarse; (*foresee*) prever.

envoy ['envoi] *n* enviado, -a *m, f.*

envy ['envi] *n* envidia *f.* *v* envidiar. **enviable** *adj* envidiable. **envious** *adj* envidioso. **enviously** *adv* con envidia.

enzyme ['enzaim] *n* enzima *f.*

epaulet ['epəlet] *n* charretera *f.*

ephemeral [i'femərəl] *adj* efímero.

epic ['epik] *n* poema épica *f.* *adj* épico.

epidemic [epi'demik] *n* epidemia. *adj* epidémico.

epilepsy ['epilepsi] *n* epilepsia *f.* **epileptic** *n, adj* epiléptico, -a. **epileptic fit** ataque epiléptico *m.*

Epiphany [i'pifəni] *n* Epifanía *f.*

episcopal [i'piskəpəl] *adj* episcopal.

episode ['episoud] n episodio m. **episodic** adj episódico.

epitaph ['epi₁ta:f] n epitafio m.

epitome [i'pitəmi] n epítome m; (fig) personificación f. **epitomize** v compendiar; ser la personificación de.

epoch ['i:pok] n época f.

equable ['ekwəbl] adj uniforme; (calm) tranquilo.

equal ['i:kwəl] n (m + f), adj igual. v igualar. **equality** n igualdad f. **equalize** v igualar; (draw) empatar.

equanimity [ekwə'nimətil] n ecuanimidad f.

equate [i'kweit] v igualar; comparar; poner en ecuación. **equation** n ecuación f.

equator [i'kweitə] n ecuador m. **equatorial** adj ecuatorial.

equestrian [i'kwestriən] adj ecuestre. n caballista m, f.

equilateral [₁i:kwi'latərəl] n figura equilátera f. adj equilátero.

equilibrium [₁i:kwi'libriəm] n equilibrio m.

equinox ['ekwinoks] n equinoccio m. **equinoctial** adj equinoccial.

equip [i'kwip] v equipar. **equipment** n equipo m; (tools) herramientas f pl.

equity ['ekwəti] n equidad f, justicia f.

equivalent [i'kwivələnt] nm, adj equivalente.

era ['iərə] n era f.

eradicate [i'radi₁keit] v erradicar. **eradication** n erradicación f.

erase [i'reiz] v borrar. **eraser** n goma de borrar f. **erasure** n borradura f.

erect [i'rekt] adj erguido. v erigir; (assemble) montar. **erection** n erección f; (building) construcción f; montaje m.

ermine ['ə:min] n armiño m.

erode [i'roud] v corroer; (wear away) erosionar. **erosion** n corrosión f; erosión f. **erosive** adj erosivo.

erotic [i'rotik] adj erótico. **eroticism** n erotismo m.

err [ə:] v errar, desviarse; (sin) pecar. **erring** adj extraviado; pecaminoso.

errand ['erənd] n recado m. **run an errand** hacer un recado. **errand boy** recadero m.

erratic [i'ratik] adj desigual; errático.

error ['erə] n (mistake) error m; (wrongdoing) extravío m.

erudite ['erudait] adj erudito. **erudition** n erudición f.

erupt [i'rupt] v estar en erupción, salir con fuerza. **eruption** n erupción f. **eruptive** adj eruptivo.

escalate ['eskə₁leit] v intensificar, agravar. **escalation** n intensificación f. **escalator** n escalera mecánica f.

escalope ['eskə₁lop] n escalope m.

escape [is'keip] n (flight) fuga f; (liquid) salida f; (gas) escape m; (responsibilities, etc.) evasión f. **escape hatch** escotilla de salvamento f. **fire escape** escalera de incendios f. v escapar de; evadir; eludir. **escape notice** pasar inadvertido. **escapism** n evasión f, escapismo m.

escort ['esko:t] n v i'sko:t] n acompañante m; (mil) escolta f. v acompañar; (mil) escoltar.

esoteric [esə'terik] adj esotérico.

especial [i'speʃəl] adj especial, particular; excepcional. **especially** adv especialmente, sobre todo.

espionage ['espiə₁na:ʒ] n espionaje m.

esplanade [₁esplə'neid] n explanada f, bulevar m, paseo m.

essay ['esei] n ensayo m; composición f; (attempt) intento m. v probar; intentar. **essayist** n ensayista m.

essence ['esns] n esencia f. **essential** adj esencial, imprescindible; fundamental. n lo esencial. **essentials** pl n elementos esenciales m pl.

establish [i'stabliʃ] v establecer. **establishment** n establecimiento m. **The Establishment** clase dirigente f.

estate [i'steit] n (property) propiedad f; (land) finca f, (S. Am.) hacienda f, estancia f; (inheritance) herencia f; (fortune) fortuna f; (social class) estado m; (of the deceased) testamentaría f. **estate agency** agencia inmobiliaria f. **estate agent** agente inmobiliario, -a m, f. **estate car** furgoneta f.

esteem [i'sti:m] v estimar, apreciar. n estima f, aprecio m.

estimate ['estimət; v 'esti₁meit] n (valuation) estimación f; (statement of cost) presupuesto m. v estimar; hacer un presupuesto de. **estimation** n juicio m; (esteem) aprecio m.

Estonia [e'stouniə] n Estonia f. **Estonian** adj estonio.

estuary ['estjuəri] n estuario m.

eternal [i'tə:nl] adj eterno. **eternity** n

eternidad f.

ether [ˈiːθə] n éter m. **ethereal** adj etéreo.

ethical [ˈeθɪkl] adj ético. **ethics** pl n ética f sing.

ethnic [ˈeθnɪk] adj étnico.

etiquette [ˈetɪket] n etiqueta f.

etymology [ˌetɪˈmɒlədʒɪ] n etimología f. **etymologist** n etimólogo, -a m, f.

EU n UE f

Eucharist [ˈjuːkərɪst] n Eucaristía f.

eunuch [ˈjuːnək] n eunuco m.

euphemism [ˈjuːfəˌmɪzəm] n eufemismo m. **euphemistic** adj eufemístico.

euphoria [juˈfoːrɪə] n euforia f. **euphoric** adj eufórico.

euro [ˈjuərou] n euro m

Europe [ˈjuərəp] n Europa f. **European** n, adj europeo, -a m, f. **European Union** Unión Europea f.

euthanasia [juːθəˈneɪzɪə] n eutanasia f.

evacuate [ɪˈvækjuˌeɪt] v evacuar. **evacuation** n evacuación f. **evacuee** n evacuado, -a m, f.

evade [ɪˈveɪd] v evadir, eludir. **evasion** n evasión f. **evasive** adj evasivo.

evaluate [ɪˈvaljuˌeɪt] v evaluar. **evaluation** n evaluación f.

evangelical [ˌiːvanˈdʒelɪkəl] adj evangélico. **evangelist** n evangelizador, -a m, f.

evaporate [ɪˈvapəˌreɪt] v evaporar; deshidratar. **evaporated milk** leche evaporada f. **evaporation** n evaporación f; deshidratación f.

eve [iːv] n víspera f. **Christmas Eve** Nochebuena f. **New Year's Eve** Noche Vieja f. **on the eve of** en vísperas de.

even [ˈiːvən] adj (surface) uniforme; (smooth) suave; (calm) ecuánime; (fair) justo; (same level) a nivel; (equal) igual; (number) par. **break even** quedar igual. **get even** desquitarse. adv siquiera; incluso. **even if** incluso si. **even so** aun así. **even though** aunque. **even-tempered** adj sereno. v nivelar; igualar. **evenly** adv uniformemente; imparcialmente.

evening [ˈiːvnɪŋ] n tarde f; anochecer m. **evening class** clase nocturna f. **evening dress** (man) traje de etiqueta m; (woman) traje de noche m. **good evening!** (early) ¡buenas tardes! (late) ¡buenas noches!

event [ɪˈvent] n (occurrence) acontecimiento m; (case) caso m; (outcome) consecuencia f; (in a programme) número m; (sport) prueba f. **in the event of** en caso de. **eventful** adj agitado; memorable. **eventual** adj final; consiguiente. **eventuality** n eventualidad f. **eventually** adv finalmente; con el tiempo.

ever [ˈevə] adv (always) siempre; nunca, jamás. **we hardly ever go out** casi nunca salimos. **not ever** nunca jamás. **ever after** desde (que).

evergreen [ˈevəgriːn] adj de hoja perenne.

everlasting [ˌevəˈlaːstɪŋ] adj eterno; perpetuo.

every [ˈevrɪ] adj (all) todo; (each) cada. **everybody** also **everyone** pron todo el mundo. **everyday** adj diario. **every other day** cada dos días. **everything** pron todo. **everywhere** adv por also en todas partes.

evict [ɪˈvɪkt] v desahuciar. **eviction** n desahucio m.

evidence [ˈevɪdəns] n evidencia f; (sign) indicio m; (law: proof) prueba f; (law: testimony) testimonio m. v evidenciar. **give evidence** declarar como testigo. **evident** adj evidente, patente.

evil [ˈiːvl] adj malo; peverso; maligno. n mal m; desgracia f. **evildoer** n malhechor, -a m, f. **evil-minded** adj malpensado.

evoke [ɪˈvouk] v evocar. **evocation** n evocación f. **evocative** adj evocador.

evolve [ɪˈvɒlv] v evolucinar; (develop) desarrollarse. **evolution** n evolución f; desarrollo m. **evolutionary** adj evolutivo.

ewe [juː] n oveja f.

exacerbate [ɪgˈzasəˌbeɪt] v exacerbar. **exacerbation** n exacerbación f.

exact [ɪgˈzakt] adj exacto. v exigir. **exacting** adj (person) exigente; (condition) severo; (work) duro. **exactly** adv exactamente; precisamente.

exaggerate [ɪgˈzadʒəˌreɪt] v exagerar; acentuar. **exaggerated** adj exagerado. **exaggeration** n exageración f.

exalt [ɪgˈzɒlt] v exaltar, elevar; (praise) glorificar. **exaltation** n exaltación f; (ecstasy) arrobamiento m. **exalted** adj exaltado, eminente.

exam [ɪgˈzam] n examen m

examine [ɪgˈzamɪn] v examinar; (search) reconocer; (by touch) analizar; (law) interrogar. **examination** n examen m; (law) interrogatorio m. **sit an exam** examinarse. **written exam** prueba escrita f. **examiner**

n examinador, -a *m*, *f*; inspector, -a *m*, *f*.

example [ig'za:mpl] *n* ejemplo *m*. **follow someone's example** tomar ejemplo de uno. **for example** por ejemplo. **set an example** dar ejemplo.

exasperate [ig'za:spə,reit] *v* exasperar. **exasperation** *n* exasperación *f*.

excavate ['ekskə,veit] *v* excavar. **excavation** *n* excavación *f*. **excavator** (*person*) excavador, -a *m*, *f*; (*tech*) excavadora *f*.

exceed [ik'si:d] *v* exceder. **exceedingly** *adv* sumamente.

excel [ik'sel] *v* superar, sobresalir. **excellence** *n* excelencia *f*. **His Excellency** su Excelencia *m*. **excellent** *adj* excelente.

except [ik'sept] *prep* excepto, salvo, con excepción de. **except for** excepto. *v* excluir, exceptuar. **exception** *n* exclusión *f*; excepción *f*. **take exception to** ofenderse por. **exceptional** *adj* excepcional.

excerpt ['eksə:pt] *n* extracto *m*. *v* extractar.

excess [ik'ses] *n* exceso *m*. *adj* excedente. **excess fare** suplemento *m*. **excess luggage** exceso de equipaje *also* peso *m*. **excessive** *adj* excesivo. **excessively** *adv* excesivamente.

exchange [iks'tʃeindʒ] *v* (*change*) cambiar; (*interchange*) intercambiar; (*courtesies*) hacerse; (*prisoners*) canjear; (*blows*) darse. *n* cambio *m*; intercambio *m*. **exchange control** control de divisas. **exchange rate** tipo de cambio *m*. **Stock Exchange** bolsa de valores *f*. **telephone exchange** central telefónica *f*.

exchequer [iks'tʃekə] *n* (*finances*) hacienda *f*; tesoro público *m*. **Chancellor of the Exchequer** Ministro de Hacienda *m*.

excise ['eksaiz] *n* impuestos sobre el consumo *m pl*.

excite [ik'sait] *v* (*stimulate*) excitar; emocionar; entusiasmar; (*irritate*) poner nervioso; (*urge*) incitar; (*imagination*) despertar; (*admiration, etc.*) provocar. **get excited** emocionarse; entusiasmarse. **excitement** *n* excitación *f*; emoción *f*; entusiasmo *m*; agitación *f*. **exciting** *adj* excitante; emocionante; apasionante.

exclaim [ik'skleim] *v* exclamar. **exclamation** *n* exclamación *f*. **exclamation mark** punto de admiración *m*.

exclude [ik'sklu:d] *v* excluir. **exclusion** *n* exclusión *f*. **exclusive** *adj* (*policy*) exclusivista; (*sole*) exclusivo; (*select*) selecto.

excommunicate [ekskə'mju:ni,keit] *v* excomulgar. **excommunication** *n* excomunión *f*.

excrete [ik'skri:t] *v* excretar. **excrement** *n* excremento *m*. **excretion** *n* excreción *f*.

excruciating [ik'skru:ʃieitiŋ] *adj* (*noise*) intolerable; (*pain*) atroz.

excursion [ik'skə:ʃən] *n* excursión *f*.

excuse [ik'skju:z] *n* excusa *f*, disculpa *f*. *v* excusar, disculpar, perdonar; (*duty*) dispensar de. **excuse me!** ¡perdón! ¡discúlpeme! **excusable** *adj* excusable, disculpable, perdonable.

ex-directory [eksdi'rektəri] el número no figura en la guía

execute ['eksi,kju:t] *v* (*order, will, criminal*) ejecutar; (*carry out*) llevar a cabo. **execution** *n* ejecución *f*; (*of order*) cumplimiento *m*. **executioner** *n* verdugo *m*.

executive [ig'zekjutiv] *adj* (*power*) ejecutivo; (*function*) dirigente; (*ability*) de ejecución. *n* (*government branch*) poder ejecutivo *m*; (*person*) ejecutivo *m*.

exemplify [ig'zempli,fai] *v* ilustrar con ejemplos. **exemplification** *n* ejemplificación *f*.

exempt [ig'zempt] *adj* exento. *v* exentar, dispensar. **exemption** *n* exención *f*.

exercise ['eksə,saiz] *n* ejercicio *m*; gimnasia *f*. **exercise book** *n* cuaderno *m*. **take exercise** hacer ejercicio. *v* (*rights, etc.*) ejercer; (*physically*) ejercitarse; (*patience*) usar de.

exert [ig'zə:t] *v* ejercer. **exert oneself** esforzarse. **exertion** *n* esfuerzo *m*; (*of strength*) empleo *m*.

exhale [eks'heil] *v* exhalar; (*breathe out*) espirar. **exhalation** *n* exhalación *f*; espiración *f*.

exhaust [ig'zo:st] *v* agotar. *n* (*system*) escape *m*. **exhaust pipe** tubo de escape *m*. **exhausting** *adj* agotador. **exhaustion** *n* agotamiento *m*. **exhaustive** *adj* exhaustivo. **exhaustively** *adv* exhaustivamente.

exhibit [ig'zibit] *v* (*display*) mostrar; (*paintings, etc.*) exponer; (*documents*) presentar. *n* objeto expuesto *m*. **exhibition** *n* exposición *f*. **make an exhibition of oneself** ponerse en ridículo. **exhibitor** *n* expositor *m*.

exhilarate [ig'zilə,reit] *v* alegrar, animar. **exhilarating** *adj* estimulante. **exhilaration** *n* alegría *f*, regocijo *m*.

exile ['eksail] *n* exilio *m*, destierro *m*;

(*person*) exiliado, -a *m, f*; desterrado, -a *m, f*.
go into exile exiliarse, exilarse, *v* exiliar, exilar, desterrar.

exist [ig'zist] *v* existir; (*live*) vivir. **existence** *n* existencia *f*. **existent** *also* **existing** *adj* existente: (*present*) actual. **existentialism** *n* existencialismo *m*. **existentialist** *n* (*m* + *f*), *adj* existencialista.

exit ['egzit] *n* salida *f*; (*theatre*) mutis *m*. *v* (*theatre*) hacer mutios.

exonerate [ig'zonə,reit] *v* (*from blame*) disculpar; (*from obligation*) dispensar de. **exoneration** *n* disculpa *f*; dispensa *f*.

exorbitant [ig'zo:bitənt] *adj* exorbitante.

exorcize ['ekso:saiz] *v* exorcizar. **exorcism** *n* exorcismo *m*. **exorcist** *n* exorcista *m, f*.

exotic [ig'zotik] *adj* exótico. **exoticism** *n* exotismo *m*.

expand [ik'spand] *v* (*cause to increase*) desarrollar; (*make larger*) dilatar; (*add to*) ampliar. **expansion** *n* expansión *f*; desarrollo *m*; dilatación *f*; ampliación *f*. **expansive** *adj* (*person*) expansivo; (*wide*) extenso. **expansiveness** *n* expansibilidad *f*.

expanse [ik'spans] *n* extensión *f*; (*wings*) envergadura *f*.

expatriate [eks'peitriət; *v* eks'peitrieit] *n*, *adj* expatriado, -a. *v* desterrar. **expatriation** *n* expatriación *f*.

expect [ik'spekt] *v* (*anticipate, hope for, require*) esperar; (*suppose*) suponer. **expectant** *adj* expectante. **expectant mother** futura madre *f*. **expectation** *n* expectación *f*; (*hope*) esperanza *f*; (*anticipation*) previsión *f*.

expedient [ik'spi:diənt] *adj* expeditivo, oportuno. *n* expediente *m*. **expedience** *also* **expediency** *n* conveniencia *f*.

expedition [,ekspi'diʃən] *n* expedición *f*.

expel [ik'spel] *v* expulsar.

expenditure [ik'spenditʃə] *n* gasto *m*. **expend** *v* gastar; (*effort*) dedicar. **expendable** *adj* (*objects*) gastable; (*people*) prescindible.

expense [ik'spens] *n* gasto *m*. **at the expense of** a costa de. **expense account** cuenta de gastos de representación *f*. **expensive** *adj* caro, costoso.

experience [ik'spiəriəns] *n* experiencia *f*. *v* experimentar; (*difficulty*) tener. **experienced** *adj* experimentado; experto.

experiment [ik'sperimənt] *n* experimento *m*. *v* hacer experimentos, experimentar.

experimental *adj* experimental.

expert ['ekspə:t] *n*, *adj* experto, -a.

expertise [,ekspə:'ti:z] *n* pericia *f*.

expire [ik'spaiə] *v* (*finish, die*) expirar; (*become void*) caducar; (*expel air*) espirar. **expiration** *also* **expiry** *n* expiración *f*; (*comm*) vencimiento *m*.

explain [ik'splein] *v* explicar. **explanation** *n* explicación *f*. **explanatory** *adj* explicativo.

expletive [ek'spli:tiv] *n* (*gramm*) expletiva *f*; (*oath*) taco *m*.

explicit [ik'splisit] *adj* explícito.

explode [ik'sploud] *v* estallar, hacer explotar; (*myth*) refutar; (*rumour*) desmentir. **explosion** *n* explosión *f*. **explosive** *nm, adj* explosivo.

exploit¹ ['eksploit] *n* hazaña *f*.

exploit² [ik'sploit] *v* explotar. **exploitation** *n* explotación *f*.

explore [ik'splo:] *v* explorar. **exploration** *n* exploración *f*. **exploratory** *adj* exploratorio. **explorer** *n* explorador, -a *m, f*.

exponent [ik'spounənt] *n* exponente *m, f*.

export ['ekspo:t; *v* ik'spo:t] *n* exportación *f*. *v* exportar. **exporter** *n* exportador, -a *m, f*.

expose [ik'spouz] *v* (*leave uncovered*) exponer; (*reveal*) revelar; (*plot, etc.*) descubrir; (*phot*) exponer. **exposure** *n* exposición *f*; revelación *f*; descubrimiento *m*; (*denunciation*) denuncia *f*; (*phot*) fotografía *f*. **exposure meter** exposímetro *m*. **indecent exposure** exhibicionismo *m*.

expound [ik'spaund] *v* exponer; comentar.

express [ik'spres] *v* expresar; (*press*) exprimir. *n* (*train*) rápido *m*; (*mail*) correo urgente *m*. *adj, adv* expreso; rápido. **expression** *n* expresión *f*. **expressive** *adj* expresivo.

expulsion [ik'spʌlʃən] *n* expulsión *f*.

exquisite ['ekswizit] *adj* exquisito; intenso.

extend [ik'stend] *v* extender, aumentar; (*widen*) ampliar; (*lengthen*) prolongar; (*stretch*) estirar; (*invitation*) enviar; (*aid*) ofrecer; (*hand*) tender; (*time-limit*) prorogar. **extension** *n* extensión *f*; prolongación *f*; aumento *m*; prórroga *f*. **telephone extension** extensión *f*. **extensive** *adj* extenso.

extent [ik'stent] *n* (*length*) extensión *f*; (*degree*) punto *m*; (*scope*) alcance *m*.

exterior [ik'stiəriə] *nm, adj* exterior.

exterminate [ik'stə:mi,neit] *v* exterminar. **extermination** *n* exterminio *m*.

external [ik'stə:nl] *adj* externo. **for external use only** sólo para uso externo.

extinct [ik'stiŋkt] *adj* extinto; (*fire, volcano*) extinguido. **extinction** *n* extinción *f*.

extinguish [ik'stiŋgwiʃ] *v* extinguir; apagar; (*hope*) destruir. **extinguisher** *n* (*fire*) extintor.

extort [ik'sto:t] *v* arrancar, sacar por fuerza. **extortion** *n* extorsión *f*. **extortionate** *adj* exorbitante.

extra ['ekstrə] *adj* extra; de más; adicional; extraordinario; no incluido. *n* (*extra charge*) recargo *m*; (*actor*) extra *m*, *f*. *adv* extraordinariamente.

extract [ik'strakt; *n* 'ekstrakt] *v* extraer; (*obtain, parts of books, etc.*) sacar. *n* extracto *m*. **extraction** *n* extracción *f*; (*descent*) origen *m*.

extradite ['ekstrə,dait] *v* conceder la extradición de; obtener la extradición de. **extradition** *n* extradición *f*.

extramural [,ekstrə'mjuərəl] *adj* para estudiantes libres.

extraordinary [ik'stro:dənəri] *adj* extraordinario; raro.

extravagant [ik'stravəgənt] *adj* (*lavish*) pródigo; (*wasteful*) despilfarrador; (*taste*) dispendioso; (*language, ideas*) extravagante. **extravagance** *n* prodigalidad *f*; despilfarro *m*; extravagancia *f*.

extreme [ik'stri:m] *nm, adj* extremo. **go to extremes** llegar a extremos. **extremist** *n* (*m* + *f*), *adj* extremista. **extremity** *n* (*end*) extremidad *f*; (*necessity*) apuro *m*.

extrovert ['ekstrəvə:t] *n, adj* extrovertido, -a.

exuberant [ig'zju:bərənt] *adj* exuberante; eufórico. **exuberance** *n* exuberancia *f*; euforia *f*.

exude [ig'zju:d] *v* exudar.

exult [ig'zʌlt] *v* exultar. **exult over** triunfar sobre. **exultant** *adj* exultante. **exultation** *n* exultación *f*.

eye [ai] *n* ojo *m*. **an eye for an eye** ojo por ojo. **private eye** detective *m*. **make eyes at** echar miradas a. **see eye to eye with** ver con los mismos ojos que. **turn a blind eye** cerrar los ojos. **be up to one's eyes in work** estar hasta aquí en trabajo. **with an eye to** con iras a. **with the naked eye** a simple vista. *v* mirar.

eyeball ['aibo:l] *n* globo del ojo *m*.

eyebrow ['aibrau] *n* ceja *f*.

eye-catching ['aikatʃiŋ] *adj* llamativo.

eyelash ['ailaʃ] *n* pestaña *f*.

eyelid ['ailid] *n* párpado *m*.

eye shadow *n* sombreador de ojos *m*.

eyesight ['aisait] *n* vista *f*.

eyesore ['aiso:] *n* algo que ofende la vista.

eyewitness ['ai,witnis] *n* testigo ocular *m*, *f*.

F

fable ['feibl] *n* fábula *f*.

fabric ['fabrik] *n* (*cloth*) tejido *m*; estructura *f*, construcción *f*. **fabricate** *v* (*invent*) fingir. **fabrication** *n* fabricación *f*; invención *f*.

fabulous ['fabjuləs] *adj* fabuloso; (*coll*) macanudo.

façade [fə'sa:d] *n* fachada *f*.

face [feis] *n* cara *f*, rostro *m*; (*side*) lado *m*; (*aspect*) aspecto *m*; (*grimace*) mueca *f*; (*surface*) superficie *f*; (*clock*) esfera *f*. **face down** boca abajo. **face up** boca arriba. **face to face** cara a cara. **on the face of it** a primera vista. **fly in the face of** burlarse de. **in the face of** frente a. **keep a straight face** mantenerse impávido. **lose face** quedar mal. **pull faces** hacer muecas. **save face** salvar las apariencias. *v* mirar hacia, dar a; estar en frente de; enfrentarse con; presentarse ante; (*consequences*) arrostrar; (*stand*) aguantar; (*resurface*) revestir.

face cloth *n* paño *m*.

facelift ['feislift] *n* (*coll*) lavado *m*.

face pack *n* mascarilla de belleza *f*.

face powder *n* polvos para la cara *m pl*.

facet ['fasit] *n* faceta *f*.

facetious [fə'si:ʃəs] *adj* chistoso; gracioso.

face value *n* (*bill*) valor nominal *m*; (*stamps*) valor facial *m*. **take something at face value** creer algo a pie juntillas.

facing ['feisiŋ] *n* (*sewing*) guarnición *f*; (*building*) revestimiento *m*. *adj* de enfrente.

facsimile [fak'siməli] *nm, adj* facsímil.

fact [fakt] *n* hecho *m*; realidad *f*. **as a matter of fact** en realidad. **in fact** *en verdad*. **factual** *adj* objetivo.

faction ['fakʃən] *n* facción *f*. **factious** *adj* faccioso.

factor ['faktə] *n* factor *m*, elemento *m*; (*comm*) agente *m*.

factory ['faktəri] *n* fábrica *f*.

faculty ['fakəlti] *n* (*university*) facultad *f*; (*gift*) facilidad *f*.

fad [fad] *n* manía *f*; novedad *f*. **faddish** *adj* maniático.

fade [feid] *v* (*colour*) descolorarse; (*light*) apagarse; (*sound*) desvanecerse; (*interest*) decaer. **faded** *adj* descolorido; marchito.

fag [fag] *n* (*coll: cigarette*) pitillo *m*. **fag end** sobras *f pl*; (*cigarette*) colilla *f*. **fagged out** rendido.

fail [feil] *v* fallar; (*not succeed*) fracasar, no lograr; (*hopes*) frustrarse; (*run out*) acabarse; (*weaken*) decaer; (*exams*) ser suspendido; (*neglect*) dejar (de). **without fail** sin falta. **failing** *n* defecto *m*; **failure** *n* fracaso *m*; fallo *m*; suspenso *m*; (*breakdown*) avería *f*.

faint [feint] *adj* (*near collapse*) mareado; (*weak*) débil; (*colour*) pálido; (*timid*) timorato; (*slight*) ligero; vago; indistinto. *v* desmayarse. *n* desmayo *m*.

fair¹ [feə] *adj* bello; hermoso; (*skin*) blanco; (*hair*) rubio; (*just*) justo; (*reputation, weather*) bueno; (*prospects*) favorable; (*play*) limpio; (*price*) razonable; (*comment*) acertado; (*average*) mediano. **by fair means or foul** por las buenas o por las malas. **fairly** *adv* con justicia; (*reasonably*) bastante. **fairness** *n* belleza *f*; justicia *f*.

fair² [feə] *n* (*amusements*) verbena *f*; (*market*) feria *f*. **fun fair** parque de atracciones *m*. **fairground** *n* real *m*.

fairy ['feəri] *n* hada *f*. *adj* de hada. **fairy lights** bombillas de colores *f pl*.

faith [feiθ] *n* confianza *f*. **have faith in** fiarse de. **religious faith** fe religiosa *f*. **faithful** *adj* fiel; exacto. **faithfulness** *n* fidelidad *f*; exactitud *f*. **faithless** *adj* desleal; infiel.

fake [feik] *n* falsificación *f*; impostor, -a *m*, *f*. *adj* falso; falsificado; (*feigned*) fingido. *v* falsificar; fingir.

falcon ['fo:lkən] *n* halcón *m*.

*fall [fo:l] *v* caer; (*prices, temperature, water*) bajar; (*wind*) amainar; (*decay*) decaer; (*task, duty, privilege*) tocar; (*accent*) recaer. **fall apart** caerse a pedazos. **fall back on** echar mano a. **fall behind** retrasarse. **fall for** (*affection*) enamorarse de, quedarse encantado con; (*trick*) dejarse engañar por. **fall in love** enamorarse. **fall out** (*quarrel*) reñir.

fall through venirse abajo. *n* (*body, earth, leaves*) caída *f*; (*prices*) baja *f*; (*slope*) declive *m*; (*US: season*) otoño *m*.

fallacy ['faləsi] *n* falacia *f*; (*deception*) engaño *m*. **fallacious** *adj* erróneo.

fallible ['faləbl] *adj* falible. **fallibility** *n* falibilidad *f*.

fallow ['falou] *adj* (*land*) en barbecho; inculto.

false [fo:ls] *adj* falso; erróneo. **false alarm** falsa alarma *f*. **false pretences** estafa *f*. **false teeth** dientes postizas *m pl*. **falsehood** *n* falsedad *f*; mentira *f*. **falseness** *n* falsedad *f*; inexactitud *f*; perfidia *f*. **falsify** *v* falsificar; desvirtuar. **falsification** *n* falsificación *f*.

falsetto [fo:l'setou] *n* falsete *m*. *adj* de falsete.

falter ['fo:ltə] *v* (*action*) vacilar; (*voice*) titubear. **faltering** *adj* vacilante; titubeante. **falteringly** *adv* con paso vacilante; con voz titubeante.

fame [feim] *n* fama *f*.

familiar [fə'miljə] *adj* familiar, conocido. **be familiar with** estar familiarizado con. **familiarity** *n* familiaridad *f*. **familiarize** *v* familiarizar.

family ['faməli] *n* familia *f*. **family allowance** subsidio familiar *m*. **family doctor** médico, -a de cabecera *m, f*. **family planning** planificación familiar *f*. **family tree** árbol genealógico *m*.

famine ['famin] *n* (*general scarcity*) escasez *f*; (*food*) hambre *f*.

famished ['famiʃt] *adj* famélico. **be famished** estar muerto de hambre.

famous ['feiməs] *adj* famoso, célebre.

fan¹ [fan] *n* (*hand*) abanico *m*; (*tech*) ventilador *m*. **fan belt** correa del ventilador *f*. *v* abanicar; agitar.

fan² [fan] *n* aficionado, -a *m, f*; admirador, -a *m, f*. **fan club** club de admiradores *m*. **fan mail** correspondencia de los admiradores *f*.

fanatic [fə'natik] *n*, *adj* fanático, -a. **fanaticism** *n* fanatismo *m*.

fancy ['fansi] *adj* de adorno; de fantasía. *n* fantasía *f*; (*whim*) capricho *m*; (*desire*) afición *f*; (*delusion*) ilusión *f*; (*taste*) gusto *m*. *v* imaginarse; suponer; gustar; (*suspect*) parecerle(a); (*desire*) apetecer. **fancy oneself** ser un creído. **fancy that!** ¡imagínate! **fancy dress** disfraz *m*. **fancied** *adj* favorito; imaginario. **fanciful** *adj* imaginario; caprichoso.

fanfare ['fænfeə] *n* fanfarria *f*.

fang [fæŋ] *n* colmillo *m*; (*snake*) diente *m*.

fantastic [fən'tæstik] *adj* fantástico.

fantasy ['fæntəsi] *n* fantasía *f*; capricho *m*.

far [faː] *adv* lejos; (*much*) mucho; muy. *adj* lejano; distante. **as far as** hasta; por lo que. **far and wide** por todas partes. **far away** lejos. **far-away** *adj* remoto. **Far East** Extremo Oriente *m*. **far-fetched** *adj* inverosímil. **far-reaching** *adj* de mucho alcance. **so far so good** hasta ahora todo va bien.

farce [faːs] *n* farsa *f*. **farcical** *adj* ridículo, absurdo.

fare [feə] *n* precio del billete *m*, tarifa *f*; (*boat*) pasaje *m*; (*passenger*) pasajero, -a; *m, f* (*in a taxi*) cliente *m, f*; (*in a bus*) viajero, -a *m, f*; (*food*) comida *f*. *v* (*get on*) **fare well** irle bien (a uno).

farewell [feə'wel] (*interj*) ¡adiós! **say farewell** decir adiós, despedirse de. *adj* de despedida.

farm [faːm] *n also* **farmhouse** granja *f*, finca *f*; (*S. Am.*) estancia *f*, hacienda *f*. **farmhand** *n* peón *m*. **farmland** *n* tierras de labrantío *f pl.* **farmyard** *n* corral *m*. *v* cultivar. **farm out** mandar hacer fuera. **farmer** *n* agricultor *m*; granjero *m*. **farming** *n* labranza *f*; agricultura *f*.

fart [faːt] (*impol*) *n* pedo *m*. *v* peerse.

farther ['faːðə] *adv* (*space*) más lejos; (*time*) más adelante. *adj* (*space, time*) más lejano.

farthest ['faːðist] *adv* más lejos. *adj* (*most distant*) más lejano; (*longest*) más largo.

fascinate ['fæsineit] *v* fascinar. **fascinating** *adj* fascinador. **fascination** *n* fascinación *f*.

fascism ['fæʃizəm] *n* fascismo *m*. **fascist** *n* (*m + f*), *adj* fascista.

fashion ['fæʃən] *n* manera *f*, modo *m*; moda *f*. **after a fashion** en cierto modo. **fashion show** desfile de modas *m*. **in fashion** de moda. **out of fashion** pasado de moda. *v* hacer; formar; (*mould*) moldear.

fast¹ [faːst] *adj* rápido, veloz; (*colour*) sólido; (*clock, etc.*) adelantado; (*secure*) seguro; firme. **fast asleep** profundamente dormido. **fast food** comida rápida *f*. **make fast** sujetar, atar. **pull a fast one** jugar una mala jugada. **stuck fast** (*in mud*) completamente atascado.

fast² [faːst] *n* ayuno *m*. *v* ayunar.

fasten ['faːsn] *v* (*fix*) fijar; (*attach*) sujetar; (*dress*) abrochar; (*close*) cerrar. **fastener** *or* **fastening** *n* corchete *m*; fijación *f*.

fastidious [fə'stidiəs] *adj* quisquilloso; (*demanding*) exigente. **fastidiousness** *n* melindre *m*.

fat [fæt] *n* grasa *f*; (*on meat*) gordo *m*. *adj* grueso; gordo. **fatten** *v* (*person*) engordar; (*animal*) cebar. **fattening** *adj* que engorda. **fatty** graso; (*person*) gordo.

fatal ['feitl] *adj* fatal, mortal. **fatality** *n* fatalidad *f*.

fate [feit] *n* destino *m*; suerte *f*. **fated** *adj* predestinado; condenado. **fateful** *adj* profético; fatal.

father ['faːðə] *n* padre *m*. **Father Christmas** Papá Noel *m*. **father-in-law** *n* suegro *m*. **fatherland** *n* patria *f*. **fatherless** *adj* huérfano de padre **fatherly** *adj* paternal.

fathom ['fæðəm] *n* braza *f*. *v* (*water depth*) sondar, sondear; (*unravel*) desentrañar. **fathomless** *adj* insondable.

fatigue [fə'tiːg] *n* fatiga *f*. *v* fatigar.

fatuous ['fætjuəs] *adj* fatuo; necio. **fatuity** *or* **fatuousness** *n* fatuidad *f*; necedad *f*.

fault [fɔːlt] *n* culpa *f*; defecto *m*; error *m*; falta *f*; (*geol*) falla *f*. **be at fault** tener la culpa. **faultiness** *n* imperfección *f*. **faultless** *adj* perfecto. **faulty** *adj* malo; erróneo; defectuoso.

fauna ['fɔːnə] *n* fauna *f*.

favour ['feivə] *n* favor *m*; favoritismo *m*; (*gift*) obsequio *m*; (*comm*) carta *f*, atenta *f*. **be in favour of** estar a favor de. *v* favorecer. **favourable** *adj* favorable. **favourite** *n*, *adj* favorito, -a.

fawn [fɔːn] *n* (*animal*) cervato *m*. (*colour*) color de gamuza *m*. **fawn on** *or* **upon** adular.

fax [fæks] *n* fax *m*. *v* mandar por fax

fear [fiə] *n* miedo *m*; temor *m*. *v* temer; tener miedo de *or* a. **fearful** *adj* (*frightening*) espantoso; (*frightened*) temeroso. **fearless** *adj* intrépido, audaz.

feasible ['fiːzəbl] *adj* factible. **feasibility** *n* viabilidad *f*.

feast [fiːst] *n* fiesta *f*; banquete *m*. **feast day** día festivo *m*.

feat [fiːt] *n* hazaña *f*.

feather ['feðə] *n* pluma *f*. **feather bed** colchón de plumas *m*.

feature ['fiːtʃə] n característica f; (*shape*) figura f; (*face*) rasgo m; (*written article*) artículo principal m. **feature film** película principal f. v presentar; representar; (*emphasize*) destacar.

February ['februəri] n febrero m.

fed [fed] V **feed**.

federal ['fedərəl] adj federal.

federate ['fedə.reit] v federar. **federation** n federación f.

fee [fiː] n (*professional*) honorarios m pl; (*club*) cuota f. **entrance fee** entrada f.

feeble ['fiːbl] adj débil; (*unconvincing*) de poco peso. **feebleness** n debilidad f.

*****feed** [fiːd] v alimentar; dar de comer; (*eat*) comer. **be fed up with** (*coll*) estar harto de. **feed on** alimentarse con. n (*for babies*) comida f; (*fodder*) foraje m; (*tech*) alimentación f. **feedback** n reaprovechamiento m; (*tech*) realimentación f.

*****feel** [fiːl] v tocar; mirar; sentir; (*realize*) darse cuenta de; (*caress*) sobar; (*think*) pensar. n tacto m; sensación f; atmósfera f; sentido m. **feeler** n antena f; tentáculo m. **feeling** n sentimiento m; sentido m; sensación f; opinión f; impresión f.

feet [fiːt] V **foot**.

feign [fein] v fingir; inventar.

feline ['fiːlain] nm, adj felino.

fell[1] [fel] V **fall**.

fell[2] [fel] v derribar; (*trees*) talar.

fellow ['felou] n hombre m; compañero m; (*coll*) tipo m; (*of a society*) miembro m. **fellowship** n comunidad f; asociación f.

felony ['feləni] n delito grave m. **felon** n criminal m.

felt[1] [felt] V **feel**.

felt[2] [felt] n fieltro m. **felt-tip pen** rotulador m.

female ['fiːmeil] adj hembra; femenino. n (*animal*) hembra f; (*person*) mujer f.

feminine ['feminin] nm, adj femenino. **femininity** n feminidad f. **feminism** n feminismo m. **feminist** n(m + f), adj feminista.

fence [fens] n cerca f, valla f. v cercar, vallar; (*sport*) practicar la esgrima. **fencing** n (*sport*) esgrima f.

fend [fend] v **fend for oneself** arreglárselas. **fend off** desviar.

fender ['fendə] n guardafuegos m invar;

(*US: car*) guardabarros m invar.

fennel ['fenl] n hinojo m.

ferment ['fəːment; 'fəːment] v fermentar. n fermento m; agitación f. **fermentation** n fermentación f.

fern [fəːn] n helecho m.

ferocious [fə'rouʃəs] adj feroz. **ferocity** n ferocidad f.

ferret ['ferit] n hurón m. **ferret out** conseguir, descubrir.

ferry ['feri] n transbordador m. v transportar.

fertile ['fəːtail] adj fértil; (*person*) fecundo. **fertility** n fertilidad f; fecundidad f. **fertilization** n fertilización f; fecundación f. **fertilize** v abonar; fecundar. **fertilizer** n abono m.

fervent ['fəːvənt] adj ferviente. **fervour** n fervor m.

fester ['festə] v supurar; (*fig*) enconarse.

festival ['festəvəl] n fiesta f. **festive** festivo. **festivity** festividad f.

festoon [fə'stuːn] v festonear. n guirnalda f.

fetch [fetʃ] v (*bring*) traer; (*procure*) buscar; (*reach*) alcanzar. **fetching** adj atractivo.

fête [feit] n fiesta f. v festejar.

fetid ['fiːtid] adj fétido.

fetish ['fetiʃ] n fetiche m.

fetter ['fetə] v encadenar. **fetters** pl n grilletes m pl; (*fig*) trabas f pl.

feud [fjuːd] n enemistad hereditaria f. v pelear, reñir.

feudal ['fjuːdl] adj feudal. **feudalism** n feudalismo m.

fever ['fiːvə] n fiebre f. **feverish** adj febril.

few [fjuː] adj poco. n pocos, -as pl. **a few** algunos, unos, unos pocos. **quite a few** bastante. **fewer** adj menos. **the fewer the better** cuantos menos mejor. **fewest** adj menos.

fiancé [fi'onsei] n novio m. **fiancée** n novia f.

fiasco [fi'askou] n fiasco m.

fib [fib] n mentirijilla f v decir una mentirijilla.

fibre ['faibə] n fibra f. **fibreglass** n fibra de vidrio f.

fickle ['fikl] adj inconstante, veleidoso.

fiction ['fikʃən] n (*stories*) narrativa f; (*invention*) ficción f. **fictional** or **fictitious** adj novelesco; ficticio.

fir

fiddle ['fidl] n violín m; (coll: trick) trampa f. v tocar el violín; (coll: cheat) camelar; (coll: falsify) amañar. **fiddle with** juguetear con. **fiddling** adj trivial; fútil.

fidelity [fi'deləti] n fidelidad f.

fidget ['fidʒit] v agitar nerviosamente. **fidgety** adj nervioso, agitado.

field [fi:ld] n campo m; (fig) esfera f. **field glasses** gemelos m pl. **field marshal** mariscal de campo m. **fieldwork** n trabajo en el terreno m.

fiend [fi:nd] n demonio m, diablo m; (coll) fanático, -a m, f. **fiendish** adj diabólico.

fierce [fiəs] adj feroz, fiero; (person) violento; (heat) intenso; (battle) encarnizado. **fierceness** or **ferocity** n ferocidad f; violencia f; furia f; intensidad f.

fiery ['faiəri] adj (burning) ardiente; (flaming) llameante; (passionate) apasionado; (temper) fogoso.

fifteen [fifti:n] nm, adj quince. **fifteenth** n, adj decimoquinto, -a.

fifth [fifθ] n, adj quinto, -a.

fifty ['fifti] nm, adj cincuenta. **go fifty-fifty** ir a medias. **fiftieth** n, adj quincuagésimo, -a. **fiftyish** adj cincuentón.

fig [fig] n (fruit) higo m; (tree) higuera f.

*fight [fait] v luchar contra, combatir. n lucha f; pelea f. **fighter** luchador m.

figment ['figmənt] n invención f.

figure ['figə] n (number) número m, cifra f; (price) precio m; (statue, design, personage) figura f; (human) línea f. **figurehead** n mascarón de proa m; (fig) testaferro m. **figure skating** patinaje artístico m. v (math) poner en cifras; (calculate) calcular. **figure out** comprender; resolver.

filament ['filəmənt] n filamento m.

file[1] [fail] n (folder) carpeta f; (card index) fichero m; (computer) archivo; m (document holder) archivador m; (dossier) expediente m. v archivar; (a claim) presentar. **file in/out** entrar/salir en fila. **file past** desfilar ante. **in single file** en fila de a uno. **filing** n clasificación f. **filing cabinet** archivo m. **filing clerk** archivero, -a m, f. archivista m, f.

file[2] [fail] n (tool) lima f. v limar. **filings** pl n limaduras f pl.

filial ['filiəl] adj filial.

fill [fil] v llenar; (space, time) ocupar; (vacancy) cubrir; (tooth) empastar; (hole) tapar;

(cookery) rellenar; (requirements) satisfacer. **fill in** (form) rellenar. **fill up** llenar. **filling** n relleno m; empaste m. **filling station** estación de servicio f.

fillet ['filit] n filete m. v cortar en filetes.

film [film] n (phot, cinema) película f; (layer) capa f; (eye) nube f; (mist, etc.) velo m. **roll of film** rollo de película m. **filmgoer** n aficionado, -a al cine m, f. **film star** astro de cine m, estrella de cine f.

filter ['filtə] n filtro m. v filtrar. **filtering** n filtración f. **filter-tipped** adj con filtro, emboquillado.

filth [filθ] n inmundicia f, suciedad f; (fig) obscenidades f pl. **filthy** adj asqueroso, inmundo; obsceno.

fin [fin] n aleta f.

final ['fainl] adj (last) último; decisivo; definitivo. n final f. **finalist** n finalista m, f. **finalize** v finalizar. **finally** adv finalmente.

finale [fi'na:li] n final f

finance [fai'næns] n finanzas f pl. v financiar. **financial** adj financiero. **financial year** año económico m. **financier** n financiero, -a m, f.

finch [fintʃ] n pinzón m.

*find [faind] v encontrar, hallar. **find out** averiguar; descubrir. n hallazgo m. **findings** pl n hallazgos m pl; resultados m pl.

fine[1] [fain] adj excelente; elegante; (pleasant) agradable; bueno; fino; delicado. **that's fine!** ¡muy bien! adv en trozos pequeños; fino; muy bien. **fine arts** bellas artes f pl. **finely** adv (small) finamente; (well) primorosamente. **finery** n galas f pl.

fine[2] [fain] n multa f. v multar.

finesse [fi'nes] n fineza f, delicadeza f; tacto m; (bridge) impás m.

finger ['fingə] n dedo m. **little finger** mañique m. v tocar. **fingernail** n uña f. **fingerprint** n huella dactilar f. **fingertip** n punta del dedo m. **have at one's fingertips** saberse al dedillo.

finish ['finiʃ] v terminar, acabar; (sport) llegar. **finish off** rematar. n fin m, conclusión f; (surface) acabado m; (sport) llegada f. **finishing line** meta f. **finishing touch** última mano f.

finite ['fainait] adj finito.

Finland ['finlənd] n Finlandia f. **Finn** n finlandés, -esa m, f. **Finnish** nm, adj finlandés.

fir [fə:] n abeto m. **fir cone** piña f.

fire ['faiə] n fuego m; (uncontrolled) incendio m; (electric or gas) estufa f. **be on fire** estar ardiendo. **catch fire** encenderse. **set on fire, set fire to** pegar fuego, incendiar. v (with enthusiasm, etc.) infundir (a); (gun) disparar; (salute) tirar; (missile) lanzar; (sack) echar. **fire on** hacer fuego sobre.

fire alarm n alarma de incendios f.

firearm ['faiə,a:m] n arma de fuego f.

fire brigade n cuerpo de bomberos m.

fire door n puerta incombustible f.

fire drill n ejercicios para casos de incendio m pl.

fire engine n bomba de incendios f.

fire-escape n escalera de incendios f.

fire-extinguisher n extintor m.

firefly ['faiəflai] n luciérnaga f.

fire-guard n guardafuego m.

firelight ['faiə,lait] n lumbre m.

fireman ['faiəmən] n bombero m.

fireplace ['faiə,pleis] n chimenea f.

fireproof ['faiə,pru:f] adj ininflamable, incombustible.

fireside ['faiə,said] n hogar m.

fire station n parque de bomberos m.

firewood ['faiə,wud] n leña f.

firework ['faiə,wə:k] n fuego de artificio m.

firing squad n pelotón de ejecución m.

firm¹ [fə:m] adj firme, sólido; estable. **firmness** n firmeza f.

firm² [fə:m] n empresa f. firma f.

first¹ [fə:st] adj primero; básico; elemental. **first aid** primeros auxilios m pl. **firstclass** adj de primera clase. **first cousin** primo hermano m. **first edition** edición principe f. **first floor** primer piso m. **first name** nombre de pila m. **first-rate** adj de primera calidad. **in the first place** en primer lugar.

first² [fə:st] adv antes, primero. **first and foremost** antes que nada. **first and last** en todos los aspectos. **travel first** viajar en primera. **you go first** usted primero.

first³ [fə:st] n primero, -a m, f; sobresaliente m. **at first** al principio. **be the first to** ser el primero en. **get a first** sacar sobresaliente.

fiscal ['fiskəl] adj fiscal.

fish [fiʃ] n (food) pescado m; (in water) pez m. **fish and chips** pescado frito con patatas fritas. v pescar. **fishy** adj (coll) sospechoso.

fishbone ['fiʃ,boun] n espina f.

fish-bowl n pecera f.

fisherman ['fiʃəmən] n pescador m.

fish finger n filete de pescado empanado m.

fish hook n anzuelo m.

fishing ['fiʃiŋ] n pesca f. **fishing line** sedal m. **fishing net** red de pesca f. **fishing rod** caña de pescar f. **fishing tackle** aparejo de pescar m. **go fishing** ir de pesca.

fish market n mercado de pescado m.

fishmonger ['fiʃ,mʌŋgə] n pescadero, -a m, f. **fishmonger's** n pescadería f.

fission ['fiʃən] n fisión f, escisión f.

fissure ['fiʃə] n grieta f.

fist [fist] n puño m. **fistful** n puñado m.

fit¹ [fit] adj conveniente; apto; adecuado; (qualified) capacitado; (competent) capaz; (worthy) digno; (healthy) sano. **it's not fit to eat** no se puede comer. **see fit** juzgar conveniente. v (try on) probar; (qualify) capacitar; (tally with) cuadrar con; adaptar; preparar; unir; (supply with) equipar con; (clothes) sentar bien a; (tailor) entallar. **fitness** n conveniencia f; salud f; aptitud f. **fitted carpet** moqueta f. **fitter** n (tailor) probador, -a m, f; (tech) ajustador m. **fitting** adj oportuno; digno; apropiado; propio. **fitting room** cuarto de pruebas m. **fittings** pl n muebles m pl; accesorios m pl.

fit² [fit] n (med) ataque m.

five [faiv] nm, adj cinco.

fix [fiks] v fijar; sujetar; (decide) establecer; (date) señalar; (hopes) poner; (coll: put right) arreglar. n aprieto m; (coll) dosis de droga f. **fixation** n obsesión f. **fixed** adj fijo; (coll: rigged) amañado. **fixture** n instalación f; (sport) partido m; (coll) permanencia f.

fizz [fiz] n burbujeo m; (coll) gaseosa f. v burbujear.

flabbergasted ['flabə,ga:stid] adj pasmado.

flabby ['flabi] adj fláccido; (spineless) blandengue. **flabbiness** n flaccidez f; blandura f.

flag¹ [flag] n bandera f; (stone) baldosa f. **flag down** detener haciendo señales. **flagpole** n asta de bandera f. **flagship** n buque insignia m.

flag² [flag] v (weaken) flaquear; (interest) decaer. **flagging** adj flojo; desmadejado.

flagon ['flagən] n (jug) jarra f; (bottle) botel-

la (de dos litros) f.
flagrant ['fleigrənt] adj flagrante; escandaloso.
flagstone ['flægstoun] n losa f
flair [fleə] n don m; instinto m; talento m.
flake [fleik] n (snow) copo m; (soap) escama f; (paint) desconchón m. v caer en copos; desconchar. **flaky** adj escamoso. **flaky pastry** hojaldre m.
flamboyant [flam,boiənt] adj llamativo. **flamboyance** n extravagancia f.
flame [fleim] n llama f. **burst into flames** incendiarse. v llamear. **flammable** adj inflamable.
flamingo [flə'miŋgou] n flamenco m.
flan [flan] n flan m.
flank [flaŋk] n (animal) ijada f; (person) costado m; (mil) flanco m. v bordear.
flannel ['flanl] n (fabric) franela f; (face cloth) pañito para lavarse la cara m. **flannels** pl n pantalones de franela m pl.
flap [flap] v (shake) sacudir; (arms) agitar; (wings) batir. n (pocket) carterita f; (envelope, etc.) solapa f; (table) ala abatible f; (coat) faldón m; (aero) alerón m; (coll) crisis f.
flare [fleə] n (blaze) llamarada f; (signal) cohete de señales m; (widening) ensanchamiento m. v llamear; ensanchar; (clothes) acampanar. **flare up** (anger) ponerse furioso.
flash [flaʃ] n destello m; (sparkle) centelleo m; (phot) flash m; (moment) instante m; (inspiration) ráfaga f; (genius) rasgo m; (hope) resquicio m. **flashback** n escena retrospectiva f. **flash bulb** bombilla de magnesio f. **flashlight** n linterna f. v despedir; lanzar; encender; destellar; centellear. **flashing** adj intermitente.
flask [flask] n frasco m; (vacuum) termo m.
flat¹ [flat] adj plano, llano, chato; horizontal; (fig) categórico; monótono; (boring) pesado; (rate) fijo; (below pitch) desafinado; (tyre) desinflado; (battery) descargado; (horse racing) sin obstáculos. **flat beer** cerveza muerta f. **flat-footed** adj de pies planos. **be flat broke** estar sin blanca. **go flat out** ir a todo gas. **flatly** adv categóricamente; completamente. n (music) bemol m; (land) llano m; (tyre) pinchazo m. **flatten** v (make flat) aplanar; (crush) aplastar; (smooth) alisar.
flat² [flat] n apartamento m. **flatlet** n piso pequeño m.

flatter ['flatə] v adular, halagar; favorecer. **flatterer** n adulador, -a m, f. **flattering** adj (words) halagüeño; (person) halagador; (clothes) favorecedor. **flattery** n halago m, adulación f.
flatulence ['flatjuləns] n flatulencia f.
flaunt [flo:nt] v ostentar. **flaunt oneself** pavonearse.
flautist ['flo:tist] n flautista m, f.
flavour ['fleivə] n sabor m, gusto m; (cookery) sazón m, sainete m. v saborear; condimentar. **flavouring** n condimento m, sainete m.
flaw [flo:] n defecto m; (error) fallo m. v (crack) agrietar; (spoil) estropear. **flawed** adj falto; imperfecto. **flawless** adj sin tacha, perfecto.
flax [flaks] n lino m. **flaxen** adj de lino; (hair) rubio.
flea [fli:] n pulga f. **fleabite** n picadura de pulga f.
fleck [flek] n (speck) mota f; (colour) mancha f; (dust) partícula f. v motear; (paint) salpicar.
fled [fled] V flee.
***flee** [fli:] v evitar; escapar de.
fleece [fli:s] n (wool) lana f; (sheared wool) velón m; (jacket) chaqueta de lana f. v (coll) pelar. **fleecy** adj (woolly) lanoso.
fleet [fli:t] n flota f; (navy) armada f. adj veloz. **fleeting** adj fugaz, breve.
Flemish ['flemiʃ] nm, adj flamenco. **Fleming** n flamenco, -a m, f.
flesh [fleʃ] n carne f. **flesh-coloured** adj de color carne. **flesh-eating** adj carnívoro. **flesh wound** herida superficial f. **in the flesh** en carne y hueso. **fleshy** adj gordo.
flew [flu:] V fly.
flex [fleks] n flexible m. v doblar. **flexibility** n flexibilidad f. **flexible** adj (pliable) flexible; (fig) elástico.
flick [flik] v dar un golpecito a. **flick through** (book) hojear. n (whip) latigazo suave m; (light stroke) golpecito m; (duster) pasada f; (wrist) movimiento rápido m. **the flicks** (coll) el cine m.
flicker ['flikə] v (light) parpadear; (flames) vacilar. n parpadeo m; (flame) llama vacilante f; (hope, etc.) resquicio m.
flight¹ [flait] n (birds) bandada f; (aircraft) escuadrilla f; (act of flying) vuelo m; (distance flown) recorrido m. **flight crew** tripu-

lación f. **flight deck** cubierta de aterrizaje f. **flight of stairs** tramo de escalera m. **flight path** trayectoria de vuelo f. **in flight** en vuelo. **flightiness** n ligereza f. **flightless** adj incapacitado para volar. **flighty** adj volátil; caprichoso.

flight² [flait] n (escape) huida f, fuga f.

flimsy ['flimzi] adj (lacking substance) poco sólido; (fragile) frágil; (weak) débil; (paper) fino; (cloth) ligero; (excuse) flojo. **flimsiness** n fragilidad f; debilidad f; finura f; ligereza f.

flinch [flintʃ] v (draw back) retroceder; (hesitate) vacilar; (muscular movement) encogerse.

*****fling** [fliŋ] v arrojar, tirar; (dash) precipitarse. **fling aside** dejar de lado. n (throw) lanzamiento f; (wild tune) juerga f.

flint [flint] n pedernal m; (of lighter) piedra de mechero f.

flip [flip] v (flick) dar un capirotazo; (coin) echar a cara o cruz. n capirotazo m. **flipper** n aleta f.

flippant ['flipənt] adj frívolo. **flippancy** n ligereza f.

flirt [flə:t] n (female) coqueta f; (male) mariposón m. v flirtear, coquetear. **flirtation** n coqueteo m.

flit [flit] v revolotear.

float [flout] v flotar; (support) hacer flotar. n flotador m; (angling) corcho m; (carnival) carroza f.

flock¹ [flok] n (sheep, goats) rebaño m; (birds) bandada f; (people) muchedumbre f. v congregarse.

flock² [flok] n (filling) borra f.

flog [flog] v (beat) azotar; (coll: sell) vender. **flogging** n paliza f; flagelación f.

flood [flʌd] v inundar; irrigar; (overflow) desbordar. n inundación f; flujo m; diluvio m. **in flood** crecido.

*****floodlight** ['flʌdlait] n foco m. v iluminar con focos. **floodlighting** n iluminación con focos f.

floor [flo:] n suelo m; piso m; (ocean) fondo m; (dance) pista f. **first floor** primer piso m. **ground floor** planta baja f. **take the floor** (speak) tomar la palabra. v (knock down) echar al suelo. **floorboard** n tabla del suelo f. **floorcloth** n trapo m. **flooring** n solado m. **floor polish** cera para el suelo f. **floor show** espectáculo de cabaret m. **floorwalker** n supervisor de división m.

flop [flop] v desplomarse; (fail) fracasar. n (coll) fracaso m. **floppy** adj flojo; colgante. **floppy disk** disquete m.

flora ['flo:rə] n flora f.

florist ['florist] n florista m, f. **florist's shop** florería f.

flounce¹ [flauns] v **flounce in/out** entrar/salir enfadado. n movimiento brusco m.

flounce² [flauns] n (of dress) volante m.

flounder ['flaundə] v forcejear; confundirse.

flour ['flauə] n harina f. v enharinar. **flour mill** molino harinero m. **floury** adj (covered with flour) enharinado; (like flour) harinoso.

flourish ['flʌriʃ] v (prosper) florecer; (wave) agitar; (brandish) esgrimir. n ostentación f; (gesture) ademán m; (writing) rasgo m. **flourishing** adj floreciente.

flout [flaut] v burlarse de.

flow [flou] v (liquid) fluir; (tears) correr; (blood in the body) circular; (blood from the body) derramarse; (tide) subir. **flow away** irse. **flow from** salir de. **flow in/out** entrar/salir a raudales. **flow into** desembocar. n circulación f; movimiento m. **flow chart** organigrama m. **flowing** adj (river) fluente; (style) fluido; (hair) suelto; (beard) largo.

flower ['flauə] n flor f. **flower arrangement** ramillete m. **flower bed** arriate m. **flowerpot** n maceta f. **flower shop** florería f. **flower show** exposición de flores f. v florecer. **flowering** adj floreciente; n florecimiento m. **flowery** adj florido.

flown [floun] V **fly**.

flu [flu:] n gripe f.

fluctuate ['flʌktjueit] v fluctuar; vacilar. **fluctuation** n fluctuación f.

flue [flu:] n chimenea f; conducto de humo m.

fluent ['fluənt] adj (language) bueno; (writing) fluido. **fluency** n facilidad f; dominio m. **fluently** adv (speech) con soltura; (writing) con fluidez.

fluff [flʌf] n pelusa f; mota f; masa esponjosa f. **fluffy** adj (pillow, cushion) mullido; (downy) velloso; (cloth) que tiene pelusa.

fluid ['fluid] nm, adj fluido.

fluke [flu:k] n chiripa f. **fluky** adj de suerte.

flung [flʌŋ] V **fling**.

fluorescent [fluə'resnt] adj fluorescente.

fond

fluorescence *n* fluorescencia *f*.

fluoride ['fluəraid] *n* fluoruro *m*. **fluoridation** *n* fluoración *f*.

flurry ['flʌri] *n* (*excitement*) agitación *f*; (*snow*) borrasca *f*; (*rain*) chaparrón *m*; (*wind*) ráfaga *f*.

flush¹ [flʌʃ] *n* (*blush*) rubor *m*; (*fever*) sofoco *m*; (*lavatory*) cisterna *f*. *v* ruborizarse; tener sofocos; (*light*) resplandecer. **flush the toilet** tirar de la cadena. **flushed** *adj* rebosante.

flush² [flʌʃ] *adj* (*abundant*) copioso; (*lavish*) liberal; (*coll: well off*) adinerado. **flush with** (*level*) a nivel con.

fluster ['flʌstə] *v* poner nervioso. *n* agitación *f*.

flute [fluːt] *n* flauta *f*.

flutter ['flʌtə] *v* (*leaves, etc.*) revolotear; (*wings*) batir; (*curtains, flags*) ondular; (*heart*) palpitar; (*flap*) agitar. *n* ondulación *f*; (*wings*) aleteo *m*; agitación *f*; (*eyelids*) parpadeo *m*; palpitación *f*.

flux [flʌks] *n* (*flow*) flujo *m*; (*changes*) cambios frecuentes *m pl*. **be in a state of flux** estar siempre cambiando.

*fly¹ [flai] *v* volar; (*escape*) huir; (*time*) pasar volando; (*kite*) echar a volar; (*aircraft*) pilotar; (*flag*) izar, enarbolar; (*go across*) atravesar; (*mileage*) recorrer. **fly away** emprender el vuelo. **fly over** sobrevolar. **fly past** desfilar. **flies** *pl n* (*trousers*) bragueta *f*.

fly² [flai] *n* mosca *f*.

fly-blown *adj* cochambroso.

fly-fishing *n* pesca con moscas *f*.

flying ['flaiiŋ] *adj* volador, volante, volando. *n* aviación *f*.

flying colours *pl n* **pass an exam with flying colours** aprobar un examen con éxito.

flying field *n* campo de aviación *m*.

flying fish *n* pez volador *m*.

flying saucer *n* platillo volante *m*, objeto volante no identificado *m*.

flying squirrel *n* ardilla volante *f*.

flying start *n* salida lanzada *f*; (*fig*) principio feliz *m*.

flyleaf ['flailiːf] *n* guarda *f*.

flyover ['flai,ouvə] *n* paso elevado *m*.

fly-paper *n* papel matamoscas *m*.

fly swatter *n* matamoscas *m invar*.

flyweight ['flaiweit] *n* peso mosca *m*.

flywheel ['flaiwiːl] *n* volante *m*.

foal [foul] *n* potro, -a *m, f*. *v* parir.

foam [foum] *n* espuma *f*. *v* espumar; (*animal*) espumajear. **foam rubber** gomaspuma *f*. **foaming** *adj* espumoso.

focal ['foukəl] *adj* focal. **focal point** punto focal.

focus ['foukəs] *n* foco *m*. **in focus** enfocado. **out of focus** fuera de foco. *v* enfocar; concentrar.

fodder ['fodə] *n* forraje *m*.

foe [fou] *n* enemigo, -a *m, f*.

foetus ['fiːtəs] *n* feto *m*. **foetal** *adj* fetal.

fog [fog] *n* niebla *f*, bruma *f*. **fogbound** *adj* (*foggy*) cubierto de niebla; (*immobilized*) detenido por la niebla. **foghorn** *n* sirena de niebla *f*. **foglamp** *or* **foglight** (*mot*) faro antiniebla *m*. **fogginess** *n* nebulosidad *f*. **foggy** *adj* nebuloso, brumoso.

foible ['foibl] *n* extravagancia *f*; (*fad*) manía *f*.

foil¹ [foil] *v* frustrar.

foil² [foil] *n* hoja fina de metal *f*; (*fig*) contraste *m*.

foil³ [foil] *n* (*fencing*) florete *m*.

foist [foist] *v* colar; meter.

fold¹ [fould] *n* (*crease*) pliegue *m*; (*wrinkle*) arruga *f*. *v* doblar, plegar; (*surround*) envolver; (*coll: close down*) liquidarse. **fold one's arms** cruzar los brazos. **folder** *n* carpeta *f*. **folding** *adj* plegable. **folding door** puerta de fuelle *f*.

fold² [fould] *n* (*sheep*) redil *m*; (*religion*) grey *f*.

foliage ['fouliidʒ] *n* follaje *m*.

folk [fouk] *pl n* gente *f sing*; pueblo *m*. **folks** *pl n* (*coll*) familia *f sing*. **folk art** arte popular *m*. **folk dance** baile folklórico *m*. **folklore** *n* folklore *m*. **folk music** música popular *f*. **folk singer** cantante de canciones populares *m, f*. **folk song** canción popular *f*.

follicle ['folikl] *n* folículo *m*.

follow ['folou] *v* seguir; (*pursue*) perseguir; (*practise*) ejercer; (*ensue*) resultar. **follow up** investigar sobre; reforzar. **follower** *n* seguidor, -a *m, f*; discípulo, -a *m, f*; aficionado, -a *m, f*. **following** *adj* siguiente. *n* partidarios *m pl*.

folly ['foli] *n* locura *f*.

fond [fond] *adj* cariñoso; indulgente. **be fond of** tenerle cariño a. **fondly** *adj* ca riñosamente. **fondness** n cariño m.

fondle ['fondl] v acariciar; mimar.

font [font] n (baptismal) pila f; (printing) fundición f, tipo de letra m.

food [fu:d] n comida f, alimento m; comestibles m pl. **food and drink** comida y bebida f. **food poisoning** intoxicación alimenticia f. **food processor** robot de cocina m. **food shop** tienda de comestibles f. **foodstuff** n producto alimenticio m.

fool [fu:l] n tonto, -a m, f; bobo, -a m, f; idiota m, f; (jester) bufón m. **foolproof** adj infalible. v (deceive) engañar; (joke) bromear. **fool about** or **around** juguetear.

foolhardy adj temerario. **foolhardiness** n temeridad f. **foolish** adj insensato; tonto. **foolishly** adv neciamente. **foolishness** n insensatez f; tontería f.

foolscap ['fu:lskap] n papel de barba m.

foot [fut] n, pl feet pie m; (animal) pata f. **from head to foot** de pies a cabeza. **on foot** a pie. **get cold feet** tener miedo.

football ['fut,bo:l] n fútbol m; (ball) pelota f. **football pools** pl n quinielas f pl.

foot brake n freno de pedal m.

footbridge ['fut,bridʒ] n pasarela f.

foothills ['fut,hilz] pl n estribaciones f pl.

foothold ['fut,hould] n punto de apoyo para el pie m; (fig) posición f.

footing ['futiŋ] n pie m, equilibrio m; condición f; posición f. **on an equal footing** en un pie de igual.

footlights ['fut,laits] pl n candilejas f pl.

footloose ['fut,lu:s] adj libre.

footnote ['fut,nout] n nota f.

footpath ['fut,pa:θ] n senda f; (pavement) acera f.

footprint ['fut,print] n pisada f.

footstep ['fut,step] n paso m.

for [fo:] prep para; por; de; (time) desde; durante; (in favour of) en favor de; (in honour of) en honor de; (in place of) en lugar de; (as regards) en cuanto a; (against) contra; (in order that) para que. conj pues, puesto que, ya que.

forage ['foridʒ] v forrajear; (fig: seek) buscar. n forraje m.

*****forbear** [fə'beə] v contenerse; abstenerse. **forbearance** n abstención f; indulgencia f; paciencia f.

*****forbid** [fə'bid] v prohibir; (prevent) impedir. **forbidding** adj impresionante;

inhóspito; severo; (threatening) amenazador.

force [fo:s] n fuerza f; (mil) cuerpo m. **in force** en vigor. **sales force** vendedores m pl. **join forces** unirse. v forzar; obligar; (tech) inyectar. **be forced to** verse obligado a. **forceful** adj fuerte; contundente.

forceps ['fo:seps] pl n fórceps m sing.

ford [fo:d] n vado m. v vadear.

fore [fo:] adj delantero; anterior. adv delante. n (naut) proa f. **come to the fore** empezar a destacar. interj (golf) ¡cuidado!

forearm ['fo:ra:m] n antebrazo m. v prevenir.

forebears ['fo:beəz] pl n antepasados m pl.

foreboding [fo:'boudiŋ] n presentimiento m.

*****forecast** ['fo:ka:st] n previsión f; pronóstico m; plan m. v pronosticar. **weather forecast** pronóstico meteorológico m.

forecourt ['fo:ko:t] n antepatio m.

forefather ['fo:fa:ðə] n antepasado m.

forefinger ['fo:fiŋgə] n dedo índice m.

forefront ['fo:frʌnt] n delantera f; sitio de mayor importancia m.

foregone ['fo:gon] adj conocido de antemano. **foregone conclusion** conclusión inevitable f.

foreground ['fo:graund] n primer plano m; primer término m.

forehand ['fo:hand] n (tennis) golpe derecho m.

forehead ['forid] n frente f.

foreign ['forən] adj extranjero; ajeno. **foreign affairs** asuntos exteriores m pl. **foreign trade** comercio exterior m. **foreign exchange** cambio exterior m. **foreign legion** legión extranjera f. **foreigner** n extranjero, -a m, f.

foreleg ['fo:leg] n pata delantera f.

foreman ['fo:mən] n capataz m.

foremost ['fo:moust] adj delantero; principal. **first and foremost** ante todo.

forename ['fo:neim] n nombre de pila m.

forensic [fə'rensik] adj forense. **forensic medicine** medicina legal f.

forerunner ['fo:rʌnə] n precursor, -a m, f; (herald) anunciador, -a m, f.

*****foresee** [fo:'si:] v prever. **foreseeable** adj previsible.

foreshadow [fo:'ʃadou] v presagiar; prefigurar.

foresight ['fɔːsait] n previsión f.

foreskin ['fɔːskin] n prepucio m.

forest ['fɒrist] n selva f; bosque m. **forester** n guardabosque m. **forestry** n silvicultura f. **Forestry Commission** administración de montes f.

forestall [fɔːˈstɔːl] v prevenir; impedir; anticiparse a.

foretaste ['fɔːteist] n anticipación f.

***foretell** [fɔːˈtel] v predecir; presagiar.

forethought ['fɔːθɔːt] n premeditación f.

forever [fɒˈevə] adv siempre, para siempre. **forever more** por siempre jamás.

forewarn [fɒˈwɔːn] v avisar, adventir. **forewarning** n aviso m, advertencia f.

foreword ['fɔːwəːd] n prefacio m; prólogo m.

forfeit ['fɔːfit] v (right) perder; (property) comisar.

forge¹ [fɔːdʒ] v (counterfeit) falsificar; (metal) fraguar. n fragua f. **forger** n falsificador m; (metal) herrero m. **forgery** n falsificación f; (thing forged) documento falsificado m; moneda falsificada f.

forge² [fɔːdʒ] v **forge ahead** hacer grandes progresos.

***forget** [fəˈget] v olvidar, olvidarse de. **forget-me-not** n nomeolvides f. **forgetful** adj olvidadizo; descuidado. **forgetfulness** n olvido m; descuido m.

***forgive** [fəˈgiv] v perdonar; dispensar. **forgiveness** n perdón m; remisión f. **forgiving** adj indulgente, clemente.

***forgo** [fɔːˈgou] v abstenerse; renunciar.

fork [fɔːk] n (cutlery) tenedor m; (gardening) horca f; (tree) horcadura f; (road) bifurcación f; (river) horcajo m. **tuning fork** diapasón m. v bifurcarse. **forked** adj bifurcado.

forlorn [fəˈlɔːn] adj desamparado; triste.

form [fɔːm] n (shape) forma f; (figure) figura f; (type) tipo m; (document) formulario m; (school year) curso m. v (make) hacer; (model) modelar; (habit) crear; (constitute) constituir; (put together) formar. **form a queue** ponerse en cola. **formation** n formación f. **formative** adj de formación, formativo.

formal ['fɔːməl] adj formal; solemne; (person) formalista; ceremonioso; de cortesía; en debida forma. **formality** n (requirement) formalidad f; ceremonia f; rigidez f.

format ['fɔːmat] n formato m. v v (computer) formatear.

former ['fɔːmə] adj (previous) anterior; (ex-) antiguo, pasado. **pron** ése, ésa, aquél, equélla, el primero, la primera. **formerly** adv anteriormente; antiguamente.

formidable ['fɔːmidəbl] adj formidable.

formula ['fɔːmjulə] n, pl -ae fórmula f.

formulate ['fɔːmjuleit] v formular. **formulation** n formulación f.

***forsake** [fəˈseik] v abandonar.

fort [fɔːt] n fuerte m, fortaleza f.

forte ['fɔːtei] n fuerte m.

forth [fɔːθ] adv en adelante. **and so forth** y así sucesivamente. **forthcoming** adj próximo; (approaching) venidero; (person) abierto. **forthright** adj franco. **forthwith** adv en seguida; en el acto.

fortify ['fɔːtifai] v (health, moral strength) fortalecer; (town) fortificar; (wine) encabezar; (argument) reforzar. **fortification** n fortalecimiento m; fortificación f; reforzamiento m.

fortitude ['fɔːtitjuːd] n fortaleza f; firmeza f.

fortnight ['fɔːtnait] n quincena f. **fortnightly** adj quincenal. adv quincenalmente.

fortress ['fɔːtris] n fortaleza f.

fortuitous [fəˈtjuːitəs] adj, adv casual.

fortunate ['fɔːtʃənət] adj afortunado; oportuno. **fortunately** adv afortunadamente.

fortune ['fɔːtʃən] n (fate) fortuna f; (luck) suerte f. **cost a fortune** costar un dineral. **stroke of fortune** golpe de suerte m. **fortune-teller** n adivino, -a m, f.

forty ['fɔːti] nm, adj cuarenta. **fortieth** nm, adj cuarentavo.

forum ['fɔːrəm] n foro m; (meeting) tribuna f.

forward ['fɔːwəd] adj (front) delantero; (movement) hacia adelante; (progressive) avanzado; (impertinent) impertinente. v (send) expedir; (promote) promover. **please forward** remítase al destinario. n (football) delantero, -a m, f. **forwards** adv adelante.

fossil ['fɒsl] nm, adj fósil. **fossilized** adj fosilizado.

foster ['fɒstə] v (child) criar; (idea) abrigar; (project) patrocinar; (favour) favorecer. adj adoptivo. **foster child** niño de acogida m. **foster family** familia de acogida f. **foster**

home hogar de acogida *m*, casa de acogida *f*.

fought [fo:t] *V* **fight**.

foul [faul] *adj* asqueroso; (*dirty*) sucio; (*air*) viciado; (*language*) grosero; (*smell*) fétido. **foul play** jugada sucia *f*. *n* falta *f*. *v* ensuciar; (*reputation*) manchar; (*sport*) cometer una falta.

found¹ [faund] *V* **find**.

found² [faund] *v* fundar; construir; (*opinion*) fundamentar. **foundation** *n* (*establishment*) fundación *f*; (*building*) cimientos *m pl*; (*fig*) fundamento *m*. **founder** fundador, -a *m, f*.

founder ['faundə] *v* (*ship*) hundirse; (*fall*) derrumbarse.

foundry ['faundri] *n* fundición *f*.

fountain ['fauntin] *n* fuente *f*. **fountainhead** *n* manantial *m*. **fountain pen** pluma estilográfica *f*.

four [fo:] *nm, adj* cuatro. **four-wheel drive** (*general*) tracción a las cuatro ruedas *f*; (*car*) todoterreno *m* . **fourth** *n, adj* cuarto, -a *m, f*.

fourteen [fo:'ti:n] *nm, adj* catorce. **fourteenth** *n, adj* decimocuarto, -a *m, f*.

fowl [faul] *n* aves de corral *f pl*; (*cock*) gallo *m*; (*hen*) gallina *f*; (*chicken*) pollo *m*.

fox [foks] *n* zorro, -a *m, f*. *v* (*baffle*) desconcertar; (*trick*) engañar. **foxglove** *n* digital *f*. **foxhound** *n* perro raposero *m*. **foxhunting** *n* caza de zorros *f*.

foyer ['foiei] *n* foyer *m*.

fraction ['frakʃən] *n* fracción *f*; pequeña parte *f*. **fractional** *adj* fraccionario.

fracture ['fraktʃə] *n* fractura *f*. *v* fracturarse.

fragile ['fradʒail] *adj* frágil. **fragility** *n* fragilidad.

fragment ['fragmənt; *v* frag'ment] *n* fragmento *m*. *v* fragmentar.

fragrant ['freigrənt] *adj* fragante. **fragrance** *n* fragancia *f*.

frail [freil] *adj* frágil; débil; delicado. **frailty** *n* fragilidad *f*; debilidad *f*; delicadez *f*.

frame [freim] *n* (*building*) armazón *f*; (*picture*) marco *m*; (*bicycle*) cuadro *m*; (*spectacles*) montura *f*; (*film*) imagen *f*. **frame of mind** estado de ánimo *m*. *v* (*enclose*) enmarcar; (*devise*) elaborar; (*shape*) formar; hacer la armazón de.

France [fra:ns] *n* Francia *f*.

franchise ['frantʃaiz] *n* derecho de voto *m*.

frank [fraŋk] *adj* franco; abierto. **frankness** *n* franqueza *f*.

frankfurter ['fraŋkfə:tə] *n* salchicha alemana *f*.

frantic ['frantik] *adj* frenético; loco.

fraternal [frə'tə:nl] *adj* fraternal. **fraternity** *n* (*brotherhood*) fraternidad *f*; (*association*) asociación *f*; (*religious*) hermandad *f*. **fraternize** *v* fraternizar.

fraud [fro:d] *n* (*law*) fraude *m*; (*deception*) engaño *m*; (*person*) impostor, -a *m, f*. **fraudulent** *adj* fraudulento.

fraught [fro:t] *adj* **fraught with** cargado de.

fray¹ [frei] *v* raer, desgastar.

fray² [frei] *n* (*brawl*) riña *f*; (*fight*) combate *m*.

freak [fri:k] *n* capricho *m*; fantasís *f*; monstruosidad *f*. *adj* imprevisto; extraño.

freckle ['frekl] *n* peca *f*. **freckled** *adj* pecoso.

free [fri:] *adj* libre; gratis; (*loose*) suelto; generoso; sincero; (*manner*) desenvuelto. **free-range** de corral.

free and easy *adj* poco ceremonioso.

freedom ['fri:dəm] *n* libertad *f*; soltura *f*.

free-for-all *n* refriega *f*.

freehand ['fri:hand] *adj* a pulso.

freehold ['fri:hould] *n* propiedad absoluta *f*.

freelance ['fri:la:ns] *n* persona que trabaja independientemente *f*.

freely ['fri:li] *adj* libremente; voluntariamente; gratuitamente.

freemason ['fri:meisn] *n* francmasón *m*. **freemasonry** *n* francmasonería *f*.

freesia ['fri:ziə] *n* fresia *f*.

freestyle ['fri:stail] *n* estilo libre *m*.

free trade *n* librecambio *m*.

free will *n* libre albedrío *m*.

*freeze [fri:z] *v* (*preserve*) congelar; (*chill*) refrigerar; (*from cold*) helarse; (*prices, etc.*) bloquear; (*turn to ice*) helar; (*stand still*) quedarse inmóvil. *n* helada *f*; bloqueo *m*. **freezer** *n* congelador *m*. **freezing** *adj* glacial. **freezing point** punto de congelación *m*.

freight [freit] *n* (*load*) carga *f*; (*transportation*) transporte *m*; (*by ship, plane*) flete *m*; (*other*) mercancías *f pl*. **freight train** tren de mercancías *m*. **freighter** *n* (*ship*) buque de carga *m*; (*aircraft*) avión de carga *m*.

French [frentʃ] *nm, adj* francés. **the French** los franceses. **French bean** judía verde *f.* **French fries** patatas fritas *f.* **French horn** trompa de llaves *f.* **French polish** barniz de muebles *m.* **French window** puerta ventana *f.*

frenzy ['frenzi] *n* frenesí *m*, delirio *m.* **frenzied** *adj* frenético.

frequent ['fri:kwənt; *v* fri'kwent] *adj* frecuente; (*usual*) común. *v* frecuentar. **frequency** *n* frecuencia *f.* **frequently** *adv* frecuentemente.

fresco ['freskou] *n* fresco *m.*

fresh [freʃ] *adj* fresco; (*bread*) tierno; (*water*) dulce; (*air*) puro; (*complexion*) de buen color; (*new*) nuevo. *adv* recientemente. **freshwater** *adj* (*fish*) de aqua dulce. **freshen up** refrescarse. **freshness** *n* frescura *f*; novedad *f.*

fret[1] [fret] *v* irritar; (*complain*) quejarse. **fretful** *adj* mal humorado; (*upset*) apenado.

fret[2] [fret] *n* (*music*) traste *m. v* adornar con calados. **fretsaw** *n* sierra de calar *f.* **fretwork** *n* calado *m.*

friar ['fraiə] *n* fraile *m*, monje *m.* **friary** *n* monasterio *m.*

friction ['frikʃən] *n* fricción *f.*

Friday ['fraidei] *n* viernes *m.* **Good Friday** Viernes Santo *m.*

fridge [fridʒ] *n* nevera *f.*

fried [fraid] *adj* frito.

friend [frend] *n* amigo, -a *m, f.* **make friends with** hacerse amigo de. **the best of friends** muy amigos. **friendliness** *n* simpatía *f.* **friendly** *adj* simpático; amistoso. **friendship** *n* amistad *f.*

frieze [fri:z] *n* friso *m.*

frigate ['frigit] *n* fragata *f.*

fright [frait] *n* susto *m*; miedo *m*; terror *m.* **frighten** *v* asustar. **be frightened** tener miedo. **frightening** *adj* espantoso. **frightful** *adj* horrible; (*fig*) tremendo.

frigid ['fridʒid] *adj* glacial; (*manner*) frío; (*med*) frígido. **frigidity** *n* frialdad *f*; (*med*) frigidez *f.*

frill [fril] *n* (*shirt*) pechera *f*; (*fluting*) encañonado *m*; (*flared edge*) volante *m*; (*ruff*) gorguera *f.* **frilly** *adj* con volantes.

fringe [frindʒ] *n* franja *f.*; (*edge*) borde *m.* **fringe benefits** beneficios complementa-

rios *m pl. v* franjar.

frisk [frisk] *v* brincar; (*coll: search*) cachear. **friskiness** *n* viveza *f.* **frisky** *adj* juguetón.

fritter[1] ['fritə] *v* **fritter away** malgastar.

fritter[2] ['fritə] *n* (*cookery*) buñuelo *m.*

frivolity [fri'voliti] *n* frivolidad *f.* **frivolous** *adj* frívolo; trivial.

frizz [friz] *v* (*hair*) rizar. **frizzy** *adj* crespo.

fro [frou] *adv* **to and fro** de un lado a otro. **go to and fro** ir y venir.

frock [frok] *n* vestido *m.*

frog [frog] *n* rana *f.* **frogman** *n* hombre rana *m.* **frogs' legs** ancas de rana *f pl.* **have a frog in one's throat** tener carraspera.

frolic ['frolik] *n* juego *m*; diversión *f. v* juguetear; divertirse. **frolicsome** *adj* juguetón.

from [from] *prep* de; desde; (*made from*) con; (*steal, buy, take, etc.*) a; (*drink, learn*) en; (*speak, act*) por; (*according to*) según.

front [frʌnt] *n* (*building*) fachada *f*; (*shop*) escaparate *m*; parte delantera *f*; principio *m*; (*face*) cara *f*; (*weather*) frente *m.* **front door** puerta principal *f.* **in front of** delante de. *adj* delantero; principal; primero.

frontier ['frʌntiə] *n* frontera *f. adj* fronterizo.

frost [frost] *n* escarcha *f*; helada *f.* **frostbite** *n* congelación *f.* **frostbitten** *adj* congelado. *v* cubrir de escarcha. **frosted glass** vidrio deslustrado *m.* **frosty** *adj* escarchado; helado.

froth [froθ] *n* espuma *f*; (*fig*) frivolidad *f. v* espumar. **frothy** *adj* espumoso; frívolo.

frown [fraun] *n* ceño *m. v* fruncir el entrecejo. **frown on** *or* **upon** desaprobar. **frowning** *adj* severo; amenazador.

froze [frouz] *V* **freeze**.

frozen ['frouzn] *adj* congelado, helado. **frozen food** comestibles congelados *m pl.*

frugal ['fru:gəl] *adj* frugal; sobrio. **frugality** *n* frugalidad *f*; sobriedad *f.*

fruit [fru:t] *n* (*on tree*) fruto *m*, (*as food*) fruta *f.* **fruit cake** pastel de fruta *m.* **fruit machine** máquina tragaperras *f.* **fruit salad** ensalada de frutas *f. v* dar fruto. **fruitful** *adj* fructífero; (*fig*) fructuoso. **fruition** *n* fruición *f*; realización *f*; (*bot*) fructificación *f.*

frustrate [frʌ'streit] *v* (*plans, etc.*) frustrar; impedir.

*fry [frai] v freír. **frying pan** sartén f.

fuchsia ['fjuːʃə] n fucsia f.

fuck [fʌk] v (impol) joder.

fudge [fʌdʒ] v fallar; inventar.

fuel ['fjuəl] n combustible m; gasolina f: (mot) carburante f. **fuel gauge** indicador del nivel de gasolina m. **fuel pump** gasolinera f. v (mot) echar gasolina a; (furnace) alimentar; (ship) abastecer de combustible.

fugitive ['fjuːdʒitiv] n, adj fugativo, -a.

fulcrum ['fulkrəm] n fulcro m.

fulfil [ful'fil] v (promise, obligation) cumplir; (ambition) realizar; (purpose) servir; (wishes) satisfacer; (function) desempeñar; (plan) llevar a cabo. **fulfilment** n cumplimiento m; realización f; satisfacción f; (instructions) ejecución f.

full [ful] adj lleno; completo; (text) íntegro; (whole) entero; (price) sin descuento; (extensive) extenso; (daylight, development) pleno; (speed) todo; (capacity) máximo; (measure, weight) exacto; (flavour) mucho. **full employment** pleno empleo m. **full up** completamente lleno. **I'm full** no puedo más. **in full colour** a todo color.

full-blooded adj (thoroughbred) de pura sangre; (robust) vigoroso; (true blue) verdadero.

full-bodied adj (wine) de mucho cuerpo.

full-dress adj de etiqueta; de gala.

full-grown adj crecido; adulto.

full-hearted adj completo.

full house n (theatre or cinema notice) no hay localidades.

full-length adj de cuerpo entero.

full-scale adj de tamaño natural.

full stop n punto m.

full-time adj de jornada completa.

fumble ['fʌmbl] v tojetear; (drop) dejar caer; (feel) hurgar; (search) buscar.

fume [fjuːm] v (fig) bufar de cólera. **fumes** pl n nhumo m.

fun [fʌn] n alegría f; gracia f; diversión f. **for fun** en broma. **funfair** n parque de atracciones m. **have fun** divertirse. **make fun of** reírse de. **what fun!** ¡qué divertido!

function ['fʌŋkʃən] n función f; acto m; recepción f. v funcionar. **functional** adj funcional.

fund [fʌnd] n fondo m; (source) fuente f.

fundamental [fʌndə'mentl] adj fundamental.

funeral ['fjuːnərəl] n funeral m; (state) exequias nacionales f pl. **funeral parlour** funeraria f. **funeral procession** cortejo fúnebre m. **funeral service** misa de cuerpo presente f.

fungus ['fʌŋgəs] n, pl **-i** (bot) hongo m; (med) fungo m.

funnel ['fʌnl] n (pourer) embudo; (smokestack) chimenea f. v verter por un embudo; (direct) encauzar.

funny ['fʌni] adj divertido; gracioso; (curious) extraño. **taste funny** tener un sabor extraño. **funny business** cosas varas f pl. **funny-bone** hueso de la alegría m. **funnily** adv graciosamente.

fur [fəː] n pelo m; (pelt) piel f; (kettle) sarro m; (tongue) saburra f. **fur coat** abrigo de pieles m. v forrar con pieles; incrustar; cubrir de sarro. **furrier** n peletero m; (shop) peletería f. **furry** adj peludo; sarroso.

furious ['fjuəriəs] adj furioso; violento.

furnace ['fəːnis] n horno m; (domestic) estufa f; (boiler) hogar m.

furnish ['fəːniʃ] v (house) amueblar; (supply) suministrar; (give) facilitar; (opportunity) dar; (proof) aducir. **furnishings** pl n muebles m pl; mobiliario m.

furniture ['fəːnitʃə] n muebles m pl. **furniture van** camión de mudanzas m.

furrow ['fʌrou] n (ploughing) surco m; (forehead) arruga f; (groove) ranura f. v surcar; arrugar.

further ['fəːðə] adj (distant, additional) otro; (another) nuevo; (later) posterior; (education) superior. adv más; más lejos, más allá; (moreover) además. v favorecer. **furtherance** n adelantamiento m; formento m. **furthermore** adv además. **furthermost** adj más lejano. **furthest** adj más lejano; extremo.

furtive ['fəːtiv] adj furtivo.

fury ['fjuəri] n furia f, furor m.

fuse¹ [fjuːz] n (elec) fusible m. **fuse box** caja de fusibles f. v (join) fusionar; (melt) fundir.

fuse² [fjuːz] n (explosives) mecha f; (detonator) espoleta f.

fuselage ['fjuːzəˌlɑːʒ] n fuselaje m.

fusion ['fjuːʒən] n fusión f.

fuss [fʌs] n (trouble) lío m; (commotion) alboroto m; (complaints) quejas f pl. **a lot of fuss about nothing** mucho ruido y pocas nueces. v agitarse; quejarse; preocuparse; molestar. **fussiness** n agitación f. **fussy** adj escrupuloso; exigente; melindroso.

futile ['fju:tail] *adj* vano; frívolo.

future ['fju:tʃə] *n* futuro *m*; porvenir *m*. *adj* futuro; venidero.

fuzz [fʌz] *n* (*on face*) vello *m*; (*fluff*) pelusa *f*. **fuzzy** *adj* velloso; (*blurred*) borroso.

G

gabble ['gabl] *v* chacharear. *n* cháchara *f*. **gabbler** *n* chacharero, -a *m*, *f*.

gable ['geibl] *n* gablete *m*.

gadget ['gadʒit] *n* aparato *m*; accesorio *m*.

Gaelic ['geilik] *adj* gaélico

gag¹ [gag] *v* amordazar. *n* mordaza *f*.

gag² [gag] *n* (*joke*) broma *f*; chiste *m*.

gaiety ['geiəti] *n* alegría *f*; jovialidad *f*.

gain [gein] *n* ganancia *f*; provecho *m*; aumento *m*, *v* ganar; avanzar.

gait [geit] *n* modo de andar *m*.

gala ['ga:lə] *n* fiesta *f*, gala *f*.

galaxy ['galəksi] *n* galaxia *f*.

gale [geil] *n* vendaval *m*.

gallant ['galənt] *adj* (*to women*) galante; (*brave*) valiente; (*stately*) elegante. **gallantry** *n* galantería *f*; valor *m*; (*courtesy*) cortesía *f*.

gall bladder ['go:l,bladə] *n* vesícula biliar *f*.

galleon ['galiən] *n* galeón *m*.

gallery ['galəri] *n* galería *f*; (*spectators*) tribuna *f*; (*theatre*) gallinero *m*.

galley ['gali] *n* (*ship*) galera *f*; (*kitchen*) cocina *f*.

gallon ['galən] *n* galón *m*.

gallop ['galəp] *n* galope *m*. *v* galopar.

gallows ['galouz] *pl n* cadalso *m sing*.

gallstone ['go:lstoun] *n* cálculo biliar *m*.

galore [gə'lo:] *adj*, *adv* en cantidad.

galvanize ['galvənaiz] *v* galvanizar.

gamble ['gambl] *v* (*bet*) apostar; (*risk*) arriesgar. **gamble on** contar con. *n* (*risky enterprise*) empresa arriesgada *f*; (*game*) jugada *f*. **gambler** *n* jugador, -a *m*, *f*. **gambling** *n* juego *m*. **gambling den** garito *m*.

game [geim] *n* juego *m*; (*sport*) deporte *m*; (*of football, tennis, etc.*) partido *m*; (*cards, chess, etc.*) partida *f*; (*hunting*) caza *f*. **game**

bird ave de caza *f*. **gamekeeper** *n* guardabosque *m*. **play the game** jugar limpio. *adj* (*coll*) valiente.

gammon ['gamən] *n* jamón ahumado *m*.

gang [gaŋ] *n* (*band*) cuadrilla *f*; (*of gangsters*) banda *f*. *v* **gang up on** conspirar contra. **gangster** *n* gángster *m*.

gangrene ['gaŋgri:n] *n* gangrena *f*. **gangrenous** *adj* gangrenoso.

gangway ['gaŋwei] *n* (*passage*) pasillo *m*; (*naut*) pasarela *f*.

gaol *V* **jail**.

gap [gap] *n* (*empty space*) vacío *m*; (*breach*) brecha *f*; (*cavity*) hueco *m*; (*in a wall*) portillo *m*; (*between hills*) quebrada *f*; (*in education*) laguna *f*; (*crack*) resquicio *m*; (*in a wood*) claro *m*. **gap year** año sabático *m*.

gape [geip] *v* (*stare*) quedarse boquiabierto; (*open wide*) abrirse mucho.

garage ['gara:dʒ] *n* garaje *m*.

garbage ['ga:bidʒ] *n* basura *f*. **garbage can** cubo de la basura *m*. **garbage disposal** vertedero de basuras *m*. **garbage man** basurero *m*.

garble ['ga:bl] *v* amañar; mutilar. **garbled** *adj* amañado; mutilado.

garden ['ga:dn] *n* jardín *m*; huerto *m*. *v* cultivar un huerto. **garden city** ciudad jardín *f*. **garden party** recepción al aire libre *f*. **garden produce** hortalizas *f pl*. **gardener** *n* jardinero, -a *m*, *f*. **gardening** *n* jardinería *f*.

gargle ['ga:gl] *v* hacer gárgaras. *n* gárgaras *f pl*.

garish ['geəriʃ] *adj* chillón

garland ['ga:lənd] *n* guirnalda *f*. *v* enguirnaldar.

garlic ['ga:lik] *n* ajo *m*.

garment ['ga:mənt] *n* prenda *f*, traje *m*, vestido *m*.

garnish ['ga:niʃ] *v* adornar, embellecer; (*cookery*) aderezar. *n* adorno *m*; aderezo *m*.

garrison ['garisn] *n* guarnición *f*. *v* guarnecer.

garter ['ga:tə] *n* liga *f*. **Order of the Garter** orden de la jarretera *f*.

gas [gas] *n* gas *m*; (*petrol*) gasolina *f*, bencina *f*. **step on the gas** (*coll*) acelerar. *v* asfixiar con gas. **gaseous** *adj* gaseoso. **gas burner** *n* mechero de gas *m*. **gas fire** *n* estufa de gas *f*. **gas main** *n* cañería maestra de gas *f*. **gas mask** *n* máscara para gases *f*. **gas**

meter *n* contador de gas *m*. **gas pipe** *n* cañería de gas *f*. **gas ring** *n* fogón de gas *m*. **gas stove** *n* cocina de gas *f*. **gasworks** *n* fábrica de gas *f*.

gash [gaʃ] *n* herida *f*; cuchillada *f*. *v* acuchillar.

gasket ['gaskit] *n* junta de culata *f*.

gasoline ['gasə‚lim] *n* gasolina *f*.

gasp [ga:sp] *n* (*breathing difficulty*) jadeo *m*; (*surprise*) boqueada *f*. *v* jadear; boquear.

gastric ['gastrik] *adj* gástrico. **gastric fever** fiebre gástrica *f*. **gastric juice** jugo gástrico. **gastric ulcer** úlcera gástrica *f*. **gastritis** *n* gastritis *f*. **gastroenteritis** *n* gastroenteritis *f*.

gastronomic [gastrə'nomik] *adj* gastronómico. **gastronomy** *n* gastronomía *f*.

gate [geit] *n* puerta *f*, entrada *f*; (*metal*) verja *f*; (*level-crossing*) barrera *f*. **gatecrash** *v* asistir sin invitación. **gatekeeper** *n* portero, -a *m*, *f*. **gatepost** *n* soporte de la puerta *m*. **gateway** *n* entrada *f*, paso *m*.

gateau ['gatou] *n pl* **-x** tarta *f*.

gather ['gaðə] *v* coger, amontonar; (*strength*) cobrar; (*harvest*) cosechar; (*understand*) colegir; (*money*) recaudar; (*sewing*) fruncir. **gather together** reunirse, congregarse. **gathering** *n* reunión *f*, afluencia *f*.

gaudy ['go:di] *adj* chillón, cursi.

gauge [geidʒ] *n* (*rail*) entrevía *f*; (*gun*) calibre *m*; (*measure*) indicador *m*; (*fig*) medida *f*. *v* medir, juzgar; calibrar. **broad/narrow gauge railway** ferrocarril de vía ancha/estrecha *m*. **pressure gauge** manómetro *m*.

gaunt [go:nt] *adj* demacrado; (*grim*) feroz; (*fig*) lúgubre.

gauze [go:z] *n* gasa *f*.

gave [geiv] *V* **give**.

gay [gei] *adj* alegre; gozoso; (*dress*) guapo; (*event*) festivo; (*coll*) homosexual. *n* (*coll*: *homosexual*) maricón *m*.

gaze [geiz] *v* mirar fijamente. *n* mirada fija *f*.

gazelle [gə'zel] *n* gacela *f*.

gazetteer [gazə'tiə] *n* gacetero *m*.

gear [giə] *n* (*mech*) engranaje *m*, juego *m*, marcha *f*; (*dress*) traje *m*; (*tackle*) utensilios *m pl*; (*naut*) aparejo *m*. **gearbox** caja de velocidades *f*. **gear lever** palanca de cambio de velocidad. **in gear** engranado. *v* aparejar; engranar; adaptar.

geese [gi:s] *V* **goose**.

gel [dʒel] *n* gomina *f*.

gelatine ['dʒelə‚ti:n] *n* gelatina *f*.

gelignite ['dʒelig‚nait] *n* gelignita *f*.

gem [dʒem] *n* joya *f*, gema *f*; (*delight*) preciosidad *f*.

Gemini ['dʒemini] *n* Géminis *m*.

gender ['dʒendə] *n* género *m*; sexo *m*.

gene [dʒi:n] *n* gene *m*.

genealogy [dʒi:ni‚alədʒi] *n* genealogía *f*. **genealogical** *adj* genealógico.

general ['dʒenərəl] *nm, adj* general. **general election** elección general *f*. **general opinion** voz común *f*. **general practitioner** médico, -a general *m*, *f*. **in general** generalmente. **generalization** *n* generalización *f*. **generalize** *v* generalizar.

generate ['dʒenəreit] *v* producir; (*elec*) generar. **generation** *n* generación *f*. **generator** *n* generador *m*; dínamo *m*.

generic [dʒi'nerik] *adj* genérico.

generous ['dʒenərəs] *adj* generoso; magnánimo. **generosity** *n* generosidad *f*; liberalidad *f*.

genetic [dʒi'netik] *adj* genético. **genetics** *n* genética *f*. **genetically modified** transgénico.

Geneva [dʒi'ni:və] *n* Ginebra *f*. **Lake Geneva** Lago de Ginebra.

genial ['dʒi:niəl] *adj* genial, cordial.

genital ['dʒenitl] *adj* genital. **genitals** *pl n* genitales *m pl*.

genitive ['dʒenitiv] *nm, adj* genitivo.

genius ['dʒi:njəs] *n* genio *m*.

genteel [dʒen'ti:l] *adj* fino; melindroso.

gentle ['dʒentl] *adj* (*light*) ligero; (*mild*) suave; (*slow*) lento; (*tame*) manso; (*moderate*) moderado; (*friendly*) amable; (*kind*) bondadoso. **gentleman** *n* caballero *m*, señor *m*. **gentlemen** *pl n* (*in correspondence*) muy señores míos, muy señores nuestros *m pl*. **gentleness** *n* amabilidad *f*; bondad *f*; suavidad *f*.

gentry ['dʒentri] *n* pequeña nobleza *f*.

gents [dʒents] *n* (*sign*) caballeros *m pl*.

genuine ['dʒenjuin] *adj* puro; genuino; verdadero; auténtico.

genus ['dʒi:nəs] *n* género *m*.

geography [dʒi'ogrəfi] *n* geografía *f*. **geographer** *n* geógrafo, -a *m*, *f*. **geographic** *adj also* **geographical** geográfico.

geology [dʒi'olədʒi] n geología f. **geological** adj geológico. **geologist** n geólogo, -a m, f.

geometry [dʒi'omətri] n geometría f. **geometrical** adj geométrico.

geranium [dʒə'reiniəm] n geranio m.

geriatric [dʒeri'atrik] adj geriátrico. **geriatrics** n geriatría f.

germ [dʒə:m] n (med) bacilo m; microbio m; (fig) germen m.

Germany ['dʒə:məni] n Alemania f. **German** n, adj alemán, -ana m, f. **German measles** rubéola f. **Germanic** adj germánico.

germinate ['dʒə:mineit] v germinar, brotar. **germination** n germinación f.

gerund ['dʒerənd] n gerundio m.

gesticulate [dʒe'stikju,leit] v gesticular. **gesticulation** n gesticulación f.

gesture ['dʒestʃə] v gesticular. n gesto m.

*get [get] v obtener; tener; recibir; (fetch) buscar; (buy) comprar; (call) llamar; (find) encontrar; (catch, reproduce) coger; (bring) llevar; (extract) sacar; (succeed) conseguir; (coll: understand) llegar a comprender; (coll: kill) matar. **get about** desplazarse. **get across** (cross) atravesar; hacer comprender. **get at** (reach) alcanzar; (tease) meterse con. **get back** (return) volver; (recover) récobrar. **get by** (manage) arreglárselas. **get down** (descend) bajar; (write) poner por escrito. **get down to** ponerse a. **get off** bajarse de; escapar. **get on** (mount) subir a; (progress) progresar; (agree) llevarse bien; (grow old) envejecer. **get out** salir; (fig) sacar. **get up** (arise) levantarse; (climb) subirse. **getaway** n huida f.

geyser ['gi:zə] n (hot spring) géiser m; (water-heater) calentador de agua m.

ghastly ['ga:stli] adj horroroso; (pale) de una palidez mortal.

gherkin ['gə:kin] n cohombrillo m.

ghetto ['getou] n gueto m; judería f.

ghost [goust] n fantasma m; espectro; (spirit) alma f. **ghost writer** escritor fantasma m. **Holy Ghost** Espíritu Santo m. **give up the ghost** entregar el alma. **ghostly** adj espectral. **ghostliness** n espiritualidad f.

giant ['dʒaiənt] nm, adj gigante.

gibberish ['dʒibəriʃ] n galimatías m invar.

gibe [dʒaib] n mofa f. v **jibe** at mofarse de.

giblets ['dʒiblits] pl n menudillos m pl.

giddy ['gidi] adj (dizzy) mareado; (height) vertiginoso; (scatter-brained) frívolo. **giddiness** n mareo m, vértigo m.

gift [gift] n regalo m; (talent) don m; (offering) ofrenda f. **gift token** vale para comprar un regalo m. **gifted** adj dotado; talentoso.

gigantic [dʒai'gantik] adj gigantesco.

giggle ['gigl] v reirse tontamente. n risita f. **the giggles** la risa tonta f sing.

gill [gil] n (fish) branquia f; (plant) laminilla f; (measure) medida de líquidos f.

gilt [gilt] nm, adj dorado. **gilt-edged** (book) con cantos dorados. **gilt-edged securities** valores de máxima garantía m pl.

gimmick ['gimik] n (coll: gadget) artefacto m; (coll: trick) truco m.

gin [dʒin] n ginebra f.

ginger ['dʒindʒə] n jengibre m. **ginger beer** gaseosa de jengibre f. **gingerbread** n pan de jengibre m. adj (hair) rojizo. v (coll) animar.

gingerly ['dʒindʒəli] adv delicadamente.

gipsy ['dʒipsi] n gitano, -a m, f.

giraffe [dʒi'ra:f] n jirafa f.

girder ['gə:də] n viga f.

girdle ['gə:dl] n (belt) cinturón m; (corset) faja f. v ceñir; (fig) rodear.

girl [gə:l] n niña f; chica f; muchacha f; señorita f. **girlfriend** n amiguita f, novia f. **girlhood** n niñez f; juventud f. **girlish** adj de niña; (of boys) afeminado.

girth [gə:θ] n circunferencia f; (waist, etc.) gordura f; (saddle) cincha f.

gist [dʒist] n esencia f, importe m.

*give [giv] v dar; (offer as a present) regalar; (deliver) entregar; (hand over) pasar; (provide with) proveer de; (grant) conceder; (infect) contagiar; (communicate) comunicar; (a speech) pronunciar; (med: administer) poner; (telephone: connect with) poner con. **give-and-take** n toma y daca m. **give away** distribuir; regalar; revelar. **giveaway** n revelación f. **give back** devolver. **give in** darse por vencido; ceder; (hand in) entregar. **give off** despedir. **give out** distribuir; emitir; anunciar; divulgar; (run out) agotarse. **give up** abandonar; renunciar a; rendirse; entregar; ceder. **give way to** retirarse ante; abandonarse a.

glacier ['glasiə] n glaciar m. **glaciation** n glaciación f.

glad [glad] *adj* feliz, alegre. **be glad** alegrarse. **gladden** *v* regocijar. **gladly** *adv* alegremente.

glamour [glamə] *n* encanto *m*. **glamorous** *adj* encantador.

glance [glaːns] *n* (*look*) vistazo *m*, ojeada *f*; (*light*) vislumbre *f*; (*projectile*) desviación *f*. *v* echar un vistazo, ojear; relumbrar; desviarse.

gland [gland] *n* glándula *f*. **glandular** *adj* glandular. **glandular fever** fiebre glandular *f*.

glare [gleə] *n* (*look*) mirada feroz *f*; (*dazzle*) deslumbramiento *m*. *v* mirar con ferocidad; deslumbrar. **glaring** *adj* feroz; deslumbrante; resplandeciente; (*conspicuous*) manifiesto.

glass [glaːs] *n* vidrio *m*; cristal *m*; (*for drinking*) vaso *m*; (*mirror*) espejo *m*; (*lens*) lente *f*. **glasses** *pl n* gafas *f pl*. **glassware** *n* cristalería *f*. **glassworks** *n* fábrica de cristal y vidrio *f*. **glassy** *adj* vitreo; (*eyes*) vidrioso; (*smooth*) liso.

glaze [gleiz] *v* (*pottery*) vidriar; (*window*) poner cristales a; (*cookery*) glasear. *n* vidriado *m*; brillo *m*. **glazier** *n* vidriero *m*.

gleam [gliːm] *n* rayo *m*. *v* relucir. **gleaming** reluciente.

glean [gliːn] *v* espigar.

glee [gliː] *n* alegría *f*. **gleeful** *adj* alegre.

glib [glib] *adj* locuaz; fácil. **glibly** *adv* con labia.

glide [glaid] *v* (*aero*) planear; (*slide*) resbalar. **glide away** escurrirse. *n* planeo *m*; (*slide*) deslizamiento *m*. **glider** *n* planeador *m*.

glimmer ['glimə] *n* luz trémula *f*; (*fig*) vislumbre *m*. *v* brillar con luz trémula.

glimpse [glimps] *v* entrever. *n* vistazo *m*. **catch a glimpse of** vislumbrar.

glint [glint] *n* destello *m*. *v* destellar.

glisten ['glisn] *v* relucir. **glistening** *adj* reluciente.

glitter ['glitə] *v* brillar. *n* brillo *m*. **glittering** *adj* brillante.

gloat [glout] *v* **gloat over** recrearse con.

globe [gloub] *n* globo *m*. **globe artichoke** alcachofa *f*. **globe-trotter** *n* trotamundos *m invar*. **global** *adj* global; mundial. **global warming** calentamiento global *m*.

gloom [gluːm] *n* oscuridad *f*; (*fig*) melancolía *f*. **gloomy** *adj* oscuro; melancólico.

glory ['gloːri] *n* gloria *f*; esplendor *m*. **glorify** *v* glorificar. **glorious** *adj* glorioso: espléndido.

gloss [glos] *n* brillo *m*; lustre *m*; (*fig*) apariencia *f*. *v* **gloss over** disculpar.

glossary ['glosəri] *n* glosario *m*.

glove [glʌv] *n* guante *m*. **boxing gloves** *pl n* guantes de boxeo *m pl*. **glove compartment** guantera *f*. **fit like a glove** sentar como anillo al dedo. **be hand in glove with** juntar diestra con diestra. *v* enguantar.

glow [glou] *v* (*shine*) brillar.

glucose ['gluːkous] *n* glucosa *f*.

glue [gluː] *n* cola *f*. *v* pegar.

glum [glʌm] *adj* deprimido, sombrío.

glut [glʌt] *n* exceso *m*. *v* hartar.

glutton ['glʌtən] *n* glotón, -ona *m, f*. **gluttonous** *adj* glotón. **gluttony** *n* glotonería *f*.

GM *n* alimentos transgénicos *m* (*pl*)

gnarled [naːld] *adj* nudoso; (*person*) curtido.

gnash [naʃ] *v* **gnash one's teeth** crujir los dientes.

gnat [nat] *n* mosquito *m*.

gnaw [noː] *v* roer. **gnawing** *adj* roedor.

gnome [noum] *n* gnomo *m*.

*go [gou] *v* ir; (*depart*) irse; (*lead to*) conducir a; (*go towards*) dirigirse a; (*leave*) dejar; (*vanish*) desaparecer; (*be removed*) quitarse; (*turn, become*) ponerse; (*function*) funcionar. **go off** (*leave*) marcharse; (*rot*) estropearse; (*gun*) dispararse. **go out** salir; (*lights, fire, etc.*) apagarse. **go round** dar la vuelta. **go with** acompañar; (*harmonize*) hacer juego con. **go without** (*manage*) arreglárselas. *n* (*coll*) energía *f*. **it's your go** te toca a ti. **on the go** ocupado. **go-between** *n* intermediario, -a *m, f*.

goad [goud] *v* aguijar; (*fig*) incitar; *n* garrocha *f*; (*fig*) estímulo *m*.

goal [goul] *n* (*structure*) meta *f*; (*score*) gol *m*; (*destination*) destinación *f*; (*purpose*) objeto *m*. **goalkeeper** *n* portero, -a *m, f*; **goalpost** *n* poste *m*.

goat [gout] *n* (*nanny*) cabra *f*; (*billy*) cabrón *m*.

gobble ['gobl] *v* engullir.

goblin ['goblin] *n* trasgo *m*, duende *m*.

god [god] *n* dios *m*. **by God!** ¡vive Dios! **for God's sake** por el amor de dios. **god-**

daughter n ahijada f. **godfather** padrino m. **godmother** n madrina f. **godsend** n don del cielo m. **godson** n ahijado m. **goddess** n diosa f.

goggles ['goglz] pl n anteojos m pl.

goings-on [,gouɪŋz'on] pl n (coll) tejemanejes m pl.

gold [gould] n oro m. **golden** adj dorado; de oro.

goldfinch ['gouldfɪntʃ] n jilguero m.

goldfish ['gouldfɪʃ] n pez de colores m. **goldfish bowl** pecera f.

goldsmith ['gouldsmiθ] n orfebre m, f.

golf [golf] n golf m. **golf course** campo de golf m. **golfer** n golfista m, f.

gondola ['gondələ] n góndola f. **gondolier** n gondolero m.

gone [gon] V go.

gong [goŋ] n gong m.

gonorrhoea [,gonə'riə] n gonorrea f.

good [gud] adj bueno; (before m sing nouns) buen; (wholesome) sano; (pleasant) amable; (genuine) legítmo; (virtuous) virtuoso. n bien m. **no good** inútil. **for good** para siempre. **goodness** n bondad f. **good-looking** adj guapo.

good afternoon interj buenas tardes f pl.

goodbye [gud'bai] interj ¡adiós!

good evening interj buenas tardes f pl.

good-for-nothing n(m + f). adj inútil.

Good Friday n Viernes Santo m.

good morning interj buenos días m pl.

good night interj buenas noches f pl.

goods [gudz] pl n (comm) artículos m pl; (possessions) bienes m pl. **goods and chattels** muebles y enseres m pl. **goods train** tren de mercancías m.

goose [gu:s] n, pl **geese** ganso m, oca f.

gooseberry ['guzbəri] n (fruit) grosella espinosa f; (bush) grosellero espinoso m.

gore[1] [go:] v cornear.

gore[2] [go:] n sangre f.

gorge [go:dʒ] n cañón m. v hartarse.

gorgeous ['go:dʒəs] adj magnífico.

gorilla [gə'rilə] n gorila m.

gorse [go:s] n tojo m.

gory ['go:ri] adj ensangrentado.

gospel ['gospəl] n evangelio m.

gossip ['gosip] n (chat) charla f; (unkind) chisme m; (person) murmurador, -a m, f; chismoso, -a m, f. **gossip column** ecos de

sociedad m pl. v (talk scandal) cotillear; (chatter) charlar.

got [got] V get.

Gothic ['goθik] adj gótico.

goulash ['gu:laʃ] n estofado húngaro m.

gourd [guəd] n calabaza f.

gourmet ['guəmei] n gastrónomo, -a m, f.

gout [gaut] n gota f.

govern ['gʌvən] v (rule) gobernar; (administer) dirigir; (determine) guiar; (restrain) dominar; (prevail) prevalecer. **governess** n aya f. **government** n gobierno m. **governor** n gobernador, -a m, f; administrador, -a m, f; (coll: boss) jefe m.

gown [gaun] n traje largo m; (law, university) toga f. **dressing gown** bata f.

GP n médico de cabecera m

grab [grab] v agarrar, arrebatar. n asimiento m, presa f; (mech) gancho m.

grace [greis] n gracia f, elegancia; (courtesy) cortesía f; (kindness) bondad f; (forgiveness) perdón m; (before meals) bendición de la mesa f; (favour) favor m; (delay) plazo m. **graceful** adj elegante; gracioso; cortés. **gracious** adj gracioso; grato.

grade [greid] n grado m; (persons, things) clase f; (mark) nota f; (gradient) pendiente f. v graduar; (goods) clasificar.

gradient ['greidiənt] n (declivity) decline m; (slope) cuesta f.

gradual ['gradjuəl] adj gradual. **gradually** (adv) gradualmente.

graduate ['gradjuət; v 'gradjueit] n, adj graduado, -a. v graduarse; diplomarse. **graduation** n graduación f.

graft [gra:ft] n injerto m. v injertarse.

grain [grein] n grano m; (wood) fibra f.

gram [gram] n gramo m.

grammar ['gramə] n gramática f. **grammar school** instituto de segunda enseñanza m. **grammatical** adj gramático.

gramophone ['graməfoun] n gramófono m; tocadiscos m invar.

granary ['granəri] n granero m.

grand [grand] adj magnífico; grande; importante; esplédido. **grandiose** adj grandioso.

granddad n also **grandpa** (coll) abuelito m.

grandchild ['grantʃaild] n nieto, -a m, f.

grandfather ['gran,fa:ðə] n abuelo m.

grandma ['granma:] *n also* **granny** (*coll*) abuelita *f*.

grandmother ['gran,mʌðə] *n* abuela *f*.

grandparent ['gran,peərənt] *n* abuelo, -a *m, f*.

grand piano *n* piano de cola *m*.

grandstand ['granstand] *n* tribuna *f*.

granite ['granit] *n* granito *m*. *adj* granítico.

grant [gra:nt] *v* conceder; (*agree to*) acceder; (*bestow*) otorgar; (*assume*) suponer. *n* concesión *f*; otorgamiento *m*; (*student*) beca *f*.

granule ['granju:l] *n* gránulo *m*. **granulated sugar** azúcar en polvo *m*.

grape [greip] *n* uva *f*. **grapevine** *n* vid *f*; (*coll*) rumores *m pl*.

grapefruit ['greipfru:t] *n* pomelo *m*.

graph [graf] *n* gráfica *f*. **graph paper** papel cuadriculado *m*. **graphic** *adj* gráfico. **graphics** gráficos *m pl*.

grapple ['grapl] *v* **grapple with** (*fight*) luchar cuerpo a cuerpo; (*fig*) intentar a resolver.

grasp [gra:sp] *v* agarrar; (*fig*) comprender. *n* agarro *m*; (*reach*) alcance *m*. **grasping** *adj* avaro.

grass [gra:s] *n* hierba *f*; (*pasture*) pasto *m*; (*lawn*) césped *m*. **grasshopper** *n* saltamontes *m*. **grass snake** culebra *f*. **grassy** *adj* cubierto de hierba; (*like grass*) herbáceo.

grate[1] [greit] *n* parrilla *f*. **grating** *n* rejilla *f*.

grate[2] [greit] *v* rallar; (*teeth*) hacer rechinar. **grater** *n* rallador *m*.

grateful ['greitful] *adj* agradecido.

gratify ['grati,fai] *v* satisfacer; (*please*) agradar. **gratifying** *adj* satisfactorio; agradable.

gratitude ['gratitju:d] *n* agradecimiento *m*.

gratuity [grə'tjuəti] *n* propina *f*.

grave[1] [greiv] *n* sepultura *f*; (*monument*) tumba *f*. **gravedigger** *n* sepulturero *m*. **gravestone** *n* lápida sepulcral *f*. **graveyard** *n* cementerio *m*.

grave[2] [greiv] *adj* grave, serio.

gravel ['gravəl] *n* grava *f*.

gravity ['gravəti] *n* (*force*) gravedad *f*; (*seriousness*) solemnidad *f*.

gravy ['greivi] *n* salsa *f*.

graze[1] [greiz] *v* (*scrape*) raspar; (*rub*) rozar. *n* rozadura *f*.

graze[2] [greiz] *v* pastar.

grease [gri:s] *n* grasa *f*. **greasepaint** *n* maquillaje *m*. **greaseproof paper** papel vegetal *m*. *v* engrasar. **greasy** *adj* grasiento; (*slippery*) resbaladizo.

great [greit] *adj* gran, grande; famoso; poderoso; magnífico. **greatly** *adv* grandemente, enormemente. **greatness** *n* grandeza *f*.

great-aunt *n* tía abuela *f*.

Great Britain *n* Gran Bretaña *f*.

Great Dane *n* perro danés *m*.

great-grandchild *n* biznieto, -a *m, f*.

great-grandfather *n* bisabuelo *m*.

great-grandmother *n* bisabuela *f*.

great-uncle *n* tío abuelo *m*.

Greece [gri:s] *n* Grecia *f*. **Greek** *n, adj* griego, -a *m, f*.

greed [gri:d] *n* avaricia *f*; (*for food*) glotonería *f*. **greedy** *adj* avaro; glotón.

green [gri:n] *adj* verde; (*inexperienced*) novato; (*fresh*) fresco; (*recent*) nuevo. *n* (*colour*) verde *m*; (*meadow*) prado *m*; (*lawn*) césped *m*. **greens** *pl n* verduras *f pl*. **greenery** *n* verdor *m*.

greenfly ['gri:nflai] *n* pulgón *m*.

greengage ['gri:ngeidʒ] *n* ciruela claudia *f*.

greengrocer ['gri:n,grousə] *n* verdulero, -a *m, f*. **greengrocery** *n* verdulería *f*.

greenhouse ['gri:nhaus] *n* invernadero *m*. **greenhouse effect** efecto invernadero *m*.

Greenland ['gri:nlənd] *n* Groenlandia *f*. **Greenlander** ['gri:nləndə] *n* groenlandés, -esa *m, f*.

greet [gri:t] *v* saludar. **greeting** *n* salutación *f*. **greetings** *pl n* recuerdos *m pl*.

gregarious [gri'geə,riəs] *adj* gregario.

grew [gru:] *V* **grow**.

grey [grei] *nm, adj* gris; (*hair*) cano. **go grey** (*hair*) encanecer. **grey-haired** *adj* canoso. **greyhound** *n* galgo *m*.

grid [grid] *n* rejilla *f*; (*elec*) red *f*.

grief [gri:f] *n* pena *f*, dolor *m*. **grief-stricken** *adj* desconsolado.

grieve [gri:v] *v* afligir; lamentar. **grieve for** echar de menos. **grievous** *adj* doloroso; grave; apenado; lamentable. **grievous bodily harm** daños corporales *m pl*.

grill [gril] *v* (*cook*) asar a la parrilla; (*interrogate*) interrogar. *n* parrilla *f*; (*meal*) asado a la parrilla *m*. **grillroom** *n* parrilla *f*.

grille [gril] *n* reja *f*; rejilla *f*.

grim [grim] *adj* feroz; severo; horrible; (*coll*) desagradable. **grimly** *adv* severamente; horriblemente.

grimace [gri'meis] *n* mueca. *v* hacer muecas.

grime [graim] *n* mugre. *f.* **grimy** *adj* mugriento.

*grind [graind] *v* (*coffee, etc.*) moler; (*sharpen*) afilar; (*teeth*) crujir. *n* (*coll*) trabajo pesado *m.* **grinder** *n* afilador *m.* **grindstone** *n* muela *f.* **keep one's nose to the grindstone** batir al yunque.

grip [grip] *n* (*of hand*) mano *f;* (*hold*) agarro *m;* (*bag*) maleta *f;* (*understanding*) comprensión *f.* *v* **asir**; (*wheels*) agarrarse; (*press*) apretar; (*the attention*) atraer. **gripping** *adj* impresionante.

gripe [graip] *v* (*med*) retortijón *m.* *v* (*coll*) quejarse.

grisly ['grizli] *adj* espantoso; horroroso; repugnante.

gristle ['grisl] *n* cartílago *m.*

grit [grit] *n* cascajo *m;* polvo *m;* (*coll: courage*) valor *m.* *v* (*teeth*) rechinar.

groan [groun] *n* gemido *m;* (*dismay*) gruñido *m.* *v* gemir; gruñir.

grocer ['grousə] *n* tendero, -a *m, f.* **groceries** *pl n* comestibles *m pl.* **grocery** *n* tienda de comestibles *f.*

groin [groin] *n* ingle *f.*

groom [gru:m] *n* (*horse*) mozo de caballos *m;* (*of bride*) novio *m.* *v* (*horse*) almohazar; (*smarten*) arreglar.

groove [gru:v] *n* ranura *f,* muesca *f;* (*record*) surco *m;* (*fig*) rutina *f.* *v* hacer ranuras en; estriar. **grooved** *adj* acanalado; estriado. **groovy** *adj* (*coll*) fenómeno.

grope [group] *v* andar a tientas. **grope for** buscar a tientas. **gropingly** *adv* a tientas.

gross [grous] *adj* (*not net*) bruto; (*coarse*) grosero; grueso, denso. *n* gruesa *f.*

grotesque [grə'tesk] *nm, adj* grotesco.

grotto ['grotou] *n* gruta *f.*

ground¹ [graund] *V* **grind**.

ground² [graund] *n* suelo *m;* (*earth*) tierra *f;* (*sport*) campo *m;* (*basis*) base *f;* (*background*) fondo *m;* (*fig*) terreno *m.* *v* poner en tierra; (*teach*) enseñar los rudimentos de. **grounds** *pl n* jardines *m pl;* (*sediment*) sedimento *m sing;* (*reason*) causa *f sing.*

ground control *n* control desde tierra *m.*

ground floor *n* planta baja *f.*

grounding ['graundiŋ] *n* **have a good grounding in** tener una buena base en.

groundless ['graundlis] *adj* sin fundamento.

ground level *n* nivel del suelo *m.*

ground rent *n* alquiler del terreno *m.*

groundsheet ['graundʃi:t] *n* tela impermeable *f.*

groundwork ['graundwə:k] *n* base *f.*

group [gru:p] *n* grupo *m.* *v* agrupar.

grouse¹ [graus] *n* ortega *f.*

grouse² [graus] *v* (*coll*) quejarse.

grove [grouv] *n* boscaje *m.*

grovel ['grovl] *v* arrastrarse; (*fig*) humillarse.

*grow [grou] *v* crecer; (*increase*) aumentar; (*become*) hacerse; (*turn*) ponerse; (*develop*) desarrollarse; (*cultivate*) cultivar. **grown-up** *n* adulto, -a *m, f.* **growth** *n* crecimiento *m;* aumento *m;* desarrollo *m;* (*med*) bulto *m;* vegetación *f.*

growl [graul] *v* gruñir. *n* gruñido *m.*

grub [grʌb] *n* larva *f;* (*coll: food*) comida *f.* *v* cavar. **grubby** *adj* sucio.

grudge [grʌdʒ] *v* envidiar. *n* rencor *m.* **bear a grudge** tener ojeriza. **grudging** *adj* mezquino. **grudgingly** *adv* de mala gana.

gruelling ['gruəliŋ] *adj* penoso; agotador.

gruesome ['gru:səm] *adj* pavoroso, macabro.

gruff [grʌf] *adj* (*manner*) brusco; (*voice*) bronco. **gruffness** *n* brusquedad *f;* bronquedad *f.*

grumble ['grʌmbl] *v* quejarse. *n* queja *f.*

grumpy ['grʌmpi] *adj* malhumorado. **grumpiness** *n* malhumor *m.*

grunt [grʌnt] *v* gruñir. *n* gruñido *m.*

guarantee [garən'ti:] *n* garantía *f.* *v* garantizar. **guarantor** *n* garante *m, f.*

guard [ga:d] *n* (*soldier*) guardia *m;* (*sentry*) centinela *m;* (*escort*) escolta *f;* (*keeper*) guardián *m;* (*train*) jefe de tren *m;* (*protection*) defensa *f;* (*watchfulness*) vigilancia *f.* **be on guard** estar de guardia. **guard dog** perro de guardia *m.* **guard's van** furgón de equipajes *m.* *v* guardar; proteger. **guard against** protegerse contra. **guarded** *adj* (*cautious*) cauteloso. **guardian** *n* (*custodian*) guardián, -a *m, f;* (*of an orphan*) tutor, -a *m, f.* **guardian angel** ángel de la guardia *m.*

guerrilla [gə'rilə] *n* guerrillero, -a *m, f.* **guerrilla warfare** guerrilla *f.*

guess [ges] *n* cálculo *m*; conjetura *f*; suposición *f*. **at a guess** a primera vista. **guesswork** *n* conjetura *f*. *v* adivinar; suponer; acertar.

guest [gest] *n* invitado, -a *m, f*; (*hotel*) huésped, -a *m, f*. **be my guest** yo invito. **guest of honour** invitado, -a de honor *m, f*. **guest-house** *n* casa de huéspedes *f*. **guest room** cuarto de huéspedes *m*.

guide [gaid] *n* guía *m, f*; (*counsellor*) consejero, -a *m, f*. **girl guide** exploradora *f*. **guidebook** *n* guía turística *f*. *v* guiar; conducir; dirigir. **guidance** *n* consejo *m*. **guided missile** projectil teledirigido *m*. **guided tour** visita acompañada *f*. **guideline** directriz *f*.

guild [gild] *v* (*association*) gremio *m*; (*craftsmen, etc.*) guilda *f*.

guillotine ['gilətiːn] *n* guillotina *f*. *v* guillotinar.

guilt [gilt] *n* culpabilidad *f*. **guilty** *adj* culpable. **plead guilty** confesarse culpable

guinea pig ['ginipig] *n* conejillo de Indias *m*.

guitar [gi'taː] *n* guitarra *f*. **guitarist** *n* guitarrista *m, f*.

gulf [gʌlf] *n* golfo *m*; (*abyss*) abismo *m*.

gull [gʌl] *n* gaviota *f*.

gullet ['gʌlit] *n* esófago *m*; (*throat*) garganta *f*.

gullible ['gʌləbl] *adj* crédulo. **gullibility** *n* credulidad *f*.

gully ['gʌli] *n* hondonada *f*.

gulp [gʌlp] *v* tragar. *n* (*drink*) trago *m*; (*food*) bocado *m*.

gum[1] [gʌm] *n* goma *f*. *v* engomar.

gum[2] [gʌm] *n* (*mouth*) encía *f*.

gun [gʌn] *n* (*weapon*) arma *f*; revólver *m*; pistola *f*; (*hunting*) escopeta *f*; rifle *m*; cañón *m*. **gunfire** *n* disparos *m pl*; cañonazos *m pl*. **gunman** *n* pistolero *m*. **gunpowder** pólvora *f*. **gun-running** *n* contrabanda de armas *f*. **gunshot** *n* disparo *m*.

gurgle ['gəːgl] *n* (*water*) borboteo *m*; (*child*) gorjeo *m*. *v* borbotear; gorjear.

gush [gʌʃ] *v* derramar. *n* chorro *m*; (*fig*) efusión *f*. **gushing** *adj* (*person*) efusivo.

gust [gʌst] *n* (*wind*) ráfaga *f*; (*smoke*) bocanada *f*; (*rain*) aguacero *m*; (*laughter, anger*) accesión *f*. **gusty** *adj* borrascoso.

gusto ['gʌstou] *n* placer *m*; brio *m*; entusiasmo *m*.

gut [gʌt] *n* (*anat*) intestino *m*, tripa *f*. **guts** *pl n* (*coll*) agallas *f pl*. *v* destripar; vaciar.

gutter ['gʌtə] *n* (*roof*) canal *m*; (*street*) arroyo *m*.

guy[1] [gai] *n* (*coll*) tipo *m*.

guy[2] [gai] *n* (*rope*) tirante *m*.

gymnasium [dʒim'neiziəm] *n* gimnasio *m*. **gymnast** *n* gimnasta *m, f*. **gymnastic** *adj* gimnástico. **gymnastics** *n* gimnasia *f*.

gynaecology [gainə'kolədʒi] *n* ginecología *f*. **gynaecological** *adj* ginecológico. **gynaecologist** *n* ginecólogo, -a *m, f*.

gypsum ['dʒipsəm] *n* yeso *m*.

gyrate [.dʒai'reit] *v* girar. **gyration** *n* giro *m*.

gyroscope ['dʒairə.skoup] *n* giroscopio *m*.

H

haberdasher ['habədaʃə] *n* mercero, -a *m, f*. **haberdashery** *n* mercería *f*.

habit ['habit] *n* costumbre *f*; (*clothes*) traje *m*. **habitual** *adj* acostumbrado.

habitable ['habitəbl] *adj* habitable.

habitat ['habitat] *n* medio *m*, habitación *f*.

hack[1] [hak] *v* acuchillar, cortar; (*kick*) dar un puntapié. (*computer*) piratear un sistema. *n* corte *m*; puntapié *m*. **hacking** *adj* (*cough*) seco.

hack[2] [hak] *n* (*horse*) rocín *m*; (*writer*) escritorzuelo, -a *m, f*; **hacker** pirata informático.

hackneyed ['haknid] *adj* usado, trillado.

had [had] *V* **have**.

haddock ['hadək] *n* eglefino *m*.

haemorrhage ['heməridʒ] *n* hemorragia *f*.

haemorrhoids ['heməroidz] *pl n* hemorriodes *f pl*.

hag [hag] *n* (*coll*) bruja *f*.

haggard ['hagəd] *adj* ojeroso; extraviado.

haggle ['hagl] *v* regatear. *n* regateo *f*.

Hague, The [heig] *n* La Haya.

hail[1] [heil] *n* granizo *m*. **hailstone** *n* granizo *m*, piedra *f*. **hailstorm** *n* granizada *f*.

hail[2] [heil] *v* (*salute*) saludar; (*coll*) llamar. **hail from** proceder de.

hair [heə] *n* pelo *m*; (*human head*) cabello

m. **comb one's hair** peinarse. **have one's hair done** ir a la peluquería. **let one's hair down** (*coll*) soltarse el pelo. **split hairs** hilar muy fino. **tear one's hair out** tirarse de los pelos. **hairy** *adj* peludo.

hairbrush ['heəbrʌʃ] *n* cepillo (para el pelo) *m.*

haircut ['heəkʌt] *n* corte de pelo *m.* **have a haircut** cortarse el pelo.

hairdresser ['heə,dresə] *n* peluquero, -a *m,* *f.* **hairdresser's** *n* peluquería *f.* **hairdressing** *n* peluquería *f.*

hair dryer *n* secador (para el pelo) *m.*

hairnet ['heənet] *n* redecilla *f.*

hairpiece ['heəpi:s] *n* postizo *m.*

hairpin ['heəpin] *n* horquilla *f.*

hair-remover *n* depilatorio *m.*

hairspray ['heəsprei] *n* fijador (para el pelo) *m.*

hairstyle ['heəstail] *n* peinado *m.*

Haiti ['heiti] *n* Haití *m.* **Haitian** *n,* *adj* haitiano, -a *m,* *f.*

half [ha:f] *n* mitad *f;* medio *m;* (*division of a match*) tiempo *m.* **by half** con mucho. **half-and-half** mitad y mitad. **in half** por la mitad. **go halves with** ir a medias con. *adj* medio. **half an hour** media hora. **half a dozen** media docena. *adv* a medias; media. **half as many** *or* **much** la mitad. **half as much again** la mitad más. **not half!** (*coll*) ¡no poco!

half-baked [,ha:f'beikt] *adj* (*coll: idea*) mal concebido; (*coll: person*) disparatado.

half-breed ['ha:f'bri:d] *n* (*impol*) mestizo, -a *m,* *f.*

half-brother ['ha:f,brʌðə] *n* hermanastro *m.*

half-hearted [,ha:f'ha:tid] *adj* poco entusiasta.

half-mast [,ha:f'ma:st] *n* **at half-mast** a media asta.

half-price [,ha:f'prais] *adj, adv* a mitad de precio.

half-sister ['ha:f,sistə] *n* hermanastra *f.*

half-time [,ha:f'taim] *n* (*sport*) descanso *m.* *adj* (*work*) de media jornada.

halfway [,ha:f'wei] *adv* a medio camino. **meet halfway** (*compromise*) partir la diferencia (con). *adj* medio.

half-wit ['ha:f'wit] *n* tonto, -a *m,* *f.*

halibut ['halibət] *n* halibut *m.*

hall [ho:l] *n* (*entrance*) vestíbulo *m;* (*room*)

sala *f.* **hall porter** conserje *m.* **hall-stand** *n* perchero *m.*

hallmark ['ho:lma:k] *n* contraste *m;* (*fig*) sello *m.* *v* contrastar.

hallowed ['haloud] *adj* santo. **hallow** *v* santificar.

Hallowe'en [halou'i:n] *n* víspera del Día de todos los Santos *f.*

hallucination [hə,lu:si'neiʃən] *n* alucinación *f.*

halo ['heilou] *n* halo *m;* (*rel*) aureola *f.*

halt [ho:lt] *n* alto *m,* parada *f.* *v* parar; interrumpir.

halter ['ho:ltə] *n* cabestro *m.*

halve [ha:v] *v* compartir; partir en dos; reducir a la mitad.

ham [ham] *n* jamón *m.*

hamburger ['hambə:gə] *n* hamburguesa *f.*

hammer ['hamə] *n* martillo *m;* (*firearm*) percursor *m.* **come under the hammer** salir a subasta. *v* martillar, martillear; (*nail*) clavar; (*iron*) batir. **hammer out** (*disputes, etc.*) elaborar.

hammock ['hamək] *n* hamaca *f.*

hamper[1] ['hampə] *v* impedir; embarazar.

hamper[2] ['hampə] *n* canasta *f.*

hamster ['hamstə] *n* hámster *m.*

hamstring ['hamstriŋ] *v* (*coll*) paralizar.

hand [hand] *n* mano *f;* (*watch, etc.*) aguja *f;* (*worker*) trabajador, -a *m, f;* (*writing*) escritura *f;* (*applause*) ovación *f;* (*measure*) palmo *m;* (*naut*) marinero *m.* **at first hand** de primera mano. **at hand** a mano. **by hand** en mano. **hand and foot** de pies y manos. **hand in hand** de la mano. **hands up!** ¡arriba las manos! **hand to hand** cuerpo a cuerpo. **keep one's hand in** no perder la práctica. **on the other hand** por otra parte. *v* dar. **hand down** transmitir. **hand in** entregar. **hand over** ceder. **handful** *n* puñado *m.*

handbag ['handbag] *n* bolso *m.*

handbook ['handbuk] *n* manual *m;* guía *f.*

handbrake ['handbreik] *n* freno de mano *m.*

handcuff ['handkʌf] *v* poner las esposas a. **handcuffs** *pl n* esposas *f pl.*

handicap ['handikap] *n* desventaja *f;* (*sport*) handicap *m.* *v* perjudicar.

handicraft ['handikra:ft] *n* mano de obra *f.*

handiwork ['handiwə:k] *n* obra *f.*

handkerchief ['haŋkətʃif] *n* pañuelo *m.*

handle ['handl] n (cup, bag, etc.) asa f; (grip of a tool) mango m; (stick, door knob) pomo m; (door lever) tirador m; (lever) brazo m. v tocar; (naut) dirigir; (mot) conducir; (tool) manejar; (lift, shift) manipular; (cope) poder con; (deal with) ocuparse de. **handle with care** frágil. **handlebars** pl n manillar m sing.

handmade [,hand'meid] adj hecho a mano.

hand-out ['handaut] n (leaflet) prospecto m; (charity) limosna f. **hand out** dar; distribuir.

hand-pick [hand'pik] v (people) escoger a dedo; (objects) escoger con sumo cuidado.

handrail ['handreil] n pasamano m.

handshake ['handʃeik] n apretón de manos m.

handsome ['hansəm] adj hermoso, bello; guapo.

handstand ['hand,stand] n pino m.

handwriting ['hand,raitiŋ] n escritura f. **handwritten** adj escrito a mano.

handy ['handi] adj (near) a mano; (skilful) mañoso; diestro; (convenient) cómodo; (manageable) manejable; (useful) útil. **come in handy** venir bien.

*hang [haŋ] v colgar, suspender; (execute) ahorcar; (head) bajar; (wallpaper) pegar; (of clothes) caer. **hang about** or **around** vagar. **hang fire** estar en suspenso. **hang-gliding** n vuelo libre m. **hangman** n verdugo m. **hang on** mantenerse firme; (remain) quedarse; (hold on) agarrarse; (depend upon) depender de. **hangover** n (slang) resaca f. **hang-up** n (coll) complejo m.

hangar ['haŋə] n hangar m.

hanker ['haŋkə] v **hanker for** or **after** anhelar. **hankering** n anhelo m.

haphazard [,hap'hazəd] adj fortuito.

happen ['hapən] v acontecer, suceder; (take place) tener lugar; (arise) sobrevenir. **happening** n suceso m, ocurrencia f.

happy ['hapi] adj feliz. alegre. **happy birthday!** ¡feliz cumpleaños! **happy Christmas!** ¡felices Pascuas! **happy-go-lucky** adj descuidado. **happiness** n alegría f. **happily** adv felizmente.

harass ['harəs] v hostigar. **harassment** n hostigamiento m. **harassment** n acoso m.

harbour ['ha:bə] n puerto m; (haven) asilo m. v dar refugio a; (cherish) abrigar.

hard [ha:d] adj duro; firme; violento; inflexible; cruel; (unjust) opresivo; (weather) severo; (stiff) tieso. adv duro; de firme; vigorosamente; (raining) a cántaros; (closely) de cerca; (badly) mal; (heavily) pesadamente. **hard-and-fast** adj (rule) inalterable. **hard-bitten** adj also **hard-boiled** (fig) duro, tenaz. **hard disk** disco duro m. **hard-hearted** adj insensible. **hard labour**. trabajos forzados m pl. **hard shoulder** cuneta f. **hard up** (coll) apurado. **hardware** n ferretería f. **harden** v endurecer; (make callous) hacer insensible. **hardness** n dureza f; inhumanidad f; tiesura f; dificultad f. **hardship** n penas f pl; sufrimiento m; privación f.

hardy ['ha:di] adj audaz; fuerte; (bot) resistente.

hare [heə] n liebre f. **hare-brained** adj casquivano. **hare-lip** n labio leporino m.

haricot ['harikou] n judía f.

harm [ha:m] n mal m; daño m. **harmful** adj malo; dañino. **harmless** adj inofensivo; inocuo.

harmonic [ha:'monik] nm, adj armónico.

harmonica [ha:'monikə] n armónica f.

harmonize ['ha:mənaiz] v armonizar.

harmony ['ha:məni] n armonía f. **harmonious** adj armonioso.

harness ['ha:nis] n guarniciones f pl. v enjaezar; (power, etc.) represar.

harp [ha:p] n arpa f. v **harp on** volver a repetir. **harpist** n arpista m, f.

harpoon [ha:'pu:n] n arpón m. v arponear.

harpsichord ['ha:psi,ko:d] n arpicordio m, clavicémbalo m.

harrowing ['harouiŋ] adj atormentado, patibulario.

harsh [ha:ʃ] adj (features) duro; (voice) ronco; (sound) discordante; (texture) áspero.

harvest ['ha:vist] n cosecha f. v cosechar.

has [haz] V **have**.

hash [haʃ] n (food) picadillo m; (coll) lío m. **make a hash of** estropear por completo. v (food) picar.

hashish ['haʃiʃ] n hachís m invar.

hassle ['hasl] n lío m, problema m

haste [heist] n prisa f. **hasten** v dar prisa a; apresurar. **hastily** adv de prisa; (rashly) a la ligera. **hasty** adj precipitado; (rash) apresurado.

hat [hat] n sombrero m. **bowler hat** som-

brero hongo *m*. **Panama hat** jipijapa *m*.
top hat sombrero de copa *m*. **take one's
hat off to** descubrirse ante.

hatch¹ [hatʃ] *v* hacer salir del cascarón;
(*coll: plot*) maquinar.

hatch² [hatʃ] *n* (*serving*) ventanilla *f*; (*naut*)
escotilla *f*; (*trapdoor*) trampa *f*.

hatchet ['hatʃit] *n* hacha *f*.

hate [heit] *v* odiar, aborrecer. *n also* **hatred**
odio *m*. **pet hate** pesadilla *f*. **hateful** *adj*
odioso.

haughty ['hoːti] *adj* altanero. **haughtiness**
n altanería *f*.

haul [hoːl] *v* (*drag*) arrastrar; (*transport*)
acarrear. *n* (*pull*) tirón *m*; (*journey*) recorrido
m; (*fish*) redada *f*; (*loot*) botín *m*. **haulage** *n*
acarreo *m*, transporte *m*.

haunt [hoːnt] *v* (*ghost*) aparecer en; (*follow*)
perseguir; (*frequent*) frecuentar; (*memories*)
obsesionar. *n* lugar predilecto *m*. **haunting**
adj obsesionante.

***have** [hav] *v* tener; (*receive*) recibir; (*drink,
food*) tomar; (*get*) conseguir; (*coll: deceive*)
engañar. **have on** (*wear*) llevar; (*coll: tease*)
tomar el pelo a. **have to** tener que.

haven ['heivn] *n* abrigo *m*; (*fig*) refugio *m*.

haversack ['havəsak] *n* mochila *f*.

havoc ['havək] *n* estragos *m pl*. **play havoc
with** hacer estragos en.

hawk [hoːk] *n* halcón *m*.

hawthorn ['hoːθoːn] *n* espino *m*.

hay [hei] *n* heno *m*. **make hay while the
sun shines** hacer su agosto. **hay fever**
fiebre del heno *f*. **haystack** *n* almiar *m*. **go
haywire** (*machine*) estropearse; (*plans*) des-
organizarse.

hazard ['hazəd] *n* peligro *m*; (*chance*) azar
m. *v* arriesgar; (*guess*) aventurar. **hazard
lights** luces de emergencia *f pl*. **hazardous**
adj arriesgado, peligroso.

haze [heiz] *n* neblina *f*; (*fig*) confusión *f*.
hazy *adj* nebuloso; (*fig*) confuso.

hazel ['heizl] *n* avellano *m*. **hazel-nut** *n*
avellana *f*. *adj* de avellano.

he [hiː] *pron* él.

head [hed] *n* cabeza *f*; (*chief*) jefe, -a *m, f*;
(*school*) director, -a *m, f*; (*bed, table, river*)
cabecera *f*; (*coin*) cara *f*; (*spear, arrows*)
punta *f*; (*steam*) presión *f*; (*hammer*) cotillo
m. *v* (*demonstration, list, etc.*) encabezar;
(*lead*) estar a la cabeza de; dirigir; conducir;
(*goal*) meter de cabeza. **head off** cortar el

paso a. **head for** dirigirse hacia. **headed**
adj (*notepaper*) con membrete. **heading** *n*
título *m*. **heady** *adj* embriagador.

headache ['hedeik] *n* dolor de cabeza *m*.

headfirst [‚hed'fəːst] *adv* de cabeza.

headlamp ['hedlamp] *or* **headlight** *n* (*mot*)
faro *m*.

headland ['hedlənd] *n* punta *f*, promontorio *m*.

headline ['hedlain] *n* (*book*) título *m*; (*newspaper*) titular *m*. **make the headlines** estar
en primera plana.

headlong ['hedlon] *adv* (*headfirst*) de
cabeza; (*rush*) precipitado.

headmaster [‚hed'maːstə] *n* director *m*.
headmistress *n* directora *f*.

head office *n* sede central *f*

head-on [‚hed'on] *adj, adv* de frente.

headphones ['hedfounz] *pl n* auriculares *m
pl*.

headquarters [‚hed'kwoːtəz] *n* (*mil*) cuartel
general *m*; (*firm*) domicilio social *m*; (*organization*) sede *f*.

headrest ['hedrest] *n* cabecero *m*, cabezal
m.

headscarf ['hedskaːf] *n* pañuelo *m*.

headstrong ['hedstron] *adj* testarudo.

headway ['hedwei] *n* progreso *m*.

heal [hiːl] *v* (*disease*) curar, sanar; (*wound*)
cicatrizar.

health [helθ] *n* salud *f*. **health certificate**
certificado médico *m*. **health food** alimentos naturales *m pl*. **health officer** inspector, -a de sanidad *m, f*. **health resort**
balneario *m*. **Ministry of Health**
Dirección General de Sanidad *f*. **public
health** sanidad pública *f*. **your health!** ¡a
su salud! **healthy** *adj* sano, saludable; salubre. **healthy appetite** buen apetito *m*.

heap [hiːp] *n* montón *m*, pila *f*; (*people*)
muchedumbre *f*. *v* amontonar, apilar.

***hear** [hiə] *v* oír; (*listen*) escuchar; (*attend*)
asistir a; (*give audience*) dar audiencia;
(*news*) enterarse de. **hear from** enterarse
de. **hear hear!** ¡¡ muy bien! **hear about** *or*
of oír hablar de. **hearing** *n* (*sense*) oído *m*;
(*act of hearing*) audición *f*. **hearing aid**
audífono *m*. **hearsay** *n* rumor *m*.

hearse [həːs] *n* coche fúnebre *m*.

heart [haːt] *n* (*anat*) corazón *m*; (*feelings*)
entrañas *f pl*; (*courage*) ánimo *m*; (*soul*) alma
f; (*cards*) copa *f*; (*lettuce*) repollo *m*. **by**

heart de memoria. **set one's heart on** poner el corazón en. **to one's heart's content** hasta quedarse satisfecho. **a man after my own heart** un hombre de los que me gustan. **hearten** v animar. **heartless** adj cruel. **hearty** adj (welcome) cordial; (meal) abundante.

heart attack n ataque cardiaco m.

heartbeat ['ha:tbi:t] n latido del corazón m.

heart-breaking ['ha:tbreikiŋ] adj desgarrador. **heart-broken** adj acongojado.

heartburn ['ha:tbə:n] n acedía f.

heart failure n colapso cardíaco m.

heartfelt ['ha:tfelt] adj de todo corazón.

hearth [ha:θ] n hogar m. **hearthrug** n alfombra f.

heart-throb ['ha:tθrob] n ídolo m.

heart-to-heart adj franco, sincero. **have a heart-to-heart talk** tener una conversación íntima.

heartwarming ['ha:two:miŋ] adj caluroso.

heat [hi:t] n calor m; (animals) celo m; (fig) vehemencia f; (passion) ardor m; (of a race) carrera eliminatoria f. v calentar; excitar; (annoy) irritar. **heatstroke** n insolación f. **heatwave** n onda de calor f. **in the heat of the moment** en el calor del momento. **heated** adj calentado; (argument) apasionado. **heater** n calentador m. **heating** n calefacción f. **central heating** calefacción central f.

heath [hi:θ] n (plant) brezo m; (land) brezal m.

heathen ['hi:ðn] n, adj pagano, -a.

heather ['heðə] n brezo m.

heave [hi:v] n (lift) gran esfuerzo m; (pull) tirón m; (sea) movimiento m; (breast) palpitación f; (retching) náusea f. v (pull) tirar de; (lift) levantar; (sigh) exhalar; (waves) subir y bajar; (retch) tener náusea; (breast) palpitar. **heave to** ponerse al pairo.

heaven ['hevn] n cielo m, paraíso m. **heavenly** adj celeste; (fig) delicioso.

heavy ['hevi] adj pesado, torpe; (slow) lento; (thick) grueso; (hard) duro; (strong) fuerte; (oppressive) opresivo; (cold) malo; (sky) anublado; (meal) abundante; (food) indigesto; (soil) recio. **heavyweight** nm, adj peso pesado. **heaviness** n peso m; torpor m; tristeza f; ponderosidad f.

Hebrew ['hi:bru:] n (people) hebreo, -a m, f; (language) hebreo m. adj hebreo.

heckle ['hekl] v interrumpir. **heckler** n perturbador, -a m, f. **heckling** n interrupción f.

hectare ['hekta:] n hectárea f.

hectic ['hektik] adj agitado.

hedge [hedʒ] n seto m. v cercar con un seto; (fig) vacilar; (a bet) compensar.

hedgehog ['hedʒhog] n erizo m.

heed [hi:d] v atender. n atención f, cuidado m. **heedless** adj desatento; negligente.

heel [hi:l] n (anat) talón m; (shoe) tacón m. v poner tacón a.

hefty ['hefti] adj (heavy) pesado; (robust) robusto.

heifer ['hefə] n novilla f.

height [hait] n altura f; (people) estatura f; (hill) colina f; (fig) colmo m; cumbre f. **heighten** v elevar; (fig) aumentar.

heir [eə] n heredero m; **heiress** n heredera f. **heirloom** n reliquia de familia f.

held [held] V **hold**.

helicopter ['helikoptə] n helicóptero m.

hell [hel] n infierno m. **go to hell!** (impol) ¡vete al infierno! **go hell for leather** ir como si se llevara el diablo. **to hell with it!** ¡qué diablos! **hellish** adj infernal; (fig) horrible.

hello [hə'lou] interj (greeting) ¡hola!; (attract attention) ¡oye!; (phone) ¡oiga!; (answering the phone) ¡diga!

helm [helm] n caña del timón f. **be at the helm** empuñar el timón.

helmet ['helmit] n casco m.

help [help] n ayuda f; socorro m; auxilio m; remedio m; (employee) empleado m; (servant) criado, -a m, f. interj ¡socorro! v ayudar; auxiliar; socorrer; (relieve) aliviar; (serve) servir; (avoid) evitar; (facilitate) facilitar; (prevent oneself from) no poder menos que. **help yourself!** ¡sírvese! **it can't be helped!** ¡no hay más remedio! **helper** n ayudante m, f. **helpful** adj útil; provechoso; amable. **helping** n porción f. **helpless** adj desamparado.

hem [hem] n dobladillo m. v hacer un dobladillo en. **hem in** (fig) rodear. **hemline** n bajo m.

hemisphere ['hemi,sfiə] n hemisferio m.

hemp [hemp] n cáñamo m.

hen [hen] n (chicken) gallina f; (female of other birds) hembra f. **henhouse** n gallinero m. **hen party** (coll) reunión de mujeres f.

henpecked *adj* dominado por su mujer.
hence [hens] *adv* por eso, por lo consiguiente; (*time*) de ahora; (*place*) de aquí.
henceforth *adv* desde aquí en adelante.
henna ['henə] *n* alheña *f*.
her [hə:] *pron* ella; (*direct object*) la; (*indirect object*) le, a ella. *adj* su (*pl* sus).
herald ['herəld] *n* heraldo *m*. *v* proclamar. **heraldic** *adj* heráldico. **heraldry** *n* heráldica *f*.
herb [hə:b] *n* hierba *f*. **herbal** *adj* herbario.
herd [hə:d] *n* rebaño *m*, manada *f*. *v* (*round up*) reunir en manada; (*drive*) conducir; (*fig*) agrupar.
here [hiə] *adv* aquí. **hereafter** *adv* en lo futuro; en adelante. **here and now** ahora mismo. **here and there** aquí y allá. **here goes!** ¡vamos a ver! **here is/are** aquí está/están.
hereditary [hi'redətəri] *adj* hereditario.
heredity [hi'redəti] *n* herencia *f*.
heresy ['herəsi] *n* herejía *f*. **heretic** *n* hereje *m*, *f*. **heretical** *adj* herético.
heritage ['heritidʒ] *n* herencia *f*.
hermit ['hə:mit] *n* ermitaño *m*.
hernia ['hə:niə] *n* hernia *f*.
hero ['hiərou] *n* héroe *m*. **heroine** *n* heroína *f*. **hero-worship** *n* culto a los héroes *m*. **heroic** *adj* heroico. **heroism** *n* heroísmo *m*.
heroin ['herouin] *n* heroína *f*.
heron ['herən] *n* garza *f*.
herring ['heriŋ] *n* arenque *m*. **red herring** (*coll*) pista falsa *f*.
hers [hə:z] *pron* suyo, suya.
herself [hə:'self] *pron* (*reflexive*) se; (*emphatic*) ella misma. **by herself** a solas.
hesitate ['heziteit] *v* vacilar. **hesitant** *adj* vacilante. **hesitation** *n* vacilación *f*.
heterosexual [hetərə'sekʃuəl] *n*(*m+f*), *adj* heterosexual.
hexagon ['heksəgən] *n* hexágono *m*. **hexagonal** *adj* hexagonal.
heyday ['heidei] *n* auge *m*, apogeo *f*.
hi [hai] hola
hiatus [hai'eitəs] *n* laguna *f*.
hibernate ['haibəneit] *v* hibernar. **hibernation** *n* hibernación *f*.
hiccup ['hikʌp] *n* hipo *m*. **have the hiccups** tener hipo. *v* hipar.
*hide¹ [haid] *v* esconder. **hide something**

from someone ocultar algo a alguien.
hide-and-seek *n* escondite *m*. **hide-out** *n* escondrijo *m*.
hide² [haid] *n* piel *f*; (*leather*) cuero *m*.
hideous ['hidiəs] *adj* horroroso.
hiding¹ ['haidiŋ] *n* **be in hiding** estar escondido. **go into hiding** esconderse. **hiding place** escondite *m*.
hiding² ['haidiŋ] *n* (*beating*) paliza *f*.
hierarchy ['haiəra:ki] *n* jerarquía *f*. **hierarchical** *adj* jerárquico.
hi-fi ['hai,fai] *n* alta fidelidad *f*.
high [hai] *adj* alto; de alto; (*speed, hopes, number*) grande; (*post*) importante; (*wind*) fuerte; (*altar, Mass*) mayor; (*voice*) agudo; (*quality*) superior; (*river*) crecido; (*noon*) pleno; (*game*) manido; (*shine, polish*) brillante; (*colour*) subido.
highbrow ['haibrau] *n*(*m + f*), *adj* intelectual.
high chair *n* silla alta para niño *f*.
high frequency *adj* de alta frecuencia.
high-heeled *adj* de tacón alto.
high jump *n* salto de altura *m*.
highland ['hailənd] *n* tierras altas *f pl*. *adj* montañoso.
highlight ['hailait] *v* destacar. *n* (*art*) toque de luz *m*; (*fig*) atracción principal *f*.
Highness ['hainis] *n* Alteza *f*.
high-pitched *adj* de tono alto.
high-rise block *n* torre *f*.
high-speed *adj* de gran velocidad.
high-spirited *adj* brioso.
high street *n* calle principal *f*.
hi(gh) tech *n* alta technología *f*.
highway ['haiwei] *n* camino real *m*, carretera *f*. **highway code** código de la circulación *m*. **highwayman** *n* salteador de caminos *m*.
hijack ['haidʒak] *v* (*aircraft*) secuestrar; (*people*) asaltar; (*goods*) robar. *n* secuestro *m*; asalto *m*.
hike [haik] *n* excursión a pie *f*. *v* ir de excursión. **hiker** *n* excursionista *m*, *f*. **hiking** *n* excursionismo *m*.
hilarious [hi'leəriəs] *adj* (*funny*) hilarante; (*merry*) alegre. **hilarity** *n* hilaridad *f*.
hill [hil] *n* colina *f*, cerro *m*; (*slope*) cuesta *f*. **hillside** *n* ladera *f*. **hilly** *adj* montañoso.
him [him] *pron* él; (*direct object*) le, lo.
himself [him'self] *pron* (*reflexive*) se; sí, sí

mismo; (*emphatic*) él mismo. **by himself** a solas.

hind [haind] *adj* trasero, posterior. **hindquarters** *pl n* cuarto trasero *m sing*. **hindsight** *n* percepción retrospectiva *f*.

hinder ['hində] *v* impedir; interrumpir. **hindrance** *n* impedimento *m*; obstáculo *m*.

Hindu [hin'du:] *n*(*m* + *f*), *adj* hindú. **Hinduism** *n* hinduismo *m*.

hinge [hindʒ] *n* bisagra *f*; (*stamps*) fijasellos *m invar. v* **hinge on** depender de.

hint [hint] *n* indirecta *f*; (*tip*) consejo *m*; (*clue*) pista *f*; indicación *f*; (*trace*) pizca *f*. **a broad hint** una insinuación muy clara. **take the hint** (*pejorative*) darse por aludido; (*follow advice*) aprovechar el consejo. *v* insinuar; soltar indirectas.

hip [hip] *n* cadera *f*.

hippopotamus [hipə'potəməs] *n* hipopótamo *m*.

hire [haiə] *v* alquilar; (*person*) contratar. **hire out** alquilar. *n* (*house, etc.*) alquiler *m*; (*engagement*) contratación *f*; (*wages*) sueldo *m*. **for hire** de alquiler; (*taxi*) libre. **hire car** coche de alquiler *m*. **hire purchase** compra a plazos *f*.

his [hiz] *adj* su (*pl* sus); de él. *pron* suyo, suya.

hiss [his] *n* silbido *m. v* silbar.

history ['histəri] *n* historia *f*. **historian** *n* historiador, -a *m, f*. **historic** *adj* histórico.

***hit** [hit] *v* golpear, pegar a; (*target*) dar en; (*wound*) herir; (*collide*) chocar con. **hit home** dar en el blanco. **hit it off with** hacer buenas migas con. *n* golpe *m*; (*mil*) impacto *m*; (*success*) exito *m*. **hit-or-miss** *adv* a la buena de Dios.

hitch [hitʃ] *n* obstáculo *m*; problema *m*; (*knot*) vuelta de cabo *m. v* (*travel*) hacerse llevar en coche; (*tie*) atar; (*link*) enganchar. **hitch-hike** *v* hacer autostop. **hitch-hiker** *n* autostopista *m, f*. **hitch-hiking** *n* autostop *m*.

hitherto [hiðə'tu:] *adv* hasta ahora.

HIV *n* VIH *m*

HIV-positive *adj* VIH-positivo *m*.

hive [haiv] *n* colmena *f*.

hoard [ho:d] *n* acumulación *f*; tesoro *m. v* acumular, amasar.

hoarding ['ho:diŋ] *n* (*fence*) valla *f*; (*advertising*) cartelera *f*.

hoarse [ho:s] *adj* ronco. **hoarsely** *adv* roncamente. **hoarseness** *n* ronquera *f*.

hoax [houks] *n* estafa *f*; engaño *m*; burla *f. v* estafar; engañar; burlar.

hobble ['hobl] *v* cojear. *n* (*gait*) cojera *f*.

hobby ['hobi] *n* pasatiempo *m*.

hock¹ [hok] *n* (*pork, etc.*) pernil *m*.

hock² [hok] *n* vino del Rín *m*.

hockey ['hoki] *n* hockey *m*. **hockey stick** bastón de hockey *m*.

hoe [hou] *n* azadón *m. v* azadonar.

hog [hog] *n* cerdo *m*, puerco *m. v* (*coll*) acaparar.

hoist [hoist] *v* (*heavy objects*) levantar; (*sails, flag*) izar. *n* (*lifting*) levantamiento *m*; (*crane*) grúa *f*; (*lift*) montacargas *m invar*; (*lifting mechanism*) cabria *f*.

***hold¹** [hould] *v* tener; mantener; agarrar; (*believe*) creer; (*keep*) guardar; (*sustain*) sostener; (*opinion*) defender. **hold back** reprimir. **hold forth** perorar. **hold on** sujetar; (*wait*) aguantar; (*grip*) agarrarse. **hold out** (*hand*) tender, ofrecer; (*last*) durar; (*resist*) resistir. **hold up** (*raise*) levantar; (*support*) sostener; (*delay*) retrasar. *n* (*grip*) asimiento *m*, agarro *m*; (*handhold*) asidero *m*; (*control*) autoridad *f*; dominio *m*. **get hold of** coger, agarrar. **hold-up** *n* interrupción *f*; (*robbery*) atraco a mano armada *m*; (*traffic jam*) embotellamiento *m*. **holder** *n* (*person*) poseedor, -a *m, f*; (*object*) receptáculo *m*.

hold² [hould] *n* (*naut*) bodega *f*.

hole [houl] *n* agujero *m*; (*from digging*) hoyo *m*; (*in garments*) boquete *m*; (*mouse*) ratonera *f*; (*rabbit*) madriguera *f*.

holiday ['holədi] *n* (*day*) fiesta *f*; (*several days*) vacaciones *f pl*. **holiday resort** centro de turismo *m*.

Holland ['holənd] *n* Holanda *f*.

hollow ['holou] *n* hueco *m*; (*in ground*) hondonada *f*. *adj, adv* hueco. *v* ahuecar.

holly ['holi] *n* acebo *m*.

hollyhock ['holihok] *n* malva loca *f*.

holster ['houlstə] *n* pistolera *f*.

holy ['houli] *adj* santo; sacro; sagrado; (*bread, water*) bendito. **holiness** *n* santidad *f*.

homage ['homidʒ] *n* homenaje *m*. **pay homage** rendir homenaje.

home [houm] *n* casa *f*; hogar *m*; domicilio *m*; (*fig*) morada *f*. **at home** en casa. **make yourself at home** está usted en su casa.

adv a casa. **go home** volver a casa. **homeless** *adj* sin casa ni hogar. **home address** dirección privada *f*. **homesick** *adj* nostálgico.

homeopathic [ˌhomiə'paθik] *adj* homeopático

home page (*internet*) *n* página principal *f*

homicide ['homisaid] *n* (*act*) homicidio *m*; (*person*) homicida *m*, *f*. **homicidal** *adj* homicida.

homogeneous [homə'dʒiːniəs] *adj* homogéneo.

homosexual [homə'sekʃuəl] *n*(*m* + *f*), *adj* homosexual. **homosexuality** *n* homosexualidad *f*.

honest ['onist] *adj* honrado; sincero; franco. **honesty** *n* honradez *f*; sinceridad *f*; rectitud *f*.

honey ['hʌni] *n* miel *f*. **honeycomb** *n* panal *m*. **honeymoon** *n* luna de miel *f*. **honeysuckle** *n* madreselva *f*.

honour ['onə] *n* honor *m*; rectitud *f*. *v* honrar. **honorary** *adj* honorario. **honourable** *adj* honorable; honrado.

hood [hud] *n* capucha *f*; (*car, pram*) capota *f*.

hoof [huːf] *n* casco *m*; (*cloven*) pezuña *f*.

hook [huk] *n* gancho *m*; (*fish*) anzuelo *m*; (*dress*) corchete *m*; (*hanger*) colgadero *m*. *v* enganchar; (*fish*) pescar; (*dress*) abrochar; colgar. **hooked** *adj* (*shaped*) ganchudo. **get hooked on** (*coll*) enviciarse en.

hooligan ['huːligən] *n* rufián *m*. **hooliganism** *n* rufianería *f*.

hoop [huːp] *n* (*toy*) aro *m*; (*barrel*) fleje *m*.

hoot [huːt] *n* (*owl*) ululato *m*; (*person*) silbato *m*; (*shout*) grito *m*; (*boat, factory*) toque de sirena *m*. *v* ulular; silbar; dar un bocinazo; gritar; dar un toque de sirena; (*boo*) abuchear.

Hoover® ['huːvə] *n* aspiradora *f*

hop¹ [hop] *v* saltar; brincar; saltar con un pie. *n* salto *m*; brinco *m*; (*coll: dance*) baile *m*; (*coll: stage in a journey*) etapa *f*.

hop² [hop] *n* (*bot*) lúpulo *m*.

hope [houp] *n* esperanza *f*. *v* esperar. **hopeful** *adj* lleno de esperanzas; confiado. **hopeless** *adj* desesperado; (*coll*) inútil.

horde [hoːd] *n* horda *f*.

horizon [hə'raizn] *n* horizonte *m*.

horizontal [hori'zontl] *adj* horizontal.

hormone ['hoːmoun] *n* hormona *f*.

horn [hoːn] *n* cuerno *m*; (*mot*) bocina *f*.

hornet ['hoːnit] *n* avispón *m*.

horoscope ['horəskoup] *n* horóscopo *m*.

horrible ['horibl] *adj* horrible, espantoso.

horrid ['horid] *adj* horroroso, odioso.

horrify ['horifai] *v* horrorizar. **horrific** *adj* horrífico, horrendo.

horror ['horə] *n* horror *m*. *adj* (*film, story, etc.*) de miedo.

hors d'œuvres [oː'dəːvr] *pl n* entremeses *m pl*.

horse [hoːs] *n* caballo *m*. **on horseback** *a* caballo. **horsepower** *n* caballo de vapor *m*. **horseradish** *n* rábano picante *m*. **horse show** concurso hípico *m*.

horticulture ['hoːtikʌltʃə] *n* horticultura *f*. **horticultural** *adj* horticultural.

hose [houz] *n* manga *f*; manguera *f*; (*stockings*) medias *f pl*. *v* regar con una manga.

hosiery ['houziəri] *n* medias *f pl*; (*business*) calcetería *f*.

hospitable [ho'spitəbl] *adj* hospitalario.

hospital ['hospitl] *n* hospital *m*. **hospitalize** *v* hospitalizar.

hospitality [ˌhospi'taliti] *n* hospitalidad *f*.

host¹ [houst] *n* huésped *m*. **hostess** *n* huéspeda *f*.

host² [houst] *n* (*crowd*) muchedumbre *f*.

hostage ['hostidʒ] *n* rehén *m*.

hostel ['hostəl] *n* hostería *f*; residencia *f*. **youth hostel** albergue juvenil *m*.

hostile ['hostail] *adj* hostil; enemigo. **hostility** *n* hostilidad *f*; enemistad *f*.

hot [hot] *adj* caliente; (*climate*) cálido; (*sun*) abrasador; (*day*) caluroso; (*spicy*) picante; (*temper*) vivo; (*issue*) controvertido; (*pursuit*) porfiado. **be hot** (*person*) tener calor; (*weather*) hacer calor. **hot dog** perro caliente *m*. **hot-house** invernadero *m*. **hotplate** *n* calientaplato *m invar*. **hot-tempered** *adj* enfadadizo. **hot-water bottle** bolsa de agua caliente *f*.

hotel [hou'tel] *n* hotel *m*.

hound [haund] *n* perro de caza *m*. *v* (*fig*) perseguir.

hour ['auə] *n* hora *f*. **after hours** fuera de horas. **by the hour** por horas. **hour by hour** de hora en hora. **peak hours** horas de mayor consumo. **rush hour** hora punta. **small hours** altas horas. **zero hour** hora H. **hourly** *adv* de cada hora.

house [haus; *v* hauz] *n* casa *f*; (*theatre*) sala

f; (*audience*) público *m*. *v* (*hold*) alojar; (*put up*) albergar.

houseboat ['hausbout] *n* casa flotante *f*.

housecoat ['hauskout] *n* bata *f*.

household ['haushould] *n* casa *f*, familia *f*. *adj* casero.

housekeeper ['haus,ki:pə] *n* (*paid*) ama de llaves *f*; (*housewife*) ama de casa *f*. **housekeeping** *n* (*work*) quehaceres domésticos *m pl*; (*money*) dinero para gastos domésticos *m*.

housemaid ['hausmeid] *n* criada *f*.

house-to-house *adj*, *adv* de casa en casa.

house-trained ['haustreind] *adj* enseñado.

house-warming ['haus,wo:miŋ] *n* **have a house-warming party** inaugurar la casa.

housewife ['hauswaif] *n* ama de casa *f*.

housing ['hauziŋ] *n* alojamiento *m*. **housing estate** urbanización *f*.

hovel ['hovəl] *n* casucha *f*.

hover ['hovə] *v* cernerse; (*fig*) rondar. **hovercraft** *n* aerodeslizador *m*.

how [hau] *adv* (*as*) como; (*in what way*) cómo; (*in exclamation before adv or adj*) qué. **how are you?** *or* **how do you do?** ¿cómo está usted? **how much?** ¿cuánto?

however [hau'evə] *conj* sin embargo. *adv* de cualquier manera que.

howl [haul] *v* (*dog, wolf*) aullar; (*wind*) bramar; (*pain*) dar alaridos; (*child*) berrear. *n* aullido *m*; bramido *m*; alarido *m*; grito *m*; berrido *m*.

hub [hʌb] *n* (*wheel*) cubo *m*; (*fig*) centro *m*. **hubcap** *n* (*mot*) tapacubos *m invar*.

huddle ['hʌdl] *v* amontonar. *n* grupo *m*.

hue [hju:] *n* color *m*.

huff [hʌf] *n* **in a huff** enojado.

hug [hʌg] *v* abrazar. *n* abrazo *m*.

huge [hju:dʒ] *adj* enorme.

hulk [hʌlk] *n* (*ship*) carraca *f*; (*derog: person*) armatoste *m*. **hulking** *adj* voluminoso.

hull [hʌl] *n* (*naut*) casco *m*.

hum [hʌm] *n* (*bees, engines*) zumbido *m*; (*a tune*) canturreo *m*. *v* zumbar; canturrear; (*fig: with activity*) hervir. **hummingbird** *n* colibrí *m*.

human ['hju:mən] *nm*, *adj* humano. **human being** ser humano *m*. **human nature** naturaleza humana *f*.

humane [hju:'mein] *adj* humano.

humanity [hju:'manəti] *n* humanidad *f*. **humanitarian** *adj* humanitario.

humble ['hʌmbl] *adj* humilde. *v* humillar

humdrum ['hʌmdrʌm] *adj* monótono.

humid ['hju:mid] *adj* húmedo. **humidity** *n* humedad *f*.

humiliate [hju:'milieit] *v* humillar. **humiliation** *n* humillación *f*.

humility [hju:'miləti] *n* humildad *f*.

humour ['hju:mə] *n* humor *m*; (*temperament*) disposición *f*. *v* complacer. **humorist** *n* humorista *m*, *f*. **humorous** *adj* humorístico.

hump [hʌmp] *n* horoba *f*. *v* (*coll: carry*) cargar con.

hunch [hʌntʃ] *v* encorvarse. *n* (*coll*) presentimiento *m*. **hunchback** *n* jorobado, -a *m*, *f*.

hundred ['hʌndrəd] *n* ciento *m*; centenar *m*; centena *f*. *adj* cien, ciento. **hundredth** *nm*, *adj* centésimo.

hung [hʌŋ] *V* **hang**.

Hungary ['hʌŋgəri] *n* Hungría *f*. **Hungarian** *n* húngaro, -a *m*, *f*.

hunger ['hʌŋgə] *n* hambre *f*. *v also* **be hungry** tener hambre, estar hambriento. **hunger for** desear. **hungrily** *adv* hambrientamente.

hunt [hʌnt] *n* caza *f*; (*search*) busca *f*. *v* cazar; buscar. **hunting** *n* caza *f*. **huntsman** *n* cazador *m*.

hurdle ['hə:dl] *n* (*sport*) valla *f*; (*fig*) obstáculo *m*. *v* vallar.

hurl [hə:l] *v* lanzar, arrojar; (*abuse*) soltar.

hurricane ['hʌrikən] *n* huracán *m*.

hurry ['hʌri] *n* prisa *f*. **be in a hurry** tener prisa. *v* dar prisa (a), apresurar. **hurried** *adj* apresurado. **hurriedly** *adj* apresuradamente.

*hurt [hə:t] *v* (*cause pain*) doler; (*wound*) herir; (*damage*) hacer daño (a); ofender; (*feelings*) mortificar. *n* herida *f*; daño *m*; mal *m*. *adj* lastimado; herido. **hurtful** *adj* dañoso; perjudicial; (*words*) hiriente.

husband ['hʌzbənd] *n* marido *m*, esposo *m*.

hush [hʌʃ] *n* silencio *m*. *interj* ¡calla! *v* silenciar. **hush up** echar tierra a. **hushed** *adj* callado.

husk [hʌsk] *n* (*cereals*) cáscara *f*; (*peas and beans*) vaina *f*; (*chestnut*) erizo *m*. *v* descascarar; desvainar; pelar.

husky ['hʌski] *n* (*dog*) perro esquimal *m*. *adj* (*hoarse*) ronco; (*strong*) fuerte. **huskily** *adv* con voz ronca. **huskiness** *n* ronquera *f*.

hussar [hə'za:] *n* húsar *m*.

hustle ['hʌsl] v empujar; (*fig*) precipitar. *n* (*energy*) empuje *m*; (*hurry*) prisa *f*; (*push*) empujón *m*. **hustle and bustle** vaivén *m*.

hut [hʌt] *n* choza *f*, cabaña *f*.

hutch [hʌtʃ] *n* (*rabbit*) conejera *f*.

hyacinth ['haiəsinθ] *n* jacinto *m*.

hybrid ['haibrid] *nm. adj* híbrido. **hybridization** *n* hibridación *f*.

hydraulic [hai'drɔ:lik] *adj* hidráulico.

hydrocarbon [‚haidrə'ka:bən] *n* hidrocarburo *m*.

hydro-electric *adj* hidroeléctrico.

hydrofoil ['haidrəfoil] *n* aerodeslizador *m*.

hydrogen ['haidrədʒən] *n* hidrógeno *m*.

hyena [hai'i:nə] *n* hiena *f*.

hygiene ['haidʒi:n] *n* higiene *f*. **hygienic** *adj* higiénico.

hymn [him] *n* himno *m*. **hymn book** or **hymnal** *n* himnario *m*.

hype [haip] *n* hiper *m*

hyperactive [haipər'aktiv] *adj* hiperactivo

hypermarket ['haipə‚ma:kit] *n* hipermercado *m*

hyphen ['haifən] *n* guión *m*.

hypnosis [hip'nousis] *n* hipnosis *f*. **hypnotic** *adj* hipnótico. **hypnotism** *n* hipnotismo *m*. **hypnotist** *n* hipnotizador, -a *m, f*. **hypnotize** v hipnotizar.

hypochondria [haipə'kondriə] *n* hipocondría *f*. **hypochondriac** *n, adj* hipocondríaco, -a *m, f*.

hypocrisy [hi'pokrəsi] *n* hipocresía *f*. **hypocrite** *n* hipócrita *m, f*. **hypocritical** *adj* hipócrita.

hypodermic [haipə'də:mik] *adj* hipodérmico. *n* jeringa hipodérmica *f*.

hypothesis [hai'poθəsis] *n, pl* -**ses** hipótesis *f*. **hypothetical** *adj* hipotético.

hysterectomy [‚histə'rektəmi] *n* histerectomía *f*.

hysteria [hi'stiəriə] *n* histeria *f*. **hysterical** *adj* histérico. **hysterics** *pl n* histerismo *m sing*; ataque histérico *m*.

I [ai] *pron* yo.

Iberian [ai'biəriən] *adj* ibérico. *n* íbero, -a *m, f*.

ice [ais] *n* hielo *m*. **iceberg** *n* iceberg *m*. **ice-breaker** *n* rompehielos *m invar*. **ice-cold** *adj* helado. **ice cream** helado *m*. **ice hockey** hockey sobre hielo. *m* **ice-skate** *n* patín de cuchilla. *m*. v (*turn into ice*) helar; (*chill*) enfriar. **icing** *n* escarchado *m*. **icing sugar** azúcar en polvo *m*, *f*. **icy** *adj* (*wind, place*) glacial; (*hand, foot*) helado.

Iceland ['aislənd] *n* Islandia *f*. **Icelander** *n* islandés, -esa *m, f*. **Icelandic** *adj* islandés.

icicle ['aisikl] *n* carámbano *m*.

icon ['aikon] *n* icono *m*.

idea [ai'diə] *n* idea *f*.

ideal [ai'diəl] *nm, adj* ideal. **idealist** *n* idealista *m, f*. **idealistic** *adj* idealista.

identical [ai'dentikəl] *adj* idéntico. **identical twins** gemelos homólogos *m pl*.

identify [ai'dentifai] v identificar. **identify with** identificarse con. **identification** *n* identificación *f*; (*papers*) documentos de identidad *m pl*.

identity [ai'dentiti] *n* identidad *f*. **identity card** carnet de identidad *m*.

ideology [aidi'olədʒi] *n* ideología *f*.

idiom ['idiəm] *n* (*expression*) idiotismo *m*; (*language*) idioma *m*. **idiomatic** *adj* idiomático.

idiosyncrasy [‚idiə'siŋkrəsi] *n* idiosincrasia *f*.

idiot ['idiət] *n* imbécil *m, f*. idiota *m, f*. **idiotic** *adj* idiota.

idle ['aidl] *adj* (*lazy*) perezoso; (*at leisure*) ocioso; (*unemployed*) desocupado; (*machine*) parado; (*talk*) frívolo; (*fears*) infundado. v (*waste time*) perder el tiempo; (*be lazy*) holgazanear; (*mechanism*) girar loco. **idleness** *n* (*laziness*) holgazanería *f*; (*leisure*) ociosidad *f*; (*unemployment*) paro *m*.

idol ['aidl] *n* ídolo *m*. **idolatry** *n* idolatría *f*. **idolize** v idolatrar.

idyllic [i'dilik] *adj* idílico.

if [if] *conj* si. **as if** como si. **if not** si no. **if only** ¡ojalá que! **if so** si es así.

ignite [ig'nait] v encender, prender fuego a.

ignition [ig'niʃən] *n* ignición *f*; (*mot*) encendido *m*. **ignition key** llave de contacto *f*. **ignition switch** interruptor del encendido *m*.

ignorant ['ignərənt] *adj* ignorante. **ignorance** *n* ignorancia *f*.

ignore [ig'no:] v (*warning*) no hacer caso de; (*person*) no hacer caso a; (*leave out*) pasar por alto.

ill [il] adj (*sick*) enfermo; (*bad*) malo. nm, adv mal. **ill-advised** adj malaconsejado. **ill-at-ease** adj molesto. **ill feeling** mal presentimiento m. **ill-mannered** adj mal educado. **ill health** mala salud f. **ill-treat** v maltratar. **ill will** mala voluntad f. **illness** n enfermedad f.

illegal [i'li:gəl] adj ilegal.

illegible [i'ledʒəbl] adj ilegible.

illegitimate [,ili'dʒitimit] adj ilegítimo. **illegitimacy** n ilegitimidad f.

illicit [i'lisit] adj ilícito.

illiterate [i'litərit] n, adj analfabeto, -a. **illiteracy** n analfabetismo m.

illogical [i'lodʒikəl] adj ilógico.

illuminate [i'lu:mi,neit] v (*light up*) iluminar; (*clear*) aclarar. **illumination** n iluminación f; aclaración f.

illusion [i'lu:ʒən] n ilusión f.

illustrate [i'lə,streit] v ilustrar; (*demonstrate*) demostrar. **illustration** n ilustración f; ejemplo m. **illustrator** n illustrador, -a m, f.

illustrious [i'lʌstriəs] adj ilustre.

image ['imidʒ] n imagen f; (*fig*) reputación f. **be the image of** ser el retrato de. **imagery** n imágenes f pl.

imagine [i'madʒin] v imaginar. **imaginary** adj imaginario. **imagination** n imaginación f. **imaginative** adj imaginativo.

imbalance [im'baləns] n desequilibrio m.

imbecile ['imbə,si:l] n imbécil m, f.

imitate ['imi,teit] v imitar. **imitation** n imitación f.

immaculate [i'makjulit] adj inmaculado.

immaterial [,imə'tiəriəl] adj indiferente; **be immaterial** no importar.

immature [,imə'tjuə] adj inmaduro. **immaturity** n inmadurez f.

immediate [i'mi:diət] adj inmediato; (*near*) cercano. **immediately** adv inmediatamente; directamente.

immense [i'mens] adj inmenso, enorme.

immerse [i'mə:s] v sumergir. **immersion** n sumersión f. **immersion heater** calentador de inmersión m.

immigrate ['imi,greit] v inmigrar. **immigrant** n (m + f), adj inmigrante. **immigration** n inmigración f.

imminent ['iminənt] adj inminente.

immobile [i'moubail] adj inmóvil. **immobilize** v inmovilizar. **immobilizer** inmovilizador m.

immoral [i'morəl] adj inmoral. **immorality** n inmoralidad f.

immortal [i'mo:tl] adj inmortal. **immortality** n inmortalidad f. **immortalize** v inmortalizar.

immovable [i'mu:vəbl] adj inmóvil; (*steadfast*) inflexible.

immune [i'mju:n] adj inmune. **immunity** n inmunidad f. **immunization** n inmunización f. **immunize** v inmunizar.

imp [imp] n diablillo m.

impact ['impakt] n impacto m.

impair [im'peə] v dañar. **impairment** n daño m.

impale [im'peil] v atravesar.

impart [im'pa:t] v (*give*) impartir; (*grant*) conceder; (*make known*) comunicar.

impartial [im'pa:ʃəl] adj imparcial. **impartiality** n imparcialidad f.

impasse [am'pa:s] n callejón m.

impassive [im'pasiv] adj impasible.

impatient [im'peiʃənt] adj impaciente. **become impatient** perder la paciencia. **impatience** n impaciencia f.

impeach [im'pi:tʃ] v acusar; (*prosecute*) encausar; (*a witness*) recusar. **impeachment** n acusación f; (*prosecution*) enjuiciamiento m; recusación f.

impeccable [im'pekəbl] adj impecable.

impede [im'pi:d] v estorbar; impedir.

impediment [im'pedimənt] n estorbo m; obstáculo m; defecto m.

impel [im'pel] v impeler; mover; (*push*) empujar; obligar.

impending [im'pendiŋ] adj inminente; próximo.

imperative [im'perətiv] adj (*peremptory*) perentorio; (*urgent*) imperioso; (*necessary*) indispensable.

imperfect [im'pə:fikt] adj imperfecto; incompleto. n (*gramm*) imperfecto m.

imperial [im'piəriəl] adj imperial; (*fig*) señorial. **imperialism** n imperialismo m.

impersonal [im'pə:sənl] adj impersonal.

impersonate [im'pə:sə,neit] v hacerse pasar por; (*theatre*) imitar. **impersonation** n imitación f.

impertinent [im'pə:tinənt] *adj* impertinente. **impertinence** *n* impertinencia *f*.

impervious [im'pə:viəs] *adj* impenetrable; (*to criticism, pain, etc.*) insensible.

impetuous [im'petjuəs] *adj* impetuoso.

impetus ['impətəs] *n* (*force*) ímpetu *m*; (*fig*) impulso *m*; estímulo *m*.

impinge [im'pindʒ] *v* **impinge on** tropezar con; usurpar.

implement ['implimənt; *v* 'impliment] *n* (*tool*) herramienta *f*; (*utensil*) utensilio *m*; **implements** *pl n* (*writing*) artículos *m pl*; (*agr*) aperos *m pl*. *v* llevar a cabo; (*law*) aplicar.

implication [impli'keiʃən] *n* implicación *f*; complicidad *f*; consecuencia *f*. **implicate** *v* implicar: comprometer.

implicit [im'plisit] *adj* implícito; absoluto.

implore [im'plo:] *v* suplicar. **imploring** *adj* suplicante.

imply [im'plai] *v* implicar; presuponer; significar; dar a entender. **implied** *adj* implícito.

impolite [impə'lait] *adj* descortés.

import ['impo:t; *v* im'po:t] *n* (*comm*) artículo importado *m*; (*meaning*) sentido *m*; importancia *f*. *v* (*comm*) importar; significar.

importance [im'po:təns] *n* importancia *f*. **important** *adj* importante.

impose [im'pouz] *v* imponer; (*tax*) gravar con. **impose on** abusar de. **imposing** *adj* imponente. **imposition** *n* imposición *f*; abuso *m*; (*tax*) impuesto *m*.

impossible [im'posəbl] *adj* imposible.

impostor [im'postə] *n* impostor, -a *m, f*.

impotent ['impətənt] *adj* impotente. **impotence** *n* impotencia *f*.

impound [im'paund] *v* confiscar.

impoverish [im'povəriʃ] *v* (*people*) empobrecer; (*land*) agotar.

impractical [im'praktikəl] *adj* poco factible

impregnate ['impreg,neit] *v* fecundar; (*saturate*) empapar. **impregnable** *adj* inexpugnable. **impregnation** *n* fecundación *f*; impregnación *f*.

impress [im'pres] *v* impresionar; (*print*) imprimir. **impression** *n* impresión *f*. **impressive** *adj* impresionante.

imprint ['imprint; *v* im'print] *n* impresión *f*. *v* imprimir.

imprison [im'prizn] *v* encarcelar. **impris-**

onment *n* encarcelamiento *m*.

improbable [im'probabl] *adj* improbable; (*story, etc.*) inverosímil.

impromptu [im'promptju:] *adv* improvisadamente. *adj* improvisado.

improper [im'propə] *adj* indecente; indecoroso; incorrecto.

improve [im'pru:v] *v* mejorar; favorecer; perfeccionar. **improvement** *n* mejora *f*; progreso *m*; reforma *f*.

improvise ['imprə,vaiz] *v* improvisar. **improvisation** *n* improvisación *f*.

impudent ['impjudənt] *adj* impudente. **impudence** *n* impudencia *f*.

impulse ['impʌls] *n* impulso *m*. **impulsive** *adj* impulsivo.

impure [im'pjuə] *adj* impuro. **impurity** *n* impureza *f*.

in [in] *prep* en; de; durante; a. *adv* dentro. **be in** (*at home*) estar en casa. **be in on** estar enterado de.

inability [inə'biləti] *n* incapacidad *f*.

inaccessible [inak'sesəbl] *adj* inaccesible. **inaccessibility** *n* inaccesibilidad *f*.

inaccurate [in'akjurit] *adj* inexacto. **inaccuracy** *n* inexactitud *f*.

inactive [in'aktiv] *adj* inactivo. **inaction** *n* inacción *f*. **inactivity** *n* inactividad *f*.

inadequate [in'adikwit] *adj* insuficiente. **inadequacy** *n* insuficiencia *f*.

inadvertent [inəd'və:tənt] *adj* inadvertido; descuidado. **inadvertently** *adv* por inadvertencia.

inane [in'ein] *adj* (*futile*) inane; (*silly*) necio. **inanity** *n* inanidad *f*; necedad *f*.

inanimate [in'animit] *adj* inanimado.

inarticulate [ina:'tikjulit] *adj* (*sound*) inarticulado; (*person*) incapaz de expresarse.

inasmuch [inaz'mʌtʃ] *adv* **inasmuch as** puesto que, visto que.

inaudible [in'o:dəbl] *adj* inaudible.

inaugurate [i'no:gju,reit] *v* inaugurar. **inaugural** *adj* inaugural. **inauguration** *n* inauguración *f*.

inborn [in'bo:n] *adj* innato; (*med*) congénito.

incapable [in'keipəbl] *adj* incapaz.

incapacitate [inkə'pasiteit] *v* incapacitar, inhabilitar

incendiary [in'sendiəri] *adj* incendiario. **incendiary bomb** bomba incendiaria *f*.

incense¹ ['insens] *n* incienso *m*.

incense² [in'sens] *v* encolerizar.

incentive [in'sentiv] *n* incentivo *m*, estímulo *m*.

incessant [in'sesənt] *adj* incesante, continuo.

incest ['insest] *n* incesto *m*. **incestuous** *adj* incestuoso.

inch [intʃ] *n* pulgada *f*. **inch by inch** poco a poco. **within an inch of** a dos pasos de. *v* **inch forward** avanzar poco a poco.

incident ['insidənt] *n* incidente *m*; (*in a story*) episodio *m*. **incidental** *adj* incidente; incidental; imprevisto; (*expense*) accesorio; (*music*) de fondo; (*secondary*) secundario; (*casual*) fortuito. **incidentally** *adv* (*by the way*) a propósito.

incinerator [in'sinə,reitə] *n* quemador de basuras *m*. **incinerate** *v* quemar. **incineration** *n* incineración *f*.

incite [in'sait] *v* incitar; provocar. **incitement** *n* incitamiento *m*; estímulo *m*.

incline [in'klain] *v* inclinar. **be inclined to** inclinarse a. **inclination** *n* pendiente *f*; (*tilt*) inclinación *f*; (*slope*) pendiente *f*; (*leaning*) tendencia *f*.

include [in'klu:d] *v* incluir; (*enclose in a letter*) adjuntar. **including** *adj* incluso. **inclusion** *n* inclusión *f*. **inclusive** *adj* inclusivo.

incognito [,inkog'ni:tou] *adv* de incógnito.

incoherent [,inkə'hiərənt] *adj* incoherente. **incoherence** *n* incoherencia *f*. **incoherently** *adv* de modo incoherente.

income ['inkʌm] *n* ingresos *m pl*. **income tax** impuesto de utilidades *m*.

incomparable [in'kompərəbl] *adj* incomparable. **incomparably** *adv* incomparablemente.

incompatible [inkəm'patəbl] *adj* incompatible. **incompatibility** *n* incompatibilidad *f*.

incompetent [in'kompitənt] *adj* incompetente. **incompetence** *n* incompetencia *f*.

incomplete [,inkəm'pli:t] *adj* incompleto; sin terminar.

incomprehensible [in,kompri'hensəbl] *adj* incomprensible.

inconceivable [inkən'si:vəbl] *adj* inconcebible.

incongruous [in'kongruəs] *adj* incongruo; incompatible. **incongruity** *n* incongruidad *f*.

inconsiderate [,inkən'sidərit] *adj* (*thoughtless*) inconsiderado; (*lacking consideration for others*) desconsiderado.

inconsistent [,inkən'sistənt] *adj* (*substance*) inconsistente; (*actions, thoughts*) inconsecuente. **inconsistency** *n* inconsistencia *f*; inconsecuencia *f*.

incontinence [in'kontinəns] *n* incontinencia *f*. **incontinent** *adj* incontinente.

inconvenient [inkən'vi:njənt] *adj* (*place*) incómodo; (*time*) inoportuno. **inconvenience** *n* inconvenientes *m pl*, molestia *f*. *v* incomodar, molestar.

incorporate [in'ko:pə,re:t] *v* incorporar, incluir; (*contain*) contener; (*comm*) constituir en sociedad.

incorrect [inkə'rekt] *adj* incorrecto; erróneo.

increase [in'kri:s; *n* 'inkri:s] *v* aumentar. *n* aumento *m*. **increasing** *adj* creciente. **increasingly** *adv* cada vez más.

incredible [in'kredəbl] *adj* increíble.

incredulous [in'kredjuləs] *adj* incrédulo. **incredulity** *n* incredulidad *f*.

increment ['inkrəmənt] *n* aumento *m*.

incriminate [in'krimineit] *v* incriminar. **incriminating** *adj* acriminador.

incubate ['inkju,beit] *v* incubar. **incubation** *n* incubación *f*. **incubator** *n* incubadora *f*.

incur [in'kə:] *v* incurrir; (*debt*) contraer; (*loss*) sufrir.

incurable [in'kjuərəbl] *adj* incurable.

indebted [in'detid] *adj* (*owing money*) endeudado (con); (*fig*) agradecido. **indebtedness** *n* deuda *f*; agradecimiento *m*.

indecent [in'di:snt] *adj* indecente. **indecency** *n* indecencia *f*.

indeed [in'di:d] *adv* en efecto; realmente. **yes indeed!** ¡ya lo creo!

indefinite [in'definit] *adj* indefinido; impreciso.

indelible [in'deləbl] *adj* indeleble.

indemnity [in'demnəti] *n* (*security*) indemnidad *f*; reparación *f*.

indent [in'dent] *v* (*dent*) abollar; (*notch*) dentar; (*comm*) pedir; (*print*) sangrar. **indentation** *n* (*notch*) muesca *f*; (*print*) sangría *f*.

independent [,indi'pendənt] *adj* independiente. **independence** *n* independencia *f*.

index ['indeks] *n* índice *m*; (*math*) expo-

nente *m*. **index finger** dedo índice *m*.
cost-of-living index índice del coste de la
vida *m*. *v* (*file*) clasificar; (*a book*) poner un
índice a.

India ['indjə] *n* India *f*. **Indian** *n* indio, -a
m, *f*; *adj* indio. **Indian ink** tinta china *f*.
Indian summer veranillo de San Martín
m. **india paper** papel de China *m*. **india
rubber** goma de borrar *f*.

indicate ['indikeit] *v* indicar, señalar. **indication** *n* indicación *f*, señal *f*. **indicative**
nm, adj indicativo. **indicator** *n* indicador
m.

indict [in'dait] *v* acusar. **indictment** *n*
acusación *f*.

indifferent [in'difrənt] *adj* indiferente;
insignificante; (*mediocre*) regular. **indifference** *n* indiferencia *f*.

indigenous [in'didʒinəs] *adj* indígena.

indigestion [,indi'dʒestʃən] *n* indigestión *f*.
indigestible *adj* indigesto.

indignant [in'dignənt] *adj* indignado. **get
indignant** indignarse. **indignantly** *adv*
con indignación. **indignation** *n* indignación *f*.

indignity [in'dignəti] *n* (*lack of dignity*)
indignidad *f*; (*outrage*) afrenta *f*.

indirect [,indi'rekt] *adj* indirecto.

indiscreet [,indi'skri:t] *adj* indiscreto. **indiscretion** *n* indiscreción *f*.

indiscriminate [,indi'skriminit] *adj* indistinto; universal; (*person*) sin criterio.

indispensable [,indi'spensəbl] *adj* indispensable.

indisposed [,indi'spouzd] *adj* (*ill*) indispuesto, enfermo; (*reluctant*) maldispuesto.
indisposition *n* indisposición *f*; aversión *f*.

individual [,indi'vidjuəl] *adj* individual; personal. *n* individuo *m*. **individuality** *n* individualidad *f*.

indoctrinate [in'doktri,neit] *v* adoctrinar.
indoctrination *n* adoctrinamiento *m*.

indolent ['indələnt] *adj* indolente. **indolence** *n* indolencia *f*.

indoor ['indo:] *adj* interior. **indoor pool**
piscina cubierta *f*. **indoors** *adv* dentro; en
casa.

induce [in'dju:s] *v* (*convince*) inducir, persuadir; (*cause*) causar, provocar. **inducement** *n* incentivo *m*; (*motive*) móvil *m*.

indulge [in'dʌldʒ] *v* (*pamper*) mimar; (*give
way to*) ceder a. **indulge in** entregarse a.

indulgence *n* indulgencia *f*; satisfacción *f*;
tolerancia *f*; (*self-indulgence*) desenfreno *m*.
indulgent *adj* indulgente.

industry ['indəstri] *n* industria *f*; diligencia
f. **industrial** *adj* industrial. **industrial
relations** relaciones profesionales *f pl*.
industrialist *n* industrial *m*. **industrialize**
v industrializar. **industrious** *adj* trabajador.

inebriated [i'ni:brieitid] *adj* ebrio.

inedible [in'edibl] *adj* incomible.

inefficient [,ini'fiʃnt] *adj* ineficaz; incompetente. **inefficiency** *n* ineficacia *f*; incompetencia *f*.

inept [i'nept] *adj* inepto.

inequality [,ini'kwoləti] *n* desigualdad *f*;
injusticia *f*.

inert [i'nə:t] *adj* inerte. **inertia** *n* inercia *f*.

inevitable [in'evitəbl] *adj* inevitable.
inevitability *n* inevitabilidad *f*.

inexpensive [,inik'spensiv] *adj* poco costoso, barato.

inexperienced [,inik'spiəriənst] *adj* inexperto.

infallible [in'faləbl] *adj* infalible.

infamous ['infəməs] *adj* de mala fama;
odioso. **infamy** *n* infamia *f*.

infancy ['infənsi] *n* infancia *f*, niñez *f*.

infant ['infənt] *n* niño, -a *m*, *f*. *adj* naciente.
infantile *adj* infantil.

infantry ['infəntri] *n* infantería *f*.

infatuate [in'fatjueit] *v* **be infatuated
with** (*person*) estar chiflado por; (*idea*) estar
encaprichado por. **infatuation** *n* enam-
oramiento *m*.

infect [in'fekt] *v* infectar; contaminar.
infection *n* infección *f*; contaminación *f*.
infectious *adj* infeccioso; contagioso.

infer [in'fə:] *v* deducir. **inference** *n* deducción *f*.

inferior [in'fiəriə] *nm, adj* inferior. **inferiority** *n* inferioridad *f*. **inferiority complex** complejo de inferioridad *m*.

infernal [in'fə:nl] *adj* infernal; (*coll*)
maldito.

infertile [in'fə:tail] *adj* infértil

infest [in'fest] *v* infestar. **infestation** *n*
infestación *f*.

infidelity [,infi'deliti] *n* infidelidad *f*.

infiltrate [in'fil,treit] *v* infiltrarse. **infiltra-
tion** *n* infiltración *f*.

infinite ['infinit] *nm, adj* infinito. **infinity**
n infinidad *f*; (*math*) infinito *m*.

infinitive [in'finitiv] *nm, adj* infinitivo.

infirm [in'fə:m] *adj* débil. **infirmity** *n* debilidad *f*; (*illness*) enfermedad *f*.

infirmary [in'fə:məri] *n* enfermería *f*; hospital *m*.

inflame [in'fleim] *v* (*set on fire*) inflamar; (*passion*) avivar; (*anger*) encender. **inflammable** *adj* inflamable. **inflammation** *n* inflamación *f*. **inflammatory** *adj* incendiario.

inflate [in'fleit] *v* hinchar; (*prices*) provocar la inflación de. **inflatable** *adj* inflable. **inflation** *n* (*air*) inflado *m*; (*comm*) inflación *f*. **inflationary** *adj* inflacionista.

inflection [in'flekʃən] *n* inflexión *f*.

inflict [in'flikt] *v* infligir, imponer. **infliction** *n* (*punishment*) castigo *m*.

influence ['influəns] *n* influencia *f*. **under the influence of** bajo los efectos de. *v* (*person*) influenciar; (*decision*) influir en. **influential** *adj* influyente.

influenza [,influ'enzə] *n* gripe *f*.

influx ['inflʌks] *n* (*gas, etc.*) entrada *f*; (*people*) afluencia *f*.

inform [in'fo:m] *v* informar. **informative** *adj* informativo. **informer** *n* denunciante *m, f*.

informal [in'fo:ml] *adj* sin ceremonia; (*person*) sencillo; (*tone*) familiar; (*unofficial*) no oficial. **informality** *n* ausencia de ceremonia *f*; sencillez *f*.

information [,infə'meiʃən] *n* información *f*. **information bureau** centro de informaciones *m*. **information desk** informaciones *f pl*. **information technology** información tecnológica *f*.

infra-red [,infrə'red] *adj* infrarrojo.

infringe [in'frindʒ] *v* infringir; violar. **infringe on** usurpar. **infringement** *n* infracción *f*; usurpación *f*.

infuriate [in'fjuəri,eit] *v* enfurecer; exasperar. **infuriating** *adj* exasperante.

ingenious [in'dʒi:njəs] *adj* ingenioso. **ingenuity** *n* ingeniosidad *f*.

ingot ['iŋgət] *n* lingote *m*.

ingratiate [in'greiʃieit] *v* tener un detalle

ingredient [in'gri:djənt] *n* ingrediente *m*.

inhabit [in'habit] *v* (*occupy*) habitar; (*live in*) vivir en. **inhabitant** *n* habitante *m, f*.

inhale [in'heil] *v* inhalar; (*smoke*) tragar. **inhaler** inhalador *m*.

inherent [in'hiərənt] *adj* inherente.

inherit [in'herit] *v* heredar. **inheritance** *n* herencia *f*; sucesión *f*.

inhibit [in'hibit] *v* (*restrain*) inhibir; (*prevent*) impedir. **inhibition** *n* inhibición *f*.

inhuman [in'hju:mən] *adj* inhumano; insensible. **inhumanity** *n* inhumanidad *f*.

iniquity [i'nikwəti] *n* iniquidad *f*. **iniquitous** *adj* inicuo.

initial [i'niʃl] *adj* inicial, primero. *n* inicial *f*; (*used as abbreviation*) siglas *f pl*. *v* poner iniciales a; marcar con las iniciales. **initially** *adv* al principio.

initiate [i'niʃi,eit] *v* iniciar; (*proceedings*) entablar; (*membership*) admitir. **initiation** *n* iniciación *f*.

initiative [i'niʃiətiv] *n* iniciativa *f*.

inject [in'dʒekt] *v* inyectar. **injection** *n* inyección *f*.

injure ['indʒə] *v* herir; lastimar; ofender. **injury** *n* herida *f*; daño *m*; ofensa *f*. **injurious** *adj* injurioso; ofensivo.

injustice [in'dʒʌstis] *n* injusticia *f*.

ink [iŋk] *n* tinta *f*. **ink-well** *n* tintero *m*. *v* entintar.

inkling ['iŋkliŋ] *n* idea *f*; algo *m*; sospecha *f*; indicio *m*.

inland ['inlənd; *adv* in'land] *adj* interior. **Inland Revenue** fisco *m*. *adv* hacia el interior.

in-laws ['in,lo:s] *pl n* (*coll*) familia política *f sing*.

***inlay** [in'lei; *n* 'inlei] *v* incrustar; adornar con marquetería. *n* incrustación *f*; (*with coloured woods*) taracea *f*.

inlet ['inlet] *n* cala *f*; brazo de mar *m*; (*tech*) entrada *f*.

inmate ['inmeit] *n* (*prison*) preso *m*; (*asylum*) internado, -a *m*, *f*; (*hospital*) enfermo, -a *m*, *f*.

inn [in] *n* posada *f*; taberna *f*. **innkeeper** *n* posadero, -a *m*, *f*; tabernero, -a *m*, *f*.

innate [i'neit] *adj* innato.

inner ['inə] *adj* interior; íntimo. **inner city** rabal *m*. **inner tube** cámara de neumático *f*.

innocent ['inəsnt] *adj* inocente. **innocence** *n* inocencia *f*.

innocuous [i'nokjuəs] *adj* inocuo; inofensivo.

innovation [inə'veiʃən] *n* innovación *f*.

innuendo [,inju'endou] *n* insinuación *f*.

innumerable [i'nju:mərəbl] *adj* innumerable.

inoculate [i'nokju,leit] *v* inocular. **inoculation** *n* inoculación *f*.

inorganic [,ino:'ganik] *adj* inorgánico.

input ['input] *n* entrada *f*; (*computer*) input *m*.

inquest ['inkwest] *n* encuesta *f*.

inquire [in'kwaiə] *v* informarse de; preguntar. **inquire into** investigar. **inquiring** *adj* (*mind*) curioso; (*look*) inquisidor. **inquiry** *n* pregunta *f*; (*official*) investigación *f*; (*request for information*) petición de información *f*. **inquiry office** oficina de informaciones *f*. **inquiries** *pl n* (*sign*) información *f sing*.

inquisition [,inkwi'ziʃən] *n* investigación *f*. **the Inquisition** la Inquisición *f*.

inquisitive [in'kwizətiv] *adj* preguntón; curioso. **inquisitiveness** *n* curiosidad *f*.

insane [in'sein] *adj* loco. **insane asylum** manicomio *m*. **insanity** *n* locura *f*.

insatiable [in'seiʃəbl] *adj* insaciable.

inscribe [in'skraib] *v* inscribir; (*engrave*) grabar. **inscription** *n* inscripción *f*.

insect ['insekt] *n* insecto *m*; (*coll*) bicho *m*. **insecticide** *n* insecticida *f*.

insecure [,insi'kjuə] *adj* inseguro; (*unstable*) inestable. **insecurity** *n* inseguridad *f*.

inseminate [in'semineit] *v* inseminar. **insemination** *n* inseminación *f*.

insensitive [in'sensətiv] *adj* insensible. **insensitivity** *n* insensibilidad *f*.

inseparable [in'sepərəbl] *adj* inseparable.

insert [in'sə:t; *n* 'insə:t] *v* introducir; (*advert*) insertar; (*between pages*) intercalar. *n* (*in a book*) encarte *m*. **insertion** *n* inserción *f*; encarte *m*; (*advert*) anuncio *m*.

inshore [,in'ʃo:] *adj* cercano a la orilla.

inside [,in'said] *adv* dentro, adentro. *prep* dentro de. *adj* interior; confidencial. *n* interior *m*; parte de adentro *f*. **inside out** al revés.

insidious [in'sidiəs] *adj* insidioso. **insidiousness** *n* insidia *f*.

insight ['insait] *n* perspicacia *f*.

insignificant [,insig'nifikant] *adj* insignificante. **insignificance** *n* insignificancia *f*.

insincere [,insin'siə] *adj* insincero; hipócrita. **insincerity** *n* insinceridad *f*; hipocresía *f*.

insinuate [in'sinjueit] *v* insinuar. **insinuation** *n* insinuación *f*.

insipid [in'sipid] *adj* insípido, soso.

insist [in'sist] *v* insistir, empeñarse. **insistence** *n* insistencia *f*, empeño *m*. **insistent** *adj* insistente. **insistently** *adv* insistentemente.

insolent ['insələnt] *adj* insolente. **insolence** *n* insolencia *f*.

insoluble [in'soljubl] *adj* insoluble.

insomnia [in'somniə] *n* insomnio *m*. **insomniac** *n*(*m* + *f*), *adj* insomne.

inspect [in'spekt] *v* inspeccionar, examinar. **inspection** *n* inspección *f*, examen *m*. **inspector** *n* inspector *m*, *f*.

inspire [in'spaiə] *v* inspirar. **inspiration** *n* inspiración *f*. **inspirational** *adj* inspirador.

instability [,instə'biləti] *n* inestabilidad *f*, instabilidad *f*.

install [in'sto:l] *v* instalar. **installation** *n* instalación *f*.

instalment [in'sto:lmənt] *n* (*payment*) plazo *m*; (*serial*) fascículo *m*. **monthly instalment** mensualidad *f*.

instance ['instəns] *n* ejemplo *m*. **for instance** por ejemplo.

instant ['instənt] *n* instante *m*, momento *m*. *adj* (*coffee, soup, etc.*) instantáneo; urgente; inmediato; inminente; (*this month*) corriente. **instantaneous** *adj* instantáneo. **instantly** *adv* al instante.

instead [in'sted] *adv* en su lugar. **instead of** en vez de.

instep ['instep] *n* empeine *m*.

instigate ['instigeit] *v* instigar, incitar; fomentar. **instigation** *n* instigación *f*. **instigator** *n* instigador, -a *m*, *f*.

instil [in'stil] *v* instilar; inculcar.

instinct ['instiŋkt] *n* instinto *m*. **instinctive** *adj* instintivo.

institute ['institju:t] *n* instituto *m*. *v* instituir, establecer; (*start*) empezar. **institution** *n* institución *f*; establecimiento *m*.

instruct [in'strʌkt] *v* (*teach*) instruir; (*order*) mandar. **instruction** *n* instrucción *f*. **instructive** *adj* instructivo. **instructor** *n* instructor, -a *m*, *f*; profesor, -a *m*, *f*; maestro, -a *m*, *f*.

instrument ['instrəmənt] *n* instrumento *m*. **instrumental** *adj* instrumental. **be instrumental in** contribuir a.

insubordinate [,insə'bo:dənət] *adj* insubordinado. **insubordination** *n* insubordinación *f*.

insufficient [,insə'fiʃənt] *adj* insuficiente.

insufficiency *n* insuficiencia *f*.

insular ['insjulə] *adj* insular; (*outlook*) estrecho de miras.

insulate ['insjuleit] *v* aislar. **insulation** *n* aislamiento *m*; (*material*) aislador *m*.

insulin ['insjulin] *n* insulina *f*.

insult [in'sʌlt; *n* 'insʌlt] *v* insultar. *n* insulto *m*.

insure [in'ʃuə] *v* asegurar. **insurance** *n* seguro *m*. **insurance broker** corredor de seguros *m*. **insurance policy** póliza de seguro *f*. **fully comprehensive insurance** seguro a todo riesgo *m*. **third party insurance** seguro contra terceros *m*. **national insurance** seguros sociales *m pl*. **take out insurance** hacerse un seguro.

intact [in'takt] *adj* intacto.

intake ['inteik] *n* (*air, water*) toma *f*; (*mot*) entrada *f*; (*fuel, steam*) válvula de admisión *f*; (*food*) ración *f*; (*school*) número de personas admitidas *m*; (*thing taken in*) consumo *m*.

intangible [in'tandʒəbl] *adj* intangible. **intangibility** *n* intangibilidad *f*.

integral ['intigrəl] *adj* (*part*) integrante; (*complete*) integral. *n* integral *f*.

integrate ['intigreit] *v* integrar. **integration** *n* integración *f*.

integrity [in'tegrəti] *n* integridad *f*.

intellect ['intilekt] *n* intelecto *m*, inteligencia *f*. **intellectual** *n*(*m* + *f*), *adj* intelectual.

intelligent [in'telidʒənt] *adj* inteligente. **intelligence** *n* inteligencia *f*; (*information*) noticia *f*; (*secret information*) información *f*.

intelligible [in'telidʒəbl] *adj* inteligible.

intend [in'tend] *v* proponerse.

intense [in'tens] *adj* intenso; fuerte; profundo; ardiente; enorme. **intensify** *v* intensificar; aumentar. **intensity** *n* intensidad *f*. **intensive** *adj* intensivo. **intensive care** asistencia intensiva *f*.

intent[1] [in'tent] *n* intención *f*, propósito *m*.

intent[2] [in'tent] *adj* atento; profundo; constante.

intention [in'tenʃən] *n* intención *f*. **intentional** *adj* intencional.

inter [in'tə:] *v* enterrar. **interment** *n* entierro *m*.

interact [,intər'akt] *v* actuar recíprocamente. **interaction** *n* interacción *f*.

interactive [intər'aktiv] *adj* interactivo

intercede [,intə'si:d] *v* interceder. **interces-**

sion *n* intercesión *f*.

intercept [,intə'sept] *v* (*message*) interceptar; (*stop someone*) parar. **interception** *n* intercepción *f*, interceptación *f*.

interchange [,intə'tʃeindʒ] *n* intercambio *m*; cambio *m*. **interchangeable** *adj* intercambiable.

intercom ['intə,kom] *n* interfono *m*.

intercourse ['intəko:s] *n* (*social*) trato *m*; (*pol, comm*) relaciones *f pl*; (*sexual*) contacto sexual *m*.

interest ['intrist] *n* interés *m*; (*advantage*) beneficio *m*. **business interests** negocios *m pl*. **interest rate** tipo de interés *m*. *v* interesar. **be interested in** interesarse en. **interesting** *adj* interesante.

interfere [,intə'fiə] *v* entrometerse. **interfere with** (*hinder*) estorbar; (*touch*) tocar; (*interests*) oponerse a. **interference** *n* intromisión *f*; obstrucción *f*; (*radio*) parásitos *m pl*. **interfering** *adj* (*person*) entrometido; interferente.

interim ['intərim] *n* ínterin *m*. *adj* provisional.

interior [in'tiəriə] *nm, adj* interior.

interjection [,intə'dʒekʃən] *n* interjección *f*.

interlude ['intəlu:d] *n* intervalo *m*; (*theatre*) entremés *m*; (*music*) interludio *m*.

intermediate [,intə'mi:diət] *adj* intermedio. **intermediary** *n* intermediario, -a *m, f*.

interminable [in'tə:minəbl] *adj* interminable.

intermission [,intə'miʃən] *n* (*interruption*) intermisión *f*; (*theatre*) entreacto *m*; (*cinema*) descanso *m*.

intermittent [,intə'mitənt] *adj* intermitente. **intermittently** *adv* a intervalos.

intern ['intə:n; *v* in'tə:n] *n* interno *m*. *v* internar. **internment** *n* internamiento *m*.

internal [in'tə:nl] *adj* interno. **internal combustion engine** motor de combustión interna *m*.

international [,intə'naʃənl] *adj* internacional. **international date line** línea de cambio de fecha *f*. **Internet** *n* internet *m*; **Internet service provider (ISP)** servidor de internet *m*.

interpose [,intə'pouz] *v* interponer; intervenir. **interposition** *n* interposición *f*.

interpret [in'tə:prit] *v* interpretar. **interpretation** *n* interpretación *f*. **interpreter** *n* intérprete *m, f*.

interrogate [in'terəgeit] v interrogar. **interrogation** n interrogatorio m. **interrogator** n interrogador, -a m, f.

interrogative [,intə'rogətiv] adj (sentence) interrogativo; (look) interrogador. n palabra interrogativa f.

interrupt [,intə'rʌpt] v interrumpir. **interruption** n interrupción f.

intersect [,intə'sekt] v cruzar; (math) cortar. **intersection** n (mot) cruce m; (math) intersección f.

intersperse [,intə'spə:s] v esparcir.

interval ['intəvəl] n (time, space, music) intervalo m; (theatre) entreacto m; (cinema) descanso m.

intervene [,intə'vi:n] v intervenir; (happen) ocurrir; (time) transcurrir; (distance) mediar. **intervention** n intervención f.

interview ['intəvju:] n entrevista f, interviú f. v entrevistar. **interviewer** n entrevistador, -a m, f.

intestine [in'testin] n intestino m. **intestinal** adj intestinal.

intimate[1] ['intimət] adj íntimo; (individual) personal; (loving) amoroso; (detailed) profundo. **intimacy** n relaciones íntimas f pl.

intimate[2] ['intimeit] v insinuar; anunciar. **intimation** n insinuación f; indicación f; indicio m.

intimidate [in'timideit] v intimidar. **intimidation** n intimidación f.

into ['intu] prep en; a; hacia; contra; dentro.

intolerable [in'tolərəbl] adj intolerable.

intolerant [in'tolərənt] adj intolerante. **intolerance** n intolerancia f.

intonation [,intə'neifən] n entonación f. **intone** v entonar.

intoxicate [in'toksikeit] v embriagar, emborrachar. **intoxicated** adj borracho, ebrio. **intoxication** n embriaguez f, borrachera f.

intransitive [in'transitiv] nm, adj intransitivo.

intravenous [,intrə'vi:nəs] adj intravenoso.

intrepid [in'trepid] adj intrépido.

intricate ['intriket] adj intrincado; complejo. **intricacy** n intrincamiento m; complejidad f.

intrigue ['intri:g; v in'tri:g] n intriga f. v intrigar.

intrinsic [in'trinsik] adj intrínseco.

introduce [,intrə'dju:s] v presentar; introducir; (acquaint) iniciar. **introduction** n presentación f; introducción f. **introductory** adj introductorio.

introspective [,intrə'spektiv] adj introspectivo. **introspection** n introspección f.

introvert ['intrə,və:t] adj introvertido, -a m, f. **introverted** adj introvertido.

intrude [in'tru:d] v imponer; meter por fuerza. **intruder** n intruso, -a m, f. **intrusion** n entremetimiento m.

intuition [,intju:'ifən] n intuición f. **intuitive** adj intuitivo.

inundate ['inʌndeit] v inundar. **inundation** n inundación f.

invade [in'veid] v invadir. **invader** n invasor, -a m, f. **invasion** n invasión f.

invalid[1] ['invəlid] nm, adj (disabled) inválido; (sick) enfermo.

invalid[2] [in'valid] adj (not valid) nulo.

invaluable [in'valjuəbl] adj inestimable.

invariable [in'veəriəbl] adj invariable. **invariably** adv invariablemente; constantemente.

invective [in'vektiv] n invectiva f.

invent [in'vent] v inventar. **invention** n invención f. **inventive** adj inventivo, ingenioso. **inventor** n inventor, -a m, f.

inventory ['invəntri] n inventario m.

invert [in'və:t] v invertir. **inverted commas** comillas f pl. **inversion** n inversión f.

invertebrate [in'və:tibrət] nm, adj invertebrado.

invest [in'vest] v invertir; (install) investir. **invest in** (fig) comprarse. **invest with** (fig) envolver en. **investment** n inversión f. **investor** n inversionista m, f.

investigate [in'vestigeit] v investigar, examinar; estudiar. **investigation** n investigación f; estudio m.

invigorating [in'vigəreitiŋ] adj tónico, estimulante. **invigorate** v vigorizar, estimular.

invincible [in'vinsəbl] adj invencible.

invisible [in'vizəbl] adj invisible. **invisibility** n invisibilidad f.

invite [in'vait] v invitar, convidar; (questions) solicitar; (ask for) pedir; (cause) provocar. **invitation** n invitación f. **inviting** adj atractivo; seductor; tentador; apetitoso.

invoice ['invois] n factura f. v facturar.

invoke [in'vouk] v invocar; (ask for) pedir;

(fall back on) recurrir. **invocation** n invocación f.

involuntary [in'vɒləntəri] *adj* involuntario. **involuntarily** *adv* sin querer.

involve [in'vɒlv] v *(concern)* concernir; *(imply)* suponer; *(affect)* afectar; *(entail)* ocasionar; *(draw somebody in)* comprometer; mezclar; *(require)* exigir; *(complicate)* complicar. **involved** *adj* complicado. **involvement** n envolvimiento m; participación f; compromiso m.

inward ['inwəd] *adj* interior, interno; *(thoughts)* íntimo. **inwardly** *adv* interiormente. **inwards** *adv* hacia dentro.

iodine ['aiədi:n] n yodo m.

ion ['aiən] n ion m.

IOU n pagaré m

IQ n CI m

irate [ai'reit] *adj* furioso.

Ireland ['aiələnd] n Irlanda f. **Irish** nm, *adj* irlandés. **the Irish** los irlandeses m pl.

iris ['aiəris] n lirio m.

irk [ə:k] v molestar. **irksome** *adj* molesto.

iron ['aiən] n *(metal)* hierro m; *(for pressing)* plancha f; *(golf)* palo de golf m. **cast iron** hierro colado m. **Iron Curtain** telón de acero m. **wrought iron** hierro forjado m. **ironmonger's** n quincallería f. v planchar. **iron out** *(fig)* allanar. **ironing** n planchado m. **ironing board** tabla de planchar f.

irony ['aiərəni] n ironía f. **ironic** *adj* irónico.

irrational [i'raʃənl] *adj* irracional. n *(math)* número irracional m.

irregular [i'regjulə] *adj* irregular. **irregularity** n irregularidad f.

irrelevant [i'reləvənt] *adj* *(remark)* fuera de propósito; *(beside the point)* no pertinente.

irreparable [i'repərəbl] *adj* irreparable.

irresistible [,iri'zistəbl] *adj* irresistible.

irrespective [,iri'spektiv] *adj* **irrespective of** sin tener en cuenta.

irresponsible [,iri'sponsəbl] *adj* irresponsable; irreflexivo.

irrevocable [i'revəkəbl] *adj* irrevocable.

irrigate ['irigeit] v irrigar. **irrigation** n irrigación f.

irritate ['iriteit] v irritar. **irritable** *adj* irritable. **irritation** n irritación f.

is [iz] V be.

island ['ailənd] n isla f; *(traffic)* refugio m.

isolate ['aisəleit] v aislar. **isolation** n aislamiento m.

issue ['iʃu:] n *(stamps, shares, etc.)* emisión f; *(publication)* publicación f; *(edition)* tirada f; *(copy)* número m; *(passport)* expedición f; *(distribution)* reparto m; *(outcome)* resultado m; *(question)* cuestión f; *(affair)* asunto m; *(offspring)* progenie f, **take issue with** estar en desacuerdo con. v salir; resultar; publicar; distribuir; *(give)* dar; emitir; *(decree)* promulgar; *(warrant, cheque)* extender; *(tickets)* expender; *(licence)* facilitar.

isthmus ['isməs] n istmo m.

it [it] *pron* él, ella ello; *(direct object)* lo, la; *(indirect object)* le.

IT n informática f

italic [i'talik] *adj* itálico. **italics** pl n bastardilla f sing.

Italy ['itəli] n Italia f. **Italian** n, *adj* italiano, -a.

itch [itʃ] n picazón f; *(desire)* ganas f pl. v picar.

item ['aitəm] n artículo m; noticia f; detalle m; punto m. **itemize** v detallar.

itinerary [ai'tinərəri] n itinerario m.

its [its] *adj* su *(pl* sus).

itself [it'self] *pron* se; él/ello mismo, ella misma; *(after prep)* sí mismo, -a. **by itself** aislado; *(alone)* solo.

ivory ['aivəri] n marfil m.

ivy ['aivi] n hiedra f, yedra f.

J

jab [dʒab] v *(stab)* pinchar; *(elbow)* dar un codazo a. n pinchazo m; codazo m; *(blow)* golpe seco m; *(coll: injection)* inyección f.

jack [dʒak] n *(mot)* gato m; *(cards)* valet m, jota f; *(Spanish cards)* sota f. v **jack up** levantar con el gato.

jackal ['dʒako:l] n chacal m.

jackdaw ['dʒakdo:] n grajilla f.

jacket ['dʒakit] n chaqueta f; *(book)* sobrecubierta f; *(tech: cylinder, pipe, etc.)* camisa f.

jackpot ['dʒakpot] n premio gordo m.

jade [dʒeid] nm, *adj* jade.

jaded ['dʒeidid] *adj* cansado.

jagged ['dʒagid] *adj* dentado.

jaguar ['dʒagjuə] n jaguar m.

jail [dʒeil] n cárcel f. v encarcelar. **jailer** n carcelero m.

jam¹ [dʒam] v (force in) meter a la fuerza; (squash) apretar; (catch) pillar; (pack) atestar; (clog) atorar; (block) bloquear; (moving part) atascar; (radio) interferir; (become wedged) atrancarse. n atasco m; (people) agolpamiento m; (traffic) embotellamiento m. **be in a jam** (coll) estar en un apuro.

jam² [dʒam] n mermelada f.

janitor ['dʒanitə] n portero m.

January ['dʒanjuəri] n enero m.

Japan [dʒə'pan] n Japón m. **Japanese** nm, adj japonés.

jar¹ [dʒaː] n (vessel) vasija f; (jam pot) tarro m; (large pot) tinaja f.

jar² [dʒaː] v (sound) chirriar; (shake) sacudir; (colours) chocar; (music) sonar mal; (nerves) irritar.

jargon ['dʒaːgən] n jerga f.

jasmine ['dʒazmin] n jazmín m.

jaundice ['dʒoːndis] n ictericia f; (fig) celos m pl.

jaunt [dʒoːnt] n paseo m.

jaunty ['dʒoːnti] adj vivaz; desenvuelto.

javelin ['dʒavəlin] n jabalina f.

jaw [dʒoː] n (person) mandíbula f; (animal) quijada f. **jawbone** n mandíbula f; quijada f.

jazz [dʒaz] n jazz m. **jazz band** orquesta de jazz f.

jealous ['dʒeləs] adj celoso; envidioso. **jealousy** n celos m pl; envidia f.

jeans [dʒiːns] pl n pantalones vaqueros m pl.

jeep [dʒiːp] n jeep m.

jeer [dʒiə] v (boo) abuchear; (mock) mofarse de. n abucheo m; mofa f.

jelly ['dʒeli] n jalea f. **jellyfish** n medusa f.

jeopardize ['dʒepədaiz] v arriesgar. **jeopardy** n riesgo m, peligro m.

jerk [dʒaːk] n sacudida f; (shove) empujón m; (pull) tirón. v sacudir; mover a tirones. **jerkily** adv con sacudidas. **jerky** adj espasmódico.

jersey ['dʒaːzi] n jersey m.

jest [dʒest] v bromear. n broma f. **jester** n bromista m, f.

jet [dʒet] n (liquid) chorro m; (flame) llama f; (plane) avión de reactor m. **jetpropelled**

adj de reacción.

jetty ['dʒeti] n muelle m.

Jew [dʒuː] n judío, -a m, f. **Jewish** adj judío.

jewel ['dʒuːəl] n joya f, piedra preciosa f; (in a watch) rubí m. **jeweller** n joyero, -a m, f. **jeweller's** n joyería f. **jewellery** n joyería f.

jig [dʒig] n giga f. v bailar la giga; dar saltitos.

jigsaw ['dʒigsoː] n (puzzle) rompecabezas m invar; (saw) sierra de vaivén f.

jilt [dʒilt] v dejar plantado a.

jingle ['dʒiŋgl] n tintineo m; (verse) copla f. v tintinear.

jinx [dʒiŋks] n (coll) maleficio m. **put a jinx on** echar mal de ojo a.

job [dʒob] n trabajo m, empleo m. **job lot** colección miscelánea f. **make a good job of (something)** hacer (algo) bien. **odd-job man** factótum m.

jockey ['dʒoki] n jinete m; jockey m.

jocular ['dʒokjulə] adj jocoso; bromista.

jodhpurs ['dʒodpəz] pl n pantalones de montar m pl.

jog [dʒog] n sacudida f; (with elbow) codazo m. **jog trot** n trote corto m. v sacudir; (memory) refrescar. **jog someone's elbow** darle en el codo a uno. **jogging** n jogging m.

join [dʒoin] v juntar, unir; (roads) ir a, dar a; (friends) reunirse con; (a company) ingresar en; (a club) hacerse socio de; (a political party) afiliarse a; (hands) darse la mano; (two pieces) ensamblar; (rivers) confluir. **join in** participar en. **join up** (mil) alistarse. **joiner** carpintero m.

joint [dʒoint] n juntura f, unión f; (anat) articulación f; (meat) corte para asar m; (slang: place) antro m. adj unido; colectivo; conjunto; mutuo. **jointly** adv en común.

joist [dʒoist] n vigueta f.

joke [dʒouk] n chiste m; (prank) broma f. v contar chistes; bromear. **joker** n chistoso, -a m, f; bromista m, f; (fool) payaso, -a m, f; (cards) comodín m.

jolly ['dʒoli] adj alegre, jovial; divertido. adv (coll: emphatic) muy. **jollity** n alegría f; jovialidad f.

jolt [dʒoult] v sacudir; (vehicle) traquetear. n sacudida f; choque m; (fig: shock) susto m.

jostle ['dʒosl] v (push) empujar; (elbow) codear. n empujones m pl.

jot [dʒɒt] n jota f. v **jot down** apuntar.

journal ['dʒəːnl] n (newspaper) periódico m; (magazine) revista f; (diary) diario m; (of a learned society) boletín m. **journalism** n periodismo m. **journalist** n periodista m, f.

journey ['dʒəːni] n viaje m. v viajar.

jovial ['dʒouviəl] adj jovial. **joviality** n jovialidad f.

joy [dʒoi] n alegría f; placer m. **joyful** or **joyous** adj alegre, gozoso. **joyriding** robo de coche m. **joystick** mando de control m.

jubilant ['dʒuːbilənt] adj jubiloso. **jubilation** n júbilo m.

jubilee ['dʒuːbiliː] n jubileo m.

Judaism ['dʒuːdeiizəm] n judaísmo m.

judge [dʒʌdʒ] n juez m; árbitro m. v juzgar; arbitrar. **judging by** a juzgar por. **judgement** n (trial) juicio; (legal sentence) sentencia f; apreciación f.

judicial [dʒuːdiʃəl] adj judicial.

judicious [dʒuːdiʃəs] adj juicioso.

judo ['dʒuːdou] n judo m.

jug [dʒʌg] n jarra f; (slang: prison) chirona f.

juggernaut ['dʒʌgənɔːt] n camión grande m.

juggle ['dʒʌgl] v hacer juegos malabares. **juggler** n malabarista m, f. **juggling** n juegos malabares m pl.

jugular ['dʒʌgjulə] nf, adj yugular.

juice [dʒuːs] n jugo m. **juicy** adj jugoso.

jukebox ['dʒuːkbɒks] n máquina de discos f.

July [dʒu'lai] n julio m.

jumble ['dʒʌmbl] v embrollar; mezclar. n embrollo m; mezcolanza f. **jumble sale** venta de caridad f.

jump [dʒʌmp] n salto m. v saltar. **jump at** (offer, etc.) aprovechar. **make someone jump** sobresaltar a uno. **jumpy** adj (coll) nervioso.

jumper ['dʒʌmpə] n (garment) jersey m.

junction ['dʒʌŋkʃən] n (join) unión f; (rail) empalme m; (road) cruce f.

juncture ['dʒʌŋkʃə] n coyuntura f. **at this juncture** en esta coyuntura.

June [dʒuːn] n junio m.

jungle ['dʒʌŋgl] n selva f.

junior ['dʒuːnjə] adj (younger) hijo; (lower rank) subalterno. n menor m, f; subalterno, -a m, f; (in school) pequeño, -a m, f.

juniper ['dʒuːnipə] n enebro m. **juniper berry** enebrina f.

junk¹ [dʒʌŋk] n trastos viejos m pl; (coll: rubbish) porquería f. **junk food** comida basura f. **junk mail** propaganda f. **junk shop** n baratillo m.

junk² [dʒʌŋk] n (naut) junco m.

jurisdiction [dʒuəris'dikʃən] n jurisdicción f.

jury ['dʒuəri] n jurado m. **juror** n jurado, -a m, f.

just [dʒʌst] adv justo; justamente; precisamente. **have just** acabar de. adj justo; exacto.

justice ['dʒʌstis] n justicia f. **Justice of the Peace** juez de paz m, f.

justify ['dʒʌstifai] v justificar. **justifiable** adj justificable. **justification** n justificación f.

jut [dʒʌt] v **jut out** sobresalir.

jute [dʒuːt] n yute m.

juvenile ['dʒuːvənail] n joven m. f, adolescente m. f, menor m, f. adj juvenil; infantil. **juvenile delinquent** delincuente juvenil m, f.

juxtapose [,dʒʌkstə'pouz] v yuxtaponer. **juxtaposition** n yuxtaposición f.

K

kaftan ['kaftan] n caftán m.

kaleidoscope [kə'laidəskoup] n calidoscopio m.

kangaroo [kaŋgə'ruː] n canguro m.

karate [kə'raːti] n karate m.

kebab [ki'bab] n pincho m.

keel [kiːl] n quilla f. **keel over** (naut) zozobrar; (coll: faint) desplomarse.

keen [kiːn] adj entusiasta; fuerte; vivo; penetrante; (prices) competitivo; (mind) agudo; (sharp) afilado. **keenly** adv con entusiasmo; profundamente. **keenness** n entusiasmo m; deseo m; profundidad f; agudeza f; finura f.

*keep [kiːp] v guardar; tener. (promise) cumplir; (appointment) acudir a; (hang on to) quedarse; (support) mantener; (hold) reservar; (detain) detener; (look after) cuidar; (continue) seguir. **keep at** seguir con. **keep**

away mantener a distancia. **keep down** contener. **keep fit** mantenerse en forma. **keep out!** ¡prohibida la entrada! **keep up with** seguir. **keeper** n guarda m, f.

keg [keg] n barril m.

kennel ['kenl] n perrera f.

kerb [kə:b] n bordillo m.

kernel ['ə:nl] n (nut) pepita f; (seed) grano m.

kerosene ['kerəsi:n] n queroseno m.

ketchup ['ketʃəp] n salsa de tomate f.

kettle ['ketl] n hervidor m. **kettledrum** n timbal m.

key [ki:] n llave f; (for a code) clave f; (music) tono m; (piano, typewriter) tecla f. **keyboard** n teclado m. **keyhole** n ojo de la cerradura m. **key ring** n llavero m. adj clave. **key (in)** (computing) (v) teclear.

khaki ['ka:ki] nm, adj caqui.

kick [kik] n patada f, puntapié m; (animal) coz f; (recoil) culatazo m; (fig: energy) fuerza f. v dar una patada a; dar una coz a. **kick off** (football) hacer el saque del centro; (fig) comenzar. **kick-off** n saque del centro m; (coll) comienzo m. **kick out** (coll) poner de patitas en la calle.

kid[1] [kid] n (goat) cabrito m; (leather) cabritilla f; (coll: child) niño, -a m, f.

kid[2] [kid] v (coll) tomar el pelo.

kidnap ['kidnap] v secuestrar, raptar. **kidnapper** n secuestrador, -a m, f. raptor, -ora m, f. **kidnapping** n secuestro m. rapto m.

kidney ['kidni] n riñón m.

kill [kil] v matar; (fig: hopes) arruinar. n muerte f; caza f. **killjoy** n aguafiestas m. f invar. **killer** n asesino, -a m, f. **killing** n (murder) asesinato m; (slaughter) matanza f.

kiln [kiln] n horno m.

kilo ['ki:lou] n kilo m.

kilobyte ['kiləbait] n kilobyte m

kilogram ['kiləgram] n kilogramo m.

kilometre ['kiləmi:tə] n kilómetro m.

kin [kin] n parientes m pl. **kinship** n parentesco m.

kindly ['kaindli] adj amablemente

kind[1] [kaind] adj amable; bueno. **kind-hearted** adj bondadoso. **kindness** n amabilidad f; bondad f.

kind[2] [kaind] n clase f, tipo m; género m; especie f. **in kind** en especie.

kindergarten ['kindəga:tn] n jardín de la infancia m.

kindle ['kindl] v encender; despertar.

kindred ['kindrid] n parientes m pl. adj (related) emparentado; (similar) semejante. **kindred spirits** almas gemelas f pl

kinetic [kin'etik] adj cinético.

king [kin] n rey m; (draughts) dama f. **kingfisher** n martin pescador m. **kingdom** n reino m. **king-size(d)** adj enorme, gigante. **king-size(d) bed** cama de matrimonio extragrande or de dos metros f

kink [kink] n (rope) retorcimiento m; (hair) rizo m. v retorcer. **kinky** adj retorcido; (coll) extraño.

kiosk ['ki:osk] n quiosco m, kiosko m.

kipper ['kipə] n arenque ahumado m.

kiss [kis] v besar. n beso m. **kiss of life** respiración boca a boca f.

kit [kit] n (tools) herramientas f pl; (sport) equipo m; (first aid) botiquín m; (model for assembling) maqueta f. **kit out** equipar.

kitchen ['kitʃin] n cocina f. **kitchen sink** fregadero m.

kite [kait] n cometa f; (bird) milano m.

kitten ['kitn] n gatito m.

kitty ['kiti] n plato m, platillo m.

kleptomania [kleptə'meiniə] n cleptomanía f. **kleptomaniac** n(m + f), adj cleptómano.

knack [nak] n facilidad f; tino m; habilidad f. **get the knack of** coger el tino de.

knapsack ['napsak] n mochila f.

knead [ni:d] v amasar.

knee [ni:] n rodilla f. **kneecap** n rótula f.

*kneel [ni:l] v arrodillarse.

knew [nju:] V **know**.

knickers ['nikəz] pl n bragas f pl.

knife [naif] n cuchillo m. v (stab) apuñalar.

knight [nait] n caballero m. v armar caballero. **knighthood** n título de caballero m.

knit [nit] v tejer. **knit together** juntar; (bones) soldarse. **knitting** n tejido de punto m. **knitting machine** máquina de hacer punto f. **knitting needle** aguja de hacer punto f.

knob [nob] n bulto m; (door) pomo m; (radio, etc.) botón m; (drawer) tirador m; (butter) pedazo m.

knobbly ['nobli] adj nudoso.

knock [nok] n golpe m, toque m. v golpear, pegar; (fig: criticize) meterse con. **knock**

down (*price*) rebajar; (*person*) atropellar; (*object*) derribar. **knock-kneed** *adj* patizambo. **knock out** (*stun*) dejar K.O.; (*from contest*) eliminar. **knockout** *n* (*boxing*) knock out *m*, K.O. *m*. **knock over** tirar. **knocker** *n* aldaba *f*, aldabón *m*.

knot [not] *n* nudo *m*. *v* anudar. **knotty** (*problem*) espinoso.

*know [nou] *v* (*facts*) saber; (*people, places*) conocer; (*recognize*) reconocer; (*distinguish*) distinguir. **know-all** *n* (*coll*) sabelotodo *m, f*. **know-how** *n* (*coll*) habilidad *f*; conocimientos *m pl*. **knowing** *adj* astuto; (*look*) de entendimiento.

knowledge ['nolidʒ] *n* conocimiento *m*. **knowledgeable** *adj* informado; erudito.

knuckle ['nʌkl] *n* nudillo *m*. **knuckle down to** ponerse seriamente a. **knuckle under** someterse.

L

lab [lab] *n* laboratorio *m*

label ['leibl] *n* etiqueta *f*. *v* poner etiqueta a.

laboratory [lə'borətəri] *n* laboratorio *m*.

labour ['leibə] *n* (*work*) trabajo *m*; (*task*) tarea *f*; (*effort*) esfuerzo *m*; (*childbirth*) parto *m*; (*manpower*) trabajadores *m pl*. **labour-saving** *adj* que ahorra trabajo. *v* trabajar; esforzarse. **laborious** *adj* laborioso. **labourer** *n* obrero *m*; peón *m*.

labyrinth ['labərinθ] *n* laberinto *m*.

lace [leis] *n* (*fabric*) encaje *m*. (*shoe*) cordón *m*. *v* atar; (*drink*) rociar.

lacerate ['lasəreit] *v* lacerar. **laceration** *n* laceración *f*.

lack [lak] *n* falta *f*, carencia *f*. **for lack of** por falta de. *v* carecer de, faltar a; necesitar.

lackadaisical [,lakə'deizikəl] *adj* apático; descuidado; tonto.

lacquer ['lakə] *n* (*hair*) laca *f*; (*paint*) pintura al duco *f*. *v* echar laca a; pintar al duco.

lad [lad] *n* (*coll*) chico *m*, muchacho *m*.

ladder ['ladə] *n* escalera de mano *f*; (*stocking*) carrera *f*. **ladderproof** *adj* indesmallable.

laden ['leidn] *adj* cargado.

ladle ['leidl] *n* cucharón *m*.

lady ['leidi] *n* señora *f*. **ladies** (*sign*) servicios de señoras *m pl*. **ladies and gentlemen!** ¡señoras y señores! **ladybird** *n* mariquita *f*. **lady-in-waiting** *n* dama de honor *f*. **ladylike** *adj* distinguida.

lag¹ [lag] *v* (*be behind time*) retrasarse; (*trail*) quedarse atrás. *n* intervalo *m*; (*delay*) retraso *m*.

lag² [lag] *v* poner un revestimiento calorifugo a. **lagging** *n* revestimiento calorifugo *m*.

lager ['la:gə] *n* cerveza dorada *f*.

lagoon [lə'gu:n] *n* laguna *f*.

laid [leid] *V* **lay¹**.

lain [lein] *V* **lie¹**.

lair [leə] *n* guarida *f*.

laity ['leiəti] *n* laicado *m*.

lake [leik] *n* lago *m*.

lamb [lam] *n* cordero *m*. **lamb chop** chuleta de cordero *f*.

lame [leim] *adj* cojo; (*excuse, etc.*) malo. **lame duck** incapaz *m, f*. *v* dejar cojo. **lamely** *adv* cojeando. **lameness** *n* cojera *f*; debilidad *f*.

lament [lə'ment] *n* lamento *m*. *v* lamentar, llorar. **lamentable** *adj* lamentable. **lamentation** *n* lamentación *f*.

laminate ['lamineit] *v* laminar. **laminated** *adj* laminado.

lamp [lamp] *n* lámpara *f*; (*street*) farol *m*; (*mot*) faro *m*. **lamppost** *n* poste de alumbrado *m*. **lampshade** *n* pantalla *f*.

lance [la:ns] *n* lanza *f*. *v* (*med*) abrir.

land [land] *n* tierra *f*; (*country*) país *m*. **landlady** *n* patrona *f*, dueña *f*. **landlord** *n* patrón *m*, dueño *m*. **landmark** *n* señal *f*. **landscape** *n* paisaje *m*. **landslide** *n* desprendimiento de tierras *m*; (*politics*) victoria aplastante *f*. *v* desembarcar; (*aircraft*) aterrizar; (*fall*) caer; (*arrive*) llegar. **landing** *n* (*passengers*) desembarco *m*; (*cargo*) desembarque *m*; aterrizaje *m*. (*staircase*) rellano *m*. **landing stage** desembarcadero *m*.

landscape ['landskeip] (*verb*) *v* ajardinar

lane [lein] *n* camino *m*; (*motorway*) banda *f*; (*running, swimming*) calle *f*.

language ['laŋgwidʒ] *n* (*means of expression*) lenguaje *m*; (*of a nation*) lengua *f*. **bad** *or* **foul language** palabrotas *f pl*.

languish ['laŋgwiʃ] *v* languidecer.

lanky ['laŋki] *adj* larguirucho.

lantern ['lantən] *n* farol *m*, linterna *f*.

lap¹ [lap] *n* (*sport*) vuelta *f*. *v* dar una vuelta; (*fold*) doblar; (*wrap*) envolver.

lap² [lap] *v* (*drink*) chapotear; beber a lengüetadas.

lap³ [lap] *n* rodillas *f pl*. **laptop** (*computing*) ordenador portátil *m*.

lapel [ləˈpel] *n* solapa *f*.

lapse [laps] *n* (*time*) lapso *m*; (*failure*) fallo *m*; (*moral error*) desliz *m*; (*fall*) caída *f*. *v* (*time*) transcurrir; cometer un desliz; caer.

larceny [ˈlaːsəni] *n* ratería *f*.

larch [laːtʃ] *n* alerce *m*.

lard [laːd] *n* manteca de cerdo *f*.

larder [ˈlaːdə] *n* despensa *f*.

large [laːdʒ] *adj* grande, amplio. **at large** libre. **large-scale** *adj* en gran escala. **largely** *adv* en gran parte.

lark¹ [laːk] (*zool*) alondra *f*.

lark² [laːk] (*coll*) *n* juerga *f*; (*joke*) broma *f*. **lark about** hacer el tonto.

larva [ˈlaːvə] *n*, *pl* **larvae** larva *f*.

larynx [ˈlarinks] *n* laringe *f*. **laryngitis** *n* laringitis *n*.

laser [ˈleizə] *n* laser *m*. **laser printer** impresora con láser *f*.

lash [laʃ] *n* (*whip*) azote *m*; (*tail*) coletazo *m*; (*waves*) embate *m*; (*eyelash*) pestaña *f*. *v* azotar; (*wind*) sacudir; (*bind*) atar. **lash out** repartir golpes a diestro y siniestro; (*coll: money*) gastar. **lashing** *n* flagelación *f*; **lashings** *pl n* (*coll*) montones *m pl*.

lass [las] *n* (*coll*) chica *f*, muchacha *f*.

lassitude [ˈlasitjuːd] *n* lasitud *f*.

lasso [laˈsuː] *n* lazo *m*. *v* coger con el lazo.

last [laːst] *adj* último. **last-minute** *adj* de última hora. **last night** anoche. *adv* el último mo, la última, lo último; por última vez; finalmente. *n* último, -a *m*, *f*; final *m*. **at least** por fin. **lastly** *adv* por último. *v* durar; permanecer; aguantar. **last out** resistir. **lasting** *adj* duradero.

latch [latʃ] *n* picaporte *m*. *v* cerrar.

late [leit] *adj* tardío; (*recent*) reciente; (*last*) último; (*delayed*) retrasado; (*former*) antiguo; (*dead*) fallecido. *adv* tarde; (*not on time*) tarde; (*after the appointed time*) con retraso; recientemente; anteriormente. **lately** *adv* hace poco. **lateness** *n* retraso *m*. **later** *adj* más tarde. **see you later!** ¡hasta luego! **latest** *adj* (*most recent*) último. **at the latest** a más tardar.

latent [ˈleitənt] *adj* latente.

lateral [ˈlatərəl] *adj* lateral.

lathe [leið] *n* torno *m*.

lather [ˈlaːðə] *n* (*soap*) espuma *f*; (*horse*) sudor *m*. *v* enjabonar.

Latin [ˈlatin] *n*. *adj* latino, -a. *n* (*language*) latín *m*.

Latin America *n* América Latina *f*. **Latin American** *n*, *adj* latinoamericano, -a *m*, *f*.

latitude [ˈlatitjuːd] *n* latitud *f*.

latrine [ləˈtriːn] *n* letrina *f*, retrete *m*.

latter [ˈlatə] *adj* último. **the latter** éste, ésta.

lattice [ˈlatis] *n* celosía *f*; enrejado *m*.

Latvia [ˈlatviə] *n* Letonia *f*; **Latvian** *adj* letón.

laugh [laːf] *v* reír, reírse. **laugh at** reírse de. *n* risa *f*. **laughable** *adj* ridículo. **it's no laughing matter** no es cosa de risa. **laughing-stock** *n* hazmerreir *m invar*. **laughter** *n* risa *f*, risas *f pl*.

launch¹ [lɔːntʃ] *v* (*ship*) botar; (*lifeboat*) echar al mar; (*missile*) lanzar; (*issue*) emitir; (*an attack*) emprender; (*a company*) fundar; (*film, play*) estrenar. **launching** *n* botadura *f*; lanzamiento *m*; fundación *f*; iniciación *f*.

launch² [lɔːntʃ] *n* lancha *f*. **motor launch** lancha motora *f*.

launder [ˈlɔːndə] *v* lavar. **launderette** *n* lavandería automática *f*. **laundry** *n* (*place*) lavandería *f*.

laurel [ˈlɔrəl] *n* laurel *m*.

lava [ˈlaːvə] *n* lava *f*.

lavatory [ˈlavətəri] *n* retrete *m*; servicios *m pl*.

lavender [ˈlavində] *n* espliego *m*.

lavish [ˈlaviʃ] *adj* pródigo; generoso; abundante; lujoso. *v* prodigar.

law [lɔː] *n* ley *f*; (*profession*) derecho *m*, leyes *f pl*. **law-abiding** *adj* respetuoso de las leyes. **lawsuit** *n* proceso *m*. **lawful** *adj* legal; lícito. **lawyer** *n* jurista *m*, *f*; abogado, -a *m*, *f*.

lawn [lɔːn] *n* césped *m*. **lawn-mower** *n* cortacéspedes *m invar*.

lax [laks] *adj* flojo; elástico; negligente. **laxity** *n* laxitud *f*; elasticidad *f*; negligencia *f*; flojedad *f*.

laxative [ˈlaksətiv] *nm*, *adj* laxante.

*lay¹ [lei] *v* (*place*) poner; (*table*) cubrir. **laid-back** *adj* (*coll*) relajado. **layabout** *n* holgazán, -ana *m*, *f*. **lay-by** *n* área de aparcamiento *f*. **lay off** (*workers*) despedir.

lay on (*provide*) proveer de. **layout** *n* (*arrangement*) disposición *f*; (*printing*) composición *f*; (*money*) gasto *m*.

lay² [lei] *adj* laico. **layman** *n* seglar *m*.

lay³ [lei] *V* **lie**.

layer ['leiə] *n* capa *f*.

lazy ['leizi] *adj* perezoso. **laze around** holgazanear. **laziness** *n* pereza *f*.

*lead¹ [li:d] *v* llevar, conducir; remitir; (*orchestra*) dirigir; ir a la cabeza. **lead on** (*encourage*) animar; (*seduce*) seducir a. **lead up to** conducir a; preparar el terreno para. *n* (*role*) primer papel *m*; supremacía *f*; (*clue*) pista *f*; ejemplo; primer lugar; (*advantage*) ventaja *f*; (*elec*) cable *m*; (*newspaper*) noticia más importante *f*. **leader** *n* guía *m*, *f*; jefe *m*, *f*; caudillo *m*; editorial *m*. **leadership** *n* dirección *f*, mando *m*; jefatura *f*. **leading** *adj* primero; principal; que encabeza.

lead² [led] *n* plomo *m*; (*pencil*) mina *f*.

leaf [li:f] *n* hoja *f*; página *f*; (*table*) hoja abatible *f*. **leaf through** hojear. **leaflet** *n* (*pamphlet*) folleto *m*.

league [li:g] *n* liga *f*; **in league with** asociado con.

leak [li:k] *n* gotera *f*; (*hole*) agujero *m*; (*gas*, *liquid*) fuga *f*, salida *f*; (*information*) filtración *f*. *v* gotear; (*boat*) hacer agua; salirse; filtrarse.

*lean¹ [li:n] *v* inclinarse. **lean back** reclinarse. **lean on** apoyarse en. **lean over backwards to** (*coll*) no escatimar esfuerzos para. **leaning** (*liking*) predilección *f*; (*tendency*) tendencia *f*.

lean² [li:n] *adj* magro, sin grasa; (*person*) flaco. *n* carne magra *f*. **leanness** *n* magrez *f*; flaqueza *f*.

*leap [li:p] *v* saltar; lanzarse. *n* salto *m*, brinco *m*. **by leaps and bounds** a pasos agigantados. **leapfrog** *n* pídola *f*. **leap year** año bisiesto *m*.

*learn [lə:n] *v* aprender. **learn of** enterarse de. **learned** *adj* instruido; erudito. **learner** *n* principiante *m*, *f*; (*driver*) aprendiz, -a *m*, *f*. **learning** *n* erudición *f*, saber *m*.

lease [li:s] *n* arrendamiento *m*. *v* arrendar. **leasehold** *adj* arrendado.

leash [li:ʃ] *n* correa *f*.

least [li:st] *adj* menor. *pron* lo menos. *adv* menos. **at least** por lo menos.

leather ['leðə] *n* cuero *m*, piel *f*. **patent leather** charol *m*. **leathery** *adj* (*meat*) correoso; (*skin*) curtido.

*leave¹ [li:v] *v* irse, marcharse; (*abandon*) dejar; (*go out of*) salir de. **be left** quedar. **leave off** dejar de. **leave out** omitir. **left-luggage office** consigna *f*. **left-overs** *pl n* sobras *f pl*.

leave² [li:v] *n* permiso *m*. **be on leave** estar de permiso. **take leave of** despedirse de.

lecherous ['letʃərəs] *adj* lascivo. **lecher** *n* lascivo, -a *m*, *f*. **lechery** *n* lascivia *f*.

lectern ['lektən] *n* atril *m*.

lecture ['lektʃə] *n* conferencia *f*. **lecture hall** sala de conferencias *f*. *v* dar una conferencia; dar clase. **lecturer** *n* conferenciante *m*, *f*; (*university*) profesor, -a *m*, *f*.

led [led] *V* **lead¹**.

ledge [ledʒ] *n* saliente *m*; (*window*) antepecho *m*; (*shelf*) repisa *f*.

ledger ['ledʒə] *n* libro mayor *m*.

lee [li:] *n* (*shelter*) abrigo *m*; (*naut*) sotavento *m*. **leeward** *adj*, *adv* a sotavento.

leech [li:tʃ] *n* sanguijuela *f*; (*person*) lapa *f*.

leek [li:k] *n* puerro *m*.

leer [liə] *v* mirar de soslayo. *n* mirada de soslayo. **leering** *adj* de soslayo.

leeway ['li:wei] *n* (*naut*) deriva *f*; (*fig*) campo *m*.

left¹ [left] *V* **leave¹**.

left² [left] *adj* izquierdo. *n* izquierda *f*. *adv* a or hacia la izquierda. **left-handed** *adj* zurdo. **left-wing** *adj* izquierdista.

leg [leg] *n* (*person*) pierna *f*; (*animal*) pata *f*; (*furniture*) pie *m*; (*trousers*) pernera *f*; (*cookery: lamb*) pierna *f*; (*chicken*) muslo *m*; (*pork*, *venison*) pernil *m*; (*sport*, *journey*) etapa *f*.

legacy ['legəsi] *n* legado *m*, herencia *f*.

legal ['li:gəl] *adj* jurídico; legal; legítimo; lícito. **legality** *n* legalidad *f*. **legalize** *v* legalizar.

legend ['ledʒənd] *n* leyenda *f*. **legendary** *adj* legendario.

legible ['ledʒəbl] *adj* legible. **legibility** *n* legibilidad *f*.

legion ['li:dʒən] *n* legión *f*.

legislate ['ledʒisleit] *v* legislar; establecer por ley. **legislation** *n* legislación *f*. **legislature** *n* legislatura *f*.

legitimate [lə'dʒitimət] *adj* legítimo; válido; auténtico. **legitimacy** *n* legitimidad *f*.

leisure ['leʒə] *n* ocio *n*; tiempo libre *m*.

leisurely ['leʒəli] (*adv*) sin prisas, despacio

lemon ['lemən] *n* (*fruit*) limón *m*; (*tree*)

limonero *m*; (*colour*) amarillo limón *m*.

lemonade *n* limonada *f*. **lemon squeezer** exprimelimones *m invar*.

*lend [lend] *v* prestar. **lending library** biblioteca de préstamo *f*.

length [leŋθ] *n* longitud *f*, largo *m*; (*distance*) distancia *f*; (*space*) espacio *m*; (*piece*) pedazo *m*; **lengthen** *v* alargar; prolongar. **lengthy** *adj* largo; prolongado.

lenient ['liːniənt] *adj* indulgente, clemente. **leniency** *n* indulgencia *f*, clemencia *f*.

lens [lenz] *n* lente *f*; (*magnifying glass*) lupa *f*; (*photo*) objetivo *m*; (*eye*) cristalino *m*. **contact lens** lente de contacto *f*.

lent [lent] *V* **lend**.

Lent [lent] *n* Cuaresma *f*.

lentil ['lentil] *n* lenteja *f*.

Leo ['liːou] *n* (*astrol*) León *m*.

leopard ['lepəd] *n* leopardo *m*.

leotard ['liːətɑːd] *n* leotardo *m*.

leper ['lepə] *n* leproso, -a *m, f*. **leprosy** *n* lepra *f*. **leprous** *adj* leproso.

lesbian ['lezbiən] *nf, adj* lesbiana. **lesbianism** *n* lesbianismo *m*.

less [les] *adj* menos; menor; inferior. *adv, prep* menos. *pron* menos **less and less** cada vez menos. **lessen** *v* disminuir, reducir. **lesser** *adj* menor.

lesson ['lesn] *n* lección *f*; clase *f*.

lest [lest] *conj* de miedo que; para no.

*let [let] *v* permitir, dejar; (*rent*) alquilar. **let down** (*lower*) bajar, descender; (*disappoint*) fallar. **let-down** *n* decepción *f*. **let go** dejar, soltar. **let in** dejar entrar; hacer entrar. **let out** dejar salir; (*clothes*) ensanchar;

lethal ['liːθəl] *adj* mortífero.

lethargy ['leθədʒi] *n* letargo *m*. **lethargic** *adj* letárgico.

letter ['letə] *n* (*character*) letra *f*; (*message*) carta *f*. **letter-box** *n* buzón *m*.

lettuce ['letis] *n* lechuga *f*.

leukaemia [luːˈkiːmiə] *n* leucemia *f*.

level ['livə] *adj* horizontal; (*flat*) llano; (*even*) a nivel; (*equal*) igual; (*spoonful*) raso; uniforme. **be level with** estar al nivel de. **level crossing** paso a nivel *m*. **level-headed** *adj* juicioso. *n* nivel *m*. **on the level** (*coll*) honrado. *v* nivelar, allanar.

lever ['liːvə] *n* palanca *f*. **leverage** *n* apalancamiento *m*.

levy ['levi] *n* exacción *f*; impuesto *m*. *v* exigir; imponer.

lewd [luːd] *adj* lascivo.

liable ['laiəbl] *adj* sujeto; (*law*) responsable. **liable to** capaz de. **liability** *n* responsabilidad *f*; inconveniente *m*; (*nuisance*) estorbo *m*.

liaison [liˈeizon] *n* enlace *m*. **liaise** *v* trabajar en colaboración con.

liar ['laiə] *n* mentiroso, -a *m, f*.

libel ['laibəl] *n* (*act*) difamación *f*; (*writing*) escrito difamatorio *m*. *v* difamar. **libellous** *adj* difamatorio.

liberal ['libərəl] *adj* liberal; libre; generoso.

liberate ['libəreit] *v* liberar. **liberation** *n* liberación *f*.

liberty ['libəti] *n* libertad *f*. **at liberty** libre.

Libra ['liːbrə] *n* Libra *f*.

library ['laibrəri] *n* biblioteca *f*. **librarian** *n* bibliotecario, -a *m, f*.

libretto [liˈbretou] *n* libreto *m*.

lice [lais] *V* **louse**.

licence ['laisəns] *n* licencia *f*, permiso *m*, autorización *f*; (*driving*) carnet de conducir *m*. **licence number** matrícula *f*. *v* conceder una licencia; autorizar. **licensed** *adj* autorizado. **licensee** *n* concesionario, -a *m, f*.

lichen ['laikən] *n* liquen *m*.

lick [lik] *v* lamer. *n* lamedura *f*, lamido *m*.

lid [lid] *n* tapa *f*, tapadera *f*.

*lie¹ [lai] *v* acostarse; echarse. **lie around** estar tirado. **lie down** acostarse. **lie in** quedarse en la cama.

lie² [lai] *n* mentira *f*. *v* mentir.

lieutenant [ləˈftenənt] *n* (*mil*) teniente *m, f*; (*deputy*) lugarteniente *m, f*.

life [laif] *n* vida *f*. **lifeless** *adj* sin vida, muerto. **lifelike** *adj* natural.

lifebelt ['laifbelt] *n* cinturón salvavidas *m*.

lifeboat ['laifbout] *n* bote salvavidas *m*.

lifebuoy ['laifboi] *n* boya salvavidas *m*.

lifebuoy ['laifboi] *n* boya salvavidas *f*

lifeguard ['laifgaːd] *n* vigilante *m, f*.

life insurance *n* seguro de vida *m*.

life-jacket *n* chaleco salvavidas *m*.

lifelike ['laiflaik] *adj* natural; parecido.

lifeline ['laiflain] *n* (*diver's*) cordel de señales *m*; (*fig*) cordón umbilical *m*.

lifelong ['laifloŋ] *adj* de toda la vida.

life-size *adj* de tamaño natural.

lifestyle ['laifstail] *n* estilo de vida *m*

lifetime ['laiftaim] *n* vida *f*.

lift [lift] *n* ascensor *m*; (*act of lifting*) levantamiento *m*; (*upward support*) empuje *m*. **give someone a lift** llevar alguien en coche. *v* levantar; alzar; coger; elevar.

ligament ['ligəmənt] *n* ligamento *m*.

*light¹ [lait] *v* (*set fire to*) encender; (*room, etc.*) iluminar, *n* luz *f*; lámpara *f*; (*mot*) faro *m*. *adj* claro; luminoso. **light bulb** bombilla *f*. **lighthouse** *n* faro *m*. **light meter** fotómetro *m*. **light-year** *n* año luz *m*. **lighten** *v* aclarar. **lighter** (*cigarette*) *n* mechero *m*. **lighting** *n* alumbrado *m*; iluminación *f*.

light² [lait] *adj* liviano; ligero. **light-headed** *adj* mareado; delirante. **light-hearted** *adj* alegre. **lightweight** *adj* ligero, de poco peso. **lighten** *v* alijerar; aliviar. **lightness** *n* ligereza *f*.

*light³ [lait] *v* **light upon** posarse en.

lightning ['laitniŋ] *n* relámpago *m*. **lightning conductor** pararrayos *m invar*.

like¹ [laik] *adj* parecido; semejante; igual; mismo. *prep* como, igual que. **be** *or* **look like** parecerse a. **liken** *v* comparar. **likeness** *n* semejanza *f*; forma *f*; retrato *m*. **likewise** *adv* del mismo modo.

like² [laik] *v* gustarle (a uno); querer a; (*want*) querer. **likeable** *adj* amable, simpático. **liking** *n* cariño *m*; simpatía *f*; gusto *m*.

likely ['laikli] *adj* probable; posible; plausible. **be likely to** ser probable que. *adv* probablemente. **likelihood** *n* probabilidad *f*.

lilac ['lailək] *n* lila *f*; (*colour*) lila *m*. *adj* de color lila.

lily ['lili] *n* azucena *f*. **lily-of-the-valley** *n* lirio de los valles *m*.

limb [lim] *n* miembro *m*.

limbo ['limbou] *n* (*rel*) limbo *m*; (*fig*) olvido *m*.

lime¹ [laim] *n* cal *f*. **limestone** *n* piedra caliza *f*.

lime² [laim] *n* (*fruit*) lima *f*; (*tree*) limero *m*. **lime juice** jugo de lima *m*.

limelight ['laim,lait] *n* **in the limelight** en el candelero.

limerick ['limərik] *n* quintilla humorística *f*.

limit ['limit] *n* límite *m*. *v* limitar. **limitation** *n* limitación *f*. **limitless** *adj* ilimitado.

limousine ['limə,ziːn] *n* limusina *f*.

limp¹ [limp] *v* cojear.

limp² [limp] *adj* flácido. **limpness** *n* flojedad *f*.

limpet ['limpit] *n* lapa *f*.

line [lain] *n* línea *f*, rayo *m*, trazo *m*; (*wrinkle*) arruga *f*; (*row*) fila *f*; (*wire*) cable *m*; (*people*) cola *f*; (*of poem*) verso *m*; (*rope*) cuerda *f*; (*flex*) cordón *m*; (*of communication*) vía *f*; (*shipping*) compañía *f*. *v* rayar; arrugar; alinearse por; bordear; (*provide an inner layer*) forrar; (*brakes*) guarnecer. **line up** poner en fila. **linear** *adj* lineal.

linen ['linin] *n* hilo *m*, lino *m*; (*sheets, etc.*) ropa blanca *f*. **linen basket** canasta de la ropa *f*.

liner ['lainə] *n* transatlántico *m*.

linger ['liŋgə] *v* (*person*) quedarse; (*memory, etc.*) persistir; (*dawdle*) rezagarse; (*loiter*) callejear.

lingerie ['lãʒəri:] *n* ropa interior *f*.

linguist ['liŋgwist] *n* lingüista *m*, *f*. **linguistic** *adj* lingüístico. **linguistics** *n* lingüística *f*.

lining ['lainiŋ] *n* (*clothes*) forro *m*; (*brakes*) guarnición *f*.

link [liŋk] *n* (*chain*) eslabón *m*; (*fig*) vínculo *m*. **links** *pl n* (*cuff*) gemelos *m pl*; *v* unir; acoplar; conectar.

linoleum [li'nouliəm] *n also* **lino** linóleo *m*.

linseed ['lin,si:d] *n* linaza *f*. **linseed oil** aceite de linaza *m*.

lint [lint] *n* hilas *f pl*.

lion ['laiən] *n* león *m*. **lioness** *n* leona *f*.

lip [lip] *n* labio *m*; (*jug*) pico *m*; (*cup*) borde *m*. **lip-read** *v* leer en los labios. **lipstick** *n* barra de labios *f*.

liqueur [li'kjuə] *n* licor *m*.

liquid ['likwid] *nm, adj* líquido. **liquidate** *v* liquidar. **liquidation** *n* liquidación *f*.

liquor ['likə] *n* bebida alcohólica *f*.

liquorice ['likəris] *n* regaliz *m*.

Lisbon ['lizbən] *n* Lisboa.

lisp [lisp] *n* ceceo *m*. *v* decir ceceando.

list¹ [list] *v* hacer una lista de; enumerar. *n* lista *f*; catálogo *m*.

list² [list] *v* (*naut*) escorar. *n* escora *f*.

listen ['lisn] *v* escuchar, oír. **listener** *n* oyente *m*, *f*.

listless ['listlis] *adj* decaído, apático.

lit [lit] *V* **light**.

litany ['litəni] *n* letanía *f*.

literacy ['litərəsi] *n* capacidad de leer y escribir *f*. **be literate** saber leer y escribir.

literal ['litərəl] *adj* literal.

literary ['litərəri] *adj* literario.

literature ['litrətʃə] *n* literatura *f*; (*advertising matter*) folletos publicitarios *m pl*.

Lithuania [liθju'einiə] *n* Lituania *f*; **Lithuanian** *adj* lituano.

litigation [liti'geiʃən] *n* litigio *m*.

litre ['li:tə] *n* litro *m*.

litter ['litə] *n* basura *f*; desorden *m*; (*zool*) camada *f*; (*bedding for animals*) pajaza *f*; (*stretcher*) camilla *f*. **litter-bin** *n* papelera *f*. *v* ensuciar; cubrir; desordenar.

little ['litl] *adj* (*small*) pequeño; (*quantity*) poco. *nm, adv* poco. **little by little** poco a poco.

liturgy ['litədʒi] *n* liturgia *f*. **liturgical** *adj* litúrgico.

live[1] [liv] *v* vivir. **live down** conseguir que se olvide. **live up to** cumplir con.

live[2] [laiv] *adj* vivo; (*broadcast*) en directo; (*coal*) en ascuas; (*elec*) cargado. *adv* en directo.

livelihood ['laivlihud] *n* sustento *m*.

lively ['laivli] *adj* vivo; enérgico; activo. **liveliness** *n* viveza *f*; animación *f*.

liven ['laivn] *v* **liven up** animar.

liver ['livə] *n* hígado *m*.

livestock ['laivstok] *n* ganado *m*.

livid ['livid] *adj* lívido; (*coll*) furioso.

living ['liviŋ] *adj* vivo, viviente. *n* vida *f*; vivos *m pl*. **living room** sala de estar *f*.

lizard ['lizəd] *n* lagarto *m*.

load [loud] *n* (*burden*) carga *f*; (*animals, vehicles*) cargamento *m*; (*fig*) peso *m*. *v* cargar. **loaded** *adj* cargado; (*coll: rich*) podrido de dinero.

loaf[1] [louf] *n* pan *m*.

loaf[2] [louf] *v* **loaf around** callejear. **loafer** *n* (*coll*) holgazán, -ana *m, f*.

loan [loun] *n* préstamo *m*. *v* prestar.

loathe [louð] *v* aborrecer. **loathing** *n* aborrecimiento *m*. **loathsome** *adj* asqueroso.

lob [lob] *v* volear. *n* volea alta *f*, lob *m*.

lobby ['lobi] *n* pasillo *m*; vestíbulo *m*; grupo de presión *m*. *v* ejercer presiones sobre.

lobe [loub] *n* lóbulo *m*.

lobster ['lobstə] *n* langosta *f*.

local ['loukəl] *adj* local; vecinal. *n* (*coll: pub*) bar del barrio *m*. **the locals** (*coll: people*) la

gente del lugar *f*. **locality** *n* (*neighbourhood*) localidad *f*; (*place*) lugar *m*. **localize** *v* localizar. **locally** *adv* localmente; en el sitio.

locate [lə'keit] *v* (*find*) encontrar; (*look for and discover*) localizar; situar. **location** *n* localización *f*; colocación *f*; situación *f*; (*cinema*) exteriores *m pl*. **film on location** *v* rodar.

lock[1] [lok] *n* (*on door, box, etc.*) cerradura *f*; (*canal*) esclusa *f*. *v* cerrarse con llave; (*mech*) bloquearse. **lock away** guardar bajo llave. **lock in** encerrar. **lock out** cerrar la puerta a. **lock up** (*house*) cerrar; (*money*) dejar bajo llave; (*imprison*) encarcelar.

lock[2] [lok] *n* (*of hair*) mecha *f*. mechón *m*.

locker ['lokə] *n* (*shelf*) casillero *m*. (*cupboard*) armario *m*.

locket ['lokit] *n* relicario *m*.

locomotive [,loukə'moutiv] *n* locomotiva *f*. *adj* locomotor. **locomotion** *n* locomoción *f*.

locust ['loukəst] *n* langosta *f*.

lodge [lodʒ] *n* (*porter's*) portería *f*; (*caretaker's*) casa del guarda *f*; (*hunting*) pabellón *m*. *v* alojar: (*place*) colocar; presentar; (*appeal*) interponer. **lodger** *n* huésped, -a *m. f*. **lodgings** *pl n* habitación *sing*. **board and lodging** pensión completa *f*.

loft [loft] *n* (*for hay*) pajar *m*; (*attic*) desván *m*. **lofty** *adj* (*high*) alto; (*principles*) elevado; (*haughty*) arrogante.

log [log] *n* tronco *m*. **logbook** *n* (*naut*) cuaderno de bitácora *m*; (*aero*) diario de vuelo *m*. *v* anotar, apuntar. **log on/off** (*computing*) conectarse/desconectarse.

logarithm ['logəriðəm] *n* logaritmo *m*.

loggerheads ['logəhedz] *pl n* **be at loggerheads** estar a mal.

logic ['lodʒik] *n* lógica *f*. **logical** *adj* lógico.

loins [loins] *pl n* lomos *m pl*.

loiter ['loitə] *v* callejear.

lollipop ['loli,pop] *n* chupón *m*.

London ['lʌndən] *n* Londres *m*.

lonely ['lounli] *adj* solo; aislado; solitario. **loneliness** *n* soledad *f*.

long[1] [loŋ] *adj* (*length*) largo; (*memory*) bueno; (*time*) mucho; (*long-lasting*) viejo. **as long as** mientras. **long-range** *adj* de larga distancia. **long-sighted** *adj* hipermétrope; (*having foresight*) previsor. **long-sleeved** *adj* de mangas largas. **long-standing** *adj* de

muchos años. **long-term** *adj* a largo plazo.
long wave (*radio*) frecuencia modulada *f*.
long-winded *adj* (*person*) prolijo; (*speech*)
interminable.

long² [lɒŋ] *v* **long for** desear con ansia.
long to tener muchas ganas de. **longing** *n*
anhelo *m*.

longevity [lɒn'dʒevəti] *n* longevidad *f*.

longitude ['lɒndʒitjuːd] *n* longitud *f*. **longitudinal** *adj* longitudinal.

loo [luː] *n* (*coll*) retrete *m*.

look [luk] *n* (*glance*) mirada *f*; (*inspection*)
ojeada *f*; aspecto *m*. *v* mirar; parecer; representar. **look after** cuidar a, cuidar de;
(*watch over*) vigilar. **look at** mirar. **look
down on** mirar despectivamente. **look for**
buscar. **look forward to** esperar. **look out**
tener cuidado. **look up** levantar los ojos;
(*improve*) ponerse mejor; (*research*) consultar, buscar. **look up to** apreciar.

loom¹ [luːm] *v* perfilarse; surgir.

loom² [luːm] *n* telar *m*.

loop [luːp] *n* lazo *m*; (*belt*) presilla *f*. *v* hacer
un lazo en.

loophole ['luːphoul] *v* (*fig*) escapatoria *f*.

loose [luːs] *adj* suelto; (*fitting*) holgado;
(*knot*) flojo; (*translation*) libre; (*tooth*) que se
mueve; **get loose** escaparse. **let loose**
soltar. **loose change** dinero suelto *m*.
loose-leaf *adj* de hojas sueltas. *v* (*free*)
soltar; (*untie*) desatar. **loosely** *adv* sin apretar; aproximadamente; vagamente. **loosen**
v aflojar, soltar.

loot [luːt] *n* botín *m*. **looter** *n* saqueador, -a
m, *f*. **looting** saqueo *m*.

lop [lɒp] *v* cortar.

lopsided [ˌlɒp'saidid] *adj* ladeado; desequilibrado.

lord [lɔːd] *n* señor *m*.

lorry ['lɒri] *n* camión *m*. **lorry-driver** *n*
camionero *m*.

***lose** [luːz] *v* perder; (*watch*, *clock*) atrasar.
loser *n* perdedor, -a *m*, *f*. **lost property**
objetos perdidos *m pl*.

loss [lɒs] *n* pérdida *f*. (*damage*) daño *m*.
(*defeat*) derrota *f*. **be at a loss** estar perdido.
sell at a loss vender con pérdida.

lost [lɒst] *V* lose.

lot [lɒt] *n* destino *m*; porción *f*; (*auction*)
lote *m*; (*ground*) parcela *f*. **a lot** mucho. **lots
of** cantidades de. **quite a lot of** bastante.

lotion ['louʃən] *n* loción *f*.

lottery ['lɒtəri] *n* lotería *f*.

lotus ['loutəs] *n* loto *m*.

loud [laud] *adj* fuerte; alto; ruidoso;
sonoro; (*colours*) chillón; vulgar. *adv* (*laugh*)
estrepitosamente. **loud-hailer** *n* megáfono
m. **loud-mouthed** *adj* fanfarrón, -ona *m*. *f*.
loudspeaker *n* altavoz *m*. **loudly** *adv* en
voz alta. **loudness** *n* fuerza *f*.

lounge [laundʒ] *n* salón *m*. **lounge suit**
traje de calle *m*. *v* (*lazy posture*) repanti-
garse; (*idle*) gandulear. **lounger** *n* tumbona
f.

louse [laus] *n*, *pl* **lice** piojo *m*. **lousy** *adj*
piojoso; (*slang*) malísimo.

lout [laut] *n* bruto *m*. **loutish** *adj* bruto.

love [lʌv] *n* amor *m*; cariño *m*; pasión *f*;
(*tennis*) cero *m*. **fall in love with** enamorarse de. **love affair** amorío *m*. **make
love** hacer el amor. **with love from** (*in letter*) abrazos *m pl*. *v* amar, querer. **lovable**
adj adorable. **lover** *n* amante *m*, *f*; (*enthusiast*) aficionado, -a *m*, *f*. **loving** *adj* cariñoso;
amoroso.

lovely ['lʌvli] *adj* encantador; delicioso; precioso.

low [lou] *adj* bajo; pequeño; (*scarce*) escaso;
(*weak*) débil; (*downhearted*) desanimado.
lowland *n* tierra baja *f*. **low-lying** *adj*
bajo. **low-fat** *adj* bajo en calorías. **low-
paid** *adj* mal pagado. **low-priced** *adj* barato. **lowly** *adj* humilde.

lower ['louə] *adj* inferior; más bajo. *v* bajar.
lower oneself rebajarse.

loyal ['lɔiəl] *adj* leal; fiel. **loyalty** *n* lealtad
f; fidelidad *f*.

lozenge ['lɒzindʒ] *n* pastilla *f*.

lubricate ['luːbrikeit] *v* lubrificar, lubricar.
lubricant *n* lubrificante *m*, lubricante *m*.
lubrication *n* lubrificación *f*, lubricación *f*,
engrase *m*.

lucid ['luːsid] *adj* lúcido; claro. **lucidity** *n*
lucidez *f*; claridad *f*.

luck [lʌk] *n* suerte *f*; destino *m*. **bad luck**
mala suerte *f*. **good luck** buena suerte *f*.
lucky *adj* afortunado; oportuno. **be lucky**
tener mucha suerte.

lucrative ['luːkrətiv] *adj* lucrativo.

ludicrous ['luːdikrəs] *adj* ridículo, absurdo.

lug [lʌg] *v* arrastrar.

luggage ['lʌgidʒ] *n* equipaje *m*; maletas *f*
pl. **luggage label** etiqueta *f*. **luggage rack**
portaequipajes *m invar*. **luggage van**

magnify

furgón de equipajes *m*.
lukewarm ['luːkwoːm] *adj* tibio.
lull [lʌl] *n* (*in storm*) calma *f*; (*fig*) tregua *f*. *v* sosegar.
lullaby ['lʌləˌbai] *n* canción de cuna *f*.
lumbago [lʌm'beigou] *n* lumbago *m*.
lumber[1] ['lʌmbə] *n* (*wood*) maderos *m pl*; (*junk*) trastos viejos *m pl*. **lumberjack** *n* leñador *m*. **lumber yard** depósito de madera *m*. *v*. **lumber with** (*coll*) hacer que cargue con.
lumber[2] ['lʌmbə] *v* moverse pesadamente.
luminous ['luːminəs] *adj* luminoso.
lump [lʌmp] *n* pedazo *m*, trozo *m*; (*mass*) masa *f*; (*clay*) pella *f*; (*stone*) bloque *m*; (*earth, sugar*) terrón *m*; (*med*) chichón *m*. **lump sum** cantidad total *f*. **lumpy** *adj* lleno de bultos.
lunar ['luːnə] *adj* lunar.
lunatic ['luːnətik] *n*, *adj* loco -a *m*, *f*. **lunacy** *n* locura *f*
lunch [lʌntʃ] *n* almuerzo *m*. *v* almorzar. **lunchtime** *n* hora de comer *f*.
lung [lʌŋ] *n* pulmón *m*.
lunge [lʌndʒ] *v* embestir, lanzarse. *n* embestida *f*.
lurch[1] [ləːtʃ] *v* dar bandazos. **lurch along** ir dando bandazos. *n* bandazo *m*.
lurch[2] [ləːtʃ] *n* **leave in the lurch** dejar en la estacada.
lure [luə] *v* atraer. *n* aliciente *m*; encanto *m*; (*decoy*) cebo *m*.
lurid ['luərid] *adj* espeluznante; sensacional.
lurk [ləːk] *v* (*lie in wait*) estar al acecho; (*be hidden*) esconderse; (*fig: be always around*) rondar. **lurking** *adj* vago; oculto.
luscious ['lʌʃəs] *adj* exquisito; apetitoso; voluptuoso.
lush [lʌʃ] *adj* lozano, exuberante.
lust [lʌst] *n* (*sexual*) lascivia *f*; (*for power, etc.*) anhelo *m*. *v* **lust after** (*object*) codiciar; (*person*) desear. **lusty** *adj* robusto, fuerte.
lustre ['lʌstə] *n* lustre *m*.
lute [luːt] *n* laúd *m*.
Luxembourg ['lʌksəmˌbəːg] *n* Luxemburgo *m*.
luxury ['lʌkʃəri] *n* lujo *m*. **luxuriant** *adj* exuberante. **luxurious** *adj* lujoso.
lynch [lintʃ] *v* linchar.
lynx [links] *n* lince *m*.
lyre [laiə] *n* lira *f*.

lyrical ['lirikəl] *adj* lírico.
lyrics ['liriks] *pl n* letra *f sing*. **lyricist** *n* autor, -a de la letra de una canción *m*, *f*.

M

mac [mak] *n* (*coll*) impermeable *m*.
macabre [mə'kaːbr] *adj* macabro.
macaroni [makə'rouni] *n* macarrones *m pl*.
mace[1] [meis] *n* (*staff*) maza *f*.
mace[2] [meis] *n* (*spice*) macis *f*.
machine [mə'ʃiːn] *n* máquina *f*. **machine-gun** *n* ametralladora *f*. **machinery** *n* maquinaria *f*; mecanismo *m*.
mackerel ['makrəl] *n* caballa *f*.
mackintosh ['makinˌtoʃ] *n* impermeable *m*.
mad [mad] *adj* loco, demente; rabioso; (*angry*) furioso. **madden** *v* enloquecer; enfurecer. **maddening** *adj* desesperante. **madly** *adv* locamente; furiosamente. **madness** *n* locura *f*; rabia *f*; furia *f*.
madam ['madəm] *n* señora *f*.
made [meid] *V* **make**.
Madeira [mə'diərə] *n* (*island*) Madera *f*; (*wine*) madera *m*.
magazine [ˌmagə'ziːn] *n* (*publication*) revista *f*; (*warehouse*) almacén *m*; (*explosives store*) polvorín *m*; (*rifle*) recámara *f*.
maggot ['magət] *n* gusano *m*, cresa *f*. **maggoty** *adj* gusanoso.
magic ['madʒik] *n* magia *f*. *adj also* **magical** mágico. **magician** *n* ilusionista *m*, *f*.
magistrate ['madʒistreit] *n* magistrado *m*; juez municipal *m*.
magnanimous [mag'naniməs] *adj* magnánimo. **magnanimity** *n* magnanimidad *f*.
magnate ['magneit] *n* magnate *m*.
magnet ['magnət] *n* imán *m*. **magnetic** *adj* magnético; atractivo. **magnetism** *n* magnetismo *m*. **magnetize** *v* magnetizar; atraer.
magnificent [mag'nifisnt] *adj* magnífico. **magnificence** *n* magnificencia *f*.
magnify ['magnifai] *v* magnificar; aumentar; exagerar. **magnifying glass** lupa *f*. **magnification** *n* aumento *m*; exageración *f*.

magnitude ['magnitju:d] *n* magnitud *f.*

magnolia [mag'nouliə] *n* magnolia *f.*

magpie ['magpai] *n* urraca *f.*

mahogany [mə'hogəni] *n* caoba *f.*

maid [meid] *n* (*servant*) criada *f*; muchacha *f.* **old maid** solterona *f.*

maiden ['meidən] *n* doncella *f. adj* virgen; soltera; inaugural. **maiden name** apellido de soltera *m.*

mail [meil] *n* (*letters*) correspondencia *f*; (*service*) correo *m.* **mailbag** *n* saca de correspondencia *f.* **mail order** pedido hecho por correo *m.*

maim [meim] *v* mutilar.

main [mein] *adj* principal. **main course** plato principal *m.* **mainland** *n* continente *m.* **main line** línea principal *f.* **main road** carretera general *f.* **mainstay** *n* estay mayor *m. n* (*gas, water*) cañería principal *f.* **mainstream** corriente principal *f.* **in the main** por lo general. **mains** *n* (*elec*) la red eléctrica *f.*

maintain [mein'tein] *v* mantener; conservar. **maintenance** *n* mantenimiento *m*; conservación *f.* **maintenance allowance** pensión alimenticia *f.*

maisonette [meizə'net] *n* casita *f.*

maize [meiz] *n* maíz *m.*

majesty ['madʒəsti] *n* majestad *f.* **majestic** *adj* majestuoso.

major ['meidʒə] *adj* mayor; principal. *n* (*mil*) comandante *m.*

majority [mə'dʒoriti] *n* mayoría *f.* **overwhelming majority** mayoría abrumadora *f.*

*make [meik] *v* hacer; efectuar; servir de; llegar a. *n* marca *f*; hechura *f.* **makebelieve** *n* simulación *f.* **make out** (*draw up*) hacer; (*cheque*) extender. **make do with** arreglárselas con. **makeover** sesión de peluquería y maquillaje *f.* **makeshift** *adj* improvisado. **make up** inventar; completar; recuperar; (*face*) maquillarse. **make-up** *n* maquillaje *m*; carácter *m.* **make up for** compensar. **maker** *n* fabricante *m.* **making** *n* fabricación *f.*

maladjusted [malə'dʒʌstid] *adj* inadaptado. **maladjustment** *n* inadaptación *f.*

malaria [mə'leəriə] *n* malaria *f*, paludismo *m.*

male [meil] *nm, adj* macho.

malevolent [mə'levələnt] *adj* malévolo.

malevolence *n* malevolencia *f.*

malfunction [mal'fʌŋkʃən] *n* funcionamiento defectuoso *m. v* funcionar defectuosamente.

malice ['malis] *n* malicia *f.* **malicious** *adj* malicioso.

malignant [mə'lignənt] *adj* malvado; malo; (*med*) maligno. **malignancy** *n* maldad *f*; malignidad *f.*

malinger [mə'liŋgə] *v* fingirse enfermo.

mall [mo:l] *n* centro comercial *m*

mallet ['malit] *n* mazo *m.*

malnutrition [malnju'triʃən] *n* desnutrición *f.*

malt [mo:lt] *n* malta *f.*

Malta ['mo:ltə] *n* Malta. **Maltese** *n, adj* maltés, -esa.

maltreat [mal'tri:t] *v* maltratar. **maltreatment** *n* maltrato *m.*

mammal ['maməl] *n* mamífero *m.*

mammoth ['maməθ] *n* mamut *m. adj* gigantesco.

man [man] *n, pl* **men** hombre *m. v* armar; ocupar. **manhood** *n* virilidad *f.* **manly** *adj* masculino.

manage ['manidʒ] *v* (*business, affairs, etc.*) dirigir; (*instrument*) manejar; (*property*) administrar. **manage to** conseguir, arreglárselas. **manageable** *adj* manejable; (*undertaking*) factible; (*animal, person*) dócil. **management** *n* gestión *f*, administración *f*, dirección *f*; (*board of directors*) junta directiva *f.* **manager** *n* gerente *m*, director *m.* **managerial** *adj* directorial. **managing director** director gerente *m.*

mandarin ['mandərin] *n* mandarín *m. adj* mandarino. **mandarin orange** mandarina *f*; (*tree*) mandarino *m.*

mandate ['mandeit] *n* mandato *m.* **mandatory** *adj* obligatorio.

mandolin ['mandəlin] *n* mandolina *f.*

mane [mein] *n* crin *f*, crines *f pl.*

mange [meindʒ] *n* sarna *f.* **mangy** *adj* sarnoso; (*coll*) asqueroso.

manger ['meindʒə] *n* pesebre *m.*

mangle¹ ['maŋgl] *n* (*wringer*) escurridor *m. v* pasar por el escurridor.

mangle² ['maŋgl] *v* despedazar; (*fig*) deformar.

mango ['maŋgou] *n* mango *m.*

manhandle [man'handl] *v* (*person*) maltratar; (*goods*) manipular.

marrow

manhole ['manhoul] n registro m.

mania ['meiniə] n manía f. **maniac** n maníaco, -a m, f; (fig) fanático, -a m, f.

manicure ['manikjuə] n manicura f. v hacer la manicura a. **manicurist** n manicuro, -a m, f.

manifest ['manifest] adj manifiesto, evidente. v mostrar, manifestarse. **manifestation** n manifestación f.

manifesto [mani'festou] n manifiesto m.

manifold ['manifould] adj múltiple; diverso. n **exhaust manifold** (mot) colector de escape m.

manipulate [mə'nipjuleit] v manipular. **manipulation** n manipulación f.

mankind [man'kaind] n raza humana f, humanidad f.

man-made [man'meid] adj sintético, artificial.

manner ['manə] n manera f, modo m; clase f; aire m. **manners** pl n modales m pl.

mannerism ['manə‚rizəm] n amaneramiento m.

manoeuvre [mə'nu:və] n maniobra f. v maniobrar.

manor ['manə] n señorío m. **manor house** casa solariega f.

manpower ['man‚pauə] n mano de obra f.

mansion ['manʃən] n (country) gran casa de campo f; (town) palacete m.

manslaughter ['man‚slɔ:tə] n homicidio sin premeditación m.

mantelpiece ['mantlpi:s] n repisa de chimenea f.

mantle ['mantl] n (cloak) capa f; (gaslamp) manguito m.

manual ['manjuəl] nm, adj manual. **manually** adv a mano.

manufacture [manju'faktʃə] n (product) producto manufacturado; (act) fabricación f. v manufacturar, fabricar. **manufacturer** n fabricante m.

manure [mə'njuə] n estiércol m, abono. v estercolar, abonar.

manuscript ['manjuskript] nm manuscrito.

many ['meni] adj muchos, mucho, un gran número de. pron muchos. **as many as** hasta. **how many?** ¿cuántos? ¿cuántas? **so many** tantos, tantas. **too many** demasiado.

map [map] n mapa m; (town) plano m. v levantar un mapa de. **map out** proyectar.

maple ['meipl] n arce m.

mar [ma:] v estropear; frustrar.

marathon ['marəθən] nm, adj maratón.

marble ['ma:bl] n mármol m; (toy) bola f. v jaspear.

march [ma:tʃ] v marchar. n marcha f.

March [ma:tʃ] n marzo m.

marchioness [ma:ʃə'nes] n marquesa f.

mare [meə] n yegua f.

margarine [ma:dʒə'ri:n] n margarina f.

margin ['ma:dʒin] n borde m, lado m; orilla f; margen m. **marginal** adj marginal. **marginally** adv por muy poco.

marguerite [ma:gə'ri:t] n margarita f.

marigold ['marigould] n caléndula f.

marijuana [mari'wa:nə] n marijuana f, marihuana f.

marina [mə'ri:nə] n puerto deportivo m.

marinade [mari'neid] n adobo m. v adobar.

marine [mə'ri:n] adj marino. n (mil) soldado de infantería de marina. **merchant marine** marina mercante f.

marital ['maritl] adj marital, matrimonial. **marital status** estado civil m.

maritime ['maritaim] adj marítimo.

marjoram ['ma:dʒərəm] n mejorana f.

mark[1] [ma:k] n marca f, señal f, mancha f; (school) nota f; calificación f; (trace) huella f. **marksman** n tirador m. v marcar, señalar; calificar. **marked** adj marcado; pronunciado; sensible.

mark[2] [ma:k] n (currency) marco m.

market ['ma:kit] n mercado m; (demand) salida f. **market day** día de mercado m. **market place** plaza de mercado f. **market research** estudio de mercados m. **market value** valor corriente m. v poner en venta, vender. **marketing** n comercialización f.

marmalade ['ma:məleid] n mermelada de naranja f.

maroon[1] [mə'ru:n] adj castaño.

maroon[2] [mə'ru:n] v abandonar.

marquee [ma:'ki:] n gran tienda de campaña f.

marquess ['ma:kwis] n marqués m.

marquetry ['ma:kətri] n marquetería f.

marriage ['maridʒ] n matrimonio m; (wedding) boda f. **marriage certificate** partida de casamiento f.

marrow ['marou] n (bone) médula f. **vegetable marrow** calabacín m.

marry ['mari] v casar; (*get married*) casarse. **married** *adj* casado. **married couple** matrimonio *m*. **married name** apellido de casada *m*.

Mars [ma:z] *n* Marte *m*. **Martian** *n, adj* marciano, -a.

marsh [ma:ʃ] *n* pantano *m*. **marshmallow** *n* (*bot*) malvavisco *m*; (*cookery*) melcocha *f*. **marshy** *adj* pantanoso.

marshal ['ma:ʃəl] *n* (*mil*) mariscal *m*; (*organizer*) maestro de ceremonias *m*. *v* poner en orden; (*mil*) formar.

martial ['ma:ʃəl] *adj* marcial.

martin ['ma:tin] *n* avión *m*.

martyr ['ma:tə] *n* mártir *m, f*. *v* martirizar. **martyrdom** *n* martirio *m*.

marvel ['ma:vəl] *n* maravilla *f*. *v* maravillarse. **marvellous** *adj* maravilloso.

marzipan [ma:zi'pan] *n* mazapán *m*.

mascara [mas'ka:rə] *n* rímel *m*.

mascot ['maskət] *n* mascota *f*.

masculine ['maskjulin] *adj* masculino. **masculinity** *n* masculinidad *f*.

mash [maʃ] *v* machacar. *n* (*animal feed*) afrecho remojado *m*.

mask [ma:sk] *n* máscara *f*, careta *f*. *v* enmascarar.

masochist ['masəkist] *n* masoquista *m, f*. **masochism** *n* masoquismo *m*. **masochistic** *adj* masoquista.

mason ['meisn] *n* albañil *m*. **masonry** *n* albañilería.

masquerade [maskə'reid] *n* (*pretence*) mascarada *f*. *v* **masquerade as** hacerse pasar por.

mass¹ [mas] *n* masa *f*. **mass media** medios informativos *m pl*. **mass meeting** mitin popular *m*. **mass-produce** *v* fabricar en serie. **mass production** fabricación en serie *f*. *v* agrupar.

mass² [mas] *n* (*rel*) misa *f*.

massacre ['masəkə] *n* matanza *f*. *v* matar en masa.

massage ['masa:ʒ] *n* masaje *m*. *v* dar un masaje. **masseur, masseuse** *n* masajista *m, f*.

massive ['masiv] *adj* sólido; masivo.

mast [ma:st] *n* (*naut*) palo *m*, mástil *m*; (*radio, etc.*) poste *m*.

master ['ma:stə] *n* (*owner*) dueño *m*; (*college*) director *m*; (*secondary school*) profesor *m*; (*primary school*) maestro; (*graduate*) licenciado, -a *m, f*; (*household*) señor *m*; (*work force*) patrón *m*; (*ship*) capitán *m*. **master copy** original *m*. **master key** llave maestra *f*. **master of ceremonies** maestro de ceremonias *m*. **masterpiece** *n* obra maestra *f*. *v* (*passions, language*) dominar; (*an animal*) domar; (*difficulties*) vencer. **mastery** *n* dominio *m*; maestría *f*.

masturbate ['mastəbeit] *v* masturbarse. **masturbation** *n* masturbación *f*.

mat [mat] *n* (*floor*) estera *f*; (*door*) esterilla *f*; (*table*) salvamanteles *m invar*; (*doily*) tapete *m*. **matted** *adj* (*hair*) enmarañado.

match¹ [matʃ] *n* fósforo *m*, cerilla *f*. **matchbox** *n* caja de fósforos *or* cerillas *f*.

match² [matʃ] *n* (*sport*) partido *m*; (*equal*) igual *m*; (*pair*) pareja *f*. *v* igualar; (*colours*) casar; (*gloves, etc.*) parear; (*clothes, furnishings*) hacer juego con; (*fit*) encajar; corresponder. **matching** a juego. **matchless** *adj* sin igual.

mate [meit] *n* (*animals*) macho, hembra *m, f*; amigo, -a *m, f*, camarada *m, f*; (*spouse*) compañero, -a *m, f*. *v* acoplar; casar; (*chess*) dar jaque mate a.

material [mə'tiəriəl] *n* material *m*; (*cloth*) tela *f*. **materials** *pl n* (*building*) materiales *m pl*; (*teaching*) material *m*; artículos *m pl*. *adj* material; esencial. **materialist** *n(m + f)*, *adj* materialista. **materialize** *v* materializar; realizar.

maternal [mə'tə:nl] *adj* maternal; (*relation*) materno.

maternity [mə'tə:nəti] *n* maternidad *f*. **maternity hospital** casa de maternidad *f*.

mathematics [maθə'matiks] *n* matemáticas *f pl*. **mathematical** *adj* matemático. **mathematician** *n* matemático, -a *m, f*.

matinée ['matinei] *n* (*cinema*) primera sesión *f*; (*theatre*) función de la tarde *f*. **matinée idol** ídolo del público *m*.

matins ['matinz] *n* maitines *m pl*.

matriarch ['meitria:k] *n* mujer que manda *f*. **matriarchal** *adj* matriarcal.

matrimony ['matriməni] *n* matrimonio *m*. **matrimonial** *adj* matrimonial.

matrix ['meitriks] *n* matriz *f*.

matron ['meitrən] *n* matrona *f*; (*hospital*) enfermera jefe *f*; (*school*) ama de llaves *f*.

matt [mat] *adj* mate.

matter ['matə] *n* materia *f*; material *m*; asunto *m*; cuestión *f*; tema *m*. **as a matter of fact** en realidad. **matter-of-fact** *adj* prosaico. **what's the matter?** ¿qué pasa? v importar. **it doesn't matter** no importa.

mattress ['matris] n colchón m. **spring-mattress** n colchón de muelles m.

mature [mə'tjuə] adj maduro. v madurar. **maturity** n madurez f.

maudlin ['mo:dlin] adj sensiblero.

maul [mo:l] v maltratar; herir gravemente.

mausoleum [mo:sə'liəm] n mausoleo m.

mauve [mouv] nm, adj malva.

maxim ['maksim] n máxima f.

maximum ['maksiməm] nm, adj máximo. **maximize** v maximizar.

***may** [mei] v poder.

May [mei] n mayo m. **May Day** primero de mayo m.

maybe ['meibi] adv quizás, quizá.

mayday ['meidei] n señal de socorro f.

mayonnaise [,meiə'neiz] n mayonesa f.

mayor [meə] n alcalde m. **mayoress** n alcaldesa f.

maze [meiz] n laberinto m.

me [mi:] pron me; (after prep) mí.

mead [mi:d] n (drink) aguamiel f.

meadow ['medou] n prado m.

meagre ['mi:gə] adj escaso, pobre.

meal¹ [mi:l] n (food) comida f.

meal² [mi:l] n (flour) harina f.

***mean¹** [mi:n] v (signify) tener la intención de, querer decir.

mean² [mi:n] adj (humble) humilde; (petty) mezquino; (stingy) agarrado; (character) vil; (unkind) malo. **meanness** n humildad f; mezquindad f; (stinginess) tacañería f; vileza f; maldad f.

mean³ [mi:n] n (average) promedio m; (math) media f. adj medio; mediano.

meander [mi'andə] v (river) serpentear; (person) vagar. n meandro m.

meaning ['mi:niŋ] n significación f; sentido m; pensamiento m. **meaningful** adj significativo. **meaningless** adj sin sentido; insignificante.

means [mi:nz] n (way) medio m, manera f; (wealth) fondos m pl. **by all means!** ¡por supuesto! **by means of** por medio de. **by no means** de ningún modo.

meanwhile ['mi:nwail] adv mientras tanto.

measles ['mi:zlz] n sarampión m.

measure ['meʒə] v medir. n medida f. **made to measure** hecho a medida. **mea-surement** n medida f.

meat [mi:t] v carne f. **cold meat** fiambre m. **meatball** n albóndiga f. **meat pie** empanada f.

mechanic [mi'kanik] n mecánico m. **mechanical** adj mecánico. **mechanics** n mecánica f sing. **mechanism** n mecanismo m. **mechanize** v mecanizar.

medal ['medl] n medalla f. **medallion** n medallón m. **medallist** n condecorado con una medalla.

meddle ['medl] v **meddle in** meterse en; **meddle with** toquetear. **meddlesome** adj entremetido.

media ['mi:diə] pl n medios m pl.

mediate ['mi:dieit] v ser mediador en; mediar. **mediation** n mediación f. **media-tor** n mediador, -a m, f.

medical ['medikəl] adj médico; de medicina. **medical consultant** médico consultor m. **medical school** facultad de medicina f. **medicate** v medicinar. **medicated** adj medicinal. **medication** (ongoing treatment) medicación f; (one-off treatment) medicamento m.

medicine ['medsən] n (art and drug) medicina f; (coll) purga f. **medicine cabinet** botiquín m. **medicinal** adj medicinal.

medieval [medi'i:vəl] adj medieval.

mediocre [mi:di'oukə] adj mediocre. **mediocrity** n mediocridad f.

meditate ['mediteit] v meditar. **medita-tion** n meditación f. **meditative** adj meditativo.

Mediterranean [,meditə'reiniən] adj mediterráneo. n Mediterráneo m.

medium ['mi:diəm] n (environment) medio ambiente m; (means) medio m; (spiritualism) médium m, f. **happy medium** justo medio m. adj mediano. **medium wave** (radio) onda media f.

medley ['medli] n mezcla f; (music) popurrí m.

meek [mi:k] adj dócil, manso; humilde. **meekness** n docilidad f, mansedumbre f.

***meet** [mi:t] v (encounter) encontrar, encontrarse a; (come together) entrevistarse con; (come across) cruzarse con; (roads) desembocar en; (correspond to) empalmar con; satisfacer; (requirement, engagement) cumplir con; (expenses) costear; (claims) acceder a. **meet someone half-way** llegar a un arreglo con alguien. **pleased to meet**

you! ¡mucho gusto! **meeting** *n* encuentro *m*; reunión *f*; sesión *f*; (*interview*) cita *f*; (*official*) entrevista *f*.

megabyte ['megabait] *n* megabyte *m*

megaphone ['megafoun] *n* megáfono *m*.

melancholy ['melənkəli] *n* melancolía *f*. *adj also* **melancholic** melancólico.

mellow ['melou] *adj* (*ripe*) maduro; (*wine*) añejo; (*voice*) suave. *v* madurar; suavizar.

melodrama ['melədra:mə] *n* melodrama *m*. **melodramatic** *adj* melodramático.

melody ['melədi] *n* melodía *f*. **melodious** *adj* melodioso.

melon ['melən] *n* melón *m*.

melt [melt] *v* fundir; derretir; (*fig*) ablandar. **melting** *n* fusión *f*. fundición *f*.

member ['membə] *n* miembro *m*. **Member of Parliament** diputado/a (*m/f*), parlamentario/a (*m/f*), Miembro del Parlamento *m*. **membership** *n* calidad de miembro *f*. **membership fee** cuota de socio *f*.

membrane ['membrein] *n* membrana *f*. **membranous** *adj* membranoso.

memento [mə'mentou] *n* recuerdo *m*.

memo ['memou] *n* (*coll*) memorándum *m*.

memoirs ['memwa:z] *pl n* memorias *f pl*.

memorable ['memərəbl] *adj* memorable.

memorandum [memə'randəm] *n* memorándum *m*.

memory ['meməri] *n* memoria *f*; (*thing remembered*) recuerdo *m*. **memorize** *v* memorizar, aprender de memoria.

men [men] *V* **man**.

menace ['menis] *n* amenaza *f*. *v* amenazar.

menagerie [mi'nadʒəri] *n* casa de fieras *f*.

mend [mend] *v* remendar; reparar; (*improve*) mejorar. **be on the mend** (*coll*) estar mejorando.

menial ['mi:niəl] *adj* (*of a servant*) doméstico; (*mean*) bajo. *n* (*servant*) criado, -a *m*, *f*.

meningitis [menin'dʒaitis] *n* meningitis *f*.

menopause ['menəpo:z] *n* menopausia *f*.

menstrual ['menstruəl] *adj* menstrual. **menstruate** *v* menstruar. **menstruation** *n* menstruación *f*.

mental ['mentl] *adj* mental; (*coll: mad*) chiflado. **mental arithmetic** cálculo mental *m*. **mental deficiency** deficiencia mental *f*. **mental home** *or* **hospital** manicomio *m*. **mentality** *n* mentalidad *f*. **mentally** *adj* mentalmente. **mentally handicapped** anormal.

menthol ['menθəl] *n* mentol *m*.

mention ['menʃən] *v* mencionar, hablar de. **don't mention it!** ¡de nada! ¡no hay de qué! **not to mention** por no decir nada de. *n* mención *f*.

menu ['menju:] *n* carta *f*, lista de platos *f*.

mercantile ['mə:kəntail] *adj* mercantil; mercante.

mercenary ['mə:sinəri] *nm, adj* mercenario.

merchandise ['mə:tʃəndaiz] *n* mercancías *f pl*. **merchandizing** *n* comercio mercantil *m*.

merchant ['mə:tʃənt] *n* comerciante *m*, *f*, negociante *m*, *f*; (*shopkeeper*) tendero, -a *m*, *f*. **merchant navy** marina mercante *f*.

mercury ['mə:kjuri] *n* mercurio *m*.

mercy ['mə:si] *n* misericordia *f*, merced *f*. **at the mercy of** a merced de. **merciful** *adj* clemente; misericordioso. **merciless** *adj* despiadado.

mere [miə] *adj* mero.

merge [mə:dʒ] *v* (*parties, companies*) fusionar; (*join*) unir; (*colours*) fundir. **merger** *n* fusión *f*; unión *f*.

meridian [mə'ridiən] *nm, adj* meridiano.

meringue [mə'raŋ] *n* merengue *m*.

merit ['merit] *n* mérito *m*. *v* merecer.

mermaid ['mə:meid] *n* sirena *f*.

merry ['meri] *adj* alegre; divertido; (*coll: slightly drunk*) achispado. **merry-go-round** *n* tiovivo *m*. **merriment** *n* alegría *f*; diversión *f*.

mesh [meʃ] *n* mella *f*; (*gears*) engranaje *m*. *v* engranar (con).

mesmerize ['mezməraiz] *v* hipnotizar.

mess [mes] *n* confusión *f*. desorden *m*; (*dirt*) porquería *f*, suciedad *f*; (*awkward situation*) lío *m*; (*mil*) comedor de la tropa *m*. **make a mess of** desordenar; ensuciar. **what a mess!** ¡qué asco! ¡qué porquería! ¡qué lío! **mess up** desordenar; ensuciar. **messy** *adj* confuso; desordenado; sucio.

message ['mesidʒ] *n* recado *m*; (*official communication*) mensaje *m*; (*errand*) encargo *m*. **messenger** *n* mensajero, -a *m*, *f*.

met [met] *V* **meet**.

metal ['metl] *n* metal *m*. *adj* de metal. **metallic** *adj* metálico. **metallurgist** *n* metalúrgico *m*. **metallurgy** *n* metalurgia *f*.

metamorphosis [metə'mo:fəsis] *n* metamorfosis *f*.

metaphor ['metəfə] *n* metáfora *f*.

metaphorical *adj* metafórico.

metaphysics [,metə'fiziks] *n* metafísica *f*. **metaphysical** *adj* metafísico. **metaphysician** *n* metafísico *m*.

meteor ['mi:tiə] *n* meteoro. **meteoric** *adj* meteórico. **meteorite** *n* meteorito *m*.

meteorology [,mi:tiə'rolədʒi] *n* meteorología *f*. **meteorological** *adj* meteorológico. **meteorologist** *n* meteorologista *m*, *f*.

meter ['mi:tə] *n* contador *m*.

methane ['mi:θein] *n* metano *m*.

method ['meθəd] *n* método *m*; técnica *f*. **methodical** *adj* metódico.

Methodist ['meθədist] *n* metodista *m*, *f*. **Methodism** *n* metodismo *m*.

methylated spirits ['meθileitid] *pl n* alcohol desnaturalizado *m*.

meticulous [mi'tikjuləs] *adj* meticuloso.

metre ['mi:tə] *n* metro *m*. **metric** *adj* métrico.

metronome ['metrənoum] *n* metrónomo *m*.

metropolis [mə'tropəlis] *n* metrópoli *f*. **metropolitan** *adj* metropolitano.

Mexico ['meksikou] *n* Méjico, México. **Mexican** *n*, *adj* mejicano, -a, mexicano, -a.

mice [mais] *V* **mouse**.

microbe ['maikroub] *n* microbio *m*.

microchip ['maikroutʃip] *n* microcircuito *m*

microfilm ['maikrə,film] *n* microfilm *m*.

microphone ['maikrəfoun] *n* micrófono *m*.

microscope ['maikrəskoup] *n* microscopio *m*. **microscopic** *adj* microscópico.

microwave ['maikrəweiv] *n* microonda *f*. **microwave oven** horno microondas *m*.

mid [mid] *adj* medio; mediados.

mid-air [,mid'eə] *n* **in mid-air** entre cielo y tierra.

midday [,mid'dei] *n* mediodía *m*.

middle ['midl] *n* medio *m*, centro *m*; mitad *f*. **in the middle** en el centro. *adj* central; mediano; de en medio; medio; intermedio. **middle-aged** *adj* de mediana edad. **the Middle Ages** Edad Media *f sing*. **middle-class** *adj* de la clase media; burgués. **Middle East** Oriente Medio *m*. **middleman** *n* intermediario *m*. **middle-of-the-road** *adj* centrista, moderado. **middle-weight** *n* peso medio *m*. **middling** *adj* regular, mediano.

midge [midʒ] *n* mosca enana *f*.

midget ['midʒit] *n* enano, -a *m*, *f*.

midnight ['midnait] *n* medianoche *f*.

midriff ['midrif] *n* diafragma *m*.

midst [midst] *n* **in our midst** entre nosotros. **in the midst of** en medio de.

midstream [,mid'stri:m] *n* **in midstream** en medio del río.

midsummer ['mid,sʌmə] *n* pleno verano *m*. **Midsummer Day** el día de San Juan *m*.

midway [,mid'wei] *adv*, *adj* a medio camino.

midweek [,mid'wi:k] *n* medio de la semana *m*.

midwife ['midwaif] *n* comadrona *f*. partera *f*. **midwifery** *n* obstetricia *f*.

midwinter [,mid'wintə] *n* pleno invierno *m*.

might¹ [mait] *V* **may**.

might² [mait] *n* poder *m*; fuerza *f*.

mighty ['maiti] *adj* poderoso; fuerte; enorme. *adv* (*coll*) muy.

migraine ['mi:grein] *n* migraña *f*.

migrant ['maigrənt] *n* emigrante *m*, *f*. *adj* migratorio

migrate [mai'greit] *v* emigrar. **migration** *n* migración. *adj* migratoria.

mike [maik] *n* (*coll: microphone*) micro *m*.

mild [maild] *adj* (*person*) dulce, apacible; (*weather*) templado; (*wind*) suave; (*disease*) benigno. **mildness** *n* dulzura *f*; suavidad *f*; benignidad *f*

mildew ['mildju:] *n* moho *m*; (*vine*) mildeu *m*; (*plants*) tizón *m*.

mile [mail] *n* milla *f*. **mileage** recorrido en millas *m*. **milestone** *n* mojón *m*; (*fig*) jalón *m*.

militant ['militənt] *adj* belicoso; (*pol*) militante. *n* militante *m*, *f*.

military ['militəri] *adj* militar.

milk [milk] *n* leche *f*. **milk chocolate** *n* chocolate con leche *m*. **milkman** *n* lechero *m*. **milk of magnesia** *n* leche de magnesia *f*. *v* ordeñar; (*fig*) exprimir. **milkiness** *n* aspecto lechoso *m*. **milking** *n* ordeño *m*. **milky** *adj* lechoso. **Milky Way** Vía Láctea *f*.

Milky Way *n* Vía Láctea *f*.

mill [mil] *n* molino *m*; (*grinder*) molinillo *m*; (*factory*) fábrica *f*. **millstone** *n* muela *f*; (*burden*) cruz *f*. *v* moler. **miller** *n* molinero, -a *m*, *f*.

millennium [mi'leniəm] *n* milenario *m*.

millet ['milit] *n* mijo *m*.

milligram ['mili,græm] *n* miligramo *m*.

millimetre ['mili,mi:tə] *n* milímetro *m*.

milliner ['milinə] *n* sombrerero, -a *m, f*. **milliner's** *n* sombrerería *f*. **millinery** *n* sombreros de señora *m pl*.

million ['miljən] *n* millón *m*. **millionaire** *n* millonario, -a *m. f*. **millionth** *n, adj* millonésimo, -a *m, f*.

mime [maim] *n* mimo *m*, pantomima *f. v* actuar de mimo.

mimic ['mimik] *adj* mímico; imitativo. *n* mimo *m*; imitador, -a *m, f. v* imitar, remedar. **mimicry** *n* mímica *f*; (*zool*) mimetismo *m*.

minaret [minə'ret] *n* minarete *m*.

mince [mins] *n* (*meat*) carne picada *f*. **mincemeat** *n* conserva de fruta picada y especias *f*. **mince pie** pastel con frutas picadas *m. v* picar; (*walk*) andar con pasos menuditos. **mince words** tener pelos en la lengua. **mincer** *n* máquina de picar carne *f*. **mincing** *adj* afectado.

mind [maind] *n* mente *f*. **bear in mind** tener en cuenta. **change one's mind** cambiar de opinión. **go out of one's mind** perder el juicio. **have a good mind to** tener ganas de. **keep in mind** acordarse de. **make up one's mind** decidirse. **read someone's mind** adivinar el pensamiento de alguien. **to my mind** a mi parecer. *v* (*look out*) tener cuidado; (*guard*) cuidar; (*rules*) cumplir; (*pay attention*) prestar atención. **do you mind?** ¿le importa? **I don't mind** a mí no me importa. **never mind** no se precocupe. **minder** escolta *f*, guardaespaldas *m pl*.

mine¹ [main] *pron* (el) mío, (la) mía, (lo) mío.

mine² [main] *n* mina *f*. **minefield** *n* campo de minas *m*. **mineshaft** *n* pozo de extracción *m*. **minesweeper** *n* dragaminas *m invar. v* minar; (*mil*) sembrar minas en. **miner** *n* minero *m*. **mining** *n* minería *f*. **mining engineer** ingeniero de minas *m*.

mineral ['minərəl] *nm, adj* mineral. **minerals** (*coll: drinks*) *pl n* gaseosas *f pl*. **mineral water** agua mineral *m*.

mingle ['miŋgl] *v* mezclar.

miniature ['minitʃə] *nf, adj* miniatura.

minibus ['minibʌs] *n* minibus *m*

minim ['minim] *n* mínima *f*, blanca *f*.

minimum ['miniməm] *nm, adj* mínimo. **minimal** *adj* mínimo. **minimize** *v* minimizar.

minister ['ministə] *n* ministro *m. v* **minister to** atender a. **ministerial** *adj* ministerial. **ministry** *n* ministerio *m*.

mink [miŋk] *n* visón *m*.

minor ['mainə] *adj* menor, más pequeño; secundario; de poca importancia. *n* menor de edad *m, f*.

minority [mai'noriti] *n* minoría *f*. **in the minority** en la minoría. *adj* minoritario.

minstrel ['minstrəl] *n* trovador *m*.

mint¹ [mint] *n* (*bot*) menta *f*.

mint² [mint] *n* casa de la moneda *f*. *adj* nuevo. *v* acuñar.

minuet [minju'et] *n* minué *m*.

minus ['mainəs] *prep* menos. *adj* negativo. **minus sign** signo menos *m*.

minute¹ ['minit] *n* minuto *m*. **minutes** *pl n* actas *f pl*.

minute² [mai'nju:t] *adj* (*tiny*) diminuto; (*detailed*) minucioso.

miracle ['mirəkl] *n* milagro *m*. **miraculous** *adj* milagroso.

mirage ['mira:ʒ] *n* espejismo *m*.

mirror ['mirə] *n* espejo *m*; (*mot*) retrovisor *m. v* reflejar.

mirth [mə:θ] *n* alegría *f*; hilaridad *f*.

misadventure [misəd'ventʃə] *n* desgracia *f*.

misanthropist [miz'ænθrəpist] *n* misántropo *m*. **misanthropic** *adj* misantrópico. **misanthropy** *n* misantropía *f*.

misapprehension [misəpri'henʃən] *n* malentendido *m*.

misbehave [misbi'heiv] *v* portarse mal. **misbehaviour** *n* mala conducta *f*.

miscalculate [mis'kælkjuleit] *v* calcular mal. **miscalculation** *n* cálculo erróneo *m*.

miscarriage [mis'kæridʒ] *n* (*med*) aborto *m*; (*plans, etc.*) fracaso *m*. **miscarriage of justice** error judicial *m*.

miscellaneous [misə'leiniəs] *adj* diverso.

mischief ['mistʃif] *n* (*evil*) maldad *f*; (*of child*) travesura *f*; (*damage*) daño *m*. **get into mischief** hacer tonterías. **make mischief** sembrar la discordia. **mischievous** *adj* malo; travieso; dañino.

misconception [miskən'sepʃən] *n* concepto falso *m*.

misconduct [mis'kondʌkt] *n* (*misbehaviour*)

mala conducta f; (*mismanagement*) mala administración f.

misconstrue [miskən'stru:] v interpretar mal.

misdeed [mis'di:d] n delito m.

misdemeanour [misdi'mi:nə] n (*law*) infracción f; (*misbehaviour*) mala conducta f.

miser ['maizə] n avaro, -a m, f. **miserly** adj mezquino.

miserable ['mizərəbl] adj (*sad*) triste; (*sick*) mal; (*unfortunate*) desgraciado; (*wretched*) miserable; (*distressing*) de pena.

misery ['mizəri] n tristeza f; (*pain*) dolor m; desgracia f; miseria f; (*coll: person*) aguafiestas m, f.

misfire [mis'faiə] v fallar; (*mot*) tener fallos. n fallo m.

misfit ['misfit] n inadaptado, -a m, f.

misfortune [mis'fo:tʃən] n desgracia f.

misgiving [mis'givin] n recelo m; inquietud f.

misguided [mis'gaidid] adj descaminado; poco afortunado.

mishap ['mishap] n contratiempo m.

misinterpret [misin'tə:prit] v interpretar mal. **misinterpretation** n interpretación errónea f.

misjudge [mis'dʒʌdʒ] v juzgar mal. **misjudgment** n estimación errónea f.

*mislay [mis'lei] v extraviar.

*mislead [mis'li:d] v engañar; equivocar. **misleading** adj engañoso.

misnomer [mis'noumə] n nombre inapropiado m.

misogynist [mi'sodʒənist] n misógino m.

misplace [mis'pleis] v colocar mal; (*lose*) extraviar.

misprint ['misprint] n errata f.

miss¹ [mis] v fallar; no dar en; (*train, bus, etc.*) perder; (*a meeting*) no asistir a; (*long for*) echar de menos. **miss out** omitir. n tiro errado m; (*failure*) fracaso m. **missing** adj (*lacking*) que falta; perdido; ausente; desaparecido.

miss² [mis] n señorita.

misshapen [miʃʃeipən] adj (*object*) deformado; (*person*) deforme.

missile ['misail] n proyectil m. **guided missile** proyectil teledirigido m.

mission ['miʃən] n misión f. **missionary** n, adj misionero, -a.

mist [mist] n (*haze*) calina f; (*fog*) neblina f; (*at sea*) bruma f; (*on glasses*) vaho m. **mist over** or **up** empañar. **misty** adj de niebla; brumoso; vago; empañado.

*mistake [mi'steik] v (*be wrong*) equivocarse en; (*the way*) equivocarse de: (*misunderstand*) entender mal. n error m; equivocación f; falta f. **by mistake** sin querer. **make a mistake** equivocarse. **mistaken** adj equivocado, erróneo; mal comprendido. **be mistaken** estar equivocado.

mistletoe ['misltou] n muérdago m.

mistress ['mistris] n (*of the house*) señora f; (*owner*) dueña f; (*lover*) amante f; (*teacher*) profesora f.

mistrust [mis'trʌst] n desconfianza f; (*suspicion*) recelo m. v desconfiar de; recelar de. **mistrustful** adj desconfiado; receloso.

*misunderstand [misʌndə'stand] v entender mal. **misunderstanding** n malentendido m.

misuse [mis'ju:s; v mis'ju:z] n mal uso m; abuso m; maltrato m; mal empleo m. v abusar de; maltratar; emplear mal.

mitigate ['mitigeit] v mitigar; aliviar; atemar. **mitigation** n mitigación f; alivio m; atenuación f.

mitre ['maitə] n (*rel*) mitra f; (*carpentry*) inglete m. v unir con ingletes.

mitten ['mitn] n mitón m.

mix [miks] v mezclar; (*drinks*) preparar; (*salad*) aliñar; (*flour, cement, etc.*) amasar. **mix up** mezclar; confundir. **mix up** n lío m; confusión f. **mixed feelings** sentimientos contradictorios m pl. **mixed grill** plato combinado m. **mixer** n (*elec*) mezclador m; (*cement*) mezcladora f. **mixture** n mezcla f; (*med*) mixtura f.

moan [moun] v gemir; (*coll: complain*) quejarse. n gemido m; queja f.

moat [mout] n foso m.

mob [mob] n multitud f; (*rabble*) chusma f. v acosar.

mobile ['moubail] nm, adj móvil. **mobile phone** teléfono móvil m. **mobility** n movilidad f. **mobilize** v movilizar.

moccasin ['mokəsin] n mocasín m.

mock [mok] v burlarse de; ridiculizar. adj simulado; falso; imitado. **mockery** n burla f; simulacro m; imitación f. **mocking** adj burlón. **mock-up** n maqueta f.

mode [moud] n modo m, manera f; (*fashion*) moda f.

model ['modl] n modelo m; (of a statue) maqueta f; (fashion) maniquí m; (dress-making pattern) patrón m. v modelar; (dress) presentar.

modem ['moudem] n módem m

moderate ['modərət; v 'modəreit] n, adj moderado, -a. v moderar; aplacar. **moderately** adv moderadamente; (fairly) mediocremente. **in moderation** con moderación.

modern ['modən] adj moderno, **modern languages** lenguas vivas f pl. **modernization** n modernización f. **modernize** v modernizar.

modest ['modist] adj modesto; discreto. **modesty** n modestia f.

modify ['modifai] v modificar. **modification** n modificación f.

modulate ['modjuleit] v modular. **modulation** n modulación f.

module ['modju:l] n módulo m.

mohair ['mouheə] n moer m.

moist [moist] adj húmedo; mojar. **moisten** v humedecer; mojar. **moisture** n humedad f. **moisturize** v humedecer. **moisturizing cream** crema hidratante f.

molasses [mə'lasiz] n melaza f.

Moldova [mol'douvə] n Moldavia

mole[1] [moul] n (on skin) lunar m.

mole[2] [moul] n (zool) topo m. **molehill** n topera f.

molecule ['molikju:l] n molécula f. **molecular** adj molecular.

molest [mə'lest] v molestar, importunar.

mollusc ['moləsk] n molusco m.

molten ['moultən] adj fundido.

moment ['moumənt] n momento m. **at the moment** de momento. **momentary** adj momentáneo. **momentarily** adv momentáneamente. **momentous** adj de gran importancia.

momentum [mə'mentəm] n momento m; ímpetu m; impulso m.

monarch ['monərk] n monarca m. **monarchist** n, adj monárquico, -a. **monarchy** n monarquía f.

monastery ['monəstəri] n monasterio m. **monastic** adj monacal.

Monday ['mʌndi] n lunes m.

money ['mʌni] n dinero m. **get one's money's worth** sacar jugo al dinero. **money-lender** n prestamista m, f. **money order** n giro postal m.

mongol ['mongəl] n, adj (med) mongol, -a. **mongolism** n mongolismo m.

mongrel ['mʌngrəl] n (dog) perro mestizo m.

monitor ['monitə] n monitor m; instructor m; (tech) radioescucha m. v controlar.

monk [mʌnk] n monje m.

monkey ['mʌnki] n mono m. **monkey around** entretenerse, perder el tiempo.

monogamy [mə'nogəmi] n monogamia f. **monogamous** adj monógamo.

monogram ['monəgram] n monograma m.

monologue ['monəlog] n monólogo m.

monopolize [mə'nopəlaiz] v monopolizar. **monopoly** n monopolio m.

monosyllable ['monəsi-ləbl] n monosílabo m. **monosyllabic** (word) monosílabo m; (statement) monosilábico.

monotone ['monətoun] n monotonía f. **monotonous** adj monótono. **monotony** n monotonía f.

monsoon [mon'su:n] n monzón m.

monster ['monstə] n monstruo m. **monstrosity** n monstruosidad f. **monstrous** adj monstruoso.

month [mʌnθ] n mes m. **calendar month** mes civil m. **monthly** n. adj mensual. adv mensualmente.

monument ['monjument] n monumento m. **monumental** adj monumental; enorme.

mood[1] [mu:d] n humor m. **moody** adj malhumorado; caprichoso.

mood[2] [mu:d] n (gramm) modo m.

moon [mu:n] n luna f. **crescent moon** media luna f. **full moon** luna llena f. **new moon** luna nueva f. **moonbeam** n rayo de luna m. **moonlight** n claro de luna m. **moonlighting** n (coll) pluriempleo m.

moor[1] [muə] n páramo m.

moor[2] [muə] v amarrar.

mop [mop] n (floor) fregona f; (hair) pelambrera f. v fregar. **mop up** limpiar.

mope [moup] v tener ideas negras.

moped ['mouped] n ciclomotor m.

moral ['morəl] adj moral; virtuoso. **moral support** apoyo moral m. n (fable) moraleja f. **morals** pl n moralidad f sing. **moralist** n moralista m, f. **moralize** v moralizar.

morale [mə'ra:l] n moral f.

morbid ['mo:bid] *adj* mórbido.

more [mo:] *adj* más; superior; mayor. *pron, adv* más. **all the more** aún más. **and what's more** y lo que es más. **even more** más; aún. **more and more** cada vez más. **more than ever** más que nunca. **once more** una vez más.

moreover [mo:'rouvə] *adv* además, también; por otra parte.

morgue [mo:g] *n* depósito de cadáveres *m*.

morning ['mo:nɪŋ] *n* mañana *f*. *adj* de la mañana. **morning coat** chaqué *m*. **morning sickness** náuseas *f pl*.

moron ['mo:ron] *n* retrasado mental *m*; (*coll*) imbécil *m*, *f*. **moronic** *adj* retrasado mental; (*coll*) idiota.

morose [mə'rous] *adj* malhumorado.

morphine ['mo:fi:n] *n* morfina *f*.

Morse code [mo:s] *n* morse *m*.

morsel ['mo:səl] *n* bocado *m*.

mortal ['mo:tl] *nm, adj* mortal. **mortality** *n* mortalidad *f*.

mortar ['mo:tə] *n* mortero *m*.

mortgage ['mo:gidʒ] *n* hipoteca *f*.

mortify ['mo:tifai] *v* mortificar. **mortification** *n* mortificación *f*.

mortuary ['mo:tʃuəri] *n* depósito de cadáveres *m*.

mosaic [mə'zeiik] *n* mosaico *m*. *adj* de mosaico.

Moscow ['moskou] *n* Moscú.

mosque [mosk] *n* mezquita *f*.

mosquito [mə'ski:tou] *n* mosquito *m*. **mosquito bite** picadura de mosquito *f*. **mosquito net** mosquitero *m*.

moss [mos] *n* musgo *m*. **mossy** *adj* musgoso.

most [moust] *adj* más; la mayoría de. *pron* la mayoría; la mayor parte; lo máximo. *adv* más; (*very*) de lo más. **at most** a lo sumo. **make the most of** sacar el mayor provecho de. **mostly** *adv* principalmente, sobre todo; en general.

motel [mou'tel] *n* motel *m*.

moth [moθ] *n* mariposa nocturna *f*. **clothes moth** polilla *f*. **mothball** bola de naftalina *f*. **moth-eaten** *adj* apolillado; (*fig*) anticuado.

mother ['mʌðə] *n* madre *f*. **mother-in-law** *n* suegra *f*. **mother-of-pearl** *n* madreperla *f*. **Mothers' Day** día de la Madre *m*. **mother-to-be** futura madre *f*. **motherhood** *n* maternidad *f*. **motherly** *adj* maternal.

motion ['mouʃən] *n* movimiento *m*; (*signal*) señas *f pl*; (*indication*) además *m*; (*of a machine*) mecanismo *m*; (*med*) deposición *f*; (*at a meeting*) moción *f*. **set in motion** poner en marcha. *v* indicar con la mano; hacer señas. **motionless** *adj* inmóvil.

motivate ['moutiveit] *v* motivar. **motivation** *n* motivo *m*.

motive ['moutiv] *n* (*reason*) motivo *m*; (*law*) móvil *m*. *adj* motor, motriz.

motor ['moutə] *n* motor *m*. **motorbike** *n* (*coll*) moto *f*. **motorboat** *n* lancha motora *f*. **motorcar** *n* automóvil *m*, coche *m*. **motorcyclist** *n* motociclista *m*, *f*. **motoring** *n* automovilismo *m*. **motorist** *n* automovilista *m*, *f*. **motorway** *n* autopista *f*.

mottled ['motld] *adj* abigarrado.

motto ['motou] *n* lema *m*.

mould¹ [mould] *n* (*container*) molde *m*; (*shape*) forma *f*; (*pattern*) modelo *m*. *v* moldear; formar.

mould² [mould] *n* (*fungus*) moho *m*. **mouldy** *adj* mohoso. **go mouldy** enmohecerse.

moult [moult] *v* mudar. *n* muda *f*.

mound [maund] *n* (*natural*) montículo *m*; (*artificial*) terraplén *m*; (*heap*) montón *m*; (*burial*) túmulo *m*.

mount¹ [maunt] *v* subir; montar a caballo. **mount up** aumentar. *n* (*horse*) montura *f*; (*base*) soporte *m*; (*phot*) borde *m*; (*drawing*) fondo *m*.

mount² [maunt] *n* monte *m*.

mountain ['mauntən] *n* montaña *f*. **mountain bike** *n* bicicleta de montaña *f*. **mountaineer** *n* montañero, -a *m*, *f*. **mountaineering** *n* montañismo *m*. **mountainous** *adj* montañoso.

mourn [mo:n] *v* lamentar. **mournful** *adj* triste; afligido. **mourning** *n* luto *m*, duelo *m*.

mouse [maus] *n*, *pl* **mice** ratón *m*. **mouse mat** *n* (*computing*) almohadilla *f*, alfombrilla *f*. **mousetrap** *n* ratonera *f*. **mousy** *adj* (*coll: hair*) pardussco; (*coll: shy*) tímido.

mousse [mu:s] *n* crema batida *f*.

moustache [mə'sta:ʃ] *n* bigote *m*.

mouth [mauθ] *n* boca *f*; (*opening*) abertura *f*; (*entrance*) entrada *f*; (*bottle*) gollete *m*; (*river*) desembocadura *f*. **mouth-piece** *n* (*music*) boquita *f*; (*phone*) micrófono *m*; (*spokesman*) portavoz *m*. **mouthwash** *n* enjuague *m*. **mouth-watering** *adj* muy apetitoso. *v* articular.

move [muːv] *v* cambiar de; mudarse de; mover; transportar; (*from one place to another*) trasladar; poner en marcha; (*emotionally*) emocionar; (*in debate*) proponer. *n* (*fig*) paso *m*; marcha *f*; medida *f*; (*house*) mudanza *f*; (*turn*) turno *m*; (*chess, etc.*) jugada *f*. **movable** *adj* movible, móvil. **movement** *n* movimiento *m*; (*gesture*) además *m*; acto *m*; tendencia *f*; transporte *m*; traslado *m*; (*vehicles*) tráfico *m*; (*tech*) mecanismo *m*; (*mil*) maniobra *f*. **moving** *adj* móvil; en movimiento; (*emotional*) conmovedor.

movie ['muːvi] *n* (*US*) película *f*. **go to the movies** ir al cine.

*mow [mou] *v* (*lawn*) cortar, segar. **mow down** barrer. **mower** cortacésped *m*.

MP *n* Dip., diputado/a *m/f*

Mr ['mistə] *n* señor *m*; Sr.

Mrs ['misiz] *n* señora *f*; Sra.

Ms [miz] *n* Srta.

much [mʌtʃ] *adj, adv, pron* mucho. **as much** tanto (*como*). **how much?** ¿cuánto? **much as** por mucho que. **so much** tanto. **too much** demasiado.

muck [mʌk] *n* (*manure*) estiércol *m*; (*dirt*) suciedad *f*. *v* **muck about** (*coll*) perder el tiempo. **mucky** *adj* asqueroso.

mucus ['mjuːkəs] *n* mucosidad *f*. **mucous** *adj* mucoso.

mud [mʌd] *n* barro *m*; (*thick mud*) fango *m*. **mudguard** *n* guardabarros *m invar*. **muddy** *adj* fangoso.

muddle ['mʌdl] *n* desorden *m*; confusión *f*. *v* confundir, embrollar. **muddle through** salir del paso. **muddleheaded** *adj* atontado.

muff [mʌf] *n* manguito *m*.

muffle ['mʌfl] *v* amortiguar. **muffle up** embozar. **muffler** *n* bufanda *f*.

mug [mʌg] *n* tazón *m*; (*slang: face*) jeta *f*; (*slang: fool*) primo, -a *m*, *f*. *v* asaltar. **mugger** *n* atracador. **mugging** *n* asalto *m*.

muggy ['mʌgi] *adj* bochornoso.

mulberry ['mʌlbəri] *n* (*fruit*) mora *f*; (*tree*) morera *f*, moral *m*.

mule¹ [mjuːl] *n* (*animal*) mulo, -a *m*, *f*. **mulish** *adj* testarudo.

mule² [mjuːl] *n* (*slipper*) babucha *f*.

multicoloured [ˌmʌltiˈkʌləd] *adj* multicolor.

multilingual [ˌmʌltiˈliŋgwəl] *adj* poligloto.

multiple ['mʌltipl] *adj* múltiple. *n* múltiplo *m*. **multiple sclerosis** esclerosis en placas *f*.

multiply ['mʌltiplai] *v* multiplicar. **multiplication** *n* multiplicación *f*. **multiplication table** tabla de multiplicar *f*.

multiracial [ˌmʌltiˈreifəl] *adj* multirracial.

multitude ['mʌltitjuːd] *n* multitud *f*, muchedumbre *f*.

mumble ['mʌmbl] *v* mascullar. *n* refunfuño *m*.

mummy¹ ['mʌmi] *n* momia *f*. **mummification** *n* momificación *f*. **mummify** *v* momificar.

mummy² ['mʌmi] *n* (*coll: mother*) mamá *f*.

mumps [mʌmps] *n* paperas *f pl*.

munch [mʌntʃ] *v* mascar.

mundane [mʌnˈdein] *adj* mundano.

municipal [mjuˈnisipəl] *adj* municipal. **municipality** *n* municipio *m*.

mural ['mjuərəl] *n*, *adj* mural.

murder ['məːdə] *n* homicidio *m*, asesinato *m*. **murderer** *n* asesino *m*. **murderess** *n* asesina *f*. **murderous** *adj* homicida, asesino.

murky ['məːki] *adj* oscuro; lóbrego.

murmur ['məːmə] *v* murmurar. *n* murmullo *m*.

muscle ['mʌsl] *n* músculo *m*. *v* **muscle in** (*coll*) meterse por fuerza en. **muscular** *adj* muscular; (*person*) musculoso.

muse [mjuːz] *n* musa *f*. *v* meditar, contemplar.

museum [mjuˈziəm] *n* museo *m*.

mushroom ['mʌʃrum] *n* hongo *m*, seta *f*; (*food*) champiñón *m*. *v* crecer como hongos.

music ['mjuːzik] *n* música *f*. **music hall** music-hall *m*. **music stand** atril *m*. **musical** *adj* de música; (*ear*) musical; (*person*) aficionado a la música. **musical** (**comedy**) *n* comedia musical *f*. **musical instrument** instrumento de música *m*. **musician** *n* músico, -a *m*, *f*.

musk [mʌsk] *n* almizcle *m*.

musket ['mʌskit] *n* mosquete *m*. **musketeer** *n* mosquetero *m*.

Muslim ['mʌzlim] *n*, *adj* musulmán, -ana.

muslin ['mʌzlin] *n* muselina *f*.

mussel ['mʌsl] *n* mejillón *m*.

*must [mʌst] v deber; tener que.

mustard ['mʌstəd] n mostaza f. **mustard pot** mostacera f.

muster ['mʌstə] v reunir; (mil) formar. n reunión f; asamblea f; (mil) revista f. **pass muster** ser aceptable.

musty ['mʌsti] adj mohoso. **smell musty** oler a cerrado.

mute [mju:t] n, adj mudo, -a; (music) sordina f. v apagar; poner sordina a. **muted** adj sordo.

mutilate ['mju:tileit] v mutilar. **mutilation** n mutilación f.

mutiny ['mju:tini] n motín m, rebelión f. v amotinarse, rebelarse. **mutinous** adj amotinado; (fig) rebelde.

mutter ['mʌtə] v murmurar. n murmullo m. **muttering** n refunfuño m.

mutton ['mʌtn] n cordero m.

mutual ['mju:tʃuəl] adj mutuo; común.

muzzle ['mʌzl] n (nose) hocico m; (device) bozal m; (gun) boca f. v abozalar.

my [mai] adj mi (pl mis), mío, mía (pl míos, mías).

myself [mai'self] pron (reflexive) me; (emphatic) yo mismo, -a; (after prep) mí. **by myself** (completamente) solo, -a.

mystery ['mistəri] n misterio m. **mysterious** adj misterioso.

mystic ['mistik] n iniciado, -a m, f; místico, -a m, f. adj also **mystical** místico; esotérico; oculto; sobrenatural.

mystify ['mistifai] v oscurecer; desconcertar; desorientar; (deceive) engañar. **mystification** n mistificación f; complejidad f; confusión f.

mystique [mi'sti:k] n mística f.

myth [miθ] n mito m. **mythical** adj mítico. **mythological** adj mitológico. **mythology** n mitología f.

N

nag [nag] v regañar. **nagging** adj gruñón. n (horse) rocín m.

nail [neil] n (metal) clavo m; (anat) uña f; (claw) garra f. **nailbrush** n cepillo de uñas m. **nail-file** n lima de uñas f. **nail polish** esmalte de uñas m. **nail-scissors** n tijeras para las uñas f pl. v clavar.

naive [nai'i:v] adj ingenuo. **naivety** n ingenuidad f.

naked ['neikid] adj desnudo. **nakedness** n desnudez f.

name [neim] n nombre m; (surname) apellido m; fama f; título m. **my name is** … me llamo …. **namesake** n tocayo, -a m, f. **what's your name?** ¿cómo se llama? v llamar; nombrar. **nameless** adj sin nombre; anónimo. **namely** adv a saber.

nanny ['nani] n niñera f.

nap¹ [nap] n sueño ligero m. v dormitar. **be caught napping** estar desprevenido.

nap² [nap] n (of cloth) lanilla f.

nape [neip] n nuca f.

napkin ['napkin] n servilleta f.

nappy ['napi] n pañal m.

narcotic [na:'kotic] nm, adj narcótico.

narrate [nə'reit] v contar. **narration** n narración f. **narrator** n narrador, -a m, f.

narrative ['narətiv] n narrativa f. adj narrativo.

narrow ['narou] adj estrecho. **narrow-gauge** adj de vía estrecha. **narrow-minded** adj de miras estrechas. v estrechar. **narrow down** reducir. **narrowly** adv (only just) por muy poco; estrechamente. **narrowness** n estrechez f.

nasal ['neizəl] adj nasal. **nasalize** v nasalizar.

nasturtium [nə'stə:ʃəm] n capuchina f.

nasty ['na:sti] adj sucio; repugnante; (unfriendly) antipático; grosero; desagradable.

nation ['neiʃən] n nación f. **national** nm, adj nacional. **national anthem** himno nacional m. **nationalism** n nacionalismo m. **nationalist** n (m+f), adj nacionalista. **nationality** n nacionalidad f. **nationalization** n nacionalización f. **nationalize** v nacionalizar. **nationwide** a nivel nacional.

native ['neitiv] adj (country, town) natal; (inhabitant) nativo; (language) materno; (product) del país. n natural m, f; nativo, -a m, f.

nativity [nə'tivəti] n nacimiento m.

natural ['natʃərəl] adj natural. **naturalism** n naturalismo m. **naturalist** n naturalista m, f. **naturally** adv naturalmente; por naturaleza.

nature ['neitʃə] n naturaleza f; (character) natural m; esencia f.

naughty ['nɔːti] adj travieso; malvado. **naughtiness** n travesura f.

nausea ['nɔːziə] n náusea f. **nauseate** v dar asco.

nautical ['nɔːtikəl] adj marítimo, náutico.

naval ['neivəl] adj naval; de marina. **naval officer** oficial de marina m.

navel ['neivəl] n ombligo m. **navel orange** naranja navel f.

navigate ['navigeit] v navegar; (steer) gobernar. **navigable** adj navegable. **navigation** n navegación f. **navigator** n navegante m.

navy ['neivi] n marina f. **navy blue** azul marino m.

near [niə] adv cerca. prep cerca de. adj cercano. v acercarse a; aproximarse a. **the near future** el futuro próximo. **nearby** adv cerca. **nearly** adv casi. **not nearly** ni con mucho. **very nearly** casi casi. **nearside** n (left side) lado izquierdo m; (right side) lado derecho m.

neat [niːt] adj limpio; bien cuidado; ordenado; (drink) solo. **neaten** v limpiar; ordenar. **neatly** adv con cuidado; (dress) con gusto; (skilfully) hábilmente. **neatness** n limpieza f; orden m; gusto m.

necessary ['nesisəri] adj necesario. **if necessary** si es preciso. **it is necessary** es preciso. **necessitate** v necesitar. **necessity** n necesidad f.

neck [nek] n (human, garment) cuello m; (animal) pescuezo m; (bottle) gollete m. **neck and neck** parejos. **necklace** n collar m.

nectar ['nektə] n néctar m.

nectarine ['nektəriːn] n nectarina f

need [niːd] n necesidad f; (lack) carencia f. v necesitar; hacer falta a uno. **needless** adj innecesario; inútil. **needy** adj necesitado. n **the needy** los necesitados m pl.

needle ['niːdl] n aguja f. **darning needle** aguja de zurcir. **knitting needle** aguja de hacer punto. **needlework** n costura f. v (coll) pinchar.

negative ['negətiv] adj negativo. n (gramm) negación f; (phot) negativo m; (reply) contestación negativa f.

neglect [ni'glekt] v no cumplir con; dejar de; no observar; descuidar; abandonar. n negligencia f; abandono m; inobservancia

f; dejadez f. **neglected** adj descuidado; abandonado.

negligée ['negliʒei] n negligé m.

negligence ['neglidʒəns] n negligencia f; descuido m. **negligent** adj negligente; descuidado.

negotiate [ni'gouʃieit] v negociar; (obstacle) franquear; (hill) subir; (bend) tomar. **negotiable** adj negociable; franqueable. **negotiation** n negociación f.

Negro ['niːgrou] nm, adj negro.

neigh [nei] v relinchar. n relincho m.

neighbour ['neibə] n vecino, -a m, f. **neighbourhood** n vecindad f; (district) barrio m. **neighbouring** adj vecino; (near) cercano. **neighbourly** adj de buena vecindad.

neither ['naiðə] adv tampoco. **neither... nor** ... ni ... ni .... conj ni, tampoco. pron ninguno, -a m, f; adj ninguno de los dos.

neon ['niːon] n neón m.

nephew ['nefjuː] n sobrino m.

nepotism ['nepətizəm] n nepotismo m.

nerve [nəːv] n nervio m; valor m; (coll: cheek) cara f. **get on someone's nerves** crisparle los nervios a uno. **lose one's nerve** (coll) rajarse. **nerve-wracking** adj crispante; horripilante. **nerves** pl (coll) nerviosismo m. **nervous** adj nervioso; (apprehensive) miedoso. **nervous breakdown** depresión nerviosa f.

nest [nest] n nido m. v anidar.

nestle ['nesl] v arrellanarse; acurrucarse.

net[1] [net] n red f; (Internet) internet m. **net curtains** visillo m sing. **network** n red f. v coger.

net[2] [net] adj neto. **net weight** peso neto m.

Netherlands ['neðələndz] pl n Países Bajos m pl.

nettle ['etl] n ortiga f. **nettle rash** urticaria f. v irritar.

neuralgia [nju'raldʒə] n neuralgia f. **neuralgic** adj neurálgico.

neurosis [nju'rousis] n neurosis f. **neurotic** n, adj neurótico, -a.

neuter ['njuːtə] nm, adj neutro.

neutral ['njuːtrəl] adj neutro. n (mot) punto muerto m. **neutrality** n neutralidad f. **neutralize** v neutralizar.

never ['nevə] adv nunca, jamás. **neverending** adj sin fin. **nevermore** adv nunca más.

nevertheless [nevəðə'les] *adv* sin embargo, no obstante.

new [nju:] *adj* nuevo; fresco.

newcomer ['nju:kʌmə] *n* recién llegado, -a *m, f*.

new-born ['nju:bo:n] *adj* recién nacido, -a *m, f*.

new-fangled ['nju:ˌfæŋgld] *adj* recién inventado.

new-laid [nju:'leid] *adj* (*egg*) recién puesto.

newly-wed ['nju:liˌwed] *adj* recién casado, -a *m, f*.

news [nju:z] *n* noticias *f pl*; actualidad *f*; (*radio*) diario hablado *m*; (*TV*) telediario *m*; (*film*) noticiario *m*. **news agency** agencia de información *f*. **newsagent** *n* vendedor de periódicos *m*. **news flash** noticia de última hora *f*. **news item** noticia *f*. **newsletter** *n* boletín *m*. **newspaper** *n* periódico *m*, diario *m*. **newsstand** *n* quiosco de periódicos *m*.

newt [nju:t] *n* tritón *m*.

New Testament *n* Nuevo Testamento *m*.

New Year *n* Año Nuevo *m*. **Happy New Year!** ¡feliz Año Nuevo! **New Year's Eve** Nochevieja *f*.

New Zealand [nju:'zi:lənd] *n* Nueva Zelanda *f*, Nueva Zelandia *f*. **New Zealander** neocelandés, -esa *m, f*, neozelandés, -esa *m, f*.

next [nekst] *adj* próximo; siguiente; que viene; (*adjoining*) vecino. *adv* luego, después; la próxima vez; ahora. *prep* junto a, cerca de. **the next day** el día siguiente *m*. **next-door** *adj* de al lado. **next to** al lado de. **next-of-kin** *n* pariente más cercano *m*. **who's next?** ¿a quién le toca?

nib [nib] *n* plumilla *f*.

nibble ['nibl] *v* mordiscar, mordisquear. *n* mordisqueo *m*.

nice [nais] *adj* (*kind*) amable; (*agreeable*) agradable; (*likeable*) simpático; (*pretty*) bonito; (*pleasant*) ameno; precioso; escrupuloso; (*weather*) bueno; (*point*) delicado. **nicely** *adv* amablemente; agradablemente; bien. **nicety** *n* precisión *f*; delicadeza *f*.

niche [nitʃ] *n* nicho *m*, hornacina *f*.

nick [nik] *n* (*notch*) muesca *f*. (*cut*) rasguño *m*. **in the nick of time** justo a tiempo. *v* hacer muescas; cortar; (*slang: steal*) birlar; (*slang: arrest*) pescar.

nickel ['nikl] *n* níquel *m*.

nickname ['nikneim] *n* apodo *m*. *v* apodar.

nicotine ['nikəti:n] *n* nicotina *f*.

niece [ni:s] *n* sobrina *f*.

niggle ['nigl] *v* ocuparse de menudencias. **niggling** *adj* de poca monta; molesto.

night [nait] *n* noche *f*. **good night!** ¡buenas noches! **last night** anoche *f*. **tomorrow night** mañana por la noche *f*.

night cap *n* (*garment*) gorro de dormir; (*coll: drink*) bebida tomada antes de acostarse *f*.

nightclub ['naitklʌb] *n* night club *m*.

nightdress ['naitdres] *n* camisón *m*, camisa de dormir *f*.

nightfall ['naitfo:l] *n* anochecer *m*.

nightingale ['naitiŋˌgeil] *n* ruiseñor *m*.

night-life ['naitlaif] *n* vida nocturna *f*.

night-light ['naitlait] *n* lamparilla *f*.

nightly ['naitli] *adj* nocturno. *adv* por las noches; todas las noches.

nightmare ['naitmeə] *n* pesadilla *f*.

night-school ['naitˌsku:l] *n* escuela nocturna *f*.

nightshade ['naitʃeid] *n* **deadly nightshade** belladona *f*.

night shift *n* turno de noche *m*.

night-watchman [ˌnait'wotʃmən] *n* guarda nocturno *m*; sereno *m*.

nil [nil] *n* nada *f*; ninguno, -a *m, f*; (*sport*) cero *m*.

nimble ['nimbl] *adj* ágil; (*mind*) vivo. **nimbleness** *n* agilidad *f*; vivacidad *f*.

nine [nain] *nm, adj* nueve. **dressed up to the nines** de punta en blanco. **ninth** *n, adj* noveno, -a.

nineteen [nain'ti:n] *nm, adj* diecinueve. **nineteenth** *n, adj* decimonoveno, -a.

ninety ['nainti] *nm, adj* noventa. **ninetieth** *n, adj* nonagésimo, -a.

nip¹ [nip] *v* (*pinch*) pellizcar; (*bite*) morder; (*coll: go quickly*) pegar un salto. **nip in the bud** cortar de raíz. *n* pellizco *m*; mordisco *m*. **nippy** *adj* rápido; (*chilly*) fresquito.

nip² [nip] *n* (*drop*) gota *f*; (*drink*) trago *m*.

nipple ['nipl] *n* (*female*) pezón *m*; (*male*) tetilla *f*; (*bottle*) tetina *f*.

nit [nit] *n* liendre *f*; (*coll*) papanatas *m invar*.

nitrogen ['naitrədʒən] *n* nitrógeno *m*.

no [nou] *adv* no. *n* ninguno. **no longer** *or*

more ya no. **no parking** prohibido aparcar. **no smoking** prohibido fumar. **no thoroughfare** calle sin salida.

noble ['noubl] n (m + f), adj noble. **nobility** n nobleza f.

nobody ['noubodi] pron nadie.

nocturnal [nok'tə:nəl] adj nocturno.

nod [nod] v inclinar; asentir con la cabeza; saludar con la cabeza; (sleepily) dar cabezadas. n inclinación de cabeza f; saludo con la cabeza m; cabezada f.

noise [noiz] n ruido m. **noiseless** adj silencioso. **noisy** adj ruidoso.

nomad ['noumad] n nómada m, f. **nomadic** adj nómada.

nominal ['nominl] adj nominal.

nominate ['nomineit] v (appoint) nombrar; (propose) designar. **nomination** n nombramiento m, designación f.

nonchalant ['nonʃələnt] adj imperturbable; indiferente. **nonchalance** n imperturbabilidad f; indiferencia f.

nonconformist [nonkən'fo:mist] n (m + f), adj disidente.

nondescript ['nondiskript] adj indescriptible.

none [nʌn] pron nadie; ninguno, -a. adv de ningún modo, de ninguna manera.

nonentity [non'entəti] n nulidad f.

nonetheless [,nʌnðə'les] adv sin embargo, no obstante.

non-existent [nonig'zistənt] adj inexistente.

non-fiction [non'fikʃən] n literatura no novelesca f.

nonplussed [non'plʌst] adj perplejo, desconcertado.

non-resident [non'rezidənt] n(m + f), adj no residente.

nonsense ['nonsəns] n tonterías f pl. **nonsensical** adj disparatado.

non-stick [non'stik] adj antiadherente.

non-stop [non'stop] adj directo; continuo; sin escalas. adv sin parar; directamente.

noodles ['nu:dlz] pl n fideos m pl.

noon [nu:n] n mediodía m.

no-one ['nouwʌn] pron nadie.

noose [nu:s] n nudo corredizo m; lazo m; (hangman's) soga f.

nor [no:] conj ni; tampoco.

norm [no:m] n norma f.

normal ['no:məl] adj normal. n lo normal m.

north [no:θ] n norte m. adj also **northerly**, **northern** del norte, norteño; (facing north) que da al norte. adv hacia el norte. **North America** Norte América. **northbound** adj de dirección norte. **north-east** nm, adj nordeste. **Northern Ireland** Irlanda del Norte. **north-west** nm, adj noroeste.

Norway ['no:wei] n Noruega f. **Norwegian** n, adj noruego, -a.

nose [nouz] n nariz f; (sense of smell) olfato m; (aircraft, car) morro m. **blow one's nose** sonarse. **have a nosebleed** sangrar por la nariz. **nosey** adj (coll) entremetido.

nostalgia [no'staldʒə] n nostalgia f. **nostalgic** adj nostálgico.

nostril ['nostrəl] n ventanilla de la nariz f; (horse) ollar m. **nostrils** pl n narices f. pl.

not [not] adv no; ni; como no; sin. **certainly not!** ¡de ninguna manera! **not at all** (acknowledging thanks) no hay de qué.

notable ['noutəbl] adj notable. **notably** adv notablemente, señaladamente.

notary ['noutəri] n notario m.

notch [notʃ] n (cut) muesca f; (degree) grado m. v hacer una muesca en.

note [nout] n nota f; (key of piano, organ) tecla f; (sound) sonido m; (money) billete m; (music) tono m; (renown) renombre m; marca. **notebook** n cuaderno m. **notepaper** n papel de escribir m. **noteworthy** adj notable. v tomar nota de; darse cuenta de; anotar, apuntar. **noted** adj notable; célebre.

nothing ['nʌθiŋ] pron nada; no ... nada. n cero m. **nothing but** sólo.

notice ['noutis] n (advert) anuncio m; (poster) cartel m; (sign) letrero m; atención f; (warning) aviso m; (dismissal) despido m; (resignation) dimisión f. **notice-board** n tablón de anuncios m. **at short notice** a corto plazo. **notice to quit** desahucio m. v darse cuenta de; fijarse en; observar; ver; prestar atención. **noticeable** adj notable; evidente.

notify ['noutifai] v avisar, notificar.

notion ['nouʃən] n idea f, concepto m.

notorious [nou'to:riəs] adj notorio. **notoriety** n notoriedad f.

notwithstanding [notwið'standiŋ] prep a pesar de. adv sin embargo. conj por más que.

nougat ['nu:ga:] n turrón de almendras m.

nought [no:t] *n* cero *m*.

noun [naun] *n* nombre *m*, sustantivo *m*.

nourish ['nʌriʃ] *v* alimentar. **nourishing** *adj* alimenticio, nutritivo. **nourishment** *n* alimento *m*.

novel[1] ['novəl] *n* novela *f*. **novelist** *n* novelista *m, f*.

novel[2] ['novəl] *adj* nuevo; original. **novelty** *n* novedad *f*.

November [nə'vembə] *n* noviembre *m*.

novice ['novis] *n* novicio, -a *m, f*.

now [nau] *adv* ahora; ya; ya ahora; actualmente; inmediatamente. **from now on** de ahora en adelante. **nowadays** *adv* hoy día. **now and again** de vez en cuando. **up to now** hasta ahora.

nowhere ['nouweə] *adv* por ninguna parte; en ninguna parte; a ninguna parte.

noxious ['nokʃəs] *adj* nocivo.

nozzle ['nozl] *n* boca *f*, boquilla *f*.

nuance [nju:ãs] *n* matiz *m*.

nuclear ['nju:kliə] *adj* nuclear.

nucleus ['nju:kliəs] *n* núcleo *m*.

nude ['nju:d] *nm, adj* desnudo. **nudism** *n* nudismo *m*. **nudist** *n(m + f)*, *adj* nudista. **nudity** *n* desnudez *f*.

nudge [nʌdʒ] *v* dar un codazo a. *n* codazo *m*.

nugget ['nʌgit] *n* pepita *f*.

nuisance ['nju:sns] *n (thing)* molestia *f*; *(person)* molesta *f*. **be a nuisance** ponerse pesado. **what a nuisance!** *(coll)* ¡qué pesadez!

null [nʌl] *adj* nulo. **null and void** nulo y sin valor.

numb [nʌm] *adj* entumecido; *(with fear)* petrificado. *v* entumecer; dejar helado. **numbness** *n* entumecimiento *m*; parálisis *f*.

number ['nʌmbə] *n* número *m*. **number plate** *(mot)* matrícula *f*. *v* numerar; contar.

numeral ['nju:mərəl] *n* número *m*, cifra *f*.

numeration [,nju:mə'reiʃn] *n* numeración *f*. **numerator** *n* numerador *m*.

numerical [nju:'merikl] *adj* numérico.

numerous ['nju:mərəs] *adj* numeroso.

nun [nʌn] *n* monja *f*.

nurse [nə:s] *n* enfermera *f*; *(nanny)* niñera *f*. *v (the sick)* cuidar; *(suckle)* criar; *(cradle)* mecer; *(hopes)* abrigar; *(plans)* acariciar. **nursing home** clínica *f*.

nursery ['nə:səri] *n (room)* habitación de los niños *f*; *(day nursery)* guardería infantil *f*; *(plants)* vivero *m*. **nursery rhyme** poesía infantil *f*. **nursery school** escuela de párvulos *f*.

nurture ['nə:tʃə] *v* nutrir, alimentar; *(rear)* criar.

nut [nʌt] *n (bot)* nuez *f*; *(tech)* tuerca *f*; *(person)* loco, -a *m, f*. **in a nutshell** en pocas palabras. **nutcracker** *n* cascanueces *m invar*. **nutmeg** *n* nuez moscada *f*.

nutrient ['nju:triənt] *n* alimento nutritivo *m*.

nutrition [nju'triʃən] *n* nutrición *f*. **nutritious** *adj* nutritivo.

nuzzle ['nʌzl] *v* hocicar.

nylon ['nailon] *n* nilón *m*.

nymph [nimf] *n* ninfa *f*.

O

oak [ouk] *n* roble *m*.

oar [o:] *n* remo *m*. **oarsman** *n* remero *m*.

oasis [ou'eisis] *n* oasis *m invar*.

oath [ouθ] *n (law)* juramento *m*; *(expletive)* blasfemia *f*. **take the oath** prestar juramento.

oats [outs] *pl n* avena *f sing*. **oatmeal** *n* harina de avena *f*.

obedient [ə'bi:diənt] *adj* obediente. **obedience** *n* obediencia *f*.

obese [ə'bi:s] *adj* obeso. **obesity** *n* obesidad *f*.

obey [ə'bei] *v* obedecer.

obituary [ə'bitjuəri] *n* necrología *f*.

object ['obʒikt; *v* əb'ʒekt] *n* objeto *m*; *(gramm)* complemento *m*; *(aim)* meta *f*. *v* oponerse; objetar; protestar. **objection** *n* objeción *m*; reparo *m*. **objectionable** *adj* censurable; desagradable. **objective** *nm, adj* objetivo.

oblige [ə'blaidʒ] *v (compel)* obligar; *(please)* complacer; *(assist)* hacer un favor. **be obliged to** *(have to)* verse obligado a; *(be grateful)* estar agradecido a. **obligation** *n* obligación *f*; *(comm)* compromiso *m*. **obligatory** *adj* obligatorio.

oblique [ə'bli:k] *adj* sesgado; indirecto.

obliterate [ə'blitəreit] v borrar; cancelar **obliteration** n borrado m; cancelación f.

oblivion [ə'bliviən] n olvido m. **oblivious** adj olvidadizo; ignorante.

oblong ['oblon] adj oblongo. n cuadrilongo m.

obnoxious [əb'nokʃəs] adj ofensivo; execrable.

oboe ['oubou] n oboe m. **oboist** n oboe m, oboísta m, f.

obscene [əb'si:n] adj obsceno. **obscenity** n obscenidad f.

obscure [əb'skjuə] adj oscuro; confuso. v oscurecer; (hide) esconder. **obscurity** n oscuridad f.

observe [əb'zə:v] v observar; ver; decir. **observant** adj observador; atento. **observation** n (remark) observación f; (of rules) observancia f. **observatory** n observatorio m.

obsess [əb'ses] v obsesionar. **obsession** n obsesión f. **obsessive** obsesivo.

obsolescent [obsə'lesnt] adj que cae en desuso. **obsolescence** n caída en desuso f.

obsolete ['obsəli:t] adj anticuado.

obstacle ['obstəkl] n obstáculo m.

obstetrics [ob'stetriks] n obstetricia f. **obstetrician** n tocólogo m.

obstinate ['obstinət] adj obstinado; terco; rebelde. **obstinacy** n obstinación f; terquedad f.

obstruct [əb'strʌkt] v obstruir; (hinder) estorbar. **obstruction** n obstrucción f; estorbo m.

obtain [əb'tein] v obtener, lograr; (acquire) adquirir; (extract) sacar.

obtrusive [əb'tru:siv] adj importuno, molesto; (meddlesome) entrometido. **obtrusion** n intrusión f.

obtuse [əb'tju:s] adj obtuso.

obverse ['obvə:s] n anverso m. adj del anverso.

obvious ['obviəs] adj obvio. **obviously** (adv) obviamente .

occasion [ə'keiʒən] n ocasión f. oportunidad f; (cause) motivo m; circunstancia f. v ocasionar; incitar. **occasional** adj ocasional. **occasionally** adv de vez en cuando.

occult ['okʌlt] adj oculto. n the occult ciencias ocultas f pl.

occupy ['okjupai] v ocupar; emplear. **occupant** n (place) ocupante m, f; (position) po-sesor, -a m, f. **occupation** n ocupación f; profesión f; trabajo m. **occupational** adj profesional. **occupational hazard** gajes del oficio m pl.

occur [ə'kə:] v (happen) ocurrir, acontecer; producirse; (opportunity) presentarse, (take place) tener lugar. **occurrence** n acontecimiento m; caso m.

ocean ['ouʃən] n océano m. **oceanic** adj oceánico.

ochre ['oukə] n ocre m.

o'clock [ə'klok] adv one o'clock la una. **two/three/etc.** o'clock las dos/tres/etc.

octagon ['oktəgən] n octágono m. **octagonal** adj octagonal.

octane ['oktein] n octano m.

octave ['oktiv] n octava f.

October [ok'toubə] n octubre m.

octopus ['oktəpəs] n pulpo m.

oculist ['okjulist] n oculista m, f.

odd [od] adj extraño, raro; (number) impar; (left over) sobrante; (occasional) alguno. **odd jobs** pequeños arreglos m pl. **oddity** n (thing) curiosidad f; (quality) singularidad f. **oddment** n saldo m. **odds** pl n (betting) apuesta f sing; (chances) posibilidades f pl. **be at odds with** estar peleado con uno. **it makes no odds** no importa. **odds and ends** pedazos m pl.

ode [oud] n oda f.

odious ['oudiəs] adj odioso.

odour ['oudə] n olor m; perfume m. **odourless** adj inodoro.

oesophagus [i:'sofəgəs] n esófago m.

of [ov] prep de.

off [of] adj (substandard) malo; (fruit, vegetables, meat, fish) pasado; (wine) agriado; (cancelled) suspendido; (elec) apagado; (water) cortado; (brake) suelto. prep de; fuera de; a … de; desde; en.

offal ['ofəl] n asadura f.

off-chance [ˌof'tʃɑːns] n on the off-chance (coll) por si acaso.

off-colour [of'kʌlə] adj be off-colour (coll) encontrarse indispuesto.

offend [ə'fend] v ofender; escandalizar; (eyes, ears) herir. **offence** n ofensa f; escándalo m; (law) delito m. **take offence** ofenderse por. **offender** n ofensor, -a m, f; delincuente m, f. **offensive** adj ofensivo; chocante; insultante.

offer ['ofə] v ofrecer; (proposal) proponer;

presentarse. *n* oferta *f*; propuesta *f*. **offer-ing** *n* (*action*) oferta *f*; (*gift*) regalo *m*. **on offer** (*adv*) en oferta.

offhand [of'hand] *adj* improvisado; brusco. *adv* sin pensarlo; bruscamente.

office ['ofis] *n* (*place*) oficina *f*; (*service*) oficio *m*; (*public office*) cargo *m*; (*function*) funciones *f pl*. **take office** entrar en funciones.

officer *n* (*mil*) oficial *m*; (*public appointee*) funcionario, -a *m, f*; (*police*) policía *f*.

official [ə'fiʃəl] *adj* oficial. *n* funcionario, -a *m, f*.

officious [ə'fiʃəs] *adj* oficioso.

offing ['ofiŋ] *n* **in the offing** en perspectiva.

off-licence ['ofiaisns] *n* bodega *f*.

off-line [of'lain] *adj* desconectado, fuera de línea.

off-peak [of'pi:k] *adj, adv* de menos tráfico; (*elec*) de menor consumo.

off-road vehicle ['ofroud] *n* vehículo todo terreno *m*.

off-season [of'si:zn] *n* estación muerta *f*. *adv, adj* fuera de temporada.

offset [of'set; *n* 'ofset] *v* compensar; desviar. *n* (*printing*) offset *m*.

offshore ['ofʃo:] *adj* de la costa.

offside [of'said] *n* (*mot: right*) lado derecho *m*; (*mot: left*) lado izquierdo *m*; (*sport*) fuera de juego *m*.

offspring ['ofspriŋ] *n* progenitura *f*; (*fig*) fruto *m*.

offstage ['ofsteidʒ] *adv, adj* entre bastidores.

off-the-cuff [ofðə'kʌf] *adj* espontáneo. *adv* de proviso.

off-white [of'wait] *adj* blancuzco.

often ['ofn] *adv* a menudo. **as often as not** la mitad de las veces. **every so often** alguna que otra vez.

ogre ['ougə] *n* ogro *m*.

oil [oil] *n* aceite *m*; petróleo *m*; (*painting*) óleo *m*; fuel *m*. **oily** *adj* (*tech*) grasiento; (*food*) aceitoso; (*skin*) graso; (*fig: manner*) zalamero.

oilcan ['oilkan] *n* aceitera *f*; (*for storage*) bidón de aceite *m*.

oilcloth ['oilklοθ] *n* hule *m*.

oil colour *n* óleo *m*.

oilfield ['oilfi:ld] *n* yacimiento pertrolífero *m*.

oil-fired [oil'faiəd] *adj* alimentado con mazut.

oilskin ['oil,skin] *n* impermeable de hule *m*.

oil stove *n* estufa de mazut *f*.

oil tanker *n* petrolero *m*.

oil well *n* pozo de petróleo *m*.

ointment ['ointmənt] *n* ungüento *m*.

O.K. [ou'kei] *interj* ¡de acuerdo!

old [ould] *adj* viejo; antiguo; (*adult*) mayor; (*clothes*) usado; (*wine*) añejo; (*other food*) pasado; (*familiar*) conocido. **I am six years old** tengo seis años. **how old is he?** ¿cuántos años tiene? **old age** vejez *f*. **old-age pensioner** pensionista *m, f*. **old-fashioned** *adj* chapado a la antigua; pasado de moda. **old maid** solterona *f*.

olive ['oliv] *n* (*fruit*) aceituna *f*, oliva *f*; (*tree*) olivo *m*. **olive green** *nm, adj* verde oliva *m*. **olive oil** aceite de oliva *m*.

Olympic [ə'limpik] *adj* olímpico. **Olympic Games** juegos olímpicos *m pl*.

omelette ['omlit] *n* tortilla *f*.

omen ['oumən] *n* presagio *m*, augurio *m*.

ominous ['ominəs] *adj* amenazador.

omit [ou'mit] *v* omitir; suprimir. **omission** *n* omisión *f*; olvido *m*.

omnipotent [om'nipətənt] *adj* omnipotente. **omnipotence** *n* omnipotencia *f*.

on [on] *pron* en, sobre; a. **oncoming** *adj* venidero; (*adv*) en desarrollo, en curso. **on-line** (*computing*) conectado, en línea. **onlooker** *n* espectador, -a *m, f*. **onset** *n* principio *m*; ataque *m*. **onshore** *adj* hacia la tierra. **onslaught** *n* ataque violento *m*. **onward(s)** *adj, adv* hacia adelante. **from now onwards** de ahora en adelante.

once [wʌns] *adv* una vez; (*formerly*) antes, hace tiempo. *conj* una vez que. **at once** en seguida. **once again** una vez más. **once and for all** de una vez para siempre.

one [wʌn] *n, pron, adj* uno, -a *m, f*. **be one up on** marcar un tanto a costa de. **one by one** uno por uno. **one-off** único intento. **one-sided** *adj* parcial; desigual. **one-way** *adj* de dirección única. **that one** ése or aquél, ésa or aquélla. **this one** éste, ésta. **which one?** ¿cuál?

oneself [wʌn'self] *pron* se; sí; sí mismo, -a; (*emphatic*) uno mismo, una misma. **by oneself** solo, -a.

onion ['ʌnjən] *n* cebolla *f*.

only ['ounli] *adj* solo; único. *adv* sólo, solamente. *conj* pero, sólo que.

onus ['ounəs] n responsabilidad f.

onyx ['oniks] n ónice m, f.

ooze [uːz] v rezumar; exudar.

opal ['oupəl] n ópalo m.

opaque [ə'paik] adj opaco; oscuro. **opacity** n opacidad f; oscuridad f.

open ['oupən] v abrir; (exhibition) inaugurar; iniciar. adj abierto; (unfolded) desplegado; (frank) franco; (meeting) público; (unsolved) pendiente; (post) vacante; (free) libre; (sea) alta. **open-air** adj al aire libre. **open-handed** adj generoso. **open-minded** adj imparcial. **open-mouthed** adj, adv boquiabierto.

opening ['oupəniŋ] n abertura f; inauguración f; oportunidad f; vacante f; principio m; (act of opening) apertura f; (breach) brecha f. adj inaugural. **opening night** noche de estreno f.

opera ['opərə] n ópera f. **opera glasses** prismáticos m pl. **opera house** ópera f. **opera singer** cantante de ópera m, f. **operatic** adj operístico. **operetta** n opereta f; zarzuela f.

operate ['opəreit] v (machine) manejar; (hacer) funcionar; (direct) dirigir; (med) operar. **operable** adj operable. **operating table** quirófano m. **operation** n funcionamiento m; manejo m; maniobra f; aplicación f; actividad f. **in operation** en vigor; en funcionamiento. **operational** adj operacional. **operative** adj en vigor; operativo; eficaz. **operator** n operario, -a m, f; maquinista m, f; telefonista m, f; (tour) agente de viajes; (wireless) radiotelegrafista m.

ophthalmic [of'θalmik] adj oftálmico.

opinion [ə'pinjən] n opinión f. **in my opinion** a mi parecer. **public opinion poll** sondeo de la opinión pública m.

opium ['oupiəm] n opio m.

opponent [ə'pounənt] n adversario, -a m, f; contrario, -a m, f.

opportune [opə'tjuːn] adj oportuno. **opportunism** n oportunismo m. **opportunist** n(m + f), adj oportunista.

opportunity [opə'tjuːnəti] n oportunidad f.

oppose [ə'pouz] v oponerse a. **opposed** adj opuesto. **be opposed to** oponerse a. **opposition** n oposición f; resistencia f.

opposite ['opəzit] adj opuesto; contrario. **the opposite sex** el otro sexo. prep enfrente de, frente a. n lo opuesto, lo contrario.

oppress [ə'pres] v oprimir. **oppression** n opresión f. **oppressive** adj opresor, opresivo; (heat) sofocante; (mentally) agobiante. **oppressor** n opresor, -a m, f.

opt [opt] v **opt out of** no meterse. **opt to** optar por.

optical ['optikl] adj óptico. **optical illusion** ilusión óptica f. **optician** n óptico m.

optimism ['optimizəm] n optimismo m. **optimist** n optimista m, f. **optimistic** adj optimista.

optimum ['optiməm] adj óptimo. n lo óptimo.

option ['opʃən] n opción f; posibilidad f; elección f. **optional** adj facultativo.

opulent ['opjulənt] adj opulento; abundante. **opulence** n opulencia f.

or [oː] conj o; (negative) ni. **or else** si no. **or not** o no.

oracle ['orəkl] n oráculo m.

oral ['oːrəl] nm, adj oral.

orange ['orindʒ] n (fruit) naranja f; (tree) naranjo m; (colour) naranja m. adj naranja. **orangeade** n naranjada f.

orator ['orətə] n orador, -a m, f. **orate** v perorar. **oration** n oración f. **oratory** n oratoria f.

orbit ['oːbit] n órbita f. v estar en órbita; dar vueltas.

orchard ['oːtʃəd] n huerto m; (apple) manzanal m; (pear) peral m.

orchestra ['oːkəstrə] n orquesta f. **orchestral** adj orquestal. **orchestrate** v orquestar. **orchestration** n orquestación f.

orchid ['oːkid] n orquídea f.

ordain [oː'dein] v (rel) ordenar; (fate) destinar. **ordination** n ordenación f.

ordeal [oː'diːl] n sufrimiento m.

order ['oːdə] n orden m; (rel) orden f; (comm) pedido m; (medal) condecoración f. **in order** (correct) en regla. **in order to** para. **out of order** no funcionar. v ordenar; organizar; clasificar; pedir; mandar.

orderly ['oːdəli] adj ordenado; metódico; disciplinado. n (mil) ordenanza m.

ordinal ['oːdinl] adj ordinal.

ordinary ['oːdənəri] adj corriente, usual; (mediocre) ordinario; simple; (average) medio. n lo corriente, lo ordinario. **out of the ordinary** extraordinario, excepcional.

ore [oː] n mineral m.

oregano [ori'ga:nou] *n* orégano *m*.

organ ['o:gən] *n* órgano *m*. **organist** *n* organista *m, f*.

organic [o:'ganik] *adj* orgánico, biológico.

organism ['o:gənizəm] *n* organismo *m*.

organize ['o:gənaiz] *v* organizar. **organization** *n* organización *f*. **organizer** *n* organizador, -a *m, f*.

orgasm ['o:gazəm] *n* orgasmo *m*.

orgy ['o:dʒi] *n* orgía *f*.

oriental [o:ri'entl] *n* (*m + f*), *adj* oriental.

orientate ['o:riənteit] *v* orientar. **orientation** *n* orientación *f*.

orifice ['orifis] *n* orificio *m*.

origin ['oridʒin] *n* origen *m*. **originate** *v* originar, provocar; comenzar. **originate from** ser descendiente de. **originator** *n* autor, -a *m, f*; creador, -a *m, f*.

original [ə'ridʒinl] *adj* original; (*first*) primero. *n* original *m*. **originally** *adv* al principio; con originalidad.

ornament ['o:nəmənt] *n* ornamento *m*. adorno *m*. *v* ornamentar, adornar. **ornamental** *adj* ornamental, de adorno.

ornate [o:'neit] *adj* recargado.

ornithology [o:ni'θolədʒi] *n* ornitología *f*. **ornithological** *adj* ornitológico. **ornithologist** *n* ornitólogo *m*.

orphan ['o:fən] *n, adj* huérfano, -a, *v* dejar huérfano. **orphanage** *n* orfanato *m*.

orthodox ['o:θədoks] *adj* ortodoxo. **orthodoxy** *n* ortodoxia *f*.

orthopaedic [o:θə'pi:dik] *adj* ortopédico.

oscillate ['osileit] *v* oscilar; fluctuar. **oscillation** *n* oscilación *f*; fluctuación *f*.

ostensible [o'stensəbl] *adj* aparente. **ostensibly** *adv* aparentemente.

ostentatious [osten'teiʃəs] *adj* ostentoso. **ostentation** *n* ostentación *f*.

osteopath ['ostiəpəθ] *n* osteópata *m, f*.

ostracize ['ostrəsaiz] *v* condenar al ostracismo. **ostracism** *n* ostracismo *m*.

ostrich ['ostritʃ] *n* avestruz *m*.

other ['ʌðə] *pron, adj* otro, -a. **other than** de otra manera que.

otherwise ['ʌðəwaiz] *adj* distinto. *adv* de otra manera; a parte de eso.

otter ['otə] *n* nutria *f*.

***ought** [o:t] *v* deber; tener que.

our [auə] *pron* nuestro, -a; el nuestro, la nuestra, *adj* nuestro.

ours [auəz] *pron* nuestro, -a; el nuestro, la nuestra.

ourselves [auə'selvz] *pron* nos; nosotros, nosotras; (*emphatic*) nosotros mismos, nosotras mismas. **by ourselves** solos, solas.

oust [aust] *v* expulsar, echar.

out [aut] *adj* fuera; (*light, fire, etc.*) apagado; (*games*) eliminado. **out loud** en voz alta. **out of** fuera de; (*through*) por; (*from*) de; (*without*) no tener, sin.

outboard ['autbo:d] *adj* fuera borda, fuera bordo.

outbreak ['autbreik] *n* (*start*) comienzo *m*; (*disease*) epidemia *f*; (*spots*) erupción *f*; (*violence, crime*) ola *f*; (*revolution*) motín *m*; (*temper*) arrebato *m*.

outbuilding ['autbildiŋ] *n* dependencia *f*.

outburst ['autbə:st] *n* explosión *f*; (*applause*) salvo *m*; (*temper*) arrebato *m*.

outcast ['autka:st] *n* proscrito, -a *m, f*; paria *m, f*.

outcome ['autkʌm] *n* resultado *m*; consecuencias *f pl*.

outcry ['autkrai] *n* (*noise*) alboroto *m*; protesta *f*.

***outdo** [aut'du:] *v* superar.

outdated [aut'deitid] *adj* anticuado, pasado de moda.

outdoor ['autdo:] *adj* al aire libre; (*clothes*) de calle. **outdoors** *adv* fuera; al aire libre.

outer ['autə] *adj* externo, exterior. **outer space** espacio exterior *m*.

outfit ['autfit] *n* (*gear*) equipo *m*; (*clothes*) ropa *f*; (*lady's costume*) conjunto *m*.

outgoing ['autgouiŋ] *adj* saliente; (*manner*) sociable. **outgoings** *pl n* gastos *m pl*.

***outgrow** [aut'grou] *v* crecer más que; (*lose*) perder con la edad. **outgrowth** *n* excrecencia *f*.

outing ['autiŋ] *n* excursión *f*; paseo *m*.

outlandish [aut'landiʃ] *adj* extraño; apartado.

outlaw ['autlo:] *n* proscrito, -a *m, f*. *v* proscribir; declarar ilegal.

outlay ['autlei] *n* gastos *m pl*.

outlet ['autlit] *n* salida *f*; (*drain*) desaguadero *m*; (*elec*) toma *f*; (*comm*) mercado *m*.

outline ['autlain] *n* contorno *m*; perfil *m*; silueta *f*; (*draft*) bosquejo *m*; (*summary*) resumen *m*; (*map*) trazado *m*; (*sketch*) esbozo *m*. *v* perfilar; bosquejar; resumir; trazar.

outlive [aut'liv] v sobrevivir.

outlook ['autluk] n vista f; punto de vista m.

outlying ['autlaiiŋ] adj exterior; remoto.

outnumber [aut'nʌmbə] v exceder en número.

out-of-date [autəv'deit] adj anticuado; pasado de moda.

outpatient ['autpeiʃənt] n paciente no internado m.

outpost ['autpoust] n puesto avanzado m

output ['autput] n producción f; (comput) resultado m; (tech) rendimiento m; (power) potencia f.

outrage ['autreidʒ] n ultraje m; m desafuero m. v ultrajar.

outrageous [aut're:dʒəs] adj ultrajante, escandaloso.

outright [aut'rait; adj 'autrait] adv francamente; (entirely) en su totalidad, (at once) en el acto. adj completo; absoluto; categórico; franco.

outset ['autset] n principio m. **at the outset** al principio.

outside [aut'said; adj 'autsaid] adv fuera, afuera. prep fuera de; más allá de. n exterior m. adj exterior, externo; al aire libre; remoto; independiente. **outsider** n (to a group) intruso, -a m, f; (to a place) forastero, -a m, f; (horse racing) caballo no favorito m.

outsize [aut'saiz] adj de talla muy grande.

outskirts ['autskə:tz] pl n afueras f pl; cercanías f pl.

outspoken [aut'spoukən] adj franco. **outspokenness** n franqueza f.

outstanding [aut'standiŋ] adj destacado, notable; (features) sobresaliente; (success) excepcional; (debt) pendiente; (still to be done) por hacer.

outstrip [aut'strip] v dejar atrás.

outward ['autwəd] adj exterior; (journey) de ida. **outward bound** que sale. **outwardly** adv exteriormente; aparentemente. **outwards** adv hacia fuera.

outweigh [aut'wei] v pesar más que; (value) valer más que.

outwit [aut'wit] v burlar.

oval ['ouvəl] adj oval, ovalado, n óvalo m.

ovary ['ouvəri] n ovario m.

ovation [ou'veiʃən] n ovación f.

oven ['ʌvn] n horno m. **ovenproof** adj de horno.

over ['ouvə] adv encima, por encima; (too much) demasiado; al otro lado. adj (finished) terminado. prep sobre, encima de; al otro lado de; superior a; durante.

overall ['ouvərɔ:l] adj de conjunto; total. adv en conjunto; por todas partes. **overalls** pl n guardapolvo m sing.

overbalance [ouvə'baləns] v (hacer) perder el equilibrio.

overbearing [ouvə'beəriŋ] adj dominante, autoritario.

overboard ['ouvəbo:d] adv (fall) por la borda. **go overboard** (coll) pasarse de la raya. **man overboard!** ¡hombre al agua!

overcast [ouvə'ka:st] adj nublado.

overcharge [ouvə'tʃa:dʒ] v cobrar un precio excesivo; (overload) sobrecargar.

overcoat ['ouvəkout] n abrigo m, sobretodo m.

*****overcome** [ouvə'kʌm] v vencer; triunfar. **be overcome by** estar muerto de.

overcrowded [ouvə'kraudid] adj atestado; superpoblado. **overcrowding** n atestamiento m; superpoblación f.

*****overdo** [ouvə'du:] v exagerar; (exhaust) fatigarse demasiado.

overdose ['ouvədous] n dosis excesiva f.

overdraft ['ouvədra:ft] n giro en descubierto m.

*****overdraw** [ouvə'dro:] v girar en descubierto. **be overdrawn** adj tener un descubierto en su cuenta.

overdue [ouvə'dju:] adj (train, etc.) atrasado; (comm) vencido y sin pagar.

overestimate [ouvə'estimeit] v sobreestimar.

overexpose [ouvəik'spouz] v (phot) sobreexponer.

overflow [ouvə'flou; n 'ouvəflou] v (flow over) derramarse; (flood) inundar. n desbordamiento m; derrame m; inundación f; (pipe) cañería de desagüe f.

overgrown [ouvə'groun] adj cubierto de hierba; (too big) demasiado crecido para su edad.

*****overhang** [ouvə'haŋ; n 'ouvəhaŋ] v sobresalir. n saliente m. **overhanging** adj saliente, sobresaliente.

overhaul [ouvə'ho:l] v investigar; revisar. n examen m, revisión f; arreglo m.

overhead [ouvə'hed] adv arriba. adj de arriba. **overheads** pl n gastos generales m pl.

*overhear [ouvə'hiə] *v* oír (por casualidad); sorprender.

overheat [ouvə'hi:t] *v* recalorar; (*fig*) acalorar.

overjoyed [ouvə'dʒoid] *adj* contentísimo.

overland [ouvə'land] *adv* por vía terrestre. *adj* terrestre.

overlap [ouvə'lap; *n* 'ouvəlap] *v* traslapar. *n* traslapo *m*.

*overlay [ouvə'lei; *n* 'ouvəlei] *v* revestir. *n* revestimiento *m*; cubierta *f*.

overleaf [ouvə'li:f] *adv* a la vuelta.

overload [ouvə'loud; *n* 'ouvəloud] *v* sobrecargar. *n* sobrecarga *f*.

overlook [ouvə'luk] *v* (*miss*) no notar; (*ignore*) no darse cuenta de; (*excuse*) perdonar; (*command a view*) dar a; dominar.

overnight [ouvə'nait] *adv* (*during the night*) por la noche; (*suddenly*) de la noche a la mañana. **stay overnight** pasar la noche. *adj* (*journey*) de noche; (*stay*) por una noche.

overpower [ouvə'pauə] *v* subyugar; (*smell, etc.*) trastornar; dominar. **overpowering** *adj* (*desire*) irresistible; abrumador.

overrated [ouvə'reitid] *adj* sobreestimado.

*override [ouvə'raid] *v* (*ride over*) pasar por encima de; dominar; (*fig*) anular, rechazar. **overriding** *adj* principal.

overrule [ouvə'ru:l] *v* denegar, no admitir.

*overrun [ouvə'rʌn] *v* (*exceed*) rebasar; (*overflow*) derramarse; (*invade*) invadir; (*flood*) inundar; (*infest*) plagar.

overseas [ouvə'sitz] *adv* en ultramar. *adj* de ultramar; (*foreign*) extranjero; (*comm*) exterior.

overseer [ouvə'siə] *n* capataz *m*; inspector, -a *m*, *f*.

overshadow [ouvə'ʃadou] *v* sombrear; (*fig*) eclipsar.

*overshoot [ouvə'ʃu:t] *v* ir más allá de.

oversight ['ouvəsait] *n* descuido *m*; omisión *f*. **through an oversight** por descuido.

*oversleep [ouvə'sli:p] *v* dormir demasiado.

overspill ['ouvəspil] *n* exceso *m*.

overt [ou'və:t] *adj* abierto; manifiesto. **overtly** *adv* evidentemente.

*overtake [ouvə'teik] *v* (*pass*) adelantar; (*catch up*) alcanzar.

*overthrow [ouvə'θrou; *n* 'ouvəθrou] *v* (*overturn*) volcar; (*plans*) desbaratar; (*government*) derrocar; (*empire*) derrumbar. *n* desbaratamiento *m*; derrocamiento *m*; derrumbamiento *m*.

overtime ['ouvətaim] *n* horas extraordinarias *f pl*.

overtone ['ouvətoun] *n* (*music*) armónico *m*; (*fig*) alusión *f*.

overture ['ouvətʃuə] *n* (*music*) obertura *f*; (*proposal*) propuesta *f*.

overturn [ouvə'tə:n] *v* (*car*) volcar; (*government, etc.*) derrocar.

overweight [ouvə'weit] *adj* **be overweight** pesar demasiado.

overwhelm [ouvə'welm] *v* (*conquer*) vencer; (*with grief*) postrar; (*work*) inundar; (*in argument*) confundir; (*joy*) rebosar. **overwhelming** *adj* (*desire*) irresistible; (*defeat*) aplastante; (*work*) abrumador.

overwork [ouvə'wə:k] *v* usar demasiado; hacer trabajar demasiado. *n* exceso de trabajo *m*.

overwrought [ouvə'ro:t] *adj* sobreexcitado, nerviosísimo.

ovulation [ovju'leiʃn] *n* ovulación *f*.

owe [ou] *v* deber; tener deudas. **owing** *adj* que se debe. **owing to** debido a.

owl [aul] *n* lechuza *f*.

own [oun] *v* tener, poseer; (*acknowledge*) reconocer. **own up** confesar. *adj* propio. **get one's own back** desquitarse. **on one's own** solo, sola. **owner** *n* dueño, -a *m*, *f*; poseedor, -a *m*, *f*. **ownership** *n* propiedad *f*; posesión *f*.

ox [oks] *n*, *pl* **oxen** buey *m*. **oxtail** *n* rabo de buey *m*.

oxygen ['oksidʒən] *n* oxígeno *m*. **oxygen tent** cámara de oxígeno *f*.

oyster ['oistə] *n* ostra *f*.

ozone ['ouzoun] *n* ozono *m*

ozone layer capa de ozono *f*.

P

pace [peis] *n* paso *m*; (*gait*) andar *m*; (*horse*) andadura *f*; (*speed*) velocidad *f*. **pacemaker** aparato del tipo de los marcapasos *m*. **keep pace with** ajustarse al paso de; (*events*) mantenerse al corriente de. *v* andar; recorrer. **pace up and down** dar vueltas.

pacific [pə'sifik] *adj* pacífico.
Pacific Ocean *n* Océano Pacífico *m*.
pacifism ['pasifizəm] *n* pacifismo *m*. **pacifist** *n*(*m* + *f*), *adj* pacifista.
pacify ['pasifai] *v* pacificar; calmar.
pack [pak] *n* (*gang*) partida *f*; (*hounds*) jauría *f*; (*cards*) baraja *f*; (*bundle*) bulto *m*; (*med*) paño *m*, compresa *f*. **packhorse** *n* caballo de carga *m*. *v* embalar; envasar; (*suitcase*) hacer; (*cram*) apretar. **pack it in** (*coll*) dejarlo. **packing** *n* embalaje *m*; envase *m*.
package ['pakidʒ] *n* paquete *m*; (*bundle*) fardo *m*. *adj* (*deal*) acuerdo global *m*; (*holiday*, *tour*) viaje todo comprendido *m*. *v* embalar; envasar.
packet ['pakit] *n* paquete *m*; (*tea*, *etc*.) sobre *m*; (*cigarettes*) cajetilla *f*.
pact [pakt] *n* pacto *m*.
pad[1] [pad] *n* (*paper*) bloc *m*; (*blotting*) carpeta *f*; (*ink*) tampón *m*; (*cushion*) almohadilla *f*; (*launching*) plataforma de lanzamiento *f*. *v* acolchar; rellenar. **pad out** (*coll*) meter paja en. **padding** *n* acolchado *m*; relleno *m*; (*fig*) paja *f*.
pad[2] [pad] *v* andar a pasos quedos.
paddle[1] ['padl] *n* (*oar*) canalete *m*; (*waterwheel*) álabe *m*. **paddle boat** *or* **steamer** vapor de ruedas *m*. *v* remar con canalete.
paddle[2] ['padl] *n* (*wade*) chapotear.
paddock ['padək] *n* paddock *m*.
padlock ['padlok] *n* candado *m*. *v* cerrar con candado.
paediatric [pi:di'atrik] *adj* pediátrico. **paediatrician** *n* pediatra *m*, pediátra *m*. **paediatrics** *n* pediatría *f*.
pagan ['peigən] *n*, *adj* pagano, -a.
page[1] [peidʒ] *n* (*book*) página *f*.
page[2] [peidʒ] *n* also **page-boy** (*hotel*) botones *m invar*; (*court*, *wedding*) page *m*. *v* (*person*) hacer llamar por un paje.
pageant ['padʒənt] *n* desfile histórico *m*. **pageantry** *n* aparato *m*, pompa *f*.
paid [peid] *V* **pay**.
pail [peil] *n* cubo *m*.
pain [pein] *n* dolor *m*. **painkiller** *n* calmante *m*. **pains** *pl n* (*effort*) esfuerzo *m*. **painstaking** *adj* concienzudo; cuidadoso. *v* doler; afligir. **painful** *adj* doloroso; (*embarrassing*) difícil. **painless** *adj* sin dolor; (*easy*) fácil.
paint [peint] *n* pintura *f*. **paintbox** *n* caja de pinturas *f*. **paintbrush** (*artist*) pincel *m*; (*house painter*) brocha *f*. **paint roller** rodillo *m*. *v* pintar; (*fig*) describir. **painter** *n* pintor, -a *m*, *f*. **painting** *n* pintura *f*; (*picture*) cuadro *m*.
pair [peə] *n* (*objects*) par *m*; (*people*, *animals*) pareja *f*; (*oxen*) yunta *f*; (*horses*) tronco *m*. *v* (*socks*, *etc*.) emparejar; (*mate*) aparearse. **pair off** (*people*) formar pareja.
Pakistan *n* Pakisten *m*; **Pakistani** *adj* Pakistaní.
Pakistan [paki'sta:n] *n* Pakistán *m*
pal [pal] *n* (*coll*) amigote *m*; camarada *m*, *f*.
palace ['paləs] *n* palacio *m*. **palatial** *adj* magnífico; suntuoso.
palate ['palit] *n* paladar *m*. **palatable** *adj* sabroso; (*fig*) agradable.
pale [peil] *adj* pálido. *v* palidecer. **paleness** *n* palidez *f*.
palette ['palit] *n* paleta *f*.
pall[1] [po:l] *v* perder el sabor; aburrirse (de).
pall[2] [po:l] *n* paño mortuorio *m*; (*smoke*) cortina *f*; (*snow*) capa *f*.
pallid ['palid] *adj* pálido.
palm[1] [pa:m] *n* (*hand*) palma *f*. **palm off** (*coll*) colar. **palmist** *n* quiromántico, -a *m*, *f*. **palmistry** *n* quiromancia *f*.
palm[2] [pa:m] *n* (*tree*) palma *f*. palmera *f*.
palpitate ['palpiteit] *v* palpitar. **palpitation** *n* palpitación *f*.
paltry ['po:ltri] *adj* miserable.
pamper ['pampə] *v* mimar.
pamphlet ['pamflit] *n* folleto *m*.
pan [pan] *n* cacerola *f*.
Panama [panə'ma:] *n* Panamá *m*. **Panama City** *n* Panamá.
pancake ['pankeik] *n* pancake *m*. **Pancake Tuesday** martes de carnaval.
pancreas ['paŋkriəs] *n* páncreas *m*. **pancreatic** *adj* pancreático.
panda ['pandə] *n* panda *m*.
pandemonium [pandi'mouniəm] *n* pandemonio *m*.
pander ['pandə] *v* **pander to** complacer.
pane [pein] *n* vidrio *m*, cristal *m*.
panel ['panl] *n* (*door*) panel *m*; (*wall*) lienzo *m*; (*dress*) paño *m*; (*control*) tablero *m*; (*experts*) grupo *m*; (*judges*) jurado *m*. *v* revestir con paneles; artesonar. **panelist** *n* miembro del jurado *m*. **panelling** *n* revestimiento de madera *m*; artesonado *m*.

pang [paŋ] n (*pain, hunger*) punzada f; (*jealousy*) angustia f; (*love*) herida f; (*conscience*) remordimiento m.

panic ['panik] n pánico m. **panic-stricken** adj preso de pánico. v asustarse.

panorama [ˌpanəˈraːmə] n panorama m. **panoramic** adj panorámico.

pansy ['panzi] n pensamiento m.

pant [pant] v jadear. n jadeo m.

panther ['panθə] n pantera f.

pantomime ['pantəmaim] n (*mime*) pantomima f.

pantry ['pantri] n despensa f.

pants [pants] pl n (*underpants*) calzoncillos m pl; (*coll: trousers*) pantalones m pl.

papal ['peipl] adj papal.

paper ['peipə] n papel m; (*news*) periódico m, diario m; (*blotting*) papel secante m; (*brown*) papel de estraza m; (*carbon*) papel carbón m; (*drawing*) papel de dibujo m; (*greaseproof*) papel vegetal m; (*tissue*) papel de seda m; (*toilet*) papel higiénico m; (*writing*) papel de escribir m; (*identity*) documentación f. v (*walls*) empapelar.

paperback ['peipəbak] n libro en rústica m.

paper bag n saco de papel m.

paper-boy n repartidor de periódicos m.

paper-clip n sujetapapeles m invar.

paper-knife n cortapapeles m invar.

paper-mill n fábrica de papel f.

paper shop n (*coll*) vendedor de periódicos m.

paperweight ['peipəweit] n pisapapeles m invar.

paperwork ['peipəwəːk] n papeleo m.

paprika ['paprikə] n paprika f.

par [paː] n igualdad f; (*comm*) par f; (*golf*) recorrido normal m. **be on a par with** correr parejas con. **feel below par** (*coll*) no sentirse bien.

parable ['parəbl] n parábola f.

parachute ['parəʃuːt] n paracaídas m invar. v saltar con paracaídas. **parachutist** n paracaidista m, f.

parade [pəˈreid] n alarde m; (*mil*) desfile m; (*promenade*) paseo público m. v (*display*) hacer alarde de; hacer desfilar; (*placard*) pasear.

paradise ['parədais] n paraíso m.

paradox ['parədoks] n paradoja f. **paradoxical** adj paradójico.

paraffin ['parəfin] n (*solid*) parafina f; (*fuel*) petróleo m.

paragon ['parəgən] n modelo m

paragraph ['parəgraːf] n párrafo m. **new paragraph** punto y aparte.

parallel ['parəlel] adj paralelo. n paralela f. **parallelogram** n paralelogramo m.

paralyse ['parəlaiz] v paralizar. **paralysis** n parálisis f. **paralytic** n. adj paralítico, -a. adj (*coll: drunk*) como una cuba.

paramedic [parəˈmedik] n médico m

paramilitary [ˌparəˈmilitəri] adj paramilitar.

paramount ['parəmaunt] adj supremo.

paranoia [ˌparəˈnoiə] n paranoia f. **paranoid** n, adj paranoico, -a.

parapet ['parəpit] n parapeto m.

paraphernalia [ˌparəfəˈneiliə] n avíos m pl.

paraphrase ['parəfreiz] n paráfrasis f. v parafrasear.

paraplegic [ˌparəˈpliːdʒik] n, adj parapléjico, -a.

parasite ['parəsait] n parásito m. **parasitic** adj parásito.

parasol ['parəsol] n parasol m.

paratrooper ['parəˌtruːpə] n soldado paracaidista m.

parcel ['paːsəl] n paquete m; (*portion*) parcela f. **parcel office** despacho de paquetes m. **parcel post** servicio de paquetes m. v also **parcel up** empaquetar.

parch [paːtʃ] v (*land*) resecar; (*person*) abrasar; **be parched with thirst** abrasarse de sed.

parchment ['paːtʃmənt] n pergamino m.

pardon ['paːdn] n perdón m; (*law*) indulto m; (*rel*) indulgencia f. v perdonar; disculpar; indultar. **pardon?** ¿cómo? **I beg your pardon** dispénseme.

pare [peə] v reducir; (*vegetables*) pelar; (*fruit*) mondar.

parent ['peərənt] n padre, madre m, f. **parents** pl n padres m pl. **parental** adj de los padres. **parenthood** n paternidad f, maternidad f.

parenthesis [pəˈrenθəsis] n paréntesis m invar. **in parentheses** entre paréntesis.

Paris ['paris] n París.

parish ['pariʃ] n parroquia f; (*civil*) municipio m. **parish church** iglesia parroquial f. **parishioner** n parroquiano, -a m, f.

parity ['pariti] n paridad f.

park [paːk] *n* parque (público) *m*. **park-and-ride** aparcamiento en estaciones periféricas conectadas con transporte urbano colectivo. **car park** aparcamiento de coches *m*. *v* aparcar. **parking** *n* estacionamiento *m*. **parking meter** parcómetro *m*. **parking ticket** multa por aparcamiento indebido *f*.

parliament ['paːləmənt] *n* parlamento *m*. **parliamentary** *adj* parlamentario.

parlour ['paːlə] *n* salón *m*; sala de recibir *f*.

parochial [pəˈroukiəl] *adj* parroquial; (*derog*) pueblerino.

parody ['parədi] *n* parodia *f*. *v* parodiar.

parole [pəˈroul] *n* libertad bajo palabra *f*.

paroxysm ['parəksizəm] *n* paroxismo *m*; (*joy, anger, etc.*) ataque *m*.

parrot ['parət] *n* loro *m*. **parrot fashion** como un loro.

parsley ['paːsli] *n* perejil *m*.

parsnip ['paːsnip] *n* pastinaca *f*.

parson ['paːsn] *n* (*priest*) cura *m*; (*Protestant*) pastor *m*. **parsonage** *n* casa del cura *f*.

part [paːt] *n* parte *f*; (*role*) papel *m*; (*tech*) pieza *f*. **on my part** de mi parte. **part exchange** cambio de un objeto por otro pagando la diferencia. **part-time** *adv* a media jornada; *adj* de media jornada. *v* dividir; separar; (*leave*) despedirse. **part one's hair** hacerse la raya. **take part in** tomar parte en. **part with** tener que separarse de. **parting** *n* separación *f*; despedida *f*; (*hair*) raya *f*. **partly** *adv* en parte.

*__partake__ [paːˈteik] *v* **partake of** compartir.

partial ['paːʃəl] *adj* parcial. **be partial to** ser aficionado a. **partiality** *n* parcialidad *f*; inclinación *f*.

participate [paːˈtisipeit] *v* participar. **participant** *n* partícipe *m, f*. **participation** *n* participación *f*.

participle ['paːtisipl] *n* participio *m*.

particle ['paːtikl] *n* partícula *f*; (*dust, etc.*) grano *m*; (*fig*) pizca *f*.

particular [pəˈtikjulə] *adj* particular; detallado; exigente. *n* detalle *m*. **in particular** particularmente. **I'm not particular** me da igual. **full particulars** información completa *f*.

partisan [paːtiˈzan] *n* partidario, -a *m, f*; (*mil*) guerrillero *m*. **partisanship** *n* partidismo *m*.

partition [paːˈtiʃən] *n* división *f*; (*section*)

parte *f*. *v* dividir; repartir.

partner ['paːtnə] *n* (*comm*) asociado, -a *m, f*, socio, -a *m, f*; (*dancing*) pareja *f*; (*cards, etc.*) compañero, -a *m, f*; (*marriage*) cónyuge *m, f*. *v* asociarse con; ser pareja de. **partnership** *n* asociación *f*; (*firm*) sociedad *f*. **go into partnership with** asociarse con.

partridge ['paːtridʒ] *n* perdiz *f*.

party ['paːti] *n* (*pol*) partido *m*; (*law*) parte *f*; (*reception*) fiesta *f*; (*gathering*) reunión *f*. **party line** (*phone*) línea telefónica compartida entre abonados *f*; (*pol*) línea política del partido *f*.

pass [paːs] *v* pasar; (*exam*) aprobar; (*be acceptable*) aceptarse; **pass away** *or* **on** (*die*) pasar a mejor vida. **pass out** (*faint*) desmayarse. **pass round** (*detour*) dar la vuelta a; (*distribute*) pasar de mano en mano. **pass up** (*decline*) rechazar. *n* (*permit*) pase *m*; (*exam*) aprobado *m*; (*mountain*) desfiladero *m*; (*sport*) pase *m*.

passage ['pasidʒ] *n* (*way*) pasaje *m*; (*alley*) callejón *m*; (*house*) corredor *m*; (*time*) paso *m*; (*literature*) trozo *m*; (*bill*) aprobación *f*; (*sea voyage*) travesía *f*.

passenger ['pasindʒə] *n* pasajero, -a *m, f*.

passer-by [paːsəˈbai] *n* transeúnte *m, f*.

passion ['paʃən] *n* pasión *f*; (*anger*) cólera *f*. **passionate** *adj* apasionado; colérico.

passive ['pasiv] *adj* pasivo. *n* (*gramm*) voz pasiva *f*. **passiveness** *also* **passivity** *n* pasividad *f*.

Passover ['paːsouvə] *n* pascua (de los Judíos) *f*.

passport ['paːspoːt] *n* pasaporte *m*.

password ['paːswaːd] *n* contraseña *f*.

past [paːst] *nm*, *adj* pasado. *prep* por delante de; (*beyond*) más allá de; (*time*) más de. **twenty past nine** las nueve y veinte. **go past** pasar.

pasta ['pastə] *n* pastas *f pl*.

paste [peist] *n* (*meat*) pasta *f*; (*glue*) engrudo *m*; (*jewellery*) estrás *m*. *v* pegar.

pastel ['pastəl] *n* pastel *m*.

pasteurize ['pastʃəraiz] *v* pasteurizar. **pasteurization** *n* pasteurización *f*.

pastime ['paːstaim] *n* pasatiempo *m*.

pastoral ['paːstərəl] *adj* pastoril; (*rel*) pastoral.

pastry ['peistri] *n* (*dough*) pasta *f*; (*cakes*) pasteles *m pl*. **puff pastry** hojaldre *m*. **pastry-cook** *n* pastelero *m*.

pasture ['pɑːstʃə] n (grass) pasto m; (field) prado m. v apacentar.

pasty¹ ['peisti] adj pastoso; (face) pálido.

pasty² ['pasti] n empanada f.

pat [pat] v dar palmaditas; (a pet) acariciar. n palmadita f; caricia f; (of butter) porción f. adj adecuado. adv oportunamente.

patch [patʃ] n (clothes) pieza f, remiendo m; (for puncture, wound, etc.) parche m; (land) parcela f. **patchwork** n labor de retazos m. v remendar; poner un parche. **patchy** adj desigual.

patent ['peitənt] adj patente, evidente; patentado. **patent leather** charol m. v patentar. n patente f. **patently** adv evidentemente.

paternal [pə'təːnl] adj paterno, paternal. **paternity** n paternidad f.

path [pɑːθ] n (way) camino m, sendero m; (star, sun) curso m.

pathetic [pə'θetik] adj patético.

pathology [pə'θɒlədʒi] n patología f. **pathological** adj patológico. **pathologist** n patólogo m.

patient ['peiʃənt] adj paciente. n enfermo, -a m, f. **patience** n paciencia f; (game) solitario m.

patio ['patiou] n patio m.

patriarchal ['peitriɑːkəl] adj patriarcal.

patriot ['patriət] n patriota m, f. **patriotic** adj patriótico. **patriotism** n patriotismo m.

patrol [pə'troul] n patrulla f. **patrol car** coche patrulla m. v patrullar.

patron ['peitrən] n patrocinador, -a m, f; (saint) patrón, -ona m, f, patrono m; (arts) mecenas m; (customer) cliente m, f. **patronage** n (sponsorship) patrocinio m; (royal) patronato m. **patronize** v (comm) patrocinar; (arts) fomentar; (artist) proteger; (be condescending) tratar con condescendencia. **patronizing** adj de superioridad.

patter¹ ['patə] v (rain) repiquetear; (footsteps) corretear. n golpecitos m pl; repiqueteo m.

patter² ['patə] n (salesman) charlatanería f. v chapurrear.

pattern ['patən] n (design) dibujo m; (needlework) patrón m; (sample) muestra f; (example) ejemplo m. v diseñar; (cloth) estampar. **patterned** adj adornado con dibujos.

paunch [pɔːntʃ] n panza f, barriga f.

pauper ['pɔːpə] n pobre m, f.

pause [pɔːz] n pausa f; silencio m. v hacer una pausa; descansar; vacilar; pararse.

pave [peiv] v empedrar, enlosar. **pave the way for** facilitar el paso de. **pavement** n acera f. **paving** n pavimento m. **paving stone** adoquín m.

pavilion [pə'viljən] n pabellón m.

paw [pɔː] n pata f; (cat) garra f. v tocar con la pata; (coll) manosear.

pawn¹ [pɔːn] v empeñar. n prenda f. **pawnbroker** n prestamista m, f. **pawnshop** n casa de empeños f.

pawn² [pɔːn] n peón m.

***pay** [pei] v pagar; dar; (compliment, visit) hacer; (attention) prestar. **pay back** (money) reembolsar; (avenge) devolver. **pay in** ingresar. **pay off** (debt) saldar; (creditor) reembolsar; (mortgage) redimir; (be worthwhile) merecer la pena; (be fruitful) dar resultado. n paga f; salario m. **pay-as-you-earn** n deducción del sueldo para los impuestos f. **payday** n día de paga m. **pay rise** aumento de sueldo m. **pay-roll** n nómina f. **pay-slip** n hoja de paga f. **payable** adj pagadero. **payee** n beneficiario, -a m, f. **payment** n pago m; recompensa f.

pea [piː] n guisante m.

peace [piːs] n paz f. **peacemaker** n pacificador, -a m, f. **peace offering** sacrificio propiciatorio m. **peaceful** adj pacífico.

peach [piːtʃ] n (fruit) melocotón m; (tree) melocotonero m.

peacock ['piːkɔk] n pavo real m.

peak [piːk] n punta f; peñasco m; (cap) visera f. **peak hours** horas punta f pl.

peal [piːl] n (bells) repiqueteo m; (laughter) carcajada f; (thunder) trueno m. v repiquetear; (thunder) retumbar; (laugh) resonar.

peanut ['piːnʌt] n cacahuete m.

pear [peə] n (fruit) pera f; (tree) peral m.

pearl [pəːl] n perla f. **pearly** adj nacarado.

peasant ['peznt] n, adj campesino, -a.

peat [piːt] n turba f.

pebble ['pebl] n guijarro m. **pebbly** adj guijarroso.

peck [pek] v picotear; picar. n picotazo m; (coll: kiss) besito m.

peckish ['pekiʃ] adj **feel peckish** (coll) tener gazuza.

peculiar [pi'kjuːljə] adj raro; extraño; carac-

terístico; propio; especial. **peculiarity** *n*
particularidad *f*; rareza *f*; característica *f*.

pedal ['pedl] *n* pedal *m*. *v* pedalear.

pedantic [pi'dantik] *adj* pedante.

peddle ['pedl] *v* vender de puerta en puerta.

pedestal ['pedistl] *n* pedestal *m*.

pedestrian [pi'destrian] *n* peatón *m*. **pedestrian crossing** paso de peatones *m*. **pedestrian precinct** zona reservada para peatones *f*. *adj* (*style*) prosaico.

pedigree ['pedigri:] *n* (*ancestry*) linaje *m*; (*animals*) pedigrí *m*. **pedigree animal** animal de raza *m*.

pedlar ['pedlə] *n* vendedor ambulante *m*.

peel [pi:l] *v* pelar. **peel off** quitar, despegar. *n* (*potatoes, oranges*) monda *f*, cáscara *f*; (*candied*) piel confitada *f*. **potato-peeler** *n* pelapatatas *m invar*. **peelings** *pl n* peladuras *f pl*.

peep [pi:p] *n* ojeada *f*. *v* echar una ojeada (a). **peeping Tom** mirón *m*. **peep out** asomar.

peer¹ [piə] *v* entornar los ojos. **peer into** mirar dentro de.

peer² [piə] *n* (*nobility*) par *m*; (*equal*) igual *m*. **peerage** *n* pares *m pl*. **peerless** *adj* sin par.

peevish ['pi:viʃ] *adj* displicente; enojadizo.

peg [peg] *n* (*hats, coats*) percha *f*; (*clothes*) pinza *f*; (*tent*) estaca *f*. **off the peg** *adj* de confección. *v* enclavijar; (*prices*) estabilizar.

pejorative [pə'dʒɔrətiv] *adj* peyorativo.

Peking [,pi:'kiŋ] *n* Pekín, Pequín.

pelican ['pelikən] *n* pelicano *m*.

pellet ['pelit] *n* bolita *f*; (*gun*) perdigón *m*; (*med*) píldora *f*.

pelmet ['pelmit] *n* galería *f*.

pelt¹ [pelt] *v* tirar, arrojar; (*with questions*) acribillar; (*rain*) llover a cántaros; (*coll: run*) ir a todo correr. **at full pelt** a toda mecha.

pelt² [pelt] *n* pellejo *m*, piel *f*.

pelvis ['pelvis] *n* pelvis *f*. **pelvic** *adj* pélvico.

pen¹ [pen] *n* pluma *f*. **penknife** *n* cortaplumas *m invar*. **pen-name** *n* seudónimo *m*.

pen² [pen] *n* (*farm animals*) corral *m*; (*sheep*) redil *m*; (*pigs*) pocilga *f*. *v* acorralar.

penal ['pi:nl] *adj* penal. **penal colony** penal *m*. **penalize** *v* penar, castigar. **penalty** *n* pena *f*; (*football*) penalty *m*; (*fig*) castigo *m*.

penance ['penəns] *n* penitencia *f*.

pencil ['pensl] *n* lápiz *m*. **pencil-sharpener** *n* sacapuntas *m invar*. *v* escribir con lápiz.

pendant ['pendənt] *n* colgante *m*.

pending ['pendiŋ] *adj* pendiente. *prep* hasta; durante.

pendulum ['pendjuləm] *n* péndulo *m*.

penetrate ['penitreit] *v* penetrar. **penetrable** *adj* penetrable. **penetration** *n* penetración *f*.

penguin ['peŋgwin] *n* pingüino *m*.

penicillin [peni'silin] *n* penicilina *f*.

peninsula [pə'ninsjulə] *n* península *f*. **peninsula** *adj* peninsular.

penis ['pi:nis] *n* pene *m*.

penitent ['penitənt] *n* (*m + f*), *adj* penitente. **penitence** *n* penitencia *f*.

pennant ['penənt] *n* (*small flag*) banderín *m*; (*naut*) gallardete *m*.

penniless ['penilis] *adj* sin dinero.

pension ['penʃən] *n* (*old age, retirement*) jubilación *f*; (*allowance*) pensión *f*. **pension fund** caja de jubilaciones *f*. *v* pensionar. **pension off** jubilar. **pensioner** *n* pensionista *m*, *f*.

pensive ['pensiv] *adj* pensativo.

pentagon ['pentəgən] *n* pentágono *m*. **pentagonal** *adj* pentagonal.

penthouse ['penthaus] *n* ático *m*.

pent-up [pent'ʌp] *adj* reprimido.

penultimate [pi'nʌltimət] *adj* penúltimo.

people ['pi:pl] *n* personas *f pl*; gente *f sing*; (*nation*) nación *f sing*; pueblo *m sing*; habitantes *m pl*; (*coll*) familia *f sing*. *v* poblar. **people carrier** (*motoring*) monovolumen *m*.

pepper ['pepə] *n* (*spice*) pimienta *f*; (*vegetable*) pimiento *m*. **peppercorn** *n* grano de pimiento *m*. **peppermint** *n* (*plant*) hierbabuena *f*; (*flavour*) menta *f*; (*sweet*) pastilla de menta *f*. **pepper-pot** *n* pimentero *m*. *v* sazonar con pimienta. **peppery** *adj* picante.

per [pə:] *prep* por. **per cent** por ciento. **percentage** *n* porcentaje *m*.

perceive [pə'si:v] *v* percibir; (*notice*) notar.

perceptible [pə'septibl] *adj* perceptible; sensible. **perceptibly** *adv* sensiblemente.

perception [pə'sepʃən] *n* percepción *f*; sensibilidad *f*. **perceptive** *adj* perceptivo; perspicaz.

perch [pə:tʃ] *n* percha *f*. *v* (*bird*) posarse; encaramar.

percolate ['pə:kəleit] *v* filtrar. **percolator** *n* cafetera de filtro *f*.

percussion [pə'kʌʃən] *n* percusión *f*.

perennial [pə'reniəl] *adj* perenne. *n* planta perenne.

perfect ['pə:fikt; *v* pə'fekt] *adj* perfecto; absoluto. *n* (*gramm*) pretérito perfecto *m*. *v* perfeccionar. **perfection** *n* perfección *f*; (*perfecting*) perfeccionamiento *m*. **perfectionist** *n*(*m* + *f*), *adj* perfeccionista.

perforate ['pə:fəreit] *v* perforar. **perforation** *n* perforación *f*.

perform [pə'fo:m] *v* llevar a cabo, ejecutar; (*duty*) cumplir; (*functions*) desempeñar; (*act*) representar. **performance** *n* ejecución *f*; cumplimiento *m*; desempeño *m*; representación *f*; (*machine*) funcionamiento *m*; *m*; celebración *f*; (*sport*) actuación *f*.

perfume ['pə:fju:m] *n* perfume *m*. *v* perfumar.

perhaps [pə'haps] *adv* quizá, quizás, tal vez.

peril ['peril] *n* peligro *m*. **perilous** *adj* peligroso.

perimeter [pə'rimitə] *n* perímetro *m*.

period ['piəriəd] *n* período *m*; época *f*; edad *f*; tiempo *m*; (*school*) clase *f*; (*menstrual*) regla *f*. **periodic** *adj* periódico. **periodical** *nm*, *adj* periódico.

peripheral [pə'rifərəl] *adj* periférico. **periphery** *n* periferia *f*. **peripheral** (*comput noun*) periférico *m*.

periscope ['periskoup] *n* periscopio *m*.

perish ['periʃ] *v* perecer. **perishable** *adj* perecedero.

perjure ['pə:dʒə] *v* **perjure oneself** perjurarse. **perjurer** *n* perjuro, -a *m*, *f*. **perjury** *n* perjurio *m*. **commit perjury** jurar en falso.

perk [pə:k] *v* **perk up** animarse. *n* (*coll: fringe benefit*) un plus. **perky** *adj* descarado; fresco.

perm [pə:m] *n* (*coll*) permanente *f*. **have a perm** hacerse la permanente.

permanent ['pə:mənənt] *adj* permanente. **permanence** *n* permanencia *f*. **permanently** *adv* permanentemente, para siempre.

permeate ['pə:mieit] *v* penetrar; (*soak*) impregnar. **permeable** *adj* permeable.

permit [pə'mit; *n* 'pə:mit] *v* permitir; dar

permiso; tolerar. *n* permiso *m*; licencia *f*; pase *m*. **permissible** *adj* permisible. **permission** *n* permiso *m*; licencia *f*. **permissive** *adj* permisivo; tolerante.

permutation [pə:mju'teiʃən] *n* permutación *f*.

pernicious [pə'niʃəs] *adj* (*med*) pernicioso; (*evil*) funesto.

perpendicular [,pə:pen'dikjulə] *nf*, *adj* perpendicular.

perpetrate ['pə:pitreit] *v* perpetrar; cometer. **perpetration** *n* perpetración *f*; comisión *f*. **perpetrator** *n* (*law*) perpetrador, -a *m*, *f*; (*author*) autor, -a *m*, *f*.

perpetual [pə'petʃuəl] *adj* perpetuo.

perpetuate [pə'petʃueit] *v* perpetuar. **perpetuation** *n* perpetuación *f*.

perplex [pə'pleks] *v* dejar perplejo, confundir. **perplexed** *adj* perplejo; confuso. **perplexing** *adj* confuso; complicado; difícil. **perplexity** *n* perplejidad *f*; confusión *f*.

persecute ['pə:sikju:t] *v* perseguir; molestar. **persecution** *n* persecución *f*.

persevere [,pə:si'viə] *v* perseverar. **perseverance** *n* perseverancia *f*. **persevering** *adj* perseverante.

persist [pə'sist] *v* persistir. **persistence** *n* persistencia *f*. **persistent** *adj* persistente; continuo.

person ['pə:sn] *n* persona *f*. **personal** *adj* personal; en persona. **personal assistant (PA)** ayudante personal *m*, *f*. **personal computer (PC)** ordenador personal *m*. **personal stereo** walkman *m*. **personality** *n* personalidad *f*. **personally** *adv* personalmente.

personify [pə'sonifai] *v* personificar. **personification** *n* personificación *f*.

personnel [pə:sə'nel] *n* personal *m*.

perspective [pə'spektiv] *n* perspectiva *f*.

perspire [pə'spaiə] *v* transpirar, sudar. **perspiration** *n* transpiración *f*, sudor *m*.

persuade [pə'sweid] *v* persuadir. **persuasion** *n* persuasión *f*. **persuasive** *adj* persuasivo; convincente.

pert [pə:t] *adj* impertinente; alegre; animado.

pertain [pə'tein] *v* pertenecer; ser propio de. **pertinent** *adj* pertinente. **pertinent to** relacionado con.

perturb [pə'tə:b] *v* perturbar. **perturbation** perturbación *f*.

Peru [pə'ru:] *n* Perú *m*.

peruse [pə'ru:z] *v* leer atentamente; examinar. **perusal** *n* lectura atenta *f*; examen *m*.

pervade [pə'veid] *v* penetrar; saturar.

perverse [pə'vəːs] *adj* obstinado; contrario; *(wicked)* perverso. **perversity** *n* obstinación *f*; perversidad *f*.

pervert [pə'vəːt; *n* 'pəːvəːt] *v (person)* pervertir; *(facts)* desnaturalizar. *n* pervertido (-a) sexual *m*, *f*. **perversion** *n* perversión *f*; desnaturalización *f*.

pessimism ['pesimizəm] *n* pesimismo *m*. **pessimist** *n* pesimista *m*, *f*. **pessimistic** *adj* pesimista.

pest [pest] *n* animal *or* insecto nocivo *m*; *(coll: person)* lata *f*. **pesticide** *n* pesticida *m*.

pester ['pestə] *v* importunar, molestar.

pet [pet] *n* animal doméstico *m*; *(person)* preferido, -a *m*, *f*. **my pet!** ¡mi cielo! *adj* mimado. **pet hate** pesadilla *f*. **pet name** nombre cariñoso *m*. **pet subject** tema preferido *m*. *v* mimar; *(caress)* acariciar.

petal ['petl] *n* pétalo *m*.

petition [pə'tiʃən] *n* petición *f*. *v* suplicar, pedir.

petrify ['petrifai] *v* petrificarse; quedarse seco.

petrol ['petrəl] *n* gasolina *f*; *(S.Am.)* nafta *f*. **petrol pump** surtidor de gasolina *m*. **petrol station** gasolinera *f*. **petrol tank** depósito de gasolina *m*.

petroleum [pə'trouliəm] *n* petróleo *m*.

petticoat ['petikout] *n* enaguas *f pl*, enagua *f*.

petty ['peti] *adj* pequeño; insignificante. **petty cash** dinero suelto *m*. **petty-minded** mezquino. **petty officer** contramaestre *m*. **pettiness** *n* pequeñez *f*; insignificancia *f*.

petulant ['petjulənt] *adj* malhumorado, irritable. **petulance** *n* mal humor *m*, irritabilidad *f*.

pew [pju:] *n* banco de iglesia *m*.

pewter ['pju:tə] *n* estaño *m*, peltre *m*.

phantom ['fantəm] *n* fantasma *m*.

pharmacy ['faːməsi] *n* farmacia *f*. **pharmaceutical** *adj* farmacéutico. **pharmacist** *n* farmacéutico, -a *m*, *f*.

pharynx ['fariŋks] *n* faringe *f*. **pharyngitis** *n* faringitis *f*.

phase [feiz] *n* fase *f*. **phase in** introducir progresivamente. **phase out** reducir progresivamente.

pheasant ['feznt] *n* faisán *m*.

phenomenon [fə'nomənən] *n, pl* -**ena** fenómeno *m*. **phenomenal** *adj* fenomenal.

phial ['faiəl] *n* frasco *m*.

philanthropy [fi'lanθrəpi] *n* filantropía *f*. **philanthropic** *adj* filantrópico. **philanthropist** *n* filántropo, -a *m*, *f*.

philately [fi'latəli] *n* filatelia *f*. **philatelic** *adj* filatélico. **philatelist** *n* filatelista *m*, *f*.

philosophy [fi'losəfi] *n* filosofía *f*. **philosopher** *n* filósofo, -a *m*, *f*. **philosophical** *adj* filosófico. **philosophize** *v* filosofar.

phlegm [flem] *n* flema *f*. **phlegmatic** *adj* flemático.

phobia ['foubiə] *n* fobia *f*.

phone [foun] *n (coll)* teléfono *m*. *v* telefonear. **phone book** guía telefónica *f*. **phone-in** *n (radio, television)* participación telefónica del público.

phonetic [fə'netik] *adj* fonético. **phonetics** *n* fonética *f*.

phoney ['founi] *adj (coll)* falso, espurio.

phosphate ['fosfeit] *n* fosfato *m*.

phosphorescence [fosfə'resəns] *n* fosforescencia *f*. **phosphorescent** *adj* fosforescente.

phosphorus ['fosfərəs] *n* fósforo *m*. **phosphorous** *adj* fosforoso.

photo ['foutou] *n (coll)* foto *f*.

photocopy ['foutou,kopi] *n* fotocopia *f*. *v* fotocopiar. **photocopier** *n* fotocopiadora *f*. **photocopying** *n* fotocopiaje *m*.

photogenic [,foutou'dʒenik] *adj* fotogénico.

photograph ['foutəgraːf] *n* fotografía *f*. **photograph album** álbum de fotografías *m*. *v* fotografiar. **photographer** *n* fotógrafo, -a *m*, *f*. **photographic** *adj* fotográfico. **photography** *n* fotografía *f*.

phrase [freiz] *n* frase *f*, expresión *f*; *(gramm)* locución *f*. **phrase-book** *n* repertorio de expresiones *m*. *v* expresar.

physical ['fizikəl] *adj* físico; *n (coll)* reconocimiento médico *m*.

physician [fi'ziʃən] *n* médico *m*.

physics ['fiziks] *n* física *f*. **physicist** *n* físico, -a *m*, *f*.

physiology [fizi'olədʒi] *n* fisiología *f*. **physiological** *adj* fisiológico *f*. **physiologist** *n* fisiólogo, -a *m*, *f*.

physiotherapy [,fiziou'θerəpi] *n* fisioterapia *f*. **physiotherapist** *n* fisioterapeuta *m. f.*

physique [fi'zi:k] *n* constitución *f*; (*appearance*) físico *m*.

piano [pi'anou] *n* piano *m*. **pianist** *n* pianista *m, f.*

pick¹ [pik] *n* elección *f*, selección *f*. **take one's pick** elegir a su gusto. *v* escoger; seleccionar; (*fruit*) recoger; (*flowers*) coger; (*lock*) abrir con ganzúa. **pick at** (*food*) picar (la comida). **pick-me-up** *n* (*coll*) tónico. *m*. **pick on** elegir, escoger. **pick out** escoger; distinguir; (*highlight*) hacer resaltar. **pickpocket** *n* ratero, -a *m, f*. **pick up** levantar; recoger; (*improve*) mejorarse; (*learn*) aprender; (*arrest*) detener.

pick² [pik] *n* (*tool*) piqueta *f*; (*music*) plectro *m*.

picket ['pikit] *n* piquete *m*; (*person*) huelguista *m, f*. *v* estar de guardia.

pickle ['pikl] *v* conservar en vinagre. *n* encurtido *m*.

picnic ['piknik] *n* merienda campestre *f*. *v* merendar en el campo.

pictorial [pik'to:riəl] *adj* pictórico, ilustrado.

picture ['piktʃə] *n* ilustración *f*; (*portrait*) retrato *m*; (*painting*) cuadro *m*; (*film*) película *f*. **picture frame** marco *m*. **picture gallery** museo de pintura *m*. **pictures** *n* (*coll*) cine *m*. *v* describir; imaginarse.

picturesque [piktʃə'resk] *adj* pintoresco.

pidgin ['pidʒən] *n* lengua macarrónica *f*.

pie [pai] *n* (*fruit*) pastel *m*; (*meat*) pastel de carne *m*.

piece [pi:s] *n* pedazo *m*, trozo *m*; parte *f*; (*material*) pieza *f*. **piecemeal** *adv* hecho por partes. **piecework** *n* trabajo a destajo *m*. *v* **piece together** juntar.

pier [piə] *n* malecón *m*; (*landing-stage*) muelle *m*.

pierce [piəs] *v* penetrar; perforar; (*go through*) traspasar. **piercing** *adj* penetrante; (*wind*) cortante.

piety ['paiəti] *n* piedad *f*.

pig [pig] *n* puerco *m*, cerdo *m*. **pigskin** *n* piel de cerdo *f*. **pigsty** *n* pocilga *f*. **pigtail** *n* coleta *f*.

pigeon ['pidʒən] *n* paloma *f*. **pigeonhole** *n* casilla *f*.

pigment ['pigmənt] *n* pigmento *m*.

pike [paik] *n* (*fish*) lucio *m*.

pilchard ['piltʃəd] *n* sardina arenque *f*.

pile¹ [pail] *n* (*heap*) pila *f*, montón *m*. *v* amontonar. **pile up** acumular. **pile-up** *n* accidente múltiple *m*.

pile² [pail] *n* (*post*) poste *m*.

pile³ [pail] *n* (*of carpet, etc.*) pelo *m*.

piles [pailz] *pl n* (*med*) hemorroides *f pl.*

pilfer ['pilfə] *v* (*coll*) sisar. **pilferage** *n* sisa *f.*

pilgrim ['pilgrim] *n* peregrino, -a *m, f*. **pilgrimage** *n* peregrinación *f.*

pill [pil] *n* píldora *f.*

pillage ['pilidʒ] *n* saqueo *m*. *v* saquear.

pillar ['pilə] *n* pilar *m*, columna *f*. **pillarbox** *n* buzón *m.*

pillion ['piljən] *n* grupa *f*. **ride pillion** ir a la grupa.

pillow ['pilou] *n* almohada *f*. **pillowcase** *n* funda de almohada *f.*

pilot ['pailət] *n* piloto *m*. **pilot-light** *n* piloto *m*. *v* guiar; conducir.

pimento [pi'mentou] *n* pimienta de Jamaica *f.*

pimp [pimp] *n* chulo *m.*

pimple ['pimpl] *n* espinilla *f*. **pimply** *adj* espinilloso.

pin [pin] *n* alfiler *m*; (*hairpin*) horquilla *f*; (*safety pin*) imperdible *m*; (*tech*) pezonera *f*; (*bolt*) perno *m*. **pincushion** *n* almohadilla *f*. **pin-money** *n* alfileres *m pl*; **pinpoint** *v* localizar con toda precisión. **pins and needles** hormigueo *m*. **pinstripe** *n* raya muy fina *f*. *v* prender con alfileres. **pin down** (*fix*) sujetar; (*find*) encontrar; (*enemy*) inmovilizar. **pin up** (*notice*) fijar.

PIN (*personal identification number*) número de identificación personal *m.*

pinafore ['pinəfo:] *n* (*apron*) delantal *m*. **pinafore dress** falda con peto *f.*

pincers ['pinsəz] *pl n* (*tool*) tenazas *f pl*; (*zool*) pinzas *f pl.*

pinch [pintʃ] *n* pellizco *m*; (*salt, etc.*) pizca *f*. **at a pinch** en caso de necesidad. **feel the pinch** empezar a pasar apuros. *v* pellizcar; (*shoes, etc.*) apretar; (*coll: steal*) mangar.

pine¹ [pain] *n* pino. *m*. **pine-cone** *n* piña *f.*

pine² [pain] *v* languidecer. **pine for** anhelar.

pineapple ['painapl] *n* ananás *m*, piña *f.*

ping-pong ['pinpon] *n* ping-pong *m*, tenis de mesa *m.*

pinion ['pinjən] *n* ala *f*. *v* maniatar.

pink [pink] *n* (*colour*) rosa *m*; (*flower*) clavel

m. adj rosa.

pinnacle ['pinəkl] *n* pináculo *m*.

pioneer [ˌpaiə'niə] *n* pionero *m*, iniciador *m*.

pious ['paiəs] *adj* pío, devoto.

pip[1] [pip] *n* (*seed*) pepita *f*.

pip[2] [pip] *n* (*phone, etc.*) señal *f*.

pipe [paip] *n* (*gas, water, etc.*) tubo *m*, tubería *f*, cañería *f*; (*tobacco*) pipa *f*; (*music*) caramillo *m*. **pipe-cleaner** limpiapipas *m invar*. **pipeline** *n* (*oil*) oleoducto *m*; (*gas*) gasoducto *m*; (*water*) tubería *f*. *v* conducir por tubería; transportar por oleoducto. **pipe down** (*coll*) callarse. **piping** *n* (*music*) sonido de la gaita *m*; (*sewing*) ribete; tubería *f*.

piquant ['pi:kənt] *adj* picante. **piquancy** *n* picante *m*.

pique [pi:k] *n* pique *m*. *v* picar; herir.

pirate ['paiərət] *n* pirata *m*. *v* piratear. **piracy** *n* piratería *f*.

pirouette [piru'et] *n* pirueta *f*. *v* hacer piruetas.

Pisces ['paisi:z] *n* Piscis *m*.

piss [pis] *n* (*impol*) meada *f*. *v* mear. **piss off!** ¡vete al cuerno! **pissed** *adj* (*drunk*) trompa. **be pissed off** estar furioso (con).

pistachio [pi'sta:ʃiou] *n* pistacho *m*.

pistol ['pistl] *n* pistola *f*.

piston ['pistən] *n* émbolo *m*, pistón *m*.

pit [pit] *n* (*hole*) pozo *m*, hoyo; mina; (*orchestra*) foso de la orquesta *m*; (*of the stomach*) boca *f*; *v* llenar de hoyitos; (*oppose*) oponer. **pit oneself against** medirse con.

pitch[1] [pitʃ] *n* (*throw*) lanzamiento *m*; (*sport*) campo *m*; (*music*) tono *m*; (*gradient*) grado de inclinación *m*; (*of a ship*) cabezada *f*. *v* lanzar, echar; entonar; (*of a ship*) cabecear; (*tent*) armar; (*fall*) caerse. **pitchfork** *n* horca *f*. *v* (*fig*) catapultar.

pitch[2] [pitʃ] *n* pez *f*, brea *f*. **pitch-black** *adj* negro como el carbón.

pitfall ['pitfɔ:l] *n* escollo *m*; trampa *f*.

pith [piθ] *n* médula *f*; (*fig*) meollo *m*. **pithy** *adj* conciso, expresivo.

pittance ['pitəns] *n* miseria *f*.

pituitary [pi'tju:itəri] *n* glándula pituitaria *f*.

pity ['piti] *n* compasión *f*; lástima *f*. **take pity on** tener lástima de. **what a pity!** ¡qué lástima! *v* compadecerse de. **pitiful**

adj lastimoso; (*bad*) lamentable. **pitiless** *adj* despiadado.

pivot ['pivət] *n* pivote *m*; eje *m*. *v* girar sobre su eje.

placard ['plaka:d] *n* cartel *m*. *v* fijar carteles.

placate [plə'keit] *v* aplacar. **placatory** *adj* placativo.

place [pleis] *n* sitio *m*, lugar *m*; (*post*) puesto *m*; local *m*; posición *f*. **all over the place** por todas partes. **in place** en su sitio. **in place of** en lugar de. **out of place** fuera de lugar. **take place** suceder, ocurrir. **take the place of** sustituir a. *v* colocar; poner; situar; (*an order*) hacer. **be well placed** estar en buena posición.

placenta [plə'sentə] *n* placenta *f*.

placid ['plasid] *adj* plácido. **placidity** *n* placidez *f*.

plagiarize ['pleidʒəraiz] *v* plagiar. **plagiarism** *n* plagio *m*. **plagiarist** *n* plagiario, -a *m, f*.

plague [pleig] *n* (*disease*) peste *f*; (*social scourge*) plaga *f*; (*nuisance*) molestia *f*. *v* importunar.

plaice [pleis] *n* platija *f*.

plaid [plad] *n* tartán *m*. *adj* escocés.

plain [plein] *adj* (*clear*) claro; simple; puro; completo; (*frank*) franco; natural; (*unattractive*) sin atractivo. **plain-clothes** *adj* en traje de calle. **plain chocolate** chocolate puro *m*. **make plain** poner de manifiesto. *n* llanura *f*.

plaintiff ['pleintif] *n* demandante *m, f*.

plaintive ['pleintiv] *adj* quejumbroso.

plait [plat] *n* (*fold*) pliegue *m*; (*hair*) trenza *f*. *v* plisar; trenzar.

plan [plan] *n* (*map*) plano *m*; (*scheme*) plan *m*, proyecto *m*. *v* (*for the future*) hacer planes para; (*holidays*) hacer el plan de; (*design*) hacer el plano de; (*action*) planear; (*production*) planificar. **planning** *n* planificación *f*.

plane[1] [plein] *n* plano *m*; (*coll: aeroplane*) avión *m*. *adj* plano.

plane[2] [plein] *n* (*tool*) cepillo *m*. *v* cepillar.

plank [plaŋk] *n* tabla *n*.

plankton ['plaŋktən] *n* plancton *m*.

plant [pla:nt] *n* (*bot*) planta *f*; (*tech*) maquinaria *f*; (*factory*) fábrica *f*; (*installation*) instalación *f*. *v* plantar. **plantation** *n* plantación *f*; hacienda *f*.

plaque [pla:k] *n* placa *f*.

plasma ['plazmə] *n* plasma *m*.

plaster ['plɑːstə] *n* (*walls*) yeso *m*; (*for wounds*) emplasto *m*. **plaster of Paris** yeso blanco *m*. *v* enyesar; cubrir. **plasterer** yesero *m*.

plastic ['plastik] *nm, adj* plástico. **plastic surgery** cirugía plástica *f*.

plate [pleit] *n* (*dish*) plato *m*; (*of metal*) chapa *f*; (*tableware*) vajilla *f*; (*in book*) lámina *f*. *v* chapar; (*silver*) platear; (*gold*) dorar. **plateful** *n* plato *m*.

plateau ['platou] *n* meseta *f*.

platform ['platfoːm] *n* plataforma *f*; (*rail*) andén *m*; (*stage*) estrado *m*; (*builders*) andamio *m*; (*pol*) programa *m*. **platform ticket** billete de andén *m*.

platinum ['platinəm] *n* platino *m*.

platonic [plə'tonik] *adj* platónico.

platoon [plə'tuːn] *n* (*mil*) pelotón *m*.

plausible ['ploːzəbl] *adj* plausible; (*person*) convincente. **plausibility** *n* plausibilidad *f*.

play [plei] *n* juego *m*, diversión *f*. (*theatre*) obra de teatro *f*; (*manoeuvre*) jugada *f*. *v* jugar. **player** *n* jugador, -a *m, f*; (*music*) intérprete *m, f*; (*theatre*) actor, actriz *m, f*. **playful** *adj* juguetón. **playfulness** *n* carácter juguetón *m*.

playback ['pleibak] *n* reproducción *f*. **play back** *v* volver a poner.

playground ['pleigraund] *n* campo de juegos *m*.

playhouse ['pleihaus] *n* teatro *m*.

playing card *n* carta *f*, naipe *m*.

playing field *n* campo de deportes *m*.

plaything ['plei,θiŋ] *n* juguete *m*.

playwright ['pleirait] *n* autor de teatro *m*.

plea [pliː] *n* súplica *f*; petición *f*; (*law*) alegato *m*.

plead [pliːd] *v* suplicar; implorar; intervenir; hacer un alegato.

pleasant ['pleznt] *adj* agradable.

please [pliːz] *v* gustar, agradar. **if you please** por favor. **pleased** *adj* contento. **pleasing** *adj* agradable.

pleasure ['pleʒə] *n* placer *m*, gusto *m*. **pleasurable** *adj* grato.

pleat [pliːt] *n* pliegue *m*. *v* plisar.

plectrum ['plektrəm] *n* plectro *m*.

pledge [pledʒ] *n* prenda *f*; promesa *f*. *v* dar en prenda; prometer.

plenty ['plenti] *n* abundancia *f*; cantidad *f*.

plenty of bastante. **plentiful** *adj* abundante, copioso.

pleurisy ['pluərisi] *n* pleuresía *f*.

pliable ['plaiəbl] *adj* flexible; (*person*) dócil. **pliability** *n* flexibilidad *f*; docilidad *f*.

pliers ['plaiəz] *pl n* alicates *m pl*.

plight [plait] *n* aprieto *m*; crisis *f*.

plimsolls ['plimsəlz] *pl n* zapatos de tenis *m pl*.

plinth [plinθ] *n* plinto *m*

plod [plod] *v* andar con paso pesado; (*coll: work*) trabajar con ahínco. **plodder** *n* empollón, -ona *m, f*.

plonk [ploŋk] *n* (*coll*) pirriaque *m*.

plop [plop] *n* plaf *m*. *v* hacer plaf.

plot[1] [plot] *n* (*story, etc.*) argumento *m*; (*conspiracy*) conspiración *f*; *v* tramar, maquinar; (*route*) trazar.

plot[2] [plot] *n* (*land*) terreno *m*; (*garden*) cuadro *m*.

plough [plau] *n* arado *m*. *v* arar. **plough one's way through** abrirse paso. **ploughman** *n* arador.

ploy [ploi] *n* truco *m*, estratagema *f*.

pluck [plʌk] *n* valor *m*; (*music*) plectro *m*; (*pull*) tirón *m*. *v* (*pull*) arrancar; (*music*) puntear; (*fruit*) coger; (*fowl*) desplumar; (*eyebrows*) depilarse. **pluck up courage** armarse de valor. **plucky** *adj* valiente.

plug [plʌg] *n* (*stopper*) taco *m*; (*sink, bath*) tapón *m*; (*elec*) enchufe *m*; (*mot*) bujía *f*. *v* taponar; tapar; enchufar; (*block up*) atascar; (*coll: advertise*) dar publicidad a. **plug away at** perseverar en. **plug in** enchufar.

plum [plʌm] *n* (*fruit*) ciruela *f*; (*tree*) ciruelo *m*.

plumage ['pluːmidʒ] *n* plumaje *m*.

plumb [plʌm] *n* plomada *f*, plomo *m*. **plumbline** *n* cuerda de plomada *f*; (*in water*) sonda *f*. *adj* vertical. *adv* a plomo. *v* aplomar; sondar. **plumber** *n* fontanero *m*. **plumbing** *n* fontanería *f*; instalación de cañerías *f*.

plume [pluːm] *n* (*feather*) pluma *f*; (*smoke*) penacho *m*. *v* emplumar.

plummet ['plʌmit] *n* plomo *m*. *v* (*bird, aircraft*) caer en picado; (*person, thing*) caer a plomo; (*prices*) caer verticalmente.

plump[1] [plʌmp] *adj* (*person*) rellenito; (*animal*) gordo. **plumpness** *n* gordura *f*.

plump[2] [plʌmp] *v* caer de golpe. **plump**

for decidirse por.

plunder ['plʌndə] v saquear; robar. n saqueo m; (loot) botín m. **plunderer** n saqueador m. **plundering** n saqueo m.

plunge [plʌndʒ] n (fall) caída f; (short dive) zambullida f; (high dive) salto m. **take the plunge** aventurarse. v (knife, etc.) meter; sumergir; (into despair) hundirse; (launch oneself) lanzarse; (fall) caer.

pluperfect [plu:'pəfikt] n pluscuamperfecto m.

plural ['pluərəl] nm, adj plural.

plus [plʌs] prep más. n cantidad positiva f; (sign) signo más m. adj positivo.

plush [plʌʃ] adj afelpado; (fig) lujoso. n felpa f.

ply[1] [plai] v (tool) manejar; (trade) ejercer; (questions) acosar; (ship, etc.) hacer el trayecto de. **ply between** hacer el servicio entre.

ply[2] [plai] n (wood) chapa f; (wool) cabo m; (fabric) capa f. **plywood** n contrachapado m.

pneumatic [nju'matik] adj neumático. **pneumatic drill** barreno neumático m.

pneumonia [nju'mouniə] n pulmonía f.

poach[1] [poutʃ] v cazar or pescar en vedado. **poacher** n cazador or pescador furtivo m. **poaching** n caza or pesca furtiva f.

poach[2] [poutʃ] v (egg) escalfar.

pocket ['pokit] n bolsillo m. **pocket-money** n dinero de bolsillo m. v embolsarse.

pod [pod] n vaina f.

podgy ['podʒi] adj (coll) gordo.

poem ['pouim] n poema m.

poet ['pouit] n poeta m. **poetess** n poetisa f. **poetic** adj poético. **poetry** n poesía f.

poignant ['poinjant] adj conmovedor.

point [point] n punto m; (sharp end) punta f; (decimal) coma f; (elec) contacto m; (meaning) sentido m; (motive) motivo; cabo m. **point of view** punto de vista m. **points** pl n (railway) agujas f pl. **beside the point** que no viene al caso. **come** or **get to the point** ir al grano. **make a point of** insistir en. **pointblank** adv (shoot) a quema ropa; (demand) sin rodeos; (refuse) categóricamente. **what's the point?** ¿para qué sirve? v señalar; (a weapon) apuntar. **point out** señalar; advertir. **pointed** adj (sharpened) afilado; (shape) puntiagudo;

(remark) directo. **pointless** adj inútil.

poise [poiz] n equilibrio m; (bearing) porte m; elegancia f; serenidad f. v poner en equilibrio; preparar. **be poised** estar en equilibrio; estar preparado.

poison ['poizn] n veneno m. v envenenar. **poisoning** n envenenamiento m. **poisonous** adj venenoso; tóxico.

poke [pouk] n empujón con el dedo; (with elbow) codazo m; (fig) hurgonada f. v dar con la punta del dedo; dar un codazo; hurgar. **poker** n hurgón m.

poker ['poukə] n (cards) póker m. **poker-faced** adj de cara inmutable.

Poland ['poulənd] n Polonia f. **Pole** n polaco, -a m, f. **Polish** nm, adj polaco.

polar ['poulə] adj polar. **polar bear** oso blanco. **polarize** v polarizar.

pole[1] [poul] n (wood) palo m; (metal) barra f; (telegraphs) poste m; (flag) asta f. **pole-vault** n salto de pértiga m.

pole[2] [poul] n (geog, elec) polo m. **pole star** estrella polar f.

police [pə'li:s] n policía f. **the police force** el cuerpo de policía m. **policeman** n policía m, guardia m. **police station** comisaría de policía f. **policewoman** n mujer policía f.

policy[1] ['poləsi] n (government) política f; principio m; táctica f.

policy[2] ['poləsi] n (insurance) póliza f.

polio ['pouliou] n polio f.

polish ['poliʃ] n (shine) brillo m; (act) pulimento m; (furniture) cera f; (shoes) betún m; (nails) esmalte m; (fig) elegancia f. v (shoes) limpiar; (metal) pulir; (floors) encerar. **polish off** zampar. **polish up** dar brillo a; (improve) perfeccionar.

polite [pə'lait] adj cortés. **politeness** n cortesía f.

politics ['politiks] n política f. **political** adj político. **politically correct** (adv) políticamente correcto. **politician** n político.

polka ['polkə] n polca f.

poll [poul] n votación f; elecciones f pl; (survey) sondeo m. v obtener; sondear. **polling booth** cabina electoral f; **polling day** día de elecciones m. **polling station** central electoral m.

pollen ['polən] n polen m. **pollen count** índice de polen m. **pollinate** v polinizar. **pollination** n polinización f.

pollute [pə'lu:t] v contaminar. **pollution** n contaminación f.

polo ['poulou] n polo m. **water polo** polo acuático m. **polo-neck** n cuello vuelto m.

polyester [,poli'estə] n poliéster m.

polygamy [pə'ligəmi] n poligamia f.

polygon ['poligən] n polígono m.

polystyrene [,poli'staiəri:n] n poliestireno m.

polytechnic [,poli'teknik] n escuela politécnica f.

polythene ['poliθi:n] n polietileno m.

pomegranate ['pomigranit] n (fruit) granada f; (tree) granado m.

pomp [pomp] n pompa f. **pompous** adj pomposo.

pond [pond] n charca f; (artificial) estanque m.

ponder ['pondə] v considerar; meditar.

pong [poŋ] n peste f

pony ['pouni] n poney m. **pony-tail** n cola de caballo f.

poodle ['pu:dl] n perro de lanas m.

poof [pu:f] n (derog) marica m.

pool[1] [pu:l] n (liquid) charco m; (swimming) piscina f.

pool[2] [pu:l] n (money) banca f; (things) recursos comunes m pl; (reserve) reserva f; (comm) fondos comunes m pl; (typing) servicio de mecanografía m. **pools** pl n (football) quinielas f pl. v aunar; reunir; poner en un fondo común.

poor [puə] adj pobre; mediocre.

poorly ['puəli] adj pobremente; mal. **be poorly** estar malo.

pop[1] [pop] n taponazo m; (drink) gaseosa f. **popcorn** n rosetas de maíz f pl. v pinchar; (cork) hacer saltar; (put) meter. **pop in** entrar un momento.

pop[2] [pop] adj popular. **pop music** música pop f.

pope [poup] n papa m.

poplar ['poplə] n álamo m.

poplin ['poplin] n popelina f.

poppy ['popi] n amapola f.

popular ['popjulə] adj popular. **popularity** n popularidad f. **popularize** v popularizar.

population [,popju'leiʃən] n población f. **populate** v poblar.

porcelain ['po:slin] n porcelana f.

porch [po:tʃ] n pórtico m.

porcupine ['po:kjupain] n puerco espín m.

pore[1] [po:] n (anat) poro m.

pore[2] [po:] v **pore over** estar absorto en.

pork [po:k] n cerdo m.

pornography [po:'nogrəfi] n pornografía f. **pornographic** adj pornográfico.

porous ['po:rəs] adj poroso.

porpoise ['po:pəs] n marsopa f.

porridge ['porid3] n gachas de avena f pl.

port[1] [po:t] n (harbour) puerto m. **port of call** puerto de escala m.

port[2] [po:t] n (naut: left) babor m.

port[3] [po:t] n (wine) oporto m.

portable ['po:təbl] adj portátil.

portent ['po:tent] n presagio m.

porter ['po:tə] n (attendant) mozo m; (doorman) portero; (in government buildings) conserje m.

portfolio [po:t'fouliou] n (folder) carpeta f; (pol) cartera f.

porthole ['po:thoul] n portilla f.

portion ['po:ʃən] n porción f; parte f.

portrait ['po:trət] n retrato m.

portray [po:'trei] v retratar; representar. **portrayal** n retrato m; representación f.

Portugal ['po:tjugl] n Portugal m. **Portuguese** nm, adj portugués. **the Portuguese** los portugueses.

pose [pouz] n postura f; afectación f. v colocar; (question) formular; (problem) plantear. **pose as** dárselas de.

posh [poʃ] adj elegante, de lujo; afectado.

position [pə'ziʃən] n posición f; sitio m; situación f; opinión f; (job) empleo m. v situar, disponer.

positive ['pozətiv] adj seguro; categórico; verdadero; afirmativo; positivo.

possess [pə'zes] v poseer. **possession** n posesión f. **possessive** nm, adj posesivo.

possible ['posəbl] adj posible. **possibility** n posibilidad f. **possibly** adv (perhaps) tal vez.

post[1] [poust] n (pole) poste m. v pegar.

post[2] [poust] n (sentry, job) puesto m. v (a sentry) apostar; (mil: send) destinar.

post[3] [poust] n (mail) correo m; (letters) cartas f pl. v mandar, enviar; echar. **postage** n franqueo m. **postage stamp** sello m. **postal** adj postal. **postal order** giro postal m.

postbox ['pousboks] n buzón m.

postcard ['pouska:d] n tarjeta postal f.

post-code *n* código postal *m*.

poster ['pousta] *n* cartel *m*.

poste restante [poust'restãt] *n* lista de correos *f*.

posterior [po'stiaria] *adj* posterior. *n* (*coll*) trasero *m*.

posterity [po'sterati] *n* posteridad *f*.

postgraduate [poust'gradjuit] *n, adj* postgraduado, -a.

post-haste *adv* a toda prisa.

posthumous ['postjumas] *adj* póstumo.

postman ['pousman] *n* cartero *m*.

postmark ['pousma:k] *n* matasellos *m invar*. *v* matasellar.

postmaster ['pousma:sta] *n* administrador de correos *m*. **postmistress** *n* administradora de correos *f*.

post-mortem *n* autopsia *f*.

post office *n* correos *m pl*.

postpone [pous'poun] *v* aplazar. **postponement** *n* aplazamiento *m*.

postscript ['pousskript] *n* posdata *f*.

postulate ['postjuleit; *n* 'postjulat] *v* postular. *n* postulado *m*.

posture ['postʃa] *n* postura *f*, actitud *f*.

pot [pot] *n* (*cooking*) olla *f*; (*flowers*) tiesto *m*; (*preserves*) tarro *m*. **pot roast** carne asada *f*. **pots and pans** batería de cocina *f*. *v* (*plant*) poner en tiesto.

potassium [pa'tasjam] *n* potasio *m*.

potato [pa'teitou] *n* patata *f*.

potent ['poutant] *adj* poderoso; (*drink*) fuerte.

potential [pa'tenʃal] *adj* posible; (*phys*) potencial. *n* posibilidad *f*; (*phys*) potencial *m*; (*elec*) voltaje *m*.

pot-hole ['pothoul] *n* (*in road*) bache *m*; (*underground*) cueva *f*. **pot-holer** *n* espeleólogo *m*. **pot-holing** *n* espeleología *f*.

potion ['pouʃan] *n* dosis *f*, poción *f*.

potter[1] ['pota] *v* (*coll*) **potter about** *or* **around** no hacer nada de particular.

potter[2] ['pota] *n* alfarero *m*. **potter's wheel** torno de alfarero *m*.

pottery ['potari] *n* (*shop, craft*) alfarería *f*; (*pots*) cacharros de barro *m pl*.

potty ['poti] *n* (*coll: baby's*) orinal *m*. *adj* (*coll: crazy*) chiflado.

pouch [pautʃ] *n* bolsa *f*; (*tobacco*) petaca *f*.

poultice ['poultis] *n* cataplasma *f*.

poultry ['poultri] *n* aves de corral *f pl*.

pounce [pauns] *v* saltar. *n* salto *m*, ataque *m*.

pound[1] [paund] *v* aporrear; martillear; azotar.

pound[2] [paund] *n* libra *f*.

pour [po:] *v* verter; echar; servir; (*rain*) diluviar; (*flow*) fluir; (*people*) salir en tropel. **pouring rain** lluvia torrencial *f*.

pout [paut] *n* mala cara *f*. *v* poner mala cara.

poverty ['povati] *n* pobreza *f*.

powder ['pauda] *n* polvo *m*; (*cosmetic*) polvos *m pl*; (*gun*) pólvora *f*. **powder puff** borla *f*. **powder room** cuarto tocador *m*. *v* pulverizar. **powdery** *adj* en polvo; pulverizado.

power ['paua] *n* poder *m*; (*elec*) potencia *f*; (*tech*) fuerza *f*; (*energy*) energía *f*. **power point** enchufe *m*, toma de corriente *f*. **power station** central eléctrica *f*. *v* accionar, impulsar. **powerful** *adj* poderoso; potente. **powerless** *adj* impotente; sin autoridad.

PR *n* Relaciones Públicas *f* (*pl*)

practicable ['praktikabl] *adj* practicable; utilizable; realizable. **practicability** *n* practicabilidad *f*.

practical ['praktikal] *adj* práctico. **practical joke** broma pesada *f*.

practice ['praktis] *n* práctica *f*; (*music*) ejercicios *m pl*; (*training*) entrenamiento *m*; (*profession*) ejercicio *m*.

practise ['praktis] *v* practicar; (*professionally*) ejercer; (*exercise*) ejercitarse; (*patience, etc.*) tener; (*music*) hacer ejercicios en.

practitioner [prak'tiʃana] *n* (*med*) médico *m*. **general practitioner** internista *m*.

pragmatic [prag'matik] *adj* pragmático; dogmático.

Prague [pra:g] *n* Praga *f*.

prairie ['preari] *n* llanura *f*, pradera *f*.

praise [preiz] *n* alabanza *f*, elogio *m*. *v* alabar, elogiar. **praiseworthy** *adj* laudable.

pram [pram] *n* cochecito de niño *m*.

prance [pra:ns] *v* caracolear, encabritarse.

prank [praŋk] *n* (*joke*) broma *f*; (*mischief*) travesura *f*.

prattle ['pratl] *v* (*chatter*) charlar; (*of a child*) balbucear. *n* chácara *f*; balbuceo *m*.

prawn [pro:n] *n* gamba *f*.

pray [prei] *v* orar, rezar. **prayer** *n* oración *f*,

rezo *m*. **prayer book** devocionario *m*.
preach [pri:tʃ] *v* predicar. **preacher** *n* predicador, -a *m, f*. **preaching** *n* predicación *f*.
precarious [pri'keəriəs] *adj* precario.
precaution [pri'kɔ:ʃən] *n* precaución *f*.
take precautions tomar precauciones.
precede [pri'si:d] *v* preceder, anteceder.
precedence *n* precedencia *f*; prioridad *f*.
precedent *n* precedente *m*.
precinct ['pri:siŋkt] *n* recinto *m*; frontera *f*; zona *f*. **shopping precinct** zona comercial *f*.
precious ['preʃəs] *adj* precioso.
precipice ['presipis] *n* precipicio *m*.
precipitate [pri'sipiteit; *adj* pri'sipitət] *v* (*throw*) precipitar, arrojar; (*hasten*) acelerar; (*cause*) causar. *adj* precipitado. **precipitation** *n* precipitación *f*.
précis ['preisi] *n* resumen *m*.
precise [pri'sais] *adj* preciso; exacto. **precision** *n* precisión *f*; exactitud *f*.
preclude [pri'klu:d] *v* excluir; evitar; impedir.
precocious [pri'kouʃəs] *adj* precoz. **precociousness** *or* **precocity** *n* precocidad *f*.
preconceive [,pri:kən'si:v] *v* preconcebir. **preconception** *n* preconcepción *f*.
precursor [,pri:'kə:sə] *n* precursor, -a *m, f*.
predator ['predətə] *n* animal de rapiña *m*; (*person*) depredador, -a *m, f*.
predecessor ['pri:disesə] *n* predecesor, -a *m, f*.
predestine [pri'destin] *v* predestinar. **predestination** *n* predestinación *f*.
predicament [pri'dikəmənt] *n* situación difícil *f*.
predicate ['predikət] *n* predicado *m*. *v* afirmar; implicar.
predict [pri'dikt] *v* predecir. **predictable** *adj* previsible. **prediction** *n* predicción *f*.
predominate [pri'domineit] *v* predominar. **predominance** *n* predominio *m*. **predominant** *adj* predominante.
pre-eminent [pri:'eminənt] *adj* preeminente. **pre-eminence** *n* preeminencia *f*.
pre-empt [pri:'empt] *v* anticiparse, adelantarse
preen [pri:n] *v* limpiar. **preen oneself** pavonearse.
prefabricate [pri:'fabrikeit] *v* prefabricar. **prefabrication** *n* prefabricación *f*. **prefab** *n* (*coll*) casa prefabricada *f*.

preface ['prefis] *n* prólogo *m*. *v* (*introduce*) introducir.
prefect ['pri:fekt] *n* (*school*) alumno/alumna responsable de disciplina *m, f*.
prefer [pri'fə:] *v* preferir. **preferable** *adj* preferible. **preference** *n* preferencia *f*. **preferential** *adj* preferente.
prefix ['pri:fiks] *n* prefijo *m*. *v* poner un prefijo; anteponer.
pregnant ['pregnənt] *adj* (*woman*) embarazada, encinta; (*animal*) preñada. **pregnancy** *n* embarazo *m*.
prehistoric [,pri:hi'storik] *adj* prehistórico.
prejudice ['predʒədis] *n* prejuicio *m*; parcialidad *f*. *v* predisponer; (*damage*) perjudicar. **prejudiced** *adj* predispuesto; parcial. **prejudicial** *adj* perjudicial.
preliminary [pri'liminəri] *adj* preliminar. **preliminaries** *pl n* preliminares *m pl*.
prelude ['prelju:d] *n* preludio *m*.
premarital [pri:'maritl] *adj* premarital.
premature [premə'tʃuə] *adj* prematuro.
premeditate [pri:'mediteit] *v* premeditar. **premeditation** *n* premeditación *f*.
premier ['premiə] *adj* primero. *n* primer ministro *m*.
première ['premieə] *n* estreno *m*.
premise ['premis] *n* premisa *f*. **premises** *pl n* local *m sing*; edificio *m sing*. **on the premises** (*adv*) in situ.
premium ['pri:miəm] *n* (*comm*) prima *f*; (*award*) premio *m*. **at a premium** a premio.
premonition [,premə'niʃən] *n* premonición *f*.
preoccupied [pri:'okjupaid] *adj* preocupado. **preoccupation** *n* preocupación *f*.
prepare [pri'peə] *v* preparar, disponer. **preparation** *n* preparación *f*. **preparations** *pl n* preparativos *m pl*. **preparatory** *adj* preparatorio; preliminar. **preparatory school** escuela preparatoria *f*.
preposition [,prepə'ziʃən] *n* preposición *f*.
preposterous [pri'postərəs] *adj* ridículo, absurdo.
prerequisite [pri:'rekwizit] *n* prerequisito *m*
prerogative [pri'rogətiv] *n* prerrogativa *f*.
prescribe [pri'skraib] *v* prescribir; (*med*) recetar. **prescription** *n* (*med*) receta *f*, prescripción *f*.
presence ['prezns] *n* presencia *f*.

present¹ ['preznt] *adj* presente. *n* presente *m*, actualidad *f*. **at present** ahora, en la actualidad. **those present** los presentes. **presently** *adv* luego.

present² [pri'zent; *n* 'preznt] *v* presentar; regalar; (*a problem*) plantear; (*an argument*) exponer. *n* regalo *m*. **presentable** *adj* presentable. **presentation** *n* presentación *f*; (*gift*) regalo *m*; (*ceremony*) entrega *f*.

preserve [pri'zə:v] *v* (*food*) conservar; (*protect*) preservar. **preserved** *adj* en conserva. **preserves** *pl n* conservas *f pl*; (*jam*) confitura *f*. **preservation** *n* conservación *f*; (*protection*) preservación *f*. **preservative** *n* producto de conservación *m*.

preside [pri'zaid] *v* presidir.

president ['prezidənt] *n* presidente, -a *m*, *f*. **presidency** *n* presidencia *f*. **presidential** *adj* presidencial.

press [pres] *n* (*newspapers*) prensa *f*; (*printing*) imprenta *f*. **press conference** rueda de prensa *f*. **press cutting** recorte de periódico *m*. *v* (*mechanical*) prensar; (*iron*) planchar; (*button*) dar a; (*squeeze*) estrujar; (*urge*) urgir. **press for** pedir con insistencia. **pressing** *adj* urgente.

pressure ['preʃə] *n* presión *f*; (*weight*) peso *m*; (*strength*) fuerza *f*; (*elec, med*) tensión *f*. **pressure cooker** olla de presión *f*. **pressure gauge** manómetro *m*. **pressure group** grupo de presión *m*. **pressurize** *v* (*cabin, etc.*) presurizar; (*coll; force*) acozar.

prestige [pre'sti:ʒ] *n* prestigio *m*.

presume [pri'zju:m] *v* suponer; permitirse. **presumably** *adv* es de suponer. **presumption** *n* presunción *f*; (*daring*) atrevimiento *m*. **presumptuous** *adj* presuntuoso; atrevido.

pretend [pri'tend] *v* fingir; (*claim*) pretender; (*imagine*) suponer. **pretence** *n* fingimiento *m*; pretensión *f*; pretexto *m*; apariencia *f*. **pretension** *n* pretensión *f*. **pretentious** *adj* pretencioso; (*showy*) presumido.

pretext ['pri:tekst] *n* pretexto *m*.

pretty ['priti] *adj* bonito, lindo. *adv* bastante.

prevail [pri'veil] *v* prevalecer, triunfar; predominar. **prevail upon** convencer. **prevailing** *adj* (*wind*) predominante, reinante; (*present*) actual. **prevalent** *adj* predominante; (*present-day*) actual; (*common*) común; extendido.

prevent [pri'vent] *v* impedir; (*avoid*) evitar. **prevention** prevención *f*; impedimento *m*. **preventive** *adj* preventivo.

preview ['pri:vju:] *n* preestreno *m*. *v* ver antes que los demás.

previous ['pri:viəs] *adj* anterior. **previously** *adv* antes.

prey [prei] *n* presa *f*; víctima *f*. **be a prey to** ser víctima de. *v* **prey on** (*animals*) alimentarse de. **prey on one's mind** preocupar mucho.

price [prais] *n* precio *m*. **fixed price** precio fijo *m*. **full price** precio fuerte *m*. **price list** tarifa *f*. **sale price** precio de venta *m*. *v* poner precio a; valorar. **priceless** *adj* inestimable.

prick [prik] *n* pinchazo *m*. *v* pinchar. **prick up one's ears** aguzar el oído.

prickle ['prikl] *n* espina. *v* picar. **prickly** *adj* espinoso.

pride [praid] *n* orgullo *m*; dignidad *f*. **pride oneself on** enorgullecerse de.

priest [pri:st] *n* sacerdote *m*. **priesthood** *n* (*office*) sacerdocio *m*; (*clergy*) clero *m*.

prim [prim] *adj* (*fussy*) remilgado; (*demure*) recatado.

primary ['praiməri] *adj* primario; básico; primero. **primarily** (*adv*) en príncipio.

primate ['praimət] *n* (*zool*) primate *m*; (*rel*) primado *m*.

prime [praim] *adj* primero; principal; original; selecto; (*math*) primo. **prime minister** primer ministro *m*. *v* preparar; (*person*) informar. **primer** *n* (*book*) cartilla *f*. **primer coat** primera mano *f*.

primitive ['primitiv] *adj* primitivo.

primrose ['primrouz] *n* primavera *f*.

prince [prins] *n* príncipe *m*. **princely** *adj* principesco. **princess** *n* princesa *f*.

principal ['prinsəpəl] *adj* principal. *n* (*school*) director, -a *m*, *f*.

principle ['prinsəpəl] *n* principio *m*. **on principle** por principio.

print [print] *n* (*finger*) huella *f*; (*impression*) marca *f*; (*phot*) prueba *f*; (*edition*) tirada *f*; (*type*) tipo *m*; (*picture*) grabado *m*. **out of print** agotado. *v* imprimir; (*phot*) sacar. **printed matter** impresos *m pl*. **printer** *n* impresor *m*; (*comput*) impresora *f*. **printing** *n* impresión *f*; (*phot*) tiraje *m*. **printing press** prensa *f*.

prior ['praiə] *adj* anterior; preferente. **prior**

to antes de. **priority** n prioridad f.

prise [praiz] v **prise off/open** abrir; levantar por fuerza.

prism ['prizm] n prisma m.

prison ['prizn] n cárcel f. **prisoner** n preso, -a m, f.

pristine ['pristi:n] adj pristino

private ['praivət] adj privado; personal; reservado; (house, car, lessons, etc.) particular; confidencial. n soldado raso m. **privacy** n intimidad f; aislamiento m. **privately** adv en privado; personalmente.

privet ['privət] n alheña f.

privilege ['privəlidʒ] n privilegio m. **privileged** adj privilegiado.

privy ['privi] n letrina f.

prize [praiz] n premio m. **prizewinner** n premiado, -a m, f. adj premiado. v estimar.

probable ['probəbl] adj probable; (credible) verosímil. **probability** n probabilidad f. **probably** adv probablemente.

probation [prə'beiʃən] n (law) libertad vigilada f; (trial period) período de prueba m. **on probation** a prueba. **probationary** adj de prueba.

probe [proub] n (act) sondeo m; (med) sonda f. v sondear; explorar.

problem ['probləm] n problema m. **problematic** adj problemático.

proceed [prə'si:d] v seguir; proceder; avanzar. **proceed to** ponerse a. **procedure** n procedimiento m. **proceedings** pl n debates m pl; (law) proceso m sing.

process ['prouses] n proceso m; procedimiento m; método m. **in the process of** en curso de. v tratar; (phot) revelar.

procession [prə'seʃən] n procesión f, desfile m.

proclaim [prə'kleim] v proclamar; declarar. **proclamation** n proclamación f; declaración f.

procrastinate [prou'krastineit] v aplazar.

procreate ['proukrieit] v procrear. **procreation** n procreación f.

procure [prə'kjuə] v conseguir.

prod [prod] n golpecito m. v punzar; (urge) estimular.

prodigal ['prodigəl] adj pródigo.

prodigy ['prodidʒi] n prodigio m. **prodigious** adj prodigioso.

produce [prə'dju:s; n 'prodju:s] v producir; (manufacture) fabricar; causar. n productos

m pl. **producer** n productor, -a m, f; (theatre) escenógrafo m. **product** m producto m. **production** n producción f; fabricación f; presentación f; (theatre) dirección f. **productive** adj productivo; fecundo. **productivity** n productividad f.

profane [prə'fein] adj profano. v profanar. **profanity** n lo profano; impiedad f.

profess [prə'fes] v (state) declarar; (claim) pretender; (affirm) afirmar.

profession [prə'feʃən] n profesión f. **professional** n(m + f), adj profesional.

professor [prə'fesə] n catedrático, -a m, f. **professorship** n cátedra f.

proficient [prə'fiʃənt] adj competente; experto. **proficiency** n competencia f; pericia f.

profile ['proufail] n perfil m; (biography) reseña f.

profit ['profit] n (financial) ganancia f; (fig) provecho m. **profit-making** adj productivo. v **profit by** or **from** beneficiarse de. **profitable** adj provechoso.

profound [prə'faund] adj profundo. **profoundly** adv profundamente.

profuse [prə'fju:s] adj profuso; abundante. **profusely** adv profusamente. **profusion** n profusión f; abundancia f.

program ['prougram] n programa m.

programme ['prougram] n programa m. v programar. **programmer** n programador, -a m, f. **programming** n programación f; adv programado.

progress ['prougres] n progreso m. **in progress** en curso. **make progress** hacer progresos. v progresar, avanzar, hacer progresos. **progression** n progresión f. **progressive** adj progresivo; (political, social) progresista.

prohibit [prə'hibit] v prohibir; impedir. **prohibition** n prohibición f.

project ['prodʒekt; v prə'dʒekt] n proyecto m. v proyectar; (protrude) hacer resaltar. **projectile** n proyectil m. **projecting** adj saliente. **projection** n proyección f; saliente m. **projector** n proyector m; (planner) proyectista m, f.

proletarian [proulə'teəriən] n, adj proletario, -a. **proletariat** n proletariado m.

proliferate [prə'lifəreit] v proliferar. **proliferation** n proliferación f.

prolific [prə'lifik] adj prolífico.

prologue ['proulog] n prólogo m.

prolong [prə'loŋ] v prolongar. **prolongation** n prolongación f.

promenade [promə'na:d] n paseo m. v pasear, pasearse.

prominent ['prominənt] adj prominente; saliente; preeminente. **prominence** n prominencia f; importancia f.

promiscuous [prə'miskjuəs] adj promiscuo; (person) libertino. **promiscuity** n promiscuidad f.

promise ['promis] n promesa f. v prometer. **promising** adj que promete.

promontory ['proməntəri] n promontorio m.

promote [prə'mout] v promover, ascender; (comm) promocionar; (encourage, stir up) fomentar; financiar. **promotion** n ascenso m; promoción f; fomento m.

prompt [prompt] adj pronto; rápido; inmediato; puntual. v incitar; inspirar; sugerir; (theatre) apuntar. **prompter** n apuntador, -a m, f.

prone [proun] adj propenso; (lying) boca abajo.

prong [proŋ] n diente m, púa f.

pronoun ['prounaun] n pronombre m.

pronounce [prə'nauns] v pronunciar; declarar. **pronouncement** n declaración f. **pronunciation** n pronunciación f.

proof [pru:f] n prueba f; (alcohol) graduación normal f. adj resistente (a); al abrigo de. **proof-read** v corregir pruebas. **proof-reading** n corrección de pruebas f.

prop¹ [prop] n puntal m; (fig) sostén m, apoyo m. v (lean) apoyar; (support) mantener.

prop² [prop] n (coll: theatre) accesorio m.

propaganda [propə'gandə] n propaganda f.

propagate ['propəgeit] v propagar. **propagation** n propagación f.

propel [prə'pel] v propulsar, impulsar. **propeller** n propulsor m; (aircraft, ship) hélice f. **propelling pencil** portaminas m invar.

proper ['propə] adj propio; correcto; decente; formal; justo; (suitable) apto; (true) verdadero; (characteristic) peculiar. **proper noun** nombre propio m. **properly** adv propiamente; bien; decentemente; correctamente.

property ['propəti] n (estate) hacienda f; (possessions) bienes m pl, propiedad f. (quality) cualidad f.

prophecy ['profəsi] n profecía f. **prophesy** v profetizar. **prophet** n profeta m. **prophetic** adj profético.

proportion [prə'po:ʃən] n proporción f; parte f. **out of proportion** desproporcionado. v proporcionar; distribuir. **proportional** adj proporcional, en proporción.

propose [prə'pouz] v proponer; (marriage) declararse; (toast) brindar; (intend) intentar. **proposal** n proposición f; (marriage) oferta de matrimonio f; (plan) proyecto m. **proposition** n proposición f; proyecto m.

proprietor [prə'praiətə] n propietario, -a m, f; dueño m, f.

propriety [prə'praiəti] n decoro m; conveniencia f; oportunidad f; corrección f.

propulsion [prə'pʌlʃən] n propulsión f.

pros and cons los pros y las contras.

prose [prouz] n prosa f.

prosecute ['prosikju:t] v proseguir; (law) procesar. **prosecution** n (of duty) cumplimiento m; (continuation) continuación f; (action of prosecuting) procesamiento m; (trial) proceso m; (party) parte acusadora f.

prospect ['prospekt; v prə'spekt] n perspectiva f; vista f. **prospects** pl n (of a job, etc.) perspectivas f pl. v prospectar. **prospective** adj eventual; futuro.

prospectus [prə'spektəs] n prospecto m.

prosper ['prospə] v prosperar. **prosperity** n prosperidad f. **prosperous** adj próspero.

prostitute ['prostitju:t] n prostituta f. v prostituir. **prostitution** n prostitución f.

prostrate ['prostreit; v pro'streit] adj (lying down) boca abajo; (exhausted) postrado. v postrar. **prostrate oneself** postrarse. **prostration** n prostración f; prosternación f.

protagonist [prou'tagənist] n protagonista m, f.

protect [prə'tekt] v proteger. **protection** n protección f. **protective** adj protector.

protégé ['protəʒei] n protegido m. **protégée** n protegida f.

protein ['prouti:n] n proteína f.

protest ['proutest; v prə'test] n protesta f. v protestar. **protester** n (on march) manifestador, -a m, f.

Protestant ['protistənt] n(m + f), adj protestante.

protocol ['proutəkol] n protocolo m.

prototype ['proutətaip] n prototipo m.

protractor [prə'traktə] *n* transportador *m*.

protrude [prə'tru:d] *v* sacar; sobresalir. **protruding** *adj* saliente, sobresaliente.

proud [praud] *adj* orgulloso; soberbio.

prove [pru:v] *v* probar; demostrar; (*show*) mostrar.

proverb [′provə:b] *n* proverbio *m*. **proverbial** *adj* proverbial.

provide [prə′vaid] *v* proveer; dar; preparar (por); proporcionar medios de vida (a). **provided that** si siempre que.

provident [′providənt] *adj* próvido. **providence** *n* providencia *f*. **providential** providencial.

province [′provins] *n* provincia *f*; esfera *f*. **the provinces** la provincia *f*. **provincial** *adj* provincial.

provision [prə′viʒən] *n* (*supply*) suministro *m*; (*providing*) provisión *f*; (*of treaty, law, etc.*) disposición *f*. **make provision for** prever. **provisions** *pl n* provisiones *f pl*. **provisional** *adj* provisional.

proviso [prə′vaizou] *n* condición *f*; estipulación *f*.

provoke [prə′vouk] *v* provocar. **provocation** *n* provocación *f*. **provocative** *adj* provocador.

prow [prau] *n* proa *f*.

prowess [′prauis] *n* valor *m*; proeza *f*.

prowl [praul] *v* rondar. **prowler** *n* rondador, -a *m, f*.

proximity [prok′siməti] *n* proximidad *f*.

proxy [′proksi] *n* poder *m*, procuración *f*. **by proxy** por poderes.

prude [pru:d] *n* mojigato, -a *m, f*. **prudish** *adj* mojigato.

prudent [′pru:dənt] *adj* prudente. **prudence** *n* prudencia *f*.

prune[1] [pru:n] *n* (*fruit*) ciruela pasa *f*.

prune[2] [pru:n] *v* podar; cortar; reducir.

pry [prai] *v* fisgar, fisgonear. **pry into** entrometerse en. **prying** *adj* fisgón.

psalm [sa:m] *n* salmo *m*.

pseudonym [′sju:dənim] *n* pseudónimo *m*.

psychedelic [,saikə′delik] *adj* psicodélico.

psychiatry [sai′kaiətri] *n* psiquiatría *f*.

psychic [′saikik] *adj* psíquico. *n* medium *m*.

psychoanalysis [,saikouə′naləsis] *n* psicoanálisis *m*. **psychoanalyse** *v* psicoanalizar. **psychoanalyst** *n* psicoanalista *m, f*.

psychology [sai′kolədʒi] *n* psicología *f*. **psychological** *adj* psicológico. **psychologist** *n* psicólogo, -a *m, f*.

psychopath [′saikəpaθ] *n* psicópata *m, f*. **psychopathic** *adj* psicopático.

psychosis [sai′kousis] *n* psicosis *f*. **psychotic** *adj* psicopático. *n* psicópata *m, f*.

psychosomatic [,saikəsə′matik] *adj* psicosomático.

psychotherapy [,saikə′θerəpi] *n* psicoterapia *f*.

pub [pʌb] *n* taberna *f*. **pub crawl** chateo *m*.

puberty [′pju:bəti] *n* pubertad *f*.

pubic [′pju:bik] *adj* púbico.

public [′pʌblik] *nm, adj* público.

publication [,pʌbli′keiʃə.] *n* publicación *f*.

publicity [pʌb′lisəti] *n* publicidad *f*.

publicize [′pʌblisaiz] *v* publicar.

public library *n* biblioteca de préstamo *f*.

public relations *n* relaciones públicas *f pl*.

public-spirited *adj* de espíritu cívico.

public transport *n* servicio de transportes *m*.

publish [′pʌbliʃ] *v* publicar. **publisher** *n* editor, -a *m, f*. **publishing** *n* publicación *f*. **publishing house** casa editora *f*.

pucker [′pʌkə] *v* (*wrinkle*) arrugar; (*pleat*) fruncir. *n* (*pleat*) frunce *m*.

pudding [′pudiŋ] *n* pudín *m*, budín *m*.

puddle [′pʌdl] *n* charco *m*.

puerile [′pjuərail] *adj* pueril.

Puerto Rico [,pwə:tou′ri:kou] *n* Puerto Rico.

puff [pʌf] *n* (*breath*) resoplido *m*; (*air*) soplo *m*; (*wind*) ráfaga *f*; (*smoke*) bocanada *f*; *v* (*blow*) soplar; (*pant*) jadear; (*smoke*) echar bocanadas. **puff out** *or* **up** hinchar. **puffy** *adj* hinchado.

pull [pul] *n* tracción *f*; (*tide*) arrastre *m*; esfuerzo *m*; (*influence*) enchufe *m*; atracción *f*. *v* (*open*) tirar de; (*drag*) arrastrar; (*uproot*) arrancar; (*tooth*) sacar; (*trigger*) apretar; (*attract*) atraer. **pull ahead** destacarse. **pull away** separar, apartar. **pull down** bajar; echar abajo. **pull in** entrar; llegar. **pull oneself together** serenarse. **pull out** (*mot*) salirse; sacar; arrancar; (*mil*) retirarse. **pull through** sacar de un apuro. **pull together** aunar sus esfuerzos. **pull up** (*mot*) parar; (*socks*) subirse; (*a chair*) acercar.

pulley [′puli] *n* polea *f*.

pullover ['pul͵ouvə] *n* jersey *m*.

pulp [pʌlp] *n* pulpa *f*. *v* reducir a pulpa.

pulpit ['pulpit] *n* púlpito *m*.

pulsate [pʌl'seit] *v* palpitar; vibrar; brillar. **pulsation** *n* pulsación *f*; vibración *f*.

pulse [pʌls] *n* (*med*) pulso *m*; (*phys*) pulsación *f*. *v* latir; vibrar.

pulverize ['pʌlvəraiz] *v* pulverizar. **pulverization** *n* pulverización *f*.

pump [pʌmp] *n* bomba *f*; (*petrol*) surtidor *m*; (*plimsoll*) zapato de lona *m*. *v* bombear; sacar. **pump up** inflar.

pumpkin ['pʌmpkin] *n* calabaza *f*.

pun [pʌn] *n* retruécano *m*.

punch¹ [pʌntʃ] *n* puñetazo *m*; golpe *m*. *v* dar un puñetazo.

punch² [pʌntʃ] *n* (*drink*) ponche *m*.

punch³ [pʌntʃ] *n* (*tool*) sacabocados *m invar*; perforadora *f*. *v* taladrar; perforar; picar.

punctual ['pʌŋktʃuəl] *adj* puntual. **punctuality** *n* puntualidad *f*.

punctuate ['pʌŋktʃueit] *v* puntuar. **punctuation** *n* puntuación *f*.

puncture ['pʌŋktʃə] *n* (*tyre*) pinchazo *m*; (*leather, skin*) perforación *f*. *v* **have a puncture** tener un pinchazo. *v* pinchar; perforar.

pungent ['pʌndʒənt] *adj* (*smell*) acre; (*taste*) picante. **pungency** *n* acritud *f*; lo picante; mordacidad *f*.

punish ['pʌniʃ] *v* castigar. **punishment** *n* castigo *m*.

punk [pʌŋk] *adj* punky

punt¹ [pʌnt] *n* (*boat*) batea *f*.

punt² [pʌnt] *v* (*bet*) apostar. **punter** *n* jugador *m*.

puny ['pju:ni] *adj* escuchimizado.

pupil¹ ['pju:pl] *n* alumno, -a *m, f*.

pupil² ['pju:pl] *n* (*eye*) pupila *f*.

puppet ['pʌpit] *n* títere *m*; marioneta *f*.

puppy ['pʌpi] *n* cachorro *m*.

purchase ['pə:tʃəs] *n* compra *f*. **purchase tax** impuesto sobre la venta *m*. *v* comprar.

pure [pjuə] *adj* puro. **purify** *v* purificar. **purist** *n* purista *m, f*. **purity** *n* pureza *f*.

purée ['pjuərei] *n* puré *m*.

purgatory ['pə:gətəri] *n* purgatorio *m*.

purge [pə:dʒ] *v* purgar; purificar. *n* purga *f*. **purgative** *nm, adj* purgante.

puritan ['pjuəritən] *n, adj* puritano, -a. **puritanical** *adj* puritano.

purl [pə:l] *v* ribetear; hacer al revés. *n* (*on lace*) puntilla *f*; (*thread*) hilo de oro o de plata *m*.

purple ['pə:pl] *nm, adj* morado.

purpose ['pə:pəs] *n* propósito *m*, objetivo *m*; destino *m*; determinación *f*; uso *m*; utilidad *f*. **on purpose** a propósito. **purposeful** *adj* decidido; (*person*) resuelto; útil.

purr [pə:] *v* ronronear. *n* ronroneo *m*.

purse [pə:s] *n* monedero *m*, portamonedas *m invar*; (*prize*) premio *m*. *v* **purse one's lips** apretar los labios.

purser ['pə:sə] *n* contador *m*.

pursue [pə'sju:] *v* perseguir. **pursuer** *n* perseguidor, -a *m, f*. **pursuit** *n* persecución *f*; profesión *f*; ocupación *f*; pasatiempo *m*.

pus [pʌs] *n* pus *m*.

push [puʃ] *n* empujón *m*; (*force*) empuje *m*. *v* empujar; presionar; (*notice on doors*) empujen. **be pushed for time** tener prisa. **pushing** *adj* ambicioso.

*put [put] *v* poner; meter; echar; (*question*) hacer; (*state*) decir. **put away** guardar; (*money*) ahorrar. **put back** volver a poner; (*clock*) atrasar. **put down** bajar; (*in writing*) apuntar; (*repress*) reprimir; (*kill*) sacrificar. **put off** (*postpone*) aplazar; (*disgust*) censar; (*revolt*) asquear; disuadir. **put on** (*clothes*) ponerse; (*a show*) representar; (*pretend*) fingir. **put up** levantar; (*hang*) colgar; (*resistance*) oponer; (*build*) construir. **put up with** aguantar; conformarse con. **put upon** engañar.

putrid ['pju:trid] *adj* pútrido; podrido.

putt [pʌt] *n* put *m*. *v* tirar al hoyo. **putter** *n* putter *m*.

putty ['pʌti] *n* masilla *f*.

puzzle ['pʌzl] *n* enigma *f*; (*game*) rompecabezas *m invar*. *v* dejar perplejo. **puzzle out** resolver; descifrar. **puzzling** *adj* enigmático; misterioso.

pyjamas [pə'dʒa:məz] *pl n* pijama *m sing*.

pylon ['pailən] *n* poste *m*.

pyramid ['pirəmid] *n* pirámide *f*.

python ['paiθən] *n* pitón *m*.

Q

quack¹ [kwak] *n* (*duck*) graznido *m*. *v* graznar.

quack² [kwak] *n* charlatán *m*.
quadrangle ['kwodraŋgl] *n* (*courtyard*) patio *m*; (*math*) cuadrángulo *m*.
quadrant ['kwodrənt] *n* cuadrante *m*.
quadrilateral [kwodrə'latərəl] *nm, adj* cuadrilátero.
quadruped ['kwodruped] *nm, adj* cuadrúpedo.
quadruple [kwod'ru:pl] *adj* cuádruple.
quadruplets [kwo'dru:plits] *pl n* cuatrillizos, -as *m, f pl*.
quagmire ['kwagmaiə] *n* pantano *m*.
quail¹ [kweil] *n* (*zool*) codorniz *f*.
quail² [kweil] *v* acobardarse.
quaint [kweint] *adj* pintoresco; excéntrico.
quake [kweik] *v* estremecerse. *n* estremecimiento. **quake with fear** temblar de miedo.
qualify ['kwolifai] *v* (*entitle*) capacitar; calificar; modificar; limitar. **qualification** *n* reserva *f*; aptitud *f*; requisito *m*. **qualifications** *pl n* títulos *m pl*. **qualified** *adj* competente; capacitado; titulado; con reservas.
quality ['kwoləti] *n* (*attribute*) cualidad *f*; calidad *f*.
qualm [kwa:m] *n* escrúpulo *m*.
quandary ['kwondəri] *n* incertidumbre *f*, dilema *m*.
quantify ['kwontifai] *v* determinar la cantidad de.
quantity ['kwontəti] *n* cantidad *f*.
quarantine ['kworəntiːn] *n* cuarentena *f*. *v* someter a cuarentena.
quarrel ['kworəl] *n* disputa *f*, pelea *f*, *v* disputar, pelear. **quarrelsome** *adj* peleador.
quarry¹ ['kwori] *n* (*stone, etc*) cantera *f*. *v* explotar una cantera.
quarry² ['kwori] *n* presa *f*.
quarter ['kwo:tə] *n* cuarto *m*; cuarta parte *f*; (*of year*) trimestre *m*; (*district*) barrio *m*. **quarter-final** *n* cuarto de final *m*. **quartermaster** *n* (*naut*) cabo de la marina *m*. **quarter past four** las cuatro y quince. **quarters** *pl n* (*mil*) cuartel *m sing*. **at close quarters** de cerca. **quarter to four** las cuatro menos cuarto. *v* dividir en cuatros; (*mil*) acuartelar. **quarterly** *adj* trimestral.
quartet [kwo:'tet] *n* cuarteto *m*.
quartz [kwo:ts] *n* cuarzo *m*.
quash [kwoʃ] *v* amular; ahogar; (*rebellion*) reprimir.

quaver ['kweivə] *n* (*music*) corchea *f*; temblor *m*. *v* temblar.
quay [ki:] *n* muelle *m*.
queasy ['kwi:zi] *adj* (*sick*) mareado; (*upset*) delicado. **queasiness** *n* náuseas *f pl*.
queen [kwi:n] *n* reina *f*; (*cards*) dama *f*. **Queen Mother** reina madre *f*.
queer [kwiə] *adj* raro; curioso; (*unwell*) indispuesto; (*slang: homosexual*) maricón. *n* (*slang*) maricón *m*, marica *f*.
quell [kwell] *v* reprimir.
quench [kwentʃ] *v* (*flames*) apagar; (*thirst*) aplacar; (*desire*) sofocar.
query ['kwiəri] *n* pregunta *f*; duda *f*. *v* preguntar; dudar (de).
quest [kwest] *n* búsqueda *f*.
question ['kwestʃən] *n* pregunta *f*; cuestión *f*; problema *m*. **begging the question** petición de principio *f*. **beside the question** que no viene al caso. **out of the question** imposible. **question mark** signo de interrogación *m*. **without question** sin duda. *v* preguntar; interrogar; poner en duda. **questionable** *adj* dudoso; discutible. **questioning** *n* interrogatorio *m*. **questionnaire** *n* cuestionario *m*.
queue [kju:] *n* cola *f*. *v* hacer cola.
quibble ['kwibl] *n* pega *f*; subterfugio *m*. *v* sutilizar; (*find fault*) ser quisquilloso.
quick [kwik] *adj* rápido; (*reply*) pronto; (*lively*) vivo; (*clever*) agudo; (*on feet*) ligero. **quicksand** *n* arena movediza *f*. **quicktempered** *adj* irascible. **quick-witted** *adj* agudo. **quicken** *v* acelerar; estimular. **quickly** *adv* rápidamente.
quid [kwid] *n* (*coll*) libra *f*.
quiet ['kwaiət] *adj* silencioso; callado; (*step*) ligero; tranquilo; (*dress*) sobrio. *n also* **quietness** tranquilidad *f*; silencio *m*; reposo *m*. **quieten** *v* callar; calmar. **quietly** *adv* silenciosamente; tranquilamente.
quill [kwil] *n* (*feather*) pluma *f*; (*pen*) cálamo *m*; (*porcupine*) púa *f*.
quilt [kwilt] *n* colcha *f*; (*eiderdown*) edredón *m*. *v* acolchar.
quince [kwins] *n* membrillo *m*.
quinine [kwi'ni:n] *n* quinina *f*.
quinsy ['kwinzi] *n* angina *f*.
quintet [kwin'tet] *n* quinteto *m*.
quirk [kwə:k] *n* peculiaridad *f*.
quit [kwit] *v* (*job*) abandonar; (*place*) dejar; (*leave*) irse de.

quite [kwait] *adv* completamente, enteramente; exactamente; verdaderamente; (*fairly*) bastante.

quiver[1] ['kwivə] *v* temblar; estremecerse. *n* temblor *m*; estremecimiento *m*.

quiver[2] ['kwivə] *n* (*for arrows*) aljaba *f*.

quiz [kwiz] *n* (*inquiry*) encuesta *f*; (*questioning*) interrogatorio *m*; examen *m*. *v* interrogar.

quizzical ['kwizikl] *adj* curioso; (*bantering*) burlón.

quota ['kwoutə] *n* cupo *m*; (*share*) cuota *f*.

quote [kwout] *v* citar; dar; (*comm*) cotizar.
quotation *n* cita *f*; (*comm*) cotización *f*.
quotation marks comillas *f pl*.

R

rabbi ['rabai] *n* rabino *m*.

rabbit ['rabit] *n* conejo *m*.

rabble ['rabl] *n* gentío *m*; (*derog*) populacho *m*.

rabies ['reibi:z] *n* rabia *f*. **rabid** *adj* rabioso.

race[1] [reis] *n* carrera *f*; (*yacht*) regata *f*.
racehorse *n* caballo de carreras *m*. **racetrack** *n* circuito de carreras *m*. *v* (*person*) competir con; (*horse*) hacer correr; (*pulse*) latir a ritmo acelerado. **racing** *n* carreras *pl*.

race[2] [reis] *n* raza *f*; familia *f*. **racial** *adj* racial. **racialism** *n also* **racism** racismo *m*. **racialist** *n* (*m + f*), *adj also* **racist** racista.

rack [rak] *n* (*shelf*) estante *m*; (*coats, etc.*) percha *f*; (*plates*) escurreplatos *m invar*; (*car roof*) baca *f*; (*torture*) potro *m*. *v* atormentar. **rack one's brains** devanarse los sesos.

racket[1] ['rakit] *n* (*sport*) raqueta *f*.

racket[2] ['rakit] *n* (*noise*) alboroto *m*, barullo *m*; (*coll: crime*) tráfico *m*; timo *m*.

radar ['reida:] *n* radar *m*.

radial ['reidiəl] *adj* radial. **radial tyre** neumático radial *m*.

radiant ['reidiənt] *adj* resplandeciente.
radiance *n* resplandor *m*.

radiate ['reidieit] *v* (*heat*) irradiar; (*rays*) emitir; (*spread*) difundir. **radiation** *n* radiación *f*. **radiator** *n* radiador *m*.

radical ['radikəl] *nm*, *adj* radical.

radio ['reidiou] *n* radio *f*. **radio beacon** radiofaro *m*. **radio contact** radiocomunicación *f*. **radio control** teledirección *f*. **radio station** emisora *f*. **radio wave** onda *f*. *v* transmitir por radio.

radioactive [reidou'aktiv] *adj* radioactivo.
radioactivity *n* radioactividad *f*.

radiography [reidi'ogrəfi] *n* radiografía *f*. **radiographer** *n* radiógrafo *m*.

radiology [reidi'olədʒi] *n* radiología *f*. **radiologist** *n* radiólogo *m*.

radiotherapy [reidiou'θerəpi] *n* radioterapia *f*.

radish ['radiʃ] *n* rábano *m*.

radium ['reidiəm] *n* radio *m*.

radius ['reidiəs] *n* radio *m*.

raffia ['rafiə] *n* rafia *f*.

raffle ['rafl] *n* rifa *f*. *v* rifar.

raft [ra:ft] *n* balsa *f*.

rafter ['ra:ftə] *n* viga *f*.

rag[1] [rag] *n* (*waste piece*) harapo *m*; (*cleaning*) trapo *m*; (*derog: newspaper*) periodicucho *m*. **regamuffin** *n* golfo *m*. **ragged** *adj* (*clothes*) hecho jirones; (*edge*) mellado.

rag[2] [rag] *v* (*coll*) tomar el pelo a. *n* payasadas *f pl*. **ragtime** *n* música sincopada *f*.

rage [reidʒ] *n* (*anger*) cólera *f*, rabia *f*; (*of elements*) furia *f*; (*fashion*) moda *f*. **be all the rage** hacer furor. *v* (*be angry*) estar furioso; (*wind, fire, beasts*) bramar; (*sea*) alborotarse. **raging** *adj* (*person*) furioso; (*pain*) muy fuerte; (*storm*) encrespado.

raid [reid] *n* (*mil*) correría *f*; (*aerial*) ataque *m*; (*police*) redada *f*; (*robbery*) asalto *m*. *v* hacer una redada; asaltar. **raider** *n* invasor *m*; (*thief*) ladrón *m*.

rail [reil] *n* (*stairs*) barandilla *f*; (*bridge*) antepecho *m*; (*balcony*) baranda *f*; (*bar*) barra *f*; (*fence*) cerco *m*; (*train, tram*) vía férrea *f*. **by rail** por ferrocarril. **railway** *or US* **railroad** *n* ferrocarril *m*. **railway line** línea ferroviaria *f*.

railings ['reilinz] *pl n* barandilla *f sing*.

rain [rein] *n* lluvia *f*. **rainbow** *n* arco iris *m*. **raincoat** *n* impermeable *m*. **raindrop** *n* gota de lluvia *f*. **rainfall** *n* precipitación *f*. **rainforest** selva tropical *f*. **rainwater** *n* agua de lluvia *f*. *v* llover. **rainy** *adj* lluvioso.

raise [reiz] *v* alzar, levantar; (*increase*) aumentar; provocar; (*problem*) plantar; (*animals*) criar.

raisin ['reizən] n pasa f.

rake [reik] n rastro m. v rastrillar. **rake together** reunir a duras penas.

rally ['rali] n reunión f; (pol) mitin político m; (mot) rallye m; (tennis) peloteo m. v reunir; (recover) recuperarse. **rally round** tomar el partido de.

ram [ram] n carnero m; (battering ram) ariete m. v (earth, etc.) apisonar; (fist, head) dar con; (pack) meter a la fuerza.

RAM [ram] RAM

ramble ['rambl] n excursión f. v pasear; (fig) divagar.

ramp [ramp] n rampa f.

rampage ['rampeidʒ] n **be on the rampage** alborotar.

rampant ['rampənt] adj (plant) exuberante; (heraldry) rampante; (aggressive) violento. **be rampant** estar difundido.

rampart ['rampa:t] n terraplén m, muralla f.

ramshackle ['ramʃakl] adj desvencijado.

ran [ran] V run.

ranch [ra:ntʃ] n rancho m; hacienda f.

rancid ['ransid] adj rancio.

rancour ['raŋkə] n rencor m.

random ['randəm] n **at random** al azar. adj hecho al azar. **random sample** muestra cogida al azar f.

rang [raŋ] V ring.

range [reindʒ] n (row) fila f; (mountains) sierra f; (area) extensión f; (distance) alcance m; (of an aircraft) autonomía f; (mil: firing) campo de tiro m; (voice) registro m; (colours, prices) gama f; (subjects) variedad f; (grazing land) dehesa f; (cooking stove) cocina económica f. v (place) colocar; (put in a row) alinear; clasificar; (wander) recorrer.

rank¹ [raŋk] n fila f; grado m; categoría f. **the rank and file** la tropa f; (ordinary people) gente del montón f. v (estimate) situar, poner; figurar; (mil) alinear.

rank² [raŋk] adj lozano; rancio.

rankle ['raŋkl] v escocer.

ransack ['ransak] v saquear; (search) registrar.

ransom ['ransəm] n rescate m. **hold to ransom** exigir rescate. v rescatar.

rap [rap] v golpear. n golpecito m; (music) rap.

rape [reip] n violación f. v violar. **rapist** n violador m.

rapid ['rapid] adj rápido. **rapids** pl n rápidos m pl. **rapidity** n rapidez f.

rapier ['reipiə] n estoque m.

rapport [ra'po:] n relación f; armonía f.

rapture ['raptʃə] n éxtasis m invar. **go into raptures over** extasiarse por.

rare¹ ['reə] adj raro. **rarity** n rareza f.

rare² ['reə] adj (cookery) poco hecho.

rascal ['ra:skəl] n bribón m, pícaro m.

rash¹ [raʃ] adj temerario. **rashness** n temeridad f.

rash² [raʃ] n (med) erupción f.

rasher ['raʃə] n loncha f.

raspberry ['ra:zbəri] n (fruit) frambuesa f; (bush) frambueso m.

rat [rat] n rata f. **rat poison** matarratas m invar. **rat race** competencia f.

rate [reit] n proporción f; índice m; velocidad f; ritmo m; precio; (discount, interest) tipo m; (pulse) frecuencia f. **at any rate** de todos modos. **ratepayer** n contribuyente m, f. **rates** pl n contribución municipal f sing. v valorar; considerar; clasificar; estimar. **rateable** adj valorable. **rating** clasificación f, valoración f. **ratings** (television) índice de audiencia m.

rather ['ra:ðə] adv más bien; bastante; (fairly) algo. **I would rather** … prefiero ….

ratify ['ratifai] v ratificar. **ratification** n ratificación f.

ratio ['reiʃiou] n razón f, relación f.

ration ['raʃən] n ración f. v racionar. **rationing** n racionamiento m.

rational ['raʃənl] adj racional; razonable; lógico. **rationale** n razón fundamental f. **rationalize** v racionalizar.

rattle ['ratl] n (toy) sonajero m; (football fan's) carraca f; ruido de sonajero; (train noise) traqueteo m; (chains) ruido metálico m; (door, window) golpe m; (teeth) castañeteo m; (machine gun) tableteo m; v hacer sonar; traquetear; hacer un ruido metálico; golpetear; castañetear; tabletear; (put off) desconcertar.

raucous ['ro:kəs] adj ronco.

ravage ['ravidʒ] n estrago m. v asolar.

rave [reiv] v delirar, desvariar. **rave over** entusiasmarse por. **raving** adj delirante.

raven ['reivən] n cuervo m.

ravenous ['ravənəs] adj hambriento. **be ravenous** tener um hambre canina.

ravine [rə'vi:n] n desfiladero m.

ravish ['ravɪʃ] v violar; raptar. **ravishing** adj encantador.

raw [rɔː] adj (uncooked) crudo; (unrefined) bruto; (inexperienced) novato; (nerves) a flor de piel; (flesh) vivo; (weather) frío y húmedo. **raw deal** (coll) injusticia f. **raw materials** materias primas f pl. **rawness** n crudeza f.

ray [rei] n rayo m; (line, fish) raya f.

rayon ['reiɒn] n rayón m.

razor ['reizə] n navaja f; (safety) maquinilla de afeitar f; (elec) máquina de afeitar eléctrica f. **razor blade** hoja de afeitar f.

re [riː] ref.

reach [riːtʃ] v (arrive at) llegar a; (achieve) lograr; (stretch out) extender; alcanzar. n alcance m; poder m; capacidad f. **out of reach** fuera del alcance. **within reach** al alcance.

react [ri'akt] v reaccionar. **reaction** n reacción f. **reactionary** n, adj reaccionario, -a. **reactor** n reactor m.

*read [riːd] v leer; estudiar; (public address) decir; (riddle) interpretar; (meter, etc.) marcar. **reader** n lector, -a m, f; (university) profesor, -a m, f; (book) libro de lectura m. **reading** n lectura f; estudio m; interpretación f. **reading-glass** n lente para leer m. **reading-lamp** lámpara de sobremesa f.

readjust [riːə'dʒʌst] v reajustar. **readjustment** n reajuste m.

ready ['redi] adj listo; pronto; a mano. **get ready** prepararse. **ready cash** dinero contante m. **ready-made** adj hecho. **readily** adv fácilmente; en seguida. **readiness** n prontitud f; facilidad f.

real [riəl] adj real, verdadero. **realism** n realismo m. **realist** n realista m, f. **reality** n realidad f, verdad f. **reality TV** telebasura f. **really** adv realmente, en verdad. **really?** ¿de veras?

realize ['riəlaiz] v (understand) darse cuenta de; (achieve) llevar a cabo; (make real) realizar. **realization** n comprensión f; realización f.

realm [relm] n reino m; (fig) esfera f.

reap [riːp] v segar; (fig) cosechar. **reaping** n siega f; cosecha f. **reaping machine** segadora mecánica f.

reappear [riːə'piə] v reaparecer. **reappearance** n reaparición f.

rear[1] [riə] adj posterior, de atrás. **rearadmiral** n contraalmirante m. **rearguard** n

retaguardia f. **rear-view mirror** retrovisor m. n parte posterior f, parte de atrás f; (of a column) cola f. **bring up the rear** cerrar la marcha.

rear[2] [riə] v (family) criar; (lift up) alzar, levantar; (horse, etc.) empinarse.

rearrange [riːə'reindʒ] v arreglar de otra manera; volver a arreglar. **rearrangement** n nuevo arreglo m.

reason ['riːzn] n razón f. v razonar. **reasonable** adj razonable. **reasoning** n razonamiento m.

reassure [riə'ʃuə] v asegurar de nuevo; confortar. **reassurance** n confianza restablecida f. **reassuring** adj tranquilizador.

rebate ['riːbeit] n rebaja f, descuento m.

rebel ['rebl] n(m+f), adj rebelde. v rebelarse. **rebellion** n rebelión f. **rebellious** adj rebelde.

rebound [ri'baund; n 'riːbaund] v rebotar. n rebote m.

rebuff [ri'bʌf] v rechazar. n desaire m.

*rebuild [riː'bild] v reedificar.

rebuke [ri'bjuːk] n censura f, reproche m. v censurar, reprochar.

recall [ri'kɔːl] v llamar; recordar. n llamada f; (dismissal) destitución f.

recant [ri'kant] v retractar.

recap ['riːkap] v (coll) recapitular. n recapitulación f.

recapture [riː'kaptʃə] v reconquistar; (recreate) hacer revivir. n reconquista f.

recede [ri'siːd] v retroceder; (tide) descender.

receipt [rə'siːt] n (act of receiving) recepción f; (slip of paper) recibo m.

receive [rə'siːv] v recibir; aceptar. **receiver** n (of loot) recibidor, -a m, f; (law) síndico m; (phone) auricular m.

recent ['riːsnt] adj reciente. **recently** adv recientemente.

receptacle [rə'septəkl] n receptáculo m.

reception [rə'sepʃən] n recepción f; acogida f. **receptionist** n recepcionista m, f. **receptive** adj receptivo.

recess [ri'ses] n (hollow) hueco m; (niche) nicho m; (parliament) período de clausura m; (rest) descanso m.

recession [rə'seʃən] n (comm) recesión f; (retreat) retroceso m.

recharge [riː'tʃɑːdʒ] v recargar.

recipe ['resəpi] n receta f.

recipient [rə'sipiənt] *n* (*receiver*) receptor, -a *m, f*; (*cheque, letter, etc.*) destinatario, -a *m, f*.

reciprocate [rə'siprəkeit] *v* corresponder; intercambiar. **reciprocating engine** motor alternativo *m*. **reciprocal** *adj* recíproco.

recite [rə'sait] *v* recitar. **recital** *n* (*a relating*) relato *m*; (*music*) recital *m*. **recitation** *n* relato *m*; recitación *f*.

reckless ['rekləs] *adj* temerario; audaz. **recklessness** *n* temeridad *f*; audacia *f*.

reckon ['rekən] *v* calcular; contar; considerar; (*coll*) creer. **reckoning** *n* cálculo *m*; cuenta *f*; (*fig*) retribución *f*.

reclaim [ri'kleim] *v* (*land*) ganar; (*reform*) reformar; (*by-product*) regenerar. **reclamation** *n* (*claiming back*) reclamación *f*; (*moral*) enmienda *f*; (*land*) aprovechamiento *m*; regeneración *f*.

recline [ri'klain] *v* apoyar; recostar.

recluse [rə'klu:s] *n* recluso, -a *m, f*.

recognize ['rekəgnaiz] *v* reconocer; confesar. **recognition** *n* reconocimiento *m*. **recognizable** *adj* identificable.

recoil [rə'koil; *n* 'ri:koil] *v* echarse atrás; (*gun*) dar culatazo; (*spring*) aflojarse. *n* culatazo *m*; aflojamiento *m*; (*repugnance*) asco *m*.

recollect [rekə'lekt] *v* acordarse de. **recollection** *n* recuerdo *m*.

recommence [rekə'mens] *v* empezar de nuevo.

recommend [rekə'mend] *v* recomendar; aconsejar. **recommendation** *n* recomendación *f*.

recompense ['rekəmpens] *n* recompensa *f*; (*law*) compensación *f*. *v* recompensar; compensar.

reconcile ['rekənsail] *v* (*dispute*) arreglar; (*individuals*) reconciliar; (*ideas*) conciliar. **reconcile oneself to** resignarse a. **reconciliation** *n* arreglo *m*; reconciliación *f*; conciliación *f*.

reconstruct [ri:kən'strʌkt] *v* (*building*) reconstruir; (*crime*) reconstituir. **reconstruction** *n* reconstrucción *f*; reconstitución *f*.

record [rə'ko:d; *n* 'reko:d] *v* registrar; tomar nota de; (*sound*) grabar. *n* registro *m*; anotación *f*; grabación *f*; disco *m*; (*account*) relación *f*; (*minutes*) actas *f pl*; (*personal history*) historial *m*; (*sport*) récord *m*. **long-playing record** disco de larga duración *m*. **record-player** *n* tocadiscos *m invar*.

recorded *adj* grabado; registrado. **recorded delivery** entrega registrada *f*. **recorder** *n* archivista *m, f*; (*music*) flauta *f*. **recording** *n* (*music*) grabación *f*.

recount [ri'kaunt; *n* 'ri:kaunt] *v* contar. *n* recuento *m*.

recoup [ri'ku:p] *v* (*recover*) recuperar; (*compensate*) indemnizar.

recover [rə'kʌvə] *v* (*get back*) recuperar; (*get well*) recobrar; ganar; obtener. **recovery** *n* recuperación *f*; (*med*) restablecimiento *m*.

recreation [rekri'eiʃən] *n* recreación *f*; (*school break*) recreo *m*.

recrimination [rəkrimi'neiʃən] *n* recriminación *f*. **recriminate** *v* recriminar.

recruit [rə'kru:t] *n* recluta *m*. *v* reclutar. **recruitment** *n* reclutamiento *m*.

rectangle ['rektaŋgl] *n* rectángulo *m*. **rectangular** *adj* rectangular.

rectify ['rektifai] *v* rectificar.

rectum ['rektəm] *n* recto *m*.

recuperate [rə'kju:pəreit] *v* recuperar; (*health*) recobrar. **recuperation** *n* recuperación *f*; (*health*) restablecimiento *m*.

recur [ri'kə:] *v* volver; repetirse. **recurrence** *n* vuelta *f*; repetición *f*; reaparición *f*. **recurrent** *adj also* **recurring** periódico; que vuelve; (*med*) recurrente.

recycle [ri:'saikl] *v* reciclar

recycling *n* reciclaje *m*.

red [red] *n* rojo *m*, colorado *m*. **in the red** deber dinero. *adj* rojo, colorado. **go red** ruborizarse. **Red Cross** Cruz Roja *f*. **redcurrant** grosella *f*. **red-handed** *adv* con las manos en la masa. **redhead** *n* pelirrojo, -a *m, f*. **red-hot** *adj* al rojo; ardiente. **red-letter day** día memorable *m*. **red-light district** barrio de mala fama *m*. **red tape** (*coll*) papeleo *m*. **redness** *n* color rojo *m*.

redeem [rə'di:m] *v* (*promise*) cumplir; (*mortgage*) amortizar; (*pawn*) desempeñar; (*fault*) expiar; (*rescue*) rescatar. **redemption** *n* cumplimiento *m*; amortización *f*; desempeño *m*; expiación *f*; rescate *m*; (*rel*) redención *f*. **beyond redemption** sin redención, irremediable.

redirect [ri:dai'rekt] *v* (*letter, etc.*) remitir al destinatario.

redress [rə'dres] *v* rectificar. *n* reparación *f*.

reduce [rə'dju:s] *v* reducir; rebajar; (*slim*) adelgazar. **reduction** *n* reducción *f*; (*length*) acortamiento *m*; (*width*) estrechamiento; (*weight*) adelgazamiento *m*; (*rank*) degradación f; (*prices*) disminución f; (*discount*) rebaja f; (*temperature*) baja f.

redundant [rə'dʌndənt] *adj* excesivo, superfluo. **be made redundant** perder su empleo. **redundancy** *n* desempleo *m*.

reed [ri:d] *n* caña f; (*of wind instrument*) lengüeta f.

reef [ri:f] *n* arrecife *m*.

reek [ri:k] *v* apestar. *n* tufo *m*.

reel[1] [ri:l] *n* (*cotton*) carrete *m*, bobina f; (*film*) cinta f; (*fishing*) carrete *m*. **reel off** (*recite*) recitar de un tirón.

reel[2] [ri:l] *v* (*sway*) hacer eses, dar vueltas.

refectory [rə'fektəri] *n* refectorio *m*.

refer [rə'fə:] *v* remitir; enviar; (*date, event*) situar; atribuir. **reference** *n* referencia f; alusión f; relación f; (*source of information*) fuente f; (*person*) fiador *m*. **reference book** libro de consulta *m*. **reference library** biblioteca de consulta f. **reference number** número de referencia *m*. **terms of reference** mandato *m*. **make reference to** referirse a. **without reference to** sin consultar. **with reference to** en cuanto a.

referee [refə'ri:] *n* árbitro *m*; (*guarantor of character*) garante *m*. *v* arbitrar.

referendum [refə'rendəm] *n* referéndum *m*.

refill [ri:'fil; *n* 'ri:fil] *v* rellenar. *n* recambio *m*; carga f.

refine [rə'fain] *v* refinar; purificar; (*technique*) perfeccionar; (*style*) pulir. **refinement** *n* (*person*) refinamiento *m*; (*manners*) finura f; (*sugar, oil*) refinado *m*; (*metal*) purificación f; (*technique*) perfeccionamiento *m*; (*style*) elegancia f. **refinery** *n* refinería f.

reflect [rə'flekt] *v* reflejar; (*think*) reflexionar. **reflection** *n* (*image*) reflejo *m*; (*act*) reflexión; meditación f; crítica f.

reflex ['ri:fleks] *nm, adj* reflejo. **reflexive** *adj* reflexivo.

reform [rə'fo:m] *v* reformar; formar de nuevo. *n* reforma f. **reformation** *n* reformación f. **reformed** *adj* reformado.

refract [rə'frakt] *v* refractar. **refraction** *n* refracción f.

refrain[1] [rə'frein] *v* abstenerse.

refrain[2] [rə'frein] *n* estribillo *m*.

refresh [rə'freʃ] *v* refrescar. **refresher course** cursillo de repaso *m*. **refreshing** *adj* refrescante. **refreshments** *pl n* refrescos *m pl*.

refrigerator [rə'fridʒəreitə] *n* refrigerador *m*, nevera f. **refrigerate** *v* refrigerar. **refrigeration** *n* refrigeración f.

refuel [ri:'fju:əl] *v* repostar(se).

refuge ['refju:dʒ] *n* refugio *m*; asilo *m*. **take refuge** refugiarse en. **refugee** *n* refugiado, -a *m, f*.

refund [ri'fʌnd; *n* 'ri:fʌnd] *v* reembolsar. *n* reembolso *m*.

refuse[1] [rə'fju:z] *v* negar. **refusal** *n* negativa f; (*rejection*) rechazo *m*.

refuse[2] ['refju:s] *n* basura f, desecho *m*, desperdicios *m pl*.

refute [ri'fju:t] *v* refutar.

regain [ri'gein] *v* recobrar; (*return to*) volver a.

regal ['ri:gəl] *adj* real, regio.

regard [rə'ga:d] *v* mirar; observar; considerar. **as regards** con respecto a. *n* mirada f; atención f; respeto *m*; aprecio *m*. **regards** *pl n* (*in a letter*) saludos *m pl*. **regarding** *prep* con respecto a. **regardless** *adv* a pesar de todo. **regardless of** sin tener en cuenta.

regatta [rə'gatə] *n* regata f.

regent ['ri:dʒənt] *n* regente *m, f*. **regency** *n* regencia f.

regime [rei'ʒi:m] *n* régimen *m*.

regiment ['redʒimənt] *n* regimiento *m*. **regimental** *adj* del regimiento.

region ['ri:dʒən] *n* región f. **regional** *adj* regional.

register ['redʒistə] *n* registro *m*; lista f. *v* registrar; (*a complaint*) presentar; (*luggage*) facturar; (*letter*) certificar; (*birth, death*) declarar. **registrar** *n* registrador *m*; (*med*) doctor, -a *m, f*. **registration** *n* (*trademark*) registro *m*; inscripción f; declaración f; certificación f; facturación f; matrícula f. **registration number** número de matrícula *m*. **registration plate** placa de matrícula f. **registry office** registro civil *m*.

regress [ri'gres] *v* retroceder. **regression** *n* regresión f.

regret [rə'gret] *v* sentir, lamentar. *n* sentimiento *m*; pesar *m*; arrepentimiento *m*; excusas *f pl*. **regrettable** *adj* lamentable; doloroso. **regretfully** (*adv*) lamentablemente.

regular ['regjulə] *adj* regular; normal; habituado. *n* (*mil*) regular; (*bar*) asiduo, -a *m, f*. **regularity** *n* regularidad f.

regulate ['regjuleit] v regular; ajustar.

regulation [regju'leiʃən] n regulación f; regla f. adj reglamentario.

rehabilitate [ri:hə'biliteit] v (reputation) rehabilitar; (for work) restaurar. **rehabilitation** n reconstrucción f; (med) reeducación f.

rehearse [rə'hə:s] v ensayar. **rehearsal** n ensayo m.

reign [rein] n reinado m; dominio m. v reinar.

reimburse [ri:im'bə:s] v reembolsar. **reimbursement** n reembolso m.

rein [rein] n rienda f; (fig) riendas f pl.

reincarnation [ri:inka:'neiʃən] n reencarnación f.

reindeer ['reindiə] n reno m.

reinforce [ri:in'fo:s] v reforzar. **reinforcement** n refuerzo m. **reinforced concrete** hormigón armado m.

reinstate [ri:in'steit] v reinstalar; restablecer. **reinstatement** n reintegración f, restablecimiento m.

reinvest [ri:in'vest] v reinvertir. **reinvestment** n reinversión f.

reissue [ri:'iʃu:] v (book) reeditar; (shares, stamps) volver a emitir.

reject [rə'dʒekt; n 'ri:dʒekt] v rechazar. n cosa defectuosa f. **rejection** n rechazamiento m; (a reject) cosa rechazada f.

rejoice [rə'dʒois] v alegrar, regocijar. **rejoicing** n alegría f, regocijo m.

rejoin [rə'dʒoin] v (reply) replicar; (club, society, etc.) reincorporarse a; (friends) reunirse con; (two objects) volver a unirse a.

rejuvenate [rə'dʒu:vəneit] v rejuvenecer. **rejuvenation** n rejuvenecimiento m.

relapse [rə'laps] n recaída f; (med) recidiva f. v recaer; reincidir.

relate [rə'leit] v (tell) contar; (be connected) relacionar. **related** adj (subjects) relacionado; (by birth or marriage) emparentado. **relating to** lo que tiene que ver con.

relation [rə'leiʃn] n (account) narración f; (relative) pariente, -a m. f; (connection) relación f. **relationship** n relación f; (kinship) parentesco m.

relative ['relətiv] adj relativo. n pariente, -a m. f. **relatively** adv relativamente. **relativity** n relatividad f.

relax [rə'laks] v relajar; (loosen) aflojar. **relaxation** n relajación f; descanso m; distracción f. **relaxing** adj relajante.

relay [ri'lei; n 'ri:lei] v transmitir. n relevo m. **relay race** carrera de relevos f.

release [rə'li:s] n liberación f; (exemption) exención f; (film, record) salida f; (information) anuncio m; (gas, steam) escape m. v liberar; (film, record) estrenar; anunciar; (let go) soltar; (mechanism) disparar.

relegate ['religeit] v relegar. **relegation** n relegación f.

relent [rə'lent] v ceder; enternecerse. **relentless** adj inexorable.

relevant ['reləvənt] adj pertinente; relativo; aplicable. **relevance** n pertinencia f; aplicabilidad f.

reliable [ri'laiəbl] adj de confianza; seguro. **reliability** n seguridad f; formalidad f.

reliance [rə'laiəns] n dependencia f; (trust) confianza f.

relic ['relik] n reliquia f; vestigio m.

relief [rə'li:f] n alivio m; (aid) socorro m; (for the poor) auxilio m; (substitute worker) relevo m; (geog, art) relieve m. adj suplementario.

relieve [rə'li:v] v aliviar; liberar; (replace) relevar; (help) socorrer.

religion [rə'lidʒən] n religión f. **religious** adj religioso.

relinquish [rə'liŋkwiʃ] v renunciar.

relish ['reliʃ] v (food) saborear; (enjoy) disfrutar. n gusto m; atracción f; entusiasmo m; (food) condimento m.

relive [ri:'liv] v volver a vivir, revivir.

relocate [ri:lou'keit] v reubicar, trasladar

reluctant [rə'lʌktənt] adj maldispuesto. **reluctance** n resistencia f. **reluctantly** adv de mala gana.

rely [rə'lai] v **rely on** contar con, confiar en.

remain [rə'mein] v quedarse. **remainder** n residuo m; resto m. **remains** pl n restos m pl; ruinas f pl.

remand [rə'ma:nd] v reencarcelar. n reencarcelamiento m. **be on remand** estar detenido.

remark [rə'ma:k] n observación f; comentario m. v observar, notar; hacer una observación. **remarkable** adj notable.

remarry [ri:'mari] v volver a casarse. **remarriage** n segundas nupcias f pl.

remedy ['remədi] n remedio m. v remediar. **remedial** adj remediador; reparador.

remember [ri'membə] v recordar, acordarse de. **remembrance** *n* recuerdo *m*.

remind [rə'maind] *v* recordar. **reminder** *n* advertencia *f*; (*comm*) notificación *f*.

reminiscence [remə'nisens] *n* reminiscencia *f*. **reminisce** *v* recordar el pasado. **reminiscent** *adj* evocador. **be reminiscent of** recordar.

remiss [rə'mis] *adj* descuidado.

remission [rə'miʃn] *n* remisión *f*, perdón *m*; exoneración *f*.

remit [rə'mit] *v* (*send*) remitir; (*forgive*) perdonar; (*return to a lower court*) devolver a un tribunal inferior. **remittance** *n* remesa *f*.

remnant ['remnənt] *n* resto *m*; (*fabric*) retal *m*.

remorse [rə'mo:s] *n* remordimiento *m*. **remorseful** *adj* arrepentido. **remorseless** *adj* sin remordimientos.

remote [rə'mout] *adj* (*distant*) lejano; (*in time or space*) remoto; (*slight*) ligero; (*out-of-the-way*) retirado; (*stand-offish*) distante. **remote control** mando a distancia *m*.

remove [rə'mu:v] *v* quitar; sacar; separar; (*move house*) mudar. **removal** *n* mudanza *f*; (*transfer*) traslado *m*; (*from office*) despido *m*.

remunerate [rə'mju:nəreit] *v* remunerar. **remuneration** *n* remuneración *f*. **remunerative** *adj* remunerador.

renaissance [rə'neisəns] *n* renacimiento *m*.

rename [ri:'neim] *v* poner un nuevo nombre a.

render ['rendə] *v* (*comm*) rendir; dar; (*a service*) hacer; (*assistance*) prestar; interpretar; (*fat*) derretir. **rendering** *n also* **rendition** interpretación *f*.

rendezvous ['rondivu:] *n* cita *f*. *v* reunir.

renegade ['renigeid] *n, adj* renegado, -a.

renew [rə'nju:] *v* renovar; (*extend*) prorrogar; (*efforts*) reanudar. **renewable** *adj* removable. **renewal** *n* renovación *f*; prórroga *f*; (*continuation after interruption*) reanudación *f*.

renounce [ri'nauns] *v* renunciar. **renunciation** *n* renunciación *f*.

renovate ['renəveit] *v* renovar; reformar. **renovation** *n* renovación *f*; reforma *f*.

renown [rə'naun] *n* renombre *m*, fama *f*. **renowned** *adj* renombrado, afamado.

rent [rent] *n* alquiler *m*. **rent-free** sin pagar alquiler. *v* alquilar. **rental** *n* alquiler *m*.

reopen [ri:'oupən] *v* volver a abrir. **reopen-**

ing *n* reapertura *f*.

reorganize [ri:'o:gənaiz] *v* reorganizar. **reorganization** *n* reorganización *f*.

rep [rep] *n* (*coll*) viajante *m*.

repair [ri'peə] *v* reparar; componer. *n* reparación *f*; compostura *f*; arreglo *m*. **beyond repair** no tener arreglo. **closed for repairs** cerrado por reformas.

repartee [repa:'ti:] *n* respuesta aguda *f*; (*coll*) dimes y diretes *m pl*.

repatriate [ri:'patrieit] *v* repatriar. **repatriation** *n* repatriación *f*.

*repay [ri'pei] *v* (*money*) devolver; (*debt*) liquidar; (*a person*) compensar; (*return*) corresponder a. **repayment** *n* devolución *f*, pago *m*; (*reward*) recompensa *f*.

repeal [ri'pi:l] *v* revocar, abrogar. *n* revocación *f*, abrogación *f*.

repeat [ri'pi:t] *v* repetir; recitar. *n* repetición *f*.

repel [ri'pel] *v* repeler; rechazar. **repellent** *adj* repelente.

repent [rə'pent] *v* arrepentirse de. **repentance** *n* arrepentimiento *m*. **repentant** *adj* arrepentido.

repercussion [ri:pə'kʌʃən] *n* repercusión *f*.

repertoire ['repətwa:] *n also* **repertory** repertorio *m*.

repetition [repə'tiʃn] *n* repetición *f*. **repetitive** *adj* reiterativo.

replace [rə'pleis] *v* (*substitute*) sustituir; (*put back*) reponer. **replacement** *n* repuesto *m*; (*person*) sustituto, -a *m, f*.

replay [ri:'plei; *n* 'ri:plei] *v* (*sport*) volver a jugar; (*music*) volver a tocar. *n* (*sport*) repetición de un partido *f*; (*television*) repetición *f*.

replenish [rə'pleniʃ] *v* rellenar. **replenishment** *n* relleno *m*.

replica ['replikə] *n* réplica *f*, copia *f*.

reply [rə'plai] *v* responder, contestar. *n* respuesta *f*, contestación *f*.

report [rə'po:t] *n* (*spoken account*) relato *m*; (*piece of news*) noticia *f*; (*official*) informe *m*; (*newspaper or broadcast story*) reportaje *m*; (*reputation*) fama *f*, (*school*) boletín *m*; (*explosion*) estampido *m*. *v* relatar; (*for a newspaper*) hacer la crónica de; (*message*) repetir; (*denounce*) denunciar; presentar un informe. **reporter** *n* reportero *m*, periodista *m, f*.

repose [rə'pouz] *n* reposo *m*, descanso *m*. *v*

reposar, descansar.

represent [reprə'zent] v representar. **representation** n representación f.

representative [reprə'zentətiv] adj representativo. n representante m, f.

repress [rə'pres] v reprimir. **repression** n represión f. **repressive** adj represivo.

reprieve [rə'priːv] n (law) indulto m; (fig: relief) alivio m. v indultar; aliviar.

reprimand ['reprimaːnd] n reprimenda f. v reprender.

reprint ['riːprint; v riː'print] n reimpresión f. v reimprimir.

reprisal [rə'praizəl] n represalia f.

reproach [rə'prəutʃ] v reprochar. n reproche m. **reproachful** adj reprensor, acusador.

reproduce [riːprə'djuːs] v reproducir. **reproduction** n reproducción f. **reproductive** adj reproductor.

reprove [rə'pruːv] v reprobar, censurar. **reproof** n reprobación f. censura f.

reptile ['reptail] n reptil m.

republic [rə'pʌblik] n república f. **republican** n. adj republicano, -a.

repudiate [rə'pjuːdieit] v (person) repudiar; (reject) rechazar; (contract) negarse a cumplir. **repudiation** n repudiación f; rechazo m; desconocimiento m.

repugnant [rə'pʌgnənt] adj repugnante. **repugnance** n repugnancia f.

repulsion [rə'pʌlʃn] n repulsión f. **repulsive** adj repulsivo. **repulsiveness** n carácter repulsivo m.

repute [rə'pjuːt] n reputación f. **reputable** adj acreditado. **reputation** n reputación f. **reputed** adj supuesto.

request [ri'kwest] n ruego m; demanda f. **at the request of** a petición de. v rogar, pedir. **request stop** parada discrecional f.

requiem ['rekwiəm] n réquiem m.

require [rə'kwaiə] v (need) requerir; (demand) exigir; (desire) desear. **requirement** n requisito m; necesidad f.

requisite ['rekwizit] adj necesario, indispensable.

requisition [ˌrekwi'ziʃən] n demanda f; pedido m. v requisar.

***reread** [riː'riːd] v releer.

re-route [riː'ruːt] v cambiar el itinerario de.

***rerun** [riː'rʌn; n 'riːrʌn] v (film) reestrenar; (race) correr de nuevo. n reestreno m.

resale [riː'seil] n reventa f.

rescue ['reskjuː] n rescate m. **rescue operations** operaciones de salvamento f pl. **go to the rescue of** ir en auxilio de. v rescatar, salvar. **rescuer** n rescatador, -a m, f; salvador, -a m, f.

research [ri'səːtʃ] n investigación f. v investigar. **researcher** n investigador, -a m, f.

***resell** [riː'sel] v revender.

resemble [rə'zembl] v parecerse a. **resemblance** n parecido m.

resent [ri'zent] v tomar a mal; ofenderse por. **resentful** adj resentido; ofendido. **resentment** n resentimiento m.

reserve [rə'zəːv] v reservar. n reserva f; (mil) reservista m. **reservation** n reserva f. **reserved** adj reservado.

reservoir ['rezəvwaː] n represa f, embalse m.

reside [rə'zaid] v residir. **residence** n (building) residencia f; (stay) permanencia f. **resident** n(m + f), adj residente. **residential** adj residencial.

residue ['rezidjuː] n residuo m. **residual** adj residual.

resign [rə'zain] v renunciar; (hand over) ceder. **resign oneself to** resignarse a. **resignation** n renuncia f; (from a post) dimisión f; resignación f. **resigned** adj resignado.

resilient [rə'ziliənt] adj elástico; (human body) resistente; (person) de carácter fuerte. **resilience** n elasticidad f; resistencia f; fuerza moral f.

resin ['rezin] n resina f.

resist [rə'zist] v resistir; (bear) aguantar; (impede) impedir. **resistance** n resistencia f; aguante f. **resistant** adj resistente.

***resit** [riː'sit] v (exam) representarse.

resolute ['rezəluːt] adj resuelto.

resolve [rə'zolv] v resolverse. **resolution** n resolución f.

resonant ['rezənənt] adj resonante. **resonance** n resonancia f. **resonate** v resonar.

resort [rə'zoːt] n estación f; centro m; recurso m. **as a last resort** como último recurso. v. **resort to** recurrir a.

resound [rə'zaund] v resonar; (fig) tener resonancias. **resounding** adj resonante; sonoro; (fig) tremendo.

resource [rə'zoːs] n recurso m; expediente m. **resourceful** adj ingenioso, inventivo.

resourcefulness *n* ingenio *m*, inventiva *f*.

respect [rə'spekt] *n* respeto *m*; consideración *f*; (*aspect*) aspecto *m*. **pay one's respects to** presentar sus respetos a. **with respect to** con respecto a. *v* respetar.

respectable *adj* respetable; decente.

respectful *adj* respetuoso. **respective** *adj* respectivo.

respiration [respə'reiʃn] *n* respiración *f*.

respite ['respait] *n* respiro *m*.

respond [rə'spond] *v* contestar; responder; reaccionar. **response** *n* respuesta *f*. **responsive** *adj* sensible.

responsible [rə'sponsəbl] *adj* responsable. **responsibility** *n* responsabilidad *f*.

rest¹ [rest] *n* descanso *m*; reposo *m*; (*music*) pausa *f*; tranquilidad *f*; (*support*) apoyo *m*. *v* descansar; (*stop*) pararse; (*stay*) quedar; (*decision*) depender de; (*lean*) apoyar. **restful** *adj* descansado; tranquilo. **restive** *adj* inquieto. **restless** *adj* desasosegado.

rest² [rest] *n* (*remainder*) resto *m*. **the rest** lo demás.

restaurant ['restront] *n* restaurant(e) *m*, restorán *m*. **restaurant car** coche restaurante *m*.

restore [rə'sto:] *v* restaurar; restablecer; (*return*) restituir; (*repair*) reformar; (*to former rank*) rehabilitar. **restoration** *n* restauración *f*; restablecimiento *m*; (*returning*) restituición *f*.

restrain [rə'strein] *v* impedir; limitar; (*repress*) contener. **restraint** *n* restricción *f*; limitación *f*; (*feelings*) represión *f*; moderación *f*.

restrict [rə'strikt] *v* restringir. **restricted** *adj* restringido; (*outlook*) estrecho. **restriction** *n* restricción *f*. **restrictive** *adj* restrictivo.

result [rə'zʌlt] *n* resultado *m*. *v* resultar. **result from** derivarse de. **result in** tener por resultado. **resultant** *adj* resultante.

resume [rə'zju:m] *v* reanudar. **resumption** *n* reanudación *f*.

résumé ['reizumei] *n* resumen *m*; (*CV (US)*) currículum *m*.

resurgence [ri'sə:dʒəns] *n* resurgimiento *m*.

resurrect [rezə'rekt] *v* resucitar. **resurrection** *n* resurrección *f*.

resuscitate [rə'sʌsəteit] *v* resucitar. **resuscitation** *n* resucitación *f*.

retail ['ri:teil] *n* venta al por menor. *adj, adv* al por menor. *v* vender al por menor; (*relate*) contar. **retailer** *n* vendedor al por menor.

retain [rə'tein] *v* (*keep*) quedarse con; conservar; retener.

retaliate [rə'talieit] *v* vengarse. **retaliation** *n* venganza *f*. **in retaliation** para vengarse.

retard [rə'ta:d] *v* retardar, retrasar. **retarded** *adj* atrasado.

retch [retʃ] *v* tener arcadas

reticent ['retisənt] *adj* reservado. **reticence** *n* reserva *f*.

retina ['retinə] *n* retina *f*.

retinue ['retinju:] *n* comitiva *f*.

retire [rə'taiə] *v* (*from work*) jubilarse; (*draw back*) retirarse; (*go to bed*) recogerse. **retired** *adj* (*trader, soldier*) retirado; (*civilian*) jubilado. **retirement** *n* retiro *m*; jubilación *f*.

retort¹ [rə'to:t] *v* replicar. *n* réplica *f*.

retort² [rə'to:t] *n* (*chem*) retorta *f*.

retrace [ri'treis] *v* volver a trazar; repasar. **retrace one's steps** desandar lo andado.

retract [rə'trakt] *v* retractar. **retraction** *n* retractación *f*, retracción *f*.

retrain [ri:'trein] *v* reconvertir

retreat [rə'tri:t] *v* retirarse; retroceder, *n* retirada *f*; (*place*) retiro *m*.

retrial [ri:'traiəl] *n* nuevo juicio *m*.

retrieve [rə'tri:v] *v* recuperar; (*from ruin*) salvar; (*hunting*) cobrar. **retrieval** *n* recuperación *f*. **retriever** *n* (*dog*) perro cobrador *m*.

retrograde ['retrəgreid] *adj* a retrógrado.

retrospect ['retrəspekt] *n* **in retrospect** retrospectivamente. **retrospective** *adj* retrospectivo.

return [rə'tə:n] *v* devolver; (*refund*) reembolsar; (*lost or stolen property*) restituir; (*investment*) dar; (*elect*) elegir; (*come back*) volver. **return a call** devolver una visita. *n* vuelta *f*, retorno *m*; (*reward*) recompensa *f*; restitución *f*; (*profit*) ganancias *f pl*; (*interest*) interés *m*; (*tax*) declaración *f*; (*ballot*) resultados *m pl*. **many happy returns!** ¡feliz cumpleaños! **return ticket** billete de ida y vuelta *m*. **in return** en recompensa. **on sale or return** en depósito.

reunite [ri:ju'nait] *v* reunir. **reunion** *n* reunión *f*.

rev [rev] (*mot*) *n* revolución *f*. **rev counter** cuentarrevoluciones *m invar*. **rev up** acelerar.

reveal [rə'viːl] v revelar, descubrir. **revealing** adj revelador. **revelation** n revelación f.

revel ['revl] v jaranear, ir de juerga. n jarana f, juerga f. **revelry** n jolgorio m.

revenge [rə'vendʒ] n venganza f. v vengar. **take revenge for** vengarse de.

revenue ['revinjuː] n (from taxes) rentas públicas f pl; (income) entrada f.

reverberate [rə'bəːbəreit] v reverberar, reflejar. **reverberation** n reverberación f.

reverence ['revərəns] n reverencia f, veneración f. **revere** v reverenciar, venerar. **reverent** adj reverente, respetuoso.

reverse [rə'vəːs] n lo contrario; (cloth) revés m; (coin) cruz f; (printed form) dorso m; (mot: gear) marcha atrás f. adj opuesto; contrario; inverso. v invertir; (turn the other way round) volver al revés; (decision) revocar; (car) dar marcha atrás. **reverse the charges** (phone) poner una conferencia a cobro revertido. **reversal** n inversión f. **reversible** adj reversible.

revert [rə'vəːt] v volver; revertir.

review [rə'vjuː] n examen m; crítica f; (mil, theatre) revista f. v examinar; volver a examinar; hacer una crítica de. **reviewer** n crítico, -a m, f.

revise [rə'vaiz] v revisar; corregir. **revision** n repaso m; corrección f.

revive [rə'vaiv] v (med) reanimar, resucitar; (trade) reactivar; (play) reponer; (custom) restablecer; (interest) renovar; (hopes) despertar. **revival** n reanimación f; resucitación f; reactivación f; restablecimiento m; (interest) renacimiento f.

revoke [rə'vouk] v revocar; (withdraw) suspender.

revolt [rə'voult] n rebelión f. v (offend) dar asco a; rebelarse. **revolting** adj asqueroso.

revolution [revə'luːʃən] n revolución f. **revolutionary** n, adj revolucionario, -a. **revolutionize** v revolucionar.

revolve [rə'volv] v girar. **revolver** n revólver m. **revolving door** puerta giratoria f.

revue [rə'vjuː] n revista f.

revulsion [rə'vʌlʃən] n repulsión f.

reward [rə'woːd] n premio m, recompensa f. v premiar, recompensar. **rewarding** adj gratificante, provechoso.

*****rewind** [riːˈwaind] v (film, tape) rebobinar.

rewinding n rebobinado m.

*****rewrite** [riːˈrait] v volver a escribir; volver a redactar.

rewire [riːˈwaiə] v reformar la instalación

rhesus ['riːsəs] n macaco de la India m. **rhesus factor** factor Rhesus m.

rhetoric ['retərik] n retórica f. **rhetorical** adj retórico.

rheumatism ['ruːmətizəm] n reumatismo m, reúma m. **rheumatic** adj reumático.

rhinoceros [rai'nosərəs] n rinoceronte m.

rhododendron [roudə'dendrən] n rododendro m.

rhubarb ['ruːbaːb] n ruibarbo m.

rhyme [raim] n rima f. v rimar.

rhythm ['riðəm] n ritmo m. **rhythmic** adj rítmico.

rib [rib] n costilla f; (umbrella) varilla f; (knitting) cordoncillo m.

ribbon ['ribən] n cinta f. **in ribbons** hecho jirones.

rice [rais] n arroz m.

rich [ritʃ] adj rico. **riches** pl n riqueza f sing. **richness** n abundancia f; fertilidad f

rickety ['rikəti] adj tambaleante.

*****rid** [rid] v librar, desembarazar. **get rid of** deshacerse de. **riddance** n libramiento m. **good riddance!** ¡menudo alivio!

riddle[1] ['ridl] n enigma m; acertijo m.

riddle[2] ['ridl] v cribar.

*****ride** [raid] v montar; (horse) montar a caballo. **ride a bicycle/motorbike** montar en bicicleta/motocicleta. n vuelta f, paseo m; (journey) viaje m. **rider** n (horse) jinete m; (addition) cláusula adicional f. **riding** n equitación f.

ridge [ridʒ] n (hills) cadena f; (crest) cumbre f; (surface) ondulación f; (roof) caballete m.

ridicule ['ridikjuːl] n ridículo m. v ridiculizar. **ridiculous** adj ridículo.

rife [raif] adj abundante.

rifle[1] ['raifl] n fusil m. **rifle range** campo de tiro m.

rifle[2] ['raifl] v saquear.

rift [rift] n (fissure) grieta f; (in clouds) claro m; (fig) ruptura f.

rig [rig] n (naut) aparejo m. v (mast) enjarciar; preparar; arreglar; equipar; (election) amañar. **rig out** ataviar. **rig up** improvisar. **rigging** n aparejo m; montaje m; equipo m.

right [rait] *adj* (*not left*) derecho; bueno; bien; justo; correcto; exacto. **be right** tener razón. *adv* a la derecha; (*straight*) derecho; bien; correctamente; exactamente; inmediatamente. *n* bien *m*; justicia *f*; (*divine, to the throne etc.*) derecho *m*; (*right hand*) derecha *f*. **civil rights** *pl n* derechos civiles *m pl*. **right angle** ángulo recto *m*. **right-handed** *adj* que usa la mano derecha. **right-of-way** *n* (*public*) servidumbre de paso *m*; (*roads*) prioridad *f*. **right-wing** *adj* (*pol*) derechista.

righteous ['raitʃəs] *adj* justo, honrado.

rightful ['raitfəl] *adj* legítimo.

rigid ['ridʒid] *adj* rígido; severo. **rigidity** *n* rigidez *f*; severidad *f*.

rigmarole ['rigməroul] *n* (*coll*) galimatías *m invar*.

rigour ['rigə] *n* rigor *m*; severidad *f*. **rigorous** *adj* riguroso; severo.

rim [rim] *m* (*cup*) borde *m*; (*wheel*) llanta *f*.

rind [raind] *n* (*fruit*) cáscara *f*; (*cheese, bacon*) corteza *f*.

ring¹ [riŋ] *n* (*finger*) anillo *m*, sortija *f*; círculo *m*; (*napkin*) aro *m*; (*keys*) llavero *m*. *v* formar círculo. **ringleader** *n* cabecilla *m*. **ring road** carretera de circunvalación *f*.

*ring² [riŋ] *v* (*bell*) sonar; llamar (por teléfono); (*ears*) zumbar. **ring off** (*phone*) colgar. **ring up** (*phone*) llamar (por teléfono); (*curtain*) subir. *n* (*phone*) llamada *f*; (*sound*) sonido *m*; (*large bell*) campaneo *m*; (*electric bell*) toque *m*; (*alarm clock*) timbre *m*; (*laughter*) cascabeleo *m*.

rink [riŋk] *n* (*ice-skating*) pista de hielo *f*; (*roller-skating*) pista de patinaje *f*.

rinse [rins] *v* aclarar. *n* aclarado *m*.

riot ['raiət] *n* revuelta *f*. **run riot** desmandarse. *v* alborotarse. **rioter** *n* alborotador, -a *m, f*. **riotous** *adj* alborotado.

rip [rip] *v* rasgar. **rip off** *or* **out** arrancar. *n* rasgón *m*, rasgadura *f*. **rip-off** *n* (*coll: swindle*) una estafa *f*.

ripe [raip] *adj* maduro. **ripen** *v* madurar. **ripeness** *n* madurez *f*.

ripple ['ripl] *n* rizo *m*; (*sound of water*) chapoteo *m*; (*conversation*) murmullo *m*. *v* rizar.

*rise [raiz] *v* (*get up*) levantarse; (*in the air*) elevarse; (*temperature, slope*) subir; (*in rank*) ascender; salir; crecer; desarrollarse; (*revolt*) sublevarse. **rising** *adj* naciente; ascendente; creciente. *n* (*sun, moon*) salida *f*; (*tide*) flujo *m*; (*water level*) crecida *f*; (*slope, temperature, curtain*) subida *f*; (*hill*) elevación *f*; (*development*) desarrollo *m*; (*prices, rate, pressure*) aumento *m*. **give rise to** provocar.

risk [risk] *n* riesgo *m*, peligro *m*. **at risk** a riesgo. *v* arriesgar. **risky** *adj* arriesgado.

rissole ['risoul] *n* croqueta *f*.

rite [rait] *n* rito *m*.

ritual ['ritʃuəl] *nm, adj* ritual.

rival ['raivəl] *n*(*m + f*), *adj* rival. *v* competir con. **rivalry** *n* rivalidad *f*, competencia *f*.

river ['rivə] *n* río *m*. **riverside** *n* ribera *f*.

River Plate *n* Río de la Plata *m*.

rivet ['rivit] *n* remache *m*, roblón *m*. *v* (*tech*) remachar; (*fig*) fijar; (*fig*) cautivar. **riveting** *adj* cautivador.

road [roud] *n* camino *m*; carretera *f*; (*in town*) calle *f*. **road-block** *n* barricada *f*. **road-side** *n* borde de la carretera *m*. **road rage** conducta agresiva de los conductores *f*. **road sign** señal de tráfico *f*. **roadway** *n* calzada *f* **roadworks** *pl n* obras *f pl*.

roam [roum] *v* rondar, vagar por.

roar [ro:] *v* (*lion*) rugir; (*bull, sea, wind*) bramar; (*engine*) zumbar; (*shout*) vociferar. **roar with anger** rugir de cólera. **roar with laughter** reírse a carcajadas. *n* rugido *m*; bramido *m*; zumbido *m*; (*crowd*) clamor *m*; vociferaciones *f pl*.

roast [roust] *v* (*meat*) asar; (*coffee*) tostar. *nm, adj* asado.

rob [rob] *v* robar, hurtar. **robber** *n* ladrón, -ona *m, f*. **robbery** *n* robo *m*, hurto *m*.

robe [roub] *n* (*judge's*) toga *f*; (*dressing gown*) bata *f*; (*costume*) traje *m*; (*monk's*) hábito *m*. *v* vestir.

robin ['robin] *n* petirrojo *m*.

robot ['roubot] *n* robot *m*.

robust [rə'bʌst] *adj* robusto, vigoroso.

rock¹ [rok] *n* roca *f*; (*in the sea*) peña *f*; (*stone*) piedra *f*; (*sweet*) pirulí *m*.

rock² [rok] *v* (*cradle*) mecer; (*move*) balancear; (*shake*) sacudir. *n* (*music*) rock *m*. **rocking chair** mecedora *f*. **rocking-horse** *n* caballito de balancín *m*.

rocket ['rokit] *n* cohete *m*. *v* (*prices*) subir vertiginosamente.

rod [rod] *n* (*pole*) barra *f*; (*fishing*) caña *f*; (*curtain*) varilla *f*.

rode [roud] *V* **ride**.

rodent ['roudənt] *n* roedor *m*.

roe [rou] n (*fish eggs*) hueva f. **soft roe** lechas f pl.

rogue [roug] n granuja m, pícaro m. **roguish** adj pícaro, picaresco. **roguishness** n picardía f.

role [roul] n papel m.

roll [roul] n (*paper, film, butter, tobacco*) rollo m; (*bread*) panecillo m; (*cloth*) pieza f; (*register*) registro m; (*list of names*) nómina f; (*thunder*) fragor m; (*drum*) redoble m. **roll-call** n lista f. **roll of honour** lista de honor f. v hacer rodar; (*cigarettes*) liar; (*waves*) arrastrar. **roll along** rodar. **roll over** dar una vuelta. **roller** n (*lawn*) rodillo m. **rollerblade** v patinar. **roller-coaster** n montaña rusa f. **roller-skate** n patín de ruedas m. **rolling-pin** n rodillo m.

romance [rou'mans] n (*love*) amores m pl; aventura amorosa f; (*story*) novela romántica f. adj (*language*) romance. v fantasear. **romantic** n, adj romántico, -a.

Rome [roum] n Roma. **Roman** n, adj romano, -a. **Roman Catholic** n, adj católico romano, católica romana. **Roman numeral** número romano m.

romp [romp] n retozo m. v retozar.

roof [ru:f] n, pl **roofs** (*building*) tejado m; (*cave, car, etc.*) techo m. **roof of the mouth** cielo de la boca m. **roof rack** baca f.

rook [ruk] n (*bird*) grajo m; (*chess*) torre f.

room [ru:m] n cuarto m; (*public*) sala f; (*hotel*) habitación de hotel f; (*space*) sitio m; (*accommodation*) alojamiento m. **double room** habitación de matrimonio f. **make room for** dejar sitio. **room and board** cama y comida f, pensión completa f. **room-mate** n compañero/compañera de habitación m, f. **room service** servicio de habitaciones m, **single room** habitación individual f. **roomy** adj espacioso.

roost [ru:st] n percha f; gallinero m. v posarse. **rooster** n gallo m.

root¹ [ru:t] n raíz f; origen m. v echar raíces; (*become fixed*) arraigar.

root² [ru:t] v (*pigs*) hozar.

rope [roup] n cuerda f; (*pearls*) sarta f. **know the ropes** estar al tanto. **learn the ropes** ponerse al tanto. v (*tie*) amarrar; (*lasso*) coger con lazo. **rope off** acordonar. **ropy** adj (*coll*) malo.

rosary ['rouzəri] n rosario m.

rose¹ [rouz] n rosa f. **rose-bush** n rosal m. **rose garden** rosaleda f. **rosewood** n pali-

sandro m. **rosy** adj rosado.

rose² [rouz] V **rise**.

rosemary ['rouzməri] n romero m.

rosette [rou'zet] n escarapela f.

*rot [rot] v pudrirse. n putrefacción f; (*substance*) podredumbre f; (*coll: rubbish*) bobadas f pl. **rotten** adj podrido; (*coll: bad*) pésimo; (*coll: ill*) fatal.

rota ['routə] n lista f.

rotate [rou'teit] v (hacer) girar, (hacer) dar vueltas; (*crops*) alternar. **rotary** adj rotatorio, rotativo. **rotation** n giro m; revolución f.

rouge [ru:ʒ] n colorete m.

rough [rʌf] adj (*surface*) áspero; (*coarse*) tosco; duro; brutal; (*draft*) aproximado. **rough-and-ready** adj improvisado. **roughage** (*for people*) fibra f; (*for animals*) forraje m. **rough copy** or **draft** borrador m. v **rough it** (*coll*) vivir sin comodidades. **roughly** adv más o menos. **roughness** n aspereza f; tosquedad f; brutalidad f; dureza f.

roulette [ru:'let] n ruleta f.

round [raund] adj redondo. prep alrededor de. n círculo m; esfera f; (*slice*) rodaja f; (*patrol, drinks*) ronda f; (*ammunition*) andanada f; (*applause*) salva f. v redondear; dar la vuelta; doblar. **round off** acabar. **round up** acorralar; reunir; (*figure*) redondear.

roundabout ['raundəbaut] n (*mot*) plaza circular f; (*fair*) tiovivo m. adj indirecto.

rouse [rauz] v despertar; animar.

route [ru:t] n ruta f, itinerario m.

routine [ru:'tim] adj rutinario. n rutina f.

rove [rouv] v vagar, errar.

row¹ [rou] n (*file*) fila f; (*knitting*) vuelta f.

row² [rou] v (*boat*) remar; (*a person*) llevar a remo. **rowing** n remo m. **rowing boat** n bote de remos m.

row³ [rou] n (*quarrel*) bronca f; (*fuss*) jaleo m; (*noise*) alboroto m. v reñir.

rowdy ['raudi] n(m + f), adj camorrista. **rowdiness** n alboroto m; ruido m.

royal ['roiəl] adj real, regio. **royalist** n monárquico, -a m, f. **royalties** pl n derechos de autor m pl. **royalty** n realeza f.

rub [rʌb] n frotamiento m. v frotar. **rubbing** n (*brass, etc.*) frotamiento m.

rubber ['rʌbə] n caucho m, goma f; (*eraser*) goma de borrar f. **rubber band** goma f.

rubber stamp sello de goma *m*. **rubber tree** gomero *m*. **rubbery** *adj* parecido a la goma.

rubbish ['rʌbiʃ] *n* (*refuse*) basura *f*; (*waste*) desperdicios *m pl*; (*derog*) porquería *f*; (*nonsense*) tonterías *f pl*.

rubble ['rʌbl] *n* escombros *m pl*.

ruby ['ru:bi] *n* rubí *m*.

rucksack ['rʌksak] *n* mochila *f*.

rudder ['rʌdə] *n* timón *m*.

rude [ru:d] *adj* (*coarse*) grosero; (*impolite*) descortés; (*rough*) tosco; (*hard*) duro; (*painful*) penoso; (*health*) robusto. **rudeness** *n* grosería *f*; descortesía *f*; indecencia *f*.

rudiment ['ru:dimənt] *n* rudimento *m*. **rudimentary** *adj* rudimentario.

rueful ['ru:fəl] *adj* contrito; vergonzoso; triste. **ruefully** *adv* tristemente. **ruefulness** *n* tristeza *f*, aflicción *f*.

ruff [rʌf] *n* (*dress*) gorguera *f*; (*on animals*) collarín *m*.

ruffian ['rʌfiən] *n* rufián *m*.

ruffle ['rʌfl] *v* (*disturb*) agitar; (*hair*) desgreñar; (*feathers*) erizar; (*cloth*) fruncir; (*wrinkle*) arrugar; (*worry*) perturbar.

rug [rʌg] *n* (*carpet*) alfombra *f*; (*small carpet*) tapete *m*; (*blanket*) manta de viaje *f*.

rugged ['rʌgid] *adj* (*rock*) escarpado; (*ground*) accidentado; (*character*) desabrido; (*face*) duro; (*climate*) riguroso. **ruggedness** *n* lo escarpado; lo accidentado; desabrimiento *m*; dureza *f*.

ruin ['ru:in] *n* ruina *f*. *v* arruinar. **ruinous** *adj* ruinoso.

rule [ru:l] *n* regla *f*; mando *m*, gobierno *m*. **as a rule** por regla general. **rule of the road** reglamento del tráfico *m*. **rules and regulations** reglamento *m sing*. *v* mandar, gobernar; (*lines*) tirar (una línea). **rule out** excluir. **ruler** *n* gobernante *m*, *f*; soberano, -a *m*, *f*; (*measuring*) regla *f*. **ruling** *n* (*law*) decisión *f*.

rum [rʌm] *n* ron *m*.

rumble ['rʌmbl] *n* mido sordo *m*; (*stomach*) borborigmo *m*. *v* retumbar; (*stomach*) sonar.

rummage ['rʌmidʒ] *v* revolver. **rummage sale** venta de prendas usadas *f*.

rumour ['ru:mə] *n* rumor *m*. **it is rumoured (that)** se rumorea (que).

rump [rʌmp] *n* (*quadruped*) ancas *f pl*; (*person*) trasero *m*; (*cookery*) cuarto trasero *m*.

*run [rʌn] *v* correr; circular; (*theatre*) estar en cartel; (*leak*) salirse; (*car*) marchar; (*machine*) funcionar; (*melt*) derretirse; (*colours*) desteñirse; (*road*) pasar; (*stockings*) hacerse una carrerilla. *n* (*race*) carrera *f*; (*short trip*) paseo *m*; (*of a train, etc.*) trayecto *m*; (*series*) serie *f*; (*ski*) pista *f*; (*print*) tirada *f*. **in the long run** a la larga.

run away *v* escaparse. **runaway** *nm*, *adj* fugitivo.

run down *v* (*knock over*) atropellar; (*criticize*) poner por los suelos. **run-down** *adj* (*exhausted*) agotado. **rundown** *n* informe detallado *m*.

rung[1] [rʌŋ] *V* **ring**.

rung[2] [rʌŋ] *n* peldaño *m*.

run in *v* (*mot*) rodar; (*arrest*) detener.

runner ['rʌnə] *n* (*athlete*) corredor, -a *m*, *f*; (*sledge*) patín *m*. **runner bean** judía escarlata *f*. **runner-up** *n* subcampeón, -ona *m*, *f*.

run out *v* acabarse.

run over *v* (*hit*) pillar; (*rehearse*) volver a ensayar; (*text*) echar un vistazo a; (*overflow*) rebosar.

run up *v* (*make quickly*) hacer rápidamente; (*flag*) izar. **run up against** tropezar con.

runway ['rʌnwei] *n* pista *f*.

rupture ['rʌptʃə] *n* ruptura *f*; (*med*) hernia *f*. *v* romper.

rural ['ruərəl] *adj* rural, campestre.

ruse [ru:z] *n* ardid *m*.

rush[1] [rʌʃ] *n* ímpetu *m*; prisa *f*; carrera precipitada *f*. *v* hacer precipitadamente; meter prisa. **rush hour** hora punta *f*.

rush[2] [rʌʃ] *n* (*bot*) junco *m*.

rusk [rʌsk] *n* galleta dura *f*.

Russia ['rʌʃə] *n* Rusia *f*. **Russian** *n*, *adj* ruso, -a.

rust [rʌst] *n* orín *m*, herrumbre *f*. *v* oxidar. **rusty** *adj* oxidado.

rustic ['rʌstik] *adj* rústico.

rustle ['rʌsl] *v* (*leaves*) susurrar; (*paper*) crujir. *n* susurro *m*; crujido *m*.

rut [rʌt] *n* rodera *f*.

ruthless ['ru:θlis] *adj* despiadado, implacable.

rye [rai] *n* centeno *m*.

S

sabbatical [sə'batikəl] *adj* sabático. **sabbatical year** año de permiso *m*.

sable ['seibl] *n* cebellina *f*.

sabotage ['sabəta:ʒ] *n* sabotaje *m*. *v* sabotear. **saboteur** *n* saboteador, -a *m*, *f*.

sabre ['seibə] *n* sable *m*.

saccharin ['sakərin] *n* sacarina *f*. *adj* sacarino.

sachet ['saʃei] *n* saquito *m*.

sack [sak] *n* saco *m*. **get the sack** (*coll*) recibir el pasaporte. *v* (*coll*) despedir.

sacrament ['sakrəmənt] *n* sacramento *m*.

sacred ['seikrid] *adj* sagrado.

sacrifice ['sakrifais] *n* sacrificio *m*. *v* sacrificar.

sacrilege ['sakrəlidʒ] *n* sacrilegio *m*. **sacrilegious** *adj* sacrílego.

sad [sad] *adj* triste. **sadden** *v* entristecer. **sadly** *adv* tristemente; (*unfortunately*) desgraciadamente. **sadness** *n* tristeza *f*.

saddle ['sadl] *n* (*horse*) silla *f*; (*bicycle*) sillín *m*. **saddle-bag** *n* (*horse*) alforja *f*; (*bicycle*) cartera *f*. **saddle with** cargar con. **saddler** *n* guarnicionero *m*. **saddlery** *n* guarniciones *f pl*.

sadism ['seidizəm] *n* sadismo *m*. **sadist** *n* sádico, -a *m*, *f*. **sadistic** *adj* sádico.

safari [sə'fa:ri] *n* safari *m*. **safari park** reserva *f*.

safe [seif] *adj* (*unhurt*) sano y salvo; (*undamaged*) intacto; (*secure*) seguro; (*harmless*) inofensivo; (*trustworthy*) de fiar. *n* caja de caudales *f*. **safekeeping** *n* custodia *f*. **be on the safe side** para mayor seguridad. **safely** *adv* a buen puerto; sin peligro. **safety** *n* seguridad *f*; salvamento *m*. **safety belt** cinturón de seguridad *m*. **safety pin** imperdible *m*.

safeguard ['seifga:d] *n* salvaguardia *f*. *v* salvaguardar.

saffron ['safrən] *n* azafrán *m*. *adj* azafranado.

sag [sag] *v* doblegarse; flaquear. *n* hundimiento *m*; flexión *f*.

saga ['sa:gə] *n* saga *f*.

sage[1] [seidʒ] *nm*, *adj* sabio.

sage[2] [seidʒ] *n* (*bot*) salvia *f*.

Sagittarius [sadʒi'teəriəs] *n* Sagitario *m*.

said [sed] *V* say.

sail [seil] *n* vela *f*; (*trip*) paseo *m*; (*wind-mill*) brazo *m*. **sailcloth** *n* lona *f*. **set sail** hacerse a la mar. *v* (*leave*) salir; (*cross*) atravesar; (*boat*) navegar. **sail through** (*coll*) hacer muy fácilmente. **sailing** *n* (*navigation*) navegación *f*; (*departure*) salida *f*. **sailing boat** barco de vela *m*. **sailor** *n* marinero *m*.

saint [seint] *n* santo, -a *m*, *f*.

sake [seik] *n* **for the sake of** por; para; por amor de.

salad ['saləd] *n* ensalada *f*. **salad cream** mayonesa *f*. **salad dressing** vinagreta *f*.

salami [sə'la:mi] *n* salchichón *m*.

salary ['saləri] *n* sueldo *m*.

sale [seil] *n* venta *f*; (*reductions*) liquidación *f*. **for** or **on sale** en venta. **sale-room** *n* sala de subasta *f*. **salesman** *n* (*shop*) dependiente *m*; (*rep*) representante *m*. **salesmanship** *n* arte de vender *m*.

saline ['seilain] *adj* salino. **salinity** *n* salinidad *f*.

saliva [sə'laivə] *n* saliva *f*. **salivary** *adj* salival. **salivate** *v* salivar.

sallow ['salou] *adj* cetrino.

salmon ['samən] *n* salmón *m*.

salon ['salon] *n* salón *m*.

saloon [sə'lu:n] *n* salón *m*; sala *f*. **saloon bar** salón interior *m*. **saloon car** coche salón *m*.

salt [so:lt] *n* sal *f*. **salt-cellar** *n* salero *m*. *v* salar. **salty** *adj* salado.

salute [sə'lu:t] *n* saludo *m*; (*gun*) salva *f*. *v* saludar.

salvage ['salvidʒ] *n* salvamento *m*; objetos salvados *m pl*. *v* salvar.

salvation [sal'veiʃən] *n* salvación *f*.

same [seim] *adj* mismo; igual. *pron* el mismo, la misma. *adv* de la misma forma. **all the same** sin embargo. **at the same time** al mismo tiempo.

sample ['sa:mpl] *n* muestra *f*; prueba *f*; ejemplo *m*. *v* probar; (*drinks*) catar.

sanatorium [sanə'to:riəm] *n* sanatorio *m*.

sanctify ['saŋktifai] *v* santificar. **sanctification** *n* santificación *f*.

sanctimonious [saŋkti'mouniəs] *adj* santurrón.

sanction ['saŋkʃən] *n* sanción *f*. *v* sancionar; autorizar.

sanctity ['saŋktəti] *n* santidad *f*; inviolabilidad *f*.

sanctuary ['saŋktʃuəri] *n* santuario *m*; (*refuge*) refugio *m*; (*animal*) reserva *f*.

sand [sand] *n* arena *f*. **sandbag** *n* saco terrero *m*. **sand dune** duna *f*. **sandpaper** *n* papel de lija *m*. *v* (*with sandpaper*) lijar. **sandy** *adj* (*beach*) arenoso; (*hair*) rubio rojizo.

sandal ['sandl] *n* sandalia *f*.

sandwich ['sanwidʒ] *n* bocadillo *m*. *v* intercalar.

sane [sein] *adj* sano; razonable. **sanity** *n* juicio *m*; (*sensibleness*) sensatez *f*.

sang [saŋ] *V* **sing**.

sanitary ['sanitəri] *adj* sanitario; higiénico. **sanitary towel** paño higiénico *m*.

sank [saŋk] *V* **sink**.

San Marino [sanmə'ri:nou] *n* San Marino

Santa Claus ['santə,klo:z] *n* San Nicolás *m*, Papá Noel *m*

sap [sap] *n* savia *f*.

sapphire ['safaiə] *n* zafiro *m*.

sarcasm ['sa:kazəm] *n* sarcasmo *m*.

sardine [sa:'di:n] *n* sardina *f*.

Sardinia [sa:'dinjə] *n* Cerdeña *f*. **Sardinian** *n*, *adj* sardo, -a *m*, *f*.

sardonic [sa:'donik] *adj* sardónico.

sash[1] [saʃ] *n* faja *f*; (*chest ribbon*) banda *f*; (*waist*) fajín *m*.

sash[2] [saʃ] *n* (*frame*) marco *m*. **sash window** ventana de guillotina *f*.

sat [sat] *V* **sit**.

Satan ['seitən] *n* Satán *m*, Satanás *m*. **satanic** *adj* satánico.

satchel ['satʃəl] *n* cartera *f*.

satellite ['satəlait] *n* satélite *m*. **satellite dish** antena parabólica *f*. **satellite TV** televisión por satélite *f*.

satin ['satin] *n* raso *m*.

satire ['sataiə] *n* sátira *f*. **satirical** *adj* satírico. **satirize** *v* satirizar.

satisfy ['satisfai] *v* satisfacer; convencer. **satisfaction** *n* satisfacción *f*. **satisfactory** *adj* satisfactorio.

saturate ['satʃəreit] *v* saturar; (*soak*) empapar. **saturation** *n* saturación *f*. **reach saturation point** llegar al punto de saturación.

Saturday ['satədi] *n* sábado *m*.

sauce [so:s] *n* salsa *f*; (*slang*) insolencia *f*. **saucy** *adj* descarado; coquetón.

saucepan ['so:spən] *n* cacerola *f*.

saucer ['so:sə] *n* platillo *m*. **flying saucer** platillo volante *m*.

sauerkraut ['sauəkraut] *n* sauerkraut *m*.

sauna [so:nə] *n* sauna *f*.

saunter [so:ntə] *v* pasearse. *n* paso lento *m*; paseo *m*.

sausage ['sosidʒ] *n* salchicha *f*. **sausage-meat** *n* carne de salchicha *f*. **sausage roll** empanadilla de salchicha *f*.

savage ['savidʒ] *adj* (*fierce*) feroz; (*primitive*) salvaje; cruel; violento. *n* salvaje *m*, *f*. *v* embestir. **savagery** *n* salvajada *f*; ferocidad *f*.

save[1] [seiv] *v* salvar; (*put aside*) ahorrar; (*keep till later*) guardar; (*protect*) proteger; (*goal*) parar. **savings** *pl n* ahorros *m pl*. **savings bank** caja de ahorros *f*.

save[2] [seiv] *prep* salvo, excepto. *conj* a no ser que.

saviour ['seivjə] *n* salvador, -a *m*, *f*.

savoir-faire [,savwa:'feə] *n* desparpajo *m*; sentido común *m*.

savour ['seivə] *v* saborear; tener sabor de. *n* sabor *m*, gusto *m*. **savoury** *adj* sabroso; salado. *n* entremés salado *m*.

saw[1] [so:] *V* **see**.

*saw[2] [so:] *n* (*tool*) sierra *f*; (*proverb*) refrán *m*. **sawdust** *n* aserrín *m*. **sawmill** *n* aserradero *m*. *v* aserrar.

saxophone ['saksəfoun] *n* saxofón *m*.

*say [sei] *v* decir; recitar. *n* **have no say** no tener ni voz ni voto. **saying** *n* (*act*) decir *m*; (*maxim*) refrán *m*.

scab [skab] *n* costra *f*, postilla *f*; (*derog: blackleg*) esquirol *m*.

scaffold ['skafəld] *n* (*platform*) tarima *f*; (*gallows*) cadalso *m*. **scaffolding** *n* andamio *m*.

scald [sko:ld] *v* escaldar; (*instruments*) esterilizar. *n* escaldadura *f*. **scalding** *adj* hirviendo, hirviente.

scale[1] [skeil] *n* (*fish, etc.*) escama *f*; (*tartar*) sarro *m*. **scaly** *adj* escamoso; sarroso.

scale[2] [skeil] *n* (*music, measurement*) escala *f*; (*damage, etc.*) amplitud *f*. **scale drawing** dibujo hecho a escala *m*. *v* (*climb*) escalar. **scale down** reducir a escala.

scales [skeilz] *pl n* balanza *f sing*.

scallop ['skaləp] *n* (*zool*) venera *f*; (*cookery*) escalope *m*; (*sewing*) festón *m*. **scallop shell** concha *f*. *v* festonear.

scalp [skalp] *n* cuero cabelludo *m*. *v* escalpar.

scalpel ['skalpəl] *n* escalpelo *m*.

scamper ['skampə] *v* corretear.

scampi ['skampi] *n* gamba grande *f*.

scan [skan] *v* recorrer con la mirada; escrutar; (*tech*) explorar; (*poetry*) escandir; (*medicine*) exploración con escáner *f*. **scanner** (*med*) (*computer*) (*airport*) escáner *m*; (*med*) ecógrafo *m*; (*radar*) antena direccional *f*.

scandal ['skandl] *n* escándalo *m*; (*gossip*) chismorreo *m*; (*law*) difamación *f*. **scandalize** *v* escandalizar. **scandalous** *adj* escandaloso.

Scandinavia [,skandi'neivjə] *n* Escandinavia *f*. **Scandinavian** *n*, *adj* escandinavo, -a.

scant [skant] *adj also* **scanty** insuficiente. **scantily** *adv* muy ligeramente.

scapegoat ['skeipgout] *n* cabeza de turco *f*.

scar [ska:] *n* cicatriz *f*. *v* cicatrizar; (*fig*) marcar.

scarce [skeəs] *adj* escaso; insuficiente; raro. **scarcely** *adv* apenas; casi. **scarcity** *n* escasez *f*.

scare [skeə] *n* susto *m*; alarma *f*. *v* asustar, espantar. **be scared** tener miedo. **scarecrow** *n* espantapájaros *m invar*.

scarf [ska:f] *m* (*woollen*) bufanda *f*; (*light*) pañuelo *m*.

scarlet ['ska:lit] *adj* escarlato. **scarlet fever** escarlatina *f*.

scathing ['skeiðiŋ] *adj* cáustico, mordaz.

scatter ['skatə] *v* esparcir; (*sprinkle*) salpicar; (*put to flight*) derrotar; dispersar; (*squander*) desparramar. **scatter-brained** *adj* atolondrado.

scavenge ['skavindʒ] *v* recoger; buscar entre. **scavenger** *n* barrendero *m*; animal que se alimenta de carroña *m*.

scene [si:n] *n* escena *f*; (*place*) lugar *m*; espectáculo *m*; vista *f*. **scenic** *adj* escénico; pintoresco.

scenery ['si:nəri] *n* (*landscape*) paisaje *m*; (*theatre*) decorado *m*.

scent [sent] *n* perfume *m*; (*smell*) olor *m*; (*track*) rastro *m*. *v* perfumar; (*smell*) oler.

sceptic ['skeptik] *n* escéptico, -a *m*, *f*. **sceptical** *adj* escéptico. **scepticism** *n* escepticismo *m*.

sceptre ['septə] *n* cetro *m*.

schedule ['ʃedju:l] *n* programa *m*; (*timetable*) horario *m*. *v* programar; fijar. **scheduled flight** vuelo regular *m*.

scheme [ski:m] *n* plan *m*; proyecto *m*,

esquema *m*; (*plot*) intriga *f*. *v* proyectar; intrigar, conspirar.

schizophrenia [,skitsə'fri:niə] *n* esquizofrenia *f*. **schizophrenic** *n*, *adj* esquizofrénico, -a.

scholar ['skolə] *n* (*learned person*) erudito, -a, *m*, *f*; (*schoolchild*) colegial, -a *m*, *f*, alumno, -a *m*, *f*; (*student*) estudiante *m*, *f*. **scholarly** *adj* erudito. **scholarship** *n* (*award*) beca *f*; erudición *f*.

scholastic [skə'lastik] *adj* escolar, escolástico.

school¹ [sku:l] *n* escuela *f*; (*private or secondary*) colegio *m*. **schoolboy** *n* alumno *m*. colegial *m*. **schoolgirl** *n* alumna *f*, colegiala *f*. **schooling** *n* educación *f*, enseñanza *f*. **schoolmaster** *n* (*primary*) maestro *m*; (*secondary*) profesor *m*. **schoolmistress** *n* maestra *f*; profesora *f*. **school-room** *n* clase *f*; sala de clase *f*.

school² [sku:l] *n* (*of fish*) banco *m*.

schooner [sku:nə] *n* goleta *f*.

sciatica [sai'atikə] *n* ciática *f*. **sciatic** *adj* ciático.

science ['saiəns] *n* ciencia *f*. **science fiction** ciencia ficción *f*. **scientific** *adj* científico. **scientist** *n* científico, -a *m*, *f*.

scintillating ['sintileitiŋ] *adj* relumbrante; (*fig*) brillante.

scissors ['sizəz] *pl n* tijeras *f pl*.

scoff¹ [skof] *v* burlarse.

scoff² [skof] *v* (*coll eat*) zamparse.

scold [skould] *v* reñir, reprender. *n* virago *f*. **scolding** *n* reprensión *f*.

scone [skon] *n* bollo *m*.

scoop [sku:p] *n* pala de mano *f*; (*press*) éxito periodístico *m*. *v* sacar con pala; (*dig*) excavar.

scooter ['sku:tə] *n* (*motor*) scooter *m*; (*child's*) patinete *m*.

scope [skoup] *n* (*range*) alcance *m*; (*opportunity*) libertad *f*; (*field of action*) esfera *f*.

scorch [sko:tʃ] *n* quemadura *f*. *v* quemar; (*singe*) chamuscar.

score [sko:] *n* (*number of points*) tanteo *m*; (*result*) resultado *m*; (*test marks*) calificación *f*; (*twenty*) veintena *f*; (*music*) partitura *f*; (*notch*) muesca *f*. **scoreboard** *n* marcador *m*. *v* (*point, goal*) marcar; orquestar; hacer una muesca en. **scorer** *n* (*scorekeeper*) tanteador *m*; (*football*) goleador *m*.

scorn [sko:n] *n* desdén *m*, desprecio *m*. *v*

desdeñar, despreciar **scornful** adj desdeñoso, despreciativo.

Scorpio ['sko:piəu] n Escorpión m.

scorpion ['sko:piən] n escorpión m

Scotland ['skotlənd] n Escocia f. **Scot** n escocés, -esa m, f. **Scotch** n whisky escocés m. **Scots** nm, adj escocés. **Scottish** adj escocés.

scoundrel ['skaundrəl] n sinvergüenza m.

scour¹ [skauə] v (clean) fregar. **scourer** n (pad) estropajo m.

scour² [skauə] v (search) recorrer, batir.

scout [skaut] n explorador m. **scoutmaster** n jefe de exploradores m.

scowl [skaul] v fruncir el entrecejo, n ceño m.

scramble ['skræmbl] v (climb) trepar; (struggle) pelearse; (mix) mezclar; (eggs) revolver. n lucha f, pelea f.

scrap [skræp] n (piece) trozo m; (metal) chatarra f; (coll: fight) pelea f. **scrapbook** n álbum de recortes m. papel para apuntes m. **scraps** pl n restos m pl, sobras f pl. **scrapyard** desgüace m. v desechar; (coll) pelear.

scrape [skreip] n (noise) chirrido m; (act) raspado m; (mark) arañazo m; (graze) rasguño m; (coll: trouble) apuro m. v raspar; (graze) arañar; (drag) arrastrar.

scratch [skrætʃ] n arañazo m; raya f; rasguño m; cero m. **scratch card** un rasca m.

scrawl [skro:l] v garabatear. n garabato m.

scream [skri:m] n grito m, chillido m. v gritar, chillar.

screech [skri:tʃ] v chillar, gritar; (brakes) chirriar. n chillido m, grito m; chirrido m.

screen [skri:n] n (TV, film) pantalla f; (folding) biombo m; (fig) cortina f. **screen-play** n guión m. **screen test** prueba cinematográfica f. v (film) proyectar; (shelter) proteger; (sift) tamizar. **screening** (med) exploración médica f. **screensaver** (comput) pantalla protectora f.

screw [skru:] n tornillo m; (propeller) hélice f. **screwdriver** n destornillador m. v atornillar. **screw up** (paper) arrugar.

scribble ['skribl] v garabatear. n garabato m.

script [skript] n (film) guión m; (theatre) argumento m; (writing) escritura f.

scripture ['skriptʃə] n (school) religión f; (holy) Sagrada Escritura f.

scroll [skrəul] n rollo m; (arch) voluta f. v (comput) desplazar, desplazarse hacia arriba/abajo.

scrounge [skraundʒ] (coll) v sablear; gorronear. **scrounger** n sablista m, f; gorrón, -ona m, f.

scrub¹ [skrʌb] n fregado m; fricción f. v fregar; restregar; (coll: cancel) cancelar. **scrubbing brush** cepillo de fregar m.

scrub² [skrʌb] n matorral m; maleza f.

scruff [skrʌf] n **by the scruff of the neck** por el cogote.

scruffy ['skrʌfi] adj desaliñado. **scruffiness** n desaliño m.

scrum [skrʌm] n melée f.

scruple ['skru:pl] n escrúpulo m. **scrupulous** adj escrupuloso.

scrutiny ['skru:təni] n escrutinio m. **scrutinize** v escudriñar.

scuffle ['skʌfl] n pelea f, refriega f. v pelear, reñir.

scull [skʌl] n remo m.

scullery ['skʌləri] n trascocina f.

sculpt [skʌlpt] v esculpir. **sculptor** n escultor, -a m, f. **sculpture** n escultura f.

scum [skʌm] n espuma f; (derog) escoria f.

scurf [skə:f] n caspa f.

scurvy ['skə:vi] n escorbuto m.

scuttle¹ ['skʌtl] n (coal) cubo del carbón m.

scuttle² ['skʌtl] v (naut) barrenar.

scuttle³ ['skʌtl] v escabullirse.

scythe [saið] n guadaña f. v guadañar.

sea [si:] n mar m, f.

sea-bed n fondo del mar m.

seaborne ['si:bo:n] adj transportado por mar.

seafood ['si:fu:d] n mariscos m pl.

seafront ['si:frʌnt] n paseo marítimo m.

seagoing ['si:ˌgəuiŋ] adj (ship) de alta mar; (person) marinero.

seagull ['si:gʌl] n gaviota f.

seahorse ['si:ho:s] n caballo de mar m.

seal¹ [si:l] n sello m. v sellar; (close) cerrar; (fate) decidir; **seal off** (area) acordonar. **sealing wax** lacre m.

seal² [si:l] n (zool) foca f. **sealskin** n piel de foca f.

sea-level n nivel del mar m.

sea-lion n león marino m.

seam [si:m] n (sewing) costura f; (coal) vena f; (geol) capa f. **seamy** adj (fig) sórdido.

seaman ['si:mən] n pl **seamen** marinero m.

séance ['seiãs] *n* sesión de espiritismo *f*.

sear [siə] *v* (*scorch*) abrasar; (*wither*) marchitar. **searing** *adj* (*pain*) punzante.

search [sə:tʃ] *n* investigación *f*; (*to find something*) búsqueda *f*; (*house, car*) registro *m*. **search engine** (*comput*) buscador *m*. **searchlight** *n* reflector *m*. **search-party** *n* equipo de salvamento *m*. **search warrant** *n* mandamiento de registro *m*. *v* buscar; registrar; investigar. **searching** *adj* (*look*) penetrante; (*examination*) minucioso.

sea shell *n* concha marina *f*.

seashore ['si:ʃo:] *n* playa *f*; costa *f*.

seasick ['si:sik] *adj* be seasick marearse. **sea sickness** mareo *m*.

seaside ['si:said] *n* playa *f*; costa *f*. **seaside resort** estación balnearia *f*.

season ['si:zn] *n* estación *f*; temporada *f*; época *f*. **season ticket** abono *m*. *v* (*food*) sazonar; (*wood*) secar. **seasonal** *adj* estacional; (*work*) temporal. **seasoning** *n* condimento *m*.

seat [si:t] *n* asiento *m*; silla *f*; localidad *f*; centro *m*. **seat-belt** *n* cinturón de seguridad *m*. *v* sentar; colocar; tener cabida para.

seawater ['si:ˌwo:tə] *n* agua de mar *f*.

seaweed ['si:wi:d] *n* alga *f*.

seaworthy ['si:ˌwə:ði] *adj* marinero. **seaworthiness** *n* navegabilidad *f*.

secluded [si'klu:did] *adj* retirado; aislado. **seclusion** *n* reclusión *f*; soledad *f*.

second¹ ['sekənd] *n* (*time*) segundo *m*. **second hand** segundero *m*.

second² ['sekənd] *n* segundo, -a *m, f.* (*gear*) segunda *f*. **seconds** *pl n* artículos de segunda clase *m pl. adj* segundo. **on second thoughts** pensándolo bien. **second-class** *adj* de segunda clase. **travel second-class** viajar en segunda. **second-hand** *adj* de segunda mano, usado. **second-rate** *adj* de segunda categoría. *v* (*in debate*) apoyar. **secondly** *adv* en segundo lugar.

secondary ['sekəndəri] *adj* secundario. **secondary school** instituto de enseñanza media *m*.

secret ['si:krit] *nm, adj* secreto. **secrecy** *n* secreto *m*. **secretive** *adj* reservado; callado. **secretly** *adv* en secreto.

secretary ['sekrətəri] *n* secretario, -a *m, f.* **secretarial** *adj* de secretario.

secrete [si'kri:t] *v* (*hide*) esconder; (*med*) secretar. **secretion** *n* secreción *f*.

sect [sekt] *n* secta *f*. **sectarian** *adj* sectario.

section ['sekʃən] *n* sección *f*; parte *f*.

sector ['sektə] *n* sector *m*.

secular ['sekjulə] *adj* profano; secular; laico.

secure [si'kjuə] *adj* seguro. *v* asegurar; cerrar firmemente; garantizar; conseguir; reservar; consolidar. **security** *n* seguridad *f*; (*for loan*) garantía *f*.

sedate [si'deit] *adj* sosegado; tranquilo. **sedation** *n* sedación *f*. **sedative** *nm, adj* sedante.

sediment ['sedimənt] *n* (*geol*) sedimento *m*; (*liquid*) poso *m*.

seduce [si'dju:s] *v* seducir. **seduction** *n* seducción *f*. **seductive** *adj* seductor.

*see¹ [si:] *v* ver; comprender; mirar; visitar; recibir. **see off** ir a despedir. **see through** (*not be deceived*) calar. **see to** ocuparse de. **see you later!** ¡hasta luego!

see² [si:] *n* (*rel*) obispado *m*.

seed [si:d] *n* semilla *f*; (*fruit*) pepita *f*; (*sperm*) semen *m*. **seedless** *adj* sin semillas; sin pepitas. **seedling** *n* plantón *m*. **seedy** *adj* granado; (*coll: ill*) pachucho.

seem [si:m] *v* parecer. **seeming** *adj* aparente; (*rel*) obispado. **seemingly** *adv* al parecer, por lo visto.

seep [si:p] *v* rezumarse. **seepage** *n* filtración *f*.

seesaw ['si:so:] *n* columpio *m*, subibaja *m*. *v* columpiarse.

seethe [si:ð] *v* borbotar. **seething** *adj* (*coll*) bufando de cólera.

segment ['segmənt] *n* segmento *m*; (*orange, etc.*) gajo *m*.

segregate ['segrigeit] *v* segregar. **segregation** *n* segregación *f*.

seize [si:z] *v* tomar; (*grab firmly*) agarrar; (*a person*) detener. **seize up** (*tech*) agarrotarse. **seizure** *n* asimiento *m*; detención *f*; (*property*) embargo *m*; (*in war*) toma *f*; (*med*) ataque *m*.

seldom ['seldəm] *adv* raramente.

select [sə'lekt] *v* escoger, elegir. *adj* escogido; (*exclusive*) selecto. **selection** *n* selección *f*. **selective** *adj* selectivo.

self [self] *n* sí mismo *m*, sí misma *f*; personalidad *f*.

self-addressed *adj* con su propia dirección.

self-adhesive *adj* autoadhesivo.

self-assured *adj* seguro de sí mismo. **self-assurance** *n* confianza en sí mismo *f*.

self-catering (*apartment*) equipado con concina

self-centred *adj* egocéntrico.

self-confident *adj* seguro de sí mismo. **self-confidence** *n* seguridad en sí mismo *f*.

self-conscious *adj* cohibido. **self-consciousness** *n* turbación *f*.

self-contained *adj* independiente.

self-control *n* dominio de sí mismo *m*. **self-controlled** *adj* sereno.

self-defence *n* (*technique*) autodefensa *f*; (*law*) legítima defensa *f*.

self-determination *n* autodeterminación *f*.

self-discipline *n* autodisciplina *f*.

self-educated *adj* autodidacto.

self-employed *adj* que trabaja por cuenta propia.

self-esteem *n* amor propio *m*.

self-evidence *adj* patente, manifiesto.

self-explanatory *adj* que se explica por sí mismo.

self-expression *n* expresión de la propia personalidad *f*.

self-interest *n* interés propio *m*.

selfish ['selfiʃ] *adj* egoísta. **selfishness** *n* egoísmo *m*.

selfless ['selflis] *adj* desinteresado.

self-made *adj* **self-made man** hijo de sus propias obras *m*.

self-opinionated *adj* obstinado.

self-pity *n* lástima de sí mismo *f*.

self-portrait *n* autorretrato *m*.

self-possessed *adj* seguro de sí mismo.

self-respect *n* dignidad *f*.

self-righteous *adj* farisaico. **self-righteousness** *n* fariseísmo *m*.

self-rule *n* autonomía *f*.

self-sacrifice *n* sacrificio de sí mismo *m*.

selfsame ['selfseim] *adj* mismísimo *m*.

self-satisfied *adj* satisfecho de sí mismo.

self-service *n* autoservicio *m*.

self-sufficient *adj* independiente. **self-sufficiency** *n* independencia *f*.

self-willed *adj* obstinado.

self-winding *adj* de cuerda automática.

*sell [sel] *v* vender(se); hacer vender. **sell off** liquidar. **seller** *n* vendedor, -a *m*, *f*;

(*dealer*) comerciante *m*.

semantic [sə'mantik] *adj* semántico. **semantics** *n* semántica *f*.

semaphore ['seməfo:] *n* semáforo *m*.

semblance ['sembləns] *n* apariencia *f*.

semen ['si:mən] *n* semen *m*.

semibreve ['semibri:v] *n* semibreve *f*.

semicircle ['semisə:kl] *n* semicírculo *m*. **semicircular** *adj* semicircular.

semicolon [semi'koulən] *n* punto y coma *m*.

semiconscious [semi'konʃəs] *adj* semiconsciente.

semi-detached house *n* casa doble *f*.

semifinal [semi'fainl] *n* semifinal *f*.

seminar ['semina:] *n* seminario *m*.

semi-precious *adj* fino; semiprecioso.

semiquaver ['semikweivə] *n* semicorchea *f*.

semi-skimmed milk leche semidesnatada *f*.

semitone ['semitoun] *n* semitono *m*.

semolina [semə'li:nə] *n* sémola *f*.

senate ['senit] *n* senado *m*. **senator** *n* senador *m*.

*send [send] *v* enviar, mandar; remitir; echar; transmitir. **send back** devolver. **send for** llamar a; (*mail-order*) escribir pidiendo.

senile ['si:nail] *adj* senil. **senility** *n* senilidad *f*.

senior ['si:njə] *adj* (*age*) mayor; (*rank*) superior. *n* (*school*) mayor *m*, *f*. **senior citizen** *n* jubilado. **seniority** *n* antigüedad *f*.

sensation [sen'seiʃən] *n* sensación *f*. **sensational** *adj* sensacional.

sense [sens] *n* sentido *m*; significado *m*; sensación *f*; sentimiento *m*; (*consensus*) sentir *m*. **senses** *pl n* (*reason*) juicio *m sing*; (*consciousness*) sentido *m*. *v* sentir. **senseless** *adj* (*unconscious*) sin sentido; (*silly*) insensato.

sensible ['sensəbl] *adj* sensato; razonable; (*clothes*) práctico.

sensitive ['sensitiv] *adj* sensible; (*easily hurt*) susceptible. **sensitivity** *n* sensibilidad *f*; susceptibilidad *f*.

sensual ['sensjuəl] *adj* sensual. **sensuality** *n* sensualidad *f*.

sensuous ['sensjuəs] *adj* sensual.

sent [sent] *V* send.

sentence ['sentəns] *n* (*gramm*) frase *f*; (*law*)

sentencia f. v sentenciar, condenar.

sentiment ['sentimənt] n sentimiento m; (sentimentality) sentimentalismo m; opinión f. **sentimental** adj sentimental.

sentry ['sentri] n centinela m.

separate ['sepərət; v 'sepəreit] adj separado; distinto; independiente; (room) particular. v separar; dividir; distinguir entre. **separation** n separación f.

September [sep'tembə] n septiembre m, setiembre m.

septic ['septik] adj séptico.

sequel ['si:kwəl] n consecuencia f; secuela f.

sequence ['si:kwəns] n sucesión f; serie f; orden m.

sequin ['si:kwin] n lentejuela f.

Serbia ['sə:biə] n Serbia f. **Serb(ian)** adj serbio.

serenade [serə'neid] n serenata f. v dar una serenata a.

serene [sə'ri:n] adj sereno. **serenity** n serenidad f.

serf [sə:f] n siervo, -a m, f.

sergeant ['sa:dʒənt] n (mil) sargento m; (police) cabo m. **sergeant-major** n sargento mayor m.

serial ['siəriəl] n serial m. adj de serie; seriado. **serialize** v publicar por entregas.

series ['siəri:z] n serie f.

serious ['siəriəs] adj serio; grave. **seriousness** n seriedad f; gravedad f.

sermon ['sə:mən] n sermón m.

serpent ['sə:pənt] n serpiente f.

serrated [sə'reitid] adj serrado; dentado.

serum ['siərəm] n suero m.

servant ['sə:vənt] n criado, -a m, f; sirviente, -a m, f; empleado, -a m, f; funcionario, -a m, f.

serve [sə:v] v servir; atender. **it serves you right** te está bien empleado. n (tennis) saque m. **server** n (comput) servidor m.

service ['sə:vis] n servicio m; favor m; (mot) revisión f; (tea) juego m; (tennis) saque m. **service charge** servicio m. **serviceman** n militar m. **service station** (mot) estación de servicio f. v (check) revisar; (maintain) mantener. **serviceable** adj utilizable; práctico. **at your service** para servirle; a su disposición.

serviette [sə:vi'et] n servilleta f.

servile ['sə:vail] adj servil. **servility** n servilismo m.

session ['seʃən] n sesión f; junta f.

***set** [set] v poner; colocar; fijar; (clock) regular; (bones) reducir; (type) componer; (to music) poner en música; (sun) ponerse. **set about** ponerse (a). **setback** n revés m; contratiempo m. **set off** (leave) partir; (explode) hacer estallar; (cause) hacer. **set out** partir; disponer. **set up** erigir; montar; establecer. n grupo m; (tools, china, etc.) juego m; (kitchen implements) batería f; (books) colección f; (people) clase f; (clothes) caída f; (sun, etc.) puesta f; (radio, etc.) aparato m; (tennis) set m; (theatre) decorado m. adj fijo; inmóvil; asignado; establecido. **setting** n (adjustment) ajuste m; (theatre) decorado m.

settee [se'ti:] n canapé m.

settle ['setl] v (solve) resolver; calmar; (country) colonizar. **settle down** instalarse; calmarse. **settle up** (bill) pagar. **settlement** n colonización f; arreglo m; liquidación f; satisfacción f. **settler** n colonizador m.

seven ['sevn] nm, adj siete. **seventh** n, adj séptimo, -a..

seventeen [sevn'ti:n] nm, adj diecisiete. **seventeenth** n, adj decimoséptimo, -a.

seventy ['sevnti] nm, adj setenta. **seventieth** n, adj septuagésimo, -a.

sever ['sevə] v cortar.

several ['sevrəl] adj, pron varios.

severe [sə'viə] adj severo; duro; (pain) agudo; (illness) grave. **severity** n severidad f; gravedad f; (weather) inclemencia f.

***sew** [sou] v coser. **sewing** n costura f. **sewing machine** máquina de coser f.

sewage ['sjuidʒ] n aguas residuales f pl.

sewer ['sjuə] n alcantarilla f, albañal m.

sex [seks] n sexo m. **sexist** adj sexista. **sexual** adj sexual. **sexual intercourse** relaciones sexuales f pl. **sexuality** n sexualidad f. **sexy** adj provocativo.

sextet [seks'tet] n sexteto m.

shabby ['ʃabi] adj andrajoso; (behaviour) mezquino.

shack [ʃak] n choza f.

shade [ʃeid] n sombra f; (lamp) pantalla f; (colour) tono m; (meaning) matiz m. v dar sombra; (art) sombrear. **shady** adj sombreado; (person) dudoso.

shadow ['ʃadou] n sombra f. **shadow cabinet** gabinete fantasma m. v (follow) seguir. **shadowy** adj indistinto; misterioso.

shaft [ʃa:ft] n (handle) mango m; (lift)

hueco *m*; (*light*) rayo *m*; (*ventilation*) pozo de ventilación *m*; (*mine*) pozo *m*; (*spear*) asta *f*.

shaggy [ˈʃagi] *adj* peludo.

*shake [ʃeik] *v* sacudir; (*bottle*) agitar; (*head*) menear; (*brandish*) esgrimir. **shake hands** darse la mano. **shake off** librarse de. *n* sacudida *f*; meneo *m*; movimiento *m*; temblor *m*. **shaky** *adj* tembloroso; (*weak*) poco sólido.

shall [ʃal] *aux translated by future tense.*

shallot [ʃəˈlot] *n* chalote *m*.

shallow [ˈʃalou] *adj* poco profundo; superficial.

sham [ʃam] *adj* fingido, simulado; falso. *n* (*person*) impostor, -a *m*, *f*; (*object*) impostura *f*. *v* fingir, simular.

shame [ʃeim] *n* vergüenza *f*; deshonra *f*; pena *f*. *v* avergonzar; deshonrar. **shame-faced** *adj* avergonzado; tímido. **shameful** *adj* vergonzoso. **shameless** *adj* desvergonzado; sinvergüenza.

shampoo [ʃamˈpuː] *n* champú *m*. *v* dar un champú a.

shamrock [ˈʃamrok] *n* trébol *m*.

shandy [ˈʃandi] *n* cerveza con gaseosa *f*.

shanty¹ [ˈʃanti] *n* (*hut*) chabola *f*. **shanty town** barrio de las latas *m*.

shanty² [ˈʃanti] *n* (*music*) saloma *f*.

shape [ʃeip] *n* forma *f*; figura *f*; aspecto *m*. *v* dar forma a; labrar; cortar; (*idea*) formular. **shapeless** *adj* informe. **shapely** *adj* bien proporcionado.

share [ʃeə] *n* parte *f*; (*comm*) acción *f*. **shareholder** *n* accionista *m*, *f*. *v* compartir.

shark [ʃaːk] *n* tiburón *m*.

sharp [ʃaːp] *adj* (*edge*) afilado; (*point*) punzante; (*bend*) brusco; (*phot*) nítido; (*outline*) definido; (*pain*) agudo; (*taste*) picante; (*clever*) vivo. *n* (*music*) sostenido *m*. **sharpen** *v* (*knife*) afilar; (*pencil*) sacar punta a. **sharpness** *n* lo afilado; agudeza *f*; (*clarity*) nitidez *f*.

shatter [ˈʃatə] *v* destrozar; (*health*) quebrantar; (*fig*) echar por tierra. **shattered** *adj* destrozado; roto; quebrantado. **shattering** *adj* demoledor; fulgurante.

shave [ʃeiv] *v* afeitarse. **shaving** *n* (*of wood, metal*) viruta *f*. **shaving brush** brocha de afeitar *f*. **shaving cream** crema de afeitar *f*.

shawl [ʃoːl] *n* chal *m*.

she [ʃiː] *pron* ella. **she who** la que, aquella que, quien.

sheaf [ʃiːf] *n* (*corn*) gavilla *f*; (*arrows*) haz *m*; (*papers*) fajo *m*.

*shear [ʃiə] *v* esquilar. **shears** *pl n* tijeras *f pl*.

sheath [ʃiːθ] *n* (*umbrella, knife, etc.*) funda *f*; (*sword*) vaina *f*. **sheathe** *v* envainar; cubrir.

*shed¹ [ʃed] *v* (*drop*) deshacerse de.

shed² [ʃed] *n* cobertizo *m*; barraca *f*.

sheen [ʃiːn] *n* brillo *m*; (*silk*) viso *m*.

sheep [ʃiːp] *n* oveja *f*. **sheepdog** *n* perro pastor *m*. **sheepskin** *n* piel de carnero *f*. **sheepish** *adj* vergonzoso.

sheer¹ [ʃiə] *adj* completo; total; puro; (*cliff*) cortado a pico; (*stockings*) diáfano.

sheer² [ʃiə] *v* (*naut*) guiñar.

sheet [ʃiːt] *n* (*bed*) sábana *f*; (*paper, glass*) hoja *f*; (*ice*) capa *f*; (*metal*) chapa *f*; (*water*) extensión *f*. **sheet lightning** fucilazo *m*. **sheet music** música en hojas sueltas *f*.

sheikh [ʃeik] *n* jeque *m*.

shelf [ʃelf] *n* estante *m*.

shell [ʃel] *n* concha *f*; (*crustacean*) caparazón *m*; (*egg, nut*) cáscara *f*; (*pea*) vaina *f*; (*cannon*) proyectil *m*. **shellfish** *pl n* mariscos *m pl*. *v* (*mil*) bombardear; (*peas, shrimps*) pelar; (*nuts*) descascarar.

shelter [ˈʃeltə] *n* abrigo *m*; asilo *m*. *v* abrigar; proteger; dar asilo.

shelve [ʃelv] *v* (*project*) dar carpetazo a. **shelving** *n* estantería *f*.

shepherd [ˈʃepəd] *n* pastor *m*.

sheriff [ˈʃerif] *n* sheriff *m*.

sherry [ˈʃeri] *n* jerez *m*.

shield [ʃiːld] *n* escudo *m*; (*fig*) defensa *f*. *v* escudar; proteger.

shift [ʃift] *n* cambio *m*; movimiento *m*; (*work*) turno *m*. **shift key** tecla de mayúsculas *f*. **shift work** trabajo por turnos *m*. *v* cambiar; mover. **shifty** *adj* furtivo.

shimmer [ˈʃimə] *v* relucir. *n* luz trémula *f*.

shin [ʃin] *n* espinilla *f*.

*shine [ʃain] *v* brillar. *n* brillo *m*, lustre *m*. **shiny** *adj* lustroso, brillante.

shingle [ˈʃingl] *n* (*pebbles*) guijarros *m pl*. **shingles** *n* (*med*) herpes *m*, *f pl*.

ship [ʃip] *n* barco *m*; navío *m*, buque *m*. **shipshape** *adj* en buen orden. **shipwreck** *n* naufragio *m*. *v* embarcar; transportar; (*send*) enviar. **shipment** *n* cargamento *m*. **shipping** *n* barcos *m pl*, buques *m pl*.

shirk [[ʃəːk] v esquivar. **shirker** n gandul, -a m, f.

shirt [[ʃəːt] n camisa f. **in one's shirt sleeves** en mangas de camisa. **shirt-tail** n faldón m.

shit [[ʃit] nf, interj (vulgar) mierda. v cagar.

shiver [[ʃivə] v temblar; estremecerse. n temblor m; estremecimiento m.

shoal [[ʃoul] n (fish) banco m.

shock [[ʃok] n choque m; (elec) descarga f. **shock absorber** amortiguador m. **shock-proof** adj a prueba de choques. v conmocionar; escandalizar. **shocking** adj escandaloso; espantoso; (news) aterrador.

shoddy [[ʃodi] adj inferior. **shoddiness** n fabricación inferior f.

*****shoe** [[ʃuː] v (horse) herrar. n zapato m. **shoelace** n cordón m. **shoemaker** n zapatero m. **shoe repairer's** zapatería de viejo f. **shoe shop** zapatería f.

shone [[ʃon] V **shine**.

shook [[ʃuk] V **shake**.

*****shoot** [[ʃuːt] v (fire) lanzar, tirar; (kill) matar; (wound) herir; (film) filmar; (hunt) cazar. n (bot) brote m. **shooting** n tiro m pl; (hunting) caza f.

shop [[ʃop] n tienda f; (larger) almacén m. **shop assistant** n dependiente, -a m, f.

shopkeeper [[ʃopkiːpə] n comerciante m, f.

shoplifter [[ʃopliftə] n ratero, -a m, f. **shoplifting** n ratería f.

shopper [[ʃopə] n comprador, -a m, f.

shopping [[ʃopiŋ] n compras f pl. **go shopping** ir de compras. **shopping bag** bolsa de la compra f. **shopping centre** centro comercial m. **shopping trolley** carrito m.

shop steward n enlace sindical m.

shore [[ʃoː] n (beach) playa f; (edge of sea) orilla f; (coast) costa f.

short [[ʃoːt] adj corto; pequeño; (not tall) bajo; (brusque) seco; (temper) vivo. **in short** en resumen. **shortage** n falta f, escasez f. **shorten** v acortar; disminuir; abreviar. **shortly** adv dentro de poco.

shortbread [[ʃoːtbred] n mantecada f.

short-circuit n cortocircuito. v ponerse en cortocircuito.

shortcoming [[ʃoːtkʌmiŋ] n defecto m.

short cut n atajo m.

shortfall [[ʃoːtfoːl] n déficit, insuficiente, falta

shorthand [[ʃoːthand] n taquigrafía f. **shorthand typist** taquimecanógrafo, -a m, f.

short list n lista de los posibles f.

short-lived adj efímero.

shorts [[ʃoːts] pl n pantalones cortos m pl.

short-sighted adj miope.

short story n novela corta f.

short-tempered adj de mal genio.

short-term adj de corto plazo.

short wave n onda corta f. adj de onda corta.

shot¹ [[ʃot] V **shoot**.

shot² [[ʃot] n bala f; tiro m; tirador, -a m, f; (sport) peso m; (med) inyección f. **shotgun** n escopeta f.

should¹ [[ʃud] v deber, tener que.

should² [[ʃud] aux translated by conditional tense.

shoulder [[ʃouldə] n hombro m. **shoulderblade** n omóplato m; (animal) paletilla f. v llevar al hombro.

shout [[ʃaut] n grito m. v gritar.

shove [[ʃʌv] n empujón m. v empujar.

shovel [[ʃʌvl] n pala f. v traspalar.

*****show** [[ʃou] v mostrar; descubrir; revelar; exhibir; indicar; demostrar; probar. n exposición f; espectáculo m; (appearance) apariencia f; (ostentation) pompa f.

show business n mundo del espectáculo m.

shower [[ʃauə] n (rain) chubasco m; (bath) ducha f. v llover; ducharse; (pour) derramar.

show in v hacer pasar.

show jumping n concurso hípico m.

show off v (coll) darse pisto.

showpiece [[ʃoupiːs] n modelo m; obra maestra f.

showroom [[ʃouruːm] n sala de muestras f.

show up v (coll: arrive) aparecer; (embarrass) poner en evidencia.

showy [[ʃoui] adj ostentoso.

shrimp [[ʃrimp] n camarón m.

shrine [[ʃrain] n capilla f; santuario m; altar m.

*****shrink** [[ʃriŋk] v (clothes) encoger. **shrink from** repugnarse de. **shrinkage** n encogimiento m.

shrivel [[ʃrivl] v secar, marchitar. **shrivel up** apergaminarse.

shroud [[ʃraud] n sudario m, mortaja f; (fig)

velo *m*. *v* amortajar; (*fig*) envolver.

Shrove Tuesday [ʃrouv] *n* martes de carnaval *m*.

shrub [ʃrʌb] *n* arbusto *m*. **shrubbery** *n* arbustos *m pl*, matorrales *m pl*.

shrug [ʃrʌg] *v* encogimiento de hombros *m*. *v* encogerse de hombros.

shudder [ˈʃʌdə] *n* repeluzno *m*; (*engine*) vibración *f*. *v* estremecerse.

shuffle [ˈʃʌfl] *n* arrastramiento de los pies *m*; (*cards*) barajada *f*. *v* arrastrar; barajar.

shun [ʃʌn] *v* evitar, rehuir.

shunt [ʃʌnt] *v* (*trains*) desviar.

*shut [ʃʌt] *v* cerrar. **shut in** encerrar. **shut out** no admitir. **shut up** (*coll*) callarse; hacer callar.

shutter [ˈʃʌtə] *n* (*window*) postigo *m*; (*phot*) obturador *m*.

shuttle [ˈʃʌtl] *n* lanzadera *f*. **shuttlecock** *n* volante *m*. **shuttle service** servicio regular de ida y vuelta *m*.

shy [ʃai] *adj* tímido. *v* (*horse*) espantarse. **shyness** *n* timidez *f*.

Siamese [saiəˈmiːz] *adj* (*cat, twin*) siamés.

sick [sik] *adj* enfermo. **be sick** vomitar. **be sick of** (*coll*) estar harto de. **feel sick** tener náuseas. **sickbed** *n* lecho de enfermo *m*. **sick benefit** subsidio de enfermedad *m*. **sicken** *v* poner enfermo. **sickening** *adj* nauseabundo; (*distressing*) deprimente. **sickly** *adj* (*person*) enfermizo; (*taste*) empalagoso. **sickness** *n* enfermedad *f*; (*sea, air*) mareo *m*.

sickle [ˈsikl] *n* hoz *f*.

side [said] *n* lado *m*; (*edge*) borde; (*team*) equipo *m*. **side with** ponerse de parte de. *adj* lateral; secundario; indirecto.

sideboard [ˈsaidboːd] *n* aparador *m*.

sideburns [ˈsaidbəːnz] *pl n* patillas *f pl*.

sidecar [ˈsaidkaː] *n* sidecar *m*.

side effects *pl n* efectos secundarios *m pl*.

sidelight [ˈsaidlait] *n* (*mot*) luz de posición *f*.

sideline [ˈsaidlain] *n* negocio accesorio *m*; (*sport*) banquillo *m*.

sidelong [ˈsaidloŋ] *adj, adv* de reojo.

side-splitting *adj* divertidísimo.

side-step *v* evitar.

side street *n* calle lateral *f*.

side-track *v* despistar.

sideways [ˈsaidweiz] *adv* oblicuamente. *adj*

de lado.

siding [ˈsaidiŋ] *n* (*rail*) vía muerta *f*.

sidle [ˈsaidl] *v* avanzar furtivamente. **sidle up to** acercarse furtivamente.

siege [siːdʒ] *n* sitio *m*, asedio *m*.

sieve [siv] *n* tamiz *m*, colador *m*. *v* tamizar.

sift [sift] *v* tamizar; (*sprinkle*) espolvorear; (*evidence*) examinar cuidadosamente. **sift out** encontrar; seleccionar. **sifter** cedazo *m*.

sigh [sai] *n* suspiro *m*. *v* suspirar.

sight [sait] *n* vista *f*; espectáculo *m*. **sightseeing** *n* turismo *m*. *v* avistar; (*aim*) apuntar.

sign [sain] *n* señal *f*; indicio *m*; (*notice*) anuncio *m*; muestra *f*. **signpost** *n* letrero *m*. *v* firmar. **sign on** *v* (*unemployment benefit*) apuntarse al paro.

signal [ˈsignəl] *n* señal *f*. *v* hacer señales; indicar.

signature [ˈsignətʃə] *n* firma *f*.

signify [ˈsignifai] *v* significar. **significance** *n* significado *m*. **significant** *adj* significativo.

silence [ˈsailəns] *n* silencio *m*. *v* callar; hacer callar. **silencer** (*mot, gun*) *n* silenciador *m*. **silent** *adj* silencioso; callado.

silhouette [siluˈet] *n* silueta *f*. **be silhouetted against** destacarse contra.

silicon chip [ˈsilikən] *n* chip de silicio *m*

silk [silk] *n* seda *f*. **silkworm** *n* gusano de seda *m*. **silky** *adj* (*fabric*) sedoso; (*voice, manner*) suave.

sill [sil] *n* antepecho *m*, alféizar *m*.

silly [ˈsili] *adj* tonto, bobo. **silliness** *n* tontería *f*, bobería *f*.

silt [silt] *n* cieno *m*, limo *m*. **silt up** encenagar.

silver [ˈsilvə] *n* plata *f*; (*coll: change*) suelto *m*. *adj* de plata; (*like silver*) plateado. **silver plate** baño de plata *m*. **silversmith** *n* platero *m*. *v* platear. **silvery** *adj* plateado; (*voice*) argentino.

similar [ˈsimilə] *adj* semejante, parecido. **similarity** *n* semejanza *f*.

simile [ˈsiməli] *n* símil *m*.

simmer [ˈsimə] *v* hervir a fuego lento; (*fig*) fermentar. **simmer down** calmarse.

simple [ˈsimpl] *adj* sencillo; natural; fácil; simple; puro; inocente; (*simple-minded*) necio. **simpleton** *n* simplón, -ona *m, f*. **simplicity** *n* sencillez *f*; simpleza *f*. **simpli-**

fy v simplificar. **simply** adv sencillamente; meramente.

simulate ['simjuleit] v similar. **simulation** n simulación f.

simultaneous [,siməl'teinjəs] adj simultáneo.

sin [sin] n pecado m. v pecar. **sinful** adj (person) pecador; pecaminoso. **sinner** n pecador, -a m, f.

since [sins] adv desde entonces. prep desde. conj desde que; (because) ya que.

sincere [sin'siə] adj sincero. **sincerity** n sinceridad f.

sinew ['sinju:] n tendón m.

*****sing** [siŋ] v cantar. **singer** n cantor, -a m, f, cantante m, f. **singing** n canto m.

singe [sindʒ] v chamuscar. n chamusquina f.

single ['siŋgl] adj solo; único; (copy) suelto; (not double) individual; (unmarried) soltero. **single bed** cama individual f. **single file** fila de a uno f. **single-handed** adv sin ayuda. **single-minded** adj resuelto. **single room** habitación individual f. **single (ticket)** billete de ida m. **single parent** padre/madre soltero/a m, f. **singles** n (sport) individual m. **single out** separar, distinguir.

singular ['siŋgjulə] nm, adj singular.

sinister ['sinistə] adj siniestro.

*****sink** [siŋk] v hundir, sumergir; (mine) cavar; (voice) bajar; (collapse) dejarse caer; (go down) descender. **sink in** (idea, etc.) darse cuenta de. n (kitchen) fregadero m; (bathroom, bedroom) lavabo m.

sinuous ['sinjuəs] adj sinuoso.

sinus ['sainəs] n seno m. **sinusitis** n sinusitis f.

sip [sip] n sorbo m. v sorber, beber a sorbos.

siphon ['saifən] n sifón m. v trasegar con sifón. **siphon off** sacar con un sifón.

sir [sə:] n señor m. caballero m.

siren ['saiərən] n sirena f.

sirloin ['sə:loin] n solomillo m.

sister ['sistə] n hermana f; (hospital) enfermera f; (nun) monja f; (religious title) sor f. **sister-in-law** n cuñada f.

*****sit** [sit] v sentar; (exam) presentarse a, (committee) ser miembro. **baby-sit** v cuidar niños. **sit down** sentarse. **sit up** incorporarse; (stay up) no acostarse. **sitting** n sentada f; sesión f; (meal) servicio m.

sittingroom n sala de estar f.

sitcom ['sitkom] n comedia f

site [sait] n lugar m, sitio m; (building) solar m; camping m

situation [sitju'eifən] n situación f; (job) empleo m. **situate** v situar.

six [siks] nm, adj seis. **sixth** n, adj sexto, -a; (date) seis m.

sixteen [siks'ti:n] nm, adj dieciséis. **sixteenth** n, adj decimosexto, -a.

sixty ['siksti] nm, adj sesenta. **sixtieth** n, adj sexagésimo, -a.

size [saiz] n tamaño m; (person, clothes) talla f; (gloves, shoes) número m. **size up** evaluar, juzgar. **sizeable** adj grande; considerable.

sizzle ['sizl] v chisporrotear. n chisporroteo m.

skate[1] [skeit] n patín m. v patinar. **skateboard** n skateboard m. **skater** n patinador, -a m, f. **skating** n patinaje m. **skating-rink** n pista de patinaje f.

skate[2] [skeit] n (fish) raya f.

skeleton ['skelitn] n esqueleto m. adj (staff, etc.) muy reducido. **skeleton key** llave maestra f.

sketch [sketf] n dibujo m; (rough) croquis m; (theatre) sketch m. v dibujar; hacer un croquis de. **sketch-book** n bloc de dibujo m. **sketchy** adj incompleto; impreciso.

skewer ['skjuə] n brocheta f. v espetar.

ski [ski:] n esquí m. **ski-lift** telesquí m. **ski slope** pista de esquí f. v esquiar. **skier** n esquiador, -a m, f. **skiing** n esquí m.

skid [skid] n patinazo m. v patinar.

skill [skil] n habilidad f; destreza f. **skilful** adj hábil; diestro. **skilled** diestro; experto; (worker) cualificado.

skim [skim] v (milk) desnatar; (surface) rozar. **skim through** hojear.

skimp [skimp] v escatimar; chapucear. **skimpy** adj escaso; pequeño; corto.

skin [skin] n piel m; (face) cutis m; (milk) nata f. **skin-diving** n natación submarina f. **skin-tight** adj muy ajustado. v (an animal) despellejar. **skinny** adj flaco, descarnado.

skip [skip] n pequeño salto m, brinco m. v saltar, brincar; saltar a la comba; (miss) saltarse.

skipper ['skipə] n capitán m.

skirmish ['skə:mif] n escaramuza f. v escaramuzar.

skirt [skə:t] *n* falda *f*. *v* dar la vuelta a. **skirting board** zócalo *m*.

skittle ['skitl] *n* bolo *m*. **skittles** *n* juego de bolos *m*.

skull [skʌl] *n* cráneo *m*. **skull and cross-bones** calavera *f*.

skunk [skʌŋk] *n* mofeta *f*.

sky [skai] *n* cielo *m*. **sky-blue** *nm, adj* azul celeste. **skylark** *n* alondra *f*. **skylight** *n* claraboya *f*. **skyline** *n* horizonte *m*. **sky scraper** *n* rascacielos *m invar*.

slab [slab] *n* (*lump*) trozo *m*; (*cake*) porción *f*; (*block*) bloque *m*; (*stone*) losa *f*; (*metal*) plancha *f*; (*chocolate*) tableta *f*.

slack [slak] *adj* (*loose*) flojo; (*lazy*) perezoso; (*trade*) encalmado. **slacken** *v* aflojar; disminuir.

slacks [slaks] *pl n* pantalones *m pl*.

slag [slag] *n* escoria *f*. **slag heap** escorial *m*.

slam [slam] *n* golpe *m*; (*door*) portazo *m*; (*bridge*) slam *m*. *v* hacer golpear; cerrar de un golpe; (*fig: criticize*) criticar severamente. **slam on the brakes** dar un frenazo.

slander ['sla:ndə] *n* calumnia *f*. (*law*) difamación *f*. *v* calumniar; difamar. **slanderous** *adj* calumnioso; difamatorio.

slang [slaŋ] *n* germanía *f*. argot *m*; jerga *f*.

slant [sla:nt] *n* inclinación *f*. sesgo *m*. *v* inclinar. **slanting** *adj* inclinado, al sesgo.

slap [slap] *n* palmada *f*.; (*on face*) bofetada *f*. *v* pegar con la mano; (*put*) poner violentamente. **slapdash** *adj* (*person*) descuidado; (*work*) chapucero. **slap-stick** *n* payasada *f*.

slash [slaʃ] *n* (*knife*) cuchillada *f*; (*whip*) latigazo *m*. *v* acuchillar; dar latigazos a; (*coll: prices*) sacrificar.

slat [slat] *n* tablilla *f*.

slate [sleit] *n* pizarra *f*. *v* empizarrar.

slaughter ['slo:tə] *n* matanza *f*. **slaughterhouse** *n* matadero *m*. *v* matar; exterminar.

slave [sleiv] *n* esclavo, -a *m, f*. *v* trabajar como un negro. **slavery** *n* esclavitud *f*.

sleazy ['sli:zi] *adj* (*place*) sórdido; (*person*) desaseado

sledge [sledʒ] *n* trineo *m*.

sledgehammer ['sledʒhamə] *n* almádena *f*.

sleek [sli:k] *adj* liso; pulcro.

*sleep [sli:p] *v* dormir; (*spend the night*) pasar la noche. *n* sueño *m*. **go to sleep** dormirse. **sleeper** (*rail*) traviesa *f*. **sleeping-bag** *n* saco de dormir *m*. **sleeping-pill** *n*

somnífero *m*. **sleepless night** noche en blanco *f*. **sleepy** *adj* soñoliento.

sleet [sli:t] *n* aguanieve *f*. *v* caer aguanieve.

sleeve [sli:v] *n* manga *f*; (*record*) funda *f*. **sleeveless** *adj* sin manga.

sleigh [slei] *n* trineo *m*.

slender ['slendə] *adj* (*thin*) delgado, fino; (*light and graceful*) esbelto; (*resources*) escaso; (*escuse*) pobre; (*hopes*) ligero.

slice [slais] *n* tajada *f*; (*bread*) rebanada *f*; (*fruit*) raja *f*; (*implement*) pala *f*. *v* cortar; partir en tajadas/rebanadas/rajas.

slick [slik] *adj* (*derog*) astuto; resbaladizo. *n* (*oil*) capa de aceite *f*.

*slide [slaid] *v* deslizar; hacer resbalar. *n* (*children's*) tobogán *m*; (*act of sliding*) deslizamiento *m*; (*microscope*) portaobjeto *m*; (*phot*) diapositiva *f*. **sliderule** *n* regla de cálculo *f*. **sliding** *adj* (*door*) corredera; (*roof*) corredizo; (*scale*) móvil.

slight [slait] *adj* pequeño; insignificante; (*person*) débil; frágil. *v* despreciar. *n* desprecio *m*. **slightest** *adj* lo más mínimo. **slightly** *adv* ligeramente.

slim [slim] *adj* delgado; esbelto. *v* adelgazar. **slimming** *adj* (*diet, etc.*) que no engorda, para adelgazar.

slime [slaim] *n* limo *m*; (*fig*) cieno *m*. **slimy** *adj* limoso: (*person*) rastrero.

*sling [sliŋ] *v* lanzar; suspender. *n* (*med*) cabestrillo *m*; (*weapon*) honda *f*.

*slink [sliŋk] *v* **slink away** escurrirse.

slip [slip] *n* (*error*) falta *f*: (*oversight*) inadvertencia *f*; (*skid*) patinazo *m*; (*stumble*) traspiés *m*; (*moral lapse*) desliz *m*; (*petticoat*) combinación *f*; (*pillow*) funda *f*; (*paper*) trozo *m*. **slip of the tongue** or **pen** lapsus *m*. *v* resbalar; pasar; poner; descorrer; escurrirse.

slipper ['slipə] *n* zapatilla *f*.

slippery ['slipəri] *adj* resbaladizo; (*person*) escurridizo.

*slit [slit] *v* cortar; rasgar. *n* cortadura *f*; resquicio *m*.

slither ['sliðə] *v* resbalar; deslizarse.

slobber ['slobə] *v* babosear. *n* baba *f*.

sloe [slou] *n* endrina *f*.

slog [slog] *n* (*coll*) pesadez *f*. *v* (*coll*) sudar tinta.

slogan ['slougən] *n* slogan *m*.

slop [slop] *v* (*splash*) salpicar; (*pour*) derramar.

slope [sloup] *n* inclinación *f*; (*hill*) falda *f*. *v* inclinarse. **sloping** *adj* inclinado; (*shoulders*) caídos.

sloppy ['slopi] *adj* (*food*) aguoso; (*garment*) muy ancho; (*careless*) chapucero; (*sentimental*) sensiblero. **sloppiness** *n* (*sentiment*) sensiblería *f*.

slot [slot] *n* ranura *f*, muesca *f*. *v* encajar; hacer una ranura.

slouch [slautʃ] *v* andar cabizbajo.

Slovakia [slou'vakiə] *n* Eslovaquia *f*; **Slovakian** *adj* eslovaco.

Slovenia [slou'vi:niə] *n* Eslovenia *f*; **Slovenian** *adj* esloveno.

slovenly ['slʌvnli] *adj* desaliñado.

slow [slou] *adj* despacio; lento; (*clock*) atrasado; (*stupid*) tardo; (*boring*) aburrido. **in slow motion** a cámara lenta. **slow down** ir más despacio.

slug [slʌg] *n* (*zool*) babosa *f*; (*bullet*) posta *f*.

sluggish ['slʌgiʃ] *adj* perezoso; lento.

sluice [slu:s] *n* esclusa *f*. *v* regar; lavar.

slum [slʌm] *n* barrio bajo *m*. **the slums** tugurios *m. pl*.

slumber ['slʌmbə] *n* sueño tranquilo *m*. *v* dormir tranquilo.

slump [slʌmp] *n* (*fig*) baja *f*; (*comm*) baja repentina *f*; depresión económica *f*. *v* desplomarse.

slung [slʌŋ] *V* **sling**.

slunk [slʌŋk] *V* **slink**.

slur [slə:] *n* baldón *m*; borrón *m*; (*music*) ligado *m*. *v* articular mal.

slush [slʌʃ] *n* nieve sucia y deshecha *f*.

slut [slʌt] *n* marrana *f*.

sly [slai] *adj* astuto; disimulado.

smack¹ [smak] *n* golpe *m*; bofetada *f*; (*sound*) chasquido *m*; *v* dar una bofetada; dar una palmada; pegar con la mano.

smack² [smak] *v* **smack of** saber a; (*fig*) oler a.

small [smo:l] *adj* pequeño; poco; chico; escaso. **small ads** anuncio por palabras *m*. **small change** dinero suelto *m*. **smallpox** *n* viruela *f*. **small talk** charla *f*. **n the small of the back** región lumbar *f*.

smart [sma:t] *adj* vivo; rápido; (*clever*) listo; de moda; majo. *v* picar. **smarten up** ponerse elegante. **smartness** *n* viveza *f*; elegancia *f*.

smash [smaʃ] *n* (*sound*) estrépito *m*; accidente *m*; (*blow*) puñetazo *m*; ruina *f*. *v* que-

brar, romper; destruir; aplastar; chocar con. **smashing** *adj* (*slang*) estupendo.

smear [smiə] *n* mancha *f*; (*med*) frotis *m*; (*fig*) calumnia *f*. *v* manchar; (*bread*) untar; calumniar. **smear campaign** campaña de difamación *f*, campaña de desprestigio *f*. **smear test** citología *f*, frotis *f*.

*smell [smel] *v* oler; tener olor. *n* olor *m*; (*sense*) olfato *m*. **smelly** *adj* maloliente.

smile [smail] *n* sonrisa *f*. *v* sonreír.

smirk [smə:k] *n* sonrisa afectada *f*. *v* sonreír afectadamente.

smock [smok] *n* blusa *f*.

smog [smog] *n* niebla espesa con humo *f*.

smoke [smouk] *n* humo *m*. **smoke-screen** *n* cortina de humo *f*. *v* humear; (*tobacco*) fumar. **smoker** *n* fumador, -a *m, f*. **no smoking** se prohíbe fumar. **smoky** *adj* que huele a humo.

smooth [smu:ð] *adj* liso; suave; llano; uniforme; (*person*) suavón. *v* alisar; suavizar. **smooth over** exculpar. **smoothly** *adv* lisamente; con suavidad.

smother ['smʌðə] *v* sofocar; apagar.

smoulder ['smouldə] *v* arder sin llama.

smudge [smʌdʒ] *n* mancha *f*; tiznón *m*. *v* manchar; tiznar.

smug [smʌg] *adj* pagado de sí mismo.

smuggle ['smʌgl] *v* pasar de contrabando; matutear. **smuggler** *n* contrabandista *m, f*. **smuggling** *n* contrabando *m*.

snack [snak] *n* bocado *m*, tentempié *m*. **snack bar** cafetería *f*.

snag [snag] *n* pega *f*, obstáculo *m*. *v* enganchar; estorbar.

snail [sneil] *n* caracol *m*.

snap [snap] *n* (*fingers*) castañeteo *m*; (*bones, teeth, mouth*) crujido *m*; (*breaking wood*) chasquido *m*; (*bite*) mordisco *m*; (*phot*) instantánea *f*. adj instantáneo; rápido. **snapdragon** *n* dragón *m*. **snapshot** *n* instantánea *f*. *v* (*bones*) romper; (*branch*) partir; (*joints*) hacer crujir; (*dog*) intentar morder; (*person*) regañar.

snare [sneə] *n* trampa *f*, lazo *m*. *v* atrapar.

snarl [sna:l] *n* gruñido *m*. *v* gruñir.

snatch [snatʃ] *n* fragmento *m*; (*theft*) robo *m*. *v* agarrar; tomar.

sneak [sni:k] *v* hacer furtivamente. **sneak in/out** entrar/salir furtivamente. *n* (*slang*) chivato, -a *m, f*.

sneer [sniə] *v* decir con desprecio. *n* desprecio *m*. **sneering** *adj* burlón.

sneeze [sni:z] *n* estornudo *m*. *v* estornudar.

sniff [snif] *n* aspiración *f*; inhalación. *f*. *v* (*smell*) oler; aspirar.

snigger ['snigə] *n* risa disimulada *f*. reírse por lo bajo.

snip [snip] *v* cortar de un tijeretazo. *n* (*coll: bargain*) ganga *f*.

snipe [snaip] *n* agachadiza *f*. *v* **snipe at** (*mil*) tirotear. **sniper** *n* paco *m*.

snivel ['snivl] *v* lloriquear. **snivelling** *adj* llorón; mocoso.

snob [snob] *n* snob *m*, esnob *m*. **snobbish** *adj* snob, esnob.

snooker ['snu:kə] *n* snooker *m*.

snoop [snu:p] *v* fisgonear; entrometerse.

snooty ['snu:ti] *adj* (*coll*) presumido.

snooze [snu:z] *n* siesta *f*; sueñecito *m*. *v* dormitar.

snore [sno:] *n* ronquido *m*. *v* roncar. **snoring** *n* ronquido *m*.

snorkel ['sno:kəl] *n* (*swimmer's*) tubo de respiración *m*; (*submarine's*) esnórquel *m*.

snort [sno:t] *n* resoplido *m*. *v* resoplar.

snout [snaut] *n* hocico *m*.

snow [snou] *n* nieve *f*. *v* nevar. **be snowed under with** estar abrumado de. **snowy** *adj* nevoso.

snowball ['snoubo:l] *n* bola de nieve *f*. *v* tirar bolas de nieve; acumularse.

snowbound ['snoubaund] *adj* bloqueado por la nieve.

snowdrift ['snoudrift] *n* ventisquero *m*.

snowdrop ['snoudrop] *n* campanilla blanca *f*.

snowfall ['snoufo:l] *n* nevada *f*.

snowflake ['snoufleik] *n* copo de nieve *m*.

snowstorm ['snousto:m] *n* tormenta de nieve *f*.

snub [snʌb] *n* repulsa *f*. *v* repulsar.

snuff [snʌf] *n* rapé *m*. **snuff-box** *n* tabaquera *f*. *v* (*extinguish*) despabilar.

snug [snʌg] *adj* cómodo; abrigadito.

snuggle ['snʌgl] *v* arrimarse; apretarse.

so [sou] *adv* así; tan; también; tanto; por lo tanto. *conj* así que, de modo que, de manera que. **and so on** y así sucesivamente. **if so** de ser así. **is that so?** ¿de veras? ... **or so** a poco más o menos .... **so as to** de manera que. **so-called** *adj* llamado. **so much** *or* **many** tanto, tantos. **so-so** *adj* (*coll*) así así.

so that para que. **so what?** ¿y qué?

soak [souk] *v* empapar. **soak in** penetrar en. **soak up** absorber. **soaking** *n* remojo *m*. **soaking wet** calado hasta los huesos.

soap [soup] *n* jabón *m*. **soap dish** jabonera *f*. **soap powder** jabón en polvo *m*. **soapsuds** *pl n* jabonaduras *f pl*. *v* jabonar. **soapy** *adj* jabonoso.

soar [so:] *v* remontarse; (*fig*) elevarse.

sob [sob] *n* sollozo *m*. *v* sollozar.

sober ['soubə] *adj* moderado; serio; (*not drunk*) sobrio. *v* **sober up** serenarse.

soccer ['sokə] *n* fútbol *m*.

sociable ['souʃəbl] *adj* sociable.

social ['souʃəl] *adj* social; (*friendly*) amistoso. **social science** sociología *f*. **social security** seguridad social *f*. **socialism** *n* socialismo *m*. **socialist** *n*(*m* + *f*), *adj* socialista. **socialize** *v* socializar.

society [sə'saiəti] *n* sociedad *f*.

sociology [sousi'olədʒi] *n* sociología *f*. **sociological** *adj* sociológico. **sociologist** *n* sociólogo, -a *m*, *f*.

sock [sok] *n* calcetín *m*.

socket ['sokit] *n* hueco *m*; (*elec*) enchufe *m*.

soda ['soudə] *n* (*chem*) sosa *f*; (*water*) agua de seltz *f*.

sodden ['sodn] *adj* empapado, saturado.

sofa ['soufə] *n* sofá *m*.

soft [soft] *adj* blando; suave; (*low*) bajo. **soft-boiled** (*egg*) pasado por agua. **software** software *m*. **soften** *v* ablandar; suavizar; bajar; **softness** *n* blandura *f*; suavidad *f*; dulzura *f*; debilidad *f*; estupidez *f*.

soggy ['sogi] *adj* empapado; (*bread*) pastoso.

soil[1] [soil] *n* tierra *f*.

soil[2] [soil] *v* ensuciar.

solar ['soulə] *adj* solar.

sold [sould] *V* **sell**.

solder ['soldə] *n* soldadura *f*. *v* soldar. **soldering-iron** *n* soldador *m*.

soldier ['souldʒə] *n* soldado *m*.

sole[1] [soul] *adj* solo, único.

sole[2] [soul] *n* (*of shoe*) suela *f*; (*of foot*) planta *f*. *v* solar.

sole[3] [soul] *n* (*fish*) lenguado *m*.

solemn ['soləm] *adj* solemne. **solemnity** *n* solemnidad *f*.

solicitor [sə'lisitə] *n* abogado, -a *m*, *f*.

solicitude [sə'lisitjuːd] n solicitud f.

solid ['solid] adj sólido; firme; continuo. n sólido m. **solids** pl n alimentos sólidos m pl. **solidarity** n solidaridad f. **solidify** v solidificarse; congelarse.

solitary ['solitəri] adj solitario; solo, único.

solitude ['solitjuːd] n soledad f.

solo ['soulou] nm, adj solo. **soloist** n. solista m, f.

solstice ['solstis] n solsticio m.

soluble ['soljubl] adj soluble.

solution [sə'luːʃən] n solución f.

solve [solv] v resolver; acertar.

solvent ['solvənt] adj (finance) solvente. n (chem) disolvente m. **solvency** n solvencia f.

sombre ['sombə] adj sombrío.

some [sʌm] adj algún, alguno, algunos; unos, varios. pron algunos; unos; un poco; parte. adv bastante; unos. **somebody** or **someone** pron alguien. **somehow** adv de algún modo; por alguna razón. **something** pron algo. **sometime** adv alguna vez, algún día. **sometimes** adv a veces, de vez en cuando. **somewhat** adv algo, algún tanto. **somewhere** adv en alguna parte. **somewhere else** en alguna otra parte.

somersault ['sʌməsoːlt] n salto mortal m. v dar un salto mortal.

son [sʌn] n hijo m. **son-in-law** n yerno m.

sonata [sə'naːtə] n sonata f.

song [soŋ] n (art) canto m; (composition) canción f.

sonic ['sonik] adj sónico.

sonnet ['sonit] n soneto m.

soon [suːn] adv pronto, dentro de poco; (early) temprano. **as soon as** tan pronto como. **sooner or later** tarde o temprano.

soot [sut] n hollín m.

soothe [suːð] v tranquilizar, calmar. **soothing** adj tranquilizador, calmante.

sophisticated [sə'fistikeitid] adj sofisticado; mundano; (machinery) complejo.

sopping ['sopiŋ] adj empapadísimo.

soprano [sə'praːnou] n soprano m, f.

sordid ['soːdid] adj sórdido.

sore [soː] adj malo; dolorido; (fig) doloroso. **sore point** tema delicado m. **sorely** adv (bitterly) profundamente; (very) muy. **soreness** n dolor m.

sorrow ['sorou] n pesar m; tristeza f. v afligirse. **sorrowful** adj afligido; triste.

sorry ['sori] adj afligido; triste; apenado; lastimoso. **feel sorry for** compadecer. interj ¡perdóneme! ¡disculpe!

sort [soːt] n clase f; especie f; tipo m; modo m; persona f. v separar de; clasificar. **sort out** apartar; (problems) arreglar **sorting office** sala de batalla f.

soufflé ['suːflei] n soufflé m.

sought [soːt] V **seek**.

soul [soul] n alma f. **soulful** adj expresivo. conmovedor.

sound¹ [saund] n (noise) sonido m, ruido m. **sound barrier** barrera del sonido f **sound effects** efectos sonoros m pl. **soundproof** adj insonoro. **sound-track** n pista sonora f. v sonar, resonar; (seem) parecer.

sound² [saund] adj sano; (reasonable) lógico; (argument) válido; (policy) prudente; (investment) seguro; (comm) solvente. **be sound asleep** estar profundamente dormido.

sound³ [saund] v (depth) sondar; (opinion) sondear.

soup [suːp] n sopa f. **clear soup** consomé m. **thick soup** puré m. **soup plate** plato sopero m. **soup spoon** cuchara sopera f.

sour [sauə] adj ácido, agrio. v agriar. **sourness** n acidez f, agrura f.

source [soːs] n fuente f; origen m.

south [sauθ] n sur m. adj also **southerly**, **southern** del sur. adv hacia el sur. **southbound** adj con rumbo al sur. **south-east** nm, adj sudeste. **south-west** nm, adj sudoeste.

South Africa Sudáfrica.

South America n Sudamérica f, América del Sur f. **South American** sudamericano, -a m, f.

souvenir [suːvə'niə] n recuerdo m.

sovereign ['sovrin] n, adj soberano, -a.

*****sow¹** [sou] v sembrar; esparcir.

sow² [sau] n cerda f, puerca f.

soya ['soiə] n soja f. **soya bean** soja f. **soy sauce** salsa picante de soja f.

spa [spaː] n balneario m; manantial mineral m.

space [speis] n espacio m; (place) sitio m; (time) temporada f. **spaceman** n astronauta m, cosmonauta m. **spacecraft** n nave espacial f. v espaciar. **spacious** adj espacioso; amplio.

spade [speid] *n* pala *f*.

spades [speidz] *pl n* (*cards*) picos *m pl*; (*Spanish cards*) espadas *f pl*.

spaghetti [spə'geti] *n* espaguetis *m pl*.

Spain [spein] *n* España *f*. **Spaniard** *n* español, -a *m, f*. **Spanish** *nm, adj* español.

spam [spam] (*internet*) *n* spam, correo basura *m*.

span [span] *n* (*time*) espacio *m*, duración *f*; (*wings*) envergadura *f*; (*space*) distancia *f*; (*bridge*) tramo *m*. *v* atravesar; medir.

spaniel ['spanjəl] *n* perro de aguas *m*; (*cocker*) sabueso *m*.

spank [spaŋk] *v* dar una azotaina. **spanking** *n* azotaina *f*.

spanner ['spanə] *n* llave *f*.

spare [speə] *adj* de reserva; de sobra; disponible. **spare part** (*mot*) recambio *m*. **spare-ribs** *pl n* (*cookery*) costillas de cerdo *f pl*. **spare room** cuarto de los invitados *m*. **spare time** ratos libres *m pl*. **spare tyre** neumático de repuesto *m*. *v* (*do without*) pasarse sin; (*avoid*) evitar; (*expense*) escatimar. **sparing** *adj* (*words*) parco; limitado; escaso; frugal.

spark [spɑːk] *n* chispa *f*. *v* chispear. **spark off** provocar. **sparking-plug** *n* bujía *f*.

sparkle ['spɑːkl] *n* centelleo *m*; (*fig*) brillo *m*. *v* centellear; (*fig*) brillar. **sparkling** *adj* (*drink*) espumoso.

sparrow ['sparou] *n* gorrión *m*.

sparse [spɑːs] *adj* escaso, poco denso. **sparsely** *adv* escasamente.

spasm ['spazəm] *n* espasmo *m*; (*fit*) ataque *m*. **spasmodic** *adj* espasmódico.

spastic ['spastik] *n, adj* espástico, -a.

spat [spat] *V* **spit**.

spate [speit] *n* avalancha *f*; torrente *m*; serie *f*

spatial ['speiʃl] *adj* espacial.

spatula ['spatjulə] *n* espátula *f*.

spawn [spɔːn] *n* (*fish*) freza *f*, hueva *f*; (*frog*) huevos *m pl*. *v* frezar; depositar.

***speak** [spiːk] *v* decir; hablar. **speak up** hablar más fuerte. **speak up for** hablar en favor de. **speaker** *n* orador, -a *m, f*; (*loudspeaker*) altavoz *m*.

spear [spiə] *n* lanza *f*. *v* traspasar. **spearhead** *n* vanguardia *f*.

special ['speʃəl] *adj* especial; particular; extraordinario. **specialist** *n* especialista *m, f*. **speciality** *n* especialidad *f*. **specialize** *v* especializar.

especializar.

species ['spiːʃiːz] *n* especie *f*.

specify ['spesifai] *v* especificar. **specific** *adj* específico. **specification** *n* especificación *f*; estipulación *f*; requisito *m*.

specimen ['spesimin] *n* (*biol*) espécimen *m*; modelo *m*; (*sample*) muestra *f*; (*example*) ejemplar *m*.

speck [spek] *n* manchita *f*; pizca *f*. **speckle** *v* motear.

spectacle ['spektəkl] *n* espectáculo *m*. **spectacles** *pl n* gafas *f pl*. **spectacular** *adj* espectacular.

spectator [spek'teitə] *n* espectador, -a *m, f*.

spectrum ['spektrəm] *n* espectro *m*.

speculate ['spekjuleit] *v* especular; conjeturar. **speculation** *n* especulación *f*; conjetura *f*. **speculative** *adj* especulativo; conjetural.

speech [spiːtʃ] *n* (*address*) discurso *m*; (*faculty*) habla *f*; (*lecture*) conferencia *f*; conversación *f*; pronunciación *f*. **speechless** *adj* mudo.

***speed** [spiːd] *v* (*mot*) ir a toda velocidad. **speed along** apresurarse. **speed up** acelerar. **speeding** *n* exceso de velocidad *m*. **speedy** *adj* veloz. *n* prisa *f*; velocidad *f*; rapidez *f*. **speedboat** *n* lancha motora *f*. **speed limit** velocidad máxima *f*. **speedometer** *n* velocímetro *m*.

***spell¹** [spel] *v* escribir; deletrear; significar. **spelling** *n* ortografía *f*.

spell² [spel] *n* (*magic*) hechizo *m*, encanto *m*. **spellbound** *adj* encantado.

spell³ [spel] *n* período *m*; turno *m*.

***spend** [spend] *v* (*money*) gastar; (*time*) pasar. **spending** *n* gasto *m*. **spending money** dinero para gastos menudos *m*.

sperm [spəːm] *n* esperma *f*.

spew [spjuː] *v* vomitar.

sphere [sfiə] *n* esfera *f*; (*province*) competencia *f*. **spherical** *adj* esférico.

spice [spais] *n* especia *f*. *v* especiar. **spicy** *adj* especiado, picante; (*fig*) sabroso.

spider ['spaidə] *n* araña *f*. **spider's web** telaraña *f*.

spike [spaik] *n* escarpia *f*.

***spill** [spil] *v* derramar. *n* (*coll: fall*) caída *f*.

***spin** [spin] *v* girar, dar vueltas; dar efecto a; (*cotton, silk, etc.*) hilar; (*web*) tejer; (*fig: a yarn*) contar. **spin-dryer** *n* secador centrífugo *m*. **spin-off** derivado. consecuencia *f*.

spin out prolongar. **spinning** n hilado m. **spinning wheel** rueca f. n giro m.

spinach ['spinidʒ] n espinaca f.

spindle ['spindl] n (axle, shaft) eje m; (of a lathe) mandril m; (of a spinning wheel) huso m. **spindly** adj largirucho.

spine [spain] n (anat) espina dorsal f; (zool) púa f; (book) lomo m. **spinal** adj espinal. **spiny** adj espinoso.

spinster ['spinstə] n soltera f.

spiral ['spaiərəl] adj espiral. n espiral f. v dar vueltas en espiral.

spire ['spaiə] n aguja f.

spirit ['spirit] n espíritu m, alma f; (ghost) fantasma m; (courage) valor m; (liveliness) ánimo; (mood) humor m; alcohol m. **spirited** adj animado, vigoroso. **spiritual** adj espiritual. **spiritualism** n espiritualismo m. **spiritualist** n(m + f), adj espiritualista.

*spit¹ [spit] v escupir. n saliva f, escupitajo m.

spit² [spit] n (cookery) espetón m, asador m; (geog) lengua de tierra f.

spite [spait] n rencor m, malevolencia f. **in spite of** a pesar de. v mortificar. **spiteful** adj rencoroso.

splash [splaʃ] n salpicadura f; (sound) chapoteo; (mark) mancha f. v salpicar.

spleen [spli:n] n (anat) bazo m; (fig) mal humor m.

splendid ['splendid] adj espléndido; excelente. **splendour** n resplandor m.

splice [splais] v empalmar; (coll: marry) unir, casar.

splint [splint] n férula f.

splinter ['splintə] n (wood) astilla f; (bomb) casco m; (bone) esquirla f; (piece) fragmento m. v astillar.

*split [split] v hender, partir; rajar; dividir; separar; (atom) desintegrar. **split up** (couple) romper. n partido m, hendido m; división f; (in cloth) rasgón m; (quarrel) ruptura f. **split second** fracción de segundo f.

splutter ['splʌtə] v (person) farfullar; (flame) chisporrotear. n farfulla f; chisporroteo m.

*spoil [spoil] v estropear, echar a perder; (child) minar; (damage) dañar. **spoil-sport** n aguafiestas m, f invar. **spoils** pl n botín m sing.

spoke¹ [spouk] V **speak**.

spoke² [spouk] n rayo m.

spokesman ['spouksmən] n portavoz m.

sponge ['spʌndʒ] n esponja f; (cake) bizcocho esponjoso m. **sponge bag** esponjera f. v limpiar con esponja; (coll: cadge) sacar de gorra. **spongy** adj esponjoso.

sponsor ['sponsə] n (for financial support) patrocinador, -a m, f; (warrantor) fiador, -a m, f; (for club membership) padrino, -a m, f. v patrocinar; fiar; apadrinar. **sponsorship** n patrocinio m.

spontaneous [spon'teinjəs] adj espontáneo. **spontaneity** n espontaneidad f.

spool [spu:l] n bobina f.

spoon [spu:n] n cuchara f. **spoonful** n cucharada f.

sporadic [spə'radik] adj esporádico.

sport [spo:t] n deporte m; (plaything) juguete m; (amusement) bula f. **sports car** coche deportivo m. **sports jacket** chaqueta de sport f. **sportsman/woman** n deportista m, f. v llevar; ostentar. **sporting** adj deportista; caballeroso. **sportive** adj juguetón; bromista.

spot [spot] n (med) grano m; espinilla f; (mark) mancha f; (pattern) lunar m; (place) sitio m; (liquid) gota f; parte f; punto m; (coll) poco m. **on the spot** en el momento; en el acto. **spot check** inspección repentina f. **spotlight** n foco m. v manchar; reconocer; notar. **spotless** adj inmaculado; **spotted** adj (speckled) moteado; con manchas; de lunares. **spotty** adj espinilloso.

spouse [spaus] n esposo, -a m, f.

spout [spaut] n (teapot) pitorro m; (jug) pico m; (rainwater pipe) caño m; (jet) chorro m; (waterspout) tromba f. v echar; (coll) soltar.

sprain [sprein] n torcedura f. v torcer.

sprawl [spro:l] n postura desgarbada f. v extender.

spray¹ [sprei] n (water) rociada f; (sea) espuma f; (sprayer) pulverizador m. v (sprinkle) rociar; pulverizar; (crops) fumigar; vaporizarse.

spray² [sprei] n (flowers) ramo m, ramillete m.

*spread [spred] v extender; (on the ground) exponer; (marmalade, butter, etc.) untar; propagar; difundir; (wings) desplegar. **spreadsheet** n hoja de cálculo f. **spread out** esparcir. n propagación f, difusión f; (town) extensión f; (span) envergadura f; (range) gama f.

spree [spri:] n juerga f.

sprig [sprig] n ramito m.

sprightly ['spraitli] *adj* despierto, vivo.

*spring [sprɪŋ] *v* saltar. **spring up** brotar; surgir. *n* (*season*) primavera *f*; (*leap*) salto *m*, brinco *m*; (*water*) fuente *f*; (*coil*) muelle *m*. **springboard** *n* trampolín *m*. **spring-cleaning** *n* limpieza general *f*. **spring onion** cebolleta *f*. **springy** *adj* elástico.

sprinkle ['sprɪŋkl] *v* (*water*) rociar; (*sugar, salt, etc.*) salpicar. **sprinkler** *n* regadera *f*; (*fire*) extintor *m*.

sprint [sprint] *n* sprint *m*, esprint *m*. *v* sprintar, esprintar.

sprout [spraut] *n* brote *m*, retoño *m*. **Brussels sprouts** coles de Bruselas *f pl*.

spruce [spruːs] *n* (*bot*) pícea *f*. *adj* elegante. **spruce up** acicalar.

spun [spʌn] *V* **spin**.

spur [spəː] *n* espuela *f*; (*fig*) estímulo *m*. **on the spur of the moment** sin pensarlo. *v* espolear. **spur on** estimular.

spurious ['spjuəriəs] *adj* espurio, falso.

spurn [spəːn] *v* desdeñar, rechazar.

spurt [spəːt] *n* (*water*) chorro *m*; (*energy*) gran esfuerzo *m*. *v* chorrear; hacer un gran esfuerzo; acelerar.

spy [spai] *n* espía *m, f. v* espiar; observar. **spying** *n* espionaje *m*.

squabble ['skwobl] *n* riña *f. v* disputar.

squad [skwod] *n* escuadra *f*; (*mil*) pelotón *m*.

squadron ['skwodrən] *n* (*mil*) escuadrón *m*; (*naut*) escuadra *f*; (*aero*) escuadrilla *f*.

squalid ['skwolid] *adj* mugriento; escuálido; miserable. **squalor** *n* mugre *f*; miseria *f*.

squall [skwoːl] *n* ráfaga *f*.

squander ['skwondə] *v* malgastar.

square [skweə] *n* (*shape*) cuadrado *m*; (*pattern*) cuadro *m*; (*chessboard*) casilla *f*; (*in a town*) plaza *f. adj* cuadrado; rectangular; (*coll: old-fashioned*) anticuado. *v* cuadrar; (*settle*) arreglar.

squash [skwoʃ] *n* (*sport*) juego de pelota *m*; (*drink*) limonada *f*, naranjada *f*; (*crushing*) aplastamiento *m. v* (*crush*) aplastar; (*squeeze*) apretar.

squat [skwot] *n* posición en cuclillas *f. adj* rechoncho. *v* agacharse. **squatter** *n* persona que ocupe ilegalmente un sitio *f*.

squawk [skwoːk] *n* graznido *m. v* graznar.

squeak [skwiːk] *n* (*mice, etc.*) chillido *m*; (*hinge*) chirrido *m. v* chillar; chirriar.

squeal [skwiːl] *n* chillido *m. v* chillar.

squeamish ['skwiːmiʃ] *adj* remilgado; delicado.

squeeze [skwiːz] *n* presión *f*; (*hug*) abrazo *m*; (*hand*) apretón *m*; (*crowd*) gentío *m. v* abrazar; apretar; (*extract*) exprimir.

squid [skwid] *n* calamar *m*.

squint [skwint] *n* (*med*) estrabismo *m* (*coll: glance*) ojeada *f. v* entrecerrar los ojos.

squirm [skwəːm] *v* retorcerse.

squirrel ['skwirəl] *n* ardilla *f*.

squirt [skwəːt] *n* chorro *m. v* lanzar; chorrear.

stab [stab] *n* puñalada. *v* apuñalar.

stabilize ['steibilaiz] *v* estabilizar. **stabilizer** *n* estabilizador *m*.

stable[1] ['steibl] *n* cuadra *f*.

stable[2] ['steibl] *adj* estable; fijo. **stability** *n* estabilidad *f*; firmeza *f*.

staccato [stə'kaːtou] *adv* staccato. *adj* (*voice, style, etc.*) entrecortado.

stack [stak] *n* (*hay, etc.*) almiar *m*; (*pile*) montón *m*; (*chimney*) cañón *m*. **stacks of** (*coll*) un montón de *m sing. v* hacinar; amontonar.

stadium ['steidiəm] *n* estadio *m*.

staff [staːf] *n* vara *f*; palo *m*; (*flag*) asta *f*; personal *m*. **staff-room** *n* (*school*) sala de profesores *f. v* proveer de personal.

stag [stag] *n* venado *m*, ciervo *m*. **stag party** reunión de hombres *f*.

stage [steidʒ] *n* (*theatre*) escenario *m*; (*platform*) estrado *m*; (*point*) etapa *f*; (*phase*) fase *f*. **stage manager** regidor de escena *m. v* representar; efectuar; organizar.

stagger ['stagə] *n* tambaleo *m. v* tambalearse; (*amaze*) asombrar; (*payments, etc.*) escalonar. **staggering** *adj* asombroso.

stagnant ['stagnənt] *adj* estancado. **stagnate** *v* estancarse. **stagnation** *n* estancamiento *m*.

staid [steid] *adj* serio; formal.

stain [stein] *n* mancha *f*; tinte *m*. **stain remover** quitamanchas *m invar. v* manchar; (*wood*) teñir. **stained-glass window** vidriera *f*.

stair [steə] *n* escalón *m*. **staircase** *n also* **stairs** *pl n* escalera *f sing*.

stake[1] [steik] *n* (*post*) poste *m*; estaca *f*; (*for plants*) rodrigón *m*; (*for execution*) hoguera *f*. *v* estacar.

stake[2] [steik] *n* (*bet*) apuesta *f*; (*investment*) intereses *m pl*. **at stake** en juego. *v* apostar.

| **stay**

stale [steil] *adj* (*bread*) duro; (*egg*) poco fresco; (*food*) rancio; (*air*) viciado. **staleness** *n* ranciedad *f*.

stalemate ['steilmeit] *n* (*chess*) ahogado *m*; (*fig*) punto muerto *m*.

stalk¹ [sto:k] *n* (*stem*) tallo *m*.

stalk² [sto:k] *v* acechar. **stalk in/out** entrar/salir con paso airado.

stall¹ [sto:l] *n* (*market*) puesto *m*; (*theatre*) butaca *f*; (*exhibition*) caseta *f*. *v* (*engine*) parar.

stall² [sto:l] *v* (*delay*) andar con rodeos. **stall off** dar largas a.

stallion ['staljən] *n* semental *m*.

stamina ['staminə] *n* vigor *m*; aguante *m*.

stammer ['stamə] *n* tartamudez *f*. *v* tartamudear.

stamp [stamp] *n* sello *m*, timbre *m*; marca *f*; impresión *f*; (*with foot*) zapatazo *m*. **stamp-collecting** *n* filatelia *f*. *v* estampar; sellar; imprimir; (*one's foot*) patear.

stampede [stam'pi:d] *n* desbocamiento *m*; desbandada *f*. *v* provocar la desbandada de.

*stand [stand] *v* (*on feet*) estar de pie; (*place*) poner; resistir; soportar; (*trial*) someterse a; (*remain*) permanecer; (*pay for*) sufragar. *n* posición *f*; plataforma *f*; (*coats, hats*) percha *f*; (*fig*) postura *f*. **standby** (*spare*) repuesto *m*; (*person*) suplente *m, f*; (*ticket*) billete de lista de espera *m*; (*plan*) contingente *m*; (*troops*) alerta *f*. **stand by** (*to be ready*) estar listo. **stand for** significar; representar. **stand out** sobresalir. **standstill** *n* parada *f*. **come to a standstill** pararse. **stand up for** defender.

standard ['standəd] *n* (*weight, length, money*) patrón *m*; (*of living*) nivel *m*; modelo *m*; criterio *m*. *adj* normal; oficial; legal; (*comm*) standard. **standard lamp** lámpara de pie *f*. **standardize** *v* estandardizar; normalizar.

standing ['standiŋ] *adj* de pie; vertical; clásico; fijo. **standing order** (*bank*) pedido regular *m*. *n* posición *f*; situación *f*; reputación *f*; duración *f*.

stank [staŋk] *V* **stink**.

stanza ['stanzə] *n* estancia *f*, estrofa *f*.

staple¹ ['steipl] *n* (*papers*) grapa *f*; (*of wool, cotton*) fibra *f*. *v* sujetar con una grapa.

staple² ['steipl] *adj* básico; principal.

star [sta:] *n* (*astron, cinema*) estrella *f*; asterisco *m*. **stars** *pl n* (*astrol*) astros *m pl*.

starfish *n* estrella de mar *f*. *v* estrellar; ser protagonista. **stardom** *n* estrellato *m*. **starry** *adj* estrellado.

starboard ['sta:bəd] *n* estribor *m*.

starch [sta:tʃ] *n* almidón *m*. *v* almidonar. **starchy** *adj* almidonado.

stare [steə] *n* mirada fija *f*. *v* mirar fijamente.

stark [sta:k] *adj* (*bleak*) desolado; (*stiff*) rígido; completo; puro; absoluto. **stark naked** completamente desnudo.

starling ['sta:liŋ] *n* estornino *m*.

start [sta:t] *n* comienzo *m*; (*of a race*) salida *f*; (*jump*) sobresalto *m*; (*fright*) susto *m*. *v* comenzar, empezar; (*clock*) poner en marcha; (*car*) arrancar; (*establish*) fundar; (*rumour*) lanzar; provocar; sobresaltar. **starter** *n* (*mot*) arranque *m*; (*meal*) entremés *m*.

startle ['sta:tl] *v* asustar. **startling** *adj* sorprendente; alarmante.

state [steit] *n* estado *m*; condición *f*; (*luxury*) lujo *m*; gran pompa *f*. **the States** Los Estados Unidos *m pl*. **statesman** *n* estadista *m*. *v* afirmar, declarar; dar; decir; consignar; exponer. **stately** *adj* majestuoso. **statement** *n* declaración *f*; informe *m*; comunicado *m*; (*bank*) balance mensual *m*.

static ['statik] *adj* estático. *n* (*radio*) parásitos *m pl*.

station ['steiʃən] *n* (*rail, radio*) estación *f*; (*position*) puesto *m*; (*place*) lugar *m*; (*social*) posición *f*. *v* apostar; estacionar.

stationary ['steiʃənəri] *adj* estacionario; inmóvil.

stationer ['steiʃənə] *n* papelero *m*. **stationer's** *n* papelería *f*. **stationery** *n* objetos de escritorio *m pl*; papel de escribir y sobres *m*.

statistics [stə'tistiks] *n* (*science*) estadística *f*. *pl n* (*data*) estadísticas *f pl*. **statistical** *adj* estadístico.

statue ['statju:] *n* estatua *f*.

stature ['statʃə] *n* estatura *f*; (*fig*) talla *f*.

status ['steitəs] *n* (*standing*) categoría *f*; (*state*) condición *f*; (*social standing*) posición *f*.

statute ['statju:t] *n* estatuo *m*. **statutory** *adj* establecido por la ley.

staunch¹ [sto:ntʃ] *adj* fiel; inquebrantable.

staunch² [sto:ntʃ] *v* restañar.

stay [stei] *n* estancia *f*; (*support*) apoyo *m*. *v* (*remain*) quedarse; (*postpone*) aplazar;

(*endure*) resistir; (*support*) apoyar.

steadfast ['stedfa:st] *adj* constante; fijo.

steady ['stedi] *adj* constante; firme; regular; continuo. *v* estabilizar; calmar; sostener. **steadily** *adv* firmemente; regularmente; sin parar. **steadiness** *n* firmeza *f*; estabilidad *f*; uniformidad *f*; regularidad *f*.

steak [steik] *n* (*beefsteak*) bistec *m*; (*of other meat or fish*) filete *m*.

***steal** [sti:l] *v* robar. **stealing** *n* robo *m*.

stealthy ['stelθi] *adj* furtivo.

steam [sti:m] *n* vapor *m*. **let off steam** (*coll*) desahogarse. *v* echar vapor; (*cookery*) cocinar al vapor.

steel [sti:l] *n* acero *m*. **steel wool** estropajo *m*. **steelworks** *pl n* acería *f sing*. **steely** *adj* acerado; inflexible.

steep¹ [sti:p] *adj* escarpado.

steep² [sti:p] *v* empapar.

steeple ['sti:pl] *n* aguja *f*. **steeplechase** *n* carrera de obstáculos *f*. **steeplejack** *n* reparador de chimeneas *m*.

steer [stiə] *v* (*ship*) gobernar; (*vehicle*) dirigir; (*bicycle*) llevar; (*course*) seguir; (*car*) manejar. **steering** *n* (*naut*) gobierno *m*; (*mot*) conducción *f*. **steering-wheel** *n* volante *m*.

stem¹ [stem] *n* tallo *m*; (*glass*) pie *m*. **stem from** derivarse de.

stem² [stem] *v* (*stop*) detener, contener.

stench [stentʃ] *n* tufo *m*.

stencil ['stensl] *n* estarcido *m*. *v* (*typing*) cliché de multicopista *m*.

step [step] *n* paso *m*; (*stairs, ladder*) peldaño *m*; (*doorway*) umbral *m*; (*degree*) escalón *m*; (*measure*) medida *f*. **stepladder** *n* escalera de tijera *f*. *v* dar un paso; ir. **step up** subir; aumentar.

stepbrother ['stepbrʌðə] *n* hermanastro *m*.

stepdaughter ['stepdɔ:tə] *n* hijastra *f*.

stepfather ['stepfa:ðə] *n* padrastro *m*.

stepmother ['stepmʌðə] *n* madrastra *f*.

stepsister ['stepsistə] *n* hermanastra *f*.

stepson ['stepsʌn] *n* hijastro *m*.

stereo ['steriou] *nf*, *adj* estéreo. **stereophonic** [stereofónico.

stereotype ['steriətaip] *n* estereotipo *m*. *v* estereotipar.

sterile ['sterail] *adj* estéril. **sterility** *n* esterilidad *f*. **sterilization** esterilización *f*. **sterilize** *v* esterilizar.

sterling ['stə:liŋ] *n* libra esterlina *f*. *adj* (*silver*) plata de ley *f*; (*character*) excelente.

stern¹ [stə:n] *adj* severo.

stern² [stə:n] *n* (*naut*) popa *f*.

stethoscope ['steθəskoup] *n* estetoscopio *m*.

stew [stju:] *n* estofado *m*. *v* (*meat*) estofar; guisar; (*fruit*) cocer.

steward ['stjuəd] *n* camarero *m*; despensero *m*. **shop steward** enlace sindical *m*. **stewardess** *n* (*ship*) camarera *f*; (*air*) azafata *f*.

stick¹ [stik] *n* madero *m*; estaca *f*; palo *m*; (*club*) garrote *m*; (*walking*) bastón *m*.

***stick²** [stik] *v* fijar; (*thrust*) clavar; (*penetrate*) pinchar; (*glue*) pegar; (*stay*) quedarse. **sticker** pegatina *f*. **stick out** sacar; sobresalir. **stick up for** (*coll*) defender. **sticky** *adj* pegajoso; (*coll*) difícil.

stickler ['stiklə] *n* **be a stickler for** dar mucha importancia a.

stiff [stif] *adj* rígido; (*manner*) distante; (*person*) severo. **stiffen** *v* atiesarse; endurecerse. **stiffness** *n* rigidez *f*; frialdad *f*; obstinación *f*.

stifle ['staifl] *v* ahogar, sofocar; (*smile, etc.*) suprimir. **stifling** *adj* sofocante.

stigma ['stigmə] *n* estigma *m*.

stile [stail] *n* portilla con escalones *f*.

still¹ [stil] *adv* todavía, aún; (*always*) siempre; (*nevertheless*) sin embargo; (*sit, stand*) quieto. *adj* tranquilo; inmóvil; silencioso. **stillborn** *adj* nacido muerto. **still life** bodegón *m*. *n* calma *f*; (*phot*) vista fija *f*.

still² [stil] *n* alambique *m*; destilería *f*.

stilt [stilt] *n* zanco *m*. **stilted** *adj* campanudo.

stimulus ['stimjuləs] *n*, *pl* **-li** estímulo *m*; incentivo *m*. **stimulant** *nm*, *adj* estimulante. **stimulate** *v* estimular. **stimulation** *n* estímulo *m*.

***sting** [stiŋ] *v* picar; herir; (*coll: overcharge*) clavar. *n* (*insect*) aguijón *m*; (*wound*) picadura *f*; (*pain*) escozor *m*.

***stink** [stiŋk] *v* heder, oler mal. *n* hedor *m*.

stint [stint] *n* sesión de trabajo *f*. *v* escatimar; limitar.

stipulate ['stipjuleit] *v* estipular. **stipulation** *n* estipulación *f*.

stir [stə:] *n* agitación *f*; sensación *f*; conmoción *f*. *v* (*tea, etc.*) revolver; mezclar; (*move*) mover; excitar. **stir up** provocar; fomentar.

stirrup ['stirəp] *n* estribo *m*.

stitch [stitʃ] *n* (*sewing*) puntada *f*; (*knitting*) punto *m*; (*med*) punto de sutura *m*; (*pain*) dolor de costado *m*. *v* coser; (*med*) suturar.

stoat [stout] *n* armiño *m*.

stock [stok] *n* (*supply*) reserva *f*; (*farm*) ganado *m*; (*cookery*) caldo *m*; (*lineage*) linaje *m*; (*race*) raza *f*; (*tree*) tronco *m*. **stockbroker** *n* corredor de Bolsa *m*. **stock exchange** Bolsa *f*. **stockpile** *n* reservas *f pl*. **stocktaking** *n* inventario *m*. *v* surtir, abastecer.

Stockholm ['stokhoum] *n* Estocolmo.

stocking ['stokiŋ] *n* media *f*.

stocky ['stoki] *adj* rechoncho.

stodge [stodʒ] *n* (*coll*) comida indigesta *f*. **stodgy** *adj* indigesto.

stoical ['stouikl] *adj* estoico.

stoke [stouk] *v* alimentar.

stole[1] [stoul] *V* **steal**.

stole[2] [stoul] *n* estola *f*.

stomach ['stʌmək] *n* estómago *m*. **stomach-ache** *n* dolor de estómago *m*. *v* soportar.

stone [stoun] *n* piedra *f*; (*fruit*) hueso *m*; (*med*) cálculo *m*. **stone-cold** *adj* helado. *v* (*throw*) apedrear. **stony** *adj* pedregoso.

stood [stud] *V* **stand**.

stool [stu:l] *n* taburete *m*.

stoop [stu:p] *n* espaldas encorvadas *f pl*. *v* encorvarse; agacharse. **stoop to** rebajarse a.

stop [stop] *n* parada *f*; cesación *f*; suspensión *f*; (*stay*) estancia *f*; (*gramm*) punto *m*. *v* parar; impedir; interrumpir; evitar; dejar de; (*a hole*) tapar; (*a gap*) rellenar; cesar. **stop over** (*stay the night*) pasar la noche. **stop-watch** *n* cronómetro *m*. **stoppage** *n* (*blockage*) obstrucción *f*; (*strike*) huelga *f*. **stopper** *n* tapón *m*.

store [sto:] *n* (*supply*) provisión *f*; (*warehouse*) depósito *m*; (*large shop*) almacén *m*; (*smaller shop*) tienda *f*. *v* (*keep*) guardar; almacenar; (*supply*) suministrar. **storage** *n* almacenaje *m*.

storey ['sto:ri] *n* piso *m*.

stork [sto:k] *n* cigüeña *f*.

storm [sto:m] *n* tempestad *f*; (*thunderstorm*) tormenta *f*. *v* (*mil*) asaltar; (*wind*) ser tempestuoso; (*fig*) fabiar. **stormy** *adj* tempestuoso; violento.

story ['sto:ri] *n* historia *f*; cuento *m*.

stout [staut] *adj* fuerte; intrépido; gordo; grueso. *n* cerveza negra *f*.

stove [stouv] *n* (*cooker*) cocina *f*; (*heater*) estufa *f*.

stow [stou] *v* colocar, meter. **stow away** guardar; esconder. **stowaway** *n* polizón *m*.

straddle ['stradl] *v* estar a caballo sobre; montar a horcajadas.

straggle ['stragl] *v* (*leg*) rezagarse; (*spread*) desparramarse. **straggler** *n* rezagado, -a *m*, *f*.

straight [streit] *adj* derecho; recto; en orden; (*hair*) lacio. *adv* derecho; directamente. **straight ahead** todo recto. **straight away** en seguida. **straightforward** *adj* sincero; (*simple*) sencillo. **straighten** *v* enderezar; arreglar.

strain[1] [strein] *n* tensión *f*; esfuerzo *m*; (*med*) torcedura *f*. *v* (*stretch*) estirar; forzar; (*sprain*) torcer; (*filter*) filtrar; (*cookery*) colar. **strainer** *n* colador *m*.

strain[2] [strein] *n* raza *f*; tendencia *f*.

strait [streit] *n* estrecho *m*.

strand[1] [strand] *n* (*hair*) trenza *f*; (*rope*) cabo *m*; (*thread*) hebra *f*.

strand[2] [strand] *n* (*shore*) playa *f*; (*river*) ribera *f*. *v* (*ship*) encallar. **be stranded** hallarse abandonado.

strange [streindʒ] *adj* extraño; raro; inesperado; (*unknown*) desconocido. **stranger** *n* desconocido, -a *m*, *f*.

strangle ['straŋgl] *v* estrangular. **stranglehold** *n* collar de fuerza *m*. **strangler** *n* estrangulador, -a *m*, *f*.

strap [strap] *n* correa *f*; (*on garment*) tirante *m*. *v* atar con correa; (*med*) vendar. **strapping** *adj* robusto.

strategy ['stratədʒi] *n* estrategia *f*. **strategic** *adj* estratégico.

stratum ['stra:təm] *n*, *pl* **-ta** estrato *m*, capa *f*.

straw [stro:] *n* paja *f*. **it's the last straw!** ¡es el colmo!

strawberry ['stro:bəri] *n* (*plant and fruit*) fresa *f*.

stray [strei] *n* animal extraviado *m*. *adj* perdido; extraviado; aislado. *v* errar; desviarse; perderse.

streak [stri:k] *n* raya *f*; vena *f*; (*light*) rayo *m*. *v* rayar; ir como un rayo. **streaky** *adj* rayado.

stream [stri:m] *n* río *m*; arroyo *m*; corriente *f*. **streamlined** *adj* aerodinámico; (*mot*) carenado; (*efficient*) eficaz. *v* correr, fluir.

streamer n serpentina f.

street [stri:t] n calle f.

strength [strenθ] n fuerza f. **strengthen** v fortalecer; reforzar; confirmar.

strenuous ['strenjuəs] adj arduo; enérgico.

stress [stres] n tensión f; presión f; (gramm) acento tónico m. v (emphasize) subrayar; insistir en; acentuar.

stretch [stretʃ] n (scope) alcance m; (of arms, distance) extensión f; (time) período m; (of road) trecho m. **home stretch** última etapa f. v estirar; tender; extender. **stretcher** n camilla f.

stricken ['strikən] adj afligido.

strict [strikt] adj severo; exacto. **strictly** adv severamente; exactamente. **strictly speaking** en realidad. **strictness** n severidad f; exactitud f.

*__stride__ [straid] v dar zancadas; andar a pasos largos. n zancada f; tranco m.

strident ['straidənt] adj estridente; llamativo.

strife [straif] n disputa f, lucha f.

*__strike__ [straik] n (industry) huelga f; (hit) golpe m; (oil, etc.) descubrimiento m. v (hit) golpear; pegar; declararse en huelga; (clock) sonar; (a bargain) cerrar; descubrir; (a match) encender. **striker** n huelguista m, f. **striking** adj impresionante; en huelga.

*__string__ [strinj] n (beads) ensartar; (hang) enristrar. n cuerda f; (of cars) fila f. **string bean** judía verde f. **string quartet** cuarteto de cuerdas m. **stringy** adj fibroso.

stringent ['strindʒənt] adj estricto, riguroso.

strip[1] [strip] v quitar; (undress) desnudar; (bed) deshacer.

strip[2] [strip] n (of land) zona f; (of wood) listón m; (tatter, scrap) tira f.

stripe [straip] n raya f; azote m. **striped** adj con rayas.

*__strive__ [straiv] v esforzarse (a).

strode [stroud] V **stride**.

stroke[1] [strouk] n golpe m, choque m; (swimming) braza f; (clock) campanada f; (mark) trazo m; (med) ataque m; (lightning) rayo m.

stroke[2] [strouk] v acariciar. n caricia f.

stroll [stroul] n vuelta f, paseo m. v dar un paseo, pasearse.

strong [stron] adj fuerte; robusto. adv muy bien. **stronghold** n fortaleza f; (fig) balu-

arte m. **strong-minded** adj resuelto. **strong-room** n cámara acorazada f.

struck [strʌk] V **strike**.

structure ['strʌktʃə] n estructura f; construcción f. **structural** adj estructural; de construcción.

struggle ['strʌgl] n lucha f. v luchar; (to escape) forcejear. **struggle in/out** entrar/salir penosamente.

strum [strʌm] v (guitar) rasguear; (other instruments) rascar. n (guitar) rasgueo m.

strung [strʌŋ] V **string**.

strut[1] [strʌt] v pavonearse.

strut[2] [strʌt] n (arch) puntal m; (aero) montante m.

stub [stʌb] n (tree) tocón m; (cigarette) colilla f; (cheque) talón m; (ticket) resguardo m; (pencil, candle) cabo m. v (toe) tropezar con. **stub out** apagar.

stubble ['stʌbl] n rastrojo m; (chin) barba f.

stubborn ['stʌbən] adj terco; inflexible. **stubbornness** n terquedad f; tenacidad f.

stuck [stʌk] V **stick**.

stud[1] [stʌd] n (collar) botón de camisa m; (boot) taco m; (nail, rivet) tachón m. v tachonar. **studded with** sembrado de, lleno de.

stud[2] [stʌd] n (place) cuadra f; (animal) semental m. **stud horse** caballo padre m.

student ['stju:dənt] n estudiante m, f; (pupil) alumno, -a m, f.

studio ['stju:diou] n estudio m.

study ['stʌdi] n estudio m; (room) gabinete m. v estudiar; examinar. **studious** adj estudioso; solícito.

stuff [stʌf] n material m, materia f; cosas f pl; (cloth) tejido m. v llenar; (cram) atestar; (cookery) rellenar. **stuffing** n (furniture) rehenchimiento m; (cookery) relleno m; (padding) paja f. **stuffy** adj mal ventilado; (person) pomposo.

stumble ['stʌmbl] v tropezar.

stump [stʌmp] n (tree) tocón m; (limb) muñón m; (pencil, etc.) cabo m; (cricket) poste m. v (fig) dejar perplejo.

stun [stʌn] v aturdir; (amaze) pasmar. **stunning** adj aturdidor; (coll) fenomenal.

stung [stʌŋ] V **sting**.

stunk [stʌŋk] V **stink**.

stunt[1] [stʌnt] v impedir el crecimiento de. **stunted** adj atrofiado.

stunt[2] [stʌnt] n hazaña f; truco publicitario

m. **stunt man** doble especial *m.*

stupid ['stju:pid] *adj* estúpido. **stupidity** *n* estupidez *f.*

stupor ['stju:pə] *n* estupor *m.*

sturdy ['stə:di] *adj* robusto, vigoroso. **sturdiness** *n* robustez *f*; vigor *m.*

sturgeon ['stə:dʒən] *n* esturión *m.*

stutter ['tʌtə] *n* tartamudeo *m. v* tartamudear.

sty [stai] *n* (*pig*) pocilga *f*; (*med*) orzuelo *m.*

style [stail] *n* estilo *m*; (*kind*) tipo *m*; manera *f*; (*fashion*) moda *f*; (*clothes*) hechura *f*; (*hair*) peinado *m. v* (*design*) diseñar. **stylish** *adj* elegante.

stylus ['stailəs] *n* (*tool*) estilete *m*; (*record player*) aguja *f.*

suave [swa:v] *adj* afable, urbano.

subconscious [sʌb'kɒnʃəs] *nm, adj* subconsciente.

subcontract [sʌbkən'trakt] *v* subcontratar. **subcontractor** *n* subcontratista *m.*

subdivide [sʌbdi'vaid] *v* subdividir(se). **subdivision** *n* subdivisión *f.*

subdue [səb'dju:] *v* (*riot. etc.*) sojuzgar; (*sound, light*) atenuar; (*voice*) bajar; (*pain*) aliviar; (*feelings*) contener. **subdued** *adj* sojuzgado; atenuado; bajo; aliviado; contenido.

subject ['sʌbdʒikt; *v* səb'dʒekt] *n* sujeto *m*; (*school*) asignatura *f*; (*theme*) tema *m*; motivo *m*; (*people*) súbdito, -a *m. f.* **subject to** sujeto a; propenso a. *v* sojuzgar; (*to an examination*) someter. **subjection** *n* sujeción *f.* **subjective** *adj* subjetivo.

subjunctive [səb'dʒʌŋktiv] *nm, adj* subjuntivo.

sublet [sʌb'let] *v* subarrendar.

sublime [sə'blaim] *adj* sublime. *n* lo sublime.

submarine ['sʌbməri:n] *n* submarino *m.*

submerge [səb'mə:dʒ] *v* sumergir. *n* sumersión *f.*

submit [səb'mit] *v* someter. **submission** *n* sumisión *f.* **submissive** *adj* sumiso.

subnormal [sʌb'no:məl] *adj* subnormal.

subordinate [sə'bo:dinət] *adj* (*gramm*) subordinado; subalterno. *n* subordinado, -a *m. f*; subalterno, -a *m. f. v* subordinar. **subordination** *n* subordinación *f.*

subscribe [səb'skraib] *v* **subscribe to** aprobar; (*newspaper*) subscribirse a. **subscriber** *n* suscriptor, -a *m. f*; abonado, -a *m, f.* **sub-**

scription *n* suscripción *f*; abono *m*; (*membership fee*) cuota *f.*

subsequent ['sʌbsikwənt] *adj* subsiguiente; posterior.

subservient [səb'sə:viənt] *adj* subordinado; servil.

subside [səb'said] *v* (*land*) hundirse; (*flood*) bajar; (*excitement*) calmarse; (*wind*) amainar. **subsidence** *n* hundimiento *m.*

subsidiary [səb'sidiəri] *adj* subsidiario; secundario; (*comm*) afiliado. *n* (*comm*) filial *f.*

subsidize ['sʌbsidaiz] *v* subvencionar. **subsidy** *n* subvención *f.*

subsist [səb'sist] *v* subsistir. **subsistence** *n* subsistencia *f.*

substance ['sʌbstəns] *n* sustancia *f.* **substantial** *adj* sustancial; sustancioso; importante.

substandard [sʌb'standəd] *adj* inferior.

substitute ['sʌbstitju:t] *n* (*person*) sustituto, -a *m. f.* substituto, -a *m. f*; (*thing*) sucedáneo *m. v* sustituir, reemplazar. **substitution** *n* sustitución *f.*

subtitle ['sʌtl] *n* subtítulo *m. v* subtitular.

subtle ['sʌtl] *adj* sutil; delicado. **subtlety** *n* sutileza *f*; delicadeza *f.*

subtract [səb'trakt] *v* restar, sustraer. **subtraction** *n* resta *f*, sustracción *f.*

suburb ['sʌbə:b] *n* suburbio *m.* **the suburbs** las afueras *f pl.* **suburban** *adj* suburbano.

subvert [səb'və:t] *v* derribar; corromper. **subversion** *n* subversión *f.* **subversive** *adj* subversivo.

subway ['sʌbwei] *n* pasaje subterráneo *m*; (*US*) metro *m.*

succeed [sək'si:d] *v* triunfar; (*follow*) suceder; (*inherit*) heredar. **succeeding** *adj* sucesivo; venidero. **success** *n* éxito *m*; triunfo *m.* **successful** *adj* que tiene éxito; próspero. **successfully** *adv* con éxito. **succession** *n* sucesión *f*; herencia *f.* **successive** *adj* sucesivo. **successor** *n* sucesor, -a *m, f.*

succinct [sək'siŋkt] *adj* sucinto.

succulent ['sʌkjulənt] *adj* suculento; (*plant*) carnoso. *n* planta carnosa *f.*

succumb [sə'kʌm] *v* sucumbir.

such [sʌtʃ] *adj* tal; semejante, parecido; tan, tanto. **such as** como. *adv* tan, tanto. *pron* los que, las que; lo que; todo lo que; esto, éste, ésta. **as such** en si.

suck [sʌk] v chupar; (*baby*) mamar. **suck up to** (*slang*) dar coba a.

sucker ['sʌkə] n (*bot*) chupón m; (*device*) émbolo m; (*slang: simpleton*) primo m.

suction ['sʌkʃən] n succión f.

sudden ['sʌdən] adj súbito; inesperado; repentino. **all of a sudden** de repente.

suds [sʌdz] pl n jabonaduras f pl.

sue [su:] v proceder contra.

suede [sweid] n ante m.

suet ['su:it] n sebo m.

suffer ['sʌfə] v sufrir, padecer; tolerar; dejar; (*undergo*) aguantar. **suffering** n sufrimiento m, padecimiento m; dolor m.

sufficient [sə'fiʃənt] adj suficiente; bastante, **suffice** v ser suficiente, bastar. **sufficiently** adv suficientemente, bastante.

suffix ['sʌfiks] n sufijo m.

suffocate ['sʌfəkeit] v ahogar, sofocar. **suffocation** n ahogo m; asfixia f.

sugar ['ʃugə] n azúcar m. **sugar bowl** azucarero m. **sugar cane** caña de azúcar f. **sugar lump** terrón de azúcar m.

suggest [sə'dʒest] v sugerir; indicar. **suggestion** n sugerencia f; indicación f. **suggestive** adj sugestivo; evocador.

suicide ['su:isaid] n (*act*) suicidio m; (*person*) suicida m, f. **commit suicide** suicidarse. **suicidal** adj suicida.

suit [su:t] n traje m; (*woman's*) conjunto m; (*law*) pleito m; (*cards*) palo m. **suitcase** n maleta f. v convenir; venir bien a. **suitable** adj conveniente; apropiado.

suite [swi:t] n (*in hotel*) suite f; (*furniture*) juego m.

sulk [sʌlk] v enfurruñarse. n enfurruñamiento m. **sulky** adj enfurruñado.

sullen ['sʌlən] adj taciturno; malhumorado. **sullenness** n taciturnidad f; mal humor m.

sulphur ['sʌlfə] n azufre m. **sulphuric** adj sulfúrico.

sultan ['sʌltən] n sultán m.

sultana [sʌl'ta:nə] n pasa de Esmirna f.

sultry ['sʌltri] adj (*weather*) sofocante; (*person*) sensual.

sum [sʌm] n suma f; cantidad f; cálculo m. v **sum up** recapitular; resumir; (*person*) evaluar.

summarize ['sʌməraiz] v resumir, recapitular. **summary** n resumen m; adj sumario.

summer ['sʌmə] n verano m. **summer holidays** vacaciones de verano f pl. **summerhouse** n cenador m.

summit ['sʌmit] n cumbre f, cima f; (*fig*) apogeo m.

summon ['sʌmən] v llamar. convocar; mandar; hacer venir. **summon up** evocar.

summons ['sʌmənz] pl n llamamiento m; (*law*) citación f. v citar.

sumptuous ['sʌmptʃuəs] adj suntuoso.

sun [sʌn] n sol m. **sunny** adj bañado de sol.

sunbathe ['sʌnbeið] v tomar el sol. **sunbathing** n baños de sol m pl.

sunbeam ['sʌnbi:m] n rayo de sol m.

sunburn ['sʌnbə:n] n (*tan*) bronceado m; (*pain*) quemadura del sol f. **sunburnt** adj bronceado; quemado por el sol.

Sunday ['sʌndi] n domingo m.

sundial ['sʌndaiəl] n reloj de sol m.

sundry ['sʌndri] adj varios. **all and sundry** todo el mundo. **sundries** pl n artículos diversos m pl.

sunflower ['sʌn,flauə] n girasol m.

sunglasses ['sʌngla:siz] pl n gafas de sol f pl.

sunk [sʌŋk] V **sink**.

sunlight ['sʌnlait] n luz del sol f.

sunrise ['sʌnraiz] n salida del sol f.

sunroof ['sʌnru:f] n techo solar m

sunset ['sʌnset] n puesta del sol f.

sunshine ['sʌnʃain] n sol m.

sunstroke ['sʌnstrouk] n insolación f.

sun-tan ['sʌntan] n bronceado m. **sun-tan lotion** loción bronceadora f.

super ['su:pə] adj (*coll*) estupendo; formidable.

superannuation [,su:pərənju'eiʃən] n jubilación f.

superb [su:'pə:b] adj soberbio; magnífico.

supercilious [,su:pə'siliəs] adj altanero; desdeñoso.

superficial [,su:pə'fiʃəl] adj superficial.

superfluous [su'pə:fluəs] adj superfluo.

superhuman [su:pə'hju:mən] adj sobrehumano.

superimpose [,su:pərim'pouz] v sobreponer. **superimposed** adj (*photo, etc.*) superpuesto.

superintendent [,su:pərin'tendənt] n superintendente m, f; director, -a m, f; (*police*) subjefe de la policía m.

superior [su:'piəriə] n, adj superior, -a.

superiority n superioridad f.

superlative [su:'pə:lətiv] adj superlativo; supremo. (gramm) nm, adj superlativo.

supermarket ['su:pə,ma:kit] n supermercado m.

supernatural [,su:pə'natʃərəl] adj sobrenatural. n lo sobrenatural.

supersede [,su:pə'si:d] v sustituir, reemplazar.

supersonic [,su:pə'sonik] adj supersónico.

superstition [su:pə'stiʃən] n superstición f. **superstitious** adj supersticioso.

supervise ['su:pəvaiz] v supervisar; vigilar. **supervision** n superintendencia f. **supervisor** n supervisor, -a m, f; director, -a m, f.

supper ['sʌpə] n cena f.

supple ['sʌpl] adj flexible, elástico. **suppleness** n flexibilidad f.

supplement ['sʌpləmənt] n suplemento m. v suplir, complementar. **supplementary** adj suplementario.

supply [sə'plai] n (stock) surtido m; provisión f; (act of supplying) suministro m. **supplier** proveedor. **supplies** pl n material m sing; provisiones pl, (stores) víveres m pl. v alimentar; proveer; abastecer; presentar.

support [sə'po:t] n apoyo m; sostén m; soporte m. v apoyar; sostener; defender; (financially) mantener. **supporter** n partidario, -a m, f; (sport) aficionado, -a.

suppose [sə'pouz] v suponer. **supposed** adj supuesto. **be supposed to** deber. **supposedly** adv según se supone. **supposing** conj si, suponiendo (que). **supposition** n suposición f.

suppress [sə'pres] v suprimir; (yawn, laugh, etc.) contener; (passion) dominar; (fact) disimular; (revolt) sofocar; (publication) prohibir; (news) ocultar. **suppression** n supresión f; dominio m; represión f; prohibición f; ocultación f.

supreme [su'pri:m] adj supremo. **supremacy** n supremacía f.

surcharge ['sə:tʃa:dʒ] n sobrecarga f.

sure [ʃuə] adj seguro, cierto. **sure enough** efectivamente. **sure-footed** adj de pie firme. **surely** adv seguramente; sin duda.

surety ['ʃuərəti] n garantía f, fianza f.

surf [sə:f] n resaca f; (foam) espuma f. **surfboard** n tabla hawaiana f. **surf** v (fig: Internet) navegar. **surfer** surfista m, f; (Internet) navegante m, f. **surfing** n surf m.

surface ['sə:fis] n superficie f. **on the surface** en apariencia. v (road) revestir; (swimmer) salir a la superficie; (submarine) sacar a la superficie.

surfeit ['sə:fit] n exceso m.

surge [sə:dʒ] n oleada f; (anger) ola f. v (sea) levantarse; (crowd) bullir.

surgeon ['sə:dʒən] n cirujano m. **surgery** n (skill) cirugía f; (place) consultorio m. **surgical** adj quirúrgico.

surly ['sə:li] adj malhumorado.

surmount [sə'maunt] v vencer, superar.

surname ['sə:neim] n apellido m.

surpass [sə'pa:s] v superar, sobrepasar.

surplus ['sə:pləs] n excedente m. adj sobrante.

surprise [sə'praiz] n sorpresa f. adj de sorpresa. v sorprender.

surrealism [sə'riəlizəm] n surrealismo m. **surrealist** n(m + f), adj surrealista. **surrealistic** adj surrealista.

surrender [sə'rendə] v rendir; (give up) ceder; entregar. n rendición f; capitulación f.

surreptitious [,sʌrəp'tiʃəs] adj subrepticio.

surround [sə'raund] v cercar, rodear. n borde m. **surrounding** adj circundante. **surroundings** pl n (environment) medio ambiente m; (environs) alrededores m pl.

surveillance [sə:'veiləns] v estar bajo vigilancía

survey ['sə:vei; v sə'vei] n inspección f; (report) informe m; (of a question) examen m; panorama m; (land) medición f. v inspeccionar; estudiar; examinar; contemplar; medir. **surveying** n inspección f; agrimensura f. **surveyor** n (land) agrimensor m; (house) inspector m.

survive [sə'vaiv] v sobrevivir a. **survival** n supervivencia f. **survivor** n sobreviviente m. f.

susceptible [sə'septəbl] adj susceptible; sensible.

suspect ['sʌspekt; v sə'spekt] n, adj sospechoso, -a. v sospechar.

suspend [sə'spend] v suspender. **suspender** n liga f. **suspense** n incertidumbre f; (book, film) suspense m. **in suspense** pendiente. **suspension** n suspensión f. **suspension bridge** puente colgante m.

suspicion [sə'spiʃən] n sospecha f. **suspicious** adj (suspecting) suspicaz; (suspected) sospechoso.

sustain [sə'stein] *v* sostener; mantener; apoyar; (*suffer*) recibir.

swab [swob] *n* (*mop*) estropajo *m*; (*med; pad*) tapón *m*. *v* fregar con estropajo; limpiar con tapón.

swagger ['swagə] *n* pavoneo *m*. *v* pavonearse; darse importancia.

swallow¹ ['swolou] *v* tragar. **swallow up** tragarse. *n* trago *m*; (*amount*) bocado *m*.

swallow² ['swolou] *n* (*bird*) golondrina *f*.

swam [swam] *V* **swim**.

swamp [swomp] *n* pantano *m*; marisma *f*. *v* sumergir; inundar. **swampy** *adj* pantanoso.

swan [swon] *n* cisne *m*.

swank [swaŋk] (*coll*) *n* fanfarronada *f*; (*person*) fanfarrón, -ona *m, f*. *v* fanfarronear. **swanky** *adj* fanfarrón.

swap *or* **swop** [swop] *n* cambio *m*. truque *m*. *v* cambiar, trocar.

swarm [swo:m] *n* (*bees*) enjambre *m*; (*fig*) multitud *f*. *v* enjambrar; (*fig*) pulular.

swarthy ['swo:ði] *adj* moreno.

swat [swot] *v* aplastar.

sway [swei] *n* balanceo *m*; oscilación *f*; dominio *m*. *v* balancearse; oscilar; (*influence*) influir.

*swear [sweə] *v* jurar. **swear in** tomar juramento a. **swear-word** *n* palabrota *f*.

sweat [swet] *n* sudor *m*. *v* sudar.

sweater *n* suéter *m*.

swede [swi:d] *n* nabo *f*.

Sweden ['swi:dn] *n* Suecia *f*. **Swede** *n* sueco, -a *m, f*. **Swedish** *nm, adj* sueco.

*sweep [swi:p] *v* deshollinar; barrer; explorar. **sweep in/out** entrar/salir rápidamente. **sweep through** difundirse. *n* (*chimney*) deshollinador *m*; (*a cleaning*) barrido *m*; (*curve*) curva *f*. **make a clean sweep** llevárselo todo. **sweeping** *adj* aplastante; demasiado general. **sweeping statement** declaración demasiado general *f*.

sweet [swi:t] *adj* (*taste*) dulce; (*air, breath, etc.*) fresco; (*smell*) bueno; (*friendly*) encantador; (*kind*) bondadoso. *n* (*toffee*) caramelo *m*; (*dessert*) postre *m*. **sweetbread** *n* mollejas *f pl*. **sweet corn** maíz tierno *m*. **sweetheart** *n* novio, -a *m, f*. **sweet potato** patata boniato *f*. **sweet-shop** *n* confitería *f*. **sweeten** *v* azucarar, endulzar. **sweetener** edulcorante *m*. **sweetly** *adv* dulcemente; (*sound*) melodiosamente. **sweetness** *n* dulzor *m*;

(*character*) dulzura *f*.

*swell [swel] *v* hinchar; inflarse. *n* inflado *m*; hinchazón *m*; curvatura *f*. **swelling** *n* inflamiento *m*.

swelter ['sweltə] *v* sofocarse de calor. **sweltering** *adj* sofocante.

swerve [swə:v] *v* desviar; (*vehicle*) dar un viraje. *n* viraje *m*.

swift [swift] *adj* rápido; pronto. *n* (*bird*) vencejo *m*. **swiftness** rapidez *f*; prontitud *f*.

swill [swil] *v* lavar con much agua; (*drink*) beber a tragos. *n* (*for pigs*) bazofia *f*.

*swim [swim] *v* nadar. *n* baño *m*. **swimmer** *n* nadador, -a *m, f*. **swimming** *n* natación *f*. **swimming baths** *or* **pool** piscina *f*. **swimming costume** traje de baño *m*.

swindle ['swindl] *n* estafa *f*. *v* estafar. **swindler** *n* estafador, -a *m, f*.

swine [swain] *n* cerdo *m*, puerco *m*; (*impol*) canalla *m, f*.

*swing [swiŋ] *v* hacer girar; balancear; oscilar; virar. *n* (*amusement*) columpio *m*; oscilación *f*; impulso *m*; (*pol*) viraje *m*. **in full swing** a toda velocidad.

swipe [swaip] (*coll*) *n* golpetazo *m*. *v* golpear con fuerza; (*steal*) afanar.

swirl [swə:l] *n* remolino *m*. *v* arremolinarse.

swish [swiʃ] *n* silbo *m*; (*of water*) susurro *m*; (*of garment*) crujido *m*. *v* (*cane*) blandir; (*tail*) menear.

Swiss [swis] *n, adj* suizo, -a. **Swiss roll** brazo de gitano *m*.

switch [switʃ] *n* (*elec*) interruptor *m*, conmutador *m*; (*change*) paso *m*; (*stick*) varilla *f*. **switchboard** *n* centralita de teléfonos *f*. *v* (*opinion, policy*) cambiar de; (*places*) cambiar; (*a train*) desviar. **switch off** desconectar. **switch on** encender.

Switzerland ['switsələnd] *n* Suiza *f*.

swivel ['swivl] *n* pivote *m*, *v* girar sobre un eje; dar una vuelta.

swollen ['swoulən] *V* **swell**.

swoop [swu:p] *n* calada *f*; redada *f*. **at one fell swoop** de un solo golpe. *v* calarse, abatirse.

swop *V* **swap**.

sword [so:d] *n* espada *f*. **swordfish** *n* pez espada *m*.

sworn [swo:n] *V* **swear**.

swot [swot] (*coll*) *n* empollón, -ona *m, f*. *v* empollar. **swotting** *n* estudio *m*.

swum [swʌm] V **swim**.

swung [swʌŋ] V **swing**.

sycamore ['sikəmɔ:] n sicomoro m.

syllable ['siləbl] n sílaba f. **syllabic** adj silábico.

syllabus ['siləbəs] n programa m.

symbol ['simbl] n símbolo m, emblema m. **symbolic** adj simbólico. **symbolism** n simbolismo m. **symbolize** v simbolizar.

symmetry ['simitri] n simetría f. **symmetrical** adj simétrico.

sympathy ['simpəθi] n pésame m; compasión f. **sympathetic** adj compasivo; comprensivo; favorable. **sympathize with** compadecerse de.

symphony ['simfəni] n sinfonía f. **symphonic** adj sinfónico.

symposium [sim'pouziəm] n simposio m.

symptom ['simptəm] n síntoma m. **symptomatic** adj sintomático.

synagogue ['sinəgog] n sinagoga f.

synchromesh ['siŋkroumeʃ] n sincronizador.

synchronize ['siŋkrənaiz] v sincronizar. **synchronization** n sincronización f.

syncopate ['siŋkəpeit] n sincopar. **syncopation** n síncopa f.

syndicate ['sindikit] n sindicato m.

syndrome ['sindroum] n síndrome m.

synonym ['sinənim] n sinónimo m. **synonymous** adj sinónimo.

synopsis [si'nopsis] n, pl **-ses** sinopsis f invar.

syntax ['sintaks] n sintaxis f.

synthesis ['sinθisis] n, pl **-ses** síntesis f invar. **synthesize** v sintetizar.

syphilis ['sifilis] n sífilis f.

syringe [si'rindʒ] n jeringa f. v jeringar.

syrup ['sirəp] n (med) jarabe m; (fruit) almíbar m. **syrupy** adj almibarado.

system ['sistəm] n sistema m; método m. **systematic** adj sistemático. **systems analyst** analista de sistemas m.

T

tab [tab] n etiqueta f. **keep tabs on** (coll) tener controlado.

tabby ['tabi] n gato atigrado m.

table ['teibl] n mesa f. **table-cloth** n mantel m. **table-mat** n salvamanteles m invar. **table-napkin** n servilleta f. **tablespoon** n cucharón m. **tablespoonful** cucharada f. **table tennis** tenis de mesa m. **clear the table** levantar la mesa. **set the table** poner la mesa.

table d'hôte [ta:blə'dout] n menú m.

tablet ['tablit] n (med, soap) pastilla f; (stone, chocolate) tableta f; (writing-paper) bloc m.

taboo [ta'bu:] nm, adj tabú.

tabulate ['tabjuleit] v tabular.

tacit ['tasit] adj tácito.

taciturn ['tasitə:n] adj taciturno.

tack [tak] n (nail) tachuela f; (sewing) hilván m; (naut: change of direction) virada f; (distance sailed) bordada f. v clavar con tachuelas; hilvanar; virar de bordo.

tackle ['takl] n (ropes) jarcias f pl; (rigging) aparejo m; (equipment) trastos m pl; (sport) placaje m. v placar; (seize) agarrar; (fig) abordar, emprender.

tact [takt] n tacto m. **tactful** adj con tacto, discreto. **tactless** adj falto de tacto, indiscreto.

tactics ['taktiks] pl n táctica f sing. **tactical** adj táctico.

tadpole ['tadpoul] n renacuajo m.

taffeta ['tafitə] n tafetán m.

tag [tag] n etiqueta f; (shoelace) herrete m; (game) pillapilla m. **tag along** (coll) seguir.

tail [teil] n cola f; rabo m; (coat, shirt) faldón m. **tailback** caravana f. **tail-end** n zaga f, rabera f. **tails** pl n (coin) cruz f sing. v (coll) seguir.

tailor ['teilə] n sastre m. v entallar; (fig) adaptar.

taint [teint] v (stain) manchar; (food) corromper; (air) viciar; (fig) mancillar. n mancha f; corrupción f; contaminación f.

*take [teik] v tomar; llevarse; (carry) cargarse; (phot) sacar; (shoe size) calzar; (occupy) ocupar; (responsibility) asumir; (bear) aguantar; (suppose) suponer. **take after** parecerse a. **take along** llevarse. **take away** quitar; (subtract) restar. **take back** (return) devolver; (retract) retirar. **take down** (pictures, curtains) descolgar; (from a shelf) bajar; (write) apuntar. **take someone down a peg** (coll) bajarle los humos a

alguien. **take in** acoger; (*situation*) entender; (*clothes*) achicar; (*coll: deceive*) engañar.
take off (*clothes*) quitarse; (*aero*) despegar.
take-off *n* despegue *m*; (*coll*) imitamonos *m invar*. **take on** (*employ*) contratar; (*challenge*) competir con. **take-over** (*comm*) adquisición *f*.

talcum powder ['talkəm] *n* talco *m*.

tale [teil] *n* cuento *m*. **fairy tales** cuentos de hadas *m pl*. **tell tales** (*coll*) contar chismes.

talent ['talənt] *n* talento *m*. **talented** *adj* talentoso, talentudo.

talk [to:k] *n* conversación *f*; charla *f*; (*lecture*) conferencia *f*; (*speech*) discurso *m*. *v* decir; hablar. **talk back** replicar. **talk down to** ponerse al alcance de. **talk into** convencer para que. **talk over** discutir. **talkative** *adj* hablador. **talking** *n* conversación *f*. **talking point** tema de conversación *m*.

tall [to:l] *adj* alto; grande. **tallboy** *n* cómoda alta *f*. **tallness** *n* altura *f*; lo alto.

tally ['tali] *n* tarja *f*; cuenta *f*. *v* tarjar; cuadrar.

talon ['talən] *n* garra *f*.

tambourine [tambə'ri:n] *n* pandereta *f*, pandero *m*.

tame [teim] *adj* manso; domesticado; (*not exciting*) aburrido. *v* domesticar; amansar.

tamper ['tampə] *v* **tamper with** (*text*) amañar; (*spoil*) estropear.

tampon ['tampon] *n* tapón *m*.

tan [tan] *n* bronceado *m*, color tostado *m*. *adj* bronceado, tostado. (*hide*) curtir; (*sun*) broncear, tostar.

tandem ['tandəm] *n* tándem *m*.

tangent ['tandʒənt] *nf*, *adj* tangente. **go off at a tangent** salirse por la tangente.

tangerine [tandʒə'ri:n] *n* (*fruit*) mandarina *f*.

tangible ['tandʒəbl] *adj* tangible.

tangle ['taŋgl] *v* enmarañar; enredar. *n* maraña *f*; enredo *m*.

tank [taŋk] *n* tanque *m*, cisterna *f*, depósito *m*; (*mil*) tanque *m*. **tanker** *n* (*lorry*) camión cisterna *m*; (*ship*) petrolero *m*.

tankard ['taŋkəd] *n* jarro *m*.

tantalize ['tantəlaiz] *v* atormentar. **tantalizing** *adj* que atormenta.

tantamount ['tantəmaunt] *adj* **be tantamount to** ser equivalente a.

tantrum ['tantrəm] *n* berrinche *m*, rabieta *f*. **fly into a tantrum** coger una rabieta.

tap¹ [tap] *n* golpecito *m*. **tap-dance** *n* zapateado *m*. *v* golpear ligeramente.

tap² [tap] *n* (*water*) grifo *m*; (*barrel*) espita *f*. *v* poner una espita a; (*phone*) interceptar; (*fig: draw on*) utilizar.

tape [teip] *n* cinta *f*; (*recording*) cinta magnetofónica *f*. **tape-measure** *n* cinta métrica *f*. **tape-recorder** *n* magnetófono *m*. **tapeworm** *n* tenia *f*. *v* (*record*) grabar; (*fasten*) atar con cinta.

taper ['teipə] *n* (*candle*) vela *f*; (*narrowing*) estrechamiento *m*. *v* estrechar. **tapering** *adj* cónico.

tapestry ['tapəstri] *n* tapiz *m*.

tapioca [tapi'oukə] *n* tapioca *f*.

tar [ta:] *n* alquitrán *m*. *v* alquitranar.

tarantula [tə'rantjulə] *n* tarántula *f*.

target ['ta:git] *n* blanco *m*; (*fig*) objeto *m*.

tariff ['tarif] *n* tarifa *f*.

tarmac ['ta:mak] *n* superficie alquitranada *f*.

tarnish ['ta:niʃ] *v* deslustrar. *n* deslustre *m*.

tarpaulin [ta:'po:lin] *n* lona alquitranada *f*.

tarragon ['tarəgən] *n* estragón *m*.

tart¹ [ta:t] *adj* agrio; ácido.

tart² [ta:t] *n* tarta *f*; (*slang*) fulana *f*.

tartar ['ta:tə] *n* (*chem*) tártaro *m*; (*on teeth*) sarro *m*.

task [ta:sk] *n* tarea *f*. **taskmaster** *n* capataz *m*.

tassel ['tasəl] *n* borla *f*.

taste [teist] *n* (*sense*) gusto *m*; sabor *m*. *v* probar; saber. **taste of** saber a. **tasteful** *adj* de buen gusto. **tasteless** *adj* insípido; (*in bad taste*) de mal gusto. **tasty** *adj* sabroso.

tattered ['tatəd] *adj* andrajoso.

tattoo¹ [tə'tu:] *n* (*on skin*) tatuaje *m*. *v* tatuar.

tattoo² [tə'tu:] *n* (*mil*) desfile militar *m*; (*drumming*) repiqueteo *m*.

tatty ['tati] *adj* (*coll*) en mal estado.

taunt [to:nt] *v* mofarse de. *n* mofa *f*. **taunting** *adj* burlón; provocante.

Taurus ['to:rəs] *n* Tauro *m*.

taut [to:t] *adj* tenso, tirante. **tautness** *n* tensión *f*, tirantez *f*.

tavern ['tavən] *n* (*bar*) taberna *f*; (*inn*) venta *f*.

tawny ['to:ni] *adj* leonado.

tax [taks] *n* impuesto *m*. contribución *f*.
tax disc (*vehicle*) pegatina del impuesto de circulación *f*. **tax-free** *adj* exento de impuestos. **tax evasion** evasión fiscal *f*. **tax haven** refugio fiscal *m*. **taxpayer** *n* contribuyente *m*, *f*. **tax return** declaración de renta *f*. *v* gravar con un impuesto; imponer contribuciones; (*try*) poner a prueba. **taxable** *adj* imponible. **taxation** *n* impuestos *m pl*; (*system*) sistema tributario *m*.

taxi ['taksi] *n* taxi *m*. **taxi-driver** *n* taxista *m*, *f*. **taximeter** *n* taxímetro *m*. **taxi rank** parada de taxis *f*. *v* (*aero*) rodar por la pista.

tea [ti:] *n* té *m*; (*snack*) merienda *f*. **teacup** *n* taza de té *f*. **teapot** *n* tetera *f*. **teaspoon** *n* cucharilla *f*. **teaspoonful** *n* cucharadita *f*. **tea towel** trapo de cocina *m*.

***teach** [ti:tʃ] *v* enseñar. **teacher** *n* (*primary*) maestro, -a *m*. *f*; (*secondary*) profesor, -a *m*. *f*. **teaching** *n* enseñanza *f*.

teak [ti:k] *n* teca *f*.

team [ti:m] *n* (*yoked animals*) yunta *f*; (*horses*) tronco *m*; (*people*) equipo *m*. **teammate** *n* compañero de equipo *m*. **team spirit** espíritu de equipo *m*. **team-work** *n* trabajo de equipo *m*. *v* **team up** agruparse.

***tear¹** [teə] *v* desgarrar; (*snatch*) arrancar. **tear along/out** ir a toda velocidad. **tear down** demoler. **tear off** (*coupon*) cortar. *n* rasgón *m*.

tear² [tiə] *n* lágrima *f*. **tear gas** gas lacrimógeno *m*. **tear-jerker** (*coll*) *n* obra sentimental *f*. **tearful** *adj* lloroso.

tease [ti:z] *v* provocar. *n* broma *f*; (*person*) bromista *m*. *f*. **teasing** *n* bromas *f pl*

teat [ti:t] *n* pezón *m*; (*animals*) teta *f*.

technique [tek'ni:k] *n* técnica *f*. **technical** *adj* técnico. **technicality** *n* detalle técnico *m*. **technician** *n* técnico, -a *m*, *f*. **technological** *adj* tecnológico. **technology** *n* tecnología *f*.

teddy bear ['tedi,beə] *n* osito de felpa *m*.

tedious ['ti:diəs] *adj* latoso. **tediousness** *n* also **tedium** pesadez *f*, tedio *m*.

tee [ti:] *n* tee *m*. *v* **tee off** dar el primer golpe.

teem [ti:m] *v* pulular, hormiguear.

teenage ['ti:neidʒ] *adj* adolescente. **teenager** *n* adolescente *m*. *f*. **teens** *pl n* adolescencia *f sing*.

teeth [ti:θ] *V* **tooth**.

teethe [ti:ð] *v* echar los dientes. **teething**

n dentición *f*.

teetotaller [ti:'toutələ] *n* abstemio, -a *m*, *f*.

telecommunications [,telikəmju:ni-'keiʃənz] *pl n* telecomunicaciones *f pl*.

telegram ['teligram] *n* telegrama *m*.

telegraph ['teligra:f] *n* telégrafo *m*. **telegraph pole** poste telegráfico *m*. *v* telegrafiar. **telegraphic** *adj* telegráfico.

telepathy [tə'lepəθi] *n* telepatía *f*. **telepathic** *adj* telepático.

telephone ['telifoun] *n* teléfono *m*. **telephone box** *or* **kiosk** cabina telefónica *f*. **telephone call** llamada telefónica *f*. **telephone directory** guía de teléfonos *f*. **telephone exchange** central telefónica *f*. **telephone number** número de teléfono *m*. **telephone operator** *or* **telephonist** telefonista *m*, *f*. *v* telefonear a.

telesales ['teliseilz] *n* televentas *f* (*pl*)

telescope ['teliskoup] *n* telescopio *m*. **telescopic** *adj* telescópico.

television ['teliviʒən] *n* televisión *f*. **television set** televisor *m*. **televise** *v* televisar.

telex ['teleks] *n* télex *m*.

***tell** [tel] *v* decir; (*story*) contar; comunicar; mandar; (*identify*) reconocer; (*distinguish*) distinguir; (*deduce*) deducir; (*observe*) notar. **tell against** perjudicar. **tell of** hablar de. **tell off** (*coll*) regañar **tell on** afectar a. **tell-tale** *adj* revelador.

temper ['tempə] *n* (*anger*) cólera *f*; temperamento *m*; humor *m*. **lose one's temper** enfadarse *v* templar.

temperament ['tempərəmənt] *n* temperamento *m*. **temperamental** *adj* caprichoso.

temperate ['tempərət] *adj* templado.

temperature ['temprətʃə] *n* temperatura *f*; (*med*) fiebre *f*.

tempestuous [tem'pestjuəs] *adj* tempestuoso.

temple¹ ['templ] *n* (*rel*) templo *m*.

temple² ['templ] *n* (*anat*) sien *f*.

tempo ['tempou] *n* (*music*) tiempo *m*; (*fig*) ritmo *m*.

temporary ['tempərəri] *adj* temporal, provisional. **temporary worker** temporario, -a *m*, *f*.

tempt [tempt] *v* tentar; seducir. **temptation** *n* tentación *f*.

ten [ten] *nm, adj* diez. **tenth** *n*, *adj* décimo, -a.

tenacious [tə'neiʃəs] *adj* tenaz. **tenacious-**

ness *also* **tenacity** *n* tenacidad *f*.

tenant ['tenənt] *n* habitante *m*, *f*. ocupante *m*, *f*. **tenancy** *n* alquiler *m*, arrendamiento *m*.

tend¹ [tend] *v* tender, tener tendencia a. **tendency** *n* tendencia *f*.

tend² [tend] *v* (*look after*) cuidar; manejar.

tender¹ ['tendə] *adj* tierno; delicado; (*kind*) cariñoso; compasivo; (*sensitive*) sensible; (*painful*) dolorido. **tenderize** *v* ablandar. **tenderness** *n* (*affection*) ternura *f* (*meat*) lo tierno.

tender² ['tendə] *v* ofertar, hacer una oferta. *n* oferta *f*. **legal tender** moneda corriente *f*.

tendon ['tendən] *n* tendón *m*.

tendril ['tendril] *n* zarcillo *m*.

tenement ['tenəmənt] *n* casa de vecindad *f*.

tennis ['tenis] *n* tenis *m*. **tennis ball** pelota de tenis *f*. **tennis court** campo de tenis *m*. **tennis player** tenista *m*, *f*. **tennis shoes** zapatos de tenis *m pl*.

tenor ['tenə] *n* (*music*) tenor *m*; (*sense*) significado *m*; (*course*) curso *m*.

tense¹ [tens] *adj* tenso; estirado. *v* tensar. **tension** *n* tensión *f*.

tense² [tens] *n* tiempo *m*.

tent [tent] *n* tienda de campaña *f*. **pitch a tent** armar una tienda de campaña.

tentacle ['tentəkl] *n* tentáculo *m*.

tentative ['tentətiv] *adj* provisional; de tanteo; indeciso.

tenterhooks ['tentəhuks] *pl n* **be on tenterhooks** estar sobre ascuas.

tenuous ['tenjuəs] *adj* tenue; delgado.

tepid ['tepid] *adj* templaducho; (*fig*) tibio. **tepidness** *n* *also* **tepidity** tibieza *f*.

term [tə:m] *n* período *m*; (*comm*) plazo *m*; (*school*) trimestre *m*; curso *m*; (*end*) término *m*. **terms** *pl n* condiciones *f pl*, (*terminology*) términos *m pl*; (*comm*) tarifa *f sing*; (*relationship*) relaciones *f pl*. **come to terms with** llegar a un acuerdo con. **on good/bad terms with** en buenas/malas relaciones con. **terms of reference** mandato *m sing*. *v* llamar, calificar.

terminal ['tə:minəl] *adj* terminal, final. *n* final de línea *m*; (*comput*) terminal *f*; (*extremity*) extremidad *f*; (*elec*) borne *m*.

terminate ['tə:mineit] *v* terminar, concluir. **termination** *n* terminación *f*.

terminology [tə:min'nolədʒi] *n* termi-

nología *f*.

terminus ['tə:minəs] *n* término *m*.

terrace ['terəs] *n* terraza *f*; (*houses*) hilera de casas *f*.

terrain [tə'rein] *n* terreno *m*.

terrestrial [tə'restriəl] *adj* terrestre.

terrible ['terəbl] *adj* terrible; atroz; horrible. **terribly** *adv* terriblemente. **terribly bad** malísimo. **terribly good** buenísimo.

terrier ['teriə] *n* terrier *m*.

terrify ['terifai] *v* aterrorizar. **terrific** *adj* (*coll: excellent*) estupendo; (*coll: extreme*) terrible; enorme.

territory ['teritəri] *n* territorio *m*. **territorial** *adj* territorial.

terror ['terə] *n* terror *m*. **terrorism** *n* terrorismo *m*. **terrorist** *n* (*m + f*), *adj* terrorista. **terrorize** *v* aterrorizar; aterrar.

terse [tə:s] *adj* conciso.

terylene ® ['terəli:n] *n* terylene ® *m*.

test [test] *n* prueba *f*; examen *m*; (*med*) análisis *m*. **test case** (*law*) juicio que hace jurisprudencia *m*. **test match** partido internacional *m*. **test paper** examen *m*. **test pilot** piloto de pruebas *m*. **test tube** tubo de ensayo *m*. *v* probar; poner un examen a; analizar; (*sight*) graduar; (*weight*) comprobar.

testament ['testəmənt] *n* testamento *m*. **the New Testament** el Nuevo Testamento *m*. **the Old Testament** el Antiguo Testamento *m*.

testicle ['testikl] *n* testículo *m*.

testify ['testifai] *v* testificar; dar testimonio.

testimony ['testiməni] *n* testimonio *m*. **testimonial** *n* testimonio *m*; recomendación *f*.

tetanus ['tetənəs] *n* tétanos *m*.

tether ['teðə] *n* traba *f*, atadura *f*. **at the end of one's tether** hartísimo. *v* trabar; atar.

text [tekst] *n* texto *m*. **textbook** *n* libro de texto *m*. **text** (*message*) mensaje de texto *m*. *v* enviar un mensaje de texto. **textual** *adj* textual.

textile ['tekstail] *nm*, *adj* textil.

texture ['tekstjuə] *n* textura *f*.

than [ðən] *conj* que; de; cuando; del que.

thank [θaŋk] *v* agradecer. **thank you** gracias. **thanksgiving** *n* acción de gracias *f*. **thanks to** gracias a. **thankful** *adj* agradecido. **thankless** *adj* desagradecido; ingrato.

that [ðat] *adj* ese, esa; aquel, aquella; el, la. *pron* ése, ésa; aquél, aquélla; (*neuter*) eso; (*neuter: farther away*) aquello; (*before relative pron or of*) el, la, lo; (*who, which*) que; el que, la que; quien; el cual, la cual; (*neuter*) lo que. *adv* así de; tan; tanto. *conj* que; de que; para que; porque.

thatch [θatʃ] *n* (*straw*) paja f; (*roof*) techo de paja *m. v* cubrir con un tejado de paja.

thaw [θɔ:] *n* (*ice*) deshielo *m*; (*snow*) derretimento *m. v* deshelar; derretir.

the [ðə] *art* el, la (*pl* los, las); (*neuter*) lo.

theatre ['θiətə] *n* teatro *m.* **theatrical** *adj* teatral, de teatro.

theft [θeft] *n* hurto, robo.

their [ðeə] *adj* su; sus; suyo, suya.

theirs [ðeəz] *pron* el suyo, la suya.

them [ðem] *pron* ellos, ellas; (*direct object*) los, las; (*indirect object*) les.

theme [θi:m] *n* tema *m.* **thematic** *adj* temático. **theme park** parque temático *m*.

themselves [ðəm'selvz] *pl pron* se; ellos mismos, ellas mismas; sí mismos, sí mismas. **by themselves** solos.

then [ðen] *adv* (*that time*) entonces; (*afterwards*) después, luego; (*furthermore*) además; (*despite that*) a pesar de eso; (*consequently*) por lo tanto. *n* entonces; ese momento. *conj* en ese caso; entonces.

theology [θi'ɒlədʒi] *n* teología f. **theologian** *n* teólogo, -a *m, f.* **theological** *adj* teológico.

theorem ['θiərəm] *n* teorema *m*.

theory ['θiəri] *n* teoría f. **theoretical** *adj* teórico.

therapy ['θerəpi] *n* terapia f. **therapeutic** *adj* terapéutico. **therapist** *n* terapeuta *m, f*.

there [ðeə] *adv* ahí; allí; allá. **thereabouts** *adv* (*place*) por ahí, por allí; (*degree*) más o menos. **thereafter** *adv* después, más tarde. **thereby** *adv* por eso, por ello. **therefore** *adv* por lo tanto. **therein** *adv* allí dentro; en eso. **there is** *or* **are** hay. **thereof** *adv* de eso; su. **thereto** *adv* a eso, a ello. **thereupon** *adv* inmediatamente después; sobre eso. **therewith** *adv* con eso. **there you are** es eso.

thermal ['θə:məl] *adj* termal; (*tech*) térmico. *n* corriente de aire caliente que sube.

thermodynamics [θə:moudai'namiks] *n* termodinámica f.

thermometer [θə'momitə] *n* termómetro *m*.

thermonuclear [θə:mou'njukliə] *adj* termonuclear.

Thermos® ['θə:məs] *n* termo® *m*, termos® *m*.

thermostat ['θə:məstat] *n* termostato *m.* **thermostatic** *adj* termostático.

thesaurus [θi'sɔ:rəs] *n* tesauro *m*

these [ði:z] *pl adj* estos, estas. *pl pron* éstos, éstas.

thesis ['θi:sis] *n, pl* **-sis** tesis *f invar*.

they [ðei] *pl pron* ellos, ellas.

thick [θik] *adj* grueso; espeso; denso; (*coll*) torpe. **thick-skinned** *adj* (*fig*) insensible. **thicken** *v* espesar(se). **thickness** *n* espesor *m*.

thief [θi:f] *n* ladrón, -ona *m, f*.

thigh [θai] *n* muslo *m*.

thimble ['θimbl] *n* dedal *m*.

thin [θin] *adj* (*person*) flaco; delgado; fino; (*hair*) ralo; (*audience*) escaso; (*air*) enrarecido; (*beer*) aguado; (*voice*) débil; (*liquid*) claro; (*excuse*) flojo. *v* adelgazar; (*dilute*) diluir. **thinness** *n* delgadez f. flaqueza f.

thing [θiŋ] *n* cosa f; objeto *m*; artículo *m*; (*coll*) chisme *m.* **things** *pl n* (*affairs, belongings*) cosas f *pl*.

*think [θiŋk] *v* pensar; meditar; imaginar. **I think so** creo que sí. **think about** pensar en. **think over** pensar bien.

third [θə:d] *adj* tercero. *n* tercero, -a *m, f*; (*fraction*) tercio *m*; (*music*) tercera f. **third-party insurance** seguro contra tercera persona *m.* **third-rate** *adj* de poca calidad.

thirst [θə:st] *n* sed f. *v* tener sed. **be thirsty** tener sed.

thirteen [θə:'ti:n] *nm, adj* trece. **thirteenth** *n, adj* decimotercero, -a *m, f*.

thirty ['θə:ti] *nm, adj* treinta. **thirtieth** *n, adj* trigésimo, -a *m, f*.

this [ðis] *adj* este, esta. *pron* éste. ésta. *adv* tan; así de.

thistle ['θisl] *n* cardo *m*.

thong [θɒŋ] *n* correa f; (*underwear*) tanga *m*.

thorn [θɔ:n] *n* espina f. **thorny** *adj* espinoso.

thorough ['θʌrə] *adj* (*search, etc.*) minucioso; (*person*) concienzudo; a fondo; completo. **thoroughbred** *n* pura sangre *m, f.* **thoroughfare** *n* vía pública f. **thoroughly** *adv* a fondo; completamente. **thorough-**

ness n minuciosidad f.

those [ðouz] adj esos, esas; aquellos, aquellas. pron ésos; ésas; aquéllos, aquéllas.

though [ðou] conj aunque. adv sin embargo. **as though** como si.

thought [θo:t] n pensamiento m; idea f; consideración f; intención f; opinión f. **thoughtful** adj pensativo; serio; (mindful) cuidadoso; (considerate) solícito. **thoughtless** adj irreflexivo; descuidado; desconsiderado.

thousand ['θauzənd] nm, adj mil. **thousandth** adj milésimo. n (fraction) milésima parte f; (position) número mil m.

thrash [θraʃ] v dar una paliza a. **thrash about** revolcarse. **thrash out** discutir a fondo. **thrashing** n paliza f.

thread [θred] n hilo m; (screw) rosca f, filete m, v ensartar, enhebrar. **threadbare** adj raído, gastado.

threat [θret] n amenaza f. **threaten** v amenazar.

three [θri:] nm, adj tres. **three-cornered** adj triangular. **three-dimensional** adj tridimensional. **threefold** adj triple. **three-legged** adj de tres patas. **three-piece suite** tresillo m. **three-ply** adj contrapachado. **three-quarter** adj tres cuartos.

thresh [θreʃ] v trillar. **threshing machine** n trilladora f.

threshold ['θreʃould] n umbral m.

threw [θru:] V **throw**.

thrift [θrift] n economía f. **thrifty** adj económico.

thrill [θril] n emoción f; (quiver) estremecimiento m. v estremecer. **thriller** n novela or película escalofriante f. **thrilling** adj emocionante; escalofriante.

thrive [θraiv] v crecer; desarrollarse; tener buena salud; prosperar. **thriving** adj lozano; próspero.

throat [θrout] n garganta f. **clear one's throat** aclararse la voz. **throaty** adj gutural.

throb [θrob] n (heart) latido m, palpitación f; (engine) zumbido m; (pulse) pulsación f; (pain) punzada f. v latir; pulsar; zumbar; dar punzadas.

thrombosis [θrom'bousis] n trombosis f invar.

throne [θroun] n trono m.

throng [θroŋ] n multitud f. muchedumbre

f. v atestar; afluir.

throttle ['θrotl] v estrangular. n (tech) regulador m; (mot) acelerador.

through [θru:] adj directo; continuo. adv de parte a parte; completamente. prep (via) por; (time) durante; (place) a través de. **no through road** calle sin salida f. **through traffic** tránsito m. **throughout** prep (place) por todo, en todo; (time) durante todo. adv hasta el final.

*throw [θrou] n tiro m, lanzamiento m; (wrestling) tumbado m. v lanzar, tirar, arrojar; (a blow) dar; (light) proyectar. **throw away** tirar; (get rid of) desechar; (money) despilfarrar. **throw off** (a habit) renunciar a; (the scent) despistar. **throw out** expulsar, echar; rechazar. **throw up** (job) dejar; (vomit) devolver.

thrush [θrʌʃ] n tordo m.

*thrust [θrʌst] v empujar; clavar; meter; poner. n empujón m; (stab) estocada f.

thud [θʌd] n ruido sordo m. v caer con un ruido sordo.

thumb [θʌm] n pulgar m. v also **thumb through** hojear. **thumb a lift** (coll) hacer autostop. **thumb index** uñeros m pl.

thump [θʌmp] n (blow) porrazo m; (noise) ruido sordo m. v (strike) golpear; (heart) latir con fuerza.

thunder ['θʌndə] n trueno m; (fig) estruendo m. **thunderstorm** n tormenta f. **thunderstruck** adj atónito. v tronar.

Thursday ['θə:zdi] n jueves m.

thus [ðʌs] adv así; de este modo.

thwart [θwo:t] v frustrar, impedir.

thyme [taim] n tomillo m.

thyroid ['θairoid] n tiroides f invar. adj tiroideo.

tiara [tϊ'a:rə] n tiara f.

tick¹ [tik] n (mark) marca f; (sound) tictac m. **tick off** (coll) reprender.

tick² [tik] n (zool) garrapata f.

ticket ['tikit] n (price) etiqueta f; (entrance) entrada f; (transport) billete m; (permit) pase m. **cloakroom ticket** número del guardarropa m. **complimentary ticket** entrada de favor f. **parking ticket** multa por aparcamiento indebido f. **return ticket** billete de ida y vuelta m. **single ticket** billete de ida m. **ticket agency** agencia de venta de billetes f. **ticket office** taquilla f.

tickle ['tikl] v hacer cosquillas a. n

cosquilleo *m*. **ticklish** *adj* cosquilloso.

tide [taid] *n* marea *f*. **tidal** de la marea. **tidal wave** maremoto *m*. **tide-mark** *n* línea de la marea alta *f*; (*coll*) lengua del agua *f*. *v* **tide over** sacar de apuro.

tidy ['taidi] *adj* ordenado; (*appearance*) arreglado; (*clean*) limpio. *v* ordenar; limpiar. **tidily** *adv* bien; aseadamente. **tidiness** *n* orden *m*; aseo *m*.

tie [tai] *v* atar; (*lace*) lacear; (*knot*) hacer; (*unite*) unir; (*link*) ligar; (*sport*) empatar. *n* (*neck*) corbata *f*; (*knot*) nudo *m*; (*bond*) lazo *m*; (*sport*) empate *m*; (*fig*) atadura *f*.

tier [tiə] *n* grada *f*; (*row*) fila *f*; (*cake*) piso *m*.

tiger ['taigə] *n* tigre *m*.

tight [tait] *adj* (*bolt, knot, etc.*) apretado; (*clothes*) ajustado; (*taut*) tirante; (*control*) estricto; (*seal*) hermético; (*bend*) cerrado; (*coll: drunk*) borracho; (*coll: mean*) agarrado. **tight-fisted** *adj* tacaño. **tight-lipped** *adj* callado. **tightrope** *n* cuerda de volatinero *f*. *adv also* **tightly** bien; herméticamente. **hold tight!** ¡agárrense bien! **tighten** (*screw, etc.*) apretar; (*rope, etc.*) tensar; (*control*) estrechar. **tighten one's belt** (*coll*) apretarse el cinturón. **tights** *pl n* mallas *f pl*.

tile [tail] *n* (*roof*) teja *f*; (*floor*) baldosa *f*. *v* tejar; embaldosar.

till[1] [til] *V* **until**.

till[2] [til] *n* caja *f*.

till[3] [til] *v* labrar, cultivar.

tiller ['tilə] *n* (*naut*) caña del timón *f*.

tilt [tilt] *n* inclinación *f*. **at full tilt** en toda mecha. *v* inclinar. **tilt at** arremeter contra.

timber ['timbə] *n* madera de construcción *f*. **timbered** (*house*) enmaderado.

time [taim] *n* tiempo *m*, momento *m*; época *f*; período *m*; (*season*) estación *f*; (*clock*) hora *f*; (*occasion*) vez *f*; (*fixed time period*) plazo *m*; (*music*) duración *f*; (*music: tempo*) compás *m*; (*sport*) final *m*. **a long time** mucho tiempo. **a short time** poco tiempo. **at the same time** al mismo tiempo. **from time to time** de vez en cuando. **in time** a tiempo. **on time** a la hora. **timeless** *adj* eternal. **timely** *adj* oportuno. **timeshare** multipropiedad *f*.

time exposure *n* exposición *f*.

time limit *n* límite de tiempo *m*.

timepiece ['taimpi:s] *n* reloj *m*.

timesaving ['taim,seiviŋ] *adj* que ahorra

tiempo.

time signal *n* señal horaria *f*.

timetable ['taimteibl] *n* horario *m*; (*transport*) guía *f*.

time zone *n* huso horario *m*.

timid ['timid] *adj* tímido. **timidity** *n* timidez *f*.

tin [tin] *n* estaño *m*; (*tinplate*) hojalata *f*; (*can*) lata *f*; (*baking*) molde *m*. **tinfoil** *n* papel de estaño *m*. **tin-opener** *n* abrelatas *m invar*. **tinny** *adj* (*sound, taste*) metálico.

tinge [tindʒ] *n* tinte *m*. *v* teñir.

tingle ['tiŋgl] *v* sentir hormigueo. *n* hormigueo *m*.

tinker ['tiŋkə] *n* calderero *m*. *v* componer, arreglar. **tinker with** jugar con.

tinkle ['tiŋkl] *n* tintineo *m*. *v* hacer tintinear.

tinsel ['tinsəl] *n* oropel *m*.

tint [tint] *n* (*hair*) tinte *m*; tono *m*; matiz *m*. *v* teñir; matizar.

tiny ['taini] *adj* diminuto.

tip[1] [tip] *n* punta *f*; (*cigarette*) filtro *m*. **on tiptoe** de puntillas.

tip[2] [tip] *v* (*tilt*) inclinar; (*pour*) verter; (*upset*) volcar.

tip[3] [tip] *n* (*hint*) consejo *m*. información *f*; (*money*) propina *f*. *v* dar una propina a. **tip-off** *n* (*coll*) información *f*.

tipsy ['tipsi] *adj* (*coll*) achispado.

tire[1] ['taiə] *v* cansar(se). **tire out** agotar. **tired** *adj* cansado. **be tired of** estar harto de. **tiredness** *n* cansancio *m*. **tiresome** *adj* pesado.

tire[2] *V* **tyre**.

tissue ['tiʃu:] *n* (*anat*) tejido *m*; (*cloth*) tisú *m*; (*handkerchief*) pañuelo de papel *m*. **tissue paper** papel de seda *m*.

title ['taitl] *n* título *m*; derecho *m*. **title deed** título de propiedad *m*. **title page** portada *f*. *v* titular. **titled** *adj* con título de nobleza.

titter ['titə] *n* risita *f*. *v* reírse nerviosamente.

to [tul] *prep* a; (*direction*) hacia; (*as far as*) hasta; (*time*) menos; (*destination, purpose*) para; (*according to*) según: (*in juxtaposition*) contra; (*compared with*) en comparación con; (*in*) por; (*in memory of*) en honor a. **to-do** *n* (*coll*) follón *m*.

toad [toud] *n* sapo *m*. **toadstool** *n* hongo venenoso *m*.

toast [toust] n pan tostado m; (speech) brindis m invar. **toast-rack** n portatostadas m invar. v tostar. **toaster** n tostador m.

tobacco [təˈbakou] n tabaco m. **tobacconist's** n estanco m.

toboggan [təˈbogən] n tobogán m. v deslizarse en tobogán.

today [təˈdei] nm. adj hoy.

toddler [ˈtodlə] n niño pequeño m; niña pequeña f.

toe [tou] n dedo del pie. **big toe** dedo gordo m. **toenail** n uña (del dedo del pie) f. **toe the line** (coll) conformarse.

toffee [ˈtofi] n caramelo m. **toffee-apple** n manzana garrapiñada f.

together [təˈgeðə] adv juntos; (at the same time) a la vez; (agreed) de acuerdo. **togetherness** n solidaridad f.

toil [toil] n trabajo agotador m. v trabajar duro.

toilet [ˈtoilit] n (lavatory) retrete m; (washing, etc.) arreglo m. **toilet paper** papel higiénico m. **toilet soap** jabón de tocador m. **toilet water** agua de Colonia f.

toiletries [ˈtoilitriz] n artículos de tocador m (pl), artículos de aseo m (pl)

token [ˈtoukən] n (sign) muestra f. prueba f; (symbol) símbolo m; (keepsake) recuerdo m; (disc) ficha f; (book, record) vale m. **as a token of** como prueba de. adj simbólico.

told [tould] V **tell**.

tolerate [ˈtoləreit] v tolerar, soportar; admitir; respetar. **tolerable** adj tolerable; (fair) mediano. **tolerance** n also **toleration** tolerancia f. **tolerant** adj tolerante.

toll[1] [toul] n (road) peaje m; (bridge) pontaje m, (victims) bajas f pl. **toll-gate** n barrera de peaje f.

toll[2] [toul] v tocar, tañer.

tomato [təˈmaːtou] n tomate m.

tomb [tuːm] n tumba f. **tombstone** n piedra sepulcral f.

tomorrow [təˈmorou] nm, adv mañana. **the day after tomorrow** pasado mañana m

ton [tʌn] n tonelada f.

tone [toun] n tono m; estilo m. v (colour) matizar. **tone down** atenuarse.

tongs [tonz] pl n (coal) tenazas f pl; (sugar) tenacillas f pl.

tongue [tʌn] n lengua f. **tongue-tied** adj mudo.

tonic [ˈtonik] adj tónico. n (med) tónico m; (music) tónica f.

tonight [təˈnait] n. adv esta noche.

tonsil [ˈtonsil] n amígdala f. **tonsillitis** n amigdalitis f.

too [tuː] adv demasiado; (also) también; (moreover) además.

took [tuk] V **take**.

tool [tuːl] n herramienta f; utensilio m. **toolbox** caja de herramientas f. **toolshed** n cobertizo para herramientas m

tooth [tuːθ] n. pl **teeth** diente m; (back tooth) muela f. **toothache** n dolor de muelas m. **tooth-brush** n cepillo de dientes m. **toothpaste** n pasta dentífrica f. **toothpick** n palillo de dientes m. **toothless** adj desdentado.

top[1] [top] n parte de arriba f, lo alto m; (of mountain) cima f; (of tin, pan, bottle, etc.) tapa f; (of page) cabeza f; (of the head) coronilla f; (surface) superficie f. adj de arriba; (best) mejor; (first) primero. v (cover) cubrir; (exceed) superar. **top up** llenar completamente.

top[2] [top] n (toy) peón m. trompo m.

topaz [ˈtoupaz] n topacio m.

topcoat [ˈtopkout] n abrigo m.

topdressing [ˈtop ˌdresin] n abono m.

top hat n chistera f.

top-heavy adj inestable.

topic [ˈtopik] n tema m, asunto m. **topical** adj de actualidad.

topless adj (person) topless.

topography [təˈpogrəfi] n topografía f. **topographical** adj topográfico.

topple [ˈtopl] v derribar, volcar, hacer caer.

top-secret adj confidencial.

topsoil [ˈtopsoil] n tierra vegetal f.

topsy-turvy [topsiˈtəːvi] adj revuelto.

torch [tottʃ] n (electric) linterna f; (burning) antorcha f.

tore [toː] V **tear**.

torment [ˈtoːment; v toːˈment] n tormento m, suplicio m. v atormentar.

tornado [toːˈneidou] n tornado m.

torpedo [toːˈpiːdou] n torpedo m. v torpedear.

torrent [ˈtorənt] n torrente m. **torrential** adj torrencial.

torso [ˈtoːsou] n torso m.

tortoise [ˈtoːtəs] n tortuga f. **tortoise-shell**

n carey *m*.

tortuous ['tɔ:tʃuəs] *adj* tortuoso.

torture ['tɔ:tʃə] *n* tortura *f*. *v* torturar. **torturer** *n* torturador *m*.

Tory ['tɔ:ri] *adj* Conservador, de derechas

toss [tos] *v* (*throw*) lanzamiento *m*; (*fall*) caída *f*; (*head*) sacudida *f*; (*coin*) sorteo a cara o cruz *m*; (*bull*) cogida *f*. *v* lanzar; sacudir; (*coin*) echar a cara o cruz; (*salad*) dar vueltas a.

tot¹ [tot] *n* (*child*) nene *m*; (*drink*) trago *m*.

tot² [tot] *v* **tot up** sumar.

total ['toutəl] *n*, *m* *adj* total. *v* (*add up*) sumar; (*add up to*) totalizar. **totalitarian** *n*. *adj* totalitario, -a.

totter ['totə] *v* bambolearse.

touch [tʌtʃ] *n* (*sense*) tacto *m*; (*contact*) contacto *m*; (*light stroke*) toque *m*; (*tap*) golpe ligero *m*; (*brush*) roce *m*. *v* tocar; rozar; (*reach*) alcanzar; (*affect*) afectar; (*move*) enternecer; (*food*) tomar. **touch up** (*improve*) retocar; (*sexually*) sobar. **touchy** *adj* susceptible.

tough [tʌf] *adj* (*hard*) duro; resistente; (*character*) tenaz; (*job*) difícil. **toughen** *v* endurecer. **toughness** *n* dureza *f*; resistencia *f*; dificultad *f*.

toupee ['tu:pei] *n* tupé *m*.

tour [tuə] *n* excursión *f*; visita *f*; viaje *m*; (*theatre*) gira *f*. **package tour** viaje todo comprendido *m*. **tour agency** agencia de viajes *f*. **tour of duty** turno de servicio *m*. *v* recorrer. **touring** *n* *also* **tourism** turismo *m*. **tourist** *n* turista *m*, *f*. **tourist** (*information*) office oficina de turismo *f*.

tournament ['tuənəmənt] *n* torneo *m*.

tousled ['tauzld] *adj* (*hair*) despeinado.

tout [taut] *v* (*ticket*) revender

tow [tou] *n* remolque *m*. *v* remolcar; (*from towpath*) sirgar. **towpath** *n* camino de sirga *m*. **tow-rope** *n* remolque *m*.

towards [tə'wo:dz] *prep* hacia; (*for*) para; (*with*) con; (*with regard to*) con respecto a.

towel ['tauəl] *n* toalla *f*; (*bath*) toalla de baño *f*; (*sanitary*) paño higiénico *m*. **towel-rail** *n* toallero *m*. **towelling** *n* felpa *f*.

tower ['tauə] *n* torre *f*. **control tower** torre de control *f*. **tower over** dominar. **towering** *adj* sobresaliente.

town [taun] *n* (*large*) ciudad *f*; (*small*) pueblo *m*. **new town** pueblo nuevo *m*. **town hall** ayuntamiento *m*. **town plan-**

-ning urbanismo *m*.

toxic ['toksik] *adj* tóxico.

toy [toi] *n* juguete *m*. *adj* de juguete. *v* **toy with** toquetear; (*idea*) acariciar.

trace [treis] *n* (*trail*) rastro *m*; (*indication*) indicio *m*; (*a little*) pizca *f*. *v* (*plan*) trazar; (*through paper*) calcar; (*trail*) rastrear; (*find*) encontrar. **tracing** *n* calco *m*. **tracing paper** papel de calcar *m*.

track [trak] *n* (*of animals, people*) huella *f*; (*of things*) rastro *m*; (*path*) sendero *m*; (*rail*) vía *f*; (*course*) curso *m*; (*racing*) pista *f*; (*tank, tractor*) oruga *f*. **tracksuit** *n* mono de entrenamiento *or* chandál *m*. *v* (*hunt*) rastrear; (*pursue*) seguir la pista de. **track down** acorralar. **tracker** *n* perseguidor *m*.

tract¹ [trakt] *n* (*region*) trecho *m*; (*anat*) aparato *m*.

tract² [trakt] *n* (*pamphlet*) folleto *m*.

tractor ['traktə] *n* tractor *m*.

trade [treid] *n* comercio *m*; (*job*) ramo *m*. **trademark** *n* marca de fábrica *f*. **tradesman** *n* comerciante *m*. **trade union** sindicato *m*. **trade unionist** sindicalista *m*, *f*. *v* comerciar; negociar; cambiar. **trade in** tomar como entrada. **trader** *n* comerciante *m*. *f*: negociante *m*. *f*.

tradition [trə'diʃən] *n* tradición *f*. **traditional** *adj* tradicional.

traffic ['trafik] *n* (*mot*) circulación *f*, tráfico *m*; (*tourist*) tránsito *m*; (*trade*) comercio *m*. **traffic jam** embotellamiento *m*. **traffic-light** *n* semáforo *m*. **traffic warden** guardián del tráfico *m*.

tragedy ['tradʒədi] *n* tragedia *f*. **tragic** *adj* trágico.

trail [treil] *n* (*path*) camino *m*, sendero; (*person or animal*) huellas *f* pl; (*smoke*) estela *f*; (*blood*) reguero *m*. *v* (*drag*) arrastrar; (*chase*) perseguir; (*an animal*) rastrear; (*lag*) ir detrás de; (*hang down*) colgar. **trailer** *n* (*mot*) remolque *m*; (*film*) trailer *m*.

train [trein] *n* (*railway*) tren *m*; (*procession*) desfile *m*; (*series*) serie *f*; (*dress*) cola *f*. *v* (*teach*) educar; (*someone for a job*) formar, capacitar; (*animal*) amaestrar; (*horse*) domar; (*sport*) entrenar. **trainee** *n* aprendiz. -a *m*. *f*. **trainer** *n* (*sport*) entrenador, -a *m*. *f*. (*boxing*) cuidador *m*: (*animals*) amaestrador, -a *m*. *f*. (*horses*) domador, -a *m*. *f*.

trait [treit] *n* rasgo *m*.

traitor ['treitə] *n* traidor. -a *m*. *f*.

tram [tram] *n* tranvía *m*.

tramp [tramp] *n* (*person*) vagabundo, -a *m. f*; (*hike*) caminata *f*; (*sound*) ruido de pasos *m. v* patear; vagabundear.

trample ['trampl] *v* pisotear. pisar.

trampoline ['trampəli:n] *n* cama elástica *f*.

trance [tra:ns] *n* trance *m*.

tranquil ['traŋkwil] *adj* tranquilo. **tranquillity** *n* tranquilidad. *f*. **tranquillize** *v* tranquilizar. **tranquillizer** *n* tranquilizante *m*.

transact [tran'zakt] *v* (*negotiate*) tratar: (*perform*) llevar a cabo. **transaction** *n* (*business*) negociación *f*; (*deal*) transacción *f*.

transcend [tran'send] *v* exceder, superar. **transcendental** *adj* trascendental.

transcribe [tran'skraib] *v* transcribir. **transcription** *n* trascripción *f*.

transept ['transept] *n* transepto *m*.

transfer [trans'fə:; *n* 'transfə:] *v* trasladar; transferir. *n* traslado *m*; (*law*) cesión *f*: (*picture*) calcomanía *f*. **transferable** *adj* transferible. **not tranferable** (*right*) inalienable; (*ticket*) intransferible.

transfix [trans'fiks] *v* traspasar.

transform [trans'fo:m] *v* transformar. **transformation** *n* transformación *f*. **transformer** *n* (*elec*) transformador *m*.

transfuse [trans'fju:z] *v* transfundir. **transfusion** *n* transfusión *f*.

transient ['tranziənt] *adj* transitorio.

transistor [tran'zistə] *n* transistor *m*. **transistorize** *v* transistorizar.

transit ['transit] *n* tránsito *m*. **in transit** de tránsito.

transition [tran'zifən] *n* transición *f*. **transitional** *adj* transitorio.

transitive ['transitiv] *adj* transitivo.

transitory ['transitari] *adj* transitorio.

translate [trans'leit] *v* traducir. **translation** *n* traducción *f*. **translator** *n* traductor, -a *m. f*.

translucent [trans'lu:snt] *adj* translúcido. **translucence** *n* translucidez *f*.

transmit [tranz'mit] *v* transmitir. trasmitir. **transmission** *n* transmisión *f*, trasmisión *f*. **transmitter** *n* (*apparatus*) transmisor *m*; (*station*) emisora *f*.

transparent [trans'peərənt] *adj* transparente. **transparency** *n* transparencia *f*; (*phot*) transparente *m*.

transplant [trans'pla:nt; *n* 'transpla:nt] *v* transplantar. *n* trasplante *m*.

transport ['transpo:t; *v* trans'po:t] *n* transporte *m. v* transportar. **transportation** *n* transporte *m*; (*convicts*) deportación *f*.

transpose [trans'pouz] *v* transponer; (*music*) transportar. **transposition** *n* transposición *f*; transporte *m*.

transverse ['tranzvə:s] *adj* transverso.

transvestite [tranz'vestait] *n* travestido *m*.

trap [trap] *n* trampa *f*; (*mice, rats*) ratonera *f*; (*vehicle*) cabriolé *m*; (*tech*) sifón de depósito *m*; (*theatre*) escotillón *m*. **trapdoor** *n* trampa *f. v* coger; coger en una trampa; rodear; pillar; bloquear.

trapeze [trə'pi:z] *n* trapecio *m*. **trapeze artist** trapecista *m, f*.

trash [traʃ] *n* basura *f*; (*coll*) cachivaches *m pl*.

trauma ['tro:mə] *n* trauma *f*. **traumatic** *adj* traumático.

travel ['travl] *v* recorrer; viajar por. **travels** *pl n* viajes *m pl*. **travel agency** agencia de viajes *f*. **travel-sickness** *n* mareo *m*. **traveller** *n* viajero, -a *m, f*; (*comm*) viajante de comercio *m*. **traveller's cheque** cheque de viaje *m*.

travesty ['travəsti] *n* parodia *f*.

trawler [tro:lə] *n* barco rastreador *m*. **trawling** *n* pesca a la rastrea *f*.

tray [trei] *n* bandeja *f*.

treachery ['tretʃəri] *n* traición *f*. **treacherous** *adj* (*person*) traidor; (*action*) traicionero.

treacle ['tri:kl] *n* melaza *f*.

*tread [tred] *v* pisar; (*walk*) andar por. **tread on** (*crush*) pisotear. *n* paso *m*; (*step of a staircase*) huella *f*; (*tyre*) banda de rodadura *f*.

treason ['tri:zn] *n* traición *f*.

treasure ['treʒə] *n* tesoro *m. v* valorar; guardar en la memoria. **treasurer** *n* tesorero, -a *m, f*. **treasury** *n* tesorería *f*.

treat [tri:t] *v* tratar; tomar; (*a patient*) atender; (*pay for*) invitar, comprar. *n* invitación *f*; placer *m*. **treatment** *n* trato *m*; (*med*) tratamiento *m*.

treatise ['tri:tiz] *n* tratado *m*.

treaty ['tri:ti] *n* tratado *m*; acuerdo *m*.

treble ['trebl] *n* (*music*) tiple *m*, soprano *m. adj* triple; (*music*) de tiple. *v* triplicar. *adv* tres veces.

tree [tri:] *n* árbol *m*.

trek [trek] v caminar trabajosamente. n expedición f; caminata f.

trellis ['trelis] n enrejado m; espaldera f. v poner un enrejado.

tremble ['trembl] v temblar. n temblor m.

tremendous [trə'mendəs] adj tremendo, enorme; extraordinario; (coll: excellent) formidable.

tremor ['tremə] n temblor m.

trench [trentʃ] n zanja f; (mil) trinchera f.

trend [trend] n tendencia f; dirección f; orientación f. **trendy** adj (coll) modernísimo.

trespass ['trespəs] n entrada ilegal f. v violar; abusar; invadir. **trespasser** n intruso, -a m. f. **trespassers will be prosecuted** prohibido el paso.

trestle ['tresl] n caballete m. **trestle table** mesa de caballete f.

trial ['traiəl] n (law) juicio m; (experiment) prueba f. ensayo m; (annoyance) molestia f; (hardship) dificultad f adj de prueba.

triangle ['traiæŋgl] n triángulo m. **triangular** adj triangular.

tribe [traib] n tribu f. **tribal** adj tribal. **tribesman** n miembro de una tribu m.

tribunal [trai'bju:nl] n tribunal m.

tributary ['tribjutəri] n afluente m. adj tributario.

tribute ['tribju:t] n tributo m.

trick [trik] n (stratagem) truco m; (ruse) astucia f; (practical joke) broma f; (cards) baza f. **trick photography** trucaje m. **trick question** pega f. v engañar. **trickery** n engaño m; astucia f. **tricky** adj difícil; delicado.

trickle ['trikl] n hilo m, chorrito m, v verter poco a poco; gotear.

tricycle ['traisikl] n triciclo m.

trifle ['traifl] n nadería f. v **trifle with** jugar con. **trifling** adj insignificante.

trigger ['trigə] n gatillo m. v accionar. **trigger off** provocar.

trigonometry [trigə'nomətri] n trigonometría f.

trill [tril] n trino m. v trinar.

trim [trim] adj aseado; (neat) arreglado; elegante. v arreglar; (reduce) cercenar; (hair) entresacar; (nails) recortar; (hedge) podar; (sails) orientar. **trimmings** pl n recortes m pl; accesorios m pl.

trinket ['triŋkit] n dije m.

trio ['tri:ou] n trío m.

trip [trip] n (voyage, effect of drugs) viaje m; (stumble) tropezón m. v dar un traspié; tropezar; (make someone fall) echar la zancadilla.

tripe [traip] n callos m pl; (coll) bobadas f pl.

triple ['tripl] nm, adj triple. v triplicar. adv tres veces.

triplet ['triplit] n (music) tresillo m; (poetry) terceto m; (person) trillizo, -a m, f.

tripod ['traipod] n trípode m.

trite [trait] adj trillado, trivial. **triteness** n lo trillado; trivialidad f.

triumph ['traiʌmf] n triunfo m. v triunfar. **triumphant** adj triunfante. **triumphantly** adv triunfantemente.

trivial ['triviəl] adj trivial. **trivia** pl n also **trivialities** trivialidades f pl.

trod [trod] V **tread**.

trolley ['troli] n (shopping) carretilla f; (tea) carrito m; (in mines) vagoneta f.

trombone [trom'boun] n trombón m.

troop [tru:p] n (people) banda f, grupo m; (animals) manada f. **troops** pl n (mil) tropas f pl. v **troop in/out** entrar/salir en tropel.

trophy ['troufi] n trofeo m.

tropic ['tropik] n trópico m. **Tropic of Cancer** Trópico de Cáncer. **Tropic of Capricorn** Trópico de Capricornio. **tropical** adj tropical.

trot [trot] n trote m. **on the trot** (coll) seguidos, seguidas. v trotar. **trotter** n mano f.

trouble ['trʌbl] n (worry) preocupación f; apuro m; pena f; (misfortune) desgracia f; problema m; disturbios m pl. **be in trouble** estar en un apuro. **look for trouble** buscar camorra. **what's the trouble?** ¿qué pasa? **troublemaker** n alborotador, -a m, f. **troubleshooter** n apaciguador. **troublesome** adj molesto. v preocupar; perturbar; afectar; molestar.

trough [trof] n (food) pesebre m; (drinking) abrevadero m; (depression) depresión f.

trousers ['trauzəz] pl n pantalón m sing.

trout [traut] n trucha f.

trowel ['trauəl] n palustre m; (gardening) desplantador m.

truant ['tru:ənt] n play **truant** hacer novillos. **truancy** n rabona f.

truce [tru:s] n tregua f. **call a truce** acordar una tregua.

truck [trʌk] *n* camión *m*; (*rail*) batea *f*. **truck driver** conductor de camión *m*

trudge [trʌdʒ] *v* andar con dificultad.

true [truː] *adj* verdadero, (*faithful*) fiel; legítimo; (*real*) auténtico; (*accurate*) exacto. **true to life** conforme a la realidad. **truly** *adv* verdaderamente

truffle ['trʌfl] *n* trufa *f*.

trump [trʌmp] *n* (*cards*) triunfo *m*. *v* fallar. **trump up** inventar.

trumpet ['trʌmpit] *n* trompeta *f*. *v* (*elephant*) barritar. **trumpeter** *n* trompetista *m*, *f*.

truncate [trʌŋ'keit] *v* truncar.

truncheon ['trʌntʃən] *n* matraca *f*; (*police*) porra *f*.

trunk [trʌŋk] *n* (*anat, bot*) tronco *m*; (*elephant*) trompa *f*; (*case*) baúl *m*. **trunk call** conferencia telefónica *f*. **trunk road** carretera principal *f*. **trunks** *pl n* calzoncillos cortos *m pl*.

truss [trʌs] *n* (*hay*) haz *m*; (*fruit*) racimo *m*; (*med*) braguero *m*. *v* atar.

trust [trʌst] *n* confianza *f*; (*law*) fideicomiso *m*; (*comm*) trust *m*; (*expectation*) esperanza *f*. **trustworthy** *adj* digno de confianza; fidedigno. *v* tener confianza en; confiar; esperar; creer. **trustee** *n* guardián *m*; (*law*) fideicomisario, -a *m*, *f*. **trusting** *adj* confiado. **trusty** *adj* leal, seguro.

truth [truːθ] *n* verdad *f*. **truthful** *adj* veraz; verdadero. **truthfulness** *n* veracidad *f*.

try [trai] *n* tentativa *f*, prueba *f*; (*rugby*) ensayo *m*. *v* probar; intentar; ensayar; (*law*) ver; (*strain*) poner a prueba; (*annoy*) molestar; (*tire*) cansar; (*afflict*) hacer sufrir. **try on** (*garment*) probarse. **try it on** (*coll*) intentar dar el pego. **trying** *adj* molesto.

tsar [zaː] *n* zar *m*.

T-shirt ['tiːʃəːt] *n* camiseta *f*.

tub [tʌb] *n* tina *f*; (*bath*) bañera *f*.

tuba ['tjuːbə] *n* tuba *f*.

tube [tjuːb] *n* tubo *m*; (*coll: underground*) metro *m*. **tubeless** *adj* (*tyre*) sin cámara.

tuber ['tjuːbə] *n* tubérculo *m*.

tuberculosis [tjubəːkjuːlousis] *n* tuberculosis *f*.

tuck [tʌk] *n* (*sewing*) alforza *f*; (*food*) comida *f*; (*sweets*) chucherías *f pl*. *v* meter; (*sheets*) remeter; (*fold*) alforzar. **tuck up** (*in bed*) arropar.

Tuesday ['tjuːzdi] *n* martes *m*.

tuft [tʌft] *n* (*plants*) mata *f*; (*feathers*) penacho *m*; (*hair*) mechón *m*.

tug [tʌg] *n* tirón *m*; (*boat*) remolcador *m*. **tug-of-war** *n* juego de la cuerda *m*. *v* (*pull*) tirar; (*tow*) remolcar; (*drag*) arrastrar.

tuition [tjuˈiʃən] *n* enseñanza *f*.

tulip ['tjuːlip] *n* tulipán *m*.

tumble ['tʌmbl] *n* caída *f*; (*acrobatics*) voltereta *f*. *v* caerse; dar volteretas; (*knock over*) derribar. **tumbledown** *adj* ruinoso. **tumble-dryer** *n* secadora al aire caliente *f*. **tumbler** *n* (*glass*) vaso *m*; (*acrobat*) volatinero, -a *m*, *f*.

tummy ['tʌmi] *n* (*coll*) barriga *f*.

tumour ['tjuːmə] *n* tumor *m*.

tumult ['tjuːmʌlt] *n* tumulto *m*. **tumultuous** *adj* tumultuoso.

tuna ['tjuːnə] *n* atún *m*.

tune [tjuːn] *n* aire *m*. in tune afinado. **out of tune** desafinado. *v* (*music*) afinar; (*mot*) poner a punto. **tune in to** (*radio*) sintonizar con. **tuneful** *adj* melodioso. **tuneless** *adj* discordante. **tuner** *n* (*person*) afinador *m*; (*radio*) sintonizador *m*. **tuning** afinación *f*; sintonización *f*; puesta a punto *f*. **tuning fork** diapasón *m*.

tunic ['tjuːnik] *n* túnica *f*.

tunnel ['tʌnl] *n* túnel *m*. *v* hacer un túnel en; (*dig*) cavar.

turban ['təːbən] *n* turbante *m*.

turbine ['təːbain] *n* turbina *f*.

turbot ['təːbət] *n* rodaballo *m*.

turbulent ['təːbjulənt] *adj* turbulento. **turbulence** *n* turbulencia *f*.

tureen [təˈriːn] *n* sopera *f*.

turf [təːf] *n* césped *m*; (*sport*) turf *m*. *v* encespedar. **turf out** (*coll*) echar.

turkey ['təːki] *n* pavo *m*.

Turkish ['təːkiʃ] *nm*, *adj* turco. **Turkish bath** baño turco *m*.

turmeric ['təːmərik] *n* cúrcuma *f*.

turmoil ['təːmoil] *n* desorden *m*; agitación *f*; alboroto *m*.

turn [təːn] *n* vuelta *f*; (*road*) curva *f*; (*body*) movimiento *m*; (*opportunity*) turno *m*; (*change*) cambio *m*; (*change in situation*) viraje *m*; (*fright*) susto *m*. **take turns** turnarse en. *v* dar vueltas; dar la vuelta a; (*body*) volver; (*corner*) doblar; (*page*) pasar; cambiar. **turn down** (*lower*) bajar; (*reject*) rechazar. **turn off** cerrar; (*light*) apagar; (*engine*) parar. **turn on** (*light, radio*) encender; (*current*) conectar; (*coll: excite*) excitar.

turn out (*end up*) resultar; (*light*) apagar. **turnover** *n* (*comm*) volumen de negocios *m*. **turn-stile** *n* torniquete *m*. **turntable** *n* (*record-player*) plato giratorio *m*. **turn up** presentarse; (*appear*) aparecer. **turning** *n* vuelta *f*; curva *f*; (*side road*) bocacalle *f*. **turning point** momento crucial *m*.

turnip ['tə:nip] *n* nabo *m*.

turpentine ['tə:pəntain] *n* trementina *f*.

turquoise ['tə:kwoiz] *n* (*stone*) turquesa *f*; (*colour*) azul turquesa *m*.

turret ['tʌrit] *n* torreón *m*; (*mil*) torreta *f*.

turtle ['tə:tl] *n* tortuga de mar *f*. **turtle-neck** *n* (*jumper collar*) cuello que sube ligeramente *m*.

tusk [tʌsk] *n* defensa *f*.

tussle ['tʌsl] *n* pelea *f*; lucha *f*. *v* pelearse.

tutor ['tju:tə] *n* (*private*) profesor particular *m*; (*university*) tutor *m*. *v* dar clases privadas.

tuxedo [tʌk'si:dou] *n* smoking *m*.

TV *n* tele *f*

tweed [twi:d] *n* tweed *m*.

tweezers ['twi:zəz] *pl n* pinzas *f pl*.

twelve [twelv] *nm*, *adj* doce. **twelfth** *n*, *adj* duodécimo, -a.

twenty ['twenti] *nm*, *adj* veinte. **twentieth** *n*. *adj* vigésimo, -a.

twice [twais] *adv* dos veces.

twiddle ['twidl] *v* dar vueltas a. **twiddle one's thumbs** estar mano sobre mano.

twig [twig] *n* ramita *f*.

twilight ['twailait] *n* crepúsculo *m*.

twin [twin] *n*, *adj* gemelo, -a. **twin beds** camas gemelas *f pl*.

twine [twain] *n* bramante *m*. *v* (*twist*) retorcer; (*interlace*) trenzar; (*embrace*) rodear con.

twinge [twindʒ] *n* (*pain*) punzada *f*; (*fig*) arrebato *m*.

twinkle ['twiŋkl] *n* centelleo *m*; (*brightness*) brillo *m*. *v* centellear; (*eyes*) brillar.

twirl [twə:l] *v* dar vueltas a. *n* vuelta *f*.

twist [twist] *v* torcer; retorcer. *n* torcimiento *m*, torsión *f*; (*tobacco*) rollo *m*: vuelta *f*; deformación *f*; contorsión *f*; inclinación *f*; (*warp*) abarquillamiento *m*; (*ankle*) torcedura *f*; (*swindle*) trampa *f*.

twit [twit] *n* (*slang*) imbécil *m*, *f*.

twitch [twitʃ] *n* (*pull*) tirón *m*; (*med*) tic *m*. *v* tirar bruscamente de; (*nervously*) crispar.

twitter ['twitə] *v* gorjear. *n* gorjeo *m*.

two [tu:] *nm*, *adj* dos. **two-faced** *adj* falso. **two-legged** *adj* bípedo.

tycoon [tai'ku:n] *n* magnate *m*.

type [taip] *n* (*sort*) tipo *m*, clase *f*; (*print*) carácter *m*, tipo *m*. **typeface** tipo de letra *m*. **typesetting** *n* composición *f*. **typewriter** *n* máquina de escribir *f*. *v* escribir a máquina. **typical** *adj* típico. **typing** *n* mecanografía *f*. **typist** *n* mecanógrafo, -a *m*, *f*.

typhoid ['taifoid] *n* fiebre tifoidea *f*.

typhoon [tai'fu:n] *n* tifón *m*.

tyrant ['tairənt] *n* tirano *m*. **tyrannical** *adj* tiránico. **tyranny** *n* tiranía *f*.

tyre *or US* **tire** ['taiə] *n* neumático *m*.

U

ubiquitous [ju'bikwitəs] *adj* ubicuo.

udder ['ʌdə] *n* ubre *f*.

UFO *n* OVNI *m*

ugly ['ʌgli] *adj* feo; repugnante. **ugliness** *n* fealdad *f*.

Ukraine *n* [ju:'krein] Ucrania *f*; **Ukrainian** *adj* ucraniano.

ulcer ['ʌlsə] *n* úlcera *f*.

ulterior [ʌl'tiəriə] *adj* ulterior. **ulterior motive** segunda intención *f*.

ultimate ['ʌltimət] *adj* último; fundamental. **ultimately** *adv* por fin, al final; esencialmente. **ultimatum** *n* ultimátum *m*.

ultrasound ['ʌltrəsaund] *n* ultrasonido *m*; (*med*) ecografía *f*

ultraviolet [ʌltrə'vaiələt] *adj* ultravioleta.

umbilical [ʌm'bilikəl] *adj* umbilical. **umbilical cord** cordón umbilical *m*.

umbrage ['ʌmbridʒ] *n* resentimiento *m*, enfado *m*. **take umbrage at** ofenderse por.

umbrella [ʌm'brelə] *n* paraguas *m invar*.

umpire ['ʌmpaiə] *n* árbitro *m*. *v* arbitrar.

umpteen [ʌmp'ti:n] (*coll*) *adj* muchísimos. **umpteenth** *adj* enésimo.

unable [ʌn'eibl] *adj* incapaz. **be unable to** (*physical*) ser incapaz de; (*due to circumstances*) no poder hacer.

unabridged [ʌnə'bridʒd] *adj* íntegro.

unacceptable [ʌnək'septəbl] *adj* inaceptable.

unaccompanied [ʌnə'kumpənid] *adj* solo,
sin compañia; (*music*) sin acompañamiento.

unaided [ʌn'eidid] *adj* sin ayuda, solo.

unadulterated [ʌnə'dʌltəreitid] *adj* no
adulterado, sin mezcla.

unanimous [ju'naniməs] *adj* unánime.
unanimity *n* unanimidad *f.*

unarmed [ʌn'aːmd] *adj* (*person*) sin armas;
desarmado.

unattached [ʌnə'tatʃt] *adj* (*loose*) suelto;
libre; independiente.

unattractive [ʌnə'traktiv] *adj* poco
atrayente, desagradable.

unauthorized [ʌn'ɔːθəraizd] *adj* no autorizado.

unavoidable [ʌnə'vɔidəbl] *adj* inevitable.

unaware [ʌnə'weə] *adj* inconsciente; ignorante. **be unaware of** ignorar. **unawares**
adv sin querer; de improviso.

unbalanced [ʌn'balənst] *adj* desequilibrado; (*mentally*) trastornado.

unbearable [ʌn'beərəbl] *adj* insoportable,
intolerable, insufrible.

unbelievable [ʌnbi'liːvəbl] *adj* increíble.

***unbend** [ʌn'bend] *v* (*straighten*) desencor-
var; (*fig*) relajar. **unbending** *adj* inflexible.

unbiased [ʌn'baiəst] *adj* imparcial.

unborn [ʌn'bɔːn] *adj*
nonato

unbreakable [ʌn'breikəbl] *adj* irrompible.

unbridled [ʌn'braidld] *adj* (*fig*) desenfrenado.

unbutton [ʌn'bʌtn] *v* desabrochar; (*fig*)
desahogarse.

uncalled-for [ʌn'kɔːldfɔː] *adj* innecesario;
injustificado; gratuito.

uncanny [ʌn'kani] *adj* extraño; misterioso.

uncertain [ʌn'səːtn] *adj* incierto. **uncertainty** *n* incertidumbre *f.*

uncle ['ʌŋkl] *n* tío *m.*

uncomfortable [ʌn'kʌmfətəbl] *adj* incómodo; (*anxious*) inquieto; (*awkward*) difícil.

uncommon [ʌn'komən] *adj* poco común,
raro.

uncompromising [ʌn'komprəmaiziŋ] *adj*
inflexible; irreconciliable.

unconditional [ʌnkən'diʃənl] *adj* incondicional.

unconscious [ʌn'konʃəs] *adj* (*med*) inconsciente; (*unaware*) ignorante.

unconventional [ʌnkən'venʃənl] *adj* poco
convencional.

uncooked [ʌn'kukt] *adj* no cocido, crudo.

uncouth [ʌn'kuːθ] *adj* grosero.

uncover [ʌn'kʌvə] *v* descubrir; (*reveal*) revelar; (*take the lid off*) destapar.

uncut [ʌn'kʌt] *adj* no cortado.

undecided [ʌndi'saidid] *adj* indeciso; irresoluto.

undeniable [ʌndi'naiəbl] *adj* incontestable.

under ['ʌndə] *adv* debajo; abajo; más
abajo; (*insufficient*) insuficiente; (*for less*)
para menos. *prep* debajo de; bajo; por debajo de; menos de; (*age*) menor de; (*lower in
rank*) por debajo de; (*repair, construction,
etc.*) en; (*according to*) según; conforme a.

underarm ['ʌndəraːm] *adj, adv* por debajo
del brazo; sobacal.

undercharge [ʌndə'tʃaːdʒ] *v* cobrar menos
de lo debido.

underclothes ['ʌndəklouðz] *pl n* ropa interior *f sing.*

undercoat ['ʌndəkout] *n* (*paint*) primera
capa *f.*

undercover [ʌndə'kʌvə] *adj* secreto; clandestino.

undercut [ʌndə'kʌt] *v* vender más barato
que.

underdeveloped [ʌndədi'veləpt] *adj* de
desarrollo atrasado; (*phot*) no revelado lo
suficiente.

underdog ['ʌndədog] *n* desvalido *m.*

underdone [ʌndə'dʌn] *adj* (*meat*) poco
hecho.

underestimate [ʌndə'estimeit] *v* tasar en
menos; menospreciar. *n also* **underestima-
tion** infravaloración *f*; menosprecio *m.*

underfoot [ʌndə'fut] *adv* debajo de los
pies.

***undergo** [ʌndə'gou] *v* sufrir, pasar por.

undergraduate [ʌndə'gradjuət] *n* estudiante no licenciado, -a *m, f.*

underground ['ʌndəgraund; *adv*
ʌndə'graund] *adj* subterráneo; oculto,
secreto. *adv* bajo tierra; clandestinamente.

undergrowth ['ʌndəgrouθ] *n* maleza *f.*

underhand [ʌndə'hand] *adj* bajo mano;
secreto.

***underlie** [ʌndə'lai] *v* estar debajo de; servir

de base a. underlying *adj* básico, fundamental.

underline [ʌndə'lain] *v* subrayar. **underlining** *n* subrayado *m*.

undermine [ʌndə'main] *v* socavar, minar.

underneath [ʌndə'ni:θ] *prep* bajo, debajo de. *adv* debajo, por debajo. *adj* inferior, de abajo.

underpaid [ʌndə'peid] *adj* mal pagado.

underpants ['ʌndəpants] *pl n* calzoncillos *m pl*.

underpass ['ʌndəpa:s] *n* paso subterráneo *m*.

underprivileged [ʌndə'privilidʒd] *adj* menesteroso.

underrate [ʌndə'reit] *v* subestimar.

underskirt ['ʌndəskə:t] *n* enaguas *f pl*.

understaffed [ʌndə'sta:ft] *adj* falto de personal.

***understand** [ʌndə'stand] *v* entender, comprender; (*believe*) creer. **understandable** *adj* comprensible. **understanding** *n* entendimiento *m*; comprensión *f*; (*reason*) razón *f*; interpretación *f*; (*knowledge*) conocimientos *m pl*; (*agreement*) acuerdo *m*.

understate *v* quitar importancia a. **make an understatement** describir sin énfasis. **that's an understatement!** ¡y usted que lo diga!

understudy ['ʌndəstʌdi] *n* suplente *m, f. v* suplir, doblar.

***undertake** [ʌndə'teik] *v* emprender; prometer. **undertaker** *n* empresario de pompas fúnebres *m*. **undertaking** *n* empresa *f*; compromiso *m*.

undertone ['ʌndətoun] *n* **in an undertone** en voz baja.

underwater [ʌndə'wo:tə] *adj* submarino.

underwear ['ʌndəweə] *n* ropa interior *f*.

underweight [ʌndə'weit] *adj* de peso insuficiente.

underworld ['ʌndəwə:ld] *n* (*criminal*) hampa *f*; (*hell*) infierno *m*.

***underwrite** [ʌndə'rait] *v* (*sign, bonds*) subscribir; (*guarantee*) garantizar; (*insure*) asegurar.

undesirable [ʌndi'zaiərəbl] *adj* no deseable; pernicioso. *n* indeseable *m, f.*

***undo** [ʌn'du:] *v* (*open*) abrir; (*knot*) desatar; (*a tie*) desanudar; (*button*) desabrochar; (*parcel*) deshacer; (*zip*) bajar; (*ruin*) arruinar. **undoing** *n* ruina *f*. **come undone** desatarse.

undoubted [ʌn'dautid] *adj* indudable.

undress [ʌn'dres] *v* desnudar(se).

undue [ʌn'dju:] *adj* excesivo; impropio. **unduly** *adv* excesivamente; impropiamente.

undulate ['ʌndjuleit] *v* ondular. **undulating** *adj* ondulante. **undulation** *n* ondulación *f.*

unearth [ʌn'ə:θ] *v* desenterrar; descubrir. **unearthly** *adj* sobrenatural; misterioso; espantoso. **unearthly hour** (*coll*) hora intempestiva *f.*

uneasy [ʌn'i:zi] *adj* inquieto; molesto; agitado; preocupado.

uneducated [ʌn'edjukeitid] *adj* ineducado.

unemployed [ʌnem'ploid] *adj* parado, desempleado. **the unemployed** los parados *m pl*. **unemployment** *n* paro *m*, desempleo *m.*

unenthusiastic [ʌnenθju:zi'astik] *adj* sin entusiasmo.

unequal [ʌn'i:kwəl] *adj* desigual; (*inadequate*) inadecuado; (*med*) irregular.

uneven [ʌn'i:vn] *adj* accidentado; (*unequal*) desigual; (*number*) impar.

uneventful [ʌni'ventfəl] *adj* sin acontecimientos.

unexpected [ʌneks'pektid] *adj* inesperado.

unfailing [ʌn'feiliŋ] *adj* infalible; (*inexhaustible*) inagotable; (*unceasing*) constante.

unfair [ʌn'feə] *adj* injusto. **unfairness** *n* injusticia *f.*

unfaithful [ʌn'feiθfəl] *adj* infiel. **unfaithfulness** *n* infidelidad *f.*

unfamiliar [ʌnfə'miljə] *adj* desconocido; extraño.

unfasten [ʌn'fa:sn] *v* (*open*) abrir; (*dress, button*) desabrochar; (*knot*) desatar; (*set free*) soltar; (*loosen*) aflojar.

unfavourable [ʌn'feivərəbl] *adj* desfavorable, adverso.

unfinished [ʌn'finiʃt] *adj* inacabado, no terminado.

unfit [ʌn'fit] *adj* incapaz; no apto; incompetente; impropio; (*ill*) enfermo, malo.

unfold [ʌn'fould] *v* desplegar; (*plans*) revelar; (*thoughts*) desarrollarse.

unforeseen [ʌnfo:'si:n] *adj* imprevisto.

unforgivable [ʌnfə'givəbl] *adj* imperdonable.

unfortunate [ʌn'fo:tʃənət] *adj* desafortunado; desgraciado.

unfounded [ʌnˈfaundid] *adj* infundado, sin fundamento.

unfriendly [ʌnˈfrendli] *adj* hostil; desfavorable.

unfurnished [ʌnˈfəːniʃd] *adj* desamueblado.

ungainly [ʌnˈgeinli] *adj* desgarbado.

ungrateful [ʌnˈgreitfəl] *adj* ingrato.

unhappy [ʌnˈhapi] *adj* infeliz; triste. **unhappiness** *n* infelicidad *f*.

unhealthy [ʌnˈhelθi] *adj* (*person*) enfermo; (*place*) malsano.

unheard-of [ʌnˈhəːdov] *adj* inaudito; sin precedente.

unhoped-for [ʌnˈhouptfoː] *adj* inesperado.

unhurt [ʌnˈhəːt] *adj* indemne, ileso.

unhygienic [ʌnhaiˈdʒiːnik] *adj* antihigiénico.

unicorn [ˈjuːnikoːn] *n* unicornio *m*.

unidentified flying object [ʌnaiˈdentifaid] *n also* **UFO** objeto volador no identificado *m*, OVNI *m*.

uniform [ˈjuːnifoːm] *nm, adj* uniforme. **uniformity** *n* uniformidad *f*.

unify [ˈjuːnifai] *v* unificar. **unification** *n* unificación *f*.

unilateral [juːniˈlatərəl] *adj* unilateral.

unimaginative [ʌniˈmadʒinətiv] *adj* poco imaginativo.

unimportant [ʌnimˈpoːtnt] *adj* poco importante.

uninhabited [ʌninˈhabitid] *adj* inhabitado.

uninhibited [ʌninˈhibitid] *adj* sin inhibición.

unintentional [ʌninˈtenʃənl] *adj* involuntario.

uninterested [ʌnˈintristid] *adj* indiferente; desinteresado. **uninteresting** *adj* poco interesante.

union [ˈjuːnjən] *n* unión *f*; (*trade*) sindicato *m*.

unique [juːˈniːk] *adj* único.

unisex [ˈjuːniˌseks] *adj* (*coll*) unisexo *invar*.

unison [ˈjuːnisn] *n* unisonancia. **in unison** al unísono.

unite [juˈnait] *v* unir; reunir; juntarse. **united** *adj* unido. **United Kingdom** Reino Unido *m*. **United Nations** Naciones Unidas *f pl*. **United States of America** Estados Unidos de América *m pl*.

unity [ˈjuːniti] *m* unidad *f*.

universe [ˈjuːnivəːs] *m* universo *m*. **universal** *adj* universal.

university [juːniˈvəːsəti] *n* universidad *f*. *adj* universitario.

unjust [ʌnˈdʒʌst] *adj* injusto.

unkempt [ʌnˈkempt] *adj* descuidado; (*hair*) despeinado.

unkind [ʌnˈkaind] *adj* poco amable; severo; cruel. **unkindness** *n* falta de amabilidad *f*; severidad *f*; crueldad *f*.

unknown [ʌn noun] *n, adj* desconocido, -a.

unlawful [ʌnˈloːfəl] *adj* ilegal; ilegítimo.

unleaded [ʌnˈledid] (*adv*) sin plomo.

unless [ʌnˈles] *conj* a no ser que, a menos que.

unlike [ʌnˈlaik] *adj* diferente, distinto. *prep* a diferencia de.

unlikely [ʌnˈlaikli] *adj* improbable; (*unexpected*) inverosímil.

unlimited [ʌnˈlimitid] *adj* ilimitado.

unload [ʌnˈloud] *v* descargar; (*get rid of*) deshacerse de.

unlock [ʌnˈlok] *v* abrir.

unlucky [ʌnˈlʌki] *adj* desgraciado; (*day, number, etc.*) funesto.

unmarried [ʌnˈmarid] *adj* soltero.

unnatural [ʌnˈnatʃərəl] *adj* antinatural; anormal; artificial.

unnecessary [ʌnˈnesəsəri] *adj* innecesario, inútil.

unnerving [ʌnˈnəːviŋ] *adj* desconcertante.

unnoticed [ʌnˈnoutist] *adv* inadvertido; desapercibido. **go** *or* **pass unnoticed** pasar desapercibido.

unobtainable [ʌnəbˈteinəbl] *adj* que no se puede conseguir.

unobtrusive [ʌnəbˈtruːsiv] *adj* discreto, modesto.

unoccupied [ʌnˈokjupaid] *adj* (*at leisure*) desocupado; (*untenanted*) deshabitado; (*seat*) libre.

unofficial [ʌnəˈfiʃəl] *adj* no oficial.

unorthodox [ʌnˈoːθədoks] *adj* poco ortodoxo.

unpack [ʌnˈpak] *v* (*box*) desembalar; (*suitcase*) deshacer.

unpaid [ʌnˈpeid] *adj* impagado; (*bill*) por pagar; (*worker*) no retribuido.

unpleasant [ʌnˈpleznt] *adj* (*weather*)

desagradable; (*unfriendly*) antipático; (*annoying*) molesto.

unplug [ʌn'plʌg] v desenchufar

unpopular [ʌn'pɒpjulə] adj impopular.

unprecedented [ʌn'presidentid] adj sin precedentes.

unpredictable [ʌnpreə'diktəbl] adj que no se puede prever; (*capricious*) antojadizo.

unqualified [ʌn'kwolifaid] adj sin título; (*without reservation*) sin reserva.

unravel [ʌn'rævəl] v (*wool*) deshacer; (*untangle*) desenredar; (*mystery*) desembrollar.

unreal [ʌn'riəl] adj irreal.

unreasonable [ʌn'ri:zənəbl] adj irrazonable; extravagante; excesivo.

unrelenting [ʌnri'lentiŋ] adj implacable.

unreliable [ʌnri'laiəbl] adj (*character*) inconstante; (*person*) poco seguro; (*machine*) poco fiable; (*service*) dudoso.

unrest [ʌn'rest] n desasosiego m, agitación f.

unruly [ʌn'ru:li] adj ingobernable; rebelde.

unsafe [ʌn'seif] adj inseguro; peligroso.

unsatisfactory [ʌnsatis'faktəri] adj poco satisfactorio.

unscrew [ʌn'skru:] v destornillar.

unscrupulous [ʌn'skru:pjuləs] adj poco escrupuloso.

unselfish [ʌn'selfiʃ] adj desinteresado; generoso.

unsettle [ʌn'setl] v perturbar; (*mentally*) desequilibrar. **unsettled** adj perturbado; agitado; desequilibrado; (*weather*) incierto.

unsightly [ʌn'saitli] adj feo, repugnante.

unskilled [ʌn'skild] adj no cualificado; no especializado. **unskilled worker** obrero no cualificado m.

unsound [ʌn'saund] adj (*unhealthy*) enfermizo; (*mentally*) demente; (*morally*) corrompido; (*goods*) imperfecto; (*foundations*) poco sólido; (*business*) poco seguro; (*argument, opinion*) falso.

unspeakable [ʌn'spi:kəbl] adj indecible.

unspecified [ʌn'spesifaid] adj no especificado.

unstable [ʌn'steibl] adj inestable.

unsteady [ʌn'stedi] adj inestable; inconstante.

unstuck [ʌn'stʌk] adj **come unstuck** despegarse; (*hopes, plans*) fracasar.

unsuccessful [ʌnsək'sesfəl] adj sin éxito;

(*person, attempt, etc.*) fracasado; (*candidate*) suspendido. **be unsuccessful** fracasar. **unsuccessfully** adv sin éxito; infructuosamente.

unsuitable [ʌn'su:təbl] adj inapropiado; inconveniente; inoportuno.

untangle [ʌn'tæŋgl] v desenmarañar.

untidy [ʌn'taidi] adj desarreglado; (*person*) desordenado. **untidiness** n desorden m.

untie [ʌn'tai] v desatar.

until [ən'til] prep hasta. conj hasta que.

untoward [ʌntə'wo:d] adj insumiso; adverso; desafortunado.

untrue [ʌn'tru:] adj falso, mentiroso; imaginario; infiel.

unusual [ʌn'ju:ʒuəl] adj desacostumbrado; extraño; excepcional.

unwanted [ʌn'wontid] adj no deseado; superfluo.

unwell [ʌn'wel] adj indispuesto, enfermo.

***unwind** [ʌn'waind] v desenrollar; (*relax*) descansar.

unwise [ʌn'waiz] adj imprudente; indiscreto.

unworthy [ʌn'wə:ði] adj indigno.

unwrap [ʌn'ræp] v desenvolver; (*parcel*) deshacer.

up [ʌp] adv arriba; hacia arriba; al aire; en el aire; (*louder*) más fuerte; (*out of bed*) levantado; (*standing*) de pie, en pie. **be up to** ser capaz de. prep arriba; en; contra; en el fondo de. **walk up and down** pasearse a lo largo y a lo ancho. **ups and downs** los altibajos m pl. **up-and-coming** adj joven y prometedor.

upbringing ['ʌpbriŋiŋ] n educación f.

update [ʌp'deit] v (*bring up to date*) poner al día; (*modernize*) modernizar.

upgrade [ʌp'greid] v modernizar; (*computer*) potenciar; (*job*) ascender

upheaval [ʌp'hi:vl] n (*geol*) levantamiento m; (*fig*) agitación f.

uphill [ʌp'hil] adj ascendente; (*struggle*) arduo.

***uphold** [ʌp'hould] v sostener; defender; confirmar.

upholster [ʌp'houlstə] v entapizar. **upholstery** n (*material*) tapicería f; (*filling*) relleno m.

upkeep ['ʌpki:p] n mantenimiento m.

uplift [ʌp'lift] n (*geol*) elevación f; (*fig*) inspiración.

upmarket [ʌp'maːkit] *adj* de categoría, de calidad superior

upon [ə'pon] *prep* sobre, encima de.

upper ['ʌpə] *adj* alto; superior. **upperclass** *adj* de la clase alta. **upper hand** dominio *m*. **uppermost** *adj* más alto; predominante.

upright ['ʌprait] *adj* vertical; derecho; (*fig*) recto. *adv* en posición vertical.

uprising ['ʌpraiziŋ] *n* sublevación *f*.

uproar ['ʌprɔː] *n* alboroto *m*, tumulto *m*. **uproarious** *adj* tumultuoso; ruidoso.

uproot [ʌp'ruːt] *v* desarraigar; (*fig*) arrancar.

****upset** [ʌp'set; *n* 'ʌpset] *v* (*knock over*) volcar; (*spill*) derramar; (*plans, etc.*) trastornar; desconcertar; (*displease*) enfadar. *adj* (*worried*) preocupado; (*ill*) indispuesto; (*nerves*) desquiciado; enfadado; (*stomach*) trastornado. *n* vuelco *m*; trastorno *m*; (*illness*) malestar *m*; dificultad *f*; (*trouble*) molestia *f*.

upshot ['ʌpʃot] *n* resultado *m*.

upside down [ʌpsai'daun] *adv, adj* al revés.

upstairs [ʌp'steəz] *adv* arriba. **go upstairs** subir. *adj* de arriba.

upstream [ʌp'striːm] *adv* río arriba, aguas arriba; (*swim*) a contracorriente.

up-to-date *adj* moderno.

upward ['ʌpwəd] *adj* ascendente. **upwards** *adv* hacia arriba.

uranium [ju'reiniəm] *n* uranio *m*.

urban ['əːbən] *adj* urbano.

urchin ['əːtʃin] *n* pilluelo *m*.

urge [əːdʒ] *v* incitar; exhortar; requerir. *n* vivo deseo *m*; impulso *m*.

urgent ['əːdʒənt] *adj* urgente; insistente. **urgency** *n* urgencia *f*; insistencia *f*.

urine ['juːrin] *n* orina *f*. **urinate** *v* orinar.

urn [əːn] *n* urna *f*.

Uruguay ['juərəgwai] *n* Uruguay *m*. **Uruguayan** *n, adj* uruguayo, -a.

us [ʌs] *pron* nos; nosotros.

usage ['juːzidʒ] *n* (*custom*) usanza *f*; (*treatment*) tratos *m pl*; (*gramm*) uso *m*.

use [juːs; *v* juːz] *n* uso *m*; empleo *m*; (*tool*) manejo *m*. **it's no use** es inútil. **what's the use?** ¿para qué? *v* usar, emplear; consumir; tomar; utilizar. **use up** agotar. **used** de segunda mano. **be used for** servir para. **be used to** estar acostumbrado a. **get used to** habituarse a. **useful** *adj* útil. **useless** *adj* inútil. **user** *n* usuario, -a *m, f*. **user-friendly** *adj* fácil de usar.

usher ['ʌʃə] *n* (*law*) ujier *m*; (*theatre*) acomodador *m*. *v* **usher in** anunciar; hacer pasar. **usherette** *n* acomodadora *f*.

usual ['juːzuəl] *adj* normal; habitual; acostumbrado. **as usual** como siempre. **usually** *adv* normalmente.

usurp [juˈzəːp] *v* usurpar.

utensil [ju'tensl] *n* utensilio *m*.

uterus ['juːtərəs] *n* útero *m*.

utility [ju'tiləti] *n* utilidad *f*. *adj* utilitario.

utilize ['juːtilaiz] *v* utilizar.

utmost ['ʌtmoust] *adj* mayor; supremo; extremo; más lejano. *n* máximo *m*. **do one's utmost** hacer todo lo posible.

utter¹ ['ʌtə] *v* decir; (*cries*) lanzar; (*sigh*) dar; (*sentiments*) expresar.

utter² ['ʌtə] *adj* absoluto; completo.

U-turn ['juːtəːn] *n* media vuelta *f*.

V

vacant ['veikənt] *adj* (*empty*) vacío; deshabitado; (*free*) libre; (*absent-minded*) distraído; vago; estúpido. **vacancy** (*job*) vacante *f*; (*room*) habitación libre *f*. **no vacancies** completo.

vacate [veɪ'keit] *v* dejar vacío.

vacation [vei'keiʃn] *n* vacaciones *f pl*.

vaccine ['vaksiːn] *n* vacuna *f*. **vaccinate** *v* vacunar. **vaccination** *n* vacunación *f*.

vacillate ['vasileit] *v* vacilar; oscilar. **vacillation** *n* vacilación *f*.

vacuum ['vakjum] *n* vacío *m*. **vacuum cleaner** aspiradora *f*. **vacuum flask** termo *m*. *v* pasar la aspiradora en.

vagina [və'dʒainə] *n* vagina *f*.

vagrant ['veigrənt] *n, adj* vagabundo, -a. **vagrancy** *n* vagabundeo *m*.

vague [veig] *adj* vago, indistinto; incierto.

vain [vein] *adj* vano, inútil; (*conceited*) vanidoso. **in vain** en vano.

valiant ['valiənt] *adj* valeroso.

valid ['valid] *adj* válido. **validity** *n* validez *f*.

valley ['vali] *n* valle *m*.

value ['valjuː] *n* valor *m*; precio *m*; importancia *f*. *v* (*appraise*) valorar, tasar; estimar; apreciar. **valuable** *adj* valioso; precioso;

costoso. **valuables** *pl n* objetos de valor *m pl.* **valuation** *n* valuación *f*; estimación *f.* **value-added tax (VAT)** impuesto sobre el valor añadido *m.*

valve [valv] *n* válvula *f.*

vampire ['vampiə] *n* vampiro *m.*

van [van] *n (road)* camión *m*; *(removal)* carro de mudanzas *m*; *(guard's)* furgón de equipajes *m*; *(leading section)* vanguardia *f.*

vandal ['vandl] *n* vándalo, -a *m, f.* **vandalism** *n* vandalismo *m.* **vandalize** *v* destrozar.

vanilla [və'nilə] *n* vainilla *f.*

vanish ['vaniʃ] *v* desaparecer.

vanity ['vanəti] *n* vanidad *f.* **vanity case** neceser *m.*

vapour ['veipə] *n* vapor *m.* **vapourize** *v* vaporizar.

varicose veins ['varikous] *pl n* varices *f pl.*

variety [və'raiəti] *n* variedad *f*; diversidad *f.* **variety show** función de variedades *f.*

various ['veəriəs] *adj* diverso; vario.

varnish ['va:niʃ] *n* barniz *m. v* barnizar.

vary ['veəri] *v* variar; cambiar; modificar. **vary from** diferenciarse de. **variable** *nf, adj* variable. **variant** *nf, adj* variante. **variation** *n* variación *f.*

vase [va:z] *n* vaso *m*; jarrón *m.*

vasectomy [və'sektəmi] *n* vasectomía *f.*

vast [va:st] *adj* vasto. **vastness** *n* inmensidad *f.*

vat [vat] *n* tinaja *f.*

VAT *n* IVA *m*

Vatican ['vatikən] *n* Vaticano *m.* **Vatican City** Ciudad del Vaticano *f.*

vault[1] [vo:lt] *n (cellar)* sótano *m*; *(arch)* bóveda *f*; *(tomb)* panteón *m*; *(bank)* cámara acorzada *f.*

vault[2] [vo:lt] *v* saltar. *n* salto *m.* **vaulting horse** potro *m.*

veal [vi:l] *n* ternera *f.*

veer [viə] *v (wind)* girar; *(ship)* virar; *(fig)* cambiar.

vegan ['vi:gən] *adj* vegeteriano estricto

vegetable ['vedʒtəbl] *n (bot)* vegetal *m*; *(cookery)* verdura *f*, legumbre *f*, *adj* vegetal. **vegetable garden** huerto *m*, huerta *f.* **vegetarian** *n, adj* vegetariano, -a. **vegetation** *n* vegetación *f.*

vehement ['vi:əmənt] *adj* vehemente; violento. **vehemence** *n* vehemencia *f*; violen-cia *f.* **vehemently** *adj* con vehemencia.

vehicle ['viəkl] *n* vehículo *m.*

veil [veil] *n* velo *m. v* velar.

vein [vein] *n* vena *f.*

velocity [və'losəti] *n* velocidad *f.*

velvet ['velvit] *n* terciopelo *m. adj* de ter-ciopelo. **velvety** *adj* aterciopelado.

vending machine ['vendiŋ] *n* distribuidor automático *m.*

veneer [və'niə] *n* chapa *f*; *(fig: gloss)* barniz *m. v* chapear.

venerate ['venəreit] *v* venerar. **venerable** *adj* venerable. **veneration** *n* veneración *f.*

venereal disease [və'niəriəl] *n* enfermedad venérea *f.*

Venetian blind [və'ni:ʃən] *n* persiana vene-ciana *f.*

Venezuela [,veni'zweilə] *n* Venezuela *f.* **Venezuelan** *n, adj* venezolano, -a.

vengeance ['vendʒəns] *n* venganza *f.* **with a vengeance** *(coll)* de verdad.

venison ['venisn] *n* venado *m.*

venom ['venəm] *n* veneno *m.* **venomous** *adj* venenoso.

vent [vent] *n (hole)* agujero *m*, abertura *f*; *(airhole)* respiradero *m*; *(tube)* conducto de ventilación *m.* **give vent to** dar libre curso a. *v* desahogar.

ventilate ['ventileit] *v* ventilar. **ventilation** *n* ventilación *f.*

ventriloquist [ven'triləkwist] *n* ventrílocuo, -a *m, f.* **ventriloquism** *n* ventriloquia *f.*

venture ['ventʃə] *n* aventura *f*, empresa arriesgada *f. v* aventurar; arriesgar.

venue ['venju:] *n* lugar de reunión *m.*

veranda [və'randə] *n also* **verandah** veran-da *f*, galería *f.*

verb [və:b] *n* verbo. **verbal** *adj* verbal.

verdict ['və:dikt] *n* veredicto *m.*

verge [və:dʒ] *n* margen *m*, borde *m*; *(lake)* orilla *f.* **on the verge of** *(fig)* a punto de, a dos dedos de. *v* **verge on** rayar en.

verify ['verifai] *v* verificar. **verification** *n* verificación *f.*

vermin ['və:min] *n (rats, mice, etc.)* bichos *m pl*; *(fleas, people)* sabandijas *f pl.* **verminous** *adj (lousy)* piojoso.

vermouth ['və:məθ] *n* vermut *m.*

vernacular [və'nakjulə] *adj* vernáculo. *n* lenguaje vulgar *m.*

versatile ['və:sətail] *adj* de talentos variados; (*mind*) flexible. **versatility** n diversos talentos m pl; flexibilidad f.

verse [vəːs] n (*poetry*) poesía f; (*stanza*) estrofa f; (*Bible*) versículo m.

version ['vəːʃən] n versión f.

versus ['vəːsəs] prep contra.

vertebra ['vəːtibrə] n, pl -brae vértebra f. **vertebral** adj vertebral. **vertebrate** nm, adj vertebrado.

vertical ['vəːtikl] nf, adj vertical.

vertigo ['vəːtigou] n vértigo m.

very ['veri] adv muy; mucho, mucha. **very much** mucho, muchísimo. adj mismo; propio; (*real*) verdadero; puro.

vessel ['vesl] n (*container*) vasija f; (*ship*) nave f.

vest [vest] n camiseta f.

vestibule ['vestibjuːl] n vestíbulo m.

vestige ['vestidʒ] n vestigio m, rastro m.

vestry ['vestri] n vestuario m, sacristía f.

vet [vet] n (*coll*) veterinario m. v (*coll*) corregir, revisar.

veteran ['vetərən] nm, adj veterano. **veteran troops** tropas aguerridas f pl.

veterinary surgeon n veterinario m.

veto ['viːtou] n veto m. v vetar, poner el veto.

vex [veks] v molestar; enfadar. **vexation** n molestia f; disgusto m.

via [vaiə] prep por, por la vía de.

viable ['vaiəbl] adj viable. **viability** n viabilidad f.

viaduct ['vaiədʌkt] n viaducto m.

vibrate [vai'breit] v vibrar. **vibration** n vibración f.

vicar ['vikə] n vicario m; (*of a parish*) cura m. **vicarage** n casa del cura f.

vicarious [vi'keəriəs] adj vicario.

vice¹ [vais] n (*evil*) vicio m; (*defect*) defecto m.

vice² [vais] n (*tool*) tornillo de banco m.

vice-chancellor [vais'tʃaːnsələ] n rector m.

vice-consul [vais'konsl] n vicecónsul m.

vice-president [vais'prezidənt] n vicepresidente m.

vice versa [vais'vəːsə] adv viceversa.

vicinity [vi'sinəti] n vecindad f; (*nearness*) cercanía f.

vicious ['viʃəs] adj (*of vice*) vicioso; (*bad*) malo; (*depraved*) pervertido; (*taste*) corrompido; (*life*) disoluto; (*crime*) atroz. **vicious circle** círculo vicioso m. **viciousness** n lo vicioso; maldad f; perversidad f.

victim ['viktim] n víctima f. **victimize** v perseguir; tomar como víctima. **victimization** n persecución f.

victory ['viktəri] n victoria f. **victorious** adj victorioso.

video n vídeo m. v grabar programas de televisión; grabar en vídeo. **video cassette** n cinta de vídeo f, **video recorder** n aparato de vídeo m. **videotape** n cinta magnética de vídeo f.

vie [vai] v competir, rivalizar.

Vienna [vi'enə] n Viena f.

view [vjuː] n vista f; panorama m; inspección f; idea f. **viewfinder** n visor m. **viewpoint** n punto de vista m. v mirar; visitar; considerar. **viewer** n (*TV*) telespectador, -a m, f; (*onlooker*) espectador, -a m, f; (*for slides*) visionadora f.

vigil ['vidʒil] n vela f, vigilia f. **vigilance** n vigilancia f. **vigilant** adj vigilante.

vigour ['vigə] n vigor m. **vigorous** adj vigoroso.

vile [vail] adj vil; horrible.

villa ['vilə] n chalet m; (*country house*) casa de campo f.

village ['vilidʒ] n aldea f, pueblo m. **villager** n aldeano, -a m, f.

villain ['vilən] n canalla m. **villainy** n villanía f.

vindictive [vin'diktiv] adj vengativo.

vine [vain] n vid f; parra f. **vineyard** n viña f.

vinegar ['vinigə] n vinagre m.

vintage ['vintidʒ] adj (*season*) vendimia f; (*crop*) cosecha f. **vintage wine** vino añejo m.

vinyl ['vainil] n vinilo m.

viola [vi'oulə] n (*music*) viola f.

violate ['vaiəleit] v (*ravish*) violar; (*desecrate*) profanar; (*infringe*) contravenir. **violation** n violación f; profanación f; contravención f.

violence ['vaiələns] n violencia f. **violent** adj violento.

violet ['vaiəlit] n (*flower, colour*) violeta. adj violado.

violin [vaiə'lin] n violín m. **violinist** n violinista m, f.

viper ['vaipə] n víbora f.

virgin ['vəːdʒin] nf, adj virgen. **virginity** n virginidad f.

Virgo ['vəːgou] n Virgo m.

virile ['virail] *adj* viril. **virility** *n* virilidad *f*.

virtual *adv* virtual. **virtually** *adv* virtualmente; prácticamente. **virtual reality** realidad virtual *f*.

virtual ['vǝ:tʃuǝl] *adj* virtual (βir'tual)

virtue ['vǝ:tju:] *n* virtud *f*; (*advantage*) ventaja *f*. **by virtue of** debido a. **virtuous** *adj* virtuoso.

virus ['vaiǝrǝs] *n* virus *m*.

visa ['vi:zǝ] *n* visado *m*.

viscount ['vaikaunt] *n* vizconde *m*. **viscountess** vizcondesa *f*.

visible ['vizǝbl] *adj* visible. **visibility** *n* visibilidad *f*.

vision ['viʒǝn] *n* (*sight, apparition*) visión *f*; (*capacity to see*) vista *f*; (*dream*) sueño *m*. **visionary** *n, adj* visionario, -a *m, f*.

visit ['vizit] *n* visita *f*. *v* (*go to, call on*) visitar; (*stay in*) pasar una temporada en. **visitor** *n* visitante *m, f*; visita *f*.

visor ['vaizǝ] *n* visera *f*.

visual ['viʒuǝl] *adj* visual. **visualize** *v* imaginarse.

vital ['vaitl] *adj* vital. **vitality** *n* vitalidad *f*. **vitally** *adv* vitalmente.

vitamin ['vitǝmin] *n* vitamina *f*.

vivacious [vi'veiʃǝs] *adj* vivo; vivaracho. **vivaciousness** *n also* **vivacity** viveza *f*, vivacidad *f*.

vivid ['vivid] *adj* vivo; (*description*) gráfico. **vividness** *n* (*colour*) viveza *f*, intensidad *f*; (*style*) fuerza *f*.

vivisection [vivi'sekʃǝn] *n* vivisección *f*.

vixen ['viksn] *n* zorra *f*, raposa *f*.

vocabulary [vǝ'kabjulǝri] *n* vocabulario *m*.

vocal ['voukǝl] *adj* vocal; (*fig*) ruidoso. **vocalist** *n* cantante *m, f*.

vocation [vou'keiʃǝn] *n* vocación *f*. **vocational** *adj* profesional.

vociferous [vǝ'sifǝrǝs] *adj* ruidoso.

vodka ['vodkǝ] *n* vodca *m*.

voice [vois] *n* voz *f*. *v* hablar; expresar. **voice mail** buzón de voz *m*.

void [void] *n* vacío *m*. *adj* (*empty*) vacío; (*job*) vacante; (*law*) nulo.

volatile ['volǝtail] *adj* (*chem*) volátil; (*fig*) voluble.

volcano [vol'keinou] *n* volcán *m*. **volcanic** *adj* volcánico.

volley ['voli] *n* (*bullets*) andanada *f*; (*arrows, stones*) lluvia *f*; (*applause*) salva *f*; (*sport*)

voleo *m*. *v* (*missile*) lanzar; (*sport*) volear.

volt [voult] *n* voltio *m*. **voltage** *n* voltaje *m*.

volume ['voljum] *n* (*space, sound*) volumen *m*; (*book*) tomo *m*, volumen *m*. **voluminous** *adj* voluminoso; abundante.

volunteer [volǝn'tiǝ] *nm, adj* voluntario. *v* ofrecer; (*remark*) hacer; (*information*) dar.

voluptuous [vǝ'lʌptʃuǝs] *adj* voluptuoso. **voluptuousness** *n* voluptuosidad *f*.

vomit ['vomit] *n* vómito *m*. *v* vomitar.

voodoo ['vu:du:] *n* vodú *m*.

voracious [vǝ'reiʃǝs] *adj* voraz. **voraciousness** *n also* **voracity** voracidad *f*.

vote [vout] *n* voto *m*; (*action*) votación *f*. **vote of confidence** voto de confianza *f*. **vote of thanks** voto de gracias *m*. *v* votar; elegir; proponer; declarar. **voter** *n* votante *m, f*; elector, -a *m, f*.

vouch [vautʃ] *v* **vouch for** (*thing*) responder de; garantizar; (*person*) responder por.

voucher ['vautʃǝ] *n* (*comm*) bono *m*, vale *m*. **luncheon voucher** vale de comida *m*.

vow [vau] *n* voto *m*; promesa solemne *f*. *v* jurar; prometer.

vowel ['vauǝl] *n* vocal *f*.

voyage ['voiidʒ] *n* viaje *m*. *v* viajar (por mar).

vulgar ['vʌlgǝ] *adj* común; ordinario; grosero. **vulgarity** *n* vulgaridad *f*; grosería *f*.

vulnerable ['vʌlnǝrǝbl] *adj* vulnerable.

vulture ['vʌltʃǝ] *n* buitre *m*.

W

wad [wod] *n* (*bung*) tapón *m*; (*notes*) rollo *m*; (*cotton wool*) bolita *f*. **wadding** *n* (*cotton wool*) guata *f*; (*filling*) relleno *m*.

waddle ['wodl] *v* anadear. *n* anadeo *m*.

wade [weid] *v* vadear. **wade through** (*book, etc.*) estudiar detenidamente.

wafer ['weifǝ] *n* (*for ices*) barquillo *m*. **wafer-thin** *adj* finísimo.

waft [woft] *v* llevar por el aire; flotar. *n* ráfaga *f*.

wag [wag] *v* agitar; (*tail*) menear. *n* (*tail*) coleada *f*; movimiento *m*; (*joker*) bromista *m, f*.

wage [weidʒ] *n* salario *m*, paga *f*. *v* **wage**

war hacer guerra.

wager ['weidʒə] n apuesta f. v apostar.

waggle ['wagl] v menear; agitar. n meneo m.

wagon ['wagən] n carro m; carreta f; (rail) vagón m.

waif [weif] n niño abandonado m.

wail [weil] n lamento m, gemido m. v lamentarse, gemir.

waist [weist] n cintura f, talle m. **waistband** n pretina f. **waistcoat** n chaleco m. **waistline** n cintura f.

wait [weit] n espera f. **lie in wait for** acechar. v esperar; (at table) atender. **waiter** n mozo m, camarero m. **waiting** n espera f; servicio m. **waiting-list** n lista de espera f. **waiting-room** n sala de espera f. **waitress** n camarera f.

waive [weiv] v renunciar a; desistir de.

wake¹ [weik] n velatorio m.

*wake² [weik] v also **wake up** despertar(se).

Wales [weilz] n el País de Gales.

walk [wo:k] n paseo m; camino m; (gait) andar m; (pace) paso m. v (go on foot) recorrer a pie; (distance) hacer a pie; (take out) pasear; (escort) acompañar. **walkout** n huelga f. **walkover** n victoria fácil f. **walker** n paseante m, f. **walking** n andar m. **walking-stick** n bastón m.

wall [wo:l] n pared f; muro m. v murar; amurallar.

wallet ['wolit] n cartera f.

wallflower ['wo:lflauə] n alhelí m. **be a wallflower** quedarse en el poyete.

wallop ['woləp] (coll) n golpazo m, trompazo m. v zurrar. **walloping** n paliza f.

wallow ['wolou] v revolcarse.

wallpaper ['wo:lpeipə] n papel pintado m. v empapelar.

walnut ['wo:lnʌt] n (nut) nuez f; (tree, wood) nogal m.

walrus ['wo:lrəs] n morsa f.

waltz [wo:lts] n vals m. v valsar.

wan [won] adj macilento.

wand [wond] n (magic) varita f; vara f.

wander ['wondə] v vagar por; (stroll) pasearse; (mentally) desvariar.

wane [wein] v (moon) menguar; (fig) decaer.

wangle ['waŋgl] v conseguir con trampas. (coll) n trampa f.

want [wont] n (lack) falta f; (need) necesi-

dad f; (poverty) miseria f; (wish) deseo m; (gap) vacío m. **for want of** por falta de. v querer; desear; necesitar; (ask) pedir; (look for) buscar. **wanted** adj buscado (por la policía). **wanting** adj (absent) ausente; (lacking) deficiente.

wanton ['wontən] adj lascivo; (promiscuous) libertino; (senseless) sin sentido. **wantonness** n libertinaje f; crueldad f; exuberancia f; (lack of moderation) desenfreno m.

war [wo:] n guerra f. **be on the warpath** (coll) estar buscando guerra. **warfare** n guerra f. **warhead** n cabeza de guerra f. **war memorial** monumento a los Caídos m. **War Office** Ministerio de la Guerra m. **warship** n buque de guerra m. **wartime** n tiempo de guerra m.

warble ['wo:bl] v gorjear, trinar. n gorjeo m, trino m.

ward [wo:d] n (hospital) sala f; (pol) distrito electoral m; (law: guardianship) custodia f; (minor) pupilo m. v **ward off** evitar.

warden ['wo:dn] n guarda m; vigilante m; director m.

warder ['wo:də] n carcelero m; guardián m.

wardrobe ['wo:droub] n guardarropa m; (theatre) vestuario m.

warehouse ['weəhaus] n almacén m. v almacenar.

wares ['weəz] n mercancías f (pl)

warm [wo:m] adj tibio; caliente; (climate) cálido; (fire) acogedor; (welcome) caluroso; (kind) cariñoso. v calentar; acalorar. **warm up** calentar; (reheat) recalentar. **warming-pan** n calentador de cama m. **warmth** n calor m; cordialidad f.

warn [wo:n] v advertir; aconsejar; (rebuke) amonestar. **warning** n advertencia f, aviso m; alarma f; ejemplo m; amonestación f. **warning light** lámpara indicadora f. **warning triangle** triángulo de seguridad m.

warp [wo:p] v (wood) alabear; (yarn) urdir; (fig) deformar. n alabeo m; urdimbre f; deformación f.

warrant ['worənt] n (police) orden f; (law) autorización legal f; justificación f; garantía f. v autorizar; justificar; garantizar. **warranty** n garantía f.

warren ['worən] n (rabbit) conejal m; (fig) colmena f.

warrior ['woriə] n guerrero m.

Warsaw ['wo:so:] ['wo:so:] n Varsovia.

wart [wo:t] *n* verruga *f.*

wary ['weəri] *adj* cauto, precavido.

was [woz] *V* **be.**

wash [woʃ] *v* lavar; (*dishes*) fregar. **wash away** quitar. **wash down** (*swallow*) tragar. **wash up** fregar. **washable** *adj* lavable. **wash-and-wear** *adj* de lava y pon. **washbasin** *n* lavabo *m.* **washboard** *n* tabla de lavar *f.* **washer** *n* arandela *f.* **washing** *n* lavado *m;* colada *f;* fregado *m.* **washing machine** lavadora *f.* **washing powder** jabón en polvo *m.* **washing-up bowl** barreño *m.* **washout** *n* (*slang*) desastre *m.*

wasp [wosp] *n* avispa *f.*

waste [weist] *n* pérdida *f;* (*food*) desperdicios *m pl;* (*rubbish*) basura *f.* **waste disposal unit** vertedero de basuras *m.* **waste land** yermo *m;* erial *m.* **waste paper** papel usado *m.* **waste-paper basket** papelera *f. v* malgastar, despilfarrar; perder; (*use up*) consumir; (*by disuse*) desperdiciar. **waste away** consumirse. **wasteful** *adj* (*person*) despilfarrador, -a *m, f;* ruinoso. **waster** *n also* **wastrel** derrochador, -a *m, f.*

watch [wotʃ] *n* (*wrist*) reloj de pulsera *m;* (*pocket*) reloj de bolsillo *m;* (*naut*) guardia *f;* vigilancia *f.* **keep watch** estar de guardia. **watch chain** cadena de reloj *f.* **watchdog** *n* perro guardián *m.* **watchmaker** *n* relojero *m.* **watchman** *n* vigilante *m.* **watch spring** muelle *m.* **watch strap** correa de reloj *f.* **watchword** *n* consigna *f. v* mirar, ver, observar; (*pay attention to*) fijarse en; (*keep an eye on*) vigilar. **watchful** *adj* atento; vigilante.

water ['wo:tə] *n* agua *f. v* (*wet*) humedecer; (*soak*) mojar; (*plants*) regar; (*eyes*) llorar. **water down** moderar. **watery** *adj* acuoso; aguado, insípido.

water-biscuit *n* galleta de harina y agua *f.*

water-closet *n* retrete *m,* wáter *m.*

water-colour *n* acuarela *f.*

watercress ['wo:təkres] *n* berro *m.*

waterfall ['wo:təfo:l] *n* cascada *f;* catarata *f.*

water-ice *n* sorbete *m.*

watering-can *n* regadera *f.*

water lily *n* nenúfar *m.*

waterline ['wo:təlain] *n* línea de flotación *f.*

waterlogged ['wo:tələgd] *adj* (*wood*) empapado; (*med*) inundado.

water main *n* cañería principal *f.*

watermark ['wo:təma:k] *n* filigrana *f;* (*tide*)

marca del nivel del agua *f.*

watermelon ['wo:təmelən] *n* sandía *f.*

waterproof ['wo:təpruf] *nm, adj* impermeable. *v* impermeabilizar.

watershed ['wo:təʃed] *n* (*fig*) momento decisivo *m;* (*geog*) línea divisora de las aguas *f.*

water-ski *v* hacer esquí acuático. **water-skiing** *n* esquí acuático *m.*

water softener *n* ablandador del agua *m.*

watertight ['wo:tətait] *adj* estanco; hermético; (*fig*) perfecto.

waterway ['wo:təwei] *n* vía navegable *f.*

waterworks ['wo:təwə:ks] *n* sistema de abastecimiento de agua *m.*

watt [wot] *n* vatio *m.*

wave [weiv] *n* (*sea*) ola *f;* (*hair*) ondulación *f;* (*physics, radio, etc.*) onda *f;* (*hand*) señal *f.* **permanent wave** permanente *f.* **waveband** *n* banda de ondas *f.* **wave-length** *n* longitud de onda *f. v* agitar; (*hair*) ondular. **wavy** *adj* ondulado.

waver ['weivə] *v* vacilar; (*falter*) flaquear; (*totter*) titubear. **wavering** *adj* vacilante; tembloroso.

wax[1] [waks] *n* cera *f.* **waxwork** *n* figura de cera *f.* **waxworks** *n* museo de figuras de cera *m. v* encerar. **waxy** *adj* ceroso.

wax[2] [waks] *v* crecer.

way [wei] *n* camino *m;* paso *m;* ruta *f;* senda *f;* dirección *f;* rumbo *m;* distancia *f;* (*journey*) viaje *m;* progreso *m;* modo *m,* manera *f;* (*means*) medio *m.* **be in the way** estar de por medio. **by the way** a propósito. **give way** ceder. **on the way** en camino. **this way** por aquí. **under way** en marcha; en preparación. **way in** entrada *f.* **way out** salida *f.*

*waylay ['wei'lei] *v* abordar.

wayside ['weisaid] *n* borde del camino *m. adj* al borde del camino.

wayward ['weiwəd] *adj* voluntarioso; díscolo.

we [wi:] *pron* nosotros, -as.

weak [wi:k] *adj* débil; flaco; flojo. **weaken** *v* debilitar. **weakling** *n* persona débil *f;* cobarde *m.* **weakness** *n* debilidad *f;* (*point*) punto flaco *m.*

wealth [welθ] *n* riqueza *f;* abundancia *f.* **wealthy** *adj* rico.

wean [wi:n] *v* (*baby*) destetar. **wean from** apartar de.

weapon ['wepən] n arma f.

*wear [weə] v llevar; poner; gastar. **wear off** pasar(se). **wear out** usarse, consumirse. n uso m; gasto m; deterioro m. **wear and tear** desgaste m.

weary ['wɪərɪ] adj fatigado, cansado, aburrido. v fatigar, cansar; aburrir. **wearily** adv cansadamente. **weariness** n fatiga f.

weasel ['wiːzl] n comadreja f.

weather ['weðə] n tiempo m. **weather-beaten** adj curtido. **weather chart** mapa meteorológico m. **weathercock** n veleta f. **weather forecast** boletín meteorológico m. v (survive) superar.

*weave [wiːv] v tejer; entrelazar; (through traffic, etc.) zigzaguear.

web [web] n (spider) tela de araña f; (fabric) tejido m; (on feet) membrana f; (network) red f; (fig) sarta f; (Internet) la Web f. **web-footed** adj palmípedo. **website** página web f.

wed [wed] v casarse con; casar. **wedding** n boda f, casamiento m. **wedding dress** traje de novia m. **wedding ring** alianza f.

wedge [wedʒ] n cuña f, calzo m. v encajar; (jam) apretar.

Wednesday ['wenzdi] n miércoles m.

weed [wiːd] n mala hierba f. **weed-killer** n herbicida m. v desherbar. **weeding** n escarda f.

week [wiːk] n semana f. **a week today/tomorrow** hoy/mañana en ocho. **weekday** n día de trabajo m. **weekend** n fin de semana m. **weekly** adv semanal. **weekly** n semanario m.

*weep [wiːp] v llorar, lamentar. **weeping willow** sauce llorón m.

weigh [wei] v pesar. **weigh down** doblar bajo un peso. **weight** n peso m. **pull one's weight** poner de su parte. **weightlifting** n halterofilia f. **weightlessness** n ingravidez f.

weird [wɪəd] adj extraño; misterioso; fantástico. **weirdness** n misterio m; lo sobrenatural.

welcome ['welkəm] adj bienvenido; grato. **be welcome** ser oportuno. **you're welcome!** ¡eres el bienvenido!; (after thanks) ¡no hay de qué! n bienvenida f. v dar la bienvenida a; recibir; alegrarse por.

weld [weld] v soldar. **welder** n soldador m. **welding** n soldadura f.

welfare ['welfeə] n bienestar m, bien m. **welfare state** estado de bienestar m.

well¹ [wel] n pozo m. **well up** brotar.

well² [wel] adj, adv bien. **as well** también.

well-advised adj juicioso.

well-behaved adj bien educado.

well-being n bienestar m.

well-born adj de buena familia.

well-bred adj (person) bien educado; (animal) de raza pura.

well-built adj bien hecho.

well-dressed adj bien vestido.

well-informed adj muy documentado.

wellington ['welɪŋtən] n bota de agua f.

well-kept adj (secret) bien guardado; (garden) bien cuidado.

well-known adj bien conocido.

well-made adj bien hecho.

well-off adj rico.

well-paid adj bien pagado.

well-read adj leído.

well-spent adj (time) bien empleado.

well-spoken adj bienhablado.

well-timed adj oportuno.

well-to-do adj rico.

well-trodden adj trillado.

well-worn adj gastado.

Welsh [welʃ] adj galés. n (language) galés m; (person) galés, -esa m, f.

went [went] V **go**.

wept [wept] V **weep**.

were [wəː] V **be**.

west [west] n oeste m. **the West** el Mundo Occidental m, adj also **westerly** del oeste, occidental. adv al oeste, hacia el oeste. **westbound** adj con rumbo al oeste. **western** adj occidental, del oeste. n (film) western m.

West Indies n Antillas f pl; **West Indian** adj antillano.

wet [wet] adj mojado; húmedo; (weather) lluvioso; (paint) fresco. **wet blanket** aguafiestas m, f invar. **wet suit** traje de buzo m, n lluvia f. v mojar; humedecer.

whack [wak] n golpe m. v golpear, pegar.

whale [weil] n ballena f.

wharf [woːf] n muelle m.

what [wot] pron lo que; (interrog, interj) qué, cuál, cómo, cánto. adj el que, la que, lo que; qué.

whatever [wot'evə] pron todo lo que; lo que; cualquier cosa que. adj cualquiera.

wicket

nothing whatever nada en absoluto.
wheat [wi:t] *n* trigo *m*.
wheel [wi:l] *n* rueda *f*; (*steering*) volante *m*.
wheelbarrow *n* carretilla *f*. **wheelchair** *n* sillón de ruedas *m*. *v* hacer rodar; empujar; dar una vuelta.
wheeze [wi:z] *n* respiración dificultosa *f*. *v* respirar con dificultad. **wheezy** *adj* asmático.
whelk [welk] *n* buccino *m*.
when [wen] *adv* cuándo, a qué hora. *conj* cuando; en que; (*as soon as*) en cuanto. **whenever** *conj* cuando; cada vez que.
where [weə] *interrog adv* dónde; adónde: de dónde; por dónde; (*in what respect*) en qué. *relative adv* donde; en donde, en que, en el cual, en la cual; adonde, a donde, al que, al cual, a la cual. *conj* donde. **whereabouts** *adv* dónde, por dónde; *n* paradero *m*. **whereas** *conj* mientras, en tanto que. **whereupon** *adv* después de lo cual. **wherever** *conj* dondequiera que; a dondequiera que.
whether [weðə] *conj* si.
which [witʃ] *interrog pron* cuál; qué. *relative pron* que; el cual, la cual, el que, la que; lo cual, lo que. *adj* qué; cuál; cuyo; cómo. **of which** del que, de la que; del cual; de la cual. **whichever** *pron* el que, la que; cualquiera que; *adj* cualquier.
whiff [wif] *n* soplo *m*; olorcillo *m*.
while [wail] *conj* mientras; (*although*) aunque. *n* rato *m*, tiempo *m*. **while away** pasar.
whim [wim] *n* capricho *m*.
whimper [w:mpə] *n* quejido *m*, gemido *m*. *v* quejarse, gemir.
whimsical [wimzikl] *adj* caprichoso; fantástico.
whine [wain] *n* (*animal*) gañido *m*; (*complaint*) queja *f*; (*pain*) quejido *m*; (*engine*) zumbido *m*. *v* gañir; quejarse; zumbar.
whip [wip] *n* azote *m*; (*riding*) látigo *m*. **whiplash** *n* latigazo *m*. **whip-round** *n* (*coll*) colecta *f*. *v* azotar; (*cookery*) batir. **whip up** avivar. **whipping** *n* azotamiento *m*.
whippet [wipit] *n* lebrel *m*.
whirl [wə:l] *n* vuelta *f*, giro *m*; (*fig*) torbellino *m*. *v* dar vueltas, girar. **whirlpool** *n* remolino *m*.
whirr [wə:] *n* (*wings*) batir *m*; (*engine*) zumbido *m*. *v* girar; zumbar.

whisk [wisk] *n* (*cookery*) batidor. *v* batir.
whisker [wiskə] *n* pelo del bigote *m*. **whiskers** *pl n* bigotes *m pl*.
whisky [wiski] *n* whisky *m*.
whisper [wispə] *n* cuchicheo *m*. *v* cuchichear.
whistle [wisl] *n* pito *m*; (*sound*) silbido *m*; pitido *m*. *v* silbar.
white [wait] *adj* blanco. **white elephant** (*fig*) objeto costoso e inútil *m*. *n* blanco *m*; (*person*) blanco, -a *m, f*. **whiten** *v* blanquear **whiteness** *n* blancura *f*.
whitewash [waitwoʃ] *n* cal *f*. *v* encalar; (*fig: cover up*) encubrir.
whiting [waitiŋ] *n* pescadilla *f*.
whittle [witl] *v* tallar. **whittle down** reducir poco a poco.
whizz [wiz] *n* zumbido *m*. **whizz-kid** *n* (*coll*) promesa *f*. **whizz past** pasar como un rayo.
who [hu:] *relative pron* quien, el quel, la que; que, el cual, la cual; que, a quien. *interrog pron* quién. **whoever** *pron* quienquiera que, cualquiera que, el que, la que, quien.
whole [houl] *adj* todo, completo, entero, total; íntegro, intacto. *n* todo *m*, total *m*, totalidad *f*. **on the whole** en general. **wholefood** alimentos integrales *m pl*, comida naturista *f*. **wholehearted** *adj* sin reservas. **wholeheartedly** *adv* incondicionalmente. **wholemeal** *adj* integral. **wholesome** *adj* saludable.
wholesale [houlseil] *n* venta al por mayor *f*. *adj, adv* al por mayor; en masa.
whom [hu:m] *relative pron* que, quien, a quien. *interrog pron* quién, a quién. **of whom** del cual, de la cual, de quien.
whooping cough [hu:piŋ] *n* tos ferina *f*.
whore [ho:] *n* (*derog*) puta *f*.
whose [hu:z] *relative pron* cuyo, cuya. *interrog pron* de quién.
why [wai] *adv* (*interrog*) por qué; (*on account of which*) por el cual, por la cual, por lo cual. *interj* ¡vaya! ¡toma! ¡pues bien!
wick [wik] *n* mecha *f*.
wicked [wikid] *adj* malo, perverso, malicioso. **wickedness** *n* maldad *f*, perversidad *f*.
wicker [wikə] *n* mimbre *m*. **wickerwork** *n* cestería *f*.
wicket [wikit] *n* (*cricket*) palos *m pl*.

wide [waid] *adj* ancho; vasto; grande. *adv* lejos; mucho. **wide awake** completamente despierto. **widespread** *adj* general. **widely** *adv* muy; mucho; generalmente.

widow ['widou] *n* viuda *f*. **be widowed** quedar viuda. **widower** *n* viudo *m*.

width [widθ] *n* anchura *f*.

wield [wi:ld] *v (tool)* manejar; *(weapon)* blandir; *(power)* ejercer.

wife [waif] *n* mujer *f*, esposa *f*.

wig [wig] *n* peluca *f*.

wiggle ['wigl] *v* menear. *n* meneo *m*. **wiggly** *adj (line)* ondulante.

wild [waild] *adj (animal, person)* salvaje; *(plant)* silvestre; *(bull)* bravo; *(character)* violento. **like wildfire** como un reguero de pólvora. **wildlife** *n* fauna *f*, vida salvaje *f*, fauna y flora *f*. **wildly** *adv* violentamente; locamente; frenéticamente; disolutamente.

wilderness ['wildənəs] *n* desierto *m*; soledad *f*.

wilful ['wilfəl] *adj (stubborn)* obstinado; *(headstrong)* voluntarioso; deliberado.

will¹ [wil] *aux translated by future tense.*

will² [wil] *n* voluntad *f*; testamento *m*. *v* disponer; desear; *(bequeath)* legar. **against one's will** de mal grado. **willpower** *n* fuerza de voluntad *f*. **willing** *adj* de buena voluntad; *(obliging)* complaciente. **be willing to** estar dispuesto a. **willingly** *adv* de buena gana. **willingness** *n* buena voluntad *f*.

willow ['w:lou] *n* sauce *m*. **willowy** *adj* esbelto.

wilt [wilt] *v* marchitar(se); *(person)* languidecer.

wily ['waili] *adj* astuto, chuzón.

***win** [win] *n* victoria *f*; *(amount won)* ganancia *f*. *v* ganar; conquistar; triunfar. **winner** *n* ganador, -a *m*, *f*; vencedor, -a *m*, *f*. **winning** *adj* ganador; *(smile, etc.)* encantador. **winnings** *pl n* ganancias *f pl*.

wince [wins] *v* hacer muecas. *n* mueca de dolor *f*.

winch [wintʃ] *n* torno *m*. *v* guindar.

wind farm *n* parque eólico *m*

wind¹ [wind] *n* viento *m*; *(breath)* aliento *m*; respiración *f*; *(med)* gases *m pl*. *v* dejar sin aliento. **windy** *adj (place)* expuesto al viento; *(day, night)* ventoso.

***wind²** [waind] *v* devanar; envolver; enrollar; *(bend)* torcer; *(road)* serpentear; *(watch)*

dar cuerda a. **wind up** terminar; *(comm)* liquidar. **winding** *adj* sinuoso; tortuoso.

wind-break *n* protección contra el viento *f*.

windfall ['windfo:l] *n* fruta caída *f*; *(fig)* ganancia inesperada *f*.

wind instrument *n* instrumento de viento *m*.

windlass ['windləs] *n* torno *m*.

windmill ['wind,mil] *n* molino de viento *m*.

window ['windou] *n* ventana *f*; *(car)* ventanilla *f*; *(cashier's)* taquilla *f*; *(shop)* escaparate *m*. **window blind** persiana *f*. **window-box** *n* jardinera *f*. **window cleaner** limpiacristales *m invar*. **window-sill** *n* antepecho *m*. **window-shopping** *n* contemplación de escaparates *f*.

windpipe ['windpaip] *n* tráquea *f*.

windproof ['windpru:f] *adj* a prueba de viento.

windscreen ['windskri:n] *n* parabrisas *m invar*. **windscreen wiper** limpiaparabrisas *m invar*.

wind-sock *n* manga de aire *f*.

windsurfing ['wind,sə:fiŋ] *n* windsurfing *m*, windsurf *m*. *v* hacer windsurf

windswept ['windswept] *adj (hair)* despeinado.

wind tunnel *n* túnel aerodinámico *m*.

wine [wain] *n* vino *m*. **wineglass** *n* copa *f*. **wine list** lista de vinos *f*. **wine-taster** *n* catavinos *m invar*. **wine waiter** bodeguero *m*.

wing [wiŋ] *n* ala *f*. **wing chair** sillón de orejas *m*. **wing commander** teniente coronel *m*. **wing-mirror** *n* retrovisor *m*. **wing nut** palometa *f*. **wings** *pl n (theatre)* bastidores *m pl*. **wingspan** *n* envergadura *f*.

wink [wiŋk] *n* guiño *m*; *(light)* parpadeo *m*. *v* guiñar; *(light)* parpadear.

winkle ['wiŋkl] *n* bígaro *m*. *v* **winkle out** sacar con dificultad.

winter ['wintə] *n* invierno *m*. *v* invernar. **wintry** *adj* de invierno; *(fig)* frío.

wipe [waip] *v* limpiar; *(mop)* enjugar; *(dry)* secar. **wipe out** destruir. *n* limpieza *f*.

wire [waiə] *n* alambre *m*; *(elec)* cordón *m*, cable *m*; hilo *m*; *(piano)* cuerda *f*; telegrama *m*. **barbed wire** alambrada *f*. **wire-brush** *n* cepillo metálico *m*. **wirecutters** *pl n* cortaalambres *m invar*. **wireless** *n* radio *f*. *v* telegrafiar; *(a house)* poner la instalación eléctrica de. **wiry** *adj* (*hair*) tieso; (*person*) enjuto y fuerte.

wise [waiz] *adj* sabio; juicioso; (*informed*) enterado. **wisdom** *n* sabiduría *f*; juicio *m*. **wisdom tooth** muela del juicio *f*.

wish [wiʃ] *v* querer; desear; gustar. *n* deseo *m*. **wishbone** *n* espoleta *f*. **wishful** *adj* deseoso. **wishful thinking** ilusiones *f pl*.

wisp [wisp] *n* (*straw*) manojo *m*; (*hair*) mechón *m*; (*smoke*) voluta *f*; (*trace*) vestigio *m*. **wispy** *adj* fino.

wistful [ˈwistfəl] *adj* triste; ansioso; pensativo. **wistfully** *adv* tristemente; con ansia.

wit [wit] *n* inteligencia *f*; agudeza *f*; (*humour*) gracia *f*; (*person*) persona aguda *f*. **be at one's wits' end** no saber qué hacer.

witch [witʃ] *n* bruja *f*. **witchcraft** *n* brujería *f*. **witch-doctor** *n* hechicero *m*. **witch-hunt** *n* persecución *f*.

with [wið] *prep* con; junto con; en manos de; más; en compañía de; (*because of*) de.

***withdraw** [wiðˈdrɔ:] *v* quitar; apartar; retirar; sacar. **withdrawal** *n* retirada *f*; (*bank*) salida *f*; renuncia *f*; retractación *f*; abandono *m*. **withdrawn** *adj* ensimismado.

wither [ˈwiðə] *v* (*plant*) marchitar(se); (*weaken*) debilitar. **withered** *adj* marchito; seco. **withering** *adj* (*look*) fulminante; (*remark*) mordaz.

***withhold** [wiðˈhould] *v* (*refuse*) negar; (*hold back*) retener; (*hide*) ocultar.

within [wiˈðin] *adv* dentro; (*at home*) en casa. *prep* dentro de; en; al alcance de; (*less than*) a menos de.

without [wiˈðaut] *prep* sin; (*outside*) fuera de. *adv* fuera.

***withstand** [wiðˈstand] *v* resistir, aguantar; oponerse a.

witness [ˈwitnis] *n* (*person*) testigo *m*; (*evidence*) prueba *f*; (*testimony*) testimonio *m*. *v* (*be present at*) asistir a; (*document*) firmar como testigo. **witness box** banco/banquillo de los testigos *m*. **witness to** atestiguar.

witty [ˈwiti] *adj* salado, gracioso, **witticism** *n* rasgo de ingenio *m*, agudeza *f*.

wizard [ˈwizəd] *n* mago *m*.

wobble [ˈwobl] *v* tambalearse. *n* tambaleo *m*. **wobbly** *adj* tambaleante.

woke [wouk] *V* **wake**.

wolf [wulf] *n* lobo *m*. **wolfhound** *n* perro lobo *m*. **wolf-whistle** *n* silbido de admiración *m*. *v* **wolf down** (*coll*) zamparse.

woman [ˈwumən] *n, pl* **women** mujer *f*. **Women's Lib** (*coll*) Movimiento de la Liberación de la Mujer *m*. **womanhood** *n* mujeres *f pl*; feminidad *f*. **womanly** *adj* femenino.

womb [wu:m] *n* matriz *f*. útero *m*.

won [wʌn] *V* **win**.

wonder [ˈwʌndə] *n* maravilla *f*; milagro *m*; admiración *f*. **no wonder** no es de extrañar. *v* preguntarse; pensar; asombrarse. **wonderful** *adj* maravilloso; (*astonishing*) asombroso.

woo [wu:] *v* cortejar; (*fig*) solicitar. **wooing** *nm, adj* galanteo.

wood [wud] *n* (*forest*) bosque *m*; (*material*) madera *f*; (*stick*) palo *m*; (*firewood*) leña *f*. **wooden** *adj* de madera; (*stiff*) estirado. **woody** *adj* arbolado; (*stem*) leñoso.

woodcock [ˈwudkok] *n* chocha *f*, becada *f*.

woodcut [ˈwudkʌt] *n* grabado en madera *m*. **woodcutter** *n* (*forester*) leñador *m*.

woodland [ˈwudlənd] *n* bosque *m*.

woodpecker [ˈwudpekə] *n* pájaro carpintero *m*.

wood-pigeon *n* paloma torcaz *f*.

woodshed [ˈwudʃed] *n* leñera *f*.

woodwind [ˈwudwind] *n* (*music*) instrumentos de viento de madera *m pl*.

woodwork [ˈwudwə:k] *n* carpintería *f*.

woodworm [ˈwudwə:m] *n* carcoma *f*.

wool [wul] *n* lana *f*. **woollen** *adj* de lana. **woolly** *adj* lanoso; de lana; (*ideas*) borroso.

word [wə:d] *n* palabra *f*; (*gramm*) vocablo *m*. **in other words** en otras palabras; es decir. *v* expresar; redactar. **wording** *n* redacción *f*; términos *m pl*. **word processing** procesamiento de textos *m*. **word processor** procesador de textos *m*. **wordy** *adj* verboso.

wore [wo:] *V* **wear**.

work [wə:k] *n* trabajo *m*, obra *f*. **men at work** obras *f pl*. **workaholic** *n* adicto al trabajo. **out of work** parado, -a. **workstation** (*comput*) terminal de trabajo *f*. *v* trabajar. **work out** resolver. **workable** *adj* (*plan*) realizable.

worker [ˈwə:kə] *n* trabajador, -a *m, f*; obrero, -a *m, f*.

work-force *n* mano de obra *f*.

working [ˈwə:kiŋ] *n* trabajo *m*; funcionamiento *m*; manejo *m*; cultivo *m*. **working-class** *adj* de la clase obrera. **workings** *pl n* excavaciones *f* pl.

workman ['wəːkmən] *n* trabajador *m*; obrero *m*. **workmanship** *n* (*skill*) artesanía *f*; ejecución *f*.

work permit *n* permiso de trabajo *m*.

workshop ['wəːkʃop] *n* taller *m*.

work-to-rule *n* trabajo a ritmo lento *m*.

world [wəːld] *n* mundo *m*. **world-wide** *adj* mundial. **World Wide Web** la Web *f*. **worldly** *adj* mundano; material.

worm [wəːm] *n* gusano *m*; (*earthworm*) lombriz *f*.

worn [woːn] *V* **wear**.

worry ['wʌri] *n* preocupación *f*. *v* preocupar(se); molestar. **don't worry!** ¡no te preocupes! **worried** *adj* preocupado.

worse [wəːs] *adj, adv* peor. **get worse** *or* **worsen** empeorar. **to make matters worse** para empeorar las cosas. *n* lo peor.

worship ['wəːʃip] *n* culto *m*; (*fig*) adoración *f*. *v* venerar; (*fig*) adorar.

worst [wəːst] *adj, adv* peor. *n* el peor *m*, la peor *f*, lo peor. **at worst** en el peor de los casos.

worsted ['wustid] *n* estambre *m*.

worth [wəːθ] *n* valor *m*; mérito *m*; valía *f*; fortuna *f*. **be worth** valer. **be worth it** merecer la pena. **worthless** *adj* sin valor; inútil. **worthwhile** *adj* que vale la pena; útil.

would ['wud] *aux translated by conditional or imperfect tense.*

wound¹ [waund] *V* **wind²**.

wound² [wuːnd] *n* herida *f*. *v* herir.

wove [wouv] *V* **weave**.

wrangle ['raŋgl] *n* disputa *f*. *v* discutir.

wrap [rap] *v* envolver; cubrir. **wrap up** abrigarse. *n* (*shawl*) chal *m*. **wrapper** *n* envoltura *f*; (*book*) sobrecubierta *f*. **wrapping** *n* envoltura *f*. **wrapping-paper** *n* papel de envolver *m*.

wreath [riːθ] *n* guirnalda *f*; (*funeral*) corona *f*. **wreathe** *v* enguirnaldar; (*wind*) enroscar.

wreck [rek] *n* (*ship*) naufragio *m*; (*train, car, plane*) restos *m* pl; (*accident*) accidente *m*; (*person*) ruina *f*. *v* (*ship*) hundir; (*building*) destruir; destrozar; (*hopes*) estropear. **wreckage** *n* restos *m* pl; (*building*) escombros *m* pl.

wren [ren] *n* reyezuelo *m*.

wrench [rentʃ] *n* (*tool*) llave inglesa *f*; (*pull*) tirón *m*; (*emotional*) dolor *m*. *v* arrancar; (*med*) torcer.

wrestle ['resl] *v* luchar con *or* contra. **wrestler** *n* luchador, -a *m, f*. **wrestling** *n* lucha *f*.

wretch [retʃ] *n* desgraciado, -a *m, f*; miserable *m, f*. **wretched** *adj* desgraciado; (*weather*) miserable; horrible.

wriggle ['rigl] *v* menear; agitar; (*fish*) colear *n* meneo *m*; serpenteo *m*.

*wring [rːŋ] *v* retorcer. **wringer** *n* escurridor *m*. **wringing wet** chorreando.

wrinkle ['riŋkl] *n* arruga *f*. *v* arrugar.

wrist [rist] *n* muñeca *f*.

writ [rit] *n* (*law*) orden *f*, mandato *m*. **issue a writ against someone** demandar a alguien en juicio.

*write [rait] *v* escribir; redactar. **writer** *n* escritor, -a *m, f*; autor, -a *m, f*. **write-off** *n* (*vehicle*) siniestro total *m*. **write off** *v* (*debt*) cancelar. **writing** *n* el escribir *m*; (*handwriting*) escritura *f*; (*something written*) escrito *m*. **in writing** por escrito. **writing-pad** *n* bloc de papel de escribir *m*. **writing-paper** *n* papel de escribir *m*.

writhe [raið] *v* retorcerse; angustiarse.

wrong [roŋ] *adj* malo; mal; (*incorrect*) equivocado; impropio; falso; erróneo. **be wrong** tener la culpa; (*mistaken*) estar equivocado. *adv* mal. *n* mal *m*; error *m*; daño *m*; injusticia *f*; ilegal. **wrongful** *adj* injusto; ilegal.

wrote [rout] *V* **write**.

wrought iron [ˌroːt'aiən] *n* hierro forjado *m*.

wry [rai] *adj* torcido; doblado; (*smile*) forzado.

X

xenophobia [ˌzenə'foubiə] *n* xenofobia *f*. **xenophobic** *adj* xenófobo.

Xerox® *n* (*machine*) Xérox® *m*, fotocopiadora *f*; (*copy*) xerografía *f*. *v* fotocopiar.

Xmas ['krisməs] *V* **Christmas**.

X-ray ['eksrei] *n* (*photo*) radiografía *f*. **X-rays** *pl n* rayos X *m* pl. *v* radiografiar.

xylophone ['zailəfoun] *n* xilófono *m*.

Y

yacht [jot] *n* yate *m*. **yachting** *n* navegación a vela *f*.

yank [jaŋk] *n* tirón *m*. *v* dar un tirón.

yap [jap] *n* ladrido *m*. *v* ladrar.

yard [ja:d] *n* patio *m*; (*site*) depósito *m*; (*repair*) taller *m*; (*rail*) estación *f*.

yardstick ['ja:dstik] *n* norma *f*

yarn [ja:n] *n* hilo *m*; (*tale*) cuento *m*.

yawn [jo:n] *v* bostezar; (*hole*) abrirse. *n* bostezo *m*.

year [jiə] *n* año *m*. **yearbook** *n* anuario *m*. **yearly** *adj* anual.

yearn [jə:n] *v* anhelar, ansiar. **yearning** *n* anhelo *m*, ansia *f*.

yeast [ji:st] *n* levadura *f*; (*fig*) fermento *m*.

yell [jel] *n* grito *m*. *v* gritar.

yellow ['jelou] *nm*, *adj* amarillo. *v* volver amarillo.

yelp [jelp] *n* gañido *m*. *v* gañir.

yes [jes] *nm*, *adv* sí.

yesterday ['jestədi] *nm*, *adv* ayer. **the day before yesterday** anteayer.

yet [jət] *adv* todavía, aún; (*already*) ya. *conj* sin embargo, no obstante; (*but*) pero.

yew [ju:] *n* tejo *m*.

yield [ji:ld] *v* producir; entregar; dar; ceder; (*interest*) devengar. *n* producción *f*; (*crop*) cosecha *f*; (*interest*) rédito *m*.

yob [job] *adj* gamberro

yodel ['joudl] *n* canción tirolesa. *v* cantar a la tirolesa.

yoga ['jougə] *n* yoga *m*.

yoghurt ['jogət] *n* yogur *m*.

yoke [jouk] *n* (*animals*) yugo *m*; (*oxen*) yunta *f*; (*dress*) canesú *m*. *v* **yoke together** trabajar juntos.

yolk [jouk] *n* yema *f*.

yonder ['jondə] *adv* allá, a lo lejos.

you [ju:] *pron* (*subject: fam*) tú *sing*; (*subject; fam*) vosotros, vosotras *pl*; (*after prep*) ti; (*direct and indirect object*) te *sing*; (*direct and indirect object*) os *pl*; (*subject and after prep; polite*) usted, ustedes; (*direct object*) le, la; (*indirect object*) le; (*indirect object with direct object pron*) se *sing, pl*.

young [jʌŋ] *adj* joven. *pl n* (*people*) los jóvenes *m pl*; (*of an animal*) cría *f sing*.

youngster *n* joven *m, f*.

your [jo:] *adj* (*fam*) tu *sing*, vuestro *pl*; (*polite*) su, sus, de usted, de ustedes. **yours** *pron* (*fam*) el tuyo, la tuya, los tuyos, las tuyas, el vuestro, la vuestra, los vuestros, las vuestras; (*polite*) el suyo, la suya, el de usted, la de usted.

yourself [jə'self] *pron* (*fam*) tú mismo *m*, tú misma *f*; (*after prep*) tí *m, f*; (*polite*) usted mismo *m*, usted misma *f*. **by yourself** tú solo, usted solo. **yourselves** *pl pron* (*fam*) vosotros mismos *m pl*; vosotras mismas *f pl*; (*polite*) ustedes mismos *m pl*, ustedes mismas *f pl*.

youth [ju:θ] *n* juventud *f*; (*boy*) joven *m*. **youth hostel** albergue de juventud *m*.

Yugoslavia [ju:gou'sla:viə] [ju:gə'sla:viə] *n* Yugoslavia *f*.

Yugoslav *n, adj* yugoslavo, -a.

Yugoslavian *n, adj* yugoslavo, -a.

Z

zap [zap] ¡zás!. *v* zapear; (*destroy*) cargarse; (*delete*) suprimir

zany ['zeini] *adj* (*coll*) estrafalario.

zeal [zi:l] *n* celo *m*. **zealous** *adj* celoso.

zebra ['zebrə] *n* cebra *f*. **zebra crossing** paso de peatones *m*.

zero ['ziərou] *n* cero *m*. **zero hour** hora H *f*, momento decisivo *m*.

zest [zest] *n* ánimo *m*; brío *m*; sabor *m*. **zestful** *adj* animado; sabroso.

zigzag ['zigzag] *n* zigzag *m*. *v* zigzaguear.

zinc [ziŋk] *n* cinc *m*, zinc *m*.

zip [zip] *n* cremallera *f*. **zip code** (*US*) código postal *m*. *v* **zip up** subir la cremallera de.

zodiac ['zoudiak] *n* zodíaco *m*.

zone [zoun] *n* zona *f*. *v* dividir en zonas.

zoo [zu:] *n* zoo *m*, parque zoológico *m*.

zoology [zou'olədʒi] *n* zoología *f*. **zoological** *adj* zoológico. **zoologist** *n* zoólogo, -a *m, f*.

zoom [zu:m] *n* zumbido *m*. **zoom lens** zoom *m*. *v* zumbar. **zoom past** (*coll*) pasar zumbando.

Spanish – Inglés

A

a [a] *prep* to, at; on, in; by, by means of.

abacero [aβa'θero] *sm* grocer. **abacería** *sf* grocery.

abad [a'βað] *sm* abbot. **abadesa** *sf* abbess. **abadía** *sf* abbey.

abadejo [aβa'ðexo] *sm* codfish.

abajo [a'βaxo] *adv* underneath, below, down. ¡**abajo** …! *interj* down with …! **de abajo** *adj* lower.

abalanzar [aβalan'θar] *v* balance; hurl. **abalanzarse a** rush at.

abandonar [aβando'nar] *v* abandon; leave; drop out. **abandonarse** *v* give way; lose heart. **abandonado** *adj* abandoned; slovenly. **abandono** *sm* abandonment; neglect.

abanicar [aβani'kar] *v* fan. **abanico** *sm* fan.

abarcar [aβar'kar] *v* take in; encompass (include); comprise; undertake.

abarrotar [aβarro'tar] *v* stow; fill up; overload.

*abastecer [aβaste'θer] *v* supply, provide with. **abastecimiento** *sm* supply. **abasto** *sm* supply of provisions.

abatir [aβa'tir] *v* knock down; kill; humble. **abatido** *adj* dejected; depressed; dismayed. **abatimiento** *sm* depression; discouragement.

abdicar [aβði'kar] *v* abdicate. **abdicación** *sf* abdication.

abdomen [aβ'ðomen] *sm* abdomen.

abedul [aβe'ðul] *sm* birch-tree.

abeja [a'βexa] *sf* bee. **abeja machiega** honey bee.

aberración [aβerra'θjon] *sf* aberration.

abertura [aβer'tura] *sf* aperture, opening; gap.

abeto [a'βeto] *sm* fir.

abierto [a'βjerto] *adj* open; candid.

abigarrar [aβigar'rar] *v* variegate; fleck. **abigarrado** *adj* flecked; mottled; variegated.

abismo [a'βismo] *sm* abyss. **abismal** *adj* abysmal.

abjurar [aβxu'rar] *v* abjure, forswear. **abjuración** *sf* abjuration.

ablandar [aβlan'dar] *v* soften. **ablandarse** *v* mellow; relent.

*abnegarse [aβne'garse] *v* deny oneself; renounce.

abobado [aβo'βaðo] *adj* stupid, silly; stupefied.

abocarse [aβo'karse] *v* approach; meet by appointment.

abochornar [aβotʃor'nar] *v* overheat; (*fig*) shame. **abochornarse** *v* blush.

abofetear [aβofete'ar] *v* slap.

abogar [aβo'gar] *v* plead; advocate.

abolengo [aβo'lengo] *sm* ancestry; inheritance.

abolir [aβo'lir] *v* abolish.

abollar [aβo'ʎar] *v* dent. **abolladura** *sf* dent. **abollonar** *v* emboss.

abominar [aβomi'nar] *v* abominate.

abominable *adj* abominable. **abominación** *sf* abomination.

abonar [aβo'nar] *v* guarantee; stand surety for; subscribe to; improve; (*agr*) manure. **abonado** *adj* safe; sure; trustworthy. *sm* subscriber; season-ticket holder. **abono** *sm* guarantee; subscription; fertilizer.

abordar [aβor'ðar] *v* approach; (*mar*) board ship; (*mar*) put into port.

aborigen [aβo'rixen] *s*(*m* + *f*), *adj* aborigine, aboriginal.

***aborrecer** [aβorre'θer] *v* hate. **aborrecimiento** *sm* hatred.

abortar [aβor'tar] *v* abort. **aborto** *sm* (*med*) abortion; (*fig*) failure.

abotonar [aβoto'nar] *v* button up.

abovedado [aβoβe'ðaðo] *adj* arched. **abovedar** *v* arch.

abrasar [aβra'sar] *v* burn; dry up. **abrasarse (de, en)** *v* (*de, en amor*) burn with. **abrasivo** *adj* abrasive.

abrazar [aβra'θar] *v* embrace, hug. **abrazo** *sm* embrace.

abrelatas [aβre'latas] *sm invar* tin-opener.

abreviar [aβreβjar] *v* abbreviate; speed up. **abreviatura** *sf* abbreviation.

abrigar [aβri'gar] *v* shelter; wrap up. **abrigo** *sm* shelter; overcoat.

abril [a'βril] *sm* April.

abrir [a'βrir] *v* open; extend; unfold; reveal.

abrochar [aβro'tʃar] *v* fasten; button.

abrogar [aβro'gar] *v* repeal. **abrogación** *sf* repeal.

abrumar [aβru'mar] *v* oppress; weigh down; overwhelm; annoy. **abrumarse** *v* become foggy. **abrumador** *adj* overwhelming; annoying.

abrupto [a'βrupto] *adj* rugged; steep; abrupt.

absceso [aβs'θeso] *sm* abscess.

ábside ['aβsiðe] *sm* apse.

absolución [aβsolu'θjon] *sf* (*rel*) absolution; (*jur*) acquittal.

absoluto [aβso'luto] *adj* absolute; complete; (*fig*) overbearing. **en absoluto** absolutely.

***absolver** [aβsol'βer] *v* absolve; acquit.

absorber [aβsor'βer] *v* absorb. **absorbente** *adj* absorbent. **absorción** *sf* absorption. **absorto** *adj* absorbed; amazed.

abstemio [aβs'temjo] *adj* abstemious.

***abstenerse** [aβste'ners] *v* abstain. **abstinencia** *sf* abstinence.

abstracto [aβ'strakto] *adj* abstract. **abstracción** *sf* abstraction. ***abstraer** *v* abstract; refrain from; become thoughtful. **abstraer de** exclude; do without. **abstraído** *adj* retired; preoccupied; absent-minded.

absurdo [aβ'surðo] *adj* absurd.

abuelo [a'βuelo] *sm* grandfather. **abuela** *sf* grandmother.

abultar [aβul'tar] *v* enlarge; increase; be bulky. **abultado** *adj* bulky; exaggerated. **abultamiento** *sm* bulkiness; exaggeration.

abundar [aβun'dar] *v* abound. **abundancia** *sf* abundance. **abundante** *adj* abundant.

aburrir [aβur'rir] *v* bore; (*fam*) spend time/money; grow bored; grow weary. **aburrido** *adj* boring; weary. **aburrimiento** *sm* boredom; wearisomeness.

abusar [aβu'sar] *v* abuse; impose upon; go too far. **abuso** *sm* abuse; misuse.

abyecto [a'βjecto] *adj* abject. **abyección** *sf* degradation; misery.

acá [a'ka] *adv* here; now. **acá y allá** here and there.

acabar [aka'βar] *v* end; complete; kill; be destroyed. **acabar de** have just. **acabarse** *v* run out. **acabado** *adj* finished; perfect. *sm* finish.

academia [aka'ðemja] *sf* academy. **académico** *adj* academic.

***acaecer** [akae'θer] *v* happen. **acaecimiento** *sm* happening.

acalorar [akalo'rar] *v* make warm; (*fig*) excite. **acalorarse** *v* become heated. **acalorado** *adj* hot.

acallar [aka'ʎar] *v* quieten; silence; (*fig*) ease.

acampar [akam'par] *v* camp.

acantilado [akanti'laðo] *adj* steep; rocky. *sm* cliff.

acaparar [akapa'rar] *v* monopolize; hoard. **acaparador** *adj* monopolistic; (*fig*) acquisitive.

acariciar [akari'θjar] *v* caress, fondle, stroke; (*fig*) cherish. **acariciador** *adj* caressing.

acarrear [akarre'ar] *v* transport; carry; (*fig*) cause; bring about.

acaso [a'kaso] *sm* chance. *adv* perhaps. **por**

si acaso just in case.

acatar [aka'tar] v respect; heed; observe. **acatable** adj worthy of respect. **acatador** adj respectful. **acatamiento** sm respect.

acaudalar [akauða'lar] v accumulate, hoard. **acaudalado** adj wealthy.

acaudillar [akauði'ʎar] v lead, command. **acaudillamiento** sm leadership.

acceder [akθe'ðer] v accede, consent. **acceder a** agree to. **accesión** sf agreement.

acceso [ak'θeso] sm access; (med) fit.

accidente [akθi'ðente] sm accident. **accidental** adj accidental.

acción [ak'θjon] sf action. **acciones** s pl shares pl, stock sing. **accionar** v work, actuate. **accionista** s(m + f) shareholder.

acebo [a'θeβo] sm holly.

acechar [aθe'tʃar] v spy on; watch; ambush; stalk. **acecho** sm observation; lying in wait.

aceite [a'θeite] sm oil. **aceite de motor** engine oil. **aceitoso** adj oily. **aceituna** sf olive.

acelerar [aθele'rar] v accelerate; quicken. **acelerarse** v hurry. **acelerador** sm accelerator.

acendrar [aθen'drar] v (metales) refine; (fig) purify.

acentuar [aθen'twar] v accentuate; stress. **acento** sm stress; stress.

aceptar [aθep'tar] v accept. **aceptable** adj acceptable, passable. **aceptación** sf acceptance.

acequia [a'θekja] sf irrigation ditch; drain.

acera [a'θera] sf pavement.

acerbo [a'θerβo] adj harsh; sharp; sour; (fig) severe.

acerar [aθe'rar] v harden with steel; strengthen; (fig) fortify.

acerca de [a'θerka ðe] adv about.

acercar [aθer'kar] v approach; bring near. **acercarse** v approach, draw near. **acercamiento** sm approach; approximation; reconciliation.

acero [a'θero] sm steel.

acérrimo [a'θerrimo] adj very strong; extremely tenacious; stalwart.

*acertar [aθer'tar] v (el blanco) hit; guess; be right; find; succeed. **acertado** adj correct; apt.

acertijo [aθer'tixo] sm riddle.

aciago [a'θjago] adj unlucky; ill-fated.

acicalar [aθika'lar] v polish; bedeck; groom; (fam) spruce oneself up. **acicalado** adj spruce; dapper; polished. **acicaladura** sf also **acicalamiento** sm polishing; grooming; dressing up.

ácido ['aθiðo] sm, adj acid.

acierto [a'θjerto] sm success; good idea; skill.

aclamar [akla'mar] v acclaim; applaud. **aclamación** sf acclamation.

aclarar [akla'rar] v explain, clarify; (color) lighten; thin out; (dudas) remove; (la ropa) rinse. **aclaración** sf explanation. **aclarado** sm rinse.

aclimatizar [aklimati'θar] v acclimatize. **aclimatación** sf acclimatization.

acné [ak'ne] sm acne.

acobardar [akoβar'ðar] v frighten; discourage.

acoger [ako'xer] v welcome; receive; shelter; accept. **acogerse** v take refuge. **acogedor** adj (persona) welcoming; (ambiente) friendly. **acogida** sf welcome.

acolchar [akol'tʃar] v pad; upholster; (fig) muffle. **acolchado** adj padded.

acólito [a'kolito] sm acolyte.

acometer [akome'ter] v attack; undertake; fill; occur to. **acometida** sf attack.

acomodar [akomo'ðar] v arrange; settle; accommodate; adjust; adapt; prepare; (fig) reconcile. **acomodación** sf arrangement; preparation. **acomodadamente** adv conveniently; easily. **acomodadizo** adj accommodating; adaptable. **acomodado** adj convenient; prepared; well-to-do. **acomodador** sm usher. **acomodamiento** sm convenience; arrangement; preparation.

acompañar [akompa'ɲar] v accompany; escort. **acompañamiento** sm accompaniment; escort; (cortejo) funeral procession.

acondicionar [akondiθjo'nar] v set up; fix; prepare; improve. **acondicionarse** v condition oneself. **acondicionado** adj equipped. **acondicionador** sm conditioner. **aire acondicionado** air-conditioning.

acongojar [akongo'xar] v sadden; distress.

aconsejar [akonse'xar] v advise. **aconsejarse** v seek advice.

*acontecer [akonte'θer] v happen. **acontecimiento** sm event.

acopiar [ako'pjar] v store; collect. **acopiamiento** sm stock.

acoplar [ako'plar] v fit; connect; couple;

(*animales*) mate. **acoplarse** *v* become friends again. **acoplado** *adj* well-matched. **acoplamiento** *sm* connection; coordination.

acorazar [akora'θar] *v* armour. **acorazado** *adj* armoured; (*fig*) hardened.

*****acordar** [akor'ðar] *v* agree; decide; remind. **acordarse** *v* remember; agree. **acordado** *adj* agreed to; wise.

acordeón [akorðe'on] *sm* accordion.

acordonar [akorðo'nar] *v* cordon off; seal off (area); (*los zapatos*) lace. **acordonado** *adj* cordoned off; ribbed.

acorralar [akorra'lar] *v* enclose; corner; round up.

acortar [akor'tar] *v* shorten; reduce. **acortarse** *v* become shorter; (*intimidarse*) be shy. **acortamiento** *sm* shortening; reduction.

acosar [ako'sar] *v* hound; pursue; harass; pester. **acoso** *sm* pursuit; harassment.

*****acostar** [akos'tar] *v* lay down; put to bed. **acostarse** *v* lie down; go to bed.

acostumbrar [akostum'brar] *v* accustom; be in the habit of. **acostumbrarse a** *v* become used to. **acostumbrado** *adj* usual.

acotar [ako'tar] *v* (*terreno*) demarcate; enclose; delimit; outline; accept. **acotado** *adj* enclosed. **acotamiento** *sm* demarcation; boundary mark; outline.

acre¹ ['akre] *adj* acrid; bitter.

acre² ['akre] *sm* acre.

*****acrecentar** [akreθen'tar] *v* increase. **acrecentamiento** *sm* increase; growth.

acreditar [akreði'tar] *v* accredit; prove; vouch for; authorize; (*com*) credit. **acreditado** *adj* reputable.

acreedor [akree'ðor] *s*(*m + f*) creditor. *adj* worthy.

acribillar [akriβi'ʎar] *v* riddle with holes.

acróbata [a'kroβata] *s*(*m + f*) acrobat.

acrónimo [a'kronimo] *sm* acronym.

acta ['akta] *sf* minutes of a meeting; official document.

actitud [akti'tud] *sf* posture, attitude.

activar [akti'βar] *v* speed up; stimulate; (*quim*) activate. **actividad** *sf* activity.

activista [akti'βista] *adj* activist.

activo [ak'tiβo] *adj* active. *sm* (*com*) assets *pl*.

acto ['akto] *n* act, deed; ceremony; (*teatro*) act. **salón de actos** *sm* assembly hall.

actor *sm* actor. **actriz** *sf* actress. **actual** *adj* present; topical; of this month. **actualmente** *adv* at present; nowadays.

actuar [ak'twar] *v* act; perform; behave. **actuación** *sf* action; performance; conduct. **actuario** *sm* (*jur*) clerk of the court.

acuarela [akwa'rela] *sf* watercolour.

acuario [a'kwario] *sm* aquarium.

acuático [a'kwatiko] *adj* aquatic.

acuciar [aku'θjar] *v* urge; pester; (*anhelar*) long for. **acucioso** *adj* urgent; diligent; desirous.

acuclillarse [akukli'ʎarse] *v* crouch, squat.

acuchillar [akutʃi'ʎar] *v* knife, stab, hack. **acuchillado** *adj* knifed; (*fig*) experienced.

acudir [aku'ðir] *v* come; go; (*a una cita*) keep; answer; attend; help; (*al médico*) consult.

acueducto [akwe'ðukto] *sm* aqueduct.

acuerdo [a'kwerðo] *sm* agreement. **¡de acuerdo!** O.K.! **ponerse de acuerdo** come to an agreement.

acumular [akumu'lar] *v* accumulate; pile; store. **acumulación** *sf* accumulation.

acuñar [aku'ɲar] *v* (*monedas*) mint; (*poner cuñas*) wedge.

acuoso [aku'oso] *adj* watery. **acuosidad** *sf* wateriness.

acurrucarse [akurru'karse] *v* curl up.

acusar [aku'sar] *v* (*jur*) accuse; charge; blame; denounce; reveal; (*com*) acknowledge. **acusación** *sf* accusation. **acusado** *sm* (*jur*) defendant.

acústico [a'kustiko] *adj* acoustic. **acústica** *sf* acoustics.

achacar [atʃa'kar] *v* attribute.

achatar [atʃa'tar] *v* flatten.

achicar [atʃi'kar] *v* reduce; (*mar*) bale; (*fig*) humiliate. **achicado** *adj* childish.

achicoria [atʃi'korja] *sf* chicory.

achicharrar [atʃitʃar'rar] *v* burn; (*molestar*) annoy. **achicharradero** *sm* furnace.

achispado [atʃis'paðo] *adj* tipsy. **achispar** *v* make tipsy.

adalid [aða'lið] *sm* leader.

adaptar [aðap'tar] *v* adapt; adjust. **adaptabilidad** *sf* adaptability. **adaptable** *adj* adaptable. **adaptación** *sf* adaptation; (*tecn*) fitting.

adecuado [aðe'kwaðo] *adj* adequate; suitable.

adefesio [aðe'fesjo] *(fam)* *sm* nonsense; *(traje)* ridiculous garment; *(persona)* ridiculously dressed person.

adelantar [aðelan'tar] *v* advance; *(reloj)* put forward; speed up; gain; *(auto)* overtake. **prohibido adelantar** no overtaking. **adelantarse** *v* go forward. **adelantado** *adj* advanced. **adelantamiento** *sm* also **adelanto** advance. **adelante** *adv* ahead, forward. **¡adelante!** come in! **de hoy en adelante** in future.

adelgazar [aðelga'θar] *v* make thin; slim. **adelgazador** *adj* slimming. **adelgazamiento** *sm* slimming. **régimen de adelgazamiento** *sm* diet.

ademán [aðe'man] *sm* expression; gesture. **ademanes** *s pl* manners.

además [aðe'mas] *adv* besides, furthermore. **además de** as well as.

adentro [a'ðentro] *adv* within, inside. **¡adentro!** come in! **mar adentro** out to sea. **tierra adentro** inland.

adepto [a'ðepto] *s(m + f)* adept; supporter.

adestrar *V* **adiestrar**.

aderezar [aðere'θar] *v* adorn; *(culin)* prepare; guide. **aderezo** *sm* adornment; cooking; seasoning; *(de ensalada)* dressing.

adeudar [aðeu'ðar] *v* owe; *(com)* charge; run into debt. **adeudado** *adj* owing; *(persona)* in debt. **adeudo** *sm* *(deuda)* debt; *(com)* charge.

*adherir [aðe'rir] *v* adhere, stick. **adherirse** adhere to. **adherencia** *sf* *(acción de pegar)* adherence. **adhesión** *sf* adhesion; *(apoyo)* support. **adhesivo** *sm, adj* adhesive.

adición [aði'θyon] *sf* addition. **adicional** *adj* additional. **adicionar** *v* add.

adicto [a'ðikto] *adj* devoted. **adicto al trabajo** *adj* workaholic. *s(m + f)* supporter; addict. **adictivo** *adj* addictive.

adiestrar [aðjes'trar] *v* train, teach. **adiestrador, -a** *sm, sf* trainer. **adiestramiento** *sm* training.

adinerado [aðine'raðo] *adj* wealthy. **adinerado, -a** *sm, sf* rich person. **adinerarse** *v* *(fam)* make one's fortune.

adiós [a'ðjos] *interj, sm* goodbye.

adivinar [aðiβi'nar] *v* foretell; guess; *(el pensamiento)* read. **adivinable** *adj* foreseeable. **adivinación** *sf* also **adivinamiento** *sm* divination; guessing. **adivinador, -a** *sm, sf* fortune-teller.

adjetivo [aðxe'tiβo] *sm* adjective.

adjudicar [aðxuði'kar] *v* award; adjudicate.

adjuntar [aðxun'tar] *v* attach; enclose; give.

adjunto [að'xunto] *adj* attached; enclosed. *sm* assistant.

administrar [aðminis'trar] *v* administer, control; *(fam)* hand out. **administración** *sf* administration. **administrativo** *adj* administrative.

admirar [aðmi'rar] *v* admire. **admirarse** *v* surprise, astonish. **admirable** *adj* admirable. **admiración** *sf* admiration.

admirador, -a *sm, sf* admirer. *adj* admiring.

admitir [aðmi'tir] *v* admit; accept; allow; acknowledge. **admisible** *adj* admissible. acceptable. **admisión** *sf* admission; acceptance.

ADN *sm* DNA.

adobar [aðo'βar] *v* pickle; season; cook.

*adolecer [aðole'θer] *v* fall ill. **adolecer de** suffer from.

adolescencia [aðoles'θenθja] *sf* adolescence. **adolescente** *s(m + f)*, *adj* adolescent.

adonde ['aðonde] *adv* where. **¿adónde?** where?

adoptar [aðop'tar] *v* adopt; assume. **adopción** *sf* adoption. **adoptivo** *adj* adoptive.

adoquín [aðo'kin] *sm* paving-stone; *(fam)* dunce. **adoquinar** *v* pave.

adorar [aðo'rar] *v* adore; worship; pray. **adorable** *adj* adorable. **adoración** *sf* adoration; worship.

*adormecer [aðorme'θer] *v* make sleepy. **adormecerse** fall asleep. **adormecerse en** give oneself up to.

adormidera [aðormi'ðera] *sf* poppy.

adornar [aðor'nar] *v* adorn, decorate; *(trajes)* trim; *(coc)* garnish; *(fig)* embellish. **adornarse** *v* dress up. **adorno** *sm* decoration; trimming; garnish.

*adquirir [aðki'rir] *v* acquire, obtain. **adquisición** *sf* acquisition; *(compra)* purchase. **adquisitivo** *adj* acquisitive.

adrede [að'reðe] *adv* on purpose.

adscribir [aðskri'βir] *v* attribute, ascribe; assign. **adscripción** *sf* attribution; assignment. **adscripto** *adj* attributed; assigned.

aduana [a'ðwana] *sf* customs *pl*. **derechos de aduana** *sm pl* customs duty *sing*. **aduanero** *sm* customs officer.

*aducir [aðu'θir] *v* (*razones*) allege; (*un texto*) quote; (*pruebas*) offer as proof.

adueñarse [aðwe'narse] *v* appropriate.

adular [aðu'lar] *v* flatter. **adulación** *sf* flattery.

adulterar [aðulte'rar] *v* adulterate; commit adultery. **adulterio** *sm* adultery. **adúltero, -a** *sm, sf* adulterer, adulteress.

adulto [a'ðulto], **-a** *s, adj* adult.

adusto [a'ðusto] *adj* very hot; (*fig*) harsh.

advenedizo [aðβene'ðiθo], **-a** *s, adj* upstart.

advenimiento [aðβeni'mjento] *sm* advent; coming.

adverbio [að'βerβjo] *sm* adverb.

adversario [aðβer'sarjo] *sm* adversary. **adversidad** *sf* adversity. **adverso** *adj* adverse; opposing.

*advertir [aðβer'tir] *v* warn; recommend; (*señalar*) point out; tell; (*comprender*) realize. **advertido** *adj* informed; experienced. **advertencia** *sf also* **advertimiento** *sm* warning.

adyacente [aðja'θente] *adj* adjacent.

aéreo [a'ereo] *adj* aerial.

aerobic [ae'roβic] *sm* aerobics.

aerodinámica [aeroði'namika] *sf* aerodynamics. **aerodinámico** *adj* aerodynamic.

aeronáutica [aero'nautika] *sf* aeronautics. **aeronáutico** *adj* aeronautical.

aeroplano [aero'plano] *sm* aeroplane.

aeropuerto [aero'pwerto] *sm* airport.

aerosol [aero'sol] *sm* aerosol.

afable [a'faβle] *adj* pleasant; genial. **afabilidad** *sf* affability.

afamado [afa'maðo] *adj* famous.

afán [a'fan] *sm* (*trabajo penoso*) toil; (*deseo*) desire; (*entusiasmo*) zeal; (*preocupación*) anxiety. **afanador** *adj* enthusiastic. **afanar** *v* work hard; (*fig: robar*) steal. **afanarse** *v* exert oneself. **afanoso** *adj* laborious; hectic.

afección [afek'θjon] *sf* (*cariño*) affection; (*med*) complaint. **afeccionarse** *v* grow fond.

afectar [afek'tar] *v* affect; pretend; adopt; (*atañer*) concern; (*dañar*) damage. **afectado** *adj* spoiled; unnatural; upset.

afecto [a'fekto] *adj* dear. **afecto a** fond of. *sm* affection.

afeitar [afei'tar] *v* shave. **afeitarse** *v* shave;

make up one's face. **afeite** *sm* make-up, cosmetics *pl*.

afeminado [afemi'naðo] *adj* effeminate. *sm* effeminate person.

*aferrar [afer'rar] *v* seize; (*mar*) moor. **aferrarse** *v* cling.

afianzar [afjan'θar] *v* reinforce; establish; restore; guarantee; seize; support. **afianzarse** *v* steady oneself; become strong. **afianzamiento** *sm* surety; guarantee; establishment.

afición [afi'θjon] *sf* inclination; fondness; (*interés*) hobby. **la afición** *sf* the fans *pl*.

aficionado [afiθjo'naðo], **-a** *sm, sf* fan. *adj* amateur; keen.

afilar [afi'lar] *v* sharpen; grind. **afilado** *adj* sharp. **afilador** *sm* (*persona*) knife-grinder; (*correa*) strop. **afilamiento** *sm* (*la nariz*) pointedness; (*los dedos*) slenderness.

afiliar [afi'ljar] *v* affiliate. **afiliación** *sf* affiliation.

afín [a'fin] *adj* adjacent; similar; related. **afinidad** *sf* similarity, affinity.

afinar [afi'nar] *v* polish; perfect; (*música*) tune. **afinarse** *v* become slimmer. **afinadura** *sf also* **afinamiento** *sm* tuning; (*fig*) refinement.

afirmar [afir'mar] *v* affirm; strengthen. **afirmarse** *v* steady oneself. **afirmación** *sf* statement; strengthening. **afirmativo** *adj* affirmative.

aflicción [aflik'θjon] *sf* affliction, grief. **afligido** *adj* distressed; (*por una muerte*) bereaved. **afligir** *v* grieve; distress; afflict.

aflojar [aflo'xar] *v* loosen, slacken; relax; (*fiebre*) abate; (*fam*) fork out, cough up. **aflojamiento** *sm* loosening, slackening; abatement; relaxation.

afluencia [aflu'enθja] *sf* crowd; (*tropel*) rush; influx; abundance.

*afluir [aflu'ir] *v* flow.

afónico [a'foniko] *adj* hoarse, voiceless. **afonía** *sf* loss of voice.

*aforar [afo'rar] *v* gauge, measure; appraise. **aforo** *sm* measurement; appraisal.

aforrar [afor'rar] *v* (*ropa, etc.*) line. **aforrarse** *v* wrap oneself up.

afortunado [afortu'naðo] *adj* fortunate; happy.

afrenta [a'frenta] *sf* insult; disgrace. **afrentar** *v* insult. **afrentarse** *v* be ashamed. **afrentador** *adj also* **afrentoso**

insulting; offensive.

África ['afrika] *sf* Africa. **africano, -a** *s, adj* African.

afrontar [afron'tar] *v* confront; bring face to face. **afrontamiento** *sm* confrontation.

afuera [a'fwera] *adv* out, outside. **¡afuera!** get out! **afueras** *s pl* suburbs *pl*.

agachar [aga'tʃar] *v* lower, bend. **agacharse** *v* bend over; crouch; (*para evitar algo*) duck. **agachada** *sf* (*fam*) trick.

agalla [a'ɡaʎa] *sf* gill; (*fam*) pluck. **agallas** *s pl* tonsils *pl*.

agarrar [aɡar'rar] *v* seize, clutch; (*comprender*) grasp; get; take; win; (*fam*) stick. **agarro** *sm* hold, grasp. **agarradero** *sm* handle.

agarrotar [aɡarro'tar] *v* tighten; strangle. **agarrotarse** *v* (*motor*) seize up; (*músculo*) go numb. **agarrotado** *adj* bound; stiff; seized up.

agasajar [aɡasa'xar] *v* welcome warmly; entertain. **agasajo** *sm* gift; welcome. **agasajos** *sm pl* hospitality *sing*.

agazapar [aɡaθa'par] *v* (*fam*) nab, catch. **agazaparse** *v* crouch; duck.

agencia [a'xenθja] *sf* agency; office. **agencia de prensa** news agency. **agencia de turismo** *or* **viajes** travel agency. **agenciar** *v* get; (*fam*) wangle. **agente** *sm* agent; policeman. **agente de bolsa** stockbroker. **agente inmobiliario** estate agent.

agenda [a'xenda] *sf* diary.

ágil ['axil] *adj* agile. **agilidad** *sf* agility.

agitar [axi'tar] *v* wave; shake; upset; stir up. **agitarse** *v* sway; fidget. **agitación** *sf* waving; shaking; movement; excitement. **agitado** *adj* agitated; rough. **agitador, -a** *sm, sf* agitator.

aglomerar [aɡlome'rar] *v* form a crowd; amass. **aglomeración** *sf* mass. **aglomeración de tráfico** traffic jam.

agobiar [aɡo'βjar] *v* weigh down; overwhelm; humiliate; depress. **agobiado** *v* bent down; overwhelmed; exhausted. **agobio** *sm* burden.

agolparse [aɡol'parse] *v* crowd together; amass. **agolpamiento** *sm* crowd; (*cosas*) pile.

agonía [aɡo'nia] *sf* (*muerte*) death; desire; agony. **agonizar** *v* be dying; suffer; annoy.

***agorar** [aɡo'rar] *v* predict. **agorero, -a** *sm, sf* fortune-teller.

agosto [a'ɡosto] *sm* August.

agotar [aɡo'tar] *v* drain; exhaust. **agotador** *adj* exhausting. **agotamiento** *sm* exhaustion.

agraciar [aɡra'θjar] *v* adorn; award; pardon. **agraciado** *adj* pretty; graceful.

agradar [aɡra'ðar] *v* please. **agradable** *adj* pleasant.

***agradecer** [aɡraðe'θer] *v* thank; be grateful for; be welcome. **agradecido** *adj* grateful. **¡muy agradecido!** much obliged! **agradecimiento** *sm* gratitude.

agrado [aɡra'ðo] *sm* pleasure; liking.

agrandar [aɡran'ðar] *v* make larger; exaggerate. **agrandamiento** *sm* enlargement.

agravar [aɡra'βar] *v* aggravate; worsen. **agravación** *sf also* **agravamiento** *sm* aggravation. **agravante** *adj* aggravating.

agraviar [aɡra'βjar] *v* offend; insult; wrong; take offence. **agravio** *sm* insult; affront; wrong.

***agredir** [aɡre'ðir] *v* assault.

agregado [aɡre'ɡaðo] *sm* aggregate; assistant; attaché; addition. **agregar** *v* join; incorporate. **agregarse** *v* be added; be incorporated.

agricultura [aɡrikul'tura] *sf* agriculture. **agrícola** *adj* agricultural.

agrietar [aɡrje'tar] *v* crack; chap.

agrio ['aɡrjo] *adj* sour; (*carácter*) bitter. *sm* (*sabor*) sourness.

agrupar [aɡru'par] *v* group; gather together. **agruparse** *v* come together.

agua [a'ɡwa] *sf* water. **agua abajo/arriba** down-/upstream. **agua dulce** fresh water. **agua mineral** *sm* mineral water. **entre dos aguas** sitting on the fence. **hacer agua** leak. **irse al agua** fall through.

aguacate [aɡwa'kate] *sm* avocado pear.

aguacero [aɡwa'θero] *sm* shower, downpour.

aguantar [aɡwan'tar] *v* tolerate, bear; (*sostener*) support; (*esperar*) wait, await; (*durar*) last. **aguante** *sm* patience; endurance.

aguar [a'ɡwar] *v* dilute; spoil. **aguarse** be ruined. **aguado** *adj* watered down.

aguardar [aɡwar'ðar] *v* wait for.

aguardiente [aɡwar'ðjente] *sm* liquor.

aguarrás [aɡwar'ras] *sm* turpentine.

aguazal [aɡwa'θal] *sm* mire.

agudeza [aɡu'ðeθa] *sf* (*de los sentidos*) sharpness; (*del dolor*) acuteness; (*ingenio*) wit. **agudizar** v sharpen; worsen. **agudo** adj sharp; acute; witty.

agüero [a'gwero] sm omen. **de buen agüero** lucky.

aguijar [agi'xar] v goad; hurry. **aguijón** sm (de un insecto) sting; stimulus. **aguijonada** sf sting; prick. **aguijonear** v goad; spur on.

águila ['agila] sf eagle. **águila ratonera** buzzard.

aguinaldo [agi'naldo] sm Christmas present.

aguja [a'guxa] sf needle; (reloj) hand; (arq) spire. **agujas** s pl points pl.

agujero [agu'xero] sm hole; (alfiletero) pincushion.

agujetas [agu'xetas] sf pl stiffness sing. **lleno de agujetas** stiff all over.

aguzar [agu'θar] v sharpen; (estimular) encourage; (el apetito) whet. **aguzado** adj sharp; sharpened. **aguzadar** adj sharpening.

ahí [a'i] adv there. **de ahí** thus, so. **por ahí** that way; thereabouts. **¡ahí es nada!** fancy that!

ahijada [ai'xaða] sf goddaughter; protégée. **ahijado** sm godson; protégé.

ahincar [ain'kar] v urge. **ahincarse** v hurry. **ahincadamente** adv tenaciously. **ahincado** adj insistent; eager. **ahínco** sm effort.

ahogar [ao'gar] v drown; flood; stifle; overwhelm. **ahogarse** v drown, be drowned. **ahogadero** sm Turkish bath. **ahogado** adj drowned; (por el gas) asphyxiated; strangled; (grito) muffled. **ahogador** adj suffocating. **ahogo** sm breathlessness; (angustia) distress.

ahora [a'ora] adv now. conj now, now then. **ahora bien** come now. **ahora mismo** right away.

ahorcar [aor'kar] v hang. **ahorcarse** v hang oneself. **ahorcadura** sf hanging.

ahorrar [ao'rrar] v save; free; avoid. **ahorrador** adj thrifty. **ahorro** sm saving; thrift.

ahuecar [awe'kar] v hollow. **¡ahueca!** (fam) scram!

ahumar [au'mar] v (culin) smoke; (llenar de humo) fill with smoke. **ahumarse** v taste smoky; (fam: emborracharse) become tipsy. **ahumado** adj smoky; smoked; (fam) tipsy.

ahuyentar [aujen'tar] v frighten off; keep at bay; (fig) dismiss. **ahuyentarse** v flee.

airado [ai'raðo] adj vexed; immoral.

aire ['aire] sm air; (parecido) likeness; (aspecto) appearance; (porte) bearing; (música) time; (auto: estrangulador) choke. **hace aire** it's windy. **aire acondicionado** air conditioning. **aireación** sf ventilation. **airear** v ventilate. **airoso** adj ventilated; windy; (fig) graceful.

aislar [ai'slar] v isolate; (elec) insulate. **aislado** adj alone; remote; insulated. **aislador** adj insulating. **cinta aisladora** sf insulating tape. **aislamiento** sm isolation; insulation.

ajar [a'xar] v crumple; wrinkle; fade; (fig) age.

ajardinar [axarði'nar] v landscape.

ajedrez [axe'ðreθ] sm chess.

ajeno [a'xeno] adj of other people; alien; free; detached; irrelevant.

ajetreo [axe'treo] sm rush; activity; bustle; exhaustion. **ajetreado** adj busy. **ajetrearse** v be busy; rush; exhaust oneself.

ajo ['axo] sm garlic. **ajo cebollino** chive. **ajo porro** leek. **diente de ajo** clove of garlic. **soltar ajos** swear.

ajuar [a'xwar] sm (de novia) trousseau; (de casa) furnishings pl.

ajustar [axus'tar] v adjust; arrange; tighten. **ajuste** sm adjustment; fitting.

ajusticiar [axusti'θjar] v execute.

al [al] contraction of **a el**.

ala ['ala] sf wing; hat brim.

alabar [ala'βar] v praise. **alabarse** v (jactarse) boast. **alabanza** sf praise.

alabastro [ala'βastro] sm alabaster.

alacena [ala'θena] sf larder; cupboard.

alacrán [ala'kran] sm scorpion.

alambicar [alambi'kar] v distil; complicate; (precio) minimize. **alambicado** adj elaborate; (estilo) subtle; affected; minimized. **alambique** sm still. **pasar algo por el alambique** examine something very carefully.

alambre [a'lambre] sm wire. **alambrada** sf (de la guerra) barbed wire; (reja) wire netting.

alameda [ala'meða] sf (avenida) tree-lined walk; (de álamos) poplar grove.

álamo ['alamo] sm poplar. **álamo temblón** aspen.

alano [a'lano] sm mastiff.

alarde [a'larðe] sm parade; display.

alardear *v* boast. **alardeo** *sm* boasting.

alargar [alar'gar] *v* lengthen, increase, enlarge; (*posponer*) defer; (*dar*) reach, hand; (*la mano*) stretch. **alargarse** *v* get longer. **alargado** *adj* elongated. **alargamiento** *sm* lengthening; extension.

alarido [ala'riðo] *sm* yell, shriek.

alarmar [alar'mar] *v* alarm; alert. **alarmarse** *v* be frightened. **alarma** *sf* alarm.

alba ['alβa] *sf* dawn.

albañil [alβa'ɲil] *sm* bricklayer.

albaricoque [alβari'koke] *sm* apricot.

albatros [alβa'tros] *sm* albatross.

albedrío [alβe'ðrio] *sm* will; (*capricho*) whim; custom. **libre albedrío** free will.

albergar [alβer'gar] *v* shelter; accommodate; (*fig*) cherish. **albergue** *sm* lodgings *pl*; (*refugio*) shelter; (*posada*) hostel.

albóndiga [al'βonðiga] *sf* rissole.

albor [al'βor] *sm* dawn; (*blancura*) whiteness.

albornoz [alβor'noθ] *sm* bathrobe.

alborotar [alβoro'tar] *v* make a noise; disturb. **alborotarse** *v* (*perturbarse*) become upset; get excited; (*una muchedumbre*) riot. **alborotado** *adj* excited; (*fig*) eventful. **alborotador** *adj* noisy; rebellious. **alboroto** *sm* disturbance, uproar.

alborozar [alβoro'θar] *v* gladden; produce laughter. **alborozarse** *v* rejoice. **alborozado** *adj* overjoyed.

álbum ['alβum] *sm* album.

alcachofa [alka'tʃofa] *sf* artichoke.

alcahuete [alka'wete] *sm* pimp; (*chismoso*) gossip. **alcahueta** *sf* procuress; gossip.

alcalde [al'kalðe] *sm* mayor. **alcaldesa** *sf* mayoress. **alcaldía** *sf* mayorship; (*oficina*) mayor's office.

alcance [al'kanθe] *sm* reach; (*sonido, arma de fuego, etc.*) range; scope; importance. **al alcance** within reach. **dar alcance a** catch up with. **alcanzar** *v* reach; catch up; understand; hit; affect; succeed; be enough; (*durar*) last.

alcantarilla [alkanta'riʎa] *sf* sewer; drain.

alcázar [al'kaθar] *sm* palace; fortress; (*mar*) quarterdeck.

alcoba [al'koβa] *sf* bedroom.

alcohol [alko'ol] *sm* alcohol. **alcohólico, -a** *s, adj* alcoholic.

alcornoque [alkor'noke] *sm* cork tree; (*fig*) nitwit.

aldaba [al'ðaβa] *sf* door knocker; (*pestillo*) latch, bolt. **tener buenas aldabas** (*fam*) have influential friends.

aldea [al'ðea] *sf* village.

aleación [alea'θjon] *sf* alloy.

alegar [ale'gar] *v* allege; state; emphasize; quote; (*jur*) plead, claim. **alegato** *sm* declaration; plea.

alegoría [alego'ria] *sf* allegory. **alegórico** *adj* allegorical.

alegrar [ale'grar] *v* gladden; make merry; be pleasing to; excite. **alegrarse** *v* be happy; (*fam*) become tipsy. **alegre** *adj* happy; bright; good; (*fam*) tipsy; (*atrevido*) daring. **alegría** *sf* joy; happiness. **¡qué alegría!** great!

alejar [ale'xar] *v* move away; keep away; avert. **alejarse** *v* go away. **alejado** *adj* far away; aloof. **alejamiento** *sm* removal; absence.

Alemania [ale'manja] *sf* Germany. **alemán, -ana** *sm, sf* German (person). **alemán** *sm* (*idioma*) German (language).

***alentar** [alen'tar] *v* breathe; (*fig*) glow; (*animar*) encourage. **alentado** *adj* encouraged; (*orgulloso*) proud; (*valiente*) brave. **alentador** *adj* encouraging.

alerce [a'lerθe] *sm* larch.

alergia [a'lerxja] *sf* allergy. **alérgico** *adj* allergic.

alero [a'lero] *sm* eaves *pl*. **estar en el alero** hang in the balance.

alerta [a'lerta] *sm* alert; standby (troops). *adv* on the alert. **¡alerta!** look out! **alertar** *v* alert, warn. **alerto** *adj* alert.

aleta [a'leta] *sf* (*peces*) fin; (*foca*) flipper.

aleve [a'leβe] *adj also* **alevoso** treacherous. **alevosía** *sf* treachery. **alevoso, -a** *sm, sf* traitor.

alfabeto [alfa'βeto] *sm* alphabet. **alfabético** *adj* alphabetical. **por orden alfabético** in alphabetical order. **alfabetizado** *adj* literate.

alfarero [alfa'rero] *sm* potter. **alfarería** *sf* pottery (art and workshop).

alférez [al'fereθ] *sm* (*mil*) second lieutenant.

alfil [al'fil] *sm* (*ajedrez*) bishop.

alfiler [alfi'ler] *sm* pin; brooch. **alfiler de la ropa** clothes-peg. **alfilerar** *v* pin. **alfilerazo** *sm* pinprick.

alfombra [al'fombra] *sf* carpet; rug. **alfom-**

brar v carpet.

alforja [al'forxa] sf rucksack.

alga ['alɣa] sf seaweed.

algarabía [alɣara'βia] sf Arabic; (fig) gibberish; (ruido) noise, row.

algazara [alɣa'θara] sf hubbub, uproar.

álgebra ['alxebra] sf algebra. **algebraico** adj also **algébrico** algebraic.

álgido ['alxiðo] adj icy cold; (fig) decisive.

algo ['alɣo] pron something; anything. adv rather, quite. sm something; (comida) snack.

algodón [alɣo'ðon] sm cotton. **algodón hidrófilo** cotton wool.

alguacil [alɣwa'θil] sm sheriff; city governor.

alguien ['alɣjen] pron someone, somebody; (interrog) anybody.

algún [al'ɣun] adj some, any. **algún tanto** a little.

alguno [al'ɣuno] adj some, any. pron one; some; someone. **algunos** ms pl some, a few.

alhaja [al'axa] sf jewel; treasure.

alhelí [ale'li] sm, pl **-líes** wallflower.

alheña [a'leɲa] sf privet; blight, mildew. **alheñar** v (secarse) wither; become mildewed.

alhucema [alu'θema] sf lavender.

aliaga [ali'aɣa] sf gorse.

aliar [ali'ar] v ally. **aliado, -a** sm, sf ally. **alianza** sf alliance.

alicaído [alika'iðo] adj depressed; weak.

alicates [ali'kates] sm pl pliers, pincers pl.

aliciente [ali'θjente] sm lure; interest; encouragement.

alienar [alje'nar] v alienate. **alienación** sf alienation. **alienado** adj insane.

aliento [a'ljento] sm breath; (fig) courage. **cobrar aliento** catch one's breath.

aligerar [alixe'rar] v lighten; shorten; alleviate. **aligerarse** v get a move on.

alimentar [alimen'tar] v feed; supply; (promover) foster. **alimentación** sf food; feeding. **alimenticio** adj nourishing. **alimento** sm food; **alimentos integrales** sm pl wholefood(s); **alimentos transgénicos** GM foods.

alinear [aline'ar] v line up. **alinearse en** join. **alineación** sf also **alineamiento** sm alignment.

aliñar [ali'ɲar] v adorn; (culin) season; prepare. **aliño** sm adornment; seasoning; preparation.

alisar [ali'sar] v smooth; polish; level. **alisaduras** sf pl shavings pl.

alistar [alis'tar] v list; recruit; prepare. **alistado** adj enlisted. **alistamiento** sm enlistment.

aliviar [ali'βjar] v lighten; alleviate; help; console. **aliviarse** v feel better, recover. **alivio** sm lightening; relief. ... **de alivio** (fam) a hell of a ...

alma ['alma] sf soul; spirit; person. **con el alma en la boca** at death's door.

almacén [alma'θen] sm warehouse; department store. **almacenaje** sm storage. **almacenero** sm storekeeper.

almanaque [alma'nake] sm almanac; diary.

almeja [al'mexa] sf clam.

almendra [al'mendra] sf almond. **almendro** sm almond tree.

almiar [al'mjar] sm haystack.

almíbar [al'miβar] sm syrup.

almidón [almi'ðon] sm starch.

almirante [almi'rante] sm admiral. **almirantazgo** sm admiralty.

almohada [almo'aða] sf pillow; cushion; (funda) pillowslip. **almohadilla** [almoa'ðiʎa] sf mouse mat.

almoneda [almo'neða] sf auction; (a bajo precio) clearance sale.

almorranas [almo'ranas] sf pl haemorrhoids pl, piles pl.

*almorzar [almor'θar] v lunch. **almuerzo** sm lunch.

alojar [alo'xar] v lodge, accommodate. **alojarse** v put up, stay. **alojamiento** sm accommodation, lodgings pl. **alojamiento y desayuno** sm bed and breakfast.

alondra [a'londra] sf lark.

alpargata [alpar'ɣata] sf rope-soled shoe. **alpargatería** sf shoe factory or shop.

Alpes ['alpes] sm pl Alps pl.

alpinismo [alpi'nismo] sm mountaineering. **alpinista** s(m + f) climber. **alpino** adj alpine.

alpiste [al'piste] sm canary seed; (fam) drink; (fam) money.

alquería [alke'ria] sf farm; (aldea) village.

alquilar [alki'lar] v rent; hire; charter. **alquilarse** v be for hire; to be let. **se alquila** (casa) to let; (coche) for hire.

alquiler *sm* renting; letting; hiring. **alquileres** *sm pl* rent *sing.* **exento de alquiler** rent-free.

alquimia [alˈkimja] *sf* alchemy.

alquitrán [alkiˈtran] *sm* tar. **alquitranado** *adj* tarred.

alrededor [alreðeˈðor] *adv* round, around. **alrededor de** about, around. **alrededores** *sm pl* environs *pl*, outskirts *pl*.

alta [ˈalta] *sf (del hospital)* discharge; *(ingreso)* enrolment. **dar de alta** pass as fit. **darse de alta** enrol.

altanero [altaˈnero] *adj* haughty, arrogant.

altar [alˈtar] *sm* altar.

alta tecnología *sf* high tech.

altavoz [altaˈβoθ] *sm* loudspeaker.

alterar [alteˈrar] *v* change, alter; disturb; *(estropear)* spoil. **alterarse** *v* go sour; change; be disturbed; get excited. **alteración** *sf* alteration; *(altercado)* quarrel.

altercar [alterˈkar] *v* argue, quarrel. **altercación** *sf* argument, quarrel.

alternar [alterˈnar] *v* alternate; be sociable. **alterno** *adj* alternating; alternate.

alternativa [alternaˈtiβa] *sf* alternative choice; *(trabajo)* shift-work; *(rotación de cosechas)* rotation. **tomar la alternativa** qualify as a bullfighter.

alto¹ [ˈalto] *adj* tall; high; upper; *(fuerte)* loud; advanced; noble. **lo alto** the top. *adv* high; high up; out loud. *sm (elevación)* hill; *(altura)* height. **alteza** *sf* height; *(título)* highness; grandeur. **altitud** *sf* altitude; *(geog)* elevation.

alto² *sm, interj* halt. **hacer alto** stop.

alubia [aˈluβja] *sf* French bean.

alucinación [aluθinaˈθjon] *sf* hallucination.

alud [aˈluð] *sm* avalanche.

aludir [aluˈðir] *v* allude, mention. **aludido** *adj* in question. **no darse por aludido** turn a deaf ear.

alumbrar [alumˈbrar] *v* light; illuminate; give light; *(descubrir)* find; *(parir)* give birth; *(brillar)* shine. **alumbrarse** *v (fam)* become tipsy. **alumbramiento** *sm* lighting; illumination. **alumbrante** *adj* illuminating; *(fig)* enlightening.

aluminio [aluˈminjo] *sm* aluminium.

alumno [aˈlumno] *sm* pupil, student.

alzar [alˈθar] *v* raise; lift. **alzarse** *v* rise; stand out. **alza** *sf* raise. **¡alza!** bravo! **alza-**

miento *sm* increase; uprising.

allá [aˈʎa] *adv* there; long ago. **más allá** farther on. **vamos allá** let's go.

allanar [aʎaˈnar] *v* level, flatten, smooth. **allanar el terreno** clear the way.

allegar [aʎeˈgar] *v* collect, reap; add; unite. **allegar fondos** raise funds. **allegarse** *v* arrive; approach. **allegarse a** become attached to.

allegado [aʎeˈgaðo], -a *sm, sf* relative; close friend. *adj* related, close. **allegamiento** *sm* collection; gathering; union; friendship; relationship.

allende [aˈʎende] *adv* beyond; besides. **allende el mar** overseas.

allí [aˈʎi] *adv* there; then. **aquí y allí** here and there. **por allí** over there.

ama [ˈama] *sf* mistress of the house; *(patrona)* landlady.

amable [aˈmaβle] *adj* kind. **amablemente** *adv* kindly. **amabilidad** *sf* kindness.

amaestrar [amaesˈtrar] *v* train.

amagar [amaˈgar] *v* threaten; show signs of. **amagarse** *v (fam)* hide.

amainar [amaiˈnar] *v* lessen; moderate. **amainarse** *v* yield.

amalgamar [amalgaˈmar] *v* amalgamate. **amalgamación** *sf* amalgamation.

amamantar [amamanˈtar] *v* suckle, nurse. **amamantador** *adj* suckling. **amamantamiento** *sm* suckling.

*amanecer [amaneˈθer] *v* dawn; arrive at break of day. *sm* dawn, daybreak.

amansar [amanˈsar] *v* break in; tame; *(fig: dolor)* ease.

amante [aˈmante] *sm, sf* lover. *adj* fond.

amañado [amaˈɲaðo] *adj* skilful; *(falso)* fake. **amañar** *v* fix; fake.

amapola [amaˈpola] *sf* poppy.

amar [aˈmar] *v* love.

amargar [amarˈgar] *v* embitter; be *or* taste bitter. **amargo** *adj* bitter. **amargor** *sm also* **amargura** *sf* bitterness.

amarillo [amaˈriʎo] *adj* yellow.

amarrar [amaˈrrar] *v* fasten; tie; moor. **amarradero** *sm* moorings *pl.* **amarro** *sm* fastening.

amartelar [amarteˈlar] *v (enamorar)* make lovesick; *(dar celos)* make jealous. **amartelarse de** *(fam)* get a crush on.

amartillar [amartiˈʎar] *v* hammer.

amasar [amaˈsar] *v* knead; mix; prepare;

(*med*) massage; (*fam*) cook up; (*fig*) amass.
amasijo *sm* (*harina*) dough; (*fam*) mixture, hotchpotch; plot.
amatista [ama'tista] *sf* amethyst.
ámbar ['ambar] *sm* amber.
ambición [ambi'θjon] *sf* ambition. **ambicioso** *adj* ambitious.
ambiente [am'bjente] *sm* atmosphere; environment. *adj* surrounding.
ambiguo [am'bigwo] *adj* ambiguous. **ambigüedad** *sf* ambiguity.
ámbito ['ambito] *sm* (*recinto*) enclosure; (*alcance*) scope; sphere; (*extensión*) expanse.
ambos ['ambos] *adj*, *pron* both.
ambulancia [ambu'lanθja] *sf* ambulance.
ambulante [ambu'lante] *adj* travelling; walking.
amedrentar [ameðren'tar] *v* frighten.
amenazar [amena'θar] *v* threaten. **amenaza** *sf* threat. **amenazador** *adj* threatening.
amenguar [amen'gwar] *v* lessen; (*deshonrar*) dishonour.
amenizar [ameni'θar] *v* make pleasant. **amenidad** *sf* pleasantness; amenity. **ameno** *adj* pleasant, delightful.
América [a'merika] *sf* America. **América del Norte/Sur** North/South America. **América Latina** Latin America. **americano, -a** *s, adj* American.
ametralladora [ametraλa'ðora] *sf* machine gun.
amianto [a'mjanto] *sm* asbestos.
amígdala [a'miɣðala] *sf* tonsil. **amigdalitis** *sf* tonsillitis.
amigo [a'miɣo] *sm* friend; boyfriend. **amiga** *sf* friend; girlfriend; mistress. **amigo por correspondencia** pen friend. **amigo** *adj* friendly.
amilanar [amila'nar] *v* frighten, terrify. **amilanarse** *v* become terrified.
aminorar [amino'rar] *v* lessen, reduce. **aminoración** *sf* lessening.
amistad [amis'tað] *sf* friendship. **amistades** *sf pl* friends *pl*. **hacer las amistades** make up. **amistar** *v* reconcile. **amistoso** *adj* friendly.
amnesia [am'nesja] *sf* amnesia.
amnistía [amnis'tia] *sf* amnesty. **amnistiar** *v* grant an amnesty to.
amo ['amo] *sm* master; overseer; employer; proprietor; (*fam*) boss.

amodorrarse [amoðor'rarse] *v* become drowsy. **amodorrado** *adj* drowsy.
amohinar [amoi'nar] *v* irritate; fret. **amohinarse** *v* become irritated *or* peevish.
*amolar [amo'lar] *v* (*cuchillo*) grind, sharpen; (*fam: fastidiar*) annoy.
amoldar [amol'ðar] *v* mould; fit; shape. **amoldarse** *v* adapt oneself.
amonestar [amones'tar] *v* warn; advise; admonish; (*anuncio de bodas*) publish the banns of. **amonestación** *sf* warning, admonition. **correr las amonestaciones** publish the banns.
amontonar [amonto'nar] *v* pile up; accumulate. **amontonarse** *v* crowd together; heap up; (*fam*) become angry.
amor [a'mor] *sm* love; devotion. **amor interesado** love of money. **amor propio** self-esteem. **amoroso** *adj* affectionate.
amoratar [amora'tar] *v* (*frío*) make purple; (*golpes*) bruise. **amoratado** *adj* purple; black and blue.
amordazar [amorða'θar] *v* gag; (*un perro*) muzzle; (*fig*) gag, silence.
amorfo [a'morfo] *adj* amorphous.
amortiguar [amorti'gwar] *v* (*luz*) dim; (*ruido*) deaden; (*fuego*) damp; (*golpe*) cushion; (*fig*) mitigate. **amortiguación** *sf also* **amortiguamiento** *sm* dimming; deadening; mitigation.
amortiguador [amortigwa'ðor] *sm* (*auto*) shock absorber. *adj* dimming; deadening; mitigating.
amortizar [amorti'θar] *v* amortize; (*una máquina*) depreciate.
amotinar [amoti'nar] *v* incite to revolt; (*fig*) disturb. **amotinarse** *v* mutiny. **amotinado** *adj also* **amotinador** mutinous, rebellious. **amotinamiento** *sm* mutiny.
amparar [ampa'rar] *v* shelter; protect; (*ayudar*) help. **ampararse** *v* seek help *or* protection. **amparo** *sm* aid; protection; refuge.
ampliar [am'pljar] *v* enlarge; lengthen; expand; increase. **amplio** *adj* wide, full; spacious. **amplitud** *sf* width; fullness; spaciousness; extent.
amplificar [amplifi'kar] *v* amplify. **amplificación** *sf* amplification. **amplificador** *sm* amplifier; *adj* amplifying.
ampolla [am'poλa] *sf* blister; (*redoma*) phial; (*frasco*) flask. **ampollar** *v* blister.
amputar [ampu'tar] *v* amputate.

amputación *sf* amputation.

amueblar [amwe'βlar] *v* furnish.

amuleto [amu'leto] *sm* amulet.

anacronismo [anakro'nismo] *sm* anachronism.

anales [a'nales] *sm pl* annals *pl*. **analista** *s(m + f)* annalist.

analfabeto [anafa'βeto], **-a** *s, adj* illiterate.

análisis [a'nalisis] *sm invar* analysis. **analista** *s(m + f)* analyst. **analista de sistemas** *sm* systems analyst. **analítico** *adj* analytical. **analizar** *v* analyse.

analogía [analo'xia] *sf* analogy. **análogo** *adj* analogous, similar.

ananás [ana'nas] *sm* pineapple.

anaquel [ana'kel] *sm* shelf. **anaquelería** *sf* shelving.

anarquía [anar'kia] *sf* anarchy. **anarquismo** *sm* anarchism. **anarquista** *s(m + f)*, *adj* anarchist.

anatomía [anato'mia] *sf* anatomy. **anatómico** *adj* anatomical.

anca ['anka] *sf* haunch; rump. **ancas** *sf pl* (*fam*) bottom *sing*.

anciano [an'θjano] *adj* old, *sm* old man. **ancianidad** *sf* old age.

ancla ['ankla] *sf* anchor. **anclar** *v also* **echar anclas** anchor.

ancho ['antʃo] *adj* wide, broad; thick; (*fig*) relieved. *sm* width. **a sus anchas** at ease. **anchura** *sf* width; fullness; (*media*) measurement; (*fig: frescura*) cheek.

anchoa [an'tʃoa] *sf* anchovy.

Andalucía [andalu'θia] *sf* Andalusia. **andaluz, -a** *s, adj* Andalusian.

andamio [an'damjo] *sm* scaffold; platform. **andamios** *sm pl* scaffolding *sing*.

*andar [an'dar] *v* walk; go; come; (*máquina*) work; (*correr*) run. **¡anda!** go on! **andar en** be engaged in; rummage in. *sm* walk, gait.

·andas ['andas] *sf pl* (*para una imagen*) portable platform *sing*; (*féretro*) bier *sing*; (*para enfermo*) stretcher *sing*.

andén [an'den] *sm* station platform; (*de autopista*) hard shoulder.

Andorra [an'dorra] *sf* Andorra. **andorrano, -a** *s, adj* Andorran.

andrajo [an'draxo] *sm* rag. **estar hecho un andrajo** be in rags. **andrajoso** *adj* ragged, tattered.

anécdota [a'nekðota] *sf* anecdote.

anecdótico *adj* anecdotal.

anegar [ane'gar] *v* flood; drown. **anegación** *sf* drowning; flooding.

anejo [a'nexo] *adj* joined, attached. *sm* annexe.

anemia [a'nemja] *sf* anaemia. **anémico** *adj* anaemic.

anestésico [anes'tesiko] *sm, adj* anaesthetic. **anestesista** *s(m + f)* anaesthetist.

anexar [anek'sar] *v* annex. **anexión** *sf* annexation.

anfibio [an'fiβjo] *sm* amphibian. *adj* amphibious.

anfiteatro [anfite'atro] *sm* amphitheatre; (*universidad*) lecture theatre; (*theatro*) gallery.

anfitrión [anfitri'on], **-ona** *sm, sf* host, hostess.

ángel ['anxel] *sm* angel. **tener ángel** be charming. **angelical** *adj also* **angélico** angelic. **angelito** *sm* cherub.

angina [an'xina] *sf* angina.

anglicano [angli'kano], **-a** *s, adj* Anglican.

angosto [an'gosto] *adj* narrow. **angostura** *sf* narrowness.

anguila [an'gila] *sf* eel.

ángulo ['angulo] *sm* angle; bend. **anguloso** *adj* angular.

angustiar [angus'tjar] *v* distress; worry. **angustia** *sf* anguish. **angustiado** *adj* distressed; miserable. **angustioso** *adj* distressing; anguished.

anhelar [ane'lar] *v* pant, gasp; (*desear*) yearn for, crave. **anhelo** *sm* panting; desire.

anidar [ani'ðar] *v* nest; (*fig*) shelter.

anillo [a'niλo] *sm* ring. **anillo de boda** wedding ring. **anillo de compromiso** *or* **pedida** engagement ring. **anillar** *v* ring.

ánima ['anima] *sf* soul.

animal [ani'mal] *sm* animal, beast. *adj* animal. **animalada** *sf* stupid thing to do *or* say; (*grosería*) bad language.

animar [ani'mar] *v* animate; entertain; encourage; comfort. **animarse** *v* cheer up. **animación** *sf* animation. **animado** *adj* lively. **animador, -a** *sm, sf* entertainer; master of ceremonies; *adj* entertaining; encouraging.

ánimo ['animo] *sm* soul; spirit; mind; courage; intention. **¡ánimo!** come on! **animoso** *adj* spirited; courageous.

aniquilar [aniki'lar] *v* annihilate.

anís [a'nis] *sm* aniseed.

aniversario [aniβer'sarjo] *sm* anniversary.

ano ['ano] *sm* anus.

anoche [a'notʃe] *adv* last night.

*anochecer [anotʃe'θer] *v* grow dark. *sm* nightfall.

anomalía [anoma'lia] *sf* anomaly. **anómalo** *adj* anomalous.

anónimo [a'nonimo] *adj* anonymous. *sm* anonymous person.

anorexia nerviosa [ano'rexja] *sf* anorexia nervosa.

anormal [anor'mal] *adj* abnormal. **anormalidad** *sf* abnormality.

anotar [ano'tar] *v* note, jot down. **anotación** *sf* note.

ansiar [an'sjar] *v* long for. **ansia** *sf* longing; (*pena*) anguish; (*fervor*) eagerness. **ansias** *sf pl* retching *sing.* **ansiedad** *sf* longing; anxiety; eagerness. **ansioso** *adj* anxious; eager; longing.

antagonismo [antago'nismo] *sm* antagonism. **antagonista** *adj* antagonistic. **antagonizar** *v* antagonize.

antaño [an'taɲo] *adv* last year; formerly.

antártico [an'tartico] *adj* antarctic. *sm* the Antarctic. **Antártica** *sf* Antarctica.

ante¹ ['ante] *prep* before; in the presence of; with regard to. **ante todo** to begin with.

ante² ['ante] *sm* suede.

anteanoche [antea'notʃe] *adv* the night before last.

anteayer [antea'jer] *adv* the day before yesterday.

antecedente [anteθe'ðente] *sm* antecedent. *adj* previous. **antecedencia** *sf* lineage. **anteceder** *v* precede.

antecesor [anteθe'sor], **-a** *sm*, *sf* predecessor; ancestor. *adj* antecedent.

antelación [antela'θjon] *sf* preference. **con antelación** in advance.

antemano [ante'mano] *adv* **de antemano** beforehand.

antena [an'tena] *sf* (*radio*) aerial; (*insecto*) antenna. **antena parabólica** *sf* satellite dish.

antenatal [antena'tal] *adj* antenatal.

anteojo [ante'oxo] *sm* small telescope. **anteojos** *sm pl* spectacles *pl*.

antepasado [antepa'saðo] *adj* previous. *sm* ancestor.

antepecho [ante'petʃo] *sm* (*de escalera*) handrail; (*de ventana*) window sill.

*anteponer [antepo'ner] *v* prefer. **anteponerse** *v* push forward.

anterior [ante'rjor] *adj* preceding, former; front.

antes ['antes] *adv* before, formerly; first; rather. **antes de** before. **antes que** rather than. **cuanto antes** as soon as possible.

antiadherente ['antiaðerente] *adj* nonstick.

antiaéreo [antja'ereo] *adj* anti-aircraft.

antibiótico [anti'bjotiko] *adj* antibiotic.

anticiclón [antiθi'klon] *sm* anticyclone.

anticipar [antiθi'par] *v* anticipate; advance. **anticiparse a hacer algo** to do something ahead of time. **anticipación** *sf* anticipation. **con anticipación** in advance. **anticipado** *adj* early, premature. **anticipo** *sm* advance payment; foretaste.

anticoncepcional [antikonθepθjo'nal] *sm*, *adj* contraceptive. **anticonceptivo** *adj* contraceptive.

anticuado [anti'kwaðo] *adj* out of date; old-fashioned.

anticuado [anti'kwaðo] *adj* outdated.

anticuario [anti'kwarjo], **-a** *sm*, *sf* antiquarian.

antidepresivo [antiðepre'siβo] *adj* antidepressant.

antídoto [an'tiðoto] *sm* antidote.

antieconómico [antieko'nomiko] *adj* uneconomic.

antiguo [an'tigwo] *adj* ancient, antique; senior; former. **de antiguo** of old. **antigualla** *sf* antique; (*persona*) old fogey; (*noticia*) stale news. **antiguamente** *adv* formerly. **antigüedad** *sf* antiquity; seniority.

Antillas [an'tiʎas] *sf pl* West Indies. **antillano** *adj* West Indian.

antílope [an'tilope] *sm* antelope.

antipatía [antipa'tia] *sf* antipathy; dislike; unfriendliness. **antipático** *adj* disagreeable; unfriendly; nasty.

antisemítico [antise'mitiko] *adj* anti-Semitic. **antisemitismo** *sm* anti-Semitism.

antiséptico [anti'septiko] *sm*, *adj* antiseptic.

antisocial [antiso'θjal] *adj* antisocial.

antítesis [an'titesis] *sf* antithesis.

antojarse [anto'xarse] *v* seem; imagine; fancy; take a fancy to. **antojársele a uno** take it into one's head to.

antojo [an'toxo] *sm* whim; (*lunar*) birthmark. **antojos** *sm pl* craving *sing.* **antojadizo** *adj* capricious.

antología [antolo'xia] *sf* anthology.

antorcha [an'tortʃa] *sf* torch.

antro ['antro] *sm* cave, den; (*fam: tasca*) low dive.

antropófago [antro'pofago], **-a** *sm, sf* cannibal. *adj* cannibalistic. **antropofagia** *sf* cannibalism.

antropología [antropolo'xia] *sf* anthropology. **antropológico** *adj* anthropological. **antropólogo**, **-a** *sm, sf* anthropologist.

anual [a'nwal] *adj* annual. **anualidad** *sf* annuity. **anuario** *sm* yearbook.

anublar [anu'βlar] *v* cloud over, obscure. **anublarse** *v* become cloudy; fade away.

anudar [anu'ðar] *v* knot; join; tie; (*empezar*) begin. **anudarse** become knotted; (*plantas*) wither. **anudadura** *sf also* **anudamiento** *sm* knotting; withering.

anular [anu'lar] *v* (*cheque*) cancel; (*ley*) repeal; (*fig: dominar*) overshadow. **anularse** *v* (*fig: renunciar*) give up everything. **anulación** *sf* cancellation; abrogation; repeal. **anulador** *adj* repealing.

anunciar [anun'θjar] *v* announce, proclaim; notify; (*hacer publicidad*) advertise; (*predecir*) foretell. **anunciador**, **-a** *sm, sf* announcer; advertiser; *adj* announcing; advertising. **anuncio** *sm* announcement; advertisement; omen; sign. **anuncio por palabras** *sm* small ads.

anzuelo [an'θwelo] *sm* fish-hook; (*fig: aliciente*) lure.

añadir [aɲa'ðir] *v* add; increase. **añadido** *sm* addition; notify. **añadidura** *sf* addition; extra. **por añadidura** furthermore, besides.

añejo [a'ɲexo] *adj* mature; (*carne*) cured; very old.

añicos [a'ɲikos] *sm pl* pieces, bits. **hacerse añicos** wear oneself out.

añil [a'ɲil] *sm* indigo plant; indigo dye.

año ['aɲo] *sm* year. **año sabático** *sm* gap year. **al año** yearly. **tener ... años** be ... years old. **todos los años** every year.

añorar [aɲo'rar] *v* long for; be homesick. **añoranza** *sf* homesickness; nostalgia; yearning.

*apacentar [apaθen'tar] *v* graze. **apacentadero** *sm* pasture. **apacentador**, **-a** *sm, sf* herdsman/woman.

apacible [apa'θiβle] *adj* mild; gentle; peaceful. **apacibilidad** *sf* mildness; peacefulness.

apaciguar [apaθi'gwar] *v* pacify; appease. **apaciguarse** *v* calm down. **apaciguador**, **-a** *sm, sf* peacemaker; troubleshooter. **apaciguamiento** *sm* pacification; appeasement.

apagar [apa'gar] *v* (*fuego*) extinguish; switch off; muffle; (*sed*) quench; (*dolor*) soothe; (*disturbio*) calm down. **apagado** *adj* extinguished; dull; lifeless; muffled. **apagaincendios** *sm invar* fire-extinguisher.

apalear [apale'ar] *v* beat; (*grano*) thresh; (*maltratar*) thrash. **apaleo** *sm* beating; winnowing; thrashing.

apañar [apa'ɲar] *v* fix; arrange; repair; (*ataviar*) dress up; (*coger*) grab; (*fam: robar*) swipe; (*fam: preparar*) get ready. **apañado** *adj* handy; dressed up.

aparador [apara'ðor] *sm* sideboard; (*escaparate*) shop window.

aparato [apa'rato] *sm* apparatus; machine; ceremony. **aparato del tipo de los marcapasos** *sm* (heart) pacemaker.

*aparecer [apare'θer] *v* appear. **aparecido** *sm* ghost.

aparejar [apare'xar] *v* prepare; (*caballos*) harness, saddle; (*cuadro*) prime. **aparejador** *sm* quantity surveyor. **aparejo** *sm* preparation; equipment; harness.

aparentar [aparen'tar] *v* pretend; feign.

aparente [apa'rente] *adj* apparent; evident; (*adecuado*) suitable.

aparición [apari'θjon] *sf* appearance; (*visión*) apparition; publication.

apariencia [apari'enθja] *sf* appearance; aspect; probability.

apartamento [aparta'mento] *sm* flat.

apartar [apar'tar] *v* separate; (*quitar*) remove; (*clasificar*) sort; (*poner a un lado*) put aside. **apartarse** *v* turn aside; (*irse*) leave. **apartado** *adj* separated; distant; *sm* paragraph; (*habitación*) spare room. **apartado de correos** post-office box. **apartamiento** *sm* separation; remoteness. **aparte** *adv* apart (from); aside.

apasionar [apasjo'nar] *v* rouse, stir. **apasionarse** *v* become excited. **apasionado** *adj* madly in love; passionate; (*ardiente*) fervent. **apasionamiento** *sm* passion.

apatía [apa'tia] *sf* apathy. **apático** *adj* apathetic.

apear [ape'ar] *v* get down, dismount. **apearse** *v* alight, get off.

apedrear [apeðre'ar] *v* stone. **apedrearse** *v* hail. **apedreo** *sm* stoning.

apelar [ape'lar] *v* appeal. **apelar a** appeal to. **apelar de** appeal against.

apellido [ape'ʎiðo] *sm* surname; (*apodo*) nickname. **apellido de soltera** maiden name.

apenar [ape'nar] *v* grieve.

apenas [a'penas] *adv* scarcely; no sooner than.

apéndice [a'pendiθe] *sm* appendix; supplement. **apendicitis** *sf* appendicitis.

apercibir [aperθi'βir] *v* prepare; (*proveer*) equip; (*advertir*) warn. **apercibirse de** equip oneself with. **apercibimiento** *sm* preparation; advice; (*jur*) summons.

aperitivo [aperi'tiβo] *sm* appetizer; apéritif. *adj* appetizing.

apero [a'pero] *sm* equipment; tools *pl.*

apertura [aper'tura] *sf* opening.

apesadumbrar [apesadum'brar] *v* grieve, afflict. **apesadumbrarse** *v* be upset.

apestar [apes'tar] *v* infect; (*fig*) vex; (*fam*) stink. **apestado** *adj* (*olor*) foul; (*que tiene peste*) plague-ridden; infested.

*apetecer [apete'θer] *v* have a hankering for, fancy; (*bienvenido*) be welcome. **apetecible** *adj* desirable, tempting. **apetencia** *sf* desire; appetite.

apetito [ape'tito] *sm* appetite.

apiadarse [apja'ðarse] *v* have pity on.

ápice ['apiθe] *sm* apex; jot, iota.

apiñar [api'ɲar] *v* squeeze together. **apiñarse** *v* crowd, throng. **apiñadura** *sf* also **apiñamiento** *sm* congestion; throng.

apio ['apjo] *sm* celery.

apisonadora [apisona'ðora] *sf* steam roller. **apisonar** *v* flatten. **apisonamiento** *sm* flattening.

aplacar [apla'kar] *v* appease; calm. **aplacable** *adj* appeasable. **aplacamiento** *sm* appeasement. **aplacador** *adj* appeasing.

aplanar [apla'nar] *v* level, flatten; (*fam*) make dejected. **aplanador** *adj* levelling. **aplanadora** *sf* leveller. **aplanamiento** *sm* levelling, flattening; (*fam*) dejection.

aplastar [aplas'tar] *v* crush, flatten.

aplaudir [aplau'ðir] *v* applaud. **aplauso** *sm* applause.

aplazar [apla'θar] *v* postpone; (*convocar*) summon; procrastinate. **aplazamiento** *sm* postponement; summons.

aplicar [apli'kar] *v* apply; attach; (*recursos, dinero*) assign. **aplicarse** *v* apply oneself; be applicable. **aplicación** *sf* application. **aplicado** *adj* studious.

aplomo [a'plomo] *sm* aplomb, self-confidence. **aplomado** *adj* self-assured.

apocar [apo'kar] *v* lessen; belittle. **apocarse** *v* become cowed. **apocado** *adj* spineless, timid. **apocamiento** *sm* timidity.

apodar [apo'ðar] *v* nickname. **apodo** *sm* nickname.

apoderar [apoðe'rar] *v* authorize. **apoderarse de** take possession of. **apoderado** *sm* agent; sports manager.

apogeo [apo'xeo] *sm* climax; summit.

apolillarse [apoli'ʎarse] *v* become motheaten. **apolilladura** *sf* moth-hole.

apoplejía [apople'xia] *sf* apoplexy. **apoplético, -a** *s, adj* apoplectic.

aportar [apor'tar] *v* bring, contribute; arrive. **aportación** *sf* contribution.

aposentar [aposen'tar] *v* lodge; give lodging to. **aposentarse** *v* take lodgings. **aposentamiento** *sm* lodging. **aposento** *sm* room; lodging.

*apostar [apos'tar] *v* bet. **apostarse** *v* bet; take up one's post. **apostador, -a** *sm, sf* punter.

apóstol [a'postol] *sm* apostle. **apostólico** *adj* apostolic.

apóstrofo [a'postrofo] *sm* (*gram*) apostrophe.

apoyar [apo'jar] *v* support; back up; lean; rest. **apoyar en** lean against. **apoyarse en** lean on. **apoyo** *sm* support; back-up.

apreciar [apre'θjar] *v* appreciate; value. **apreciar en mucho** value highly. **apreciable** *adj* appreciable; estimable; (*ruido*) audible. **apreciación** *sf* appreciation; (*valoración*) appraisal. **apreciativo** *adj* appreciative. **aprecio** *sm* appraisal; esteem.

aprehender [apreen'der] *v* seize; understand. **aprehensible** *adj* understandable. **aprehensión** *sf* capture, arrest; understanding.

apremiar [apre'mjar] *v* press, urge; (*obligar*) force; (*dar prisa*) hurry. **apremiador** *adj* urgent. **apremio** *sm* urgency; compulsion.

aprender [apren'der] *v* learn. **aprendiz, -a** *sm, sf* apprentice. **aprendizaje** *sm* apprenticeship.

aprensión [apren'sjon] *sf* apprehension, fear. **aprensivo** *adj* apprehensive.

apresar [apre'sar] *v* seize, arrest. **apresamiento** *sm* seizure.

aprestar [apres'tar] *v* prepare; (*telas*) size. **aprestarse** *v* get ready. **apresto** *sm* preparation.

apresurar [apresu'rar] *v* hurry, quicken. **apresuradamente** *adv* hastily. **apresurado** *adj* hurried. **apresuramiento** *sm* haste.

*apretar [apre'tar] *v* squeeze; grip; tighten; (*botón*) press; (*la mano*) shake; (*dolor*) get worse; (*comprimir*) press down. **apretarse** *v* crowd together; huddle together. **apretado** *adj* tight; (*colchón*) hard; cramped; cluttered; difficult; (*tacaño*) miserly. **apretón** *sm* squeeze; (*fam: aprieto*) tight spot; (*fam: necesidad natural*) call of nature. **aprieto** *sm* awkward situation.

aprisa [a'prisa] *adv* quickly.

aprisionar [aprisjon'ar] *v* imprison.

*aprobar [apro'βar] *v* approve; approve of; (*examen*) pass. **aprobación** *sf* approval; pass. **aprobado** *adj* approved. *sm* pass.

apropiar [apti'pjar] *v* appropriate; adapt. **apropiarse de algo** appropriate something. **apropiado** *adj* appropriate, suitable.

aprovechar [aproβe'tʃar] *v* profit by; be useful; make progress. **aprovecharse de** take advantage of. **aprovechado** *adj* thrifty; (*apañado*) resourceful; studious; (*egoísta*) selfish. **aprovechamiento** *sm* profit; exploitation; benefit.

aproximar [aproksi'mar] *v* bring nearer. **aproximarse** *v* approach. **aproximación** *sf* approximation; nearness. **aproximado** *adj* approximate.

aptitud [apti'tuð] *sf* aptitude; capacity. **apto** *adj* apt; suitable.

apuesta [a'pwesta] *sf* bet.

apuesto [a'pwesto] *adj* smart, spruce.

apuntar [apun'tar] *v* (*señalar*) point at; (*arma*) aim; (*sugerir*) point out; (*anotar*) make a note of; (*demostrar*) display; (*sacar punta*) sharpen; (*jugar*) bet; (*teatro*) prompt. **apuntarse** *v* put one's name down; (*fam*) enrol; **apuntarse al paro** *v* sign on (as unemployed). **apuntado** *adj* pointed. **apunte** *sm* (*nota*) note; (*puesta*) stake;

prompter; (*teatro*) cue; (*dibujo*) sketch.

apuñalar [apuɲa'lar] *v* stab.

apurar [apu'rar] *v* purify; (*acabar*) exhaust; (*vaciar*) drain; examine in detail; (*dar prisa*) rush, hurry. **apurarse** *v* (*preocuparse*) worry; hurry up. **apuradamente** *adv* with difficulty; (*ser indigente*) in want; (*fam*) exactly. **apurado** *adj* (*pobre*) hard up; (*agotado*) worn out; (*avergonzado*) embarrassed. **apuro** *sm* (*dificultad*) tight spot; embarrassment.

aquejar [ake'xar] *v* afflict. **aquejoso** *adj* afflicted.

aquel, aquella [a'kel, a'keʎa] *adj* that. **aquellos, aquellas** *pl* those. **aquél, aquélla** *pron* that; the one; the former.

aquí [a'ki] *adv* here. **de aquí en adelante** from now on. **heme aquí** here I am. **por aquí** this way.

aquietar [akje'tar] *v* quieten.

aquilatar [akila'tar] *v* test, examine closely.

Arabia [a'raβja] *sf* Arabia. **árabe** *adj* Arab, Arabian, Arabic; *sm, sf* Arab, Arabian; *sm* (*lengua*) Arabic. **arábico** *adj also* **arábigo** Arabic.

arancel [aran'θel] *sm* tariff, duty.

araña [a'raɲa] *sf* spider; (*luz*) chandelier.

arañar [ara'ɲar] *v* scratch. **arañada** *sf* scratch. **arañador** *adj* scratching, scraping. **arañazo** *sm* scratch.

arar [a'rar] *v* plough. **arado** *sm* plough.

arbitrar [arβi'trar] *v* arbitrate; referee. **arbitraje** *sm* arbitration. **arbitrario** *adj* arbitrary. **árbitro** *sm* referee, umpire.

arbitrio [ar'βitrjo] *sm* (*voluntad*) will; (*recurso*) means; (*jur*) judgment. **arbitrios** *sm pl* taxes *pl*.

árbol ['arβol] *sm* tree; (*tecn*) shaft; (*palo*) mast. **árbol de Navidad** Christmas tree. **arboleda** *sf* wood, spinney.

arbusto [ar'βusto] *sm* bush.

arca ['arka] *sf* box, chest. **arca de agua** reservoir.

arcada [ar'kaða] *sf* arcade. **arcadas** *sf pl* nausea *sing*.

arcaico [ar'kaiko] *adj* archaic. **arcaísmo** *sm* archaism.

arce ['arθe] *sm* maple.

arcilla [ar'θiʎa] *sf* clay.

arco ['arko] *sm* arc; arch; (*arma, música*) bow. **arco iris** rainbow.

archiduque [artʃi'ðuke] *sm* archduke.

archiduquesa *sf* archduchess.
archipiélago [artʃi'pjelago] *sm* archipelago.
archivo [ar'tʃiβo] *sm* file; archives; (*computadora*) file. *pl.* **archivador** *sm* filing cabinet. **archivar** *v* file. **archivero, -a** *sm, sf also* **archivista** *s(m + f)* archivist.
arder [ar'ðer] *v* burn; (*estiércol*) rot; (*fig*) seethe. **arderse** *v* burn up. **ardiente** *adj* ardent, burning; feverish.
ardid [ar'ðið] *sm* trick, ruse.
ardilla [ar'ðiʎa] *sf* squirrel.
ardor [ar'ðor] *sm* ardour; (*quemazón*) burn; (*fig*) enthusiasm. **ardorosamente** *adv* ardently. **ardoroso** *adj* burning; feverish; fervent.
arduo [ar'ðuo] *adj* arduous, difficult.
área ['area] *sf* area.
arena [a'rena] *sf* sand; (*en el circo*) arena; (*ruedo*) bullring. **arena movediza** quicksand. **arenal** *sm* stretch of sand. **arenar** *v* sand.
arengar [aren'gar] *v* harangue. **arenga** *sf* harangue.
arenque [a'renke] *sm* herring.
argamasa [arga'masa] *sf* mortar. **argamasar** *v* mortar.
Argentina [arxen'tina] *sf* Argentina. **argentino** *adj* (*de plata*) silvery; Argentinian. **argentino, -a** *sm, sf* Argentine, Argentinian.
argolla [ar'goʎa] *sf* large metal ring, hoop.
argucia [ar'guθja] *sf* fallacy; subtlety.
***argüir** [ar'gwir] *v* (*alegar*) argue; indicate; demonstrate; (*delatar*) accuse; infer.
aria ['arja] *sf* aria.
argumento [argu'mento] *sm* argument; (*cuento*) plot. **argumentador** *adj* argumentative.
aridez [ari'ðeθ] *sf* dryness. **aridecer** *v* dry up. **aridecerse** *v* become dry. **árido** *adj* arid. **medida de áridos** *sf* dry measure.
arisco [a'risko] *adj* (*tímido*) shy; (*huraño*) unfriendly; (*animales*) wild.
aristocracia [aristo'kraθja] *sf* aristocracy. **aristócrata** *s(m + f)* aristocrat. **aristocrático** *adj* aristocratic.
aritmética [arit'metika] *sf* arithmetic. **aritmético** *adj* arithmetic, arithmetical.
armada [ar'maða] *sf* navy, fleet.
armar [ar'mar] *v* arm; prepare; reinforce; (*proveer*) provide; organize. **armarse** *v* arm oneself; prepare oneself; (*estallar*) break

out. **arma** *sf* weapon. **armado** *adj* armed.
armadura *sf* armour; framework. **armamento** *sm* armament.
armario [ar'marjo] *sm* cupboard; (*para ropa*) wardrobe.
armazón [arma'θon] *sm* (*anat*) skeleton. *sf* (*conjunto de piezas*) framework.
armería [arme'ria] *sf* gunsmiths; (*heráldica*) heraldry.
armisticio [armis'tiθjo] *sm* armistice.
armonía [armo'nia] *sf* harmony. **armónico** *adj also* **armonioso** harmonious.
armónica [ar'monika] *sf* harmonica.
aro ['aro] *sm* (*argolla*) iron ring; (*de tonel*) hoop.
aroma [a'roma] *sm* aroma. **aromático** *adj* aromatic, fragrant. **aromatizante** *adj* flavouring. **aromatizar** *v* flavour.
arpa ['arpa] *sf* harp. **arpista** *s(m + f)* harpist.
arpón [ar'pon] *sm* harpoon.
arquear [arke'ar] *v* arch, curve. **arqueo** *sm* arching.
arqueología [arkeolo'xia] *sf* archaeology. **arqueológico** *adj* archaeological. **arqueólogo** *sm* archaeologist.
arquero [ar'kero] *sm* archer; (*com*) cashier.
arquitectura [arkitek'tura] *sf* architecture. **arquitecto** *sm* architect.
arrabal [arra'βal] *sm* suburb. **arrabales** *sm pl* outskirts *pl*.
arraigar [arrai'gar] *v* take root. **arraigarse** *v* settle down. **arraigado** *adj* deep-rooted. **arraigo** *sm* roots *pl*; influence.
arrancar [arran'kar] *v* root up, tear out, force out; (*las flemas*) expectorate; (*suspiro*) heave; (*agarrar*) snatch; (*auto*) start. **arrancarse** *v* begin. **arrancada** *sf* sudden start; jerk. **arrancado** *adj* uprooted; (*fam*) broke. **arrancadura** *sf* pulling; uprooting; (*dientes*) extraction. **arranque** *sm* (*auto*) starting; (*carretera*) beginning; (*energía*) burst; origin.
arrasar [arra'sar] *v* (*llenar*) fill to the brim; (*edificio*) demolish; (*allanar*) level. **arrasarse** *v* clear up. **arrasadura** *sf* levelling. **arrasamiento** *sm* levelling; demolition.
arrastrar [arras'trar] *v* pull, haul, drag; (*viento*) blow away; (*provocar*) give rise to; attract. **arrastrarse** *v* crawl, creep. **arrastre** *sm* dragging; haulage. **ser de mucho**

arrastre be highly influential.

arrebatar [arreβa'tar] *v* snatch; (*viento*) blow away; carry away; (*arrancar*) rip off; enrage; captivate. **arrebatarse** *v* get overcooked. **arrebatadamente** *adv* hurriedly. **arrebatadizo** *adj* short-tempered. **arrebatamiento** *sm* seizure; (*éxtasis*) rapture. **arrebato** *sm* (*furor*) rage; rapture.

arrebujarse [arreβu'xarse] *v* wrap oneself up.

arreciar [arre'θjar] *v* grow worse *or* stronger; increase in intensity.

arrecife [arre'θife] *sm* reef.

arreglar [arre'glar] *v* organize, regulate; (*poner en orden*) tidy; (*disponer*) arrange; (*componer*) mend; get ready; (*rectificar*) put right. **arreglarse** *v* be content; (*vestirse*) dress; (*ponerse de acuerdo*) agree; (*ir tirando*) get by. **arreglado** *adj* regulated; tidy; (*bien vestido*) smart; reasonable; (*conducta*) good. **arreglo** *sm* agreement; arrangement; repair.

arremeter [arreme'ter] *v* attack. **arremetida** *sf* assault.

*arrendar [arren'dar] *v* let; (*alquilar*) rent. **arrendador** *sm* landlord; (*que toma en alquiler*) tenant. **arrendadora** *sf* landlady; tenant. **arrendamiento** *sm* letting; rent.

arreo [ar'reo] *sm* adornment. **arreos** *sm pl* harness *sing*.

*arrepentirse [arrepen'tirse] *v* repent. **arrepentimiento** *sm* repentance.

arrestar [arres'tar] *v* arrest. **arrestarse** *v* rush boldly. **arrestado** *adj* imprisoned; (*audaz*) bold. **arresto** *sm* arrest; imprisonment. **arrestos** *sm pl* boldness *sing*.

arriar [ar'rjar] *v* (*vela, bandera*) strike, lower; (*cable*) slacken. **arriarse** *v* (*inundarse*) be flooded.

arriba [ar'riβa] *adv* up; upstairs; above. **de arriba abajo** from head to foot. **¡mano arriba!** hands up! **arriba** *prep* above.

arribar [arri'βar] *v* arrive. **arribar a** reach. **arribada** *sf* arrival.

arriendo [ar'rjendo] *sm* letting; renting; hiring.

arriesgar [arrjes'gar] *v* risk. **arriesgarse** *v* take a risk. **arriesgarse en** venture on. **arriesgado** *adj* dangerous.

arrimar [arri'mar] *v* (*acercar*) get near *or* close; put away. **arrimarse** *v* draw up; gather together; live together.

arrinconar [arrinko'nar] *v* corner; (*desechar*) discard; (*fam: vivir solo*) live in isolation. **arrinconado** *adj* (*olvidado*) forgotten; (*abandonado*) forsaken.

arroba [ar'roβa] *sf* weight of 11.5 kg.

arrobar [arro'βar] *v* entrance. **arrobado** *adj* in ecstasy. **arrobador** *adj* bewitching. **arrobamiento** *sm* also **arrobo** ecstasy, rapture.

arrodillarse [arroði'ʎarse] *v* kneel. **arrodillamiento** *sm* kneeling.

arrogancia [arro'ganθja] *sf* arrogance. **arrogante** *adj* arrogant.

arrojar [arro'xar] *v* throw, hurl; emit. **arrojarse** *v* hurl oneself. **arrojado** *adj* bold. **arrojo** *sm* boldness, daring.

arrollar [arro'ʎar] *v* (*enrollar*) roll up; (*llevarse*) sweep away; (*atropellar*) run over; (*aniquilar*) crush.

arropar [arro'par] *v* (*abrigarse*) wrap up; (*en una cama*) tuck up; cover.

arrostrar [arros'trar] *v* face up to, confront.

arroyo [ar'roʎo] *sm* stream; (*calle*) gutter.

arroz [ar'roθ] *sm* rice.

arrugar [arru'gar] *v* wrinkle; (*ropa*) crease. **arruga** *sf* wrinkle; crease.

arruinar [arrui'nar] *v* ruin; destroy; blight.

arrullar [arru'ʎar] *v* lull to sleep; (*paloma*) coo. **arrullo** *sm* cooing.

arrumbar [arrum'bar] *v* discard; (*fig*) ignore.

arrurruz [arrur'ruθ] *sm* arrowroot.

arsenal [arse'nal] *sm* arsenal; (*astillero*) shipyard.

arsénico [ar'seniko] *sm* arsenic.

arte ['arte] *sm, sf* art; (*hechura*) workmanship; (*astucia*) cunning. **no tener arte ni parte en** have nothing to do with. **por buenas o malas artes** by fair means or foul.

artefacto [arte'fakto] *sm* device, appliance.

artejo [ar'texo] *sm* knuckle.

arteria [ar'terja] *sf* artery.

artesano [arte'sano] *sm* craftsman. **artesanía** *sf* craftsmanship.

ártico ['artiko] *adj* arctic. **Ártico** *sm* the Arctic. **Círculo Polar Ártico** *sm* Arctic Circle.

articular [artiku'lar] *v* articulate, join together. **articulación** *sf* articulation.

artículo [ar'tikulo] *sm* article; item; (*diccionary*) entry. **artículos** *sm pl* goods *pl*. **artículos de aseo/de tocador**

sm pl toiletries.

artificial [artifi'θjal] *adj* artificial.

artificio [arti'fiθjo] *sm* device; skill; (*truco*) trick.

artillería [artiʎe'ria] *sf* artillery. **artillero** *sm* gunner.

artimaña [arti'maɲa] *sf* (*trampa*) trap; (*astucia*) trick.

artista [ar'tista] *s(m + f)* artist; actor, actress. **artístico** *adj* artistic.

artritis [ar'tritis] *sf* arthritis.

arzobispo [arθo'βispo] *sm* archbishop.

as [as] *sm* ace.

asa ['asa] *sf* handle.

asado [a'saðo] *sm* (*culin*) roast (meat). *adj* roast, roasted. **asador** *sm* spit. **asar** *v* roast; (*fam*) pester.

asalariado [asala'rjaðo], **-a** *sm, sf* wage-earner. *adj* paid, wage-earning.

asaltar [asal'tar] *v* assault, attack; (*banco*) raid; (*fig: idea*) cross one's mind. **asalto** *sm* attack; (*boxeo*) round.

asamblea [asam'blea] *sf* assembly, meeting.

asbesto [as'βesto] *sm* asbestos.

ascendencia [asθen'ðenθja] *sf* ancestry; origin; (*predominio*) influence.

***ascender** [asθen'der] *v* ascend; (*subir a*) add up; (*empleo*) be promoted; promote. **ascendiente** *sm* influence. **ascendientes** *sm pl* ancestors *pl*, ancestry *sing*. **ascensión** *sf* ascent; promotion. **ascensor** *sm* lift. **ascensorista** *s(m + f)* lift attendant.

asco ['asko] *sm* disgust, loathing. **dar asco** disgust. **hacer asco** turn one's nose up.

ascua ['askwa] *sf* ember. **estar sobre ascuas** be on tenterhooks.

asear [ase'ar] *v* clean; wash; decorate; (*arreglar*) tidy up. **asearse** *v* have a wash; spruce oneself up. **aseado** *adj* clean; tidy. **aseo** *sm* cleanliness; tidiness.

asechar [ase'tʃar] *v* ambush. **asecho** *sm* trap.

asediar [ase'ðjar] *v* besiege; (*fig*) bother. **asedio** *sm* siege.

asegurar [asegu'rar] *v* secure; safeguard; (*consolidar*) strengthen; (*confortar*) reassure; insure; assure. **asegurarse** *v* make sure. **asegurado** *adj* insured; assured. **asegurador** *sm* underwriter. **aseguramiento** *sm* securing; insurance; assurance.

asemejarse [aseme'xarse] *v* resemble, be alike.

***asentar** [asen'tar] *v* place; seat; (*cimientos*) lay; (*polvo*) settle; (*campamento*) pitch; (*establecer*) found; (*afilar*) sharpen; (*convenir*) agree; (*acalmar*) calm down; (*ir bien*) be suitable. **asentarse** *v* sit down; settle down.

***asentir** [asen'tir] *v* agree, assent. **asentimiento** *sm* assent.

asequible [ase'kiβle] *adj* reasonable; (*alcanzable*) obtainable; affable.

***aserrar** [aser'rar] *v* saw. **aserradero** *sm* sawmill. **aserrado** *adj* serrated. **aserrín** *sm* sawdust.

asertivo [aser'tiβo] *adj* assertive.

aserto [a'serto] *sm* assertion.

asesinar [asesi'nar] *v* murder; assassinate. **asesinato** *sm* murder; assassination. **asesino** *adj* murderous.

asesorar [aseso'rar] *v* advise; take advice. **asesoramiento** *sm* advising; opinion.

asestar [ases'tar] *v* (*arma*) aim; (*golpe*) strike. **asestadura** *sf* aiming.

asfalto [as'falto] *sm* asphalt. **asfaltado** *adj* covered with asphalt. **asfaltar** *v* asphalt.

asfixiar [asfik'sjar] *v* suffocate. **asfixia** *sf* suffocation.

así [a'si] *adv* so, thus, in this way, in that way. **así así** so-so. **así como** just as; as well as. **así que** as soon as; therefore. **así sea** so be it.

Asia ['asja] *sf* Asia. **asiático, -a** *s, adj* Asiatic, Asian.

asidero [asi'ðero] *sm* handle; (*fig*) excuse.

asiduo [a'siðwo] *adj* assiduous, hardworking; frequent.

asiento [a'sjento] *sm* seat, chair; place; (*de botellas, etc.*) base, bottom; (*tratado*) treaty; note; stability; (*sentido común*) common sense. **asientos** *sm pl* seat *sing*, bottom *sing*. **asiento de estómago** attack of indigestion. **tomar asiento** sit down.

asignar [asig'nar] *v* assign; attribute; allocate. **asignación** *sf* (*atribución*) allocation; (*cita*) appointment; (*subsidio*) grant; (*sueldo*) wages.

asignatura [asigna'tura] *sf* (*scholastic*) subject.

asilo [a'silo] *sm* asylum; refuge; home; shelter.

asimilar [asimi'lar] *v* assimilate; compare. **asimilarse** *v* be assimilated; (*asemejarse*) resemble. **asimilación** *sf* assimilation; comparison.

asimismo [asiˈmismo] *adv* in like manner, in the same way.

*asir [aˈsir] *v* grasp; grip; (*plantas*) take root. **asirse de** hang on to.

asistir [asisˈtir] *v* help; attend; be present; (*testigo*) witness. **assistencia** *sf* assistance; attendance; (*teatro, etc.*) audience; (*muchedumbre*) crowd; (*médica*) care; presence. **asistencias** *sf pl* maintenance *sing*. **asistenta** *sf* charlady; (*hotel*) chambermaid. **asistente** *sm* assistant; (*mil*) orderly; member of an audience.

asma [ˈasma] *sf* asthma.

asno [ˈasno] *sm* donkey, ass; (*fig*) idiot.

asociar [asoˈθjar] *v* associate; (*com*) enter into partnership. **asociarse** *v* associate oneself, share. **asociación** *sf* association; (*com*) partnership. **asociado** *sm* member.

asolar [asoˈlar] *v* destroy; (*arrasar*) flatten; (*calor*) parch. **asolador** *adj* devastating. **asolamiento** *sm* devastation.

asolear [asoleˈar] *v* put in the sun. **asolearse** *v* sunbathe.

asomar [asoˈmar] *v* show, appear. **asomarse** *v* lean out; (*fam: achisparse*) become tipsy. **asomada** *sf* brief appearance. **asomo** *sm* appearance; (*sombra*) shadow; (*indicio*) hint.

asombrar [asomˈbrar] *v* astonish; (*dar sombra*) shade; (*color*) darken. **asombrador** *adj* astonishing. **asombramiento** *sm* also **asombro** *sm* astonishment; (*fam: aparecido*) ghost. **asombroso** *adj* astonishing; stupefying.

aspecto [asˈpekto] *sm* aspect; appearance.

áspero [ˈaspero] *adj* (*tosco*) rough; (*agrio*) sour; (*persona*) gruff; (*voz*) harsh; (*clima*) hard; (*terreno*) rugged. **aspereza** *sf* roughness; sourness; harshness.

aspersión [asperˈsjon] *sf* sprinkling; spraying. **asperjar** *v* sprinkle.

aspirar [aspiˈrar] *v* inhale; (*fig*) aspire. **aspiración** *sf* inhalation; aspiration. **aspiradora** *sf* vacuum cleaner.

aspirina [aspiˈrina] *sf* aspirin.

asqueroso [askeˈroso] *adj* disgusting; vile; dirty; repulsive. **asquerosidad** *sf* filth; obscenity.

asta [ˈasta] *sf* (*arma*) spear; (*palo*) shaft; (*de la bandera*) staff; (*cuerno*) horn. **a media asta** at half mast.

asterisco [asteˈrisko] *sm* asterisk.

astil [asˈtil] *sm* handle; (*pluma*) quill.

astillar [astiˈʎar] *v* splinter; smash.

astillero [astiˈʎero] *sm* shipyard.

astringir [astrinˈxir] *v* constrict; (*sujetar*) blind. **astringente** *sm, adj* astringent.

astro [ˈastro] *sm* star.

astrología [astroloˈxia] *sf* astrology. **astrólogo** *sm* astrologer.

astronauta [astroˈnauta] *s(m + f)* astronaut. **astronáutica** *sf* astronautics.

astronomía [astronoˈmia] *sf* astronomy. **astronómico** *adj* astronomical. **astrónomo** *sm* astronomer.

astucia [asˈtuθja] *sf* (*habilidad*) cleverness; (*ingenio*) cunning. **astuto** *adj* clever; cunning.

asumir [asuˈmir] *v* assume.

asunto [aˈsunto] *sm* (*tema*) subject; (*cosa*) affair; (*negocio*) business; (*caso*) fact; (*cuestión*) matter. **asuntos a tratar** *pl* agenda *sing*. **asuntos exteriores** foreign affairs.

asustar [asusˈtar] *v* frighten.

atacar [ataˈkar] *v* attack; (*recalcar*) stuff; (*un botón*) fasten. **atacador, -a** *sm, sf* assailant. **ataque** *sm* attack; (*med*) fit. **ataque cardíaco** heart attack. **ataque fulminante** (*med*) stroke.

atado [aˈtaðo] *sm* bundle. *adj* shy.

atajar [ataˈxar] *v* intercept; (*detener*) check; (*impedir*) obstruct; (*tomar el camino más corto*) take a short cut. **atajador, -a** *sm, sf* interceptor. **atajo** *sm* short cut.

atar [aˈtar] *v* tie; lace; bind. **loco de atar** raving mad. **atarse** *v* become confused. **atador** *adj* binding. **atadura** *sf* binding; (*cuerda*) rope; (*fig: vínculo*) bond.

*atardecer [ataðeˈθer] *v* get late; grow dark. *sm* dusk.

atareado [atareˈaðo] *adj* very busy. **atarear** *v* load with work.

atascar [atasˈkar] *v* plug, stop (a leak); obstruct. **atascadero** *sm* mire; (*fig*) stumbling-block. **atasco** *sm* obstruction.

ataúd [ataˈuð] *sm* coffin.

ataviar [ataˈβjar] *v* dress up, adorn. **ataviarse en** or **de** dress oneself up in. **atavío** *sm* attire.

ateísmo [ateˈismo] *sm* atheism. **ateísta** *s(m + f)* atheist. **ateo, -a** *sm, sf* atheist.

atemorizar [atemoriˈθar] *v* frighten.

atención [atenˈθjon] *sf* attention; courtesy;

interest; (*cariño*) kindness. **prestar atención** pay attention. **atenciones** *sf pl* business affairs. **atento** *adj* attentive; kind; careful; special; (*consciente*) aware.

*atender [aten'der] *v* attend to; (*cuidar*) look after; serve; (*una máquina*) service; (*un aviso*) listen to.

*atenerse [ate'nerse] *v* abide, adhere; (*a una persona*) rely on.

atentar [aten'tar] *v* attempt; offend.

atenuar [ate'nwar] *v* attenuate; lessen; (*la luz*) dim. **atenuación** *sf* attenuation.

*aterrar¹ [ater'rar] *v* demolish.

aterrar² [ater'rar] *v* frighten, terrify. **aterrador** *adj* terrifying.

aterrizar [aterri'θar] *v* (*aviac*) land. **aterrizaje** *sm* landing.

aterrorizar [aterrori'θar] *v* terrify; terrorize. **aterrorizador** *adj* terrifying.

atesorar [ateso'rar] *v* hoard; (*fig*) possess. **atesoramiento** *sm* hoarding.

*atestar [ates'tar] *v* (*llenar*) stuff; (*un tren*) crowd, pack; (*desordenar*) clutter up. **atestado** *adj* full up; packed.

atestiguar [atesti'gwar] *v* testify.

ático ['atiko] *sm* attic.

atisbar [atis'βar] *v* (*mirar*) spy on; (*vislumbrar*) distinguish; (*vigilar*) watch for. **atisbo** *sm* spying; (*fig*) hint.

atizar [ati'θar] *v* (*el fuego*) poke, stir; (*fig*) stir up, incite. **atizador** *sm* poker.

Atlántico [at'lantiko] *sm* Atlantic. **atlántico** *adj* Atlantic.

atlas ['atlas] *sm* atlas.

atleta [at'leta] *s(m + f)* athlete. **atlético** *adj* athletic. **atletismo** *sm* athletics.

atmósfera [at'mosfera] *sf* atmosphere. **mala atmósfera** atmospherics *pl.* **atmosférico** *adj* atmospheric.

atolondrar [atolon'drar] *v* confuse; (*aturdir*) stun. **atolondrarse** *v* lose one's head. **atolondradamente** *adv* recklessly. **atolondramiento** *sm* recklessness; confusion.

atolladero [atoʎa'ðero] *sm* bog; (*fig*) impasse. **atollarse** *v* get bogged down.

átomo ['atomo] *sm* atom. **atómico** *adj* atomic.

atónito [a'tonito] *adj* astonished.

atontar [aton'tar] *v* (*golpe*) stun, daze; (*dejar sin habla*) dumbfound; (*embrutecer*) deaden; (*drogas*) make stupid. **atontado** *adj* stunned; bewildered; dumbfounded; stupid.

atormentar [atormen'tar] *v* torment; torture. **atormentador** *sm* tormentor; torturer.

atornillar [atorni'ʎar] *v* screw in/on/down.

atosigar [atosi'gar] *v* poison; (*molestar*) pester. **atosigarse** *v* toil. **atosigador** *adj* poisoning; pestering. **atosigamiento** *sm* poisoning; pestering.

atracar [atra'kar] *v* (*robar*) hold up; moor; (*fam*) gorge. **atracarse** *v* gorge oneself. **atracada** *sf* docking; (*pelea*) scuffle. **atracador** *sm* bandit; mugger.

atracción [atrak'θjon] *sf* attraction. **atracciones** *sf pl* entertainment *sing.* **atractivo** *adj* attractive.

*atraer [atra'er] *v* attract. **atracción** *sf* attraction. **atracciones** *sf pl* entertainment *sing.*

atrancar [atran'kar] *v* (*puerta*) bar; block up. **atrancarse** *v* become blocked/stuck/jammed.

atrapar [atra'par] *v* catch, trap.

atrás [a'tras] *adv* behind; in the rear; back; backwards; previously. **¡atrás!** get back!

atrasado *adj* late; behind; in arrears; (*reloj*) slow; backward; in debt. **atrasar** *v* (*diferir*) postpone; put back; slow down; lose (time). **atrasarse** lag behind; be late; be slow. **atraso** *sm* delay; backwardness; slowness.

*atravesar [atraβe'sar] *v* (*poner*) place or put across; (*traspasar*) pierce; penetrate; cross; (*apostar*) bet. **atravesarse** *v* stand or lie across; get stuck; interfere; quarrel. **atravesado** *adj* lying across; pierced; (*fig*) wicked.

atreverse [atre'βerse] *v* dare; venture; be insolent. **atrevido, -a** *sm, sf* daredevil; cheeky person. **atrevimiento** *sm* boldness; effrontery.

*atribuir [atriβu'ir] *v* attribute. **atribución** *sf* attribution. **atributo** *sm* attribute.

atrocidad [atroθi'ðað] *sf* atrocity. **atroz** *adj* atrocious. **atrozmente** *adv* atrociously.

atrofia [a'trofja] *sf* atrophy. **atrofiar** *v* atrophy.

atropellar [atrope'ʎar] *v* knock down; (*pisotear*) trample on; (*ultrajar*) offend; (*agraviar*) bully; (*trabajo*) rush. **atropellar por** ignore. **atropellarse** *v* hurry. **atropelladamente** *adv* hurriedly. **atropellado**

adj hasty. **atropellador** *adj* precipitate.
atropello *sm* jostling, pushing; accident; outrage.

atún [a'tun] *sm* tunny, tuna.

aturdir [atur'ðir] *v* stun, daze; (*marear*) make dizzy; bewilder. **aturdido** *adj* dazed; (*imprudente*) thoughtless. **aturdidor** *adj* deafening. **aturdimiento** *sm* daze; giddiness; amazement.

aturrullar [aturru'ʎar] *v* confuse, bewilder. **aturrullarse** *v* become confused; panic.

atusar [atu'sar] *v* (*cortar*) trim; (*alisar*) smooth; (*acariciar*) stroke. **atusarse** *v* spruce oneself up.

audacia [au'ðaθja] *sf* audacity. **audaz** *adj* audacious.

audible [au'ðiβle] *adj* audible. **audibilidad** *sf* audibility.

audición [auði'θjon] *sf* hearing; (*prueba*) audition.

audiencia [au'ðjenθja] *sf* audience; hearing; (*tribunal*) court.

audífono [au'ðifono] *sm* hearing aid.

audiovisual [auðjoβi'swal] *adj* audiovisual.

auge ['auxe] *sm* peak; progress.

augurar [augu'rar] *v* predict. **augurio** *sm* augury, omen.

aula ['aula] *sf* lecture hall; (*escuela*) classroom. **aula magna** assembly hall.

aullar [au'ʎar] *v* howl. **aullido** *sm* howl.

aumentar [aumen'tar] *v* increase; (*sueldo*) raise; magnify; (*mejorar*) get better; (*empeorar*) get worse. **aumento** *sm* increase; rise; magnification.

aun [a'un] *adv* even. **aun así** even so. **aun cuando** although. **aún** *adv* still, yet. **aún no** not yet.

aunque [a'unke] *conj* even though, although.

áureo ['aureo] *adj* gold(en).

aureola [aure'ola] *sf* halo.

auricular [auriku'lar] *adj* of the ear, aural. *sm* (*dedo*) little finger; (*teléfono*) telephone receiver. **auriculares** *sm pl* headphones *pl*.

aurora [au'rora] *sf* dawn.

ausencia [au'senθja] *sf* absence. **ausente** *adj* absent; missing.

auspicio [aus'piθjo] *sm* auspice, omen; (*patrocinio*) patronage.

austero [aus'tero] *adj* austere. **austeridad** *sf* austerity.

austral [aus'tral] *adj* southern.

Australia [aus'tralja] *sf* Australia. **australiano, -a** *s, adj* Australian.

Austria ['austrja] *sf* Austria. **austriaco, -a** *s, adj* Austrian.

auténtico [au'tentiko] *adj* authentic. **autenticar** *v* authenticate. **autenticidad** *sf* authenticity.

autismo [au'tismo] *sm* autism. **autístico** *adj* autistic.

auto¹ ['auto] *sm* (*fam*) car. **auto de choque** dodgem car.

auto² *sm* (*jur*) sentence; (*de un pleito*) judgment. **autos** *sm pl* proceedings *pl*.

autobiografía [autoβjogra'fia] *sf* autobiography. **autobiográfico** *adj* autobiographical.

autobús [auto'βus] *sm* bus.

autocar [auto'kar] *sm* motor coach.

autocaravana *sf* camper (van).

autodominio [autoðo'minjo] *sm* self-control.

autoescuela [autoes'kwela] *sf* driving school.

autoexpresión [autoekspre'sjon] *sf* self-expression.

autógrafo [au'tografo] *sm, adj* autograph.

autómata [au'tomata] *sm* robot.

automático [auto'matiko] *adj* automatic. **automatización** *sf* automation.

automóvil [auto'moβil] *sm* motorcar. **automovilista** *s(m + f)* motorist.

autonomía [autono'mia] *sf* autonomy. **autónomo** *adj* autonomous.

autopista [auto'pista] *sf* motorway.

autopsia [au'topsja] *sf* autopsy, postmortem.

autor [au'tor], **-a** *sm, sf* author; creator.

autorizar [autori'θar] *v* authorize; approve. **autoridad** *sf* authority. **autoritario** *adj* authoritarian. **autorización** *sf* authorization. **autorizado** *adj* authorized, official; (*seguro*) reliable.

autorretrato [autorre'trato] *sm* self-portrait.

autoservicio [autoser'βiθjo] *sm* self-service restaurant; supermarket.

autostop [auto'stop] *sm* hitchhiking. **hacer el autostop** hitchhike. **autostopista** *s(m + f)* hitchhiker.

auxiliar [auksi'ljar] *v* help; attend. *sm, adj* assistant; auxiliary.

avalancha [aβa'lantʃa] *sf* avalanche.

avalorar [aβalo'rar] *v* (*realzar*) enhance; (*fig*) inspire.

avaluar [aβalu'ar] *v* value, appraise.

avanzar [aβan'θar] *v* advance, progress. **avance** *sm* advance; (*com*) balance. **avanzada** *sf* (*mil*) outpost.

avaricia [aβa'riθja] *sf* avarice. **avaricioso** *adj* greedy; miserly. **avaro** *adj* miserly, mean.

avasallar [aβasa'ʎar] *v* subjugate; dominate. **avasallarse** *v* submit.

ave ['aβe] *sf* bird. **aves de corral** *pl* poultry *sing*.

avecinarse [aβeθi'narse] *v* approach.

avellana [aβe'ʎana] *sf* hazelnut.

avena [a'βena] *sf* sing oats *pl*.

avenencia [aβe'nenθja] *sf* agreement; (*arreglo*) compromise.

avenida [aβe'niða] *sf* avenue.

***avenir** [aβe'nir] *v* reconcile, bring together; (*suceder*) happen. **avenirse** *v* agree; adapt; correspond to. **avenimiento** *sm* agreement.

aventajar [aβenta'xar] *v* lead; come in front of; (*sobresalir*) surpass; prefer. **aventajado** *adj* outstanding; favourable.

aventura [aβen'tura] *sf* adventure; (*riesgo*) risk; (*amor*) affair. **aventurado** *adj* risky. **aventurar** *v* risk; venture. **aventurero** *adj* adventurous.

***avergonzar** [aβergon'θar] *v* shame; (*poner en un apuro*) embarrass. **avergonzarse** *v* be ashamed. **avergonzado** *adj* ashamed; embarrassed.

avería¹ [aβe'ria] *sf* aviary.

avería² [aβe'ria] *sf* (*coche*) breakdown; (*daño*) damage. **averiar** *v* damage; break down.

averiguar [aβeri'gwar] *v* investigate; (*examinar*) verify. **averiguación** *sf* investigation; verification. **averiguador** *adj* investigating; inquiring.

aversión [aβer'sjon] *sf* aversion.

avestruz [aβes'truθ] *sm* ostrich.

aviación [aβja'θjon] *sf* aviation; air force. **aviador, -a** *sm, sf* aviator.

ávido ['aβiðo] *adj* avid; (*con ganas*) eager. **avidez** *sf* avidity; eagerness.

avinagrar [aβina'grar] *v* sour, make bitter. **avinagrado** *adj* sour; (*fam*) peevish.

avión¹ [a'βjon] *sm* aircraft. **avión a reacción** jet plane. **por avión** by airmail.

avión² *sm* swift; martin.

avisar [aβi'sar] *v* inform; advise; admonish. **avisado** *adj* prudent. **mal avisado** rash. **avisador, -a** *sm, sf* adviser; informer; messenger. **aviso** *sm* notice; announcement; advice; (*advertencia*) warning; prudence.

avispa [a'βispa] *sf* wasp.

avivar [aβi'βar] *v* enliven; (*acelerar*) hasten; revive. **avivador** *adj* hastening; enlivening.

ay ['ai] *interj* alas!

aya ['aja] *sf* governess.

ayer [a'jer] *adv* yesterday; (*fig*) formerly, lately. *sm* the recent past. **de ayer acá** since yesterday.

ayo ['ajo] *sm* tutor.

ayudar [aju'ðar] *v* help. **ayudarse** *v* help each other; make use of. **ayuda** *sf* help. **ayudante, -a** *sm, sf* assistant. **ayudante personal** *s(m+f)* personal assistant.

ayunar [aju'nar] *v* fast. **ayuno** *sm* fast, fasting.

ayuntamiento [ajunta'mjento] *sm* union; joint; (*cópula*) copulation; (*institución*) town council; (*edificio*) town hall.

azada [a'θaða] *sf* hoe; spade.

azafata [aθa'fata] *sf* air hostess.

azafrán [aθa'fran] *sm* saffron.

azahar [aθa'ar] *sm* orange blossom; lemon blossom.

azar [a'θar] *sm* chance, accident; (*desgracia*) misfortune. **al azar** at random.

azogue [a'θoge] *sm* mercury.

azorar [aθo'rar] *v* upset, embarrass. **azorarse** *v* become flustered. **azoramiento** *sm* embarrassment; (*miedo*) fear.

azotar [aθo'tar] *v* beat; (*a un niño*) spank; (*látigo*) whip. **azote** *sm* whip; spanking; (*fig: verdugo*) scourge.

azotea [aθo'tea] *sf* flat roof.

azúcar [a'θukar] *sm or sf* sugar. **azúcar en terrón** lump sugar. **azúcar extra fina** castor sugar. **azúcar morena** brown sugar. **azucarado** *adj* sugary. **azucarero, -a** *sm, sf* sugar bowl.

azucena [aθu'θena] *sf* white lily.

azufre [a'θufre] *sm* sulphur.

azul [a'θul] *sm, adj* blue. **azul marino** navy blue. **azulado** *adj* blue, bluish.

azulejo [aθu'lexo] *sm* tile.

azuzar [aθu'θar] *v* (*fig*) incite; urge; cause trouble. **azuzador, -a** *sm, sf* trouble-maker.

B

baba ['baβa] *sf* saliva, spit. **babero** *sm* bib.

Babia ['baβja] *sf* estar en Babia have one's head in the clouds.

babor [ba'βor] *sm* (*mar*) port side.

babosa [ba'βosa] *sf* slug.

bacalao [baka'lao] *sm* cod.

bacía [ba'θia] *sf* (*de barbero*) shaving-bowl; (*recipiente*) metal basin.

bacteria [bak'teria] *sf* germ. **bacterias** *sf pl* bacteria *pl*.

bache ['batʃe] *sm* pothole.

bachiller [batʃi'ʎer] *s*(*m + f*) holder of a school-leaving certificate; (*universidad*) holder of a bachelor's degree. **bachillerato** *sm* school-leaving certificate; bachelor's degree.

bagaje [ba'gaxe] *sm* (*mil*) baggage; (*animal*) beast of burden.

bahía [ba'ia] *sf* bay.

bailar [bai'lar] *v* dance. **bailarín, -ina** *sm, sf* ballet dancer. **baile** *sm* dancing; dance; ball. **baile de disfraces** or **trajes** fancy-dress ball.

bajamar [baxa'mar] *sf* low tide.

bajar [ba'xar] *v* get down; lower; let down; take or bring down; (*computadora*) download. **bajar de categoría** *v* demote. **baja** *sf* fall, drop. **bajada** *sf* (*caída*) drop; (*pendiente*) slope; (*descendimiento*) descent.

bajo ['baxo] *adj* (*estatura*) short; low; lowered; (*sonido*) soft; (*conducta*) disgraceful. *adv* low; below; quietly, softly. **bajo en calorías** *adj* low-fat. *prep* under. **bajeza** *sf* base act; lowness.

bajón [ba'xon] *sm* (*música*) bassoon; (*bajada*) fall.

bala ['bala] *sf* (*proyectil*) bullet; (*algodón*) bale. **balazo** *sm* (*tiro*) shot; (*herida*) wound.

balada [ba'laða] *sf* ballad.

baladí [bala'ði] *adj* trivial, unimportant.

baladrón [bala'ðron], **-ona** *sm, sf* boaster, braggart. *adj* boastful.

balancear [balanθe'ar] *v* balance; (*barco*)

roll; (*vacilar*) hesitate. **balancearse** *v* roll; (*en un columpio*) swing. **balance** *sm* (*com*) balance sheet; (*inventario*) stocktaking. **balanceo** *sm* balancing; (*oscilación*) swaying. **balanza** *sf* scales *pl*.

balar [ba'lar] *v* bleat.

balaustrada [balau'straða] *sf* balustrade.

balbucear [balβuθe'ar] *v* stammer, stutter. **balbuceo** *sm* stammer.

balcón [bal'kon] *sm* balcony.

baldar [bal'ðar] *v* cripple; (*naipes*) trump; (*molestar*) inconvenience. **baldarse** *v* wear oneself out. **baldado, -a** *sm, sf* cripple. **baldadura** *sf* infirmity.

balde¹ ['balðe] *sm* bucket.

balde² *adv* de balde free of charge. **en balde** in vain.

baldío [bal'ðio] *sm* wasteland. *adj* uncultivated; (*fig*) useless.

baldón [bal'ðon] *sm* (*afrenta*) affront; (*deshonra*) disgrace.

baldosa [bal'ðosa] *sf* paving tile.

baliza [ba'liθa] *sf* bollard.

balneario [balne'arjo] *sm* spa.

balón [ba'lon] *sm* ball, football; (*com*) bale. **baloncesto** *sm* basketball. **balonvolea** *sm* volleyball.

balsa¹ ['balsa] *sf* balsa.

balsa² *sf* raft.

balsa³ *sf* (*agua*) pond.

bálsamo ['balsamo] *sm* balsam; (*fig*) balm.

Báltico ['baltiko] *sm* Baltic Sea. **báltico** *adj* Baltic.

ballena [ba'ʎena] *sf* whale.

ballesta [ba'ʎesta] *sf* crossbow. **ballestero** *sm* archer.

ballet [ba'le] *sm* ballet.

bambolear [bambole'ar] *v* sway.

bambolla [bam'boʎa] *sf* show, ostentation. **darse bambolla** show off.

bambú [bam'bu] *sm* bamboo.

banana [ba'nana] *sf* banana. **banano** *sm* banana tree.

banasta [ba'nasta] *sf* large basket.

banca ['banka] *sf* (*asiento*) bench; (*com*) banking.

bancarrota [bankar'rota] *sf* bankruptcy. **hacer bancarrota** go bankrupt.

banco ['banko] *sm* bench; (*iglesia*) pew; (*colegio*) desk; (*com*) bank.

banda ['banda] *sf* group; (*pandilla*) gang;

(faja) sash; *(cinta)* ribbon; *(lado)* side; *(orilla)* river bank. **bandada** *sf* flock.

bandeja [ban'dexa] *sf* tray.

bandera [ban'dera] *sf* flag, banner. **a banderas desplegadas** openly. **banderilla** *sf* bullfighter's dart. **banderillero** *sm* one who thrusts banderillas into the bull.

bandido [ban'diðo] *sm* bandit.

bando ['bando] *sm* proclamation; *(facción)* faction; party; *(pez)* shoal (of fish).

bandolero [bando'lero], **-a** *sm*, *sf* bandit.

banjo ['banxo] *sm* banjo.

banquete [ban'kete] *sm* banquet, feast.

bañar [ba'ɲar] *v* bathe. **bañarse** *v (en la bañera)* have a bath; *(en el mar)* bathe. **bañera** *sf* bathtub. **bañero** *sm* lifeguard. **bañista** *s(m + f)* bather. **baño** *sm* bath; *(en el agua)* dip, swim; *(cubierta)* coating. **cuarto de baño** bathroom.

baquetear [bakete'ar] *v (incomodar)* bother; *(maltratar)* treat harshly. **baquetazo** *sm* blow, knock. **baqueteo** *sm (traqueteo)* jolting; *(molestia)* bother.

bar [bar] *sm* bar.

baraja [ba'raxa] *sf* pack of cards. **barajar** *v* shuffle.

barandilla [baran'diʎa] *sf* rail, railing.

barato [ba'rato] *adj* cheap. **dar de barato** take for granted. **baratear** *v* undersell. **baratija** *sf* trinket. **baratijas** *sf pl* junk *sing.* **baratura** *sf* cheapness.

baraúnda [bara'unda] *sf (alboroto)* uproar; *(confusión)* chaos.

barba ['barβa] *sf* beard. **barba a barba** face to face. **barbado** *adj* bearded. **barbería** *sf* barber's shop. **barbero** *sm* barber. **barbudo** *adj* having a full beard.

bárbaro ['barβaro], **-a** *sm*, *sf* barbarian; *(fig)* lout. *adj* barbarous, barbaric; *(bruto)* rough; *(fam)* fantastic. **barbaridad** *sf* barbarity; *(ultraje)* outrage. **¡qué barbaridad!** fancy that! how terrible!

barbecho [bar'βetʃo] *sm* fallow land. **barbechar** *v* leave fallow.

barbilla [bar'βiʎa] *sf* chin.

barca ['barka] *sf* boat. **barca de pasaje** ferry boat.

barco ['barko] *sm* ship, boat. **ir en barco** go by boat.

barnizar [barni'θar] *v (madera)* varnish; *(cerámica)* glaze. **barniz** *sm* varnish; glaze.

barómetro [ba'rometro] *sm* barometer.

barométrico *adj* barometric.

barón [ba'ron] *sm* baron. **baronesa** *sf* baroness. **baronet** *sm* baronet.

barquillo [bar'kiʎo] *sm* thin sweet wafer.

barra ['barra] *sf (metal, madera, chocolate, jabón, etc.)* bar; *(vara)* rod; *(joya)* pin; *(palanca)* lever; *(pan)* loaf; *(jur)* dock; *(mar)* tiller.

barraca [bar'raka] *sf* cabin, hut; *(feria)* stall.

barranco [bar'ranko] *sm* ravine, gully; *(fig)* obstacle.

barrenar [barre'nar] *v* drill, bore; *(leyes)* violate; *(una empresa)* foil. **barrena** *sf* drill.

barrer [bar'rer] *v* sweep.

barrera [bar'rera] *sf* barrier; obstacle; gate. **barrera de peaje** tollgate.

barricada [barri'kada] *sf* barricade.

barriga [bar'riga] *sf* belly.

barril [bar'ril] *sm* barrel.

barrio ['barrjo] *sm* district, quarter.

barro ['barro] *sm* mud. **barroso** *adj* muddy.

barroco [bar'roko] *sm* baroque period. *adj* baroque.

barruntar [barrun'tar] *v* have a feeling; *(suponer)* suppose. **barruntador** *adj* prophetic. **barrunte** *or* **barrunto** *sm* feeling; supposition; *(indicio)* sign.

bártulos ['bartulos] *sm pl* belongings, odds and ends. **liar los bártulos** pack one's bags.

barullo [ba'ruʎo] *sm* confusion; *(alboroto)* row. **a barullo** galore.

basar [ba'sar] *v* found; base. **basarse en** be based on. **base** *sf* base, basis. **base de datos** *sf* database. **a base de** by. **alimento base** staple food. **básico** *adj* basic, essential.

bastante [bas'tante] *adj* enough. *adv* enough, sufficiently; *(algo)* rather, fairly. **bastar** *v* suffice. **¡basta!** that's enough!

bastardo [bas'tardo], **-a** *s*, *adj* bastard. **bastardear** *v* degenerate. **bastardilla** *sf* italics *pl.* **bastardillo** *adj* italic.

bastidor [basti'ðor] *sm* frame; *(ventana)* sash. **entre bastidores** behind the scenes.

basto¹ ['basto] *adj* coarse, crude.

basto² *sm (arnés)* pack-saddle.

basto³ *sm (naipes)* ace of clubs. **bastos** *sm pl* clubs.

bastón [bas'ton] *sm* cane, stick.

basura [ba'sura] *sf* rubbish, litter. **basurero**

sm dustman.

bata ['bata] *sm* (*de cama*) dressing gown; (*de médico, etc.*) overall.

batalla [ba'taʎa] *sf* battle. **campo de batalla** battlefield.

batata [ba'tata] *sf* sweet potato.

batea [ba'tea] *sf* (*barco*) punt; (*bandeja*) tray; (*vagón*) open wagon.

batería [bate'ria] *sf* battery; (*teatro*) footlights; (*música*) percussion. **batería de cocina** kitchen utensils *pl*.

batir [ba'tir] *v* (*huevos*) beat; (*las manos*) clap; (*vencer*) defeat; (*derribar*) knock down; (*culin*) whisk. **batirse** *v* flight. **batido** *sm* (*leche*) milk shake; (*culin*) batter. **batidor** *sm* whisk.

batuta [ba'tuta] *sf* (*música*) baton. **llevar la batuta** rule the roost.

baúl [ba'ul] *sm* trunk.

bautizar [bauti'θar] *v* baptize, christen; (*fam: vino, etc.*) water down. **bautismo** *sm* baptism, christening. **bautista** *sm* Baptist.

baya ['baja] *sf* berry.

bayeta [ba'jeta] *sf* baize; floorcloth; rag.

bayoneta [bajo'neta] *sf* bayonet.

baza ['baθa] *sf* (*naipes*) trick. **meter baza** intervene.

bazar [ba'θar] *sm* bazaar.

bazo ['baθo] *sm* spleen. *adj* brownish yellow.

beato [be'ato] *adj* pious; blessed; (*fam*) sanctimonious.

beber [be'βer] *v* drink. **beberse** *v* drink up. **bebida** *sf* drink.

beca ['beka] *sf* grant; scholarship.

becerro [be'θerro] *sm* yearling calf.

bedel [be'ðel] *sm* porter; beadle.

befar [be'far] *v* mock, taunt. **befa** *sf* jeer, taunt.

béisbol ['beisβol] *sm* baseball.

Belén [be'len] *s* Bethlehem. **belén** *sm* Nativity scene; (*fam*) bedlam.

Bélgica ['belxika] *sf* Belgium. **belga** *s*(*m* + *f*), *adj* Belgian.

bélico ['beliko] *adj* warlike. **belicosidad** *sf* bellicosity. **belicoso** *adj* bellicose.

beligerante [belixe'rante] *s*(*m* + *f*), *adj* belligerent. **beligerancia** *sf* belligerence.

bellaco [be'ʎako] *-a sm, sf* rogue. *adj* cunning; wicked.

belleza [be'ʎeθa] *sf* beauty. **bellísimo** *adj* gorgeous. **bello** *adj* beautiful; noble.

bellota [be'ʎota] *sf* acorn.

bemol [be'mol] *sm, adj* (*música*) flat.

bencina [ben'θina] *sf* benzine.

***bendecir** [bende'θir] *v* bless; praise. **bendición** *sf* benediction; grace. **bendito** *adj* blessed; saintly; (*fam*) wretched.

beneficiar [benefi'θjar] *v* benefit; profit. **benefactor, -a** *sm, sf also* **beneficiador, -a** benefactor. **beneficencia** *sf* charity; welfare. **beneficiado, -a** *sm, sf also* **beneficiario, -a** beneficiary. **beneficio** *sm* benefit; gain. **beneficioso** *adj* beneficial.

benemérito [bene'merito] *adj* worthy, well-deserving.

beneplácito [bene'plaθito] *sm* consent, approval.

benevolencia [benevo'lenθja] *sf* benevolence. **benevolente** *or* **benévolo** *adj* benevolent.

benignidad [benigni'ðað] *sf* kindness; (*clima*) mildness. **benigno** *adj* kind; mild.

beodo [be'oðo], **-a** *sm, sf* drunkard. *adj* drunk.

berberecho [berβe'retʃo] *sm* cockle.

berenjena [beren'xena] *sf* aubergine.

bermejo [ber'mexo] *adj* vermilion; (*cabellos*) ginger.

bermellón [berme'ʎon] *sm* vermilion.

berrear [berre'ar] *v* bellow; yell. **berrearse** *v* (*fam*) spill the beans. **berrido** *sm* bellow; yell.

berrinche [ber'rintʃe] *sm* (*fam*) tantrum.

berro ['berro] *sm* watercress.

berza ['berθa] *sf* cabbage.

besar [be'sar] *v* kiss. **beso** *sm* kiss.

bestia ['bestja] *sf* beast, animal. *sm, sf* (*persona*) beast; idiot. **bestial** *adj* bestial; beastly; (*fam*) smashing; enormous. **bestialidad** *sf* bestiality; beastliness.

best-seller [best'seler] *sm* bestseller.

betún [be'tun] *sm* shoe polish; bitumen.

biblia ['biβlja] *sf* Bible. **bíblico** *adj* biblical.

bibliografía [biβliogra'fia] *sf* bibliography. **bibliográfico** *adj* bibliographic(al). **bibliógrafo, -a** *sm, sf* bibliographer.

biblioteca [biβlio'teka] *sf* library. **bibliotecario, -a** *sm, sf* librarian.

bíceps ['biθeps] *sm invar* biceps.

bicicleta [biθi'kleta] *sf* bicycle. **bicicleta de montaña** *sf* mountain bike.

bicho ['bitʃo] *sm* small animal; insect; (*fam*) odd character; (*fam*) ugly person.

bieldo ['bjelðo] *sm* pitchfork.

Bielorrusia [bjelo'rrusja] *sm* Belarus.

bien [bjen] *adv* well; right; properly; very; fully; easily; gladly. **ahora bien** nevertheless. **o bien** or else. **¿y bien?** so what? *sm* good; welfare; advantage: gain; darling. **bien que** *conj also* **si bien** although. **no bien** no sooner. **bienes** *sm pl* property *sing*, riches. **bienes inmuebles** real estate *sing*.

bienal [bje'nal] *sf, adj* biennial.

bienaventurado [bjenaβentu'raðo] *adj* happy; blessed; (*fig*) naïve.

bienestar [bjenes'tar] *sm* well-being; comfort.

bienhechor [bjene'tʃor], **-a** *sm, sf* benefactor.

bienio ['bjenjo] *sm* period of two years.

bienvenida [bjenβe'niða] *sf* welcome. **dar la bienvenida a** welcome.

biftec [bif'tek] *sm* steak.

bifurcarse [bifur'karse] *v* fork; branch off. **bifurcación** *sf* fork; junction.

bigamia [bi'gamja] *sf* bigamy. **bígamo, -a** *sm, sf* bigamist.

bigote [bi'gote] *sm* moustache.

bilingüe [bi'lingwe] *adj* bilingual.

bilis ['bilis] *sf* bile; (*fig*) bad temper.

billar [bi'ʎar] *sm* billiards. **billar ruso** snooker.

billete [bi'ʎete] *sm* ticket; (*dinero*) banknote; (*carta*) letter. **billete de abono** season ticket. **billete de ida** single ticket. **billete de ida y vuelta** return ticket. **billete de lista de espera** standby ticket. **sacar un billete** buy a ticket.

billón [bi'ʎon] *sm* billion.

binóculo [bi'nokulo] *sm* binoculars *pl*.

biodegradable [bjoðegra'ðaβle] *adj* biodegradable.

biografía [biogra'fia] *sf* biography. **biográfico** *adj* biographical. **biógrafo, -a** *sm, sf* biographer.

biología [biolo'xia] *sf* biology. **biológico** *adj* biological. **biólogo** *sm* biologist.

biombo ['bjombo] *sm* folding screen.

bióxido [bi'oksiðo] *sm* dioxide. **bióxido de carbono** carbon dioxide.

biplano [bi'plano] *sm* biplane.

birlar [bir'lar] *v* (*fam: robar*) pinch. swipe;

(*fam: matar*) bump off.

bisabuela [bisa'βwela] *sf* great-grandmother. **bisabuelo** great-grandfather.

bisagra [bi'sagra] *sf* hinge.

bisiesto [bi'sjesto] *adj* **año bisiesto** leap year.

bisoño [bi'soɲo], **-a** *sm, sf* greenhorn, novice; (*mil*) rookie.

bizarría [biθar'ria] *sf* (*valor*) bravery; generosity.

bizcar [biθ'kar] *v* squint. **bizco** *adj* crosseyed. **dejar bizco** (*fam*) dumbfound.

bizcocho [biθ'kotʃo] *sm* sponge cake. **bizcocho borracho** rum baba.

bizma ['biθma] *sf* poultice.

blanco ['blanko], **-a** *adj* white; blank; (*fam*) cowardly. *sm, sf* white man/woman; white colour; *sm* (*de tiro*) target. **blanca** *sf* (*música*) minim. **no tener blanca** be completely broke. **blancura** *sf* whiteness. **dar en el blanco** be on target. **quedarse en blanco** be disappointed. **blanquear** *v* whiten; whitewash. **blanquecer** *v* whitewash; bleach.

blandir [blan'dir] *v* flourish, brandish.

blando ['blando] *adj* soft; mild; gentle. *adv* softly; gently. **blandura** *sf* softness; tenderness; (*carácter*) weakness.

blasfemar [blasfe'mar] *v* blaspheme; (*fig*) curse. **blasfemia** *sf* blasphemy; curse. **blasfemo, -a** *sm, sf* blasphemer.

blasón [bla'son] *sm* heraldry; (*escudo*) coat of arms. **hacer blasón de** boast about.

blindaje [blin'daxe] *sm* armour. **blindado** *adj* armoured; armour-plated.

bloquear [bloke'ar] *v* block; obstruct; (*mil*) blockade. **bloque** *sm* block; bloc. **bloqueo** *sm* blockade.

blusa ['blusa] *sf* blouse; (*guardapolvo*) overall.

boa ['boa] *sf* boa constrictor.

boato [bo'ato] *sm* pomp; show.

bobada [bo'baða] *sf* nonsense; foolish thing. **bobería** *sf* stupidity. **bobo, -a** *sm, sf* fool, idiot.

bobina [bo'bina] *sf* reel, spool.

boca ['boka] *sf* mouth; opening. **a boca de jarro** point-blank. **a boca de noche** at dusk. **boca abajo/arriba** face down/up. **¡punto en boca!** mum's the word!

bocacalle [boka'kaʎe] *sf* intersection.

bocadillo [boka'ðiʎo] *sm* sandwich; snack.

bocado *sm* mouthful; bite.

boceto [bo'θeto] *sm* (*dibujo*) sketch; (*escrito*) draft.

bocina [bo'θina] *sf* trumpet; (*aut*) horn, hooter.

bochorno [bo'tʃorno] *sm* sultry weather; (*vergüenza*) embarrassment; (*mareo*) giddiness. **sufrir un bochorno** feel embarrassed. **bochornoso** *adj* sultry; thundery; embarrassing.

boda ['boða] *sf* wedding, marriage.

bodega [bo'ðega] *sf* wine cellar; wine shop; bar.

bofetada [bofe'taða] *sf* slap; blow.

boga ['boga] *sf* (*mar*) rowing; (*fig*) vogue. **estar en boga** be in fashion. **bogador, -a** *sm*, *sf* rower.

bohemio [bo'emjo], **-a** *s*, *adj* Bohemian; (*gitano*) gipsy.

boicotear [boikote'ar] *v* boycott. **boicot** or **boicoteo** *sm* boycott.

boina ['boina] *sf* beret.

bola ['bola] *sf* ball; (*canica*) marble; (*betún*) shoe polish; (*del mundo*) globe; (*fig*) fib. **bola de naftalina** mothball. **bolear** *v* fib; throw.

boleta [bo'leta] *sf* ticket; pass; (*vale*) voucher; (*votación*) ballot paper.

boleto [bo'leto] *sm* lottery ticket; betting slip; (*fam*) fib. **boletín** *sm* bulletin. **boletín de noticias** news bulletin. **boletín de precios** price list. **boletín meteorológico** weather forecast.

bolígrafo [bo'ligrafo] *sm* ballpoint pen; Biro.

Bolivia [bo'liβja] *sf* Bolivia. **boliviano, -a** *s*, *adj* Bolivian.

bollo ['boʎo] *sm* bun, roll, small loaf.

bolsa ['bolsa] *sf* bag; purse. **bolsillo** *sm* pocket.

bomba ['bomba] *sf* pump, bomb. **bomba de gasolina** petrol pump.

bombardear [bombarðe'ar] *v* bombard.

bombilla [bom'biʎa] *sf* (*elec*) light bulb; (*tecn*) small pump; glass tube.

bombo ['bombo] *sm* big drum; great praise. *adj* surprised.

bombón [bom'bon] *sm* sweet, chocolate.

bonachón [bona'tʃon] *adj* (*fam*) genial.

bondad [bon'dað] *sf* goodness; kindness. **tenga la bondad de ...** please .... **bondadoso** *adj* warm-hearted; good.

bonete [bo'nete] *sm* academic cap. **gran bonete** important person.

bonito [bo'nito] *adj* pretty, nice, graceful.

bono ['bono] *sm* voucher; certificate; bond. **bono postal** money-order.

boquear [boke'ar] *v* gasp; utter; be dying. **boqueada** *sf* gasp.

boquerón [boke'ron] *sm* large opening; anchovy; whitebait. **boquete** *sm* small hole; gap.

boquiabierto [bokja'βjerto] *adj* openmouthed; gaping.

boquilla [bo'kiʎa] *sf* mouthpiece; nozzle; pipe stem.

borboll(e)ar [borβo'ʎar] *v* bubble. **borbolleo** *sm* bubbling. **borbollón** *sm* bubble.

borbotar [borβo'tar] *v* bubble; boil; gush. **borbotón** *sm* bubbling; boiling.

bordar [bor'ðar] *v* embroider. **bordado** *sm* embroidery.

borde ['borðe] *sm* border, edge; rim. **bordear** *v* skirt, edge round.

bordillo [bor'ðiʎo] *sm* kerb.

bordo ['borðo] *sm* (*mar*) side of a ship; tack. **a bordo** on board. **de alto bordo** oceangoing.

boreal [bore'al] *adj* northern.

bornear [borne'ar] *v* bend, turn, twist; warp.

borra ['borra] *sf* coarse wool; nap; waste; (*fam*) idle chatter.

borracho [bor'ratʃo] *adj* drunk; (*fam*) crazy. **borrachera** or **borrachería** *sf* drunkenness; drunken spree, binge.

borrador [borra'ðor] *sm* rough copy; blotter; scribbling pad.

borrar [bor'rar] *v* cross out; erase; blot. **goma de borrar** rubber. **borrable** *adj* erasable.

borrasca [bor'raska] *sf* storm; squall. **borrascoso** *adj* stormy; squally; (*fig*) boisterous.

borrico [bor'riko] *sm* ass. **puesto en el borrico** hellbent.

borrón [bor'ron] *sm* blot, smudge; blemish; stain. **borronear** *v* scribble (on). **borroso** *adj* blurred; smudged; stained; illegible.

bosque ['boske] *sm* forest, wood.

bosquejar [boske'xar] *v* make a rough sketch of. **bosquejo** *sm* outline; sketch.

bostezar [boste'θar] *v* yawn. **bostezo** *sm* yawn.

bota¹ ['bota] sf boot. **ponerse las botas a** do justice to (something).

bota² sf wineskin.

botánica [bo'tanika] sf botany. **botánico** adj botanical. **botanista** s(m + f) botanist.

botar [bo'tar] v throw, fling; launch.

bote¹ ['bote] sm thrust; blow; jump; bounce.

bote² sm jar; can.

bote³ sm boat. **bote salvavidas** lifeboat.

botella [bo'teʎa] sf bottle.

botica [bo'tika] sf chemist's shop; medicine chest; medicines pl; shop, store. **hay de todo como en botica** there is everything under the sun. **boticario** sm chemist.

botija [bo'tixa] sf earthenware pot. **botijo** sm earthenware jug.

botín [bo'tin] sm booty, loot.

botón [bo'ton] sm button; (flor) bud; (puerta) knob. **botonar** v bud.

bóveda ['boβeða] sf vault. **bóveda de jardín** bower.

bovino [bo'βino] adj bovine.

boxear [bokse'ar] v box. **boxeador** sm boxer. **boxeo** sm boxing.

boya ['boja] sf buoy. **boya salvavidas** sf lifebuoy. **boyante** adj buoyant.

bozal [bo'θal] sm muzzle. s(m + f) (fam) greenhorn. adj (fam) stupid; foolish; untamed.

bracero [bra'θero], **-a** sm, sf hired hand; labourer.

braga ['braga] sf (cuerda) guy-rope; (de mujer) knickers pl; (de niño) nappy. **calzarse las bragas** wear the trousers.

bramar [bra'mar] v roar, bellow. **bramido** sm roar, bellow.

brasa ['brasa] sf live coal. **estar en brasas** be on edge. **brasero** sm brazier.

Brasil [bra'sil] sm Brazil. **brasileño, -a** s, adj Brazilian.

bravío [bra'βio] adj wild; fierce. sm fierceness.

bravo ['braβo] adj brave; fierce; (fam) rough; (fam) rude; (fam) luxurious. **mar bravo** rough sea. **¡bravo!** interj bravo! well done! **bravura** sf ferocity; courage; manliness.

brazada [bra'θaða] sf arm movement; stroke. **brazado** sm armful.

brazalete [braθa'lete] sm bracelet.

brazo ['braθo] sm arm; branch; (fig) strength, power. **brazo a brazo** hand to hand. **a brazo partido** with bare fists. **brazo derecho** right-hand man. **tener brazo** be tough.

brea ['brea] sf pitch, tar.

brebaje [bre'βaxe] sm concoction, potion.

brecol ['brekol] sm broccoli.

brecha ['bretʃa] sf breach, opening.

bregar¹ [bre'gar] v struggle; fight. **brega** sf struggle; quarrel. **andar a la brega** (fig) slog away.

bregar² v (amasar) knead.

Bretaña [bre'tana] sf Britain; Brittany. **Gran Bretaña** Great Britain. **bretón, -ona** s, adj Breton.

breve ['breβe] adj brief, short. **en breve** before long. sf (música) breve. **brevedad** sf brevity.

brezal [bre'θal] sm heath. **brezo** sm heather.

bribón [bri'βon], **-ona** sm, sf rascal; rogue; vagabond. adj rascally.

brida ['briða] sf bridle; rein; horsemanship. **a toda brida** hell for leather.

brigada [bri'gaða] sf brigade; gang; squad. sm sergeant-major.

brillar [bri'ʎar] v shine; sparkle; gleam. **brillante** adj brilliant; shining; glossy. **brillo** sm brilliance; brightness; glitter.

brincar [brin'kar] v bounce; jump; hop. **brinco** sm jump; hop; skip; bounce.

brindar [brin'ðar] v offer; drink someone's health. **brindis** sm invar toast.

brío ['brio] sm spirit; vigour; determination. **brioso** adj spirited; vigorous; determined; elegant.

brisa ['brisa] sf breeze.

británico [bri'taniko], **-a** sm, sf Briton. adj British. **los británicos** the British.

brocha ['brotʃa] sf paintbrush; (afeitar) shaving brush.

broche ['brotʃe] sm brooch; clasp, clip. **broche de oro** finishing touch.

broma ['broma] sf joke; fun; trick. **broma pesada** practical joke. **en broma** as a joke. **sin broma** joking apart. **bromear** v joke. **bromista** s(m + f) practical joker; funny person.

bromuro [bro'muro] sm bromide.

bronca ['bronka] sf (fam) row; brawl; ticking off. **echar una bronca** tick off.

bronce ['bronθe] *sm* bronze. **bronceado** *adj* bronzed; sun-tanned.

bronco ['bronko] *adj* rough; brittle; (*voz*) harsh; (*carácter*) hard, rude.

bronquial [bronki'al] *adj* bronchial. **bronquitis** *sf* bronchitis.

brotar [bro'tar] *v* grow; bud; germinate; spring forth. **brote** *sm* bud; shoot; (*agua*) gushing; (*fiebre*) rise; (*fig*) outbreak.

bruja ['bruxa] *sf* witch. **brujo** *sm* sorcerer.

brújula ['bruxula] *sf* compass. **perder la brújula** lose one's grip.

bruma ['bruma] *sf* mist. **brumoso** *adj* misty.

bruno ['bruno] *adj* dark brown.

bruñir [bru'ɲir] *v* polish. **bruñido** *sm* shine, polish. **bruñidor** *sm* polisher.

brusco ['brusko] *adj* brusque; abrupt; rough.

Bruselas [bru'selas] *sf* Brussels.

bruto ['bruto] *adj* coarse; brutish; rough; gross. *sm* brute; beast. **en bruto** gross; rough; uncut. **brutal** *adj* brutal; savage. **brutalidad** *sf* brutality; brutishness.

bucear [buθe'ar] *v* dive; swim underwater. **buceo** *sm* dive; diving; skin diving.

bucle ['bukle] *sm* curl; ringlet.

buche ['butʃe] *sm* craw; crop; stomach; (*fam*) belly; (*fam*) bosom, breast.

budismo [bu'ðismo] *sm* Buddhism. **budista** *s*(*m* + *f*), *adj* Buddhist.

buenaventura [bwenaβen'tura] *sf* good luck, fortune.

bueno ['bweno] *adj also* **buen** good; right; sound; fine; (*fam*) funny; (*fam*) amazing. *interj, conj* well; all right. **a buenas** of one's own accord. **buena voluntad** goodwill. **de buena gana** willingly. **¡buenas!** hello! **buenas noches** good night. **buenas tardes** good afternoon; good evening. **buenos días** good morning. **de buenas a primeras** without warning; at first sight; straight away. **estar de buenas** be in a good mood.

buey [bwej] *sm* ox. **a paso de buey** at a snail's pace.

búfalo ['bufalo] *sm* buffalo.

bufanda [bu'fanda] *sf* scarf, muffler.

bufar [bu'far] *v* spit; snort; puff and blow.

bufete [bu'fete] *sm* (*mesa*) writing-desk; (*despacho*) solicitor's office; clientele.

buhardilla [bwar'ðiʎa] *sf* attic, garret; skylight.

búho ['buo] *sm* owl; (*fam*) recluse.

buhonero [bwo'nero] *sm* pedlar, hawker. **buhonería** *sf* hawking, peddling.

buitre ['bwitre] *sm* vulture.

bujía [bu'xia] *sf* candle; candlepower; (*aut*) sparking-plug.

bulbo ['bulβo] *sm* (*bot*) bulb. **bulboso** *adj* bulbous.

Bulgaria [bul'garja] *sf* Bulgaria. **búlgaro, -a** *s, adj* Bulgarian.

bulimia [bu'limja] *sf* bulimia.

bulto ['bulto] *sm* bulk, size; shape, form; bale, package; piece of luggage; (*med*) lump, swelling. **a bulto** approximately. **de bulto** obvious. **escoger a bulto** pick at random.

bulla ['buʎa] *sf* noise; bustle. **meter bulla** kick up a racket.

bullir [bu'ʎir] *v* boil; swarm; stir; bustle; abound; itch. **bullicio** *sm* bustle; uproar. **bullicioso** *adj* lively; noisy; bustling.

buñuelo [bu'ɲwelo] *sm* fritter; doughnut; (*fam*) mess.

buque ['buke] *sm* ship, vessel. **buque de guerra** warship. **buque cargero** freighter.

burbujear [burβuxe'ar] *v* bubble. **burbuja** *sf* bubble.

burdel [bur'ðel] *sm* brothel.

burdo ['burðo] *adj* clumsy; coarse; crude.

burgués [bur'ges] *adj* bourgeois, middle-class. **burguesía** *sf* bourgeoisie, middle class.

burla ['burla] *sf* hoax; joke; trick; taunt. **burlar** *v* hoax; trick; mock. **burlarse de** make fun of. **burlería** *sf* fun; artifice; deceit; ridicule.

burocracia [buro'kraθja] *sf* bureaucracy. **burócrata** *s*(*m* + *f*) bureaucrat. **burocrático** *adj* bureaucratic.

burro ['burro] *sm* donkey; (*fam*) fool. **burro cargado de letras** pompous ass.

buscar [bus'kar] *v* search for, look for. **busca** *sf* search. **en busca de** in search of. **buscador, -a** *sm, sf* seeker; search engine (computer). **búsqueda** *sf* search.

busto ['busto] *sm* bust.

butaca [bu'taka] *sf* theatre seat; armchair.

buzo ['buθo] *sm* diver. **campana de buzo** diving-bell.

buzón [bu'θon] *sm* pillar box, letter box; plug, bung. **buzón de voz** *sm* voice mail.

byte ['bait] *sm* byte.

C

cabal [ka'βal] *adj* exact; complete; perfect. *adv* exactly; perfectly.

cábala ['kaβala] *sf* (*fig*) intrigue; divination.

cabalgar [kaβal'gar] *v* ride. **cabalgada** *sf* raid; cavalcade. **cabalgador** *sm* horseman.

caballa [ka'βaʎa] *sf* mackerel.

caballero [kaβa'ʎero] *sm* horseman; gentleman; knight. **caballeresco** *adj* chivalrous. **caballería** *sf* cavalry.

caballete [kaβa'ʎete] *sm* ridge; trestle; easel; bridge of the nose.

caballo [ka'βaʎo] *sm* horse; (*ajedrez*) knight; (*naipes*) queen. **a caballo** on horseback. **caballo de vapor** horsepower. **caballo entero** stallion. **caballito** *sm* pony.

cabaña [ka'βaɲa] *sf* cabin; herd, flock.

cabaret [kaβa're] *sm* cabaret; nightclub.

cabecear [kaβeθe'ar] *v* nod; shake one's head. **cabecera** *sf* (*de mesa, cama, etc.*) head; river's source.

cabello [ka'βeʎo] *sm* hair. **traído por los cabellos** far-fetched. **cabelludo** *adj* hairy; shaggy; downy.

*caber [ka'βer] *v* fit, find room; befall; be possible. **no cabe duda** there is no doubt.

cabestro [ka'βestro] *sm* halter; leading ox. **llevar del cabestro** lead by the nose. **cabestrillo** *sm* arm sling.

cabeza [ka'βeθa] *sf* head; chief; summit; capital. **cabeza de turco** scapegoat. **cabeza torcida** hypocrite. **cabezudo** *adj* big-headed.

cabida [ka'βiða] *sf* capacity, space. **dar cabida a** make room for. **tener cabida** be appropriate.

cabildo [ka'βildo] *sm* town council; (*rel*) chapter.

cabina [ka'βina] *sf* cabin; telephone kiosk.

cabizbajo [kaβiθ'βaxo] *adj* downcast.

cable ['kaβle] *sm* cable, rope; cable(gram). **cablegrafiar** *v* cable. **cablegrama** *sm* cable(gram).

cabo ['kaβo] *sm* cape, headland; end; stump; handle; rope; corporal; bit, piece. **al cabo de** at the end of. **llevar a cabo** carry out.

cabotaje [kaβo'taxe] *sm* coastal navigation.

cabra ['kaβra] *sf* goat.

cabria ['kaβrja] *sf* crane, hoist.

cabriola [ka'βrjola] *sf* gambol; hop; jump. **cabriolar** *v* jump; caper.

cacahuete [kaka'wete] *sm* peanut.

cacao [ka'kao] *sm* cocoa; cacao.

cacarear [kakare'ar] *v* crow, cackle; boast. **cacareo** *sm* crowing, cackling; boasting.

cacería [kaθe'ria] *sf* hunting; hunt.

cacerola [kaθe'rola] *sf* saucepan.

caché [ka'tʃe] *sm* cache.

cacique [ka'θike] *sm* political boss; tyrant.

caco ['kako] *sm* pickpocket; thief; (*fam*) coward.

cacto ['kakto] *sm* cactus.

cacharrería [katʃarre'ria] *sf* crockery. **cacharro** *sm* earthenware vessel; thing; piece of junk. **lavar los cacharros** do the washing-up.

cachemir [katʃe'mir] *sm* cashmere.

cachete [ka'tʃete] *sm* blow, slap; cheek; swollen cheek. **cachetear** *v* slap.

cachivache [katʃi'βatʃe] *sm* pot; thing; utensil; bauble.

cacho ['katʃo] *sm* piece, chunk, slice.

cachorro [ka'tʃorro], **-a** *sm, sf* pup; cub; kitten.

cada ['kaða] *adj invar* each, every. **cada vez más** more and more.

cadáver [ka'ðaβer] *sm* corpse.

cadena [ka'ðena] *sf* chain. **cadena perpetua** life imprisonment. **estar en cadena** be in prison.

cadencia [ka'ðenθja] *sf* cadence, rhythm.

cadera [ka'ðera] *sf* hip.

cadete [ka'ðete] *sm* cadet.

caducar [kaðu'kar] *v* expire, lapse; become senile. **caduco** *adj* senile; in decline.

*caer [ka'er] *v* fall, drop, tumble; decline, fall due; fade; fit, suit; realize, understand; be located, lie. **caer en** *or* **sobre** fall upon. **caer en la cuenta** understand. **caer en saco roto** fall on deaf ears. **caída** *sf* fall; downfall; lapse.

café [ka'fe] *sm* coffee; café. **café con leche** white coffee. **café solo** black coffee. **cafeína** *sf* caffeine. **cafetera** *sf* coffee pot.

cafetería *sf* coffee bar.

caimán [kai'man] *sm* alligator.

caja ['kaxa] *sf* box, case; safe; coffin; frame; hole, slot; cash box; cashier's office; cash; (*música*) drum; (*auto*) body. **caja de ahorros** savings bank. **caja de herramientas** *sf* toolbox. **cajero, -a** *sm, sf* cashier. **cajero automático** *sm* cash dispenser, ATM. **cajetilla** *sf* packet; small box. **cajón** *sm* large box; crate, chest; drawer; coffin.

cal [kal] *sm* lime.

calabaza [kala'βaθa] *sf* pumpkin; gourd; (*fam*) fool. **dar calabazas a** (*examen*) fail; jilt. **llevar calabazas** be jilted. **calabazada** *sf* (*fam*) blow on the head.

calabozo [kala'βoθo] *sm* prison cell; pruning knife.

calamar [kala'mar] *sm* squid.

calambre [ka'lambre] *sm* cramp.

calamidad [kalami'ðað] *sf* calamity.

calar [ka'lar] *v* soak; perforate; slice; size up; (*fam*) pick pockets. **calarse hasta los huesos** get soaked to the skin.

calavera [kala'βera] *sf* skull. **calaverada** *sf* wild escapade, tomfoolery. **calaverear** *v* act recklessly; live it up.

calcar [kal'kar] *v* trace; copy; trample upon. **calco** *sm* tracing; copy.

calce ['kalθe] *sm* (*de rueda*) rim; wedge.

calceta [kal'θeta] *sf* stocking; fetter. **hacer calceta** knit. **calcetero, -a** *sm, sf* hosier. **calcetín** *sm* sock.

calcinar [kalθi'nar] *v* burn, blacken.

calcio ['kalθjo] *sm* calcium.

calcular [kalku'lar] *v* calculate. **calculadora** *sf* calculation. **calculadora** *sf* calculating machine. **cálculo** *sm* calculation; estimate; (*med*) gallstone.

calda ['kalða] *sf* heating. **caldas** *sf pl* thermal springs *pl*.

caldera [kal'ðera] *sf* cauldron, boiling pan. **calderilla** *sf* small change.

caldo ['kalðo] *sm* broth; soup; salad dressing. **caldos** *sm pl* liquid foodstuffs *pl*; wines *pl*.

calefacción [kalefak'θjon] *sf* heating. **calefacción central** central heating.

calendario [kalen'darjo] *sm* calendar.

*calentar [kalen'tar] *v* heat, warm; (*fam*) thrash. **calentarse** *v* warm oneself; become excited. **calentador** *sm* heater. **calentamiento global** *sm* global warming.

calentura *sf* fever. **caliente** *adj* hot, warm.

caletre [ka'letre] *sm* (*fam*) good sense, sound judgment.

calibrar [kali'βrar] *v* calibrate; gauge; measure. **calibre** *sm* calibre; gauge; (*fig*) importance.

calidad [kali'ðað] *sf* quality; (*med*) fever. **calidades** *sf pl* conditions *pl*; rules *pl*. **a calidad de que** on condition that. **en calidad de** in the capacity of.

cálido ['kaliðo] *adj* hot, warm.

calificar [kalifi'kar] *v* qualify; judge; distinguish; prove worthy. **calificación** *sf* appreciation; distinction; judgment. **calificado** *adj* distinguished; suitable.

calina [ka'lina] *sf* mist, fog.

cáliz ['kaliθ] *sm* chalice, cup.

calmante [kal'mante] *adj* soothing. *sm* sedative.

calmar [kal'mar] *v* calm; be calm. **calmarse** *v* quieten down. **calma** *sf* calm, lull. **calmoso** *adj* calm.

calor [ka'lor] *sm* heat, warmth; fervour; fever. **hacer calor** (*temperatura*) be hot. **tener calor** (*persona*) be hot. **caluroso** *adj* hot, warm; (*fig*) ardent.

caloría [kalo'ria] *sf* calorie.

calvo ['kalβo] *adj* bald; bare; threadbare. **calvez** *sf also* **calvicie** baldness.

calzar [kal'θar] *v* put shoes on; wear (shoes, gloves, spurs); wedge. **calza** *sf* chock; (*fam*) stocking. **calzada** *sf* roadway.

calzón [kal'θon] *sm* trousers *pl*; safety belt. **calzones** *sm pl* trousers *pl*. **calzoncillos** *sm pl* underpants *pl*.

callar [ka'ʎar] *v* be silent; shut up. **callado** *adj* silent; reserved; secret. **de callado** quietly.

calle ['kaʎe] *sf* street, road. **dejar en la calle** leave penniless. **hacer calle** clear the way. **callejón** *sm* alley. **callejón sin salida** cul-de-sac. **callejuela** *sf* back street; (*fig*) loophole.

callo ['kaʎo] *sm* (*med*) corn, callus. **callos** *sm pl* tripe *sing*. **calloso** *adj* hard, callous.

cama ['kama] *sf* bed; litter; floor. **caer en cama** fall ill. **cama de campaña/matrimonio/soltero** camp/double/single bed.

camafeo [kama'feo] *sm* cameo.

camaleón [kamale'on] *sm* chameleon.

camandulero [kamandu'lero] *adj* (*fam*) sly;

hypocritical.

cámara ['kamara] *sf* room; loft; chamber; cine *or* TV camera; inner tube. **ayuda de cámara** *sf* valet. **música de cámara** *sf* chamber music.

camarada [kama'raða] *sm* comrade; colleague.

camarero [kama'rero] *sm* waiter; steward. **camarera** *sf* waitress; stewardess; chambermaid.

camarilla [kama'riʎa] *sf* clique; parliamentary lobby.

camarón [kama'ron] *sm* shrimp.

camarote [kama'rote] *sm* cabin.

cambiar [kam'bjar] *v* change; exchange. **cambiar de opinión** *v* change one's mind. **cambiante** *sm* moneychanger. **cambio** *sm* change; alteration; small change. **a cambio de** in exchange for. **en cambio** on the other hand.

camelar [kame'lar] *v* (*fam*) flatter; woo. **cameleo** *sm* (*fam*) flattery.

camello [ka'meʎo] *sm* camel.

camilla [ka'miʎa] *sf* stretcher; litter; couch.

caminar [kami'nar] *v* walk; travel; move along. **caminante** *s*(*m + f*) traveller. **camino** *sm* path; road; route; way. **abrirse camino** make one's way. **camino adelante** straight on. **ponerse en camino** set out.

camión [ka'mjon] *sm* lorry. **camión de bomberos** fire engine.

camisa [ka'misa] *sf* shirt; fruit skin; casing; lining; dust jacket; paper wrapper. **camisa de dormir** nightdress. **camisa de fuerza** straightjacket. **dejar sin camisa** ruin (someone). **camiseta** *sf* vest. **camisón** *sm* nightdress; nightshirt.

camorra [ka'morra] *sf* (*fam*) quarrel, fight. **buscar camorra** look for trouble.

campamento [kampa'mento] *sm* camp. **campar** *v* camp; excel.

campana [kam'pana] *sf* bell; mantelpiece; parish (church); curfew.

campante [kam'pante] *adj* proud; pleased; (*fam*) relaxed, cool.

campaña [kam'paɲa] *sf* plain; campaign.

campechano [kampe'tʃano] *adj* (*fam*) genial; frank. **campechanía** *sf* good nature; frankness.

campeón [kampe'on], **-ona** *sm, sf* champion. **campeón de venta** bestseller. **campe-**

onato *sm* championship. **de campeonato** (*fig, fam*) fantastic.

campista [kam'pista] *s*(*m+f*) camper (person).

campo ['kampo] *sm* field; countryside; camp; pitch; background. **campo de aviación** airfield. **campo raso** open country. **campesino, -a** *s, adj* peasant, rustic.

can [kan] *sm* dog; trigger.

cana ['kana] *sf* white *or* grey hair. **peinar canas** be getting old.

Canadá [kana'ða] *sm* Canada. **canadiense** *s*(*m + f*), *adj* Canadian.

canal [ka'nal] *sm* canal; channel; ditch; tube. *sf* carcass. **canalón** *sm* drainpipe; gutter.

canalla [ka'naʎa] *sf* rabble, mob. *sm* swine, scoundrel.

canapé [kana'pe] *sm* couch, sofa; (*culin*) canapé.

Canarias [ka'narjas] *sf pl* Canary Islands *pl*. **canario, -a** *sm, sf* inhabitant of the Canary Islands.

canario [ka'narjo] *sm* canary.

canasta [ka'nasta] *sf* basket.

cancelar [kanθe'lar] *v* cancel, annul. **cancelación** *sf* cancellation.

cáncer ['kanθer] *sm* (*med*) cancer.

Cáncer *sm* (*astron*) Cancer.

canciller [kanθi'ʎer] *sm* chancellor.

canción [kan'θjon] *sf* song; tune; rhyme. **mudar de canción** change one's tune. **cancionero** *sm* song-book.

cancha ['kantʃa] *sf* football ground; tennis court; racecourse.

candado [kan'daðo] *sm* padlock.

candela [kan'dela] *sf* candle; candlestick; fire; blossom; (*fam*) light. **candelero** *sm* candlestick; oil lamp. **poner en el candelero** make popular.

candente [kan'dente] *adj* red-hot, burning.

candidato [kandi'ðato] *sm* candidate. **candidatura** *sf* candidature.

cándido ['kandiðo] *adj* innocent, pure; gullible; candid. **candidez** *sf* candour; gullibility; stupid remark.

candil [kan'ðil] *sm* oil lamp.

candor [kan'dor] *sm* innocence; candour; simplicity. **candoroso** *adj* ingenuous; innocent; frank.

canela [ka'nela] *sf* cinnamon.

canelón [kane'lon] *sm* gutter; spout; icicle.

cangrejo [kan'grexo] *sm* crab.

canguro [kan'guro] *sm* kangaroo; *s(m+f)* baby-sitter.

caníbal [ka'niβal] *s(m+f)*, *adj* cannibal. **canibalismo** *sm* cannibalism.

canilla [ka'niʎa] *sf (tecn)* bobbin, spool; *(med)* shinbone; tap, spout.

canino [ka'nino] *adj* canine. **hambre canina** ravenous hunger.

canjear [kanxe'ar] *v* exchange. **canje** *sm* exchange.

cano ['kano] *adj* white-haired, greyhaired; *(fig)* ancient.

canoa [ka'noa] *sf* canoe.

canon ['kanon] *sm* rule; levy; perfect example; *(rel, música)* canon.

canónigo [ka'nonigo] *sm (rel)* canon. **canónico** *adj* canonical. **canonización** *sf* canonization. **canonizar** *v* canonize.

cansar [kan'sar] *v* tire, fatigue. **cansado** *adj* tired, weary; tiresome. **vista cansada** weak eyesight. **cansancio** *sm* weariness, fatigue.

cantar [kan'tar] *v* sing; chant; praise; *(fam)* squeal, confess. *sm* song; tune; poem. **cantante** *s(m + f)* singer.

cántara ['kantara] *sf* pitcher; liquid measure.

cántaro ['kantaro] *sm* pitcher. **llover a cántaros** rain cats and dogs.

cantera [kan'tera] *sf* quarry; *(fig)* breeding ground, source. **cantería** *sf* masonry; building made of hewn stone. **cantero** *sm* stonemason; crust of bread; strip of land.

cantidad [kanti'ðað] *sf* quantity, amount.

cantimplora [kantim'plora] *sf* siphon; water bottle.

cantina [kan'tina] *sf* buffet; canteen; wine cellar; picnic basket.

canto¹ ['kanto] *sm* song; singing. **cantor, -a** *sm*, *sf* singer.

canto² *sm* edge; border; crust; corner; pebble. **al canto** *(fam)* in support. **de canto** edgeways.

caña ['kaɲa] *sf* cane; reed; walking stick; beer glass; shin bone. **caña de azúcar** sugar-cane. **caña de pescar** fishing-rod.

cañada [ka'ɲada] *sf* glen, ravine.

cáñamo ['kaɲamo] *sm* hemp.

caño ['kaɲo] *sm* pipe; sewer, **cañería** *sf* drain; piping.

cañón [ka'ɲon] *sm* canyon; cannon, gun; gun barrel; pipe, tube.

caoba [ka'oβa] *sf* mahogany.

caos ['kaos] *sm* chaos. **caótico** *adj* chaotic.

capa ['kapa] *sf* cloak; cape; covering; lid.

capacidad [kapaθi'ðað] *sf* capacity; ability; opportunity.

capacha [ka'patʃa] *sf also* **capacho** *sm* shopping basket.

capar [ka'par] *v* castrate; *(fam)* reduce.

capataz [kapa'taθ] *sm* foreman; overseer.

capaz [ka'paθ] *adj* capable; able; spacious.

capellán [kape'ʎan] *sm* chaplain.

capilar [kapi'lar] *sm*, *adj* capillary.

capilla [ka'piʎa] *sf* chapel; choir; hood. **estar en capilla** *(fam)* be in suspense.

capital [kapi'tal] *sm (com)* capital. *sf* capital city. *adj* principal.

capitán [kapi'tal] *sm* captain, leader. **capitanear** *v* command; lead.

capitular [kapitu'lar] *v* capitulate; make an agreement. **capitulación** *sf* capitulation; agreement.

capítulo [ka'pitulo] *sm (libro)* chapter; town council meeting; *(rel)* chapter.

capón [ka'pon] *sm* capon; eunuch; gelding; bundle of sticks.

capote [ka'pote] *sm* cape; greatcoat. **capotear** *v (fig, fam)* shirk.

capricho [ka'pritʃo] *sm* caprice, whim. **caprichoso** *adj* capricious.

cápsula ['kapsula] *sf* capsule; cartridge case; metal cap.

captar [kap'tar] *v* win over; gain; grasp.

capturar [kaptu'rar] *v* capture; arrest. **captura** *sf* capture.

capucha [ka'putʃa] *sf* hood; circumflex accent.

capuchina [kapu'tʃina] *sf* nasturtium.

capullo [ka'puʎo] *sm* cocoon; bud, **en capullo** in embryo.

cara ['kara] *sf* face; appearance; surface. **cara adelante/atrás** forwards/backwards. **cara o cruz** heads or tails. **dar la cara** face the music. **hacer cara a** face up to. **tener cara de** look like.

carabina [kara'βina] *sf* carbine; rifle. **carabinero** *sm* rifleman.

caracol [kara'kol] *sm* snail; spiral.

carácter [ka'rakter] *sm* character; nature; condition; sign, mark. **característica** *sf* characteristic. **característico** *adj* characteristic. **caracterización** *sf* characterization; *(teatro)* make-up. **caracterizar** *v* characterize; confer an honour on; *(teatro)* make up.

¡caramba! [ka'ramba] *interj* damn it!

caramelo [kara'melo] *sm* sweet, toffee; caramel.

carapacho [kara'patʃo] *sm* shell, carapace.

carátula [ka'ratula] *sf* mask; *(fam)* theatre, stage.

caravana [kara'βana] *sf* caravan; group, crowd; camper (van); tailback.

carbohidrato [karβoi'ðrato] *sm* carbohydrate.

carbón [kar'βon] *sm* coal; charcoal; carbon; carbon paper. **carbonera** *sf* coal cellar; coal scuttle; charcoal burner. **carbonería** *sf* coalyard. **carbono** *sm* carbon.

carbunclo [kar'βunklo] *sm also* **carbunco** *(med)* carbuncle.

carburador [karβura'ðor] *sm* carburettor.

carcajada [karka'xaða] *sf* burst of laughter.

cárcel [ˈkarθel] *sf* prison. **carcelero, -a** *sm, sf* jailer, warder.

carcomer [karko'mer] *v* corrode, eat away; undermine.

cardar [kar'ðar] *v (tecn)* card, comb, **carda** *sf (tecn)* card, carding; *(fam)* reprimand.

cardenal [karðe'nal] *sm* cardinal; bruise.

cardíaco [kar'ðiako] *adj* cardiac.

cardinal [karði'nal] *adj* principal; cardinal.

cardo [ˈkarðo] *sm* thistle.

carear [kare'ar] *v* confront; compare; come face to face. **carearse** *v* meet.

*carecer [kare'θer] *v* lack, need. **carencia** *sf* lack, shortage; deficiency.

carestía [kares'tia] *sf* shortage, scarcity; high price.

careta [ka'reta] *sf* mask. **careta antigás** gasmask.

carey [ka'rej] *sm* turtle; tortoiseshell.

cargar [kar'gar] *v* load; burden; charge; tax; blame; attack; *(fam)* vex; lean, incline. **cargarse** *v* become full; be overburdened; *(fam)* be fed up; *(cielo)* become dark. **carga** *sf* load, burden; charge; tax; pressure. **cargadero** *sm* loading bay. **cargador** *sm* freighter; loader; carrier. **cargamento** *sm* cargo, load.

cargo [ˈkargo] *sm* post; accusation; responsibility; *(com)* charge; freighter. **cuenta a**

cargo *sf* charge account.

cariarse [ka'rjarse] *v* decay. **caries** *sf invar* caries.

caribe [ka'riβe] *s(m + f)*, *adj* Caribbean. **Mar Caribe** *sm* Caribbean Sea. **caribeño** *adj* Caribbean.

caricatura [karika'tura] *sf* caricature.

caricia [ka'riθja] *sf* caress. **caricioso** *adj* caressing.

caridad [kari'ðað] *sf* charity. **caritativo** *adj* charitable.

cariño [ka'riɲo] *sm* love, affection, **cariñoso** *adj* affectionate, loving.

carisma [ka'risma] *sm* charisma. **carismático** *adj* charismatic.

cariz [ka'riθ] *sm* appearance, aspect.

carmesí [karme'si] *sm, adj* crimson.

carmín [kar'min] *sm, adj* carmine.

carnada [kar'naða] *sf* bait.

carnaval [karna'βal] *sm* carnival.

carne [ˈkarne] *sf* meat, flesh, **carne magra** lean meat. **carnal** *adj* carnal. **carnicería** *sf* butcher's shop. **carnicero** *sm* butcher.

carnero [kar'nero] *sm* sheep; ram; mutton; cemetery.

carpa [ˈkarpa] *sf* carp.

caro [ˈkaro] *adj* expensive; dear, beloved.

carpeta [kar'peta] *sf* folder, file; portfolio; briefcase; tablecloth. **dar carpetazo a** shelve.

carpintería [karpinte'ria] *sf* carpentry; carpenter's shop. **carpintero** *sm* carpenter, joiner.

carrera [ka'rrera] *sf* race; road; career; course; line; *(media)* ladder. **carreras** *sm* racing. **circuito de carreras** racetrack. **de carrera** swiftly. **hacer carrera** succeed.

carreta [ka'rreta] *sf* cart, wagon. **carretear** *v* cart, haul.

carrete [ka'rrete] *sm* reel, spool, bobbin.

carretera [karre'tera] *sf* road, highway. **carretera de circunvalación** by-pass. **carretera de doble calzada** *sf* dual carriageway.

carril [ka'rril] *sm* furrow, rut; narrow road; rail.

carro [ˈkarro] *sm* cart; car; typewriter carriage. **carro blindado** armoured car. **carro de mudanzas** removal van.

carroña [ka'rroɲa] *sf* carrion.

carroza [ka'rroθa] *sf* carriage; state coach;

float.

carta ['karta] sf letter; chart; map; playing card; charter, document, **carta certificada** registered letter. **carta de venta** bill of sale. **tomar cartas en** (fam) take part in.

cartel [kar'tel] sm placard, poster. **cartelera** sf hoarding.

cartera [kar'tera] sf wallet; purse; briefcase; notebook; portfolio; office of a cabinet minister.

cartero [kar'tero] sm postman.

cartílago [kar'tilago] sm cartilage.

cartón [kar'ton] sm cardboard; carton; cartoon.

cartucho [kar'tutʃo] sm cartridge; paper cone.

casa ['kasa] sf house, home; household; business; building; flat. **casa de empeños** pawnshop. **casa de huéspedes** boarding-house. **casa pública** brothel. **casa y comida** board and lodging. **en casa** at home. **un amigo de casa** a friend of the family.

casar [ka'sar] v give in marriage; join. **casarse con** marry, get married. **casamiento** sm marriage.

cascabel [kaska'βel] sm small bell. **serpiente de cascabel** sf rattlesnake. **cascabelada** sf (fam) foolish action.

cascada [kas'kaða] sf waterfall.

cascar [kas'kar] v crack; burst; split; break; (fam) beat up; (fam) cough up; (fam) chatter; (fam) kick the bucket.

cáscara ['kaskara] sf shell; peel; rind; husk; bark.

cascarón [kaska'ron] sm egg-shell.

casco ['kasko] sm skull; helmet; skin; segment; shrapnel. **cascotes** sm pl rubble sing.

caserío [kase'rio] sm group of houses; settlement; country house.

casero [ka'sero] adj home-made; familiar; informal; (fam) domestic. sm landlord; tenant; caretaker.

casi ['kasi] adv nearly, almost.

casilla [ka'siʎa] sf hut, cabin; lodge; pigeon-hole; section.

caso ['kaso] sm case, matter; event; chance; occasion. **el caso es** the fact is. **en tal caso** in such a case. **en todo caso** in any case. **hacer caso a** pay attention to.

caspa ['kaspa] sf dandruff.

casta ['kasta] sf caste; breed; class.

castaño [kas'taɲo] sm chestnut-tree; chestnut brown. adj chestnut. **castaña** sf chestnut; hair bun.

castañuela [kasta'ɲwela] sf castanet.

castellano [kaste'ʎano], **-a** s, adj Castilian. sm (lengua) Castilian.

castidad [kasti'ðað] sf chastity.

castigar [kasti'gar] v punish, chastise. **castigo** sm punishment.

Castilla [kas'tiʎa] sf Castile.

castillo [kas'tiʎo] sm castle.

castizo [kas'tiθo] adj pure; pure-blooded; traditional.

casto ['kasto] adj chaste, pure.

castor [kas'tor] sm beaver.

castrar [kas'trar] v castrate; (agr) prune. **castrado** sm eunuch.

castrense [kas'trense] adj military.

casual [ka'swal] adj chance, coincidental. **casualidad** sf chance; coincidence; accident. **por casualidad** by chance.

casucha [ka'sutʃa] sf also **casuca** hovel.

cataclismo [kata'klismo] sm cataclysm.

catacumbas [kata'cumbas] sf pl catacombs pl.

catadura¹ [kata'ðura] sf tasting. **catador** sm taster, sampler. **catar** v taste, sample.

catadura² sf (fam) expression, look.

catalejo [kata'lexo] sm telescope.

catálogo [ka'talogo] sm catalogue. **catalogar** v catalogue; classify.

Cataluña [kata'luɲa] sf Catalonia.

cataplasma [kata'plasma] sf poultice.

catarata [kata'rata] sf waterfall; (med) cataract.

catarro [ka'tarro] sm catarrh, common cold. **catarro pradial** hay fever. **coger un catarro** catch cold.

catástrofe [ka'tastrofe] sf catastrophe. **catastrófico** adj catastrophic.

catecismo [kate'θismo] sm catechism.

cátedra ['kateðra] sf lecture room; senior teaching post; (puesto) chair.

catedral [kate'ðral] sf cathedral.

categoría [katego'ria] sf category; class; rank. **categórico** adj categorical; strict.

caterva [ka'terβa] sf crowd; heap.

cátodo ['katoðo] sm cathode.

católico [ka'toliko], **-a** s, adj (Roman) Catholic. **catolicismo** sm (Roman) Catholicism.

catorce [ka'torθe] sm, adj fourteen.

catorceno *adj* fourteenth.

catre ['katre] *sm* camp-bed; cot.

cauce ['kauθe] *sm* river bed; ditch.

caución [kau'θjon] *sf* caution; pledge; bail.

caucho ['kautʃo] *sm* rubber.

caudal [kau'ðal] *sm* wealth; abundance.

caudillo [kau'ðiʎo] *sm* leader, chief.

causar [kau'sar] *v* cause, create, occasion. **causa** *sf* cause, reason, motive; (*jur*) trial. **a causa de** owing to. **causa pública** public welfare.

cáustico ['kaustiko] *adj* caustic, burning; scathing.

cautela [kau'tela] *sf* care, caution; cunning. **cauteloso** *adj* cautious; cunning. **cauto** *adj* cautious, wary.

cautivar [kauti'βar] *v* capture; captivate; charm. **cautividad** *sf* captivity. **cautivo, -a** *sm, sf* captive.

cavar [ka'βar] *v* dig; excavate; (*agr*) dress; ponder. **cava** *sf* cultivation. **cavadura** *sf* digging; dressing.

caverna [ka'βerna] *sf* cavern, cave. **cavernoso** *adj* cavernous; (*fig*) deep.

cavidad [kaβi'ðað] *sf* cavity.

cavilar [kaβi'lar] *v* think deeply, meditate. **caviloso** *adj* pensive; worried.

cayado [ka'jaðo] *sm* shepherd's crook; walking-stick.

cazar [ka'θar] *v* hunt; chase; shoot; catch. **caza** *sf* hunt; chase; game. **cazador, -a** *sm, sf* hunter.

cazo ['kaθo] *sm* ladle; saucepan; gluepot. **cazo eléctrico** electric kettle.

cazoleta [kaθo'leta] *sf* small pan; pipe bowl.

cazuela [ka'θwela] *sf* casserole; (*teatro*) the gods.

CD *sm* CD.

CD-ROM *sm* CD-ROM.

cebada [θe'βaða] *sf* barley. **cebadar** *v* feed (animals).

cebar [θe'βar] *v* feed, fatten up; prime, charge; penetrate; long for. **cebarse en** vent one's rage on; gloat over.

cebolla [θe'βoʎa] *sf* onion; flower bulb. **cebollana** *sf* chive. **cebolleta** *sf* leek.

cebra ['θeβra] *sf* zebra. **paso de cebra** *sm* zebra crossing.

cecear [θeθe'ar] *v* lisp. **ceceo** *sm* lisp. **ceceoso** *adj* lisping.

ceder [θe'ðer] *v* give up; yield; sag.

cedro ['θeðro] *sm* cedar.

cédula ['θeðula] *sf* charter; certificate; form; patent.

***cegar** [θe'gar] *v* blind; go blind; block up; cover. **cegador** *adj* blinding. **cegarra** *adj* (*fam*) short-sighted. **cegarrita** *adj* (*fam*) peering. **ceguedad** *or* **ceguera** *sf* blindness.

ceja ['θexa] *sf* eyebrow; mountain top; rim; cloud-cap. **fruncir las cejas** knit one's brows. **quemarse las cejas** burn the midnight oil. **tener entre ceja y ceja** (*fam*) concentrate on.

celada [θe'laða] *sf* helmet; trick; ambush.

celar [θe'lar] *v* check on; watch; conceal; protect. **celador** *sm* watchman.

celda ['θelða] *sf* cell.

celebrar [θele'βrar] *v* celebrate; praise; acclaim; conduct; (*rel*) say mass. **celebrarse** *v* take place. **celebración** *sf* celebration; acclamation. **celebrante** *sm* celebrant priest. **célebre** *adj* famous. **celebridad** *sf* fame; celebration.

celeridad [θeleri'ðað] *sf* speed.

celeste [θe'leste] *adj* heavenly.

celibato [θeli'βato] *sm* celibacy; (*fam*) bachelor. **célibe** *s(m + f)* single person; bachelor; spinster.

celo ['θelo] *sm* zeal; heat, rut. **celos** *sm pl* jealousy *sing*. **dar celos a** make jealous. **tener celos** be jealous. **celosía** *sf* window lattice; venetian blind; jealousy. **celoso** *adj* zealous; jealous.

celta ['θelta] *s(m + f)* Celt. *sm* (*lengua*) Celtic.

célula ['θelula] *sf* cell.

celuloide [θelu'lojðe] *sm* celluloid.

celulosa [θelu'losa] *sf* cellulose.

cementerio [θemen'terjo] *sm* cemetery.

cemento [θe'mento] *sm* cement. **cemento armado** reinforced concrete.

cenagal [θena'gal] *sm* marsh, swamp; (*fam*) tight spot, mess.

cenar [θe'nar] *v* dine on, have for supper/dinner. **cena** *sf* evening meal, supper, dinner.

cenefa [θe'nefa] *sf* border; edging; frieze.

ceniza [θe'niθa] *sf* ash, cinder. **convertir en cenizas** reduce to ashes. **cenicero** *sm* ashtray.

censo ['θenso] *sm* census; tax; annuity; pension; ground rent; (*fig*) burden. **censar**

v take a census of. **censor** *sm* censor; auditor.

censurar [θensu'rar] *v* censor; censure; condemn. **censura** *sf* censoring; censorship. **censurable** *adj* blameworthy. **censurador** *sm* censor. **censurista** *s(m + f)* critic; fault-finder.

centellear [θenteλe'ar] *v also* **centellar** sparkle; flash; twinkle; flicker. **centella** *sf* flash; spark. **centelleo** *sm* gleam; glitter; sparkle.

centavo [θen'taβo] *sm* cent.

centena [θen'tena] *sf* hundred. **centenada** *sf also* **centenar** *sm* hundred. **a** *or* **por centenares** by the hundred. **centenario** *sm* centenary.

centeno¹ [θen'teno] *sm* rye.

centeno² *adj* hundred.

centésimo [θen'tesimo] *adj* hundredth. *sm* cent.

centígrado [θen'tiɣraðo] *adj* centigrade.

centímetro [θen'timetro] *sm* centimetre.

céntimo ['θentimo] *adj* hundredth. *sm* cent.

centinela [θenti'nela] *s(m + f)* guard, sentry.

centrar [θen'trar] *v* centre. **central** *adj* central. **central** *sf* head office; headquarters; power station; switchboard. **centro** *sm* centre, middle; aim, goal, objective. **centro comercial** *sm* (shopping) mall.

centrífugo [θen'trifuɣo] *adj* centrifugal.

centroamérica [θentroa'merika] *sf* Central America. **centroamericano** *adj* Central American.

centuria [θen'turja] *sf* century.

*****ceñir** [θe'ɲir] *v* gird, surround, encircle; crown; frame; shorten, take in; be a tight fit for. **ceñirse** *v* limit; adapt oneself to; cling. **ceñido** *adj* tight-fitting. **ceñidor** *sm* belt.

ceño ['θeɲo] *sm* frown. **fruncir el ceño** frown. **ceñudo** *adj* frowning.

cepa ['θepa] *sf* tree stump; stock; root; origin.

cepillar [θepi'λar] brush; plane. **cepillarse** *v (fam)* fail an exam; *(fam)* polish off. **cepillo** *sm* brush; plane.

cepo ['θepo] *sm* branch; stocks *pl*; collecting box; *(tecn)* clamp, socket.

cera ['θera] *sf* wax.

cerámico [θe'ramiko] *adj* ceramic. **cerámica** *sf* ceramics; pottery.

cerca ['θerka] *adv* near, close, nearby. **cerca de** close by; almost; about. **de cerca** closely. **cercanía** *sf* nearness. **cercanía** *sf pl* vicinity *sing*, neighbourhood *sing*. **cercano** *adj* near, close.

cercar [θer'kar] *v* enclose; fence; surround; encompass. **cerca** *sf* enclosure, wall, fence. **cercado** *sm* enclosure.

cerco ['θerko] *sm* ring; circle; enclosure; frame; siege.

cerda ['θerda] *sf (zool)* sow; bristle. **cerdear** *v (animales)* be lame, limp. **cerdo** *sm* pig; pork. **cerdoso** *adj* bristly.

Cerdeña [θer'ðeɲa] *sf* Sardinia.

cereal [θere'al] *sm, adj* cereal.

cerebro [θe' reβro] *sm* brain. **cerebral** *adj* cerebral.

ceremonia [θere'monja] *sf* ceremony. **ceremonial** *adj* ceremonial. **ceremonioso** *adj* ceremonious.

cereza [θe'reθa] *sf* cherry. **cerezo** *sm* cherry tree.

cerilla [θe' riλa] *sf* match.

*****cerner** [θer'ner] *v* sift; sieve; examine carefully; drizzle. **cernerse** *v* sway; waddle; hover; threaten.

cero ['θero] *sm* zero, nothing.

*****cerrar** [θer'rar] *v* shut, close, seal off. **cerrarse** *v* close up; stand firm; heal; cloud over. **cerrar con llave** lock. **cerrar la boca** shut up. **cerrar la marcha** bring up the rear. **cerrado** *adj* closed; secretive; obtuse; overcast. **cerradura** *sf* lock; locking up. **cerraje** *sm* lock.

cerril [θer'ril] *adj* rough, rocky; wild; ill-bred.

cerro ['θerro] *sm* hill, ridge; animal's neck.

cerrojo [θer'roxo] *sm* bolt.

certeza [θer'teθa] *sf also* **certidumbre** certainty.

certificar [θertifi'kar] *v* certify; register; guarantee. **certificado** *sm* certificate; registered letter.

cervato [θer' βato] *sm (zool)* fawn.

cerveza [θer' βeθa] *sf* beer.

cerviz [θer' βiθ] *sf* nape of the neck, cervix. **bajar la cerviz** bow one's head.

cesar [θe'sar] *v* cease, stop; leave one's job. **cesación** *sf* cessation, stoppage. **cesante** *adj* out of office, unemployed. **cesantía** *sf* suspension from office.

cesárea [θe'sarea] *sf* Caesarean.

cesión [θe'sjon] *sf* transfer; assignment; conveyance; resignation.

césped [' θespeð] *sf* turf, lawn. **césped inglés** lawn.

cesta ['θesta] *sf* basket, hamper. **cestería** *sf* basketwork, wickerwork. **cesto** *sm* basket.

cetro ['θetro] *sm* sceptre; (*fig*) power.

CI *sm* IQ.

cía ['θia] *sf* hip-bone.

cianuro [θja'nuro] *sm* cyanide.

ciática [θi'atika] *sf* sciatica. **ciático** *adj* sciatic.

ciberespacio [θiβeres'paθjo] *sm* cyberspace.

cicatería [θikate' ria] *sf* stinginess.

cicatriz [θika'triθ] *sf* scar.

ciclismo [θi'klismo] *sm* cycling. **ciclista** *s*(*m* + *f*) cyclist.

ciclo ['θiklo] *sm* cycle. **cíclico** *adj* cyclical.

ciclón [θi'klon] *sm* cyclone.

cidra ['θiðra] *sf* citron. **cidro** *sm* citron tree.

ciego ['θjeɣo], **-a** *sm*, *sf* blind person. *adj* blind.

cielo ['θjelo] *sm* sky; heaven; ceiling; climate. **¡cielos!** good heavens!

ciempiés [θjem' pjes] *sm invar* centipede.

ciénaga ['θjenaɣa] *sf* bog, marsh, swamp.

ciencia ['θjenθja] *sf* science; knowledge, learning. **ciencia ficción** science fiction.

científico [θjen'tifiko], **-a** *sm*, *sf* scientist. *adj* scientific.

cieno ['θjeno] *sm* mud. **cienoso** *adj* muddy.

ciento ['θjento] *sm*, *adj also* **cien** hundred.

cierre ['θjerre] *sm* closing; fastening; lock.

cierto ['θjerto] *adj* certain. *adv* certainly. **de cierto** certainly. **por cierto** of course.

ciervo ['θjerβo] *sm* deer; stag. **cierva** *sf* hind, doe.

cierzo ['θjerθo] *sm* north wind.

cifra ['θifra] *sf* number, figure; cipher; code; abbreviation. **en cifra** in short. **cifrar** *v* summarize; cipher; enclose. **cifrar las esperanzas en** set one's hopes on.

cigarro [θi'ɣarro] *sm* cigar. **cigarrillo** *sm* cigarette.

cigüeña [θi'ɣweɲa] *sf* stork.

cilindro [θi'lindro] *sm* cylinder. **cilíndrico** *adj* cylindrical.

cima ['θima] *sf* top; summit. **dar cima a** finish off. **por cima** at the top; superficially.

címbalo ['θimbalo] *sm* cymbal.

cimbrar [θim'brar] *v also* **cimbrear** vibrate; bend; sway.

***cimentar** [θimen'tar] *v* found; establish. **cimiento** *sm* foundation.

cinc [θink] *sm* zinc.

cincel [θin'θel] *sm* chisel. **cincelador** *sm* engraver; stonecutter.

cinco ['θinko] *sm*, *adj* five.

cincuenta [θin'kwenta] *sm*, *adj* fifty.

cinchar [θin'tʃar] *v* girth; fasten with hoops. **cincha** *sf* girth, cinch. **cincho** *sm* belt; hoop.

cine ['θine] *sm* cinema.

cínico ['θiniko], **-a** *sm*, *sf* cynic. *adj* cynical; shameless. **cinismo** *sm* cynicism.

cínife ['θinife] *sm* mosquito.

cinta ['θinta] *sf* ribbon; strip; tape; tape-measure. **cinta de vídeo** *sf* video film. **cinteado** *adj* beribboned.

cintura [θin'tura] *sf* waist; belt. **meter a uno en cintura** make someone behave. **cinturón** *sm* belt; zone; circle. **cinturón de seguridad** safety belt.

ciprés [θi'pres] *sm* cypress.

circo ['θirko] *sm* circus.

circuito [θir'kwito] *sm* circuit.

circular [θirku'lar] *v* circulate; circularize; move. *adj* round, circular. **circulación** *sf* circulation; traffic.

circuncidar [θirkunθi'ðar] *v* circumcise. **circuncisión** *sf* circumcision. **circunciso** *adj* circumcised.

circundar [θirkun'dar] *v* surround, encircle.

circunferencia [θirkunfe'renθja] *sf* circumference.

circunflejo [θirkun'flexo] *sm* circumflex.

circunscribir [θirkunskri' βir] *v* circumscribe.

circunspecto [θirkun' spekto] *adj* circumspect. **circunspección** *sf* circumspection.

circunstancia [θirkun'stanθja] *sf* circumstance; condition; incident. **circunstancial** *adj* circumstantial. **circunstante** *adj* surrounding; present.

circunvecino [θirkunβe' θino] *adj* neighbouring.

ciruela [θiˈrwela] *sf* plum. **ciruelo** *sm* plum-tree.

cirugía [θiruˈxia] *sf* surgery. **cirujano** *sm* surgeon.

cisco [ˈθisko] *sm* coal dust; (*fam*) hubbub.

cisma [ˈθisma] *sm* schism; discord.

cisne [ˈθisne] *sm* swan.

cisterna [θisˈterna] *sf* cistern, water tank.

cita [ˈθita] *sf* citation; appointment; quotation. **citar** *v* make an appointment; quote; (*jur*) summons.

ciudad [θjuˈðað] *sf* city. **ciudadanía** *sf* citizenship. **ciudadano, -a** *sm, sf* citizen. **ciudadela** *sf* citadel.

cívico [ˈθiβiko] *adj* civic; patriotic.

civilizar [θiβiliˈθar] *v* civilize. **civil** *adj* civil. **civilización** *sf* civilization.

cizalla [θiˈθaʎa] *sf* shears *pl*; metal shavings *pl*.

clamar [klaˈmar] *v* cry out; beseech.

clamor [klaˈmor] *sm* shout; cry. **clamorear** *v* cry out for; beseech. **clamoroso** *adj* noisy.

clandestino [klandesˈtino] *adj* secret.

clara [ˈklara] *sf* white of egg; bald patch

claraboya [klaraˈβoja] *sf* skylight

clarear [klareˈar] *v* clear; dawn; grow light; be transparent; (*fam*) reveal secrets.

clarete [klaˈrete] *sm* claret.

clarificar [klarifiˈkar] *v* clarify. **clarificación** *sf* clarification.

clarín [klaˈrin] *sm* bugle.

clarinete [klariˈnete] *sm* clarinet.

claro [ˈklaro] *adj* light; clear; distinct. *adv* clearly. *sm* opening, space; clearing. **claro que** of course. **claro que sí** certainly. **claridad** *sf* clarity; light; brightness.

clase [ˈklase] *sf* class, type; lesson; classroom. **clase media** middle class. **clase particular** private lesson.

clásico [ˈklasiko] *adj* classic(al). *sm* classic.

clasificar [klasifiˈkar] *v* classify. **clasificación** *sf* classification.

claudicar [klauðiˈkar] *v* limp; (*fam*) yield; (*fig*) shirk; (*fig*) falter. **claudicación** *sf* limping; yielding; shirking.

claustro [ˈklaustro] *sm* cloister; teaching staff. **claustral** *adj* cloistered.

claustrofobia [klaustroˈfoβja] *sf* claustrophobia.

cláusula [ˈklausula] *sf* clause.

clavar [klaˈβar] *v* nail; fasten, fix; (*fam*) cheat. **clava** *sf* club, cudgel. **clavado en la cama** bed-ridden. **clavija** *sf* peg, pin. **clavo** *sm* nail; spike.

clave [ˈklaβe] *sf* key; clue; clef. *sm* harpsichord.

clavel [klaˈβel] *sm* carnation.

clavícula [klaˈβikula] *sf* collar bone.

clemencia [kleˈmenθja] *sf* mercy. **clemente** *adj* merciful.

clérigo [ˈklerigo] *sm* clergyman, priest. **clerical** *adj* clerical. **clericato** *sm* also **clero** clergy.

cliente [ˈkljente] **, -a** *sm, sf* client, customer; patient. **clientela** *sf* clients *pl*, customers *pl*; practice.

clima [ˈklima] *sm* climate. **climático** *adj* climatic.

clínica [ˈklinika] *sf* clinic. **clínico** *adj* clinical.

clisé [kliˈse] *sm* (*foto*) negative; (*fig*) cliché.

cloaca [kloˈaka] *sf* sewer, drain.

clonar [kloˈnar] *v* clone.

cloro [ˈkloro] *sm* chlorine.

clorofila [kloroˈfila] *sf* chlorophyll.

cloroformo [kloroˈformo] *sm* chloroform. **cloroformar** *v* chloroform.

club [kluβ] *sm* club. **club de noche** night-club.

coacción [koakˈθjon] *sf* coercion **coactivo** *adj* coercive.

coagular [koaguˈlar] *v* coagulate; curdle; clot. **coagulación** *sf* coagulation; clotting.

coalición [koaliˈθjon] *sf* coalition.

coartada [koarˈtaða] *sf* alibi.

coartar [koarˈtar] *v* hinder; prevent; limit; restrict

cobarde [koˈβarðe] *s(m + f)* coward. *adj* cowardly. **cobardía** *sf* cowardice.

cobertizo [koβerˈtiθo] *sm* garage; shed.

cobertura [koβerˈtura] *sf* covering.

cobijar [koβiˈxar] *v* cover, shelter. **cobijo** *sm* shelter

cobrar [koˈβrar] *v* charge; earn; gain. **cobrarse** *v* (*med*) recover. **cobradero** *adj* recoverable. **cobrador, -a** *sm, sf* collector; conductor; receiver. **cobranza** *sf* collection; receipt.

cobre [ˈkoβre] *sm* copper. **batirse el cobre** (*fam*) get on with it. **cobres** *sm pl* (*música*) brass.

*cocer [koˈθer] v cook. **cocido** sm stew.

cocinar [koθiˈnar] v cook. **cocina** sf kitchen; cookery. **cocinero, -a** sm, sf cook.

coco [ˈkoko] sm coconut; coconut palm; grub, larva; (fam) face; (fam) head. **hacer cocos** make faces.

cocodrilo [kokoˈðrilo] sm crocodile.

cóctel [ˈkoktel] sm cocktail.

coche [ˈkotʃe] sm car; coach; carriage. **coche cama** sleeper. **coche de alquiler** hire car, self-drive car. **coche fúnebre** hearse.

cochino [koˈtʃino], **-a** sm, sf pig, swine. adj (fam) rotten; filthy; disgusting. **cochinada** sf filth; filthy thing. **cochinera** sf pigsty.

codear [koðeˈar] v nudge, elbow. **codearse** v rub shoulders with. **codazo** sm nudge. **codo** sm elbow; bend.

codeína [koðeˈina] sf codeine.

codelincuente [koðelinˈkwente] s(m + f) accomplice. **codelincuencia** sf complicity.

códice [ˈkoðiθe] sm codex.

codiciar [koðiˈθjar] v covet. **codicia** sf greed. **codicioso** adj greedy.

codificar [koðifiˈkar] v codify. **codificación** sf codification.

código [ˈkoðiɣo] sm code. **código de barras** sm bar code. **código de carreteras** highway code.

codillo [koˈðiλo] sm forearm; (culin) shoulder.

codorniz [koðorˈniθ] sf quail.

coercer [koerˈθer] v coerce. **coerción** sf coercion.

coexistir [koeksisˈtir] v coexist. **coexistencia** sf coexistence.

cofia [ˈkofja] sf coif; hair-net.

cofradía [kofraˈðia] sf fraternity; society.

cofre [ˈkofre] sm chest.

coger [koˈxer] v get; take; catch; seize; fit; collect. **cogida** sf gathering; (tauromaquia) goring. **cogido** sm fold, pleat.

cogote [koˈɣote] sm nape of the neck. **ser tieso de cogote** be stiff-necked.

cohete [koˈete] sm rocket.

cohibir [koiˈβir] v inhibit; embarrass. **cohibidor** adj inhibiting. **cohibición** sf inhibition. **cohibido** adj restricted.

cohombrillo [koomˈbriλo] sm gherkin. **cohombro** sm cucumber.

coincidencia [koinθiˈðenθja] sf coincidence. **coincidente** adj coincidental.

cojear [koxeˈar] v limp; hobble; (fig) waver; (fig) lapse. **cojera** sf lameness. **cojo** adj lame; lopsided.

cojín [koˈxin] sm cushion. **cojinete** sm small pillow; pad; (tecn) bearing. **cojinete de bolas** ball-bearing.

cok [kok] sm coke.

col [kol] sf cabbage. **coles de Bruselas** Brussels sprouts pl.

cola [ˈkola] sf tail; end; (vestido) train; queue; glue. **hacer cola** form a queue.

colaborar [kolaβoˈrar] v collaborate. **colaboración** sf collaboration. **colaborador, -a** sm, sf collaborator.

colapso [koˈlapso] sm collapse, breakdown.

*colar [koˈlar] v strain; filter; wash; confer; (fig, fam) slip through. **colarse** v slip; gate-crash; jump the queue; err. **colada** sf washing. **coladero** sm colander, sieve.

colcha [ˈkoltʃa] sf bedspread.

colchón [kolˈtʃon] sm mattress.

colear [koleˈar] v wag the tail.

colección [kolekˈθjon] sf collection. **colectivo** adj collective. **colectividad** sf collectivity; community.

colega [koˈleɣa] sm colleague.

colegio [koˈlexjo] sm college, school. **colegial** sm schoolboy.

colegir [koleˈxir] v infer, conclude.

cólera [ˈkolera] sf anger. sm cholera. **colérico** adj angry.

colesterol [kolesteˈrol] sm colesterol.

coleta [koˈleta] sf pigtail; postscript.

*colgar [kolˈɣar] v hang, hang up, hang out. **colgadero** sm hook; peg; hanger. **puente colgante** sm suspension bridge.

coliflor [koliˈflor] sf cauliflower.

colilla [koˈliλa] sf cigarette stub.

colina [koˈlina] sf hill.

colindar [kolinˈdar] v adjoin. **colindante** adj adjacent.

colisión [koliˈsjon] sf collision.

colmar [kolˈmar] v fill to overflowing. **colmado** adj plentiful.

colmena [kolˈmena] sf beehive.

colmillo [kolˈmiλo] sm tooth; fang; tusk. **enseñar los colmillos** (fam) threaten.

colmo [ˈkolmo] sm highest point; limit.

colocar [koloˈkar] v place; put in position; arrange; find employment for. **colocarse** v get a job. **colocación** *sf* employment; position; investment.

Colombia [ko'lombja] *sf* Colombia. **colombiano, -a** *s, adj* Colombian.

colonia [ko'lonja] *sf* colony. **colonial** *adj* colonial; imported. **colonialismo** *sm* colonialism. **colonización** *sf* colonization. **colonizar** *v* colonize. **colonizador** *sm* settler. **colono** *sm* colonist, colonial.

coloquio [ko'lokjo] *sm* conversation.

color [ko'lor] *sm* colour; dye; paint; complexion. **colorado** *sm, adj* coloured; red. **ponerse colorado** blush. **colorar** *v* colour, dye. **colorear** *v* colour, dye; grow red; ripen, **colorete** *sm* rouge. **colorido** *sm* colour, colouring, **colorín** *sm* goldfinch; (*fam*) measles.

colosal [kolo'sal] *adj* colossal.

columbrar [kolum'brar] *v* glimpse; (*fig*) suspect.

columna [ko'lumna] *sf* column. pillar.

columpiar [kolum'pjar] *v* swing. **columpiarse** *v* sway; (*fam*) waddle; blunder. **columpio** *sm* swing.

collado [ko'λaðo] *sm* hill; fell.

collar [ko'λar] *sm* necklace; collar.

coma¹ [ˈkoma] *sf* (*gram*) comma.

coma² *sm* (*med*) coma.

comadre [ko'maðre] *sf* midwife; god-mother; (*fam*) neighbour, friend. **comadrear** *v* gossip. **comadreo** *sm* gossip.

comadreja [koma'ðrexa] *sf* weasel.

comadrona [koma'ðrona] *sf* midwife.

comandante [koman'dante] *sm* commander. **comandar** *v* command.

comandita [koman'dita] *sf* sleeping partnership. **socio comanditario** *sm* sleeping partner.

comarca [ko'marka] *sf* region, district.

comba [ˈkomba] *sf* bend, curve; camber; sag. **combadura** *sf* curvature; camber.

combatir [komba'tir] *v* combat, fight, **combate** *sm* combat, battle, struggle, **combatiente** *sm* fighter; soldier.

combinar [kombi'nar] *v* combine; plan. arrange. **combinación** *sf* combination; project; permutation. **combinatorio** *adj* combining.

combustible [kombus'tiβle] *adj* combustible. *sm* fuel.

comedero [kome'ðero] *adj* edible. *sm* dining-room; feeding-trough.

comedia [ko'meðja] *sf* play; comedy; theatre. **comediante, -a** *sm, sf* actor/actress.

comediar [kome'ðjar] *v* divide into equal shares.

comedido [kome'ðiðo] *adj* polite, courteous; moderate. **comedir** *v* prepare. **comedirse** *v* restrain oneself.

comedor [kome'ðor] *sm* dining-room.

comensal [komen'sal] *sm* table companion.

comentar [komen'tar] *v* comment on; discuss. **comentario** *sm* commentary. **comentarista** *s(m + f)* commentator. **comento** *sm* comment.

*comenzar [komen'θar] *v* commence. **comienzo** *sm* beginning.

comer [ko'mer] *v* eat; corrode; erode. **no tener qué comer** have nothing to eat. **ser de buen comer** have a good appetite. **comerse** *v* swallow; eat up. **comestible** *adj* edible. **comestibles** *sm pl* food *sing*; groceries *pl*. **comida** *sf* food; meal; lunch.

comercio [ko'merθjo] *sm* commerce; trade; shop. **comercio al por mayor/menor** wholesale/retail trade. **comercio electrónico** *sm* e-commerce.**comerciante** *sm* shopkeeper; merchant; tradesman. **comerciar** *v* trade. **comercial** *s(m+f)* commercial.

cometa [ko'meta] *sf* kite. *sm* comet.

cometer [kome'ter] *v* commit. **cometido** *sm* task; assignment; mission.

comezón [kome'θon] *sf* itch; itching.

cómico [ˈkomiko] *adj* comic(al). *sm* comedian.

comida basura *sf* junk food.

comida naturista *sf* wholefood(s).

comida rápida *sf* fast food.

comilón [komi'lon], **-ona** *sm, sf* glutton. *adj* gluttonous, *sf* feast.

comillas [ko'miλas] *sf pl* inverted commas *pl*.

comisaría [komisa'ria] *sf* police station. **comisario** *sm* commissary; commissioner; police inspector.

comisión [komi'sjon] *sf* commission; mission; committee.

comiso [ko'miso] *sm* (*jur*) confiscation.

comité [komi'te] *sm* committee.

comitiva [komi'tiβa] *sf* retinue.

como [ˈkomo] *adv* how; as; as if; why; when; so that; about, approximately. *conj* as, since, because; if. **así como** as soon as;

in the same way that. **como quiera que sea** in one way or another. **tan pronto como** as soon as. **¿cómo?** *adv* how? why? in what way? ¡cómo! *interj* what! why! eh! **el cómo y el porqué** the how and the why.

cómoda [ˈkomoða] *sf* chest of drawers.

cómodo [ˈkomoðo] *adj* convenient; comfortable. **comodidad** *sf* convenience, comfort. **a su comodidad** at your earliest convenience.

compacto [komˈpakto] *adj* compact, close.

****compadecer** [kompaðeˈθer] *v* pity. **compadecerse** *v* sympathize; agree.

compadre [komˈpaðre] *sm* godfather; pal, crony.

compaginar [kompaxiˈnar] *v* arrange; combine; join; match; agree.

compañero [kompaˈɲero], **-a** *sm, sf* companion, partner; one of a pair. **compañerismo** *sm* fellowship. **compañía** *sf* company, society.

comparar [kompaˈrar] *v* compare. **comparación** *sf* comparison. **comparativo** *adj* comparative.

****comparecer** [kompareˈθer] *v* appear in court. **orden de comparecer** *sm* summons.

compartimiento [kompartiˈmjento] *sm* compartment; section; division. **compartir** *v* divide; share.

compás [komˈpas] *sm* (*mar*) compass; (*mat*) pair of compasses; rhythm; pattern, standard. **llevar el compás** beat time. **compasado** *adj* orderly, moderate. **compasar** *v* measure; regulate.

compasión [kompaˈsjon] *sf* compassion. **compasivo** *adj* compassionate.

compatible [kompaˈtiβle] *adj* compatible. **compatibilidad** *sf* compatibility.

compatriota [kompaˈtrjota] *s(m + f)* compatriot.

compeler [kompeˈler] *v* compel.

compendio [komˈpendjo] *sm* compendium; summary, précis. **en compendio** briefly. **compendiar** *v* summarize.

compensar [kompenˈsar] *v* compensate; offset; make amends. **compensación** *sf* compensation. **compensatorio** *adj* compensatory.

****competir** [kompeˈtir] *v* compete; contest. **competencia** *sf* competition; concern; competence. **competente** *adj* competent;

able. **competición** *sf* competition. **competidor, -a** *sm, sf* competitor.

compilar [kompiˈlar] *v* compile. **compilación** *sf* compilation.

compinche [komˈpintʃe] *s(m + f)* pal, chum; accomplice.

****complacer** [komplaˈθer] *v* please; oblige; humour. **complacerse** *v* be pleased, be glad (to). **complacencia** *sf* pleasure; indulgence. **complaciente** *adj* helpful; obliging.

complejo [komˈplexo] *adj, sm* complex. **complejidad** *sf* complexity.

complementario [komplemenˈtarjo] *adj* complementary. **complemento** *sm* complement.

completar [kompleˈtar] *v* complete. **completo** *adj* complete.

complicar [kompliˈkar] *v* complicate; be complicated *or* confused. **complicarse** *v* become confused *or* complicated. **complicación** *sf* complication. **complicado** *adj* complicated.

cómplice [ˈkompliθe] *s(m + f)* accomplice. **complicidad** *sf* complicity.

complot [komˈplot] *sm* plot; intrigue; (*fam*) understanding.

****componer** [kompoˈner] *v* compose; form; repair; adjust; write. **componerse** *v* compose oneself; tidy oneself up; dress up; agree. **componerse de** consist of. **componedor, -a** *sm, sf* compositor; repairer; arbitrator. **componente** *sm* component; ingredient. **componible** *adj* adjustable.

comportar [komporˈtar] *v* tolerate; involve. **comportarse** *v* behave. **comportamiento** *sm* behaviour. **comporte** *sm* behaviour; bearing.

composición [komposiˈθjon] *sf* composition; mixture; agreement; settlement. **compositor, -a** *sm, sf* composer.

compostura [komposˈtura] *sf* composition, structure; repair; neatness; adornment; agreement; composure; adjustment.

compota [komˈpota] *sf* (*culin*) compote.

comprar [komˈprar] *v* buy; bribe. **compra** *sf* purchase. **comprador, -a** *sm, sf* shopper.

comprender [komprenˈder] *v* understand; include. **comprensibilidad** *sf* intelligibility. **comprensible** *adj* understandable. **comprensión** *sf* understanding; inclusion. **comprensivo** *adj* understanding; comprising.

comprimir [kompriˈmir] *v* squeeze; com-

press. **comprimirse** v control oneself.
compresa sf compress; sanitary towel.
compresión sf compression.

*comprobar [kompro'βar] v verify, check.
comprobación sf verification. **comprobante** adj verifying. sm voucher; receipt.

comprometer [komprome'ter] v risk; compromise; commit. **comprometido** adj embarrassing; committed; implicated.
compromiso sm commitment; agreement; compromise.

compuesto [kom'pwesto] sm compound.
adj compound; repaired; dressed-up.

compunción [kompun'θjon] sf compunction; contrition.

computar [kompu'tar] v compute, calculate. **computadora** sf computer.

comulgar [komul'gar] v give/take communion; (fig) share.

común [ko'mun] adj common; ordinary; vulgar. sm community, public toilet. **por lo común** generally. **comunal** adj communal.

comunicar [komuni'kar] v communicate; convey; transmit; (dos cuartos) connect.
comunicarse v spread; keep in touch with; exchange. **comunicación** sf communication; message. **comunicativo** adj talkative; catching.

comunidad [komuni'ðað] sf community.

comunión [komu'njon] sf communion.

comunismo [komu'nismo] sm communism. **comunista** s(m + f). adj communist.

con [kon] prep with; by; in spite of; to, towards. **con que** conj whereupon; and so. **con tal que** provided that.

cóncavo ['konkaβo] adj concave. **concavidad** sf hollow, cavity.

*concebir [konθe'βir] v conceive; imagine; understand; take; (med) conceive. **concebible** adj conceivable, imaginable. **concepción** sf conception, idea; (med) conception. **concepto** sm concept; idea; opinion; witticism.

conceder [konθe'ðer] v concede, grant; allow; spare; award. **concesión** sf concession; grant.

concejo [kon'θexo] sm council. **concejal** sm councillor. **concejil** adj municipal.

concentrar [konθen'trar] v concentrate.
concentración sf concentration.

concerniente [konθer'njente] adj concerning, regarding. **concernir** v concern.

*concertar [konθer'tar] v harmonize; agree; adjust; compare. **concertado** adj concerted.

conciencia [kon'θjenθja] sf conscience; consciousness; mind; conscientiousness.
concienzudo adj conscientious.

concierto [kon'θjerto] sm concert; concerto; agreement; (fig) harmony. **de concierto** in agreement.

conciliar [konθi'ljar] v conciliate; reconcile; gain. adj of a council. sm councillor.
concilio sm councillor; council.

conciso [kon'θiso] adj concise.

concitar [konθi'tar] v stir up.

*concluir [konklu'ir] v conclude; deduce; settle; convince. **conclusión** sf conclusion.

*concordar [konkor'ðar] v agree. **concordancia** sf agreement. **concorde** adj in agreement. **concordia** sf harmony.

concretar [konkre'tar] v bring together; limit; specify; state explicitly. **concretarse** v confine oneself; be definite; keep; take shape. **concreto** adj concrete, specific. **en concreto** in brief.

concubina [konku'βina] sf concubine.

concurrir [konkur'rir] v meet; attend; go; coincide; contribute; concur; compete.
concurrido adj popular; crowded. **concurso** sm meeting; cooperation; help; competition.

concusión [konku'sjon] sf concussion.

concha ['kontʃa] sf shell.

condado [kon'daðo] sm earldom; county.
conde sm earl. **condesa** sf countess.

condecorar [kondeko'rar] v (persona) decorate. **condecoración** sf medal, decoration.

condenar [konde'nar] v condemn; sentence; block up. **condena** sf sentence; conviction. **cumplir condena** serve a sentence. **condenación** sf condemnation; damnation. **condenado, -a** sm, sf; condemned person; wretch.

condensar [konden'sar] v condense. **condensación** sf condensation. **condensador** sm condenser.

*condescender [kondesθen'der] v condescend; yield; comply **condescendencia** sf condescension; compliance. **condescendiente** adj condescending; obliging.

condicionar [kondiθjo'nar] v condition; determine. **condición** sf condition; quality; temperament.

condimentar [kondimen'tar] v season.
 condimento sm seasoning, condiment.

condolerse [kondo'lerse] v condole, sympathize. **condolencia** sf condolence.

condonar [kondo'nar] v pardon, condone;
 (deuda) cancel. **condonación** sf pardon.

*__conducir__ [kondu'θir] v conduct; transport;
 guide; manage; (auto) drive; be suitable.
 conducirse v behave. **conducción** sf transport; guidance; direction, management.
 conducción a izquierda lefthand drive.
 permiso de conducción sm driving
 licence. **conducta** sf transport; conduct;
 direction; behaviour. **conducta agresiva
 de los conductores** sf road rage.

conducto [kon'dukto] sm conduit; pipe.
 conductor sm (tecn) conductor.

conectar [konek'tar] v connect; switch on.
 conectarse v log on (computer). **conectado** adj on-line. **conectador** sm connector.
 conexión sf connection.

conejo [ko'nexo] sm rabbit. **coneja** sf doe.

confabularse [konfaβu'larse] v plot. **con-
 fabulación** sf conspiracy.

confeccionar [konfekθjon'ar] v make,
 make up. **confección** sf making; tailoring;
 clothing. **confeccionado** adj readymade,
 ready-to-wear.

confederar [konfeðe'rar] v confederate.
 confederación sf confederation, confeder-
 acy.

conferenciar [konferen'θjar] v talk, discuss. **conferencia** sf conference; lecture;
 telephone call. **conferencia a cobro
 revertido** reverse-charge call. **conferencia
 en la cumbre** summit conference. **conferencia interurbana** trunk call.

*__conferir__ [konfe'rir] v confer, consult;
 award, grant.

*__confesar__ [konfe'sar] v confess, admit. **con-
 fesar de plano** own up. **confesión** sf confession.

confeti [kon'feti] sm pl confetti sing.

confiar [kon'fjar] v entrust; trust; rely. **con-
 fiable** adj trustworthy. **confiado** adj confident; trusting. **confianza** sf confidence;
 reliability; informality.

confidencia [konfi'ðenθja] sf secret; confidence. **confidencial** adj confidential. **con-
 fidente** adj faithful.

confinar [konfi'nar] v confine; banish. **confinar con** border on. **confín** sm border,
 limit.

confirmar [konfir'mar] v confirm. **confir-
 marse** v be confirmed. **confirmación** sf
 confirmation.

confiscar [konfis'kar] v confiscate. **confiscación** sf confiscation.

confitar [konfi'tar] v coat with sugar; preserve in syrup. **confite** sm sweet. **confitería** sf sweet-shop. **confitura** sf candied
 fruit.

conflicto [kon'flikto] sm conflict.

*__confluir__ [konflu'ir] v converge, meet.

conformar [konfor'mar] v conform. **conformarse** v resign oneself. **conforme** adj
 in agreement; alike; according. **conforme
 a** in accordance with. **según y conforme**
 it all depends.

confortar [konfor'tar] v comfort; encourage. **confortable** adj comfortable. **con-
 forte** sm solace, comfort.

confrontar [konfron'tar] v confront; compare. **confrontar con** border on; confront.
 confrontación sf confrontation.

confundir [konfun'dir] v confuse; mistake.
 confusión sf confusion. **confuso** adj confused; embarrassed.

congelar [konxe'lar] v freeze; congeal. **congelación** sf freezing. **congelación de
 salarios** wage freeze. **congelador** sm freezer.

congénito [kon'xenito] adj congenital.

congestionar [konxestjo'nar] v congest.
 congestión sf congestion.

conglomerarse [konglome'rarse] v conglomerate. **conglomeración** sf conglomeration.

congoja [kon'goxa] sf agony; distress.

congratular [kongratu'lar] v congratulate.
 congratularse v be delighted. **congratu-
 lación** sf congratulation; delight.

congregar [kongre'gar] v congregate. **congregación** sf congregation.

congreso [kon'greso] sm congress; assembly; conference.

congrio ['kongrjo] sm conger eel.

congruente [kongru'ente] adj congruent;
 suitable. **congruencia** sf congruence;
 suitability.

cónico ['koniko] adj conical.

conífero [ko'nifero] adj coniferous.
 conífera sf conifer.

conjeturar [konxetu'rar] v conjecture,
 guess. **conjetura** sf conjecture, guess.

conjugar [konxu'gar] v combine; (gram) conjugate. **conjugación** sf conjugation.

conjunto [kon'xunto] sm whole. adj joint. **en conjunto** as a whole. **conjunción** sf (gram) conjunction.

conjurar [konxu'rar] v bind by oath; implore; ward off; conspire; exorcise. **conjura** sf also **conjuración** conspiracy. **conjurador** sm exorcist. **conjuro** sm exorcism; entreaty.

conmemorar [konmemo'rar] v commemorate. **conmemoración** sf commemoration. **conmemorativo** adj commemorative.

conmigo [kon'migo] pron with me, with myself.

conminar [konmi'nar] v threaten; warn. **conminativo** adj threatening; compulsory.

conmiseración [konmisera'θjon] sf commiseration.

conmoción [konmo'θjon] sf commotion; upheaval; shock. **conmoción cerebral** concussion.

conmover [konmo'βer] v disturb; touch. **conmoverse** v be moved. **conmovedor** adj moving, touching.

conmutar [konmu'tar] v exchange. **conmutador** sm switch.

connivencia [konni'βenθja] sf connivance.

connotar [konno'tar] v imply. **connotación** sf connotation.

cono ['kono] sm cone.

***conocer** [kono'θer] v know; understand; recognize. **conocer de** know about. **conocer de or en** (jur) try (a case). **conocer de nombre** know by name. **conocerse** v meet; be acquainted with. **se conoce que** it is clear that. **conocedor, -a s,** adj expert. **conocido, -a sm,** sf acquaintance. **conocimiento** sm knowledge; good sense; consciousness; (com) bill of lading; proof of identity. **perder el conocimiento** lose consciousness.

conque ['konke] conj so. sm (fam) condition. **conqué** sm (fam) means.

conquistar [konkis'tar] v conquer; win; win over. **conquista** sf conquest. **conquistador, -a sm,** sf conqueror.

consabido [konsa'βiðo] adj traditional; well known; aforementioned.

consagrar [konsa'grar] v consecrate; dedicate. **consagración** sf consecration; dedication.

consanguíneo [konsan'gineo] adj related by blood. **consanguinidad** sf blood relationship.

consciente [kons'θjente] adj conscious.

consecuencia [konse'kwenθja] sf consequence; outcome; consistency; spin-off. **en or por consecuencia** consequently. **ser de consecuencia** be of importance. **traer como consecuencia** result in. **consecuente** adj consequent; consistent.

consecutivo [konseku'tiβo] adj consecutive.

***conseguir** [konse'gir] v get; attain; procure; bring about; manage. **dar por conseguido** take for granted.

consejo [kon'sexo] sm advice, counsel; council. **consejo de guerra** court-martial. **entrar en consejo** begin consultation. **consejero** sm adviser; member of board of directors.

***consentir** [konsen'tir] v allow; believe; tolerate; spoil; agree. **consentir en** consent to. **consentirse** v begin to crack; come loose. **consentido** adj pampered.

conserje [kon'serxe] sm porter, doorkeeper.

conservar [konser'βar] v conserve; preserve. **conservarse** v last, wear well. **conserva** sf preserved food; jam; pickles pl. **conservación** sf conservation; preserving. **conservador, -a sm,** sf (pol) Conservative; (museo) curator.

considerar [konsiðe'rar] v consider. **considerable** adj considerable; substantial. **consideración** sf consideration. **por consideración a** out of respect for. **ser de consideración** be important. **tener or guardar consideraciones** show consideration.

consignar [konsig'nar] v consign; assign; deposit; send. **consignación** sf consignment. **consigna** sf left-luggage office; password; slogan.

consigo [kon'sigo] pron with him/her/you/one.

consiguiente [konsi'gjente] adj consequent.

consistir [konsis'tir] v consist. **consistir en** consist of. **consistencia** sf consistency. **consistente** adj consistent.

***consolar** [konso'lar] v console. **consolación** sf consolation.

consolidar [konsoli'ðar] v consolidate; strengthen. **consolidación** sf consolidation.

consonante [konso'nante] *sm* consonant. *adj* rhyming; harmonious. **consonancia** *sf* rhyme; harmony. **consonar** *v* rhyme; harmonize.

consorte [kon'sorte] *s(m + f)* consort; accomplice; companion. **consorcio** *sm* association; fellowship; consortium.

conspicuo [kons'pikwo] *adj* conspicuous.

conspirar [konspi'rar] *v* conspire, plot. **conspiración** *sf* conspiracy, plot.

constante [kons'tante] *adj* constant. **constancia** *sf* constancy.

constar [kons'tar] *v* be clear; be evident; be on record. **constar de** consist of. **constar en** appear; be recorded.

constelación [konstela'θjon] *sf* constellation; climate.

consternarse [konster'narse] *v* be dismayed. **consternación** *sf* consternation, dismay.

constiparse [konsti'parse] *v* catch a cold. **constipación** *sf* cold. **estar constipado** have a cold.

***constituir** [konstitu'ir] *v* constitute; establish; compose. **constitución** *sf* constitution.

constreñir [konstre'nir] *v* constrain; force; constipate. **constreñimiento** *sm* constraint. **constricción** *sf* constriction.

***construir** [konstru'ir] *v* construct. **construcción** *sf* construction. **constructor, -a** *sm, sf* builder, constructor.

consuelo [kon'swelo] *sm* consolation.

cónsul ['konsul] *sm* consul. **consulado** *sm* consulate.

consultar [konsul'tar] *v* consult. **consulta** *sf* consultation.

consumado [konsu'maðo] *adj* consummate; accomplished. **consumación** *sf* consummation; completion. **consumar** *v* accomplish; complete.

consumir [konsu'mir] *v* consume. **consumirse** *v* languish; be uneasy. **consumido** *adj* consumed; (*fam*) lean; (*fam*) timid. **consumo** *sm* consumption.

contabilidad [kontaβili'ðað] *sf* accounting; bookkeeping. **contable** *sm* bookkeeper; accountant.

contacto [kon'takto] *sm* contact.

contagiar [konta'xjar] *v* infect, contaminate; corrupt. **contagio** *sm* contagion. **contagioso** *adj* contagious.

contaminar [kontami'nar] *v* contaminate. **contaminación** *sf* contamination.

***contar** [kon'tar] *v* count; relate. **contar con** count on; expect; possess. **contado** *adj* counted, limited. **al contado** cash down. **de contado** immediately. **por de contado** certainly. **contador** *sm* counter; cashier; (*tecn*) meter. **contador de aparcamiento** parking meter.

contemplar [kontem'plar] *v* contemplate. **contemplación** *sf* contemplation. **contemplativo** *adj* contemplative.

contemporáneo [kontempo'raneo], **-a** *s, adj* contemporary.

***contender** [konten'der] *v* contend; struggle; argue. **contención** *sf* contention. **contencioso** *adj* contentious. **contendedor** *sm* contender, antagonist. **contendiente** *s(m + f)* litigant. **contienda** *sf* contest; dispute.

***contener** [konte'ner] *v* contain; control; suppress; stop. **contenedor de vidrio** *sm* bottle bank.

contenido [konte'niðo] *adj* reserved; moderate; contained. *sm* contents *pl*.

contentar [konten'tar] *v* satisfy, content. **contentarse** *v* be pleased. **contentamiento** *sm* contentment. **contento** *adj* content, satisfied.

contestar [kontes'tar] *v* answer; confirm; agree. **contestador automático** *sm* answering machine. **contestable** *adj* questionable. **contestación** *sf* reply; dispute.

contexto [kon'teksto] *sm* context.

contigo [kon'tigo] *pron* (*fam*) with you.

contiguo [kon'tigwo] *adj* contiguous; adjoining. **contigüidad** *sf* contiguity.

continente [konti'nente] *sm* continent; bearing; container. *adj* containing; continent. **continencia** *sf* continence. **continental** *adj* continental.

contingente [kontin'xente] *adj* contingent, accidental. *sm* contingent; standby (plan). **contingencia** *sf* contingency.

continuar [konti'nwar] *v* continue; remain; endure. **continuación** *sf* continuation. **a continuación de** following. **continuo** *adj* continuous.

contorno [kon'torno] *sm* contour, outline.

contornos *sm pl* environs *pl*. **en contorno** round about.

contra ['kontra] *prep* against; opposite; facing. **el pro y el contra** the pros and cons. **en contra de** in opposition to.

contrabajo [kontra'βaxo] *sm* double bass.
contrabando [kontra'βando] *sm* contraband; smuggling.
contracción [kontrak'θjon] *sf* contraction.
*contradecir [kontraðe'θir] *v* contradict. **contradicción** *sf* contradiction.
*contraer [kontra'er] *v* contract; enter into; be infected with. **contraer matrimonio con** marry.
contrafuerte [kontra'fwerte] *sm* buttress.
*contrahacer [kontraa'θer] *v* counterfeit; copy. **contrahacerse** *v* feign.
contrahecho [kontra'etʃo] *adj* deformed.
contramaestre [kontrama'estre] *sm* foreman; (*mar*) boatswain.
contramandar [kontraman'dar] *v* countermand.
contrapelo [kontra'pelo] *adv* **a contrapelo** against the grain.
contrapesar [kontrape'sar] *v* counterpoise, counterbalance; offset. **contrapeso** *sm* counterpoise.
contraponer [kontrapo'ner] *v* set against; oppose; contrast.
contrapunto [kontra'punto] *sm* counterpoint.
contrariar [kontra'rjar] *v* oppose. **contrariedad** *sf* opposition; setback; annoyance.
contrario [kon'trarjo], **-a** *sm*, *sf* opponent. **al contrario** on the contrary. **de lo contrario** otherwise. *adj* contrary, opposite.
contrarrestar [kontrarres'tar] *v* counteract; oppose; resist; (*la pelota*) return.
contrarrevolución [kontrarreβolu'θjon] *sf* counter-revolution. **contrarrevolucionario, -a** *s, adj* counter-revolutionary.
contrasentido [kontrasen'tiðo] *sm* contradiction; nonsense; mistranslation; misinterpretation.
contraseña [kontra'seɲa] *sf* countersign; password.
contrastar [kontras'tar] *v* contrast; resist; inspect. **contraste** *sm* contrast; opposition; hallmark; inspector. **en contraste con** in contrast to.
contrato [kon'trato] *sm* contract; covenant.
contraveneno [kontraβe'neno] *sm* antidote.
*contravenir [kontraβe'nir] *v* contravene. **contravención** *sf* contravention.
*contribuir [kontri'βwir] *v* contribute; pay

tax. **contribución** *sf* contribution; tax. **contribuyente** *s(m + f)* tax-payer.
contrición [kontri'θjon] *sf* contrition.
contrincante [kontrin'kante] *sm* competitor; rival.
controlador de tráfico aéreo *sm* air traffic controller.
controversia [kontro'βersja] *sf* controversy. **controvertible** *adj* controversial. **controvertir** *v* dispute, argue.
contumacia [kontu'maθja] *sf* stubbornness, obstinacy; (*jur*) contempt of court. **contumaz** *adj* stubborn; perverse.
conturbar [kontur'βar] *v* perturb; disturb. **conturbación** *sf* perturbation.
contusión [kontu'sjon] *sf* contusion, bruise. **contusionar** *v* bruise.
*convalecer [konβale'θer] *v* convalesce. **convalecencia** *sf* convalescence.
convecino [konβe'θino] *adj* neighbouring.
convencer [konβen'θer] *v* convince. **convencedor** *adj* convincing. **convencimiento** *sm* conviction.
*convenir [konβe'nir] *v* agree, be agreed; arrange; be convenient; be advisable. **me conviene** it suits me. **convención** *sf* convention; agreement; assembly. **convencional** *adj* conventional. **convenible** *adj* docile. **conveniencia** *sf* convenience; conformity; usefulness; advantage. **conveniente** *adj* convenient; expedient; proper. **convenio** *sm* agreement; compact.
convento [kon'βento] *sm* convent.
converger [konβer'xer] *v also* **convergir** converge; (*fig*) agree. **convergencia** *sf* convergence. **convergente** *adj* convergent.
conversar [konβer'sar] *v* converse. **conversar con** talk to. **conversar sobre** talk about. **conversador** *adj* sociable. **conversación** *sf* conversation.
*convertir [konβer'tir] *v* convert. **convertidor catalítico** *sm* catalytic converter. **convertirse** *v* become, turn into. **conversión** *sf* conversion. **convertible** *adj* convertible.
convexo [kon'βekso] *adj* convex. **convexidad** *sf* convexity.
convicción [konβik'θjon] *sf* conviction. **convicto** *adj* convicted.
convidar [konβi'ðar] *v* invite. **convidarse** *v* offer one's services. **convidada** *sf* (*fam*) invitation to a drink. **pagar la convidada** (*fam*) treat to a drink. **convidado, -a** *sm, sf*

guest. **convidador, -a** *sm, sf* host/hostess.

convincente [konβin'θente] *adj* convincing.

convivir [konβi'βir] *v* coexist. **convivencia** *sf* coexistence.

convocar [konβo'kar] *v* convoke. **convocación** *sf* convocation. **convocador, -a** *sm, sf* convener. **convocatoria** *sf* summons.

convoy [kon'βoi] *sm* convoy. **convoyar** *v* convoy.

convulsión [konβul'sjon] *sf* convulsion. **convulsivo** *adj* convulsive.

conyugal [konju'gal] *adj* conjugal. **cónyuge** *s(m + f)* spouse.

coñac [ko'nak] *sm* cognac, brandy.

cooperar [koope'rar] *v* cooperate. **cooperación** *sf* cooperation. **cooperativa** *sf* cooperative.

coordinar [koorði'nar] *v* coordinate. **coordinación** *sf* coordination.

copa ['kopa] *sf* glass; cup; goblet. **sombrero de copa** top-hat. **tomar una copa** have a drink. **copas** *sf pl* (*naipes*) hearts. **copado** *adj* (*árbol*) bushy. **copera** *sf* cupboard; sideboard.

Copenhague [kope'nage] *sf* Copenhagen.

copete [ko'pete] *sm* tuft of hair; bun; (*pájaro*) crest; summit; (*fig*) haughtiness. **de alto copete** aristocratic.

copiar [ko'pjar] *v* copy; record. **copia** *sf* copy; duplicate; image; abundance. **copia de seguridad** *sf* back-up (computer). **copiador, -a** *sm, sf* copier. **copiante** *s(m + f)* copyist.

copla ['kopla] *sf* verse; song; ballad. **coplas de ciego** doggerel.

copo ['kopo] *sm* flake; ball of wool; clot; lump.

coque ['koke] *sm* coke.

coquetear [kokete'ar] *v* flirt. **coqueta** *sf* flirt. **coqueteo** *sm* flirtation. **coquetón** *sm* (*fam*) philanderer.

coraje [ko'raxe] *sm* courage; anger. **corajinoso** *adj* irate.

coral [ko'ral] *sm* coral. *adj* choral.

coraza [ko'raθa] *sf* armour.

corazón [kora'θon] *sm* heart. **de corazón** sincerely.

corbata [kor'βata] *sf* necktie.

corcovado [korko'βaðo], **-a** *sm, sf* hunchback. *adj* hunchbacked.

corchea [kor'tʃea] *sf* (*música*) quaver.

corchete [kor'tʃete] *sm* clasp.

corcho ['kortʃo] *sm* cork.

cordel [kor'ðel] *sm* thin rope, line. **a cordel** in a straight line.

cordero [kor'ðero] *sm* lamb.

cordial [kor'ðjal] *adj* invigorating, stimulating; cordial, friendly, **dedo cordial** *sm* middle finger. **cordialidad** *sf* cordiality.

cordillera [korði'ʎera] *sf* mountain range.

cordón [kor'ðon] *sm* string; cord; braid.

cordura [kor'ðura] *sf* prudence; discretion.

coreografía [koreogra'fia] *sf* choreography.

cornada [kor'nada] *sf* goring. **cornear** *v* gore.

corneja [kor'nexa] *sf* crow.

corneta [kor'neta] *sf* bugle; hunting horn. **corneta de llaves** cornet.

cornudo [kor'nuðo] *adj* horned; cuckolded. *sm* cuckold.

coro ['koro] *sm* chorus.

coronar [koro'nar] *v* crown. **corona** *sf* crown. **coronación** *sf* coronation.

coronel [koro'nel] *sm* colonel.

coronilla [koro'niʎa] *sf* crown of the head.

corporal [korpo'ral] *adj* corporal. **corporación** *sf* corporation. **corpóreo** *adj* corporeal. **corpulencia** *sf* corpulence. **corpulento** *adj* corpulent.

corporativo [korpora'tiβo] *adj* corporate.

corpúsculo [kor'puskulo] *sm* corpuscle.

corral [kor'ral] *sm* yard; courtyard; corral; enclosure.

correa [kor'rea] *sf* leather strap; belt. **correa de ventilador** fan belt.

corredor [korre'ðor] *sm* corridor; runner; (*com*) broker.

*****corregir** [korre'xir] *v* correct. **corregirse** *v* reform oneself. **correción** *sf* correction; punishment. **correccional** *adj* reformatory. **correctivo** *sm, adj* corrective. **correcto** *adj* correct; well-bred.

correo [kor'reo] *sm* mail, post; post office; courier. **correo basura** *sm* spam (Internet). **correo certificado** registered post. **correo electrónico** *sm* e-mail. **a vuelta de correo** by return of post.

correr [kor'rer] *v* run; flow; pass; sail; cover; travel over. **correrse** *v* move; (*fam*) talk too much.

corresponder [korrespon'der] *v* correspond; concern; reply; repay; be grateful;

belong to; match; suit; fit. **a quien corresponda** to whom it may concern. **corresponderse** v correspond; agree; like each other. **correspondencia** sf correspondence, letters pl; agreement; reciprocation. **corresponsal** s(m + f) newspaper correspondent.

corrida [kor'riða] sf sprint. **corrida de toros** bullfight.

corrido [kor'riðo] adj abashed; experienced; over the specified weight.

corriente [kor'rjente] sf current, flow. adj current; running; everyday; standard; fluent. **agua corriente** running water. **al corriente** informed, up-to-date. **corriente alterna/continua** alternating/direct current. **corriente de aire** draught. **corriente principal** sf mainstream.

corroborar [korroβo'rar] v corroborate; strengthen. **corroboración** sf corroboration.

*corroer [korro'er] v corrode. **corrosión** sf corrosion.

corromper [korrom'per] v corrupt; ruin; bribe. **corromperse** v putrefy; be corrupted. **corrupción** sf corruption; stink; bribery.

corsé [kor'se] sm corset.

cortabolsas [korta'bolsas] sm invar (fam) pickpocket.

cortacésped [korta'θespeð] sm mower.

cortaplumas [korta'plumas] sm invar penknife.

cortar [kor'tar] v cut; cut short; break in on; stop; switch off. **cortarse** v cut oneself; become embarrassed. **cortante** adj cutting; sharp. **corte** sm cut; cutting edge.

corte ['korte] sf (royal) court.

cortejar [korte'xar] v court; accompany. **cortejo** sm courtship; accompaniment; homage.

cortesía [korte'sia] sf courtesy. **cortés** adj courteous.

corteza [kor'teθa] sf bark; rind; crust.

cortijo [kor'tixo] sm farmhouse and farm.

cortina [kor'tina] sf curtain; screen; dregs pl. **cortina de hierro** iron curtain. **cortina de humo** smokescreen.

corto ['korto] adj short; defective; stupid; timid. **corto circuito** sm short circuit. **corto de vista** short-sighted.

corvo ['korβo] adj curved; bent; crooked.

cosa ['kosa] sf thing; something; affair. **cosa de oír/ver** something worth listening to/seeing. **no sea cosa que** lest.

cosecha [ko'setʃa] sf harvest. **cosechar** v reap, harvest.

coser [ko'ser] v sew; stitch; join. **coserse la boca** (fam) keep mum.

cosquillas [kos'kiʎas] sf tickling; ticklishness. **hacer cosquillas a** tickle. **cosquillear** v tickle. **cosquilloso** adj ticklish.

costa¹ ['kosta] sf coast. **costear** v sail along the coast. **costera** sf slope, hill. **costero** adj coastal.

costa² sf cost; expense. **a toda costa** at all costs. **costar** v cost; cause. **coste** sm cost, price.

costilla [kos'tiʎa] sf rib; chop, cutlet. **costillas** sf pl shoulders pl.

costra ['kostra] sf scab; crust; (fam) filthiness.

costumbre [kos'tumbre] sf custom. **de costumbre** usual; usually.

costura [kos'tura] sf sewing; seam; dressmaking. **costurera** sf seamstress.

cotejar [kote'xar] v compare. **cotejo** sm comparison.

cotidiano [koti'ðjano] adj daily.

coto ['koto] sm enclosure; reserve; limit. **coto de caza** hunting reserve.

cotorra [ko'torra] sf parrot; magpie; (fam) chatterbox.

coyuntura [konjun'tura] sf joint; opportunity.

coz [koθ] sf recoil; kick.

cráneo ['kraneo] sm skull.

cráter ['krater] sm crater.

crear [kre'ar] v create; make; invent; found. **creación** sf creation. **creador, -a** sm, sf creator; inventor. **creativo** adj also **creador** creative.

*crecer [kre'θer] v grow. **crecerse** v become conceited; take courage. **creces** sf pl increase sing. **con creces** amply, with interest. **crecido** adj grown; high; large; in flood. **crecimiento** sm growth; increase; flooding.

credenciales [kreðen'θjales] sf pl credentials pl.

crédito ['kreðito] sm credit; credence; reputation. **carta de crédito** sf credit card.

credo ['kreðo] *sm* creed.

crédulo ['kreðulo] *adj* credulous.

***creer** [kre'er] *v* believe; think. **¡créamelo!** believe me! **¡ya lo creo!** of course! **creíble** *adj* credible.

crema ['krema] *sf* cream; custard.

cremación [krema'θjon] *sf* cremation.

cremallera [krema'ʎera] *sf* zip-fastener.

crepúsculo [kre'puskulo] *sm* twilight.

crespo ['krespo] *adj* crispy; fuzzy; crinkled; *(fig)* obscure; *(fig)* angry.

cresta ['kresta] *sf* crest, comb; tuft.

creta ['kreta] *sf* chalk.

criar [kri'ar] *v* breed; create; beget. **criarse** *v* grow up; be raised *or* reared. **cría** *sf* act of breeding; litter; brood; young. **cría intensiva** *sf* battery farming. **criada** *sf* maid. **criadero** *sm* (*plants*) nursery. **criado** *sm* manservant. **crianza** *sf* breeding; nursing. **buena/mala crianza** good/bad upbringing. **criatura** *sf* creature; infant.

cribar [kri'βar] *v* sieve; sift. **criba** *sf* sieve; screen.

crimen ['krimen] *sm* crime. **criminal** *sm, adj* criminal.

criollo [kri'oʎo], **-a** *s, adj* Creole.

cripta ['kripta] *sf* crypt.

crisálida [kri'saliða] *sf* chrysalis.

crisantemo [krisan'temo] *sm* chrysanthemum.

crisis ['krisis] *sf invar* crisis (*pl* -ses).

crisol [kri'sol] *sm* crucible.

crispar [kris'par] *v* cause to contract *or* twitch; contort; irritate. **crisparse** *v* twitch.

cristal [kirs'tal] *sm* crystal; glass; window; mirror. **cristal de contacto** contact lens. **cristal tallado** cut glass. **cristal trasero** (*auto*) rear window. **cristalería** *sf* glassworks; glassware. **cristalero, -a** *sm, sf* glazier; glassblower. **cristalino** *adj* crystalline; *(fig)* limpid.

Cristo ['kristo] *sm* Christ. **cristiandad** *sf* Christianity. **cristianismo** *sm* Christianity. **cristiano, -a** *s, adj* Christian.

criterio [kri'terjo] *sm* criterion (*pl* -a); point of view; opinion.

criticar [kriti'kar] *v* criticize. **crítica** *sf* criticism; review.

crítico ['kritiko] *sm* critic, *adj* critical.

Croacia [kro'aθja] *sf* Croatia. **croata** *adj* Croatian.

cromo ['kromo] *sm* chromium, chrome; picture card.

crónica ['kronika] *sf* chronicle; report. **cronista** *sm* chronicler; correspondent.

crónico ['kroniko] *adj* chronic.

cronología [kronolo'xia] *sf* chronology. **cronológico** *adj* chronological.

cronómetro [kro'nometro] *sm* chronometer; stopwatch.

croqueta [kro'keta] *sf* croquette.

croquis ['krokis] *sm invar* sketch, rough draft.

crucero [kru'θero] *sm* cruiser; cruise; crossroads *pl.*

crucificar [kruθifi'kar] *v* crucify. **crucifijo** *sm* crucifix. **crucifixión** *sf* crucifixion.

crucigrama [kruθi'grama] *sm* crossword puzzle.

crudo ['kruðo] *adj* crude; raw; immature; *(fam)* boastful.

cruel [kru'el] *adj* cruel. **crueldad** *sf* cruelty.

cruento [kru'ento] *adj* bloody.

crujir [kru'xir] *v* creak; rustle; crackle. **crujido** *sm* creak; rustle; crackle.

crustáceo [krus'taθeo] *sm, adj* crustacean.

cruz [kruθ] *sf* cross. **en cruz** crosswise. **cruzada** *sf* crusade; crossroads *pl.* **cruzado** *sm* crusader; knight. **cruzar** *v* cross; cross oneself; pass *or* place across; dub. **cruzarse** *v* pass each other; exchange. **Cruz Roju** *sf* Red Cross.

cuaderno [kwa'ðerno] *sm* notebook; exercise book; *(fam)* pack of cards.

cuadra ['kwaðra] *sf* stable; hut; large hall; hospital ward.

cuadragésimo [kwaðra'xesimo] *adj* fortieth.

cuadrante [kwa'ðrante] *adj* squaring. *sm* quadrant.

cuadrar [kwa'ðrar] *v* square. **cuadrado** *adj* square; stocky; perfect.

cuadrilla [kwa'ðriʎa] *sf* gang. **cuadrillero** *sm* foreman.

cuadro ['kwaðro] *sm* square; picture; sight, scene. **en cuadro** in a square.

cuadrúpedo [kwa'ðrupeðo] *sm, adj* quadruped.

cuajar [kwa'xar] *v* coagulate; congeal; clot; settle; fill with; *(fam)* catch on. **cuajado** *adj* curdled; congealed; *(fig)* dumbfounded. **cuajadura** *sf* curdling; congealing; coagulation.

cual [kwal] *pron* which; who, *adv* such as. **a cual más** equally. **¿cuál?** *pron interrog* which? what?

cualidad [kwali'ðað] *sf* quality.

cualquier [kwal'kjer] *adj* (*con sustantivo*) any. **cualquiera** *pron, pl* **cualesquiera** any; anyone; anybody.

cuan [kwan] *adv* how; as.

cuando ['kwando] *adv* when. **de vez en cuando** from time to time. **hasta cuando** until. **¿cuándo?** *adv interrog* when?

cuantía [kwan'tia] *sf* quantity.

cuanto ['kwanto] *adj* as much as; all; whatever, *adv* **en cuanto** as soon as. **en cuanto a** as to. **¿cuánto?** *pron interrog* how much? how long?

cuarenta [kwa'renta] *sm, adj* forty.

cuaresma [kwa'resma] *sf* Lent.

cuartear [kwarte'ar] *v* quarter; cut into joints. **cuartearse** *v* crack.

cuartel [kwar'tel] *sm* quarter; barracks.

cuarto ['kwarto] *adj* fourth. *sm* quarter; room. **cuarto de baño** bathroom. **cuarto de estar** livingroom.

cuarzo [kwarθo] *sm* quartz.

cuatro ['kwatro] *sm, adj* four.

cuba ['kuba] *sf* barrel; tub; drunkard. **estar como una cuba** (*fam*) be drunk.

Cuba *sf* Cuba. **cubano, -a** *s, adj* Cuban.

cúbico [ku'βiko] *adj* cubic. **raíz cúbica** *f* cube root.

cubículo [ku'βikulo] *sm* cubicle.

cubo ['kuβo] *sm* bucket.

cubrir [ku'βrir] *v* cover; drown; repay. **cubrirse** *v* cover oneself; put on one's hat; cloud over. **cubierta** *sf* cover; roof; tyre; bedspread; (*mar*) deck. **cubierto** *sm* cover; place-setting; menu. **bajo cubierto** under cover. **precio del cubierto** *sm* cover charge.

cucaracha [kuka'ratʃa] *sf* cockroach.

cuclillas [ku'kliʎas] *adv* **en cuclillas** squatting, on one's haunches.

cuclillo [ku'kliʎo] *sm* cuckoo; cuckold.

cuchara [ku'tʃara] *sf* spoon; ladle; trowel. **cucharada** *sf* spoonful. **cucharadita** *sf* teaspoonful. **cucharita** *sf* teaspoon; coffeespoon. **cucharón** *sm* ladle; scoop.

cuchichear [kutʃitʃe'ar] *v* whisper. **cuchicheo** *sm* whisper; whispering.

cuchilla [ku'tʃiʎa] *sf* kitchen knife; chopper;

razor blade; range of mountains. **patines de cuchilla** *sm pl* ice skates *pl.* **cuchillada** *sf* slash; stab; knifing. **andar a cuchilladas** be at daggers drawn. **cuchillería** *sf* cutlery; cutlery shop. **cuchillo** *sm* knife.

cuello ['kweʎo] *sm* collar; neck; throat. **cuello de pico** V-neck. **cuello vuelto** polo neck.

cuenca ['kwenka] *sf* wooden bowl; eye socket; (*geog*) basin.

cuenta ['kwenta] *sf* account; bill; count; report. **a cuenta** on account. **¿a cuenta de qué?** why? **tener en cuenta** bear in mind.

cuento ['kwento] *sm* tale; fib; fuss. **cuento chino** nonsense.

cuerda ['kwerða] *sf* cord; rope; string; chain; (*anat*) chord. **cuerdas vocales** vocal chords *pl.*

cuerdo ['kwerðo], **-a** *sm, sf* sane person. *adj* sane.

cuerno ['kwerno] *sm* horn; antler; feeler.

cuero ['kwero] *sm* skin; hide; leather.

cuerpo ['kwerpo] *sm* body; piece, section; stage; corps. **cuerpo de casa** housework. **cuerpo entero** full-length. **cuerpo muerto** (*mar*) mooring buoy.

cuervo ['kwerβo] *sm* raven.

cuesta ['kwesta] *sf* slope; hill. **a cuestas** on one's back. **cuesta abajo/arriba** down/uphill.

cuestión [kwes'tjon] *sf* question, issue; dispute. **cuestionar** *v* question; argue.

cueva ['kweβa] *sf* cave; cellar, den.

cuidar [kwiðar] *v* take care of; pay attention to. **cuidar de que** take care that. **no cuidarse de** take no notice of. **cuidado** *sm* care; carefulness; affair; worry. **¡cuidado!** beware! **cuidador** *adj* careful. **cuidadora** *sf* child-minder.

cuita ['kwita] *sf* worry; sorrow. **cuitado** *adj* worried; bashful.

culebra [ku'leβra] *sf* snake; (*fam*) practical joke. **culebrear** *v* wriggle; zigzag.

culinario [kuli'narjo] *adj* culinary.

culminar [kulmi'nar] *v* culminate. **culminación** *sf* culmination. **culminante** *adj* culminating.

culo ['kulo] *sm* (*fam*) bottom, arse. **ir de culo** go downhill.

culpar [kul'par] *v* blame. **culparse** *v* take the blame. **culpa** *sm* blame; fault; guilt. **echar la culpa a** lay the blame on.

culpabilidad *sf* culpability. **culpable** *adj* guilty.

cultivar [kulti'βar] *v* cultivate; grow; develop. **cultivador, -a** *sm, sf* farmer; grower; *sf* (*máquina*) cultivator. **cultivación** *sf* cultivation; culture, **cultivo** *sm* cultivation; culture.

culto ['kulto] *adj* cultivated; cultured; civilized. *sm* worship; cult. **rendir culto a** worship. **cultura** *sf* culture, learning.

cumbre ['kumbre] *sf* peak, summit.

cumpleaños [kumple'aɲos] *sm invar* birthday. **feliz cumpleaños** happy birthday.

cumplir [kum'plir] *v* fulfil; reach; end; do one's duty. **cumplirse** *v* be realized. **cumplir años** have a birthday. **por cumplir** as a matter of form. **cumplido** *adj* plentiful; faultless; polite. **cumplimentar** *v* compliment, fulfil. **cumplimentero** *adj* excessively formal. **cumplimiento** *sm* compliment, fulfilment, politeness.

cúmulo [kumulo] *sm* heap; large amount, (*nube*) cumulus.

cuna ['kuna] *sf* cradle; (*fig*) origin; birthplace.

cundir [kun'dir] *v* spread; increase; grow.

cuneta [ku'neta] *sf* ditch; gutter; hard shoulder

cuña ['kuɲa] *sf* wedge; chock. **tener cuña** (*fam*) have friends at court.

cuñado [ku'ɲado] *sm* brother-in-law

cuño ['kuɲo] *sm* die; die-stamp; (*fig*) impression

cuota ['kwota] *sf* quota; contribution; dues *pl.*

cupón [ku'pon] *sm* coupon; ticket.

cúpula ['kupula] *sf* dome.

cura¹ ['kura] *sm* priest. **cura párroco** parish priest.

cura² *sf* cure; healing; remedy; treatment; dressing. **primera cura** first aid **curación** *sf* cure. **curador, -a** *sm, sf* guardian; tutor; curator. **curativo** *adj* healing.

curioso [ku'rjoso] *adj* curious; neat; attentive *sm* bystander **curiosidad** *sf* curiosity.

cursar [kur'sar] *v* attend; study; frequent. **cursado** *adj* skilled. **cursante** *s*(*m + f*) student.

currículum [ku'rrikulum] *sm* curriculum; résumé. **currículum vítae** *sm* curriculum vitae.

cursi ['kursi] *adj* pretentious; affected; vulgar. *s*(*m + f*) pretentious person; snob.

curso ['kurso] *sm* course; direction; school year. **curso acelerado** crash course.

cursor [kur'sor] *sm* cursor.

curtir [kur'tir] *v* tan; harden. **curtirse** *v* become tanned, become hardened; accustom oneself. **curtidor** *sm* tanner. **curtiduría** *sf* tannery. **curtimiento** *sm* tanning.

curva ['kurβa] *sf* curve, bend. **curvar** *v* curve, bend. **curvatura** *sf* curvature. **curvo** *adj* curved, bent.

cúspide ['kusp:ðe] *sf* peak, summit.

custodiar [kusto'ðjar] *v* take care of; guard, defend. **custodia** *sf* custody. **custodio** *sm* custodian.

cutis ['kut:s] *sm invar* skin, complexion.

cuyo ['kujo] *pron* whose; of which; of whom.

CH

chabacano [tʃaβa'kano] *adj* vulgar, common. **chabacanería** *sf* vulgarity; vulgar remark.

chacal [tʃa'kal] *sm* jackal.

chafar [sʃa'far] *v* flatten; crush; crease; (*en una discusión*) stump.

chal [tʃal] *sm* shawl.

chalado [tʃa'laðo] *adj* (*fam*) crazy, dotty.

chalán [tʃa'lan] *sm* horse dealer; shady businessman.

chaleco [tʃa'leko] *sm* waistcoat.

chalupa [tʃa'lupa] *sf* canoe; launch.

chambelán [tʃambe'lan] *sm* chamberlain.

champaña [tʃam'paɲa] *sm* champagne.

champú [tʃam'pu] *sm* shampoo.

chamuscar [tʃamus'kar] *v* singe, scorch.

chancear [tʃanθe'ar] *v* joke. **chancearse** *v* make fun of. **chanza** *sf* joke.

chanchullo [tʃan'tʃuʎo] *sm* (*fam*) crooked deal.

chantaje [tʃan'taxe] *sm* blackmail. **chantajista** *s*(*m + f*) blackmailer.

chapa ['tʃapa] *sf* metal sheet; rouge; (*fam*) common sense.

chaparro [tʃa'parro] *adj* (*fam*) tubby.

chaparrón [tʃapar'ron] *sm* downpour, cloudburst.

chapón [tʃa'pon] *sm* ink blot.

chapotear [tʃapote'ar] *v* sponge; moisten; splash. **chapoteo** *sm* sponging; moistening; splashing.

chapucero [tʃapu'θero], **-a** *sm, sf* bungler; liar. *adj* crude, clumsy. **chapucear** *v* botch. bungle.

chapuzar [tʃapu'θar] *v* duck, plunge into water.

chaqueta [tʃa'keta] *sf* jacket. **chaqueta de lana** *sf* fleece (jacket).

charca [tʃarka] *sf* pool.

charco [tʃarko] *sm* puddle.

charcutería [tʃarkute'ria] *sf* delicatessen.

charlar [tʃar'lar] *v* (*fam*) chat, chatter; gossip. **charla** *sf* (*fam*) chatter, talk. **charlador, -a** *sm, sf also* **charlatán, -ana** *sm, sf* chatterbox. **charladuría** *sf* chatter; gossip.

charol [tʃa'rol] *sm* varnish; patent leather, **darse charol** boast. **charolar** *v* varnish.

charro [tʃarro] *adj* (*fam*) churlish; illbred; tawdry. **charrada** *sf* boorishness.

chasquear [tʃaske'ar] *v* trick; disappoint. **chasco** *sm* trick; disappointment.

chato [tʃato] *adj* flat-nosed; flat. *sm* small glass.

chaval [tʃa'βal] *sm* (*fam*) lad; kid. **chavala** *sf* (*fam*) lass; girl.

Checoslovaquia [tʃekoslo'βakja] *sf* Czechoslovakia. **checoslovaco, -a** *s, adj* Czechoslovak(ian).

cheque [tʃeke] *sm* cheque. **cheque de viajero** traveller's cheque.

chicle [tʃ:kle] *sm* chewing gum.

chico [tʃiko] *adj* small. *sm* boy. **chica** *sf* girl.

chichón [tʃi'tʃon] *sm* lump, bump.

chiflar [tʃi'flar] *v* whistle; hiss; (*fam*) swig. **chiflarse por** be crazy about. **chifla** *sf* whistle; hissing. **chiflado, -a** *sm, sf* (*fam*) crackpot; (*fam: aficionado*) fan; *adj* (*fam*) crazy.

chile [tʃile]. *sm* chili, chilli.

Chile [tʃile] *sm* Chile. **chileno, -a** *s, adj* Chilean.

chillar [tʃi'ʎar] *v* scream; howl; squeak; blare. **chillador** *adj* screaming; shrieking. **chillería** *sf* screaming; scolding. **chillido** *sm* scream; howl; squeak.

chillón [tʃi'ʎon] *adj* garish.

chimenea [tʃime'nea] *sf* chimney; fireplace.

chimpancé [tʃimpan'θe] *sm* chimpanzee.

china [tʃina] *sf* porcelain; china.

China *sf* China. **chino, -a** *s, adj* Chinese.

chinche [tʃ:ntʃe] *sf* bedbug.

chingar [tʃin'gar] *v* (*fam*) drink; (*fam*) pester.

chip de silicio [tʃip de si'liθjo] *sm* silicon chip.

Chipre [tʃipre] *sm* Cyprus. **chipriota** *s*(*m* + *f*), *adj* Cypriot.

chiripa [tʃi'ripa] *sf* fluke, lucky accident.

chirriar [tʃirri'ar] *v* creak; squeak; chatter. **chirrido** *sm* creaking; squeaking; chattering.

chisme [tʃisme] *sm* gadget; contrivance; knick-knack. **chismes** *sm pl* gossip *sing*. **chismear** *v* gossip. **chismería** *sf* tittle-tattle. **chismoso** *adj* gossiping.

chispear [tʃispe'ar] *v* spark; sparkle; drizzle. **chispa** *sf* spark; little bit. **chispeante** *adj* sparkling.

chisporrotear [tʃisporrote'ar] *v* spark; sizzle. **chisporroteo** *sm* sparking; sizzling.

chistar [tʃis'tar] *v* speak; open one's lips. **no chistar** say not a word. **¡chite!** *interj* hush!

chiste [tʃiste] *sf* joke. **tener chiste** be funny. **chistoso** *adj* funny; joking.

chivo [tʃiβo], **-a** *sm, sf* (*zool*) kid.

chocar [tʃo'kar] *v* surprise; shock; collide. **choque** *sm* shock; jolt; crash; dispute.

chocolate [tʃoko'late] *sm* chocolate. **chocolatería** chocolate shop.

chochear [tʃotʃe'ar] *v* be in one's dotage. **chochera** *sf* dotage. **chocho** *adj* doddering.

chofer [tʃofer] *sm* chauffeur.

chorizo [tʃo'riθo] *sm* spicy sausage.

chorrear [tʃorre'ar] *v* gush; spout; drip. **chorreo** *sm* gushing; spouting; dripping. **chorro** *sm* jet; gush; flow; stream.

choza [tʃoθa] *sf* hut, hovel.

chubasco [tʃu'βasko] *sm* shower; squall; (*fig*) setback.

chuleta [tʃu'leta] *sf* chop, cutlet; (*fam*) slap.

chulo [tʃulo] *sm* pimp; (*fam*) ruffian; (*fam*) spiv. *adj* cheeky; flashy; insolent. **chulada** *sf* cheek; vulgar thing; funny thing. **chulear** *v* get cheeky with.

chungar [tʃun'gar] *v* (*fam*) tease; tell jokes. **chunga** *sf* banter, fun.

chupar [tʃu'par] *v* suck; absorb. **chuparse** *v* become worn to a shadow. **chupada** *sf* suck, sucking. **chupadero** *also* **chupador** *adj* sucking; absorbent. **chupete** *sm* (*para niños*) dummy. **chupetear** *v* suck at.

churro ['tʃurro] *sm* deep-fried batter; (*fam*) dead loss.

chusco ['tʃusko], **-a** *sm, sf* wag, wit. *adj* funny.

chusma ['tʃusma] *sf* rabble, riffraff.

chuzo ['tʃuθo] *sm* (*arma*) pike. **llover a chuzos** pour down.

D

dactilógrafo [dakti'lografo], **-a** *sm, sf* typist. **dactilografía** *sf* typing.

dádiva ['daðiβa] *sf* gift. **dadivoso** *adj* generous.

dado ['daðo] *sm* die (*pl* dice).

daga ['daga] *sf* dagger.

dama ['dama] *sf* lady; mistress; (*ajedrez*) queen; (*juego de damas*) king. **damas** *sf pl* draughts.

damasco [da'masko] *sm* damask.

damnificar [damnifi'kar] *v* injure, harm.

danés [da'nes], **-esa** *sm, sf* Dane. *sm* (*lengua*) Danish. *adj* Danish.

danzar [dan'θar] *v* dance. **danza** *sf* dance, dancing. **danzante**, **-a** *sm, sf* dancer.

dañar [da'ɲar] *v* harm; damage; spoil. **dañino** *adj* destructive. **daño** *sm* injury; damage; loss.

*dar [dar] *v* give; grant; yield; (*reloj*) strike; (*naipes*) deal. **dar a** face; overlook. **dar como** *or* **por** declare; consider. **dar con** meet. **lo mismo da** it makes no difference. **darse** *v* regard oneself; devote oneself; matter; occur. **darse cuenta** realize.

dardo ['darðo] *sm* dart.

dársena ['darsena] *sm* dock.

dátil ['datil] *sm* (*fruto*) date.

dato ['dato] *sm* fact; piece of information.

de [de] *prep* of; from.

debajo [de'βaxo] *adv* underneath. **debajo de** *prep* under, beneath, below.

debatir [deβa'tir] *v* debate, discuss. **debate** *sm* debate.

deber [de'βer] *v* owe; must; ought. *sm* duty; debt. **debidamente** *adv* fittingly. **debido** *also* fitting; just. **debido a** due to. **débito** *sm* debt.

debilitar [deβili'tar] *v* weaken. **débil** *adj* weak. **debilidad** *sf* weakness.

*decaer [deka'er] *v* decline; decay. **decadencia** *sf* decadence; decline. **decadente** *adj* decadent.

decano [de'kano] *sm* dean.

decapitar [dekapi'tar] *v* decapitate. **decapitación** *sf* decapitation.

decena [de'θena] *sf* unit of ten.

decencia [de'θenθja] *sf* decency; modesty; cleanliness. **decente** *adj* decent; modest; clean.

decenio [de'θenjo] *sm* decade.

decepción [deθep'θjon] *sf* disappointment.

decidir [deθi'ðir] *v* decide. **decidirse** *v* make up one's mind. **decisión** *sf* decision. **decisivo** *adj* decisive.

décima ['deθima] *sf* tenth; tithe. **decimal** *adj* decimal. **décimo** *adj* tenth. **decimoctavo** *adj* eighteenth. **decimocuarto** *adj* fourteenth. **decimonono** *or* **decimonoveno** *adj* nineteenth. **decimoquinto** *adj* fifteenth. **decimoséptimo** *adj* seventeenth. **decimosexto** *adj* sixteenth. **decimotercio** *adj* thirteenth.

*decir [de'θir] *v* say; tell; speak; call. **¿diga?** (*teléfono*) hello!

declamar [dekla'mar] *v* declaim; speak out; recite. **declamación** *sf* declamation; oration. **declamador**, **-a** *sm, sf* orator.

declarar [dekla'rar] *v* declare; state; explain. **declararse** *v* declare oneself; (*fuego, etc.*) break out; (*amor*) propose. **declaración** *sf* declaration.

declinar [dekli'nar] *v* decay; fade; depart; (*gram*) decline. **declinación** *sf* decline; (*gram*) declension.

declive [de'kliβe] *sm* slope; (*com*) slump.

decorar [deko'rar] *v* decorate. **decoración** *sf* decoration. **decorador**, **-a** *sm, sf* decorator. **decorativo** *adj* decorative.

decoro [de'koro] *sm* decorum; dignity; respect.

*decrecer [dekre'θer] *v* decrease. **decremento** *sm* diminution.

decrépito [de'krepito] *adj* decrepit.

decretar [dekre'tar] *v* decree. **decreto** *sm*

decree.

dedal [de'ðal] *sm* thimble.

dédalo ['deðalo] *sm* maze.

dedicar [deði'kar] *v* dedicate, devote. **dedicación** *sf* dedication. **dedicatoria** *sf* (*libro*) dedication.

dedillo [de'ðiλo] *sm* **al dedillo** at one's fingertips.

dedo ['deðo] *sm* finger; toe. **dedo del corazón** middle finger. **dedo índice** forefinger. **dedo meñique** little finger. **dedo pulgar** thumb.

*deducir [deðu'θir] *v* deduce; allege; deduct. **deducción** *sf* deduction. **deductivo** *adj* deductive.

defectible [defek'tiβle] *adj* fallible; defective. **defecto** *sm* defect. **defectuoso** *adj* defective.

*defender [defen'der] *v* defend; prohibit; oppose. **defendible** *adj* defensible. **defendido, -a** *sm, sf* (*jur*) defendant. **defensa** *sf* defence; shelter. **defensa pasiva** civil defence. **defensivo** *adj* defensive. **defensor, -a** *sm, sf* protector; counsel.

deferencia [defe'renθja] *sf* deference. **deferente** *adj* deferential.

*deferir [defe'rir] *v* defer; delegate.

deficiencia [defi'θjenθja] *sf* deficiency. **deficiente** *adj* deficient.

definir [defi'nir] *v* define. **definición** *sf* definition. **definido** *adj* definite. **definitivo** *adj* definitive. **en definitiva** in short.

deformar [defor'mar] *v* deform; disfigure. **deformación** *sf* deformation; distortion. **deforme** *adj* deformed; abnormal. **deformidad** *sf* deformity; (*fig*) perversion.

defraudar [defrau'dar] *v* defraud; evade; disappoint; frustrate. **defraudar al fisco** evade taxes. **defraudación** *sf* fraud; deceit. **defraudador, -a** *sm, sf* tax evader; swindler.

defunción [defun'θjon] *sf* decease.

degenerar [dexene'rar] *v* degenerate. **degeneración** *sf* degeneration.

deglutir [deglu'tir] *v* swallow. **deglución** *sf* swallowing.

*degollar [dego'λar] *v* cut the throat of; behead; (*fig*) ruin. **degollación** *sf* throat-cutting; decapitation. **degolladero** *sm* slaughter-house; scaffold. **degollador, -a** *sm, sf* executioner.

degradar [degra'ðar] *v* degrade.

degradación *sf* degradation.

degustación [degusta'θion] *sf* tasting; sampling.

dehesa [de'esa] *sf* pasture.

deificar [deifi'kar] *v* deify. **deidad** *sf* deity. **deificación** *sf* deification.

dejar [de'xar] *v* leave; yield; drop; let, allow. **dejar de** leave off, stop; fail to. **dejarse** *v* neglect oneself. **dejarse vencer** give in to. **dejarse de** cease to. **dejarse engañar por** *v* fall for (trick).

del [del] *contraction of* **de el**.

delantal [delan'tal] *sm* apron.

delante [de'lante] *adv* before, in front, ahead. **delante de** before, in front of. **delantera** *sf* front; advantage; lead. **delantero** *adj* front; foremost.

delatar [dela'tar] *v* denounce; betray. **delator, -a** *sm, sf* informer.

delegar [dele'gar] *v* delegate. **delegación** *sf* delegation. **delegado** *adj* delegated.

deleitar [delei'tar] *v* delight; please. **deleitarse** *v* take delight. **deleite** *sm* delight; pleasure. **deleitoso** *adj* delightful.

deletrear [deletre'ar] *v* spell out; interpret. **deletreo** *sm* spelling out; decipherment.

deleznable [deleθ'naβle] *adj* brittle; fragile; frail.

delfín [del'fin] *sm* dolphin.

delgado [del'gaðo] *adj* thin; delicate; ingenious. **delgadez** *sf* thinness.

deliberar [deliβe'rar] *v* deliberate, consider. **deliberación** *sf* deliberation. **deliberado** *adj* deliberate.

delicado [deli'kaðo] *adj* delicate; tender; touchy. **delicadez** *sf* delicacy; tenderness; touchiness; frailty; squeamishness.

delicioso [deli'θjoso] *adj* delicious; delightful. **delicia** *sf* delight.

delimitar [delimi'tar] *v* delimit. **delimitación** *sf* delimitation.

delincuencia [delin'kwenθja] *sf* delinquency. **delincuente** *s(m + f)* delinquent, criminal.

delinear [deline'ar] *v* delineate; outline; sketch. **delineación** *sf* delineation. **delineante** *sm* draughtsman.

delirar [deli'rar] *v* be delirious; rave. **delirio** *sm* delirium.

delito [de'lito] *sm* crime.

delta ['delta] *sm* delta.

demacrarse [dema'krarse] *v* waste away.

demacración sf emaciation. **demacrado** adj emaciated.

demagogia [dema'goxja] sf demagogy. **demagogo** sm demagogue.

demandar [deman'dar] v request; desire; (jur) sue. **demanda** sf demand; appeal; petition; question. **demandado, -a** sm, sf (jur) defendant. **demandante** s(m + f) (jur) plaintiff.

demarcar [demar'kar] v demarcate. **demarcación** sf demarcation.

demás [de'mas] adj other; rest; remaining. **los demás, las demás** the others. **estar demás** be unwanted. **y demás** etcetera. **demasía** sf excess; outrage; insolence. **demasiado** adj, adv too much.

demencia [de'menθja] sf insanity. **demente** adj insane.

democracia [demo'kraθja] sf democracy. **demócrata** adj democratic. s(m + f) democrat. **democrático** adj democratic.

***demoler** [demo'ler] v demolish. **demolición** sf demolition.

demonio [de'monjo] sm demon. **demoniaco** adj demoniac.

demorar [demo'rar] v delay; remain. **demora** sf delay.

***demostrar** [demos'trar] v demonstrate; prove. **demostrable** adj demonstrable. **demostración** sf demonstration. **demostrativo** adj demonstrative.

***denegar** [dene'gar] v deny, refuse. **denegación** sf denial, refusal.

denigrar [deni'grar] v denigrate; slander; insult. **denigración** sf denigration; disgrace.

denominar [denomi'nar] v name. **denominación** sf denomination.

denotar [deno'tar] v denote; indicate.

denso ['denso] adj dense. **densidad** sf density

dentado [den'taðo] adj toothed; jagged; (tecn) cogged. **dentadura** sf set of teeth. **dental** adj dental. **dentar** v furnish with teeth; cut one's teeth. **dentellar** v (dientes) chatter. **dentellear** v bite **dentífrico** sm toothpaste. **dentista** s(m + f) dentist.

dentro ['dentro] adv inside, within. **dentro de poco** shortly

denudar [denu'ðar] v denude

denunciar [denun'θjar] v denounce; inform, accuse **denuncia** sf denunciation; accusation.

departamento [departa'mento] sm department.

depender [depen'der] v depend. **dependencia** sf dependence; reliance. **dependiente, -a** sm, sf shop assistant. **dependiente de** dependent on.

deplorar [deplo'rar] v deplore; regret. **deplorable** adj deplorable.

***deponer** [depo'ner] v lay down, lay aside; remove from office; depose; (jur) give evidence; defecate. **deponente** s(m + f) witness.

deportar [depor'tar] v deport. **deportación** sf deportation.

deporte [de'porte] sm sport. **deportismo** sm sport; enthusiasm for sport. **deportista** s(m + f) sportsman/woman. **coche deportivo** sports car.

depositar [deposi'tar] v deposit. **depósito** sm deposit; store; tank; tip.

depravar [depra'βar] v deprave; corrupt. **depravación** sf depravity. **depravado** adj depraved

depreciar [depre'θjar] v depreciate, lessen in value. **depreciación** sf depreciation.

deprimir [depri'mir] v depress. **depresión** sf depression. **depresivo** adj depressing.

depurar [depu'rar] v purify. **depuración** sf purification.

derecha [de'retʃa] sf right; right hand. **a la derecha** on the right. **derecho** sm law; adj right; straight; upright.

derivar [deri'βar] v derive. **derivación** sf derivation. **derivado** [deri'βaðo] sf spinoff.

derogar [dero'gar] v repeal; abolish; cancel. **derogación** sf repeal; abolition.

derramar [derra'mar] v spill; overflow; scatter; spread. **derramarse** v be scattered; overflow. **derrame** sm spilling; leakage; overflow; slope.

***derretir** [derre'tir] v melt; dissipate. **derretirse** v be deeply in love; (fam) be impatient. **derretimiento** sm melting; (fam) consuming passion.

derribar [derri'βar] v tear down; knock down; throw down. **derribarse** v fall down **derribo** sm demolition. **derribos** sm pl rubble sing.

derrocar [derro'kar] v hurl down; ruin.

derrochar [derro'tʃar] v squander; dissipate. **derrochador, -a** s, adj prodigal; spendthrift.

derrotar [derro'tar] v defeat; ruin; put to flight. **derrota** sf defeat; failure. **derrotado** adj defeated; shabby.

derrumbar [derrum'bar] v knock down, hurl down, pull down. **derrumbarse** v collapse. **derrumbo** sm collapse; overthrow; demolition.

desabotonar [desaβoto'nar] v unbutton; blossom. **desabotonarse** v come undone.

desabrigar [desaβri'gar] v uncover; leave without shelter; take off clothing. **desabrigado** adj uncovered; unprotected; exposed. **desabrigo** sm uncovering; exposure.

desabrochar [desaβro'tʃar] v unfasten; undo. **desabrocharse** v come undone.

desacatar [desaka'tar] v be disrespectful; disobey. **desacato** sm disrespect; contempt.

*****desacertar** [desaθer'tar] v be wrong; act foolishly. **desacertado** adj mistaken; ill-advised; unsuccessful; unfortunate; clumsy. **desacierto** sm mistake, blunder.

desacomodar [desakomo'ðar] v inconvenience; dismiss. **desacomodarse** v lose one's job. **desacomodado** adj poor; inconvenient; unemployed. **desacomodamiento** sm also **desacomodo** sm discomfort; inconvenience.

desaconsejado [desakonse'xaðo] adj ill-advised. **desaconsejar** v advise against.

*****desacordar** [desakor'ðar] v put out of tune. **desacordarse** v get out of tune; be forgetful. **desacordado** adj discordant.

desacostumbrar [desakostum'brar] v break a habit. **desacostumbrado** adj unusual.

desacreditar [desakreði'tar] v discredit.

desactivar [desakti'βar] v defuse.

desacuerdo [desa'kwerðo] sm discord; disagreement; unconsciousness.

desafecto [desa'fekto] adj disaffected; indifferent; adverse.

desafinar [desafi'nar] v be out of tune; (fig) speak out of turn.

desafío [desa'fio] sm challenge.

desagradar [desagra'ðar] v displease; be unpleasant. **desagradable** adj unpleasant.

desagradecido [desagraðe'θiðo], **-a** sm, sf ingrate. adj ungrateful.

desagraviar [desagra'βjar] v make amends for. **desagravio** sm indemnity; compensa-

tion.

desaguar [desa'gwar] v drain. **desaguadero** sm drain; channel. **desagüe** sm drainage; outlet.

desahogar [desao'gar] v ease; console. **desahogarse** v recover; free oneself; speak one's mind; get out of debt. **desahogado** adj impudent; well-off; spacious; uncluttered. **desahogo** sm ease; comfort; relief.

desahuciar [desau'θjar] v evict; despair of. **desahucio** sm eviction.

desairar [desai'rar] v disregard; snub. **desairado** adj spurned; unattractive; awkward. **desaire** sm snub; rebuff; gracelessness.

desajustar [desaxus'tar] v disarrange. **desajustarse** v break down. **desajuste** sm breakdown.

desalado [desa'laðo] adj impatient; hasty; unsalted.

*****desalentar** [desalen'tar] v make breathless; discourage. **desalentarse** v lose heart.

desaliñar [desali'nar] v disturb; ruffle. **desaliñado** adj slovenly. **desaliño** sm slovenliness; uncleanness; negligence.

desalojar [desalo'xar] v remove; eject. **desalojarse** v move out. **desalojamiento** sm ejection.

desalquilado [desalki'laðo] adj vacant. **desalquilar** v vacate.

desamor [desa'mor] sm indifference; ingratitude.

desamparar [desampa'rar] v abandon. **desamparo** sm abandonment; helplessness.

desangrar [desan'grar] v bleed; impoverish. **desangrarse** v lose much blood.

desanimar [desani'mar] v discourage. **desanimarse** v become discouraged. **desánimo** sm discouragement.

desanudar [desanu'ðar] v untie; disentangle.

desapacible [desapa'θiβle] adj disagreeable. **desapacibilidad** sf unpleasantness.

*****desaparecer** [desapare'θer] v disappear; hide; wear off. **desaparecido** adj missing. **desaparecimiento** sm disappearance.

desapegarse [desape'garse] v lose interest in. **desapego** sm lack of interest; coldness.

desapercibido [desaperθi'βiðo] adj unnoticed. **coger desapercibido** catch unawares.

desapoderar [desapoðe'rar] *v* dispossess; dismiss.

*****desapretar** [desapre'tar] *v* loosen.

*****desaprobar** [desapro'βar] *v* disapprove of. **desaprobación** *sf* disapproval.

desaprovechar [desaproβe'tʃar] *v* waste; lose ground. **desaprovechado** *adj* unprofitable; backward. **desaprovechamiento** *sm* waste; misuse.

desapuntar [desapun'tar] *v* unstitch.

desarmar [desar'mar] *v* disarm; disband; dismantle; calm. **desarme** *sm* disarmament.

desarraigar [desarrai'gar] *v* uproot. **desarraigado** *adj* uprooted; rootless.

desarreglar [desarre'glar] *v* upset; disarrange. **desarreglado** *adj* slovenly; faulty. **desarreglo** *sm* disorder; untidiness; trouble.

desarrollar [desarro'ʎar] *v* unfold; develop. **desarrollo** *sm* development.

desarrugar [desarru'gar] *v* smooth out.

desasear [desase'ar] *v* soil; disarrange. **desaseo** *sm* dirtiness; disorder.

*****desasir** [desa'sir] *v* loosen, undo. **desasirse de** get rid of.

*****desasosegar** [desasose'gar] *v* disturb. **desasosiego** *sm* disquiet; restlessness.

desastre [de'sastre] *sm* disaster. **desastrado** *adj* unlucky; dirty; disorderly. **desastroso** *adj* disastrous.

desatar [desa'tar] *v* undo; unravel. **desatarse** *v* break out; lose all reserve. **desatadura** *sf* untying.

*****desatender** [desaten'der] *v* ignore; slight. **desatención** *sf* inattention; discourtesy. **desatentado** *adj* absent-minded. **desatento** *adj* discourteous.

desatinar [desati'nar] *v* bewilder; rave; blunder. **desatinado** *adj* silly; rash. **desatino** *sm* absurdity; blunder; tactlessness.

*****desavenir** [desaβe'nir] *v* cause to quarrel. **desavenirse** *v* quarrel. **desavenido** *adj* incompatible.

desaventajado [desaβenta'xaðo] *adj* unfavourable; inferior.

desaviar [desa'βjar] *v* lead astray; deprive of necessities; inconvenience. **desavío** *sm* inconvenience; lack of means.

desayunar [desaju'nar] *v* breakfast. **desayuno** *sm* breakfast.

desazonar [desaθo'nar] *v* render tasteless; displease. **desazón** *sm* insipidity; displeasure. **desazonado** *adj* tasteless; displeased.

desbandarse [desβan'darse] *v* disband; disperse.

desbarajustar [desβaraxus'tar] *v* confuse. **desbarajuste** *sm* confusion.

desbaratar [desβara'tar] *v* ruin; spoil; waste; talk rubbish. **desbaratarse** *v* fall apart; get carried away. **desbaratado** *adj* wrecked; dissipated. **desbaratamiento** *sm* waste; disorder; wrecking.

desbordar [desβor'ðar] *v* flood; overflow; (*fig*) lose one's self-control. **desbordamiento** *sm* overflow.

descabezar [deskaβe'θar] *v* behead. **descabezarse** *v* rack one's brains. **descabezado** *adj* headless; rash.

descafeinado [deskafej'naðo] *adj* decaffeinated.

descalabrar [deskala'βrar] *v* wound (in the head); maltreat; defeat. **descalabro** *sm* setback; defeat.

descalificar [deskalifi'kar] *v* disqualify. **descalificación** *sf* disqualification.

descalzar [deskal'θar] *v* take off one's shoes. **descalzo** *adj* barefoot.

descamisado [deskami'saðo] *adj* destitute. *sm* tramp.

descansar [deskan'sar] *v* rest; sleep; lean; depend. **descansado** *adj* rested. **descanso** *sm* rest; repose.

descarado [deska'raðo] *adj* brazen; cheeky; blatant.

descargar [deskar'gar] *v* unload; discharge; free; absolve. **descarga** *sf* discharge; unloading. **descargado** *adj* (*batería*) flat. **descargo** *sm* unloading; discharge of debt. **descargue** *sm* unloading of goods.

descartar [deskar'tar] *v* discard; leave out. **descartarse** *v* get out of. **descarte** *sm* discarding; rejection.

*****descender** [desθen'der] *v* descend; flow; lower. **descendencia** *sf* lineage. **descendiente** *s(m + f)* descendant. **descenso** *sm* descent; fall; decline.

descentralizar [desθentrali'θar] *v* decentralize.

descifrar [desθi'frar] *v* decipher. **decifrable** *adj* decipherable.

*****descolgar** [deskol'gar] *v* lower; (*teléfono*) pick up; take down. **descolgarse** *v* come down; slip; drop; surprise.

descodificar [deskoðifi'kar] *v* decode.

descolorar [deskolo'rar] *v* discolour, **descolorido** *adj* discoloured.

descomedido [deskome'ðiðo] *adj* immoderate; disproportionate; rude. **descomedirse** *v* go too far.

***descomponer** [deskompo'ner] *v* decompose; disturb. **descomponerse** *v* rot; become upset. **descomposición** *sf* decomposition. **descompuesto** *adj* broken; faulty; insolent.

***desconcertar** [deskonθer'tar] *v* disconcert; damage. **desconcierto** *sm* disorder; confusion.

desconectar [deskonek'tar] *v* disconnect. **desconectado** *adj* off-line. **desconectarse** *v* log off (computer).

desconfiar [deskon'fjar] *v* lack confidence. **desconfiar de** distrust. **desconfiado** *adj* distrustful. **desconfianza** *sf* mistrust, suspicion.

desconformar [deskonfor'mar] *v* disagree, dissent.

***desconocer** [deskono'θer] *v* fail to recognize; ignore; deny; disown. **desconocido** *adj* unknown; unrecognized; ungrateful. **desconocimiento** *sm* ignorance; ingratitude; repudiation.

desconsiderado [deskonside'raðo] *adj* inconsiderate.

***desconsolar** [deskonso'lar] *v* grieve, distress. **desconsolado** *adj* disconsolate. **desconsuelo** *sm* grief; affliction.

***descontar** [deskon'tar] *v* discount; deduct; take for granted.

descontento [deskon'tento] *adj* dissatisfied.

descontinuar [deskontinu'ar] *v* discontinue.

descorazonar [deskorazo'nar] *v* discourage.

descorchar [deskor'tʃar] *v* uncork. **descorchador** *sm* corkscrew.

descortés [deskor'tes] *adj* discourteous. **descortesía** *sf* discourtesy.

descreer [deskre'er] *v* disbelieve; discredit. **descrédito** *sm* discredit.

describir [deskri'βir] *v* describe. **descripción** *sf* description. **descriptivo** *adj* descriptive.

descuajar [deskwa'xar] *v* liquefy; uproot; dishearten.

descubrir [desku'βrir] *v* discover; uncover; publish. **descubierto** *adj* exposed; manifest; hatless. **descubridor, -a** *sm, sf* discoverer. **descubrimiento** *sm* discovery.

descuento [des'kwento] *sm* discount.

descuidar [deskwi'ðar] *v* neglect; release; distract. **descuidar de** forget to. ¡**descuida!** don't worry! **descuidarse** *v* be careless; neglect one's health. **descuidado** *adj* neglectful; careless; casual. **descuido** *sm* negligence; carelessness; thoughtlessness.

desde ['desðe] *prep* from; since; after. **desde luego** of course; immediately.

***desdecir** [desðe'θir] *v* gainsay; be unworthy of. **desdecirse** *v* retract.

desdeñar [desðe'ɲar] *v* disdain; scorn. **desdén** *sm* disdain; scorn. **al desdén** nonchalantly. **desdeñoso** *adj* disdainful.

desdicha [des'ðitʃa] *sf* misfortune; misery. **desdichado** *adj* unfortunate; wretched.

desdoblar [desðo'βlar] *v* unfold; split.

desdorar [desðo'rar] *v* tarnish. **desdoro** *sm* stain; dishonour.

desear [dese'ar] *v* wish, desire. **deseable** *adj* desirable. **deseo** *sm* desire. **deseoso** *adj* desirous.

desecar [dese'kar] *v* dry up.

desechar [dese'tʃar] *v* refuse; reject. **desecho** *sm* residue; rubbish; contempt.

desembalar [desemba'lar] *v* unpack.

desembarazar [desembara'θar] *v* clear; extricate; vacate. **desembarazarse** *v* get rid of. **desembarazo** *sm* freedom; naturalness.

desembarcar [desembar'kar] *v* unload; disembark. **desembarcadero** *sm* landing-stage. **desembarco** *sm* disembarkation; landing.

desembocar [desembo'kar] *v* flow; empty. **desembocadura** *sf* mouth; outlet; opening.

desembolsar [desembol'sar] *v* pay out. **desembolso** *sm* payment. **desembolsos** *sm pl* expenses *pl*.

desembragar [desembra'gar] *v* disengage; release; (*auto*) declutch. **desembrague** *sm* disengaging; (*auto*) declutching; (*auto*) clutch pedal.

desembrollar [desembro'ʎar] *v* disentangle; sort out.

desempate [desem'pate] *sm* (*fútbol*) play-off.

desempeñar [desempe'ɲar] *v* (*teatro*) play

a role; release from debt. **desempeño** *sm* redemption of a pledge; freedom from an obligation.

desempleado [desemple'aðo] *adj* unemployed. **desempleo** *sm* unemployment

desencantar [desenkan'tar] *v* disillusion. **desencanto** *sm* disillusionment.

desenchufar [desentʃu'far] *v* unplug.

desenfadar [desenfa'ðar] *v* appease. **desenfadarse** *v* calm down. **desenfadado** *adj* free, unencumbered **desenfado** *sm* freedom; naturalness.

desenfrenar [desenfre'nar] *v* unbridle. **desenfrenarse** *v* give way to passion. **desenfrenado** *adj* unbridled. **desenfreno** *sm* licentiousness.

desenganchar [desengan'tʃar] *v* unfasten, unhook.

desengañar [desenga'ɲar] *v* disabuse, disillusion. **desengaño** *sm* disillusionment.

desenlace [desen'laθe] *sm* dénouement; outcome.

desenredar [desenre'ðar] *v* disentangle, straighten out. **desenredo** *sm* disentanglement.

desenrollar [desenro'ʎar] *v* unroll; unwind.

*****desentenderse** [desenten'derse] *v* pretend to be ignorant (of); take no part in.

*****desenterrar** [desenter'rar] *v* disinter; unearth; recall. **desenterramiento** *sm* disinterment; recollection.

desentonar [desento'nar] *v* be out of tune; humiliate; behave badly. **desentono** *sm* discord; bad behaviour.

desentrañar [desentra'ɲar] *v* disembowel; (*fig*) unravel.

desenvainar [desenβai'nar] *v* unsheath; (*fig*) bring into the open.

*****desenvolver** [desenβol'βer] *v* unwrap; unwind; develop; expand. **desenvolverse** *v* become unwrapped; fend for oneself; prosper. **desenvoltura** *sf* naturalness; cheerfulness; eloquence.

deseo [de'seo] *V* desear.

desequilibrar [desekili'βrar] *v* unbalance. **desequilibrado** *adj* off balance; mentally unbalanced. **desequilibrio** *sm* imbalance.

desertar [deser'tar] *v* desert. **desertor, -a** *sm, sf* deserter.

desesperar [desespe'rar] *v* (cause to) despair; exasperate. **desesperación** *sf* desperation; despair; anger. **desesperado** *adj* desperate; hopeless. **desesperanza** *sf* despair.

desestimar [desesti'mar] *v* undervalue; reject. **desestima** *sf* lack of esteem.

desfachatado [desfatʃa'taðo] *adj* brazen; shameless. **desfachatez** *sf* brazenness; impudence

desfalcar [desfal'kar] *v* embezzle. **desfalco** *sm* embezzlement.

*****desfallecer** [desfaʎe'θer] *v* faint; weaken. **desfallecido** *adj* faint; weak. **desfallecimiento** *sm* weakness; faintness.

desfavorable [desfaβo'raβle] *adj* unfavourable.

desfigurar [desfigu'rar] *v* disfigure; disguise; distort. **desfiguramiento** *sm* disfigurement; distortion.

desfilar [desfi'lar] *v* parade. **desfiladero** *sm* gorge, defile. **desfile** *sm* parade. **desfile de modas** fashion show.

desgajar [desga'xar] *v* tear off; break off.

desganar [desga'nar] *v* spoil the appetite of **desganarse** *v* lose one's appetite. **desgana** *sf* loss of appetite; reluctance. **desganado** *adj* lacking appetite; reluctant.

desgarbado [desgar'βaðo] *adj* gawky; ungainly.

desgarrar [desgar'rar] *v* rend; tear; (*fig: corazón*) break. **desgarrado** *adj* dissolute. **desgarro** *sm* tear; impudence.

desgastar [desgas'tar] *v* wear away; corrode; ruin. **desgaste** *sm* wear; corrosion; ruin.

desgraciar [desgra'θjar] *v* displease; prevent; spoil. **desgraciarse** *v* fail; lose favour. **desgracia** *sf* misfortune; accident; grief; disgrace; unfriendliness. **por desgracia** unfortunately. **desgraciado** *adj* unlucky; unhappy; in disgrace.

deshabitado [desaβi'taðo] *adj* uninhabited.

*****deshacer** [desa'θer] *v* undo; cancel; destroy; frustrate. **deshacerse** *v* get rid of; break; go to pieces. **deshacerse por** strive to

*****deshelar** [dese'lar] *v* thaw; melt. **deshelamiento** *sm* de-icing. **deshielo** *sm* thawing; melting.

desheredar [desere'ðar] *v* disinherit. **desheredado** *adj* disinherited; underprivileged. **desheredamiento** *sm* disinheritance.

deshidratar [desiðra'tar] *v* dehydrate.

deshidratación *sf* dehydration.

deshilar [desi'lar] *v* unravel. **deshilado** *adj* unravelled; frayed.

deshilvanado [desilβa'naðo] *adj* (*fig: discurso*) disjointed; disconnected.

deshinchar [desin't∫ar] *v* deflate; give vent to. **deshincharse** *v* go down; go flat; (*fig*) come off one's high horse. **deshinchado** *adj* flat; deflated. **deshinchadura** *sf* deflation.

deshojar [deso'xar] *v* defoliate.

deshollinar [desoλi'nar] *v* sweep chimneys. **deshollinador** *sm* chimney-sweep.

deshonesto [deso'nesto] *adj* dishonest; indecent.

deshonrar [deson'rar] *v* dishonour. **deshonra** *sf* dishonour; affront. **deshonroso** *adj* shameful, disgraceful.

deshora [des'ora] *adv* **a deshora** at an inconvenient time.

deshuesar [deswe'sar] *v* (*carne*) bone; (*fruta*) stone.

desidia [de'siðja] *sf* carelessness; inertia. **desidioso** *adj* lazy.

desierto [de'sjerto] *sm* desert. *adj* deserted.

designar [desig'nar] *v* designate. **designación** *sf* designation. **designio** *sm* intention, idea.

desigual [desi'gwal] *adj* unequal; uneven; changeable; different. **desigualdad** *sf* inequality.

desilusionar [desilusjo'nar] *v* disillusion. **desilusión** *sf* disillusionment.

desinfectar [desinfek'tar] *v* disinfect. **desinfección** *sf* disinfection. **desinfectante** *sm, adj* disinfectant.

desinflar [desin'flar] *v* deflate.

desinterés [desinte'res] *sm* disinterest. **desinteresado** *adj* disinterested.

desistir [desis'tir] *v* desist.

desleal [desle'al] *adj* disloyal. **deslealtad** *sf* disloyalty.

deslenguado [deslen'gwado] *adj* foul-mouthed; shameless. **deslenguarse** *v* (*fam*) use foul language.

desligar [desli'gar] *v* loosen; untie; (*fig*) absolve. **desligarse** *v* break away.

deslindar [deslin'dar] *v* define the limits of. **deslinde** *sm* delimitation.

deslizar [desli'θar] *v* slip; glide; slide. **desliz** *sm* skid; (*fig*) indiscretion. **deslizadero** *sm* slippery place.

deslucir [deslu'θir] *v* tarnish.

deslumbrar [deslum'βrar] *v* dazzle; (*fig*) bewilder. **deslumbrador** *adj* dazzling. **deslumbramiento** *sm* dazzle; glare.

desmán [des'man] *sm* excess; misconduct; outrage.

desmandar [desman'dar] *v* countermand. **desmandarse** *v* stray; get out of hand.

desmantelar [desmante'lar] *v* dismantle.

desmayar [desma'jar] *v* falter; discourage. **desmayarse** *v* faint. **desmayado** *adj* faint, fainting. **desmayo** *sm* swoon.

*****desmedirse** [desme'ðirse] *v* forget oneself; lose self-control. **desmedido** *adj* excessive.

desmejorar [desmexo'rar] *v* weaken; impair. **desmejorarse** *v* deteriorate.

*****desmembrar** [desmem'brar] *v* dismember; divide. **desmembración** *sf* dismemberment.

*****desmentir** [desmen'tir] *v* contradict; deny; belie. **desmentirse** *v* go back on one's word.

desmenuzar [desmenu'θar] *v* crumble; sift.

desmerecer [desmere'θer] *v* be unworthy of; be inferior. **desmerecimiento** *sm* demerit.

desmesurado [desmesu'raðo] *adj* disproportionate; excessive. **desmesurarse** *v* go too far.

desmontar [desmon'tar] *v* clear; level; (*árbol*) fell; dismantle.

desmoralizar [desmorali'θar] *v* demoralize. **desmoralización** *sf* demoralization.

desmoronar [desmoro'nar] *v* cause to crumble away. **desmoronarse** *v* crumble.

desnatar [desna'tar] *v* (*leche*) skim; (*fig*) take the best of.

desnivel [des'niβel] *sm* unevenness; gradient; difference of level.

desnudar [desnu'ðar] *v* strip, denude. **desnudez** *sf* nakedness. **desnudo** *adj* naked.

*****desobedecer** [desoβeðe'θer] *v* disobey. **desobediencia** *sf* disobedience. **desobediente** *adj* disobedient.

desocupar [desoku'par] *v* vacate. **desocuparse** *v* leave work; retire. **desocupación** *sf* leisure; unemployment. **desocupado** *adj* idle; unemployed; free.

desolar [deso'lar] *v* lay waste; afflict. **desolarse** *v* grieve. **desolación** *sf* desolation. **desolado** *adj* desolate; disconsolate.

desodorante [desoðo'rante] *sm, adj* deodorant.

desorden [des'orden] *sm* disorder. **desordenado** *adj* disordered.

desorganizar [desorgani'θar] *v* disorganize. **desorganización** *sf* disorganization.

desorientar [desorjen'tar] *v* mislead; (*fig*) confuse. **desorientarse** *v* lose one's bearings. **desorientación** *sf* disorientation; perplexity.

despabilado [despaβi'laðo] *adj* wide awake; alert. **despabilarse** *v* wake up.

despacio [des'paθjo] *adv* slowly; gradually; leisurely.

despachar [despa'tʃar] *v* dispatch; attend to; dismiss. **despacharse** *v* get rid of; finish; hurry. **despacho** *sm* dispatch; customs clearance; study; office; warrant; telegram.

despachurrar [despatʃur'rar] *v* (*fam*) crush; squash; (*fig*) make a mess of.

desparpajo [despar'paxo] *sm* self-assurance; nonchalance. **desparpajado** *adj* self-assured. **desparpajar** *v* disarrange; (*fam*) prattle.

desparramar [desparra'mar] *v* scatter; squander.

despavorido [despaβori'ðo] *adj* terrified.

despectivo [despek'tiβo] *adj* contemptuous, scornful.

despechar [despe'tʃar] *v* drive to despair; slight; enrage; (*fam*) wean. **despecharse** *v* despair. **despecho** *sm* despair. **a despecho de** in spite of.

despedazar [despeða'θar] *v* tear to pieces; smash.

*despedir [despe'ðir] *v* dismiss; see off; give off; escort. **despedirse** *v* say good-bye. **despedida** *sf* dismissal; farewell.

despegar [despe'gar] *v* unstick. **despegarse** *v* become detached; become indifferent. **despegado** *adj* unstuck; (*fig*) cold.

despeinar [despei'nar] *v* disarrange the hair.

despejar [despe'xar] *v* free from obstructions. **despejarse** *v* be free and easy. **despejado** *adj* bright; clear. **despejo** *sm* brightness; self-confidence.

despellejar [despeʎe'xar] *v* skin, flay.

despensa [des'pensa] *sf* pantry; store of food.

despeñadero [despeɲa'ðero] *sm* precipice; (*fam*) risk. **despeñadizo** *adj* steep.

despeñar *v* precipitate. **despeño** *sm* fall.

desperdiciar [desperði'θjar] *v* waste. **desperdiciador, -a** *sm, sf* squanderer.

desperezarse [despere'θarse] *v* stretch oneself; rouse oneself.

*despertar [desper'tar] *v* awaken; arouse. **despertarse** *v* wake up. **despertador** *sm* alarm clock; warning. **despertamiento** *sm* awakening. **despierto** *adj* awake; watchful.

despiadado [despja'ðaðo] *adj* cruel, pitiless.

despilfarrar [despilfar'rar] *v* squander. **despilfarrado** *adj* wasteful; shabby. **despilfarro** *sm* waste; slovenliness.

despintar [despin'tar] *v* take paint off; fade.

despistar [despis'tar] *v* throw off the scent. **despistarse** *v* get lost. **despiste** *sm* absent-mindedness.

desplazar [despla'θar] *v* (*computadora*) scroll.

*desplegar [desple'gar] *v* unfold; reveal; display. **desplegadura** *sf* unfolding.

desplomarse [desplo'marse] *v* tilt; collapse; drop. **desplomo** *sm* (*pared, etc.*) bulge.

despojar [despo'xar] *v* deprive; dispossess. **despojarse** *v* divest oneself. **despojo** *sm* plunder. **despojos** *sm pl* scraps *pl*, leavings *pl*.

desposado [despo'saðo] *adj* newly-wed. **desposanda** *sf* bride. **desposando** *sm* bridegroom. **desposar** *v* marry. **desposarse** *v* become engaged; get married.

desposeer [despose'er] *v* dispossess.

déspota ['despota] *sm* despot. **despótico** *adj* despotic. **despotismo** *sm* despotism.

despreciar [despre'θjar] *v* reject; ignore; despise. **despreciarse de** not deign to. **despreciable** *adj* despicable. **desprecio** *sm* scorn; contempt; snub.

desprender [despren'der] *v* separate, remove; give off. **desprenderse** *v* withdraw; renounce; be deduced. **desprendimiento** *sm* disinterestedness; generosity; separation. **desprendimiento de tierras** landslide.

desprevenido [despreβe'niðo] *adj* unprepared. **desprevención** *sf* lack of foresight.

desproporción [despropor'θjon] *sf* disproportion. **desproporcionado** *adj* disproportionate.

después [des'pwes] *adv* afterwards, after, next, later; since. **después de** after. **después que** after.

desquiciar [deski'θjar] *v* unhinge; disconnect. **desquiciarse** *v* lose control. **desquiciado** *adj* off balance; (*fam*) crazy.

desquitar [deski'tar] *v* compensate. **desquitarse** *v* recoup; get one's revenge. **desquite** *sm* compensation; revenge.

destacar [desta'kar] *v* (*mil*) detach; stand out. **destacarse** *v* be conspicuous. **destacado** *adj* outstanding.

destajo [des'taxo] *sm* piecework. **destajar** *v* settle the terms for a job.

destapar [desta'par] *v* uncover. **destaparse** *v* reveal oneself.

destartalado [destarta'laðo] *adj* (*casa*) tumbledown; rambling.

destello [des'teλo] *sm* sparkling. **destellar** *v* sparkle.

destemplar [destem'plar] *v* disconcert. **destemplarse** *v* get out of tune; lose one's temper. **destemplado** *adj* out of tune; inharmonious.

*desteñir [deste'ɲir] *v* discolour; fade.

*desterrar [deste'rrar] *v* banish; (*fig*) discard. **desterrarse** *v* go into exile. **destierro** *sm* exile.

destilar [desti'lar] *v* distil; filter; ooze. **destilación** *sf* distillation. **destilador** *sm* still.

destinar [desti'nar] *v* destine; assign. **destino** *sm* destiny; destination; job. **con destino a** bound for. **destinatario** *sm* addressee.

*destituir [desti'twir] *v* dismiss; deprive of. **destitución** *sf* removal; dismissal.

destornillar [destorni'λar] *v* unscrew. **destornillarse** *v* (*fam*) go crazy. **destornillador** *sm* screwdriver.

destreza [des'treθa] *sf* skill, dexterity.

destronar [destro'nar] *v* dethrone; depose. **destronamiento** *sm* dethronement.

destrozar [destro'θar] *v* destroy; squander. **destrozo** *sm* destruction.

*destruir [destru'ir] *v* destroy. **destruirse** *v* (*mat*) cancel out. **destrucción** *sf* destruction. **destructivo** *adj* destructive. **destructor** *adj* destructive.

desunir [desu'nir] *v* separate; disunite. **desunión** *sf* separation.

desusar [desu'sar] *v* be unaccustomed to. **desusarse** *v* become obsolete. **desusado**

adj obsolete. **desuso** *sm* disuse.

desvalido [desβa'liðo] *adj* helpless; destitute.

desvalijar [desβali'xar] *v* rifle; rob.

desván [des'βan] *sm* attic.

*desvanecer [desβane'θer] *v* make disappear; remove. **desvanecerse** *v* evaporate; disappear; faint. **desvanecido** *adj* smug; vain; (*med*) faint. **desvanecimiento** *sm* disappearance; smugness; faint.

desvariar [desβa'rjar] *v* rave. **desvarío** *sm* delirium.

desvelar [desβe'lar] *v* stop from sleeping. **desvelarse** *v* stay awake; (*fig*) dedicate oneself. **desvelo** *sm* insomnia; effort; devotion. **gracias a mis desvelos** thanks to my efforts.

desventaja [desβen'taxa] *sf* disadvantage. **desventajoso** *adj* disadvantageous.

desventura [desβen'tura] *sf* misfortune. **desventurado** *adj* unfortunate; fainthearted.

desvergonzado [desβergon'θaðo], **-a** *sm, sf* shameless person. *adj* shameless.

desviar [des'βjar] *v* deviate; turn aside; deflect. **desviarse** *v* branch off. **desvío** *sm* detour; deviation.

desvirtuar [desβir'twar] *v* impair; decrease in strength *or* merit.

desvivirse [desβi'βirse] *v* long for; go out of one's way to.

detallar [deta'λar] *v* (*com*) retail; tell in detail. **detalle** *sm* detail; nice gesture. **vender al detalle** sell retail. **detalladamente** *adv* in detail. **detallista** *s(m + f)* retailer.

detective [detek'tiβe] *s(m + f)* detective.

*detener [dete'ner] *v* detain. **detenerse** *v* linger. **detención** *sf* arrest; delay; thoroughness. **detenido** *adj* under arrest; careful.

detergente [deter'xente] *sm, adj* detergent.

deteriorar [deterjo'rar] *v* deteriorate; damage. **deterioración** *sf also* **deterioro** *sm* deterioration.

determinar [determi'nar] *v* determine. **determinarse** *v* make up one's mind. **determinación** *sf* determination; decision. **determinado** *adj* determined; decided; definite.

detestar [detes'tar] *v* detest. **detestable** *adj* detestable. **detestación** *sf* detestation.

detonar [deto'nar] *v* detonate. **detonación**
sf detonation.

detractar [detrak'tar] *v* defame. **detrac-
ción** *sf* defamation.

*detraer [detra'er] *v* denigrate; withdraw

detrás [de'tras] *adv* behind. **detrás de** *prep*
behind. **por detrás de uno** behind someone's back.

detrimento [detri'mento] *sm* detriment;
damage. **en detrimento de** to the detriment of.

deuda ['deuða], *sf* debt; trespass. **deudor, -
a** *sm, sf* debtor.

deudo ['deuðo], **-a** *sm, sf* relative. *sm* relationship.

devanar [deβa'nar] *v* wind, coil. **devanarse los sesos** (*fam*) rack one's brains.

devanear [deβane'ar] *v* rave. **devaneo** *sm*
delirium; flirtation.

devastar [deβas'tar] *v* devastate. **devastación** *sf* devastation.

devengar [deβen'gar] *v* have due; (*intereses*) yield.

devoción [deβo'θjon] *sf* devotion. **devocionario** *sm* prayer book.

*devolver [deβol'βer] *v* return. **devolución**
sf return; refund.

devorar [deβo'rar] *v* devour.

devoto [de'βoto], **-a** *sm, sf* devotee. *adj*
devout; devoted.

día ['dia] *sm* day; daytime. **¡buenos días!**
good morning! **del día** fresh. **ocho días** a
week. **todos los días** every day.

diablo ['djaβlo] *sm* devil. **diabólico** *adj*
diabolical.

diafragma [dja'fragma] *sm* diaphragm.

diagnosticar [diagnosti'kar] *v* diagnose
diagnosis *sf invar* diagnosis. **diagnóstico**
adj diagnostic.

diagonal [diago'nal] *sf, adj* diagonal.

diagrama [dia'grama] *sm* diagram.

dialecto [dia'lekto] *sm* dialect.

diálogo [di'alogo] *sm* dialogue.

diamante [dia'mante] *sm* diamond.

diámetro [di'ametro] *sm* diameter. **diame-
tral** *adj* diametric.

diario [di'arjo] *sm* daily newspaper; diary.
diario hablado news bulletin. *adj* daily.
de diario for everyday use.

diarrea [diar'rea] *sf* diarrhoea.

dibujar [diβu'xar] *v* draw. **dibujante** *s(m* +

f) artist; designer; cartoonist; draughtsman. **dibujo** *sm* drawing; sketch; design.

dicción [dik'θjon] *sf* diction; word.

diccionario [dikθjo'narjo] *sm* dictionary.

diciembre [di'θjembre] *sm* December.

dictado [dik'taðo] *sm* dictation; title. **dicta-
dos** *sm pl* dictates *pl.* **dictador** *sm* dictator.
dictadura *sf* dictatorship. **dictar** *v* dictate.

dictamen [dik'tamen] *sm* opinion; advice;
report.

dicha ['d:tʃa] *sf* happiness; good luck. **por
dicha** luckily. **dichoso** *adj* happy; lucky;
(*fam*) boring.

dicho ['ditʃo] *V* decir. *sm* saying; remark;
proverb. **dicho y hecho** no sooner said
than done.

diente ['djente] *sm* tooth.

diestra ['djestra] *sf* right hand. **diestro** *adj*
right; skilful; sly.

dieta ['djeta] *sf* diet.

diez [djeθ] *sm, adj* ten. **diecinueve** *sm, adj*
nineteen. **dieciocho** *sm, adj* eighteen.
dieciséis *sm, adj* sixteen. **diecisiete** *sm, adj*
seventeen. **diezmar** *v* decimate.

diferencia [dife'renθ ja] *sf* difference. **a
diferencia de** unlike. **diferenciar** *v* differentiate; differ. **diferenciarse** be different.
diferente *adj* different.

*diferir [dife'rir] *v* defer; differ.

difícil [di'fiθ il] *adj* difficult. **dificultad** *sf*
difficulty. **dificultar** *v* make difficult; hinder.

difidente [difi'ðente] *adj* mistrustful. **difi-
dencia** *sf* mistrust.

difundir [difun'dir] *v* diffuse; broadcast;
divulge; spread. **difusión** *sf* spread; broadcast; diffusion.

difunto [di'funto] *adj* dead. *sm* deceased
person.

*digerir [dixe'rir] *v* digest; (*fig*) endure.
digestible *adj* digestible. **digestión** *sf*
digestion.

digital [dixi'tal] *adj* digital.

dignarse [dig'narse] *v* deign, condescend.

dignidad [digni'ðað] *sf* dignity; rank. **dignatario** *sm* dignitary. **digno** *adj* worthy.

digresión [digre'sjon] *sf* digression.

dilación [dila'θ jon] *sf* delay.

dilatar [dila'tar] *v* dilate; expand; delay.

dilatarse *v* speak at great length. **dilatación** *sf* extension; delay. **dilatado** *adj* numerous; long-winded. **dilatorio** *adj* dilatory.

dilema [di'lema] *sm* dilemma.

diligencia [dili'xenθja] *sf* diligence; *(fam)* job.

dilucidar [diluθi'ðar] *v* elucidate; solve.

diluir [dilu'ir] *v* dilute. **dilución** *sf* dilution.

diluvio [di'luβjo] *sm* deluge.

dimanar [dima'nar] *v* arise from; flow.

dimensión [dimen'sjon] *sf* dimension.

diminutivo [diminu'tiβo] *adj* diminutive. **diminuto** *adj* tiny.

dimitir [dimi'tir] *v* resign. **dimisión** *sf* resignation.

Dinamarca [dina'marka] *sf* Denmark. **dinamarqués, -esa** *sm, sf* Dane; *adj* Danish.

dinamita [dina'mita] *sf* dynamite.

dínamo ['dinamo] *sm* dynamo. **dinámico** *adj* dynamic.

dinastía [dinas'tia] *sf* dynasty.

dinero [di'nero] *sm* money. **de dinero** rich. **dinero suelto** loose change. **estar mal de dinero** be hard up.

dintel [din'tel] *sm* lintel.

dio [djo] *V* **dar**.

diócesi(s) [di'oθesi(s)] *sf invar* diocese.

dios [djos] *sm* god, idol. **diosa** *sf* goddess.

diploma [di'ploma] *sf* diploma.

diplomacia [diplo'maθja] *sf* diplomacy. **diplomático** *sm* diplomat; *adj* diplomatic.

diputado [dipu'taðo] *sm* deputy, delegate, representative.

dique ['dike] *sm* dike; dam; dry dock.

dirigir [diri'xir] *v* direct; govern; steer; regulate. **dirigirse** *v* go; speak; write. **dirección** *sf* direction; directorship; management; postal address. **directivo** *adj* directive; guiding. **directo** *adj* direct; straight. **director, -a** *sm, sf* director; editor. **directorio** *sm* directory. **directriz** *sf* guideline.

***discernir** [disθer'nir] *v* discern. **discernimiento** *sm* discernment.

disciplina [disθip'lina] *sf* discipline; doctrine; obedience. **disciplinar** *v* discipline; train.

discípulo [dis'θipulo], **-a** *sm, sf* disciple; pupil.

disco ['disko] *sm* disc; record; discus. **disco compacto** *sm* compact disc. **disco duro** *sm* hard disk.

disconforme [diskon'forme] *adj* in disagreement. **disconformidad** *sf* disagreement.

discontinuar [disconti'nwar] *v* discontinue. **discontinuación** *sf* discontinuation. **discontinuo** *adj* discontinuous.

discordia [dis'korðja] *sf* discord. **discordante** *adj also* **discorde** discordant.

discoteca [disko'teka] *sf* disco; record library.

discreción [diskre'θjon] *sf* discretion. **a discreción** optional, at will.

discrepancia [diskre'panθja] *sf* discrepancy.

discreto [dis'kreto] *adj* discreet; moderate; sober; witty.

disculpar [diskul'par] *v* excuse; forgive. *v* apologize. **disculpa** *sf* excuse; apology.

discurrir [diskur'rir] *v* ponder; speak; roam; invent.

discurso [dis'kurso] *sm* discourse; reasoning; passage of time. **discursivo** *adj* discursive.

discutir [disku'tir] *v* discuss; debate. **discusión** *sf* discussion; argument. **discutido** *adj* controversial.

disecar [dise'kar] *v* dissect. **disección** *sf* dissection.

diseminar [disemi'nar] *v* scatter. **diseminarse** *v* spread. **diseminación** *sf* dissemination.

disentería [disente'ria] *sf* dysentery.

***disentir** [disen'tir] *v* dissent; differ. **disensión** *sf* dissent; disagreement; quarrel.

diseñar [dise'ɲar] *v* sketch; design. **diseñador, -a** *sm, sf* designer. **diseño** *sm* sketch; design. **de diseño** *adj* designer.

disfrazar [disfra'θar] *v* disguise. **disfraz** *sm* disguise; fancy dress.

disfrutar [disfru'tar] *v* possess; enjoy; receive. **disfrute** *sm* enjoyment.

disgregar [disgre'gar] *v* disintegrate; separate. **disgregación** *sf* disintegration; separation.

disgustar [disgus'tar] *v* upset; displease. **disgustarse** *v* become angry. **disgustado** *adj* annoyed; displeased; disappointed. **disgusto** *sm* annoyance; displeasure; repugnance; trouble.

disidente [disi'ðente] *s(m + f)*, *adj* dissident. **disidir** *v* dissent.

disimular [disimu'lar] *v* pretend; dissemble;

hide; tolerate. **disimulable** *adj* excusable. **disimulo** *sm* concealment; indulgence.

disipar [disi'par] *v* dissipate. **disiparse** *v* disperse; vanish; clear up. **disipación** *sf* dissipation. **disipado** *adj* dissipated.

dislocar [dislo'kar] *v* dislocate. **dislocación** *sf* dislocation.

***disminuir** [disminu'ir] *v* diminish. **disminución** *sf* decrease; reduction.

disociar [diso'θjar] *v* dissociate. **disociación** *sf* dissociation.

***disolver** [disol'βer] *v* dissolve. **disoluble** *adj* dissoluble. **disolución** *sf* dissolution; (*fig*) dissoluteness. **disoluto** *adj* dissolute.

***disonar** [diso'nar] *v* disagree; be inharmonious. **disonancia** *sf* discord. **disonante** *adj* discordant.

disparar [dispa'rar] *v* fire; shoot; throw. **dispararse** *v* explode; fly off; race. **disparadamente** *adv* hurriedly; foolishly. **disparo** *sm* firing; shot; attack.

disparatado [dispara'taðo] *adj* absurd. **disparatar** *v* talk nonsense; act foolishly. **disparate** *sm* absurdity.

disparidad [dispari'ðað] *sf* disparity.

dispensar [dispen'sar] *v* dispense; pardon. **dispense usted** forgive me. **dispensa** *sf* dispensation; exemption. **dispensable** *adj* dispensable. **dispensario** *sm* dispensary.

dispersar [disper'sar] *v* disperse. **dispersión** *sf* dispersal. **disperso** *adj* dispersed, scattered.

***disponer** [dispo'ner] *v* dispose; arrange; decide; prepare. **disponer de** dispose of; have. **disponerse a** get ready. **disponible** *adj* disposable; available. **disposición** *sf* disposition; instruction; inclination; determination. **tomar disposiciones** take steps. **última disposición** last will and testament. **dispuesto** *adj* arranged; disposed; ready; willing.

disputar [dispu'tar] *v* dispute; debate. **disputa** *sf* dispute, argument.

disquete [dis'kete] *sm* floppy disk.

distancia [dis'tanθja] *sf* distance. **distante** *adj* distant.

distinguir [distin'gir] *v* distinguish; esteem. **distinción** *sf* distinction; politeness. **distinguido** *adj* distinguished. **distintivo** *adj* distinctive. **distinto** *adj* distinct; different.

***distraer** [distra'er] *v* distract; entertain. **distracción** *sf* distraction. **distraído** *adj* absent-minded; entertaining.

***distribuir** [distriβu'ir] *v* distribute; deliver; allot. **distribución** *sf* distribution. **cuadro de distribución** *sm* switchboard. **distribuidor** *sm* (*auto*) distributor; agent. **distribuidor automático** slot machine.

distrito [dis'trito] *sm* district.

disturbar [distur'βar] *v* disturb. **disturbio** *sm* disturbance.

disuadir [diswa'ðir] *v* dissuade.

diurno [di'urno] *adj* daily.

divagar [diβa'gar] *v* digress; roam. **divagación** *sf* digression.

diván [di'βan] *sm* divan.

divergir [diβer'xir] *v* diverge; disagree. **divergencia** *sf* divergence. **divergente** *adj* divergent.

diverso [di'βerso] *adj* diverse. **diversos** *adj pl* various; many. **diversidad** *sf* diversity.

***divertir** [diβer'tir] *v* entertain; divert. **divertido** *adj* amusing; entertaining.

dividir [diβi'ðir] *v* divide; split. **división** *sf* division; (*gram*) hyphen, dash. **divisor** *sm* divider. **divisorio** *adj* dividing.

divino [di'βino] *adj* divine. **divinidad** *sf* divinity.

divisa [di'βisa] *sf* emblem; (*com*) currency. **divisas** *sf pl* (*com*) foreign exchange *sing*. **control de divisas** (*com*) exchange control.

divisar [diβi'sar] *v* distinguish, discern.

divorciar [diβor'θjar] *v* divorce. **divorciarse** *v* get divorced. **divorciado, -a** *sm, sf* divorcee. **divorcio** *sm* divorce.

divulgar [diβul'gar] *v* divulge; circulate; spread. **divulgarse** *v* come out. **divulgación** *sf* disclosure.

doblar [do'βlar] *v* double; fold; bend; (*fig*) persuade; (*fig*) submit. **doblarse** *v* fold; buckle; stoop; yield. **dobladillo** *sm* hem; trouser turn-up. **dobladura** *sf* crease, fold. **doble** *adj also* **doblado** double; dual; stocky; deceitful. **el doble** twice as much.

doce ['doθe] *sm, adj* twelve. **docena** *sf* dozen.

docente [do'θente] *adj* educational. **personal docente** teaching staff.

dócil ['doθil] *adj* docile; obedient. **docilidad** *sf* docility.

doctor [dok'tor] **-a** *sm, sf* doctor. **docto** *adj* learned. **doctorado** *sm* doctorate.

doctrina [dok'trina] *sf* doctrine. **doctrinal** *adj* doctrinal.

documentar [dokumen'tar] *v* document. **documentación** *sf* documentation; identity papers *pl*.

dogal [do'gal] *sm* halter.

dogma ['dogma] *sm* dogma. **dogmático** *adj* dogmatic. **dogmatismo** *sm* dogmatism.

dogo ['dogo] *sm* bulldog.

dólar ['dolar] *sm* dollar.

*doler [do'ler] *v* hurt; ache; grieve. **dolerse de** feel the effects of; regret; pity. **dolor** *sm* pain; grief; repentance. **dolorido** *adj* in pain; grief-stricken. **doloroso** *adj* painful; pitiful; sorrowful.

domar [do'mar] *v* tame; train. **doma** *sf* training.

doméstico [do'mestiko], **-a** *sm, sf* servant. *adj* domestic. **domesticar** *v* domesticate. **domesticidad** *sf* domesticity.

domiciliar [domiθi'ljar] *v* domicile. **domiciliarse** *v* take up residence. **domiciliado** *adj* resident. **domicilio** *sm* home. **domiciliación bancaria** *sf* direct debit.

dominar [domi'nar] *v* dominate; master. **dominación** *sf* domination; authority. **dominador** *adj* dominating. **dominante** *adj* dominating; dominant. **dominio** *sm* dominion; authority; supremacy.

domingo [do'mingo] *sm* Sunday. **hacer domingo** take a day off.

dominó [domi'no] *sm* (*juego*) dominoes *pl*.

don¹ [don] *sm* (*con nombre de pila*) Mr.

don² *sm* gift; talent. **donación** *sf* donation. **donador, -a** *sm, sf* donor. **donar** *v* give, bestow. **donativo** *sm* offering.

donaire [do'naire] *sm* charm, grace; wit. **donairoso** *adj* graceful; witty.

donde ['donðe] *adv* where. **dondequiera** *adv* wherever. **¿dónde?** where? **¿por dónde?** which way?

doña ['doɲa] *sf* (*con el nombre de pila de una señora o una viuda*) Mrs.

dorar [do'rar] *v* gild; (*culin*) brown. **dorado** *adj* gilt; golden.

*dormir [dor'mir] *v* sleep. **dormirse** *v* go to sleep. **dormilón, -ona** *sm, sf* sleepyhead. **dormitorio** *sm* dormitory.

dorso ['dorso] *sm* back. **dorsal** *adj* dorsal.

dos [dos] *sm, adj* two. **dos veces** twice. **las dos** two o'clock. **los dos** both.

dosis ['dosis] *sf invar* dose. **dosificación** *sf* dosage. **dosificar** *v* dose.

dotar [do'tar] *v* endow; equip; staff. **dotación** *sf* endowment; foundation; personnel. **dotado** *adj* endowed; gifted. **dotador, -a** *sm, sf* donor. **dote** *sf* dowry. **dotes** *sf pl* endowments *pl*, talents *pl*.

draga ['draga] *sf* dredge. **dragado** *sm* dredging. **dragar** *v* dredge; (*minas*) sweep.

dragón [dra'gon] *sm* dragon.

drama ['drama] *sm* drama. **dramática** *sf* dramatic art. **dramático** *adj* dramatic. **dramatizar** *v* dramatize. **dramaturgo, -a** *sm, sf* playwright.

drenaje [dre'naxe] *sm* drainage. **drenar** *v* drain.

droga ['droga] *sf* drug. (*fam, fig*) trick, practical joke, fib. **drogadicto, -a** *s, adj* drug addict. **drogar** *v* drug, dope.

dual [dwal] *adj* dual. **dualidad** *sf* duality. **dualismo** *sm* dualism.

ducado [du'kaðo] *sm* duchy.

dúctil ['duktil] *adj* ductile; malleable.

ducha ['dutʃa] *sf* shower. **ducharse** *v* have *or* take a shower.

dudar [du'ðar] *v* doubt. **duda** *sf* doubt. **sin duda** doubtless. **dudoso** *adj* doubtful; dubious.

duelo¹ ['dwelo] *sm* sorrow; mourning.

duelo² *sm* duel.

duende ['dwende] *sm* imp; goblin; elf.

dueño ['dweɲo], **-a** *sm, sf* owner; master/mistress; landlord/landlady.

dulce ['dulθe] *sm* sweet. *adj* sweet; mild; gentle; soft; (*agua*) fresh. **dulcería** *sf* confectionery. **dulzura** *sf* sweetness; mildness.

dúo ['duo] *sm* duet.

duodécimo [duo'ðeθimo] *sm, adj* twelfth.

duplicar [dupli'kar] *v* duplicate. **duplicarse** *v* double. **duplicación** *sf* duplication; doubling. **duplicado** *sm, adj* duplicate. **duplicador** *sm* duplicator.

duplicidad [dupliθi'ðað] *sf* duplicity.

duque ['duke] *sm* duke. **duquesa** *sf* duchess.

durar [du'rar] *v* last, endure. **durable** *adj* durable. **duración** *sf* duration. **durante** *adv* during.

durazno [du'raθno] *sm* peach; peach tree.

durmiente [dur'mjente] *adj* sleeping.

duro ['duro] *adj* hard; firm. **dureza** *sf* hardness; severity.

DVD *sm* DVD.

E

e [e] *conj* and.

ébano ['eβano] *sm* ebony.

ebrio ['eβrjo] *adj* drunk.

eclesiástico [ekle'sjastiko] *adj, sm* ecclesiastic.

eclipse [e'klipse] *sm* eclipse. **eclipsar** *v* eclipse.

eco ['eko] *sm* echo.

ecografía [ekogra'fia] *sf* ultrasound. **ecógrafo** *sm* scanner (medical).

economía [ekono'mia] *sf* economy. **económico** *adj* economical. **economista** *s(m + f)* economist. **economizar** *v* economize.

ecuador [ekwa'ðor] *sm* equator.

ecuestre [e'kwestre] *adj* equestrian.

echar [e'tʃar] *v* throw; emit; (*naipes*) deal/pour out; dismiss; begin; perform. **echar a** start to. **echar abajo** demolish. **echar a perder** spoil. **echar de ver** notice. **echarse** *v* lie down.

edad [e'ðað] *sf* age. **edad madura** middle age.

edicto [e'ðikto] *sm* edict.

edificar [eðifi'kar] *v* build; (*fig*) edify. **edificio** *sm* edifice.

editar [eði'tar] *v* publish. **edición** *sf* edition. **editor, -a** *sm, sf* publisher.

edredón [eðre'ðon] *sm* eiderdown.

educar [eðu'kar] *v* educate; bring up; train. **educación** *sf* education; upbringing. **educado** *adj* educated; well-mannered.

edulcorante [eðulko'rante] *sm* sweetener.

efectivo [efek'tiβo] *adj* effective; real. **dinero efectivo** *sm* cash. **efecto** *sm* effect; result; (*com*) document. **efectos** *sm pl* effects *pl*, assets *pl*. **efectos en cartera** holdings *pl*. **efectuar** *v* carry out.

efecto invernadero *sm* greenhouse effect.

efervescencia [eferβes'θenθja] *sf* effervescence. **efervescente** *adj* effervescent.

eficacia [efi'kaθja] *sf* efficacy; efficiency. **eficaz** *adj* efficacious; efficient. **eficiencia** *sf* efficiency. **eficiente** *adj* efficient.

efigie [e'fixje] *sf* effigy.

efímero [e'fimero] *adj* ephemeral.

efusión [efu'sjon] *sf* effusion.

Egipto [e'xipto] *sm* Egypt. **egipcio, -a** *s. adj* Egyptian.

egoísmo [ego'ismo] *sm* egoism. **egoísta** *s(m + f)* egoist. **egotismo** *sm* egotism. **egotista** *s(m + f)* egotist.

egregio [e'grexjo] *adj* eminent.

eje ['exe] *sm* axis; axle; (*fig*) core, hub. **eje del mundo** earth's axis.

ejecutar [exeku'tar] *v* execute; put to death; seize; perform. **ejecución** *sf* execution. **ejecutivo** *sm, adj* executive. **ejecutor, -a** *sm, sf* executor; executioner.

ejemplar [exem'plar] *sm* copy; model; specimen; example. *adj* exemplary. **ejemplificar** *v* exemplify. **ejemplo** *sm* example. **dar ejemplo** set an example. **sin ejemplo** unprecedented.

ejercer [exer'θer] *v* practise; exercise. **ejercicio** *sm* exercise.

ejército [e'xerθito] *sm* army.

el [el] *art m* the.

él [el] *pron* he, it.

elaborar [elaβo'rar] *v* elaborate; make; manufacture. **elaboración** *sf* elaboration. **elaborado** *adj* elaborate.

elástico [e'lastiko] *sm, adj* elastic. **elasticidad** *sf* elasticity.

elección [elek'θjon] *sf* election; choice, selection. **elector, -a** *sm, sf* elector. **electorado** *sm* electorate. **electoral** *adj* electoral.

eléctrico [e'lektriko] *adj* electric(al). **electricidad** *sf* electricity. **electrizar** *v* electrify. **electrocutar** *v* electrocute. **electrodo** *sm* electrode. **electrónico** *adj* electronic.

elefante [ele'fante] *sm* elephant.

elegancia [ele'ganθja] *sf* elegance. **elegante** *adj* elegant.

*elegir [ele'xir] *v* elect, choose. **elegible** *adj* eligible.

elemental [elemen'tal] *adj* elementary. **elemento** *sm* element. **elementos** *sm pl* elements; rudiments.

elevar [ele'βar] *v* elevate, lift, raise. **elevarse** *v* rise; soar; be elated. **elevación** *sf* elevation; rapture; pride. **elevado** *adj* lofty; sublime.

eliminar [elimi'nar] *v* eliminate. **eliminación** *sf* elimination.

elocución [eloku'θjon] *sf* elocution. **elocuencia** *sf* eloquence. **elocuente** *adj* eloquent.

elogiar [elo'xjar] *v* praise. **elogio** *sm* praise. **elogioso** *adj* laudatory.

elucidar [eluθi'ðar] *v* elucidate. **elucidación** *sf* elucidation.

eludir [elu'ðir] *v* elude.

ella ['eʎa] *pron* she, it.

ello ['eʎo] *pron* it.

emanar [ema'nar] *v* emanate. **emanación** *sf* emanation.

emancipar [emanθi'par] *v* emancipate. **emancipación** *sf* emancipation.

embajada [emba'xaða] *sf* embassy; *(fig)* errand. **embajador** *sm* ambassador.

embalar [emba'lar] *v* pack, bale. **embalaje** *sm* packing; bale.

embarazar [embara'θar] *v* embarrass; hinder; make pregnant. **embarazarse** *v* become pregnant. **embarazada** *adj* pregnant. **embarazo** *sm* embarrassment; obstacle; pregnancy. **embarazoso** *adj* embarrassing; awkward.

embarcar [embar'kar] *v* embark; ship; *(fam)* involve. **embarcarse** *v* go on board. **embarcación** *sf* boat; embarkation; voyage. **embarcadero** *sm* landing-stage. **embarco** *sm* embarkation.

embargar [embar'gar] *v* *(jur)* seize; *(fig)* overcome; blunt. **embargo** *sm* embargo. **sin embargo** nevertheless.

embarque [em'barke] *sm* shipment.

embarrar [embar'rar] *v* smear; cover with mud. **embarrarse** *v* get dirty.

embeber [embe'βer] *v* absorb, soak up; shrink. **embebecerse** *v* *(fig)* immerse oneself.

*embellecer [embeʎe'θer] *v* embellish.

*embestir [embes'tir] *v* attack; charge. **embestida** *sf* onslaught; charge.

emblema [em'blema] *sm* emblem. **emblemático** *adj* emblematic.

embobar [embo'βar] *v* stupefy; fascinate.

embocar [embo'kar] *v* put in the mouth; enter; *(fig)* swallow. **embocadura** *sf* mouth of a river; *(vino)* taste; *(caballo)* bit.

embolsar [embol'sar] *v* pocket.

emborrachar [emborra'tʃar] *v* intoxicate. **emborracharse** *v* get drunk.

emboscar [embos'kar] *v* ambush. **emboscarse** *v* lie in ambush. **emboscada** *sf* ambush.

embotar [embo'tar] *v* blunt, dull; pack in a jar. **embotarse** *v* become enervated. **embo-**

tadura *sf* also **embotamiento** *sm* bluntness, dullness.

embotellar [embote'ʎar] *v* bottle. **embotellarse** *v* learn by heart. **embotellado** *adj* bottled; jammed. **embotellamiento** *sm* bottling; traffic jam.

embozar [embo'θar] *v* muffle; wrap up. **embozadamente** *adv* secretly. **embozo** *sm* fold; *(fig)* disguise. **quitarse el embozo** bare one's face.

embragar [embra'gar] *v* *(auto)* engage the clutch. **embrague** *sm* *(auto)* clutch.

embriagarse [embrja'garse] *v* get drunk. **embriagado** *adj* drunk.

embrión [em'brjon] *sm* embryo. **embriología** *sf* embryology.

embrollar [embro'ʎar] *v* muddle, confuse. **embrollarse** *v* get mixed up. **embrollo** *sm* confusion.

embrujar [embru'xar] *v* bewitch.

*embrutecer [embrute'θer] *v* brutalize; stupefy.

embudo [em'buðo] *sm* funnel; crater; *(fig)* trick.

embuste [em'buste] *sm* lie; trick. **embustear** *v* lie; cheat. **embustería** *sf* deceit; imposture. **embustero, -a** *sm, sf* liar; cheat; *adj* lying; deceitful.

embutir [embu'tir] *v* stuff; cram; *(tecn)* inlay. **embutido** *sm* sausage.

emergencia [emer'xenθja] *sf* emergence; emergency. **emergente** *adj* emergent; resultant. **emerger** *v* emerge.

emigrar [emi'grar] *v* emigrate; migrate. **emigración** *sf* emigration; migration. **emigrado, -a** *sm, sf* emigrant. **emigrante** *s(m + f)*, *adj* emigrant.

eminencia [emi'nenθja] *sf* eminence; height. **eminente** *adj* eminent.

emisario [emi'sarjo], **-a** *sm, sf* emissary.

emitir [emi'tir] *v* emit; broadcast; transmit. **emisión** *sf* emission; broadcast; programme. **emisor** *sm* transmitter. **emisora** *sf* radio station.

emoción [emo'θjon] *sf* emotion; thrill. **emocionante** *adj* moving; exciting. **emotivo** *adj* emotive.

empachar [empa'tʃar] *v* satiate; give indigestion; sicken; conceal; *(fig)* hinder. **empacharse** *v* have indigestion; become confused; get fed up. **empachado** *adj* clumsy; sick; fed up. **empacho** *sm* indigestion; *(fig)* embarrassment.

empadronar [empaðro'nar] v register.
empadronamiento sm census.

empalagar [empala'gar] v cloy; vex.
empalagarse v get fed up. **empalagoso**
adj cloying.

empalar [empa'lar] v impale.

empalizada [empali'θaða] sf stockade.
empalizar v fence.

empalmar [empal'mar] v splice; couple;
join. **empalme** sm joint; junction.

empanada [empa'naða] sf meat pie.

empañar [empa'ɲar] v tarnish; swathe;
obscure. **empañarse** v cloud over.
empañado adj misty.

empapar [empa'par] v soak; drench.
empapamiento sm soaking.

empapelar [empape'lar] v paper; wrap in
paper.

empaquetar [empake'tar] v pack, package.
empaque sm packing.

emparejar [empare'xar] v match; pair;
draw level; catch up. **emparejadura** sf
matching; levelling.

empastar [empas'tar] v paste; fill. **empas-
tado** adj filled; (libro) clothbound.

empatar [empa'tar] v (juegos) tie, draw.
empate sm tie, draw.

*****empedernir** [empeðer'nir] v harden.
empedernido adj hardened; inveterate.

*****empedrar** [empe'ðrar] v pave. **empedra-
do** adj paved; cobbled.

empeine [em'peine] sm groin; instep; (med)
impetigo.

empeñar [empe'ɲar] v pawn, pledge; commit; get involved. **empeñarse** v start;
strive; get into debt. **empeñado** adj insistent. **empeño** sm pledge; contract; insistence; yearning. **casa de empeño** sf
pawnshop. **en empeño** in pawn.

empeorar [empeo'rar] v make worse; wors-
en. **empeoramiento** sm deterioration.

*****empequeñecer** [empekeɲe'θer] v dwarf;
belittle.

emperador [empera'ðor] sm emperor.
emperatriz sf empress.

*****empezar** [empe'θar] v begin.

empinar [empi'nar] v straighten; exalt.
empinarse v rear up; stand on tiptoe;
tower. **empinado** adj erect; on tiptoe;
haughty.

empírico [em'piriko] adj empirical.
empirismo sm empiricism.

emplazar [empla'θar] v summon; locate.
emplazamiento sm (jur) summons.

emplear [emple'ar] v employ; use; invest;
spend. **empleado, -a** sm, sf employee.
empleador, -a sm, sf employer. **empleo** sm
employment; job; use.

*****empobrecer** [empoβre'θer] v impoverish.
empobrecimiento sm impoverishment.

empollar [empo'ʎar] v hatch; (fam) swot,
mug up.

emponzoñar [emponθo'ɲar] v poison.
emponzoñamiento sm poisoning.

empotrar [empo'trar] v embed. **empo-
tramiento** sm embedding.

emprender [empren'der] v undertake;
start; attack. **emprender con** accost.
emprendedor adj enterprising.

empresa [em'presa] sf enterprise; (com)
company; management. **empresario, -a**
sm, sf impresario; contractor.

empréstito [em'prestito] sm loan.

empujar [empu'xar] v push; press; (fig)
urge. **empuje** sm push; enterprise. **a empu-
jes** by fits and starts.

empuñar [empu'ɲar] v seize; take up.
empuñadura sf hilt.

emular [emu'lar] v emulate.

emulsión [emul'sjon] sf emulsion. **emulsionar** v emulsify.

en [en] prep on; in; into; onto. **en casa** at
home. **en donde** where. **en tren** by train.

enaguas [e'nagwas] sf pl petticoat sing.

enajenar [enaxe'nar] v alienate; transfer;
drive mad; enrapture. **enajenarse** v lose
one's self-control. **enajenación** sf also **ena-
jenamiento** sm alienation; absent-mindedness; rapture; panic.

enamorar [enamo'rar] v court; win the
love of. **enamorarse** v fall in love. **enamorado, -a** sm, sf sweetheart.

enano [e'nano], **-a** sm, sf dwarf.

enarbolar [enarβo'lar] v hoist. **enarbo-
larse** v rear; lose one's temper.

*****enardecer** [enarðe'θer] v inflame.
enardecerse v become excited.

encabestrar [enkaβes'trar] v put a halter
on.

encabezar [enkaβe'θar] v lead; head; take a
census of; put a title to. **encabezamiento**
sm headline; heading; census.

encadenar [enkaðe'nar] v chain, shackle.
encadenamiento sm chaining; (fig)

linking.

encajar [enka'xar] *v* fit; join; bear; pocket; drop; land. **encajarse** *v* get stuck; squeeze in. **encajadura** *sf (hueso)* setting; socket. **encaje** *sm* joint; setting; socket; lace.

encallar [enka'ʎar] *v* run aground. **encallarse** *v* harden. **encalladero** *sm* sandbank; reef.

encaminar [enkami'nar] *v* direct; guide. **encaminarse** *v* set out for.

encandilar [enkandi'lar] *v* dazzle; stimulate. **encandilarse** *v (ojos)* sparkle.

encantar [enkan'tar] *v* enchant; charm. **encantado** *adj* charmed; haunted. **¡encantado!** pleased to meet you! **encantador** *adj* charming. **encanto** *sm* charm; delight.

encapotar [enkapo'tar] *v* cover with a cloak. **encapotarse** *v* cloak oneself; look sullen; cloud over. **encapotado** *adj* overcast.

encapricharse [enkapri'tʃarse] *v* set one's mind on. **encapricharse por** *or* **con** become infatuated with.

encarar [enka'rar] *v* face up to; aim; confront. **encaramiento** *sm* encounter.

encarcelar [enkarθe'lar] *v* imprison. **encarcelamiento** *sm* imprisonment.

*encarecer [enkare'θer] *v* raise the price of; praise; urge. **encarecidamente** *adv* earnestly. **encarecido** *adj* highly recommended. **encarecimiento** *sm* price increase; emphasis; recommendation.

encargar [enkar'gar] *v (com)* order; commission; entrust; charge; advise. **encargarse de** take charge of. **encargado** *sm* agent. **encargo** *sm* errand; job; order.

encarnar [enkar'nar] *v* personify; heal; pierce the flesh; bait. **encarnarse** *v* mix, join in. **encarnación** *sf* incarnation. **encarnado** *adj* incarnate; red; *(uña)* ingrowing.

encarnizar [enkarni'θar] *v* infuriate. **encarnizarse** *v* devour. **encarnizado** *adj* inflamed; bloody.

encasillar [enkasi'ʎar] *v* classify.

encauzar [enkau'θar] *v* channel; direct. **encauzamiento** *sm* channelling; *(fig)* guidance.

Encefalopatía Espongiforme Bovina *sf* Bovine Spongiform Encaphalopathy (BSE).

*encender [enθen'der] *v* light; set on fire; turn on; arouse. **encendedor** *sm* lighter. **encendido** *adj* lit; burning; flushed.·

encendimiento *sm* burning; ardour.

*encerrar [enθer'rar] *v* shut up; enclose; contain. **encerrarse** *v* live in seclusion. **encerramiento** *sm* enclosure; lock-up. **encierro** *sm* enclosure; prison.

enchufe [en'tʃufe] *sm* power point.

encía [en'θia] *sf (anat)* gum.

enciclopedia [enθiklo'peðja] *sf* encyclopaedia. **enciclopédico** *adj* encyclopaedic.

encima [en'θima] *adv* above; overhead. **por encima** over; quickly; superficially, **encima de** on top of.

encina [en'θina] *sf* ilex, holm oak.

encinta [en'θinta] *adj* pregnant.

enclavar [enkla'βar] *v* locate; nail; pierce. **enclave** *sm* enclave; situation.

enclenque [en'klenke] *adj* sickly; feeble; skinny.

encoger [enko'xer] *v* shrink. **encogerse de hombros** shrug one's shoulders. **encogido** *adj* shrunk; *(fig)* timid. **encogimiento** *sm* shrinkage; shyness.

encolar [enko'lar] *v* glue. **encolamiento** *sm* gluing.

*encomendar [enkomen'ðar] *v* entrust. **encomendarse** *v* commend oneself. **encomienda** *sf* assignment; tribute; land concession.

encomiar [enko'mjar] *v* praise. **encomiador** *adj* laudatory.

enconar [enko'nar] *v* inflame; infect. **enconarse** *v* become inflamed; become infected; get angry.

encontrar [enkon'trar] *v* find; meet. **encontrarse** *v* find oneself; quarrel. **encontrado** *adj* opposed.

encopetado [enkope'taðo] *adj* of noble birth; aristocratic; presumptuous.

encorvar [enkor'βar] *v* curve. **encorvarse** *v* become bent; *(caballo)* buck. **encorvado** *adj* bent; stooped. **encorvamiento** *sm* bend; stoop.

encrespar [enkres'par] *v* curl; make rough; excite; irritate. **encresparse** *v* curl; become rough; become entangled.

encrucijada [enkruθi'xaða] *sf* crossroads *pl.*

encuadernar [enkwaðer'nar] *v (libro)* bind. **encuadernación** *sf* bookbinding.

encuadrar [enkwa'ðrar] *v* frame; insert. **encuadre** *sm* frame.

*encubrir [enku'βrir] *v* conceal; *(jur)*

receive stolen goods. **encubierto** *adj* concealed. **encubrimiento** *sm* concealment.

encuentro [en'kwentro] *sm* encounter; collision.

encumbrar [enkum'brar] *v* raise; ascend; exalt. **encumbrado** *adj* high, lofty. **encumbramiento** *sm* height; praise.

enchufar [entʃu'far] *v* plug in; connect. **enchufado, -a** *sm*, *sf (fam)* wirepuller. **enchufe** *sm* electric plug; joint; *(fam)* cushy job. **enchufismo** *sm (fam)* wirepulling.

endeble [en'deβle] *adj* frail. **endeblez** *sf* frailty.

endémico [en'demiko] *adj* endemic.

enderezar [endere'θar] *v* straighten; guide; put right. **enderezarse** *v* stand up straight. **enderezado** *adj* favourable.

endeudarse [endeu'ðarse] *v* get into debt.

endiablado [endja'βlaðo] *adj* devilish. **endiablar** *v* bedevil.

endiosar [endjo'sar] *v* deify. **endiosarse** *v* be conceited. **endiosado** *adj* deified; conceited.

endosar [endo'sar] *v also* **endorsar** endorse. **endoso** *sm also* **endorso** *sm* endorsement.

endulzar [endul'θar] *v* sweeten. **endulzadura** *sf* sweetening.

*****endurecer** [endure'θer] *v* harden. **endurecido** *adj* hardened. **endurecimiento** *sm* hardening.

enebro [e'neβro] *sm* juniper.

enemigo [ene'migo], **-a** *sm*, *sf* enemy. *adj* hostile. **enemistar** *v* make an enemy of.

energía [ener'xia] *sf* energy. **enérgico** *adj* energetic; vigorous; drastic.

enero [e'nero] *sm* January.

enfadar [enfa'ðar] *v* anger. **enfado** *sm* anger; annoyance. **enfadoso** *adj* annoying.

énfasis ['enfasis] *s(m or f)* emphasis. **enfático** *adj* emphatic.

enfermar [enfer'mar] *v* make ill; fall ill. **enfermedad** *sf* illness. **enfermedad profesional** occupational disease. **enfermería** *sf* infirmary. **enfermera, -o** *sf*, *sm* nurse. **enfermo** *adj* ill.

enfilar [enfi'lar] *v* line up.

*****enflaquecer** [enflake'θer] *v* weaken; make thin; grow thin. **enflaquecimiento** *sm* weakening; emaciation.

enfocar [enfo'kar] *v* focus; approach, tack-

le. **enfoque** *sm* focus; approach.

enfrascar [enfras'kar] *v* bottle. **enfrascarse** *v* become involved; become engrossed.

enfrentar [enfren'tar] *v* confront; face; resist. **enfrentarse** *v* face up to. **enfrente** *adv* opposite. **enfrente de** *prep* opposite.

enfriar [enfri'ar] *v* cool. **enfriarse** *v* cool down. **enfriadero** *sm* coldroom. **enfriamiento** *sm* cooling.

*****enfurecer** [enfure'θer] *v* infuriate. **enfurecerse** *v* rage. **enfurecimiento** *sm* fury.

enganchar [engan'tʃar] *v* hook; hitch; hang up; harness. **enganche** *sm* hook; coupling; harnessing; enlistment.

engañar [enga'nar] *v* deceive. **engaño** *sm* deceit. **engañoso** *adj* deceitful.

engatusar [engatu'sar] *v* coax; flatter. **engatusamiento** *sm* coaxing.

engendrar [enxen'drar] *v* engender; breed. **engendrador** *adj* generating. **engendramiento** *sm* generating. **engendro** *sm* foetus; abortion; monster; brainchild.

englobar [englo'βar] *v* include; embrace.

engordar [engor'ðar] *v* fatten; gain weight. **engorde** *sm (animales)* fattening up.

engorro [en'gorro] *sm* nuisance. **engorroso** *adj* troublesome.

engranar [engra'nar] *v* put in gear, mesh, interlock. **engranaje** *sm* gear; cogs; connection.

*****engrandecer** [engrande'θer] *v* enlarge; exaggerate; promote. **engrandecimiento** *sm* enlargement; increase; exaggeration.

engrasar [engra'sar] *v* grease. **engrase** *sm* greasing.

engreído [engre'iðo] *adj* conceited. **engreimiento** *sm* conceit. **engreír** *v* make conceited.

*****engrosar** [engro'sar] *v* fatten; thicken; increase. **engrosarse** *v* enlarge. **engrosamiento** *sm* fattening; thickening.

*****engullir** [engu'ʎir] *v* gobble; gulp down.

enhiesto [e'njesto] *adj* erect; upright. **enhestar** *v* erect. **enhestarse** *v* rise; straighten oneself up.

enhorabuena [enora'βwena] *sf* congratulations *pl*. **dar la enhorabuena** congratulate. **enhoramala** *adv* inopportunely.

enigma [e'nigma] *sm* enigma. **enigmático** *adj* enigmatic.

enjabonar [enxaβo'nar] *v* soap. **enjabonadura** *sf* lathering.

enjambre [en'xambre] *sm* swarm. **enjambrar** *v* swarm.

enjaular [enxau'lar] *v* cage.

enjuagar [enxwa'ɣar] *v* rinse. **enjuague** *sm* rinse, rinsing; (*fig*) plot.

enjugar [enxu'ɣar] *v* dry; wipe; cancel. **enjugador** *sm* clothes-drier.

enjuiciar [enxwi'θjar] *v* (*jur*) sue; try; prosecute; judge. **enjuiciamiento** *sm* trial; lawsuit; judgment.

enlace [en'laθe] *sm* link; connection; liaison; marriage. **enlazar** *v* join; connect; relate. **enlazarse** *v* marry.

*enloquecer [enloke'θer] *v* madden. **enloquecido** *adj* mad. **enloquecimiento** *sm* madness.

enlosar [enlo'sar] *v* tile; pave. **enlosado** *sm* tiling; paving.

*enlucir [enlu'θir] *v* plaster; polish. **enlucido** *sm* plaster. **enlucimiento** *sm* plastering; polishing.

enlutar [enlu'tar] *v* dress in mourning; (*fig*) sadden. **enlutado** *adj* in mourning.

enmarañar [enmara'ɲar] *v* entangle; muddle; confuse. **enmarañamiento** *sm* tangle; confusion.

enmascarar [enmaska'rar] *v* mask. **enmascararse** *v* go in disguise. **enmascaramiento** *sm* camouflage.

*enmendar [enmen'dar] *v* amend; correct; reform. **enmendadura** *sf* correction. **enmienda** *sf* rectification; repair; amendment.

*enmohecer [enmoe'θer] *v* rust; make mouldy. **enmohecerse** *v* get rusty; grow mouldy. **enmohecimiento** *sm* rusting; mouldering.

*enmudecer [enmuðe'θer] *v* silence. **enmudecerse** *v* fall silent; become dumb.

ennoblecer [ennoβle'θer] *v* ennoble; do honour to. **ennoblecimiento** *sm* ennobling.

enojar [eno'xar] *v* annoy; offend. **enojarse** *v* get cross. **enojado** *adj* angry. **enojo** *sm* annoyance; anger.

*enorgullecer [enorɡuʎe'θer] *v* make proud. **enorgullecerse** *v* grow proud. **enorgullecerse de** pride oneself on. **enorgullecimiento** *sm* pride.

enorme [e'norme] *adj* enormous. **enormidad** *sf* hugeness; enormity.

*enrarecer [enrare'θer] *v* make rare; rarefy.

enrarecerse *v* become scarce. **enrarecido** *adj* rarefied. **enrarecimiento** *sm* scarcity.

enredar [enre'ðar] *v* catch; entangle; compromise; involved. **enredarse** *v* become involved. **planta enredadera** *sf* climbing plant. **enredador** *adj* mischievous. **enredo** *sm* tangle; mess; love affair. **enredoso** *adj* complicated; mischievous.

enrevesado [enreβe'saðo] *adj* complicated, involved.

*enriquecer [enrike'θer] *v* enrich.

*enrojecer [enroxe'θer] *v* redden; cause to blush. **enrojecerse** *v* blush. **enrojecimiento** *sm* glowing; blush.

enrollar [enro'ʎar] *v* coil up. **enrollamiento** *sm* rolling up; coiling.

*enronquecer [enronke'θer] *v* make hoarse. **enronquecimiento** *sm* hoarseness.

enroscar [enros'kar] *v* twist, curl. **enroscarse** *v* curl up. **enroscadura** *sf* twisting, curling.

ensalada [ensa'laða] *sf* salad.

ensalmar [ensal'mar] *v* (*huesos*) set; cure. **ensalmador, -a** *sm, sf* quack; bonesetter. **ensalmado** *sm* quack remedy.

ensalzar [ensal'θar] *v* praise. **ensalzarse** *v* boast. **ensalzamiento** *sm* praise.

ensamblar [ensam'blar] *v* assemble; join. **ensamblado** *sm* joint. **ensamblador** *sm* joiner. **ensamblaje** *sm* joining; joint.

ensanchar [ensan'tʃar] *v* grow broader; enlarge; stretch. **ensancharse** *v* put on airs. **ensanche** *sm* enlargement; extension; new suburb.

ensañar [ensa'ɲar] *v* infuriate. **ensañarse** *v* be merciless.

ensayar [ensa'jar] *v* test; try; rehearse. **ensayarse** *v* practise; rehearse. **ensayo** *sm* test; trial; essay; rehearsal. **ensayo general** dress rehearsal.

ensenada [ense'naða] *sf* cove; inlet.

enseñar [ense'ɲar] *v* show; teach. **bien/mal enseñado** well/ill-bred. **enseñanza** *sf* teaching; education.

enseres [en'seres] *sm pl* goods and chattels; equipment *sing*.

ensillar [ensi'ʎar] *v* saddle.

ensimismarse [ensimis'marse] *v* become lost in thought. **ensimismado** *adj* lost in thought. **ensimismamiento** *sm* pensiveness.

*ensordecer [ensorðe'θer] *v* deafen. **ensor-**

decerse *v* grow deaf. **ensordecedor** *adj* deafening. **ensordecimiento** *sm* deafness.

ensuciar [ensu'θjar] *v* dirty. **ensuciador** *adj* dirtying. **ensuciamiento** *sm* dirtiness, dirt.

ensueño [en'sweɲo] *sm* dream; fantasy. ¡ni por ensueño! not likely!

entablar [enta'βlar] *v* begin; open; establish; board up; put in a splint; (*juegos*) set up. **entablado** *sm* planking; wooden floor.

entallar [enta'ʎar] *v* carve; notch; engrave; fit to the body. **entalladura** *sf* notch; mortise; carving.

ente ['ente] *sm* entity; (*fam*) fellow.

*****entender** [enten'der] *v* understand; believe; mean. **entenderse** *v* make oneself understood. **entendedor, -a** *sm, sf* expert. **entendidamente** *adv* cleverly. **entendido** *adj* understood; well informed; clever. ¡entendido! O.K.!

enterar [ente'rar] *v* inform; instruct. **enterarse** *v* become aware. **enterado** *adj* aware.

*****enternecer** [enterne'θer] *v* soften. **enternecerse** *v* be moved; relent.

entero [en'tero] *adj* entire, whole; perfect; pure; strong. **por entero** completely. **enteramente** *adv* entirely.

*****enterrar** [enter'rar] *v* bury. **entarrador** *sm* gravedigger. **entierro** *sm* burial; funeral.

entidad [enti'ðað] *sf* society; company; significance; entity.

entonar [ento'nar] *v* tune; intone; sing in tune. **entonación** *sf* intonation. **entonado** *adj* in tune; haughty.

entonces [en'tonθes] *adv* then; in that case; and so.

entornar [entor'nar] *v* (*ojos, puerta*) half close; tilt.

*****entorpecer** [entorpe'θer] *v* benumb; obstruct. **entorpecimiento** *sm* numbness; sluggishness; obstruction.

entrada [en'traða] *sf* entrance; doorway; admission; (*deporte*) gate; ticket; income; takings *pl*. **derechos de entrada** *sm pl* import duty *sing*. **de entrada** to begin with. **entrar** *v* enter; flow into; fit; join; introduce; invade. **el año que entra** the coming year.

entrambos [en'trambos] *pl adj* both.

entraña [en'traɲa] *sf* essence; core; disposition. **entrañas** *sf pl* entrails, bowels. **no tener entrañas** be heartless. **entrañable** *adj* dear, beloved; endearing. **entrañar** *v*

bury deep; involve. **entrañarse** *v* penetrate to the core.

entre ['entre] *prep* between; among. **entre-semana** on weekdays. **entretanto** *adv* meanwhile.

entreabierto [entrea'βjerto] *adj* half-open.

entrecejo [entre'θexo] *sm* frown.

entregar [entre'gar] *v* deliver; surrender. **entrega** *sf* delivery; (*fascículo*) instalment.

entrelazar [entrela'θar] *v* entwine.

entremés [entre'mes] *sm* (*culin*) hors d'oeuvre; (*teatro*) short farce.

entremeter [entreme'ter] *v* also **entrometer** mix; insert. **entremeterse** also **entrometerse** *v* interfere. **entremetido, -a** *sm, sf* also **entrometido, -a** busybody.

entrenar [entre'nar] *v* train; coach. **entrenador, -a** *sm, sf* trainer; coach. **entrenamiento** *sm* training; coaching.

entresacar [entresa'kar] *v* select; prune; thin out.

entresuelo [entre'swelo] *sm* mezzanine.

entretejer [entrete'xer] *v* interweave.

*****entretener** [entrete'ner] *v* entertain; delay; maintain. **entretenerse** *v* pass the time. **entretenido** *adj* entertaining; busy. **entretenimiento** *sm* entertainment; pastime; delaying.

*****entrever** [entre'βer] *v* make out; foresee.

entrevista [entre'βista] *sf* interview. **entrevistar** *v* interview. **entrevistarse** *v* hold an interview.

*****entristecer** [entriste'θer] *v* sadden. **entristecerse** *v* grow sad. **entristecimiento** *sm* sadness.

*****entumecer** [entume'θer] *v* numb. **entumecerse** *v* go numb; (*mar*) surge. **entumecido** *adj* numb. **entumecimiento** *sm* numbness.

enturbiar [entur'βjar] *v* make cloudy; muddy. **enturbiarse** *v* be in disorder.

entusiasmar [entusjas'mar] *v* fill with enthusiasm. **entusiasmarse** *v* be very keen. **entusiasmo** *sm* enthusiasm. **entusiasta** *s*(*m + f*) enthusiast; *adj* enthusiastic. **entusiástico** *adj* enthusiastic.

enumerar [enume'rar] *v* enumerate. **enumeración** *sf* enumeration.

enunciar [enun'θjar] *v* enunciate, state. **enunciación** *sf* statement, enunciation.

envainar [enβai'nar] *v* sheathe.

*****envanecer** [enβane'θer] *v* make vain.

envanecimiento *sm* vanity.

envasar [enβa'sar] *v* pack; wrap; bottle. **envasador** *sm* packer; large funnel. **envase** *sm* packing; bottling; container.

*envejecer [enβexe'θer] *v* age. **envejecerse** *v* grow old. **envejecido** *adj* aged. **envejecimiento** *sm* ageing.

envenenar [enβene'nar] *v* poison. **envenenador** *adj* poisonous. **envenenamiento** *sm* poisoning; pollution.

envergadura [enβerga'ðura] *sf* wingspan; (*fig*) scope.

enviar [en'βjar] *v* send. **enviar un mensaje de texto** *v* text (a message). **enviado, -a** *sm, sf* messenger; representative; envoy.

envidiar [enβi'ðjar] *v* envy. **envidia** *sf* envy. **envidioso** *adj* envious.

*envilecer [enβile'θer] *v* debase. **envilecimiento** *sm* debasement; degradation.

envío [en'βio] *sm* dispatch; shipment; remittance.

*envolver [enβol'βer] *v* envelop; wrap up; involve; imply; (*mil*) encircle. **envoltura** *sf* wrapping; envelope.

enzarzar [enθar'θar] *v* cover with brambles; set at odds. **enzarzarse** *v* get caught up in brambles; (*fig*) squabble.

enzima [en'θima] *sf* enzyme.

épico ['epiko] *adj* epic.

epidemia [epi'ðemja] *sf* epidemic. **epidémico** *adj* epidemic.

epígrafe [e'piɣrafe] *sm* epigraph.

epílogo [e'piloɣo] *sm* epilogue.

episcopado [episko'paðo] *sm* bishopric; episcopate. **episcopal** *adj* episcopal.

episodio [epi'soðjo] *sm* episode.

epitafio [epi'tafjo] *sm* epitaph.

época ['epoka] *sf* epoch.

equidad [eki'ðað] *sf* equity; fairness.

equilibrar [ekili'βrar] *v* balance. **equilibrio** *sm* equilibrium; balance; poise. **equilibrismo** *sm* acrobatics. **equilibrista** *s(m + f)* acrobat.

equinoccio [eki'nokθjo] *sm* equinox. **equinoccial** *adj* equinoctial.

equipar [eki'par] *v* equip. **equipado con concina** *sm* self-catering (apartment). **equipaje** *sm* luggage; equipment. **equipo** *sm* team; equipment; trousseau.

equitación [ekita'θjon] *sf* riding; horsemanship.

equitativo [ekita'tiβo] *adj* fair, equitable.

equivalencia [ekiβa'lenθja] *sf* equivalence. **equivalente** *adj* equivalent. **equivaler** *v* be equivalent.

equivocar [ekiβo'kar] *v* mistake. **equivocarse** *v* be mistaken. **equivocación** *sf* mistake. **equívoco** *adj* ambiguous.

era¹ ['era] *sf* era.

era² ['era] *V* **ser**.

eremita [ere'mita] *sm also* **ermitaño** *sm* hermit.

eres ['eres] *V* **ser**.

*erguir [er'gir] *v* raise, erect. **erguirse** *v* straighten up. **erguimiento** *sm* raising.

erigir [eri'xir] *v* erect; build; establish. **erigirse** *v* set oneself up. **erección** *sf* erection; establishment. **erecto** *adj* erect.

erizar [eri'θar] *v* bristle. **erizarse** *v* bristle; (*pelo*) stand on end. **erizado** *adj* bristly.

erizo [e'riθo] *sm* hedgehog.

erradicar [erraði'kar] *v* eradicate; uproot. **erradicación** *sf* eradication.

*errar [er'rar] *v* miss; fail; wander. **errarse** *v* be mistaken. **erradizo** *adj* wandering. **errado** *adj* mistaken. **errante** *adj* wandering; nomadic. **erróneo** *adj* erroneous, mistaken. **error** *sm* error.

eructar [eruk'tar] *v* belch. **eructo** *sm* belch.

erudición [eruði'θjon] *sf* erudition. **erudito, -a** *sm, sf* scholar; *adj* erudite.

erupción [erup'θjon] *sf* eruption; (*med*) rash. **eruptivo** *adj* eruptive.

esbelto [es'βelto] *adj* slim. **esbeltez** *sf* slimness.

esbozar [esβo'θar] *v* sketch. **esbozo** *sm* sketch.

escabechar [eskaβe'tʃar] *v* (*culin*) pickle; (*fam*) fail an exam; (*fam*) bump off. **escabeche** *sm* pickle.

escabroso [eska'βroso] *adj* rough; crude; harsh; (*fig*) difficult. **escabro** *sm* (*med*) scab. **escabrosidad** *sf* roughness; crudity; harshness.

*escabullirse [eskaβu'ʎirse] *v* sneak away or out.

escala [es'kala] *sf* ladder; scale; port of call. **en gran escala** on a large scale. **escala franca** free port. **hacer escala en** put in at. **escalar** *v* climb; escalate. **escalamiento** *sm* escalation.

escaldar [eskal'ðar] *v* scald; make red hot. **escaldado** *adj* scalded; cautious.

escalera [eska'lera] *sf* stairs *pl.* **escalera**

móvil escalator.

escalfar [eskal'far] v (culin) poach. **escalfado** adj poached. **escalfador** sm poacher.

escalofrío [eskalo'frio] sm shiver. **escalofriante** adj bloodcurdling.

escalón [eska'lon] sm rung; step. **escalonar** v space; stagger. **escalonado** adj spread out; staggered. **escalonamiento** sm spacing; staggering.

escalonia [eska'lonja] sf also **escaloña** shallot.

escalpelo [eskal'pelo] sm scalpel.

escama [es'kama] sf (jabón) flake; (animal) scale. **escamado** adj (fam) suspicious. **escamar** v scale; (fam) make suspicious. **escamarse** v (fam) become suspicious. **escamoso** adj scaly; (fam) suspicious.

escamot(e)ar [eskamo't(j)ar] v make disappear; shirk. **escamoteo** sm (fam) swindle. **escamoteador, -a** sm, sf conjurer; (fam) swindler.

escampar [eskam'par] v clear out; stop raining. **escampada** sf clear spell.

escándalo [es'kandalo] sm scandal; uproar; viciousness. **dar un escándalo** make a scene. **escandalizar** v scandalize. **escandalizarse** v be shocked. **escandaloso** adj scandalous; turbulent.

escáner [es'kaner] sm scanner.

escaño [es'kaɲo] sm bench; seat in Parliament.

escapar [eska'par] v escape. **escaparse** v escape; leak. **escapada** sf escape; escapade. **escape** sm escape; leakage. **a escape** at full speed. **tubo de escape** exhaust pipe. **escapismo** sm escapism.

escaparate [eskapa'rate] sm shop window.

escarabajo [eskara'βaxo] sm beetle; (fam) dwarf.

escaramuza [eskara'muθa] sf skirmish. **escaramucear** v skirmish.

escarbar [eskar'βar] v scratch; scrape; pry into. **escarbo** sm scraping; scratching.

escarcha [es'kartʃa] sf frost.

escarlata [eskar'lata] sf, adj scarlet.

*escarmentar [eskarmen'tar] v punish; learn from experience; be warned. **escarmiento** sm punishment; warning.

*escarnecer [eskarne'θer] v mock. **escarnecimiento** sm scorn; derision.

escarola [eska'rola] sf endive.

escarpa [es'karpa] sf slope.

escasear [eskase'ar] v skimp; be scarce. **escasamente** adv scantily. **escasez** sf scarcity. **escaso** adj scarce; skimpy.

escena [es'θena] sf scene; stage. **poner en escena** stage. **escénico** adj scenic.

escéptico [es'θeptiko] s. adj sceptic(al). **escepticismo** sm scepticism.

*esclarecer [esklare'θer] v brighten; clear; dawn. **esclarecido** adj illustrious. **esclarecimiento** sm illumination; splendour; dawn.

esclavitud [esklaβi'tuð] sf slavery. **esclavizar** v enslave. **esclavo, -a** sm, sf slave.

esclusa [es'klusa] sf lock; floodgate. **esclusa de aire** airlock.

escoba [es'koβa] sf broom, brush. **escobar** v sweep, brush.

*escocer [esko'θer] v smart, sting. **escocerse** v chafe. **escocedor** adj painful. **escocedura** sf sting.

escoger [esko'xer] v choose. **escogido** adj chosen, choice. **escogimiento** sm choice, selection.

escolar [esko'lar] s(m + f) schoolboy/girl. adj scholastic. **escolástica** sf scholasticism. **escolástico** adj scholastic.

escolta [es'kolta] sf escort; (guardaespaldas) minder, bodyguard. **escoltar** v escort.

escollo [es'koʎo] sm reef; difficulty; danger.

escombro [es'kombro] sm mackerel; débris; rubbish.

esconder [eskon'der] v hide. **esconderse** v conceal oneself. **escondidamente** adv secretly. **escondite** sm hiding place; (juego) hide-and-seek.

escopeta [esko'peta] sf shotgun; rifle. **escopeta de aire comprimido** airgun.

escoplo [es'koplo] sm chisel. **escoplear** v chisel; gouge.

escoria [es'korja] sf slag; dross; (fig) scum. **escorial** sm slag heap.

escorpión [eskor'pjon] sf scorpion.

escotado [esko'taðo] adj (vestido) low-cut. **escotar** v lower the neckline; scoop out.

escotilla [esko'tiʎa] sf (mar) hatch.

escribano [eskri'βano] sm clerk; notary.

*escribir [eskri'βir] v write. **escribir a máquina** type. **escribirse** v spell. **escribido** adj (fam) well read. **escribiente** s(m + f) clerk. **escrito a mano** handwritten. sm writing; document; letter. **escritor,**

-a *sm, sf* writer. **escritorio** *sm* bureau; office. **escritura** *sf* writing; script; (*jur*) deed.

escrúpulo [es'krupulo] *sm* scruple; conscientiousness. **escrupuloso** *adj* scrupulous.

escrutinio [eskru'tinjo] *sm* scrutiny. **escrutar** *v* scrutinize.

escuadra [es'kwaðra] *sf* carpenter's square; (*mil*) squad; (*mil*) corporal; (*mar*) squadron; (*fig*) gang. **a escuadra** at right angles. **escuadrar** *v* square.

escuálido [es'kwaliðo] *adj* squalid; weak; skinny. **escualidez** *sf* squalor; weakness; emaciation.

escuchar [esku'tʃar] *v* listen to; hear. **escucharse** *v* pay too much attention to oneself. **escucha** *sf* listening; sentry; chaperone. **a la escucha** on the alert. **escuchador, -a** *sm, sf* listener.

escudero [esku'ðero] *sm* squire, page. **escudar** *v* shield. **escudo** *sm* shield.

escudriñar [eskuðri'nar] *v* scrutinize. **escudriñador** *adj* examining; curious. **escudriñamiento** *sm* investigation; search.

escuela [es'kwela] *sf* school.

esculpir [eskul'pir] *v* sculpture; engrave. **escultor, -a** *sm, sf* sculptor. **escultura** *sf* sculpture.

escupir [esku'pir] *v* spit. **escupidura** *sf* spittle.

escurrir [esku'rrir] *v* drain; wring out; drip; slip; ooze. **escurrirse** *v* drain; sneak off. **escurridizo** *adj* slippery. **escurridor** *sm* plate rack; colander; draining board; wringer. **escurriduras** *sf pl* dregs *pl*. **escurrimiento** *sm* draining; dripping.

ese ['ese] *adj also* **esa** that.

ése ['ese] *pron also* **ésa** that one; the former.

esencia [e'senθja] *sf* essence. **esencial** *adj* essential.

esfera [es'fera] *sf* sphere. **esférico** *adj* spherical.

esfinge [es'finxe] *sf* sphinx.

*esforzar [esfor'θar] *v* invigorate; strengthen; encourage. **esforzarse** *v* make an effort. **esforzado** *adj* vigorous. **esfuerzo** *sm* effort.

esgrimir [esgri'mir] *v* brandish; fence. **esgrima** *sf* fencing. **esgrimidor, -a** *sm. sf* fencer.

eslabón [esla'βon] *sm* link. **eslabonamiento** *sm* linking. **eslabonar** *v* link.

Eslovaquia [eslo'βakja] *sf* Slovakia. **eslovaco** *adj* Slovakian.

Eslovenia [eslo'βenja] *sf* Slovenia. **esloveno** *adj* Slovenian.

esmaltar [esmal'tar] *v* enamel; (*las uñas*) varnish. **esmalte** *sm* varnish.

esmerado [esme'raðo] *adj* careful, painstaking. **esmerar** *v* polish; take great pains.

esmeralda [esme'ralða] *sf* emerald.

esnórquel [es'norkel] *sm* snorkel.

eso ['eso] *pron* that, that thing. **en eso** at that moment. **eso es** that's right. **eso mismo** just so. **por eso** because of that. **esos** *adj pl also* **esas** those. **ésos** *pron pl also* **ésas** those; the former.

espabilar [espaβi'lar] *v* (*vela*) snuff. **espabilarse** *v* (*fam*) look sharp.

espaciar [espa'θjar] *v* space out; spread. **espaciarse** *v* expatiate; enjoy oneself. **espacial** *adj* space. **nave espacial** spaceship. **espaciamiento** *sm* spacing. **espacio** *sm* space. **espacioso** *adj* spacious.

espada [es'paða] *sf* sword; swordsman. *sm* matador. **pez espada** swordfish.

espalda [es'palða] *sf* shoulder; back. **a espaldas** behind someone's back. **volver las espaldas** turn tail.

espantapájaros [espanta'paxaros] *sm invar* scarecrow.

espantar [espan'tar] *v* scare. **espantarse** *v* take fright. **espanto** *sm* fright; terror. **espantoso** *adj* frightful; amazing.

España [es'paɲa] *sf* Spain.

español [espa'ɲol], **-a** *sm, sf* Spaniard. *sm* (*lengua*) Spanish. *adj* Spanish.

*esparcir [espar'θir] *v* scatter; spread. **esparcirse** *v* amuse oneself. **esparcidamente** *adv* separately. **esparcido** *adj* cheerful; amusing; scattered. **esparcimiento** *sm* scattering: pastime.

espárrago [es'parrago] *sm* asparagus.

espasmo [es'pasmo] *sm* spasm. **espasmódico** *adj* spasmodic.

especia [es'peθja] *sf* spice.

especial [espe'θjal] *adj* special; particular. **en especial** especially. **especialidad** *sf* speciality. **especialista** *s(m + f)*, *adj* specialist. **especializarse** *v* specialize.

especie [es'peθje] *sf* species; kind; affair; appearance.

específico [espe'θifiko] *adj* specific. *sm*

(*med*) patent medicine. **especificación** *sf* specification. **especificación normalizada** standard specification. **especificar** *v* specify.

espectáculo [espek'takulo] *sm* spectacle; entertainment. **espectacular** *adj* spectacular. **espectador, -a** *sm*, *sf* spectator.

espectro [es'pektro] *sm* spectre.

espejo [es'pexo] *sm* mirror. **espejo retrovisor** (*auto*) rear-view mirror. **espejismo** *sm* mirage.

esperar [espe'rar] *v* hope; expect; await. **esperar a que** wait until. **espera** *sf* waiting; expectation; delay. **sala de espera** waiting room. **esperanza** *sf* hope. **esperanzador** *adj* encouraging.

esperpento [esper'pento] *sm* fright; grotesqueness; absurdity.

espesar [espe'sar] *v* thicken; tighten. **espeso** *adj* thick; greasy. **espesamiento** *sm* thickening.

espetar [espe'tar] *v* (*culin*) skewer; pierce. **espetarse** *v* be pompous.

espía [es'pia] *s(m + f)* spy. **espiar** *v* spy upon. **espionaje** *sm* espionage.

espiga [es'piga] *sf* (*bot*) ear, spike. **espigado** *adj* gone to seed. **espigar** *v* glean.

espín [es'pin] *sm* porcupine.

espina [es'pina] *sf* thorn; spine; splinter; fishbone. **espina dorsal** backbone.

espinaca [espi'naka] *sf* spinach.

espiral [espi'ral] *sf, adj* spiral.

espíritu [es'piritu] *sm* spirit; soul; ghost; wit; breathing. **espiritado** *adj* possessed; (*fam*) skinny. **espiritismo** *sm* spiritualism. **espiritista** *s(m + f)* spiritualist. **espiritoso** *adj* spirited. **espiritual** *adj* spiritual. **espiritualidad** *sf* spirituality.

espléndido [es'plendiðo] *adj* splendid; magnificent. **esplendor** *sm* splendour.

espliego [es'pljego] *sm* lavender.

esplín [es'plin] *sm* spleen.

espolear [espole'ar] *v* spur, spur on. **espoleo** *sm* spurring.

esponja [es'ponxa] *sf* sponge. **esponjar** *v* make spongy; puff up. **esponjarse** *v* become spongy; (*fig*) become puffed up with pride; glow with health.

esponsales [espon'sales] *sm pl* betrothal *sing*.

espontáneo [espon'taneo] *adj* spontaneous. **espontaneidad** *sf* spontaneity.

esporádico [espo'raðiko] *adj* sporadic.

esposa [es'posa] *sf* wife. **esposas** *sf pl* handcuffs. **esposado** *adj* newly married; handcuffed.

espuela [es'pwela] *sf* spur. **echar la espuela** have one for the road.

espuma [es'puma] *sf* foam; froth; lather. **espumadera** *sf* strainer. **espumajear** *v* foam at the mouth. **espumajoso** *adj* foaming; frothy. **espumar** *v* skim; froth; lather; sparkle. **espumoso** *adj* frothy; sparkling.

esquela [es'kela] *sf* note; short letter; obituary.

esqueleto [eske'leto] *sm* skeleton.

esquema [es'kema] *sm* scheme. **esquemático** *adj* schematic.

esquí [es'ki] *sm, pl* **esquíes** *or* **esquís** ski. **esquiador, -a** *sm*, *sf* skier. **esquiar** *v* ski.

esquilar [eski'lar] *v* shear, clip. **sin esquilar** unshorn.

esquimal [eski'mal] *sm, adj* Eskimo.

esquina [es'kina] *sf* (*afuera*) corner. **doblar la esquina** turn the corner. **esquinar** *v* form a corner with.

esquirol [eski'rol] *sm* (*fam*) strike-breaker, blackleg.

esquivar [eski'βar] *v* avoid, shun; disappear. **esquivarse** *v* shy away. **esquivo** *adj* unsociable.

estabilidad [estaβili'ðað] *sf* stability. **estabilizar** *v* stabilize. **estable** *adj* stable.

*****establecer** [estaβle'θer] *v* establish. **establecerse** *v* settle down; set up. **establecido** *adj* established. **establecimiento** *sm* establishment.

establo [es'taβlo] *sm* cowshed.

estaca [es'taka] *sf* stake, post. **estacada** *sf* fence; stockade. **estacar** *v* fence; stake out.

estación [esta'θjon] *sf* station; season. **estacionamiento** *sm* parking. **estacionar** *v* park.

estadio [es'taðjo] *sm* stadium; (*med*) phase.

estado [es'taðo] *sm* state; status; order; estate; statement. **estado civil** marital status. **estado de ánimo** state of mind. **estar en estado** be pregnant. **hombre de estado** statesman.

Estados Unidos [es'taðos u'niðos] *sm pl* United States (of America). **estadounidense** *s(m + f)*, *adj* American.

estafa [es'tafa] *sf* swindle. **estafador, -a** *sm*, *sf* swindler. **estafar** *v* swindle.

estafeta [esta'feta] *sf* courier; sub-post office.

estallar [esta'ar] *v* explode; burst; erupt. **estallido** *sm* explosion; crash.

estampar [estam'par] *v* stamp; print; imprint. **estampa** *sf* print; engraving; impression; footprint.

estampida [estam'piða] *sf* stampede; explosion, bang. **estampido** *sm* explosion, bang.

estancar [estan'kar] *v* stem; block; delay; monopolize. **estancarse** *v* stagnate. **estancación** *sf* stagnation. **estancado** *adj* stagnant; blocked. **estanco** *sm* monopoly; state tobacco shop. **estanquero, -a** *sm, sf* tobacconist.

estandarte [estan'darte] *sm* banner.

estanque [es'tanke] *sm* reservoir; ornamental pond.

estante [es'tante] *sm* shelf. **estantería** *sf* shelving; bookcase.

estaño [es'taɲo] *sm* tin. **estañar** *v* solder.

*estar [es'tar] *v* be. **está bien** (it's) all right. **estar para** be about to. **no está** he *or* she is not at home. **ya que estamos** while we're at it.

estático [es'tatiko] *adj* static.

estatua [es'tatwa] *sf* statue.

estatura [esta'tura] *sf* stature, height.

estatuto [esta'tuto] *sm* statute. **estatuario** *adj* statutory.

este¹ ['este] *adj also* **esta** this; the latter.

este² *sm, adj* east.

éste ['este] *pron also* **ésta** this.

estela [es'tela] *sf* (*mar*) wake; trail.

estelar [este'lar] *adj* stellar.

estepa [es'tepa] *sf* steppe.

estera [es'tera] *sf* matting.

estereofónico [estereo'foniko] *adj* stereophonic.

estereotipo [estereo'tipo] *sm* stereotype.

estéril [es'teril] *adj* sterile; pointless. **esterelizar** *v* sterilize.

esterlina [ester'lina] *adj* sterling. **libra esterlina** pound sterling.

estético [es'tetiko] *adj* aesthetic. **estética** *sf* aesthetics.

estetoscopio [esteto'skopjo] *sm* stethoscope.

estiércol [es'tjerkol] *sm* manure.

estigma [es'tigma] *sm* stigma. **estigmatizar** *v* stigmatize.

estilar [esti'lar] *v* be accustomed; (*documento*) draw up; be in use; be in fashion. **estilístico** *adj* stylistic. **estilizado** *adj* stylized. **estilo** *sm* style; type; fashion. **estilo de vida** *sm* lifestyle.

estimar [esti'mar] *v* esteem; estimate. **estima** *sf* esteem. **estimable** *adj* estimable. **estimación** *sf* estimate; estimation.

estimular [estimu'lar] *v* stimulate. **estimulante** *adj* stimulating; *sm* (*med*) stimulant. **estímulo** *sm* stimulus.

estipular [estipu'lar] *v* stipulate. **estipulación** *sf* stipulation.

estirar [esti'rar] *v* stretch; extend. **estirado** *adj* affected; miserly. **estirón** *sm* jerk.

estirpe [es'tirpe] *sf* lineage; stock.

esto ['esto] *pron* this. **en esto** whereupon.

estofa [es'tofa] *sf* (*fig*) quality; class; brocade. **estofado** *adj* quilted; (*culin*) stewed. **estofar** *v* quilt; stew.

estoico [es'toiko], **-a** *s, adj* stoic. **estoicismo** *sm* stoicism.

estómago [es'tomago] *sm* stomach. **estomagar** *v* give indigestion.

Estonia [es'tonja] *sm* Estonia. **estonio** *adj* Estonian.

estorbar [estor'βar] *v* hinder; be in the way. **estorbo** *sm* hindrance; obstruction.

estornino [estor'nino] *sm* starling.

estornudar [estornu'ðar] *v* sneeze. **estornudo** *sm* sneeze.

estoy [es'toi] *V* **estar**.

estrafalario [estrafa'larjo] *adj* outlandish; extravagant; slovenly.

estrada [es'traða] *sf* road, highway.

estragar [estra'gar] *v* corrupt; destroy. **estrago** *sm* ruin, havoc. **hacer estragos** wreak havoc.

estrangular [estrangu'lar] *v* strangle. **estrangulación** *sf* strangulation. **estrangulador** *sm* strangler; (*auto*) choke.

estratagema [estrata'xema] *sf* stratagem. **estrategia** *sf* strategy. **estratégico** *adj* strategic.

estrechar [estre'tʃar] *v* make smaller; tighten; bring closer together. **estrecharse** *v* become narrower; squeeze together; shake hands; make economies. **estrechamente** *adv* narrowly. **estrechamiento** *sm* narrowing; taking-in; tightening; handshake. **estrecho** *adj* narrow; cramped; tight; strict.

estrella [es'trea] *sf* star. **estrellado** *adj* starry.

estrellar [estre'ar] *v* smash (to pieces).

*estremecer [estreme'θer] *v* shake; startle. **estremecerse** *v* shudder; tremble. **estremecimiento** *sm* shake; shudder; tremble.

estrenar [estre'nar] *v* wear for the first time; (*teatro*) perform for the first time. **estreno** *sm* inauguration; first night; dress rehearsal.

estrenuo [es'trenwo] *adj* strong; courageous.

estreñido [estre'niðo] *adj* constipated. **estreñimiento** *sm* constipation.

estrépito [es'trepito] *sm* noise, din; fuss. **estrepitoso** *adj* noisy; resounding.

estribo [es'triβo] *sm* stirrup; step; running-board. **perder los estribos** lose one's head.

estribor [estri'βor] *sm* (*mar*) starboard.

estricto [es'trikto] *adj* strict.

estridente [estri'ðente] *adj* strident.

estropajo [estro'paxo] *sm* scourer; rubbish. **estropajoso** *adj* thick; stringy; slovenly.

estropear [estrope'ar] *v* spoil; break; maim; age.

estructura [estruk'tura] *sf* structure; framework. **estructural** *adj* structural. **estructurar** *v* organize; construct.

estruendo [estru'endo] *sm* din; uproar; bustle; pomp. **estruendoso** *adj* noisy.

estrujar [estru'xar] *v* squeeze; crush. **estrujadura** *sf* pressure. **estrujón** *sm* squeeze.

estuario [es'twarjo] *sm* estuary.

estuche [es'tutʃe] *sm* box; case; casket; sheath.

estudiar [estu'ðjar] *v* study. **estudiante** *s(m + f)* student. **estudio** *sm* study; research; studio. **estudioso** *adj* studious.

estufa [es'tufa] *sf* stove; fire; hothouse.

estupefacto [estupe'fakto] *adj* stupefied; astonished. **estupefacción** *sf* stupefaction; astonishment.

estupefaciente [estupefa'θjente] *adj* stupefying; astonishing. *sm* (*med*) narcotic.

estupendo [estu'pendo] *adj* stupendous.

estúpido [es'tupiðo] *adj* stupid. **estupidez** *sf* stupidity. **estupor** *sm* stupor.

esturión [estu'rjon] *sm* sturgeon.

etapa [e'tapa] *sf* (*de un viaje*) stage; period.

éter ['eter] *sm* ether. **etéreo** *adj* ethereal.

eternidad [eterni'ðað] *sf* eternity. **eternal** *adj* eternal. **eternizar** *v* perpetuate.

ética ['etika] *sf* ethics. **ético** *adj* ethical.

etimología [etimolo'xia] *sf* etymology. **etimológico** *adj* etymological.

etiqueta [eti'keta] *sf* etiquette; label; tag. **etiquetero** *adj* formal.

eucalipto [euka'lipto] *sm* eucalyptus.

eufemismo [eufe'mismo] *sm* euphemism. **eufemístico** *adj* euphemistic.

eunuco [eu'nuko] *sm* eunuch.

euro ['euro] *sm* euro.

Europa [eu'ropa] *sf* Europe. **europeo, -a** *s, adj* European.

Eurotúnel [euro'tunel] *sm* Channel tunnel.

eutanasia [euta'nasja] *sf* euthanasia.

evacuar [eβa'kwar] *v* evacuate; fulfil. **evacuación** *sf* evacuation. **evacuado, -a** *sm, sf* evacuee.

evadir [eβa'ðir] *v* evade. **evadirse** *v* escape. **evadido, -a** *sm, sf* fugitive. **evasión** *sf* escape; flight. **evasivo** *adj* evasive.

evaluar [eβa'lwar] *v* evaluate; value. **evaluación** *sf* evaluation.

evangélico [eβan'xeliko] *adj* evangelical. **evangelio** *sm* gospel. **evangelista** *sm* evangelist.

evaporar [evapo'rar] *v* evaporate. **evaporación** *sf* evaporation.

evento [e'βento] *sm* (unforeseen) event.

eventual [even'twal] *adj* temporary; possible; accidental. **eventualidad** *sf* contingency.

evidencia [evi'ðenθja] *sf* certainty; proof; evidence. **evidenciar** *v* make evident. **evidente** *adj* evident.

evitar [eβi'tar] *v* avoid. **evitable** *adj* avoidable.

evocar [evo'kar] *v* evoke. **evocación** *sf* evocation. **evocativo** *adj* evocative.

evolución [evolu'θjon] *sf* evolution. **evolucionar** *v* evolve. **evolutivo** *adj* evolutionary.

exacerbar [eksaθer'βar] *v* exacerbate, exasperate. **exacerbación** *sf* exacerbation.

exactitud [eksakti'tuð] *sf* exactitude; accuracy. **exacto** *adj* exact; correct.

exagerar [eksaxe'rar] *v* exaggerate. **exagerado** *adj* exaggerated. **exageración** *sf* exaggeration.

exaltar [eksal'tar] *v* exalt; raise; praise.

exaltarse v get worked up; get heated.
exaltación sf exaltation. **exaltado** adj hotheaded.

examinar [eksami'nar] v examine; inspect; test. **examinarse** v take an examination. **examen** sm examination; inquiry; investigation. **examen de conductor** driving test. **examinador, -a** sm, sf examiner.

exangüe [ek'sangwe] adj bloodless; weak.

exánime [ek'sanime] adj lifeless; unconscious; weak. **caer exánime** fall in a faint.

exasperar [eksaspe'rar] v exasperate; vex. **exasperarse** v become annoyed. **exasperación** sf exasperation. **exasperante** adj exasperating.

excavar [ekska'βar] v excavate; dig. **excavación** sf excavation.

exceder [eksθe'ðer] v exceed. **excederse** v forget oneself. **excedente** adj exceeding; excessive.

excelencia [eksθe'lenθja] sf excellence. **excelente** adj excellent; first-rate.

excéntrico [eks'θentriko] adj, sm eccentric. **excentricidad** sf eccentricity.

excepción [eksθep'θjon] sf exception. **a excepción de** with the exception of. **estado de excepción** state of emergency. **excepcional** adj exceptional. **excepto** prep excepting.

excerpta [ek'θerpta] sf excerpt.

excesivo [eksθe'siβo] adj excessive. **exceso** sm excess; surplus. **exceso de equipaje** excess luggage.

excitar [eksθi'tar] v excite; stir up. **excitabilidad** sf excitability. **excitable** adj excitable. **excitante** adj exciting.

exclamar [ekskla'mar] v exclaim. **exclamarse contra** protest against. **exclamación** sf exclamation. **exclamativo** adj exclamatory.

*excluir [eksklu'ir] v exclude. **exclusivo** adj exclusive. **exclusión** sf exclusion.

excomulgar [ekskomul'gar] v excommunicate. **excomulgación** sf excommunication. **excomulgado** adj excommunicated; (fam) accused.

excreción [ekskre'θjon] sf excretion. **excremento** sm excrement. **excretar** v excrete.

excursión [ekskur'sjon] sf excursion. **excursión a pie** hike. **ir de excursión** go on an outing. **excursionista** s(m + f) tripper; hiker.

excusar [eksku'sar] v excuse; avoid;

exempt. **excusarse** v apologize. **excusa** sf excuse; apology. **excusable** adj pardonable. **excusadamente** adv unnecessarily. **excusado** adj excused; unnecessary; exempt; concealed; private. **excusado es decir** needless to say. **excusado** sm toilet.

exentar [eksen'tar] v exempt. **exención** sf exemption. **exento** adj exempt.

exequias [ek'sekjas] sf pl funeral rites.

exhalar [eksa'lar] v exhale; emit; utter. **exhalación** sf exhalation; vapour; shooting star; lightning flash.

exhausto [ek'sausto] adj exhausted. **exhaustivo** adj exhaustive.

exhibir [eksi'βir] v exhibit. **exhibición** sf exhibition. **exhibicionismo** sm exhibitionism. **exhibicionista** s(m + f) exhibitionist.

exhortar [eksor'tar] v exhort. **exhortación** sf exhortation.

exigir [eksi'xir] v demand. **exigencia** sf demand; requirement. **exigente** adj exacting; demanding.

exiguo [ek'sigwo] adj scanty. **exigüidad** sf scantiness.

eximir [eksi'mir] v exempt; excuse. **eximente** adj exempting.

existir [eksis'tir] v exist. **existencia** sf existence. **en existencia** in stock. **existente** adj existent; extant; in stock.

éxito ['eksito] sm success; result. **éxito de ventas** sm bestseller. **tener éxito** be successful.

éxodo ['eksoðo] sm exodus, emigration.

exonerar [eksone'rar] v exonerate; relieve; dismiss. **exoneración** sf exoneration; relief.

exorbitante [eksorβi'tante] adj exorbitant, excessive.

exorcizar [eksorθi'θar] v exorcize. **exorcismo** sm exorcism. **exorcista** sm exorcist.

exótico [ek'sotiko] adj exotic.

expansión [ekspan'sjon] sf expansion; recreation. **expansionarse** v give vent to one's feelings. **expansivo** adj expansive.

expatriar [ekspatri'ar] v exile. **expatriación** sf banishment.

expectación [ekspekta'θjon] sf expectation. **expectante** adj expectant.

expedición [ekspeði'θjon] sf expedition; party; shipment; dispatch; speed.

*expedir [ekspe'ðir] v send, dispatch; issue. **expediente** sm (jur) proceedings pl; dossier;

inquiry; record. **expediente** *adj* expedient.

expendedor [ekspende'ðor], **-a** *sm, sf* dealer; retailer; ticket agent. *adj* spending.

experiencia [ekspe'rjenθja] *sf* experience; experiment.

experimentar [eksperimen'tar] *v* experiment; test; feel. **experimentado** *adj* experienced. **experimental** *adj* experimental. **experimento** *sm* experiment.

experto [eks'perto] *sm, adj* expert.

expiar [eks'pjar] *v* atone for. **expiación** *sf* atonement.

expirar [ekspi'rar] *v* expire; die; die down. **expiración** *sf* expiration.

explanar [ekspla'nar] *v* level; (*fig*) explain. **explanación** *sf* levelling; (*fig*) explanation.

explicar [ekspli'kar] *v* explain; justify; lecture. **explicarse** *v* speak plainly; understand. **explicación** *sf* explanation. **explicativo** *adj* explanatory.

explícito [eks'pliθito] *adj* explicit.

explorar [eksplo'rar] *v* explore, investigate. **exploración** *sf* exploration. **exploración con escáner** *sf* scan (medical). **exploración médica** *sf* (medical) screening. **explorador** *sm* explorer; (*mil*) scout; boy scout; *adj* exploratory.

explosión [eksplo'sjon] *sf* explosion. **explosivo** *sm, adj* explosive.

explotar [eksplo'tar] *v* exploit; develop; cultivate; explode. **explotación** *sf* exploitation; operation; development; cultivation.

*exponer [ekspo'ner] *v* expose; set out; explain. **exponerse** *v* lay oneself open. **exponente** *s*(*m* + *f*) exponent; example; proof.

exportar [ekspor'tar] *v* export. **exportación** *sf* export. **exportador, -a** *sm, sf* exporter.

exposición [exposi'θjon] *sf* exhibition; display; statement; explanation; risk; (*foto*) exposure. **sala de exposición** showroom.

exprés [eks'pres] *sm* (*tren*) express; (*café*) espresso.

expresar [ekspre'sar] *v* express, convey. **expresarse** *v* express oneself; state. **expresamente** *adv* specifically; explicitly. **expresión** *sf* expression. **expresiones** *sf pl* greetings; regards. **expresivamente** *adv* expressively; affectionately. **expresivo** *adj* expressive; affectionate. **expreso** *adj* expressed; express.

exprimir [ekspri'mir] *v* squeeze; exploit. **exprimidor** *sm* squeezer.

expuesto [eks'pwesto] *adj* on display; exposed; explained.

expulsar [ekspul'sar] *v* expel, throw out.

exquisito [ekski'sito] *adj* exquisite; delightful; refined.

éxtasis ['ekstasis] *sm invar* ecstasy.

*extender [eksten'der] *v* extend; spread. **extenderse** *v* spread; range; enlarge. **extendido** *adj* extended; widespread; outstretched. **extensamente** *adv* at length. **extensible** *adj* extending. **extensión** *sf* extension; expanse; extent; area. **extensiones** *sf pl* (hair) braid. **extensivo** *adj* extendible. **extenso** *adj* extensive; large; widespread; full.

éxtasis ['ekstasis] *sm* ecstasy (drug).

extenuar [ekste'nwar] *v* weaken; exhaust. **extenuación** *sf* emaciation; extenuation.

exterior [ekste'rjor] *adj* exterior, external; foreign. **asuntos exteriores** *sm pl* foreign affairs. *sm* outside, exterior; appearance. **al exterior** outside. **del exterior** from abroad.

exterminar [ekstermi'nar] *v* exterminate. **exterminación** *sf* extermination. **exterminador, -a** *sm, sf* exterminator.

externo [eks'terno], **-a** *sm, sf* day pupil. *adj* external; outward. **externado** *sm* day school.

extinguir [ekstin'gir] *v* extinguish; wipe out; put down. **extinguirse** *v* die out. **extinción** *sf* extinction. **extinto** *adj* extinct. **extintor** *sm* fire extinguisher.

extirpar [ekstir'par] *v* uproot; remove. **extirpación** *sf* uprooting; extraction.

extra ['ekstra] *adj invar* extra; best-quality. *sm* (*cine, teatro*) extra.

*extraer [ekstra'er] *v* extract; release. **extracción** *sf* extraction; birth. **extracto** *sm* extract; excerpt; abstract.

extranjero [ekstran'xero], **-a** *sm, sf* foreigner; foreign countries *pl. adj* foreign.

extrañar [ekstra'ɲar] *v* be surprised; surprise; be shy; banish. **extrañarse** *v* go into exile. **extrañamiento** *sm* surprise; banishment. **extrañeza** *sf* strangeness; surprise. **extraño, -a** *sm, sf* stranger. **extraño** *adj* strange; peculiar; foreign.

extraordinario [ekstraorði'narjo] *adj* extraordinary. *sm* (*diario*) special edition.

extravagancia [ekstraβa'ganθja] *sf* extravagance; strangeness. **extravagante** *adj* extravagant; eccentric.

extraviar [ekstra'βjar] v lose; mislay; mislead. **extraviarse** v get lost; be missing; go astray.

extremar [ekstre'mar] v take to extremes. **extremarse** v do one's best.

extremo [ek'stremo] adj extreme, last. **en caso extremo** as a last resort. sm extreme; end; point. **al extremo de** to the point of. **de extremo a extremo** from end to end. **Extremo Oriente** Far East. **extremidad** sf extremity; end; limit.

exuberancia [eksuβe'ranθja] sf exuberance; abundance. **exuberante** adj exuberant.

exudar [eksu'ðar] v exude. **exudación** sf exudation.

exultar [eksul'tar] v exult. **exultación** sf exultation.

F

fábrica ['faβrika] sf factory; manufacture. **fabricación** sf manufacture. **de fabricación casera** home-made. **fabricación en serie** mass production. **fabricante** s(m + f) manufacturer. **fabricar** v manufacture; make; build.

fábula ['faβula] sf fable; story; gossip. **fabuloso** adj fabulous; incredible.

facción [fak'θjon] sf faction; gang. **facciones** sf pl features.

faceta [fa'θeta] sf facet.

facial [fa'θjal] adj facial.

fácil ['faθil] adj easy; simple; likely; well-behaved. **fácil de usar** adj user-friendly. **facilidad** sf facility; ease; fluency; gift. **facilitar** v facilitate; supply; provide; arrange. **fácilmente** adv easily.

facsímil [fak'simil] sm, adj also **facsímile** facsimile.

factible [fak'tiβle] adj feasible.

factor [fak'tor] sm factor; agent.

facturar [faktu'rar] v invoice; (ferrocarril) register luggage. **factura** sf invoice. **facturación** sf invoicing.

facultad [fakul'taθ] sf faculty; authority; school. **facultar** v commission; authorize. **facultativo** adj optional.

facha ['fatʃa] sf (fam) appearance, looks;

(fam) mess.

fachada [fa'tʃaða] sf façade.

faena [fa'ena] sf task; (fam) dirty trick. **estar de faena** be at work. **faenas domésticas** housework.

fagot [fa'got] sm bassoon.

faisán [fai'san] sm pheasant.

faja ['faxa] sf bandage; sash; belt; wrapper; strip of land. **fajar** v wrap; bandage.

falaz [fa'laθ] adj fallacious; deceitful.

falda ['falda] sf skirt; side of a hill; hat brim; lap.

falsear [false'ar] v falsify. **falseador, -a** sm, sf forger; counterfeiter. **falseamiento** sm misrepresentation. **falsedad** sf falsity. **falseo** sm bevelling. **falso** adj false; treacherous; sham.

falsificar [falsifi'kar] v falsify; forge; adulterate. **falsificación** sf falsification; adulteration.

falta ['falta] sf lack, want, need; shortage; failure; (deporte) foul. **faltar** v be lacking; fail; be absent; be untrue. **falto** sm shortage; deficiency; fault. **falto** adj short; deficient; incomplete.

fallar [fa'ʎar] v (jur) judge; sentence; fail; (naipes) trump. **no falla** it's always the same. **sin falla** without fail.

***fallecer** [faʎe'θer] v die. **fallecido** adj deceased. **fallecimiento** sm death.

fallido [fa'ʎiðo] sm bankrupt. adj bankrupt; unsuccessful. **fallo** sm (jur) sentence, judgment; failure; fault; (naipes) trump.

fama ['fama] sf fame; reputation. **es fama que** it is rumoured that. **famoso** adj famous.

familia [fa'milja] sf family; household. **familia de acogida** sf foster family. **familiar** adj family; familiar; simple. **familiar** sm friend; relative. **familiaridad** sf familiarity. **familiarizar** v familiarize.

fanático [fa'natiko] adj, sm fanatic(al). **fanatismo** sm fanaticism.

fanfarrón [fanfar'ron], **-ona** sm, sf bully; braggart. adj boastful. **fanfarronear** v brag.

fango ['fango] sm mire, mud. **fangal** sm quagmire. **fangoso** adj muddy.

fantasía [fanta'sia] sf fantasy; fancy; whim. **joyas de fantasía** imitation jewellery.

fantasma [fan'tasma] sm ghost. **fantasmal** adj ghostly.

fantástico [fan'tastiko] *adj* fantastic; wonderful; vain.

fantoche [fan'totʃe] *sm* puppet; foolish figure.

fardo ['farðo] *sm* bundle, pack; burden.

fariseo [fari'seo] *sm* Pharisee; (*fam*) hypocrite. **farisaico** *adj* (*fam*) hypocritical.

farmacia [far'maθja] *sf* chemist's shop. **farmacia de guardia** all-night chemist's. **farmacéutico** *adj* pharmaceutical.

faro ['faro] *sm* lighthouse; beacon; (*auto*) headlamp.

farol [fa'rol] *sm* lantern; lamp; street lamp; (*fam*) swank.

farsa ['farsa] *sf* farce; humbug. **farsante** *sm* charlatan.

fas [fas] *adv* (*fam*) **por fas o por nefas** rightly or wrongly; by hook or by crook.

fascinar [fasθi'nar] *v* fascinate. **fascinación** *sf* fascination. **fascinador** *adj* fascinating.

fascismo [fas'θismo] *sm* fascism. **fascista** *s*, *adj* fascist.

fase ['fase] *sf* phase.

fastidiar [fasti'ðjar] *v* annoy; bore; upset. **¡no fastidies!** don't talk rot! **fastidio** *sm* annoyance; nuisance. **fastidioso** *adj* annoying; tedious.

fastuoso [fas'twoso] *adj* magnificent, grand, splendid.

fatal [fa'tal] *adj* fatal; inevitable; (*fam*) awful. **fatalidad** *sf* fatality; bad luck; destiny; disaster. **fatalista** *s* (*m* + *f*) fatalist. **fatalismo** *sm* fatalism.

fatigar [fati'gar] *v* weary; annoy. **fatigarse** *v* get tired. **fatiga** *sf* fatigue. **fatigas** *sf pl* troubles. **fatigoso** *adj* tiring; tiresome; laboured.

fatuidad [fatwi'ðað] *sf* fatuity; vanity.

fausto ['fausto] *adj* lucky; happy. *sm* display; pomp.

favor [fa'βor] *sm* favour; gift; grace; help. **a favor de** in favour of. **de favor** complimentary. **hacer el favor de** be so kind as to. **por favor** please. **favorable** *adj* favourable. **favorecer** *v* favour; help. **favoritismo** *sm* favouritism. **favorito, -a** *s*, *adj* favourite.

fax ['faks] *sm* fax. *v* **mandar por fax** fax.

faz [faθ] *sf* face; obverse.

fe [fe] *sf* faith; faithfulness; trust; witness; certificate. **a fe de** on the word of. **dar fe de** certify. **prestar fe a** believe in.

fealdad [feal'ðað] *sf* ugliness.

febrero [fe'βrero] *sm* February.

febril [fe'βril] *adj* feverish; (*fig*) anxious.

fecundar [fekun'dar] *v* fertilize. **fecundación** *sf* fertilization. **fecundidad** *sf* fertility; fruitfulness. **fecundizar** *v* fertilize. **fecundo** *adj* fertile; fruitful; prolific. **fecundo en** full of.

fecha ['fetʃa] *sf* date. **hasta la fecha** to date. **fechar** *v* date.

federación [feðera'θjon] *sf* federation. **federal** *adj* federal. **federalismo** *sm* federalism. **federar** *v* federate. **federativo** *adj* federative.

fehaciente [fea'θjente] *adj* (*jur*) authentic; irrefutable; reliable.

felicidad [feliθi'ðað] *sf* happiness; success. **¡felicidades!** congratulations! **feliz** *adj* happy; fortunate.

felicitar [feliθi'tar] *v* congratulate. **felicitación** *sf* congratulation; compliment.

feligrés [feli'gres], **-esa** *sm*, *sf* parishioner. **feligresía** *sf* parish.

felino [fe'lino] *sm*, *adj* feline.

felpa ['felpa] *sf* plush; towelling; (*fam*) beating. **felpar** *v* cover with plush. **felpudo** *adj* plushy.

femenino [feme'nino] *adj* feminine; female. **feminismo** *sm* feminism. **feminista** *s*, *adj* feminist.

*fenecer [fene'θer] *v* die; end. **fenecimiento** *sm* death; end.

fenómeno [fe'nomeno] *sm* phenomenon; freak. *adj* fantastic.

feo ['feo] *adj* ugly.

féretro ['feretro] *sm* coffin; bier.

feria ['ferja] *sf* fair; show; festival; holiday. **feria de muestras** trade fair.

fermentar [fermen'tar] *v* ferment; agitate. **fermentación** *sf* fermentation.

ferocidad [feroθi'ðað] *sf* ferocity; fury. **feroz** *adj* savage; wild; fierce.

férreo ['ferreo] *adj* iron; ferrous; (*fig*) stern. **ferretería** *sf* ironmonger's shop; hardware shop. **ferretero** *sm* ironmonger.

ferrocarril [ferrokar'ril] *sm* railway. **ferroviario** *adj* railway.

fértil ['fertil] *adj* fertile; abundant. **fertilidad** *sf* fertility. **fertilizante** *sm* fertilizer. **fertilizar** *v* fertilize.

ferviente [fer'βjente] *adj* fervent. **fervor**

sm fervour. **fervoroso** *adj* fervid, ardent.

festejar [feste'xar] *v* entertain; feast; celebrate; woo. **festejo** *sm* entertainment; celebration; courtship.

festival [festi'βal] *sm* festival. *adj* festive. **festividad** *sf* festivity. **festivo** *adj* festive.

fétido ['fetiðo] *adj* fetid, stinking.

feto ['feto] *sm* foetus. **fetal** *adj* foetal.

feudal [feu'ðal] *adj* feudal. **feudalismo** *sm* feudalism.

fiado ['fjaðo] *sm* trust. **comprar al fiado** buy on credit. **fiador, -a** *sm, sf* guarantor. **fiador** *sm* press stud; pin; bracket; tumbler; safety catch. **salir fiador de** go bail for. **fianza** *sf* deposit; guarantor; surety. **libertad bajo fianza** release on bail. **fiar** *v* guarantee; go bail for; sell on credit; trust. **no se fía** no credit given.

fiambre ['fjambre] *sm* cold cooked meat; (*coll*) corpse.

fiasco [fi'asko] *sm* fiasco; flop.

fibra ['fiβra] *sf* fibre; (*fig*) vigour. **fibra de vidrio** fibreglass.

ficción [fik'θjon] *sf* fiction; invention. **ficticio** *adj* fictitious.

ficha ['fitʃa] *sf* counter, chip; (*juegos*) piece; filing card.

fidedigno [fiðe'ðigno] *adj* trustworthy. **fidelidad** *sf* loyalty, fidelity. **alta fidelidad** hi-fi.

fideos ['fiðeos] *sm pl* noodles.

fiebre ['fjeβre] *sf* fever. **tener fiebre** be feverish.

fiel [fjel] *adj* faithful; true; accurate; reliable; honourable. *sm* good Christian; inspector; scale pointer.

fieltro ['fjeltro] *sm* (*tejido*) felt; felt hat.

fiera ['fjera] *sf* wild beast; (*persona*) brute. **casa de fieras** menagerie. **fiero** *adj* wild.

fiesta ['fjesta] *sf* feast day; holiday; party. **estar de fiesta** be in high spirits. **hacer fiestas a uno** make a fuss over someone.

figurar [figu'rar] *v* shape; adorn; figure; pretend. **figurarse** *v* imagine, seem. **figura** *sf* shape; figure; face; (*música*) note; (*naipes*) court card; (*fig*) personality; (*fam*) unpleasant person. **figurado** *adj also* **figurativo** figurative.

fijar [fi'xar] *v* fasten; fix; stick; secure; draw up. **fijarse** *v* settle; take notice; look. **¡fíjate!** just think! **¡fijamos en esto!** that's settled! **fijación** *sf* setting; fixing; sticking.

fijador *sm* fixative. **fijeza** *sf* fixity; certainty; firmness. **fijo** *adj* fixed; permanent; steady.

fila ['fila] *sf* row; line; file; column. **en fila india** in single file.

filantropía [filantro'pia] *sf* philanthropy. **filantrópico** *adj* philanthropic. **filántropo, -a** *sm, sf* philanthropist.

filete [fi'lete] *sm* sirloin; fillet; (*ropa*) edging; (*tecn*) screw thread.

filiación [filja'θjon] *sf* filiation; relationship; association; personal description.

filial [fi'ljal] *adj* filial. *sf* subsidiary.

filigrana [fili'grana] *sf* filigree work; watermark; delicate object.

filo ['filo] *sm* cutting edge; dividing line. **dar un filo** a sharpen. **por filo** exactly.

filón [fi'lon] *sm* (*mineral*) vein, seam; (*fam*) cushy job.

filosofía [filoso'fia] *sf* philosophy. **filosofar** *v* philosophize. **filósofo, -a** *sm, sf* philosopher. **filosófico** *adj* philosophic(al).

filtrar [fil'trar] *v* filter; strain. **filtrarse** *v* seep through. **filtración** *sf* filtration; (*fig*) leak. **filtrador** *sm* filter. **filtro** *sm* filter; strainer; love potion.

fin [fin] *sm* end; death; aim. **a fin de** in order to. **a fines de** at the end of. **al fin y al cabo** when all is said and done. **por fin** at last.

final [fi'nal] *adj* final. *sm* end; finale. **al final de** at the end of. **finalidad** *sf* aim; purpose; finality. **finalizar** *v* finalize.

financiar [finan'θjar] *v* finance. **financiero** *sm* financier. **financiero** *adj* financial. **finanzas** *sf pl* finances.

finca ['finka] *sf* property; estate; farm.

fineza [fi'neθa] *sf* refinement; kindness; gift.

fingir [fin'xir] *v* pretend; sham. **fingirse** *v* pretend to be. **fingimiento** *sm* pretence; deceit.

Finlandia [fin'landja] *sf* Finland. **finlandés, -esa** *s, adj* Finn(ish).

fino ['fino] *adj* fine; refined; delicate; sharp; shrewd; elegant; precious; select; pure.

firmar [fir'mar] *v* sign. **firma** *sf* signature; (*negocio*) firm.

firme ['firme] *adj* firm; steady; rigid; hard; settled. *sm* firm ground; foundation; roadbed. **de firme** steadily. **oferta en firme** firm offer. **¡firmes!** (*mil*) attention!

firmeza *sf* firmness; steadfastness.

fiscal [fis'kal] *adj* fiscal; tax. *sm* treasury official; (*jur*) public prosecutor. **fiscalizar** *v* control; criticize; pry into. **fisco** *sm* exchequer.

física ['fisika] *sf* physics. **físico** *sm* physician; physique. **físico** *adj* physical. **físico, -a** *sm, sf* physicist.

fisiología [fisjolo'xia] *sf* physiology. **fisiológico** *adj* physiological. **fisiólogo, -a** *sm, sf* physiologist.

fisionomía [fisjono'mia] *sf* physiognomy.

fisioterapia [fisjote'rapja] *sf* physiotherapy. **fisioterapeuta** *s(m + f)* physiotherapist.

flaco ['flako] *adj* thin; weak; (*memoria*) short. *sm* weak point. **flaquear** *v* weaken; slacken; flag; fail. **flaqueza** *sf* thinness; frailty.

flagrante [fla'grante] *adj* flagrant, blatant. **en flagrante** in the act.

flamante [fla'mante] *adj* blazing; brand-new.

flamenco¹ [fla'menko] *adj* Flemish; gypsy; flamenco.

flamenco² *sm* flamingo.

flanco ['flanko] *sm* flank. **coger por el flanco** catch unawares.

flauta ['flauta] *sf* flute. **flautista** *s(m + f)* flautist.

fleco ['fleko] *sm* fringe.

flecha ['fletʃa] *sf* arrow. **flecha de dirección** traffic indicator. **flecha de mar** squid. **subir en flecha** shoot up. **flechar** *v* shoot with an arrow; (*fam*) inspire love at first sight; (*fam*) rush. **flechero** *sm* archer.

fletar [fle'tar] *v* charter; hire. **fletamento** *also* **fletamiento** *sm* charter. **flete** *sm* freight.

flexible [flek'siβle] *adj* flexible. *sm* flex. **flexibilidad** *sf* flexibility. **flexión** *sf* flexing; (*gram*) inflexion.

flojo ['floxo] *adj* loose; weak; meagre; lazy. **flojear** *v* slacken; grow weak. **flojedad** *sf* slackness; weakness; carelessness.

flor [flor] *sf* flower; blossom. **a flor de tierra** at ground level. **echar flores** flatter. **en flor** in bloom. **flor de lis** lily. **floral** *adj* floral. **florar** *v* flourish; flower. **florecerse** *v* mildew. **florería** *sf* florist's shop. **florero** *sm* vase. **florido** *adj* flowery; florid. **florista** *s(m + f)* florist.

flotar [flo'tar] *v* float; flutter; stream. **flota** *sf* fleet. **flotable** *adj* buoyant. **flotación** *sf* floatation; fluttering. **flotante** *adj* floating; flowing. **flote** *sm* floatation. **a flote** afloat.

fluctuar [fluk'twar] *v* fluctuate. **fluctuación** *sf* fluctuation.

*fluir [flu'ir] *v* flow. **fluente** *adj* fluid; flowing. **fluidez** *sf* fluidity; fluency. **fluido** *sm, adj* fluid. **flujo** *sm* stream; flow; rising tide. **flujo de vientre** diarrhoea.

fluorescencia [fluores'θenθja] *sf* fluorescence. **fluorescente** *adj* fluorescent.

fluoruro [flwo'ruro] *sm* fluoride.

fobia ['foβja] *sf* phobia.

foca ['foka] *sf* (*zool*) seal.

foco ['foko] *sm* focus; centre; source. **focal** *adj* focal.

fogata [fo'gata] *sf* blaze; bonfire.

fogón [fo'gon] *sm* fireplace; stove.

fogoso [fo'goso] *adj* fiery; impetuous.

follaje [fo'ʎaxe] *sm* foliage; excessive decoration.

folletín [foʎe'tin] *sm* serial story; newspaper article. **folleto** *sm* pamphlet. **folletista** *s(m + f)* pamphleteer.

follón [fo'ʎon] *adj* lazy; arrogant; blustering; cowardly. **follón, -ona** *sm, sf* good-for-nothing; coward; loafer.

fomentar [fomen'tar] *v* foment; warm; incubate; (*fig*) encourage.

fonda ['fonda] *sf* inn, boarding house.

fondear [fonde'ar] *v* anchor; sound; search.

fondo ['fondo] *sm* bottom; depth; essence; capital; fund; character; disposition. **a fondo** thoroughly. **artículo de fondo** leading article. **en el fondo** at heart. **estar en fondos** be well off.

fontanero [fonta'nero] *sm* plumber. **fontanar** *sm* spring. **fontanería** *sf* plumbing.

forajido [fora'xiðo], **-a** *sm, sf* outlaw; fugitive.

forastero [foras'tero], **-a** *sm, sf* stranger; alien. *adj* strange.

forcejear [forθexe'ar] *v* struggle, strive. **forcej(e)o** *sm* struggle.

forense [fo'rense] *adj* forensic; strange.

forjar [for'xar] *v* forge; beat into shape; invent. **forja** *sf* forge; forging.

formal [for'mal] *adj* formal; regular; methodical; serious; steady; reliable. **formalidad** *sf* formality; seriousness; orderliness; propriety. **formalismo** *sm* formalism.

formalizar v formulate; legalize. **formalizarse** v take seriously.

formar [for'mar] v form; educate; train. **formarse** v be trained; develop. **forma** sf form; shape; manner; convention; mould. **de forma que** so that. **tener buenas formas** be polite.

formatear [formate'ar] v (*computadora*) format.

formidable [formi'ðaβle] adj formidable; tremendous. **¡formidable!** great!

fórmula ['formula] sf formula; (*med*) prescription.

fornicar [forni'kar] v fornicate. **fornicación** sf fornication. **fornicador, -a** sm, sf fornicator.

fornido [for'niðo] adj robust, husky.

foro ['foro] sm forum; legal profession; leasehold; (*teatro*) back.

forraje [for'raxe] sm fodder; forage; (*fam*) hodgepodge. **forrajeador** sm forager. **forrajear** v forage.

forrar [for'rar] v line; pad; put a cover on. **forrarse** v line one's pockets. **forro** sm lining; cover.

*fortalecer [fortale'θer] v strengthen; encourage. **fortalecimiento** sm fortification; strengthening. **fortaleza** sf fortress; fortitude; vigour. **fortificación** sf fortification. **fortificar** v fortify; strengthen. **fortificarse** v gain strength.

fortuito [for'twito] adj fortuitous; accidental.

fortuna [for'tuna] sf fortune, wealth; good luck; happiness; fate. **por fortuna** luckily. **probar fortuna** try one's luck.

*forzar [for'θar] v force; rape. **forzadamente** adv forcibly. **forzado** adj forced; hard; far-fetched. **forzosamente** adv unavoidably. **forzoso** adj unavoidable; necessary.

fosa ['fosa] sf grave; (*anat*) cavity.

fosfato [fos'fato] sm phosphate. **fosforescencia** sf phosphorescence. **fosforescente** adj phosphorescent. **fósforo** sm phosphorus; match.

fósil ['fosil] sm fossil. **fosilizarse** v fossilize.

foso ['foso] sm hole; ditch; (*teatro*) pit; (*mil*) trench.

fotocopiar [fotoko'pjar] v photocopy. **fotocopia** sf photocopy. **fotocopiadora** sf copier.

fotografía [fotogra'fia] sf photography; photograph. **fotografiar** v photograph. **fotográfico** adj photographic. **fotógrafo, -a** sm, sf photographer.

frac [frak] sm dress coat, tails pl.

fracasar [fraka'sar] v fail. **fracaso** sm failure.

fracción [frak'θjon] sf (*mat*) fraction; portion; fragment. **fraccionamiento** sm breaking-up. **fraccionar** v break up; divide.

fractura [frak'tura] sf (*med*) fracture. **robo con fractura** sm burglary. **fracturar** v fracture.

fragancia [fra'ganθja] sf fragrance. **fragante** adj fragrant; flagrant.

fragata [fra'gata] sf frigate.

frágil ['fraxil] adj fragile; weak. **fragilidad** sf fragility; weakness.

fragmento [frag'mento] sm fragment. **fragmentar** v fragment. **fragmentario** adj fragmentary.

fragor [fra'gor] sm row, noise. **fragoroso** adj deafening.

fraguar [fra'gwar] v (*hierro*) forge; concoct; (*cemento*) harden. **fragua** sf forge. **fraguador, -a** sm, sf schemer, plotter.

fraile ['fraile] sm friar, monk.

frambuesa [fram'bwesa] sf raspberry. **frambueso** sm raspberry bush.

Francia ['franθja] sf France. **francés, -esa** sm, sf Frenchman/woman. **francés** sm, adj French.

francmasón [frankma'son] sm freemason. **francmasonería** sf freemasonry.

franco ['franko] adj frank, open; generous; free; (*com*) post or duty free.

franela [fra'nela] sf flannel.

franja ['franxa] sf fringe; border. **franjar** v fringe, trim.

franquear [franke'ar] v free; clear; exempt; grant. **franquearse** v open one's heart. **franqueo** sm franking, stamping; postage.

franqueza [fran'keθa] sf frankness; generosity; freedom.

frasco ['frasko] sm flask.

frase ['frase] sf (*gram*) sentence; phrase; expression. **frase hecha** cliché. **fraseología** sf phraseology.

fraternal [frater'nal] adj fraternal. **fraternidad** sf fraternity. **fraternizar** v fraternize. **fraterno** adj fraternal.

fraude ['frauðe] *sm* fraud; deception. **fraudulencia** *sf* dishonesty. **fraudulento** *adj* fraudulent.

fray [fraj] *sm* (*rel*) friar, brother.

frecuencia [fre'kwenθja] *sf* frequency. **frecuencia modulada** *sf* long wave. **con frecuencia** often. **frecuentar** *v* frequent. **frecuente** *adj* frequent.

***fregar** [fre'gar] *v* rub; scrub; wash up. **fregadero** *sm* sink. **fregado** *sm* rubbing; scrubbing; washing; (*fam*) intrigue. **fregador, -a** *sm, sf* dishwasher; *sm* sink, dishcloth.

***freír** [fre'ir] *v* fry; (*fam*) bother. **freidura** *sf* frying. **freiduría** *sf* fish shop.

fréjol ['frexol] *sm* kidney bean.

frenar [fre'nar] *v* brake; check. **freno** *sm* brake; bridle. **freno de mano** handbrake. **poner/soltar el freno** apply/release the brake.

frenesí [frene'si] *sm* frenzy.

frente ['frente] *sm* front; face; façade. **al frente** at the head. **de frente** forward. **en frente** opposite. *sf* forehead; head. **frente a frente** face to face.

fresa ['fresa] *sf* strawberry.

fresco ['fresko] *adj* cool; fresh; new; calm. **frescura** *sf* coolness; freshness; fertility; calmness; indifference; (*fam*) insolence.

fresno ['fresno] *sm* (*bot*) ash.

fricción [frik'θjon] *sf* friction; (*med*) massage. **friccionar** *v* rub; massage.

frigidez [frixi'ðeθ] *sf* frigidity. **frígido** *adj* frigid. **frigorífico** *sm* refrigerating; refrigerator.

frijón [fri'xon] *sm* bean.

frío ['frio] *adj* cold; cool; indifferent. *sm* cold. **coger frío** catch cold. **tener frío** be cold. **frialdad** *sf* coldness; indifference; impotence.

friolera [frjo'lera] *sf* triviality, trifle.

frisar [fri'sar] *v* frizz, curl. **frisar en** (*edad*) border on.

frito ['frito] *V* **freír**. *adj* fried. **estar frito** be fed up. **patatas fritas** chips. **quedarse frito** (*fam*) nod off.

frívolo ['friβolo] *adj* frivolous. **frivolidad** *sf* frivolity.

frondoso [fron'doso] *adj* leafy; lush. **frondosidad** *sf* leafiness; lushness.

frontera [fron'tera] *sf* frontier.

frotar [fro'tar] *v* rub; (*cerilla*) strike.

frotación *sf* rubbing; friction. **frote** *sm* rub.

fructífero [fruk'tifero] *adj* fruit-bearing; fruitful.

frugal [fru'gal] *adj* frugal. **frugalidad** *sf* frugality.

fruncir [frun'θir] *v* wrinkle; gather; pleat. **fruncir el ceño** frown. **fruncido** *adj* gathered; wrinkled. **fruncimiento** *sm* gathering; wrinkling.

frustrar [frus'trar] *v* frustrate. **frustrarse** *v* fail.

fruta ['fruta] *sf* fruit. **fruta de sartén** fritter. **frutal** *adj* fruit. **frutería** *sf* fruiterer's. **frutero, -a** *sm, sf* fruiterer. **fruto** *sm* fruit; product; result; offspring; profit. **frutos civiles** (*jur*) unearned income.

fue¹ ['fue] *V* **ir**.

fue² ['fue] *V* **ser**.

fuego ['fwego] *sm* fire; light; burner; heat; rash; passion; zeal. **apagar el fuego** put out the fire. **arma de fuego** firearm. **cocer a fuego lento/vivo** cook slowly/quickly. **fuegos artificiales** fireworks. **prender fuego a** set fire to.

fuelle ['fweλe] *sm* bellows.

fuente ['fwente] *sf* fountain; spring; source; serving dish.

fuera ['fwera] *adv* outside; out; abroad. **aquí/allí fuera** out here/there. **estar fuera** be away. **¡fuera!** get out! **ir fuera** go outside. **por fuera** on the outside.

fuero ['fwero] *sm* law; code of laws; jurisdiction.

fuerte ['fwerte] *adj* strong; large; heavy; concentrated. **precio fuerte** full price. *sm* (*mil*) fort; stronghold. **fuerza** *sf* strength; loudness; power; effort; electric current. **fuerza pública** police force.

fugarse [fu'garse] *v* run away; escape. **fuga** *sf* escape; elopement; (*gas, etc.*) leak; (*música*) fugue. **ponerse en fuga** take flight. **fugaz** *adj* fleeting. **fugitivo, -a** *s, adj* fugitive.

fulano [fu'lano] *sm* so-and-so, what's-his-name. **fulana** *sf* whore.

fulcro ['fulkro] *sm* fulcrum.

fulgor [ful'gor] *sm* glow; sparkle; brilliance. **fulgente** *also* **fúlgido** *adj* brilliant. **fulgir** *v* shine. **fulgurante** *adj* shining; glowing. **fulgurar** *v* flash; shine; glow.

fulminante [fulmi'nante] *adj* explosive; thundering; (*med*) grave; (*med*) mortal. **ful-**

minar *v* strike (by lightning); thunder; explode.

fumar [fu'mar] *v* smoke. **prohibido fumar** no smoking. **fumarse** *v* squander. **fumada** *sf* (*de humo*) puff.

fumigar [fumi'gar] *v* fumigate. **fumigación** *sf* fumigation. **fumigador** *sm* fumigator.

funcionar [funθjo'nar] *v* function, work, go. **no funciona** out of order. **función** *sf* function; performance; party; duty. **funcional** *adj* functional. **funcionamiento** *sm* functioning; operation; performance. **funcionario, -a** *sm, sf* public official.

funda ['funda] *sf* case, cover. **funda de almohada** pillowcase.

fundar [fun'dar] *v* found; establish; base. **fundarse** *v* be based. **fundación** *sf* foundation. **fundado** *adj* founded; justified. **fundamental** *adj* fundamental. **fundamento** *sm* foundation; basis; reason; reliability.

fundir [fun'dir] *v* cast; smelt; melt; merge. **fundición** *sf* melting; smelting; foundry.

fúnebre ['funeβre] *adj* funeral; mournful. **coche fúnebre** hearse.

funesto [fu'nesto] *adj* ill-fated; disastrous; fatal.

furgón [fur'gon] *sm* wagon; truck; van. **furgón de cola** guard's van. **furgoneta** *sf* van. **furgoneta familiar** station wagon.

furia ['furja] *sf* fury; violence; frenzy. **furioso** *adj* furious; raging; enormous. **furor** *sm* fury; passion; fever. **con furor** furiously. **hacer furor** be all the rage.

furtivo [fur'tiβo] *adj* furtive; sly.

furúnculo [fu'runkulo] *sm* (*med*) boil.

fusible [fu'siβle] *adj* fusible. *sm* fuse.

fusil [fu'sil] *sm* rifle.

fusión [fu'sjon] *sf* fusion; melting; thawing. **fusionar** *v* fuse; merge. **fusionamiento** *sm* merger.

fuste ['fuste] *sm* wood; (*fig*) importance. **gente de fuste** people of consequence.

fútbol ['futβol] *sm* football. **futbolista** *sm* footballer.

fútil ['futil] *adj* futile, trivial. **futilidad** *sf* futility; triviality.

futuro [fu'turo] *sm, adj* future. **futurista** *adj* futuristic.

G

gabán [ga'βan] *sm* overcoat.

gabardina [gaβar'ðina] *sf* raincoat.

gabinete [gaβi'nete] *sm* (*pol*) cabinet; study; studio.

gacela [ga'θela] *sf* gazelle.

gaceta [ga'θeta] *sf* gazette; journal. **gacetero** *sm* journalist; **gacetilla** *sf* gossip column.

gachas ['gatʃas] *sf pl* porridge *sing*; slops *pl*.

gacho ['gatʃo] *adj* drooping.

gaélico [ga'eliko] *adj* Gaelic.

gafas ['gafas] *sf pl* spectacles. **gafas de sol** sunglasses.

gajo ['gaxo] *sm* (*de horcas*) prong; (*de naranja*) segment; (*de frutas*) cluster.

gala ['gala] *sf* full dress; pomp; elegance. **de gala** in full dress. **hacer gala de** show off. **tener a gala** pride oneself in.

galán [ga'lan] *sm* gallant; suitor; handsome man; (*teatro*) leading man. **galante** *adj* gallant; flirtatious. **galantear** *v* woo; flirt; flatter. **galanteo** *sm* flirtation; courting; flattery. **galantería** *sf* gallantry; elegance.

galardón [galar'ðon] *sm* reward. **galardonar** *v* reward.

galeón [gale'on] *sm* galleon.

galera [ga'lera] *sf* (*mar*) galley; wagon.

galería [gale'ria] *sf* gallery.

Gales ['gales] *sm* Wales. **galés, -esa** *sm, sf* Welshman/woman. **galés** *sm* (*lengua*) Welsh.

galgo ['galgo] *sm* greyhound.

galón¹ [ga'lon] *sm* braid; (*mil*) stripe. **quitar los galones** demote.

galón² *sm* gallon.

galopar [galo'par] *v* gallop. **galope** *sm* gallop. **a medio galope** at a canter.

galvanizar [galβani'θar] *v* galvanize.

gallardo [ga'ʎarðo] *adj* elegant; gallant. **gallardía** *sf* elegance; charm. **gallardear** *v* behave gracefully.

galleta [ga'ʎeta] *sf* biscuit.

gallina [ga'ʎina] *sf* hen, chicken. **gallo** *sm* cock, rooster.

gamuza [ga'muθa] *sf* chamois; (*trapo*) duster.

gana ['gana] *sf* desire; wish; appetite. **de**

buena/mala gana willingly/unwillingly. **tener ganas de** want to.

ganadería [ganaðe'ria] *sf* cattle-raising; cattle farm; cattle; breed. **ganadero. -a** *sm, sf* cattle-raiser; stockbreeder. **ganado** *sm* cattle; livestock.

ganar [ga'nar] *v* gain, get; earn; take; surpass. **ganar en peso** put on weight. **ganancia** *sf* profit. **ganancias** *sf pl* earnings; winnings.

gancho ['gantʃo] *sm* hook; (fam) decoy; (fam) pimp; (fam) sex appeal.

ganga ['ganga] *sf* (fam) bargain; (fam) cushy job.

gangrena [gan'grena] *sf* gangrene. **gangrenoso** *adj* gangrenous.

ganso ['ganso] *sm* goose, gander; (fam) boor. **gansada** *sf* (fam) stupid thing.

garabatear [garaβate'ar] *v* scribble; (fam) beat about the bush. **garabateo** *sm* scribbling. **garabato** *sm* scribble; doodle.

garaje [ga'raxe] *sm* garage.

garantizar [garanti'θar] *v* guarantee. **garantía** *sf* guarantee.

garbanzo [gar'βanθo] *sm* chickpea.

garbo ['garβo] *sm* grace; generosity; jauntiness. **garboso** *adj* graceful; generous; jaunty.

garganta [gar'ganta] *sf* throat. **tener buena garganta** have a good voice. **gargantear** *v* warble.

gargarizar [gargari'θar] *v* gargle. **gárgara** *sf* gargle.

gárgola ['gargola] *sf* gargoyle.

garita [ga'rita] *sf* sentry box; lavatory; porter's lodge. **garita de señales** signal-box.

garra ['garra] *sf* claw.

garrafa [gar'rafa] *sf* decanter.

garrapata [garra'pata] *sf* (zool) tick.

garrote [gar'rote] *sm* stick, club; garotte; (med) tourniquet. **dar garrote a** execute.

garza ['garθa] *sf* heron.

gas [gas] *sm* gas. **a todo gas** flat out.

gasa ['gasa] *sf* gauze.

gaseosa [gase'osa] *sf* lemonade.

gasolina [gaso'lina] *sf* petrol. **gasolinera** *sf* petrol pump.

gastar [gas'tar] *v* spend; waste; wear out or away. **gasto** *sm* expense; outlay. **gastos** *sm pl* expenses; costs. **gastos generales** overheads.

gatillo [ga'tiʎo] *sm* trigger; dentist's forceps; (tecn) jack.

gato ['gato] *sm* cat; (tecn) jack; (fam) hoard. **a gatas** on all fours. **gatear** *v* clamber; (fam) crawl. **gatearse** *v* scratch.

gavilán [gaβi'lan] *sm* hawk; (pluma) nib; (bot) thistle.

gavilla [ga'βiʎa] *sf* sheaf; bundle; (fam) gang.

gaviota [ga'βjota] *sf* seagull.

gazapo [ga'θapo] *sm* young rabbit; slip of the tongue; blunder; misprint.

gazpacho [gaθ'patʃo] *sm* cold vegetable soup.

gelatina [xela'tina] *sf* gelatine.

gelignita [xelig'nita] *sf* gelignite.

gemelo [xe'melo] *sm, adj* twin. *sm pl* cufflinks; opera glasses.

*gemir [xe'mir] *v* groan. **gemido** *sm* groan; wail.

genealogía [xenealo'xia] *sf* genealogy. **genealógico** *adj* genealogical. **árbol genealógico** family tree.

generación [xenera'θjon] *sf* generation. **generador** *sm* (tecn) generator. **generar** *v* generate.

generalizar [xenerali'θar] *v* generalize. **general** *adj* general. **general** *sm* (mil) general. **generalidad** *sf* majority. **generalización** *sf* generalization.

genérico [xe'neriko] *adj* generic. **género** *sm* race; kind; style; material; article; gender. **géneros** *sm pl* goods, merchandise *sing*.

generoso [xene'roso] *adj* generous. **generosidad** *sf* generosity.

genética [xe'netika] *sf* genetics. **genético** *adj* genetic.

genial [xe'njal] *adj* brilliant; outstanding; pleasant. **genio** *sm* genius; character. **estar de mal genio** be in a bad temper.

genital [xeni'tal] *adj* genital. **genitales** *sm pl* genitals.

gente ['xente] *sf* people. **gente baja** lower classes. **gente menuda** children.

gentil [xen'til] *adj* charming; genteel; civil; gentile; heathen. *sm* gentile; heathen; pagan. **gentileza** *sf* grace; elegance; gentility; civility.

gentío [xen'tio] *sm* crowd.

genuino [xe'nwino] *adj* genuine.

geografía [xeogra'fia] *sf* geography.

geográfico adj geographic(al). **geógrafo** sm geographer.

geología [xeolo'xia] sf geology. **geológico** adj geological. **geólogo** sm geologist.

geometría [xeome'tria] sf geometry. **geométrico** adj geometric.

geranio [xe'ranjo] sm geranium.

gerencia [xe'renθja] sf management. **gerente** sm manager.

germinar [xermi'nar] v germinate. **germen** sm germ.

gesticular [xestiku'lar] v gesticulate. **gesticulación** sf gesticulation; grimace.

gestión [xes'tjon] sf arrangement; measure; management. **gestionar** v negotiate; get hold of.

gesto ['xesto] sm expression; countenance; gesture.

geyser ['xejser] sm geyser.

gigante [xi'gante] sm giant. adj gigantic.

gimnasia [xim'nasja] sf gymnastics. **gimnasio** sm gymnasium. **gimnasta** s(m + f) gymnast.

ginebra [xi'neβra] sf gin.

ginecología [xinekolo'xia] sf gynaecology. **ginecólogo, -a**, sm, sf gynaecologist.

gira ['xira] sf tour; excursion; picnic.

giralda [xi'ralða] sf weathercock.

girar [xi'rar] v turn; swivel; send; (com) draw. **girar dinero** remit money. **giratorio** adj gyratory. **puerta giratoria** revolving door. **giro** sm turn; (com) draft. **giro postal** sm postal order; money order.

girasol [xira'sol] sm sunflower.

gitano [xi'tano], **-a** s, adj gypsy.

glacial [gla'θjal] adj freezing.

glaciar [gla'θjar] sm glacier.

gladio ['glaðjo] sm (bot) gladiolus.

glándula ['glandula] sf gland. **glandular** adj glandular.

glicerina [gliθe'rina] sf glycerine.

global [glo'βal] adj global; comprehensive; total. **globo** sm globe, sphere. **en globo** all in all. **globo ocular** eyeball. **globular** adj globular. **glóbulo** sm globule.

gloriarse [glo'rjarse] v boast; glory. **gloria** sf glory; (culin) custard tart. **glorificación** sf glorification. **glorificar** v glorify. **glorioso** adj glorious; conceited.

glosar [glo'sar] v annotate. **glosa** sf annotation. **glosario** sm glossary.

glotón [glo'ton], **-ona** sm, sf glutton. adj gluttonous.

glucosa [glu'kosa] sf glucose.

*gobernar [goβer'nar] v govern; control; manage. **gobernación** sf government. **gobernador** sm governor. **gobierno** sm (pol) government; guidance.

goce ['goθe] sm enjoyment.

gol [gol] sm (deporte) goal. **golear** v score a goal.

golfo ['golfo] sm gulf; (geog) bay; guttersnipe.

golondrina [golon'drina] sf (zool) swallow.

golosina [golo'sina] sf sweet; delicacy; (fig) desire; (fig) greed. **goloso** adj sweet-toothed; appetizing; greedy.

golpear [golpe'ar] v strike, hit. **golpe** sm blow; coup; large amount; attack. **golpe de estado** coup d'état. **golpe de gracia** coup de grâce.

goma ['goma] sf rubber; gum; rubber band; elastic. **goma de borrar** eraser. **goma espuma** foam rubber.

gomina [go'mina] sf gel.

gordo ['gorðo] sm, adj fat. **gordura** sf fatness, obesity.

gorila [go'rila] sf gorilla.

gorjear [gorxe'ar] v chirp, trill; twitter. **gorjeo** sm chirping; trilling; twittering.

gorra ['gorra] sf peaked cap; bonnet; (fam) sponger. **de gorra** free. **vivir de gorra** sponge.

gorrión [gor'rjon] sf sparrow.

gorro ['gorro] sm cap.

gotear [gote'ar] v drip; trickle; leak. **gota** sf drop. **gotera** sf leak; gutter. **goteras** sf pl (fig) aches and pains.

gótico ['gotiko] adj Gothic.

gozar [go'θar] v enjoy; possess. **gozarse** v rejoice. **gozo** sm joy. **gozoso** adj joyful.

gozne ['goθne] sm hinge.

grabar [gra'βar] v engrave; carve; imprint; record. **grabado** sm engraving; picture; recording. **grabador de cinta** sm tape recorder.

gracia ['graθja] sf grace; favour; charm; joke. **me hace gracia** it amuses me. **tener gracia** be amusing.

gracias ['graθjas] sf pl thanks. **acción de gracias** thanksgiving. **dar gracias** thank. **muchas gracias** many thanks.

gracioso [gra'θjoso] adj graceful; amusing;

gracious. *sm* (*teatro*) buffoon.

grada ['graða] *sf* step; stair. **gradería** *sf* flight of steps; row of seats.

grado ['graðo] *sm* grade; degree; rank; pleasure. **de grado** willingly. **graduación** *sf* graduation. **gradual** *adj* gradual. **gradualmente** *adv* gradually. **graduando, -a** *sm, sf* undergraduate. **graduar** *v* graduate; award a degree to. **graduarse** *v* gain a degree.

gráfico ['grafiko] *adj* graphic. *sm* graph; diagram. *sm pl* graphics.

grajo ['graxo] *sm* (*zool*) rook.

gramática [gra'matika] *sf* grammar. **gramático** *adj* grammatical.

gramo ['gramo] *sm* gramme.

gramófono [gra'mofono] *sm* gramophone.

gran [gran] *V* **grande.**

grana¹ ['grana] *sf* small seed; seeding time.

grana² *sf, adj* scarlet.

granada [gra'naða] *sf* pomegranate.

grande ['grande] *adj also* **gran** large, big, great. **grandeza** *sf* greatness; size. **grandioso** *adj* grandiose; grand.

granel [gra'nel] *adv* **a granel** in bulk.

granero [gra'nero] *sm* granary.

granito [gra'nito] *sm* granite.

granizar [grani'θar] *v* hail. **granizo** *sm* hail.

granja ['granxa] *sf* farm. **granja avícola** poultry farm. **granjero, -a** *sm, sf* farmer.

grano ['grano] *sm* grain; bean; pimple. **ir al grano** come to the point. **granoso** *adj* granular.

grapa ['grapa] *sf* clamp; staple; dowel.

grasa ['grasa] *sf* grease; fat. **grasera** *sf* dripping pan. **grasiento** *adj* greasy; oily; filthy. **graso** *adj* fatty.

gratificar [gratifi'kar] *v* gratify; reward; tip. **gratificación** *sf* reward; gratuity; bonus; gratification. **gratificante** *adj* rewarding.

gratis ['gratis] *adv* free.

gratitud [grati'tuð] *sf* gratitude.

grato ['grato] *adj* pleasing; pleasant; welcome. **me es grato ...** I am pleased ....

gratuito [gra'twito] *adj* free; gratuitous.

gravamen [gra'βamen] *sm* charge; obligation; burden; tax. **gravar** *v* burden; oppress. **gravar impuestos a** *or* **sobre** tax.

grave ['graβe] *adj* grave, serious; weighty. **ponerse grave** become gravely ill. **gravedad** *sf* gravity, seriousness.

gravitar [graβi'tar] *v* gravitate. **gravitación** *sf* gravitation, gravity.

graznar [graθ'nar] *v* croak; cackle. **graznido** *sm* croak; cackle.

Grecia ['greθja] *sf* Greece. **griego** *s, adj* Greek. **griego** *sm* (*idioma*) Greek; (*fam*) gibberish.

greda ['greða] *sf* clay. **gredoso** *adj* clayey.

gregario [gre'garjo] *adj* gregarious.

gremio ['gremjo] *sm* guild; fraternity; union. **gremio obrero** trade union.

greña ['grena] *sf* tangled hair. **andar a la greña** (*fam*) squabble.

grey [grej] *sf* congregation; flock, herd.

grieta ['grjeta] *sf* crack.

grifo ['grifo] *sm* tap. **al grifo** on draught.

grillo ['griλo] *sm* (*zool*) cricket. **grillos** *sm pl* shackles, fetters.

gringo ['gringo], **-a** *sm, sf* (*fam*) foreigner.

gripe ['gripe] *sf* (*med*) influenza, flu.

gris [gris] *adj* grey.

gritar [gri'tar] *v* shout, scream, yell. **grito** *sm* shout, scream, yell. **el último grito** the latest fashion.

grosella [gro'seλa] *sf* currant. **grosella espinosa/negra/roja** gooseberry/blackcurrant/redcurrant.

grosería [grose'ria] *sf* vulgarity. **grosero** *adj* vulgar.

grotesco [gro'tesko] *adj* grotesque; absurd.

grúa ['grua] *sf* (*tecn*) crane.

grueso [gru'eso] *adj* thick; large; heavy; dull; slow; coarse. *sm* thickness; heaviness. **gruesa** *sf* (*número*) gross.

grulla ['gruλa] *sf* (*zool*) crane.

grumete [gru'mete] *sm* cabin boy.

*****gruñir** [gru'nir] *v* growl. **gruñido** *sm* growl.

gruñón [gru'non] *adj* nagging.

grupo ['grupo] *sm* group. **grupo de presión** *sm* pressure group. **grupo sanguíneo** blood group.

gruta ['gruta] *sf* grotto; cave.

guadaña [gwa'ðana] *sf* scythe.

guante ['gwante] *sm* glove. **guantear** *v* slap.

guapo ['gwapo] *adj* handsome; pretty; flashy. *sm* boaster; bully; (*fam*) lover.

guardar [gwar'ðar] *v* guard; keep; protect; respect. **guarda** *s*(*m + f*) guard; keeper. **guarda** *sf* custody; protection. **guarda-**

costas *sm invar* coastguard. **guardafuego** *sm* hearth fender. **guardapolvo** *sm* dustcover. **guardarropa** *sm* wardrobe; cloakroom. **guardería** *sf* crèche. **guardia** *sf* guard; police force. **guardia civil** Civil Guard.

guardián [gwar'ðjan], **-a** *sm, sf* guardian; keeper; caretaker.

guardilla [gwar'ðiʎa] *sf* attic.

guarida [gwa'riða] *sf* den, lair; haunt; shelter.

*guarnecer [gwarne'θer] *v* equip; provide; furnish; adorn; garnish; plaster. **guarnición** *sf* adornment; provision; (*mil*) garrison. **guarnicionar** *v* garrison.

guasa ['gwasa] *sf* joke. **sin guasa** seriously. **guasearse** *v* (*fam*) joke; tease. **guaseo** *sm* leg-pull.

gubernamental [guβernamen'tal] *adj* governmental.

guerra ['gerra] *sf* war. **guerra mundial** world war. **guerrear** *v* wage war. **guerrero, -a** *sm, sf* warrior. **guerrilla** *sf* guerrilla band; guerrilla warfare. **guerrillero** *sm* guerrilla fighter.

guiar [gi'ar] *v* guide; steer; drive. **guía** *sm* (*persona*) guide. **guía** *sf* (*libro*) guide, guidebook. **guía sonora** soundtrack. **guía telefónica** *sf* phone book.

guija ['gixa] *sf* pebble.

guillotina [giʎo'tina] *sf* guillotine. **guillotinar** *v* guillotine.

guiñar [gi'ɲar] *v* wink. **guiño** *sm* wink.

guión [gi'on] *sm* hyphen; film script; outline; subtitle.

guisa ['gisa] *sf* way, manner. **a guisa de** like. **de tal guisa** in such a manner.

guisado [gi'saðo] *sm* stew. **guisar** *v* cook; prepare. **guiso** *sm* cooked dish; stew.

guisante [gi'sante] *sm* pea. **guisante de olor** sweet pea.

guitarra [gi'tarra] *sf* guitar. **guitarrista** *s(m + f)* guitarist.

gula ['gula] *sf* greed.

gusano [gu'sano] *sm* worm; maggot; caterpillar. **gusano de seda** silkworm.

gustar [gus'tar] *v* please; like; taste; try. **gustar de** enjoy. **¡así me gusta!** that's what I like! **gusto** *sm* pleasure; fancy; style; taste; flavour. **de buen/mal gusto** in good/bad taste. **con mucho gusto** with great pleasure. **¡mucho gusto!** how do you do? **gustoso** *adj* tasty; pleasant.

gutural [gutu'ral] *adj* guttural.

H

haba ['aβa] *sf* broad bean; swelling; bruise.

*haber [a'βer] *v* have. **haber de** have to. **hay que** one must. **no hay de que** don't mention it. **haberes** *sm pl* assets; property *sing*; income *sing*.

habichuela [aβi'tʃwela] *sf* bean. **habichuela verde** French bean.

hábil ['aβil] *adj* clever; able. **habilidad** *sf* cleverness; ability.

habilitar [aβili'tar] *v* qualify; enable. **habilitación** *sf* qualification.

habitar [aβi'tar] *v* inhabit. **habitable** *adj* habitable. **habitación** *sf* habitation; room; lodgings *pl*. **habitante** *s(m + f)* inhabitant.

hábito ['aβito] *sm* habit; attire. **habitual** *adj* habitual. **habituar** *v* accustom. **habituarse** *v* become accustomed to.

hablar [a'βlar] *v* speak, talk. **¿quién habla?** (*al teléfono*) who's speaking? **se habla español** Spanish spoken. **habla** *sf* language; speech. **hablador, -a** *sm, sf* chatterbox. **hablilla** *sf* rumour; gossip.

hacedero [aθe'ðero] *adj* feasible. **hacedor, -a** *sm, sf* creator.

hacendado [aθen'daðo] *sm* landowner.

*hacer [a'θer] *v* do; make; perform; produce. **hacer calor/frío** be hot/cold. **hacer fiesta** take a holiday. **hace mucho tiempo que** it is a long time since. **hacer para** make an effort to. **hacer rappel** *v* abseil. **hacerse** *v* become.

hacia ['aθja] *prep* towards; about. **hacia atrás** backwards.

hacienda [a'θjenda] *sf* estate; ranch.

hacina [a'θina] *sf* stack, rick. **hacinar** *v* stack; amass.

hacha ['atʃa] *sf* axe.

hada ['aða] *sf* fairy. **hada madrina** fairy godmother. **cuento de hadas** *sm* fairy tale.

hado ['aðo] *sm* fate.

halagar [ala'gar] *v* flatter. **halago** *sm* flattery. **halagüeño** *adj* flattering.

halcón [al'kon] *sm* falcon. **halconería** *sf*

falconry.
hálito ['alito] *sm* breath.
hallar [a'ʎar] *v* find; find out. **hallarse** *v* be situated. **hallarse bien con** be pleased with. **hallazgo** *sm* discovery.
hamaca [a'maka] *sf* hammock.
hambre ['ambre] *sf* hunger; starvation. **pasar hambre** go hungry. **tener hambre** be hungry. **hambriento** *adj* hungry.
hamburguesa [ambur'gesa] *sf* hamburger; beefburger.
haragán [ara'gan] *adj* lazy. **haraganear** *v* idle.
harapiento [ara'pjento] *adj* ragged. **harapo** *sm* rag.
harina [a'rina] *sf* flour. **harinero** *adj* also **harinoso** floury.
hartar [ar'tar] *v* stuff; gorge; weary; bore. **harto** *adj* satiated. **hartura** *sf* satiety.
hasta ['asta] *prep* until; up to; as much as; as far as. *adv* even. **hasta ahora** up to now. **hasta aquí** so far. **hasta luego** (*interj*) so long, good-bye. **hasta que** until.
hastío [as'tio] *sm* disgust; weariness. **hastiar** *v* disgust; bore.
hato ['ato] *sm* herd; flock; gang.
hay [aj] there is; there are. **hay que** one must.
haya ['aja] *sf* beech.
haz¹ [aθ] *sm* bunch; bundle; sheaf.
haz² *sf* face; surface. **a sobre haz** on the surface.
hazaña [a'θaɲa] *sf* deed; feat; exploit.
hazmerreír [aθmerre'ir] *sm* laughing-stock.
hebilla [e'βiʎa] *sf* buckle; clasp.
hebra ['eβra] *sf* fibre; thread; (*de madera*) grain.
hebreo [e'βreo] *s, adj* Hebrew. *sm* (*lengua*) Hebrew.
hechicero [etʃi'θero] *sm* sorcerer; wizard. **hechicera** *sf* sorceress; witch. **hechicería** *sf* witchcraft; sorcery; enchantment. **hechizar** *v* bewitch. **hechizo** *sm* magic spell.
hecho ['etʃo] *V* hacer. *adj* mature; finished; cooked. **hecho y derecho** in every sense of the word. **muy/poco hecho** overdone/underdone. *sm* fact; deed; feat; matter; event. **de hecho** in fact. **hechura** *sf* making; making-up; shape; workmanship.
hediondo [e'ðjondo] *adj* stinking; repul-

sive. **heder** *v* stink; vex. **hedor** *sm* stink.
***helar** [e'lar] *v* freeze. **helada** *sf* frost. **helado** *sm* ice cream.
helecho [e'letʃo] *sm* fern.
hélice ['eliθe] *sf* helix; spiral; propeller.
helicóptero [eli'koptero] *sm* helicopter.
hembra ['embra] *sf* female; clasp; socket; (*de tornillo*) nut.
hemisferio [emis'ferjo] *sm* hemisphere. **hemisférico** *adj* hemispheric, hemispherical.
hemorragia [emor'raxja] *sf* haemorrhage.
hemorroides [emor'rojðes] *sf pl* haemorrhoids.
***henchirse** [en'tʃirse] *v* swell up; stuff oneself. **henchidura** *sf* filling.
***hender** [en'der] *v* split. **hendidura** *sf* split; crack.
heno ['eno] *sm* hay.
heraldo [e'raldo] *sm* herald. **heráldica** *sf* heraldry. *adj* heraldic.
herbaje [er'βaxe] *sm* pasture. **herbario** *adj* herbal. **herbicida** *sm* weedkiller. **herbívoro, -a** *sm, sf* herbivore. **herbívoro** *adj* herbivorous. **herbolario** *sm* herbalist. **herboso** *adj* grassy.
heredar [ere'ðar] *v* inherit. **heredad** *sf* estate. **heredero, -a** *sm, sf* heir/heiress. **hereditario** *adj* hereditary.
hereje [e'rexe] *s(m + f)* heretic. **herejía** *sf* heresy. **herético** *adj* heretic.
herencia [e'renθja] *sf* inheritance; heredity.
***herir** [e'rir] *v* wound. **herida** *sf* wound. **herido** *sm* casualty.
hermano [er'mano] *sm* brother. **hermano de leche** *sm* foster brother. **hermana** *sf* sister. **hermandad** *sf* brotherhood. **hermanastro, -a** *sm, sf* stepbrother/stepsister.
hermético [er'metiko] *adj* hermetic.
hermoso [er'moso] *adj* beautiful; handsome. **hermosura** *sf* beauty; handsomeness.
héroe ['eroe] *sm* hero. **heroico** *adj* heroic. **heroína** *sf* heroine. **heroísmo** *sm* heroism.
heroína [ero'ina] *sf* heroin.
herramienta [erra'mjenta] *sf* tool; implement.
***herrar** [er'rar] *v* (*caballo*) shoe. **herradura** *sf* horseshoe. **camino de herradura** bridle path. **herrería** *sf* smithy, forge. **herrero** *sm* blacksmith.
herrumbre [er'rumbre] *sf* rust. **herrum-

brar v rust. **herrumbroso** adj rusty.

*hervir [er'βir] v boil. **hervidero** sm boiling; bubbling; (fig) swarm, crowd; hot-bed. **hervidor** sm kettle. **hervor** sm boiling; fervour.

hesitar [esi'tar] v hesitate. **hesitación** sf hesitation.

hez [eθ] sf, pl **heces** dregs pl; scum.

hibernar [iβer'nar] v hibernate. **hibernación** sf hibernation.

híbrido [i'βriðo] sm, adj hybrid. **hibridación** sf hybridization. **hibridizar** v hybridize.

hidalgo [i'ðalgo] sm nobleman. adj noble. **hidalguía** sf nobility.

hidráulico [i'ðrauliko] adj hydraulic. **freno hidráulico** sm hydraulic brake.

hidroala [iðro'ala] sf hovercraft.

hidroavión [iðroa'βjon] sm seaplane.

hidroeléctrico [iðroe'lektriko] adj hydro-electric.

hidrofobia [iðro'foβja] sf hydrophobia.

hidrógeno [i'ðroxeno] sm hydrogen.

hidropesía [idrope'sia] sf dropsy.

hiedra [i'jeðra] sf ivy.

hielo ['jelo] sm ice.

hiena ['jena] sf hyena.

hierba ['jerβa] sf grass; herb. **mala hierba** weed.

hierbabuena [jerβa'βwena] sf mint.

hierro ['jerro] sm iron. **hierro colado** cast iron. **hierro forjado** wrought iron.

hígado ['igaðo] sm liver.

higiene [i'xjene] sf hygiene. **higiénico** adj hygienic. **paños higiénicos** sm pl sanitary towels.

higo ['igo] sm fig. **higuera** sf fig-tree.

hijo ['ixo] sm son. **hijos** sm pl children. **hija** sf daughter. **hijo/hija político, -a** son/daughter-in-law.

hilar [i'lar] v spin; infer. **hiladora** sf spinning wheel. **hilandería** sf spinning. **hilandero, -a** sm, sf (persona) spinner.

hilarante [ila'rante] adj hilarious. **hilaridad** sf hilarity.

hilera [i'lera] sf row; rank; file.

hilo ['ilo] sm thread; yarn; wire. **hilo de coser** sewing thread. **hilo de perlas** string of pearls. **telegrafía sin hilos** sf wireless telegraphy.

himno ['imno] sm hymn; anthem. **himno nacional** national anthem. **himnario** sm hymn book.

hincapié [inka'pje] sm foothold; emphasis. **hacer hincapié en** insist on.

hincar [in'kar] v drive in; sink; plunge. **hincarse de rodillas** kneel down.

hinchar [in't∫ar] v inflate; swell. **hincharse** v puff up; (fam) become bigheaded. **hinchazón** sm (med) swelling; arrogance.

hinojo [i'noxo] sm fennel. **hinojos** sm pl knees.

hiper ['iper] sm hype.

hiperactivo [iperak'tiβo] adj hyperactive.

hipermercado [ipermer'kaðo] sm hypermarket.

hípico ['ipiko] adj equine. **hipismo** sm show-jumping. **hipódromo** sm race course.

hipnosis [ip'nosis] sm hypnosis. **hipnótico** adj hypnotic. **hipnotismo** sm hypnotism. **hipnotizador, -a** sm, sf hypnotist. **hipnotizar** v hypnotize.

hipo ['ipo] sm hiccup; longing; grudge. **tener hipo** have the hiccups.

hipocondría [ipokon'dria] sf hypochondria. **hipocondríaco, -a** sm, sf hypochondriac.

hipocresía [ipokre'sia] sf hypocrisy. **hipócrita** adj hypocritical. **hipócrita** s(m + f) hypocrite.

hipodérmico [ipo'ðermiko] adj hypodermic.

hipopótamo [ipo'potamo] sm hippopotamus.

hipotecar [ipote'kar] v mortgage. **hipoteca** sf mortgage.

hipótesis [i'potesis] sf hypothesis. **hipotético** adj hypothetical.

hirsuto [ir'suto] adj hairy.

hirviente [ir'βjente] adj boiling.

hispánico [is'paniko] adj Hispanic.

hispanoamericano [ispanoameri'kano] s, adj Spanish American.

histerectomía [isterekto'mia] sf hysterectomy.

histeria [i'sterja] sf hysteria. **histérico** adj hysterical.

historia [is'torja] sf history; story; fib; gossip; trouble. **armar historias** (fam) make trouble. **historiador, -a** sm, sf historian. **histórico** adj historical; historic.

hockey sobre hielo sm ice hockey.

hogar [o'gar] sm hearth; home. **hogar de**

acogida *sf* foster home.

hoguera [o'gera] *sf* bonfire.

hoja ['oxa] *sf* leaf; petal; sheet; layer; flake; blade; newspaper; (*formulario*) form. **hoja de afeitar** razor blade. **hoja de cálculo** spreadsheet. **hoja de paga** payroll.

hojalata [oxa'lata] *sf* tinplate; tin.

hojear [oxe'ar] *v* leaf through.

hola ['ola] *interj* hi.

Holanda [o'landa] *sf* Holland. **holandés** *adj* Dutch. **holandés** *sm* Dutchman; (*lengua*) Dutch. **holandesa** *sf* Dutchwoman.

*****holgar** [ol'gar] *v* rest; be idle; be unnecessary. **holgarse** *v* enjoy oneself. **holgazán** *adj* idle. **holgazanear** *v* idle. **holgura** *sf* roominess; comfort.

*****hollar** [o'ʎar] *v* tread; trample down.

hollín [o'ʎin] *sm* soot. **hollimiento** *adj* sooty.

hombre ['ombre] *sm* man. **hombre bueno** arbiter. **hombre de negocios** businessman. **¡hombre!** good heavens, man! **hombrear** *v* act the man.

hombro ['ombro] *sm* (*anat*) shoulder. **echarse al hombro** shoulder.

homenaje [ome'naxe] *sm* homage. **homenajear** *v* pay homage to.

homeópata [ome'opata] *s*(*m* + *f*) homeopath. **homeopático** *adj* homeopathic. **homeopatía** *sf* homeopathy.

homicida [omi'θiða] *s*(*m* + *f*) murderer. *adj* homicidal. **homicidio** *sm* murder.

homogéneo [omo'xeneo] *adj* homogeneous. **homogeneidad** *sf* homogeneity, homogeneousness.

homólogo [o'mologo] *adj* corresponding; synonymous.

honda ['onda] *sf* catapult; sling.

hondo ['ondo] *adj* deep. *sm* bottom. **hondonada** *sf* depression; hollow. **hondura** *sf* depth.

honesto [o'nesto] *adj* honest; modest; chaste. **honestidad** *sf* honesty; modesty; chastity.

hongo ['ongo] *sm* mushroom; bowler hat.

honor [o'nor] *sm* honour. **honorable** *adj* honourable. **honorario** *adj* honorary. **honorario** *sm* honorarium. **honra** *sf* honour; reputation; dignity; respect. **tener a mucha honra** be very proud of. **honradez** *sf* honesty; uprightness. **honrado** *adj* hon-

est; upright. **honrar** *v* honour; be a credit to. **honrarse** *v* be honoured. **honroso** *adj* honourable.

hora ['ora] *sf* hour. **pedir hora** make an appointment. **¿qué hora es?** what time is it? **horario** *adj* hour. **horario** *sm* hours of work; timetable.

horca ['orka] *sf* gallows *pl*; pitchfork. **horcado** *adj* forked.

horda ['rða] *sf* horde.

horizonte [ori'θonte] *sm* horizon. **horizontal** *adj* horizontal.

hormiga [or'miga] *sf* ant; itch. **hormigoso** *adj* ant-eaten; itchy. **hormiguear** *v* swarm; creep; itch. **hormigueo** *sm* itching; swarming. **hormiguero** *sm* anthill; swarm.

hormigón [ormi'gon] *sm* concrete. **hormigón armado** reinforced concrete.

hormona [or'mona] *sf* hormone.

hornero [or'nero], **-a** *sm*, *sf* baker. **hornear** *v* bake. **hornería** *sf* baking.

horno ['orno] *sm* oven; furnace. **horno microondas** *sm* microwave oven. **hornillo** *sm* stove, cooker; gas or electric ring.

horóscopo [o'roskopo] *sm* horoscope.

horquilla [or'kiʎa] *sf* pitchfork; hairpin; rowlock.

horrible [or'riβle] *adj* horrible.

horror [or'ror] *sm* horror. **horrendo** *adj* hideous; horrible. **horrífico** *adj* horrific, horrifying. **horrorizar** *v* horrify. **horroroso** *adj* horrid, horrible.

hortaliza [orta'liθa] *sf* green vegetable. **hortelano, -a** *sm*, *sf* gardener. **hortelano** *adj* market-gardening.

horticultura [ortikul'tura] *sf* horticulture. **hortícola** *adj* horticultural.

hosco ['osko] *adj* grim; surly; gloomy. **hoscoso** *adj* bristly.

hospedar [ospe'ðar] *v* lodge, put up. **hospedarse** *v* have lodgings. **hospedaje** *sf* lodging. **hospedería** *sf* inn, hostelry.

hospicio [os'piθjo] *sm* orphanage; poorhouse.

hospital [ospi'tal] *sm* hospital. **hospitalario** *adj* hospitable. **hospitalidad** *sf* hospitality. **hospitalización** *sf* hospitalization. **hospitalizar** *v* hospitalize.

hostelero [oste'lero], **-a** *sm*, *sf* innkeeper. **hostería** *sf* inn.

hostia ['ostja] *sf* (*rel*) wafer; (*fam*) bashing.

hostigar [osti'gar] *v* whip; harass; molest.

hostigamiento *sm* harassing; molesting; lashing. **hostigo** *sm* lash.

hostil [os'til] *adj* hostile. **hostilidad** *sf* hostility.

hotel [o'tel] *sm* hotel; villa. **hotelería** *sf* hotel-keeping. **hotelero, -a** *sm, sf* hotelkeeper.

hoy [oj] *adv* today; now. **de hoy en adelante** from now on. **hoy en día** nowadays. **hoy por hoy** for the time being.

hoya ['oja] *sf* hole; valley.

hoyo ['ojo] *sm* pit; hole; dent; grave. **hoyuelo** *sm* small hole; dimple.

hoz [oθ] *sf* sickle; ravine.

hueco ['weko] *adj* hollow; empty; vain; resonant. *sm* hollow; gap; cavity; vacancy.

huelga ['welga] *sf* (*de obreros*) strike. **huelguista** *s*(*m + f*) striker.

huelgo ['welgo] *sm* breath; (*tecn*) play.

huella ['weʎa] *sf* footprint; tread; impression. **huella digital** fingerprint. **huella de sonido** soundtrack.

huérfano ['werfano], **-a** *sm, sf* orphan.

huerta ['werta] *sf* vegetable garden; orchard; irrigated land. **huerto** *sm* orchard; kitchen garden.

hueso ['weso] *sm* bone; stone; pip; (*fam*) drudgery. **dar con sus huesos** end up. **estar en los huesos** be very thin. **huesudo** *adj* bony.

huésped ['wespeð], **-a** *sm, sf* guest; lodger **casa de huéspedes** boarding house.

hueva ['weβa] *sf* roe. **huevas** *sf pl* spawn.

huevo ['weβo] *sm* egg. **huevo de Pascua** Easter egg. **huevo duro** hard-boiled egg. **huevo escalfado** poached egg. **huevo frito** fried egg. **huevo pasado por agua** soft-boiled egg. **huevo revuelto** scrambled egg.

*huir [wir] *v* flee. **huida** *sf* flight; escape.

hule¹ ['ule] *sm* oilskin; rubber.

hule² *sm* (*cornada*) goring.

hulla ['uʎa] *sf* coal.

humano [u'mano] *adj* human; humane. *sm* human being. **humanar** *v* humanize. **humanidad** *sf* humanity. **humanismo** *sm* humanism. **humanista** *s*(*m + f*) humanist. **humanitario, -a** *s, adj* humanitarian.

húmedo ['umeðo] *adj* humid, damp, moist, **humedad** *sf* humidity, dampness. **humedecer** *v* dampen, moisten.

humillar [umi'ʎar] *v* humiliate; shame.

humildad *sf* humility. **humilde** *adj* humble. **humillación** *sf* humiliation.

humo ['umo] *sm* smoke; fumes *pl*. **vender humos** boast. **humear** *v* smoke. **humoso** *adj* smoky.

humor [u'mor] *sm* humour; temper; mood. **buen/mal humor** good/bad temper. **humorada** *sf* witticism. **humorista** *s*(*m + f*) humorist. **humorístico** *adj* humorous.

hundir [un'dir] *v* sink; drive in; crush. **hundirse** *v* go under; collapse. **hundimiento** *sm* sinking; collapse.

Hungría [un'gria] *sf* Hungary. **húngaro** *s, adj* Hungarian.

huracán [ura'kan] *sm* hurricane.

hurgar [ur'gar] *v* poke; stir; pick. **hurgón** *sm* poker.

hurón [u'ron] *sm* ferret. **huronear** *v* hunt with a ferret, (*fam*) pry.

hurtadillas [urta'ðiʎas] *adv* **a hurtadillas** slyly, stealthily.

hurtar [ur'tar] *v* steal; remove; cheat. **hurtar el cuerpo** dodge. **hurtador, -a** *sm, sf* thief. **hurto** *sm* theft; thing stolen.

husmear [usme'ar] *v* scent; track; (*fam*) pry; (*fam: carne*) smell high. **husmeo** *sm* scenting; smelling; prying.

huso ['uso] *sm* spindle; (*avión*) fuselage.

I

íbice ['iβiθe] *sm* ibex.

ictericia [ikte'riθja] *sf* jaundice.

ida ['iða] *sf* departure; journey. **idas y venidas** coming and going.

idea [i'ðea] *sf* idea; intention. **tener idea de** intend to. **ideal** *adj* ideal; imaginary. **idealismo** *sm* idealism. **idealista** *s, adj* idealist. **idealizar** *v* idealize. **idear** *v* imagine; plan.

idéntico [i'ðentiko] *adj* identical. **identidad** *sf* identity. **identificación** *sf* identification. **identificar** *v* identify.

ideología [iðeolo'xia] *sf* ideology. **ideológico** *adj* ideological.

idilio [i'ðiljo] *sm* idyll. **idílico** *adj* idyllic.

idioma [i'ðjoma] *sm* language. **idiomático** *adj* idiomatic; linguistic.

idiosincrasia [iðjosin'krasja] *sf* idiosyncrasy. **idiosincrásico** *adj* idiosyncratic.

idiota [i'ðjota] *s(m + f)* idiot. *adj* idiotic. **idiotez** *sf* idiocy. **idiótico** *adj* idiotic.

ídolo ['iðolo] *sm* idol. **idólatra** *s(m + f)* idolater. **idólatra** *adj* idolatrous. **idolatrar** *v* idolize. **idolatría** *sf* idolatry.

idóneo [i'ðoneo] *adj* apt, fit. **idoneidad** *sf* aptness, fitness.

iglesia [i'glesja] *sf* church.

ignición [igni'θjon] *sf* ignition. **ignito** *adj* ignited.

ignominia [igno'minja] *sf* ignominy. **ignominioso** *adj* ignominious.

ignorar [igno'rar] *v* be unaware of; refuse to know. **ignorancia** *sf* ignorance. **ignorante** *adj* ignorant.

igual [i'gwal] *adj* same; equal; even. **por igual** evenly. **es igual** it makes no difference. **igualar** *v* equalize. **igualación** *sf* equalization. **igualdad** *sf* equality.

ijada [i'xaða] *sf* flank. **ijadear** *v* pant.

ilegal [ile'gal] *adj* illegal. **ilegalidad** *sf* illegality.

ilegible [ile'xiβle] *adj* illegible.

ilegítimo [ile'xitimo] *adj* illegitimate. **ilegitimidad** *sf* illegitimacy.

ileso [i'leso] *adj* unharmed.

ilícito [i'liθito] *adj* illicit.

ilógico [i'loxiko] *adj* illogical.

iluminar [ilumi'nar] *v* illuminate, **iluminación** *sf* illumination.

ilusión [ilu'sjon] *sf* illusion; delusion; expectation. **ilusionado** *adj* eager. **ilusionar** *v* fascinate. **ilusionarse** *v* delude oneself; build up hopes. **ilusionismo** *sm* conjuring trick. **ilusionista** *s(m + f)* conjurer. **iluso** *adj* deceived; deluded. **ilusorio** *adj* illusory.

ilustrar [ilu'strar] *v* illustrate. **ilustración** *sf* illustration; enlightenment. **ilustrador, -a** *sm, sf* illustrator.

imaginar [imaxi'nar] *v* imagine. **imagen** *sf* image. **imaginación** *sf* imagination. **imaginario** *adj* imaginary. **imaginativo** *adj* imaginative.

imán [i'man] *sm* magnet **imanar** *v* also **imantar** magnetize. **imantación** *sf* magnetization.

imbécil [im'βeθil] *adj* imbecile. **imbecilidad** *sf* imbecility.

imborrable [imbor'raβle] *adj* unforgettable.

*imbuir [imbu'ir] *v* imbue.

imitar [imi'tar] *v* imitate, copy. **imitable** *adj* imitable. **imitación** *sf* imitation. **imitador, -a** *sm, sf* imitator. **imitativo** *adj* imitative.

impaciente [impa'θjente] *adj* impatient. **impaciencia** *sf* impatience. **impacientarse** *v* become impatient.

impacto [im'pakto] *sm* impact.

impar [im'par] *adj (mat)* odd. **número impar** odd number.

imparcial [impar'θjal] *adj* impartial. **imparcialidad** *sf* impartiality.

impartir [impar'tir] *v* impart.

impasible [impa'siβle] *adj* impassive. **impasibilidad** *sf* impassivity.

impávido [im'paβiðo] *adj* fearless, dauntless. **impavidez** *sf* fearlessness, dauntlessness.

impecable [impe'kaβle] *adj* impeccable. **impecabilidad** *sf* impeccability.

*impedir [impe'ðir] *v* impede; prevent. **impediente** *adj* obstructing. **impedimento** *sm* impediment.

impeler [impe'ler] *v* impel; drive; propel.

impenetrable [impene'traβle] *adj* impenetrable.

impenitente [impeni'tente] *adj* impenitent.

imperar [impe'rar] *v* rule; prevail. **imperativo** *adj* imperative; commanding.

imperceptible [imperθep'tiβle] *adj* imperceptible.

imperdible [imper'ðiβle] *sm* safety pin.

imperdonable [imperðo'naβle] *adj* unforgivable.

imperfecto [imper'fekto] *adj* imperfect. **imperfección** *sf* imperfection.

imperio [im'perjo] *sm* empire. **imperial** *adj* imperial. **imperialismo** *sm* imperialism. **imperialista** *s, adj* imperialist.

impermeable [imperme'aβle] *adj* waterproof. *sm* mackintosh.

impersonal [imperso'nal] *adj* impersonal.

impertinente [imperti'nente] *adj* impertinent. **impertinencia** *sf* impertinence.

imperturbable [impertur'βaβle] *adj* imperturbable. **imperturbabilidad** *sf* imperturbability.

ímpetu ['impetu] *sm* impetus. **impetuosidad** *sf* impetuosity.

impío [im'pio] *adj* godless, impious. **impiedad** *sf* impiety.

implacable [impla'kaβle] *adj* implacable. **implacabilidad** *sf* implacability.

implantar [implan'tar] *v* implant.

implicar [impli'kar] *v* imply; implicate; entail. **implicación** *sf* implication; contradiction. **implicatorio** *adj* contradictory.

implícito [im'pliθito] *adj* implicit.

implorar [implo'rar] *v* implore, beg. **imploración** *sf* entreaty.

*imponer [impo'ner] *v* impose; inflict; acquaint; inspire; deposit; impute falsely. **imponerse** *v* dominate. **imponente** *adj* imposing; striking; (*fam*) sensational, smashing.

impopular [impopu'lar] *adj* unpopular. **impopularidad** *sf* unpopularity.

importante [impor'tante] *adj* important. **importancia** *sf* importance. **importar** *v* matter, concern. **no importa** it doesn't matter.

importunar [importu'nar] *v* importune, pester. **importunidad** *sf* importunity. **importuno** *adj* importunate, pestering.

imposible [impo'siβle] *adj* impossible. **imposibilidad** *sf* impossibility. **imposibilitar** *v* make impossible.

imposición [imposi'θjon] *sf* imposition; tax.

impostor [impos'tor], **-a** *sm, sf* impostor.

impotente [impo'tente] *adj* impotent; powerless. **impotencia** *sf* impotence.

impracticable [imprakti'kaβle] *adj* impracticable.

imprecar [impre'kar] *v* curse. **imprecación** *sf* curse. **imprecatorio** *adj* abusive.

impreciso [impre'θiso] *adj* imprecise. **imprecisión** *sf* imprecision.

impregnar [impreg'nar] *v* impregnate; saturate. **impregnable** *adj* absorbent. **impregnación** *sf* impregnation.

imprescindible [impresθin'diβle] *adj* indispensable.

impreso [im'preso] *adj* printed. **imprenta** *sf* press; printing. **impresión** *sf* impression; imprint; stamp; print; printing; edition. **impresionable** *adj* impressionable. **impresionar** *v* impress; shock. **impresionarse** *v* be deeply moved. **impresionismo** *sm* impressionism. **impresionista** *s(m + f)* impressionist. **impresor** *sm* printer.

impresora *sf* printer (computer). **impresora con láser** *sf* laser printer.

imprevisto [impre'βisto] *adj* unexpected.

imprimir [impri'mir] *v* print; implant.

improbable [impro'βaβle] *adj* improbable. **improbabilidad** *sf* improbability.

ímprobo ['improβo] *adj* wicked; arduous. **improbidad** *sf* dishonesty.

improcedente [improθe'ðente] *adj* improper; inappropriate; (*jur*) inadmissible. **improcedencia** *sf* impropriety; inappropriateness; (*jur*) inadmissibility.

improductivo [improduk'tiβo] *adj* unproductive.

impropio [im'propjo] *adj* improper; unbecoming. **impropiedad** *sf* impropriety.

imprévido [im'proβiðo] *adj* improvident. **improvidencia** *sf* improvidence.

improvisar [improβi'sar] *v* improvise. **improvisación** *sf* improvisation.

improvisto [improβ'βisto] *adj* unforeseen. **a la improvista** without warning.

imprudente [impru'ðente] *adj* imprudent. **imprudencia** *sf* imprudence.

impúdico [im'puðiko] *adj* shameless, immodest.

impuesto [im'pwesto] *sm* tax; duty. **impuesto sobre el valor añadido (IVA)** *sm* value-added-tax (VAT).

impugnar [impug'nar] *v* impugn; oppose; refute.

impulsar [impul'sar] *v* impel; drive; move. **impulsión** *sf* impulse; impetus. **impulso** *sm* impulse; drive; momentum.

impune [im'pune] *adj* unpunished. **impunidad** *sf* impunity.

impuro [im'puro] *adj* impure; lewd. **impureza** *sf* impurity; lewdness. **impurificación** *sf* defilement. **impurificar** *v* defile.

imputar [impu'tar] *v* impute; ascribe. **imputable** *adj* chargeable. **imputación** *sf* imputation; accusation.

inacabable [inaka'βaβle] *adj* endless.

inaccesible [inakθe'siβle] *adj* inaccessible. **inaccesibilidad** *sf* inaccessibility.

inaceptable [inaθep'taβle] *adj* unacceptable.

inacostumbrado [inakostum'braðo] *adj* unaccustomed.

inactivo [inak'tiβo] *adj* inactive. **inactividad** *sf* inactivity.

inadecuado [inaðe'kwaðo] *adj* inadequate.

inadecuación *sf* inadequacy.

inadmisible [inaðmi'siβle] *adj* inadmissible.

inadvertido [inaðβer'tiðo] *adj* inadvertent. **inadvertencia** *sf* inadvertence, carelessness.

inagotable [inago'taβle] *adj* inexhaustible.

inaguantable [inagwan'taβle] *adj* unbearable.

inajenable [inaxe'naβle] *adj* inalienable.

inalterable [inalte'raβle] *adj* unalterable; imperturbable. **inalterabilidad** *sf* immutability; imperturbability. **inalterado** *adj* unchanged.

inanición [inani'θjon] *sf* starvation; weakness; exhaustion.

inanimado [inani'maðo] *adj* inanimate, lifeless.

inapagable [inapa'gaβle] *adj* unquenchable.

inaplicable [inapli'kaβle] *adj* inapplicable. **inaplicado** *adj* indolent.

inapreciable [inapre'θjaβle] *adj* priceless; invaluable.

inapto [in'apto] *adj* unsuitable; incapable.

inasequible [inase'kiβle] *adj* unattainable.

inaudible [inau'ðiβle] *adj* inaudible.

inaudito [inau'ðito] *adj* unheard of; outrageous.

inaugurar [inaugu'rar] *v* inaugurate. **inauguración** *sf* inauguration.

incalculable [inkalku'laβle] *adj* incalculable.

incandescente [inkandes'θente] *adj* incandescent. **incandescencia** *sf* incandescence.

incansable [inkan'saβle] *adj* indefatigable, untiring.

incapacitar [inkapaθi'tar] *v* incapacitate; disable; disqualify. **incapacidad** *sf* incapacity; incompetence; disability. **incapaz** *adj* unfit; incapable.

incautarse [inkau'tarse] *v* (*jur*) confiscate. **incautación** *sf* confiscation.

incauto [in'kauto] *adj* incautious; gullible.

incendiar [inθen'djar] *v* set on fire. **incendiarse** *v* catch fire. **incendiario, -a** *sm, sf* arsonist. **incendiario** *adj* incendiary. **incendio** *sm* fire. **incendio provocado** arson.

incentivo [inθen'tiβo] *sm* incentive. **incentivar** *v* incite.

incertidumbre [inθerti'ðumbre] *sf* uncertainty.

incesante [inθe'sante] *adj* incessant.

incesto [in'θesto] *sm* incest. **incestuoso** *adj* incestuous.

incidente [inθi'ðente] *sm* incident. *adj* incidental. **incidencia** *sf* incident; incidence. **incidental** *adj* incidental.

incienso [in'θjenso] *sm* incense.

incierto [in'θjerto] *adj* uncertain; untrue.

incinerar [inθine'rar] *v* incinerate; cremate. **incineración** *sf* incineration; cremation.

incipiente [inθi'pjente] *adj* incipient.

incisivo [inθi'siβo] *adj* incisive; cutting. *sm* (*diente*) incisor. **incisión** *sf* incision, cut. **inciso** *adj* cut.

incitar [inθi'tar] *v* incite; instigate. **incitación** *sf* incitement; enticement. **incitador, -a** *sm, sf* instigator.

incivil [inθi'βil] *adj* uncivil, impolite.

inclemente [inkle'mente] *adj* inclement; harsh. **inclemencia** *sf* inclemency; harshness.

inclinar [inkli'nar] *v* incline; lean; influence; induce; lower. **inclinarse** *v* feel disposed; bow; stoop. **inclinación** *sf* inclination; leaning; slope; dip. **inclinado** *adj* inclined; sloping.

*****incluir** [inklu'ir] *v* include. **inclusión** *sf* inclusion. **inclusivo** *adj* inclusive. **incluso** *adj* included; enclosed. **incluso** *adv* even.

incógnito [in'kognito] *adj* unknown. **de incógnito** incognito.

incoherente [inkoe'rente] *adj* incoherent. **incoherencia** *sf* incoherence.

incoloro [inko'loro] *adj* colourless.

incombustible [inkombus'tiβle] *adj* incombustible, fireproof.

incomodar [inkomo'ðar] *v* disturb, annoy, molest. **incomodidad** *sf* inconvenience; discomfort. **incómodo** *adj* uncomfortable; annoying.

incomparable [inkompa'raβle] *adj* incomparable.

incompatible [inkompa'tiβle] *adj* incompatible. **incompatibilidad** *sf* incompatibility.

incompetente [inkompe'tente] *adj* incompetent. **incompetencia** *sf* incompetence.

incompleto [inkom'pleto] *adj* incomplete. **incompletamente** *adv* incompletely.

incomprensible [inkompren'siβle] *adj* incomprehensible. **incomprensibilidad** *sf*

incomprehensibility. **incomprensión** *sf*
lack of understanding.

incomunicado [inkomuni'kaðo] *adj* isolated. **incomunicable** *adj* incommunicable. **incomunicación** *sf* isolation. **incomunicar** *v* isolate.

inconcebible [inkonθe'β iβle] *adj* inconceivable.

inconcluso [inkon'kluso] *adj* unfinished; inconclusive.

incondicional [inkondiθjo'nal] *adj* unconditional. *s(m + f)* staunch supporter.

inconfundible [inkonfun'diβle] *adj* unmistakable.

incongruente [inkongru'ente] *adj* incongruous; incongruent. **incongruencia** *sf* incongruousness; incongruity.

inconmensurable [inkonmensu'raβle] *adj* immeasurable.

inconmovible [inkonmo'βiβle] *adj* unshakable; firm.

inconsciente [inkons'θjente] *adj* unconscious; unaware; thoughtless. **inconsciencia** *sf* unconsciousness; unawareness; thoughtlessness.

inconsecuente [inkonse'kwente] *adj* inconsequential; inconsistent. **inconsecuencia** *sf* inconsistency.

inconsiderado [inkonsiðe'raðo] *adj* illconsidered. **inconsideración** *sf* inconsiderateness.

inconstante [inkon'stante] *adj* inconstant, fickle. **inconstancia** *sf* inconstancy, fickleness.

incontable [inkon'taβle] *adj* innumerable.

incontestable [inkontes'taβle] *adj* incontestable, indisputable.

incontinente [inkonti'nente] *adj* incontinent. **incontinencia** *sf* incontinence.

inconveniente [inkonβe'njente] *adj* inconvenient, impolite. *sm* objection; trouble; obstacle. **inconveniencia** *sf* inconvenience; impropriety; unsuitability.

incorporar [inkorpo'rar] *v* incorporate. **incorporarse** *v* sit up; become a member. **incorporación** *sf* incorporation. **incorporado** *adj* incorporated.

incorrecto [inkor'rekto] *adj* incorrect. **incorrección** *sf* inaccuracy. **incorregibilidad** *sf* incorrigibility. **incorregible** *adj* incorrigible.

incorrupto [inkor'rupto] *adj* incorrupt,

pure. **incorruptible** *adj* incorruptible.

incrédulo [in'kreðulo] *adj* incredulous, sceptical. **incredulidad** *sf* incredulity, scepticism. **increíble** *adj* incredible.

incremento [inkre'mento] *sm* increase.

increpar [inkre'par] *v* reproach; rebuke. **increpación** *sf* rebuke.

incriminar [inkrimi'nar] *v* incriminate; exaggerate. **incriminación** *sf* incrimination.

incrustar [inkrus'tar] *v* encrust. **incrustación** *sf* encrustation.

incubar [inku'βar] *v* incubate; (*med*) be sickening for. **incubación** *sf* incubation. **incubadora** *sf* incubator.

inculcar [inkul'kar] *v* inculcate. **inculcarse** *v* be obstinate. **inculcación** *sf* inculcation.

inculpable [inkul'paβle] *adj* blameless. **inculpabilidad** *sf* blamelessness.

inculto [in'kulto] *adj* uncouth; uneducated. **incultura** *sf* lack of culture.

incumbencia [inkum'benθja] *sf* responsibility, duty. **incumbir** *v* be incumbent upon.

incurable [inku'raβle] *adj* incurable.

incurrir [inkur'rir] *v* incur; fall; commit.

incursión [inkur'sjon] *sf* incursion, raid.

indagar [inda'gar] *v* investigate. **indagación** *sf* investigation. **indagador, -a** *sm, sf* investigator.

indebido [inde'βiðo] *adj* unjust; improper.

indecente [inde'θente] *adj* indecent; foul; wretched. **indecencia** *sf* indecency; obscenity.

indecible [inde'θiβle] *adj* indescribable; unspeakable.

indecisión [inde'θisjon] *sf* indecision. **indeciso** *adj* indecisive.

indecoroso [indeco'roso] *adj* indecorous. **indecoro** *sm* lack of propriety.

indefectible [indefek'tiβle] *adj* unfailing.

indefenso [inde'fenso] *adj* defenceless. **indefendible** *adj* indefensible.

indefinible [indefi'niβle] *adj* indefinable. **indefinido** *adj* indefinite.

indeleble [inde'leβle] *adj* indelible.

indelicado [indeli'kaðo] *adj* indelicate. **indelicadeza** *sf* indelicacy.

indemne [in'demne] *adj* unhurt. **indemnidad** *sf* indemnity. **indemnización** *sf* compensation. **indemnizar** *v* indemnify, compensate.

independencia [indepen'denθja] *sf* independence. **independiente** *adj* independent.

indescifrable [indeθi'fraβle] *adj* indecipherable.

indescriptible [indescrip'tiβle] *adj* indescribable.

indeseable [indese'aβle] *adj* undesirable.

indestructible [indestruk'tiβle] *adj* indestructible. **indestructibilidad** *sf* indestructibility.

indeterminado [indetermi'naðo] *adj* indeterminate; undetermined.

India ['indja] *sf* India. **indio, -a** *s, adj* Indian.

indicar [indi'kar] *v* indicate; show; suggest. **indicación** *sf* indication. **indicado** *adj* suitable; recommended. **indicador** *sm* pointer; gauge. **indicativo** *adj* indicative. *sm* (*gram*) indicative.

índice ['indiθe] *sm* index.

indicio [in'diθjo] *sm* sign; trace. **indicios** *sm pl* (*jur*) evidence *sing*.

indiferencia [indife'renθja] *sf* indifference. **indiferente** *adj* indifferent.

indígena [in'dixena] *s(m + f)*, *adj* native.

indigestión [indixes'tjon] *sf* indigestion. **indigestible** *adj* indigestible.

indignar [indig'nar] *v* anger, annoy. **indignarse** *v* become indignant. **indignación** *sf* indignation. **indignidad** *sf* indignity. **indigno** *adj* unworthy; disgraceful.

indirecta [indi'rekta] *sf* innuendo. **indirecto** *adj* indirect.

indisciplina [indisθi'plina] *sf* indiscipline. **indisciplinado** *adj* undisciplined.

indiscreción [indiskre'θjon] *sf* indiscretion. **indiscreto** *adj* indiscreet.

indisculpable [indiskul'paβle] *adj* inexcusable.

indiscutible [indisku'tiβle] *adj* unquestionable.

indisoluble [indiso'luβle] *adj* indissoluble.

indispensable [indispen'saβle] *adj* indispensable.

*indisponer [indispo'ner] *v* upset; render unfit. **indisponerse** *v* become ill. **indisposición** *sf* indisposition. **indispuesto** *adj* indisposed, poorly.

indisputable [indispu'taβle] *adj* indisputable.

indistinto [indis'tinto] *adj* indistinct; vague.

individual [indiβi'ðwal] *adj* individual. **individualidad** *sf* individuality. **individualismo** *sm* individualism. **individualista** *s(m + f)* individualist. **individualizar** *v* individualize. **individuo, -a** *sm, sf* individual.

indivisible [indiβi'siβle] *adj* indivisible. **indiviso** *adj* undivided.

índole ['indole] *sf* nature.

indolente [indo'lente] *adj* indolent; painless. **indolencia** *sf* indolence; painlessness.

indómito [in'domito] *adj* untamed; indomitable.

indubitable [induβi'taβle] *adj* indubitable.

*inducir [indu'θir] *v* persuade; lead; infer. **inducción** *sf* induction. **inducimiento** *sm* inducement.

indudable [indu'ðaβle] *adj* unquestionable.

indulgente [indul'xente] *adj* indulgent. **indulgencia** *sf* indulgence.

indultar [indul'tar] *v* pardon; excuse. **indulto** *sm* mercy; reprieve; exemption.

indumento [indu'mento] *sm* apparel.

industria [in'dustrja] *sf* industry; business; ingenuity. **de industria** on purpose. **industrial** *adj* industrial. **industrial** *sm* industrialist. **industrialismo** *sm* industrialism. **industrializar** *v* industrialize. **industrioso** *adj* industrious.

inédito [i'neðito] *adj* unpublished.

inefable [ine'faβle] *adj* ineffable.

ineficaz [inefi'kaθ] *adj* inefficient. **ineficacia** *sf* inefficiency.

ineludible [inelu'ðiβle] *adj* inevitable.

inepto [i'nepto] *adj* inept. **ineptitud** *sf* ineptitude.

inequívoco [ine'kiβoko] *adj* unmistakable.

inercia [i'nerθja] *sf* inertia; lifelessness.

inerme [i'nerme] *adj* unarmed.

inerte [i'nerte] *adj* inert.

inesperado [inespe'raðo] *adj* unexpected, unforeseen.

inestable [ines'taβle] *adj* unstable. **inestabilidad** *sf* instability.

inestimable [inesti'maβle] *adj* invaluable.

inevitable [ineβi'taβle] *adj* inevitable.

inexacto [inek'sakto] *adj* inaccurate. **inexactitud** *sf* inaccuracy.

inexcusable [ineksku'saβle] *adj* inexcusable; essential.

inexorable [inekso'raβle] *adj* inexorable.

inexperto [ineks'perto] *adj* inexperienced.

inexplicable [inekspli'kaβle] *adj* inexplicable.

infalible [infa'liβle] *adj* infallible. **infalibilidad** *sf* infallibility.

infamar [infa'mar] *v* dishonour. **infamación** *sf* defamation. **infame** *adj* infamous. **infamia** *sf* infamy.

infante [in'fante] *sm, adj* infant. *sm* prince. **infancia** *sf* infancy. **infantil** *adj* infantile.

infantería [infante'ria] *sf* infantry.

infatigable [infati'gaβle] *adj* indefatigable.

infausto [in'fausto] *adj* ill-omened; ill-famed.

infectar [infek'tar] *v* infect. **infección** *sf* infection. **infeccioso** *adj* infectious.

infeliz [infe'liθ] *adj* unhappy. *s(m + f)* luckless person.

inferior [infe'rjor] *adj* inferior; lower. *sm* inferior. **inferioridad** *sf* inferiority.

***inferir** [infe'rir] *v* infer; inflict. **inferirse** *v* follow.

infernal [infer'nal] *adj* infernal.

infértil [in'fertil] *adj* infertile.

infestar [infes'tar] *v* infest; overrun. **infestación** *sf* infestation.

infiel [in'fjel] *adj* unfaithful. *s(m + f)* infidel.

infierno [in'fjerno] *sm* hell.

ínfimo [ˈinfimo] *adj* lowest; vilest.

infinito [infiˈnito] *adj* infinite. **infinidad** *sf* infinity. **infinitivo** *sm* (*gram*) infinitive.

inflamar [inflaˈmar] *v* inflame. **inflamable** *adj* inflammable. **inflamación** *sf* inflammation.

inflar [inˈflar] *v* inflate. **inflable** *adj* inflatable. **inflación** *sf* inflation; swelling.

inflexible [inflekˈsiβle] *adj* inflexible. **inflexibilidad** *sf* inflexibility.

infligir [infliˈxir] *v* inflict.

***influir** [influˈir] *v* influence; affect. **influencia** *sf* influence; authority. **influente** *adj* *also* **influyente** influential. **influjo** *sm* influence; flood.

informal [inforˈmal] *adj* informal; unreliable. **informalidad** *sf* informality; unreliability.

informar [inforˈmar] *v* inform; notify. **informarse** *v* find out. **información** *sf*
information; judicial inquiry. **información tecnológica** *sf* information technology. **informador, -a** *sm, sf* informant. **informe** *sm* report; testimonial. **informe** *adj* shapeless.

informática [inforˈmatika] *sf* IT.

infortunio [inforˈtunjo] *sm* misfortune. **infortunado** *adj* unfortunate.

infracción [infrakˈθjon] *sf* breach; infringement. **infractor, -a** *sm, sf* transgressor.

infranqueable [infrankeˈaβle] *adj* impassable; insurmountable.

infringir [infrinˈxir] *v* infringe; violate.

infructuoso [infrukˈtwoso] *adj* fruitless.

infundado [infunˈdaðo] *adj* unfounded.

infundir [infunˈdir] *v* instil. **infusión** *sf* inspiration.

ingeniería [inxenjeˈria] *sf* engineering. **ingeniero** *sm* engineer.

ingenio [inˈxenjo] *sm* talent; wit; ingenuity; device. **ingeniosidad** *sf* ingenuity. **ingenioso** *adj* ingenious; inventive.

ingenuo [inˈxenwo] *adj* naïve; frank; simple. **ingenuidad** *sf* frankness; credulity.

***ingerir** [inxeˈrir] *v* (*comida*) consume. **ingerirse** *v* meddle. **ingerencia** *sf* interference.

Inglaterra [inglaˈterra] *sf* England. **inglés** *adj* English; *sm* Englishman; (*idioma*) English. **inglesa** *sf* Englishwoman.

ingrato [inˈgrato] *adj* ungrateful; unpleasant. **ingratitud** *sf* ingratitude.

ingrediente [ingreˈðjente] *sm* ingredient.

ingresar [ingreˈsar] *v* enter; join; (*hospital*) be admitted; (*dinero*) deposit. **ingreso** *sm* entrance; (*com*) deposit; admission. **derecho de ingreso** *sm* entrance fee.

inhábil [iˈnaβil] *adj* incompetent; tactless. **día inhábil** non-working day. **inhabilidad** *sf* incompetence; inability. **inhabilitar** *v* disqualify; disable.

inhabitable [inaβiˈtaβle] *adj* uninhabitable. **inhabitado** *adj* uninhabited.

inhalar [inaˈlar] *v* inhale. **inhalación** *sf* inhalation. **inhalador** *sm* inhaler.

inherente [ineˈrente] *adj* inherent. **inherencia** *sf* inherence.

inhibir [iniˈβir] *v* inhibit. **inhibirse** *v* refrain. **inhibición** *sf* inhibition. **inhibitorio** *adj* inhibitive.

inhospitalario [inospitaˈlarjo] *adj* inhospitable. **inhospitalidad** *sf* inhospitableness.

inhumano [inu'mano] *adj* inhuman. **inhumanidad** *sf* inhumanity.

inhumar [inu'mar] *v* bury.

inicial [ini'θjal] *adj*, *sf* initial. **iniciación** *sf* initiation. **iniciado, -a** *sm*, *sf* initiate. **iniciador, -a** *sm*, *sf* initiator. **iniciar** *v* initiate; (*computadora*) boot up. **iniciativa** *sf* initiative.

inicuo [i'nikwo] *adj* wicked. **iniquidad** *sf* iniquity.

injertar [inxer'tar] *v* graft. **injerto** *sm* graft, grafting.

injuriar [inxuri'ar] *v* insult; damage; injure. **injuria** *sf* offence; harm. **injuriador** *adj* offensive. **injurioso** *adj* insulting.

injusticia [inxus'tiθja] *sf* injustice. **injusto** *adj* unjust.

inmediato [inme'ðjato] *adj* immediate. **de inmediato** immediately.

inmejorable [inmexo'raβle] *adj* unsurpassable.

inmemorial [inmemo'rjal] *adj* immemorial.

inmenso [in'menso] *adj* immense.

inmerecido [inmere'θiðo] *adj* undeserved.

inmigrar [inmi'grar] *v* immigrate. **inmigración** *sf* immigration. **inmigrante** *s*(*m + f*), *adj* immigrant.

inminente [inmi'nente] *adj* imminent. **inminencia** *sf* imminence.

inmoderado [inmoðe'raðo] *adj* excessive. **inmoderación** *sf* excess.

inmodestia [inmodes'tia] *sf* immodesty. **inmodesto** *adj* immodest.

inmolar [inmo'lar] *v* sacrifice. **inmolación** *sf* sacrifice.

inmoral [inmo'ral] *adj* immoral. **inmoralidad** *sf* immorality.

inmortal [inmor'tal] *adj*, *s*(*m + f*) immortal. **inmortalidad** *sf* immortality. **inmortalizar** *v* immortalize.

inmóvil [in'moβil] *adj* motionless. **inmovible** *adj* immovable. **inmovilidad** *sf* immobility. **inmovilizador** *sm* immobilizer. **inmovilizar** *v* immobilize.

inmueble [in'mweβle] *sm* property; real estate.

inmundo [in'mundo] *adj* filthy; impure. **inmundicia** *sf* filth; impurity.

inmune [in'mune] *adj* immune; exempt. **inmunidad** *sf* immunity; exemption. **inmunización** *sf* immunization. **inmunizar** *v* immunize.

inmutar [inmu'tar] *v* change. **inmutarse** *v* change one's expression. **inmutabilidad** *sf* immutability. **inmutable** *adj* immutable.

innato [in'nato] *adj* innate.

innecesario [inneθe'sarjo] *adj* unnecessary.

innegable [in'negaβle] *adj* undeniable.

innoble [in'noβle] *adj* ignoble.

innocuo [in'nokwo] *adj also* **inocuo** innocuous.

innovar [inno'βar] *v* innovate. **innovación** *sf* innovation. **innovador, -a** *sm*, *sf* innovator. **innovador** *adj* innovative. **innovamiento** *sm* innovation.

innumerable [innume'raβle] *adj* innumerable.

inobediente [inoβe'ðjente] *adj* disobedient. **inobediencia** *sf* disobedience.

inocente [ino'θente] *adj* innocent. **inocencia** *sf* innocence.

inocular [inoku'lar] *v* inoculate; contaminate. **inoculación** *sf* inoculation.

inodoro [ino'ðoro] *adj* odourless.

inofensivo [inofen'siβo] *adj* harmless.

inolvidable [inolβi'ðaβle] *adj* unforgettable.

inoperable [inope'raβle] *adj* inoperable.

inopinado [inopi'naðo] *adj* unexpected.

inoportuno [inopor'tuno] *adj* inopportune.

inoxidable [inoksi'ðaβle] *adj* rustless; stainless. **acero inoxidable** *sm* stainless steel.

inquebrantable [inkeβran'taβle] *adj* unbreakable; unyielding.

inquietar [inkje'tar] *v* disturb; disquiet. **inquietador** *adj* disquieting. **inquietante** *adj* disquieting. **inquieto** *adj* restless. **inquietud** *sf* restlessness.

inquilino [inki'lino], **-a** *sm*, *sf* tenant, **inquilinato** *sm* lease.

__*inquirir__ [inki'rir] *v* investigate; examine.

inquiridor , **-a** *sm*, *sf* inquirer. **inquisición** *sf* inquisition; inquiry. **inquisidor** *sm* inquisitor. **inquisitivo** *adj* inquisitive.

insaciable [insa'θjaβle] *adj* insatiable.

insalubre [insa'luβre] *adj* unhealthy. **insalubridad** *sf* unhealthiness.

insanable [insa'naβle] *adj* incurable.

insano [in'sano] *adj* insane; unhealthy. **insania** *sf* insanity.

inscribir [inskri'βir] *v* inscribe; register. **inscripción** *sf* inscription; registration.

insecto [in'sekto] *sm* insect. **insecticida** *sm* insecticide. **insectólogo, -a** *sm, sf* entomologist.

inseguro [inse'guro] *adj* insecure; unsafe; uncertain. **inseguridad** *sf* insecurity; uncertainty.

insensato [insen'sato] *adj* senseless; wild. **insensatez** *sf* folly.

insensible [insen'siβle] *adj* insensible; insensitive; imperceptible. **insensibilidad** *sf* insensibility; insensitiveness.

insertar [inser'tar] *v* insert. **inserto** *sm* insertion.

inservible [inser'βiβle] *adj* useless.

insidioso [insi'ðjoso] *adj* insidious.

insigne [in'signe] *adj* illustrious, distinguished.

insignia [in'signja] *sf* badge; banner. **insignias** *sf pl* insignia.

insignificante [insiɣnifi'kante] *adj* insignificant. **insignificancia** *sf* insignificance.

insincero [insin'θero] *adj* insincere. **insinceridad** *sf* insincerity.

insinuar [insinu'ar] *v* insinuate, suggest. **insinuarse** *v* work one's way (into); make advances. **insinuación** *sf* insinuation; suggestiveness. **insinuante** *adj* insinuating; suggestive.

insípido [in'sipiðo] *adj* insipid, tasteless. **insipidez** *sf* tastelessness.

insistir [insis'tir] *v* insist; persist. **insistencia** *sf* insistence; persistence. **insistente** *adj* insistent; persistent.

insociable [inso'θjaβle] *adj* unsociable. **insociabilidad** *sf* unsociability, unsociableness.

insolación [insola'θjon] *sf* sunstroke. **insolar** *v* expose to the sun. **insolarse** *v* get sunstroke.

insolente [inso'lente] *adj* insolent. **insolencia** *sf* insolence.

insólito [in'solito] *adj* unusual.

insolvente [insol'βente] *adj* insolvent, penniless. **insoluble** *adj* insoluble. **insolvencia** *sf* insolvency.

insomne [in'somne] *s(m + f)*, *adj* insomniac. **insomnio** *sm* insomnia.

insondable [inson'daβle] *adj* unfathomable.

insoportable [insopor'taβle] *adj* intolerable.

inspeccionar [inspekθjo'nar] *v* inspect.

inspección *sf* inspection. **inspector, -a** *sm, sf* inspector.

inspirar [inspi'rar] *v* inhale; inspire. **inspiración** *sf* inhalation; inspiration. **inspirador** *adj* inspirational.

instable [in'staβle] *adj* unstable. **instabilidad** *sf* instability.

instalar [insta'lar] *v* install; establish. **instalación** *sf* installation; (*fábrica*) plant **instalador** *sm* fitter.

instancia [instan'θja] *sf* petition; application form.

instante [in'stante] *sm* instant; moment. *adj* insistent. **instantánea** *sf* snapshot. **instantáneo** *adj* instantaneous. **instantemente** *adv* insistently.

instaurar [instau'rar] *v* set up; restore. **instauración** *sf* restoration. **instaurativo** *adj* restorative.

instigar [insti'gar] *v* instigate; incite. **instigación** *sf* instigation. **instigador, -a** *sm, sf* instigator.

instintivo [instin'tiβo] *adj* instinctive. **instinto** *sm* instinct.

*****instituir** [institu'ir] *v* institute. **institución** *sf* institution. **instituto** *sm* institute; state secondary school.

*****instruir** [instru'ir] *v* instruct. **instrucción** *sf* instruction; education; knowledge. **instructivo** *adj* instructive. **instructor, -a** *sm, sf* instructor. **instruido** *adj* educated.

instrumento [instru'mento] *sm* instrument. **instrumentación** *sf* orchestration. **instrumental** *adj* instrumental. **instrumentar** *v* orchestrate. **instrumentista** *s(m + f)* instrumentalist; instrument-maker.

insubordinar [insuβorði'nar] *v* incite to rebellion. **insubordinarse** *v* rebel. **insubordinación** *sf* insubordination. **insubordinado** *adj* insubordinate.

insubstancial [insuβstan'θjal] *adj* insubstantial.

insuficiente [insufi'θjente] *adj* insufficient; inadequate. **insuficiencia** *sf* insufficiency; inadequacy.

insufrible [insu'friβle] *adj* insufferable.

insular [insu'lar] *adj* insular.

insulso [in'sulso] *adj* dull; tasteless. **insulsez** *sf* tastelessness.

insultar [insul'tar] *v* insult. **insultador** *adj also* **insultante** insulting. **insulto** *sm* insult.

insuperable [insupe'raβle] *adj* insuperable.

insurgente [insur'xente] *s(m + f)* rebel. *adj* rebellious. **insurrección** *sf* rebellion. **insurreccionarse** *v* rebel. **insurrecto, -a** *s, adj* insurgent.

intacto [in'takto] *adj* intact.

intachable [inta'tʃaβle] *adj* irreproachable.

intangible [intan'xiβle] *adj* intangible. **intangibilidad** *sf* intangibility.

integrar [inte'grar] *v* integrate; compose; complete; repay. **integración** *sf* integration. **integral** *adj* integral. **pan integral** *sm* wholemeal bread. **integrante** *adj* integral. **integridad** *sf* integrity. **íntegro** *adj* entire, whole.

intelecto [inte'lekto] *sm* intellect. **intelectual** *s(m + f), adj* intellectual. **intelectualidad** *sf* intelligentsia. **intelectualismo** *sm* intellectualism.

inteligente [inteli'xente] *adj* intelligent. **inteligencia** *sf* intelligence; knowledge; comprehension. **inteligibilidad** *sf* intelligibility. **inteligible** *adj* intelligible.

intemperante [intempe'rante] *adj* intemperate. **intemperancia** *sf* intemperance.

intemperie [intem'perje] *sf* bad weather. **estar a la intemperie** be out in the open.

intempestivo [intempes'tiβo] *adj* inopportune.

intención [inten'θjon] *sf* intention. **primera intención** frankness. **segunda intención** duplicity. **intencionadamente** *adv* deliberately. **intencionado** *adj* deliberate. **intencional** *adj* intentional.

intenso [in'tenso] *adj* intense. **intensidad** *sf* intensity. **intensificar** *v* intensify. **intensión** *sf* intensity. **intensivo** *adj* intensive.

intentar [inten'tar] *v* try. **intento** *sm* attempt.

interactivo [interak'tiβo] *adj* interactive.

intercalar [interka'lar] *v* insert.

intercambio [inter'kambjo] *sm* interchange. **intercambiar** *v* interchange, exchange. **intercambiable** *adj* interchangeable.

interceder [interθe'ðer] *v* intercede. **intercesión** *sf* intercession.

interceptar [interθep'tar] *v* intercept; block. **intercepción** *sf* interception.

interdecir [interðe'θir] *v* prohibit. **interdicción** *sf also* **interdicto** *sm* prohibition.

interesante [intere'sante] *adj* interesting.

interesar [intere'sar] *v* interest. **interés** *sm* interest. **llevar interés** bear interest. **interesante** *adj* interesting.

*interferir [interfe'rir] *v* interfere. **interferencia** *sf* interference.

ínterin ['interin] *sm* interim. **interino** *adj* provisional; acting.

interior [inte'rjor] *adj* interior; internal; inner; home. *sm* interior; inside; inland.

interjección [interxek'θjon] *sf* interjection.

intermedio [inter'meðjo] *sm* interval; interlude. *adj* intermediate. **intermediar** *v* mediate. **intermediario, -a** *s, adj* intermediary.

interminable [intermi'naβle] *adj* interminable.

intermisión [intermi'sjon] *sf* intermission.

intermitente [intermi'tente] *adj* intermittent.

internacional [internaθjo'nal] *adj* international. **internacionalismo** *sm* internationalism. **internacionalista** *s(m + f)* internationalist.

internar [inter'nar] *v* intern; confine. **internarse** *v* penetrate; intrude. **internamiento** *sm* internment. **interno** *adj* internal; domestic. **escuela interna** *sf* boarding school.

internet [inter'net] *sm* Internet. **servidor de internet** Internet service provider.

interpelar [interpe'lar] *v* appeal to, implore. **interpelación** *sf* appeal.

*interponer [interpo'ner] *v* interpose. **interponerse** *v* intervene. **interposición** *sf* intervention; *(jur)* lodging of an appeal.

interpretar [interpre'tar] *v* interpret. **interpretación** *sf* interpretation. **intérprete** *s(m + f)* interpreter.

interrogar [interro'gar] *v* question. **interrogación** *sf* question; question mark. **interrogativo** *adj* interrogative. **interrogatorio** *sm* interrogation.

interrumpir [interrum'pir] *v* interrupt. **interrupción** *sf* interruption. **interruptor** *sm* electrical switch.

intervalo [inter'βalo] *sm* interval; gap.

*intervenir [interβe'nir] *v* intervene; interfere; participate; happen; control; *(med)* operate on; *(com)* audit. **intervención** *sf* intervention; control; operation; audit. **interventor** *sm* auditor; inspector; supervisor.

intestado [intes'taðo] *adj* intestate.

intestino [intes'tino] *adj* internal. *sm* intestine. **intestinal** *adj* intestinal.

intimar [inti'mar] *v* intimate; become close friends. **intimación** *sf* declaration. **intimidad** *sf* intimacy. **en la intimidad** privately. **íntimo** *adj* intimate.

intimidar [intimi'ðar] *v* intimidate. **intimidación** *sf* intimidation.

intolerable [intole'raβle] *adj* intolerable. **intolerancia** *sf* intolerance. **intolerante** *adj* intolerant.

intoxicar [intoksi'kar] *v* poison. **intoxicación** *sf* poisoning.

intraducible [intraðu'θiβle] *adj* untranslatable.

intranquilo [intran'kilo] *adj* restless. **intranquilidad** *sf* restlessness.

intransigente [intransi'xente] *adj* intransigent. **intransigencia** *sf* intransigence.

intransitable [intransi'taβle] *adj* impassable.

intransitivo [intransi'tiβo] *adj* (*gram*) intransitive.

intratable [intra'taβle] *adj* intractable; unsociable.

intrépido [in'trepiðo] *adj* brave. **intrepidez** *sf* valour.

intrigar [intri'gar] *v* intrigue. **intriga** *sf* intrigue. **intrigante** *adj* intriguing.

intrincado [intrin'kaðo] *adj* intricate; entangled.

intrínseco [in'trinseko] *adj* intrinsic.

***introducir** [introðu'θir] *v* introduce. **introducción** *sf* introduction. **introductor** *adj* introductory.

intruso [in'truso], **-a** *sm, sf* intruder. *adj* intrusive. **intrusarse** *v* intrude. **intrusión** *sf* intrusion.

intuición [intwi'θjon] *sf* intuition. **intuir** *v* feel; sense. **intuitivo** *adj* intuitive.

inundar [inun'dar] *v* flood. **inundación** *sf* flood. **inundante** *adj* flooding.

inusitado [inusi'taðo] *adj* unusual.

inútil [i'nutil] *adj* useless. **inutilidad** *sf* uselessness. **inutilizar** *v* render useless.

invadir [inβa'ðir] *v* invade. **invasión** *sf* invasion. **invasor, -a** *sm, sf* invader.

invalidar [inβali'ðar] *v* invalidate. **invalidación** *sf* invalidity. **inválido, -a** *sm, sf* invalid. *adj* invalid, void.

invariable [inva'rjaβle] *adj* invariable.

invencible [inβen'θiβle] *adj* invincible. **invencibilidad** *sf* invincibility.

inventar [inβen'tar] *v* invent. **invención** *sf* invention. **inventivo** *adj* inventive. **invento** *sm* invention. **inventor, -a** *sm, sf* inventor.

inventario [inβen'tarjo] *sm* inventory.

invernáculo [inβer'nakulo] *sm also* **invernadero** greenhouse, hothouse.

***invernar** [inβer'nar] *v* winter; hibernate. **invernada** *sf* winter; hibernation. **invernal** *adj* wintry.

inverosímil [inβero'simil] *adj* improbable. **inverosimilitud** *sf* improbability.

invertebrado [inβerte'βraðo] *sm, adj* invertebrate.

***invertir** [inβer'tir] *v* invert; (*com*) invest. **inversión** *sf* inversion; investment. **inverso** *adj* inverse, inverted. **por la inversa** the other way round.

investigar [inβesti'gar] *v* investigate. **investigación** *sf* investigation. **investigador, -a** *sm, sf* investigator; researcher.

***investir** [inβes'tir] *v* invest; confer upon. **investidura** *sf* investiture.

inveterado [inβete'raðo] *adj* inveterate, confirmed.

invicto [in'βikto] *adj* undefeated.

invierno [in'βjerno] *sm* winter.

inviolable [inβjo'laβle] *adj* inviolable. **inviolado** *adj* inviolate.

invisible [inβi'siβle] *adj* invisible. **invisibilidad** *sf* invisibility.

invitar [inβi'tar] *v* invite; call on. **invitar a una copa** stand a drink. **invitación** *sf* invitation. **invitado, -a** *sm, sf* guest.

invocar [inβo'kar] *v* invoke. **invocación** *sf* invocation.

involuntario [inβolun'tarjo] *adj* involuntary.

invulnerable [inβulne'raβle] *adj* invulnerable. **invulnerabilidad** *sf* invulnerability.

inyectar [injek'tar] *v* inject. **inyección** *sf* injection. **inyectado** *adj* congested.

***ir** [ir] *v* go; walk; come; suit. **irse** *v* go away. **ir a medias** go halves. **ir tirando** get by.

ira ['ira] *sf* anger. **iracundia** *sf* wrath. **iracundo** *adj* wrathful.

iris ['iris] *sm* (*anat*) iris. **arco iris** *sm* rainbow.

Irlanda [ir'landa] *sf* Ireland. **irlandés** *adj*

Irish. *sm* Irishman; (*idioma*) Irish. **irlandesa** *sf* Irishwoman.

ironía [iro'nia] *sf* irony. **irónico** *adj* ironic(al).

irracional [irraθjo'nal] *adj* irrational. **irracionalidad** *sf* irrationality.

irradiar [irra'ðjar] *v* irradiate, radiate. **irradiación** *sf* irradiation.

irrazonable [irraθo'naβle] *adj* unreasonable.

irreal [irre'al] *adj* unreal. **irrealidad** *sf* unreality.

irreconciliable [irrekonθi'ljaβle] *adj* irreconcilable.

irrecuperable [irrekupe'raβle] *adj* irretrievable.

irreemplazable [irreempla'θaβle] *adj* irreplaceable.

irreflexión [irreflek'sjon] *sf* hastiness; thoughtlessness. **irreflexivo** hasty; thoughtless.

irrefrenable [irrefre'naβle] *adj* uncontrollable.

irrefutable [irrefu'taβle] *adj* irrefutable.

irregular [irregu'lar] *adj* irregular. **irregularidad** *sf* irregularity.

irreligioso [irreli'xjoso] *adj* irreligious.

irremediable [irreme'ðjaβle] *adj* incurable.

irreprimible [irrepri'niβle] *adj* irrepressible.

irresistible [irresis'tiβle] *adj* irresistible.

irresoluto [irreso'luto] *adj* irresolute. **irresoluble** *adj* unsolvable. **irresolución** *sf* irresolution. indecision.

irrespetuoso [irrespe'twoso] *adj* disrespectful.

irresponsable [irrespon'saβle] *adj* irresponsible. **irresponsabilidad** *sf* irresponsibility.

irrigar [irri'gar] *v* irrigate. **irrigación** *sf* irrigation. **irrigador** *sm* sprinkler.

irritable [irri'taβle] *adj* irritable. **irritabilidad** *sf* irritability. **irritación** *sf* irritation. **irritante** *sm, adj* irritant. **irritar** *v* irritate.

isla ['isla] *sf* island. **en isla** isolated. **isleño, -a** *sm, sf* islander.

Islandia [is'landja] *sf* Iceland. **islandés, -esa** *sm, sf* Icelander; *sm* (*idioma*) Icelandic. **islandés** *adj* Icelandic.

istmo ['istmo] *sm* isthmus.

Italia [i'talja] *sf* Italy. **italiano, -a,** *s, adj* Italian.

itinerario [itine'rarjo] *sm* itinerary.

IVA ['iβa] *sm* VAT.

izar [i'θar] *v* hoist.

izquierda [iθ'kjerða] *sf* left; left hand; left wing. **mantenerse a la izquierda** keep left. **izquierdo** *adj* left; left-handed.

J

jabalí [xaβa'li] *sm* wild boar.

jabalina [xaβa'lina] *sf* javelin; (*zool*) wild sow.

jabón [xa'βon] *sm* soap. **jabón de tocador** toilet soap. **jabonar** *v* soap. **jabonera** *sf* soap-dish. **jabonoso** *adj* soapy.

jaca ['xaka] *sf* pony.

jacinto [xa'θinto] *sm* hyacinth.

jactarse [xak'tarse] *v* boast. **jactancia** *sf* boasting. **jactancioso** *adj* boastful.

jadear [xaðe'ar] *v* pant. **jadeante** *adj* panting. **jadeo** *sm* pant; panting.

jalear [xale'ar] *v* urge on. **jaleo** *sm* row, din. **armar un jaleo** start a row.

jamás [xa'mas] *adv* never. **nunca jamás** never ever.

jamón [xa'mon] *sm* ham. **jamón serrano** cured ham.

Japón [xa'pon] *sm* Japan. **japonés** *s(m + f)*, *adj* Japanese.

jaque ['xake] *sm* (*ajedrez*) check.

jaqueca [xa'keka] *sf* migraine. **dar jaqueca a** (*fam*) pester.

jarabe [xa'raβe] *sm* syrup.

jarana [xa'rana] *sf* spree; rumpus; trick. **dar jarabe a uno** (*fam*) butter someone up.

jardín [xar'ðin] *sm* garden. **jardinería** *sf* gardening. **jardinero, -a** *sm, sf* gardener.

jarra ['xarra] *sf* jug, pitcher. **jarro** *sm* jug; jar. **jarrón** *sm* vase.

jaula ['xaula] *sf* cage; crate; playpen.

jazmín [xaθ'min] *sm* jasmine.

jefe ['xefe] *sm* chief; head; leader. **jefa** *sf* head; manageress. **jefatura** *sf* leadership; managership; chieftaincy. **jefatura de policía** police headquarters.

jengibre [xen'xiβre] *sm* ginger.

jeque ['xeke] *sm* sheikh.

jerarquía [xerar'kia] *sf* hierarchy.
jerárquico *adj* hierarchical.

jerez [xe'reθ] *sm* cherry.

jerga ['xerga] *sf also* **jerigonza** jargon.

jeringa [xe'ringa] *sf* syringe. **jeringar** *v*
syringe; *(fam)* annoy.

jeroglífico [xero'glifiko] *s, adj* hieroglyphic.

jersey [xer'sei] *sm* jersey.

jesuita [xesu'ita] *sm, adj* Jesuit. **jesuítico**
adj jesuitical.

jeta ['xeta] *sf* snout; thick lips; *(fam)* face,
mug. **poner jeta** pull a face.

jilguero [xil'gero] *sm* goldfinch.

jinete [xi'nete] *sm* horseman; saddle horse;
thoroughbred horse. **jinetear** *v* ride on
horseback.

jirafa [xi'rafa] *sf* giraffe.

jocoso [xo'koso] *adj* amusing. **jocosidad** *sf*
humour.

jofaina [xo'faina] *sf* washbowl.

jornada [xor'naða] *sf* journey; working day;
session; expedition; *(teatro)* act. **al fin de
la jornada** at the end of the day. **jornal**
sm day's wage. **jornalero** *sm* day labourer.

joroba [xo'roβa] *sf* hump; *(fam)* pest.
jorobado, -a *s, adj* hunchback.

jota ['xota] *sf* letter *j*; jot; Spanish dance.

joven ['xoβen] *adj* young. **jóvenes** *s(m + f)
pl* youth.

joya ['xoja] *sf* jewel. **joyería** *sf* jewellery.
joyero *sm* jeweller.

jubilar [xuβi'lar] *v* retire; pension off. **jubilarse** *v* retire; rejoice. **jubilación** *sf* pension; retirement; jubilation. **jubilado** *adj*
retired.

jubileo [xuβi'leo] *sm* jubilee; comings and
goings *pl*.

júbilo ['xuβilo] *sm* jubilation, rejoicing.
jubiloso *adj* jubilant.

judía [xu'ðia] *sf* bean. **judía blanca** haricot
bean. **judía escarlata** runner bean. **judía
verde** French bean.

judicial [xuði'θjal] *adj* judicial. **judicatura**
sf judicature.

judío [xu'ðio], **-a** *sm, sf* Jew. *adj* Jewish.
judaico *adj* Jewish. **judaísmo** *sm* Judaism.

juego ['xwego] *sm* game; sport; gambling;
play; *(platos, tazas, etc.)* set; service.

juerga ['xwerga] *sf (fam)* spree, binge. **juer-
gista** *s(m + f)* reveller.

jueves ['xweβes] *sm* Thursday.

juez [xweθ] *sm* judge, justice. **juez de
hecho** juror.

*jugar [xu'gar] *v* play; bet; gamble. **jugarse**
v bet; risk. **jugada** move; throw; stroke;
shot; play. **mala jugada** dirty trick.
jugador, -a *sm, sf* player; gambler.

juglar [xu'glar], **-a** *sm, sf* minstrel.

jugo ['xugo] *sm* juice; sap. **jugoso** *adj* juicy.

juguete [xu'gete] *sm* toy; plaything.
juguetear *v* frolic. **jugueteo** *sm* frolicking,
juguetería *sf* toyshop.

juicio ['xwiθjo] *sm (jur)* trial; judgment;
opinion; sense. **a juicio de** in the opinion
of. **perder el juicio** lose one's mind.
juicioso *adj* judicious.

julio ['xuljo] *sm* July.

jumento [xu'mento] *sm* ass.

junco¹ ['xunko] *sm (bot)* reed.

junco² *sm (mar)* junk.

jungla ['xungla] *sf* jungle.

junio ['xunjo] *sm* June.

junquera [xun'kera] *sf (bot)* rush.

junquillo [xun'kiʎo] *sm (bot)* jonquil.

juntar [xun'tar] *v* join; assemble; unite; collect. **juntarse** *v* meet; join; gather; live
together. **junta** *sf* meeting; session; board;
council; junta. **junto** *adj* joined, united,
together. *adv* **junto a** near. **muy junto**
very close.

juramentar [xuramen'tar] *v* swear in. **jura-
mentarse** *v* take an oath. **jura** *sf* oath;
swearing. **jurado** *adj* sworn; *sm* jury. **jurado de cuentas** chartered accountant. **juramento** *sm* oath; curse. **juramento falso**
perjury. **jurar** *v* swear. **jurar al cargo** take
the oath of office.

jurídico [xu'riðiko] *adj* juridical, legal.

jurisconsulto [xuriskon'sulto] *sm* legal
expert. **jurisdicción** *sf* jurisdiction.
jurisprudencia *sf* jurisprudence. **jurista**
sm jurist, lawyer.

justa ['xusta] *sf* joust; contest.

justificar [xustifi'kar] *v* justify. **justificarse**
v clear oneself. **justamente** *adv* justly;
exactly. **¡justamente!** precisely! **justicia** *sf*
justice; execution. **justiciable** *adj* action-
able. **justiciero** *adj* just. **justificable** *adj*
justifiable. **justificación** *sf* justification.
justificado *adj* justified.

justo ['xusto] *adj* just; lawful; precise. *adv*
exactly; tightly.

juvenil [xuβe'nil] *adj* youthful. *s(m + f)*

junior. **juventud** *sf* youth.
juzgar [xuθ'gar] *v* judge; consider. **juzgar mal** misjudge. **juzgado** *sm* court.

K

kaki ['kaki] *sm, adj* khaki.
kilo ['kilo] *sm* kilo.
kilobyte [kilo'βait] *sm* kilobyte.
kilogramo [kilo'gramo] *sm* kilogramme.
kilolitro [kilo'litro] *sm* kilolitre.
kilómetro [ki'lometro] *sm* kilometre. **kilométrico** *adj* kilometric.
kilovatio [kilo'βatjo] *sm* kilowatt.
kiosco ['kjosko] *sm* kiosk.

L

la [la] *art f* the. *pron* her, it.
laberinto [laβe'rinto] *sm* labyrinth; maze.
labio ['laβjo] *sm* lip. **labial** *adj* labial.
labor [la'βor] *sf* work; labour. **laborador** *sm* worker; farmer. **laborar** *v* work; till. **laborear** *v* work; till; mine. **laboreo** *sm* working; tilling; mining. **laborioso** *adj* industrious; laborious. **laborismo** *sm* (*pol*) Labour party. **laborista** *s(m+f)* Labour-party member.
laboratorio [laβora'torjo] *sm* laboratory.
labrar [la'βrar] *v* fashion; carve; work; cultivate; build; bring about. **labradero** *adj* workable; arable. **labrador, -a** *sm, sf* peasant. **labranza** *sf* farming; farmland. **labriego** *sm* peasant; farmhand.
laburno [la'βurno] *sm* laburnum.
laca ['laka] *sf* lacquer, varnish.
lacayo [la'kajo] *sm* lackey.
lacerar [laθe'rar] *v* lacerate; harm; (*fruta*) damage. **laceración** *sf* laceration; damage.
lacio ['laθjo] *adj* limp; lank; withered.
lacónico [la'koniko] *adj* laconic.
lacrar¹ [la'krar] *v* infect; damage. **lacra** *sf* blemish.
lacrar² *v* seal. **lacre** *sm* sealing wax.

lacrimoso [lakri'moso] *adj* tearful.
lácteo ['lakteo] *adj* milky. **vía láctea** *sf* Milky Way. **productos lácteos** *sm pl* dairy products. **lactante** *adj* suckling, nursling. **lactar** *v* suckle.
ladear [laðe'ar] *v* tip, tilt, overturn; deviate; skirt. **ladeo** *sm* tipping, tilting.
ladera [la'ðera] *sf* slope; hillside.
ladino [la'ðino] *adj* multilingual; crafty.
lado ['laðo] *sm* side; way; space; direction; protection. **lado izquierdo** *sm* nearside. **al lado** close. **al lado de** beside. **por el lado de** in the direction of.
ladrar [la'ðrar] *v* bark. **ladrido** *sm* bark; barking.
ladrillo [la'ðriʎo] *sm* brick, tile.
ladrón [la'ðron], **-a** *sm, sf* thief, robber. *sm* sluice gate; multiple socket.
lagarto [la'garto] *sm* lizard.
lago ['lago] *sm* lake.
lágrima ['lagrima] *sf* tear; drop. **verter lágrimas** shed tears. **lagrimoso** *adj* tearful.
laguna [la'guna] *sf* lagoon; pond; gap.
laico ['laiko] *adj* lay, secular.
lamentar [lamen'tar] *v* lament; regret; grieve. **lamentarse** *v* complain. **lamentable** *adj* deplorable. **lamentablemente** *adv* regretfully. **lamentación** *sf* lamentation, lament. **lamento** *sm* lament; mourning. **lamentoso** *adj* lamentable, mournful.
lamer [la'mer] *v* lick.
lámina ['lamina] *sf* metal sheet; picture; engraving. **laminar** *v* laminate.
lámpara ['lampara] *sf* lamp; light; valve.
lana ['lana] *sf* wool; fleece. **lana de vidrio** fibreglass. **lanudo** *adj* woolly; shaggy.
lance ['lanθe] *sm* throw; event; move; stroke. **lance de fortuna** chance. **de lance** second-hand.
lanceta [lan'θeta] *sf* lancet.
lancha ['lantʃa] *sf* launch; flagstone. **lancha salvavidas** lifeboat. **lanchero** *sm* boatman.
langosta [lan'gosta] *sf* lobster; locust.
*languidecer [langiðe'θer] *v* languish. **languidez** *sf* languor. **lánguido** *adj* languid.
lanza ['lanθa] *sf* spear; lance; pike; nozzle.
lanzar [lan'θar] *v* throw; fling; evict. **lanzarse** *v* spring. **lanzamiento** *sm* launching.

lápida ['lapiða] sf stone slab; tablet.

lápiz ['lapiθ] sm pencil. **lapicero** sm pencil-holder.

lapso ['lapso] sm lapse.

lar [lar] sm hearth; home.

largar [lar'gar] v loosen; free. **largarse** v go away.

largo ['largo] adj long; (fam) generous. sm length. **a lo largo de** the length of. **dar largas a** delay. **largueza** sf length; generosity.

laringe [la'rinxe] sf larynx.

larva ['larβa] sf larva.

lascivo [las'θiβo] adj lascivious. **lascivia** sf lasciviousness.

laso ['laso] adj weary. **lasitud** sf lassitude.

lástima ['lastima] sf pity; complaint. **¡qué lástima!** what a pity! **lastimar** v hurt. **lastimarse** v pity; complain. **lastimoso** adj pitiable, pitiful.

lastre ['lastre] sm ballast.

lata ['lata] sf tin, can; (fam) nuisance. **dar la lata** (fam) pester.

latente [la'tente] adj latent.

lateral [late'ral] adj lateral, side.

látigo ['latigo] sm whip. **latigazo** sm whiplash.

latín [la'tin] sm Latin. **latinoamericano, -a** s, adj Latin American.

latir [la'tir] v beat; throb. **latido** sm heartbeat; throb.

latitud [lati'tuð] sf latitude; breadth. **lato** adj broad.

latón [la'ton] sm brass.

latoso [la'toso] adj (fam) annoying; boring.

latrocinio [latro'θinjo] sm theft.

laúd [la'uð] sm lute.

laudable [lau'ðaβle] adj praiseworthy.

laurel [lau'rel] sm laurel; laurel wreath. **laureado** adj laureate. **laurear** v honour; reward. **lauro** sm (fig) glory.

lava ['laβa] sf lava.

lavar [la'βar] v wash. **lavable** adj washable. **lavabo** sm washing-basin. **lavación** sf lotion; wash. **lavadero** sm washing-place. **lavado** sm wash; washing. **lavadora** sf washing machine. **lavandería** sf laundry.

laxante [lak'sante] sm laxative. **laxidad** sf laxity.

lazo ['laθo] sm lasso; loop; bow; knot; snare; link.

leal [le'al] adj loyal. **lealtad** sf loyalty.

lebrel [le'βrel] sm greyhound.

lección [lek'θjon] sf lesson. **lector, -a** sm, sf reader; lecturer. **lectura** sf reading matter.

leche ['letʃe] sf milk. **leche semidesnatada** sf semi-skimmed milk. **lechería** sf dairy. **lechero** sm milkman.

lecho ['letʃo] sm bed; layer.

lechuga [le'tʃuga] sf lettuce.

lechuza [le'tʃuθa] sf owl.

*leer [le'er] v read.

legación [lega'θjon] sf legation. **legado** sm legacy; ambassador.

legal [le'gal] adj legal; lawful. **legalidad** sf legality. **legalización** sf legalization. **legalizar** v legalize.

legar [le'gar] v bequeath; depute.

legendario [lexen'darjo] adj legendary.

legible [le'xiβle] adj legible.

legión [le'xjon] sf legion.

legislar [lexis'lar] v legislate. **legislación** sf legislation. **legislador, -a** sm, sf legislator. **legislativo** adj legislative. **legislatura** sf legislature.

legitimar [lexiti'mar] v prove; justify. **legitimidad** sf legitimacy. **legítimo** adj legitimate.

lego ['lego] adj lay. sm layman.

legua ['legwa] sf league.

legumbre [le'gumbre] sf vegetable.

lejía [le'xia] sf bleach.

lejos ['lexos] adv far away. **a lo lejos** in the distance. sm perspective; background. **lejanía** sf distance. **lejano** adj far-away.

lema ['lema] sf motto.

lencería [lenθe'ria] sf linen goods; lingerie.

lengua ['lengwa] sf tongue; language. **trabarse la lengua** become tongue-tied. **lenguaje** sm language; speech; style.

lenguado [len'gwaðo] sm (zool) sole.

lengüeta [len'gweta] sf (de zapato) tongue.

lenidad [leni'ðað] sf lenience; mildness.

lente ['lente] s(m+f) lens. **lente de aumento** magnifying glass. **lentes** pl glasses, spectacles. **lentes de contacto** contact lenses.

lenteja [len'texa] sf lentil.

lento ['lento] adj slow. **lentitud** sf slowness.

leña ['leɲa] sf firewood.

león [le'on] sm lion. **leona** sf lioness. **leoni-**

no *adj* leonine.

lepra ['lepra] *sf* leprosy. **leproso** *adj* leprous.

lesión [le'sjon] *sf* injury. **lesionar** *v* injure. **lesivo** *adj* injurious.

letanía [leta'nia] *sf* litany; long list.

letargo [le'targo] *sm* lethargy. **letárgico** *adj* lethargic.

Letonia [le'tonja] *sf* Latvia. **letón** *adj* Latvian.

letra ['letra] *sf* letter; handwriting; lyric; (*com*) draft. **Letras** *sf pl* literature; Arts. **letra mayúscula** capital letter. **letra minúscula** lower-case letter. **letrado** *sm* lawyer. **letrero** *sm* label; sign.

leva ['leβa] *sf* (*tecn*) cam; lever. **árbol de levas** camshaft.

levadizo [leβa'ðiθo] *adj* that can be lifted. **puente levadizo** *sm* drawbridge.

levadura [leβa'ðura] *sf* leaven, yeast.

levantar [leβan'tar] *v* lift; raise; erect. **levantarse** *v* rise, get up. **levantamiento** *sm* raising; insurrection. **levantado** *adj* raised; lofty.

leve ['leβe] *adj* slight; trifling. **levedad** *sf* lightness; slightness.

léxico ['leksiko] *adj* lexical. *sm* dictionary; vocabulary.

ley [lej] *sf* law; loyalty; standard. **a toda ley** according to rule. **tener ley a** be very fond of.

leyenda [le'jenda] *sf* legend.

liar [ljar] *v* bind; tie up; (*fam*) involve. **liarlas** *v* (*fam*) clear off. **liarse** *v* (*fam*) join; start an affair; get involved.

libélula [li'βelula] *sf* dragonfly.

liberal [liβe'ral] *adj* generous. **liberalidad** *sf* generosity.

libertar [liβer'tar] *v also* **liberar** liberate, free. **libertad** *sf* freedom; independence. **libertador, -a** *sm, sf* liberator.

libertinaje [liβerti'naxe] *sm* licentiousness. **libertino, -a** *s, adj* libertine.

libra ['liβra] *sf* (*peso*) pound. **libra esterlina** pound sterling.

librar [li'βrar] *v* free; exempt; deliver; despatch; expedite; (*com*) draw; pass sentence. **librador, -a** *sm, sf* liberator. **libramiento** *sm* delivery; rescue; (*com*) draft. **libranza** *sf* (*com*) draft. **libre** *adj* free; vacant; isolated; loose.

librería [liβre'ria] *sf* bookshop; bookselling;

bookcase. **librero, -a** *sm, sf* bookseller.

libreta [li'βreta] *sf* notebook; cashbook; one-pound loaf.

libro ['liβro] *sm* book. **libro diario** journal. **libro mayor** ledger.

licenciar [liθen'θjar] *v* license. **licenciarse** *v* graduate. **licencia** *sf* licence; degree; (*mil*) leave. **licenciado, -a** *sm, sf* graduate; *sm* lawyer; discharged soldier. **licenciatura** *sf* Bachelor's degree.

licencioso [liθen'θjoso] *adj* licentious.

liceo [li'θeo] *sm* lyceum; secondary school.

licitar [liθi'tar] *v* (*subasta*) bid. **licitación** *sf* bid. **licitador, -a** *sm, sf* bidder.

lícito ['liθito] *adj* authorized.

licor [li'kor] *sm* liquor; liqueur.

líder ['liðer] *sm* leader.

lidiar [li'ðjar] *v* (*toros*) fight. **lidia** *sf* bull-fight. **lidiador** *sm* bullfighter.

liebre ['ljeβre] *sf* hare. **coger una liebre** (*fam*) come a cropper.

lienzo ['ljenθo] *sm* canvas; linen.

liga ['liga] *sf* garter; league; alloy. **ligadura** *sf* ligature; bond. **ligamento** *sm* ligament; bond. **ligar** *v* bind; tie; unite; alloy. **ligarse** *v* join; band together.

ligero [li'xero] *adj* light; swift; frivolous. **ligereza** *sf* lightness; swiftness; frivolousness.

lija ['lixa] *sf* sandpaper; (*zool*) dogfish. **lijar** *v* sandpaper.

lila ['lila] *sf* (*bot*) lilac. *sm* (*color*) lilac. *adj* (*fam*) foolish.

lima[1] ['lima] *sf* file; polish. **limar** *v* file; polish; undermine. **limadura** *sf* filing.

lima[2] *sf* lime; lime tree.

limaza [li'maθa] *sf* slug.

limitar [limi'tar] *v* limit. **limitación** *sf* limitation. **límite** *sm* limit; boundary.

limón [li'mon] *sm* lemon; lemon tree. **limonada** *sf* lemonade. **limonero** *sm* lemon tree.

limosna [li'mosna] *sf* alms *pl*.

limpiabotas [limpja'βotas] *sm invar* bootblack.

limpiadera [limpja'ðera] *sf* clothes brush.

limpiadientes [limpja'ðjentes] *sm invar* toothpick.

limpiar [lim'pjar] *v* clean; clear; wipe; prune; weed. **limpiador, -a** *sm, sf* cleaner. **limpiadura** *sf* cleaning. **limpieza** *sf* cleanness. **limpio** *adj* clean; clear; pure. **jugar limpio** play fair. **poner en limpio** copy out.

linaje [li'naxe] *sm* lineage. **linaje humano** mankind.

linaza [li'naθa] *sf* linseed.

lince ['linθe] *sm* lynx.

linchar [lin'tʃar] *v* lynch. **linchamiento** *sm* lynching.

lindar [lin'dar] *v* **lindar con** border; adjoin. **linde** *sf* boundary. **lindero** *sm* limit.

lindo ['lindo] *adj* pretty; handsome; nice. **de lo lindo** a great deal. **lindeza** *sf* beauty; niceness. **lindura** *sf* prettiness.

línea ['linea] *sf* line; boundary; class. **línea aérea** airline. **línea ferroviaria** railway line. **lineal** *adj* linear.

lingüista [lin'gwista] *s(m + f)* linguist. **lingüística** *sf* linguistics. **lingüístico** *adj* linguistic.

linimento [lini'mento] *sm* liniment.

lino ['lino] *sm* linen.

linóleo [li'noleo] *sm* linoleum.

linterna [lin'terna] *sf* lantern; lamp; torch; lighthouse.

lío ['lio] *sm* parcel; trouble; mess; hassle. **armar un lío** raise a rumpus.

liquidar [liki'ðar] *v* liquefy; liquidate, settle up. **liquidez** *sf* fluidity. **líquido** *sm, adj* liquid; (*com*) net. **líquido imponible** net taxable amount.

lira ['lira] *sf* lyre; inspiration.

lírica ['lirika] *sf* lyric poetry. **lírico** *adj* lyric.

lirio ['lirjo] *sm* lily.

lirón [li'ron] *sm* dormouse. **dormir como un lirón** sleep like a log.

lisiar [li'sjar] *v* cripple. **lisiado** *adj* crippled.

liso ['liso] *adj* smooth.

lisonjear [lisonxe'ar] *v* flatter. **lisonja** *sf* flattery. **lisonjero** *adj* flattering.

lista ['lista] *sf* list; stripe; band. **a listas** striped. **lista de correos** poste restante. **lista de platos** menu.

listo ['listo] *adj* ready; finished; clever.

litera [li'tera] *sf* berth; bunk; (*cama*) litter. **literas** *sf pl* bunk beds.

literato [lite'rato], **-a** *sm, sf* literary person. *adj* literary. **literatura** *sf* literature.

litigar [liti'gar] *v* go to law, litigate. **litigación** *sf* litigation. **litigio** *sm* lawsuit. **litigioso** *adj* contentious.

litografía [lito'grafja] *sf* lithograph; lithography. **litográfico** *adj* lithographic.

litoral [lito'ral] *adj* coastal. *sm* shore.

litro ['litro] *sm* litre.

liturgia [litur'xia] *sf* liturgy. **litúrgico** *adj* liturgical.

liviano [li'βjano] *adj* light; trivial; lewd. **liviandad** *sf* lightness; triviality; lewdness.

lívido ['liβiðo] *adj* livid.

lo [lo] *art m* him, it; that, what.

loable [lo'aβle] *adj* praiseworthy. **loa** *sf* praise. **loador** *adj* praising. **loar** *v* praise.

lobo ['loβo] *sm* wolf. **lobo marino** seal. **lobero** *adj* wolfish.

lóbrego ['loβrego] *adj* gloomy, murky. **lobreguecer** *v* darken; grow dark. **lobreguez** *sf* gloom; murk.

lóbulo ['loβulo] *sm* lobe.

local [lo'kal] *adj* local. *sm* place. **localidad** *sf* locality; (*teatro*) seat. **sacar localidades** get tickets. **localizar** *v* localize.

loción [lo'θjon] *sf* lotion.

loco ['loko], **-a** *adj* mad; excessive. *sm, sf* mad person. **volverse loco** go mad. **locura** *sf* madness; folly. **hacer locuras** act madly.

locomoción [lokomo'θjon] *sf* locomotion. **locomotora** *sf* locomotive.

locuaz [lo'kwaθ] *adj* talkative. **locuacidad** *sf* talkativeness.

locutor [loku'tor], **-a** *sm, sf* radio announcer; commentator.

lodo ['loðo] *sm* mud. **lodoso** *adj* muddy.

lógica ['loxika] *sf* logic. **lógico** *adj* logical. **lógicamente** *adv* logically; naturally. **logística** *sf* logistics.

lograr [lo'grar] *v* get; achieve. **lograrse** *v* succeed. **logrería** *sf* profiteering. **logro** *sm* success; profit; usury.

loma ['loma] *sf* hill; slope.

lombriz [lom'briθ] *sf* worm; earthworm. **lombriz solitaria** tapeworm.

lomo ['lomo] *sm* (*carne*) loin; (*animal*) back; (*libro*) spine.

lona ['lona] *sf* canvas.

Londres ['londres] *sm* London.

longaniza [longa'niθa] *sf* pork sausage.

longevidad [lonxeβi'ðað] *sf* longevity.

longitud [lonxi'tuð] *sf* longitude. **longitudinal** *adj* longitudinal.

lonja ['lonxa] *sf* (*de carne*) slice; grocer's shop; strap; church porch.

loro ['loro] *sm* parrot.

losa ['losa] *sf* stone slab; flagstone; tile.

lote ['lote] *sm* (*com*) lot; share; prize.

loza ['loθa] *sf* crockery; pottery.

lozano [lo'θano] *adj* luxuriant; lush; robust; sprightly. **lozanía** *sf* luxuriance.

lubrificar [luβrifi'kar] *v also* **lubricar** lubricate. **lubricación** *sf also* **lubrificación** lubrication. **lubricante** *sm, adj also* **lubrificante** lubricant.

lúcido ['luθiðo] *adj* lucid; shining. **lucidez** *sf* lucidity; brilliance.

luciérnaga [lu'θjernaga] *sf* glow-worm.

*lucir [lu'θir] *v* shine; gleam; excel; show off. **lucirse** *v* be successful; dress up.

lucro ['lukro] *sm* profit, gain. **lucros y daños** profit and loss.

luchar [lu'tʃar] *v* fight, struggle. **lucha** *sf* fight, struggle. **lucha libre** all-in wrestling. **luchador, -a** *sm, sf* fighter.

luego ['lwego] *adv* then; next; later; presently. *conj* as; therefore. **luego que** as soon as. **desde luego** of course. **hasta luego** so long.

lugar [lu'gar] *sm* place; occasion; chance; opportunity. **en lugar de** instead of. **tener lugar** take place.

lugarteniente [lugarte'njente] *sm* lieutenant.

lúgubre ['luguβre] *adj* lugubrious.

lujo ['luxo] *sm* luxury. **de lujo** de luxe. **lujoso** *adj* luxurious.

lujuria [lu'xurja] *sf* lust; lechery. **lujuriar** *v* lust. **lujurioso** *adj* lustful; lecherous.

lumbago [lum'bago] *sm* lumbago.

lumbre ['lumbre] *sf* fire; brightness; light; skylight. **echar lumbres** spark. **lumbrera** *sf* luminary; skylight; air vent; (*fig*) leading light.

luminoso [lumi'noso] *adj* bright; luminous.

luna ['luna] *sf* moon. **luna de miel** honeymoon. **lunar** *adj* lunar. **lunático, -a** *s, adj* lunatic.

lunar [lu'nar] *sm* mole; beauty spot; blemish.

lunes ['lunes] *sm* Monday.

lupa ['lupa] *sf* magnifying glass.

lupanar [lupa'nar] *sm* brothel.

lustrar [lus'trar] *v* polish; purify. **lustre** *sm* lustre; gloss; splendour.

luto ['luto] *sm* mourning; bereavement. **ir**

de luto be in mourning.

Luxemburgo [luksem'burgo] *sm* Luxembourg.

luz [luθ] *sf* light; daylight; window. **luces de emergencia** *sf pl* hazard lights. **a todas luces** clearly. **dar la luz** put the light on.

LL

llaga ['ʎaga] *sf* ulcer; sore; wound. **llagar** *v* ulcerate; wound.

llama¹ ['ʎama] *sf* (*fuego*) flame. **estar en llamas** burst into flames. **llamear** *v* blaze.

llama² *sf* (*pantano*) swamp.

llama³ *sf* (*zool*) llama.

llamar [ʎa'mar] *v* call; appeal to; name; attract. **llamarse** *v* be called. **¿cómo se llama?** what is your name? **llamado** *adj* so-called. **llamada** *sf* call; summons. **llamador, -a** *sm, sf* caller; messenger.

llana ['ʎana] *sf* trowel.

llano ['ʎano] *adj* flat; plain; straightforward. **número llano** Roman numeral. *sm* plain; flatness. **llanura** *sf* evenness; flat land.

llanta ['ʎanta] *sf* iron hoop; rim.

llanto ['ʎanto] *sm* lament; crying.

llave ['ʎaβe] *sf* key; spanner. **llave maestra** skeleton key. **llave inglesa** adjustable spanner.

llegar [ʎe'gar] *v* arrive; reach; suffice; happen. **llegarse** *v* come *or* go round. **llegar a** end up at. **llegar a ser** become. **llegada** *sf* arrival. **a la llegada** on arrival.

llenar [ʎe'nar] *v* fill; be satisfied. **lleno** *adj* full; covered; complete. **de lleno** completely. **llenura** *sf* abundance.

llevar [ʎe'βar] *v* take; carry; wear; deal with; sever; charge; manage; (*tiempo*) spend. **llevar a cabo** carry out. **llevarse** *v* take away. **llevarse bien con** get on well with.

llorar [ʎo'rar] *v* weep, cry; mourn. **llorón, -ona** *adj* weepy. **lloroso** *adj* tearful.

llover [ʎo'βer] *v* rain. **llover a cántaros** pour down. **lloverse** *v* (*tejado*) leak. **lloviznar** *v* drizzle. **llovizna** *sf* drizzle. **lluvia** *sf* rain. **lluvia ácida** *sf* acid rain. **lluvia torrencial** *sf* pouring rain. **lluvioso** *adj* rainy.

M

macabro [ma'kaβro] *adj* macabre.

macarrón [makar'ron] *sm* macaroon. **macarrones** *sm pl* macaroni *sing*.

macanudo [maka'nuðo] *adj (fam)* terrific.

maceta [ma'θeta] *sf* flowerpot.

macilento [maθi'lento] *adj* lean; wan.

macizo [ma'θiθo] *adj* solid. *sm* mass; flowerbed. **macizar** *v* fill up.

mácula ['makula] *sf* spot, stain. **macular** *v* spot, stain.

machacar [matʃa'kar] *v* pound; crush; bombard; *(fig)* harp on. **machacón, -ona** *sm, sf* bore; swot. **machaconería** *sf* tiresomeness. **machaqueo** *sm* pounding; crushing; harping.

machete [ma'tʃete] *sm* machete; hunting-knife.

macho ['matʃo] *adj* male; masculine; virile. *sm (fam)* he-man; sledgehammer; he-mule. **machismo** *sm* virility.

machucar [matʃu'kar] *v* beat; pound; bruise.

madeja [ma'ðexa] *sf* skein; mop of hair.

madera [ma'ðera] *sf* wood, timber; horn. **tener madera de** have the makings of. **maderería** *sf* timber yard. **madero** *sm* beam; log.

madrastra [ma'ðrastra] *sf* stepmother.

madre ['maðre] *sf* mother. **madre política** mother-in-law. **madre de acogida** *sf* foster mother.

madreselva [maðre'selβa] *sf* honeysuckle.

madriguera [maðri'gera] *sf* den; warren.

madrina [ma'ðrina] *sf* godmother; patroness. **madrina de boda** bridesmaid.

madrugar [maðru'gar] *v* rise early. **madrugada** *sf* early morning. **madrugador, -a** *sm, sf* early riser.

madurar [maðu'rar] *v* mature, ripen. **madurez** *sf* maturity; wisdom. **maduro** *adj* ripe; middle-aged.

maestría [maes'tria] *sf* mastery. **maestrar** *v* direct; conduct; domineer. **maestra** *sf* mistress; schoolmistress. **maestro** *sm* master; teacher; *adj* master, main, chief. **magistral** *adj* masterly.

magia ['maxja] *sf* magic. **mágico** *adj* magic(al). **magico** *sm* magician.

magistrado [maxi'straðo] *sm* magistrate. **magistratura** *sf* judicature.

magnánimo [mag'nanimo] *adj* magnanimous. **magnanimidad** *sf* magnanimity.

magnético [mag'netiko] *adj* magnetic. **magnetismo** *sm* magnetism. **magnetizar** *v* magnetize.

magnetofón [magneto'fon] *sm also* **magnetófono** tape recorder. **cinta magnetofónica** recording tape.

magnífico [mag'nifiko] *adj* magnificent. **magnificencia** *sf* magnificence.

magnitud [magni'tuð] *sf* size, magnitude.

mago ['mago] *sm* magician, wizard.

magro ['magro] *adj* thin, lean. *sm* lean meat.

magullar [magu'ʎar] *v* bruise. **magulladura** *sf* bruise.

maíz [ma'iθ] *sm* maize. **harina de maíz** *sf* cornflour.

majadero [maxa'ðero] *adj* silly; boring. *sm* pestle. **majadería** *sf* nonsense. **majadura** *sf* crushing, pounding. **majar** *v* crush, pound.

majestad [maxes'tað] *sf* majesty; royalty; grandeur. **majestuoso** *adj* majestic; stately; solemn.

majo ['maxo], **-a** *sm, sf* dandy. *adj* sporty; swaggering; genial, nice.

mal [mal] *adj V* **malo**. *adv* badly; poorly; wrongly. *sm* wrong; evil; illness; harm. **de mal en peor** from bad to worse. **echar a mal** despise; waste. **llevar a mal** take offence at. **mal presentimiento** *sm* ill feeling. **mal que bien** somehow or other.

malaconsejado [malakonse'xaðo] *adj* ill-advised.

malacostumbrado [malakostum'braðo] *adj* spoiled.

malaventura [malaβen'tura] *sf* misfortune. **malaventurado** *adj* unlucky.

malbaratar [malβara'tar] *v* squander; undersell.

malcontento [malkon'tento], **-a** *sm, sf* malcontent. *adj* discontented.

malcriado [malkri'aðo] *adj* ill-bred. **malcriar** *v* spoil.

maldad [mal'ðað] *sf* wickedness.

*maldecir [malðe'θir] *v* curse. **maldecir de** speak ill of. **maldición** *sf* curse. **maldito** *adj* accursed.

maleable [male'aβle] *adj* malleable.

maleabilidad *sf* maleability.

malear [male'ar] *v* damage; spoil. **malearse** *v* go wrong.

maleficio [male'fiθjo] *sm* injury; witchcraft. **maleficiar** *v* hurt; bewitch.

malestar [males'tar] *sm* uneasiness.

maleta [ma'leta] *sf* suitcase; (*auto*) boot. **hacer la maleta** pack up.

malévolo [ma'leβolo] *adj* malevolent. **malevolencia** *sf* malevolence.

maleza [ma'leθa] *sf* thicket; weeds *pl*.

malgastar [malgas'tar] *v* squander, waste. **malgastador, -a** *s, adj* spendthrift.

malhablado [mala'βlaðo] *adj* foulmouthed.

malhechor [male'tʃor], **-a** *sm, sf* wrongdoer. **malhecho** *sm* misdeed.

malhumorado [malumo'raðo] *adj* ill-tempered.

malicia [ma'liθja] *sf* malice; slyness; mischievousness. **maliciable** *adj* suspicious. **maliciarse** *v* go bad. **malicioso** *adj* malicious; shrewd; sly.

maligno [ma'ligno] *adj* malignant; malicious. **maliguidad** *sf* malignity; malice.

malintencionado [malintenθjo'naðo] *adj* ill-disposed.

malo ['malo] *adj also* **mal** bad; evil; wrong; poor; difficult; sick. **estar malo** be ill. **mala fama** ill fame. **venir de malas** have bad intentions.

malograr [malo'grar] *v* waste; miss. **malograrse** *v* fail; fall through. **malogrado** *adj* abortive. **malogro** *sm* failure.

*malquerer [malke'rer] *v* hate. **malquerencia** *sf* ill-will; hatred.

malsano [mal'sano] *adj* unhealthy; sick; insanitary.

malta ['malta] *sf* malt.

Malta ['malta] *sf* Malta. **maltés, -esa** *s, adj* Maltese; *sm* (*idioma*) Maltese.

maltraer [maltra'er] *v* hurt; abuse.

maltratar [maltra'tar] *v* ill-treat. **maltrato** *sm* ill-treatment.

malva ['malβa] *sf* mallow. **malva real** hollyhock.

malvado [mal'βaðo], **-a** *sm, sf* evildoer. *adj* wicked.

malla ['maʎa] *sf* mesh; network; (*de metal*) mail. **mallas** *sf pl* tights.

mallo ['maʎo] *sm* mallet.

mamá [ma'ma] *sf also* **mama** mum(my), mother.

mamar [ma'mar] *v* suck; acquire. **mamarse** *v* get drunk; fiddle, wangle. **mamoso** *adj* sucking.

mamífero [ma'mifero] *sm* mammal.

mampostería [mamposte'ria] *sf* masonry. **mampuesto** *sm* rubble.

manada [ma'naða] *sf* herd, flock; crowd. **manadero** *sm* herdsman; shepherd.

manantial [manan'tjal] *sm* spring; source, origin. **manar** *v* flow; issue.

mancebo [man'θeβo] *sm* youth; shop assistant; bachelor.

manco ['manko] *adj* one-handed; one-armed; crippled; faulty. **mancar** *v* cripple.

mancomunar [mankomu'nar] *v* join, unite. **mancomún** *adv* jointly. **mancomunarse** *v* merge. **mancomunidad** *sf* association, confederation.

manchar [man'tʃar] *v* stain; mark. **mancha** *sf* stain; mark; dishonour.

mandar [man'dar] *v* order; command; send; bequeath. **mandarse** *v* manage by oneself. **mandadero, -a** *sm, sf* messenger. **mandado** *sm* order; errand. **mandamiento** *sm* commandment, order.

mandatario [manda'tarjo] *sm* attorney; agent; mandatary. **mandato** *sm* commandment; mandate. **mandato judicial** writ.

mandíbula [man'diβula] *sf* jawbone.

mando ['mando] *sm* command; power; authority. **mando de control** *sm* joystick.

manejar [mane'xar] *v* operate; handle; manage. **manejable** *adj* manageable. **manejo** *sm* operation; handling; control; stratagem.

manera [ma'nera] *sf* manner; mode; way; fashion. **a manera de** by way of. **de ninguna manera** by no means. **de todas maneras** by all means. **manera de ver** outlook.

manga ['manga] *sf* sleeve; hosepipe; waterspout. **manga de agua** shower. **manga de viento** whirlwind. **manguera** *sf* garden hose.

mango¹ ['mango] *sm* (*bot*) mango.

mango² *sm* handle; stock.

manía [ma'nia] *sf* mania, craze. **maníaco** *adj, sm* maniac.

maniatar [manja'tar] *v* manacle.

manicomio [mani'komjo] *sm* lunatic asylum.

*manifestar [manifes'tar] *v* show; declare; manifest. **manifestación** *sf* manifestation. **manifestante** *s(m + f)* demonstrator. **manifiesto** *adj* clear, evident. **manifiesto** *sm* manifesto.

maniobrar [manjo'βrar] *v* manoeuvre; operate; manipulate; plot. **maniobra** *sf* manoeuvre; stratagem; handling.

manipular [manipu'lar] *v* manipulate. **manipulación** *sf* manipulation. **manipulador, -a** *sm, sf* manipulator.

maniquí [mani'ki] *sm* tailor's dummy; puppet. *sf* mannequin; model.

manivela [mani'βela] *sf (auto)* crank.

mano ['mano] *sf* hand; paw; *(pintura)* coat; *(juego)* hand, round, turn. **a mano** by hand. **a mano salva** without risk. **de segunda mano** secondhand. **darse las manos** shake hands. **mano a mano** in a friendly way. **manojo** *sm* handful.

manosear [manose'ar] *v* handle; paw; fondle. **manoseado** *adj* hackneyed.

mansión [man'sjon] *sf* mansion.

manso ['manso] *adj* tame; gentle; meek. **mansedumbre** *sf* tameness; meekness.

manta ['manta] *sf* blanket; rug; *(fam)* thrashing.

manteca [man'teka] *sf* grease; lard; butter; cream. **mantecada** *sf* slice of bread and butter.

mantecado [mante'kaðo] *sm* ice-cream; bun.

mantel ['mantel] *sm* tablecloth.

*mantener [mante'ner] *v* maintain; hold; defend; feed; sustain. **mantenimiento** *sm* maintenance.

mantequilla [mante'kiʎa] *sf* butter. **mantequera** *sf* churn; butter-dish. **mantequería** *sf* dairy.

mantilla [man'tiʎa] *sf* mantilla, shawl.

manto ['manto] *sm* cloak. **mantón** *sm* shawl.

manual [ma'nwal] *sm* handbook. *adj* manual.

manubrio [manu'βrio] *sm* handle; crank.

manufactura [manufak'tura] *sf* manufacture; factory. **manufacturado** *adj* manufactured. **manufacturar** *v* manufacture.

manuscrito [manu'skrito] *sm* manuscript.

manzana [man'θana] *sf* apple; block of flats. **manzano** *sm* apple tree.

maña ['maɲa] *sf* skill; bad habit; cunning. **mañoso** *adj* clever; crafty.

mañana [ma'ɲana] *sf* morning. *sm, adv* tomorrow. **de mañana** early. **hasta mañana** see you tomorrow. **pasado mañana** the day after tomorrow.

mapa ['mapa] *sm* map; chart.

maqueta [ma'keta] *sf* mock-up.

máquina ['makina] *sf* machine; locomotive; engine; car; bicycle. **a toda máquina** at full speed. **máquina de coser** sewing machine. **máquina de escribir** typewriter. **máquina registradora** cash register.

maquinación [makina'θjon] *sf* machination; plotting. **maquinal** *adj* automatic; mechanical. **maquinar** *v* plot.

mar [mar] *s(m + f)* sea. **alta mar** high seas. **baja mar** low tide.

maraña [ma'raɲa] *sf* thicket; tangle; perplexity. **marañar** *v* tangle. **marañoso** *adj* entangling.

maravillar [maraβi'ʎar] *v* wonder; amaze. **maravilla** *sf* marvel; wonder. **maravilloso** *adj* wonderful.

marcar [mar'kar] *v* mark; brand; show; dial; score. **marca** *sf* mark; make; gauge; label. **marca registrada** registered trademark.

marcial [mar'θjal] *adj* martial; warlike.

marco ['marko] *sm* frame; setting; *(moneda)* mark.

marchar [mar'tʃar] *v* march; go; run; work; depart. **marcharse** *v* go away. **marcha** *sf* march; course; movement; departure. **poner en marcha** set in motion.

marchitar [martʃi'tar] *v* fade; wither; shrivel. **marchitable** *adj* perishable. **marchito** *adj* faded.

marea [ma'rea] *sf* tide; light breeze; dew. **marea creciente/menguante** flood/ebb tide.

marearse [mare'arse] *v* feel (sea) sick. **mareado** *adj* (sea) sick; dizzy. **mareo** *sm* sickness; *(fam)* nuisance.

maremoto [mare'moto] *sm* tidal wave.

marfil [mar'fil] *sm* ivory.

margarina [marga'rina] *sf* margarine.

margarita [marga'rita] *sf* daisy; pearl.

margen [mar'xen] *sm* border; margin; verge; shoulder; fringe. **al margen de** in addition to. *sf* river bank; seashore.

marica [ma'rika] *sf* magpie. *sm (fam)* sissy. **maricón** *sm* homosexual.

marido [ma'riðo] *sm* husband.

mariguana [mari'gwana] *sf also* **marihuana** marijuana.

marina [ma'rina] *sf* navy; shore; seamanship. **marinero** *sm* sailor. **marinero** *adj* seafaring; seaworthy. **marino** *sm* sailor. **marino** *adj* marine.

mariposa [mari'posa] *sf* butterfly.

mariquita [mari'kita] *sf* ladybird.

mariscal [maris'kal] *sm* marshal. **mariscal de campo** field marshal.

marisco [ma'risko] *sm* seafood; shellfish.

marítimo [ma'ritimo] *adj* maritime.

marmita [mar'mita] *sf* stewpot.

mármol ['marmol] *sm* marble, **marmóreo** *adj* marble.

marqués [mar'kes] *sm* marquis. **marquesa** *sf* marchioness.

marrano [mar'rano] *sm* pig. *adj* filthy.

marrón [mar'ron] *adj* brown; maroon. *sm* (*color*) chestnut.

marsopa [mar'sopa] *sf* porpoise.

martes ['martes] *sm invar* Tuesday.

martillar [marti'ʎar] *v* hammer. **martillo** *sm* hammer.

martín pescador [mar'tin peska'ðor] *sm* kingfisher.

mártir ['martir] *s(m + f)* martyr. **martirio** *sm* martyrdom.

marxista [mark'sista] *s(m + f)* Marxist. **marxismo** *sm* Marxism.

marzo ['marθo] *sm* March.

mas [mas] *conj* but; yet. **mas que** although.

más [mas] *adv* more; most. **nada más** nothing else. **es más** moreover. **más bien** rather. **por más que** however much. *sm* plus.

masa ['masa] *sf* mass; volume; dough; mortar.

masaje [ma'saxe] *sm* massage. **masajista** *s(m + f)* masseur, masseuse.

mascar [mas'kar] *v* chew; (*fam*) mumble. **mascadura** *sf* chewing.

máscara ['maskara] *sf* mask. **mascarada** *sf* masquerade.

masculino [masku'lino] *adj* masculine, male. *sm* (*gram*) masculine. **masculinidad** *sf* masculinity.

masón [ma'son] *sm* freemason. **masonería** *sf* freemasonry.

masoquismo [maso'kismo] *sm* masochism. **masoquista** *s(m + f)* masochist. **masoquista** *adj* masochistic.

masticar [masti'kar] *v* chew. **masticación** *sf* mastication.

mástil ['mastil] *sm* (*mar*) mast; pole; post.

mastín [mas'tin] *sm* mastiff. **mastín danés** Great Dane.

masturbación [masturβa'θjon] *sf* masturbation. **masturbarse** *v* masturbate.

mata ['mata] *sf* bush; shrub; grove; mop of hair.

matafuego [mata'fwego] *sm* fire extinguisher.

matar [ma'tar] *v* kill, slaughter; tire out; put out. **matadero** *sm* slaughterhouse. **matador** *sm* bullfighter. **matanza** *sf* slaughter.

matamoscas [mata'moskas] *sm invar* flyswatter.

matarratas [matar'ratas] *sm invar* rat poison.

mate¹ ['mate] *sm* (check) mate.

mate² *adj* mat, dull.

matemáticas [mate'matikas] *sf* mathematics. **matemático, -a** *sm, sf* mathematician. **matemático** *adj* mathematical.

materia [ma'terja] *sf* matter; stuff; subject. **materia prima** raw material. **en materia de** as regards. **material** *adj* material. **material** *sm* stuff, material. **materiales de derribo** rubble *sing*. **materialismo** *sm* materialism. **materialista** *s(m + f)* materialist. **materialista** *adj* materialistic. **materializar** *v* materialize.

maternal [mater'nal] *adj* maternal. **maternidad** *sf* maternity. **casa de maternidad** maternity hospital. **materno** *adj* maternal.

matinal [mati'nal] *adj* morning.

matiz [ma'tiθ] *sm* tint; hue; shade; shade of meaning. **matizado** *adj* variegated. **matizar** *v* blend; shade.

matorral [mator'ral] *sm* bush; thicket; scrubland.

matricular [matriku'lar] *v* enrol; register; matriculate. **matricularse** *v* register; (*contienda*) enter. **matrícula** *sf* register; enrolment; matriculation; (*auto*) licence plate.

matrimonio [matri'monjo] *sm* matrimony, marriage; (*fam*) married couple.

matriz [ma'triθ] *sf* matrix; womb. *adj* mother; chief. **casa matriz** headquarters.

matrona [ma'trona] *sf* matron; midwife.

matute [ma'tute] *sm* smuggling; contraband. **matutear** *v* smuggle. **matutero, -a** *sm, sf* smuggler.

matutino [matu'tino] *adj also* **matutinal** morning.

maullar [mau'ʎar] *v* mew. **maullido** *sm* mewing.

mausoleo [mauso'leo] *sm* mausoleum.

máxima ['maksima] *sf* maxim.

máxime ['maksime] *adv* especially; principally. **máximo** *adj, sm* maximum.

maximizar [maksimi'θar] *v* maximize.

maya ['maja] *sf* daisy.

mayo ['majo] *sm* May; maypole.

mayonesa [majo'nesa] *sf* mayonnaise.

mayor [ma'jor] *sm* head, chief. *adj* older, elder; major, main; larger; adult. **calle mayor** high street. **al por mayor** wholesale. **mayoral** *sm* foreman; farm manager.

mayorazgo [majo'raθgo] *sm* primogeniture; first born son; entailed estate.

mayordomo [major'ðomo] *sm* butler; steward.

mayoría [majo'ria] *sf* majority; coming of age.

mayorista [majo'rista] *sm* wholesaler. *adj* wholesale.

mayúscula [ma'juskula] *sf* capital letter.

maza ['maθa] *sf* mace; club; butt. **mazada** *sf* blow with a club.

mazapán [maθa'pan] *sm* marzipan.

mazmorra [maθ'morra] *sf* dungeon.

me [me] *pron* me, myself.

mear [me'ar] *v* (*vulgar*) piss. **mearse** *v* wet oneself. **meadero** *sm* urinal.

mecánica [me'kanika] *sf* mechanics; machinery. **mecánico** *sm* mechanic; driver. **mecanismo** *sm* mechanism. **mecanizar** *v* mechanize.

mecanógrafo [meka'nografo], **-a** *sm, sf* typist. **mecanografía** *sf* typewriting. **mecanografiar** *v* type.

mecer [me'θer] *v* rock; swing; shake; stir. **mecedor** *sm* swing. **mecedora** *sf* rocking-chair.

mecha ['metʃa] *sf* wick; fuse; match.

mechera [me'tʃera] *sf* (*fam*) shoplifter.

mechero [me'tʃero] *sm* cigarette lighter; gas burner.

medalla [me'ðaʎa] *sf* medal.

media ['meðja] *sf* stocking.

mediado [me'ðjaðo] *adj* half-full; half-way through; half-finished. **a mediados de** in *or* about the middle of.

mediano [me'ðjano] *adj* medium; average; mediocre. **medianero** *adj* intermediate; interceding.

medianoche [meðja'notʃe] *sf* midnight.

mediante [me'ðjante] *adj* intervening. *prep* by means of. **mediar** *v* intervene; mediate; elapse.

medicina [meði'θina] *sf* medicine. **medicación** *sf* medication. **medicamento** *sm* medicine. **medicar** *v* medicate. **medicinal** *adj* medicinal. **médico** *sm* doctor. **médico** *adj* medical. **médico de cabecera** *sm* GP.

medio ['meðjo] *sm* middle; half; medium; way. **de medio a medio** completely. **medios** *sm pl* means, resources. *adv* half; partly. **medidas a medias** half-measures. *adj* half; middle; average; medium. **de medio cuerpo** half-length.

mediocre [me'ðjokre] *adj* mediocre. **mediocridad** *sf* mediocrity.

mediodía [meðjo'ðia] *sm* midday, noon; south.

medioeval [meðjoe'βal] *adj* medieval.

***medir** [me'ðir] *v* measure; scan. **medirse** *v* act prudently. **medida** *sf* measure(ment); step; moderation. **a medida que** according as.

meditar [meði'tar] *v* meditate (on). **meditabundo** *adj* pensive. **meditación** *sf* meditation.

mediterráneo [meðiter'raneo] *adj* Mediterranean.

medrar [me'ðrar] *v* prosper, thrive; grow. **medra** *sf* prosperity; growth. **medro** *sm* progress; improvement.

medroso [me'ðroso] *adj* fearful; timid; frightening.

médula ['meðula] *sf also* **medula** marrow; (*fig*) essence.

medusa [me'ðusa] *sf* jellyfish.

megabyte [mega'bait] *sm* megabyte.

megáfono [me'gafono] *sm* megaphone.

megalómano [mega'lomano], **-a** *sm, sf* megalomaniac. **megalomanía** *sf* megalomania.

mejilla [me'xiʎa] *sf* cheek.

mejor [me'xor] *adj* better; best. *adv* better; best; rather. **a lo mejor** probably. **mejor**

que mejor better still. **tanto mejor** so much the better. **mejora** sf improvement.

mejorar v improve; surpass. **mejorarse** v get better.

melancólico [melan'koliko] adj melancholy. **melancolía** sf melancholy.

melandro [me'landro] sm badger.

melaza [me'laθa] sf molasses; treacle.

melena [me'lena] sf mane; long hair.

melindroso [melin'droso] adj finicky; squeamish.

melocotón [meloko'ton] sm peach; peach tree.

melodía [melo'ðia] sf melody; tune. **melodioso** adj melodious.

melodrama [melo'ðrama] sm melodrama. **melodramático** adj melodramatic.

melón [me'lon] sm melon.

meloso [me'loso] adj honeyed; mild; sickly.

mella ['meʎa] sf notch; dent; impression. **hacer mella a** make a deep impression on.

mellizo [me'ʎiθo], **-a** s, adj twin.

membrana [mem'brana] sf membrane.

membrillo [mem'briʎo] sm quince; quince tree.

memorable [memo'raβle] adj memorable. **memorar** v remember. **memoria** sf memory; record. **de memoria** by heart. **memorial** sm memorial; petition.

mencionar [menθjo'nar] v mention, name. **mención** sf mention.

mendigar [mendi'gar] v beg. **mendicación** sf begging. **mendicante** adj begging. **mendigante** sm beggar. **mendigo, -a** sm, sf beggar.

menear [mene'ar] v stir; shake; sway; manage; run. **meneo** sm wag; shake.

menester [menes'ter] sm need; want; occupation. **ser menester** be necessary. **menesteroso** adj needy.

menguar [men'gwar] v lessen; decline. **mengua** sf lessening; decline. **menguado** adj impaired; diminished; wretched.

menopausia [meno'pausja] sf menopause.

menor [me'nor] adj minor; lesser; least; younger; youngest; smaller; smallest. **al por menor** retail.

menos ['menos] adj less, fewer. adv less; minus; except. **al, a lo o por lo menos** at least. **echar de menos** miss.

menoscabar [menoska'βar] v lessen; impair; discredit. **menoscabo** sm reduc-

tion; impairment.

menospreciar [menospre'θjar] v underrate; despise. **menospreciable** contemptible. **menosprecio** sm contempt; scorn; disrespect; undervaluation.

mensaje [men'saxe] sm message. **mensaje de texto** sm text (message). **mensajero, -a** sm, sf messenger.

menstruar [menstru'ar] v menstruate. **menstruación** sf menstruation. **menstrual** adj menstrual.

mensual [men'swal] adj monthly. **mensualidad** sf monthly salary.

mensurar [mensu'rar] v measure. **mensura** sf measure. **mensural** adj measuring.

menta ['menta] sf mint; peppermint.

mental [men'tal] adj mental; intellectual. **mentalidad** sf mentality. **mente** sf mind. **irse de la mente** slip one's mind.

mentecato [mente'kato]. **-a** sm. sf simpleton. adj foolish; half-witted.

*mentir [men'tir] v lie. **mentir con** disagree with. **mentira** sf lie; error. **parece mentira** it's hard to believe.

menudear [menuðe'ar] v repeat frequently; happen often. **menudencia** sf detail; minuteness; pettiness. **menudencias** sf pl or **menudas** sm pl offal sing. **menudos** adj small, tiny; petty. **a menudo** often.

meñique [me'ɲike] sm little finger. adj tiny.

meollo [me'oʎo] sm (anat) marrow; brains pl; (fig) essence.

meple ['meple] sm maple.

mercado [mer'kaðo] sm market. **Mercado Común** Common Market. **mercadear** v trade. **mercader** sm merchant. **mercadería** sf merchandise. **mercadillo** sm car boot sale. **mercancía** sf goods; wares pl. **mercante** adj merchant. **mercantil** adj mercantile.

mercancías [merkan'θias] sf pl wares.

merced [mer'θeð] sf mercy; favour. **merced a** thanks to.

mercenario [merθe'narjo], **-a** s, adj mercenary.

mercero [mer'θero], **-a** sm, sf haberdasher. **mercería** sf haberdashery.

mercurio [mer'kurjo] sm mercury. **mercurial** adj mercurial.

*merecer [mere'θer] v deserve; be worthy of **merecer la pena** be worthwhile. **merecimiento** sm merit.

*merendar [meren'dar] *v* take afternoon tea; have an afternoon snack. **merendarse** a get the better of. **merendero** *sm* open-air café. **merienda** *sf* afternoon snack.

merengue [me'renge] *sm* meringue.

meridiano [meri'ðjano] *sm, adj* meridian. **meridiana** *sf* couch. **meridional** *adj* southern.

mérito ['merito] *sm* merit; value. **hacer mérito de** mention. **meritorio** *adj* meritorious.

merla ['merla] *sf* blackbird.

merluza [mer'luθa] *sf* hake.

mermar [mer'mar] *v* decrease, reduce. **merma** *sf* reduction; wastage; loss.

mermelada [merme'laða] *sf* marmalade; jam.

mero ['mero] *adj* mere, pure.

merodear [meroðe'ar] *v* maraud. **merodeador, -a** *sm, sf* marauder.

mes [mes] *sm* month. **al mes** per month.

mesa ['mesa] *sf* table; desk. **mesa de cambios** bank. **alzar la mesa** clear the table.

meseta [me'seta] *sf* plateau; staircase landing.

mesón [me'son] *sm* inn; hostelry. **mesonero, -a** *sm, sf* innkeeper.

mestizo [mes'tiθo], **-a** *s, adj* half-caste.

mesura [me'sura] *sf* dignity; politeness; moderation.

meta ['meta] *sf* goal; aim; destination. **guardameta** *sm* goalkeeper.

metabolismo [metabo'lismo] *sm* metabolism.

metafísica [meta'fiska] *sf* metaphysics. **metafísico** *adj* metaphysical.

metáfora [me'tafora] *sf* metaphor. **metafórico** *adj* metaphorical.

metal [me'tal] *sm* metal; (*música*) brass; (*voz*) timbre. **metálico** *adj* metallic. **metalurgia** *sf* metallurgy.

meteoro [mete'oro] *sm* meteor. **meteórico** *adj* meteoric. **meteorito** *sm* meteorite. **meteorología** *sf* meteorology.

meter [me'ter] *v* insert, put in; smuggle; produce; reduce. **meterse** *v* interfere; intervene. **meterse a** turn to. **meterse con** quarrel with. **metido** *adj* compressed.

meticuloso [metiku'loso] *adj* meticulous.

metodista [meto'ðista] *s(m + f)*, *adj* Methodist. **metodismo** *sm* Methodism.

método ['metoðo] *sm* method, manner. **metódico** *adj* methodical.

métrico ['metriko] *adj* metric(al). **metro** *sm* metre; underground railway.

metrónomo [me'tronomo] *sm* metronome.

metrópoli [me'tropoli] *sf* metropolis. **metropolitano** *adj* metropolitan.

mezclar [meθ'klar] *v* mix; blend. **mezclarse** *v* mingle; intermarry. **mezcla** *sf* mixture; medley. **mezcladora** *sf* mixer, blender. **mezcolanza** *sf* hotchpotch.

mezquino [meθ'kino] *adj* mean. **mezquindad** *sf* meanness.

mezquita [meθ'kita] *sf* mosque.

mi [mi] *adj* my. **mí** *pron* me.

miaja ['mjaxa] *sf* crumb; bit.

mico ['miko] *sm* monkey.

microbio [mi'kroβjo] *sm* microbe. **microbiología** *sf* microbiology.

microcircuito [mikroθir'kwito] *sm* microchip.

micrófono [mi'krofono] *sm* microphone.

microscopio [mikro'skopjo] *sm* microscope. **microscópico** *adj* microscopic.

miedo [mi'eðo] *sm* fear. **dar miedo a** frighten. **tener miedo** be afraid. **miedoso** *adj* frightened.

miel [mi'el] *sf* honey. **miel de caña** molasses.

miembro ['mjembro] *sm* member; limb.

miente [mi'jente] *sf* mind; thought. **caer en mientes** come to mind. **¡ni por mientes!** not on your life! **parar mientes en** consider.

mientras ['mjentras] *adv, conj* while; meanwhile; so long as. **mientras tanto** meanwhile.

miércoles [mi'erkoles] *sm* Wednesday. **miércoles de ceniza** Ash Wednesday.

mierda ['mjerða] *sf* (*impol*) shit; muck. **¡váyase a la mierda!** go to hell!

mies [mjes] *sf* corn. **mieses** *sf pl* cornfield.

miga ['miga] *sf* crumb; substance. **hacer buenas migas con** get on well with.

migración [migra'θjon] *sf* migration. **migratorio** *adj* migratory.

migraña [mi'graɲa] *sf* migraine.

mil [mil] *sm, adj* thousand. **milésimo** *adj* thousandth. **miles de** masses of.

milagro [mi'lagro] *sm* miracle; wonder. **milagroso** *adj* miraculous.

milano [mi'lano] *sm (ave)* kite.

mildeu [mil'deu] *sm* mildew.

milicia [mi'liθja] *sf* militia; military service. **militar** *adj* military. *sm* soldier.

miligramo [mili'gramo] *sm* milligramme.

milla ['miʎa] *sf* mile.

millar [mi'ʎar] *sm* thousand. **a millares** in thousands.

millón [mi'ʎon] *sm* million. **millonésimo** *adj* millionth. **millonario, -a** *sm, sf* millionaire.

mimar [mi'mar] *v* spoil; pamper.

mimbre ['mimbre] *s(m + f)* wicker.

minar [mi'nar] *v* mine. **mina** *sf* mine; store; pencil lead. **minador** *sm* miner; *(mar)* minelayer. **minero** *sm* miner; mine-owner.

minarete [mina'rete] *sm* minaret.

mineral [mine'ral] *sm, adj* mineral. **mineralogía** *sf* mineralogy.

miniatura [minja'tura] *sf* miniature.

minibus [mini'βus] *sm* minibus.

mínimo ['minimo] *sm, adj* minimum.

ministerio [mini'sterjo] *sm* ministry; office. **ministerial** *adj* ministerial. **ministrador** *sm* administrator. **ministrar** *v* minister; administer. **ministro** *sm* minister; judge. **primer ministro** prime minister.

minoría [mino'ria] *sf* minority. **minorar** *v* diminish.

minucioso [minu'θjoso] *adj* meticulous; minute.

minué [minu'e] *sm* minuet.

minúscula [mi'nuskula] *sf* small letter.

minuta [mi'nuta] *sf* memo; menu; list. **minutar** *v* make notes on.

minutía [minu'tia] *sf* carnation.

minuto [mi'nuto] *sm* minute.

mío ['mio] *adj, pron pers* mine.

miope [mi'ope] *adj* shortsighted. **miopía** *sf* myopia.

miosotis [mjo'sotis] *sm* forget-me-not.

mirar [mi'rar] *v* look; consider. **mira** *sf* sight. **estar a la mira** be on the lookout. **con miras a** with a view to. **mirada** *sf* look; glance. **miradero** *sm* centre of attention; vantage point. **mirado** *adj* circumspect. **mirador** *sm* bay window. **miramiento** *sm* look; consideration; respect.

mirasol [mira'sol] *sm* sunflower.

mirlo ['mirlo] *sm* blackbird.

mirra ['mirra] *sf* myrrh.

mirto ['mirto] *sf* mass. **misal** *sm* missal.

miserable [mise'raβle] *adj* wretched, miserable. **miseria** *sf* misery; poverty. **misericordia** *sf* mercy; compassion. **misericordioso** *adj* merciful; compassionate. **mísero** *adj* wretched.

misión [misi'on] *sf* mission.

mismo ['mismo] *adj* same; own; very; just; right. **aquí mismo** right here. **lo mismo con** the same goes for. **yo mismo** I myself.

misterio [mis'terjo] *sm* mystery. **misterioso** *adj* mysterious. **misticismo** *sm* mysticism. **místico, - a, s, adj** mystic. **mistificación** *sf* falsification; trick. **mistificar** *v* falsify; deceive.

mitad [mi'tað] *sf* half; middle.

mítico ['mitiko] *adj* mythical. **mito** *m* myth. **mitología** *sf* mythology. **mitológico** *adj* mythological.

mitigar [miti'gar] *v* mitigate; relieve. **mitigación** *sf* mitigation. **mitigante** *adj* mitigating.

mitin ['mitin] *sm* political rally.

mitón [mi'ton] *sm* mitten.

mitra ['mitra] *sf* mitre.

mixto ['miksto] *adj* mixed. *sm* compound. **mixtura** *sf* mixture. **mixturar** *v* mix.

mobiliario [moβili'arjo] *sm* furniture.

mocasín [moka'sin] *sm* moccasin.

mocero [mo'θero] *adj* sensual. **mocear** *v* act like a youngster. **mocedad** *sf* youth; youthful prank.

moción [mo'θjon] *sf* motion.

moco ['moko] *sm* mucus. **mocoso** *adj* mucous.

mochila [mo'tʃila] *sf* rucksack.

mocho ['motʃo] *adj* shorn; lopped; *(sin cuernos)* hornless.

moda ['moða] *sf* fashion. **de moda** in fashion. **pasado de moda** old-fashioned.

modales [mo'ðales] *sm pl* manners.

modelo [mo'ðelo] *sm, adj* model; paragon. **modela** *sf* fashion model. **modelar** *v* model.

módem ['moðem] *sm (computadora)* modem.

moderar [moðe'rar] *v* moderate; restrain. **moderación** *sf* moderation. **moderado** *adj* moderate. **moderador, -a** *sm, sf* moderator. **moderativo** *adj* moderating.

moderno [mo'ðerno] *adj* modern. **modernidad** *sf* modernity. **modernizar** *v* modernize. **modernizarse** *v* get up-to-date.

modesto [mo'ðesto] *adj* modest. **modestía** *sf* modesty.

módico ['moðiko] *adj* moderate. **modicidad** *sf* moderateness.

modificar [moðifi'kar] *v* modify. **modificación** *sf* modification.

modismo [mo'ðismo] *sm* idiom.

modista [mo'ðista] *sf* dressmaker.

modo ['moðo] *sm* mode; manner; method. **de modo que** so that. **de todos modos** in any case.

modorra [mo'ðorra] *sf* drowsiness. **modorro** *adj* drowsy.

modular [moðu'lar] *v* modulate. **modulación** *sf* modulation.

mofar [mo'far] *v* scoff; mock. **mofarse de** jeer at. **mofa** *sf* mockery. **mofador** *adj* mocking.

mohín [mo'in] *sm* grimace. **mohino** *adj* sulky.

moho ['moo] *sm* mould; rust. **mohoso** *adj* mouldy; rusty. **ponerse mohoso** go mouldy; go rusty.

mojar [mo'xar] *v* wet; moisten; soak. **mojado** *adj* wet; damp.

mojigato [moxi'gato], **-a** *sm*, *sf* hypocrite; prude. *adj* hypocritical; prudish.

mojón [mo'xon] *sm* landmark.

moldar [mol'ðar] *v also* **moldear** mould. **molde** *sm* mould. **moldura** *sf* moulding.

molécula [mo'lekula] *sf* molecule. **molecular** *adj* molecular.

*moler [mo'ler] *v* grind; crush; (*fig*) bore, weary. **moledura** *sf* grinding; milling; exhaustion.

molestar [moles'tar] *v* annoy; bother; disturb. **molestarse** *v* worry. **no se moleste** don't bother. **molestia** *sf* trouble. **molesto** *adj* tiresome; embarrassing.

molinero [moli'nero] *sm* miller. **molino** *sm* mill.

molusco [mo'lusko] *sm* mollusc.

mollera [mo'ʎera] *sf* crown of the head; (*fig*) brains. **cerrado de mollera** dense; obstinate.

momentáneo [momen'taneo] *adj* momentary. **momento** *sm* moment; momentum. **al momento** immediately.

momia ['momja] *sf* (*cadáver*) mummy. **momificación** *sf* mummification. **momificar** *v* mummify.

monada [mo'naða] *sf* kindness; flattery. **¡qué monada!** how lovely!

monarca [mo'narka] *sm* monarch. **monarquía** *sf* monarchy. **monárquico** *adj* monarchic(al).

monasterio [monas'terjo] *sm* monastery. **monástico** *adj* monastic.

mondar [mon'dar] *v* clean; prune; strip; trim; peel. **monda** *sf* pruning; trimming; cleaning. **mondadientes** *m invar* toothpick. **mondador, -a** *sm*, *sf* pruner; peeler; cleaner. **mondo** *adj* pure; bare; clean.

moneda [mo'neða] *sf* money; coin. **monedero** *sm* purse. **monedero falso** counterfeiter.

monitor ['monitor], **-a** *sm*, *sf* monitor.

monja ['monxa] *sf* nun. **monje** *sm* monk.

mono¹ ['mono] *sm* monkey; ape.

mono² *adj* lovely; cute.

monólogo [mo'nologo] *sm* monologue.

monopolizar [monopoli'θar] *v* monopolize. **monopolio** *sm* monopoly.

monosílabo [mono'silaβo] *sm* monosyllable.

monótono [mo'notono] *adj* monotonous. **monotonía** *sf* monotony.

monovolumen [monoβo'lumen] *sm* people carrier.

monóxido de carbono *sm* carbon monoxide.

monstruo ['monstruo] *sm* monster. **monstruosidad** *sf* monstrosity. **monstruoso** *adj* monstrous.

monta ['monta] *sf* mounting; amount. **montacargas** *sm invar* service lift. **montaje** *sm* mounting.

montaña [mon'taɲa] *sf* mountain. **montañés** *adj* mountain. **montañismo** *sm* mountaineering. **montañoso** *adj* mountainous. **monte** *sm* mountain; mount.

montar [mon'tar] *v* mount; ride; assemble; establish; frame; mounting. **montura** *sf* mount; saddle; frame; mounting.

montera [mon'tera] *sf* cloth cap; bullfighter's hat; skylight. **montero** *sm* hunter.

montón [mon'ton] *sm* heap, pile. **a montones** lots of.

monumento [monu'mento] *sm* monument; memorial. **monumental** *adj* monumental.

moño ['moɲo] *sm* bun, topknot. **ponerse moños** put on airs.

moqueta [mo'keta] *sf* fitted carpet.

mora[1] ['mora] *sf* blackberry; mulberry.

mora[2] *sf* delay.

morada [mo'raða] *sf* abode; sojourn. **morar** *v* dwell.

morado [mo'raðo] *adj* purple; violet. **ponerse morado** stuff oneself.

moral [mo'ral] *adj* moral. **morales** *sf pl* morals. **moraleja** *sf* (*de un cuento*) moral. **moralidad** *sf* morality. **moralista** *s*(*m* + *f*) moralist. **moralizar** *v* moralize.

mórbido ['morβiðo] *adj* morbid; delicate. **morbidez** *sf* tenderness. **morbilidad** *sf* morbidity. **morboso** *adj* morbid; diseased.

morcilla [mor'θiʎa] *sf* black pudding.

mordaz [mor'ðaθ] *adj* mordant; pungent.

mordaza [mor'ðaθa] *sf* (*en la boca*) gag.

***morder** [mor'ðer] *v* bite. **mordedura** *sf* bite. **mordiente** *adj* biting. **mordiscar** *v* nibble. **mordiscón** *sm* nibble; mouthful.

moreno [mo'reno] *adj* brown; tanned; dark.

morera [mo'rera] *sf* mulberry tree.

morfina [mor'fina] *sf* morphine.

moribundo [mori'βundo] *adj* moribund.

***morir** [mo'rir] *v* die; end; fade. **morirse por** crave.

mormón [mor'mon], **-a** *sm*, *sf* Mormon. **mormonismo** *sm* Mormonism.

moro ['moro], **-a** *sm*, *sf* Moor. *adj* Moorish.

moroso [mo'roso] *adj* slow; sluggish; late. **morosidad** *sf* slowness; inactivity.

morralla [mor'raʎa] *sf* rubbish; (*fig*) rabble.

morriña [mor'riɲa] *sf* nostalgia; homesickness.

mortaja [mor'taxa] *sf* shroud.

mortal [mor'tal] *adj* mortal; lethal; awful. *s*(*m* + *f*) mortal. **mortalidad** *sf* mortality.

mortero [mor'tero] *sm* mortar.

mortífero [mor'tifero] *adj* deadly, fatal.

mortificar [mortifi'kar] *v* mortify. **mortificación** *sf* mortification.

mosca ['moska] *sf* fly. **papar moscas** gape. **moscarda** *sf* bluebottle. **moscardón** *sm* blowfly; hornet.

mosquete [mos'kete] *sm* musket. **mosquetero** *sm* musketeer.

mosquito [mos'kito] *sm* mosquito; gnat.

mosquitero *sm* mosquito net.

mostaza [mos'taθa] *sf* mustard.

***mostrar** [mos'trar] *v* show; exhibit; point out. **mostrable** *adj* demonstrable. **mostrador** *sm* (*reloj*) dial: (*tienda*) counter.

mote ['mote] *sm* nickname. **motejar** *v* label; name.

motín [mo'tin] *sm* uprising; mutiny.

motivar [moti'βar] *v* cause, give rise to; justify; explain. **motivación** *sf* motivation. **motivo** *sm* motive; grounds *pl*. **con motivo de** owing to.

motocicleta [motoθi'kleta] *sf* motorcycle. **motociclista** *s*(*m* + *f*) motor-cyclist.

motor ['motor] *sm* motor; engine. **motorista** *s*(*m* + *f*) motorcyclist. **motorizar** *v* motorize.

motriz [mo'triθ] *adj* motive.

mover [mo'βer] *v* move; shake; stir; incite. **moverse** *v* move; get a move on. **movedizo** *adj* movable; inconstant. **movible** *adj* mobile. **móvil** *adj* mobile; fickle. **movilidad** *sf* mobility. **movilizar** *v* mobilize. **movilización** *sf* mobilization. **movimiento** *sm* movement; motion; activity.

mozo ['moθo] *sm* youth, lad; waiter. **moza** *sf* girl; servant.

mucoso [mu'koso] *adj* mucous. **mucosidad** *sf* mucus.

muchacho [mu'tʃatʃo] *sm* boy; chap. **muchacha** *sf* girl; servant.

muchedumbre [mutʃe'ðumbre] *sf* crowd; (*fig*) a lot.

mucho ['mutʃo] *adj* a lot of; much; great; many. *pron* many; a lot. *adv* much; a lot; a long time. **con mucho** by far. **por mucho que** however much.

mudar [mu'ðar] *v* change; remove; shed. **mudarse** *v* move house; change one's clothes. **muda** *sf* change; moulting. **mudable** *adj* changeable; variable. **mudanza** *sf* change; removal. **camión de mundanzas** *sm* removal van.

mudo ['muðo] *adj* dumb, mute. **mudez** *sf* dumbness.

mueble ['mweβle] *sm* piece of furniture. **muebles** *sm pl* furniture *sing*.

mueca ['mweka] *sf* grimace.

muela ['mwela] *sf* molar. **muela del juicio** wisdom tooth.

muelle ['mweʎe] *adj* soft; luxurious. *sm* wharf; embankment; spring.

muérdago [mu'erðaɣo] *sm* mistletoe.

muerte ['mwerte] *sf* death; murder. **de mala muerte** (*fam*) rotten; lousy.

muerto ['mwerto] *V* **morir**. *adj* dead. *sm* corpse.

muestra ['mwestra] *sf* sample, example; specimen; sign.

mugir [mu'xir] *v* roar; bellow; low. **mugido** *sm* roar; bellow; lowing.

mujer [mu'xer] *sf* woman; wife.

muleta [mu'leta] *sf* crutch; bullfighter's cape.

mulo ['mulo] *sm* mule.

multar [mul'tar] *v* fine. **multa** *sf* fine.

múltiple ['multiple] *adj* multiple; many. **multiplicación** *sf* multiplication. **multiplicar** *v* multiply, increase.

multipropiedad [multipro'pjeðað] *sf* time-share (house, apartment).

multitud [multi'tuð] *sf* multitude, crowd.

***mullir** [mu'ʎir] *v* beat; break up; loosen. **mullido** *adj* soft; fluffy.

mundo ['mundo] *sm* world; (*fam*) crowd. **todo el mundo** everybody. **mundanal** *adj* worldly. **mundanería** *sf* worldliness. **mundial** *adj* world; worldwide. **mundovisión** *sf* broadcasting by satellite.

municipal [muniθi'pal] *adj* municipal. *sm* policeman. **municipalidad** *sf* municipality. **municipio** *sm* town council.

munífico [mu'nifiko] *adj* munificent; liberal. **munificencia** *sf* munificence; liberality.

muñeca [mu'neka] *sf* doll; dressmaker's dummy; wrist.

muralla [mu'raʎa] *sf* wall; rampart. **mural** *adj*, *sm* mural. **murar** *v* wall. **muro** *sm* wall.

murciélago [murθi'elaɣo] *sm* (*zool*) bat.

murmullo [mur'muʎo] *sm* murmur; whisper; rustle.

murmurar [murmu'rar] *v* murmur; whisper; mutter; gossip. **murmuración** *sf* gossiping. **murmurio** *sm* murmuring.

músculo ['muskulo] *sm* muscle. **muscular** *adj* muscular.

muselina [muse'lina] *sf* muslin.

museo [mu'seo] *sm* museum; art gallery.

musgo ['musɣo] *sm* moss.

música ['musika] *sf* music. **musical** *adj* musical. **músico, -a** *sm*, *sf* musician. **musicología** *sf* musicology.

muslo ['muslo] *sm* thigh.

mustio ['mustjo] *adj* withered; sad. **mustiarse** *v* wither.

mutación [muta'θjon] *sf* mutation; change. **mutabilidad** *sf* mutability. **mutante** *sm*, *adj* mutant.

mutilar [muti'lar] *v* mutilate; cripple. **mutilación** *sf* mutilation. **mutilado, -a** *sm*, *sf* cripple.

mutual ['mutwal] *adj* mutual. **mutuo** *adj* mutual; joint.

muy [mwi] *adv* very; quite; too; much. **muy señor mío** (*carta*) Dear Sir.

N

nabo ['naβo] *sm* turnip.

nácar ['nakar] *sm* mother-of-pearl.

***nacer** [na'θer] *v* be born; originate. **nacido** *adj* born. **naciente** *adj* growing. **nacimiento** *sm* birth; origin.

nación [na'θjon] *sf* nation. **nacional** *adj* national. *s*(*m* + *f*) national; native. **nacionalidad** *sf* nationality. **nacionalismo** *sm* nationalism. **nacionalizar** *v* nationalize.

nada ['naða] *sf* nothing. *adv* by no means. **de nada** don't mention it. **nada más** only.

nadar [na'ðar] *v* swim. **nadador, -a** *sm*, *sf* swimmer.

nadie ['naðje] *pron* nobody, no one.

naipe ['naipe] *sm* playing-card.

nalga ['nalɣa] *sf* buttock.

naranja [na'ranxa] *sf* orange. **naranjada** *sf* orangeade. **naranjo** *sm* orange tree.

narciso [nar'θiso] *sm* narcissus. **narcisismo** *sm* narcissism.

narcótico [nar'kotiko] *sm*, *adj* narcotic.

nariz [na'riθ] *sf*, *pl* **narices** nose.

narrar [nar'rar] *v* narrate. **narración** *sf* narration. **narrador, -a** *sm*, *sf* narrator. **narrativa** *sf* narrative.

nasal [na'sal] *adj* nasal.

nata ['nata] *sf* cream; curd; (*fig*) the best. **natillas** *sf pl* custard *sing*.

natación [nata'θjon] *sf* swimming.

natal [na'tal] *adj* natal; native. *sm* birth; birthday. **natalidad** *sf* birthrate.

nativo [na'tiβo], **-a** *s, adj* native. **natividad** *sf* nativity. **nato** *adj* born.

natural [natu'ral] *s(m + f)* native; citizen. *sm* nature. *adj* natural; lifelike. **naturaleza** *sf* nature; nationality. **naturalidad** *sf* naturalness; citizenship.

naufragar [naufra'gar] *v* sink; be shipwrecked. **naufragio** *sm* shipwreck. **náufrago** *adj* shipwrecked.

náusea ['nausea] *sf* nausea. **nauseabundo** *adj* nauseous; nauseating.

náutico ['nautiko] *adj* nautical. **náutica** *sf* navigation.

navaja [na'βaxa] *sf* penknife; razor. **navajada** *sf* stab; gash.

naval [na'βal] *adj* naval. **nave** *sf or* **navío** *sm* ship. **nave espacial** *sf* spacecraft. **navegable** *adj* navigable. **navegación** *sf* navigation; sailing. **navegador** *sm* browser (Internet). **navegante** *sm* navigator; *s(m+f)* surfer (Internet). **navegar** *v* browse; surf (Internet).

neblina [ne'βlina] *sf* mist, fog. **nebulosidad** *sf* nebulosity; haziness. **nebuloso** *adj* nebulous.

necedad [neθe'ðað] *sf* foolishness; nonsense. **necio** *adj* foolish.

necesario [neθe'sarjo] *adj* necessary. **necesidad** *sf* necessity; poverty. **necesitado** *adj* needy. **necesitar** *v* need.

néctar ['nektar] *sm* nectar.

nectarína [necta'rina] *sf* nectarine.

nefario [ne'farjo] *adj* nefarious.

nefasto [ne'fasto] *adj* ill-omened; unlucky.

*negar [ne'gar] *v* deny; refuse. **negarse** *v* decline; refuse. **negación** *sf* negation. **negativa** *sm (foto)* negative; *sf* refusal.

negligencia [negli'xenθja] *sf* negligence. **negligente** *adj* negligent.

negociar [nego'θjar] *v* trade; negotiate. **negociable** *adj* negotiable. **negociación** *sf* transaction; negotiation. **negociado** *sm* bureau; division. **negociador, -a** *sm, adj* negotiator; agent. **negociante** *sm* businessman; merchant. **negocio** *sm* business; trade; negotiation.

negro ['negro], **-a** *s, adj* black. **negrita** *adj, sf* bold (typeface). **negrura** *sf* blackness.

nene ['nene], **-a** *sm, sf* baby.

nenúfar [ne'nufar] *sm* waterlily.

neón [ne'on] *sm* neon.

nepotismo [nepo'tismo] *sm* nepotism.

nervio ['nerβjo] *sm* nerve; *(de una hoja)* rib; sinew. **crisparle los nervios a uno** get on someone's nerves. **tener los nervios en punta** be on edge. **nerviosidad** *sf* nervousness. **nervioso** *adj* nervous. **crisis nerviosa** *sf* nervous breakdown.

neto ['neto] *adj* pure; clear; *(com)* net.

neumático [neu'matiko] *sm* tyre. *adj* pneumatic.

neumonía [neumo'nia] *sf* pneumonia.

neuralgia [neu'ralxja] *sf* neuralgia. **neurálgico** *adj* neuralgic.

neurótico [neu'rotiko] *adj* neurotic. **neurosis** *sf* neurosis.

neutro ['neutro] *adj* neutral; *(gram)* neuter. **neutral** *s(m + f)* , *adj* neutral. **neutralidad** *sf* neutrality. **neutralizar** *v* neutralize.

*nevar [ne'βar] *v* snow. **nevada** *sf* snow storm. **nevasca** *sf* snowfall. **nevera** *sf* refrigerator. **nevisca** *sf* light snowfall. **neviscar** *v* snow lightly. **nevoso** *adj* snowy.

nexo ['nekso] *sm* link, tie.

ni [ni] *conj* neither; nor; or: not even, **ni uno ni otro** neither one nor the other

nicotina [niko'tina] *sf* nicotine.

nicho ['nitʃo] *sm* niche.

nido [ni'ðo] *sm* nest. **cunas de nido** pull-out beds. **nidada** *sf* brood; clutch. **nidal** *sm* nest; nest egg.

niebla [ni'eβla] *sf* fog; mist; mildew.

nieto [ni'eto] *sm* grandson. **nieta** *sf* granddaughter.

nieve [ni'eβe] *sf* snow.

nilón [ni'lon] *sm* nylon.

ninfa ['ninfa] *sf* nymph.

ninguno [nin'guno] *adj also* **ningún** no; not one. **ninguna manera** in no way. *pron* nobody.

niña ['niŋa] *sf* little girl; *(del ojo)* pupil. **niñada** *sf* childishness. **niñera** *sf* nanny. **niñez** *sf* childhood. **niño** *sm* little boy; child. **desde niño** from childhood. **Niña Exploradora** *sf* Brownie Guide.

níquel ['nikel] *sm* nickel. **niquelar** *v* nickel-plate.

níspero ['nispero] *sm* medlar tree. **níspola** *sf* medlar.

nítido [ni'tiðo] *adj* clear; bright. **nitidez** *sf* brightness; neatness.

nitrógeno [ni'troxeno] *sm* nitrogen. **nitrato** *sm* nitrate. **nítrico** *adj* nitric. **nitro** *sm* nitre; saltpetre. **nitroso** *adj* nitrous.

nivelar [niβe'lar] *v* level; balance. **nivelarse** *v* become level. **nivelarse con** get even with. **nivel** *sm* level; standard. **nivel de aire** spirit-level. **nivel de vida** standard of living. **paso a nivel** level-crossing. **nivelación** *sf* levelling.

no [no] *adv* no; not. **no bien** no sooner. **no más** only. **no obstante** in spite of. **que no** if only.

noble ['noβle] *adj* noble. *sm* nobleman. **nobleza** *sf* nobility.

noción [no'θjon] *sf* notion; idea. **nociones** *sf pl* smattering *sing*; rudiments.

nocivo [no'θiβo] *adj* noxious; harmful.

nocturno [nok'turno] *adj* nocturnal; night. **noctámbulo, -a** *sm, sf* sleepwalker.

noche ['notʃe] *sf* night; evening. **por la noche** at night. **Nochebuena** *sf* Christmas Eve.

nódulo ['noðulo] *sm* nodule.

nogal [no'gal] *sm* also **noguera** *sf* walnut tree.

nómada ['nomaða] *s(m + f)* nomad. *adj* nomadic.

nombrar [nom'brar] *v* name; nominate; mention. **nombradía** *sf* reputation. **nombramiento** *sm* naming; nomination. **nombre** *sm* name; title. **nombre de pila** Christian name. **nomenclatura** *sf* nomenclature; terminology; catalogue. **nómina** *sf* list; payroll. **nominación** *sf* nomination. **nominal** *adj* nominal. **nominativo** *sm* (*gram*) nominative.

non [non] *adj* (*mat*) odd. *sm* odd number.

nonagésimo [nona'xesimo] *adj* ninetieth. **nonagenario, -a** *s, adj* nonagenarian.

norabuena [nora'βwena] *sf* congratulations *pl. adv* by good fortune. **noramala** *adv* unfortunately.

nordeste [nor'ðeste] *sm* north-east; (*viento*) northeaster. *adj* north-east.

noria [no'ria] *sf* waterwheel.

norma ['norma] *sf* norm; rule. **normal** *adj* normal. **normalidad** *sf* normality. **normalizar** *v* normalize.

noroeste [noro'este] *sm* north-west; (*viento*) northwesterly. *adj* north-west.

norte ['norte] *sm, adj* north. **perder el norte** lose one's bearings. **norteño** *adj* northern.

Noruega [nor'wega] *sf* Norway. **noruego, -a** *sm, sf* (*persona*) Norwegian; *sm* (*idioma*) Norwegian.

nos [nos] *pron* us, ourselves.

nosotros [no'sotros] *pron* we; us, ourselves.

nostalgia [nos'talxja] *sf* nostalgia. **nostálgico** *adj* nostalgic; homesick.

notar [no'tar] *v* note; notice; note down. **nota** *sf* (*música, etc.*) note; mark; report; repute. **notabilidad** *sf* notability. **notable** *adj* notable. **notación** *sf* notation.

notario [no'tarjo] *sm* notary. **notaría** *sf* notary's office.

noticiar [noti'θjar] *v* notify. **noticia(s)** *sf* (*pl*) news *sing*. **noticiario** *sm* news bulletin. **noticiero, -a** *sm, sf* reporter. **notición** *sm* (*fam*) big news. **noticioso** *adj* well-informed. **notificación** *sf* notification.

notorio [no'torjo] *adj* notorious. **notoriedad** *sf* notoriety.

novato [no'βato], **-a** *s, adj* novice.

novecientos [noβe'θjentos] *adj, s* nine hundred.

novedad [noβe'ðað] *sf* novelty; change. **novedades** *sf pl* latest models.

novela [no'βela] *sf* novel. **novelista** *s(m + f)* novelist.

noveno [no'βeno] *adj* ninth. **noventa** *adj* ninety.

novia ['noβja] *sf* girlfriend; fiancée; bride. **traje de novia** wedding dress. **novio** *sm* boyfriend; fiancé; bridegroom.

novicio [no'βiθjo] *sm* beginner; apprentice. **noviciado** *sm* novitiate; apprenticeship.

noviembre [no'βjembre] *sm* November.

novilla [no'βiʎa] *sf* heifer. **novillada** *sf* bullfight with young bulls. **novillero** *sm* novice bullfighter. **novillo** *sm* young bull. **hacer novillos** play truant.

nube ['nuβe] *sf* cloud. **estar por las nubes** (*precios*) be sky-high. **poner por las nubes** praise to the skies. **nublado** *adj* overcast. **nublar** *v* cloud over. **nubloso** *adj* cloudy; ill-fated.

núcleo ['nukleo] *sm* nucleus; core; (*bot*) stone. **nuclear** *adj* nuclear.

nudillo [nu'ðiʎo] *sm* knuckle.

nudo¹ ['nuðo] *sm* knot; bond; tumour.

nudo² *adj* nude.

nuera ['nwera] *sf* daughter-in-law.

nuestro ['nwestro] *adj* our. *pron* ours.

nueva ['nweβa] *sf* news. **nuevo** *adj* new. **de nuevo** again. **nuevo flamante** brand new.

nueve ['nweβe] *adj, sm* nine.

nuez [nweθ] *sf* nut; walnut. **nuez de la garganta** Adam's apple.

nulo ['nulo] *adj* null; void; (*fig*) hopeless.

numerar [nume'rar] *v* number. **numeral** *sm, adj* numeral. **numérico** *adj* numerical. **número** *sm* number; size; quantity. **número de identificación personal** *sm* PIN number. **numeró no figura en la guía** ex-directory number. **numeroso** *adj*

nunca ['nunka] *adv* never; ever. **casi nunca** hardly ever.

nuncio ['nunθjo] *sm* nuncio; (*fig*) omen.

nupcial [nup'θjal] *adj* nuptial. **nupcias** *sf pl* nuptials.

nutria [nu'tria] *sf also* **nutra** *sf* otter.

nutrir [nu'trir] *v* nourish. **nutrición** *sf* nutrition. **nutrimento** *sm* nutriment. **nutritivo** *adj* nourishing.

Ñ

ñaque ['nake] *sm* odds and ends *pl*.

ñoño ['nono] *adj* insipid; prudish; fussy. **ñoñería** *sf also* **ñoñez** *sf* insipidity; prudery; fussiness.

ñu [nu] *sm* gnu.

O

o [o] *conj* or. **o ... o** either ... or. **o sea** in other words.

obcecar [oβθe'kar] *v* blind; deceive. **obcecarse** *v* become blind; be dazzled. **obcecado** *adj* blind; obdurate.

obduración [oβðura'θjon] *sf* obduracy; obstinacy.

*****obedecer** [oβeðe'θer] *v* obey. **obediencia** *sf* obedience. **obediente** *adj* obedient.

obertura [oβer'tura] *sf* (*música*) overture.

obesidad [oβesi'ðað] *sf* obesity. **obeso** *adj* obese.

obispo [o'βispo] *sm* bishop. **obispado** *sm* bishopric.

obituario [oβi'twarjo] *sm* obituary.

objetar [oβxe'tar] *v* object (to). **objeción** *sf* objection. **objetivo** *sm* objective. **objeto** *sm* object.

oblicuo [o'βlikwo] *adj* oblique. **oblicuar** *v* slant.

obligar [oβli'gar] *v* oblige; force. **verse obligado a** be forced to. **obligación** *sf* obligation. **obligado** *adj* essential. **obligatorio** *adj* compulsory.

obliterar [oβlite'rar] *v* obliterate; obstruct.

oblongo [o'βlongo] *adj* oblong.

obrar [o'βrar] *v* work; operate; make; build; behave. **obra** *sf* work. **obra maestra** masterpiece. **obrero, -a** *sm, sf* worker.

obsceno [oβs'θeno] *adj* obscene. **obscenidad** *sf* obscenity.

*****obscurecer** [oβskure'θer] *v also* **oscurecer** obscure, darken. **obscuridad** *sf* obscurity. **obscuro** *adj* obscure.

obsequiar [oβseki'ar] *v* entertain; treat; present. **obsequio** *sm* courtesy; gift. **obsequioso** *adj* obsequious; attentive.

observar [oβseki'var] *v* observe. **observación** *sf* observation. **observador, -a** *sm, sf* observer. **observancia** *sf* observance. **observante** *adj* observant. **observatorio** *sm* observatory.

obsesión [oβse'sjon] *sf* obsession. **obsesionante** *or* **obsesivo** *adj* obsessive. **obseso** *adj* obsessed.

obsoleto [oβso'leto] *adj* obsolete.

obstáculo [oβ'stakulo] *sm* obstacle.

obstante [oβ'stante] *prep* in spite of. *adv* **no obstante** notwithstanding; nevertheless. **obstar** *v* hinder; oppose.

obstetricia [oβste'triθja] *sf* obstetrics. **obstétrico** *adj* obstetric.

obstinarse [oβsti'narse] *v* be obstinate; persist. **obstinación** *sf* obstinacy. **obstinado** *adj* obstinate.

*****obstruir** [oβstru'ir] *v* obstruct. **obstrucción** *sf* obstruction. **obstructivo** *adj* obstructive.

*****obtener** [oβte'ner] *v* obtain. **obtención** *sf* attainment.

obturar [obtu'rar] *v* stop up, plug. **obturación** *sf* plugging; sealing. **velocidad de obturación** (*foto*) shutter speed. **obturador** *sm* plug; (*foto*) shutter.

obtuso [oβ'tuso] *adj* obtuse.

obús [o'βus] *sm* howitzer.

obvio ['oββjo] *adj* obvious. **obviamente** *adv* obviously. **obviar** *v* obviate.

oca ['oka] *sf* goose.

ocasión [oka'sjon] *sf* occasion; opportunity; reason. **ocasional** *adj* occasional; chance. **ocasionalmente** *adv* occasionally; accidentally. **ocasionar** *v* cause.

ocaso [o'kaso] *sm* sunset; decline; west.

occidental [okθiðen'tal] *adj* western, occidental. **occidente** *sm* west.

océano [o'θeano] *sm* ocean.

ocio ['oθjo] *sm* leisure; idleness. **ociosidad** *sf* idleness. **ocioso** *adj* idle.

ocre ['okre] *sm* ochre.

octágono [ok'tagono] *adj* octagonal. *sm* octagon.

octava [ok'taβa] *sf* octave. **octavo** *adj* eighth. **octogenario, -a** *sm, sf* octogenarian. **octogésimo** *adj* eightieth.

octubre [ok'tuβre] *sm* October.

ocular [oku'lar] *adj* ocular. **testigo ocular** eyewitness. *sm* eyepiece. **oculista** *s(m + f)* oculist.

ocultar [okul'tar] *v* hide. **ocultación** *sf* concealment; dissimulation. **oculto** *adj* secret; hidden; occult.

ocupar [oku'par] *v* occupy; employ; take over. **ocuparse (de)** look after; do; employ. **ocupación** *sf* occupation. **ocupado** *adj* occupied; **taken**; engaged. **ocupante** *s(m + f)* occupant.

occurrir [okur'rir] *v* occur. **ocurrencia** *sf* occurrence; (*fig*) witticism; idea. **ocurrente** *adj* witty.

ochenta [o'tʃenta] *sm, adj* eighty. **ocho** *sm, adj* eight.

oda ['oða] *sf* ode.

odiar [o'ðjar] *v* hate. **odio** *sm* hate, hatred. **tener odio a uno** hate someone. **odiosidad** *sf* hatefulness; odiousness. **odioso** *adj* odious; hateful.

odorífero [oðo'rifero] *adj* odoriferous, fragrant.

oeste [o'este] *sm* west.

ofender [ofen'der] *v* offend; insult. **ofenderse** *v* resent. **ofensa** *sf* offence; insult. **ofensiva** *sf* attack. **ofensivo** *adj* offensive; insulting. **ofensor, -a** *sm, sf* offender.

oferta [o'ferta] *sf* offer; bid; tender; gift. **ley de la oferta y la demanda** law of supply and demand.

oficial [ofi'θjal] *adj, sm* official. **oficialía** *sf* clerkship. **oficina** *sf* office; agency; laboratory. **oficina de turismo** *sf* tourist office. **oficio** *sm* job; appointment; calling. **oficioso** *adj* diligent; meddlesome.

****ofrecer** [ofre'θer] *v* offer. **ofrecerse** *v* volunteer. **¿qué se le ofrece a usted?** may I help you? **ofrecimiento** *sm* offer. **ofrendar** *v* contribute. **ofrenda** *sf* offer.

ofuscar [ofus'kar] *v* bewilder; dazzle.

ogro ['ogro] *sm* ogre.

oigo [o'igo] *V* **oír**

****oír** [o'ir] *v* hear; listen to. **oírse** *v* be heard. **oír decir que** hear that. **oída** *sf* hearing. **oíble** *adj* audible. **oído** *sm* hearing; ear. **dolor de oídos** earache.

ojal [o'xal] *sm* buttonhole.

ojalá [oxa'la] *interj* let's hope so! would to God! *conj* if only.

ojear[1] [oxe'ar] *v* look at. **ojeada** *sf* glance.

ojear[2] *v* (*en la caza*) start game; (*espantar*) scare off.

ojo ['oxo] *sm* eye; opening; hole; keyhole; (*puente*) span. **¡ojo!** look out!

ola ['ola] *sf* wave. **ola de calor** heatwave.

olé [o'le] *interj* bravo!

oleandro [ole'andro] *sm* oleander.

óleo ['oleo] *sm* oil. **pintura al óleo** *sf* oil painting. **oleoducto** *sm* pipeline. **oleosidad** *sf* oiliness. **oleoso** *adj* oily.

****oler** [o'ler] *v* smell. **oler bien/mal** smell good/bad. **olfatear** *v* smell; sniff; sniff out. **olfato** *sm* sense of smell. **olfatorio** *adj* olfactory. **oliente** *adj* smelling. **olor** *sm* smell. **oloroso** *adj* fragrant.

oligarquía [oligar'kia] *sf* oligarchy.

olímpico [o'limpiko] *adj* Olympic. **juegos olímpicos** Olympic games.

oliva [o'liβa] *sf* olive; olive tree. **olivar** *sm* olive grove. **olivo** *sm* olive tree.

olmo ['olmo] *sm* elm tree. **olmeda** *sf* elm grove.

olvidar [olβi'ðar] *v* forget. **olvidadizo** *adj* forgetful. **olvido** *sm* forgetfulness.

olla ['oʎa] *sf* pot; kettle; stew; (*remolino*) eddy. **olla exprés** pressure cooker. **olla podrida** hotpot.

ombligo [om'bligo] *sm* navel; (*fig*) core.

ominoso [omi'noso] *adj* ominous.

omitir [omi'tir] *v* omit; neglect. **omisión** *sf* omission. **omiso** *adj* careless. **hacer caso omiso de** ignore; overlook.

ómnibus ['omniβus] *sm* omnibus.

omnipotencia [omnipo'tenθja] *sf* omnipotence. **omnipotente** *adj* omnipotent.

omnisciencia [omni'sθjenθja] *sf* omniscience. **omniscio** *adj* omniscient.

omnívoro [om'niβoro] *adj* omnivorous.

once ['onθe] *sm, adj* eleven.

onda ['onda] *sf* wave; ripple. **onda corta/larga/media** short/long/medium wave. **onda luminosa** light wave. **onda sonora** sound wave. **ondear** *v* wave. **ondearse** *v* swing. **ondulación** *sf* undulation. **ondulado** *adj* wavy. **ondulante** *adj* undulating. **ondular** *v* undulate; wriggle.

oneroso [one'roso] *adj* onerous.

ónice ['oniθe] *sm also* **ónique, ónix** onyx.

onza ['onθa] *sf (peso y animal)* ounce.

opaco [o'pako] *adj* opaque; dull. **opacidad** *sf* opacity.

opción [op'θjon] *sf* option. **opcional** *adj* optional.

ópera ['opera] *sf* opera.

operar [ope'rar] *v* operate. **operación** *sf* operation. **operador, -a** *sm, sf* operator; surgeon; projectionist. **operante** *adj* operative. **operario, -a** *sm, sf* operative, worker. **operativo** *adj* operative.

opinar [opi'nar] *v* think; judge. **opinión** *sf* opinion.

opio ['opjo] *sm* opium.

***oponer** [opo'ner] *v* oppose; hinder; contradict. **oponerse -a** compete for. **oposición** *sf* opposition. **opositor, -a** *sm, sf* opponent; competitor.

oportunidad [oportuni'ðað] *sf* opportunity. **oportunista** *adj* opportunist. **oportuno** *adj* opportune.

oprimir [opri'mir] *v* oppress; depress. **opresión** *sf* oppression. **opresivo** *adj* oppressive. **opresor, -a** *sm, sf* oppressor.

oprobio [o'proβjo] *sm* opprobrium, disgrace. **oprobioso** *adj* disgraceful.

optar [op'tar] *v* opt, choose.

óptico ['optiko] *adj* optic, optical. **sm** optician.

optimismo [opti'mismo] *sm* optimism. **optimista** *s(m + f)* optimist.

óptimo ['optimo] *adj* optimum, best.

opuesto [o'pwesto] *adj* opposed; against.

opulento [opu'lento] *adj* opulent. **opulencia** *sf* opulence.

oquedad [oke'ðað] *sf* hole; hollow.

ora ['ora] *conj* now.

oráculo [o'rakulo] *sm* oracle.

orangután [orangu'tan] *sm* orangutan.

orar [o'rar] *v* pray; plead; make a speech. **oración** *sf* oration; prayer. **partes de la oración** parts of speech. **orador, -a** *sm, sf* orator. **orador sagrado** preacher. **oral** *adj* oral.

orbe ['orβe] *sm* orb, globe.

órbita ['orβita] *sf* orbit. **orbitar** *v* orbit.

ordenar [orðe'nar] *v* order. command; tidy; direct; ordain. **ordenarse** *v* become ordained. **orden** *sm* order, sequence. **por su orden** successively. **ordenación** *sf* arrangement; ordination. **ordenanza** *sf* arrangement; ordinance.

ordenador [orðe'nador] *sm* computer. **ordenador personal** personal computer. **ordenador portátil** laptop.

ordeñar [orðe'ɲar] *v* milk.

ordinal [orði'nal] *adj* ordinal.

ordinario [orði'narjo] *adj* ordinary; common. **de ordinario** usually.

orear [ore'ar] *v* air, ventilate. **orearse** *v* get a breath of fresh air.

oreja [o'rexa] *sf* ear. **bajar las orejas** knuckle under.

orfebre [or'feβre] *sm* goldsmith; silversmith. **orfebrería** *sf* goldwork; silverwork.

orfeón [orfe'on] *sm* choral society.

orgánico [or'ganiko] *adj* organic. **organismo** *sm* organism. **organista** *s(m + f)* organist. **organización** *sf* organization. **organizador, -a** *sm, sf* organizer. **organo** *sm* organ.

orgasmo [or'gasmo] *sm* orgasm.

orgía [or'xia] *sf* orgy.

orgulloso [orgu'loso] *adj* proud. **sm** pride.

orientarse [orjen'tarse] *v* find one's bearings. **orientación** *sf* orientation. **oriental** *adj* oriental, eastern. **oriente** *sm* orient, east. **Extremo Oriente** Far East. **Oriente Medio** Middle East.

orificio [ori'fiθjo] *sm* orifice, hole.

origen [o'rixen] *sm* origin; native country. **original** *adj* original. **originalidad** *sf* originality. **originar** *v* originate. **originarse** *v* arise.

orilla [o'riʎa] *sf* edge; bank; shore. **a orillas de** on the banks of.

orín [o'rin] *sm* rust.

orina [o'rina] *sf* urine. **orinal** *sm* chamber

pagar

pot. **orinar** *v* urinate.

oriundo [o'rjundo] *adj* native of.

orlar [or'lar] *v* border, edge. **orla** *sf* border, trimming.

ornamentar [ornamen'tar] *v* adorn, decorate. **ornamentación** *sf* ornamentation. **ornamental** *adj* ornamental. **ornamento** *sm* ornament. **ornar** *v* adorn. **ornato** *sm* adornment.

ornitología [ornitolo'xia] *sf* ornithology. **ornitólogo** *sm* ornithologist.

oro ['oro] *sm* gold. **oro batido** gold leaf. **oro en bruto** bullion. **oropel** *sm* tinsel.

orquesta [or'kesta] *sf* orchestra. **orquestación** *sf* orchestration. **orquestar** *v* orchestrate.

orquídea [or'kiðea] *sf* orchid.

ortega [or'tega] *sf* grouse.

ortodoxo [orto'ðokso] *adj* orthodox. **ortodoxia** *sf* orthodoxy.

ortografia [ortogra'fia] *sf* orthography, spelling.

ortopédico [orto'peðiko], -a, *sm, sf* orthopedist. *adj* orthopedic.

oruga [o'ruga] *sf* caterpillar.

os [os] *pron pl* you.

osa ['osa] *sf* she-bear. **oso** bear. **oso blanco** polar bear.

osar [o'sar] *v* dare. **osadía** *sf* daring. **osado** *adj* daring.

oscilar [osθi'lar] *v* oscillate, swing. **oscilación** *sf* oscillation.

oscuro [os'kuro] *adj* dark, obscure. **oscurecer** *v* darken; confuse. **oscuridad** *sf* obscurity.

ostensible [osten'siβle] *adj* ostensible; apparent. **ostentación** *sf* ostentation. **ostentar** *v* show off. **ostentativo** *adj* also **ostentoso** ostentatious.

ostra ['ostra] *sf* oyster.

otear [ote'ar] *v* make out; watch; scan.

otoño [o'toɲo] *sm* autumn. **otoñada** *sf* autumn season. **otoñal** *adj* autumnal. **otoñarse** *v* be seasoned.

otorgar [otor'gar] *v* grant; award; confer. **otorgamiento** *sm* granting; authorization.

otro ['otro] *adj* other; another. **otra vez** again. **otro tanto** the same (again). *pron* another. **algún otro** some other.

ovación [oβa'θjon] *sf* ovation. **ovacionar** *v* give an ovation to.

óvalo ['oβalo] *sm* oval; ellipse. **oval** *adj* oval.

ovario [o'βarjo] *sm* ovary.

oveja [o'βexa] *sf* ewe; sheep.

ovillo [o'βiʎa] *sm* (*de lana*) ball; heap.

OVNI ['oβni] *sm* (*objete volante no identificado*) UFO (unidentified flying object).

oxidar [oksi'ðar] *v* oxidize. **óxido** *sm* oxide. **oxígeno** *sm* oxygen.

oye ['oje] *V* **oír**.

oyente [o'jente] *adj* hearing. *s(m + f)* listener.

ozono [o'θono] *sm* ozone.

ozono [o'θono] *sm* ozone. **capa de ozono** ozone layer.

P

pabellón [paβe'ʎon] *sm* pavilion; bell tent; summerhouse; hospital block; flag.

*pacer [pa'θer] *v* graze, pasture.

paciencia [pa'θjenθja] *sf* patience. **paciente** *s(m + f)*, *adj* patient. **pacienzudo** *adj* long-suffering.

pacificar [paθifi'kar] *v* pacify. **pacificación** *sf* pacification. **pacificador** *adj* pacifying. **pacífico** *adj* pacific, peaceful. **Oceano Pacífico** Pacific Ocean. **pacifismo** *sm* pacifism. **pacifista** *s(m + f)* pacifist.

pacotilla [pako'tiʎa] *sf* inferior goods *pl*. **de pacotilla** shoddy.

pactar [pak'tar] *v* make a pact, agree. **pacto** *sm* pact, agreement.

pachorra [pa'tʃorra] *sf* sluggishness; indolence.

*padecer [paðe'θer] *v* suffer; endure. **padecer de** suffer from. **padecimiento** *sm* suffering; ailment.

padre ['paðre] *sm* father. **padres** *sm pl* parents. **padrastro** *sm* stepfather. **Padre Nuestro** Lord's Prayer. **padrino** *sm* godfather; second; sponsor. **padrino de boda** best man.

padrón [pa'ðron] *sm* census; pattern; memorial; (*fam*) indulgent father.

pagano [pa'gano], -a *sm, sf, adj* pagan.

pagar [pa'gar] *v* pay. **pagarse de** take a liking to. **paga** *sf* payment; salary. **pagadero** *adj* payable. **pagador**, -a *sm, sf* payer.

pagaduría sf pay office. **pagaré** sm IOU. **pago** sm payment; reward.

página ['paxina] sf page. **página principal** sf home page (Internet). **página web** sf website.

país [pa'is] sm country. **paisaje** sm landscape; countryside. **paisanaje** sm peasantry. **paisano, -na** sm, sf compatriot; peasant.

Países Bajos [pa'ises'βaxos] sm pl The Netherlands.

paja ['paxa] sf straw. **echar pajas** draw lots. **pajita** sf drinking straw.

pájaro ['paxaro] sm bird. **pajarera** sf birdcage.

paje ['paxe] sm (niño) page.

Pakistán [pakis'tan] sm Pakistan. **pakistaní** adj Pakistani.

pala ['pala] sf shovel; spade; scoop; dustpan; bat. **palazo** sm blow with a stick.

palabra [pa'laβra] sf word. **de palabra** by word of mouth. **faltar a la palabra** break one's word. **palabreo** sm verbiage. **palabrista** s(m + f) chatterbox. **palabrota** sf swear word.

palacio [pa'laθjo] sm palace; mansion. **en palacio** at court.

paladar [pala'ðar] sm palate. **paladear** v taste, relish.

palanca [pa'lanka] sf crowbar; lever; (fam) influence.

palangana [palan'gana] sf washbasin.

palco ['palko] sm (teatro) box.

paleta [pa'leta] sf shovel; trowel; (de pintor) palette; (de hélice) blade; (anat) shoulder blade.

paliar [pali'ar] v alleviate. **paliativo** adj palliative.

*palidecer [paliðe'θer] v become pale. **palidez** paleness. **pálido** adj pale.

palillo [pa'liʎo] sm toothpick; small stick.

paliza [pa'liθa] sf beating, hiding.

palma ['palma] sf palm tree; (anat) palm. **palmada** sf slap; applause. **palmar** adj clear, obvious. **palmatoria** sf candlestick; cane. **palmear** v clap hands. **palmera** sf palm tree.

palmo ['palmo] sm (medida) span, handbreadth. **palmotear** v applaud. **palmoteo** sm applause.

palo ['palo] sm stick; pole; handle; blow with a stick; mast. **dar de palos** thrash.

paloma [pa'loma] sf dove; pigeon. **palomar** sm dovecote. **palomino** sm young pigeon.

palpable [pal'paβle] adj palpable.

palpar [pal'par] v feel, touch. **palparse** v grope.

palpitar [palpi'tar] v palpitate, throb. **palpitación** sf palpitation. **palpitante** adj palpitating, throbbing.

paludismo [palu'ðismo] sm malaria.

palurdo [pa'lurðo] sm, adj rustic.

palustre[1] [pa'lustre] adj marshy.

palustre[2] sm trowel.

pan [pan] sm bread; loaf; dough. **pan ácimo** unleavened bread. **panadería** sf bread shop. **panadero, -a** sm, sf baker.

pana ['pana] sf corduroy. **pana lisa** velvet.

panal [pa'nal] sm honeycomb.

panamá [pana'ma] sm Panama hat.

panamericano [panameri'kano] adj pan-American.

pancarta [pan'karta] sf placard.

pandereta [pande'reta] sf tambourine.

pandilla [pan'diʎa] sf gang; clique.

panfleto [pan'fleto] sm pamphlet. **panfletista** s(m + f) pamphleteer.

pánico ['paniko] sm, adj panic.

pantalón [panta'lon] sm also **pantalones** m pl trousers.

pantalla [pan'taʎa] sf lampshade; screen. **pantalla protectora** sf screensaver.

pantano [pan'tano] sm marsh; bog, **pantanal** sm marshland. **pantanoso** adj swampy.

panteísta [pante'ista] s(m + f) pantheist. **panteísmo** sm pantheism.

pantera [pan'tera] sf panther.

pantomima [panto'mima] sf pantomime.

pantorrilla [pantor'riʎa] sf (anat) calf.

pantufla [pan'tufla] sf or **pantuflo** sm slipper.

panza ['panθa] sf belly. **panzada** sf bellyful.

pañal [pa'nal] sm nappy.

pañería [pane'ria] sf drapery. **pañero** sm draper. **pañete** sm light cloth. **paño** sm cloth. **paños menores** underclothes. **pañuelo** sm handkerchief.

papa[1] ['papa] sm pope. **papado** sm papacy. **papal** adj papal.

papa[2] sf potato.

parilla

papá [pa'pa] *sm* daddy.

papada [pa'paða] *sf* double chin.

papagayo [papa'gajo] *sm* parrot.

papar [pa'par] *v* eat; gulp. **papamoscas** *m invar* flycatcher; (*fig*) simpleton. **papar moscas** gape.

papel [pa'pel] *sm* paper. **papel de forrar** brown paper. **papel de fumar** cigarette paper. **papeleo** *sm* paperwork; (*fam*) red tape. **papelera** *sf* wastepaper basket. **papelería** *sf* stationer's.

papera [pa'pera] *sf* goitre. **paperas** *sf pl* mumps *sing*.

papiro [pa'piro] *sm* papyrus.

paquete [pa'kete] *sm* packet.

par [par] *sm* pair. *adj* equal. **sin par** matchless.

para ['para] *prep* for; towards. **para mañana** by tomorrow. **¿para qué?** why?

parábola [pa'raβola] *sf* parable; parabola.

parabrisas [para'βrisas] *sm invar* windscreen.

paracaídas [paraka'iðas] *sm invar* parachute. **paracaidista** *s(m + f)* parachutist.

parochoques [para'ʃtokes] *sm invar* (*auto*) bumper.

parada [pa'raða] *sf* stop; stopping; (*taxi*) rank; pause; parade; dam. **paradero** *sm* whereabouts; destination; home. **parado** *adj* motionless; unemployed.

paradoja [para'ðoxa] *sf* paradox. **paradójico** *adj* paradoxical.

parador [para'ðor] *sm* tourist hotel.

parafina [para'fina] *sf* paraffin.

paráfrasis [pa'rafrasis] *sf invar* paraphrase. **parafrasear** *v* paraphrase.

paraguas [pa'ragwas] *sm invar* umbrella.

paraíso [para'iso] *sm* paradise; (*teatro*) gallery.

paralela [para'lela] *sf* parallel. **paralelas** *sf pl* parallel bars. **paralelo** *sm*, *adj* parallel.

parálisis [pa'ralisis] *sf* paralysis. **paralítico** *sm*, *adj* paralytic. **paralizar** *v* paralyse.

páramo ['paramo] *sm* wilderness; bleak plateau. **paramera** *sf* desert.

parangón [paran'gon] *sm* comparison. **parangonar** *v* compare.

parapeto [para'peto] *sm* parapet; railing.

parar [pa'rar] *v* stop; check. **pararse** *v* stay; end up. **parar en mal** come to a bad end.

pararrayos [parar'rajos] *sm invar* lightning conductor.

parásito [pa'rasito] *sm* parasite. *adj* parasitic.

parasol [para'sol] *sm* parasol.

parcela [par'θela] *sf* (*de tierra*) plot. **parcelar** *v* parcel out.

parcial [par'θjal] *adj* partial. **parcialidad** *sf* partiality.

parco ['parko] *adj* frugal; mean; sparing.

parche ['partʃe] *sm* plaster; patch; drumhead.

pardo ['parðo] *adj* dark; brown.

parear [pare'ar] *v* match, pair.

*****parecer** [pare'θer] *v* seem; appear. **parecerse** *v* resemble. **parecido** *adj* similar. **bien parecido** good-looking.

pared [pa'reð] *sf* wall. **paredón** *sm* large wall.

pareja [pa'rexa] *sf* pair; couple. **parejo** *adj* even; equal.

parentela [paren'tela] *sf* kindred. **parentesco** *sm* kinship.

paréntesis [pa'rentesis] *sm* parenthesis; bracket.

paridad [pari'ðað] *sf* comparison; parity.

pariente [pa'rjente] *sm* relation.

parir [pa'rir] *v* give birth to.

París [pa'ris] *s* Paris.

parla ['parla] *sf* gossip; chatter. **parlador**. **-a** *sm*, *sf* talker. **parlanchín** *adj* talkative. **parlante** *adj* chattering. **parlar** *v* chatter. **parleta** *sf* small talk.

parlamento [parla'mento] *sm* parliament. **parlamentario** *adj* parliamentary.

paro ['paro] *sm* stoppage; unemployment.

parodiar [paro'ðjar] *v* parody. **parodia** *sf* parody.

paroxismo [parok'sismo] *sm* paroxysm.

parpadear [parpaðe'ar] *v* blink; wink. **parpadeo** *sm* blinking; winking. **párpado** *sm* eyelid.

parque ['parke] *sm* park. **parque eólico** *sm* wind farm. **parque temático** *sm* theme park.

parra ['parra] *sf* vine. **hoja de parra** figleaf. **parra virgen** Virginia creeper.

párrafo ['parrafo] *sm* paragraph.

parricida [parri'θiða] *s(m + f)* (*criminal*) parricide. **parricidio** *sm* (*crimen*) parricide.

parrilla [par'riʎa] *sf* grill; gridiron; grate; grillroom.

párroco ['parroko] *sm* parish priest. **parroquia** *sf* parish; parish church. **parroquial** *adj* parochial. **parroquiano, -a** *sm, sf* parishioner; regular customer.

parsimonia [parsi'monja] *sf* parsimony; frugality; calmness.

parte ['parte] *sf* part; share; point; side; way; party; role; actor. **en otra parte** elsewhere. **por todas partes** everywhere. **por una parte y por otra** on the one hand and on the other.

partera [par'tera] *sf* midwife.

partición [parti'θjon] *sf* partition; division. **partible** *adj* divisible.

participar [partiθi'par] *v* participate; partake; invest; inform; announce. **participación** *sf* participation; share; announcement. **participante** *s(m + f)* participant; informant; competitor. **partícipe** *s(m + f)* participant.

participio [parti'θipjo] *sm* (*gram*) participle.

partícula [par'tikula] *sf* particle.

particular [partiku'lar] *adj* particular; peculiar; individual; personal. **casa particular** private house. *sm* matter; individual; civilian. **particularidad** *sf* peculiarity. **particularizar** *v* specify; distinguish; prefer. **particularizarse** *v* stand out. **particularamente** *adv* in particular.

partida [par'tiða] *sf* departure; certificate; (*com*) entry; item; party; game. **partida de campo** picnic. **partida doble** double entry. **partidario, -a** *sm, sf* follower; partisan.

partido [par'tiðo] *sm* (*deporte*) match; (*pol*) party. *adj* divided. **darse a partido** give in. **sacar partido** benefit from.

partir [par'tir] *v* leave, depart; divide; share. **a partir de hoy** from today on. **partirse** *v* differ in opinion; depart. **partidor** *sm* distributor.

partitura [parti'tura] *sf* (*música*) score.

parto ['parto] *sm* childbirth; delivery; (*fig*) brainchild.

parvo ['parβo] *adj* little. **párvulo** *adj* very small.

pasa ['pasa] *sf* raisin. **pasa de Corinto** currant.

pasada [pa'saða] *sf* passage; (*aves*) flight. **de pasada** in passing. **mala pasada** dirty trick. **pasadero** *adj* tolerable.

pasado [pa'saðo] *sm, adj* past. **lo pasado,** let bygones be bygones. **pasado mañana** the day after tomorrow. **pasado de moda** *adj* outdated.

pasador [pasa'ðor], **-a** *sm, sf* smuggler. *sm* filter; colander; bolt; pin; fastener. **pasadores** *sm pl* cufflinks *pl*.

pasaje [pa'saxe] *sm* passage; fare; ticket; voyage; passengers *pl*. **pasajero, -a** *sm, sf* passenger.

pasamano [pasa'mano] *sm* bannister; handrail.

pasapasa [pasa'pasa] *sm* sleight-of-hand.

pasaporte [pasa'porte] *sm* passport.

pasar [pa'sar] *v* pass; give; spend; take; send; run; cross; penetrate. **pasar de moda** go out of fashion. **pasar el muerto** *v* pass the buck. **pasarlo bien/mal** have a good/bad time. **pasar por** be considered. **pasar por alto** overlook. **¿qué pasa?** what's up? **pasarse** pass off; be over; miss. **pasarse de** be too. **pasarse por** call in at.

pasarela [pasa'rela] *sf* footbridge; gangway.

pasatiempo [pasa'tjempo] *sm* pastime, amusement.

pascua ['paskwa] *sf* (*rel*) feast; Christmas; Easter; Epiphany; Passover. **¡felices pascuas y próspero año nuevo!** merry Christmas and a happy New Year!

pase ['pase] *sm* invitation; permission; (*autorización*) pass.

pasear [pase'ar] *v* go for a walk; take for a walk; go for a ride. **paseo** *sm* walk; drive; ride.

pasillo [pa'siʎo] *sm* corridor, passage.

pasión [pasi'on] *sf* passion. **pasional** *adj* passionate.

pasivo [pa'siβo] *adj* passive. *sm* (*com*) liabilities *pl*. **pasividad** *sf* passivity.

pasmar [pas'mar] *v* chill; stun; amaze. **pasmo** *sm* amazement; convulsion. **pasmoso** *adj* wonderful.

paso ['paso] *sm* step; pace; walk; passage; situation. **paso a nivel** level-crossing. **paso a paso** step by step. **salir del paso** get out of a difficulty.

pasta ['pasta] *sf* pasta; dough; paste. **pastas** *sf pl* noodles.

pastar [pas'tar] *v* graze, pasture.

pastel [pas'tel] *sm* cake, pastry; (*color*) pastel. **pastel de carne** meat pie. **pastelería** *sf* cake shop; cakes *pl*; confectionery. **pastelero, -a** *sm, sf* pastrycook.

pastilla [pas'tiʎa] *sf* bar; piece; tablet.

pastinaca [pasti'naka] *sf* (*bot*) turnip; (*zool*) stingray.

pasto ['pasto] *sm* grass; pasture. **a pasto** galore. **pastor** *sm* shepherd; pastor. **pastoral** *adj* pastoral. **pastorear** *v* pasture.

pastura [pas'tura] *sf* pasture; fodder.

pata ['pata] *sf* (*de animal*) foot; leg; paw. **meter la pata** (*fam*) put one's foot in it. **tener mala pata** (*fam*) be unlucky. **patada** *sf* kick; stamp. **patalear** *v* stamp; kick about. **pataleo** *sm* kicking.

patán [pa'tan] *sm* lout. *adj* churlish. **patanería** *sf* boorishness.

patata [pa'tata] *sf* potato. **patatas fritas** chips.

patear [pate'ar] *v* kick; stamp.

patente [pa'tente] *sm* (*com*) patent. *adj* obvious.

paternal [pater'nal] *adj* paternal. **paternidad** *sf* paternity. **paterno** *adj* paternal.

patético [pa'tetiko] *adj* pathetic.

patíbulo [pa'tiβulo] *sm* gallows *pl*.

patillas [pa'tiʎas] *sf pl* whiskers *pl*, sideboards *pl*.

patín [pa'tin] *sm* skate. **patín de ruedas** roller skate. **patinadero** *sm* skating rink. **patinador, -a** *sm* skater. **patinaje** *sm* skating. **patinar** *v* skate; skid; rollerblade. **patinazo** *sm* skid; (*fam*) blunder. **patinete** *sm* child's scooter.

patio ['patjo] *sm* patio; yard.

pato ['pato] *sm* duck. **pagar el pato** (*fam*) carry the can.

patochada [pato'tʃaða] *sf* blunder.

patología [patolo'xia] *sf* pathology. **patológico** *adj* pathological. **patólogo, -a** *sm, sf* pathologist.

patraña [pa'traɲa] *sf* cock-and-bull story; fib.

patria ['patrja] *sf* native land. **patriota** *s* (*m + f*) patriot. **patriótico** *adj* patriotic. **patriotismo** *sm* patriotism.

patriarca [pa'trjarka] *sm* patriarch. **patriarcal** *adj* patriarchal.

patricio [pa'triθjo], **-a** *sm, sf, adj* patrician.

patrimonio [patri'monjo] *sm* patrimony, birthright. **patrimonial** *adj* patrimonial.

patrocinar [patroθi'nar] *v* patronize; sponsor. **patrocinador, -a** *sm, sf* patron; sponsor. **patrocinio** *sm* patronage; sponsorship.

patrón [pa'tron] *sm* patron; owner; landlord; pattern. **patronato** *sm* patronage; board of trustees; society.

patrono [pa'trono] *sm* boss; patron saint; owner.

patrulla [pa'truʎa] *sf* patrol. **patrullar** *v* patrol.

paulatino [paula'tino] *adj* slow, gradual. **paulatinamente** *adj* gradually; little by little.

pausa ['pausa] *sf* pause; (*música*) rest. **pausado** *adj* slow; deliberate. **pausar** *v* pause; interrupt.

pauta ['pauta] *sf* rule; model; lines *pl*. **pautar** *v* rule; give instructions. **papel pautado** ruled paper.

pávido ['paβiðo] *adj* timid.

pavimentar [paβimen'tar] *v* pave; surface. **pavimento** *sm* pavement.

pavo ['paβo] *sm* turkey. **pavo real** peacock. **pavonear** *v* show off.

pavor [pa'βor] *sm* terror; dread. **pavorido** *adj* terror-stricken. **pavoroso** *adj* dreadful; awful. **pavura** *sf* fear; dread.

payaso [pa'jaso] *sm* clown. **payasada** *sf* clowning.

paz [paθ] *sf* peace. **hacer las paces** make it up. **¡paz!** hush!

peaje [pe'axe] *sm* toll. **peajero** *sm* toll-collector.

peatón [pea'ton] *sm* pedestrian.

peca ['peka] *sf* spot; freckle. **pecoso** *adj* freckled.

pecar [pe'kar] *v* sin. **pecado** *sm* sin. **pecador, -a** *sm, sf* sinner. **pecaminoso** *adj* sinful.

pécora ['pekora] *sf* sheep; (*fam*) slut.

peculiar [peku'ljar] *adj* peculiar; special. **peculiaridad** *sf* peculiarity. **peculiarmente** peculiarly.

pechera [pe'tʃera] *sf* bib; shirt-front.

pecho ['petʃo] *sm* chest; bosom; breast; courage; tax. **dar el pecho** suckle. **enfermo del pecho** consumptive. **pechuga** *sf* (*de ave*) breast.

pedagogía [peðago'xia] *sf* pedagogy. **pedagógico** *adj* teaching. **pedagogo, -a** *sm, sf* teacher.

pedal [pe'ðal] *sm* pedal. **pedalear** *v* pedal.

pedante [pe'ðante] *s* (*m + f*) pedant. *adj* pedantic. **pedantería** *sf* pedantry.

pedazo [pe'ðaθo] *sm* piece. **hacerse pedazos** be smashed to bits.

pedernal [peðer'nal] *sm* flint.
pedestal [peðe'stal] *sm* pedestal.
pedestre [pe'ðestre] *adj* pedestrian.
pediatría [peðja'tria] *sf* paediatrics. **pediatra** *or* **pediatra** *sm, sf* paediatrician.
pedicuro [peði'kuro], **-a** *sm, sf* chiropodist. *sf* chiropody.
*pedir [pe'ðir] *v* ask; ask for; order. **pedir limosna** beg. **pedir prestado** borrow. **pedido** *sm* demand; (*com*) order. **pedimento** *sm* petition.
pedo ['peðo] *sm* (*vulgar*) fart.
pedregal [peðre'gal] *sm* stony ground. **pedrea** *sf* stoning; hailstorm. **pedregoso** *adj* stony. **pedrería** *sf* jewels *pl*. **pedrero** *sm* stone-cutter. **pedrisco** *sm* hailstorm.
pegar [pe'gar] *v* hit; glue; (*med*) infect; take effect; give; let out; fire; sew on. **pegar fuego a** set fire to. **pegar un tiro** fire a shot. **pega** *sf* difficulty; hoax; snag. **poner pegas a** find fault with. **pegajoso** *adj* sticky; infectious. **pegatina** *sf* sticker.
peinar [pei'nar] *v* comb. **peinado** *sm* hairstyle. **peinador, -a** *sm, sf* hairdresser; *sm* bathrobe. **peine** *sm* comb.
pelar [pe'lar] *v* cut; peel; shear; skin; shell. **pelar la pava** woo. **pelado** *adj* shorn; peeled; bare. **pelaje** *sm* fur. **pelambre** *sm* (*de animales*) hair. **pelambrera** *sf* fleece.
peldaño [pel'ðaɲo] *sm* stair; step.
pelear [pele'ar] *v* fight. **pelearse con alguien** fight somebody. **pelea** *sf* fight. **peleador** *sm* fight.
pelele [pe'lele] *sm* puppet; dummy.
peliagudo [pelja'guðo] *adj* (*fig*) difficult, tough.
pelícano [pe'likano] *sm* pelican.
película [pe'likula] *sf* film. **película de vídeo** *sf* video cassette.
peligro [pe'ligro] *sm* danger. **peligrarse** *v* be in danger. **peligroso** *adj* dangerous.
pelmazo [pel'maθo] *sm* also **pelma** *sf* bore; crushed mass.
pelo ['pelo] *sm* hair; (*en madera*) grain; nap. **de medio pelo** low-class. **soltarse el pelo** show one's true colours. **pelón** *adj* bald.
pelota [pe'lota] *sf* ball. **echarse la pelota** pass the buck. **en pelota** naked.
pelotón [pelo'ton] *sm* platoon; squad.
peltre ['peltre] *sm* pewter.
peluca [pe'luka] *sf* wig.
peludo [pe'luðo] *adj* hairy.

peluquero [pelu'kero], **-a** *sm, sf* hairdresser. **peluquería** *sf* hairdresser's.
pelusa [pe'lusa] *sf* down; fuzz; (*fam*) jealousy.
pelleja [pe'ʎexa] *sf* also **pellejo** *sm* hide, skin. **jugarse el pellejo** risk one's neck.
pellizcar [peʎiθ'kar] *v* nip, pinch. **pellizco** *sm* nip, pinch.
pello ['peʎo] *sm* fur jacket.
pena ['pena] *sf* pain; grief; hardship; penalty; effort. **pena capital** capital punishment. **¡qué pena!** what a shame! **penable** *adj* punishable. **penado** *adj* painful. **penal** *adj* penal. **penalidad** *sf* penalty. **penar** *v* punish; suffer. **penarse** *v* grieve.
pender [pen'der] *v* hang; (*jur*) be pending. **pendiente** *adj* hanging; pending. **estar pendiente de** depend on.
péndulo ['pendulo] *sm* pendulum.
pene ['pene] *sm* penis.
penetrar [pene'trar] *v* penetrate; comprehend. **penetrarse** *v* become aware of; imbibe. **penetrable** *adj* penetrable. **penetración** *sf* penetration. **penetrante** *adj* penetrating.
penicilina [peniθi'lina] *sf* penicillin.
península [pe'ninsula] *sf* peninsula. **peninsular** *adj* peninsular.
penique [pe'nike] *sm* penny.
penitencia [peni'tenθja] *sf* penitence. **hacer penitencia** (*fam*) take pot-luck. **penitencial** *adj* penitential. **penitenciaría** *sf* penitentiary. **penitente** *adj* penitent.
penoso [pe'noso] *adj* painful; difficult.
*pensar [pen'sar] *v* think; think over; intend. **pensar en** think about. **pensado** *adj* deliberate. **de pensado** on purpose. **pensador, -a** *sm, sf* thinker. **pensamiento** *sm* thought. **pensativo** *adj* thoughtful.
pensión [pensi'on] *sf* pension; boarding house; hardship. **pensionado, -a** *sm, sf* pensioner. **pensionar** *v* pension. **pensionista** *s(m + f)* pensioner; boarder.
pentágono [pen'tagono] *sm* pentagon.
penúltimo [pe'nultimo] *adj* penultimate.
penumbra [pe'numbra] *sf* half-light.
penuria [pe'nurja] *sf* penury; shortage.
peña ['peɲa] *sf* crag; rock; cliff; group of friends. **peñasco** *sm* large rock. **peñascoso** *adj* rocky. **peñón** *sm* rocky mountain. **el Peñón de Gibraltar** the Rock of Gibraltar.
peón [pe'on] *sm* unskilled labourer; pedes-

trian; foot-soldier; (*ajedrez*) pawn.

peonía [peo'nia] *sf* peony.

peor [pe'or] *adj, adv* worse; worst. **peoría** *sf* worsening.

pepino [pe'pino] *sm* cucumber. **no valer un pepino** not be worth a damn. **pepinillo** *sm* gherkin.

pepita [pe'pita] *sf* seed, pip; (*oro*) nugget.

pequeño [pe'keɲo] *adj* small; humble. **pequeñez** *sf* smallness; pettiness.

pera ['pera] *sf* pear; light-switch; (*barba*) goatee; sinecure. **peral** *sm* pear tree.

perca ['perka] *sf* (*zool*) perch.

percance [per'kanθe] *sm* mishap; profit.

percatarse [perka'tarse] *v* notice.

percibir [perθi'βir] *v* perceive; collect. **percepción** *sf* perception; collection. **perceptible** *adj* perceptible. **perceptivo** *adj* perceptive. **perceptor, -a** *sm, sf* perceiver. **percibo** *sm* collecting.

percusión [perku'sjon] *sf* percussion.

percha ['pertʃa] *sf* perch; pole; hat-stand; coat-rack.

*****perder** [per'ðer] *v* lose; spoil; waste. **perderse por** be inordinately fond of. **perdición** *sf* loss; perdition. **pérdida** *sf* damage; waste. **perdido** *adj* lost; dissolute.

perdiz [per'ðiθ] *sf* partridge.

perdonar [perðo'nar] *v* pardon; excuse. **pardón** *sm* pardon; mercy. **con perdón** by your leave. **perdonable** *adj* pardonable. **perdonavidas** *m invar* (*fam*) bully.

perdurar [perðu'rar] *v* endure. **perdurable** *adj* everlasting.

*****perecer** [pere'θer] *v* perish. **perecerse por** crave. **perecedero** *adj* perishable.

peregrinar [peregri'nar] *v* travel; go on a pilgrimage. **peregrinación** *sf* pilgrimage. **peregrino, -a** *sm, sf* pilgrim.

perejil [pere'xil] *sm* parsley.

perenne [pe'renne] *adj* perennial.

perentorio [peren'torjo] *adj* peremptory; urgent.

perezoso [pere'θoso] *adj* lazy. **pereza** *sf* laziness.

perfecto [per'fekto] *adj* perfect. **perfección** *sf* perfection. **perfeccionamiento** *sm* improvement; perfection. **perfeccionar** *v* perfect; improve.

pérfido ['perfiðo] *adj* perfidious. **perfidia** *sf* perfidy.

perfilar [perfi'lar] *v* outline. **perfil** *sm* pro-file; outline.

perforar [perfo'rar] *v* perforate; drill; puncture. **perforación** *sf* perforation. **perforadora** *sf* drill.

perfumar [perfu'mar] *v* perfume. **perfume** *sm* perfume. **perfumería** *sf* perfume shop.

perfunctorio [perfunk'torjo] *adj* perfunctory.

pericial [peri'θjal] *adj* expert. **pericia** *sf* skill.

perico [pe'riko] *sm* parakeet; toupee.

periferia [peri'ferja] *sf* periphery. **periférico** *sm* peripheral (computer).

perímetro [pe'rimetro] *sm* perimeter.

periódico [peri'odiko] *sm* periodical; newspaper. *adj* periodic. **periodicidad** *sf* recurrence. **periodismo** *sm* journalism. **periodista** *s(m + f)* journalist. **periodístico** *adj* journalistic. **período** *or* **periodo** *sm* period. **período de prácticas** probationary period.

peripecia [peri'peθja] *sf* vicissitude; incident; adventure.

periscopio [peris'kopjo] *sm* periscope.

perjudicar [perxuði'kar] *v* prejudice; harm. **perjudicial** *adj* harmful. **perjuicio** *sm* prejudice; damage.

perjurar [perxu'rar] *v* perjure oneself. **perjurio** *sm* perjury. **perjuro, -a** *sm, sf* perjurer.

perla ['perla] *sf* pearl. **de perlas** perfectly.

*****permanecer** [permane'θer] *v* stay, remain. **permanencia** *sf* stay; permanence. **permanente** *adj* permanent.

permitir [permi'tir] *v* permit. ¿**me permite?** may I? **permisible** *adj* permissible. **permisivo** *adj* permissive. **permiso** *sm* permission; permit; leave; licence. **con permiso** if I may.

permutar [permu'tar] *v* permute; exchange. **permuta** *sf* exchange; permutation. **permutación** *sf* permutation.

perniabierto [pernia'βjerto] *adj* bandy-legged.

pernicioso [perni'θjoso] *adj* pernicious.

pernoctar [pernok'tar] *v* spend the night.

pero[1] ['pero] *conj* but; yet. ¡**pero bueno!** why!

pero[2] *sm* pear tree.

perogrullada [perogru'ʎaða] *sf* platitude.

perorar [pero'rar] *v* make a speech. **peroración** *sf* peroration.

peróxido [per'oksiðo] *sm* peroxide.
perpendicular [perpendiku'lar] *sf, adj* perpendicular.
perpetrar [perpe'trar] *v* perpetrate. **perpetración** *sf* perpetration.
perpetuar [perpe'twar] *v* perpetuate. **perpetuación** *sf* perpetuation. **perpetuidad** *sf* perpetuity. **perpetuo** *adj* perpetual.
perplejo [per'plexo] *adj* perplexed; perplexing. **perplejidad** *sf* perplexity.
perro ['perro] *sm* dog; (*fam*) penny. **perra** *sf* bitch. **perrera** *sf* kennel; dog pound; dogcatcher's wagon. **perrero** *sm* dog-catcher.
*****perseguir** [perse'gir] *v* pursue; persecute. **persecución** *sf* pursuit; persecution. **perseguidor, -a** *sm, sf* pursuer; persecutor.
perseverar [perseβe'rar] *v* persevere. **perseverancia** *sf* perseverance. **perseverante** *adj* persevering.
persiana [per'sjana] *sf* slatted shutter. **persiana veneciana** venetian blind.
persistir [persis'tir] *v* persist. **persistencia** *sf* persistence. **persistente** *adj* persistent.
persona [per'sona] *sf* person. **persona a persona** man to man. **personaje** *sm* personage; (*teatro*) character. **personal** *adj* personal. **personalidad** *sf* personality. **personalismo** *sm* partiality. **personalizar** *v* personalize. **personarse** *v* appear in person. **personificar** *v* personify.
perspectiva [perspek'tiβa] *sf* perspective; outlook.
perspicaz [perspi'kaθ] *adj* perspicacious. **perspicacia** *sf* perspicacity.
persuadir [perswa'ðir] *v* persuade. **persuasión** *sf* persuasion. **persuasivo** *adj* persuasive.
*****pertenecer** [pertene'θer] *v* belong. **perteneciente** *adj* belonging. **pertenencia** *sf* ownership; property; membership.
pértiga ['pertiga] *sf* pole. **salto de pértiga** pole vault.
pertiguero [perti'gero] *sm* verger.
pertinaz [perti'naθ] *adj* pertinacious. **pertinacia** *sf* pertinacity.
pertinente [perti'nente] *adj* pertinent. **pertinencia** *sf* pertinence.
pertrechar [pertre'tʃar] *v* supply; equip. **pertrechos** *sm pl* equipment *sing*; munitions *pl*.
perturbar [pertur'βar] *v* perturb. **perturbación** *sf* perturbation. **perturbador** *adj* perturbing.

*****pervertir** [perβer'tir] *v* pervert. **perversidad** *sf* perversity. **perversión** *sf* perversion. **perverso** *adj* perverse.
pesa ['pesa] *sf* weight. **pesas y medidas** weights and measures. **pesadez** *sf* heaviness; drowsiness; hardship.
pesadilla [pesa'ðiʎa] *sf* nightmare.
pesado [pe'saðo] *adj* heavy; sluggish. *sm* bore. **pesadumbre** *sf* grief.
pésame ['pesame] *sm* condolence.
pesar [pe'sar] *v* weigh. **a pesar de** in spite of. **me pesa mucho** I'm very sorry.
pescar [pes'kar] *v* fish. **pesca** *sf* fishing. **pescada** *sf* hake. **pescadería** *sf* fish shop; fish market. **pescadero** *sm* fishmonger. **pescado** *sm* fish. **pescador** *sm* fisherman. **pescador de caña** angler.
pescuezo [pes'kweθo] *sm* neck.
pesebre [pe'seβre] *sm* crib; manger.
pesimista [pesi'mista] *s(m + f)* pessimist. *adj* pessimistic. **pesimismo** *sm* pessimism.
pésimo ['pesimo] *adj* worthless.
peso ['peso] *sm* weight; balance; scales *pl*; peso. **en peso** bodily. **peso específico** specific gravity.
pesquisa [pes'kisa] *sf* inquiry.
pestañear [pestaɲe'ar] *v* blink. **pestaña** *sf* eyelash; fringe; hem. **pestañeo** *sm* blink.
peste ['peste] *sf* plague; corruption; poison. **echar pestes** curse. **pesticida** *sf* pesticide. **pestilencia** *sf* pestilence. **pestilente** *adj* pestilent; stinking.
pestillo [pes'tiʎo] *sm* bolt; latch.
petaca [pe'taka] *sf* tobacco pouch; cigarette case.
pétalo ['petalo] *sm* petal.
petardo [pe'tarðo] *sm* firework; (*fam*) swindle.
petición [peti'θjon] *sf* petition; plea. **peticionario, -a** *sm, sf* petitioner.
petirrojo [petir'roxo] *sm* robin.
peto ['peto] *sm* bib; breastplate.
petrificar [petrifi'kar] *v* petrify. **pétreo** *adj* stony.
petróleo [pe'troleo] *sm* petroleum. **petrolero** *sm* oil-tanker.
petulante [petu'lante] *adj* petulant; insolent. **petulancia** *sf* petulance; insolence.
peyorativo [pejora'tiβo] *adj* pejorative.

pez [peθ] *sm* fish. *sf* pitch, tar.

pezón [pe'θon] *sm* (*bot*) stalk; (*anat*) nipple.

pezuña [pe'θuɲa] *sf* hoof.

piadoso [pja'ðoso] *adj* pious; merciful.

piano ['pjano] *sm* piano. **pianista** *s*(*m* + *f*) pianist.

piar [pjar] *v* chirp.

piara ['pjara] *sf* herd.

pica ['pika] *sf* lance, pike; goad; pick; magpie.

picadillo [peka'ðiʎo] *sm* minced meat.

picante [pi'kante] *adj* hot; spicy; pungent; biting.

picaporte [pika'porte] *sm* door handle; latch; knocker; latch-key.

picar [pi'kar] *v* prick, pierce; sting; burn; punch; bite, eat; chop up. **picado** *adj* bitten; stung; minced; sour; bad. **picadura** *sf* bite; sting; peck.

picardear [pikar'ðjar] *v* corrupt; get up to mischief. **picardía** *sf* dirty trick; craftiness; mischief. **picaresco** *adj* roguish. **pícaro, -a** *sm, sf* rogue.

pico ['piko] *sm* beak; peak; pickaxe. **darse el pico** kiss. **pico carpintero** woodpecker. **son las cuatro y pico** it is just after four.

picotear [pikote'ar] *v* peck; chatter. **picotearse** *v* wrangle. **picotada** *sf also* **picotazo** *sm* peck. **picotero, -a** *sm, sf* chatterbox.

pichón [pi'tʃon] *sm* pigeon. **pichona** *sf* (*fam*) darling.

pie [pje] *sm* foot; base; stem. **a cuatro pies** on all fours. **dar pie a** give cause for. **de pies a cabeza** from head to foot.

piedad [pje'ðað] *sf* piety; pity.

piedra ['pjeðra] *sf* stone.

piel [pjel] *sf* skin.

pienso ['pjenso] *sm* fodder. **ni por pienso** not likely.

pierna ['pjerna] *sf* leg.

pieza ['pjeθa] *sf* piece; part; room. **dejar de una pieza** leave speechless.

pífano ['pifano] *sm* fife.

pigmento [pig'mento] *sm* pigment.

pigmeo [pig'meo], **-a** *s, adj* pygmy.

pijama [pi'xama] *sm* pyjamas *pl*.

pila[1] ['pila] *sf* heap; battery.

pila[2] *sf* basin; trough; font. **nombre de pila** Christian name.

pilar [pi'lar] *sm* pillar; pier; milestone; basin.

píldora ['pilðora] *sf* pill.

pilón [pi'lon] *sm* basin; trough; mortar; pylon.

piloto [pi'loto] *sm* pilot; (*auto*) rear light, parking light.

piltrafa [pil'trafa] *sf* gristly meat. **piltrafas** *sf pl* scraps *pl*.

pillar [pi'ʎar] *v* pillage; get; run over; (*fam*) catch. **pillaje** *sm* pillage.

pillo ['piʎo], **-a** *sm, sf* scoundrel. *adj* villainous. **pillastre** *sm or* **pillastron** *sm* rogue. **pillería** *sf* gang of villains; knavery.

pimienta [pi'mjenta] *sf* pepper. **pimiento** *sm* (*planta*) pepper. **pimentón** *sm* paprika.

pimpollo [pim'poʎo] *sm* sprout; sapling; (*fam*) handsome boy, pretty girl.

pináculo [pi'nakulo] *sm* pinnacle.

pinar [pi'nar] *sm* pine forest.

pincel [pin'θel] *sm* paintbrush. **pincelada** *sf* brush-stroke. **pincelar** *v* paint.

pinchadiscos [pintʃa'ðiskos] *s*(*m*+*f*) disc jockey.

pinchar [pin'tʃar] *v* puncture. **pincharse** *v* have a puncture. **pinchazo** *sm* puncture. **pincho** *sm* point; prickle; spine.

pingo ['pingo] *sm* rag; devil. **pingos** *sm pl* (*fam*) togs.

pingüe ['pingwe] *adj* fatty; abundant.

pingüino [pin'gwino] *sm* penguin.

pino ['pino] *sm* pine tree. **pinocha** *sf* pine needle.

pintar [pin'tar] *v* paint. **pintarse** *v* make oneself up. **pinta** *sf* spot. **tener buena/mala pinta** look good/bad. **pintor, -a** *sm, sf* painter. **pintoresco** *adj* picturesque; scenic. **pintorrear** *v* (*fam*) daub. **pintura** *sf* painting; picture.

pinzas ['pinθas] *sf pl* tweezers; pincers; forceps; tongs; clothes pegs.

pinzón [pin'θon] *sm* finch.

piña ['piɲa] *sf* pineapple; pine cone.

piñón [pi'ɲon] *sm* pinion.

pío[1] ['pio] *sm* chirp.

pío[2] *adj* pious; merciful.

piojo ['pjoxo] *sm* louse. **piojoso** *adj* lousy.

pipa ['pipa] *sf* pipe; pip.

pique ['pike] *sm* pique; resentment. **echar a pique** sink; ruin.

piqueta [pi'keta] *sf* pickaxe.

piquete [pi'kete] *sm* picket; squad;

sting; hole.

piragua [pi'ragwa] *sf* canoe.

pirámide [pi'ramiðe] *sf* pyramid. **piramidal** *adj* pyramidal.

pirata [pi'rata] *sm, adj* pirate. **pirata informático** *adj* hacker (computer). **piratear un sistema** *v* hack (computer).

Pirineos [piri'neos] *sm pl* Pyrenees *pl*.

piropear [pirope'ar] *v* (*fam*) compliment. **piropo** *sm* compliment.

pirotecnia [piro'teknja] *sf* fireworks *pl*.

pirueta [pi'rweta] *sf* pirouette. **piruetear** *v* pirouette.

pisar [pi'sar] *v* tread; trample. **pisada** *sf* footprint; step. **pisapapeles** *sm invar* paperweight.

piscina [pis'θina] *sf* swimming pool.

piscolabis [pisko'laβis] *sm invar* (*fam*) snack.

piso ['piso] *sm* floor; storey; flat. **piso bajo** ground floor.

pisotear [pisote'ar] *v* trample. **pisoteo** *sm* trampling.

pista ['pista] *sf* track; trail; runway; court; ring; rink. **pista de baile** dance floor. **pista de esquí** *sf* ski slope.

pistola [pis'tola] *sf* pistol. **pistolera** *sf* holster. **pistolero** *sm* gunman.

pistón [pis'ton] *sm* piston.

pitar [pi'tar] *v* whistle at; blow a whistle; boo, hiss. **pitada** *sf* whistle.

pitón [pi'ton] *sm* python.

pizarra [pi'θarra] *sf* blackboard; slate.

pizca ['piθka] *sf* (*fam*) crumb; drop; pinch.

placa ['plaka] *sf* plate; badge; plaque. **placa de matrícula** (*auto*) number plate.

*placer [pla'θer] *v* please. *sm* pleasure. **a placer** at one's leisure.

plácido ['plaθiðo] *adj* placid; pleasant.

plagar [pla'gar] *v* plague. **plaga** *sf* plague.

plagiar [pla'xjar] *v* plagiarize. **plagio** *sm* plagiarism.

plan [plan] *sm* plan; project.

plana ['plana] *sf* (*imprenta*) page; (*llanura*) plain.

planchar [plan'tʃar] *v* iron, press. **mesa de planchar** *sf* ironing board. **plancha** *sf* iron. **planchado** *sm* ironing.

planear [plane'ar] *v* plan; glide. **planeo** *sm* gliding.

planeta [pla'neta] *sf* planet. **planetario** *sm* planetarium.

planincie [pla'niθje] *sf* plain; plateau.

planificar [planifi'kar] *v* plan. **planificación** *sf* planning.

plano ['plano] *adj* flat; level; smooth. *sm* map; plan; plane. **de plano** directly. **plano acotado** contour map. **primer plano** close-up.

plantar [plan'tar] *v* plant; erect. **plantarse** *v* stop; settle; stand firm. **planta** *sf* plant; (*pie*) sole; plan; floor. **plantación** *sf* plantation. **plante** *sm* strike; mutiny. **plantío** *sm* field; vegetable plot. **plantón** *sm* seedling.

plantear [plante'ar] *v* expound; create; institute; introduce. **planteamiento** *sm* exposition; introduction; layout.

plantel [plan'tel] *sm* (*bot*) nursery.

plantilla [plan'tiʎa] *sf* model, pattern; sole (of shoe); (*com*) payroll.

plasma ['plasma] *sm* plasma.

plasmar [plas'mar] *v* mould. **plasmarse** *v* materialize.

plástico ['plastiko] *sm, adj* plastic. **plasticidad** *sf* plasticity.

plata ['plata] *sf* silver; (*fig*) money. **hablar en plata** speak frankly.

plataforma [plata'forma] *sf* platform; flatcar; oilrig. **plataforma de lanzamiento** launching pad.

plátano ['platano] *sm* banana; banana tree; plane tree.

platea [pla'tea] *sf* (*teatro*) stalls *pl*.

platear [plate'ar] *v* silverplate. **platero** *sm* silversmith.

plática ['platika] *sf* chat; sermon.

platija [pla'tixa] *sf* plaice.

platillo [pla'tiʎo] *sm* saucer. **platillo volante** flying saucer.

platino [pla'tino] *sm* platinum.

plato ['plato] *sm* plate; course; dish. **hacer plato** serve a meal.

platónico [pla'toniko] *adj* platonic.

plausible [plau'siβle] *adj* plausible; praiseworthy. **plausibilidad** *sf* plausibility; praiseworthiness.

playa ['plaja] *sf* beach; seaside.

plaza ['plaθa] *sf* town square; market; town; position. **¡plaza!** make way!

plazo ['plaθo] *sm* time limit; instalment. **comprar a plazos** buy on hire-purchase.

pleamar [plea'mar] *sf* high tide.

plebe ['pleβe] *sf* common people *pl.* **plebeye** *adj* plebeian.

plebiscito [pleβis'θito] *sm* plebiscite.

***plegar** [ple'gar] *v* fold; bend; pleat. **plegable** *adj* folding; collapsible; pliable. **plegadera** *sf* paper-knife. **pliegue** *sm* crease; tuck; pleat.

pleitear [pleite'ar] *v* litigate; plead. **pleito** *sm* lawsuit.

pleno ['pleno] *adj* complete; full. **plenamente** *adv* fully. **plenitud** *sf* fullness; abundance.

pliego ['pljeɣo] *sm* sheet of paper; sealed letter. **pliego de condiciones** specifications *pl.*

plinto ['plinto] *sm* plinth.

plomo ['plomo] *sm* lead; fuse. **a plomo** straight down. **plomada** *sf* lead pencil; plumb line. **plomería** *sf* plumbing. **plomero** *sm* plumber.

pluma ['pluma] *sf* feather; pen. **pluma estilográfica** fountain pen. **plumaje** *sm* plumage.

plural [plu'ral] *sm, adj* plural. **pluralidad** *sf* majority.

plus [plus] *sm* bonus. **plus de carestía de vida** cost-of-living bonus.

pluscuamperfecto [pluskwamper'fekto] *sm* pluperfect.

plusmarca [plus'marka] (*deporte*) *sm* record. **plusmarquista** *s*(*m* + *f*) record-holder.

***poblar** [po'βlar] *v* populate, inhabit; stock; colonize; plant. **poblarse** *v* bud; leaf. **población** *sf* population; town. **poblado** *sm* town; village. **poblador, -a** *sm, sf* settler.

pobre [po'βre] *adj* poor. *sm* pauper. **¡pobre de tí!** you poor thing! **pobrete** *adj* wretched. **pobretón** *adj* very poor. **pobreza** *sf* poverty.

pocilga [po'θilɣa] *sf* pigsty.

poción [po'θjon] *sf* potion.

poco ['poko] *adj* (*cantidad*) little; small. *adv* little; not very; not long. **un poco a** little. **pocos** *adj pl* few. **poco antes** shortly before. **poco factible** *adj* impractical. **poco a poco** little by little. **por poco** nearly.

podar [po'ðar] *v* prune. **poda** *sf* pruning. **podadera** *sf* pruning shears *pl.*

podenco [po'ðenko] *sm* hound.

***poder¹** [po'ðer] *v* can, be able to; be possible. **hasta más no poder** as much as one can. **no poder más** be exhausted. **puede ser** perhaps.

poder² *sm* power; capacity; possession. **casarse por poderes** marry by proxy. **hacer un poder** make an effort. **poder disuasivo** deterrent. **poderío** *sm* authority; wealth. **poderoso** *adj* powerful.

poema [po'ema] *sm* poem. **poesía** *sf* poetry. **poeta** *sm* poet. **poético** *adj* poetic. **poetisa** *sf* poetess.

***podrir** *V* **pudrir.**

polaco [po'lako] *adj* Polish. *sm* Pole; (*idioma*) Polish.

polar [po'lar] *adj* polar. **polaridad** *sf* polarity. **polarizar** *v* polarize.

polea [po'lea] *sf* pulley.

polémica [po'lemika] *sf* polemic; polemics *pl.* **polémico** *adj* polemical.

polen [po'len] *sm* pollen.

policía [poli'θia] *sf* police force. *sm* policeman. **policiaco** *adj* police. **novela policiaca** detective novel.

poligamia [poli'ɣamja] *sf* polygamy. **polígamo** *adj* polygamous.

polígono [po'liɣno] *sm* polygon. **polígono industrial** industrial estate. **poligonal** *adj* polygonal.

polilla [po'liʎa] *sf* moth.

pólipo ['polipo] *sm* polyp.

política [po'litika] *sf* politics; policy. **político** *sm* politician. **políticamente correcto** *adj* politically correct. **padre político** father-in-law.

póliza ['poliθa] *sf* policy; contract; stamp. **póliza de seguros** insurance policy.

polizón [poli'θon] *sm* stowaway.

polo ['polo] *sm* (*geog*) pole; (*tecn*) terminal; (*deporte*) polo; ice lolly. **polo acuático** water polo. **Polo Norte/Sur** North/South Pole.

Polonia [po'lonja] *sf* Poland. **polonesa** *sf* polonaise.

poltrona [pol'trona] *sf* easy chair. **poltrón** *adj* lazy.

polvo ['polβo] *sm* powder; dust. **café en polvo** instant coffee. **polvos** *sm pl* powder *sing.* **polvos de talco** talcum powder. **polvareda** *sf* dust cloud; (*fig*) to-do. **polvera** *sf* powder compact. **pólvora** *sf* gunpowder.

polla ['poʎa] *sf* pullet. **pollo** *sm* chicken.

polluelo *sm* chick.

pómez ['pomeθ] *sf* pumice.

pomo ['pomo] *sm* pommel; doorknob.

pompa ['pompa] *sf* pomp; bubble; display. **pomposidad** *sf* pomposity. **pomposo** *adj* pompous.

pómulo ['pomulo] *sm* cheekbone.

ponche ['pontʃe] *sm* (*bebida*) punch.

poncho ['pontʃo] *sm* poncho. *adj* listless.

ponderar [ponde'rar] *v* weigh up; praise highly. **ponderable** *adj* praiseworthy. **ponderación** *sf* weighing up; exaggerated praise. **ponderado** *adj* measured; prudent. **ponderativo** *adj* excessive; deliberative.

ponente [po'nente] *sm* reporter. **ponencia** *sf* report.

***poner** [po'ner] *v* put; set. **poner al día** bring up to date. **poner casa** move (house). **poner de comer** feed. **ponerse** *v* turn oneself; dress; get down to; arrive. **ponerse bueno** recover. **ponerse guapo** smarten oneself up.

poniente [po'njente] *sm* west.

pontificado [pontifi'kaðo] *sm* papacy. **pontifical** *adj* pontifical. **pontífice** *sm* pope.

pontón [pon'ton] *sm* (*puente*) pontoon.

ponzoña [pon'θoɲa] *sf* poison. **ponzoñoso** *adj* poisonous.

popa ['popa] *sf* stern. **a popa** astern.

popelina [pope'lina] *sf* poplin.

populacho [popu'latʃo] *sm* rabble.

popular [popu'lar] *adj* popular. **popularidad** *sf* popularity. **popularizar** *v* popularize.

por [por] *prep* for; by; through; during; in exchange for. **por ciento** per cent. **por más que** however. **¿por qué?** why? **por si acaso** in case. **por supuesto** of course.

porcelana [porθe'lana] *sf* porcelain.

porcentaje [porθen'taxe] *sm* percentage.

porción [por'θjon] *sf* portion.

porche ['portʃe] *sm* porch.

pordiosero [porðjo'sero], **-a** *sm, sf* beggar.

porfiar [por'fjar] *v* insist; persist; argue. **porfia** *sf* insistence. **porfiado** *adj* stubborn.

pormenor [porme'nor] *sm* detail. **al pormenor** retail.

pornografía [pornogra'fia] *sf* pornography.

poro ['poro] *sm* pore. **poroso** *adj* porous.

porque ['porke] *conj* because.

porqué [por'ke] *sm* reason.

porquería [porke'ria] *sf* disgusting mess; muck.

porra ['porra] *sf* club; truncheon. **porrazo** *sm* blow.

porro ['porro] *sm* leek.

porrón [por'ron] *adj* dull, stupid. **a porrones** (*fam*) galore.

portador [porta'ðor] *sm* (*com*) bearer. **portar** *v* bear, carry. **portarse** *v* behave oneself. **portátil** *adj* portable.

portal [por'tal] *sm* entrance hall, portal.

portamonedas [portamo'neðas] *sm invar* wallet.

portavoz [porta'βoθ] *sm* megaphone; spokesman.

portazgo [por'taθgo] *sm* toll.

portazo [por'taθo] *sm* slam. **dar un portazo** slam the door.

porte ['porte] *sm* transport; carriage; conduct.

portento [por'tento] *sm* marvel. **portentoso** *adj* marvellous.

portería [porte'ria] *sf* porter's lodge. **portero, -a** *sm, sf* porter.

portezuela [porte'θwela] *sf* (*auto*) door.

pórtico ['portiko] *sm* portico.

portilla [por'tiʎa] *sf* porthole.

Portugal [portu'gal] *sm* Portugal. **portugués, -esa** *s, adj* Portuguese; *sm* (*idioma*) Portuguese.

porvenir [porβe'nir] *sm* future. **sin porvenir** without prospects.

pos [pos] *sm* **en pos de** behind.

posada [po'saða] *sf* inn; lodging. **posadero, -a** *sm, sf* innkeeper.

posar [po'sar] *v* alight; pose; lodge; lay down. **posarse** *v* settle; land.

***poseer** [pose'er] *v* possess; hold; master. **posesión** *sf* possession. **posesiones** *sf pl* property *sing*.

posible [po'siβle] *adj* possible. **posibilidad** *sf* possibility. **posibilitar** *v* facilitate.

posición [posi'θjon] *sf* position.

positivo [posi'tiβo] *adj, sm* positive.

***posponer** [pospo'ner] *v* postpone; value less.

postal [pos'tal] *adj* postal. *sf* postcard. **giro postal** *sm* money order; postal order.

postdata [post'ðata] *sf* postscript.

poste ['poste] *sm* pole; pillar; post. **poste**

indicador signpost.

postergar [poster'gar] *v* pass over; postpone; adjourn. **postergación** *sf* postponement; adjournment.

posteridad [posteri'ðað] *sf* posterity. **posterior** *adj* posterior; subsequent; later.

postizo [pos'tiθo] *adj* false; artificial; assumed. *sm* hairpiece. **pierna postiza** *sf* artificial leg.

postrar [pos'trar] *v* prostrate. **postrarse** *v* kneel down; weaken. **postración** *sf* prostration. **postrado** *adj* prostrate.

postre ['postre] *sm* dessert.

postremo [pos'tremo] *adj* last. **postrimería** *sf* end, death.

postular [postu'lar] *v* postulate; request; apply for; collect. **postulación** *sf* collection. **postulado** *sm* postulate. **postulante, -a** *sm, sf* collector; applicant.

póstumo ['postumo] *adj* posthumous.

postura [pos'tura] *sf* posture; attitude.

potable [po'taβle] *adj* drinkable.

potaje [po'taxe] *sm* stew; soup.

potasio [po'tasjo] *sm* potassium.

pote ['pote] *sm* jar; jug.

potencia [po'tenθja] *sf* power; ability; potential. **potencial** *adj* potential. **potentado** *sm* potentate. **potente** *adj* powerful.

potestad [potes'tað] *sf* authority; power.

potro ['potro] *sm* colt; instrument of torture.

pozo ['poθo] *sm* hole; well; shaft; bilge.

práctica ['praktika] *sf* practice; method. **practicabilidad** *sf* practicability. **practicable** *adj* practicable. **practicante** *s(m + f)* nurse; practitioner. **practicar** *v* practise; play; perform. **práctico** *adj* practical; experienced.

pradera [pra'ðera] *sf* meadow; prairie. **prado** *sm* field, meadow.

pragmático [prag'matiko] *adj* pragmatic. **pragmatismo** *sm* pragmatism.

preámbulo [pre'ambulo] *sm* preamble.

precario [pre'karjo] *adj* precarious. **precariedad** *sf* precariousness.

precaución [prekau'θjon] *sf* precaution. **con precaución** cautiously. **precaver** *v* forestall. **precaverse** *v* be on one's guard (against).

preceder [preθe'ðer] *v* precede. **precedencia** *sf* precedence; preference. **precedente** *sm* precedent.

precepto [pre'θepto] *sm* precept; regulation. **preceptivo** *adj* compulsory.

preciar [pre'θjar] *v* value. **preciarse** *v* boast. **preciado** *adj* prized; boastful. **precio** *sm* price; esteem. **preciosidad** *sf* excellence. **precioso** *adj* precious; witty.

precipicio [preθi'piθjo] *sm* precipice.

precipitar [preθipi'tar] *v* precipitate. **precipitarse** *v* rush. **precipitación** *sf* precipitation; haste. **precipitado** *adj also* **precipitoso** hasty, rash.

precisar [preθi'sar] *v* need; be necessary; define; fix. **precisamente** *adv* precisely; necessarily. **precisión** *sf* precision; necessity. **preciso** *adj* necessary.

*preconcebir [prekonθe'βir] *v* preconceive. **preconcebido** *adj* preconceived.

preconizar [prekoni'θar] *v* praise; recommend; suggest. **preconización** *sf* recommendation; praise.

precoz [pre'koθ] *adj* precocious. **precocidad** *sf* precocity.

precursor [prekur'sor] *sm* forerunner.

predecesor [preðeθe'sor], **-a** *sm, sf* predecessor.

*predecir [preðe'θir] *v* predict. **predicción** *sf* prediction.

predestinar [preðesti'nar] *v* predestine. **predestinación** *sf* predestination.

prédica ['preðika] *sf* sermon; preaching. **predicación** *sf* preaching. **predicaderas** *sf pl (fam)* eloquence *sing.* **predicador, -a** *sm, sf* preacher. **predicar** *v* preach.

predicado [preði'kaðo] *sm (gram)* predicate.

predicamento [preðika'mento] *sm* predicament; prestige.

predilección [preðilek'θjon] *sf* predilection.

*predisponer [preðispo'ner] *v* predispose. **predisponer contra** prejudice against. **predisposición** *sf* predisposition.

predominar [preðomi'nar] *v* predominate. **predominancia** *sf* predominance. **predominante** *adj* predominant.

preeminente [preemi'nente] *adj* pre-eminent. **preeminencia** *sf* pre-eminence.

prefabricar [prefaβri'kar] *v* prefabricate. **prefabricación** *sf* prefabrication.

prefacio [pre'faθjo] *sm* preface.

prefecto [pre'fekto] *sm* prefect. **prefectura** *sf* prefecture.

*preferir [prefe'rir] *v* prefer. **preferencia** *sf* preference. **preferente** *adj* preferential; preferable. **preferible** *adj* preferable. **preferido** *adj* favourite.

prefigurar [prefigu'rar] *v* prefigure, foreshadow. **prefiguración** *sf* prefiguration.

prefijo [pre'fixo] *adj* prefixed. *sm* prefix. **prefijar** *v* prefix; prearrange.

pregonar [prego'nar] *v* proclaim, announce. **pregón** *sm* proclamation. **pregonero** *sm* town crier.

preguntar [pregun'tar] *v* ask; query; inquire. **preguntarse** *v* wonder. **pregunta** *sf* question. **preguntador, -a** *sm, sf* questioner.

prehistórico [preis'toriko] *adj* prehistoric.

prejuicio [pre'xwiθjo] *sm* prejudice. **prejuzgar** *v* prejudge.

prelado [pre'laðo] *sm* prelate.

preliminar [prelimi'nar] *adj, sm* preliminary. **preliminares** *sm pl* preliminaries *pl.*

preludio [pre'luðjo] *sm* prelude.

prematuro [prema'turo] *adj* premature.

premeditar [premeði'tar] *v* premeditate. **premeditación** *sf* premeditation.

premiar [pre'mjar] *v* reward. **premio** *sm* reward; prize; (*com*) premium. **premio gordo** first prize.

premisa [pre'misa] *sf* premise, assumption.

premonición [premoni'θjon] *sf* premonition.

premura [pre'mura] *sf* urgency; tightness.

prenatal [prena'tal] *adj* antenatal.

prenda ['prenda] *sf* pledge; (*com*) security; garment; darling. **en prenda** as a token of. **prendar** *v* pledge; pawn; please. **prendarse de** fall in love with. **prendería** *sf* second-hand shop. **prendero, -a** *sm, sf* second-hand dealer; pawnbroker.

prensa ['prensa] *sf* press; printing press. **dar a la prensa** publish. **prensar** *v* press.

prensil [pren'sil] *adj* prehensile.

preñado [pre'naðo] *adj* pregnant; bulging; full. **preñar** *v* become pregnant; impregnate. **preñez** *sf* pregnancy.

preocupar [preoku'par] *v* preoccupy; worry; get worried. **¡no se preocupe!** don't worry! **preocupación** *sf* preoccupation; prejudice; worry. **preocupado** *adj* preoccupied; worried.

preparar [prepa'rar] *v* prepare. **preparación** *sf* preparation. **preparativo**

adj also **preparatorio** preparatory.

preponderar [preponde'rar] *v* preponderate, prevail. **preponderancia** *sf* preponderance. **preponderante** *adj* preponderant.

preposición [preposi'θjon] *sf* (*gram*) preposition.

prerequisito [prereki'sito] *sm* prerequisite.

prerrogativa [prerroga'tiβa] *sf* prerogative.

presa¹ ['presa] *sf* capture; prey; victim; quarry; seizure. **presas** *sf pl* fangs *pl*; talons *pl.* **ave de presa** *sf* bird of prey.

presa² *sf* dam; weir. **presa de contención** reservoir.

presagiar [presa'xjar] *v* presage. **presagio** *sm* omen.

présbita ['presβita] *adj also* **présbite** longsighted. **presbicia** *sf* longsightedness.

presbítero [pres'βitero] *sm* priest. **presbiterado** *sm* priesthood.

prescindir [presθin'dir] *v* do without. **prescindible** *adj* dispensable.

prescribir [preskri'βir] *v* prescribe; determine. **prescripción** *sf* prescription. **prescrito** *adj* prescribed.

presenciar [presen'θjar] *v* attend; witness. **presencia** *sf* presence; appearance. **presencia de ánimo** presence of mind.

presentar [presen'tar] *v* present; introduce; submit; propose; tender. **le presento a** may I introduce you to. **presentarse** *v* present oneself; arise; turn up; report; apply. **presentable** *adj* presentable. **presentación** *sf* presentation; introduction. **presente** *adj* present. **mejorando lo presente** present company excepted.

*presentir [presen'tir] *v* have forebodings of. **presentimiento** *sm* presentiment.

preservar [preser'βar] *v* preserve; protect. **preservación** *sf* preservation; protection. **preservador** *adj* preservative. **preservativo** *sm* condom.

presidencia [presi'ðenθja] *sf* presidency. **presidente** *sm* president.

presidiario [presi'ðjarjo] *sm* convict. **presidio** *sm* prison; penal servitude.

presidir [presi'ðir] *v* preside over; dominate.

presilla [pre'siʎa] *sf* loop; fastener.

presión [pre'sjon] *sf* pressure.

preso ['preso] , **-a** *sm sf* prisoner. *adj* captured.

prestar [pres'tar] *v* lend. **prestación** *sf*

lending. **prestado** *adj* loaned. **dar/pedir prestado** lend/borrow. **prestador, -a** *sm, sf* lender. **prestamista** *s(m + f)* money-lender. **préstamo** *sm* loan. **prestario, -a** *sm, sf* borrower.

presteza [pres'teθa] *sf* promptness.

prestidigitador [prestiðixita'ðor] *sm* conjurer; magician. **prestidigitación** *sf* conjuring; magic.

prestigio [pres'tixjo] *sm* prestige; trick. **prestigiado** *adj also* **prestigioso** prestigious.

presto ['presto] *adj* prompt; ready. *adv* promptly.

presumir [presu'mir] *v* presume, assume. **según cabe presumir** presumably. **presumirse** *v* swank; be presumptuous. **presumible** *adj* presumable. **presunción** *sf* assumption; presumptuousness. **presunto** *adj* presumed. **presuntuosidad** *sf* conceit. **presuntuoso** *adj* conceited.

***presuponer** [presupo'ner] *v* presuppose; budget. **presupuesto** *sm* budget; reason; supposition.

presura [pre'sura] *sf* promptness; persistence. **presuroso** *adj* prompt; hasty.

pretender [preten'der] *v* claim; aspire to; seek; want; apply for; allege; pretend. **pretendiente** *sm* pretender; claimant; suitor. **pretensión** *sf* pretension; claim.

pretérito [pre'terito] *sm* (*gram*) past.

pretexto [pre'teksto] *sm* pretext.

***prevalecer** [preβale'θer] *v* prevail. **prevaleciente** *adj* prevailing.

prevaricar [preβari'kar] *v* prevaricate. **prevaricación** *sf* prevarication; breach of trust. **prevaricador, -a** *sm, sf* prevaricator.

***prevenir** [preβe'nir] *v* prevent; warn; prepare; foresee. **prevención** *sf* prevention; warning; preparation; prejudice; police station. **prevenido** *adj* prepared; forewarned. **bien prevenido** full. **preventivo** *adj* preventive.

***prever** [pre'βer] *v* foresee; anticipate. **previsión** *sf* foresight; forecast. **caja de previsión** *sf* social security.

previo ['preβjo] *adj* previous. **previo pago** after payment.

prieto ['prjeto] *adj* dark; mean.

prima ['prima] *sf* premium; bonus.

primado [pri'maðo] *sm* (*rel*) primate.

primario [pri'marjo] *adj* primary.

primavera [prima'βera] *sf* spring.

primer [pri'mer] *adj* first. **primeramente** *adv* first; mainly. **primero** *adj* first; best; principal. **de primera** first-class.

primitivo [primi'tiβo] *adj* primitive; original.

primo ['primo] *adj* prime. *sm* cousin.

primogénito [primo'xenito] *adj* first-born.

primor [pri'mor] *sm* beauty; delicacy; skill. **primoroso** *adj* exquisite; skilful.

princesa [prin'θesa] *sf* princess.

principal [prinθi'pal] *adj, sm* principal.

príncipe ['prinθipe] *sm* prince.

principiar [prinθi'pjar] *v* start. **principiante** *s(m + f)* novice. **principio** *sm* beginning.

pringar [prin'gar] *v* stain with grease; wound; involve; slander. **pringarse** *v* embezzle. **pringón** *adj* greasy. **pringoso** *adj* fatty, greasy. **pringue** *s(m + f)* grease stain; dripping.

prior [pri'or] *sm* (*rel*) prior. *adj* prior. **priora** *sf* prioress. **priorato** *sm* priory. **prioridad** *sf* priority.

prisa ['prisa] *sf* hurry. **darse prisa** hurry. **tener prisa** be in a hurry.

prisión [pri'sjon] *sf* prison; imprisonment. **prisionero, -a** *sm, sf* prisoner.

prisma ['prisma] *sm* prism. **prismático** *adj* prismatic.

pristino [pris'tino] *adj* pristine.

privar¹ [pri'βar] *v* deprive; prohibit. **privación** *sf* deprivation. **privado** *adj* private.

privar² *v* be in favour; be popular.

privilegiar [priβile'xjar] *v* grant a favour to. **privilegio** *sm* privilege.

pro [pro] *sm* benefit, profit. **en pro de** on behalf of. **hombre de pro** *sm* honest man.

proa ['proa] *sf* (*mar*) prow, bow, bows *pl*. **mascarón de proa** *sm* figurehead.

probable [pro'βaβle] *adj* probable. **probabilidad** *sf* probability.

***probar** [pro'βar] *v* test; try; taste; prove. **probarse** *v* try on. **probador** *sm* fitting room. **probanza** *sf* proof. **probeta** *sf* test tube.

probidad [proβi'ðað] *sf* probity, integrity.

problema [pro'βlema] *sm* problem.

proceder [proθe'ðer] *v* proceed; behave; originate. **procedencia** *sf* origin; port of departure. **procedente** *adj* originating; reasonable; proper. **procedimiento** *sm* process.

procesador de textos *sm* word processor.

procesamiento de textos *sm* word processing.

procesar [proθe'sar] *v* prosecute. **procesado, -a** *sm*, *sf* accused. **procesal** *adj* procedural. **procesamiento** *sm* prosecution.

procesión [proθe'sjon] *sf* procession.

proclamar [prokla'mar] *v* proclaim. **proclama** *sf also* **proclamación** *f* proclamation.

procrear [prokre'ar] *v* procreate. **procreación** *sf* procreation. **procreador, -a** *sm*, *sf* procreator.

procurar [proku'rar] *v* cause; attempt; obtain; succeed; give. **procura** *sf* power of attorney. **procurador, -a** *sm*, *sf* lawyer.

prodigar [proði'gar] *v* squander; lavish. **prodigalidad** *sf* prodigality.

prodigio [pro'ðixjo] *sm* prodigy. **prodigioso** *adj* prodigious.

pródigo ['proðigo] *adj* prodigal; wasteful.

***producir** [proðu'θir] *v* produce. **producirse** *v* happen. **producción** *sf* production. **productivo** *adj* productive. **producto** *sm* product. **productor, -a** *sm*, *sf* producer.

proeza [pro'eθa] *sf* deed; feat.

profanar [profa'nar] *v* profane. **profanación** *sf* profanation. **profano** *adj* profane.

profecía [profe'θia] *sf* prophecy. **profeta** *sm* prophet. **profético** *adj* prophetic. **profetisa** *sf* prophetess. **profetizar** *v* prophesy.

***proferir** [profe'rir] *v* utter.

profesar [profe'sar] *v* profess; manifest; practise a profession. **profesión** *sf* profession. **profesional** *adj* professional. **profesor, -a** *sm*, *sf* professor, teacher. **profesorado** *sm* professorship; teaching staff.

prófugo ['profugo], **-a** *s*, *adj* fugitive.

profundizar [profundi'θar] *v* deepen. **profundidad** *sf* depth. **profundo** *adj* deep.

profusión [profu'sjon] *sf* profusion. **profuso** *adj* profuse.

progenie [pro'xenje] *sf* progeny. **progenitor** *sm* progenitor. **progenitores** *sm pl* ancestors *pl*; parents *pl*. **progenitura** *sf* off-spring.

programa [pro'grama] *sm* program(me). **programa basura** *sm* chat show. **programador** *s(m+f)* programmer.

progresar [progre'sar] *v* progress. **progresión** *sf* progression. **progresivo** *adj* progressive. **progreso** *sm* progress.

prohibir [proi'βir] *v* prohibit. **se prohibe fumar** no smoking. **prohibición** *sf* prohibition. **prohibitivo** *adj* prohibitive.

prohijar [proi'xar] *v* adopt. **prohijamiento** *sm* adoption.

prójimo ['proximo] *sm* fellow man; neighbour; (*fam*) bloke.

prole ['prole] *sf* offspring.

prolapso [pro'lapso] *sm* prolapse.

proletario [prole'tarjo], **-a** *s*, *adj* proletarian.

prolífico [pro'lifiko] *adj* prolific.

prolijo [pro'lixo] *adj* tedious; long-winded. **prolijidad** *sf* long-windedness.

prólogo ['prologo] *sm* prologue.

prolongar [prolon'gar] *v* prolong. **prolongación** *sf* prolongation. **prolongado** *adj* prolonged.

promediar [prome'ðjar] *v* bisect; average out; mediate. **promedio** *sm* middle; average.

promesa [pro'mesa] *sf* promise. **prometer** *v* promise. **prometerse** *v* expect; become engaged. **prometérselas felices** have high hopes. **prometida** *sf* fiancée. **prometido** *sm* fiancé.

prominencia [promi'nenθja] *sf* prominence; projection; bulge. **prominente** *adj* prominent.

promiscuo [pro'miskwo] *adj* promiscuous; ambiguous.

promontorio [promon'torjo] *sm* promontory.

***promover** [promo'βer] *v* promote. **promoción** *sf* promotion. **promotor, -a** *sm*, *sf* promoter.

promulgar [promul'gar] *v* promulgate. **promulgación** *sf* promulgation.

pronombre [pro'nombre] *sm* pronoun.

pronosticar [pronosti'kar] *v* prognosticate. **pronosticación** *sf* prognostication, forecast. **pronóstico** *sm* prediction.

prontitud [pronti'tuð] *sf* promptness. **pronto** *adv* quickly, at once. **¡hasta pronto!** see you soon!

pronunciar [pronun'θjar] *v* pronounce. **pronunciarse** *v* rebel. **pronunciación** *sf* pronunciation. **pronunciamiento** *sm* rising; (*jur*) pronouncement.

propagar [propa'gar] *v* propagate. **propagación** *sf* propagation. **propaganda** *sf* propaganda; junk mail.

propalar [propa'lar] *v* publish; divulge.

propenso [pro'penso] *adj* prone. **propender** *v* incline. **propensión** *sf* inclination.

propicio [pro'piθjo] *adj* propitious. **propiciación** *sf* propitiation. **propiciar** *v* propitiate.

propiedad [propje'ðað] *sf* property; ownership; propriety; resemblance. **propietario, -a** *sm, sf* landlord/lady.

propina [pro'pina] *sf* (*dinero*) tip.

propio ['propjo] *adj* proper; own; particular. **nombre propio** *sm* proper noun. **ser propio de** be typical of. **sus propias palabras** his very words. **propiamente** *adv* properly.

*proponer [propo'ner] *v* propose. **proponente** *s(m + f)* proposer. **proposición** *sf* proposition; proposal.

proporción [propor'θjon] *sf* proportion. **proporcionado** *adj* proportionate. **bien proporcionado** well proportioned. **proporcional** *adj* proportional. **proporcionar** *v* supply; cause; adapt.

propósito [pro'posito] *sm* purpose; intention. **a propósito** by the way. **a propósito de** with regard to. **de propósito** on purpose.

propuesta [pro'pwesta] *sf* proposal.

propulsar [propul'sar] *v* propel. **propulsión** *sf* propulsion. **propulsor** *sm* propeller.

prorrata [pro'rrata] *sf* quota. **a prorrata** pro rata.

prórroga ['prorroga] *sf* prorogation, extension. **prorrogar** *v* prorogue, adjourn.

prorrumpir [prorrum'pir] *v* break out.

prosa ['prosa] *sf* prose. **prosaico** *adj* prosaic.

proscribir [proskri'βir] *v* proscribe, ban. **proscripción** *sf* proscription, prohibition. **proscrito** *adj* outlawed, banished.

prosecución [proseku'θjon] *sf* pursuit; continuation. **proseguir** *v* pursue; continue.

prosélito [pro'selito] *sm* proselyte.

prospecto [pros'pekto] *sm* prospectus.

prosperar [prospe'rar] *v* prosper. **prosperi-** dad *sf* prosperity. **próspero** *adj* prosperous.

prosternarse [proster'narse] *v* prostrate oneself.

*prostituir [prostitu'ir] *v* prostitute. **prostíbulo** *sm* brothel. **prostitución** *sf* prostitution. **prostituta** *sf* prostitute.

protagonista [protago'nista] *s(m + f)* protagonist.

proteger [prote'xer] *v* protect. **protección** *sf* protection. **protector** *adj* protective. **protegido, -a** *sm, sf* protégé.

proteína [prote'ina] *sf* protein.

protestar [protes'tar] *v* protest. **protesta** *sf* protest. **protestación** *sf* protestation. **protestante** *s(m + f)*, *adj* Protestant. **protestantismo** *sm* Protestantism.

protocolo [proto'kolo] *sm* protocol.

prototipo [proto'tipo] *sm* prototype.

protuberancia [protuβe'ranθja] *sf* protuberance. **protuberante** *adj* protuberant.

provecho [pro'βetʃo] *sm* advantage; profit. **de provecho** useful. **sacar provecho de** benefit from. **provechoso** *adj* profitable.

proveer [proβe'er] *v* provide; deal with; decide; fill. **proveedor, -a** *sm, sf* supplier.

*provenir [proβe'nir] *v* originate. **proveniente** *adj* originating.

proverbio [pro'βerβjo] *sm* proverb. **proverbial** *adj* proverbial.

providencia [proβi'ðenθja] *sf* providence; foresight. **providencial** *adj* providential. **providente** *adj* provident.

provincia [pro'βinθja] *sf* province. **provincial** *adj* provincial. **provincialismo** *sm* provincialism.

provisión [proβisi'on] *sf* provision. **provisional** *adj* provisional. **provisionalmente** *adv* provisionally. **provisor** *sm* purveyer. **provisto** *adj* supplied.

provocar [proβo'kar] *v* provoke; cause. **provocación** *sf* provocation. **provocador** *adj* provocative. **provocante** *adj* provoking.

próximo ['proksimo] *adj* next; neighbouring. **la semana próxima** next week. **proximamente** *adv* closely; soon. **proximidad** *sf* proximity.

proyectar [projek'tar] *v* project; plan; throw. **proyección** *sf* projection. **proyectil** *sm* projectile. **proyecto** *sm* project. **proyector** *sm* projector; searchlight; spotlight.

prudencia [pru'ðenθja] *sf* prudence. **pru-**

dencial adj (fam) moderate. **prudente** adj prudent.

prueba ['prweβa] sf test; proof; tasting; (deporte) event. **a prueba** on trial. **a prueba de** proof against.

prurito [pru'rito] sm itch; urge.

psicoanálisis [psikoa'nalisis] sm invar psychoanalysis. **psicoanalista** s(m + f) psychoanalyst. **psicoanalizar** v psychoanalyse.

psicología [psikolo'xia] sf psychology. **psicológico** adj psychological. **psicólogo, -a** sm, sf psychologist.

psiquiatría [psikja'tria] sf psychiatry. **psiquiatra** s(m + f) psychiatrist. **psiquiátrico** adj psychiatric.

púa ['pua] sf prong; barb; thorn; sharp point.

pubertad [puβer'taθ] sf puberty.

publicar [puβli'kar] v publish. **publicación** sf publication. **publicidad** sf publicity; advertising. **público** sm, adj public. **dar al público** publish.

puchero [pu'tʃero] sm stew; cooking-pot. **ganarse el puchero** earn one's daily bread.

pucho [putʃo] sm cigarette or cigar end; fag-end.

púdico [puðiko] adj chaste; modest. **pudicia** sf chastity; modesty.

pudiente [pu'ðjente] adj rich.

pudín [pu'ðin] sm pudding.

pudor [pu'ðor] sm modesty; shame. **pudoroso** adj modest.

*pudrir [pu'ðrir] v rot, decay. **pudrición** sf putrefaction. **pudrimiento** sm rotting.

pueblo ['pweβlo] sm people; town; village. **de pueblos** from the country.

puente ['pwente] sm bridge. **puente colgante** suspension bridge.

puerco [pwerko] sm pig. adj filthy. **puerca** sf sow. **puerco espín** porcupine.

pueril [pue'ril] adj childish. **puerilidad** sf childishness.

puerro ['pwerro] sm leek.

puerta ['pwerta] sf door; entrance. **puerta principal** front door. **puerta trasera** back door.

puerto ['pwerto] sm port; harbour; mountain pass.

puerto de escala sm port of call.

pues [pwes] adv, conj then; since; because; well; so; yes. **pues bien** OK. **¡pues claro!** of course! **¿pues qué?** so what?

puesta ['pwesta] sf (del sol) setting; bet;

putting. **puesta en escena** staging.

puesto ['pwesto] sm small shop; place; stall; job. **puesto de periódicos** newspaper stand.

pugnar [pug'nar] v fight; struggle. **pugna** sf fight. **pugnaz** adj pugnacious.

pujar [pu'xar] v strain; strive; outbid. **pujante** adj strong. **pujanza** sf strength.

pulcritud [pulkri'tuθ] sf neatness; care. **pulcro** adj neat, tidy.

pulga ['pulga] sf flea. **pulgoso** adj flea-ridden.

pulgada [pul'gaða] sf inch. **pulgar** sm thumb.

pulir [pu'lir] v polish; adorn. **pulidez** sf polish; neatness. **pulido** adj polished; smooth; neat. **pulidor** sm polisher. **pulimentar** v polish. **pulimento** sm polish, shine.

pulmón [pul'mon] sm lung. **pulmonía** sf pneumonia.

pulpa ['pulpa] sf pulp.

púlpito ['pulpito] sm pulpit.

pulpo ['pulpo] sm octopus.

pulsar [pul'sar] v pulsate. **pulso** sm pulse; wrist; steady hand.

pulsera [pul'sera] sf bracelet; watch strap. **reloj de pulsera** sm wristwatch.

pulverizar [pulβeri'θar] v pulverize; spray. **pulverización** sf pulverization. **pulverizador** sm spray; atomizer.

pulla ['puʎa] sf taunt; obscenity.

punción [pun'θjon] sf (med) puncture.

punición [puni'θjon] sf punishment. **punible** adj punishable. **punitivo** adj punitive.

punky adj punk.

punta ['punta] sf point; tip; head; end; nail. **horas punta** sf pl rush hours pl. **sacar punta a** sharpen. **velocidad punta** sf top speed.

puntada [pun'taða] sf stitch.

puntapié [punta'pje] sm kick. **echar a puntapiés** kick out.

puntear [punte'ar] v stitch; tick off; perforate. **punteado** sm (música) plucking.

puntería [punte'ria] sf aim; marksmanship. **puntero** adj outstanding.

puntilla [pun'tiʎa] sf tack; nib; fine lace. **de puntillas** on tiptoe.

punto ['punto] sm point; full stop; stitch; mark; honour; matter; item. **punto com** sm dotcom. **punto de vista** sm point of view. **al punto** at once. **dos puntos** colon. **en punto** on the dot. **¡punto en boca!** mum's the word!

puntual [puntu'al] *adj* punctual; reliable. **puntualidad** *sf* punctuality; reliability.

puntualizar [puntwali'θar] *v* arrange; determine; perfect; settle.

puntuar [pun'twar] *v* punctuate. **puntuación** *sf* punctuation. **signos de puntuación** *sm pl* punctuation marks *pl*.

punzar [pun'θar] *v* pierce. **punzada** *sf* prick; twinge. **punzante** *adj* sharp. **punzón** *sm* awl, punch.

puñado [pu'naðo] *sm* handful. **puñada** *sf also* **puñetazo** *sm* blow, clout. **puño** *sm* fist; cuff. **de propio puño** in one's own handwriting.

puñal [pu'ɲal] *sm* dagger. **puñalada** *sf* stab.

pupila [pu'pila] *sf* (*anat*) pupil.

pupilaje [pupi'laxe] *sm* boarding-house; tutelage.

pupitre [pu'pitre] *sm* desk.

puré [pu're] *sm* purée. **puré de patatas** mashed potatoes *pl*.

pureza [pu'reθa] *sf* purity. **purificación** *sf* purification. **purificar** *v* purify. **purista** *s(m + f)* purist. **puro** *adj* pure; simple.

purgar [pur'gar] *v* purge; purify. **purgante** *sm* purgative. **purgativo** *adj* purgative. **purgatorio** *sm* purgatory.

puritano [puri'tano], **-a** *s, adj* puritan. **puritanismo** *sm* puritanism.

púrpura ['purpura] *sf* purple.

pus [pus] *sm* pus, matter.

pusilánime [pusi'lanime] *adj* cowardly. **pusilanimidad** *sf* cowardliness.

pústula ['pustula] *sf* (*med*) pustule, pimple.

puta ['puta] *sf* (*fam*) whore, prostitute. **puto** *sm* (*fam*) bugger.

putrefacción [putrefak'θjon] *sf* putrefaction. **putrefacto** *adj* rotten. **pútrido** *adj* putrid.

puya ['puja] *sf* goad; (*fig*) gibe.

Q

que [ke] *pron* who; whom; that; which. *conj* that; because; than. **que sí** of course.

más que more than.

qué [ke] *pron, adj* what. **¿qué pasa?** what's going on? **¡qué miedo!** what a fright! **¡qué raro!** how extraordinary!

*****quebrar** [ke'βrar] *v* break; go bankrupt. **quebrado** *adj* broken; bankrupt. **quebradura** *sf* crack; gap. **quebrantar** *v* shatter. **quebranto** *sm* exhaustion.

queda ['keða] *sf* curfew.

quedar [ke'ðar] *v* stay; remain; sojourn. **quedarse** *v* stay behind. **quedarse encantado con** *v* fall for (affection). **quedar en nada** come to nothing.

quedo ['keðo] *adj* quiet; still. *adv* quietly.

quehaceres [kea'θeres] *sm pl* chores; duties.

quejarse [ke'xarse] *v* complain; moan. **queja** *sf* complaint. **quejido** *sm* groan. **quejoso** *adj* plaintive; complaining.

quemar [ke'mar] *v* burn; scorch. **quema** *sf* burning; fire. **quemadura** *sf* burn; scald. **quemante** *adj* burning; burn. **quemazón** *sf* burning; burn.

querella [ke'reʎa] *sf* quarrel; (*jur*) complaint. **querellarse** *v* lodge a complaint.

*****querer** [ke'rer] *v* love; want; try; determine. *sm* affection. **querido** *adj* dear.

queso ['keso] *sm* cheese. **queso rallado** grated cheese.

quiá [ki'a] *interj* never! surely not!

quicio ['kiθjo] *sm* hinge. **fuera de quicio** out of order.

quiebra [ki'eβra] *sf* bankruptcy; slump; fissure.

quien [ki'en] *pron* who; whom; whoever. **quién** *pron interrog* who. **¿quién sabe?** who knows? **quienquiera** *pron* whoever, whosoever.

quieto [ki'eto] *adj* still, quiet, **quietud** *sf* stillness.

quijote [ki'xote] *sm* quixotic person; idealist.

quilate [ki'late] *sm* carat.

quilla ['kiʎa] *sf* keel.

quimera [ki'mera] *sf* hallucination; quarrel. **quimérico** *adj* fantastic.

química ['kimika] *sf* chemistry. **químico** *adj* chemical.

quincalla [kin'kaʎa] *sf* hardware; iron-mongery. **quincallero, -a** *sm, sf* ironmonger.

quince ['kinθe] *sm, adj* fifteen. **quincena** *sf* fortnight. **quincuagésima** *adj* fiftieth.

quinientos *adj invar* five hundred.

quinta ['kinta] *sf* country house; conscription; (*música*) fifth.

quintal [kin'tal] *sm* hundredweight.

quinto ['kinto] *adj* fifth.

quiosco [ki'osko] *sm* kiosk.

quirúrgico [ki'rurxiko] *adj* surgical.

quisquilla [kis'kiʎa] *sf* quibble; trifle; (*zool*) shrimp.

quiste ['kiste] *sm* (*med*) cyst.

quitamanchas [kita'mantʃas] *sm invar* stain-remover.

quitar [ki'tar] *v* remove; take off; take away. **quitarse** *v* get rid of; withdraw; abstain. **de quita y pon** easily detachable.

quitasol [kita'sol] *sm* parasol, sunshade.

quizá(s) [ki'θa(s)] *adv* perhaps, maybe.

R

rabal [ra'bal] *sm* inner city.

rábano ['raβano] *sm* radish.

rabiar [ra'βjar] *v* rave, rage. **rabiar por** long for. **rabia** *sf* rage, fury; (*med*) rabies. **rabioso** *adj* rabid.

rabino [ra'βino] *sm* rabbi.

rabo ['raβo] *sm* tail; stalk. **hacer rabona** play truant.

racial [ra'θjal] *adj* racial.

racimo [ra'θimo] *sm* bunch; cluster.

raciocinar [raθoθi'nar] *v also* **racionar** ration. **ración** *sf* portion, ration.

racional [raθjo'nal] *adj* rational. **racionalidad** *sf* rationality. **racionalista** *adj* rationalist.

racista [ra'θista] *s(m + f)* racist.

racha ['ratʃa] *sf* gust of wind; streak of luck; split.

radiactivo [radjak'tiβo] *adj* radioactive. **radioactividad** *sf* radioactivity.

radiar [ra'ðjar] *v* radiate; broadcast. **radiación** *sf* radiation; broadcasting. **radiador** *sm* radiator. **radiante** *adj* radiant.

radicar [raði'kar] *v* take root; settle. **radicación** *sf* taking root.

radical [raði'kal] *adj* radical, fundamental. **radicalismo** *sm* radicalism.

radio¹ ['raðjo] *sm* radius.

radio² *sm* radium.

radio³ *sf* radio. **radiodifusión** *sf* broadcasting. **radiomisora** *sf* radio station. **radioyente** *s(m + f)* listener.

***raer** [ra'er] *v* scrape; erase.

raíz [ra'iθ] *sf* root. **bienes raíces** real estate sing.

rajar [ra'xar] *v* slit; crack; slice. **raja** *sf* crack; slice.

ralea [ra'lea] *sf* sort; breed.

rallar [ra'ʎar] *v* grate. **rallador** *sm* grater. **rallo** *sm* rasp.

rama ['rama] *sf* (*bot*) branch, bough.

rambla ['rambla] *sf* avenue; gully.

ramificarse [ramifi'karse] *v* branch out. **ramificación** *sf* ramification.

ramillete [rami'ʎete] *sm* bunch of flowers; posy; cluster.

ramo ['ramo] *sm* (*bot*) branch; cluster; bouquet.

rampa ['rampa] *sf* ramp.

ramplón [ram'plon] *adj* coarse, vulgar.

rana ['rana] *sf* frog.

rancio ['ranθjo] *adj* rancid, rank, stale.

rancho ['rantʃo] *sm* (*comida*) mess; farm; ranch. **ranchero** *sm* rancher.

rango ['rango] *sm* class, rank.

ranura [ra'nura] *sf* groove.

rap ['rap] *adj* rap (music).

rapaz [ra'paθ] *adj* rapacious. **rapacidad** *sf* rapacity.

rapé [ra'pe] *sm* snuff.

rápido [ra'piðo] *adj* rapid. **rapidez** *sf* speed.

rapiña [ra'piɲa] *sf* robbery with violence.

rapsodia [rap'soðja] *sf* rhapsody.

raptar [rap'tar] *v* carry off, abduct; kidnap. **rapto** *sm* abduction. **raptor, -a** *sm, sf* kidnapper.

raquero [ra'kero] *sm* beachcomber.

raqueta [ra'keta] *sf* racket.

raro ['raro] *adj* rare. **rareza** *sf* rarity.

ras [ras] *sm* level. **a ras de tierra** at ground level.

rascacielos [raska'θjelos] *sm invar* skyscraper.

rascar [ras'kar] *v* scratch; scrape. **rascadura** *sf* scratching.

rasgar [ras'gar] *v* tear; rip; slash.

rasgo ['rasgo] *sm* feature; feat; (*de*

pluma) stroke.
raso ['raso] *adj* flat; level; smooth.
raspar [ras'par] *v* rasp. **raspa** *sf* rasp. **raspadura** *sf* rasping.
rastra ['rastra] *sf* trail; trace; sledge.
rastrear [rastre'ar] *v* trace; track; rake.
rastrillar [rastri'ʎar] *v* rake. **rastrillo** *sm* rake.
rastro ['rastro] *sm* track; trail.
rastrojo [ras'troxo] *sm* stubble.
rasurar [rasu'rar] *v* shave. **rasura** *sf* shaving.
rata ['rata] *sf* rat.
ratería [rate'ria] *sf* larceny, petty thieving. **ratero, -a** *sm, sf* petty thief.
ratificar [ratifi'kar] *v* ratify. **ratificación** *sf* ratification.
rato ['rato] *sm* a little while, short period of time. **al poco rato** shortly after.
ratón [ra'ton] *sm* mouse. **ratonera** *sf* mousetrap.
rayar [ra'jar] *v* rule; draw lines on; underline. **raya** *sf* line; stripe; limit. **a raya** within bounds. **rayado** *adj* lined; striped.
rayo ['rajo] *sm* beam, ray of light; flash of lightning.
raza ['raθa] *sf* race; lineage; breed.
razón [ra'θon] *sf* reason; rationale. **tener razón** be right. **razonable** *adj* reasonable. **razonar** *v* reason; justify.
reacción [reak'θjon] *sf* reaction. **reaccionar** *v* react. **reaccionario** *s(m + f)* reactionary. **reactor** *sm* reactor.
reacio [re'aθjo] *adj* obstinate.
real¹ [re'al] *adj* real.
real² *adj* royal.
realce [re'alθe] *sm* (*arte*) relief; highlight; importance.
realizar [reali'θar] *v* realize; make; perform.
realzar [real'θar] *v* raise; emboss; dignify.
reanimar [reani'mar] *v* revive; encourage.
reanudar [reanu'ðar] *v* renew. **reanudarse** *v* start again.
*reaparecer [reapare'θer] *v* reappear. **reaparición** *sf* reappearance.
rebajar [reβa'xar] *v* lessen, reduce; lower; allow discount; (*bebida*) weaken. **rebajarse** *v* demean oneself. **rebaja** *sf* reduction.
rebanada [reβa'naða] *sf* slice. **rebanar** *v* slice.
rebaño [re'βaɲo] *sm* flock; herd.

rebasar [reβa'sar] *v* go beyond, exceed; overtake; overflow.
rebatir [reβa'tir] *v* rebut, refute; repel. **rebato** *sm* (*mil*) alarm, call to arms; surprise attack.
rebeca [re'βeka] *sf* cardigan.
rebelarse [reβe'larse] *v* rebel. **rebelde** *adj* rebellious. **rebeldía** *sf* rebelliousness. **rebelión** *sf* rebellion.
rebosar [reβo'sar] *v* overflow. **rebosadura** *sf* overflowing.
rebotar [reβo'tar] *v* bend back; rebound; bounce. **rebotación** *sf* bouncing. **rebote** *sm* bounce.
rebozar [reβo'θar] *v* muffle. **rebozo** *sm* muffler. **sin rebozo** openly.
rebuscar [reβus'kar] *v* search for. **rebusca** *sf* search. **rebuscado** *adj* elaborate.
rebuznar [reβuθ'nar] *v* bray. **rebuzno** *sm* bray.
recado [re'kaðo] *sm* errand; message. **recadista** *s(m + f)* messenger.
*recaer [reka'er] *v* relapse. **recaída** *sf* relapse.
recalcar [rekal'kar] *v* cram; pack; stress. **recalcadura** *sf* pressing; packing.
recalcitrante [rekalθi'trante] *adj* recalcitrant.
*recalentar [rekalen'tar] *v* reheat; rekindle. **recalentarse** *v* overheat.
recambio [re'kambjo] *sm* re-exchange. **piezas de recambio** *sf pl* spare parts.
recargar [rekar'gar] *v* reload; overload; increase; recharge. **recarga** *sf* refill. **recargable** *adj* refillable. **recargo** *sm* additional load; surcharge.
recatarse [reka'tarse] *v* be cautious. **recatar** *v* cover up. **recatado** *adj* prudent. **recato** *sm* prudence.
recaudar [rekau'ðar] *v* collect. **recaudación** *sf* collection. **recaudador** *sm* tax collector. **a buen recaudo** in safe keeping.
recelar [reθe'lar] *v* suspect; fear. **recelo** *sm* mistrust. **receloso** *adj* suspicious.
recepción [reθep'θjon] *sf* reception; receipt; admission.
receptáculo [reθep'takulo] *sm* receptacle.
receptor [reθep'tor] *sm* recipient, receiver.
recesión [reθe'sjon] *sf* recession.
receta [re'θeta] *sf* formula; recipe; prescription.
recibir [reθi'βir] *v* receive. **recibidor, -a**

sm, sf receiver. **recibo** *sm* reception; (*com*) receipt. **acusar recibo** (*com*) acknowledge receipt.

reciclar [reθi'klar] *v* (m) recycle. **reciclaje** *sm* recycling.

recién [re'θjen] *adv* recently, lately, just. **recién llegado** *sm* newcomer. **reciente** *adj* recent, new.

recinto [re'θinto] *sm* enclosure; precinct, district.

recio ['reθjo] *adj* tough, strong. *adv* loudly.

recipiente [reθi'pjente] *sm* receptacle; recipient.

reciprocar [reθipro'kar] *v* reciprocate. **recíproco** *adj* reciprocal.

recitar [reθi'tar] *v* recite. *sm* recital. **recitación** *sf* recitation.

reclamar [rekla'mar] *v* claim; demand; appeal. **reclamación** *sf* claim; protest. **reclamo** *sm* call; advertisement.

reclinar [rekli'nar] *v* lean, recline. **reclinación** *sf* leaning.

reclusión [reklu'sjon] *sf* seclusion; imprisonment. **recluso, -a** *sm* recluse; convict.

recluta [re'kluta] *sm* recruit; conscript. **reclutamiento** *sm* recruitment. **reclutar** *v* recruit; conscript.

recobrar [reko'βrar] *v* recover; recuperate; regain. **recobro** *sm* recovery.

recoger [reko'xer] *v* pick up; gather; collect; confiscate; take in; shrink. **recogerse** *v* withdraw within oneself. **recogida** *sf* collection; harvest; withdrawal. **recogido** *adj* short; small; secluded. **recogimiento** *sm* withdrawal.

recolección [rekolek'θjon] *sf* gathering; harvest; recollection; compilation. **recolectar** *v* harvest.

*****recomendar** [rekomen'dar] *v* recommend; commend. **recomendación** *sf* recommendation. **recomendado, -a** *sm, sf* protégé/protégée.

recompensar [rekompen'sar] *v* recompense, reward. **recompenso** *sf* compensation; recompense.

reconciliarse [rekonθi'ljarse] *v* reconcile oneself. **reconciliación** *sf* reconciliation.

recóndito [re'kondito] *adj* secret; obscure.

*****reconocer** [rekono'θer] *v* recognize; acknowledge; examine closely. **reconocible** *adj* recognizable. **recononcimiento** *sm* recognition; acknowledgement; examination.

reconquista [rekon'kista] *sf* reconquest. **reconquistar** *v* reconquer.

reconsiderar [rekonside'rar] *v* reconsider.

*****reconstituir** [rekonstitu'ir] *v* reconstitute. **reconstitución** *sf* reconstitution.

*****reconstruir** [rekonstru'ir] *v* reconstruct.

*****reconvenir** [rekonβe'nir] *v* reproach; rebuke. **reconvención** *sf* reproach.

recopilar [rekopi'lar] *v* compile; summarize. **recopilación** *sf* compilation; summary. **recopilador** *sm* compiler.

*****recordar** [rekor'ðar] *v* remember; commemorate; remind. **recordarse** *v* wake up. **para recordar** in memory. **recordable** *adj* memorable. **recordativo** *adj* reminiscent.

recorrer [reko'rer] *v* go over; traverse; examine; survey; repair. **recorrido** *sm* journey; run; revision.

recortar [rekor'tar] *v* cut out; cut down; clip; trim; stand out. **recorte** *sm* cutting; outline.

recoveco [reko'βeko] *sm* bend; nook; recess.

recrearse [rekre'arse] *v* amuse oneself. **recreación** *sf* recreation. **recreo** *sm* recreation; amusement.

recreativos [rekrea'tiβos] *sm pl* amusement arcade.

recriminar [rekrimi'nar] *v* recriminate. **recriminación** *sf* recrimination.

*****recrudecer** [rekruðe'θer] *v* recur; break out again.

rectángulo [rek'tangulo] *sm* rectangle. **rectangular** *adj* rectangular.

rectificar [rektifi'kar] *v* rectify; correct. **rectificación** *sf* rectification.

rectitud [rekti'tuð] *sf* rectitude; rightness. **recto** *adj* right; just; straight.

rector [rek'tor] *sm* rector; principal; governor. **rectoría** *sf* rectory.

recua ['rekwa] *sf* drove, herd; (*fig*) gang.

recuento [re'kwento] *sm* recount; calculation; inventory.

recuerdo [re'kwerðo] *sm* recollection; memory. **recuerdos** *sm pl* regards *pl*.

recular [reku'lar] *v* recoil. **reculada** *sf* recoil.

recuperar [rekupe'rar] *v* recuperate. **recuperación** *sf* recovery.

recurrir [reku'rir] *v* revert; resort (to). **recurrir a** have recourse to. **recurso** *sm* recourse; appeal.

recusar [reku'sar] v refuse; reject. **recusación** sf refusal; rejection.

rechazar [retʃa'θar] v repel; deny. **rechazamiento** sm repulsion. **rechazo** sm rebound; rejection.

rechinar [retʃi'nar] v creak; squeak; (*los dientes*) gnash. **rechinamiento** sm creaking; squeaking.

rechoncho [re'tʃontʃo] adj squat; chubby.

red [reð] sf net; grid; grille; grating; snare. **caer en la red** fall into the trap. **red ferroviaria** railway system.

redactar [reðak'tar] v edit. **redacción** sf editing; journalism. **redactor, -a** sm, sf editor; writer.

redención [reðen'θjon] sf redemption; help; salvation. **redentor, -a** sm, sf redeemer.

redimir [reði'mir] v redeem; ransom. **redimible** adj redeemable.

rédito ['reðito] sm income. **rédito imponible** taxable income.

redoblar [reðo'βlar] v double; redouble; repeat. **redobladura** sf redoubling.

redondear [reðonde'ar] v round; round off. **redondo** adj round; spherical. **negocio redondo** sm square deal.

*reducir [reðu'θir] v reduce; lessen; compress; scale down **reducción** sf reduction. **reducido** adj reduced; abridged.

redundar [reðun'dar] v redound; overflow.

reembolsar [reembol'sar] v reimburse, repay. **reembolso** sm reimbursement; refund. **contra reembolso** cash on delivery.

reemplazar [reempla'θar] v replace. **reemplazable** adj replaceable. **reemplazo** sm replacement.

referencia [refe'renθja] sf reference; account; allusion. **referente** adj referring. **referido** adj aforementioned; in question.

referéndum [refe'rendum] sm referendum.

*referir [refe'rir] v refer; narrate; describe.

refinar [refi'nar] v refine; polish; perfect. **refinación** sf refinement. **refinado** adj refined; slick. **refinadura** sf refinement. **refinería** sf refinery.

reflectar [reflek'tar] v reflect. **reflector** sm reflector; searchlight.

reflejar [refle'xar] v reflect; show. **refleja** sf reflection. **reflejo** sm reflection; reflex; glare.

reflexión [refle'ksjon] sf reflection. **reflexionar** v reflect. **reflexivo** adj (*gram*) reflexive.

reflujo [re'fluxo] sm ebb.

reformar [refor'mar] v reform; amend; remake; improve; repair. **reformar la instalación** v rewire. **reforma** sf reform, reformation. **reformación** sf reformation. **reformador, -a** sm, sf reformer. **reformativo** adj reformative. **reformatorio** sm reformatory.

*reforzar [refor'θar] v reinforce; strengthen; encourage; boost. **reforzado** adj reinforced.

refractario [refrak'tarjo] adj refractory. **refracción** sf refraction. **refractar** v refract.

refrán [re'fran] sm proverb, saying.

*refregar [refre'gar] v rub; scour; scold. **refregadura** sf rubbing, friction.

refrenar [refre'nar] v curb, control. **refrenamiento** sm restraint.

refrescar [refres'kar] v refresh; cool; repeat; revise. **refrescadura** sf refreshing. **refrescante** adj refreshing; cooling. **refresco** sm refreshment; cold drink.

refuerzo [re'fwerθo] sm reinforcement; backing; help.

refugiarse [refu'xjarse] v shelter. **refugio** sm refuge. **refugio de peatones** traffic island. **refugiado, -a** sm, sf refugee.

refulgir [reful'xir] v shine, gleam. **refulgencia** sf brilliance. **refulgente** adj brilliant.

refundir [refun'dir] v recast; adapt; refurbish. **refundición** sf recasting; adaptation.

refunfuñar [refunfu'ɲar] v grumble. grouse. **refunfuñadura** sf also **refunfuño** sm grumbling.

refutar [refu'tar] v refute. **refutable** adj refutable. **refutación** sf refutation.

regadera [rega'ðera] sf watering-can; channel; irrigation ditch. **regadero** sm irrigation ditch. **regadío** sm irrigated land. **regadizo** adj irrigable. **regadura** sf irrigation. **regar** v water; irrigate; sprinkle.

regalar [rega'lar] v give; treat; regale; entertain. **regalador, -a** sm, sf entertainer. **regalo** sm gift; pleasure; treat; entertainment.

regaliz [rega'liθ] sm liquorice.

regañar [rega'ɲar] v scold; quarrel; growl; grumble. **regaño** sm scolding; quarrel;

growl; grumble.

regata [re'gata] *sf* regatta.

regatear [regate'ar] *v* haggle; bargain; retail; begrudge; dodge. **regate** *sm* dodge. **regateo** *sm* haggling. **regatería** *sf* retail. **regatero, -a** *sm, sf* retailer.

regazo [re'gaθo] *sm* lap.

regencia [re'xenθja] *sf* regency.

regenerar [rexene'rar] *v* regenerate. **regeneración** *sf* regeneration. **regenerativo** *adj* regenerative.

regentar [rexen'tar] *v* manage; govern; boss. **regente** *sm* regent; director; professor. **regentear** *v* domineer.

régimen ['reximen] *sm* regime; system; rate; diet; performance.

regimiento [rexi'mjento] *sm* regiment; administration; government; town council. **regimentación** *sf* regimentation. **regimental** *adj* regimental. **regimentar** *v* regiment.

región [re'xjon] *sf* region; territory; area; space. **regional** *adj* regional.

*regir [re'xir] *v* govern; manage; control; obtain; prevail; steer.

registrar [rexis'trar] *v* register; inspect; record; search; show. **registración** *sf* registration. **registrado** *adj* registered; examined. **registrador** *sm* registrar; inspector. **registradora** *sf* cash register. **registro** *sm* register; registry; inspection.

reglar [re'glar] *v* rule; regulate; control. **reglarse** *v* conform; reform. **regla** *sf* rule; method; discipline; menstruation. **a regla** by rule. **regla de cálculo** slide rule. **regladamente** *adv* regularly. **reglado** *adj* regular; regulated; temperate. **reglamentación** *sf* regulation. **reglamentar** *v* regulate. **reglamentario** *adj* statutory. **reglamento** *sm* statute; rules and regulations *pl*.

regocijar [regoθi'xar] *v* rejoice; gladden. **regocijarse** *v* rejoice; exult. **regocijador** *adj* cheering. **regocijo** *sm* joy, gladness.

regresar [regre'sar] *v* return.

regular [regu'lar] *adj* regular; average; ordinary. **por lo regular** as a rule. *v* regulate; control; adjust. **regulación** *adj* regulation; control. **regulación a distancia** remote control. **regulado** *adj* regulated; regular. **regulador** *sm* regulator; throttle. **regulador de volumen** volume control. **regularidad** *sf* regularity; ordinariness.

regularización *sf* regularization. **regularizar** *v* regularize.

rehabilitar [reaβili'tar] *v* rehabilitate. **rehabilitación** *sf* rehabilitation.

*rehacer [rea'θer] *v* remake; recover; renovate; repair. **rehacerse** *v* recuperate. **rehecho** *adj* remade; squat.

rehén [re'en] *sm* hostage.

*rehuir [re'wir] *v* flee; shrink from; avoid; shirk. **rehuida** *sf* flight.

rehusar [reu'sar] *v* refuse; reject.

reimprimir [reimpri'mir] *v* reprint. **reimpresión** *sf* reprint. **reimpreso** *adj* reprinted.

reinar [rei'nar] *v* reign; prevail. **reina** *sf* queen. **reinante** *adj* reigning. **reinado** *sm* reign. **reino** *sm* kingdom, reign. **reino animal** animal kingdom.

reincidir [reinθi'ðir] *v* backslide; relapse into; reiterate. **reincidencia** *sf* backsliding; reiteration. **reincidente** *adj* backsliding; relapsing; reiterating.

reintegrar [reinte'grar] *v* reintegrate; reimburse; recover. **reintegrarse** *v* recoup oneself. **reintegrable** *adj* reimbursable. **reintegración** *sf* reintegration; restoration. **reintegro** *sm* recovery; reimbursement.

*reír [re'ir] *v* laugh. **reírse de** make fun of.

reiterar [reite'rar] *v* reiterate. **reiteración** *sf* reiteration.

reivindicar [reiβindi'kar] *v* reclaim; claim; rehabilitate. **reivindicación** *sf* claim; recovery.

reja ['rexa] *sf* grating; grille; ploughshare; lattice. **rejado** *sm* grating; railing. **rejería** *sf* ornamental ironwork. **rejilla** *sf* small grating; *(tren)* luggage rack.

*rejuvenecer [rexuβene'θer] *v* rejuvenate. **rejuvenecimiento** *sm* rejuvenation.

relación [rela'θjon] *sf* relation; connection; report; narrative; intercourse; relationship. **relaciones** *sf pl* courtship *sing*; engagement *sing*. **relacionado** *adj* related. **relacionar** *v* relate; report; connect. **relacionarse** *v* be related; be connected. **relaciones públicas** *sf pl* PR.

relajar [rela'xar] *v* relax; remit; loosen; debauch. **relajación** *sf* relaxation; loosening; laxity; rupture. **relajadamente** *adv* loosely, dissolutely. **relajado** *adj* lax; ruptured; laid-back. **relajador** *adj* relaxing.

relámpago [re'lampago] *sm* lightning. **relámpago difuso** sheet lightning.

relatar [rela'tar] v report; relate; tell. **relatador, -a** sm, sf narrator.

relatividad [relatiβi'ðað] sf relativity.

relevar [rele'βar] v relieve; absolve; replace; free; emboss. **relevación** sf relief; liberation; remission. **relevante** adj outstanding. **relevo** sm relay race. **relieve** sm relief; prominence. **en relieve** embossed.

relicario [reli'karjo] sm reliquary, shrine; locket.

religión [reli'xjon] sf religion; faith; creed.

religioso [reli'xjoso] sm friar, monk; religious person. adj religious.

reliquia [re'likja] sf relic; memento; ailment. **reliquia de familia** heirloom.

reloj [re'lox] sm clock; watch. **reloj de caja** grandfather clock. **reloj de cuclillo** cuckoo clock. **reloj despertador** alarm clock. **reloj pulsera** wristwatch. **relojería** sf watchmaker's shop. **relojero** sm watchmaker.

*relucir [relu'θir] v shine; excel. **sacar a relucir** show off. **reluciente** adj gleaming.

reluctante [reluk'tante] adj reluctant.

relumbrar [relum'brar] v dazzle; glare. **relumbrante** adj dazzling. **relumbre** sm sparkle; flash. **relumbro** sm glare; tinsel. **relumbroso** adj dazzling.

rellenar [reʎe'nar] v refill; fill; stuff; cram. **rellenable** adj refillable. **relleno** sm filling; stuffing; packing.

remachar [rema'tʃar] v rivet; stress. **remachado** adj riveted; (fam) quiet. **remache** sm rivet.

remanente [rema'nente] sm remains pl.

remanso [re'manso] sm backwater; sluggishness.

remar [re'mar] v row; toil.

rematar [rema'tar] v finish; kill; knock down at auction. **rematado** adj completely ruined. **rematante** sm highest bidder. **remate** sm end; finishing touch; highest bid.

remediar [reme'ðjar] v remedy; help; prevent. **remediable** adj remediable. **remedio** sm remedy. **no hay remedio** it can't be helped.

*remendar [remen'dar] v repair; patch; darn. **remendado** adj spotty; patched. **remendón, -ona** sm, sf mender; repairer. **remiendo** sm repair; patch. **echar un remiendo a** put a patch on.

remero [re'mero] sm oarsman.

remesa [re'mesa] sf remittance; consignment; shipment. **remesar** v remit; ship.

remilgado [remil'gaðo] adj mincing; prim; squeamish. **remilgarse** v simper. **remilgo** sm smirk; primness.

reminiscencia [remini'sθenθja] sf reminiscence.

remirado [remi'raðo] adj considerate; cautious; discreet. **remirar** v review. **remirarse** v take great pains; enjoy looking over.

remisión [remi'sjon] sf remission; pardon; reference. **remisible** adj pardonable. **remiso** adj remiss.

remitir [remi'tir] v send; pardon; adjourn; abate. **remitirse a** quote from. **remitido** sm dispatch.

remo ['remo] sm oar; paddle; rowing. **remos** sm pl limbs pl.

remojar [remo'xar] v soak; steep. **remojo** sm soaking; steeping.

remolacha [remo'latʃa] sf beetroot.

remolcar [remol'kar] v tow; haul. **remolcador** sm tug.

remolino [remo'lino] sm whirlwind; whirlpool; (fig) throng. **remolinar** v eddy.

remontar [remon'tar] v remount; mend; go back in time; raise; frighten. **remonte** sm repair; remounting; rising.

remordimiento [remorði'mjento] sm remorse.

remoto [re'moto] adj remote; improbable.

*remover [remo'βer] v remove; move; stir; discharge. **removimiento** sm removal.

remunerar [remune'rar] v remunerate. **remuneración** sf remuneration. **remunerativo** adj remunerative.

*renacer [rena'θer] v be reborn; recover. **renacimiento** sm rebirth; renaissance.

renacuajo [rena'kwaxo] sm tadpole.

rencilla [ren'θiʎa] sf squabble; feud. **rencilloso** adj quarrelsome.

rencor [ren'kor] sm rancour. **rencoroso** adj rancorous.

*rendir [ren'dir] v conquer; yield; surrender. **rendirse** v wear oneself out. **rendición** sf surrender; (com) profit. **rendido** adj submissive. **rendimiento** sm humility; weariness; output.

*renegar [rene'gar] v disown; detest; curse. **renegado, -a** sm, sf renegade. **renegador,**

-a *sm, sf* blasphemer.

renglón [ren'glon] *sm* written or printed line. **leer entre renglones** read between the lines.

reno ['reno] *sm* reindeer.

renombre [re'nombre] *sm* renown; surname. **renombrado** *adj* renowned.

*renovar [reno'βar] *v* renovate; renew. **renovable** *adj* renewable. **renovación** *sf* renovation; renewal. **renuevo** *sm* renewal; sprout.

rentar [ren'tar] *v* yield an income or profit. **renta** *sf* income; profit. **rentero, -a** *sm. sf* tenant farmer. **rentista** *s(m + f)* stockholder. **rentístico** *adj* financial.

renunciar [renun'θjar] *v* renounce; resign. **renuncia** *sf* renunciation; resignation.

*reñir [re'ɲir] *v* scold; quarrel. **reñido** *adj* on bad terms. **reñidor** *adj* quarrelsome.

reo ['reo], **-a** *sm, sf* defendant. *adj* guilty.

reojo [re'oxo] *sm* **mirar de reojo** look askance.

reorganizar [reorgani'θar] *v* reorganize. **reorganización** *sf* reorganization.

reparar [repa'rar] *v* repair; restore; correct; make amends for; observe; parry. **reparable** *adj* noteworthy. **reparador, -a** *sm, sf* repairer; faultfinder. **reparo** *sm* repair; remedy; observation; protection.

repartir [repar'tir] *v* share; distribute. **repartición** *sf* distribution. **repartidor, -a** *sm, sf* distributor. **reparto** *sm* distribution; (*teatro*) cast.

repasar [repa'sar] *v* revise; review; retrace. **repaso** *sm* review; (*fam*) reprimand.

repatriar [repa'trjar] *v* repatriate. **repatriación** *sf* repatriation. **repatriado, -a** *sm, sf* repatriate.

repeler [repe'ler] *v* repel. **repelente** *adj* repellent.

repente [re'pente] *sm* sudden impulse. **de repente** suddenly.

repercutir [reperku'tir] *v* re-echo; rebound. **repercusión** *sf* repercussion; reverberation. **repertorio** [reper'torjo] *sm* repertory; repertoire.

*repetir [repe'tir] *v* repeat; recite. **repetición** *sf* repetition; recital.

repisa [re'pisa] *sf* shelf; ledge; bracket. **repisa de chimenea** mantelpiece. **repisa de ventana** window sill.

*replegar [reple'gar] *v* refold; (*mil*) retreat.

replegable *adj* folding. **repliegue** *sm* fold, crease; retreat.

repleto [re'pleto] *adj* replete; plump.

réplica ['replika] *sf* answer; replica. **replicar** *v* argue; answer back. **replicato** *sm* argument; answer.

repoblación [repoβla'θjon] *sf* repopulation; restocking; reforestation. **repoblar** *v* repopulate; restock; reforest.

repollo [re'poλo] *sm* cabbage.

*reponer [re'poɲer] *v* replace; restore. **reponerse** *v* recover.

reportar [repor'tar] *v* restrain; obtain; bring. **reportarse** *v* contain oneself. **reportamiento** *sm* restraint.

reposar [repo'sar] *v* rest; lie down; settle; lie buried. **reposo** *sm* repose.

repostería [reposte'ria] *sf* pastry shop; pantry. **repostero, -a** *sm, sf* pastrycook; confectioner.

reprender [repren'der] *v* reprimand. **reprensible** *adj* reprehensible. **reprensor** *adj* reproachful.

represalia [repre'salja] *sf* reprisal.

representar [represen'tar] *v* represent; signify; describe; express; perform; appear to have. **representarse** *v* imagine. **representable** *adj* representable; performable. **representación** *sf* representation; performance. **representante** *s(m + f)* representative; actor, actress. **representativo** *adj* representative.

represión [repre'sjon] *sm* repression; control. **represivo** *adj* repressive.

reprimenda [repri'menda] *sf* reprimand.

reprimir [repri'mir] *v* repress; suppress. **reprimible** *adj* repressible.

*reprobar [repro'βar] *v* reprove; condemn; (*examen*) fail. **reprobable** *adj* reprehensible. **reprobación** *sf* reproof; failure. **reprobado, -a** *sm, sf* also **réprobo, -a** *sm, sf* reprobate.

reprochar [repro'tʃar] *v* reproach; challenge. **reprochable** *adj* reproachable; reproachful. **reprochador, -a** *sm, sf* reproacher.

*reproducir [reproðu'θir] *v* reproduce. **reproducible** *adj* reproducible. **reproducción** *sf* reproduction. **reproductor, -a** *sm, sf* breeder.

reptil [rep'til] *sm* reptile.

república [re'puβlika] *sf* republic. **republi-**

canismo *sm* republicanism. **republicano, -a** *sm*, *sf* republican.

repudiar [repu'ðjar] *v* repudiate. **repudiación** *sf* repudiation.

repuesto [re'pwesto] *sm* supply; store; standby; sideboard. **de repuesto** spare, extra. *adj* replaced; secluded; recovered.

repugnar [repug'nar] *v* contradict; object to; be repugnant. **repugnarse** *v* conflict. **repugnancia** *sf* repugnance; opposition. **repugnante** *adj* repugnant.

repulsivo [repul'siβo] *adj* repulsive. **repulsa** *sf* refusal; rebuke. **repulsar** *v* reject; refuse. **repulsión** *sf* rejection; refusal.

reputar [repu'tar] *v* repute; consider; esteem. **reputación** *sf* reputation. **reputado** *adj* reputed.

*requebrar [reke'βrar] *v* woo; flatter; flirt with. **requebrador, -a** *sm*, *sf* flirt.

requemar [reke'mar] *v* scorch; inflame; overcook. **requemarse** *v* smoulder; become tanned. **requemado** *adj* burnt; tanned. **requemamiento** *sm* bite; sting. **requemante** *adj* burning; stinging.

*requerir [reke'rir] *v* request; require; urge; notify; summon; examine. **requeriente** *adj* requiring. **requerimiento** *sm* requisition; summons; notification; request.

requesón [reke'son] *sm* curd; cottage cheese.

requisar [reki'sar] *v* requisition. **requisa** *sf* tour of inspection; requisition. **requisición** *sf* requisition. **requisito** *adj* requisite.

res [res] *sf* head of cattle; animal.

resabio [re'saβjo] *sm* bad habit; unpleasant aftertaste. **resabiado** *adj* crafty; wicked; spoiled. **resabiar** *v* pervert; become vicious. **resabiarse** *v* become annoyed.

resaca [re'saka] *sf* undertow; surf; surge.

resaltar [resal'tar] *v* rebound, stand out. **resalte** *sm* projection. **resalto** *sm* rebound.

resarcir [resar'θir] *v* compensate. **resarcirse de** make up for. **resarcimiento** *sm* compensation.

resbalar [resβa'lar] *v* slide; skid; slip. **resbaladero** *also* **resbaladizo**, **resbalante** *adj* slippery. **resbalador** *adj* sliding. **resbaladura** *sf* skid mark. **resbalón** *sm* slide; slip; skid.

rescatar [reska'tar] *v* rescue; recover; save; ransom; make up for. **rescate** *sm* redemption; rescue; ransom.

rescindir [resθin'dir] *v* rescind. **rescisión** *sf* annulment.

rescoldo [res'kolðo] *sm* misgiving; embers *pl*.

resecar [rese'kar] *v* dry thoroughly. **reseco** *adj* desiccated.

*resentirse [resen'tirse] *v* feel the effects; be weakened.

reseñar [rese'nar] *v* review; outline. **reseña** *sf* review; outline.

reservar [reser'βar] *v* reserve; preserve; conceal. **reserva** *sf* reserve; reservation. **a reserva de** with the intention of. **reserva de asiento** reservation. **sin reserva** frankly. **reservado** *adj* reserved; discreet.

resfriar [resfri'ar] *v* cool; turn cold. **resfriarse** *v* catch cold. **resfriado** *m* (*med*) cold.

resguardar [resgwar'ðar] *v* defend; preserve. **resguardarse** *v* protect oneself. **resguardo** *sm* defence; protection; guarantee. **reguardo de correos** postal receipt.

residencia [resi'ðenθja] *sf* residence; boarding house. **residencial** *adj* residential. **residente** *s*(*m* + *f*) resident. **residir** *v* reside.

residuo [re'siðwo] *sm* residue. **residuos** *sm pl* refuse *sing*. **residual** *adj* residual.

resignar [resig'nar] *v* resign; renounce. **resignarse** *v* resign oneself. **resigna** *sf* renunciation. **resignación** *sf* resignation.

resina [re'sina] *sf* resin.

resistir [resis'tir] *v* resist; refuse. **resistencia** *sf* resistance; stamina. **resistente** *adj* resistant.

resolución [resolu'θjon] *sf* resolution; decision. **resoluto** *adj* resolute; skilled.

*resolver [resol'βer] *v* resolve; decide; analyse. **resolverse** *v* make up one's mind.

*resollar [reso'ʎar] *v* pant; puff; snort.

*resonar [reso'nar] *v* resound. **resonancia** *sf* resonance. **resonante** *adj* resonant.

resoplar [reso'plar] *v* snort; puff. **resoplido** *sm* snort; puff.

resorte [re'sorte] *sm* resort; means; motive; (*mec*) spring; elasticity.

respaldar [respal'ðar] *v* back; support; endorse. **respaldarse** *v* lean. **respaldo** *sm* chair back; support.

respecto [re'spekto] *sm* respect. **con respecto a** with regard to.

respetar [respe'tar] *v* respect. **respetabilidad** *sf* respectability. **respetable** *adj* respectable. **respetador** *adj* respectful. **respeto** *sm* respect. **respetuoso** *adj* respectful.

respirar [respi'rar] v breathe. **respiración** sf respiration, breath. **respiro** sm breathing. **respiradero** sm ventilator.

*resplandecer [resplanðe'θer] v glitter. **resplandeciente** adj glittering. **resplandor** sm glitter.

responder [respon'der] v respond. **responder por** vouch for. **respondón** adj saucy. **responsivo** adj responsive. **respuesta** sf reply; refutation.

responsable [respon'saβle] adj responsible. **responsabilidad** sf responsibility.

*resquebrajar [reskeβra'xar] v also **resquebrar** split; crack. **resquebra(ja)dura** sf crack.

resquemar [reske'mar] v sting the tongue. sm sting in the mouth; remorse; resentment.

resquicio [res'kiθjo] sm crack; chink; (fig) slight chance.

*restablecer [restaβle'θer] v re-establish. **restablecerse** v recover from illness. **restablecimiento** sm re-establishment; recovery.

restallar [resta'λar] v crack; crackle.

restante [re'stante] adj remaining. sm remainder.

restar [res'tar] v subtract; remain.

restaurante [restau'rante] sm restaurant. **restauración** sf restoration. **restaurar** v restore; recover; repair.

*restituir [restitu'ir] v restore; pay back. **restituirse** v return. **restitución** sf restitution.

resto ['resto] sm rest, remainder.

*restregar [restre'gar] v rub; scrub; wipe. **restregón** sm rubbing; scrubbing; wiping.

restricción [restrik'θjon] sf restriction. **restrictivo** adj restrictive.

restringir [restrin'xir] v restrict.

resucitar [resuθi'tar] v resuscitate. **resucitación** sf resuscitation.

resuello [re'sweλo] sm breathing.

resuelto [re'swelto] adj resolute; resolved; firm.

resultar [resul'tar] v result; happen; turn out; go. **resulta** sf result, effect. **resultado** sm result; (computadora) output. **resultante** adj resultant.

resumir [resu'mir] v summarize; abbreviate. **resumen** sm summary. **en resumen** in brief. **resumido** adj summarized.

retablo [re'taβlo] sm altarpiece.

retaguardia [reta'gwarðja] sf rearguard.

retal [re'tal] sm remnant.

retama [re'tama] sf (bot) broom.

retardar [retar'ðar] v retard, delay; (reloj) put back. **retardación** sf delay. **retardo** sm delay.

retén [re'ten] sm spare, reserve.

*retener [rete'ner] v retain; deduct; detain; arrest. **retención** sf retention; deduction; detention. **retentiva** sf memory. **retentivo** adj retentive.

retina [re'tina] sf retina.

retintín [retin'tin] sm jingle.

retirar [reti'rar] v withdraw. **retirarse** v go into seclusion. **retirada** sf retreat. **retirado** adj retired; remote. **retiro** sm retirement; retreat.

reto ['reto] sm challenge.

retocar [reto'kar] v retouch. **retoque** sm retouching.

*retorcer [retor'θer] v twist; distort. **retorcerse** v writhe. **retorcimiento** sm contortion.

retórica [re'torika] sf rhetoric. **retórico** adj rhetorical.

retornar [retor'nar] v return. **retorno** sm return; remuneration.

retractar [retrak'tar] v retract. **retracción** sf retraction. **retractable** adj also **retráctil** retractable.

*retraer [retra'er] v dissuade; bring again. **retraerse** v shelter; retreat. **retraído** adj retiring; unsociable. **retraimiento** sm retirement; retreat.

retrasar [retra'sar] v delay; put back; (reloj) be slow. **retrasarse** v be late. **retraso** sm delay; lateness.

retratar [retra'tar] v portray. **retratista** s(m + f) portrait painter. **retrato** sm portrait.

retrete [re'trete] sm lavatory.

*retribuir [retriβu'ir] v recompense; repay. **retribución** sf retribution; recompense.

retroceder [retroθe'ðer] v recede; fall back. **retroceso** sm retreat; (com) slump. **retrogresión** sf retrogression.

retruécano [retru'ekano] sm pun.

retumbar [retum'bar] v resound. **retumbante** adj resounding. **retumbo** sm rumble.

reuma ['reuma] sm rheumatism. **reumáti-**

co *adj* rheumatic. **reumatismo** *sm* rheumatism.

reunir [reu'nir] *v* reunite; unite; gather; reconcile. **reunión** *sf* meeting.

revalidar [reβali'ðar] *v* ratify; confirm. **revalidación** *sf* ratification.

revancha [re'βantʃa] *sf* revenge.

revelar [reβe'lar] *v* reveal; (*foto*) develop. **revelación** *sf* revelation. **revelador** *adj* revealing.

revendedor [reβende'ðor], **-a** *sm*, *sf* retailer. **revender** *v* retail; tout (tickets).

*reventar [reβen'tar] *v* burst. **reventarse** *v* blow up. **reventón** *sm* burst; blowout.

reverberar [reβerβe'rar] *v* reverberate. **reverberación** *sf* reverberation. **reverbero** *sm* reverberation; reflector.

*reverdecer [reβerðe'θer] *v* grow green again; revive.

reverenciar [reβeren'θjar] *v* reverence, venerate. **reverencia** *sf* reverence. **reverendo** *adj* reverend. **reverente** *adj* reverent.

reversión [reβer'sjon] *sf* reversion. **reversible** *adj* revertible. **reverso** *adj* reverse.

revés [re'βes] *sm* reverse; back; setback. **al revés** upside down; inside out; back to front. **revesado** *adj* complicated; unruly.

revisar [reβi'sar] *v* revise; review. **revisión** *sf* revision; review; (*com*) audit. **revista** *sf* review; journal.

revivir [reβi'βir] *v* revive. **revivificar** *v* revive.

revocar [reβo'kar] *v* revoke; dissuade.

*revolcar [reβol'kar] *v* knock down; defeat; (*fam*) fail an exam. **revolcarse** *v* wallow.

revoltillo [reβol'tiʎo] *sm also* **revoltijo** jumble; mess.

revoltoso [reβol'toso] *adj* mischievous; unruly.

revolución [reβolu'θjon] *sf* revolution. **revolucionario, -a** *sm*, *sf* revolutionary.

*revolver [reβol'βer] *v* revolve; stir; disturb. **revolverse** *v* turn round.

revólver [re'βolβer] *sm* revolver.

revoque [re'βoke] *sm* plaster; stucco; whitewash.

revuelta [re'βwelta] *sf* revolt; turn; bend; change. **revuelto** *adj* difficult; unruly; upside down; disturbed.

rey [rej] *sm* king.

reyerta [re'jerta] *sf* quarrel; brawl.

rezagar [reθa'gar] *v* defer; postpone; leave behind. **rezagarse** *v* straggle. **rezagado** *sm* (*mil*) straggler. **rezago** *sm* remainder.

rezar [re'θar] *v* pray, pray for. **rezo** *sm* prayer; prayers *pl*.

rezumarse [reθu'marse] *v* ooze, drip; leak out.

riachuelo [rja'tʃwelo] *sm* brook. **ría** *sf* estuary.

ribera [ri'βera] *sf* river bank; shore.

ribete [ri'βete] *sm* (*de ropa*) border, edging; trimmings *pl*. **ribetear** *v* border; edge.

ricino [ri'θino] *sm* castor-oil plant. **aceite de ricino** *sm* castor oil.

rico ['riko], **-a** *sm*, *sf* rich person. *adj* rich; handsome; tasty.

ridiculizar [riðikuli'θar] *v* ridicule. **ridículo** *adj* ridiculous.

riego ['rjego] *sm* irrigation.

riel [rjel] *sm* ingot; (*ferro*) rail.

rienda ['rjenda] *sf* rein. **a rienda suelta** at full speed. **llevar las riendas** be in control.

riesgo ['rjesgo] *sm* risk.

rifar [ri'far] *v* raffle. **rifa** *sf* raffle.

rifle ['rifle] *sm* rifle.

rígido ['rixiðo] *adj* rigid. **rigidez** *sf* rigidity.

rigor [ri'gor] *sm* severity; rigour. **rigorismo** *sm* austerity. **riguroso** *adj* rigorous.

rimar [ri'mar] *v* rhyme. **rima** *sf* rhyme.

rimbombante [rimbom'bante] *adj* grandiloquent; bombastic. **rimbombancia** *sf* grandiloquence.

rincón [rin'kon] *sm* corner. **rinconada** *sf* corner table.

rinoceronte [rinoθe'ronte] *sm* rhinoceros.

riña ['riɲa] *sf* brawl; fight; quarrel.

riñón [ri'ɲon] *sm* kidney.

río ['rio] *sm* river. **río arriba** upstream.

ripio ['ripjo] *sm* rubble; refuse; residue. **no perder ripio** not to miss a trick.

riqueza [ri'keθa] *sf* wealth.

risa ['risa] *sf* laughter; laugh. **risueño** *adj* smiling; happy.

ristre ['ristre] *sm* **en ristre** at the ready.

ritmo ['ritmo] *sm* rhythm. **rítmico** *adj* rhythmic.

rito ['rito] *sm* rite. **ritual** *sm* ritual. **ritualismo** *sm* ritualism. **ritualista** *adj* ritualistic.

rival [ri'βal] *s(m + f)*, *adj* rival. **rivalidad** *sf* rivalry. **rivalizar** v vie. **rivalizar con** rival.

rizar [ri'θar] v (*pelo*) curl. **rizado** sm curling. **rizador** sm curling-iron. **rizo** adj curly.

robar [ro'βar] v rob, steal; kidnap. **robo** sm robbery.

roble ['roβle] sm oak.

***robustecer** [roβuste'θer] v strengthen. **robustecerse** v gain strength. **robustecimiento** sm strengthening. **robustez** sf robustness. **robusto** adj robust.

robo ['roβo] sm break-in. **robo de coche** sm joyriding.

robot de cocina sm food processor.

roca ['roka] sf rock.

roce ['roθe] sm friction; rubbing; chafing.

rociar [ro'θjar] v sprinkle; spray; strew; moisten. **rociada** sf sprinkling; spraying; dew. **rociadera** sf watering can. **rociador** sm sprinkler.

rocín [ro'θin] sm nag; hack.

rodapié [roða'pje] sm skirting-board.

***rodar** [ro'ðar] v roll; revolve; rotate. **rodado** adj (*auto*) run-in. **tránsito rodado** sm road traffic. **rodaja** sf small wheel. **rodaje** sm wheels pl.

rodear [roðe'ar] v encircle; enclose; encompass; go round. **rodearse** v surround oneself. **rodeo** sm detour; evasion; rodeo.

rodezno [ro'ðeθno] sm waterwheel; cogwheel.

rodilla [ro'ðiλa] sf knee. **de rodillas** kneeling.

rodillo [ro'ðiλo] sm rolling pin; roller; mangle.

***roer** [ro'er] v gnaw; nibble. **roerse** v bite. **roedor** adj gnawing.

***rogar** [ro'gar] v beg; pray. **rogación** sf petition. **rogativa** sf supplication.

rojo ['roxo] adj red. sm red; rouge. **rojear** v redden. **rojizo** adj reddish.

rollizo [ro'λiθo] adj chubby; plump.

rollo ['roλo] sm roll; cylinder; (*foto*) film.

romance [ro'manθe] sm, adj romance. sm ballad. **romancero** sm ballad collection; ballad singer. **romántico** adj romantic.

romería [rome'ria] sf pilgrimage. **romero, -a** sm, sf pilgrim; sm rosemary.

romo ['romo] adj snub-nosed; blunt; dull.

rompecabezas [rompeka'βeθas] sm invar puzzle; jigsaw; riddle.

rompeolas [rompe'olas] sm invar breakwater.

romper [rom'per] v break; fracture; separate (couple); breakout. **rompimiento** sm break; breach.

romper [rom'per] v split up (a couple).

ron [ron] sm rum.

roncar [ron'kar] v snore; roar; boast. **ronca** sf bellow. **ronquido** sm snore.

ronco ['ronko] adj hoarse. **ronquedad** sf hoarseness.

rondar [ron'dar] v patrol; go round; pursue; haunt; serenade. **rondador** sm patrolman. **ronda** sf patrol; round of drinks.

ronronear [ronrone'ar] v purr.

ronzal [ron'θal] sm halter.

roña ['rona] sf filth; mange; rust; (*fam*) meanness. adj stingy. **roñoso** adj mangy; filthy; stingy.

ropa ['ropa] sf clothes pl, clothing. **ropa de cama** bed linen. **ropa interior** underclothes. **ropero** sm wardrobe.

roque ['roke] sm (*ajedrez*) rook.

rosa ['rosa] sf rose. **novela rosa** sf romantic novel. **rosado** adj rose-coloured. **rosal** sm rosebush.

rosario [ro"sarjo] sm rosary.

rosca ['roska] sf thread of a screw; doughnut; bread roll.

rostro ['rostro] sm countenance, face. **hacer rostro a** face.

rotación [rota'θjon] sf rotation. **rotativo** adj rotary.

roto ['roto] adj broken; torn. sm hole.

rotular [rotu'lar] v label. **rótulo** sf label; placard.

rotundo [ro'tundo] adj round; (*fig*) emphatic. **rotundidad** sf roundness.

roturar [rotu'rar] v (*tierra*) break up. **rotura** sf breaking.

rozar [ro'θar] v graze; scrape. **rozarse** v be tongue-tied; trip over one's feet. **rozamiento** sm rubbing, friction.

rubí [ru'βi] sm, pl **rubíes** ruby.

rubio ['ruβjo] sm, adj blond. **rubia** sf blonde.

rubor [ru'βor] sm blush. **ruborizarse** v blush. **ruboroso** adj blushing.

rúbrica ['ruβrika] sf rubric; heading; flourish after a signature. **rubricar** v sign with a flourish.

rudeza [ru'ðeθa] *sf* roughness, rudeness. **rudo** *adj* rough; coarse; crude.

rudimento [ruði'mento] *sm* rudiment.

rueca [ru'eka] *sf* distaff.

rueda [ru'eða] *sf* wheel. **rueda de recambio** spare wheel.

ruedo [ru'eðo] *sm* edge; hem; round mat.

ruego [ru'ego] *sm* request; supplication.

rugir [ru'xir] *v* roar; bellow; howl. **rugido** *sm* roar; bellow; howl.

rugoso [ru'goso] *adj* wrinkled.

ruibarbo [rui'βarβo] *sm* rhubarb.

ruido [ru'iðo] *sm* noise; rumour. **meter ruido** make a noise. **ruidoso** *adj* noisy.

ruin [ru'in] *adj* mean; foul; puny. **ruindad** *sf* meanness; villainy.

ruina [ru'ina] *sf* ruin; ruins *pl.* **ruinoso** *adj* ruinous.

ruiseñor [ruise'ɲor] *sm* nightingale.

rumbo ['rumbo] *sm* course; direction; *(fam)* pomp. **hacer rumbo** set a course. **rumboso** *adj* splendid; lavish.

rumiar [ru'mjar] *v* ruminate; chew; grumble. **rumiante** *sm* ruminant.

rumor [ru'mor] *sm* rumour; noise; murmur. **rumorear** *v* rumour. **rumoroso** *adj* murmuring.

ruptura [rup'tura] *sf* rupture; break.

rural [ru'ral] *adj* rural.

Rusia ['rusja] *sf* Russia. **ruso, -a** *sm, sf* Russian.

rústico ['rustiko] *adj* rustic.

ruta ['ruta] *sf* route; road.

rutina [ru'tina] *sf* routine. **rutinario** *adj* routine; unimaginative.

S

sábado ['saβaðo] *sm* Saturday.

sabana [sa'βana] *sf* savannah.

sábana ['saβana] *sf* sheet.

sabanilla [saβa'niʎa] *sf* small cloth, napkin.

sabañón [saβa'ɲon] *sm* chilblain.

*saber [sa'βer] *v* know; know how to; be aware of. **a saber** namely. **sabedor** *adj* well-informed. **sabidillo, -a** *sm, sf (fam)* know-all. **sabido** *adj* known; learned. **sabiduría** *sf* knowledge; wisdom. **sabio** *adj* wise.

sabor [sa'βor] *sm* taste; flavour. **saborear** *v* taste; savour. **saborearse** *v* smack one's lips. **saboroso** *adj* tasty; savoury.

sabotear [saβote'ar] *v* sabotage. **saboteador, -a** *sm, sf* saboteur. **sabotaje** *sm* sabotage.

sabroso [sa'βroso] *adj* delicious; tasty; pleasant; racy.

sabueso [sa'βweso] *sm* bloodhound.

sacabocados [sakaβo'kaðos] *sm invar (tecn)* punch.

sacacorchos [saka'kortʃos] *sm invar* corkscrew.

sacamanchas [saka'mantʃas] *sm invar* stain-remover.

sacar [sa'kar] *v* get out; put out; draw; publish; take out; buy tickets; *(tenis)* serve. **saca** *sf* extraction; exportation.

sacarina [saka'rina] *sf* saccharine.

sacerdote [saker'ðote] *sm* priest. **sacerdocio** *sm* priesthood. **sacerdotal** *adj* priestly. **sacerdotisa** *f* priestess.

saciar [sa'θjar] *v* satiate. **saciedad** *sf* satiety.

saco ['sako] *sm* sack; bag; plunder. **entrar a saco** plunder.

sacramento [sakra'mento] *sm* sacrament. **sacramental** *adj* sacramental.

sacrificar [sakrifi'kar] *v* sacrifice. **sacrificadero** *sm* slaughterhouse. **sacrificio** *sm* sacrifice; slaughter.

sacrilegio [sakri'lexjo] *sm* sacrilege. **sacrílego** *adj* sacrilegious.

sacro ['sakro] *adj* sacred. **sacrosanto** *adj* sacrosanct.

sacudir [saku'ðir] *v* shake, jolt. **sacudirse** *v* shake off; repel. **sacudida** *sf* shake, jolt.

sádico ['saðiko] *adj* sadistic. **sadismo** *sm* sadism. **sadista** *s (m + f)* sadist.

saeta [sa'eta] *sf* arrow; watch *or* clock hand. **saetada** *sf* arrow wound. **saetera** *sf* loophole. **saetero** *sm* bowman.

sagacidad [sagaθi'ðað] *sf* shrewdness. **sagaz** *adj* shrewd, wise.

sagrado [sa'graðo] *adj* sacred, holy. *sm* sanctuary.

sajón [sa'xon], **-ona** *s, adj* Saxon.

sal [sal] *sf* salt; wit; charm. **salero** *sm* salt cellar; wit; charm. **saleroso** *adj (fam)* witty; charming.

sala ['sala] *sf* hall; drawing-room; (*med*) ward; (*teatro*) house. **sala de conferencias** lecture hall. **sala de espera** waiting-room.

salacidad [salaθi'ðað] *sf* lechery.

salar [sa'lar] *v* salt. **salado** *adj* salty; witty.

salario [sa'larjo] *sm* salary, pay.

salchicha [sal'tʃitʃa] *sf* sausage. **salchichón** *sm* salami.

saldar [sal'ðar] *v* settle; liquidate; pay off. **saldo** *sm* payment; balance; bargain sale.

salida [sa'liða] *sf* departure; exit; start; outskirts *pl*; pretext; (*del sol*) rising; outcome; projection; witticism. **calle sin salida** *sf* cul-de-sac. **dar salida a** sell. **tener buenas salidas** be full of witty remarks. **saliente** *adj* projecting.

salina [sa'lina] *sm* salt mine. **salino** *adj* saline.

*salir [sa'lir] *v* leave; emerge; (*astron*) rise; happen. **salir para** leave for. **salir por alguien** vouch for someone. **salirse** *v* leak; overflow; escape.

saliva [sa'liβa] *sf* saliva. **salivar** *v* salivate.

salmo ['salmo] *sm* psalm. **salmista** *s(m + f)* psalmist. **salmodia** *sf* psalmody.

salmón [sal'mon] *sm* salmon.

salmuera [sal'mwera] *sf* brine.

salón [sa'lon] *sm* large hall; drawingroom.

salpicar [salpi'kar] *v* splash; sprinkle. **salpicadura** *sf* splash; spatter.

salpimentar [salpimen'tar] *v* season with salt and pepper.

salpullido [salpu'ʎiðo] *sm* (*med*) rash.

salsa ['salsa] *sf* sauce, gravy.

saltamontes [salta'montes] *sm invar* grasshopper.

saltar [sal'tar] *v* jump; skip; break; explode. **salto** *sm* jump; hop; chasm. **salto de agua** waterfall. **salto de altura** high jump. **salto con garrocha** pole vault. **salto mortal** somersault.

saltear [salte'ar] *v* rob; assault. **salteador** *sm* highwayman. **salteamiento** *sm* highway robbery.

salubre [sa'luβre] *adj* salubrious, healthy. **salubridad** *sf* wholesomeness. **salud** *sf* health. **¡salud!** cheers! **saludable** *adj* salutary. **saludador** *sm* quack doctor.

salvado [sal'βaðo] *sm* bran.

salvaguardar [salβagwar'ðar] *v* safeguard. **salvaguardia** *sf* safeguard.

saludar [salu'ðar] *v* salute; greet. **le saluda**

atentamente yours faithfully. **saludo** *sm* greeting; salute. **saludos** *sm pl* regards *pl*. best wishes *pl*. **salutación** *sf* greeting.

salvaje [sal'βaxe] *adj* wild; uncultivated; savage. **salvajada** *sf* barbarity. **salvajería** *sf* savagery.

salvamanteles [salβaman'teles] *sm invar* table mat.

salvar [sal'βar] *v* save, rescue; except; cross; overcome. **salvarse** *v* escape. **salvamento** *sm* salvation; salvage. **salvador** *adj* healing; saving.

salvavidas [salβa'βiðas] *sm invar* lifebelt; life buoy; lifeboat.

salvedad [salβe'ðað] *sf* proviso; reservation; distinction.

salvia ['salβja] *sf* sage.

salvo ['salβo] *adv* except, saving. *adj* safe. **a salvo** safe. **poner a salvo** rescue. **salvo qué** unless.

salvoconducto [salβokon'dukto] *sm* safeconduct.

san [san] *adj* saint; holy. *V* **santo**.

sanar [sa'nar] *v* heal; cure; get better. **sanable** *adj* curable. **sanatorio** *sm* sanatorium.

sanción [san'θjon] *sf* sanction. **sancionar** *v* sanction.

sandalia [san'dalja] *sf* sandal.

sandía [san'dia] *sf* watermelon.

sanear [sane'ar] *v* guarantee; drain; repair. **saneado** *adj* unencumbered; nett. **saneamiento** *sm* surety; drainage.

sangrar [san'grar] *v* bleed; drain off. **sangradera** *sf* lancet. **sangre** *sf* blood. **a sangre fría** in cold blood. **sangriento** *adj* bloody. **sanguinario** *adj* bloodthirsty. **sanguinolento** *adj* bloody.

sangría [san'gria] *sf* bleeding; drink made of fruit and red wine.

sanguijuela [sangi'xwela] *sf* leech.

sanidad [sani'ðað] *sf* health; sanitation. **sanitario** *adj* sanitary. **sano** *adj* healthy; wholesome; sound; good.

santiamén [santja'men] *sm* instant. **en un santiamén** in a jiffy.

santificar [santifi'kar] *v* sanctify, consecrate. **santificación** *sf* sanctification.

santiguar [santi'gwar] *v* bless. **santiguarse** *v* cross oneself.

santo ['santo], **-a** *sm*, *sf* saint. *adj* sacred; saintly; holy. **santo y bueno** all well and good.

santuario [san'twarjo] *sm* sanctuary, shrine.

saña ['saɲa] *sf* rage; cruelty. **sañoso** *adj* furious; cruel.

sapo ['sapo] *sm* toad.

saquear [sake'ar] *v* plunder. **saqueo** *sm* plunder. **saqueador, -a** *sm, sf* looter.

sarampión [saram'pjon] *sm* measles.

sarcasmo [sar'kasmo] *sm* sarcasm. **sarcástico** *adj* sarcastic.

sarcófago [sar'kofaɣo] *sm* sarcophagus.

sardina [sar'ðina] *sf* sardine.

sardónico [sar'ðoniko] *adj* sardonic.

sargento [sar'xento] *sm* sergeant.

sarna ['sarna] *sf* scabies; itch. **sarnoso** *adj* mangy.

sartén [sar'ten] *sf* frying pan.

sastre ['sastre] *sm* tailor. **sastrería** *sf* tailoring; tailor's shop.

satélite [sa'telite] *sm* satellite.

sátira ['satira] *sf* satire. **satírico** *adj* satirical. **satirizar** *v* satirize.

***satisfacer** [satisfa'θer] *v* satisfy; please. **satisfacerse** *v* satisfy oneself; take revenge. **satisfacción** *sf* satisfaction. **satisfactorio** *adj* satisfactory. **satisfecho** *adj* satisfied.

saturar [satu'rar] *v* saturate. **saturación** *sf* saturation.

sauce ['sauθe] *sm* willow.

saúco [sa'uko] *sm* (*bot*) elder.

savia ['saβja] *sf* sap.

saxófono [sak'sofono] *sm* saxophone.

saya ['saja] *sf* skirt, petticoat. **sayo** *sm* smock.

sazonar [saθo'nar] *v* (*culin*) season; ripen. **sazón** *sf* season; (*culin*) flavour; mellowness. **a la sazón** at the time. **sazonado** *adj* tasty; well seasoned.

se [se] *pron* himself; herself; yourself; oneself; itself; themselves; yourselves; one another; each other. **se dice** they say. **se habla inglés** English is spoken.

sebo ['seβo] *sm* grease. **seboso** *adj* greasy.

secar [se'kar] *v* dry. **secarse** *v* dry oneself; dry up. **seca** *sf* drought; sandbank. **secador** *sm* hair-dryer. **secadora** *sf* clothes-dryer. **secano** *sm* dry land. **secante** *sm* blotting paper. **seco** *adj* dry; lean; hoarse. **en seco** high and dry.

sección [sek'θjon] *sf* section.

secretario [sekre'tarjo], **-a** *sm, sf* secretary.

secretaría *sf* secretariat.

secreto [se'kreto] *adj* secret; private; hidden. *sm* secrecy, secret knowledge. **secreto a voces** open secret. **secreteo** *sm* private conversation.

secta ['sekta] *sf* sect. **sectario, -a** *sm, sf* sectarian.

secuaz [se'kwaθ] *sm* follower, supporter.

secuestrar [sekwes'trar] *v* kidnap; hijack. **secuestrador, -a** *sm, sf* kidnapper; hijacker. **secuestro** *sm* kidnap; hijack.

secular [seku'lar] *adj* secular. **secularizar** *v* secularize.

secundar [sekun'dar] *v* second, support.

sed [seð] *sf* thirst. **tener sed** be thirsty. **sediento** *adj* thirsty.

seda ['seða] *sf* silk. **sedoso** *adj* silky.

sedante [se'ðante] *sm* sedative. *adj* calming.

sede ['seðe] *sf* (*rel*) see; (*de gobierno*) seat. **sede central** *sf* head office. **Santa Sede** Holy See.

sedentario [seðen'tarjo] *adj* sedentary.

sedería [seðe'ria] *sf* silk trade; drapery.

sedición [seði'θjon] *sf* sedition. **sedicioso** *adj* seditious.

sedimento [seði'mento] *sm* sediment. **sedimentar** *v* deposit.

***seducir** [seðu'θir] *v* seduce; attract. **seducción** *sf* seduction. **seductivo** *adj* seductive. **seductor, -a** *sm, sf* seducer.

***segar** [se'ɣar] *v* reap; mow. **segadora** *sf* mower; reaper.

seglar [se'ɣlar] *sm* layman. *adj* secular.

segmento [seɣ'mento] *sm* segment.

segregar [seɣre'ɣar] *v* segregate. **segregación** *sf* segregation.

***seguir** [se'ɣir] *v* follow; pursue; continue. **seguida** *sf* continuation. **en seguida** at once. **seguido** *adj* successive; straight. **cuatro días seguidos** four days running. **seguimiento** *sm* pursuit; following.

según [se'ɣun] *prep* according to. *adv* it all depends. *conj* as.

segundo [se'ɣundo] *adj*, *sm* second.

segundón [seɣun'don] *sm* second son.

seguro [se'ɣuro] *adj* sure; safe. *sm* safety catch; insurance. **seguridad** *sf* safety; certainty.

seis ['seis] *sm*, *adj* six.

selección [selek'θjon] *sf* selection. **selec-**

cionar *v* select. **selectivo** *adj* selective. **selecto** *adj* select.

selva ['selβa] *sf* forest; jungle. **selva tropical** *sf* rainforest. **selvoso** *adj* wooded, forested.

sello ['seλo] *sm* stamp; seal. **selladura** *sf* sealing. **sellar** *v* stamp; seal.

semáforo [se'maforo] *sm* semaphore; traffic lights *pl*.

semana [se'mana] *sf* week. **semanal** *adj* weekly. **semanario** *sm* weekly publication.

semblante [sem'blante] *sm* face; appearance.

*sembrar [sem'brar] *v* sow; scatter, **sembradera** *sf* seed-drill. **sembrador, -a** *sm, sf* sower.

semejar [seme'xar] *v* resemble. **semejante** *adj* similar. **semejanza** *sf* similarity.

semen ['semen] *sm* semen. **semental** *sm* sire. **sementera** *sf* sowing; seed-time.

semestre [se'mestre] *sm* semester. **semestral** *adj* half-yearly.

semicírculo [semi'θirkulo] *sm* semicircle. **semicircular** *adj* semicircular.

semilla [se'miλa] *sf* seed. **semillero** *sm* seedbed.

seminario [semi'narjo] *sm* seminary; seminar; seedbed.

senado [se'naðo] *sm* senate. **senador** *sm* senator.

sencillo [sen'θiλo] *adj* simple; easy. **sencillez** *sf* simplicity.

senda ['senda] *sf* path. **sendero** *sm* path.

sendos ['sendos] *adj pl* each.

senectud [senek'tuð] *sf* old age.

senil [se'nil] *adj* senile. **senilidad** *sf* senility.

seno ['seno] *sm* bosom, breast; haven; refuge.

sensación [sensa'θjon] *sf* sensation. **sensacional** *adj* sensational.

sensatez [sensa'teθ] *sf* good sense. **sensato** *adj* sensible.

sensibilidad [sensiβili'ðað] *sf* sensibility; sensitivity. **sensible** *adj* sensitive; sensible; considerable.

sensiblería [sensiβle'ria] *sf* sentimentality. **sensiblero** *adj* sentimental.

sensitivo [sensi'tiβo] *adj* relating to the senses; sensitive.

sensual [sen'swal] *adj* sensual. **sensualidad** *sf* sensuality.

*sentar [sen'tar] *v* seat; place; locate; establish; press; suit; fit. **sentarse** *v* sit down; settle. **sentada** *sf* sit-in. **sentado** *adj* seated; established.

sentencia [sen'tenθja] *sf* (*jur*) sentence. **sentenciar** *v* (*jur*) sentence. **sentencioso** *adj* sententious.

sentido [sen'tiðo] *sm* sense; meaning; direction; feeling. **sin sentido** meaningless. **tener sentido** make sense. *adj* heartfelt; moving; sincere.

sentimiento [senti'mjento] *sm* feeling; emotion; sentiment; grief. **sentimental** *adj* sentimental.

*sentir [sen'tir] *v* feel; hear; regret. **lo siento mucho** I am very sorry. **sentirse** *v* feel; suffer from. **sentirse enfermo** feel ill. **sentirse obligado a** feel obliged to.

seña ['seɲa] *sf* mark; sign; signal; password. **señas** *sf pl* address *sing*.

señal [se'ɲal] *sf* signal; sign; mark. **en señal de** in proof of. **señaladamente** *adv* signally. **señalado** *adj* famous. **señalar** *v* mark; signal; point out; denote. **señalarse** *v* distinguish oneself.

señor [se'ɲor] *sm* mister; gentleman; lord; master. **El Señor** the Lord. **señora** *sf* lady; wife; mistress; madam. **la señora de García** Mrs García. **señorear** *v* domineer. **señorearse** *v* take possession. **señoría** *sf* lordship. **señorío** *sm* dominion; stateliness. **señorita** *sf* miss; young lady.

separar [sepa'rar] *v* separate; divide; discharge. **separable** *adj* separable. **separación** *sf* separation; dismissal. **separado** *adj* separate. **por separado** separately.

septentrional [septentrjo'nal] *adj* northern.

séptico ['septiko] *adj* septic.

septiembre [sep'tjembre] *sm* September.

séptimo ['septimo] *adj* seventh.

septuagésimo [septwa'xesimo] *adj* seventieth.

sepulcro [se'pulkro] *sm* tomb, grave.

sepultar [sepul'tar] *v* bury. **sepultura** *sf* grave; burial. **sepulturero** *sm* gravedigger.

sequedad [seke'ðað] *sf* dryness; curtness. **sequía** *sf* drought.

séquito ['sekito] *sm* entourage, followers *pl*.

*ser [ser] *v* be; exist; occur. **a no ser por** but for. **sea lo que sea** come what may. **si no es que** unless.

seráfico [se'rafiko] *adj* seraphic. **serafín** *sm* seraph.

Serbia ['serβja] *sf* Serbia. **serbio** *adj* Serb.

serenar [sere'nar] *v* calm; settle. **sereno** *adj* serene; calm. **serenidad** *sf* serenity; calmness.

serenata [sere'nata] *sf* serenade.

serie ['serje] *sf* series. **fabricación en serie** *sf* mass production.

serio ['serjo] *adj* serious. **tomar en serio** take seriously. **seriedad** *sf* seriousness; sincerity.

sermón [ser'mon] *sm* sermon.

serpiente [ser'pjente] *sf* serpent. **serpiente de cascabel** rattlesnake. **serpentear** *v* wriggle. **serpentino** *adj* serpentine.

serrano [ser'rano] *adj* of the mountains. *sm* highlander. **serranía** *sf* mountainous country.

***serrar** [ser'rar] *v* saw. **serrado** *adj* serrated. **serrín** *sm* sawdust.

servicio [ser'βiθjo] *sm* service; attendance. **estar de servicio** be on duty. **servicios** *sm pl* toilet *sing*. **servible** *adj* serviceable. **servidor, -a** *sm*, *sf* servant; (*computadora*) server. **su seguro servidor** yours faithfully. **servidumbre** *sf* household staff; servitude. **servil** *adj* servile. **servilismo** *sm* servility.

servilleta [serβi'ʎeta] *sf* napkin.

***servir** [ser'βir] *v* serve. **para servir a usted** at your service. **servir de** act as. **servirse** *v* help oneself. **servirse de** make use of.

sesenta [se'senta] *sm*, *adj* sixty.

sesgar [ses'gar] *v* slant; twist. **sesgo** *sm* slant; twist.

sesión [se'sjon] *sf* session; conference. **sesión de peluquería y maquillaje** *sf* makeover.

seso ['seso] *sm* brain; sense, understanding, wisdom. **perder el seso** go mad.

seta ['seta] *sf* mushroom.

setenta [se'tenta] *sm*, *adj* seventy.

setiembre *V* septiembre.

seto ['seto] *sm* fence.

seudónimo [seu'ðonimo] *sm* pseudonym. **seudo** *adj* (*fam*) pseudo.

severo [se'βero] *adj* severe; harsh. **severidad** *sf* severity.

sexagésimo [seksa'xesimo] *adj* sixtieth. **sexagenario, -a** *sm*, *sf* sexagenarian.

sexista [sek'sista] *adj* sexist.

sexo ['sekso] *sm* sex. **sexual** *adj* sexual. **sexualidad** *sf* sexuality.

sexto ['seksto] *adj* sixth. **sexteto** *sm* sextet.

si [si] *conj* if; whether. **si bien** although.

sí¹ [si] *adv* yes; indeed. **eso sí que es** yes, that's it. *sm* consent. **dar el sí** agree.

sí² *pron* himself; herself; itself; yourself; oneself; themselves; yourselves. **de por sí** in itself. **entre sí** among themselves. **metido en sí** pensive.

sibilante [siβi'lante] *adj* sibilant.

siderurgia [siðe'rurxja] *sf* iron and steel industry.

sidra ['siðra] *sf* cider.

siega ['sjega] *sf* reaping, harvesting.

siembra ['sjembra] *sf* sowing.

siempre ['sjempre] *adv* always. **siempre jamás** for ever and ever. **siempre que** whenever; provided that.

sien [sjen] *sf* (*anat*) temple.

sierra ['sjerra] *sf* saw; mountain range.

siervo ['sjerβo] *sm* slave; servant.

siesta ['sjesta] *sf* siesta.

siete ['sjete] *adj*, *sm* seven.

sífilis ['sifilis] *sm* syphilis. **sifilítico, -a** , *s*, *adj* syphilitic.

sifón [si'fon] *sm* soda water; syphon.

sigilar [sixi'lar] *v* conceal. **sigilo** *sm* secrecy. **sigiloso** *adj* secretive.

siglo ['siglo] *sm* century. **siglo de oro** golden age.

signar [sig'nar] *v* sign, seal. **signarse** *v* cross oneself. **signatura** *sf* signature.

significar [signifi'kar] *v* signify; notify. **significado** *sm* meaning; significance. **significativo** *adj* significant.

signo ['signo] *sm* sign; symbol.

siguiente [si'gjente] *adj* following, next.

sílaba ['silaβa] *sf* syllable.

silbar [sil'βar] *v* whistle; hiss. **silbido** *sm* whistle, hiss.

silencio [si'lenθjo] *sm* silence. **silenciador** *sm* (*de arma*) silencer. **silenciar** *v* silence. **silencioso** *adj* silent.

silueta [si'lweta] *sf* silhouette, outline.

silvestre [sil'βestre] *adj* wild. **silvicultura** *sf* forestry.

silla ['siʎa] *sf* chair; seat; saddle. **silla de paseo** *sf* buggy. **silla de tijera** deck chair. **sillón** *sm* armchair.

sima ['sima] *sf* abyss.

símbolo ['simbolo] *sm* symbol. **simbólico** *adj* symbolic. **simbolismo** *sm* symbolism. **simbolizar** *v* symbolize.

simetría [sime'tria] *sf* symmetry. **simétrico** *adj* symmetrical.

simiente [si'mjente] *sf* seed.

símil ['simil] *adj* similar. *sm* comparison; simile. **similar** *adj* similar. **similitud** *sf* similarity.

simpatía [simpa'tia] *sf* affection; sympathy; friendliness; charm. **simpático** *adj* charming; endearing; friendly; nice. **simpatizar** *v* sympathize; get on.

simple ['simple] *adj* simple; pure; naïve. **simplemente** *adv* merely. **simpleza** *sf* simplicity; simpleness; silly thing. **simplicidad** *sf* simplicity. **simplificar** *v* simplify. **simplón, -ona** *sm*, *sf* simpleton.

simulacro [simu'lakro] *sm* image; semblance.

simular [simu'lar] *v* simulate. **simulación** *sf* pretence. **simulado** *adj* sham.

simultáneo [simul'taneo] *adj* simultaneous. **simultaneidad** *sf* simultaneousness.

sin [sin] *prep* without; but for; apart from. **sin embargo** nevertheless. **sin falta** without fail. **sin plombo** *adj* unleaded. **sin que** without.

sinagoga [sina'goɣa] *sf* synagogue.

sincero [sin'θero] *adj* sincere. **sinceridad** *sf* sincerity.

síncopa ['sinkopa] *sf* syncopation. **sincopar** *v* syncopate.

sindicato [sindi'kato] *sm* trade union; syndicate. **sindical** *adj* trade-union. **sindicalismo** *sm* trade-unionism. **síndico** *sm* trustee.

Síndrome de Down *sm* Down's Syndrome.

sinfín [sin'fin] *sm* endless number.

sinfonía [sinfo'nia] *sf* symphony. **sinfónico** *adj* symphonic.

singular [singu'lar] *adj* singular; exceptional; unique; excellent. **singularidad** *sf* singularity; excellence. **singularizar** *v* single out. **singularizarse** *v* distinguish oneself.

siniestro [si'njestro] *adj* (*dirección*) left; sinister. *sm* catastrophe. **siniestrado, -a** *sm*, *sf* victim of an accident.

sinnúmero [sin'numero] *sm* endless number.

sino¹ ['sino] *conj* but, except. **no sólo ...**

sino ... not only ... but also ....

sino² *sm* fate.

sinónimo [si'nonimo] *sm* synonym. *adj* synonymous.

sinopsis [si'nopsis] *sf* synopsis (*pl* -ses).

sinrazón [sinra'θon] *sf* injustice.

sinsabor [sinsa'βor] *sm* trouble.

sintaxis [sin'taksis] *sf* syntax. **sintáctico** *adj* syntactic.

síntesis ['sintesis] *sf* synthesis (*pl* -ses). **sintético** *adj* synthetic.

síntoma ['sintoma] *sm* symptom. **sintomático** *adj* symptomatic.

sintonizar [sintoni'θar] *v* (*radio*) tune in. **sintonía** *sf* signature tune.

sinvergüenza [sinβer'ɣwenθa] *adj* shameless. *s*(*m* + *f*) cad.

siquiera [si'kjera] *adv* at least; even; just. **ni siquiera** not at all. *conj* even if; even though. **siquiera ... siquiera ...** whether ... or whether ....

sirena [si'rena] *sf* (*ninfa*) siren, mermaid; (*tecn*) siren, fog-horn.

sirviente [sir'βjente] *sm* servant.

sisar [si'sar] *v* pilfer; cheat. **sisa** *sf* theft, pilfering.

sísmico ['sismiko] *adj* seismic. **sismógrafo** *sm* seismograph.

sistema [sis'tema] *sm* system, method. **sistemático** *adj* systematic.

sitiar [si'tjar] *sm* besiege; surround.

sitio ['sitjo] *sm* place; room, space; siege. **no hay sitio** there is no room.

situar [si'twar] *v* situate; put. **situación** *sf* situation.

so [so] *prep* under. **so pena de** under penalty of.

sobaco [so'βako] *sm* armpit.

sobado [so'βaðo] *adj* kneaded; (*fam*) shabby, well-worn. **sobar** *v* knead; thrash; crumple; fondle.

soberanía [soβera'nia] *sf* sovereignty. **soberano, -a** *s*, *adj* sovereign.

soberbia [so'βerβja] *sf* pride; magnificence; pomp. **soberbio** *adj* proud; superb.

sobornar [so'βor'nar] *v* bribe. **soborno** *sm* bribe; bribery.

sobrar [so'βrar] *sf* surplus. **de sobra** in excess. **sobras** *sf pl* remains *pl*. **sobradamente** *adv* excessively. **sobrado** *adj* abundant; superfluous. **sobrancero** *adj* unemployed. **sobrante** *adj* spare.

sobre¹ ['soβre] *prep* on; upon; over; above; about. **sobre las diez** about ten o'clock. **sobre todo** above all.

sobre² *sm* envelope.

sobrecama [soβre'kama] *sm* bedspread.

sobrecargar [soβrekar'gar] *v* overload. **sobrecarga** *sf* extra burden. **sobrecargo** *sm* purser.

sobrecejo [soβre'θexo] *sm* frown.

sobrecoger [soβreko'xer] *v* surprise, take aback. **sobrecogerse** *v* be startled.

sobredicho [soβre'ðitʃo] *adj* aforesaid.

sobrehumano [soβreu'mano] *adj* superhuman.

sobremanera [soβrema'nera] *adv* exceedingly.

sobremesa [soβre'mesa] *sf* dessert; table cover; after-dinner chat.

sobrenatural [soβrenatu'ral] *adj* supernatural.

sobrepasar [soβrepa'sar] *v* surpass.

*sobreponer [soβrepo'ner] *v* superimpose. **sobreponerse a** overcome. **sobrepuesto** *adj* superimposed.

sobreprecio [soβre'preθjo] *sm* surcharge.

*sobresalir [soβresa'lir] *v* excel. **sobresaliente** *adj* outstanding.

sobresaltar [soβresal'tar] *v* attack; frighten. **sobresalto** *sm* sudden attack; shock. **de sobresalto** suddenly.

sobrescrito [soβre'skrito] *sm* (*en un sobre*) address.

sobretodo [soβre'toðo] *sm* overcoat.

*sobrevenir [soβreβe'nir] *v* happen suddenly.

sobrevivir [soβreβi'βir] *v* survive. **sobreviviente** *s(m + f)* survivor.

sobriedad [soβrie'ðað] *sf* sobriety. **sobrio** *adj* sober, moderate.

sobrino [so'βrino] *sm* nephew. **sobrina** *sf* niece.

socarrón [sokar'ron] *adj* sarcastic; sly. **socarronería** *sf* sarcasm; slyness.

socavar [soka'βar] *v* undermine. **socavón** *sm* excavation.

sociable [so'θjaβle] *adj* sociable. **sociabilidad** *sf* sociability.

social [so'θjal] *adj* social. **socializar** *v* socialize. **socialismo** *sm* socialism. **socialista** *s(m + f)* socialist.

sociedad [soθje'ðað] *sf* society. **socio, -a** *sm, sf* associate.

sociología [soθjolo'xia] *sf* sociology. **sociólogo, -a** *sm, sf* sociologist.

socorrer [sokor'rer] *v* help. **socorrido** *adj* helpful; handy. **socorro** *sm* succour; relief. **¡socorro!** help!

soda ['soða] *sf* soda-water.

soez [so'eθ] *adj* obscene; vulgar.

sofá [so'fa] *sf* sofa, settee.

sofocar [sofo'kar] *v* suffocate. **sofocación** *sf* suffocation. **sofocado** *adj* breathless. **sofoco** *sm* suffocation.

software *sm* software.

soga ['soga] *sf* rope, cord. **hacer soga** lag behind.

soja ['soxa] *sf* soya.

sojuzgar [soxuθ'gar] *v* subdue.

sol [sol] *sm* sun; sunlight. **hace sol** it's sunny. **tomar el sol** sunbathe.

solamente [sola'mente] *adv* only. **no solamente** not only.

solapa [so'lapa] *sf* flap; lapel; (*fig*) pretext. **solapado** *adj* sly. **solapar** *v* overlap; (*fig*) cover up, hide.

*solar [so'lar] *adj* solar. *sm* lot; plot; building site.

solaz [so'laθ] *sm* recreation; solace. **a solaz** with pleasure. **solazar** *v* distract; amuse; solace.

soldado [sol'daðo] *sm* soldier.

*soldar [sol'ðar] *v* solder; weld; (*huesos*) knit. **soldador** *sm* soldering iron. **soldadura** *sf* welding.

soledad [sole'ðað] *sf* loneliness, solitude.

solemne [so'lemne] *adj* solemn. **solemnidad** *sf* solemnity. **solemnizar** *v* solemnize.

*soler [so'ler] *v* be in the habit of; usually be *or* do. **suele comer mucho** he usually eats a lot.

solera [so'lera] *sf* prop; stone pavement; tradition; strong old wine.

solicitar [soliθi'tar] *v* request; pursue; canvass. **solicitación** *sf* solicitation; application. **solicitador, -a** *sm, sf or* **solicitante** *sm* petitioner; applicant. **solícito** *adj* solicitous. **solicitud** *sf* solicitude.

solidaridad [soliðari'ðað] *sf* solidarity. **solidar** *v* consolidate. **solidario** *adj* mutual. **solidez** *sf* solidity. **solidificar** *v* solidify. **sólido** *adj* solid.

solitario [soli'tarjo], -a *sm*, *sf* hermit, recluse. *adj* lonely; solitary; alone; single.

solo ['solo] *adj* alone; single; unique; only; (*música*) solo. *sm* (*música*) solo.

sólo ['solo] *adv* only, merely.

*soltar [sol'tar] *v* release; free; loosen; break; shed. **soltarse** *v* break loose; become unscrewed; lose one's inhibitions.

soltero [sol'tero] *sm* bachelor. *adj* single. **soltera** *sf* spinster. **soltería** *sf* celibacy. **solterona** *sf* old maid.

soltura [sol'tura] *sf* looseness; agility; fluency. **con soltura** fluently.

soluble [so'luβle] *adj* soluble. **solubilidad** *sf* solubility. **solución** *sf* solution. **solucionar** *v* solve.

solvencia [sol'βenθja] *sf* solvency; settlement. **solvente** *adj* solvent.

sollo ['soʎo] *sm* sturgeon.

sollozar [soʎo'θar] *v* sob. **sollozo** *sm* sob.

sombra ['sombra] *sf* shadow; shade. **dar sombra a** shade.

sombrero [som'brero] *sm* hat.

sombrilla [som'briʎa] *sf* parasol.

sombrío [som'brio] *sm* shady spot. *adj* shady; gloomy. **sombroso** *adj* shady.

somero [so'mero] *adj* superficial.

someter [some'ter] *v* submit; subdue. **sometimiento** *sm* submission.

somnífero [som'nifero] *sm* sleeping pill.

somnolencia [somno'lenθja] *sf* sleepiness. **somnámbulo**, -a *sm*, *sf* sleepwalker. **somnolente** *adj* sleepy.

son [son] *sm* sound; rumour; manner. **por este son** by this means.

*sonar [so'nar] *v* sound; ring; chime. **sonarse** *v* blow one's nose. **sonante** *adj* sounding; ringing.

sondear [sonde'ar] *v* fathom; sound out.

soneto [so'neto] *sm* sonnet.

sonido [so'niðo] *sm* sound.

sonoro [so'noro] *adj* sonorous; resonant. **sonoridad** *sf* sonority.

*sonreír [sonre'ir] *v* smile. **sonriente** *adj* smiling. **sonrisa** *sf* smile.

sonrojar [sonro'xar] *v* blush; flush. **sonrojo** *sm* blush.

*soñar [so'ɲar] *v* dream. **soñador**, -a *sm*, *sf* dreamer. **soñera** *sf* drowsiness. **soñoliento** *adj* drowsy.

sopa ['sopa] *sf* soup. **como una sopa** soaked to the skin. **sopero** *sm* soup plate.

sopapo [so'papo] *sm* (*fam*) blow, punch. **sopapear** *v* chuck under the chin; punch.

soplar [so'plar] *v* blow; blow out; blow away; prompt. **sopladura** *sf* blowing. **soplillo** *sm* fan; blower. **soplo** *sm* blowing; puff of wind. **soplón**, -ona *sm*, *sf* informer.

sopor [so'por] *sm* drowsiness.

soportar [sopor'tar] *v* support; tolerate; endure. **soporte** *sm* support; stand.

sor [sor] *sf* (*rel*) sister.

sorber [sor'βer] *v* sip; suck; soak up. **sorbete** *sm* sherbet; water ice. **sorbetón** *sm* large draught. **sorbo** *sm* sip; swallow; gulp.

sordera [sor'ðera] *sf* deafness. **sordo** *adj* deaf; muffled.

sórdido ['sorðiðo] *adj* squalid. **sordidez** *sf* squalor.

sordomudo [sorðo'muðo], -a *sm*, *sf* deaf-mute. *adj* deaf and dumb.

sorprender [sorpren'der] *v* surprise. **sorprendente** *adj* surprising. **sorpresa** *sf* surprise.

sortear [sorte'ar] *v* cast lots for; avoid, get round. **sorteable** *adj* avoidable. **sorteo** *sm* raffle; casting of lots; dodging.

sortija [sor'tixa] *sf* ring; (*de pelo*) curl.

sortilegio [sorti'lexjo] *sm* sorcery; charm. **sortílega** *sf* sorceress. **sortílego** *sm* sorcerer.

*sosegar [sose'gar] *v* calm, quieten. **sosiego** *sm* calm, quiet.

soslayar [sosla'jar] *v* place obliquely; dodge; avoid. **soslayo** *adj* oblique.

soso ['soso] *adj* tasteless; dull.

sospechar [sospe'tʃar] *v* suspect. **sospecha** *sf* suspicion. **sospechoso** *adj* suspicious, suspect.

*sostener [soste'ner] *v* support; sustain. **sostén** *sm* support; brassière. **sostenedor**, -a *sm*, *sf* supporter. **sostenido** *adj* sustained; constant.

sota ['sota] *sf* (*deporte*) jack; (*fam*) hussy.

sotana [so'tana] *sf* cassock.

sótano ['sotano] *sm* basement, cellar.

soto ['soto] *sm* thicket, copse.

soviet [so'βjet] *sm* Soviet. **soviético** *adj* Soviet.

spaghettis [spa'getis] *sm pl* spaghetti *sing*.

spam ['spam] *sm* spam (Internet).

su [su] *adj* his; her; its; your; their; one's.

suave ['swaβe] *adj* smooth; soft; mild. **suavidad** *sf* smoothness; softness. **suavizar** *v* soften; smooth; strop.

***subarrendar** [suβarren'dar] *v* sublet, sublease. **subarriendo** *sm* subletting.

subasta [su'βasta] *sf* auction. **subastar** *v* auction.

subcampeón [subkam'pjon], **-ona** *sm*, *sf* runner-up.

subconsciencia [subkons'θjenθja] *sf* subconscious. **subconsciente** *adj* subconscious.

subdesarrollado [suβðesarro'λaðo] *adj* underdeveloped. **subdesarrollo** *sm* underdevelopment.

súbdito ['suβðito] *sm* subject, citizen.

subdividir [suβðiβi'ðir] *v* subdivide. **subdivisión** *sf* subdivision.

subir [su'βir] *v* climb; go up; rise; lift; promote. **subir al coche** get into the car. **subirse** *v* rise; become conceited. **subida** *sf* ascent. **subido** *adj* (*color*) bright.

súbito ['suβito] *adj* sudden. **adv** suddenly.

subjuntivo [subxun'tiβo] *sm* (*gram*) subjunctive.

sublevar [suβle'βar] *v* incite to rebellion. **sublevarse** *v* rebel. **sublevación** *sf* rebellion.

sublime [su'βlime] *adj* sublime, lofty. **sublimación** *sf* sublimation. **sublimidad** *sf* sublimity.

submarino [suβma'rino] *adj* underwater. *sm* submarine.

subordinado [suβorði'naðo] *adj* subordinate. **subordinar** *v* subordinate.

subproducto [suβpro'ðukto] *sm* by-product.

subrayar [suβra'jar] *v* underline, underscore; emphasize. **subrayado** *sm* underlining; emphasis.

subsanar [suβsa'nar] *v* excuse; redeem.

subscribir [suβskri'βir] *v* subscribe; sign. **subscripción** *sf* subscription.

***subseguir** [suβse'gir] *v* follow. **subsiguiente** *adj* subsequent.

subsidiario [suβsi'ðjarjo] *adj* subsidiary.

subsidio [suβ'siðjo] *sm* subsidy, grant, allowance.

subsistir [suβsis'tir] *v* subsist; exist. **subsistencia** *sf* permanence; subsistence. **subsistente** *adj* subsisting.

substancia [suβ'staθja] *sf* substance. **en**

substancia briefly. **substancial** *adj* substantial. **substanciar** *v* summarize; substantiate. **substancioso** *adj* substantial.

***substituir** [suβstitu'ir] *v* substitute. **substitución** *sf* substitution. **substitutivo** *adj* substitute.

***substraer** [suβstra'er] *v* subtract; remove; steal. **substraerse** *v* evade; withdraw. **substracción** *sf* subtraction; stealing.

subterfugio [suβter'fuxjo] *sm* subterfuge.

subterráneo [suβter'raneo] *adj* subterranean.

subtítulo [suβ'titulo] *sm* subtitle.

suburbio [suβ'urβjo] *sm* outskirts *pl*; slum. **suburbano** *adj* suburban.

subvención [suββen'θjon *sf* subsidy. **subvencionar** *v* subsidize.

subvertir [suββer'tir] *v* subvert. **subversión** *sf* subversion. **subversivo** *adj* subversive.

subyugar [suβju'gar] *v* subjugate. **subyugación** *sf* subjugation.

suceder [suθe'ðer] *v* succeed; follow; happen. **sucedido** *sm* event. **sucediente** *adj* following. **sucesión** *sf* succession; offspring. **sucesivamente** *adv* successively. **sucesivo** *adj* successive. **en lo sucesivo** hereafter. **suceso** *sm* event; outcome.

suciedad [suθje'ðað] *sf* dirt, dirtiness. **sucio** *adj* dirty; vile, mean.

sucinto [su'θinto] *adj* succinct, brief.

sucumbir [sukum'bir] *v* succumb.

sucursal [sukur'sal] *sm* branch.

sud [suð] *adj*, *sm* south.

Sudáfrica [suð'afrika] *s* South Africa.

Sudamérica [suda'merika] *s* South America. **sudamericano, -a** *s*, *adj* South American.

sudar [su'ðar] *v* sweat. **sudar tinta** (*fam*) sweat blood. **sudor** *sm* sweat. **sudoroso** *adj* sweaty.

sudeste [su'ðeste] *adj*, *sm* south-east.

sudoeste [suðo'este] *sm*, *adj* south-west.

Suecia ['sweθja] *sf* Sweden.

sueco ['sweko], **-a** *sm*, *sf* Swede. *sm* (*idioma*) Swedish. *adj* Swedish.

suegro ['swegro] *sm* father-in-law.

suela ['swela] *sf* (*de zapato*) sole. **suelas** *sf pl* sandals *pl*.

sueldo ['swelðo] *sm* salary; wage; pay. **a sueldo** paid.

suelo ['swelo] *sm* ground; soil; floor. **echar al suelo** demolish.

suelto ['swelto] *adj* free; loose; separate; agile.

sueño ['sweɲo] *sm* dream; sleep. **tener sueño** be sleepy.

suero ['swero] *sm* serum; whey.

suerte ['swerte] *sf* luck; fate; chance; kind; manner; quality. **¡buena suerte!** good luck! **de otra suerte** otherwise. **de tal suerte que** in such a way that.

suéter ['sweter] *sm* sweater.

suficiencia [sufi'θjenθja] *sf* sufficiency; ability; self-importance. **suficiente** *adj* sufficient; capable.

sufragar [sufra'gar] *v* help; finance. **sufragar por** vote for. **sufragio** *sm* suffrage.

sufrir [suf'rir] *v* suffer; endure. **sufrido** *adj* long-suffering. **sufrimiento** *sm* **suffering**; patience.

*sugerir [suxe'rir] *v* suggest, hint. **sugerencia** *sf* suggestion. **sugerente** *adj* suggestive. **sugestión** *sf* suggestion. **sugestionable** *adj* suggestible. **sugestionar** *v* influence. **sugestivo** *adj* suggestive; stimulating.

suicidarse [swiθi'ðarse] *v* commit suicide. **suicida** *s(m + f)* (*persona*) suicide. **suicidio** *sm* suicide.

Suiza ['swiθa] *sf* Switzerland. **suizo, -a** *s, adj* Swiss.

sujetar [suxe'tar] *v* secure; hold; fasten; seize; tie; restrain; subordinate. **sujetarse** *v* hang on; hold up; subject oneself to; abide by. **sujeción** *sf* subjection; control. **sujetapapeles** *sm invar* paperclip. **sujeto** *sm* subject; individual.

sumar [su'mar] *v* add, add up. **sumarse** *v* join in. **suma** *sf* sum; summary; essence. **en suma** in short. **sumadora** *sf* adding machine. **sumamente** *adv* extremely.

sumaria *sf* (*jur*) indictment. **sumario** *sm* summary.

sumergir [sumer'xir] *v* submerge, plunge. **sumersión** *sf* submersion.

suministrar [suminis'trar] *v* supply, provide. **suministro** *sm* supply. **suministros** *sm pl* supplies *pl*, provisions *pl*.

sumir [su'mir] *v* submerge; sink.

sumisión [sumi'sjon] *sf* submission. **sumiso** *adj* submissive.

sumo ['sumo] *adj* greatest; supreme. **tribunal supremo** *sm* supreme court.

suntuoso [sun'twoso] *adj* sumptuous. **suntuosidad** *sf* sumptuousness.

supeditar [supeði'tar] *v* subdue. subordinate. **supeditación** *sf* subjection.

superar [supe'rar] *v* surpass; overcome. **superable** *adj* surmountable. **superación** *sf* overcoming.

superávit [supe'raβit] *sm* surplus.

superchería [supertʃe'ria] *sf* fraud; swindle.

superficial [superfi'θjal] *adj* superficial. **superficie** *sf* surface; area.

superfluo [super'fluo] *adj* superfluous. **superfluidad** *sf* superfluity.

superior [supe'rjor] *adj* better; superior. *sm* superior.

superlativo [superla'tiβo] *adj* superlative.

supermercado [supermer'kaðo] *sm* supermarket.

supersecreto [superse'kreto] *adj* top secret.

superstición [supersti'θjon] *sf* superstition. **supersticioso** *adj* superstitious.

supervivencia [superβi'βenθja] *sf* survival. **superviviente** *s(m+f)* survivor.

supino [su'pino] *adj* supine.

suplantar [suplan'tar] *v* supplant; forge.

suplemento [suple'mento] *sm* supplement. **suplementario** *adj* supplementary; extra. **horas suplementarias** *sf pl* overtime *sing*.

suplente *s(m+f)* substitute, standby (person).

súplica ['suplika] *sf* supplication; petition. **suplicación** *sf* supplication; wafer biscuit. **suplicante** *s(m+f)* supplicant. **suplicar** *v* implore; beseech.

suplicio [su'pliθjo] *sm* torture.

suplir [su'plir] *v* make up for; substitute.

*suponer [supo'ner] *v* suppose; believe; mean; guess. **suposición** *sf* supposition; slander.

supremo [su'premo] *adj* supreme. **supremacía** *sf* supremacy.

suprimir [supri'mir] *v* suppress; delete; omit; eliminate. **supresión** *sf* suppression; deletion.

supuesto [su'pwesto] *adj* supposed; so-called; hypothetical; feigned. **¡por supuesto!** of course! **supuesto que** since; if. *sm* hypothesis (*pl* -ses).

sur [sur] *adj* southern. *sm* south.

surcar [sur'kar] *v* plough; cleave.

surfista *s(m+f)* surfer.

surgir [sur'xir] *v* rise; spring forth; appear; anchor. **surgidero** *sm* anchorage.

surrealista [surreal'ista] *s(m+f)* surrealist. **surrealismo** *sm* surrealism.

surtido [sur'tiðo] *adj* assorted. **bien surtido** well stocked. *sm* stock; range; assortment. **surtidor** *sm* jet; fountain; petrol pump. **surtir** *v* supply. **surtir un pedido** fill an order.

susceptibilidad [susθeptiβili'ða ð] *sf* susceptibility. **susceptible** *adj* susceptible.

suscitar [susθi'tar] *v* agitate, stir up. **suscitar interés** arouse interest.

suscribir *V* subscribir.

susodicho [suso'ðitʃo] *adj* aforementioned.

suspender [suspen'der] *v* suspend; adjourn; hang; fail; interrupt. **suspensión** *sf* suspension. **suspenso** *sm* (*examen*) failure.

suspicacia [suspi'kaθja] *sf* suspicion; misgiving. **suspicaz** *adj* suspicious.

suspirar [suspi'rar] *v* sigh. **suspirado** *adj* longed for, wished for, **suspiro** *sm* sigh.

sustancia *V* substancia.

sustentar [susten'tar] *v* sustain; maintain. **sustentamiento** *sm* sustenance; maintenance. **sustento** *sm* sustenance.

***sustituir** *V* substituir.

susto ['susto] *sm* fright. **dar susto a** frighten.

susurrar [susur'rar] *v* whisper; murmur. **susurrarse** *v* be rumoured. **susurrante** *adj* whispering. **susurro** *sm* whisper; murmur.

sutil [su'til] *adj* subtle; sharp; slender; delicate. **sutileza** *sf* subtlety; thinness; sharpness. **sutilizar** *v* thin down; polish; sharpen.

sutura [su'tura] *sf* suture.

suyo ['sujo] *adj* of his; of hers; of yours; of theirs. *pron* his; hers; yours; its; theirs. **lo suyo** one's share. **muy suyo** typical of one.

T

tabaco [ta'βako] *sm* tabacco. **tabacalero**, **-a** *sm, sf* tobacconist.

tábano ['taβano] *sm* horsefly.

taberna [ta'βerna] *sf* tavern; public house.

tabique [ta'βike] *sm* partition; dividing wall. **tabicar** *v* wall up.

tabla ['taβla] *sf* board, plank; tablet; slab; index; vegetable plot. **tablas** *sf pl* (*teatro*) stage *sing*. **pisar las tablas** go on the stage. **tablado** *sm* wooden platform; bedstead; gallows. **tablaje** *sm* boards *pl*. **tablajería** *sf* gambling. **tablear** *vb* saw into planks. **tablero** *sm* planking; blackboard; gambling den. **tableta** *sf* tablet. **tablilla** *sf* notice-board. **tablón** *sm* beam.

tabú [ta'βu] *sm* taboo.

tabular [tabu'lar] *adj* tabular. *v* tabulate.

taburete [taβu'rete] *sm* stool.

tacaño [ta'kaɲo] *adj* mean, stingy. **tacañería** *sf* meanness.

tácito ['taθito] *adj* tacit. **taciturnidad** *sf* taciturnity. **taciturno** *adj* taciturn.

taco ['tako] *sm* wad; plug; billiard cue; draught; oath. **soltar un taco** utter an oath.

tacón [ta'kon] *sm* heel. **taconazo** *sm* blow *or* tap with the heel.

tacto ['takto] *sm* touch; sense of touch; tact.

tachar [ta'tʃar] *v* accuse; erase. **tacha** *sf* fault; tack, small nail. **poner tacha** find fault. **tachón** *sm* (*carpintería*) stud. **tachonado** *adj* studded. **tachonar** *v* stud. **tachoso** *adj* defective. **tachuela** *sf* small tack.

tahona [ta'ona] *sf* bakery.

taimado [tai'maðo] *adj* sly, crafty; sullen.

tajar [ta'xar] *v* cut; hew; cleave. **taja** *sf* incision. **tajada** *sf* slice. **sacar tajada** profit. **tajadero** *sm* chopping-block. **tajador** *sm* chopper.

tal [tal] *adj* such; such a. **el tal** that fellow. **tal como** such as. **tal vez** perhaps. *pron* someone; such a person *or* thing. **como tal** as such. *adv* so; as though.

taladrar [tala'ðrar] *v* bore, drill. **taladro** *sm* bore, drill.

talante [ta'lante] *sm* mood; look; grace. **de buen/mal talante** in a good/bad mood.

talar¹ [ta'lar] *v* cut down, fell.

talar² *adj* full-length.

talco ['talko] *sm* tinsel; talcum powder.

talega [ta'lega] *sf* money bag; nappy.

talento [ta'lento] *sm* talent. **talentoso** *adj* talented. **talentudo** *adj* over-talented.

talón [ta'lon] *sm* heel; counterfoil; voucher; coupon.

talud [ta'luð] *sm* slope.

tallar [ta'ʎar] *v* carve; appraise; deal cards.

tallarín [taʎa'rin] *sm* noodle.

talle ['taʎe] *sm* figure; waist.

taller [ta'ʎer] *sm* workshop; studio.

tallo ['taʎo] *sm* stem, stalk.

tamaño [ta'maɲo] *sm* size. **de tamaño natural** life-size.

tambalearse [tambale'arse] *v* stagger; wobble; sway.

también [tam'bjen] *adv* also, too.

tambor [tam'bor] *sm* drum. **tambormayor** drum major.

Támesis ['tamesis] *sm* Thames.

tamiz [ta'miθ] *sm* sieve. **pasar por tamiz** sift.

tampoco [tam'poko] *adv* neither.

tan [tan] *adv* so. **tan siquiera** even if only.

tanda ['tanda] *sf* turn; shift; relay; gang.

tanga ['tanga] *sm* thong (underwear).

tangente [tan'xente] *sm, adj* tangent.

tangerina [tanxe'rina] *sf* tangerine.

tangible [tan'xiβle] *adj* tangible.

tanque ['tanke] *sm* tank.

tantear [tante'ar] *v* try; test; sound; keep score. **tantearse** *v* think carefully. **tanteo** *sm* calculation; score.

tanto ['tanto] *adj* as much; so much; as great; so great. *adv* so much; as much; so; thus. **tanto como** as much as. **por lo tanto** therefore. *sm* amount; sum. **otro tanto** as much again.

***tañer** [ta'ɲer] *v* (*música*) play. **tañido** *sm* tune; twanging.

tapacubo [tapa'kuβo] *sm* hub-cap.

tapar [ta'par] *v* cover up; plug; cap; cork. **tapa** *sf* lid; cover. **tapadero** *sm* stopper. **taparrabo** *sm* loincloth. **tapón** *sm* cork; stopper.

tapia ['tapja] *sf* garden wall. **tapiar** *v* wall up.

tapicería [tapiθe'ria] *sf* tapestry; upholstery. **tapicero, -a** *sm, sf* upholsterer. **tapiz** *sm* tapestry. **tapizar** *v* hang with tapestry; upholster.

taquigrafía [takigra'fia] *sf* shorthand. **taquígrafo, -a** *sm, sf* stenographer.

taquilla [ta'kiʎa] *sf* box office; till.

tararear [tarare'ar] *v* hum.

tardar [tar'ðar] *v* delay; take a long time. **tardanza** *sf* slowness.

tarde ['tarðe] *sf* afternoon; evening. *adv* late. **se hace tarde** it's getting late. **tardecer** *v* grow late.

tarea [ta'rea] *sf* task; homework.

tarifa [ta'rifa] *sf* tariff; price list; rate.

tarima [ta'rima] *sf* stand; platform.

tarjeta [tar'xeta] *sf* card. **tarjeta de crédito** *sf* charge card. **tarjeta postal** postcard.

tarro ['tarro] *sm* jar.

tarta ['tarta] *sf* cake, tart.

tartamudear [tartamuðe'ar] *v* stammer, stutter. **tartamudeo** *sm* stammer, stutter. **tartamudo, -a** *sm, sf* stutterer.

tasar [ta'sar] *v* appraise; value. **tasa** *sf* rate; valuation. **sin tasa** without limit. **tasación** *sf* valuation.

tatarabuelo [tatara'βwelo] *sm* great-greatgrandfather. **tatarabuela** *sf* great-greatgrandmother.

tatuaje [ta'twaxe] *sm* tattoo. **tatuar** *v* tattoo.

tauromaquia [tauro'makja] *sf* bullfighting.

taxidermia [taksi'ðermja] *sf* taxidermy. **taxidermista** *s(m+f)* taxidermist.

taxi ['taksi] *sm* taxi. **taxímetro** *sm* taximeter. **taxista** *s(m + f)* taxi-driver.

taza ['taθa] *sf* cup.

te [te] *pron* you; to you; yourself; to yourself.

té [te] *sm* tea.

teatro [te'atro] *sm* theatre. **teátrico** *adj* theatrical. **teatrero, -a** *sm, sf* theatre-goer.

tecla ['tekla] *sf* key. **teclado** *sm* keyboard. **teclear** *v* strum; try; (*computadora*) key (in).

técnica ['teknika] *sf* technique. **técnico, -a** *sm, sf* technician. **tecnología** *sf* technology. **tecnólogo, -a** *sm, sf* technologist.

techado [te'tʃaðo] *sm* roof; ceiling. **bajo techado** under cover. **techar** *v* put a roof on. **techo** *sm* roof; ceiling. **techo solar** *sm* sunroof.

tedio ['teðjo] *sm* tedium. **tedioso** *adj* tedious.

teja ['texa] *sf* tile. **tejado** *sm* tiled roof. **tejar** *v* tile. **tejaroz** *sm* eaves *pl*.

tejer [te'xer] *v* knit; weave. **tejedor, -a** *sm, sf* weaver. **tejedura** *sf* texture; weaving.

tejón [te'xon] *sm* (*zool*) badger.

tela ['tela] *sf* cloth; material. **tela de araña** spider's web. **telar** *sm* loom.

telaraña [tele'raɲa] *sf* cobweb.

tele ['tele] *sf* TV. **telebasura** *sf* reality TV.

telefonear [telefone'ar] *v* telephone. **teléfono** *sm* telephone. **teléfono móvil** *sm* mobile phone.

telegrafiar [telegra'fjar] *v* telegraph. **telegrafía** *sf* telegraphy. **telégrafo** *sm* telegraph.

telegrama [tele'grama] *sm* telegram.

telemando [tele'mando] *sm* remote control.

telepatía [telepa'tia] *sf* telepathy. **telepático** *adj* telepathic.

telescopio [tele'skopjo] *sm* telescope. **telescópico** *adj* telescopic.

telestudio [tele'stuðjo] *sm* television studio.

televentas [tele'βentas] *sf pl* telesales.

televisión [teleβi'sjon] *sf* television. **televisar** *v* televise. **televisor** *sm* television set. **televisión por cable** *sf* cable television. **televisión por satélite** *sf* satellite television.

telina [te'lina] *sf* clam.

telón [te'lon] *sm* curtain. **telón de acero** Iron Curtain.

tema ['tema] *sm* theme. **temático** *adj* thematic.

*temblar [tem'blar] *v* tremble, shiver, shake. **temblor** *sm* shudder. **temblor de tierra** earthquake. **tembloroso** *adj* trembling, shuddering.

temer [te'mer] *v* fear, be afraid. **temeridad** *sf* temerity. **temeroso** *adj* fearful. **temor** *sm* fear.

temperamento [tempera'mento] *sm* temperament, nature. **temperancia** *sf* temperance. **temperar** *v* temper.

temperatura [tempera'tura] *sf* temperature.

tempestad [tempes'tað] *sf* storm. **tempestuoso** *adj* stormy.

templar [tem'plar] *v* temper; moderate. **templado** *adj* temperate.

temple ['temple] *sm* temperature; mood; distemper. **pintura al temple** *sf* painting in distemper.

templo ['templo] *sm* temple.

temporada [tempo'raða] *sf* space of time, season, period.

temporal [tempo'ral] *adj also* **temporáneo** temporary; temporal, worldly, secular. *sm* bad weather.

temprano [tem'prano] *adj, adv* early.

tenaz [te'naθ] *adj* tenacious. **tenacidad** *sf* tenacity. **tenazas** *sf pl* pincers pl.

tendedero [tende'ðero] *sm* clothes line; place for drying clothes.

tendencia [ten'denθja] *sf* tendency.

*tender [ten'der] *v* spread out; extend; hang up; lay; set.

tendero [ten'dero], **-a** *sm, sf* shopkeeper.

tendón [ten'don] *sm* (*anat*) tendon.

tenebroso [tene'βroso] *adj* dark, gloomy. **tenebrosidad** *sf* gloom.

tenedor [tene'ðor] *sm* fork; holder. **tenedor de libros** bookkeeper. **teneduría** *sf* bookkeeping.

tenencia [te'nenθja] *sf* tenancy, occupancy; tenure.

*tener [te'ner] *v* have; possess; hold; spend. **tener en mucho** esteem. **tener para sí** think. **tener puesto** wear.

tenería [tene'ria] *sf* tannery.

tenia ['tenja] *sf* tapeworm.

teniente [te'njente] *sm* lieutenant. **teniente coronel** *sm* lieutenant-colonel.

tenis ['tenis] *sm* tennis.

tenor¹ ['tenor] *sm* tenor.

tenor² *sm* meaning, purport.

tenso ['tenso] *adj* tense, taut. **tensión** *sf* tension. **tensión arterial** blood pressure.

*tentar [ten'tar] *v* tempt; feel; attempt; examine. **tentación** *sf* temptation. **tentador** *sm* tempter. **tentadora** *sf* temptress. **tentativa** *sf* attempt. **tentativo** *adj* tentative.

tentáculo [ten'takulo] *sm* tentacle.

tentempié [tentempi'e] *sm* (*fam*) snack.

tenue ['tenwe] *adj* tenuous; faint; subdued. **tenuidad** *sf* slightness.

*teñir [te'ɲir] *v* dye, stain, colour. **teñidura** *sf* dyeing.

teología [teolo'xia] *sf* theology. **teólogo** *sm* theologian.

teorema [teo'rema] *sf* theorem.

teoría [teo'ria] *sf* theory. **teórico** *adj* theoretical. **teorizar** *v* theorize.

teosofía [teoso'fia] *sf* theosophy.

tercero [ter'θero] *adj, sm* third.

terapéutico [tera'peutiko] *adj* therapeutic. **teurapéutica** *sf* therapeutics.

terciar [ter'θjar] *v* tilt sideways; divide into three; mediate. **tercio** *adj* third.

terciopelo [terθjo'pelo] *sm* velvet. **terciopelado** *adj* velvety.

terco ['terko] *adj* stubborn.

tergiversar [terxiβer'sar] *v* misrepresent; distort. **tergiversación** *sf* distortion.

térmico ['termiko] *adj* thermal (underwear).

terminar [termi'nar] *v* finish, end; complete. **terminación** *sf* end. **terminal** *adj* terminal. **terminal de trabajo** *sf* workstation.

terminante *adj* decisive. **terminología** *sf* terminology.

término ['termino] *sm* end. **dar término a** bring to an end. **término medio** average.

termita [ter'mita] *sf also* **termite** *sm* termite.

termo ['termo] *sm* vacuum flask.

termodinámica [termoði'namika] *sf* thermodynamics.

termómetro [ter'mometro] *sm* thermometer.

termonuclear [termonukle'ar] *adj* thermonuclear.

termostato [termo'stato] *sm* thermostat.

ternero [ter'nero] *sm* calf; veal.

terneza [ter'neθa] *sf* tenderness; endearment.

ternilla [ter'niʎa] *sf* gristle.

terquedad [terke'ðað] *sf* stubbornness, obstinacy.

terraplén [terra'plen] *sm* terrace; embankment.

terraza [ter'raθa] *sf* terrace.

terremoto [terre'moto] *sm* earthquake.

terreno [ter'reno] *sm* terrain; land. **ceder terreno** give ground.

terrestre [ter'restre] *adj* terrestrial.

terrible [ter'riβle] *adj* terrible. **terrífico** *adj* terrifying.

territorial [territo'rjal] *adj* territorial. **territorio** *sm* territory.

terrón [ter'ron] *sm* lump of sugar; clod of earth.

terror [ter'ror] *sm* terror. **terrorismo** *sm* terrorism. **terrorista** *s(m + f)* terrorist.

terso ['terso] *adj* smooth; glossy; polished. **tersar** *v* smooth. **tersura** *sf* smoothness.

tertulia [ter'tulja] *sf* social gathering; company.

tesauro [te'sauro] *sm* thesaurus.

tesis ['tesis] *sf invar* thesis.

tesón [te'son] *sm* tenacity; persistence; inflexibility. **tesonería** *sf* doggedness.

tesoro [te'soro] *sm* treasure. **tesorería** *sf* treasury. **tesorero, -a** *sm, sf* treasurer.

testa ['testa] *sf* head.

testar [tes'tar] *v* make a will. **testamento** *sm* will, testament.

testarudo [testa'ruðo] *adj* stubborn, obstinate. **testarudez** *sf* obstinacy.

testificar [testifi'kar] *v* testify; witness. **testigo** *sm* witness. **testimonial** *adj* bearing witness. **testimoniar** *v* bear witness to. **testimonio** *sm* witness; testimony.

testículo [tes'tikulo] *sm* testicle.

teta ['teta] *sf* teat, nipple; mammary gland; udder.

tetera [te'tera] *sf* teapot.

tétrico ['tetriko] *adj* gloomy; grave; sullen.

textil [teks'til] *sm, adj* textile.

texto ['teksto] *sm* text; textbook.

textura [teks'tura] *sf* texture.

tez [teθ] *sf* complexion, skin.

ti [ti] *pron (fam)* you. **de ti para mi** between you and me.

tía ['tia] *sf* aunt; old mother; *(fam)* tart. **no hay tu tía** nothing doing.

tibio ['tiβjo] *adj* lukewarm. **tibieza** *sf* tepidity.

tiburón [tiβu'ron] *sm* shark.

tiempo ['tjempo] *sm* time; weather; *(gram)* tense. **al poco tiempo** soon after. **tiempo atrás** some time ago. **tiempo de perros** filthy weather.

tienda ['tjenda] *sf* shop, store; tent. **tienda de modas** boutique.

tienta ['tjenta] *sf* probe. **andar a tientas** feel one's way.

tiento ['tjento] *sm* feel, tough; tact. **a tiento** by touch.

tierno ['tjerno] *adj* tender; fresh. **pan tierno** fresh bread.

tierra ['tjerra] *sf* earth; land; country; ground. **echar por tierra** wreck. **tierra vegetal** topsoil.

tieso ['tjeso] *adj* stiff; firm. *adv* strongly. **tiesura** *sf* stiffness.

tiesto ['tjesto] *sm* flower pot.

tifo ['tifo] *sm* typhus.

tifoideo [tifoi'ðeo] *adj* typhoid. **fiebre tifoidea** *sf* typhoid fever.

tifón [ti'fon] *sm* typhoon.

tigre ['tigre] *sm* tiger.

tijeras [ti'xeras] *sf pl* scissors; shears.

tilín [ti'lin] *sm* ting-a-ling. **en un tilín** in a flash.

tilo ['tilo] *sm* lime, linden tree.

timar [ti'mar] *v* cheat. **timador** *sm* swindler.

timbrar [tim'brar] *v* stamp; seal. **timbre** *sm* bell; postage stamp.

tímido ['timiðo] *adj* timid. **timidez** *sf* timidity.

timo ['timo] *sm* cheat; swindle.

timón [ti'mon] *sm* helm; rudder. **timonear** *v* (*mar*) steer. **timonero** *sm* helmsman.

tímpano ['timpano] *sm* (*anat*) eardrum; (*música*) kettledrum.

tina ['tina] *sf* tub. **tinaja** *sf* large earthen jar.

tinglado [tin'glaðo] *sm* shed; platform.

tinieblas [ti'njeβlas] *sf pl* darkness *sing*; (*fig*) confusion *sing*.

tino ['tino] *sm* tact; moderation; skill, **sin tino** stupidly.

tinta ['tinta] *sf* ink; hue, colour. **tinte** *sm* dye; stain; shade. **tintero** *sm* inkstand, inkwell. **tintorería** *sf* dyeing; dry-cleaning. **tintorero, -a** *sm, sf* dyer; dry-cleaner. **tintura** *sf* dye; rouge.

tintín [tin'tin] *sm* tinkle. **tintinear** *v* tinkle.

tinto ['tinto] *adj* dyed. **vino tinto** *sm* red wine.

tiña ['tiɲa] *sf* ringworm.

tío ['tio] *sm* uncle.

tiovivo [tjo'βiβo] *sm* merry-go-round.

típico ['tipiko] *adj* typical; characteristic.

tiple ['tiple] *sm* (*música*) treble. *sf* soprano.

tipo ['tipo] *sm* type, pattern; model; standard; (*fam*) fellow. **tipo de cambio** rate of exchange. **tipo de interés** interest rate. **tipo de letra** font (type).

tipografía [tipogra'fia] *sf* printing. **tipógrafo** *sm* printer.

tira ['tira] *sf* long strip, band.

tirada [ti'raða] *sf* throw; stretch; circulation. **tirador** *sm* marksman; handle.

tirado [ti'raðo] *adj* streamlined; (*fam*) dead easy; (*fam*) dirt cheap.

tiranía [tira'nia] *sf* tyranny. **tirano, -a** *sm, sf* tyrant. **tiranizar** *v* tyrannize.

tirante [ti'rante] *adj* taut. **tirantez** *sf* tautness.

tirar [ti'rar] *v* throw, fling; pull. **tirar por una calle** turn down a street.

tiritar [tiri'tar] *v* shiver. **tiritón** *sm* shiver.

tiro ['tiro] *sm* throw; shot; discharge; report; blow; practical joke. **tiro al blanco** target practice.

tiroides [ti'rojðes] *sm* thyroid.

tirón [ti'ron] *sm* haul, jerk; cramp; tyro, beginner. **de un tirón** straight off.

tiroteo [tiro'teo] *sm* firing, crossfire. **tirotear** *v* snipe at.

tisis ['tisis] *sf* tuberculosis.

títere ['titere] *sm* puppet; marionette.

titubear [tituβe'ar] *v* vacillate; totter, stagger; stammer. **titubeo** *sm* staggering; hesitation.

título ['titulo] *sm* title; license, diploma; degree. **titular** *adj* titular.

tiza ['tiθa] *sf* chalk.

tiznar [tiθ'nar] *v* stain, tarnish. **tiznado** *adj* stained, grimy. **tiznajo** *sm* smudge.

toalla [to'aʎa] *sf* towel. **toalla de baño** bathtowel. **toallero** *sm* towel-rail.

tobillo [to'βiʎo] *sm* ankle.

tobogán [toβa'gan] *sm* slide; chute.

tocadiscos [toka'ðiskos] *sm invar* record-player.

tocado [to'kaðo] *sm* coiffure.

tocador [toka'ðor] *sm* dressing-table.

tocar [to'kar] *v* touch; feel; (*música*) play; belong; concern; border on; be one's turn. **tocarse** *v* put on one's hat.

tocino [to'θino] *sm* bacon; salt pork.

todavía [toða'βia] *adv* yet, still; nevertheless. **todavía más** even more.

todo ['toðo] *adj* all; entire; every; each. **todo el mundo** everybody. **todo o nada** all or nothing.

todoterreno *sm* four-wheel drive (vehicle).

toldo ['tolðo] *sm* awning.

tolerar [tole'rar] *v* tolerate; bear. **tolerable** *adj* tolerable. **tolerancia** *sf* tolerance. **tolerante** *adj* tolerant.

toma de corriente *sf* power point.

tomar [to'mar] *v* take; hold; get; gather. **tomarse** *v* get rusty. **tomada** *sf* capture. **tomadura** *sf* taking.

tomate [to'mate] *sm* tomato. **tomatera** *sf* tomato plant.

tomillo [to'miʎo] *sm* thyme.

tomo ['tomo] *sm* tome, volume; bulk.

ton [ton] *sm* motive; occasion. **sin ton ni son** without rhyme or reason.

tonada [to'naða] *sf* song. **tonalidad** *sf* tonality.

tonel [to'nel] *sm* cask, barrel.

tonelada [tone'laða] *sf* ton. **tonelaje** *sm* tonnage.

tónico [to'niko] *sm, adj* (*música*) tonic. **tonificar** *v* (*med*) tone up.

tono ['tono] *sm* (*música*) pitch; tone; manner. **darse tono** put on airs.

tontería [tonte'ria] *sf* foolishness, nonsense. **tonto** *adj* foolish, silly; stupid; ignorant.

topacio [to'paθjo] *sm* topaz.

topar [to'par] *v* collide with; strike against; encounter; meet by chance.

tope ['tope] *sm* top, summit; end. **al tope** end to end.

tópico ['topiko] *sm* topic. *adj* topical.

topless ['toples] *adj* topless.

topo ['topo] *sm* mole. **topera** *sf* molehill.

topografía [topogra'fia] *sf* topography. **topográfico** *adj* topographical.

toque ['toke] *sm* touch; peal of bells; test, trial.

tórax ['toraks] *sm* thorax.

torbellino [torβe'ʎino] *sm* whirlwind; whirlpool.

***torcer** [tor'θer] *v* twist; turn; wrench; bend. **torcedura** *sf* twisting; sprain. **torcido** *adj* twisted; bent. **torcimiento** *sm* distortion.

tordo ['torðo] *sm* thrush.

torear [tore'ar] *v* fight the bull. **torero** *sm* bullfighter.

tormenta [tor'menta] *sf* storm. **tormentoso** *adj* stormy.

tormentar [tormen'tar] *v* torment. **tormento** *sm* torment; affliction; pain.

tornar [tor'nar] *v* turn; return; do again. **torna** *sf* return. **tornarse** *v* become.

tornasol [torna'sol] *sm* (*bot*) sunflower; litmus.

torneo [tor'neo] *sm* tournament.

tornillo [tor'niʎo] *sm* screw.

torniquete [torni'kete] *sm* tourniquet; turnstile.

toro ['toro] *sm* bull. **toros** *sm pl* bullfight.

toronja [to'ronxa] *sf* grapefruit.

torpe ['torpe] *adj* clumsy; indecent. **torpeza** *sf* clumsiness; indecency.

torpedo [tor'peðo] *sm* torpedo. **torpedero** *sm* torpedo-boat.

tórpido ['torpiðo] *adj* torpid. **torpor** *sm* torpor.

torre ['torre] *sf* tower.

torrente [tor'rente] *sm* torrent. **torrencial** *adj* torrential.

tórrido ['torriðo] *adj* torrid.

torta ['torta] *sf* cake; pie. **tortada** *sf* meat pie. **tortera** *sf* pie dish.

tortilla [tor'tiʎa] *sf* omelette.

tortuga [tor'tuga] *sf* tortoise; turtle.

tortura [tor'tura] *sf* torture. **tortuoso** *adj* tortuous.

tos [tos] *sf* cough. **tos ferina** whooping-cough. **toser** *v* cough.

tosco ['tosko] *adj* coarse; crude; clumsy. **tosquedad** *sf* roughness; crudeness.

***tostar** [tos'tar] *v* toast; roast; tan. **tostada** *sf* piece of toast.

total [to'tal] *sm* total. **totalidad** *sf* totality. **totalitario** *adj* totalitarian. **totalizar** *v* total.

tóxico ['toksiko] *sm* poison. *adj* poisonous. **toxicar** *v* poison.

toxicómano [toksi'komano], **-a** *sm, sf* drug-addict. **toxicomanía** *sf* drug-addiction.

tozudo [to'θuðo] *adj* stubborn.

traba ['traβa] *sf* link; fetter; hindrance. **poner trabas** hinder. **trabadura** *sf* bond. **trabamiento** *sm* joining. **trabar** *v* join; fetter; strike up. **trabar amistad** become friends. **trabón** *sm* fetter.

trabajar [traβa'xar] *v* work; work on; elaborate; trouble; deal in. **trabajado** *adj* elaborate. **trabajador, -a** *sm, sf* worker. **trabajo** *sm* work; toil; exertion; hardship. **trabajoso** *adj* laborious.

trabalenguas [traβa'lengwas] *sm invar* tongue-twister.

tracción [trak'θjon] *sf* traction. **tractor** *sm* tractor.

tradición [traði'θjon] *sf* tradition. **tradicional** *adj* traditional.

***traducir** [traðu'θir] *v* translate; interpret. **traducción** *sf* translation. **traductor, -a** *sm, sf* translator.

***traer** [tra'er] *v* bring; carry; fetch; result in; wear. **traer a mal traer** treat roughly. **traer a cuento** mention. **traerse** *v* be dressed; behave.

traficar [trafi'kar] *v* trade; travel. **trafi-**

cante s(m + f) dealer. **tráfico** sm trade; traffic.

tragaluz [traga'luθ] sf skylight.

tragar [tra'gar] v swallow. **no puedo tragarle** I can't stand him. **tragadero** sm gullet. **trago** sm swallow; gulp.

tragedia [tra'xeðia] sf tragedy. **trágico** adj tragic.

traicionar [traiθjo'nar] v betray. **traición** sf treason; treachery. **traicionero** adj treacherous. **traidor, -a** sm, sf traitor.

traje ['traxe] sm dress; suit; costume. **traje de etiqueta** evening dress. **baile de trajes** sm fancy-dress ball.

trajín [tra'xin] sm haulage; coming and going. **trajinante** sm (com) carrier.

tramar [tra'mar] v weave; plan, plot. **trama** sf weft; plot.

tramitar [trami'tar] v negotiate, arrange. **tramitación** sf arrangements pl. **trámite** sm procedure; formality.

tramo ['tramo] sm (puente) span; (escaleras) flight; (terreno) strip.

trampa ['trampa] sf trap; trapdoor; fraud. **tramposo** adj deceitful.

trampear [trampe'ar] v defraud; scrape by. **trampeador, -a** sm, sf swindler.

trampolín [trampo'lin] sm ski jump; springboard.

trancar [tran'kar] v (puerta) bar; stride. **tranca** sf stick; club; (fam) drunkenness. **tranco** sm stride.

trance ['tranθe] sm trance; critical situation. **a todo trance** at all costs.

tranquilizar [trankili'θar] v tranquillize. **tranquilidad** sf tranquillity. **tranquilo** adj tranquil.

transacción [transak'θjon] sf transaction.

transatlántico [transat'lantiko] adj transatlantic. sm (mar) liner.

transbordar [transβor'ðar] v transfer. **transbordo** sm transfer.

transcribir [transkri'βir] v transcribe. **transcripción** sf transcription.

transcurrir [transkur'rir] v elapse, pass. **transcurso** sm course or lapse of time.

transeúnte [transe'unte] adj transitory, transient. s(m + f) transient, passer-by.

***transferir** [transfe'rir] v transfer. **transferible** adj transferable.

transfigurar [transfigu'rar] v transfigure. **transfiguración** sf transfiguration.

transformar [transfor'mar] v transform. **transformación** sf transformation.

tránsfuga ['transfuga] sm deserter.

***transgredir** [transgre'ðir] v transgress, violate. **transgresión** sf transgression. **transgresor, -a** sm, sf transgressor.

transgénico [trans'xeniko] adj genetically modified.

transición [transi'θjon] sf transition.

transido [tran'siðo] adj overwhelmed; stricken.

transigir [transi'xir] v compromise. **transigencia** sf tolerance. **transigeate** adj tolerant.

transistor [transis'tor] sm transistor.

transistar [transi'tar] v travel; pass. **transitivo** adj (gram) transitive. **tránsito** sm transit; passage; transition. **transitorio** adj transitory.

transmitir [transmi'tir] v transmit. **transmisión** sf transmission. **transmisor** sm transmitter.

transparencia [transpa'renθja] sf transparency. **transparente** adj transparent.

transpirar [transpi'rar] v perspire; transpire. **transpiración** sf perspiration.

***transponer** [transpo'ner] v transpose; transplant. **transponerse** v get down; get sleepy.

transportar [transpor'tar] v transport; (música) transpose. **transportarse** get carried away. **transporte** sm transport. **transposición** sf transposition.

tranvía [tran'βia] sm tramway; tram.

trapaza [tra'paθa] sf swindle, fraud; trick. **trapacear** v defraud. **trapacista** s(m + f) swindler.

trapecio [tra'peθjo] sm trapeze.

trapo ['trapo] sm rag. pl old clothes.

traquetear [trakete'ar] v shake up; rattle. **traqueteo** sm rattling; jolting.

tras [tras] prep after; behind; beyond. **tras de** in addition to.

***trascender** [trasθen'der] v transcend; leak out; spread. **trascendencia** sf transcendence. **trascendental** adj momentous. **trascendente** adj transcendent.

***trasegar** [trase'gar] v decant; upset.

trasero [tra'sero] adj rear. sm behind. **trasera** sf back; rear.

trasladar [trasla'ðar] v transfer; translate; postpone. **trasladarse** v go; move.

traslación *sf* transfer; translation. **traslado** *sm* copy; transfer.

***traslucirse** [traslu'θirse] *v* shine; show through. **traslúcido** *adj* translucent.

traslumbrar [traslum'brar] *v* dazzle.

trasmutar [trasmu'tar] *v* transmute. **trasmutación** *sf* transmutation.

trasnochar [trasno'tʃar] *v* be up all *or* most of the night.

traspasar [traspa'sar] *v* transfer; transfix; transgress. **traspasador, -a** *sm, sf* transgressor. **traspaso** *sm* transfer; transgression.

traspié [tras'pje] *sm* stumble.

trasplantar [trasplan'tar] *v* transplant. **trasplantarse** *v* migrate. **trasplante** *sm* transplant.

trasquilar [traski'lar] *v* shear, snip, clip. **trasquilado** *adj* sheared; cropped.

traste ['traste] *sm* (*música*) fret. **ir al traste** fall through, fail.

trasto ['trasto] *sm* tool; weapon; equipment; piece of furniture.

trastornar [trastor'nar] *v* upset; turn upside down. **trastornado** *adj* unbalanced. **trastorno** *sm* upheaval; inconvenience.

trasunto [tra'sunto] *sm* copy, reproduction; likeness. **trasuntar** *v* copy.

tratar [tra'tar] *v* treat; deal with; handle. **tratable** *adj* manageable. **tratamiento** *sm* treatment. **trato** *sm* treatment; behaviour; bargain. **mal trato** ill-treatment.

través [tra'βes] *sm* slant; bias; reverse. **a través de** across.

travesero [traβe'sero] *adj* transverse. **travesía** *sf* crossroad.

travesura [traβe'sura] *sf* trick, prank.

traviesa [tra'βjesa] *sf* (*ferrocarril*) sleeper; (*arq*) rafter; bet.

travieso [tra'βjeso] *adj* transverse, cross; lively; mischievous. **a campo traviesa** cross-country.

trayecto [tra'jekto] *sm* route; fare stage; distance; way; itinerary. **trayectoria** *sf* trajectory.

trazar [tra'θar] *v* draw; plot; trace; design. **traza** *sf* sketch. **bien/mal trazado** good/bad looking. **trazador, -a** *sm, sf* designer.

trébol ['treβol] *sm* clover.

trece ['treθe] *adj, sm* thirteen.

trecho ['tretʃo] *sm* space; distance; lapse; stretch.

tregua ['tregwa] *sf* truce; respite.

treinta ['treinta] *adj, sm* thirty.

tremendo [tre'mendo] *adj* tremendous.

trémulo ['tremulo] *adj* tremulous.

tren [tren] *sm* train. **tren botijo** excursion train.

trenzar [tren'θar] *v* braid. **trenza** *sf* plait, braid.

trementina [tremen'tina] *sf* turpentine.

trepar [tre'par] *v* climb. **trepa** *sf* climbing. **trepadoras** *sf pl* climbing plants.

trepidar [trepi'ðar] *v* shake, tremble. **trepidación** *sf* tremor.

tres [tres] *adj, sm* three.

triángulo [tri'angulo] *sm* triangle. **triangular** *adj* triangular.

triángulo de seguridad *sm* warning triangle.

tribu ['triβu] *sf* tribe.

tribuna [tri'βuna] *sf* tribune; gallery; grandstand. **tribunal** *sm* tribunal.

tributar [triβu'tar] *v* pay. **tributable** *adj* tributary. **tributación** *sf* tax. **tributante** *s(m + f)* taxpayer. **tributo** *sm* tribute; tax.

triciclo [tri'θiklo] *sm* tricycle.

tricotar [triko'tar] *v* knit.

trigo ['trigo] *sm* wheat. **trigal** *sm* wheatfield.

trigésimo [tri'xesimo] *adj* thirtieth.

trigonometría [trigonome'tria] *sf* trigonometry.

trillar [tri'ʎar] *v* thresh; beat. **trilla** *sf* threshing. **trillador, -a** *sm, sf* threshing machine.

trimestre [tri'mestre] *sm* three-month term. **trimestral** *adj* quarterly.

trinar [tri'nar] *v* trill. **trinado** *sm* trill.

trincar [trin'kar] *v* break; bind; hold down.

trinchar [trin'tʃar] *v* carve. **trinchante** *sm* carving-knife. **trinchero** *adj* carving.

trinchera [trin'tʃera] *sf* trench.

trineo [tri'neo] *sm* sledge, sled, sleigh.

trinidad [trini'ðað] *sf* trinity.

trinitaria [trini'tarja] *sf* pansy.

tripa ['tripa] *sf* intestine. **tener malas tripas** be cruel.

triple ['triple] *adj* triple.

trípode ['tripoðe] *sm* tripod.

tripulación [tripula'θjon] *sf* crew. **tripulante** *sm* member of the crew.

triscar [tris'kar] *v* mingle; stamp; frisk.

trisca *sf* crunch.

triste ['triste] *adj* sad, mournful, gloomy. **tristeza** *sf* sadness.

triturar [tritu'rar] *v* grind, crush. **trituración** *sf* grinding.

triunfar [triun'far] *v* triumph. **triunfador, -a** *sm, sf* victor. **triunfal** *adj* triumphal. **triunfante** *adj* triumphant. **triunfo** *sm* triumph.

trivial [tri'βjal] *adj* trivial. **trivialidad** *sf* triviality.

triza ['triθa] *sf* shred; particle, fragment.

trocar [tro'kar] *v* exchange. **trocarse** *v* change into. **trocamiento** *sm* exchange.

trochemoche [trotʃe'motʃe] *adv* higgledy-piggledy.

trofeo [tro'feo] *sm* trophy.

trole ['trole] *sm* trolley.

tromba ['tromba] *sf* waterspout.

trombón [trom'bon] *sm* trombone.

trompa ['trompa] *sf* hunting horn; (*elefante*) trunk; proboscis.

trompada [trom'paða] *sf* bump; thump.

trompeta [trom'peta] *sf* trumpet. **trompetero** *sm* trumpeter.

*tronar [tro'nar] *v* thunder. **tronada** *sf* thunderstorm. **tronante** *adj* thunderous. **tronido** *sm* thunderclap.

tronco ['tronko] *sm* tree trunk; stalk; stern.

tronchar [tron'tʃar] *v* bring down; break up.

trono ['trono] *sm* throne.

tropa ['tropa] *sf* troop.

tropel [tro'pel] *sm* crowd. **en tropel** in a rush. **tropelía** *sf* rush, hurry.

*tropezar [trope'θar] *v* stumble; run into. **tropiezo** *sm* stumble.

trópico ['tropiko] *sm* tropic. **tropical** *adj* tropical.

trotar [tro'tar] *v* trot. **trote** *sm* trot.

trozo ['troθo] *sm* piece, fragment, bit.

truco ['truko] *sm* trick.

trucha ['trutʃa] *sf* trout; (*mec*) crane.

trueno [tru'eno] *sm* thunder.

trueque [tru'eke] *sm* exchange, barter.

trufa ['trufa] *sf* truffle.

truncar [trun'kar] *v* truncate, abridge. **truncado** *adj* truncated.

tu [tu] *adj* (*fam*) your.

tú [tu] *pron* (*fam*) you.

tubérculo [tu'βerkulo] *sm* tubercle; tuber.

tuberculosis *sf* tuberculosis. **tuberculoso** *adj* tubercular.

tubo ['tuβo] *sm* tube, pipe. **tubería** *sf* tubing. **tubular** *adj* tubular.

tuerca ['twerka] *sf* (*mec*) nut. **tuerca a mariposa** wing nut.

tuerto, -a ['twerto] *sm, sf* one-eyed person. *adj* one-eyed.

tuétano [tu'etano] *sm* (*anat*) marrow.

tufo ['tufo] *sm* vapour; fume; stench. **tufarada** *sf* whiff.

tul [tul] *sm* tulle.

tulipán [tuli'pan] *sm* tulip.

tullido [tu'ʎiðo] *adj* cripple. **tullirse** *v* be crippled.

tumba¹ ['tumba] *sf* tomb.

tumba² *sf* tumble. **tumbar** *v* knock down; tumble.

tumor [tu'mor] *sm* tumour.

tumulto [tu'multo] *sm* tumult. **tumultuoso** *adj* tumultuous.

tunante [tu'nante] *s(m + f)* rascal, crook. *adj* rascally. **tunantería** *sf* crookedness.

túnel ['tunel] *sm* tunnel.

túnica ['tunika] *sf* tunic.

tuno ['tuno] *sm* rogue.

tupé [tu'pe] *sm* toupee.

tupido [tu'piðo] *adj* thick; dense.

turba ['turβa] *sf* crowd; heap; peat. **turbal** *sm* peat bog.

turbante [tur'βante] *sm* turban.

turbar [tur'βar] *v* disturb. **turbarse** *v* be embarrassed.

turbina [tur'βina] *sf* turbine.

turbulento [turβu'lento] *adj* turbulent, disorderly. **turbulencia** *sf* turbulence.

turismo [tu'rismo] *sm* tourism. **turista** *s(m + f)* tourist.

turnar [tur'nar] *v* alternate, take turns. **turno** *sm* turn, shift. **por turno** in turn.

turón [tu'ron] *sm* polecat.

turquesa [tur'kesa] *sf* turquoise.

turrón [tur'ron] *sm* nougat.

tutear [tute'ar] *v* address as *tú*.

tutela [tu'tela] *sf* protection; tutelage. **tutelar** *adj* guardian.

tutor [tu'tor] *sm* tutor; guardian. **tutoría** *sf* guardianship.

tuyo ['tujo] *pron* (*fam*) yours; of yours.

TVCC *sf* CCTV.

U

u [u] *conj* or (before words beginning with *o* or *ho*).

ubicar [uβi'kar] *v* be situated; (*auto*) park. **ubicarse** *v* place oneself. **ubicuidad** *sf* ubiquity. **ubicuo** *adj* ubiquitous.

ubre ['uβre] *sf* udder.

Ucrania [u'kranja] *sf* Ukraine. **ucraniano** *adj* Ukrainian.

UE *sf* EU.

ufanarse [ufa'narse] *v* boast. **ufano** *adj* proud, conceited. **ufanía** *sf* pride, arrogance.

ujier [u'xjer] *sm* usher.

úlcera ['ulθera] *sf* ulcer. **ulcerado** *adj* ulcer-ed.

ulterior [ulte'rjor] *adj* further, farther; ulterior. **ulteriormente** *adj* later.

ultimar [ulti'mar] *v* conclude, finish. **ultimación** *sf* conclusion. **últimamente** *adv* finally; recently. **ultimátum** *sm* ultimatum. **último** *adj* last; latest. **por último** finally.

ultrajar [ultra'xar] *v* outrage; insult. **ultraje** *sm* outrage. **ultrajoso** *adj* outrageous.

ultramarino [ultrama'rino] *adj* overseas. **ultramar** *sm* overseas countries *pl*. **ir a ultramar** go abroad.

ultranza [ul'tranθa] *adv* **a ultranza** to the death; at all costs.

ultrasonido [ultraso'niðo] *sm* ultrasound.

umbral [um'bral] *sm* threshold. **pisar los umbrales** cross the threshold.

umbrío [um'brio] *adj also* **umbroso** shady.

un [un] *art also* **una** a; one. *adj* one.

unánime [u'nanime] *adj* unanimous. **unanimidad** *sf* unanimity.

unción [un'θjon] *sf* anointing, unction. **extremaunción** *sf* (*rel*) extreme unction.

uncir [un'θir] *v* yoke.

undécimo [un'deθimo], **-a** *s*, *adj* eleventh.

undoso [un'doso] *adj* wavy. **undulación** *sf* undulation. **undulante** *adj* undulating. **undular** *v* undulate.

ungir [un'xir] *v* anoint. **ungimiento** *sm* unction. **ungüento** *sm* ointment.

único ['uniko] *adj* only, sole, single; unique. **únicamente** *adv* only, solely. **único intento** one-off.

unicornio [uni'kornjo] *sm* unicorn.

unidad [uni'ðað] *sf* unity; union; unit. **unidad de disco** *sf* disk drive. **unido** *adj* united. **unificación** *sf* unification. **unificar** *v* unify.

uniformar [unifor'mar] *v* make uniform; standardize. **uniforme** *adj*, *sm* uniform. **uniformidad** *sf* uniformity.

unión [u'njon] *sf* union; unity; marriage. **unir** *v* join; mix. **unirse** *v* join; mingle.

Unión Europea *sf* European Union.

Unión Soviética [u'njon so'βjetika] *sf* Soviet Union.

unísono [u'nisono] *adj* harmonious. **al unísono** in unison; unanimously.

universidad [uniβersi'ðað] *sf* university. **universitario** *adj* of a university.

universo [uni'βerso] *sm* universe. **universal** *adj* universal. **universalidad** *sf* universality.

uno ['uno] *adj* one; only. *pron* one; someone. **unos** *pron pl* some; a few. **unos y otros** all.

untar [un'tar] *v* grease; smear; stain; spread. **unto** *sm* grease; ointment.

uña ['uɲa] *sf* (*anat*) nail; talon, claw; hoof. **esconder las uñas** hide one's feelings. **uñero** *sm* ingrowing toenail.

uranio [u'ranjo] *sm* uranium.

urbano [ur'βano] *adj* urban; urbane. **urbanidad** *sf* urbanity. **urbanístico** *adj* urban. **urbanización** *sf* town planning. **urbe** *sf* large city.

urdir [ur'ðir] *v* warp; (*fig*) plot, scheme.

urgencia [ur'xenθja] *sf* urgency; emergency. **urgente** *adj* urgent. **urgir** *v* be urgent; urge. **me urge el tiempo** I am pressed for time.

urinario [uri'narjo] *sm* urinal.

urna ['urna] *sf* urn; ballot box.

urogallo [uro'ɣaʎo] *sm* (*zool*) grouse.

urraca [u'raka] *sf* magpie.

usar [u'sar] *v* use; employ; be accustomed. **usado** *adj* used; worn. **usanza** *sf* custom; usage. **uso** *sm* use; wear; custom; enjoyment; fashion. **al uso de** in the style of.

usted [u'steð] *pron also* **Vd** you. **¡a usted!** thank you!

usual [u'swal] *adj* usual.

usufructo [u'sufrukto] *sm* use; enjoyment.

usura [u'sura] *sf* usury. **usurero, -a** *sm*, *sf* usurer.

usurpar [usur'par] *v* usurp. **usurpación** *sf* usurpation. **usurpador, -a** *sm, sf* usurper.

utensilio [uten'siljo] *sm* utensil; implement, tool.

útero ['utero] *sm* uterus. **uterino** *adj* uterine.

útil ['util] *sm* tool. *adj* useful; fit. **utilidad** *sf* utility, usefulness. **utilitario** *adj* utilitarian. **utilizar** *v* utilize, use.

uva ['uβa] *sf* grape. **uva pasa** raisin.

V

vaca ['βaka] *sf* cow; beef.

vacaciones [baka'θjones] *sf pl* vacation *sing*; holidays *pl*. **irse de vacaciones** go on holiday.

vacante [βa'kante] *adj* vacant. *sf* vacancy. **vacar** *v* fall vacant.

vacilar [βaθi'lar] *v* hesitate. **vacilante** *adj* unstable, unsteady. **vacilación** *sf* vacillation.

vacío [βa'θio] *adj* empty. *sm* void; vacuum. **vaciar** *v* empty; pour out. **vacuo** *adj* empty; vacuous.

vacunar [βaku'nar] *v* vaccinate. **vacunación** *sf* vaccination.

vadear [βaðe'ar] *v* wade; surmount, overcome. **vadeable** *adj* fordable.

vagar [βa'gar] *v* wander, move about. *sm* leisure; ease. **vagabundo, -a** *sm, sf* vagabond. **vagante** *adj* vagrant.

vago ['βago] *adj* vague; indolent. *sm* tramp; loafer. **vaguedad** *sf* vagueness.

vagón [βa'gon] *sm* railway carriage; wagon. **vagón restaurante** dining-car. **vagoneta** *sf* small truck.

vahear [βae'ar] *v* steam. **vaho** *sm* vapour.

vahído [βa'iðo] *sm* vertigo, dizziness.

vaina ['βaina] *sf* sheath; scabbard; pod.

vainilla [βai'niʎa] *sf* vanilla.

vaivén [βai'βen] *sm* fluctuation; sway; swinging movement.

vajilla [βa'xiʎa] *sf* tableware, dishes *pl*.

vale ['βale] *sm* voucher; receipt; IOU.

valedero [βale'ðero] *adj* valid.

valentía [βalen'tia] *sf* valour, courage; brave *or* courageous act; bragging. **valen-**

tón, -ona *sm, sf* braggart.

***valer** [βa'ler] *v* be worth; cost; be equal to. **vale la pena** be worthwhile. **válgame la frase** if you dont't mind my saying so. **valerse** *v* make use of. **valía** *sf* value, worth.

valeroso [βale'roso] *adj* brave; valuable.

validar [βali'ðar] *v* validate; make binding. **validación** *sf* validation; ratification. **válido** *adj* valid. **validez** *sf* validity.

valiente [βa'ljente] *adj* valiant, courageous; strong; first-rate.

valija [βa'lixa] *sf* valise; case; mail bag.

valimiento [βali'mjento] *sm* value; good will; protection; favour.

valor [βa'lor] *sm* value, worth; price; valour, courage. *adj* valuable. **valoración** *sf* valuation. **valorar** *v* value, appraise.

valsar [βal'sar] *v* waltz. **vals** *sm* waltz.

valuar [βalu'ar] *v* value, appraise, assess. **valuación** *sf* valuation.

válvula ['βalβula] *sf* valve.

vallar [βa'ʎar] *v* fence in, enclose. **valla** *sf* fence. **vallado** *sm* enclosure.

valle ['βaʎe] *sm* valley.

vampiro [βam'piro] *sm* vampire.

vanagloriarse [βanaglo'rjarse] *v* boast. **vanagloria** *sf* boasting, vainglory.

vándalo ['βandalo] *sm, adj* vandal **vandalismo** *sm* vandalism.

vanguardia [βan'gwarðja] *sf* vanguard; avant-garde.

vano ['βano] *adj* vain; idle. **en vano** in vain. **vanidad** *sf* vanity. **vanidoso** *adj* vain.

vapor [βa'por] *sm* vapour; steam; (*mar*) steamer. **vaporización** *sf* evaporation. **vaporizar** *v* evaporate.

vaquero [βa'kero] *sm* cowboy. **vaquería** *sf* herd of cows.

vaqueta [βa'keta] *sf* cowhide.

vara ['βara] *sf* rod, pole, staff; (*medida*) yard. **tener vara alta** have the upper hand.

varar [βa'rar] *v* launch; run aground.

variar [βa'rjar] *v* vary, change. **variable** *adj* variable. **variación** *sf* variation. **variado** *adj* varied. **variante** *sf* variant; version.

varice [βa'riθe] *sf also* **várice** varicose vein.

varilla [βa'riʎa] *sf* small stick; jawbone; curtain rail.

vario ['βarjo] *adj* varied, diverse. **varios** *adj* several.

varón [βa'ron] *sm, adj* male. **varonil** *adj* manly, virile.

vaselina® [βase'lina] *sf* Vaseline®.

vasija [βa'sixa] *sf* vessel; bowl; dish. **vaso** *sm* glass, tumbler.

vástago ['βastaɣo] *sm* stem, shoot, sprout; scion, offspring.

vasto ['βasto] *adj* vast. **vastedad** *sf* vastness.

vaticinar [βatiθi'nar] *v* predict, foretell. **vaticinador, -a** *sm, sf* prophet, seer. **vaticinio** *sm* divination, prophecy.

vatio ['βatjo] *sm* (*elec*) watt.

vecino [βe'θino], **-a** *sm, sf* neighbour. **vecinal** *adj* local. **vecindad** *sf* neighbourhood.

vedar [βe'ðar] *v* veto; prohibit; hinder. **veda** *sf* prohibition. **vedado** *sm* game preserve.

vega ['βeɣa] *sf* plain; tract of fertile ground.

vegetación [βexeta'θjon] *sf* vegetation. **vegetal** *adj* vegetable. **vegetar** *v* grow; (*fig*) vegetate. **vegetariano, -a** *sm, sf* vegetarian. **vegeteriano estricto** *s, adj* vegan.

vehemencia [βee'menθja] *sf* vehemence. **vehemente** *adj* vehement.

vehículo [βe'ikulo] *sm* vehicle. **vehículo todo terreno** *sm* off-road vehicle.

veinte ['βeinte] *sm, adj* twenty.

vejar [βe'xar] *v* vex, harass, annoy. **vejación** *sf* vexation. **vejatorio** *adj* vexatious.

vejez [βe'xeθ] *sf* old age.

vejiga [βe'xiɣa] *sf* blister; bladder.

vela ['βela] *sf* vigil, watch; candle; sail. **velar** *v* keep watch; stay awake.

veleidad [βelei'ðað] *sf* whim; fickleness. **veleidoso** *adj* fickle.

velero [βe'lero] *sm* sailing ship; glider.

velo ['βelo] *sm* veil.

velocidad [βeloθi'ðað] *sf* velocity. **velocímetro** *sm* speedometer. **veloz** *adj* fast, quick.

vello ['βeλo] *sm* soft hair, down; fluff. **velloso** *adj* dowry.

vena ['βena] *sf* vein; scan. **trabajar por venas** work in fits and starts.

venablo [βe'naβlo] *sm* javelin.

venado [βe'naðo] *sm* deer; (*culin*) venison.

venal [βe'nal] *adj* venal.

vencer [βen'θer] *v* defeat; win; (*com*) fall due. **vencerse** *v* control oneself. **vencible** *adj* beatable. **los vencidos** the losers.

vencimiento *sm* victory; (*com*) expiration, falling due.

vendar [βen'dar] *v* bandage. **venda** *sf* also **vendaje** *sm* bandage.

vendaval [βenda'βal] *sm* gale.

vender [βen'der] *v* sell. **vendedor** *sm* seller; vendor; salesperson. **vendible** *adj* saleable.

vendimia [βen'ðimja] *sf* grape harvest; vintage.

veneno [βe'neno] *sm* venom, poison. **venenoso** *adj* poisonous.

venerar [βene'rar] *v* venerate. **venerable** *adj* venerable. **veneración** *sf* veneration.

venéreo [βe'nereo] *adj* venereal.

venero [βe'nero] *sm* spring of water; source, origin, root.

vengar [βen'gar] *v* avenge. **vengador, -a** *sm, sf* avenger. **venganza** *sf* vengeance. **vengativo** *adj* vindictive.

venia ['βenja] *sf* forgiveness, pardon; permission, leave.

*venir [βe'nir] *v* come. **venir bien** be suitable *or* convenient. **venirse** *v* come *or* go back. **venida** *sf* arrival, coming; return. **venidero** *adj* coming, future.

venta ['βenta] *sf* sale, market; inn. **venta a plazos** hire purchase. **ventero, -a** *sm, sf* innkeeper.

ventaja [βen'taxa] *sf* advantage. **ventajoso** *adj* advantageous.

ventana [βen'tana] *sf* window.

ventilar [βenti'lar] *v* ventilate. **ventilación** *sf* ventilation. **ventilador** *sm* ventilator; fan.

ventosa [βen'tosa] *sf* vent.

ventoso [βen'toso] *adj* windy. **ventosidad** *sf* flatulence.

ventrílocuo [βen'trilokwo] *sm* ventriloquist. **ventriloquia** *sf* ventriloquism.

ventura [βen'tura] *sf* joy, happiness; good luck. **mala ventura** ill luck. **venturado**, **venturero** *or* **venturoso** *adj* lucky; happy.

*ver [βer] *v* see. *sm* view; aspect; opinion; looks *pl*, appearance. **echar de ver** notice. **estar viendo** have a feeling. **vamos a ver** let's see.

vera ['βera] *sf* border, edge.

verano [βe'rano] *sm* summer. **veranear** *v* spend the summer. **veraneo** *sm* summer holiday.

veras ['βeras] *sf pl* truth *sing.* **de veras** indeed, really. **veracidad** *sf* veracity. **veraz**

adj truthful.

verbo [ˈβerβo] *sm* verb. **verbosidad** *sf* verbosity. **verboso** *adj* verbose.

verdad [βerˈðað] *sf* truth. **verdadero** *adj* true; real, authentic; sincere; truthful.

verde [ˈβerðe] *adj* green; immature; fresh; young; immodest, obscene. **darse un verde** amuse oneself.

verdugo [βerˈðugo] *sm* executioner; hangman; scourge. **verdugón** *sm* weal (from whiplash).

verdulero [βerðuˈlero] *sm* greengrocer. **verdulería** *sf* greengrocer's. **verdura** *sf* greenness. **verduras** *sf pl* vegetables.

veredicto [βereˈðikto] *sm* verdict.

vergüenza [βerˈgwenθa] *sf* shame; affront; disgrace; shyness, timidity. **sin vergüenza** shameless. **vergonzoso** *adj* shy; shameful.

verídico [βeˈriðiko] *adj* truthful.

verificar [βerifiˈkar] *v* verify; examine, inspect; check. **verificarse** *v* prove true; be verified. **verificación** *sf* verification. **verificativo** *adj* corroborative.

verosímil [βeroˈsimil] *adj* likely, probable. **verosimilitud** *sf* probability.

verruga [βerˈruga] *sf* wart.

versado [βerˈsaðo] *adj* versed, experienced; skilful.

versar [βerˈsar] *v* go round; spin. **versar sobre** to treat of, deal with.

versátil [βerˈsatil] *adj* versatile; variable; inconstant. **versatilidad** *sf* versatility; changeableness.

versículo [βerˈsikulo] *sm* verse. **versificar** *v* versify. **verso** *sm* verse. **verso suelto** blank verse.

versión [βerˈsjon] *sf* version.

vértebra [ˈβerteβra] *sf* vertebra. **vertebrado** *sm, adj* vertebrate.

***verter** [βerˈter] *v* spill, empty; pour; interpret, translate. **vertedero** *sm* drain. **vertedor** *sm* sewer.

vertical [βertiˈkal] *adj* vertical.

vértice [ˈβertiθe] *sm* apex.

vértigo [ˈβertigo] *sm* vertigo. **vertiginoso** *adj* giddy.

vesícula [βeˈsikula] *sf* (*anat*) vesicle; blister.

vestíbulo [βesˈtiβulo] *sm* vestibule, entrance hall; lobby.

vestigio [βesˈtixjo] *sm* vestige; footstep; trace.

***vestir** [βesˈtir] *v* dress; clothe. **vestirse** get

dressed. **vestido** *sm* dress.

veta [ˈβeta] *sf* vein of ore, etc.; grain in wood; streak.

veterano [βeteˈrano] *sm, adj* veteran.

veterinaria [βeteriˈnarja] *sf* veterinary science. **veterinario** *sm* vet.

veto [ˈβeto] *sm* veto.

vez [βeθ] *sf* turn; time; occasion. **a la vez** at once. **a veces** sometimes. **otra vez** once more. **tal vez** perhaps.

vía [ˈβia] *sf* road; way; track. **vía aérea** air mail. **en vías de** in the process of. **Vía Láctea** Milky Way.

viable [ˈβjaβle] *adj* viable.

viaducto [βjaˈðukto] *sm* viaduct.

viajar [βjaˈxar] *v* travel. **viajante** *s(m + f)* traveller. **viaje** *sm* trip, journey. **viajero, -a** *sm, sf* traveller; passenger.

víbora [ˈβiβora] *sf* viper.

vibrar [βiˈβrar] *v* vibrate, shake. **vibración** *sf* vibration. **vibrador** *sm* vibrator. **vibrante** *adj* vibrating; vibrant.

vicario [βiˈkarjo] *sm* vicar.

viciar [βiˈθjar] *v* vitiate; corrupt. **vicio** *sm* vice; defect. **de vicio** for no reason at all. **vicioso** *adj* vicious.

vicisitud [βiθisiˈtuð] *sf* vicissitude, mishap.

víctima [ˈβiktima] *sf* victim; sacrifice.

victoria [βikˈtorja] *sf* victory. **victorioso** *adj* victorious.

vid [βið] *sf* vine.

vida [ˈβiða] *sf* life. **en mi vida** never in my life. **nivel de vida** *sm* standard of living.

vídeo [ˈβiðeo] *sm* video (film/recorder). **videocámara** *sf* camcorder.

vidriar [βiˈðrjar] *v* glaze. **vidriera** *sf* stained glass. **vidrio** *sm* glass. **vidrioso** *adj* glassy.

viejo [ˈβjexo] *adj* old. *sm* old man. **vieja** *sf* old woman.

viento [ˈβjento] *sm* wind.

vientre [ˈβjentre] *sm* abdomen, belly; womb; bowels *pl*.

viernes [ˈβjernes] *sm* Friday. **Viernes Santo** Good Friday.

viga [ˈβiga] *sf* beam; timber.

vigente [βiˈxente] *adj* (*jur*) in force, valid. **vigencia** *sf* validity. **en vigencia** in effect; in force.

vigésimo [βiˈxesimo] *adj* twentieth.

vigilar [βixiˈlar] *v* watch over. **vigilancia** *sf* vigilance. **vigilante** *adj* vigilant. **vigilia** *sf* watchfulness; vigil.

vigor [βi'gor] *sm* vigour. **vigoroso** *adj* vigorous.

VIH *sm* HIV. **VIH-positivo** *adj* HIV-positive.

vil [βil] *adj* vile. **vileza** *sf* vileness.

vilo ['βilo] *adv* **en vilo** aloft; suspended; (*fig*) on tenterhooks.

villa ['βiʎa] *sf* villa; town.

villancico [βiʎan'θiko] *sm* Christmas carol.

villanía [βiʎa'nia] *sf* villainy; coarse expression.

vinagre [βi'nagre] *sm* vinegar. **vinagroso** *adj* vinegary.

vínuclo ['βinkulo] *sm* link; chain; tie.

vindicar [βindi'kar] *v* vindicate. **vindicación** *sf* vindication.

vino ['βino] *sm* wine. **vino tinto** red wine. **vino de solera** vintage wine. **vinícola** *adj* relating to wine *or* wine production. **viña** *sf* vineyard.

viñeta [βi'neta] *sf* vignette.

violar [βjo'lar] *v* violate; rape. **violación** *sf* violation; rape. **violador** *sm* rapist.

violencia [βjo'lenθja] *sf* violence. **violentar** *v* force, open by force; violate; do violence to.

violeta [βjo'leta] *adj, sf* violet.

violín [βjo'lin] *sm* violin. **violinista** *s(m + f)* violinist. **violón** *sm* double-bass.

virar [βi'rar] *v* veer; change direction; (*mar*) tack.

virgen [βir'xen] *adj, sf* virgin. **virginidad** *sf* virginity.

viril [βi'ril] *adj* virile. **virilidad** *sf* virility.

virtual [βir'twal] *adj* virtual; potential. **realidad virtual** virtual reality.

virtud [βir'tuð] *sf* virtue. **virtuoso** *adj* virtuous. **virtuosidad** *sf* virtuosity.

viruela [βi'rwela] *sf* smallpox.

virulencia [βiru'lenθja] *sf* virulence. **virulento** *adj* virulent.

visado [βi'saðo] *sm* visa.

visaje [βi'saxe] *sm* smirk, grimace. **visajero** *adj* grimacing.

vísceras ['βisθeras] *sf pl* viscera *pl*.

viscoso [βis'koso] *adj* viscous. **viscosidad** *sf* viscosity.

visera [βi'sera] *sf* visor.

visible [βi'siβle] *adj* visible. **visibilidad** *sf* visibility.

visión [βi'sjon] *sf* vision, eyesight; dream,

fantasy; view. **visionario, -a** *sm, sf* visionary.

visitar [βisi'tar] *v* visit; inspect. **visita** *sf* visit; visitor. **hacer una visita** pay a visit.

vislumbrar [βislum'brar] *v* catch a glimpse of. **vislumbre** *sf* glimpse; glimmer.

viso ['βiso] *sm* aspect, appearance; gleam.

víspera ['βispera] *sf* eve; (*fig*) approach. **en vísperas de** on the eve of.

vista ['βista] *sf* view; eyesight; appearance, look; gaze. **a primera vista** at first sight. **con vistas de** with a view to. **¡hasta la vista!** good-bye!

visto ['βisto] *adj* seen; obvious. **bien visto** approved of. **visto bueno** authorized. **visto que** seeing that.

vistoso [βis'toso] *adj* showy; (*fam*) loud.

visual [βi'swal] *adj* visual.

vital [βi'tal] *adj* vital. **vitalidad** *sf* vitality.

vitamina [βita'mina] *sf* vitamin.

vitela [βi'tela] *sf* vellum.

vitorear [βitore'ar] *v* shout, cheer, acclaim. **¡vítor!** bravo!

vítreo [βi'treo] *adj* vitreous. **vitrina** *sf* showcase.

vitriólico [βi'trjoliko] *adv* vitriolic. **vitriolo** *sm* vitriol.

vituperar [βitupe'rar] *v* vituperate; abuse; insult. **vituperación** *sf* blame.

viuda ['βjuða] *sf* widow. **viudo** *sm* widower. **viudez** *sf* widowhood.

vivaz [βi' βaθ] *adj* vivacious. **vivacidad** *sf* vivacity.

víveres ['βiβeres] *sm pl* provisions *pl*.

vivero [βi'βero] *sm* fishpond.

viveza [βi'β eθa] *sf* gaiety, liveliness.

vivienda [βi'βjenda] *sf* housing; dwelling; lodgings *pl*. **vivienda de protección oficial, VPO** *sf* council house. **vividero** *adj* habitable.

vivificar [βiβifi'kar] *v* animate, bring to life.

vivir [βi'βir] *v* live. **¿quién vive?** who goes there? *sm* way of life.

vivisección [βi βisek'θjon] *sf* vivisection.

vivo ['βiβo] *adj* living, alive; vivid. **al vivo** to the life.

vizconde [βiθ'konde] *sm* viscount. **viscondesa** *sf* viscountess.

vocablo [βo'kaβlo] *sm* word. **vocabulario** *sm* vocabulary.

vocación [βoka'θjon] *sf* vocation.

vocal [βo'kal] *adj* vocal. *sm* voter. *sf* vowel.

vocear [βoθe'ar] *v* bawl. **vocerío** *sm* bawling. **vocero** *sm* spokesman.

vociferar [βoθife'rar] *v* bawl; shout.

vocinglero [βoθin'glero] *adj* vociferous; loud-mouthed; talkative. **vocinglería** *sf* clamour, uproar.

volante [βo'lante] *adj* flying. *sm* steering-wheel; shuttlecock.

*volar [βo'lar] *v* fly; blow up, explode. **volarse** *v* become furious.

volátil [βo'latil] *adj* volatile.

volcán [βol'kan] *sm* volcano. **volcánico** *adj* volcanic.

*volcar [βol'kar] *v* upset; capsize. **volcarse** *v* fall over; bend over backwards.

volear [βole'ar] *v* volley. **voleo** *sm* volley.

volición [βoli'θjon] *sf* volition.

voltaje [βol'taxe] *sm* voltage. **voltio** *sm* volt.

voltear [βolte'ar] *v* overturn; revolve; tumble. **volteador, -a** *sm*, *sf* tumbler. **volteo** *sm* somersault.

voluble [βo'luβle] *adj* changeable. **volubilidad** *sf* changeable.

volumen [βolu'men] *sm* volume. **voluminoso** *adj* voluminous.

voluntad [βolun'tað] *sf* volition; affection. **a voluntad** at will. **buena voluntad** good-will.

voluntario [βolun'tarjo] *adj* voluntary. **voluntariedad** *sf* free will.

voluptuoso [βolup'twoso] *adj* voluptuous. **voluptuosidad** *sf* voluptuousness.

*volver [βol'βer] *v* return; turn; turn over. **volver sobre sí** pull oneself together. **volverse** *v* become; go back. **volverse loco** go mad.

vomitar [βomi'tar] *v* vomit. **vómito** *sm* vomit.

voraz [βo'raθ] *adj* voracious. **voracidad** *sf* voracity.

vórtice [βor'tiθe] *sm* vortex.

vosotros [βo'sotros] *pron pl (fam)* you.

votar [βo'tar] *v* vote. **votante** *s(m + f)* voter. **voto** *sm* vote; vow.

voz [βoθ] *sf* voice; shout; report. **a media voz** in a whisper. **dar voces** call out.

vuelco ['βwelko] *sm* upset; overturning.

vuelo ['βwelo] *sm* flight; flying; wing. **vuelo regular** *sm* scheduled flight. **al vuelo** in flight. **en un vuelo** in a jiffy.

vuelta ['βwelta] *sf* turn; return; bend; reverse; recompense. **dar una vuelta** take a stroll. **estar de vuelta** be back.

vuestro ['βwestro] *pron* yours. *adj* your.

vulcanizar [βulkani'θar] *v* vulcanize.

vulgar [βul'gar] *adj* common; ordinary; vulgar. **el hombre vulgar** the common man.

vulnerar [βulne'rar] *v* wound. **vulnerabilidad** *sf* vulnerability. **vulnerable** *adj* vulnerable.

xilófono [ksi'lofono] *sm* xylophone.

y [i] *conj* and.

ya [ja] *adv* already; now; yet; later. **ya que** since. **ya voy** I'm just coming.

yacimiento [jaθi'mjento] *sm* (*minerales*) bed. **yacente** *adj* recumbent.

yanqui [jan'ki] *adj*, *sm* (*fam*) Yankee.

yarda ['jarða] *sf* yard.

yate ['jate] *sm* yacht.

yedra ['jeðra] *sf* ivy.

yegua ['jegwa] *sf* mare.

yelmo ['jelmo] *sm* helmet.

yema ['jema] *sf* yolk; bud; button. **yema del dedo** tip of the finger.

yerba ['jerβa] *sf* grass; herb.

yermo ['jermo] *sm* waste land. *adj* barren; desert.

yerno ['jerno] *sm* son-in-law.

yerro ['jerro] *sm* error; mistake.

yeso ['jeso] *sm* gypsum; plaster; plaster cast.

yo [jo] *pron* I; myself; me; ego.

yodo ['joðo] *sm* iodine.

yogur [jo'gur] *sm* yoghurt.

yugo ['jugo] *sm* yoke.

yugular [jugu'lar] *adj* jugular.

yunque ['junke] *sm* anvil.

yunta ['junta] *sf* couple, pair; (*de bueyes*) yoke.

yute ['jute] *sm* jute.

***yuxtaponer** [jukstapo'ner] *v* juxtapose. **yuxtaposición** *sf* juxtaposition. **yuxtapuesto** *adj* juxtaposed.

Z

zafar [θa'far] *v* loosen; free; clear; lighten. **zafarse** *v* run away.

zafio ['θafjo] *adj* uncouth.

zafiro [θa'firo] *sm* sapphire.

zaga ['θaga] *sf* rear; back.

zaguán [θa'gwan] *sm* entrance hall.

***zaherir** [θae'rir] *v* censure; mock; reproach.

zahurda [θa'urða] *sf* pigsty.

zalamería [θalame'ria] *sf* flattery. **zalamero, -a** *sm, sf* flatterer.

zamarra [θa'marra] *sf* sheepskin jacket.

zambo ['θambo] *adj* knock-kneed. *sm* half-breed; monkey.

***zambullir** [θambu'ʎir] *v* dive. **zambullida** *sf* dive.

zampar [θam'par] *v* polish off; shove in; devour. **zamparse** *v* rush.

zanahoria [θana'orja] *sf* carrot.

zancada [θan'kaða] *sf* long stride. **en dos zancadas** in a trice. **zancadilla** *sf* trip; trap. **echar la zancadilla** trip up.

zanco ['θanko] *sm* stilt.

zancudo [θan'kuðo] *adj* long-legged.

zángano ['θangano] *sm* (*insecto*) drone; (*fig*) loafer; fool.

zangolotear [θangolote'ar] *v* shake; fidget; rattle. **zangoloteo** *sm* shaking; rattling.

zanja ['θanxa] *sf* ditch; trench. **abrir las zanjas** lay the foundations.

zapa ['θapa] *sf* spade; trench. **zapapico** *sm* pickaxe. **zapar** *v* undermine.

zapatear [θapate'ar] *v* kick; ill-treat; tap-dance. **zapateado** *sm* Andalusian dance. **zapatería** *sf* shoe shop; shoe factory.

zapatero, -a *sm, sf* shoemaker. **zapatilla** *sf* slipper. **zapato** *sm* shoe.

zar [θar] *sm* tsar.

zarandear [θarande'ar] *v* sift; winnow; shake. **zaranda** *sf* sieve.

zaraza [θa'raθa] *sf* chintz.

zarcillo [θar'θiλo] *sm* hoe; barrel hoop; vine tendril; ear-ring.

zarco ['θarko] *adj* (*ojos*) light blue.

zarpa ['θarpa] *v* claw; paw. **echar la zarpa** grab hold. **zarpar** *v* weigh anchor. **zarpazo** *sm* whack.

zarza ['θarθa] *sf* bramble, blackberry bush. **zarzamora** *sf* (*fruto*) blackberry.

zarzo ['θarθo] *sm* hurdle.

zarzuela [θar'θwela] *sf* light *or* comic opera.

zeta ['θeta] *sf* letter z.

zigzaguear [θigθage'ar] *v* zigzag. **zigzag** *sm* zigzag.

zinc [θink] *sm* zinc.

zócalo ['θokalo] *sm* plinth; skirting board.

zodiaco [θo'ðjako] *sm* zodiac.

zona ['θona] *sf* zone; area. **zona edificada** built-up area. **zonas verdes** green belt *sing*.

zoología [θoolo'xia] *sf* zoology. **zoológico** *adj* zoological. **parque zoológico** *sm* zoological gardens *pl*, zoo. **zoólogo, -a** *sm, sf* zoologist.

zoquete [θo'kete] *sm* chunk of wood; piece of stale bread; (*fam*) blockhead.

zorro ['θorro] *sm* fox. **zorra** *sf* vixen. **zorrera** *sf* foxhole.

zozobrar [θoθo'βrar] *v* wreck; capsize; founder; (*fig*) worry. **zozobra** *sf* foundering; worry.

zueco ['θweko] *sm* clog; galosh.

zumbar [θum'bar] *v* buzz; hum; strike; whack. **zumbarse de** make fun of. **zumbido** *sm* humming; buzzing.

zumbón [θum'bon] **, -a** *sm, sf* jester; tease. *adj* waggish.

zumo ['θumo] *sm* juice. **zumoso** *adj* juicy.

zurcir [θur'θir] *v* darn. **zurcido** *sm* darn; stitch. **zurcidura** *sf* darning.

zurdo, -a ['θurðo] *sm, sf* left-handed person. *adj* left-handed.

zurrar [θur'rar] *v* thrash; (*cuero*) dress; curry. **zurra** *sf* tanning; thrashing. **zurrador** *sm* tanner.

zurrón [θur'ron] *sm* leather bag; husk.

zutano [θu'tano] **, -a** *sm, sf* so-and-so. **fulano, zutano y mengano** Tom, Dick, and Harry.